**Foreign Relations of the
United States, 1961–1963**

Volume XII

American Republics

Editors	Edward C. Keefer
	Harriet Dashiell Schwar
	W. Taylor Fain III
General Editor	Glenn W. LaFantasie

United States Government Printing Office
Washington
1996

DEPARTMENT OF STATE PUBLICATION 10318

OFFICE OF THE HISTORIAN

BUREAU OF PUBLIC AFFAIRS

For sale by the U.S. Government Printing Office
Superintendent of Documents, Mail Stop: SSOP, Washington, DC 20402–9328
ISBN 0–16–045178–7

Preface

The *Foreign Relations of the United States* series presents the official documentary historical record of major foreign policy decisions and significant diplomatic activity of the United States Government. The series documents the facts and events that contributed to the formulation of policies and includes evidence of supporting and alternative views to the policy positions ultimately adopted.

The Historian of the Department of State is charged with the responsibility for the preparation of the *Foreign Relations* series. The staff of the Office of the Historian, Bureau of Public Affairs, plans, researches, compiles, and edits the volumes in the series. This documentary editing proceeds in full accord with the generally accepted standards of historical scholarship. Official regulations codifying specific standards for the selection and editing of documents for the series were first promulgated by Secretary of State Frank B. Kellogg on March 26, 1925. These regulations, with minor modifications, guided the series through 1991.

A new statutory charter for the preparation of the series was established by Public Law 102–138, the Foreign Relations Authorization Act, Fiscal Years 1992 and 1993, which was signed by President George Bush on October 28, 1991. Section 198 of P.L. 102–138 added a new Title IV to the Department of State's Basic Authorities Act of 1956 (22 USC 4351, *et seq.*).

The statute requires that the *Foreign Relations* series be a thorough, accurate, and reliable record of major United States foreign policy decisions and significant United States diplomatic activity. The volumes of the series should include all records needed to provide comprehensive documentation of major foreign policy decisions and actions of the United States Government, including facts that contributed to the formulation of policies and records that provided supporting and alternative views to the policy positions ultimately adopted.

The statute confirms the editing principles established by Secretary Kellogg: the *Foreign Relations* series is guided by the principles of historical objectivity and accuracy; records should not be altered or deletions made without indicating in the published text that a deletion has been made; the published record should omit no facts that were of major importance in reaching a decision; and nothing should be omitted for the purposes of concealing a defect in policy. The statute also requires that the *Foreign Relations* series be published not more than 30 years after the events recorded.

III

The editors of this volume, which was compiled in 1993, are convinced that it meets all regulatory, statutory, and scholarly standards of selection and editing. Although this volume records policies and events of more than 30 years ago, the statute of October 28, 1991, allows the Department until 1996 to reach the 30-year line in the publication of the series.

Structure and Scope of the Foreign Relations Series

This volume is part of a subseries of volumes of the *Foreign Relations* series that documents the most important issues in the foreign policy of the 3 years (1961–1963) of the administration of John F. Kennedy. The subseries presents in 25 print volumes and 5 microfiche supplements a documentary record of major foreign policy decisions and actions of President Kennedy's administration.

This volume presents documentation on U.S. policy toward countries of the Caribbean (Dominican Republic and Haiti), Central America (Panama), South America (Argentine, Brazil, Peru, and the British colony of British Guiana (later Guyana)), and regional issues such as the Alliance for Progress, Latin American security, and the threat of Cuban subversion. U.S. policy toward and relations with Cuba and management of the Cuban missile crisis are documented separately in volumes X and XI. A separate microfiche supplement to volumes X, XI, and XII presents documentation on U.S. policy toward and relations with Bolivia, Chile, Colombia, Costa Rica, Ecuador, El Salvador, Guatemala, Honduras, Jamaica, Mexico, and Venezuela, as well as additional documentation on Cuba.

Sources for the Foreign Relations Series

The *Foreign Relations* statute requires that the published record in the *Foreign Relations* series include all records needed to provide comprehensive documentation on major foreign policy decisions and actions of the U.S. Government. It further requires that government agencies, departments, and other entities of the U.S. Government cooperate with the Department of State Historian by providing full and complete access to records pertinent to foreign policy decisions and actions and by providing copies of selected records. The editors believe that in terms of access this volume was prepared in accordance with the standards and mandates of this statute.

The editors had complete access to all the retired records and papers of the Department of State: the central files of the Department; the special decentralized files ("lot files") of the Department at the bureau, office, and division levels; the files of the Department's Executive Secretariat, which contain the records of international conferences and high-level official visits, correspondence with foreign leaders by the President and Secretary of State, and memoranda of conversations between the President and Secretary of State and foreign officials; and the files of overseas diplomatic posts. Certain intelligence-related files maintained in the Bureau of Intelligence and Research became available to the Department historians only after this volume was compiled. Arrangements have been made for Department historians to have full and timely access to these records for future volumes. Department historians will endeavor to select documentation from these files that provides information on policy decisions during 1961–1963 as background to the policy deliberations of the Johnson administration.

The editors of the *Foreign Relations* series also have full access to the papers of Presidents Kennedy and Johnson and other White House foreign policy records. Presidential papers maintained and preserved at the Presidential libraries include some of the most significant foreign affairs-related documentation from other federal agencies including the National Security Council, the Central Intelligence Agency, the Department of Defense, and the Joint Chiefs of Staff. Also of special value at the Kennedy Library are the papers of Arthur M. Schlesinger, Jr., Special Assistant to the President.

Department of State historians also have access to records of the Department of Defense, particularly the records of the Secretary of Defense and his major assistants, and to the Maxwell Taylor Papers at the National Defense University. The Chester B. Bowles Papers at Yale University were also consulted and proved useful.

Since 1991, the Central Intelligence Agency has provided expanded access to Department historians to high-level intelligence documents from those records still in the custody of that Agency. Department historians' expanded access is arranged by the History Staff of the Center for the Study of Intelligence, Central Intelligence Agency, pursuant to a May 1992 memorandum of understanding. This access arrangement coincided with the research of volumes for the 1961–1963 triennium. Department of State and CIA historians continue to work out the procedural and scholarly aspects of this access, and the variety of documentation made available and selected for publication in the volumes has expanded. The editors made particular use of the files of Director John A. McCone as well as finished intelligence from the registry of the Deputy Directorate for Intelligence.

All of this documentation has been made available for use in the *Foreign Relations* series thanks to the consent of these agencies, the assistance of their staff, and especially the cooperation and support of the National Archives and Records Administration. The List of Sources, pages XV–XX, lists the particular files and collections consulted and cited in this volume.

Principles of Document Selection for the Foreign Relations Series

In preparing each volume of the *Foreign Relations* series, the editors are guided by some general principles for the selection of documents. Each editor, in consultation with the General Editor and other senior editors, determines the particular issues and topics to be documented either in detail, in brief, or in summary. Some general decisions are also made regarding issues that cannot be documented in the volume but will be addressed in a microfiche supplement or in bibliographical notes.

The following general selection criteria are used in preparing volumes in the *Foreign Relations* series. Individual compiler-editors vary these criteria in accordance with the particular issues and the available documentation. The editors also tend to apply these selection criteria in accordance with their own interpretation of the generally accepted standards of scholarship. In selecting documentation for publication, the editors gave priority to unpublished classified records, rather than previously published records (which are accounted for in appropriate bibliographical notes).

Selection Criteria (in general order of priority):

1. Major foreign affairs commitments made on behalf of the United States to other governments, including those that define or identify the principal foreign affairs interests of the United States;

2. Major foreign affairs issues, commitments, negotiations, and activities, whether or not major decisions were made, and including dissenting or alternative opinions to the process ultimately adopted;

3. The decisions, discussions, actions, and considerations of the President, as the official constitutionally responsible for the direction of foreign policy;

4. The discussions and actions of the National Security Council, the Cabinet, and special Presidential policy groups, including the policy options brought before these bodies or their individual members;

5. The policy options adopted by or considered by the Secretary of State and the most important actions taken to implement Presidential decisions or policies;

6. Diplomatic negotiations and conferences, official correspondence, and other exchanges between U.S. representatives and those of other governments that demonstrate the main lines of policy implementation on major issues;

7. Important elements of information that attended Presidential decisions and policy recommendations of the Secretary of State;

8. Major foreign affairs decisions, negotiations, and commitments undertaken on behalf of the United States by government officials and representatives in other agencies in the foreign affairs community or

other branches of government made without the involvement (or even knowledge) of the White House or the Department of State;

9. The main policy lines of intelligence activities if they constituted major aspects of U.S. foreign policy toward a nation or region or if they provided key information in the formulation of major U.S. policies;

10. The role of the Congress in the preparation and execution of particular foreign policies or foreign affairs actions;

11. Economic aspects of foreign policy;

12. The main policy lines of U.S. military and economic assistance as well as other types of assistance;

13. The political-military recommendations, decisions, and activities of the military establishment and major regional military commands as they bear upon the formulation or execution of major U.S. foreign policies;

14. Documentation that illuminates special decision-making processes that accomplished the policies recorded in particular volumes;

15. Diplomatic appointments that reflect major policies or affect policy changes.

Scope and Focus of Documents Researched and Selected for Foreign Relations, 1961–1963, Volume XII

The documentation printed in this volume focuses on U.S. policy toward the American Republics of the Caribbean, Central, and South America. The guiding principle for selection was high-level interest within the Kennedy administration in policy and relations toward a specific country. This focus tends to give more coverage to countries in which there were crisis or specific problems and de-emphasizes countries that had basically good relations with the United States during the period. Documents were selected that highlight policy discussions within the U.S. Government, with particular emphasis on the highest level at which policy on a particular subject was determined, that revealed policy positions and internal differences over policy, and that summarized developments or positions regarding an issue. Records of conversations with foreign leaders both abroad and in Washington were selected to illuminate U.S. relations with those countries. Embassy reportage is limited to particularly significant cables that may have influenced or contributed to the making of U.S. policy at critical points. A number of relevant documents that conveyed finished intelligence to U.S. policymakers, in particular National Intelligence Estimates and Special National Intelligence Estimates, are included.

President Kennedy, with advice from his key advisers, made the major foreign policy decisions during his Presidency, and the editors tried to document his role as much possible. The role of White House and National Security Council Staff members in providing information and advice to the President grew during this period. The editors accordingly selected memoranda that presented to the President the views and recommendations of his White House advisers. Formal approved policy papers were rare in the Kennedy administration, and internal discussions between the President and his advisers were not always recorded. The editors sought to document Presidential decisions by drawing upon the best material available.

The Department of State, which continued to play a leading role in formulating foreign policy and providing advice on foreign policy matters to the President, also played the principal role in the implementation of those policies and in negotiations on policy matters with foreign governments. While President Kennedy determined the major outlines of U.S. policy toward the American Republics and on occasion involved himself in the details of formulation and implementation of policy with respect to particular countries or issues, the Department of State and other government agencies managed the day-to-day aspects of protecting U.S. interests in the area.

Editorial Methodology

The documents are presented chronologically in each compilation according to Washington time or, in the case of conferences, in the order of individual meetings. Incoming telegrams from U.S. Missions are placed according to time of receipt in the Department of State or other receiving agency, rather than the time of transmission; memoranda of conversation are placed according to the time and date of the conversation, rather than the date the memorandum was drafted.

Editorial treatment of the documents published in the *Foreign Relations* series follows Office style guidelines, supplemented by guidance from the General Editor and the chief technical editor. The source text is reproduced as exactly as possible, including marginalia or other notations, which are described in the footnotes. Texts are transcribed and printed according to accepted conventions for the publication of historical documents in the limitations of modern typography. A heading has been supplied by the editors for each document included in the volume. Spelling, capitalization, and punctuation are retained as found in the source text, except that obvious typographical errors are silently corrected. Other mistakes and omissions in the source text are corrected by bracketed insertions: a correction is set in italic type; an addition in roman type. Words or phrases underlined in the source text are printed in italics. Abbreviations and contractions are preserved as found in the source text, and a list of abbreviations is included in the front matter of each volume.

Bracketed insertions are also used to indicate omitted text that deals with an unrelated subject (in roman type) or that remains classified after declassification review (in italic type). The amount of material not declassified has been noted by indicating the number of lines or pages of source text that were omitted. Entire documents withheld for security reasons have been accounted for and are listed by headings, source notes, and number of pages not declassified in their chronological place. The amount of material omitted from this volume because it was unrelated to the subject of the volume, however, has not been delineated. All brackets that appear in the source text are so identified by footnotes.

An unnumbered source note to each document indicates the document's source, original classification, distribution, and drafting information. This note also provides the background of important documents and policies and indicates if the President or his major policy advisers read the document. Every effort has been made to determine if a document has been previously published, and this information has been included in the source footnote.

Editorial notes and additional annotation summarize pertinent material not printed in the volume, indicate the location of additional documentary sources, provide references to important related documents printed in other volumes, describe key events, and provide summaries of and citations to public statements that supplement and elucidate the printed documents. Information derived from memoirs and other first-hand accounts have been used when appropriate to supplement or explicate the official record.

Advisory Committee on Historical Diplomatic Documentation

The Advisory Committee on Historical Diplomatic Documentation, established under the *Foreign Relations* statute, reviews records, advises, and makes recommendations concerning the *Foreign Relations* series. The Advisory Committee monitors the overall compilation and editorial process of the series and advises on all aspects of the preparation and declassification of the series. Although the Advisory Committee does not attempt to review the contents of individual volumes in the series, it does monitor the overall process and makes recommendations on particular problems that come to its attention.

The Advisory Committee reviewed the compilation on U.S. policy toward British Guiana, as noted below.

Declassification Review

The final declassification review of this volume, completed in 1995, resulted in the decision to withhold 2.7 percent of the documentation originally selected for publication; 7 documents were denied in full. The Department of State and the Central Intelligence Agency initially determined that major portions of the compilation on policy toward British Guiana should not be declassified. This declassification review decision would clearly have resulted in an incomplete and inaccurate published record. The Advisory Committee on Historical Diplomatic Documentation agreed and strongly recommended declassification. The issue was reconsidered at the highest levels of the Department of State and other concerned agencies. A determination was made to declassify all but those portions of documents and whole documents indicated in the text printed in the compilation on British Guiana. The Advisory Committee concurred in the decision of the Historian's Office to publish this volume with the compilation on British Guiana as restored during the declassification appeal process.

The Division of Historical Documents Review of the Office of Freedom of Information, Privacy, and Classification Review, Bureau of Administration, Department of State, conducted the declassification review of the documents published in this volume. The review was conducted in accordance with the standards set forth in Executive Order 12356 on National Security Information, which was superseded by Executive Order 12958 on April 20, 1995, and applicable laws.

Under Executive Order 12356, information that concerns one or more of the following categories, and the disclosure of which reasonably could be expected to cause damage to the national security, requires classification:

1) military plans, weapons, or operations;
2) the vulnerabilities or capabilities of systems, installations, projects, or plans relating to the national security;
3) foreign government information;
4) intelligence activities (including special activities), or intelligence sources or methods;
5) foreign relations or foreign activities of the United States;
6) scientific, technological, or economic matters relating to national security;
7) U.S. Government programs for safeguarding nuclear materials or facilities;
8) cryptology; or
9) a confidential source.

The principle guiding declassification review is to release all information, subject only to the current requirements of national security as embodied in law and regulation. Declassification decisions entailed concurrence of the appropriate geographic and functional bureaus in the Department of State, other concerned agencies of the U.S. Government, and the appropriate foreign governments regarding specific documents of those governments.

Acknowledgements

The editors wish to acknowledge the assistance of officials at the John F. Kennedy Library, in particular Suzanne Forbes; the National Archives and Records Administration; and other specialized repositories who assisted in the collection of documents for this volume.

W. Taylor Fain III collected, selected, and edited the compilations on the Alliance for Progress, Brazil, British Guiana, the Dominican Republic, and Peru; Harriet Dashiell Schwar collected, selected, and edited the compilations on Latin American security, the question of Cuban subversion, and Panama; and Edward C. Keefer collected, selected, and edited the compilations on Argentina and Haiti. David W. Mabon planned the volume and conducted the review under the general supervision of Editor in Chief Glenn W. LaFantasie. Edward C. Keefer oversaw the final steps in the editorial and publication process. Rita Baker, Deb Godfrey, and Vicki E. Futscher did the copy and technical editing and Barbara-Ann Bacon of the Publishing Services Division oversaw the production of the volume. Juniee Oneida prepared the index.

William Z. Slany
The Historian
Bureau of Public Affairs

May 1996

Contents

List of Sources

Department of State

Decimal Central Files. Through January 1963 the Department of State continued to use the decimal central file system familiar to users of previous volumes of the *Foreign Relations* series. Most of the documents in this volume through January 1963 were selected from the following files:

120.1520: Stevenson trip to Latin America
123 Jones, J. Wesley: personnel matters relating to J. Wesley Jones
371.04: Meetings of Consultation of OAS Foreign Ministers
371.05: Council of the Organization of American States
371.8: OAS Committee on Economic Cooperation
411.39: trade between the United States and the Dominican Republic
611.19: U.S. relations with Panama
611.15: U.S. relations with Honduras
611.20: U.S. relations with Latin America
611.23: U.S. relations with Peru
611.32: U.S. relations with Brazil
611.35: U.S. relations with Argentina
611.38: U.S. relations with Haiti
611.39: U.S. relations with the Dominican Republic
612.37: Mexican relations with Cuba
635.00: international relations of Argentina
710.5–MSP: U.S. military assistance to the Western Hemisphere
711.11–KE: files relating to President Kennedy
713.00: Central American political affairs
713.20: political affairs in South and Central America
713.5: Central American defense affairs
720.5: Latin American defense affairs
720.5–MSP: U.S. military assistance to Latin America
721.00: Colombian internal political affairs
723.00: Peruvian internal political affairs
723.5–MSP: U.S. military assistance to Peru
731.5–MSP: U.S. military assistance to Venezuela
732.00: Brazilian internal political affairs
732.5–MSP: U.S. military assistance to Brazil
735.00: Argentine internal political affairs
736.5–MSP: U.S. military assistance to the West Indies
737.00: Cuban internal political affairs
738.11: U.S. political relations with Haiti
739.00: Dominican Republic internal political affairs
741.D: British Guiana political affairs
811.20: economic relations between the U.S. and South and Central America
811.0032: economic relations between the U.S. and Brazil
812.00: internal economic relations in Mexico

Subject-Numeric Central Files. In February 1963 the Department adopted a subject-numeric central file system.

AID (US) 9 PAN: U.S.-Panama economic aid negotiations
CSM 10 LAT AM: communism in Latin America

DEF 12 CUBA: Cuban armaments
DEF 19 US–LAT AM: U.S. military aid to Latin America
PET 6 PERU: Peruvian oil companies
PET 15 ARG: industrial organization and control of Argentine petroleum industry
POL ARG–US: U.S.-Argentine relations
POL BR GU: British Guiana political affairs
POL BR GU–US: U.S.-British Guiana relations
POL BRAZ: Brazilian political affairs
POL DOM REP–HAI: Dominican Republic-Haitian relations
POL HAI–US: U.S.-Haitian relations
POL PERU–US: U.S.-Peruvian relations
POL 1 BR GU–US: U.S.-British Guiana relations, general policy and background
POL 1 BRAZ–US: U.S.-Brazilian relations, general policy and background
POL 1 US: U.S. political affairs, general policy and background
POL 2 DOM REP: general political reporting on the Dominican Republic
POL 3 COAS–IA: Council of the Organization of American States
POL 7 ARG: visits and meetings with Argentine leaders
POL 7 COSTA RICA: President Kennedy's meeting with Central American Presidents
POL 7 PERU: visits and meetings with Peruvian leaders
POL 14 ARG: Argentine elections
POL 14 PERU: Peruvian elections
POL 15 DOM REP: Dominican Republic Government
POL 15 HAI: Haitian Government
POL 16 DOM REP: recognition of Dominican Republic
POL 17–1 DOM REP–US: U.S.-Dominican Republic diplomatic representation
POL 19 BR GU: colonial government of British Guiana
POL 26 ARG: coups in Argentina
POL 26 DOM REP: coups in the Dominican Republic
POL 26 HAI: coups and rebellions in Haiti
POL 26 LAT AM: coups in Latin America
POL 27–1 HAI: invasion of Haiti
POL 36 CUBA: travel between Cuba and other countries
POL PANAMA–US: U.S. relations with Panama

Lot Files. These are the special decentralized files of the policymaking level of the Department of State, including the Executive Secretariat, overseas Foreign Service posts, and U.S. special missions. A list of the lot files used or consulted for this volume follows.

ARA/IPA Files: Lot 69 D 211

Files of Inter-American conferences, both specialized and sponsored by the Organization of American States, 1956–1965.

ARA/NC Files: Lot 67 D 77

Subject files for British Guiana, 1950–1964.

Conference Files: Lot 65 D 366

Records of official visits by heads of government and foreign ministers to the United States and international conferences attended by the President or Secretary of State, 1961, as maintained by the Executive Secretariat.

Conference Files: Lot 65 D 533

Records of official visits by heads of government and foreign ministers to the United States and international conferences attended by the President or Secretary of State, 1962, as maintained by the Executive Secretariat.

Conference Files: Lot 66 D 110

Records of official visits by heads of government and foreign ministers to the United States and international conferences attended by the President or Secretary of State, 1961–1964, as maintained by the Executive Secretariat.

Interdepartmental Committee on Foreign Economic Policy Files: Lot 65 D 68

Records of the Interdepartmental Committee of Under Secretaries on Foreign Economic Policy, 1961–1963.

Latin America Task Force Files: Lot 61 D 298

Minutes of the Task Force on Latin America, 1961.

NSAM Files: Lot 72 D 316

Department of State master file of NSAMs 1–371, 1961–1968.

Policy Guidelines: Lot 67 D 396

Master file of Guidelines for Policy and Operations papers, 1961–1966.

Presidential Correspondence: Lot 66 D 204

Correspondence between the President and Secretary of State and heads of government and foreign ministers for 1953–1964, as maintained by the Executive Secretariat.

Presidential Memoranda of Conversation: Lot 66 D 149

Memoranda of conversation between the President and foreign visitors, 1956–1964, as maintained by the Executive Secretariat.

Presidential Memoranda of Conversation: Lot 66 D 476

Memoranda of conversation between the President and foreign visitors, October 1963–October 1966, as maintained by the Executive Secretariat.

Rusk Files: Lot 72 D 192

Files of Secretary of State Dean Rusk, 1961–1969, including texts of speeches and public statements, miscellaneous correspondence files, White House correspondence, chronological files, and memoranda of telephone conversations.

Secretary's Memoranda of Conversation: Lot 65 D 330

Memoranda of the Secretary's and Acting Secretary's conversations, 1961–1964.

Secretary's Staff Meetings: Lot 66 D 147

Minutes of the Secretary of State's staff meetings and memoranda of Chester Bowles telephone conversations, as maintained by the Executive Secretariat.

S/P Files: Lot 69 D 121

Files of the Policy Planning Council, 1962.

S/P Files: Lot 70 D 199

Files of the Policy Planning Council, 1963–1964.

S/P–NSC Files: Lot 62 D 1

Serial and subject master file of National Security Council documents and correspondence for 1948–1961, as maintained by the Policy Planning Staff.

S/PC Files: Lot 71 D 273

Files of Policy Planning Staff member Ernest K. Lindley, 1962–1968.

S/S–NSC (Miscellaneous) Files: Lot 66 D 95

Miscellaneous files of the National Security Council, including records of actions, 1947–1963, as maintained by the Executive Secretariat.

S/S–NSC Files: Lot 70 D 265

Files pertaining to National Security Council meetings, including policy papers, position papers, administrative documents, but not minutes of the meetings themselves, for 1961–1966, as maintained by the Executive Secretariat.

S/S–NSC Files: Lot 72 D 316

File of National Security Action Memoranda (NSAMs), 1961–1968, as maintained by the Executive Secretariat.

State–JCS Meetings: Lot 70 D 328

Records of the meetings of the Joint Chiefs of Staff and representatives of the Department of State for 1959–1963, as maintained by the Executive Secretariat.

National Archives and Records Administration, Washington, D.C.

Record Group 59, General Records of the Department of State

S/P Files: Lot 67 D 548

Records of the Policy Planning Council for 1957–1961.

S/P Files: Lot 69 D 121

Records of the Policy Planning Council for 1962.

S/S–NSC Files: Lot 63 D 351

Master file of National Security Council documents, correspondence, and related Department of State memoranda for 1947–1961, maintained by the Executive Secretariat.

Dwight D. Eisenhower Presidential Library, Abliene, Kansas

Whitman File

Papers of Dwight D. Eisenhower as maintained by his personal secretary, Ann C. Whitman.

Lyndon Baines Johnson Presidential Library, Austin, Texas

National Security File:
  Agency Files
  Aides' Files

Rusk Appointment Books

Vice Presidential Security File

John F. Kennedy Presidential Library, Boston, Massachusetts

Ball Papers

Papers of George W. Ball, Under Secretary of State for Economic Affairs, 1961, and Under Secretary of State, 1961–1963, consisting of records of telephone conversations during his tenure as Under Secretary.

National Security Files:

    Chester V. Clifton Series

    Countries Series: Argentina, Brazil, British Guiana, Dominican Republic, Haiti, Panama, Peru

    Departments and Agencies Series

    Meetings and Memoranda Series

    Regional Security Series

    Subjects Series

    Trip and Conference Series

    William H. Brubeck Series

President's Appointment Books

President's Office Files

    Countries Series

Schlesinger Papers

    Papers of Arthur M. Schlesinger, Jr., Special Assistant to the President.

Library of Congress Manuscript Division, Washington, D.C.

Harriman Papers

    Papers of Averell W. Harriman, Ambassador at Large, 1961; Assistant Secretary of State for Far Eastern Affairs, 1961–1963; Under Secretary of State for Political Affairs, 1963.

National Defense University, Washington, D.C.

Lemnitzer Papers

    Papers of General Lyman L. Lemnitzer, Chairman of the Joint Chiefs of Staff, 1960–1962.

Taylor Papers

    Papers of General Maxwell D. Taylor, Military Adviser to the President 1961–1962; and Chairman of the Joint Chiefs of Staff, 1962–1964.

Princeton University, Seeley G. Mudd Manuscript Library, Princeton, New Jersey

Stevenson Papers

    Papers of Adlai E. Stevenson, Representative at the United Nations, 1961–1963.

Washington National Records Center, Suitland, Maryland

Record Group 330, Records of the Office of the Secretary of Defense

McNamara Files: FRC 71 A 3470

    Files of Secretary of Defense Robert S. McNamara for 1961–1968.

OSD Files: FRC 65 A 3464

Files of the Secretary and Deputy Secretary of Defense and their assistants for 1961.

OSD Files: FRC 66 A 3542

Files of the Secretary and Deputy Secretary of Defense and their assistants for 1962.

OASD/ISA Files: FRC 64 A 2382

General and country files of the Assistant Secretary of Defense for International Security Affairs for 1961.

OASD/ISA Files: FRC 65 A 3501

General and country files of the Assistant Secretary of Defense for International Security Affairs for 1962.

OASD/ISA Files: FRC 67 A 4564

General and country files of the Assistant Secretary of Defense for International Security Affairs for 1963.

OASD/ISA Files: FRC 69 A 926

Top Secret files of the Assistant Secretary of Defense for International Security Affairs for 1961–1963.

OASD/(C) A Files: FRC 71 A 2896

Files of the Secretary of Defense relating to the Cuban missile crisis, 1961–1963.

Agency for International Development, Washington, D.C.

Administrator Files: Lot 286 65 481

Files of the AID Administrator for 1961–1962.

Administrator Files: Lot 286 67 1530

Files of the AID Administrator for 1962–1965.

Central Intelligence Agency

Files of John A. McCone, 1962–1965, Job 80–B01258A

Office of the Deputy Director of Intelligence Registry, Job 79–R01012A

Yale University, New Haven, Connecticut

Bowles Papers

List of Abbreviations

AD, Accion Democratica, Venezuelan political party
AFL–CIO, American Federation of Labor–Congress of Industrial Organizations
AFP, Alliance for Progress
AID, Agency for International Development
ALCAN, Aluminium Company of Canada
A.P., Accion Popular, Peruvian political party
APRA, Alianza Popular Revolucionaria Americana, Peruvian political party
ARA, Bureau of Inter-American Affairs, U.S. Department of State
ARA/BR, Bureau of Inter-American Affairs, Office of Brazilian Affairs
ARA/CCA, Bureau of Inter-American Affairs, Office of the Coordinator of Cuban Affairs
ARA/CMA, Bureau of Inter-American Affairs, Office of Caribbean and Mexican Affairs
ARA/EST, Bureau of Inter-American Affairs, Office of East Coast Affairs
ARA/OAP, Bureau of Inter-American Affairs, Office of Central American and Panamanian Affairs
ARA/REA, Bureau of Inter-American Affairs, Office of Inter-American Regional Economic Affairs
ARA/RPA, Bureau of Inter-American Affairs, Office of Inter-American Regional Political Affairs
ARA/WST, Bureau of Inter-American Affairs, Office of West Coast Affairs
ARs, American Republics
ARS, aerial reconnaissance and security

B/FAC, Deputy Coordinator for Foreign Assistance, Office of the Under Secretary of State for Economic Affairs
BG, British Guiana
BWI$, British West Indies dollar

CA, Central America
CAS, Controlled American source
CI, counter insurgency
CIA, Central Intelligence Agency
CIAP, Inter-American Committee on the Alliance for Progress
CINCARIB, Commander in Chief, Caribbean
CINCLANT, Commander in Chief, Atlantic
CINCSO, Commander in Chief, Southern Command
Cirtel, Circular telegram
COAS, Council of the Organization of American States
COMAP, Commerce Committee for the Alliance for Progress
COMIBOL, Corporacion Minera de Bolivia
Contel, Consulate telegram

DCM, Deputy Chief of Mission
Deptel, Department of State telegram
DOD, Department of Defense
DOD/ISA, Department of Defense, Office of the Assistant Secretary for International Security Affairs
DR, Dominican Republic

ECLA, United Nations Council on Latin America
Embdes, Embassy despatch

Embtel, Embassy telegram
EUR/WE, Bureau of European Affairs, Office of Western European Affairs
Eximbank, Export Import Bank of the United States

FBI, Federal Bureau of Investigation
FM, Foreign Minister
FY, fiscal year
FYI, for your information

GAWU, Guiana Agricultural Workers Union
GOA, Government of Argentina
GOB, Government of Bolivia; Government of Brazil
GOC, Government of Chile; Government of Colombia
GODR, Government of the Dominican Republic
GOH, Government of Haiti
GOP, Government of Panama; Government of Peru
GUS, Government of the United States

HMG, His/Her Majesty's Government

IA, Inter-American
IADB, Inter-American Development Bank
IA–ECOSOC, Inter-American Economic and Social Council
IAPC, Inter-American Peace Committee
IBRD, International Bank for Reconstruction and Development (World Bank)
ICA, International Cooperation Administration
IDB, Inter-American Development Bank
IFC, International Finance Corporation
IMF, International Monetary Fund
INR, Bureau of Intelligence and Research, Department of State
INR/DDC, Bureau of Intelligence and Research, Deputy Director for Coordination
INR/RAR, Bureau of Intelligence and Research, Office of Research and Analysis for American Republics
IPC, International Petroleum Company
ITT, International Telephone and Telegraph Corporation

LA, Latin America
LAFTA, Latin American Free Trade Association
LAPC, Latin American Policy Committee

MAAG, Military Assistance Advisory Group
MAP, Military Assistance Program
MATS, Military Air Transport Service
MFM, meeting of Foreign Ministers
MPCA, Man Power Citizens Association, British Guiana
MPD, Movimiento Popular Dominicano, Dominican political party

niact, night action, communications indicator requiring action by the recipient at any hour of the day or night
NIE, National Intelligence Estimate
NSC, National Security Council
NSAM, National Security Action Memorandum
NSP, National Security Paper

OARS, ocean area reconnaissance satellite
OAS, Organization of American States
OASD/ISA, Office of the Assistant Secretary of Defense for International Security Affairs
ODECA, Organizacion de Estados Centro-Americanos
OIC, Office of International Conferences, Bureau of International Organization Affairs

P.L.–480, Public Law 480, Food for Peace
PNC, People's National Congress, British Guiana political party
POLAD, Political Adviser
PPP, People's Progressive Party, British Guiana political party
PR, proportional representation
PRD, Partido Revolucionario Dominicano, Dominican political party
PRSC, Partido Revolucionario Social Cristiano, Dominican political party
PWO, People's Women Organization, suborganization of the People's Progressive Party
PYO, People's Youth Organization, suborganization of the People's Progressive Party

SCCS, Special Consultative Committee on Security
SIM, Trujillo's secret police
SNIE, Special National Intelligence Estimate
S/P, Policy Planning Council, Department of State
S/S, Executive Secretariat, Department of State
SUDENE, Superintendency for the Development of the Northeast (Brazil)

TTM, Ton Tons Macoutes (Haiti)
TWI, The West Indies

UF, United Front, British Guiana political party
UCN, Union Civica Nacional, Dominican political party
UCRP, Union Civica Radical del Pueblo, Argentine political party
UN, United Nations
UNCLA, United Nations Economic Commission on Latin America
UNCRI, Union Civica Radical Intransigenta, Argentine political party
UNCTAD, United Nations Conference on Trade and Development
UNESCO, United Nations Educational, Scientific and Cultural Organization
USAID, United States Agency for International Development
USG, United States Government
USIA, United States Information Agency
USIS, United States Information Service
USMC, United States Marine Corps
USUN, United States Mission to the United Nations
UWI, University of the West Indies

WAT, Washington Assessment Team
WIROM, telegram indicator for Department of State administrative telegrams

YPF, Yacimientos Petroliferos Fiscales (national petroleum company of Argentina)

List of Persons

Abbes, "Johnny" Garcia, Chief of the Dominican Secret Police under Trujillo

Abbuhl, Forest E., officer in charge Haitian Affairs, Office of Caribbean and Mexican Affairs, Bureau of Inter-American Affairs, from January 22, 1961

Achilles, Theodore C., Member, Task Force on Latin America; Counselor of the Department of State to February 15, 1961; Director, Department of State Operations Center

Alemann, Dr. Roberto T., Argentine Minister of Economy, April 1961–April 1962; Ambassador to the United States after June 1962

Alessandri Rodriguez, Jorge, President of Chile

Allen, Ward P., Director, Office of Inter-American Regional Political Affairs, Bureau of Inter-American Affairs from June 24, 1962

Alsogaray, Alvaro, Argentine Minister of Economy, May 1962–October 1963

Amiama Tio, Luis, member, Dominican Council of State

Atila Luna, General Miguel, Chief of Staff, Dominican Air Force

Baez, Porfirio Herrera, Dominican Foreign Minister in Balaguer government

Balaguer, Joaquin, President of the Dominican Republic to January 1, 1962; President of the Council of State to January 16, 1962

Ball, George W., Under Secretary of State for Economic and Agricultural Affairs, January 30–December 3, 1961; Under Secretary of State from December 4, 1961

Barall, Milton, Deputy Assistant Secretary of State for Inter-American Affairs

Barbot, Clement, Former head of the Haitian Ton Ton Macoutes and opponent of the Duvalier government

Battle, Lucius D., Executive Secretary of the Department of State, March 16, 1961–May 2, 1962

Belaúnde Terry, Fernando, President of Peru from July 28, 1963

Belcher, Taylor G., Director, Office of West Coast Affairs, Bureau of Inter-American Affairs from August 20, 1961

Bell, David E., Adminstrator, Agency for International Development, from December 21, 1961

Bell, John O., Deputy Coordinator for Foreign Assistance, Department of State, to November 4, 1961; Ambassador to Guatemala from November 10, 1961

Beltran Espantoso, Pedro, Prime Minister, Minister of Finance, and Minister of Commerce of Peru to July 18, 1962

Berle, Adolf A., Chairman, Task Force on Immediate Latin American Problems, November–December 1960; Chairman, Task Force on Latin America, January 2–July 7, 1961

Betancourt, Romulo, President of Venezuela

Bonilla Atiles, Dr. Jose, Dominican Secretary of State for Foreign Affairs under the Council of State

Bonnelly, Rafael F., President of the Dominican Council of State, January 18, 1962–February 27, 1963

Bosch, Juan, President of the Dominican Republic, February 27, 1962–September 25, 1963

Bowdler, William G., Office of Regional Political Affairs, Bureau of Inter-American Affairs

Bowles, Chester B., Under Secretary of State, January 25–December 3, 1961; President's Special Adviser on Africa, Asia, and Latin America, December 4, 1961–June 9, 1963

Bracken, Katherine W., Director, Office of Central American and Panamanian Affairs, Bureau of Inter-American Affairs to November 11, 1961

Briz(z)ola, Leonel, Governor of Rio Grande do Sul Province, Brazil; brother-in-law of President Goulart

Brubeck, William H., Executive Secretary of the Department of State, May 14, 1962–July 20, 1963

Bundy, McGeorge, Special Assistant to the President for National Security Affairs

Bundy, William P., Deputy Assistant Secretary of Defense for International Security Affairs

Burke, Admiral Arleigh A., USN, Chief of Naval Operations to August 1, 1961

Burnham, Forbes, leader of the People's National Congress of British Guiana

Cabell, General Charles P., Deputy Director of Central Intelligence to November 1961

Cabot, John M., Ambassador to Brazil to August 17, 1961

Califano, Joseph A., Jr., Special Assistant to the Secretary of the Army

Camilion, Oscar, Argentine Under-Secretary of Foreign Affairs to March 1962

Carcano, Miguel Angel, Argentine Foreign Minister to March 1962

Carril, Bonifacio del, Argentine Ambassador to the United States to March 1962; Foreign Minister to October 1963

Carillo Flores, Antonio, Mexican Ambassador to the United States

Cassini, Igor, reporter, Hearst Newspapers; unregistered agent of the Dominican Government

Castro Ruz, Fidel, Premier of Cuba

Chayes, Abram J., Legal Adviser, Department of State from February 6, 1961

Chiari, Roberto F., President of Panama

Cleveland, J. Harlan, Assistant Secretary of State for International Oganization Affairs from February 21, 1961

Coerr, Wymberly De R., Deputy Assistant Secretary of State for Inter-American Affairs to June 1962; Ambassador to Uruguay from July 27, 1962

Collins, V. Lansing, Director, Office of Central American and Panamanian Affairs, Bureau of Inter-American Affairs, from January 20, 1963

Cottrell, Sterling J., Deputy Assistant Secretary of State for Inter-American Affairs from April 14, 1963

Crimmins, John H., Director, Office of Caribbean and Mexican Affairs, Bureau of Inter-American Affairs, April 7, 1962–January 16, 1963

Crockett, Kennedy M., Deputy Director, Office of Caribbean and Mexican Affairs, Bureau of Inter-American Affairs, from November 11, 1962

D'Aquiar, Peter, leader of the United Front political party of British Guiana

Dantas, Francisco Clementino San Tiago, Brazilian Minister of Foreign Relations; later Minister of Finance

Dearborn, Henry V., Consul General, Ciudad Trujillo to May 27, 1961; Counselor, Embassy in Bogota from September 1961

Dillon, C. Douglas, Secretary of the Treasury

Dulles, Allen W., Director of Central Intelligence to November 1961

Dungan, Ralph A., Special Assistant to President Kennedy

Duvalier, Francois, President of Haiti

Echavarria, General Rafael Rodriguez, Commander, Dominican Air Force; leader of coup against the Council of State, January 16, 1962

Enemark, General W.A., USA, Regional Director, Western Hemisphere Affairs, Office of the Assistant Secretary of Defense for International Security Affairs

Falcón Briceño, Marcos, Foreign Minister of Venezuela

Farland, Joseph S., Ambassador to Panama until August 1963

Fiallo, Viriato A., Presidential candidate of the UCN in the Dominican election of 1962

Fignole, Daniel, political opponent of the Duvalier government in Haiti

Fisher, John W., Director, Office of Central American and Panamanian Affairs from June 10, 1962

Fitzgerald, Dennis A., Deputy Director for Operations, International Cooperation Administration

Fleming, Robert J., Jr., U.S. Governor of the Panama Canal Zone

Framini, Andres, Argentine Peronist labor leader; elected governor of Buenos Aires Province, March 1962 (election annulled by Guido government in April 1962)

Fraser, Hugh, British Under Secretary of State for the Colonies, 1960–1962

Freeman, Fulton, U.S. Ambassador to Colombia from June 15, 1961

Freites Barrera, Andres, Dominican Ambassador to the United States under the Council of State; Foreign Minister under the Bosch government

Frigerio, Rogelio, adviser to Argentine President Frondizi

Frondizi, Arturo, President of Argentina to March 29, 1962

Fulbright, J. William, Senator (D–Arkansas); Chairman, Senate Foreign Relations Committee

Gilpatric, Roswell L., Deputy Secretary of Defense from January 24, 1961

Goodwin, Richard N., Assistant Special Counsel to President Kennedy until November 1961; Deputy Assistant Secretary of State for Inter-American Affairs November 1961–January 1963; Secretary General, International Peace Corps Secretariat, from January 1963

Gordon, A. Lincoln, member, Task Force on Immediate Latin American Problems, November–December 1960; Ambassador to Brazil from October 19, 1961

Goulart, Jaoa, President of Brazil from September 7, 1961

Grey, Sir Ralph, Governor of British Guiana

Guevara de la Serna, Major Ernesto "Che," Cuban Minister of Industry

Guido, Jose Maria, Provisional President of Argentina, March 1962–October 1963

Hamilton, Fowler, Administrator of the Agency for International Development, September 30–December 20, 1961

Harriman, W. Averell, Ambassador at Large, February 13–December 3, 1961; Assistant Secretary of State for Far Eastern Affairs, December 4, 1961–April 3, 1963; Under Secretary of State for Political Affairs from April 4, 1963

Hartwick, Tobias, officer in charge US–OAS Delegation Matters, Office of Regional Political Affairs, Bureau of Inter-American Affairs

Haya de la Torre, Victor Raul, President-elect of Peru June 1962; prevented from taking office; candidate for President June 1963

Hemba, Alton W., Deputy Director, Office of East Coast Affairs, Bureau of Inter-American Affairs, until March 1962

Henderson, Douglas, Deputy Chief of Mission, Lima, Peru to July 25, 1962; Chargé d'Affaires, July 26–November 29, 1962

Hill, John Calvin, Consul General, Ciudad Trujillo, Dominican Republic, May 28, 1961–January 5, 1962; Chargé d'Affaires ad interim, January 6–March 9, 1962

Hilsman, Roger, Jr., Assistant Secretary of State for Intelligence and Research, February 19, 1961–April 25, 1963; Assistant Secretary of State for Far Eastern Affairs from May 9, 1963

Home, Alexander Frederick Douglas, British Secretary of State for Foreign Affairs until October 1963; thereafter Prime Minister

Hoyt, Henry A., Minister Counselor and Counselor General, Embassy in Argentina, from January 1961; Chargé d'Affaires ad interim, October 1961–February 1962

Hughes, Thomas L., Deputy Assistant Secretary of State for Intelligence and Research to April 27, 1963; Assistant Secretary of State for Intelligence and Research from April 28, 1963

Hurwitch, Robert A., Deputy Director, Office of Caribbean and Mexican Affairs, Bureau of Inter-American Affairs, February–June 1962; Special Assistant for Cuban Affairs, June 1962–August 1963

Illia, Arturo, President of Argentina from October 1963
Imbert Barrera, Antonio, member, Dominican Council of State

Jagan, Cheddi, Prime Minister of British Guiana from September 5, 1961
Jagan, Janet, Minister of the Interior of British Guiana from June 17, 1963
Jamison, Edward A., Director, Office of Inter-American Regional Political Affairs, Bureau of Inter-American Affairs, until June 10, 1962
Johnson, U. Alexis, Deputy Under Secretary of State for Political Affairs from May 2, 1961
Jones, J. Wesley, Ambassador to Peru from February 1963
Jumelle, Gaston, political opponent of President Duvalier of Haiti

Katzenbach, Nicholas deB., Deputy Attorney General of the United States
Kaysen, Carl, Deputy Special Assistant to the President for National Security Affairs from November 1961
Kennedy, John F., President of the United States
Kennedy, Robert F., Attorney General of the United States
Khrushchev, Nikita S., Chairman of the Council of Ministers of the Soviet Union
Kitchen, Jeffrey C., Deputy Assistant Secretary of State for Politico-Military Affairs from May 1961
Krulak, Major General Victor H., Special Assistant, Director of the Joint Staff for Counter-Insurgency and Special Activities; Chairman, Committee on Cuban Subversion from February 27, 1963
Kubitscheck, Juscelino, former President of Brazil
Kyle, Joseph B., Office of the Deputy Coordinator for Foreign Assistance, Agency for International Development

Lancaster, Bruce M., officer in charge Argentine Affairs, Office of East Coast Affairs, Bureau of Inter-American Affairs, from June 1962
Lane, Samuel O., Deputy Director, Office of West Coast Affairs, Bureau of Inter-American Affairs to January 1962
Leddy, John M., member, Task Force on Latin America; Assistant Secretary of the Treasury for International Affairs
Legere, Colonel Lawrence J., Assistant to the President's Military Representative
Lemnitzer, General Lyman L., USA, Chairman, Joint Chiefs of Staff to September 30, 1962
Linder, Harold, U.S. Governor, Inter-American Development Bank; President, Export-Import Bank of the United States
Lindley Lopez, General Nicolas, Leader of Peruvian military junta, March–July 1963
Lleras Camargo, Alberto, President of Colombia until 1962
Llosa, Admiral Luis Edgardo, Minister of Foreign Affairs under the Peruvian military junta
Loeb, James I., Jr., Ambassador to Peru, May 23, 1961–July 26, 1962
Lopez Mateos, Adolfo, President of Mexico

MacLeod, Iain N., British Secretary of State for Colonies until October 9, 1961
Magloire, Paul E., President of Haiti, 1950–1956
Mann, Thomas C., Assistant Secretary of State for Inter-American Affairs to April 20, 1961;. Ambassador to Mexico from May 8, 1961
Margolies, Daniel F., Deputy Director, Office of East Coast Affairs, Bureau of Inter-American Affairs from January 1963
Mariani, Clemente, Brazilian Minister of Finance
Martin, Edwin M., Assistant Secretary of State for Economic and Business Affairs until May 17, 1962; Assistant Secretary of State for Inter-American Affairs from May 18, 1962

Martin, John Bartlow, special envoy to the Dominican Republic, September 1961; Ambassador to the Dominican Republic, March 1962–September 1963

Maulding, Reginald, British Secretary of State for Colonies, October 9, 1961–July 16, 1962

May, Herbert K., Chief, Latin America Division, Department of the Treasury to May 15, 1962; Deputy Assistant Secretary of State for Inter-American Affairs from May 16, 1962

Mazzili, Ranieri, interim President of Brazil, August 26, 1961–September 7, 1961

McClintock, Robert M., Ambassador to Argentina from February 1962

McCone, John A., Director of Central Intelligence from November 29, 1961

McGhee, George C., Counselor, Department of State, February 16–December 3, 1961; Director, Policy Planning Staff, February 13–November 29, 1961; Under Secretary of State for Political Affairs, November 29, 1961–March 27, 1963; Ambassador to the Federal Republic of Germnay from May 18, 1963

McGovern, George, Director, Food for Peace, 1961

McNamara, Robert S., Secretary of Defense

Melby, Everett K., Consul in Georgetown, British Guiana until January 1, 1962; Consul General until September 2, 1963

Miolan, Angel, Party Chief, Partido Revolucionairo Dominicano

Mora, Jose A., Uruguayan, Secretary General of the Organization of American States

Morales-Carrion, Arturo, member, Task Force on Latin America; Deputy Assistant Secretary of State for Inter-American Affairs from February 14, 1961

Moreira Salles, Walther, special emissary from Brazilian President Quadros to the United States, March 1961; Finance Minister from September 7, 1961

Morrison, DeLesseps S., Permanent Representative to the Organization of American States

Morse, Wayne L., Senator (D–Oregon), Chairman, Senate Foreign Relations Subcommittee on American Republics Affairs

Moscoso, Teodoro, member, Task Force on Latin America; Ambassador to Venezuela, May–November 1961; Assistant Administrator for Latin America, Agency for International Development, U.S. Coordinator for the Alliance for Progress

Moskowitz, Sam, officer in charge Colombian Affairs, Office of West Coast Affairs, Bureau of Inter-American Affairs, October 1961–February 1963

Muniz, Carlos Manuel, Argentine Foreign Minister, October 1962–October 1963

Murphy, Robert D., adviser to President Kennedy on matters concerning the Dominican Republic

Murrow, Edward R., Director, United States Information Agency

Musich, Arnaldo, adviser to Argentine President Frondizi

Neves, Tancredo, Prime Minister of Brazil, September 1961–January 1963

Newbegin, Robert, Ambassador to Haiti to December 1961

O'Connor, James F., officer in charge Argentine Affairs, Office of East Coast Affairs, Bureau of Inter-American Affairs, until July 1961

Odriá, Manuel, former President of Peru; candidate for the Peruvian Presidency, June 1962, June 1963

Oduber, Daniel, Foreign Minister of Costa Rica

O'Meara, General Andrew P., Commander in Chief, Caribbean

Perez Godoy, General Ricardo, leader of the Peruvian coup of July 18, 1962; leader of the Peruvian military junta to March 1963

Peron, Juan Domingo, former President of Argentina exiled to Spain

Perrete, Carlos Humberto, Vice President of Argentina from October 1963

Pico, Rafael, temporary adminstrator of U.S. financial assistance to the Dominican Republic in early 1962

Poole, Richard A., offficer in charge Peruvian Affairs, Office of West Coast Affairs, Bureau of Inter-American Affairs, from June 1962
Prado y Ugarteche, Manuel, President of Peru until July 18, 1962

Quadros, Janio, President of Brazil, January 31–August 25, 1961

Read, Benjamin H., Executive Secretary of the Department of State from August 4, 1963
Reid Cabral, Donald, Second Vice President of the Dominican Council of State, Foreign Minister under the Triumvirate
Rostow, Walt W., President's Deputy Special Assistant for National Security Affairs until November 29, 1961; thereafter Counselor of the Department of State and Chairman, Policy Planning Council
Rubin, Seymour J., General Counsel, International Cooperation Administration
Rubirosa, Porfirio, son-in-law of Generalissimo Rafael Trujillo
Rubottom, Roy R., Jr., Ambassador to Argentina until February 1962
Rusk, Dean, Secretary of State

Santos, Emilio de los, member of the Dominican Triumvirate
Sayre, Robert M., Executive Secretary of the Task Force on Latin America, officer in charge Mexican Affairs, Office of Caribbean and Mexican Affairs, Bureau of Inter-American Affairs, September 1961–April 1962; thereafter Special Assistant to the President
Schlesinger, Arthur M., Jr., Special Assistant to the President
Schwalb Lopez Aldana, Fernando, Foreign Minister of Peru under the Belaunde government
Shriver, Sargent, Director of the Peace Corps
Sloan, Frank K., Deputy Assistant Secretary of Defense for International Security Affairs
Smith, Bromley K., Acting Executive Secretary of the National Security Council until August 1961; thereafter Executive Secretary
Solis, Galileo, Foreign Minister of Panama
Sparks, Edward J., Ambassador to Venezuela until April 15, 1961; Ambassador to Uruguay from May 24, 1961
Spencer, George O., officer in charge Inter-American Security and Military Assistance, Office of Inter-American Regional Political Affairs, Bureau of Inter-American Affairs
Stephansky, Ben Solomon, Ambassador to Bolivia, June 29, 1961–October 15, 1963
Stevenson, Adlai E., U.S. Permanent Representative to the United Nations
Stewart, C. Allen, Counselor, Embassy at Caracas to February 1962; thereafter, Ambassador to Venezuela
Swank, Emory C., Special Assistant to the Secretary of State

Tapia, Ramone, member of the Dominican Triumvirate
Tavares, Manuel, member of the Dominican Triumvirate
Taylor, General Maxwell D., USA, President's Military Representative, June 1961–September 1962; Chairman, Joint Chiefs of Staff from October 1, 1962
Thurston, Raymond L., Ambassador to Haiti, January 1962–May 1963
Trujillo, Arismendi, brother of Generalissimo Rafael Trujillo
Trujillo, Hector Bienvenido, brother of Generalissimo Rafael Trujillo
Trujillo, Rafael Leonidas Martinez, Jr. ("Ramfis"), son of Generalissimo Trujillo
Trujillo y Molina, General Rafael Leonidas, Generalissimo and Commander in Chief, Dominican armed forces
Turnage, William V., Director, Office of Inter-American Regional Economic Affairs, Bureau of Inter-American Affairs, from June 11, 1961
Tyler, William R., Deputy Assistant Secretary of State for European Affairs until August 1962; thereafter Assistant Secretary

Ulloa, Manuel, special envoy of Peruvian President Belaunde to Washington, November 1963

Vance, Cyrus R., General Counsel of the Department of Defense, January 29, 1961–June 30, 1962; Secretary of the Army from July 5, 1962

Wellman, Harvey R., Director, Office of East Coast Affairs, Bureau of Inter-American Affairs, April 1961–August 1963

Wessin y Wessin, Colonel Elias, leader of Dominican coup of September 25, 1963

Wheeler, General Earle G., Chief of Staff, U.S. Army

Wheeler, Richard S., Deputy Director, Office of International Conferences, Bureau of International Organization Affairs, Department of State

Whiteman, Marjorie M., Assistant Legal Adviser for Inter-American Affairs, Office of the Legal Adviser

Whittaker, Arthur P., historian; member, Task Force on Immediate Latin American Problems

Williams, Haydn, Deputy Assistant Secretary of Defense for International Security Affairs

Williams, Newell F., Director, USAID mission to the Dominican Republic, spring 1962–September 28, 1963

Wilson, Jackson W., officer in charge Brazilian Affairs, Office of East Coast Affairs, Bureau of Inter-American Affairs, until October 1962

Woodward, Robert F., Assistant Secretary of State for Inter-American Affairs, July 17, 1961–May 17, 1962

ALLIANCE FOR PROGRESS

1. Editorial Note

Senator John F. Kennedy made his first address on Latin American affairs at a Democratic Party dinner in San Juan, Puerto Rico on December 15, 1958. In that speech he expressed solidarity with the Latin American peoples in their efforts to oppose Communist subversion in the region, endorsed the creation of an Inter-American Development Bank, the establishment of commodity agreements, land reform in Latin America, and expanded cultural and educational ties between the Latin American nations and the United States. For text of this speech, see the Kennedy Library, Pre-Presidential Papers, Speech File.

In September 1960, Presidential candidate Kennedy sought to establish a Latin American policy that distanced him from the Eisenhower–Nixon administration's regional diplomacy while stating affirmatively his intentions for the hemisphere. On a campaign trip through Texas in September 1960, Kennedy aide Richard N. Goodwin was struck by the title of the magazine *Alianza*, a Spanish language periodical published in the United States, as the possible basis for a phrase to describe Kennedy's views on a new U.S. policy toward Latin America. Further consideration and refinement led Goodwin to coin the phrase *Alianza para Progreso* (later *Alianza para el Progreso* or Alliance for Progress in English). Kennedy used the phrase for the first time in public during a campaign speech in Tampa, Florida, on October 18. (For a more complete discussion of the origins of the term Alliance for Progress, see Richard N. Goodwin, *Remembering America: A Voice From the Sixties*, Little Brown, 1988.) The text of Kennedy's Tampa speech is in the Kennedy Library, Pre-Presidential Papers, Tampa, Florida.

Following Kennedy's election in November, Goodwin coordinated Kennedy's establishment of a Task Force on Immediate Latin American Problems. It was chaired by former Assistant Secretary of State Adolf Berle and composed of Goodwin, Arturo Morales-Carrion and Teodoro Moscoso of the Puerto Rican Government, economist and Latin Americanist Lincoln Gordon of Harvard, political scientist Robert Alexander, and historian Arthur P. Whittaker. The Task Force was charged with evaluating U.S.-Latin American relations and prioritizing the tasks of the new administration in the region. It submitted its report to the President on January 4, 1961 (see Document 2).

Kennedy repeated his calls for an alliance for progress between the United States and its Latin American neighbors in his inaugural address of January 20. For text of the address, see *Public Papers of the Presidents of the United States: John F. Kennedy, 1961*, pages 1–3. In his first State of the

1

Union address on January 30, President Kennedy reemphasized his commitment to the Alliance for Progress. He urged the Congress to appropriate the $500 million pledged by the September 13, 1960, Act of Bogotá, and expressed his intention to appoint an interdepartmental task force on Latin America, strengthen the authority of the Organization of American States, abolish illiteracy in the hemisphere, and send a Food for Peace mission to Latin America (ibid., pages 19–28). For text of the Act of Bogotá, see Department of State *Bulletin*, October 3, 1960, pages 537–540.

The new Task Force on Latin America, again chaired by Berle, convened its first meeting on February 2; see Document 4.

---

2.   Report From the Task Force on Immediate Latin American Problems to President-elect Kennedy

Washington, January 4, 1961.

The Task Force on Immediate Problems of Latin America reports as follows:

I. Position of the new Administration: Basic Assumptions

Your campaign aroused high hopes in Latin America, based on your statements, on the cooperation achieved under President Roosevelt, and on prospects that the conflicts in the area (possibly approaching climax—an "historical moment") may find new solutions. Exaggerated visions have also been raised by the Communist press, perhaps to produce chaos-making disillusionment later. This offers opportunity for dramatic moves for the better.

In Moscow and Peiping revolutionary seizure of parts of Latin America appears to have been agreed on as an early target in the "Cold War" now active in the Caribbean littoral.

Substantial Latin American apprehension exists that the incoming Administration, while justifiably upgrading Asia and Africa, may continue to leave Latin America a step-child.

Source: Kennedy Library, Pre-Presidential Papers, Transition Series, Task Force Reports 1960, Latin America. No classification marking.

We think the incoming Administration promptly on inauguration should

(a) emphasize its vivid interest in Latin America,
(b) outline forcefully a line of approach,
(c) provide, administratively, top-level direction for Latin American problems.

Doctrine and Principle

We are agreed that the greatest single task of American diplomacy in Latin America is to divorce the inevitable and necessary Latin American social transformation from connection with and prevent its capture by overseas Communist Power politics. The specific offensive plan of the Soviet Union and China, measurably successful to date, has been to convert the Latin American social revolution into a Marxist attack on the United States itself. On its side, the United States has stated no clear philosophy of its own, and has no effective machinery to disseminate such a philosophy.

We recommend that the policy of the United States be erected on four basic propositions (the "philosophical principle" so sought by Latin Americans). These are:

(a) The imperative principle of human freedom. From this proceeds the obligation to maintain decent human rights, standards of conduct in dealing with individuals.
(b) Recognition that genuine freedom necessitates advancing social and economic well-being for everyone. Men are not free when enslaved by disease, ignorance, poverty, and inhuman conditions, or where their creative energies are thwarted by hopelessness.
(c) The principle that governments take their legitimacy from the free assent of their peoples and therefore can from time to time be changed without force. This carries with it the general conclusion that the only legitimate governments are freely elected governments.
(d) The principle that American governments shall not become either prisoners or tools of extra-American Power politics. The Western Hemisphere must remain master in its own house.

While transformations almost invariably involve economic problems affecting the United States, these can be resolved among men of good-will. Our experience with the Mexican and Bolivian revolutions proves this.

Basic Assumptions

1. That Latin America is and will continue to be an area of primary concern to the United States.

2. That the new Administration will undertake a new approach in dealing with the serious problems that already confront the United States in the Latin American field, and others that may arise.

3. That such an approach ought to be sought with confidence in the new Administration's success in improving substantially on the

approach followed by its predecessor, but also with recognition of the fact that the United States is neither omnipotent nor omniscient; that it cannot solve, but can only help the Latin Americans try to solve, most of the problems of their highly diversified region in their own way, and that its freedom of choice in this matter is subject to the limitations indicated below.

4.   That it is and will continue to be the policy of the United States to maintain and develop the O.A.S. within the framework of the United Nations and to respect its obligations as a member of both organizations.

5.   That the present ferment in Latin America, which facilitates Communist penetration, is the outward sign of a tide of social and political change the United States cannot and should not check. The United States can help well-disposed Americans (of whom there are many) to direct the transformation into channels that are, or ought to be, acceptable to it as well as beneficial to the people involved.

6.   That from the United States point of view, the present Communist challenge in Latin America resembles, but is more dangerous than, the Nazi-Fascist threat of the Franklin Roosevelt period and demands an even bolder and more imaginative response.

[Here follow Sections II, "Latin America in the Cold War," III, "Personnel Changes," IV, "Emergency Situations Requiring Immediate Action," V, "Approach to Economic and Social Policy," and VI, "American Orientation."]

3.   **Editorial Note**

In late January 1961 President Kennedy identified the need for a major Presidential address on Latin America and the Alliance for Progress. Assistant Special Counsel to the President Richard Goodwin was charged with drafting the speech, which was to be a distillation of the recommendations being made by the Task Force on Latin America. Following a series of informal meetings in the White House "fish room" (so-called because Franklin Roosevelt had kept his aquariums there) with members of the Task Force and representatives of other agencies associated with the administration's Latin America policy, and after numerous suggestions, both substantive and stylistic, by other members of the White House staff and Secretary of State Dean Rusk, Goodwin drafted the speech at his Washington home between March 7 and 10. Editorial revisions were made by the President on March 11. (See Goodwin, *Remembering America,* pages 146–159, and Arthur M. Schlesinger, Jr., *A Thousand Days: John F. Kennedy in the White House,* Boston, 1965, pages 202–205.)

---

4.   Memorandum of Meeting

LATF–M/1   Washington, February 2, 1961, 4:15 p.m.

TASK FORCE ON LATIN AMERICA

PARTICIPANTS

Adolf A. Berle, Jr., Chairman
Thomas C. Mann, Assistant Secretary of State for Inter-American Affairs
John M. Leddy, Assistant Secretary of the Treasury for International Affairs
Theodore C. Achilles, Counselor of Department of State
Lincoln Gordon, Consultant
Haydn Williams, Deputy Assistant Secretary of Defense for International Security Affairs
Wymberly Coerr, Deputy Assistant Secretary of State for Inter-American Affairs
Robert M. Sayre, Executive Secretary

The meeting commenced at 4:15 p.m.

Mr. Berle briefly explained the purpose of the Task Force. It is an action and not a study group, acting under the direction of the Secretary of State and the President. The Task Force does not supersede the Bureau of Inter-American Affairs which remains responsible for foreign policy operations with respect to Latin America. The Task Force is to insure that problems get the prompt attention of the Secretary of State and the President and that the decisions taken are carried out. It has the longer range responsibility of obtaining general agreement on policies and launching those policies.

[Here follows section 1, "Assistance to Brazil."]

2.   *Financial Resources for Latin American Area*

It was agreed that the request to the Congress for appropriations of $500 million to fulfill the U.S. commitment under the Act of Bogotá

Source: Department of State, Latin America Task Force Files: Lot 61 D 298, Task Force on Latin America, Minutes. Secret. Drafted by Sayre.

should be handled separately and not be included in the Mutual Security Program.

The Task Force discussed the question as to whether there should be included in a request for a contingency appropriation soon to be submitted to the Congress a request for $50 million to initiate the program. It was stated that ICA now has ready some $78 million in projects it can initiate immediately. No decision was reached.

The Task Force discussed the distribution of the $500 million fund between the Inter-American Bank and ICA. It had been tentatively agreed within the Executive Branch that $375 million would go to the Inter-American Bank. The Task Force agreed to seek a new decision from the present Administration which would either confirm or modify this division.

(Mr. Leddy departed at this time.)

[Here follow sections 3, "Arms Traffic in the Caribbean" and 4, "Cuba."]

---

5.   Draft Memorandum From the Consultant to the Task Force on Latin America (Gordon) to the President's Assistant Special Counsel (Goodwin)

Washington, March 6, 1961.

SUBJECT

  Key Issues for Presidential Address on the Inter-American Alliance for Progress

1. *Central Theme.* The keynote of the Alliance for Progress is a sustained effort for economic development and social progress, combining vigorous measures of self-help with the provision of complementary outside resources under the guidance and stimulation of greatly strengthened agencies for regional cooperation. We should embark on a decade of democratic progress, to demonstrate in this Hemisphere that economic growth, social equity, and the democratic development of societies can proceed hand-in-hand.

2. *Comparison with the Marshall Plan.* The concept of a long-term development program for Latin America inevitably brings to mind the

---

Source: Kennedy Library, National Security Files, Subjects, Alliance for Progress. Official Use Only.

post-war European Recovery Program. Many people, indeed, have spoken of the need for a "Latin American Marshall Plan." In most respects, this is a misleading analogy. The problems of overcoming an ancient heritage of poverty, widespread illiteracy, and grave social, economic and geographical imbalances in the development process are fundamentally different from those of engendering economic recovery in industrially advanced nations temporarily crippled by war. In Latin America, much greater emphasis must be placed on the necessarily slow processes of institutional reform. The effort will take much longer. The volume of annual outside assistance measured in financial terms will be smaller and technical cooperation in various fields will play a greater role.

Yet in by far the larger part of the Hemisphere, the physical and human resources make possible the achievement within a decade of self-sustaining economic and social development on a democratic basis. And in one major respect, the analogy of the Marshall Plan is fully applicable. That Plan served to focus the constructive energies of Europe on the urgent tasks of economic recovery and to replace despair by hope—a hope richly rewarded by the Plan's success. The Alliance for Progress must likewise energize the great reservoir of human talent in Latin America for the challenging task of securing growth with justice and freedom.

3. *Historical Background.* This program has not been conceived in a vacuum. For many years, various problems of Latin American economic and social development have been closely studied by the Latin American governments and private organizations immediately concerned, by agencies of the United Nations and the Organization of American States, and by United States officials, foundations, private enterprises, and individual citizens. Special studies made by members of Congress or commissioned by Congressional Committees have helped to lay a firm foundation for a new concerted effort. The Brazilian initiative for Operation Pan America gave special stimulus to Hemisphere-wide attention to these problems.[1]

The culmination thus far of these previous endeavors was the Act of Bogotá, subscribed by representatives of 19 of the 21 American Republics on September 12 of last year. This Act calls for a new and vigorous program of inter-American cooperation to achieve accelerated economic and social progress and thereby to strengthen free and democratic institutions. As a first step, acting in accordance with Congressional authority embodied in the American Republics Cooperation Act, the United States Government proposed to establish a special Inter-American Fund for Social Progress. Within a few days, we shall present to the Congress a

---

[1] For details of Operation Pan America, see *Foreign Relations*, 1958–1960, volume V.

specific request for the appropriation of $500 million to bring this Fund into being. Prompt and favorable action on this program is a matter of urgency.

Our further immediate task is to work out with our sister Republics the other programs of action to make a reality of the high purposes set forth in the Act of Bogotá.

4. *Country Programs for Economic and Social Development.* The foundation stones of the Alliance for Progress must be integrated country development programs which establish broad targets and priorities among and within the major sectors of the economy, paying due attention to public investment for social as well as economic purposes, which provide for internal monetary stability and external payments equilibrium, and which include the necessary legislative and administrative measures for mobilization of domestic resources and for improvements in such fields as tax structures, land tenure, credit institutions, and educational facilities. Only on such a foundation can outside resources be efficiently applied to complement the measures of self-help which must constitute the great bulk of the effort.

Some governments will be in a position to prepare such programs with their own resources; in some cases, indeed, excellent work in this direction has already been done. In other cases, governments will desire outside assistance for this purpose. This should be a primary task of the strengthened staff of the Inter-American Economic and Social Council, working in intimate association with the staffs of the Economic Commission for Latin America and the Inter-American Development Bank. The review and analysis of these programs, and of progress toward their implementation, should be the central objective of the annual consultative meetings of the Inter-American Economic and Social Council called for by Chapter IV of the Act of Bogotá.

[Here follow sections 5–11, "Functional Targets for Hemispheric Progress," "Trade Policy—Markets and Commodity Stabilization," "Latin American Economic Integration," "Inter-American Annual Reviews," "Operating Agencies for the Program," "Additional Resources from the United States," and "The Role of Private Enterprise."]

6.   **Memorandum From the President's Special Assistant (Schlesinger) to the President's Assistant Special Counsel (Goodwin)**

Washington, March 8, 1961.

SUBJECT

Latin American Speech

While the body of the speech must obviously deal with programs and purposes in the economic field, it is extremely important, in my judgment, that the speech *not* leave the broad impression that we regard economics as the be-all and end-all of existence. The Latinos want economic aid all right; but they resent the idea that money solves everything or that the major problems of life can be comprehended in material terms. So I hope that the economic matter can be put into a framework which makes it clear (a) that we are concerned with economics, not for its own sake, but to promote the higher aims of culture and the spirit, and (b) that, in our zest for economic growth, we do not propose to remake the other nations of the hemisphere in our own image.

To do this, it will be necessary to go in for a certain amount of high-flown corn. This will, I am sure, leave the President cold, but it will thrill the audience south of the border, where metahistorical disquisitions are inordinately admired.

I am attaching a few pages[1] in the hope that they may suggest something to you (but, if they don't fit your line of thought, please file them forthwith in the nearest wastebasket).

One other problem: I think it important not to make it all sound too easy. I doubt very much, for example, whether any aid program can put every child in the hemisphere effectively in school in ten years. At present, I gather, half those of school age never get to school at all; of those who do, half drop out at the end of the first year. Probably half the people in Latin America are presently illiterate. (On the other hand, excessive emphasis on mass illiteracy will offend Latin American sensibilities unless offset by recognition that Costa Rica and Uruguay are 90% literate, Chile and Argentina 80%, etc.)

The speech should suggest (a) the President's realistic understanding of the hard complexities of the problem, (b) the resources of will and material assistance which the US and the Latin American republics mean

---

Source: Kennedy Library, Schlesinger Papers, White House Files, Latin America, March 8, 1961–April 30, 1961. No classification marking.

[1] Not found.

to bring to the solution, and (c) the rather realistic goals which a massive coordination and concentration of effort might hopefully attain.

Arthur Schlesinger, jr.[2]

---

[2] Printed from a copy that bears this typed signature.

---

7.   Memorandum From the President's Special Assistant (Schlesinger) to President Kennedy

Washington, March 10, 1961.

Attached you will find a report on my recent visit to Latin America.[1] Because it is a long document, I will herewith summarize its main points.

The argument is that Latin America is irrevocably committed to the quest for modernization. This process of modernization cannot take place without a drastic revision of the semi-feudal agrarian structure of society which still prevails through much of the subcontinent. That revision can come about in two ways—through a middle-class revolution or through a "workers-and-peasants" (i.e., Communist or Peronista) revolution. It is obviously to the US interest to promote the middle-class revolution. Unfortunately the Latin America's landed oligarchy does not understand the gravity of its own situation. It constitutes the chief barrier to the middle-class revolution and, by thwarting the middle-class revolution, may well bring about the proletarian revolution.

The paper discusses the changes we should make in US policies in order to help the middle-class revolution. It then describes the forces arrayed against the attempt of the middle class from bringing about a peaceable reconstruction of Latin American society. Pages 11–13 contain an evaluation of Castro's present strength in Latin America.

Two appendices contain notes on the Latin American statesmen interviewed and on the US diplomats consulted along the way.

Arthur Schlesinger, jr.[2]

Source: Kennedy Library, Schlesinger Papers, White House Files, Latin America Report, March 10, 1961. Confidential. Copies were distributed to McGeorge Bundy, Walt W. Rostow, and Allen Dulles.

[1] Schlesinger accompanied Food for Peace Director George McGovern on a mission to Argentina, Brazil, Peru, Bolivia, Panama, and Venezuela.

[2] Printed from a copy that bears this typed signature.

Attachment

REPORT TO THE PRESIDENT ON LATIN AMERICAN MISSION
February 12–March 3, 1961

Part I. The Current Crisis in Latin America

In a famous quotation, German Arciniegas, the Colombian historian, once wrote, "There are two (Latin) Americas: the visible and the invisible." The invisible Latin America, Arciniegas said, is the Latin America of presidents, embassies, armies, navies, business offices, haciendas. This is, on the whole, manageable and predictable. It is the invisible Latin America which constitutes the mystery. This is "the mute, repressed America which is a vast reservoir of revolution. . . . Nobody knows exactly what these 150,000,000 silent men and women think, feel, dream or await in the depths of their being."

The problem of political ferment in Latin America is the consequence of the struggle of the invisible Latin America to move into the 20th century. To put the question less rhetorically, it is the problem of the peaceful incorporation into their national economic and political societies of a vast submerged population, largely Indian, which has existed for centuries *outside* both the money economy and party politics but which is now uneasily stirring with (and being ruthlessly stirred by) new aspirations and new expectations. To put it most concisely, it is the problem of the *modernization* of Latin American society.

The chief obstacle to modernization is the existence in many Latin American countries of an agrarian, semi-feudal economic structure. The chief guardians of this backward economic structure are the classes which benefit from it—the so-called landholding oligarchy which still more or less governs most of the continent, including especially the Andean nations of Chile, Peru, Ecuador and Colombia. So long as this structure exists, half the population of these countries will be excluded from their national societies and kept in poverty and illiteracy; and, so long as this structure exists, industrializations, economic growth and social mobility will be impossible.

What are the means of breaking the agrarian system? The most favorable means from the US viewpoint would be the *middle-class revolution* where the processes of economic modernization carry the new urban middle class into power and produce, along with it, such necessities of modern technical society as constitutional government, honest public administration, a responsible party system, a rational land system, an efficient system of taxation, mass education, social mobility, etc.

These middle-class revolutions arise typically out of a combination of technological change, entrepreneurial initiative (often set off by foreign capital) and statist doctrine. They are often accompanied by deceptively lurid nationalist-populist rhetoric. They range along the ideological spectrum from the Brazil of Kubitschek, where the bonds of the old agrarian society were burst by the sheer momentum of economic growth, to the Mexican Revolution of 1910, where the state broke the bonds under the banner of extreme revolutionary sloganeering. Betancourt is currently trying to carry out a middle-class revolution in Venezuela; Haya de la Torre has one in mind for Peru if he can win the election in 1962.

None of these Latin American revolutions has been complete. Even Mexico and Brazil, economically the two most dynamic countries, still have great areas of poverty, illiteracy and stagnation. Nonetheless in the last forty years the middle class has increased from 10 percent to perhaps 25–30 percent of the Latin American population—an increase reflected in the swing away from dictatorship and personalism and the increasing demand for stable free governments.

The pressing need in Latin America is to promote the middle-class revolution as speedily as possible. The corollary is that, *if the possessing classes of Latin America make the middle-class revolution impossible, they will make a "workers-and-peasants" revolution inevitable;* that is, if they destroy a Betancourt, they will guarantee a Castro or a Peron.

Part II. US Policy and the Middle-Class Revolution

The problem for US policy is to do what it can *to hasten the middle-class revolution.*

This task now has an extremely high degree of urgency. The main reasons for this urgency are as follows:

1) *Because population has been growing faster than output, in recent years, Latin America has begun to lose ground in the struggle for development.* Population has been increasing at a faster rate in Latin America in the last decade than in any other region in the world. In most Latin American countries the rate of increase during the fifties was two to three times that of the US. During this decade, the population of the 20 Latin American republics, which was about 132 million in 1945, rushed ahead of that of the US. Every indication is that this population explosion will continue. It is currently estimated that by 1975 Latin America will have a population of 303 million as against 240 million for Northern America, and that by 2000 the difference will be between 592 million and 312 million.

In the meantime, production has failed to keep pace with population growth. Latin American statistics are generally unreliable; but it would seem that, while per capita gross domestic product increased in the period 1948–56, it has since then begun to decline. Certainly so far as agricultural products are concerned, the per capita production may have fallen by as much as 6 percent. In general, Latin America will have to *double* its real income in the next thirty years to stay as poor as it is today.

Moreover, the disparity between the rich and the poor has increased, and—with the influx of the desperately poor into the cities—the contrast between luxury and squalor is becoming more visible and explosive than ever.

2) *The Soviet Union, in association with Cuba, is exploiting the situation and providing the US with unprecedented serious competition.* The hemisphere level of expectation continues to rise—stimulated both by the increase in conspicuous consumption and by the spread of the Castro idea of taking matters into one's own hand. At the same time, as living standards begin to decline, many people tend toward Communism both as an outlet for social resentment and as a swift and sure technique for social modernization. Meanwhile, the Soviet Union hovers in the wings, flourishing large development loans and presenting itself as the model for achieving modernization in a single generation.

3) *Time is running out for the parties of the middle-class revolution.* For a generation, the essential struggle in Latin America has been between the old oligarchy and the new proponents of middle-class society (including men in the social-democratic tradition like Betancourt, Figueres and Haya de la Torre as well as men in the liberal tradition like Lleras Camargo and Galo Plaza). This has been an indecisive fight. In the main, the landed classes have succeeded in blocking basic structural change. The democratic parties, in short, have thus far failed to deliver the goods to the satisfaction of the younger and more impatient members of the middle and working classes.

As a consequence, I found a disturbing tendency on the part of the younger intellectuals, for example, to regard parties like Accion Democratica (Venezuela) or APRA (Peru) as tired, played-out, irrelevant, the parties of the older generation—at the same time that the oligarchy in these countries continues to regard them as parties of red revolution. My guess is that, if the middle-class parties don't go over the goal line in the next decade, they will be finished, and the initiative will pass to parties committed to a drastic and violent radicalism.

4) *Latin America is waiting expectantly for new initiatives from Washington.* The election of President Kennedy and the return of the Democrats to power have given rise to enormous expectations throughout Latin America. The Inaugural Address evoked particular admiration. People are looking on JFK as a reincarnation of FDR. To a surprising degree, the slate has been wiped clean of past neglect and error. The atmosphere is set for miracles. There is consequently real danger that the intensity of present expectations may lead to future disappointments— though I am sure that, if the US government comes up with any reasonably developed interest and program, the present mood will continue.

The US must act very soon, in short, to reverse the recent decline in Latin America's economic position, to counter the increasingly adroit efforts of the Communists to exploit this situation and to reinforce the middle-class parties before their credit runs out.

What can the US do to hasten the middle-class revolution?

The policies may be divided for convenience into three categories: political; economic; and social. Obviously the more that these policies can be carried out through the OAS rather than as unilateral US decisions, the better. And obviously the applicability of these proposals will vary considerably from country to country.

Political. Here the main thing is familiar enough—to make it absolutely clear that we regard dictatorship and the suppression of popular rights as ultimately incompatible with the principles of the hemisphere. We can't start off on an anti-dictatorship crusade, and no doubt we will continue to have short-run dealings with dictators; but no one in the hemisphere should be under any illusion how the US feels about dictatorships in the long run. We should give every dictator a sense of impermanence. Along with this, we should encourage the OAS to concern itself with the ways and means of guaranteeing regular free elections in all countries of the hemisphere.

Moreover, we should give our positive and particular support to governments which seem likely to bring about the sort of middle-class revolution we regard as favorable to our own interests—countries where social reform and economic development promise to be attained through democratic means. Full backing for the Betancourt government of Venezuela, for example, might be the best possible way of convincing aspiring Latin Americans that the democratic road to national fulfillment is both more reliable and more agreeable than the Castro road.

Economic. Here we must place our main emphasis on *development*. This may not sound like a new departure; but for several Latin American countries, it will represent a radical change in US policy.

During the fifties the US Government, under the baleful influence of the International Monetary Fund, committed itself to the view in a number of cases that the first requirement was, not economic development, but financial stabilization. The consequences for Argentina, Chile and Bolivia were drastic deflationary programs which induced economic stagnation, lowered living standards and finally brought about an entirely predictable pro-Communist reaction. Today Frondizi is politically on the ropes in Argentina; the pro-Communist parties are making impressive gains in Chile; and Communist penetration of the MNR party in Bolivia has proceeded apace. Of course, each country presented its own problems; the case for catharsis after the Peron years in Argentina was much stronger than the case for austerity in Bolivia, a country where there are no savings to be protected from inflation. An unchecked inflation is obviously a grave social danger. But the point is the prevailing belief of the fifties that stabilization and development were competing alternatives. As a US Assistant Secretary of State for Inter-American Affairs told the House Committee on Foreign Relations with regard to Bolivia in testifying on the Mutual Security Act of 1960, "We had to tell the Bolivian Government that they couldn't put their money into it (the development program) and we weren't going to put ours into it."

The IMF argument, of course, is that stabilization will ultimately bring about development by attracting foreign capital. Unfortunately this process hasn't worked in any of the three countries mentioned. On the other hand, Brazil, which defied the Fund in the fifties, has had, along with a serious inflation, a genuine economic expansion. Today Brazilian GNP is probably about four times that of Argentina.

In short, the IMF policy has *not* produced economic growth. It has probably retarded the middle-class revolution. It has certainly increased anti-US feeling, since the Fund's location in Washington means that many people in Latin America assume it to be an arm of the US Government. Its programs have demonstrably resulted in political gains for the far left. It is surely time to dissociate US policy from the Fund and its mechanical application of deflationary remedies. (It would be better still to begin to moderate the policy of the Fund; a good first step would be to appoint someone like Seymour Harris as US Executive Director.)

Development, of course, is a broad term. It requires a substantial capital outlay from the US; it also requires careful consideration of the uses to which that capital outlay should be put. We must, for example, be prepared to give more assistance than we have in the past to *industrialization*. For one thing, industrialization is the shortest way to promote the rise of the new middle class on which our political hopes in Latin America must rest. Also, in the long run industrialization, far from destroying the market for US industrial exports, will probably (if the experience of other markets holds true) enrich the countries industrialized and *increase* their purchases from the US. Our policies have been geared too long to the thesis that Latin America should be essentially a producer and exporter of primary commodities—a thesis which, of course, gratifies the landholding oligarchy and convinces the apostles of modernization that we plan to keep Latin America in perpetual colonial servitude. In this connection, we must surely abandon the doctrinaire position that we will make loans to private corporations but that, when a Latin American government wishes to develop its own petroleum or electric power resources, the United States can make no loans to state-owned enterprise. Private enterprise has a most important role to play in Latin America. But we complicate our life immeasurably if we regard it as the *sole* engine of economic development and thereby appear to convert our own government into an instrument of American business interests.

Industrialization is only one part of the strategy of development. It must be accompanied by simultaneous action on a number of other fronts if it is not to aggravate economic disparities and social tensions. For example, industrialization at the expense of necessary investment in agriculture and transportation can cause dangerous imbalance in a national economy. To maintain this balance—and to introduce a larger measure of predictability into economic calculations—it would seem useful to explore the possibilities of commodity stabilization agreements to protect countries whose whole foreign exchange position depends on one or two export crops. Moreover, since most of the increase in GNP will go to feed new mouths, these countries can accumulate capital for investment only if they can sell their primary commodities to industrial countries at adequate prices.

The problem of industrialization is closely related to the structure of land ownership. Through much of Latin America, the existing land system, as we have seen, is a main barrier against the modernization of society. In effect, the land system imprisons a large part of the population, cutting it off from effective participation in the economic or political life of the nation. For generations, people accepted this condition as a law of nature. Now increasing numbers refuse to take it any longer. In Peru the Indians are moving onto the large estates and squatting on land sites. In northeast Brazil the *Ligas Camponeses* of Francisco Juliao are mobilizing the peasants and urging them to assert their "rights." In Brazil, Venezuela, Peru and other countries, people are flocking out of the country into the shocking shanty-towns which already ring Rio, Caracas and Lima and which promise to become extremely dangerous centers of political unrest.

The only way to control such movements is to set in motion effective programs of *land reform*. But unadorned land reform—i.e., the redistribution of land to the peasants—by itself may do more harm than good. It must be accompanied by programs to increase the productivity of small farms—which means especially *"supervised credit"*, a combination of credit and agricultural extension work, along the lines of the Farm Security Administration in the thirties and of the Japanese land reform in the late forties. If land reform programs threaten to reduce output for a year or two until the new system begins to take hold, the US Food for Peace program can play a valuable role in supplying food for the period of transition.

The problem of land reform is closely bound up with the need for a *reform in tax systems*. The typical Latin American tax system is based on (a) import duties and (b) excise and sale taxes. In recent years, there have been rather rudimentary efforts to impose income taxes, largely evaded. There has also been some use of export duties (as in Chile, Salvador and Guatemala). Corporate income taxes are generally below US levels.

The obvious omission in this recital is land. In most countries tax on land is nonexistent or negligible. The result is a highly regressive system in which the landed oligarchy pays an exceedingly small proportion of its income in taxation. Because the tax on land is so inconsiderable, capital naturally rushes into land, which bids up land values and results in artificially high land prices. This means that the poor can never afford to buy land. It means also that expropriation with compensation at prevailing rates would result in terrifically inflated claims against the national treasury.

Tax reform thus is potentially a most significant key to agrarian change. An effective land tax could do much to reduce resistance to land reform. The state of Sao Paulo in Brazil recently enacted a law imposing a tax on landholders whose land was not in efficient cultivation; the idea, of course, was to induce them either to put their land into cultivation or else to divest themselves of it to small-holders. It is interesting to note that this law had the strong support of the Sao Paulo business community.

All these necessities—industrialization, land reform, tax reform— are thus intimately connected and require simultaneous action. The result of action on these fronts would be to encourage economic diversification, lay the basis for a small farmer class in the country and a business class in the city, and thereby advance the middle-class revolution.

Social. Activity in a number of areas is required to give the middle-class revolution logistic support. Transport, public health and housing are all essential. For example, Brazil today has (I am told) fewer miles of paved roads than Vermont. There is need in every Latin American republic, except Argentina, for speedy development of internal transportation—not only railroads but farm-to-market and other access roads. The needs in public health and housing are too evident to call for elaboration.

Most important of all is education. At present (despite such countries as Costa Rica, Uruguay and Argentina), Latin America remains 40 percent illiterate. Half of the children of school age never get to school; of those who do, half drop out at the end of the first year. Only about 5 percent complete primary school. The institutions of higher education are handicapped by a tradition of university organization which gives excessive control to the students and depends to a considerable degree on a part-time faculty. Of those students who do get to the universities, too many become lawyers and accountants; too few become engineers, scientists, agronomists, metallurgists, veterinarians. The condition of technical education is abysmally low throughout the continent. Argentina's economy, for example, has been organized for generations around livestock; but its universities offer no degrees in animal husbandry. Public administration, business administration, industrial engineering—all are virtually unknown. Obviously modernization requires a massive redevelopment with US and OAS help of the Latin American educational system, not only because literacy is indispensable to a middle-class society, but because trained technical personnel are indispensable to rapid economic growth.

It is extremely important to keep a proper balance between the programs of economic and social investment. We encountered repeatedly in Latin America the fear that the creation of the Bogota social fund meant that US interest was shifting from economic to social investment. When we pointed out that economic growth resulted in the main from improved productivity and that productivity depended on education and research and that therefore schools, for example, were a good thing, the answer came obstinately back that steel mills were more important. It is no doubt true that some countries, like Bolivia, have overdone their provisions for social investment at the expense of heavy capital investment. Yet social investment remains of fundamental importance in the advance toward a middle-class society.

Beyond the specific issues of social investment, there remains the broader question of the cultural setting in which these policies seek to operate. The Latin Americans tend to regard the United States as a materialistic nation, a paradise of Babbits. At the turn of the century the Uruguayan Jose Enrique Rodo in his influential book *Ariel y Caliban* argued that the Latin role was to play Ariel to the US Caliban. Rodo wrote of the US, "Its prosperity is as immense as its incapability of satisfying even a mediocre view of human destiny. Titanic in its concentration of human will-power, with unprecedented triumphs in all spheres of material aggrandizement, its civilization yet produces as a whole a singular impression of insufficiency, of emptiness." The Latins see themselves as Greeks, the North Americans as Romans.

Our policies, to have their full effect, must take account of this Latin American attitude. We must take every opportunity to show that we do *not* regard economics as the be-all and end-all of existence. We must make it clear that we are concerned with material abundance, not for its own sake, but to promote the higher aims of culture and civilization. We must also make it clear that, in our zest for economic growth and the middle-class revolution, we do not propose to remake the other nations of the hemisphere in our own image. We must show our respect for the distinctive cultures and traditions of the other American republics. Our proposals should derive ultimately from a generous vision of the diverse spiritual potentialities of a united hemisphere.

[Here follow Part III, "Obstacles to the Middle Class Revolution" and an appendix conveying Schlesinger's personal impressions of the Latin American heads of state with whom he met.]

Arthur Schlesinger, jr.[3]

---

[3] Printed from a copy that bears this typed signature.

8.   Editorial Note

On March 13, 1961, in the East Room of the White House, President Kennedy addressed the assembled diplomatic representatives of the Latin American countries in Washington and a bipartisan group of U.S. Congressmen to outline a 10-year, 10-point program for the Alliance for Progress. For text of the address, see *Public Papers of the Presidents of the United States: John F. Kennedy, 1961*, pages 170–175. The following day Kennedy delivered a special message to Congress requesting the appropriation of the $500 million U.S. commitment to the Act of Bogotá and the Inter-American Fund for Social Progress. (Ibid., pages 176–181)

---

9.   Memorandum by the Acting Executive Secretary of the National Security Council (Smith)

Washington, March 20, 1961.

CHECKLIST OF PROGRAMS AND ACTIONS TO IMPLEMENT THE TEN-YEAR PLAN FOR THE AMERICAS

1.   Initiate the massive planning effort required by the 10-year plan.

a.   Convoke a Ministerial meeting of the Inter-American Economic and Social Council promptly.

b.   Greatly strengthen the Council in order that it may become the central planning body for the plan.

c.   Formulate for early presentation to the Council detailed procedures for developing for each Latin American state its long-range economic plan.

(1) Such country plans will:

(a) Establish targets and priorities;
(b) Ensure monetary stability;
(c) Establish machinery for vital social change;
(d) Stimulate private activity and initiative; and
(e) Provide for a maximum national effort.

(2) Such plans will be the foundation of all development efforts.
(3) Such plans will provide the basis for the allocation of outside resources.

d.   Assemble under the direction of the Council, working with the Economic Commission for Latin America and the Inter-American Bank, the leading economists and experts of the Hemisphere, who will:

Source: Kennedy Library, National Security Files, Latin America. No classification marking.

(1) Help each country devise its own development plans, and;

(2) Provide a continuing review of economic progress in the Hemisphere.

2. Attack the social barriers which block economic progress by committing, as soon as appropriated, the $500 million Inter-American Fund for Social Progress (the Bogota fund) to:

a. Combat illiteracy;
b. Improve the productivity and use of land;
c. Wipe out disease;
d. Attack archaic tax and land tenure structures;
e. Provide educational opportunities; and
f. Initiate projects designed to make the benefits of increasing abundance available to all.

3. Support the economic integration of Latin America in order to create larger markets and competitive opportunity:

a. Provide full backing for the Central American common market; and
b. Promote the creation of free trade areas in South America.

4. Initiate the cooperative case-by-case examinations of Latin American commodity market problems for the purpose of finding practical methods of ending frequent violent changes in prices of commodities produced in Latin America.

5. Expand the Food for Peace emergency program by:

a. Helping to establish food reserves in areas of recurrent drought;
b. Providing school lunches; and
c. Offering feed grains for use in rural development.

6. Develop programs to ensure that all people of the Hemisphere share in the expanding benefits of modern science:

a. Invite Latin American scientists:

(1) To work with American scientists in new projects, such as in medicine, agriculture, physics and astronomy;

(2) To help plan regional research laboratories.

b. Strengthen cooperation between American universities and laboratories.
c. Expand existing science teacher-training programs to include Latin American instructors.
d. Assist in establishing science teacher-training programs in other American countries.
e. Translate and make available new teaching materials in physics, chemistry, biology and mathematics.

7. Rapidly expand the training of those needed to man the economies of rapidly developing countries by:

a. Expanding the technical training programs, using the Peace Corps wherever needed; and

b. Assisting Latin American universities and research institutions.

8. Actively seek to increase confidence in the collective security system of the Organization of American States in order to permit a sensible limitation of arms.

a. Devote to constructive use a share of those Latin American resources now spent on arms; and
b. Use existing Latin American armies not only to defend their countries, but to build them.

9. Invite Latin Americans to contribute to the enrichment of life and culture of the U.S. by:

a. Obtaining Latin American teachers to teach their literature, history and tradition in U.S. educational institutions;
b. Increasing opportunities for U.S. students to attend Latin American universities; and
c. Increasing access to Latin American music, art and philosophy.

10. Develop ways of making clear to the Latin Americans that:

a. Assistance from the social fund will depend not merely on need, but on the demonstrated readiness of each government to make the institutional improvements which promise lasting social progress.
b. Outside resources will be focussed on projects which have the greatest multiplying effect on (1) mobilizing domestic resources; (2) contributing to institutional reform; and (3) reducing the major obstacles to a development in which all can share. To this end:

(1) Provide assistance for improving land usage only to those nations in which the benefits will accrue to the great mass of rural workers.

(2) Increase housing for middle income groups through improved credit mechanisms.

(3) Expand mass housing through self-help projects by:

(a) Providing low cost materials, land and technical guidance:
(b) Using the owner's labor to construct his house; and
(c) Repaying costs of materials with long term mortgages.

(4) Broaden educational opportunities by

(a) Self-help school construction, and
(b) Use of local people as part-time teachers.

(5) Improve rural living conditions by encouraging higher and more diversified agricultural production; better distribution of wealth and income, and wider sharing in the process of development:

(a) Establish rural credit facilities;
(b) Help finance resettlement in new lands;
(c) Construct access roads to new settlement sites;

(d) Conduct agricultural surveys; and

(e) Introduce agricultural extension surveys.

11. Develop specific guidance for the administration of funds by the Inter-American Development Bank to reflect the principles stated in paragraph 10.

a. Administer $394 million of the Bogota Fund under a special trust agreement with the U.S.

b. Insure that most of these funds will be used to make loans with flexible terms, including low interest rates for repayment in local currency.

c. Insure that the bank's major fields of activity will be:

(1) Land settlement and improved land use.

(2) Housing.

(3) Water supply.

(4) Sanitation.

(5) Technical assistance related to the mobilizing of domestic financial resources.

12. Direct the International Cooperation Administration to develop specific criteria for administration of its funds to reflect the principles stated in paragraph 10.

a. Program $100 million for activities which are generally not self-liquidating by developing grants for:

(1) Education and training;

(2) Public health projects; and

(3) Strengthening general governmental services in fields related to economic and social development.

ASSIGNMENTS TO CARRY OUT THE NEW LATIN AID PROGRAM

1. Assign the responsibility for this program to a senior officer or group of officers in the government through whom Presidential authority and responsibility may be exercised and whom the President can hold responsible for the execution of the program which involves such a tremendous variety of public and private organizations and resources.

2. See that State, USIA and CIA pull out all the stops on an information program built around the Kennedy speech at the White House reception and the aid message. The output of all the official and unattributed media in Latin America should be reviewed in light of the new effort—objectives, courses of action, slogans, program emphases, should be cranked into the output. This information program must be in depth and ways should be found to getting all of the official and unofficial spokesmen for the government and the country to be coherently together on a continuing basis. The "Alliance for Progress" must become

as well-known as the "Monroe Doctrine" and the "Good Neighbor Policy."

3. See that instructions are issued through proper channels to the Departments of Health, Education and Welfare; Labor; Agriculture; Commerce; Interior; Defense and the National Science Foundation so that they can participate constructively in planning, program execution, and staffing.

4. In addition, the above agencies must undertake activities in the U.S. directed towards mobilizing the private components of the program—the foundations, universities and U.S. business enterprises—to play their part.

---

10.   Memorandum From the Chairman of the Task Force on Latin America (Berle) to President Kennedy

Washington, April 25, 1961.

SUBJECT

Hemispheric Policy

After reviewing all the apparent possibilities in the hemispheric situation, I suggest the following policy:

I. *Isolation of Cuba*, now to be considered a Communist bloc country.

1. Maintain close Navy patrol with orders to stop suspicious shipping.
2. Work out political bilateral defense pacts with those governments in the Caribbean area we believe subject to possible attack. Such agreements should provide for

(a) immediate military assistance in case of attack from outside these countries or attacks from the inside determined by either party to be inspired, stimulated or directed by the Communist bloc, in which Cuba must presently be included,

(b) prompt continuing cooperation in police arrangements to prevent, interrupt or seize arms, agitation and break up bloc organization and financing from within the Communist bloc.

Source: Department of State, Latin America Task Force Files: Lot 61 D 298, The President. Secret. Sent through Goodwin.

3. Invoke the *Trading with the Enemy Act*[1] in respect of Cuba. Revive measures under which the United States in the pre-World War II period, controlled trade in Latin America so that American trade shall not benefit Communist sympathizers or agents. Hemisphere-wide machinery for this purpose will have to be re-established.

4. Guardedly treat American financial aid to Latin American governments on a case by case basis so that in general we help our friends.

5. Call a meeting of O.A.S. and lay down a doctrine.

Alliance for Progress

II. *Call the IA–ECOSOC meeting* to organize the Alianza para el Progreso as soon as possible.[2] Consideration should be given Montevideo as meeting place; Uruguay has already intimated to us that it would be glad to be host to such a meeting.

In this invitation, emphasis should be given to three heads:

(a) education,
(b) social measures,
(c) economic development,

in that order.

Behind this is a great deal of detailed information and calculation. It implies a commitment to do a great deal of work in American organization. The mobilization of Latin American political parties presently in progress is one very hopeful line. On our side, we must also reorganize our propaganda so that it is more than mere "information"; our cultural work so that American books can be bought as cheaply as Communist books; our educational exchanges so that they reach into the high schools as well as the universities under men actually interested in students and capable of choosing the ablest, and generally capable of making contact with youth. Possibly the Peace Corps could be of help here. Our embassies in general are not so staffed at present.

Appropriations

This, I think, is the time to ask a very large fund at discretion of the President. I should suggest $2 billion. I think the Congress is in a mood to consider such a proposal.

Organization

This also is the time to free the financial and economic machinery we now have from a tremendous cobweb of legislation, agreements with

---

[1] P.L. 91, approved October 6, 1917; for text and revisions, see 40 Stat. 411 as amended.

[2] For details of the planning of the IA–ECOSOC extraordinary meeting, see Document 12.

Congressional committees and so forth, which for practical purposes inhibit rapid motion in any direction.

In practice this would mean:

(a) Discretion of the President to direct loans from the EXIM Bank;

(b) Discretion of the President to direct uses to be made of the ICA money and the PL 480 money, and the handling of the military assistance program;

(c) The President should have power to allocate from his discretionary fund money for use by these agencies in reorganized form;

(d) Consideration should be given to appointing a Chief of Hemispheric Operations who as deputy for the President might give instructions, directions and authorizations. Preferably he should be operating in policy matters under your general direction.

This, though not all-inclusive, covers some immediate steps which I think should be taken. It puts our operation in the hemisphere on a Cold War basis—thereby recognizing the actual situation.

In the current situation, it appears easiest to reach for the guns. But military operation now would obviously be a very bloody business and the losses in hemisphere support might be greater even than the gains of victory.

At the moment, hemisphere anti-Castrista sentiment is rising. The pro-Castro and Communist demonstrations have been turned out to be surprisingly weak. Faced with possibility of lack of defense by or in conjunction with the United States, and the reality of living undefended against the Communist bloc, Latin American sentiment is rather rapidly swinging towards the United States. In a period of time (it might possibly be a year or less) measures could be taken which are not practical today. I do not anticipate any immediate moves from Cuba against anyone; they would justify military intervention on a scale which the Cubans could not remotely meet, and they are clearly unsure how far the bloc would go in supporting them (so, I think, is the bloc). Khrushchev's letter strongly suggests behind its bluster endeavor to give assurance that the bloc would not establish missile bases—though it is difficult to say whether the assurances are worth anything or not.

The polarization between the Soviet bloc and the Alianza para el Progreso has been forced by the Cuban failure.[3] Everyone now knows what the alternatives are. I am clear the Alianza para el Progreso will polarize an already great and growing support.

A. A. Berle[4]

---

[3] Reference is to the attempted Bay of Pigs invasion; for documentation, see volume X.

[4] Printed from a copy that bears this typed signature.

11.   Memorandum of Conversation

Washington, May 24, 1961.

SUBJECT

Ambassador Stevenson's Trip to Latin America

PARTICIPANTS

The President
The Secretary of State
Ambassador Adlai E. Stevenson
Assistant Secretary Harlan Cleveland

The following is a summary of consensus and action and not a detailed record of a meeting which lasted about an hour and a half on several subjects.

The President expressed the view that Ambassador Stevenson should take the proposed trip to Latin America. He made or agreed to the following arrangements regarding the trip:

Purpose.

The purpose of the trip is *not* to encourage common action against Cuba nor to explain about the Cuban episode. The announced purposes will be to consult with our South American neighbors on the policy and proposals set forth in the President's speech to the Latin American Ambassadors at the White House, on the Alianza para Progreso, and the speech by President Kennedy to the Council of the Organization of American States at the Pan American Union on April 14.[1]

The purposes of the trip are therefore to (a) lay the groundwork for the meeting of IA–ECOSOC in Montevideo; (b) to seek ways to improve economic and social and political cooperation in a hemisphere which needs to be more tightly bound together through cooperation in all spheres and (c) to consult with our Latin American friends on a wide range of matters of special interest to Governor Stevenson as the U.S. Ambassador to the United Nations.

Both the announcement and the background guidance given to the press should stress that this trip is not for the purpose of developing a hemispheric conference of Foreign Ministers to mobilize against Cuba, or anything of the sort. It was agreed that political action of this type and

---

Source: Kennedy Library, National Security Files, Stevenson Trip to Latin America. Secret. Drafted by Cleveland on May 25 and approved by M. Manfull of S/S the same day. A note on the source text reads: "not cleared by the President or the Secretary." The meeting was held at the White House.

[1] For text, see *Public Papers of the Presidents of the United States: John F. Kennedy, 1961,* pp. 276–279.

at this level is not in the cards for the time being, at least before the ECO-SOC meeting. The President emphasized that the purpose of U.S. policy was not in any sense "retaliation" against Cuba; that he looked to the future, not the past; and that the less said for the time being about Cuba the better.

In the course of the discussion of the idea that the President might personally visit the ECOSOC meeting, the President expressed the view that such a visit should be at the end of the Conference, and not decided on and announced beforehand in order to avoid a confrontation with Castro which would be to Castro's benefit. The Secretary of State recommended, and the President agreed that no decision whatever should be made about the President's participation in the Montevideo Conference until about July 1, after Ambassador Stevenson had returned from his trip.

There was a brief discussion of the tractors-for-prisoners proposal.[2] The President directed that a collection of editorials in the hemisphere press on the subject, which Edward R. Murrow had showed him, should be made available to the American press.

---

[2] This was a plan to supply American-built tractors to the Cuban Government in exchange for the release of prisoners taken during the failed Bay of Pigs invasion. See volume X.

---

12.   Memorandum From the President's Assistant Special Counsel (Goodwin) to President Kennedy

Washington, June 12, 1961.

RE

Planning for the Alliance for Progress Meeting

The planning for the Alliance for Progress Meeting in Montevideo has proceeded along the following major lines.

1.   On March 13 you proposed the Alliance for Progress and called for an IA–ECOSOC Meeting as the first major step in its implementation.[1]

Source: Kennedy Library, President's Office Files, Staff Memoranda, Goodwin. No classification marking.

[1] See Document 8.

2. On April 14 you said that the meeting should be held early this summer; and shortly thereafter your delegate to the OAS proposed July 14.[2]

3. During the same week in April, Lincoln Gordon and I met in Rio with Jorge Sol (Chief of the IA–ECOSOC staff), Raul Prebisch (Chief of the UN Commission for Latin America), and Felipe Herrera (President of the Inter-American Bank). Out of this intensive series of discussions, lasting a week, emerged a general consensus on the objectives of the July meeting—what we hoped to accomplish, a proposed agenda, and the manner in which the preparatory work would be organized.

4. Immediately thereafter this agreed agenda was presented by the U.S. to the O.A.S. and adopted with minor modifications.[3]

5. At the same time the White House requested our own economic people to prepare some specific plans for commodity price stabilization to be ready for the July meeting.

6. Pursuant to the agreements reached at Rio a series of OAS–ECLA–Inter-American Bank task forces were assembled to do the work preparatory to the meeting. I believe it can be said that this was the best Inter-American group of economists ever assembled; including Gerhard Colm and Al Hirschman from the U.S. and leading economists from almost every country in Latin America. The coordination from the U.S. side was done by Lincoln Gordon and I worked closely with Gordon. (When Gordon had to leave I asked Dick Ruggles of Yale to take over, which he did.)

7. The task forces have now completed work on papers for nearly all the points on the agenda. They are first rate.

8. Last Thursday[4] there was a White House meeting with representatives from State and Treasury. At this meeting it was agreed that we would proceed—on the basis of these papers—to draft the "Charter of Montevideo"—a four or five page statement which we would want the meeting to adopt as its final result, setting forth the framework for the Alliance, goals, commitments, and machinery for planning.

9. This paper is now being circulated and should be in final form—for your approval—shortly.

10. We would hope to circulate this document to Latin American governments in advance of the July 15 meeting.

Richard N. Goodwin[5]

---

[2] These meetings were apparently conducted during the week the governors of the Inter-American Development Bank met in Rio de Janeiro. Information about that week's activities is in Department of State, Central File 033.1100–Di.

[3] The agenda was adopted unanimously by the Council of the OAS on May 31 as described in Circular CA–10391 of the same day. (Ibid., 371.8/5–3161)

[4] June 8.

[5] Printed from a copy that bears this typed signature.

13.   **Memorandum From the President's Special Assistant (Schlesinger) to President Kennedy**

Washington, June 27, 1961.

SUBJECT

Bureau of Inter-American Affairs, Department of State

I had a long talk yesterday with Dr. Arturo Morales-Carrion, Deputy Assistant Secretary of State for Inter-American Affairs. Morales is an intelligent and balanced man who discussed his Bureau with reluctance but in the conviction that he owed the White House a frank report on the situation.

The Foreign Service officers in Latin American affairs, according to Morales, constitute a tightly-knit club of men who believe that they alone know Latin America, who have enjoyed an undisturbed monopoly for a long time and who now keenly resent the intervention of "outsiders" in the field. Their attitudes are entrenched, their minds are set, and they regard new approaches and ideas with automatic skepticism. They are predominantly out of sympathy with the *Alianza*.

"The President's vision of Latin American policy," Morales says, "is bound to be defeated when the men running the day-to-day operations are unsympathetic with that vision. To get change in Latin America, you must have people committed to change. Among this group there is no joy, no purpose, no drive. 'What is our headache today?' is their attitude. They form a sullen knot of resistance to fresh approaches. They have no realization of the forces at work in Latin America today. They do not understand that our policy can succeed only as it enlists the support of the democratic left. They have no sympathy for the democratic left. They are uninterested in the intellectual community of Latin America or in the labor movement. They very rarely even see Latin Americans in Washington except on formal and bureaucratic occasions.

"All they do is sit around the table discussing things. When something comes up, they talk for hours and end up with ten reasons for doing it and twelve for not doing it. They have no instinct for decision or action.

"We have been striving for a new look in Latin America. But, if our operating people exhibit the same old attitudes and use the same old clichés, we are going to look in Latin America like the same old crowd."

Morales says that, so far as he himself is concerned, he feels practically immobilized. He says that he has "pleaded" for a definition of his

Source: Kennedy Library, Schlesinger Papers, White House Subject File, Alliance for Progress. Confidential. Copies were sent to Goodwin and Attorney General Kennedy.

area of responsibility, but has never received any serious statement of functions. At first, he feared that he was being discriminated against as a Puerto Rican; but, as he saw the attitude of the regulars toward Goodwin, Gordon and Schlesinger, he realized that he was being discriminated against as an intruder. He says that his personal relations have been cordial and courteous. He is coming to feel, however, that he will probably be more useful to the *Alianza* outside the government than within. I urged him to wait for a few more months and see whether the situation does not improve.

Recommendation. When Bob Woodward[1] comes, you might want to consider calling him in, telling him that the *Alianza* is the heart of our Latin American policy, that you expect ARA to overflow with affirmative commitment to the *Alianza,* and that those who think it is all nonsense should be transferred to some place where they will be happier.

Arthur Schlesinger, jr.[2]

---

[1] Reference is to Robert F. Woodward who became Assistant Secretary of State for Inter-American Affairs on July 17.

[2] Printed from a copy that bears this typed signature.

---

14.   Report From the Representative to the United Nations (Stevenson) to President Kennedy

Washington, June 27, 1961.

REPORT TO THE PRESIDENT ON SOUTH AMERICAN MISSION, JUNE 4–22, 1961

I.   *Introduction*

During the period of June 4–22, 1961, I visited each of the ten capitals of South America to consult with the Presidents and leading government officials on plans for advancing the "Alliance for Progress" and possibilities of collective action to defend the Western hemisphere against Communist penetration and subversion, including indirect aggression through Cuba. I was accompanied by Ambassador Ellis O. Briggs, Pro-

---

Source: Department of State, Central Files, 033.1100–ST. Secret. Transmitted to the President under cover of a June 28 memorandum from Stevenson.

fessor Lincoln Gordon, and a supporting staff from the Department of State.

Our mission received everywhere remarkably effective support from our resident Ambassadors and their staffs, as well as excellent briefing and background materials prepared in advance in the Department of State. I should like also to express my gratitude for the way in which our travels were handled by Major Conover and the crew of MATS Constellation 254.

[Here follow Parts II, "Political Appreciation" and III, "Communist Castro Influence."]

IV. *Preparations for Economic Conference and Alliance for Progress*

We encountered a unanimous and intense interest in the Alliance for Progress. Your March 13 address was described as having created a profound impression in Latin America—the most favorable since Franklin Roosevelt's announcement of the "Good Neighbor" policy. Without exception, governments emphasized the critical importance of making the Uruguay meeting of the Inter-American Economic and Social Council a "success", and not merely another in the long line of inter-American meetings.

On the other hand, there was no clear or uniform definition of what would constitute "success". There was wide variety in the concept of the meeting's objective and procedures, and great disparity in the intensity and character of national preparations for the program.

A few governments, actually that of Peru, appeared to believe that the meeting would be the occasion for the cutting of an aid "melon," with little regard to self-help measures or structural reforms in such fields as land tenure and taxation. But all paid at least lip-service to the concept of self-help, and several were in deadly earnest on this front. In terms of technical work on long-term programming for national economic and social development, Colombia, Chile, Brazil and perhaps Venezuela, seemed to be well in advance of their sister nations. Several others handed us "shopping lists" of public investment projects on which they looked for loans or other aid. Argentina and Chile emphasized the importance for them of economic development as contrasted with social investment. Many governments advanced claims for "special consideration" on political or other grounds.

In several cases, less emphasis was placed on outside aid for public investment than on trade and commodity price policies. Argentina, Uruguay, and Chile declared their strong interest in American policy support for their commercial negotiations with the European Common Market. There was the most intense interest in joint action to stabilize primary commodity markets and to raise prices of key export items, notably coffee.

I believe that our mission greatly clarified the thinking of the South American governments on the types of results which we hope might be achieved at the Uruguay conference, especially in the fields of investment programming and the coordination of outside aid. We must clearly expect active discussion of commercial policy and commodity markets, and we should have well-defined positions on these issues. A forthcoming attitude in these fields would do much to overcome the disappointments which are likely with respect to the amounts and conditions of financial aid.

As to aid, it is a fact that the needs are large, the desire for accelerated growth is great, and the capacity for effective use of aid is being rapidly augmented by the systematic programming of public investments, often for the first time. In most cases, the general concepts of needs and priorities are not far out of line with our own thinking. It is evident that large increases in the rate of economic and social public investment and United States aid, as compared with recent years, are expected. Fortunately, most of the governments appear to be thinking mainly in terms of hard loans, which can be financed by the World Bank, Inter-American Development Bank, and Export-Import Bank to the extent that the real credit-worthiness permits. (This in turn may be largely dependent on action in the commercial policy and commodity market areas.) If Congress furnishes the authority you have requested for making long-term commitments, there is no question but that the ability of the Latin American governments to carry through sustained development efforts, including the needed structural reforms, will be greatly enhanced.

On the question of the timing of the meeting, Brazil strongly desired a one-month postponement to enable more adequate national and international preparatory work to be completed. Most of the other governments favored a two or three week postponement, although a few emphasized their own readiness to meet on July 15 as scheduled. I understand that the OAS Council is now about to agree on a revised date of August 5 for the meeting of Ministers, to be preceded by an expert-level meeting on August 1. This seems to me a sound conclusion. The publicity concerning the deferred date should of course make it clear that the purpose is solely to permit the completion of more adequate preparations and thus to contribute to a successful outcome.

[Here follows section V. "Collective Political Action Against Indirect Aggression and Communist Penetration Based on Cuba."]

Respectfully submitted,

Adlai E. Stevenson[1]

---

[1] Printed from a copy that bears this typed signature.

15.   Summary Guidelines Paper

Washington, July 3, 1961.

UNITED STATES POLICY TOWARD LATIN AMERICA

Background

Latin America today is in a state of deep unrest. Most of its countries are economically underdeveloped and socially backward. The distribution of land and other forms of national wealth greatly favors the propertied classes. The masses suffer from poor housing, malnutrition and illiteracy. In many countries large rural groups, which include most of the Indian peoples, are not integrated into the economic and social life of the nation. The poor and underprivileged, stimulated by the example of the Cuban revolution, are now demanding opportunities for a decent living. Meanwhile, the population is increasing much more rapidly than the rate of production. International communism, encouraged by its success in Cuba and assisted by the Castro regime, is trying to take advantage of this explosive situation to subvert other countries of the hemisphere.

The Organization of American States has not thus far demonstrated much ability, or interest, in protecting its members from communist subversion and most of them have tended to regard Cuba as more a United States problem than a hemisphere one. The governments generally are alive to the need for economic and social progress, and look to the United States for help in this direction. Apart from Cuba there are few dictatorships left in the area, though it cannot be said that the seeds of representative democracy have yet taken deep root in most countries. In meeting the two-fold challenge to Latin America from rising economic expectations of the masses and from communist subversion, the Latin American military will have an important role to play. But the challenge is also, and mainly, to the United States.

Objectives

The central objectives of the United States in Latin America are:

1. The achievement by each of the countries of the area of permanently democratic and fully representative governments, supported by broadly based viable economies, in order that they may become active

Source: Kennedy Library, National Security Files, Latin America, April–August 1961. Secret. Drafted by Braddock. The full text of the paper, dated May 25, is in Department of State, Central Files, 611.20/6–261. It was discussed at the Secretary's Policy Planning meeting on June 8. (Ibid., S/PC Files: Lot 71 D 273, Latin America)

participants in the world community and firmly established on the side of western democracy in the world power struggle.

2. Satisfaction of the basic aspirations of the peoples of Latin America for economic and social justice and welfare, and association of the United States with progress toward these ends.

3. Awareness by the governments and peoples of the area of the threat of international communism and of its subversive nature, particularly as exemplified in Cuba, and the determination and ability, with United States assistance, to defeat it.

For the accomplishment of the aforementioned objectives two major lines of action by the United States are indicated:

1. Strike at the causes of unrest by assisting strongly, through the Alliance for Progress, those countries which are genuinely striving toward economic and social progress; and

2. Strengthen the will and the capability of governments, with emphasis on internal security, to defeat attempts at a take-over by forces supported by or allied with international communism or Castroism.

Other important guidelines of action are as follows:

Political

1. Maintain correct relations with all recognized governments but give special encouragement to democratic governments.

2. Make a planned effort in each country, directed by the Ambassador, to influence leaders and representative groups to initiate or support development and reform programs, using democratic processes.

3. Make clear that the United States is interested in the improvement of living conditions of working people and in the education and health of their children. Encourage and assist non-communist local labor organizations. Help in building up technical skills in the labor force.

4. Strengthen hemispheric solidarity by providing effective United States leadership, living up to all our inter-American commitments, strongly supporting the OAS, consulting with Latin American States before taking any actions which will affect them, and by bringing Canada and later the West Indies into closer relationship with the inter-American system.

5. Seek the resolution of disputes between American States in accordance with OAS procedures.

6. Encourage individual and collective action by the other American Republics against Sino-Soviet bloc influence and subversion through suitable controls on communist representation, activities, entry and trade.

7. Increase awareness of the threats to Latin America from communism by exposing communist activities, exchanging information, and explaining the fallacies of communist doctrine.

8. Seek by all legitimate means available to us, including all feasible measures in the OAS, to weaken, isolate and promote the downfall of the Castro-communist dictatorship in Cuba and establish security arrangements, especially in the Caribbean area, to defeat possible attempts by the Castro regime to subvert governments in that area.

9. Apply pressure and persuasion, unilaterally and through the OAS, on the President of the Dominican Republic to bring about the full restoration of civil rights in that country, the preparation and carrying out in 1962 of free and open elections, and the elimination of all vestiges of the Trujillo dictatorship.

10. Remove so far as possible sources of friction between Panama and the United States. Seek to develop attitudes in Panama and throughout Latin America favorable to United States construction and operation of a sea level successor to the present canal by 1980.

Economic and Social

1. Give priority help to Latin America, especially during the next ten years, for improvement in health and education, reform of tax systems and administration, housing improvement, better and more equitable land utilization, construction of roads and other public facilities, establishment of productive enterprises and for better distribution of income.

2. Devote special attention to the improvement of rural areas and of living conditions of subsistence Indian and campesino groups.

3. Urge and assist all countries to establish long-term, balanced development plans.

4. Encourage the Latin American nations to base their economies on a system of progressive free enterprise, and create a climate conducive to responsible private investment, particularly local investment. Help them develop measures to prevent abuses of the system. Encourage governments to develop as official projects those service enterprises and industries which are important to the economy but are neglected by private investors.

5. Urge and help governments to take all steps possible to encourage the maximum supply of capital from domestic sources, and advise them on how to accumulate domestic capital. Encourage them to look to private investors and to international regional lending institutions as the major sources for external development capital. Negotiate tax agreements, investment guarantee agreements, and Treaties of Friendship, Commerce and Navigation, as needed and feasible, to provide incentives for private investment.

6. Extend financial assistance, consistent with United States loan policy considerations, for Latin American economic development and for budgetary and balance of payments purposes.

7. Encourage other free world countries to provide capital and technical assistance to Latin America.

8. Continue to negotiate sales and grants of surplus United States agricultural commodities.

9. Expand and improve technical cooperation, and program it on a long-term basis. Provide technical assistance especially in rural areas, for development of rural extension services and for support of schools teaching elementary farming methods.

10. Utilize the Peace Corps for improving economic and social conditions, particularly in rural areas, and getting elementary knowledge to the population.

11. Encourage the use of selected military personnel and units in development projects, when circumstances permit, and the formation and training of engineering-type military units which could be used in such projects.

12. Try to maintain stable long-term trading policies and to avoid restrictive practices which adversely affect Latin American exports to the United States. Encourage the establishment of Latin American customs unions which conform to GATT criteria.

13. Seek cooperative practical methods of bringing an end to the pattern of violent changes in commodity prices, and of encouraging the development of the first stages of processing raw materials. Encourage and assist sound programs aimed at diversification of production.

Informational, Cultural and Scientific

1. Provide strong informational support for the Alliance for Progress, with emphasis on the principle of self-help.

2. Increase the output, especially in Latin America, of informational material designed to expose the communist conspiracy in Cuba and its betrayal of the Cuban revolution.

3. Increase the student exchange program. Encourage the enrollment in Latin American universities of American students selected for their ability to propagate democracy, financing this program mainly through student loans, not grants.

4. Make available at give-away-prices books in appropriate languages by American and other authors that explain the concepts, ideals and methods of democracy.

5. Seek through technical assistance and other appropriate programs to help Latin American educational institutions, and encourage American institutions of learning to cooperate in this effort.

6. Promote greater cooperation in the scientific field through such means as the establishment of science teacher training programs, and the provision to Latin American institutions of new teaching materials.

7. Emphasize throughout Latin America the non-military character and objectives of United States space programs, in order to obtain Latin American cooperation for the implementation of such programs.

Military

1. Assume primary responsibility for military operations in the Atlantic and Pacific Oceans and the Caribbean Sea, and seek Latin American acceptance of this arrangement.

2. Encourage acceptance that each of the Latin American countries is responsible for contributing to the defense of the hemisphere by maintaining internal security against communist-Castroist guerrilla and subversive threats, and security of its coasts, territorial waters, bases and strategic areas against external aggression.

3. Make available to Latin American countries, on a grant basis if necessary, the training and military equipment they need to carry out the aforementioned missions according first priority to assistance for internal security.

4. Encourage standardization of military doctrine, unit organization and training along United States lines.

5. Seek to discourage or prevent the acquisition of military equipment or training by an American State from communist governments.

6. Encourage Latin American countries, particularly in the Caribbean area, to enter into special security arrangements with the United States, consistent with the Rio Treaty, designed to thwart communist attempts at infiltration or subversion.

7. Encourage Latin American countries to limit their armaments to the levels and types required for the missions described in paragraph 2 above.

8. Seek to make the Latin American military ever conscious of its role of protectors of the people in their constitutional rights.

16.   Letter From the Chairman of the Task Force on Latin America (Berle) to President Kennedy

Washington, July 7, 1961.

MY DEAR MR. PRESIDENT: I transmit herewith the report of the Task Force on Latin America whose creation you directed shortly after your inauguration.

The Task Force was conceived as a mechanism of transition. With the appointment of the new Secretary of State for Latin American Affairs, the period of transition has substantially ended. The emergency problems pending solution on January 20 last have been or are in process of being dealt with. Under your leadership, the new direction of policy, I am convinced, offers good opportunity and prospect of success. I therefore ask that the Task Force be now discharged.

Prior to your inauguration, you constituted an informal group to report on Latin American policy.[1] That group made one suggestion not yet acted on. It proposed the creation in the Department of State of the post of Undersecretary of State for Latin American Affairs. This would provide a high level straight line channel through the Secretary of State, by which the widely scattered activities of the government affecting Latin American affairs could be coordinated. This recommendation I venture to renew. Management of hemispheric affairs, comprising a continent and a half organized as a regional alliance, is a huge task. It is difficult to carry out so great an enterprise from a subordinate bureaucratic position.

The Task Force report suggests enlargement of the education-information-propaganda effort. An informal working group headed by Assistant Secretary of State Philip Coombs has been studying this possibility. Copies of their preliminary reports have been delivered to Mr. Richard Goodwin.

Let me pay special tribute to the effective cooperation and support of Assistant Secretary of the Treasury John M. Leddy and Assistant Secretary of Defense Haydn Williams. We are indebted to both for their wisdom and unstinting effort.

Source: Department of State, Latin America Task Force Files: Lot 61 D 298, Report to the President. Confidential.

[1] See Document 1.

With the discharge of the Task Force, my own assignment comes to an end. Please feel free to call on me if at any time hereafter I can be of assistance.

Respectfully yours,

A.A. Berle[2]

Enclosure

REPORT OF THE PRESIDENT'S TASK FORCE ON
LATIN AMERICA

I report herewith on the operations of the President's Task Force on Latin America. Being a task force and not a committee, this report is made on my responsibility as Chairman. Though a small hard core of individuals were continuously members of the Task Force, others were added for specific problems, so that its personnel varied with the problems encountered.

As stated at its first meeting,

"the Task Force is an action and not a study group, acting under the direction of the Secretary of State and the President. The Task Force does not supersede the Bureau of Inter-American Affairs which remains responsible for foreign policy operations with respect to Latin America."

Its function was to assure that urgent problems were brought to the attention of the Secretary of State and through him or at his direction to the President, and to expedite action in accordance with decisions taken.

The Task Force held its first meeting on February 2, 1961. It has met regularly thereafter at intervals of two weeks. Informal sub-groups reporting to it have worked on aspects of the chief matters under consideration, and on a number of special questions.

From the outset it was assumed that the Task Force would not be permanent. It was designed to deal with problems raised by transition from the previous to the present Administration, and by certain substantial changes in Latin American policy attendant upon its entrance, and to coordinate action on them.

The most important single function, as it has been the most important single result, of the Task Force activities has been to focus attention

---

[2] Printed from a copy that bears this typed signature.

on the importance of Latin America to the United States, on the urgent nature of its problems, and on assuring that these problems receive prompt and adequate consideration. This appears to have happened. The inter-American world no longer considers Latin America as a step-child of American official thinking.

A number of substantial tasks, some of them of emergency nature, required immediate action. The more important of these were:

1. Securing legislation appropriating $500 million to implement commitments made by the Government of the United States at the Conference of Bogota held on September 5–14, 1960.

Members of the Task Force, notably Professor Lincoln Gordon, Assistant Secretary of the Treasury John Leddy and myself, under supervision of the Secretary of State and the Secretary of the Treasury, made the presentation in behalf of this legislation before the committees of the House of Representatives and the Senate, respectively. The appropriation was passed by the House of Representatives on April 25, 1961, by the Senate on May 9, 1961, and became law on May 27, 1961.[3]

2. Financial assistance to Brazil.

The financial condition of Brazil when President Janio Quadros assumed office and took over administration of its government on February 1, 1961, was under strain. The Task Force proposed initiation of financial aid to that government, both in the form of a possible emergency loan (which later proved unnecessary) and recommended negotiations looking toward readjustment of Brazil's external debt, together with additional financing so that it might more readily normalize its economic condition. This proved to be a large job. The figures are somewhat misleading, since the large portion of the financing involved rescheduling of already outstanding loans due to the United States and to American banks, rather than new money. A group was constituted, functioning under the Secretary of the Treasury, headed by Assistant Secretary Leddy. The operation, so far as it related directly to the United States, comprised $338 million of new financing, and rescheduling of $559 million of outstanding debt due to the Export-Import Bank, the International Monetary Fund and American banks. Assistance was also given in rescheduling Brazilian debt outstanding in Europe and elsewhere amounting to nearly $300 million, and in securing certain European credits. This is being concluded now.

3. Financial assistance to Venezuela.

A somewhat similar problem was presented by the request of the Venezuelan government for financial assistance. The Task Force agreed that prompt attention should be given to the Venezuelan request. A

---

[3] 75 Stat. 86, P.L. 87–41.

group was constituted for that purpose. This task has been completed in substantial part and the emergency phase of this assistance has been taken care of. Certain additional phases, more especially the financing of projects which will tend to relieve the burden of unemployment in and about Caracas and at the same time strengthen the social-economic conditions in Venezuela are moving forward in channels.

4. Expediting Colombian projects.

The Task Force considered certain economic projects of social and military importance previously agreed upon with the government of Colombia but which had encountered difficulties in execution. Obstacles were overcome. Arrangements in respect of certain of them were expedited, and they are being or have been carried out.

5. Latin American defense policy.

The Task Force has had for consideration a redraft of the paper covering United States defense policy in respect of Latin America. This involved preparation of a new paper for submission to the President through the National Security Council. The Department of Defense, represented on the Task Force by the Assistant Secretary of Defense, Mr. Haydn Williams, undertook to prepare such a draft—a substantial piece of work. This was done; concurrence of the interested agencies was secured; the draft was approved by the Task Force on May 19, 1961 and through the Department of State has been forwarded to the National Security Council.[4]

6. The Bolivian economic situation.

The Task Force considered the situation in Bolivia whose economic situation had become precarious with attendant political problems. Informally the Task Force stimulated decision to organize a special interdepartmental group to deal immediately with that problem, comprising the representatives of the various interested agencies. The group was constituted, went to Bolivia, worked out a program, returned, and the program in large measure has already been implemented. Full implementation will follow in due course, conditions in Bolivia permitting.

7. Communist bloc offers to Latin American countries.

The Task Force considered a suggestion that the United States cease to discourage Latin American governments from accepting preferred Soviet economic aid. After examination, the Task Force recommended no change in current policy of dealing with each of these situations on its merits.

---

[4] Reference is to a paper entitled "U.S. Policy for the Security of Latin America in the Sixties." (Department of State, Latin America Task Force Files: Lot 61 D 298, Task Force Materials including Basic Documents)

8. The 11th Inter-American Conference.

The 11th regular Inter-American Conference was scheduled to have been held at Quito, Ecuador, on May 24, 1961. It was, however, clear that substantial sentiment existed among Latin American governments for postponement, certainly until after the Special Meeting of the Inter-American Economic and Social Council proposed by the Government of the United States. Taken on the initiative of a number of Latin American governments, the situation was resolved by action of the Organization of American States in favor of postponement of the conference.

The foregoing list scarcely reflects the amount of patient, difficult and devoted work required to bring these affairs to conclusion within the comparatively short period of five months. Trips to Latin America were carried out by four members of the Task Force.

In addition to these matters (which are either concluded or in such shape that they will be concluded in due course), the Task Force has considered and recommended action on a number of other less extensive problems of significant importance. In a number of these, action was secured.

9. Education-information-propaganda: an unfinished task.

The Task Force has under study and consideration one subject of major importance, namely, expansion to adequate proportions of the United States education-information-propaganda-cultural program and facilities in Latin America.

Criticism of existing agencies is not here implied. They work with the money and tools given them. But there is general agreement (shared by the agencies themselves) that the present program is inadequate, and that its various elements have tended to become disparate. Its extent should be increased; and its depth of impact must be intensified. Under current conditions, probably its conception needs to be changed. An adequate program must develop the Western World thesis of political, economic and social progress under freedom; must demonstrate how this is done; must educate students in its theory and practice; must produce substantial numbers of men and women in each country in each year trained to carry theory into practice; must create a climate through mass media supporting the development of a socially effective free society.

Low priced books and educational materials at high school and university levels must be provided. Expanded contact must be developed with student groups from high school through university. Mass media must support the Western World thesis and the many Latin American parties, organizations and groups of men who hold that thesis and are endeavoring to give it reality.

American effort must compete with and defend against a Communist-bloc program presently organized, and operating on a scale approximately seven times that of current United States efforts, measured by comparative expenditures. (All United States agencies combined spend about $15 million. The Communist-bloc countries are spending in the neighborhood of $100 million.) In many Latin American countries the stratum of intellectuals and politically conscious people is narrow. Communist-bloc educational and propaganda agencies thus can infiltrate educational systems, select groups for special training, and over-run the intellectually conscious life of the less developed countries. Absent any other system, by providing a few hundred or (as planned in the case of Brazil) a few thousand trained Communists each year, the Communist-bloc effort can, after a few years of operation, virtually take over the functioning of the country. Underdeveloped countries with adequate educational systems are ready targets for this kind of imperialism. There is no reason why a vacuum should be left to be filled by our enemies.

Development of a plan for an education-information-propaganda organization, and outlining legislation to make it effective, will take some time. The subject ranks with that of political or military defense. I believe it goes beyond the function of the Task Force. I therefore suggest that a special White House-sponsored group be constituted to take it over.

A final word. It must be taken as personal.

The present struggle will not be won, and can be lost, by opportunist support of transitory power-holders or forces whose objectives are basically hostile to the peoples they dominate. Success of the American effort in Latin America requires that at all times its policy be based on clear, consistent, moral democratic principles. I do not see that any other policy can be accepted or indeed stands any real chance of ultimate success. The forces sweeping Latin America today demand progress, and a better life for the masses of their people, through evolution if possible, or through revolution if that price must be paid. A preponderance of these forces want the resulting forms to provide liberty, rejecting tyranny whether from the right or from the left. This deep current corresponds to the principles outlined in the President's speech of March 13, 1961, elaborating the "Alliance for Progress."

Respectfully submitted,

Adolf A. Berle[5]
Chairman
Task Force on Latin America

---

[5] Printed from a copy that indicates Berle signed the original.

17.   Memorandum From the Under Secretary of State (Bowles) to Secretary of State Rusk

Washington, July 25, 1961.

SUBJECT

The Montevideo Conference

I am concerned lest the momentum generated by the Act of Bogota and the Alliance for Progress be dissipated by a conference at Montevideo which is so heavily dedicated to financial and technical measures that the human element gets lost in the shuffle.

Expectations are very high in Latin America. Yet if the primary test of the Alliance's success is to be the number of dollars that are made available by the U.S.A. we may end up with every country dissatisfied with its share of our necessarily limited funds.

Since our financial capabilities are not inexhaustible, we must seek constantly to identify the United States with other less costly aspects of the process of economic and social change which are of equal or even greater importance to the development of prosperous, stable, democratic societies.

It seems to me, speaking in the most general terms, that we can identify three major elements in the development complex where we can be most effective.

The first of these is providing resources for economic *growth*. We have many instruments for doing this, most of which are expensive. Moreover, massive investments in infrastructure and industrial facilities, essential though we know them to be, may in fact create additional tensions within a society by failing to meet immediate consumer expectations and by increasing the disparity between the wealthy and the poor.

Greater emphasis, therefore, should be applied to bringing about basic reforms in the *distribution* of wealth. This means promoting social justice through changes in tax systems, land tenure patterns, credit arrangements, which in addition to their obvious political implications, can help release domestic resources and talents for more productive utilization.

For the United States this is a dramatic, necessary and yet virtually costless exercise. Moreover, such reforms will make sense to the American people because they stem from such well-accepted convictions as to

Source: Department of State, Central Files, 371.8/7–2561. Official Use Only. Copies were distributed to Woodward, Goodwin, and Schlesinger.

the proper nature of society as that a man should own his land and home and that the burden of taxation should be distributed on the basis of ability to pay. Sometimes there are suggestions that pushing for social reform abroad means espousing some "radical", un-American doctrine; in fact quite the opposite is true.

A third area where we can assist, also at relatively little financial expense, is in *promoting the welfare of the rural areas,* where 70% of the people of Latin America live. An integrated approach to rural poverty through extension services, cooperatives, land reform, self-help schools, roads, and so forth, can yield an enormous return not only in better living conditions but in the immeasurable elements of hope and self respect which are the strongest bulwarks against Castro-Communism. Yet for all of Northeast Brazil, probably the most poverty-stricken part of Latin America, the *dollar* needs are estimated at only $76 million over the next five years.

Integration, it seems to me, must be the essential element of our efforts to stimulate rural development not only in Latin America but throughout the underdeveloped world. I have drafted a memorandum[1] (now being circulated for comment within the Department) which discusses this coordinated approach and suggests ways in which it can be furthered. A firm expression of our interest along these lines would not be amiss at the Punta del Este meeting.

I hope that our delegation to Montevideo will bear constantly in mind these three inter-related aspects of United States involvement in Latin American economic and social progress and will lose no opportunity to reemphasize our concern with the last two elements as well as the first. It will help re-inspire many of our Latin American friends as well as reassure our own citizens that "foreign aid" need not consist solely of an ever-increasing stream of dollars.

---

[1] Not found.

18.   Memorandum From Secretary of the Treasury Dillon to President Kennedy

Washington, August 1, 1961.

SUBJECT

IA–ECOSOC Conference at Montevideo

Our preparations for this Conference have now been completed.

Our major objective will be to reach a comprehensive inter-American agreement along the lines of the draft "Accord Establishing an Alliance for Progress," with which you are familiar.

Preliminary reactions to our draft Accord from a number of Latin American countries, including Brazil, Mexico and the Central Americans indicate a strong desire to include in the Accord chapters on Basic Primary Products and Economic Integration. We can agree to this, depending on the nature of the commitments.

The main substantive problems I foresee at the Conference are these:

(1) There is strong Latin American support for a U.S. commitment to arrangements to provide compensatory financing to offset price declines for Latin American exports. A specific plan—costing $1 billion, of which not more than $200 million could come from Latin America—was put forward by the OAS group of experts which prepared the documentation for the Conference. Apart from its initial cost, we do not yet know whether a plan like this could work on a self-sustaining basis—i.e., without degenerating into a scheme for repeated injections of each. Hence, we can express interest in the plan and agree to study it, but my present feeling is that we must resist accepting the plan in principle until further study is made.

(2) The Argentines have urged U.S. financial support for a regional fund to permit the Latin Americans to extend export guarantees to promote their exports to each other, particularly of capital equipment (some of which Argentina produces) and other manufactures. This particular kind of financing would be very hard for Congress to swallow, since we would, in effect, be subsidizing Latin American exports in direct competition with our own exports. We would have less difficulty with arrangements whereby the Latin Americans themselves provided export financing as a part of their over-all development programs, with U.S. assistance being related to these programs as a whole rather than to the export financing aspect. It is not clear how far the other Latin Americans will support the Argentine proposals since they are only of interest to those few countries with some capacity to export manufactured goods.

Source: Kennedy Library, National Security Files, Trips and Conference Series, Montevideo, August 1961. Official Use Only.

(3) A number of countries have raised questions about the proposal for an Export Committee on Development to evaluate individual development programs, a proposal which we are supporting. Argentina has strongly opposed the idea and Mexico has urged the Committee not be "compulsory." The fear expressed is that the Committee would represent interferences with national sovereignty. This, of course, would not be the case and I suspect that the real reason for opposition to the Committee is the belief that the United States will really use it in order to assure adequate self-help efforts on the part of recipient nations, just as we now rely on the IMF to induce countries to adopt satisfactory fiscal and monetary measures, I am confident that some useful machinery can be agreed upon but we will have to make concessions of form.

(4) The Latin Americans will want from us a much stronger statement on U.S. public assistance to their development than it is possible to provide in the formal language of the draft Accord. Accordingly, I propose in my major statement to include language along the following lines: In the first 12 months following the invitation by President Kennedy to join in an Alliance for Progress, we foresee public U.S. assistance to Latin America exceeding $1 billion—more than three times the amount for 1960 and more than double the average for 1950–60. It is not possible to predict a precise range of assistance for future years since this will vitally depend on efforts of the Latin American countries themselves in preparing and executing effective development programs. However, I wish to reaffirm and re-emphasize the pledge of President Kennedy that if the Latin Americans are ready to do their part, then the U.S. would help to provide resources of a scope and magnitude sufficient to make this bold development program a success—just as the U.S. helped to provide the resources adequate to help rebuild the economies of Western Europe. As the President stated, "only an effort of towering dimensions can ensure fulfillment of our plan for a decade of progress."

A statement on these lines would square with ICA projections of U.S. public assistance to Latin America and is acceptable to Secretary Rusk.

Undoubtedly many other problems will arise in the course of the meeting, but these are the principal ones which can now be foreseen.

I have discussed our approach to the Montevideo Conference, including the foregoing points, with the House Foreign Affairs and Senate Foreign Relations Committees. They appeared to be entirely satisfied.

Douglas Dillon[1]

---

[1] Printed from a copy that indicates Dillon signed the original.

19.   Editorial Note

The extraordinary meeting of the Inter-American Economic and Social Council convened in Punta del Este on August 5, 1961. The United States delegation was led by Secretary of the Treasury C. Douglas Dillon. At the meeting's opening session, Robert A. Conrads, Assistant Secretary General of the Conference, read a message from President Kennedy that reiterated the commitment of the United States to the Alliance for Progress and hemispheric development. For text, see *Public Papers of the Presidents of the United States: John F. Kennedy, 1961*, pages 548–549.

20.   Telegram From the Embassy in Uruguay to the Department of State

Montevideo, August 6, 1961, 8 p.m.

100. IA–ECOSOC.

"Dear Mr. President:

Opening day of conference went well. We have had full talks with Brazil, Uruguay, Argentina, Chile and Peru and shorter talks with others. Single overriding preoccupation of all is extent of US commitment. Latins point out they must take drastic steps in tax reform and land reform and devote more funds to development. This process will be greatly facilitated if they can feel confident that once they have done their part adequate foreign aid will be available. Your statement was most helpful in this regard and was very well received. I will have to go as far as possible Monday in indicating magnitude of long range availabilities of aid, assuming necessary steps by Latins. If Latins can be reasonably satisfied on this point, other difficulties will rapidly fade away.[1]

Source: Kennedy Library, National Security Files, Trips and Conference Series, Montevideo, August 1961. Confidential; Niact; Eyes Only. A marginal notation indicates that the President saw it.

[1] In his August 5 address, Secretary Dillon announced that the United States would allocate at least $1 billion in development assistance to Latin America during the first year of the Alliance for Progress. The text of the address is in Department of State *Bulletin*, August 28, 1961, pp. 356–360. According to telegram 110 from Montevideo, the address was "received by large audience with prolonged applause." (Department of State, Central Files, 371.8/8–861)

Guevara so far has not done well. In private session he made strong attack on Beltran for mentioning Alliance for Progress favorably and further declared that Cuba was non-Christian, atheistic government and therefore it improper to refer to religion in conference speeches. This did not go down well with anybody. Unfortunately press is playing him up. Example was inaccurate story of our arrival at Montevideo where pro-Castro crowd numbered not more than 500 at outside despite free bus transportation from town. Communists had hoped for 5,000 and result considered by Uruguayan Government as evidence sharp decline in Castro prestige. Guevara reportedly has thirty resolutions to introduce. We will see.

We have agreed to work closely with Brazil, Argentina, Chile, and Peru in preparing draft for final act. Committee work starts Wednesday and should finish Friday or Saturday. I have been asked by Frondizi to call on him in Buenos Aires. Am planning to fly over Thursday with Alemann. Feel this is wise in order to balance off talk with Quadros.

While Haedo still very much hopes you can visit conference at end, as he said in his telegram to you, other delegations have not mentioned matter and seem to be fully satisfied with your decision. Although a visit by you would naturally be well received by all delegations, I do not as of now see any reason for change in original decision.

Faithfully yours,

Douglas"

Sparks

---

21.   **Telegram From the Embassy in Uruguay to the Department of State**

Montevideo, August 9, 1961, 9 a.m.

113. IA–ECOSOC. Guevara, Cuban delegate, in speech today read from documents apparently purloined in Caracas. Photostats were later circulated all delegates with Spanish translations accompanying.

Documents were (1) office memo of 12 June 1961 to Ambassador Moscoso from Irving Tragen and Robert Cox via John Gates classified

---

Source: Kennedy Library, National Security Files, Trips and Conference Series, Montevideo, August 1961. Official Use Only. Repeated to Caracas.

Official Use Only,[1] and (2) INR contribution to NIE 80/90–61 "Latin American Reactions to Developments in and with Respect to Cuba" classified Secret.[2]

Guevara read first paragraph page three of first document on Venezuelan administrative defects and most of penultimate paragraph on severe choices to be faced by oligarchy. He said [*read?*] extensively from other document.

Document well prepared and reflects sincere interest of US in LA development although nationalistic sentiments will be offended by extent to which US participation in widespread improvements is suggested.

Venezuelans will be irritated by "constructive criticism" but we do not anticipate significant adverse effects. Dillon seeing Venezuelans August 9. Revelation of other document does no harm.

Sparks

---

[1] For text, see telegram 117 from Montevideo, August 9. (Department of State, Central Files, 731.5–MSP/8–961)

[2] Dated July 18. (Central Intelligence Agency Files, Job 79–R01012A, ODDI Registry)

---

22.   Telegram From the Embassy in Uruguay to the Department of State

Montevideo, August 9, 1961, 9 p.m.

123. Please deliver following message to President:

"Dear Mr. President:

Guevara speech was masterful presentation of Communist point of view. He clearly identified Cuba as full-fledged member of bloc talking of our 'sister Socialist Republic.' Since he attacked Alliance for Progress in its entirety and everything conference is trying to do, he made little substantive impression on delegates. However, he was aiming over their heads at people of Latin America, and we cannot from here estimate how successful he was in this effort.

Since Guevara speech frankly political and so characterized by him and since conference chairman has requested all delegates to avoid polit-

---

Source: Department of State, Central Files, 371.8/8–961. Secret; Priority.

ical comments and stick to business we do not feel it proper to dignify Guevara performance by entering into argument with him here. What State Department may care to say in answer to Guevara is another matter which I think should depend on reaction to his speech throughout hemisphere. I have, however, put out statement designed to bolster Betancourt re document from our Embassy in Venezuela.[1] This statement prepared in collaboration with Venezuelan delegation and at their request. They view publication of document as Cuban attempt to undermine Betancourt at home.

Effect of my speech on delegates has been generally very good. Sole exception was Argentina which annoyed at lack of mention of programs for Argentine meat and wheat. We have reached agreement on preliminary draft of final act which has been submitted to conference under sponsorship Argentina, Brazil, Chile, Mexico and Peru. Draft does not contain chapter on commodities or integration which being worked on separately. So far no real problems in sight. Expect that in due course and after disposing of numerous suggested resolutions, including many from Cuba, main document will be approved by 20 to 1 vote. All statements made to plenary session friendly to us except possibly Ecuador. Conference schedule calls for working parties to meet during next three days with general committee of whole convening on Saturday to consider reports of committees and draft final act.

Faithfully yours,

Douglas Dillon."

Sparks

---

[1] See Document 21.

---

23.   Telegram From the Embassy in Uruguay to the Department of State

Montevideo, August 9, 1961, 11 p.m.

126. Please transmit following message to President:

"Dear Mr. President:

We have noted some feeling among smaller countries that Brazil and Argentina are working together to dominate conference. There is

Source: Department of State, Central Files, 371.8/8–961. Secret; Niact.

also some concern that my stop in Brasilia and my visit tomorrow with Frondizi are an indication that US is aiding and abetting this effort. Chilean Minister strongly urged that I stop in some other capital, not necessarily Santiago, on way back to Washington and that this be announced before conference ends.

I think there is considerable merit in Chilean suggestion. Most convenient stop over would be Caracas, which could substitute for planned overnight at Ramey. In view of document affair such a stop might be particularly useful. Accordingly, after talking matter over with Woodward who fully concurs I told Mayobre that if Venezuelan Government felt it would be helpful I would be glad to stop overnight at Caracas on way home, visiting with Betancourt that night and/or following morning. Mayobre thought this a fine idea and said he would consult his government and let me know. Had one hour meeting with Venezuelans who expressed great appreciation for our prompt action in putting out statement re document. In addition to Venezuelans and those mentioned in earlier message have now had full scale meetings with Mexico and Colombia.

Faithfully yours,

Douglas Dillon"

Sparks

---

24.   Telegram From the Embassy in Uruguay to the Department of State

Montevideo, August 9, 1961.

124. In Committee Two today Cuba (Guevara) made clear its desire have Montevideo Treaty discussed as of interest to non signatories considering joining Common Market. Noted Cuba isolated economically from Latin American countries by special circumstances but had factories which could expand production if free to export. Cuba and trading partners could benefit by economic specialization and exchange. However without guarantees against economic boycotts specialization would entail risk Cuba hurt by such boycott. Hence Cuba would insist

Source: Kennedy Library, National Security Files, Trips and Conference Series, Montevideo, August 1961. Unclassified.

on guarantees against economic aggression. Under the economic integration agreement (LAFTA) there should be according Guevara provision for long term contracts as safeguard against: (a) interruption of trade as result political pressure and (b) planned production in excess of amounts that could be sold [sic] wanted fundamental discussion here of expansion such exchanges between Cuba and Latin America countries especially those in LAFTA.

Sparks

---

25.   Telegram From the Embassy in Uruguay to the Department of State

Montevideo, August 11, 1961, 1 a.m.

148. From Dillon. It would be very helpful here if at appropriate moment near end of conference we could announce that supposedly secret document read by Guevara had previously been furnished to and discussed with Venezuelan Government. Such a revaluation would be of major help in discrediting Guevara. Recognize problem posed by difference in two versions. If Department and Ambassador agree, suggest Ambassador discuss matter frankly with Betancourt to see whether anything along these lines would be practical. Would need decision promptly so as to be in position to act by Monday.[1]

Sparks

Source: Department of State, Central Files, 371.8/8–1161. Confidential. Repeated to Caracas.

[1] August 14.

---

26.   Telegram From the Embassy in Uruguay to the Department of State

Montevideo, August 11, 1961, midnight.

155. From Dillon. Would appreciate Department's thinking on best tactics for handling Cubans in closing meetings of conference. Cubans

---

Source: Department of State, Central Files, 371.8/8–1161. Confidential; Niact.

can be expected to ask us whether or not they will be eligible for assistance under alliance. Unless Department has other views I would intend reply that Cuba not member of IDB or IBRD, that Cuba did not approve Act of Bogota and therefore not eligible for social progress fund loans, that US in any event has no intention aiding Cuba as long as Cuban Government controlled by international Communism.

With such an answer we can expect Cuban reply that this proves conference was politically organized to split Cuba from other Latin American Governments and that although Cuba has been prepared to sign final act this made it impossible for her to do so.

Alternatively Cuba may announce firm intention to sign document and then try to imply that by signature they somehow gain right to be assisted. This could pose problem of US and Cuba signing same document. If this should come up I feel we should go ahead and sign making same statement as indicated above. We cannot allow Cuba to wreck conference by tactical act of signature of document satisfactory to US and others.

If neither of these events occur and Cuba remains silent which highly unlikely, I would nevertheless be inclined to include in final statement a paragraph on Cuba along following lines:

"The US Delegation feels that conference is to be congratulated as it has not allowed itself to be turned aside from its [work?] by the attempt of one delegation to inject political issues into this conference. While the opening statement of the Cuban delegate was full of inaccuracies and untruths, in particular regarding the United States, I do not wish to burden this conference with a detailed reply to these false charges. I merely take this opportunity to categorically deny all charges of aggression against the Cuban people. I wish to emphasize that this meeting is not the place to discuss political matters. There is a proper place in our American organization for such discussions. We all know what it is. If the present government of Cuba truly wishes to discuss the Cuban situation they are perfectly aware that the proper forum is the Council of the OAS, and not this meeting."

Particularly desire guidance on challenge to Cuba to take case to OAS.

There is distinct possibility that there may be a public session of some sort on final draft during course of Monday. Therefore prompt reply required for receipt here at conference site no later than 8:00 A.M. Monday. Woodward concurs.

Sparks

27.   Telegram From the Department of State to the Embassy in Uruguay

Washington, August 12, 1961, 6:19 p.m.

183. IA–ECOSOC for Dillon. Embtel 155.[1] Dept. approves your general approach and suggests following revision your statement to be used your discretion.

Begin Verbatim Text. US delegation has noted politically motivated statements Cuban delegate, replete with inaccuracies and untruths, in particular with regard to US. I do not wish burden this conference with reply these false charges. However, I feel I must reply to the question raised by Cuban delegation as to whether GOC eligible for assistance.

Under Alliance for Progress, there will be drawn together and concentrated for LA substantially increased aid from both US and the battery of aid mechanisms available free world. US does not decide alone eligibility for assistance except with respect to its own agencies. Other free world sources of financing can determine for themselves whether Cuba eligible for assistance and whether meets their separate criteria. However, so long as Cuba is under domination of communism, a system alien and inimical to our own inter-American system, US will oppose access by Cuba to funds provided by US for Alliance for Progress.

Whether GOC signs final document is matter of indifference to GUS. Certainly US delegation has right to question motives of GOC whose delegate, at very inception this conference, charged that entire Alliance for Progress "is a vehicle conceived to separate the people of Cuba from the other peoples of the Americas." GOC has publicly and continuously disavowed its ties to the OAS and has deliberately converted itself into communist state responsive to imperialist designs of Sino-Soviet Bloc. If GOC is now separated from peoples of Americas it has only itself to blame. When Cuba has demonstrated by concrete action its willingness to accept principles and obligations of OAS Charter and remaining solemn agreements of IA system, it can expect assume its place as respected member American family of nations.

US delegation feels conference is to be congratulated for not having allowed itself to be turned aside from its work by attempt of one delegation to inject political issues into this conference. *End Verbatim Text.*

Source: Kennedy Library, National Security Files, Trips and Conference Series, Montevideo, August 1961. Confidential; Niact. Drafted by Barall, Jamison, and Braddock; cleared by Kerr, Fowler, Sternfeld, Wallner, Coerr, and Korn; and approved by U. Alexis Johnson. A handwritten notation on the source text indicates the telegram was sent to Hyannis Port.
[1] Document 26.

FYI. Department believes challenge to Cuba to take case against US to OAS should be avoided. Our basic position is that real issue (Communism) is one between rest of hemisphere and Cuba which should be dealt with on initiative members OAS other than Cuba along lines Colombian or other suitable proposal. Moreover, challenge to Cuba use appropriate OAS forum such as ad hoc committee created by 7th MFM long since made and systematically rejected or ignored by Castro regime. Renewal at this time could give impetus to tendency treat problem as one between Cuba and US and weaken efforts toward hemispheric solution.

Since $20 billion figure mentioned in conference encompasses many potential sources of financing including private European capital, recommend you not mention any specific institution or component and avoid impression US unilaterally controls access to all. End FYI.

Rusk

---

28.   Telegram From the Embassy in Uruguay to the Department of State

Montevideo, August 12, 1961, noon.

165. Please pass following message to President.

"Dear Mr. President:

For last four days we have been going through hectic merry-go-round typical of Latin American economic conferences which must be seen to be believed. There have been four committees at work each of which has split into two or three subcommittees and they have been considering not only the basic act of Punta del Este to which there have been submitted 79 written amendments, but also 71 other resolutions covering just about every subject under the sun. Decisions made in subcommittee one day are reversed the next and then changed further by full committee. This is same process we went through at Buenos Aires economic conference of 57 but then it took over three weeks compared to ten days for this conference.

Daylight is now appearing and reports of working committees should hopefully be completed late tonight, Saturday, reproduced on

---

Source: Department of State, Central Files, 371.8/8–1361. Secret; Priority; Eyes Only. Received in the Department at 7:15 a.m. August 13.

Sunday and be considered by general committee of heads of delegations beginning Monday. Results generally follow very closely substance of US draft but with considerable language changes so that each nation can have something it can call its own.

There have only been two points of major substantive importance, the composition of the group of experts and a statement regarding scope of immediate US assistance. Argentina attacked original group of experts as US attempt to infringe sovereignty of Latin Americans. This effectively tied our hands so we backed off, said this was matter for Latins to settle and told our friends among smaller countries that we would favor strongest set-up they could get. Result was small country revolt against Argentina which eventually found herself completely alone. Then came final compromise which is practically identical in substance with our original proposal except that group increased from seven to nine and provision for chairman eliminated. Specific provision also made for use of panels of three so that committee can work on as many as three country plans at once. We had envisaged just such a procedure for our committee of seven.

Problem of US commitment for immediate assistance proved more difficult. This was Uruguayan idea, specifically that of President Haedo whose year in office ends in March and who wants a monument to his term of office. Uruguayan actions have taken on color of pure blackmail and even led to Haedo press statement that Uruguay would withdraw from conference if they could not get satisfaction. They started with proposal that US agree to commit one billion dollars to emergency projects in Latin America between now and end of year. Figure apparently picked because there was US commitment of $500 million at Bogota and this conference at least twice as important as Bogota. They rounded up support from El Salvador, which has behaved poorly here, Bolivia, Haiti, Paraguay and Ecuador although none of others would be problem without Uruguayan push. We said no and negotiated indirectly with Uruguayans for two days using Argentina, Chile, Mexico and El Salvador as go-betweens at various times. Finally I met for two hours this afternoon with Uruguayan Finance Minister and reached agreement which I hope will stick during committee consideration tonight. Substance of agreement is general statement on US willingness to help in short-term projects followed by reference to your message to conference regarding one billion dollars from all US sources in first year of Alliance. There is also statement that US will take prompt action (pro or con) on projects submitted during next sixty days by countries in emergency difficulties. There is understanding that this means only smaller countries and specifically does not include Argentina, Brazil or Mexico. In practice it should mean assignment this fall of about $10 million to Uruguay for schools, health centers and road building. Haedo at one time sent me word that his real price was $20 million but I am sure $10 million will be ample. This whole negotiation was disagreeable in the extreme but Uruguay as host country was in position exert pressure and chose to do so. I imagine part of it may have been Haedo personal pique at your decision not to attend conference.

Cuban resolutions have taken time to handle but have not been serious problem. They have only succeeded in getting in two or three bits of objectionable language which we shall remove during general committee consideration.

Information report was also a problem since experts' draft of general principles was poorly written, objectionable to US and full of political statements which gave Cubans fine opportunity for numerous speeches on political motivation of conference. Final results, however, are satisfactory and meet fundamental US objectives.

In short, conference is proceeding about as we expected roughly on schedule, although Uruguayans today were talking of closing up Thursday instead of Wednesday. Result should be fully satisfactory document and enthusiasm from all sides, but leaving all concerned with hard and continuing task of converting Alianza into concrete action. Final Senate action Monday on foreign aid would be substantial added attraction to conference windup.

Faithfully yours,

Douglas Dillon"

Sparks

---

29.   Telegram From the Embassy in Uruguay to the Department of State

Montevideo, August 14, 1961, 10 p.m.

179. Please transmit following message to President:

"Dear Mr. President:

The various committees have now completed their work and the general committee consisting of the heads of delegations will meet at seven tonight, Monday, to arrive at the final conference document. We have been meeting steadily for the past 24 hours with other heads of

---

Source: Department of State, Central Files, 371.8/8–1561. Secret; Eyes Only.

delegations except for the Cubans in an attempt to clean up the various documents and resolutions and tonight we will have to formalize this action with the Cubans present. In addition, Beltran of Peru, with the strong support of a number of other delegations has prepared a brief hard hitting résumé of our work which will be very effective from a public relations point of view. For this reason it will be highly objectionable to the Cubans and since they have not had a chance to see it as yet we can expect a violent explosion from them when it comes up.

We hope to keep to the original schedule and complete our work Wednesday but we will have to have luck with us. Despite what our friends from Uruguay may have been feeding to the press there are no new promises of US aid or new funds and no abandonment of the self-help concept.

Faithfully yours,

Douglas Dillon"

Sparks

30.   Telegram From the Embassy in Uruguay to the Department of State

Montevideo, August 16, 1961, 11 p.m.

188. Please transmit following message to President.

"Dear Mr. President:

Conference wound up its substantive work at 3:15 a.m. Wednesday when the general committee completed its approval of short declaration of Punta del Este which was prepared for public consumption in view of length and complexity of basic charter of Punta del Este.[1] Cubans made four or five efforts to amend the declaration but all their amendments were voted down unanimously, except for Bolivia, whose delegation has followed straight communist line throughout conference, clearly taking guidance from the Cubans. Head of Bolivian delegation was sick and out of action throughout conference and this comment does not reflect upon him personally. I was particularly pleased when the conference at my urging accepted unchanged a strong paragraph on promotion of private enterprise rejecting Bolivian motion to substitute the words 'public and

Source: Department of State, Central Files, 371.8/8–1761. Secret; Priority; Eyes Only.
[1] For text of the Declaration to the Peoples of America and the Charter of Punta del Este, see Department of State *Bulletin*, September 11, 1961, pp. 462–469.

private' for 'private'. The close of the conference was remarkable show of solidarity on the part of all except Cuba and Boliva. Final result is, I think, everything we could have hoped for and the Alliance for Progress has now been fully and successfuly launched.

Chapter on basic commodities sounds in places like very strong medicine but in every case where it refers to US there are the usual escape hatches which have come to be well recognized in inter-American Conference language. We abstained on two resolutions, one on meat and one on wool, which are in annex of main document, and in each case we were joined in abstention by Mexico. Guevara has had no success in upsetting conference but I do not believe this was his primary purpose. He has by maintaining relatively moderate position during working sessions of conference made it considerably more difficult for any early action along lines of Colombian initiative. I am convinced that his primary purpose here was to forestall such action. In this I am afraid he has had considerable success.

In the substantive work of the conference we received our most continuous and useful support from the large Brazilian delegation which was very strong and which on all substantive issues had no hesitancy in standing with us against Cuban amendments. The Brazilian delegation tried to offset this support by dining and lunching with Guevara a number of times. However they never once supported a Cuban initiative of any sort. We also had fine and helpful relations throughout conference with the Argentine and Mexican delegations. The Mexicans were very helpful on number of occasions which contrasted very favorably with their completely passive attitude at Bogota. Alemann of Argentina was outstanding among Latin Ministers in helping direct course of conference. Beltran of Peru and chief Chilean delegate Figueroa were also most helpful throughout, although Peruvian delegation as a whole was weak and unreliable. We also had help at important moments from Colombian and Venezuelan delegations both of which were of a high order. The other delegations, with the exception of Bolivia and Uruguay, were all friendly and behaved about as could be expected. The Uruguayans while not at all pro-Castro were extremely difficult on all sorts of items throughout the conference. The unsuccessful efforts to blackmail us into a promise of definite sums of short term aid marked low point of conference as far as I was concerned.

We will be leaving Montevideo early Friday and I will see Betancourt Saturday morning and lunch with him. We will arrive Washington Saturday evening.

Faithfully yours,

Douglas Dillon"

Sparks

31.   Editorial Note

At 2 a.m. on August 17, 1961, the head of the Cuban delegation to the IA–ECOSOC conference, Ernesto "Che" Guevara, contrived to meet the Assistant Special Counsel to President Kennedy, Richard N. Goodwin, at a party given by a Brazilian diplomat in Montevideo. The two spoke for approximately 3 hours. Goodwin made clear to Guevara that he had no authority to speak for the United States Government but would convey Guevara's ideas to the appropriate people in Washington. Guevara expounded on the nature and problems of U.S.-Cuban relations. He repeated his condemnation of the Alliance for Progress. The previous day at the closing session of the conference, he had characterized the Alliance as an instrument of U.S. economic imperialism, which was doomed to failure by its reliance on the privileged governing classes in Latin America to implement reforms. For Goodwin's account of the meeting, contained in his August 22 memorandum to President Kennedy, see volume X, and *Remembering America*, pages 195–202.

---

32.   Memorandum From Secretary of the Treasury Dillon to President Kennedy

Washington, August 25, 1961.

SUBJECT

Immediate Steps in Furthering the Alliance for Progress

In order to maintain the momentum of the Alliance for Progress created at Punta del Este, and also to make good on the commitments which were made to act promptly on emergency and short-term projects, I believe there are several steps which should be taken so that we can exercise the necessary leadership over the next few months while the new aid agency is being established. These recommendations reflect not only my views but also those of Secretary Rusk and ICA Director Labouisse.

1. It is of primary importance that the quality of U.S. personnel working on our aid programs in Washington and in the field be

---

Source: Kennedy Library, National Security Files, Alliance for Progress. Official Use Only.

improved, starting with the selection of an imaginative, knowledgeable and energetic person to serve as the head of the Latin American Bureau of the new aid agency. Meanwhile, I believe that the actions outlined below should serve to maintain the momentum which is required.

2. We should immediately inform all our missions in the participating Latin American countries of the understandings reached at Punta del Este so that they can effectively work with the other governments, especially in the field of emergency and short-term measures. The draft of a circular message is now under discussion between State, Treasury, and ICA/AID. When the aid legislation has been enacted, there should probably be a regional meeting of senior Washington and field personnel involved in carrying out the Alliance for Progress so that our objectives and methods can be fully explained and considered.

3. We should begin immediately to press the Secretary General of the OAS, the President of the Inter-American Development Bank and the Executive Secretary of ECLA to prepare the list of experts on the basis of which IA–ECOSOC will elect the new 9-man committee of development experts, which is to evaluate and make recommendations on long-term development programs. I believe it would be very helpful if the process of reviewing long-term programs could be started within the next two or three months for one or two countries where such programs are well advanced. I suggest that Mr. Labouisse, Assistant Secretary Woodward, and Ambassador Morrison might give this matter their personal attention.

4. The Charter of Punta del Este states that the United States stands ready to act promptly on applications for emergency financial assistance and urges the Latin Americans to make their applications for such assistance, to meet existing situations, within the next 60 days. There is already a temporary inter-agency committee under the chairmanship of Assistant Secretary Martin to coordinate views on requests for assistance, pending establishment of the aid agency. This committee should be retained, with the addition of the U.S. Executive Director of the IDB, Mr. Cutler. To assure that applications for assistance are given appropriate political consideration and that bureaucratic delays will be overcome as rapidly as possible, the group should be supplemented by a policy committee under the chairmanship of Under Secretary Ball, including Messrs. Woodward, Leddy, Linder, Martin, Coffin and Goodwin.

5. These emergency needs will have to be met out of Contingency Funds unless the applications meet the legislative criteria for Development Loans or Development Grants or qualify for Export-Import Bank loans.

6. A directive should be issued requiring that this committee be informed of all Latin American aid requests of any kind to U.S. officials.

7. I suggest that the Martin group should make a prompt survey of basic projects in a few of the smaller countries which might be moved quite rapidly.

8. We should inform the U.S. Executive Director of the Inter-American Development Bank that the U.S. will strongly support the large-scale self-help housing program, of the order of perhaps as much as $100 million, which the Bank's staff is now considering. We should support a promotional effort by the Bank to secure good applications and prompt arrangements to expand technical assistance for the carrying out of such projects.

9. Within the next few weeks we should negotiate with the Secretary General of the OAS an over-all agreement enabling us to finance, with the $6 million social progress money earmarked for OAS activities, the various task forces on education, health, land reform and other self-help measures which were provided for in one of the resolutions adopted at Punta del Este. Ambassador Morrison, with the assistance of ICA and ARA, should be requested to take the lead in this matter, under the general guidance of the Martin Committee.

10. We should request our missions to report on the status of self-help measures in the participating Latin American countries as well as long-term development programs which may be approaching the stage of financing. I suggest that the Martin Committee be asked to take the lead in preparing the necessary questionnaire and in keeping one up-to-date record of actions in this field. Meanwhile, the interested agencies must continue work already started so that we can most effectively relate our aid to progress in self-help and reform measures in the recipient countries.

11. The introduction of self-help measures, such as taxes and land reform, will be an extended process requiring continuous representational efforts and negotiations by our field personnel. This will require reorienting field staffs from the purely Point IV approach that has largely characterized our Latin American missions by increasing their competence in broad economic and social problems and policies. It will mean recruiting people with new kinds of skills and making more efficient use of officers with a capacity for this effort.

Douglas Dillon[1]

---

[1] Printed from a copy that indicates Dillon signed the original.

33.   Memorandum From the President's Assistant Special Counsel (Goodwin) to President Kennedy

Washington, September 28, 1961.

If the world emerges relatively unscathed from the current series of crises, then one of the most important long-range activities of your Administration will be to place the Alliance for Progress on a sound footing. We have already discussed the desirability of establishing a special fund for Latin America sometime early next year. It is clear that current appropriations will not be adequate to do the job which has to be done. Thus, it is absolutely essential that the next three or four months see this program get off to a good start. We cannot raise living standards in a few months, but we can begin on soundly conceived plans and projects; we can work to ensure that some of the Latin American nations show signs of significant self-help and social reform activity; and we can re-shape the procedures and thinking of our Latin American aid personnel.

All these things—and especially signs of activity on the part of the Latins themselves—are vital if we are to get anywhere with an Alianza fund. This means good people to run the program—especially the regional director in the Aid Agency. This regional director should be more than an area chief for A.I.D. He should be the "Coordinator of the Alliance for Progress"—with authority to direct the U.S. representatives on the Inter-American Bank, to be consulted on ExIm Bank activity, and to run, as far as possible, all the varied aspects of Latin American economic development programs.

It is, as we well know, very difficult to get capable enough people to do this. Nothing is more discouraging than to compare the caliber of people who were drafted into the Marshall Plan effort with those who now run our Latin American Aid program—a program which you have said is comparable in "scope and magnitude" to the Marshall Plan. However, there is one fellow now in the government—John Leddy of Treasury—who could probably do this job. Except for Linc Gordon he is the one person I know of who I would be confident could handle the Alianza in its early stages. It is very possible that there are people on the outside who might even be better, but appointing someone from outside would be an act of faith. In addition, if this program is to get off the ground immediately, Leddy's knowledge of the intricacies of our government (he also worked for Dillon in State), and the vagaries of Latin American economics (he worked on the Act of Bogota as well as the Charter of

Source: Kennedy Library, President's Office Files, Staff Memoranda, Goodwin. No classification marking.

Punta del Este) would be invaluable. This is by far the best fellow I, or anyone else, knows of for the job.

Doug Dillon would not want him to leave Treasury. He regards him as an invaluable assistant. I am convinced Leddy would take the job if pressed, although his loyalty to Dillon as well as the importance of his present post as Assistant Secretary of the Treasury would make him reluctant. You would have to draft him and that depends on the priority you give to this task.

2. As you know, I am very deeply involved in the day-to-day conduct of Latin American affairs. This involvement is inevitable as long as I am acting as an agent of yours in your effort to re-energize a long dormant and ineffective area of our policy. But such involvement is bound to create some difficulties. My relationship with Woodward is, I strongly believe, of the best; and there remains little, if any, resentment in the Bureau of Inter-American Affairs. He regards me as an aid to his policy, not an obstacle.

However, as long as I deal with Cuban exiles and with other Latins I am bound to be the object of some criticism and even personal abuse. I do not mind this in the slightest. It does not bother me or affect my work. I only point it out as a possible potential source of some embarrassment to you. I attach, as an example, a column which appeared in the *Northern Virginia Sun*.[1] The story itself is a complete fabrication. I never saw this fellow. In fact, I never heard of him until this story appeared. The quote from an "aide of Woodward" is also mythical. I also get word that the Tom Dodd–HUAC–Human Events crowd has been "looking into my background." Fortunately I was born too late to join anything incriminating.

Dick

---

[1] Not attached.

34.   Telegram From the Embassy in Mexico to the Department of State

Mexico City, October 19, 1961, 10 p.m.

Secun 26. For President, Secretary, Ball and Hamilton from Bowles. Although I am reporting separately on over-all results of regional meetings our Chiefs of Mission in Lima and San Jose, I would like to add some special comments on the dilemma we face in regard to the Alliance for Progress.

1) The Act of Bogota, Declaration of Punta del Este, and our own recent aid legislation called for no less than an economic and social revolution throughout Latin America.

2) The prestige and integrity of the Kennedy Administration are deeply committed to an all out effort to make this program successful. Indeed many Latin Americans already refer to the program not as the "Alliance for Progress" but as the "Kennedy Plan".

3) Opposition in Latin America to the determined effort which is required will be more formidable than has been generally assumed in Washington. The governments of most Latin American countries have not yet grasped what this program calls for in the way of economic and social change, nor do the economically privileged groups understand the sacrifices which will be required of them.

The obstacles to change vary from country to country but they are all deep-seated and each will be extremely difficult to remove. Some governments, for instance, feel it is impossible even to consider really basic land reform programs. Whatever they propose to do in this direction is likely to be no more than a gesture. Others are persuaded that a progressive tax system is antagonistic to their tradition, interest and in any event is no one's business but their own. Some others, noticeably Venezuela, which have taken important first steps in land reform and tax reform, will vigorously oppose any proposal to adjust the purchasing power of their currency to that of other trading nations, much less to take measures necessary to stop the flight of their capital overseas. When government officials in these countries are asked why the US should be asked to replace with our dollars those dollars and pounds sterling which their own well-to-do people have been transferring to banks in Switzerland, they show little comprehension.

4) As we press reluctant governments for economic, fiscal and social reforms and reorient our defense policy in Latin America toward

---

Source: Kennedy Library, National Security Files, Countries Series, Mexico, General, January 1961–May 1962. Confidential; Priority.

greater emphasis on internal security measures and less on old-fashioned prestige building military establishments, we will face strong criticism. Diminished political cooperation from many US oriented governments whose leaders do not in fact accept the need for rapid evolutionary change is inevitable. Many of our Missions are likely to become less effective in government-to-government dealings and support from some Latin American representatives in the United Nations will become less assured.

5) If we carry through with our commitment to this democratic revolution as I believe we must, we will be subjected in country after country to powerful attacks by the local oligarchy which will equate every reform we propose with radicalism. At the other extreme will be the Communists and Castroites who will attempt to equate our reform efforts with some new form of Yankee imperialism. In between will be the bulk of the people, in many cases with able and dedicated leaders, who will support our efforts but who lack funds, organization, and access to radio and news media.

6) With a few exceptions, our Chiefs of Mission and their associates are keenly aware of the implications of this situation. Due in large measure to the straight talk which characterized our meetings, they are convinced of need for a firm and consistent US position and determined to carry their share of the burden in spite of difficulties which they know will be created for them personally. Many of those present with long Latin American experience have been arguing for years in favor of the very approach to which we are now committed. Everyone agrees there will be need occasionally for compromise and expediency. But it is felt that these must be kept to a minimum.

7) Nearly all Ambassadors, however, expressed concern that their efforts to induce even at a reasonable pace social and economic reforms as quid pro quo for US loans, grants and technical assistance may not be backed up from Washington. In other words, they fear that the predictably strong reaction from entrenched conservative Latin American interests will cause us to back away when chips are down, in order to avoid the displeasure of politically friendly governments now in office.

8) The challenge that confronts us is a formidable one. I am more than ever convinced that we have an opportunity in Latin America which conceivably may prove to be a turning point in the whole global situation. If we have the courage and insight to stick to our stated objectives, an increasing number of liberal, strongly anti-Communist Latin American leaders with growing public support will begin to line up beside us. If we exert a great effort now to build fruitful relationships with the rising new political generation, we may even, after a few years of extremely frustrating and explosive change, be able to stand on a

much more solid political structure in this hemisphere which will be of inestimable value in dealing with the rest of the world.

9) Assuming that we are in fact determined to carry out the democratic role in which we have presented ourselves, there are several important requirements.

(A) The choice of the regional aid administrator for Latin America under Fowler Hamilton is, in my opinion, one of the most important appointments we will make in a long time.

(B) Closer coordination between all the lending and aid agencies must be assured. Efforts will be made to play the aid against the inter-American Bank, the inter-American Bank against the EXIM Bank, etc. It is essential that these agencies reach agreement on terms of operations, interpretations of the Act of Bogota, the Declaration of Punta del Este, as well as the legislation under which they are operating.

(C) In order to assure this essential coordination and to provide the utmost support for each Ambassador in his negotiations with his host government, we should place a high priority on the development of detailed standards which reflect the Act of Bogota, the Declaration of Punta del Este, and our own legislation. Every effort should be made to secure agreement on these standards, not only in aid but in the inter-American Bank, and other aid groups dealing with Latin America.

(D) Increased attention should be given to the military in all Latin American countries. If they can be persuaded that their support for economic and social reform is essential to the establishment of democratic, anti-Communist, secure societies, they can go far to assure the success of this program. If they fail to see the issues and side with the land-owning oligarchies, the result will be either an end to reform, civil war, or both. Haydn Williams has been a great strength in outlining this situation to the Mission Chiefs. He is confident that we can count on Pentagon understanding and assistance.

(E) There has been much too little emphasis in this area on the food for peace program. This can be a major element in the Alliance, particularly in the rural areas where sixty to seventy percent of the people live. The potentiality of this program in Latin America has scarcely been tapped.

(F) As opposition to economic and social reforms called for by the Act of Bogota develops from Latin American sources, we may expect to see similar criticism develop among conservative groups in the US. I believe that we can deal effectively with this sort of criticism by stressing the fact that we Americans have always believed that every farmer has a right to his own land, that a progressive income tax system which we advocate for Latin America has been well established for half a century in our own country. Why should we heavily taxed Americans be asked to contribute to help nations and governments which are unwilling to help themselves?

(G) Every effort should be made to assist our Ambassadors to meet the difficult pressures which they will surely encounter. Wide publicity for the detailed standards which we must develop in cooperation with the other agencies will be helpful in this respect. They will permit our Ambassadors to stress that we are acting solely on the basis of agreements in the Act of Bogota, the Declaration of Punta del Este which each Latin American Government signed, as well as on the instructions from the US Congress with regard to carrying out these objectives.

Even with such precise standards to which they can point we may and probably will see some Ambassadors declared persona non grata if they do their jobs well. These meetings convinced me that our Ambassadors in Latin America face the toughest assignments during the next few years to be found anywhere in the world. We must be certain they do not personally suffer in their careers for carrying out hard assignments just too well.

A personal letter from the President to each Ambassador in Latin America expressing his understanding of the difficulties they will be called upon to face and assuring them of his support would be most helpful. Such a letter from the President would also be an ideal vehicle for the concise, authoritative statement of our long and short range political objectives under the Alliance which, I believe, is urgently needed. I shall draft such a letter upon my return for your consideration.

Murat Williams' experience in El Salvador made a deep impression on all Mission Chiefs. The new government there is making an earnest if mild effort to carry out the objectives of the Declaration of Punta del Este. As a result it is under extreme pressure from the oligarchy in El Salvador which is centered around fourteen major land-owning families, plus some US citizens with major business interests. This group has started rumors that Williams has been forced to resign, that he has exceeded his instructions, that he has been rebuked by Washington, etc. Williams bluntly stated that although he is willing personally to meet whatever pressures may be involved, he would like my assurance that he would not someday receive a telegram from Washington suggesting that he was taking his job too seriously. I assured him this would not occur and after telephone consultation with Ed Gudeman in Washington asked Jay Cerf, Deputy Assistant Secretary of Commerce, to return briefly to Salvador with Williams to demonstrate that the latter has the administration's full support and to attempt to persuade the American businessmen to adopt a more realistic position.

I am convinced that the Alliance for Progress is one of the most important political and economic opportunities since the Marshall Plan. But it is far more complex, however, than any we have tackled before and a great deal of courage and insight will be required to carry it out. If we effectively meet this challenge we will succeed in bringing about peaceful economic and social revolution in Latin America of enormous worldwide consequence. Most Latin Americans whom I have met do not think we have the guts to do it. I have assured him that we have.

Mann

35. Summary Minutes of Meeting

Washington, November 29, 1961.

INTERDEPARTMENTAL COMMITTEE OF UNDER SECRETARIES ON FOREIGN ECONOMIC POLICY

[Here follows a list of participants 1-1/2 pages long.]

Alliance for Progress

Under Secretary Bowles presided at the meeting and made the presentation on the Alliance for Progress.

Reviewing the history of US relations with Latin America, he said that one of our difficulties has been that we have continued to think in European terms. We considered that world stability depended on European stability. When we finally realized that Europe was no longer the place where all policy decisions were made, we adapted ourselves to the new look in Asia and Africa, but we continued to take Latin America for granted. We can no longer do that, for a real revolution has come to this area.

The Act of Bogota was a historic document of great importance. It makes clear that Latin American development puts responsibilities on the Latin Americans as well as on us. We will put in money only if those countries have development plans and only if they will take action in such fields as taxes, land reform, prevention of capital flight. Congress

Source: Department of State, Interdepartmental Committee on Foreign Economic Policy Files: Lot 65 D 68, Interdepartmental Committee of Under Secretaries on Foreign Economic Policy, Alliance for Progress. Confidential.

has made it clear that it is authorizing us to carry the program forward under the conditions and framework outlined at Bogota.

Mr. Bowles doubts that we have considered in depth the requirements and the implications of the Alliance for Progress. Revolution in depth does not take place just by swapping one set of masters for another. What we are asking is that the philosophy of Jefferson and the social reforms of F.D.R. be telescoped into a few years in Latin America. And these steps will have to be taken against the wills of the rich and influential Latin Americans and the people in power. If the tremendous difference between the rich and poor is allowed to continue, Castro-like movements will rise to power. There will be explosions unless we can help create a liberal centrist dynamism that can operate free of the Left and the Right.

The reforms we want them to make appear very radical to them. We take progressive income tax for granted, but this is shockingly radical to those countries. We also take it for granted that there will be governmental interference in our economy whenever there is a clear need for it such as in time of war. We expect the government to stop capital outflow if it is leaving the country at such a rate as to jeopardize our economy. Those countries allow capital flight until their financial resources are all gone and then they ask us to replace them. Our whole system of land ownership is radical by their standards.

The Under Secretary wondered if we realize the full implications of what we are doing when we ask for these reforms. If this program works out, we will have really independent thinkers on the part of Latin American countries. They will not do whatever we want them to do. We will not always be able to rely on their votes in the UN. What will the US reaction be then? Will we say the whole thing was a mistake? Or will we realize that these are the growing pains of independence?

Mr. Bowles mentioned the cable he sent back from Mexico City[1] (distributed). In it he pointed out some of the problems we will face and said that our Ambassadors would face a hard test as the programs they espouse run afoul of the best families in the countries to which they are assigned. It is very important that our Ambassadors know they can depend on the Department to back them up. "We have a real bear by the tail," Mr. Bowles said, "and I hope we realize it."

The Under Secretary emphasized that this is not a job for any one agency but involves almost every one in Washington. There must be close coordination. We need to develop standard criteria, otherwise the Latin Americans will play off one agency against another. These criteria must be worked out from the Act of Bogota, the Punta del Este confer-

---

[1] Document 34.

ence, and from our Congressional mandate. Mr. Bowles touched briefly on the roles of some of the agencies—State, USIA, Labor, Commerce, Defense and Treasury.

General Discussion

The major points which emerged in the discussion that followed Mr. Bowles' remarks are summarized below:

Tax Reform. A good deal of the discussion centered on tax reform. Income taxes will be particularly difficult to establish. Tax collections must be improved. Career services should be established to make tax collections. It was pointed out that Argentina has almost doubled its tax revenue without raising taxes one cent—merely by tightening up on collections. We need a good rationale for tax reform which will help sell it to the wealthy and powerful Latin Americans.

The Time Element. The program cannot be implemented and reforms cannot happen overnight, but lots of the Latin Americans expect this.

Preventing Capital Flight. Latin Americans should be given tax privileges for productive investment at home, but it should be made difficult for investment capital to go abroad. This means tighter exchange controls.

How to Bring About Reform. Persuasion—with finesse—will be needed as Latin Americans do not like to be told how to run their economies. Such persuasion can be exerted by utilizing forces other than the US Government, such as the OAS, the Inter-American Development Bank, and the Harvard group which will be having another tax conference in Latin America this year.

Reforms have to be built into the country programs and it must be clear that the financing of the plan is dependent on the reforms being carried out. The panel of nine experts will be most important in this regard. In the course of their review, the experts can say if a plan is inadequate with respect to tax or land reform. If it is, we can then say that the panel's recommendation is not favorable, so we can't finance the plan. This is an important new instrument.

The idea that external financing will be in some ratio to internal resource contribution could be an incentive for the governments to collect taxes and encourage local investment. As plans are developed and the Latin Americans realize what has to be done, they will start thinking of the means for generating the money to accomplish the objectives. The Bell report on the Philippines was cited as an example of how to get reforms. We offered the Philippines $50 million a year for five years, but we conditioned our aid on a minimum wage law, land reform, tighter control over foreign exchange, and a progressive income tax. President Magsaysay told US officials later that if the US hadn't put those conditions on its aid, he couldn't have built a reform program.

Use of ECLA. The UN Economic Commission for Latin America should have an important role in the Alliance for Progress. It will take some time for the US to live down its previous negative attitude toward ECLA, but the Latin Americans have great respect for it. Strengthening ECLA is one way of bringing about some of the changes without the onus being on the US. Also, ECLA is a promising place to build up a supply of technicians.

US Private Investment. US private investment is important in the Alliance for Progress. The type of an operation Americans run in a foreign country is one of the most important factors in that country's attitude toward the US. Bringing in know-how is an important contribution. But Latin Americans are worried for fear the repatriation of earnings will be too large.

An excellent example of investment was cited in the Sears operation in El Salvador. Five years ago Sears opened a store there. When it opened, zero percent of the products sold were made in El Salvador. Today 42 per cent are made there. As a consequence of this investment, a furniture factory and a plastics factory have been established, with Sears lending part of the money for those operations. All the employees in the Sears store are locals except the manager, and the pride in the operation is something to behold. Every clerk operates a cash register, and the loss due to theft is no greater than in Sears stores here. Local art is exhibited in the store and is sold without profit to the store so that it serves as an art gallery as well.

The Commerce Department indicated that it is thinking of having a hemisphere conference in one of the countries which has led in social reform. Private investors could show their products and demonstrate what they are doing for the countries in which they are operating.

Need for Point in US Government for Private Investors to Come. Under Secretary of Treasury Fowler said there should be one place in the US Government where private intrepreneurs can come and get an answer to their questions—whether they should make a joint-company approach; whether there should be a veering away from raw material to consumer goods local manufacturing, etc. He thought State the logical place.

Need for a Political Base. A political base must be established which allows reforms to go ahead. The labor unions can be a force for good or a force for the other side. It is not easy to get the labor movements in these countries to move in the right direction, but the Labor Department is giving a lot of thought to this. Social Security and other benefits of a welfare state cannot precede economic development. The question is what kind of priorities are to be established—and what political support can be mustered for them.

Task Force to Formulate Agreed Concepts. It was agreed that there should be uniform standards and criteria for use by AID, the Eximbank, and US representatives on international bodies such as the Inter-American Development Bank, the panel of nine experts, etc. There was concurrence that an inter-agency task force should be established immediately to concern itself with formulating agreed concepts which our agencies and representatives could follow with conformity. AID was asked to take the leadership in this matter.

Joseph D. Coppock[2]
Executive Secretary

---

[2] Printed from a copy that bears this typed signature.

---

36.   Memorandum From the Under Secretary of State (Ball) to the Assistant Secretary of State for Inter-American Affairs (Woodward)

Washington, January 8, 1962.

When I saw the Attorney General this morning, he made a strong point of asking that on any statements made by the United States at the Foreign Ministers' meeting in Punta del Este[1] we should emphasize the positive approach through the Alliance for Progress and our concern for the Latin American people, rather than merely the negative approach of our apprehension over the threat of Castroism. I told him that I was sure this was being planned, but he asked me if I would make a special effort to see that this was done. He said that "It would be extremely helpful in several quarters if this could be accomplished."

Source: Department of State, Central Files, 611.20/1–862. No classification marking. Copies were sent to Swank, Dutton, Jamison, Tully, and Moscoso. A marginal notation indicates the memorandum was intended to be circulated to Goodwin.

[1] Reference is to the Eighth Meeting of Foreign Ministers of the Organization of American States convened at Punta del Este, January 21–31.

37.   Highlights of the First Meeting of the Working Group on Problems of the Alliance for Progress

Washington, January 16, 1962.

PRESENT

AID—Mr. Chenery, Mr. Moscoso, Mr. Rubin
E—Mr. Trezise
ARA—Mr. Goodwin
S/P—Mr. Rostow
S/P—Mr. Fried
S/P—Mr. Johnson
S/P—Mr. Ramsey
S/P—Mr. Wriggins
Ambassador Stephansky
Treasury—Mr. Leddy
OAS Committee of Wise Men—Mr. Perloff

The working paper prepared by S/P[1] appeared to be a useful starting point, raising among other questions, (1) the usefulness of attempting to locate Latin American countries in one of four identifiable stages of modernization and (2) the necessity of taking the political (and other non-economic) characteristics of recipients into account when Alliance assistance programs are to be considered.

Latin America is a peculiarly useful area for examination of the problem of assistance on this combined basis because political and economic factors are closer to being dominant than in other areas where military factors are more urgent. Also economic and political development has proceeded far enough in some cases to reveal major structural imbalances.

In our explorations it is important to remember that aid is only one element of foreign policy, and trade, commodity stabilization, traditional diplomacy and other forms of direct influence may be as useful.

Because up till now the criteria for aid have been explained to Congress in broad terms, emphasizing the need for long term aid, our hands may be unnecessarily tied unless we are able this year to explain with much greater sophistication the uses and limits of the present aid criteria. With Congress we must discuss candidly the underlying problems of effecting a turn-around in aid policy, which demands a turn-around in the policies of the recipient governments themselves. Since we must bring the recipient countries along with our own changing concepts, it

---

Source: Department of State, S/P Files: Lot 69 D 121, American Republics, 1962. Confidential.

[1] Not printed. (Ibid.)

takes time. Often there are signs of change—notably the early formulation of plans—which do not strike the casual observer and are not yet affecting official policy in recipient countries. Accordingly, we have reason to attempt to persuade Congress that our aid policies in Latin America are not in as disheveled a condition as it may appear.

What are the most urgent reforms which we should insist upon?

We should distinguish reforms urged for essentially political reasons from those aimed at promoting economic development. The former might be designed to shift the locus of power from backward-looking to forward-looking groups, to prevent the defection of important groups, or to bring the government closer to the people. Land reform in many countries might serve such purposes. Tax reforms may serve a more exclusively developmental purpose, although certain types of tax reforms might work against development if they were mainly political in their intent.

What techniques have we for applying political pressures in order to induce conformance to reform criteria? There are some countries where the politically dominant groups are not interested in reform, where their power remains for the present relatively unimpaired—either because change has not yet challenged their traditional base of power or because they can count upon the loyalty of the military. We cannot expect to influence such regions very much toward reform, unless they face urgent financial or other crises.

How can we develop the skills, organizational and other know-how, for promoting the strength, unity and constructiveness of the middle and left of center political elements who are likely to be the best guarantors of the kind of orderly yet expeditious change which the Alliance sets as its model? Often such political groupings exist in latent form but lack organization.

Where aid must be given for political reasons, such as to prevent a diplomatically friendly regime from falling, we should endeavor to (a) give it some economically sensible purpose, and (b) strengthen the hand of those who want to press forward toward development. Military aid in the past has often served the purpose of shoring up an unpopular regime and, unfortunately, it has often been given to men with little interest in development, whereas we should use aid to enhance the influence and prestige of those who are interested in development.

The term "political aid" is regularly used in two different senses: (a) aid designed to have a favorable impact upon our relations with a particular country (e.g. aid to Panama designed to reduce demands for unacceptable changes in our Panama Canal relationship); and (b) aid designed to have an effect upon the political structure or political process of the country aided. In actual fact, of course, the distinction is often not so clear-cut. It is clear that Congress objects to political aid in the first of these two senses; it is less certain whether Congressmen could not be convinced of the value of the second kind of political aid.

Alliance as at present formulated lacks an illuminating overall political objective for the hemisphere and its place in US grand strategy. The last Administration made the promotion of a free enterprise community our objective. That was simple and it had an appeal to certain groups. It contained a self-help element. Is our present objective the creation of some new kind of inter-American system? Lacking a clear objective, we are not clear where we must . . . trim developmental objectives in order to insure survival of friendly regimes, or where we can sacrifice a regime friendly in the short run so long as it is likely to be replaced by one more determined to bring rapid political and economic change.

Bolivia has passed through the Punta del Esta barrier, but it poses profoundly difficult problems. Commitment and promise have outrun capacity to perform: mass organizations have leaped forward in their ability to swing power while government administration, the political system, economic productivity and the balance of payments position have all fallen far short. On the other hand, Bolivia's leaders are well-endowed with that indispensable precondition for development—the will to modernize—and this may be the most important ingredient of all.

Particularly here, there may be very real merit in concentrating efforts on a few cases which can become demonstrations of what we are able to do when we set our minds to it. Too much dispersion may lead to inconspicuous results; concentration of effort may make demonstrations possible.

Can we appropriately discuss "criteria" and expect to have them operative when we are in fact within an "alliance" in which the recipients, too, presumably have something to say about what they require? When others are as deeply involved in the planning as they are presumed to be, criteria defined by the US may not be applicable.

Some insurance in cases of risky policy. If we could assure countries that we could stand behind them if they undertook policies with some economic risk, such as land reform, tax reform, etc., it might be a useful inducement to bolder development initiatives.

Despite our talk of "self-help", many government leaders in Latin America just don't take us seriously. In part this is because they do not see how they can insist upon further measures of self-help and still remain in power. In part, too, they believe our assistance to be largely politically motivated. We must be alert to the demonstration effect of our assistance policies. They must have it demonstrated that those who try to meet the criteria will obtain more resources for development. If we shore up too many friendly regimes for political reasons without putting due weight on economic development criteria, they will not take our talk of self-help and reform seriously.

Perhaps the most difficult problem is finding ways of engaging the local political system in the development enterprise. Unless there develop local political pressures working toward self-help, reform and development, US efforts to insist on aid criteria will be diplomatic liabilities. This may be the most important task facing us.

Some important cautions were expressed on the way work should be conducted: (1) an unduly elaborate analytical scheme may not be applicable for lack of data, the margins for statistical error in many cases being so large as to more than outweigh any possible increments of resources forthcoming from abroad; (2) since each situation was unique, and fraught with intangibles, generalized propositions would not be likely to be applicable in more than one or two cases, and each one country would have to be examined independently in any case.

For instance, too rapid tax reforms can cause disinvestment and flight of capital, land reform initially produces a fall in production and balance of payments difficulties. Therefore, one must be able to reach an equation combining political growth, social gains and economic development. Each country's equation will be different. On the other hand, an unstructured empirical analysis of individual countries was not likely to be fruitful.

It was decided to proceed along the following lines:

(1) A smaller working group would be established, combining AID and S/P personnel, to formulate a set of questions which would, if answered, get at the key economic and political problems in carrying forward the Alliance criteria in individual countries. These, when refined, would provide a working framework for some country studies.

(2) Five or six studies would then be undertaken, in considerable depth, on countries of major importance to the US which represent different characteristic Alliance problems.

(3) The criteria problem would then be re-assessed and the possibilities of extending this method to other countries in Latin America and elsewhere.

38.   Research Memorandum Prepared in the Bureau of Intelligence and Research

RAR–11   Washington, January 17, 1962.

LATIN AMERICAN POLITICAL STABILITY AND THE ALLIANCE FOR PROGRESS

Abstract

Broadly-based political stability is a goal sought by the United States in the Alliance for Progress.[1] Some Latin American countries have already made real headway toward this goal, especially Mexico, Uruguay, and Costa Rica, and to a lesser extent, Venezuela and Argentina. The governments in these countries are oriented toward middle class interests and are based on fairly wide popular support; their political institutions provide means of articulating the interests of important groups in the population. Thus they are reasonably well protected against internal subversion and foreign intrigue, despite weaknesses and stresses in their systems of government.

For other Latin American countries to reach this degree of political stability involves their making a series of changes to which serious obstacles exist in their social patterns and in pressures from right and left against orderly reform. Some of the governments, even though they are organized on a narrow interest base, respond in a measure to popular needs, but by and large the ruling groups lack zeal for reform, with all its hazards. The military institution, a key element, is inclined to the status quo. Organized labor, often the major popular sector, is generally disoriented and vulnerable to the appeals of the revolutionary left. The growing middle class sector has generally not been a stabilizing force. However, the Alliance for Progress can provide the framework for enlist-

---

Source: Department of State, S/P Files: Lot 69 D 121, American Republics, 1962. Limited Official Use; Noforn. Drafted by Bushnell. Sent to the members of the Secretary's Policy Planning Committee under cover of a February 9 memorandum from Rostow. It was intended as the basis for a discussion by the Committee at a meeting held on February 13; see Document 40.

[1] This paper was prepared in response to questions raised by Research Memorandum RAR–6 of November 17, 1961, "Alliance for Progress Goals Linked with Presidential Upsets", which described blocks to reform in countries with narrowly-based governments. [Footnote in the source text. RAR–6 suggested that the leaders of Latin American countries attempting to implement Alliance for Progress reforms had drawn the wrath of both the extreme right and revolutionary left in their nations. This resulted in destabilizing political pressures that led to the ouster of the Presidents of El Salvador, Brazil, and Ecuador. (Department of State, S/P Files: Lot 69 D 121, American Republics, 1961)]

ing middle class elements in support of evolutionary reform, permitting a mutation from the present narrowly-based political systems to more broadly-based but still moderate governments.

Progress Toward Stability

Not all Latin American governments suffer from chronic instability. In some countries there are organized bases of popular support for constitutional authority and substantial immunity to subversive movements of the left and right. Included among these countries are Mexico, Uruguay, Costa Rica, and perhaps Venezuela and Argentina. In their societies the danger of subversion from the right has been greatly reduced. Political action by the military is curbed because of the strength and influence of well-organized popular forces which are relatively immune to propaganda from the revolutionary left.

Costa Rica and Uruguay have developed greater political stability because of their cultural and social unity and the evolution over a long period of a large middle class. The stability of the other countries (Mexico, Venezuela, Argentina), which are more complex and less unified, is the end product of radical reform or revolution carried out under the leadership of mass-based political parties. In Mexico the reorganization of political life on a popular base took a generation of civil war and revolution. Argentina and Venezuela achieved means of articulating and providing representation for the interests of broader groups in the community through less violent, far-reaching and long-drawn-out progress toward the new political order.

The broadening of the political base in these countries of radical reform is not to be looked upon wholly in terms of modern western (Anglo-American) experience either as to methods or results. These societies have emphasized national sovereignty, popular welfare, and industrial development rather than personal political and economic liberties. The middle class reformers or revolutionary leadership proclaimed these goals and made it their first order of business to pursue them and thereby to consolidate a mass following. Political change was accomplished by a greater centralization of government authority, with strong overtones of fascism in the Argentine experience under Peron. The governments created by the Mexican PRI, the Argentine Peronists, and the Venezuelan AD were designed to manipulate and shape their countries through playing a large role in both political and economic affairs. They were to be directly responsible for the strategy of achieving national goals. Achievements in turn were to strengthen their claim to continuing leadership in the society.

The record of stabilization in the new pattern suggests hazards as well as advantages in Latin-style democracy. The balancing of wider interests may cause new rigidities even while it brings stability. Very large bureaucracies have grown up to carry out economic missions as well as to serve the functions of patron to the humble and broker between multiplying pressure groups. In Argentina, while carefully balancing the forces of labor and the military, the Frondizi regime is attempting to bring about a resumption of economic growth and to move Argentina off the dead center eventually reached by the Peronist regime with its deficit financing, overblown bureaucracy, feather-bedding unions, business monopoly, and neglect of agriculture. In Venezuela there is great danger that the abuses and corruption of the dictatorship will be translated into abuses of economic democracy if large numbers of citizens come to rely on government support instead of productive work. In Mexico the new social system has yet to embrace much more than half the population in its benefits.

The essential common factor among the broadly-based moderate governments is that they are middle class governments with relatively good linkages to the mass of the population. The mass support for these regimes goes beyond the enthusiasm conjured up by heated election campaigns. The continuity of popular support which defends them against movements from the political extremes reflects the development of mass organizations that are either keyed into the dominant political system or are able to articulate popular interests and make good their claims to obtain benefits for the people through established means of communication with the government. Not all middle class governments with broad bases of support, however, are stable and moderate. In Bolivia and Cuba the overthrow of the established order by middle class radical groups destroyed capital resources, caused an exodus of technicians and entrepreneurs, and made both countries dependent upon foreign aid for their basic necessities. Moreover, the Mexican Revolution and to a lesser degree the Peronist reforms that effected the transfer of power to the middle class were severely wasteful of national resources and capabilities.

Obstacles to Stability

What are the prospects that other Latin American countries will reach political stability through widened popular participation and support of authority? Can the transition proceed without leading into a harsh totalitarian system as in Cuba or a breakdown as in Bolivia? The answer may be in doubt for all except a few of the other thirteen Latin American republics.

With luck and good planning this few could include Brazil, Chile, and Colombia. Even in these countries the prospects for achieving a broadened and strengthened base of authority while maintaining stability are far in the future if they have to be realized through the slow-moving processes of gradual, evolutionary social and economic change. On the other hand, forcing the pace by political action of the type applied in Mexico or Argentina could open the way for excesses of the Cuban type, associated with Soviet intervention. It could lead to civil war even without foreign support of the revolutionary left. Venezuela, with its large petroleum revenues, is not a model for the poorer countries of the area. The cultural and social endowments of Uruguay and Costa Rica simply have no parallel elsewhere.

Some Latin American governments with a narrow political base are sensitive to popular pressures and undertake piecemeal reforms. But significant reform is barred by the difficulty of the problems to be solved or the reluctance of ruling groups to push essential measures. Most governments appear to be paralyzed for fear of offending propertied interests and precipitating action by vested interests in conjunction with the military on the one hand, or of encouraging the revolutionary left on the other. The feeling that radical change is foolhardy has doubtless been reinforced by the experience of reform-inclined executives in Brazil and Ecuador. In any case, the present leadership finds maintenance of the status quo the lesser of two evils.

The military may be torn between their traditional alignment with the propertied class and, on the other hand, their growing fear of revolution if reform lags, and in some cases the aspirations of personnel drawn from reform-minded sectors of society. However, the overriding fear may well be apprehension that once the mob is out of control its new leadership will liquidate the military. The tighter the lid has been held down, the stronger will be anticipations of reaction tending to take an extreme form. Thus, in the absence of a strong responsible civilian leadership to furnish a lead toward reform, the military may be incapable of playing a positive role. Whether the leadership is in the hands of reaction or reform, they tend to stand with constitutional authority.

The main organizational focus that commonly exists amongst the people in general is the trade unions; this sector of labor is subject to a confusion of impulses. A strong stand against Castro/communist penetration will be found amongst labor groups in Mexico, Argentina, Venezuela, Colombia, and Uruguay, but in most of the countries these groups have no effective reformist leadership around which to rally. Meanwhile communist forces are strengthening their political thrust and gaining the confidence of revolutionary leftwing and campesino groups—although these groups are still limited in numbers. Throughout the area many labor organizations remain passive against a threat to government authority.

The example of Cuba has the effect more of reinforcing the determination of propertied groups to maintain a tighter control than of stimulating an impulse among them to sponsor reform. Their inclination to maintain the status quo is increased by their inability to appease popular pressures and to gain organized mass support through half measures and programs of change that are limited in scope. They may be further confirmed in this immobilism by their ability to count on military backing against radical reform movements. In these circumstances the propertied groups offer less than effective partnership in prosecuting reforms under the Alliance for Progress. They even offset foreign financial aid by removing their capital to safe havens abroad. Such reforms as they sponsor tend to be hesitant and badly executed, and in the long run the reforms can serve little purpose in achieving political stability.

In most of those countries where it lacks the force to take over the governments, the middle class still plays a disturbing role in the political system. It has grown rapidly in recent years with the expansion of the urban complex, greater educational opportunities, and the area-wide burst of economic growth following World War II. Usually dominant in the management of mass-based political parties, trade unions, campesino organizations, communications media, the educational system, and the military, middle class leaders have key but still subordinate roles in the society. They are inclined to be dissatisfied with their secondary position and relatively humble status. The rank and file of the middle class, dependent salaried personnel and small business men, is under pressure from inflation, the housing shortage, and monopoly pricing. Many are only slightly above a decent subsistence level. Thus the Latin American middle class is not comparable to the moderate, propertied middle class of either Western European or US tradition. Its loudest voices are chauvinistic, anti-capitalist, and resentful of a status quo that limits its horizons and seems to deny the possibility of rapid progress for the nation as a whole. The middle class in many countries of Latin America where it has not yet achieved dominance in the society represents a most serious danger to the present order of things.

Role of the Alliance for Progress

In the charged political atmosphere of these years, pressure for Alliance for Progress reforms may actually feed extremist strength since propertied groups are not ready to give way without a struggle to governments that propose rapid social change. Nevertheless, despite its immediate effect in stirring up political discords, the Alliance for Progress may carry with it means to resolve the conflict between middle class aspirations and mass hopes as against the status quo. Its goals presuppose a whole range of social operations that require the services of hundreds of thousands of members of the middle class, ranging from individuals with no more than vocational training to intellectuals skilled in the arts of communication, and also including the military. These tasks include services to labor unions, rural education, rural extension, cadastral surveys, conservation, cooperative organizations, as well as employment in the growing industrial and modern service sector. Most of the proposed reforms will be labor intensive since many individuals are needed to organize the new social and economic units and to act as intermediaries for the dissemination of techniques already well understood but not now practiced outside the urban areas or in a relatively small urban sector.

These civilian activities performed by the military would also spread the rule of law and order and increase respect for government in rural areas. All these programs for the military would have a dual purpose—they would directly contribute to the development of the country and to the improvement of living standards at the same time that they involved the military in the Alliance, increased popular respect for the military, and indoctrinated the military in the benefits of widespread socio-economic progress.

All Latin American armed forces will not be eager to participate in such development programs. They would prefer prestigious modern fighting equipment to bulldozers and surveying equipment; but the supply of military equipment can be made dependent at least in part on the execution of civil action programs. The military, especially the officers, may be unwilling to spend long periods of time in the backward rural areas, but some officers may find satisfying careers in civil action programs once they are started. In Bolivia many recruits would like to stay in the military if more than private's pay were available for men engaged in civil action work.

Students and Teachers

To involve university students and teachers in the Alliance for Progress is difficult because these groups do not generally have continuing organizations with widespread support. Failure to enlist their support, however, may doom the program because these groups reject moderate reform and students provide the infantry for the violence of the revolutionary left. Moreover, in pursuing its aim of promoting self-help, one of the main targets of the Alliance must be education. Improvement in the quality and quantity of education can contribute powerfully to weaning students from extreme leftist philosophies if aid is directed to strengthening universities and faculties which have moderate political leanings. In general the politically moderate pro-United States universities are also those which do outstanding work in education—for example, the University of Concepcion (Chile), which is located in an agricultural area and emphasizes agricultural technology; the University of Minas Gerais (Brazil), which is noted for its advanced work in the social sciences; or the University of Valle (Colombia), which is reported to have a full-time faculty of 172 for a student body of 250 in medicine, 240 in engineering, 100 in economics, 50 in nursing, and 500 in part-time extension courses in the same fields.

There are many factors underlying the widespread leftist political action among students and teachers, of which some of the most important follow. Students almost universally attend only part-time, as does the faculty. The students and frequently even the faculty are not required to attend class. Students concentrate in law and liberal arts faculties far beyond the possibility of remunerative employment in activities other than politics. Students control the universities through their representation on governing councils. Facilities are usually lacking for study, especially libraries and laboratories.

Support from the Alliance can help to remove these basic conditions which lead to extremist political activity. In some cases new universities, including regional universities, could be established. New schools and faculties to strengthen studies in agricultural technology, social sciences, and other neglected disciplines could be created under the Alliance. Aid should also be directed to those institutions and faculties which include the fewest far left agitators.

How effective a serious approach to education can be in discouraging irresponsible political activity may be gauged from the University Center (faculty) of General Studies at the National University of Honduras. This faculty was recently organized to provide general subjects in preparation for the specialized faculties and to introduce needed new professional courses. A difficult curriculum and a disciplined approach to practical education are the hallmarks of the new faculty. In the elections of July, 1961, for leadership of the student federation the students of the new faculty ran up a large enough majority for the democratic candidates to offset the small majorities won by the communist-inclined candidates in each of the six other faculties, although the leftists still control the federation through the faculty representatives.

Careful distribution of aid to education can weaken the universities and faculties which are politically oriented to the left by building up universities and faculties which, because of their own participation in the Alliance, will tend to support it. There may, to be sure, be less political organization and activity in schools which devote themselves to preparing technical personnel for work in the development effort. Yet it is to be anticipated that, as these graduates grow into their work of construction and leadership, they will swell the ranks of the moderate, centrist minded groups on the political stage of the nation.

39.   Research Memorandum From the Director of the Bureau of Intelligence and Research (Hughes) to the Assistant Secretary of State for Inter-American Affairs (Woodward)

INR–35   Washington, January 19, 1962.

SUBJECT

> Creating Allies for Socio-Economic Progress With Political Stability in Latin America

Since RAR–6 on the polarization of political forces presented a rather bleak picture,[1] we have tried to do some thinking which may be of interest to you on the positive aspects of the Alliance.

Abstract

Organized political forces in most Latin American countries are polarized on the status quo right and the far left. There is an uneasy balance between left and right which is unfavorable to prospects for orderly advancement. Success of the Alliance for Progress may therefore depend on the ability of the Alliance to build its own organized support of moderate groups by directing a substantial part of the available foreign funds to projects that specifically aim at strengthening major groups and institutions in the center at the same time that they contribute directly to socio-economic progress. Organized groups that may with particularly successful results be involved in the process of development are moderate labor unions and military organizations. The power of the revolutionary left among students may be reduced if AID can involve chosen educational institutions more fully in its program. The disbursing of aid through organizations somewhat independent of the government also minimizes US reliance on the current government as the only purveyor of evolutionary change.

The Problem

In Latin America the United States desires to promote orderly evolution avoiding the extremes of castrista revolution and maintenance of the status quo. For such evolution to proceed in changing the face of Latin America the Alliance for Progress must have strong, well-organized local allies. Yet, in most countries the organized politico-economic groups tend to polarize at the extremes of the revolutionary left and the status quo right (see RM–RAR–61–6, 8, and 10). These poles are especially powerful because each is based on a hard-core of experienced

---

Source: Department of State, S/P Files: Lot 69 D 121, American Republics, 1962. Limited Official Use; Noforn. Also sent to the members of the Secretary's Policy Planning Committee under cover of a February 9 memorandum from Rostow. It was intended to serve as the basis for a discussion by the Committee held February 13; see Document 40.

[1] See footnote 1, Document 38.

political tacticians: the left on the communists, the right on the less formally organized but for the time being more powerful socio-economic landowning and business interests. To offset these extremes the Alliance for Progress needs support from other organized power groups in the community.

The Proposal

Four potential allies in most Latin American countries are the labor unions, the military, the universities and secondary schools, and the church. Now the extreme power groups usually control most of these institutions or at least make them ineffective in political power. In general the military and the church are strongly influenced by the vested interests of the right, while extreme leftists have gained leadership in many universities and labor unions. Yet these groups are potentially centrist; and, if the Alliance for Progress can wean them from the control of the extremists and strengthen their independence and power, it can build its own consistent reliable support.

The possible methods of using the Alliance for Progress to build support for evolutionary development vary enormously among the countries and among various groups. The basic method would be to channel financial assistance through actual or potential allies in labor, the military, and the educational system, when such assistance would strengthen the underlying bases of moderate political action at the same time that it served specific goals of the Alliance for Progress. The church, which is not considered in detail in this paper, could be counted on more and more to push social action favoring political stability as the programs of other responsible agencies gained momentum. As a general rule Alliance funds will be just one additional means of steering crucial elements toward support of moderate but steady socio-economic progress. The many other programs, like information, educational exchange, and direct personal contact, could also be speeded and coordinated. Not only the church but numerous other private groups in Latin America, both national and foreign, are ready to join in these programs if given a lead in the right direction.

Some US financial and technical aid now goes to labor and military groups in Latin America. What is proposed is a very high priority to these groups as a means of directly improving the political environment for the Alliance for Progress.

In those Latin American countries—Mexico, Argentina, Venezuela—where substantial socio-economic change has occurred during the last three decades, the process has involved a bureaucratic centralization of power in the government, accompanied by Parkinsonian inefficiency (see RM–RAR–62–11). The decentralization suggested here for some development efforts is not an attempt to stop centralization of power altogether, for centralization is essential for rapid development in the

Latin American cultural and economic environment. Rather, the building of moderate centrist groups will supplement and modify the inevitable concentration of power in three ways: (1) by providing articulate political demands for creation and use of desirable central government power, (2) by reducing slightly the strain of increasing demands on the civilian central bureaucracy through dispersion of control over a small part of the development program to independent power centers, (3) by providing independent guidance and criticism of the dominant central authority so as to limit inefficiency and diversion from the central task of development.

Selection of Aid Recipients

U.S. aid to Latin America has been directed through the local civil authorities except for substantial quantities to selected local businesses of either foreign or domestic ownership. Aid directed to or through the government tends to gain immediate support for US policy, but it also tends to build animosity among those groups that oppose the government, because they find US aid supporting (directly or indirectly) the political "ins." In the past, when the opposition assumed power, it quickly turned to the United States despite past bad feeling, because there was no alternative source of the aid necessary to maintain the new government in power. Now, however, as its economic power increases, the USSR becomes an alternative source of economic aid—and a source whose ideology appeals to the far leftists more than the American politico-economic ideology appeals to the status quo right.

To strengthen the supporters of present governments exclusively is by no means vital to long-term interests of the United States. In fact, the United States is best able to work with a country where any government will be backed and controlled by a selection of moderate groups. Thus, to create and strengthen moderate groups in a society serves the United States long-term interests, whether or not these groups are in power at a given moment. To the extent that aid is not controlled by the political "ins" the United States avoids building potential enemies among the political opposition. It remains true, of course, that much aid must in any case be channeled through the existing government because in many fields it is the only organization which can carry out the programs. In some countries such as Chile, Peru, Paraguay, and Nicaragua aid to the governments may be needed as a lever to gain permission for the United States to extend aid to groups or institutions that are not controlled by the political incumbents.

Labor unions and the military are the two groups which may most easily be built into strong auxiliaries of the Alliance for Progress in Latin America. Both the unions and the military influence large numbers of people. Both are usually lower-class organizations with middle-class leadership. Both have continuing organizations and patterns of leadership, an established continuing function, and a desire to maintain at least some independence from the politicians of the current government. The course of the Cuban revolution is making the leaders of both groups realize that non-communist labor leaders and the traditional armed forces are among the first to be liquidated by a Castro-communist regime.

Labor

Programs to build moderate labor unions might center on making loans and grants directly to selected union federations and locals for cooperative socio-economic projects that benefit their members. An example is the project now under way through which AID will contribute $350,000 toward constructing, furnishing, and operating labor temples in Guayaquil and Quito, Ecuador. The labor centers will house headquarters of individual unions, provide meeting places, and offer services such as training courses and legal aid. In some cases directly productive investments can be channeled through labor organizations. For example, the Inter-American Bank recently loaned $640,000 to a cooperative of 4000 meat-packing workers in Montevideo to expand the operations of a plant abandoned by private enterprise and reopened by the workers' cooperative. The cooperative has been under attack from a rival communist-controlled union.

Such projects as union housing cooperatives might receive IDB loans. A combination of AID loans and grants might finance such community projects as worker clinics, trade schools, and meeting halls. Export-Import Bank loans might provide tools of the trade to such unions as those of taxi drivers—for example the dynamic but moderate Chauffeurs of the First of May in Bolivia. The DLF, IDB, or IFC might finance worker cooperatives that have been taking over various enterprises previously owned by governments. Similar financing might be available for union cooperative stores, whose buying power can effectively reduce living costs for workers as they have in Argentina. Technical and financial assistance could be given to members of farm unions who purchase their own land and equipment, and to marketing cooperatives.

Increasing support for unions would primarily be a matter of giving selected unions priority in the disbursement of AID and IDB assistance for housing, health, education, and cooperative productive enterprises. (Financial assistance to unions is supported in item III,4,b of the Latin American Guidelines for Policy and Operations.) Careful selection of the unions to receive Alliance aid would be essential to insure that only strongly based unions with non-communist but dynamic leadership are assisted in extending their benefits and thus their membership and strength. There are many unions in Latin America that deserve US support, as, for example, Aprista unions in Peru (like the Federation of Textile Workers and the Lima Union of Bus Workers), democratic unions in

Argentina (General Confederation of Commercial Employees and Confederation of Municipal Workers), progressive industrial unions in El Salvador (Cigarette Factory Union and Brewery Union), and budding moderate unions in Brazil (the São Paulo clothing workers and metallurgical workers). The labor attaché and other members of the Embassy and USOM staff should be able to select such unions and in many cases informally to generate planning and preparation of project plans and loan or grant applications.

The increase in cooperative socio-economic activity will in itself lessen the importance to unions of activity in politics as the main means of accomplishing union goals. The improvement of living standards through cooperative action will give immediate meaning to union membership and tend to direct union interest to productive activity. Moreover, by actually participating in the Alliance unions will tend to become supporters for other aspects of the Alliance program in their country.

All the financing would not have to be furnished by the United States; as loans to union cooperatives become accepted, local banks, government agencies, and employers will find it desirable and even necessary to assist.

The Military

The possible military role in the Alliance for Progress is quite different from that of free trade unions. At present, military support for the Alliance is fostered by the US information program, trips to the United States, attendance at US service schools, and the work of US attachés; this military support can be increased if the military becomes directly involved in bringing the benefits of the Alliance to the people, especially in rural areas. A program of this sort would require a large-scale expansion of the present limited civil action programs (as suggested in item 62 of the Latin American guidelines and supported by General Lemnitzer in his November 9 and November 30 memos to the President).

Bolivia now has a civil action program of this sort under way. About one-third of its small army is said to be engaged in colonization and road building in eastern Bolivia and another one-third is working on agricultural projects in the Altiplano. However, the effectiveness of military civil action programs in Bolivia is severely limited by the lack of trained personnel and necessary equipment.

Development loans from the IDB and AID loans and grants as well as technical assistance from the US military might be used to train and equip construction battalions to build roads, irrigation facilities, schools, and other public works in rural areas. Small military groups might be trained and equipped to conduct on behalf of civilian ministries the cadastral surveys which are a vital part of any agrarian reform program. Training of military recruits might include teaching in elementary agricultural skills. In conjunction with their public works programs in rural areas the military might conduct adult education courses and thus contribute to spreading literacy and elementary agricultural techniques.

It may well be that a most valuable return from Alliance for Progress reforms, once they are underway, will be in terms of political stability—with an indirect byproduct in confidence favoring continued economic growth. Social pressures would be much reduced if the use of middle class energies in the execution of reforms should expand the proportionate size of those middle class elements which subscribe to moderate political action and take a responsible part in national political life. In political terms it would mean new opportunities to effect peaceful evolution from the present narrowly-based political systems to government based on more active cooperation of classes and wider agreement on national goals. The political system produced by such a mutation could in many ways be more in accord with US interests than one achieved by radical change which forced the propertied class to hand over their dominant position to the middle class as the leader of extremist mass-supported organizations.

---

40. Highlights of Discussion at the Secretary of State's Policy Planning Committee Meeting

Washington, February 13, 1962, 10 a.m.

SUBJECT

Three INR Papers on Aspects of Political Change in Latin America

PRESENT

S—the Secretary	S/P—Mr. Fried
AID—Mr. Chenery	S/P—Mr. Wriggins
AID—Mr. Coerr	INR—Mr. Hilsman
USIA—Mr. Murrow	P—Mr. Rowan
B—Mr. McGhee	CU—Mr. Coombs
G—Mr. Johnson	AF—Mr. Herz
S/R—Mr. Thomson	ARA—Mr. Goodwin
S/P—Mr. Morgan	EUR—Mr. Elting
S/P—Mr. Ramsey	FE—Mr. Usher
	NEA—Mr. Cottam

The INR papers were found to be provocative and stimulating.[1] There was some question whether the examples chosen in RAR–6 in fact

---

Source: Department of State, Secretary's Memoranda of Conversation: Lot 65 D 330. Secret. Drafted by Wriggins.

[1] RAR–6, RAR–11, and INR–35; see Document 38 and footnote 1 thereto and Document 39.

represented examples of the useful hypothesis of the paper. It was explained that these were all preliminary papers intended as suggestive for those concerned with the Alliance and background for a larger, long-term study of "political development" now under external contract.

The Alliance for Progress, it was pointed out, was primarily political in nature, ultimately designed to encourage the growth of reasonably stable governments capable of absorbing reform and change, secure from both the extreme Left and the extreme Right. In Latin America we seek more than we seek in Asia, i.e., neutral countries capable of maintaining their own stability. Rather, we hope the Alliance for Progress will increase the strength of the free world alliance as these countries industrialize and develop over the next twenty years. The danger is that many Latin American countries may fall not merely into neutralism but all the way into the Communist orbit. Bolivia, Ecuador and one or two others could well become Cubas.

Alliance for Progress reforms may work primarily to reduce political and social tensions or they may contribute to improving output by accumulating more resources and directing them into more productive channels. The former should buy us more time to assist governments and political systems to make the difficult adjustments necessary as they move to greater productivity and ultimately to political viability.

There are four main difficulties. Firstly, the entrenched oligarchies in many countries are resistant to change and refuse to face the facts of political life. In some countries, the Alliance is very likely to fail because of the inflexible attitudes of the oligarchic leaders. Secondly, a stable and responsible middle class is not yet developed. Thirdly, there is danger that in our efforts to ease the way for reforms and changes which we consider to be inevitable, we will so arouse mass impatience that we will release forces we cannot control. Che Guevara believes this will be the outcome of the Alliance. The fourth difficulty concerns the lack of qualified people in the U.S. and Latin America, capable of economic planning and possessing the necessary political skills to manage political and economic transitions. At the moment, no single sound development project is lacking funds. The real shortage is lack of planned projects.

It is difficult to determine how much self-help and reform we can insist upon in relation to the political limitations facing a recipient government. S/P is heading up a study on this problem.[2] At present, there is no correlation between per capita assistance received by countries and their performance in terms of self-help and reform criteria. Indeed, the most irresponsible countries, those which get into balance-of-payments or other major financial difficulties, are the ones which have received most assistance. We thus reward the irresponsible and discriminate against the responsible.

---

[2] Not found.

While some stressed the importance of concentrating on the oligarchy and finding ways of persuading it to change its ways, others emphasized the importance of doing what we could now to multiply production and increase the opportunity and achievement of the masses. Well thought-out technical assistance programs focusing on crucial sectors, such as improved seeds and agricultural methods, are one way to do this. Undue preoccupation with the oligarchies will lead to a flight of capital and political disruption which the Communists and other extremists can use to their advantage. We should draw on our experience and recall that not by leveling down have we progressed in the United States, but by leveling up. We should, therefore, attempt to combine indigenous and foreign resources to find the quickest means of progress, which can be experienced by ordinary people, as in agricultural production, eliminating debilitating diseases and in education. Seed corn projects in Mexico, the Puerto Rican rural health service, and the U.S. Extension Service were examples. We must, it was held, concentrate on what we can do now to work with the people on the bottom and help them to get on with their own development.

It was also felt that the problem posed to us by the oligarchies was not so much to limit their high privilege, but to induce them, with our assistance, to encourage greater participation of the middle and lower social strata in national life. The symbolic importance for us of not being too closely identified with the oligarchies was stressed. We should not forget the very important role played by intellectuals, teachers, students and journalists in the formation of opinions for the future. We seek to induce them to overcome their alienation and to play a more constructive role in society. Mr. Achilles is conducting a study in this connection, in Communist tactics toward youth and education and how we can deal with these problems more energetically.

Prior to the Alliance, we allowed the Communists to hold the monopoly of sympathy toward change. Only lately—and with the Alliance—have we begun to demonstrate our interest in change.

We must persuade the home offices of U.S. business to encourage their field staffs to get behind the Alliance. For those interested in the mass Latin American market, there is no difficulty but extractive industries need more attention on our part. The good work already undertaken through Advisory Councils and the like, to explain in the long-run U.S. interest in the success of the Alliance, should be stepped up.

Latin Americans are fighters, and they will fight two things: dictatorship and intervention. We must be wary not to become tarred with the brush of "intervention" even as we attempt to induce governments to follow our aid criteria. A broadening of U.S. contacts with the area will improve our chances of encouraging a fight on dictatorship through reforms and of avoiding the charge of governmental intervention.

41.   Memorandum of Conversation

Washington, February 16, 1962, 4:17–5:50 p.m.

SUBJECT

Alliance for Progress

PARTICIPANTS

The President
Mr. Dungan, Assistant to the President
Mr. Coffin, Acting Administrator of AID
Mr. Moscoso, United States Coordinator of the Alliance for Progress
Mr. Woodward, Assistant Secretary—ARA
Mr. Goodwin, Deputy Assistant Secretary—ARA
Mr. Bissell, Deputy Director—CIA
Mr. Hansen, Assistant Director—BOB
Mr. Coombe, Assistant Secretary—CU
Mr. Rostow, Councilor
Mr. Morales Carrion, Deputy Assistant Secretary—ARA
Mr. Hilsman, Director of INR
Mr. Linder, President—Ex-Im Bank
Mr. Shriver, Director—Peace Corps
Mr. Nitze, Assistant Secretary of Defense—ISA
Mr. Haydn Williams, Deputy Assistant Secretary of Defense
Mr. Sternfeld, Director, Office of Development Planning—AID

The discussion was opened by Mr. Woodward, indicating to the President that a message addressed to Latin America telling of the forward strides that have been taken domestically in the fields of integration, housing and education would have a tremendous impact on the Latin American populace. Mr. Woodward also indicated that of tremendous significance to L.A. would be the results of the forthcoming commodity discussions, particularly the coffee stabilization agreement, which, if preliminary discussions are successful in March, will be taken up in the U.N. in June.

Mr. Goodwin then presented a series of papers to the President.[1] The President questioned the drop-off in commitments of U.S. aid to Latin America in January and also wishes to know who was responsible for the Inter-American Bank since its disbursements have been so low in comparison to the commitments. He was informed that the lag in IDB disbursements was probably related to the long lead time connected with the individual projects. As to the low level of commitments in the month

---

Source: Department of State, Presidential Memoranda of Conversation: Lot 66 D 149, January–March 1962. Confidential. Drafted by Sternfeld on February 26. The time of the meeting is from the President's Appointment Book. (Kennedy Library)

[1] See Document 40.

of January, there was no complete explanation possible. Mr. Linder of the Export-Import Bank indicated that he had several projects in the pipeline and that he expected to make available about 300–350 million dollars in loans to Latin America in the next year.

The President discussed the situation in Argentina and raised a number of questions relating to the 1963 proposed program for Argentina and Ecuador and total Alliance for Progress requests. (It appears that the President will wish to review the individual country proposals within the next 10 days.) He indicated that the $3 billion authorization request should be over and above the amounts available for lending in L.A. under the 5-year commitment authority. This would indicate to the Congress that we were not attempting to use the funds previously justified for Latin America to be spread among the other countries of the world.

The President expressed some concern that the justifications to the Congress should not be too vague, that specific projects be set forth to justify our fund request. He suggested that Mr. Moscoso receive a complete briefing on the tactics of Representative Passman in conducting hearings.

The President indicated his strong view that the fate of the whole aid program rests on the success of the Alliance for Progress and that operations and activities connected with the Alliance for Progress should be given the highest priority (five to one), notwithstanding the requirements of the other areas in AID for staff and other sources.

The President indicated he did not wish Mr. Moscoso to be called an Assistant Administrator. He believed within the AID organization he should be called Director or Coordinator for the Alliance program.

The President inquired into the status of the proposed contract with the National Academy of Science on the hoof and mouth disease problem in Argentina. He directed that action be taken to consummate the contract and that no publicity be given to the possible effect eradication of this disease would have on imports by the U.S. from Argentina.

Action: AA/LA with White House Science Adviser

The President inquired as to the low level of PL 480 in Latin America and requested a memorandum as to the possibility of expanding these programs. He also inquired as to the large amounts of PL 480 going to Egypt and the reasons therefor.

Action: AA/LA with A/MR and White House Coordinator of Food for Peace

The President approved the establishment of a Latin American Policy Committee under the chairmanship of ARA, with membership of USIA, AID, CIA and Defense. He requested that this Committee review on a weekly basis the over-all political problems and economic programs by country and that a report be furnished him each week.

Action: ARA

The President directed that Mr. Moscoso conduct a thorough study of all procedures which may be hampering the program and that AID make available the services of Mr. William Parks for this purpose. He also directed that ways be found to fill current job vacancies in the LA Bureau and that steps be taken to bring in small numbers of highly qualified men, with in-service training being used as the means of increasing their utility. He asked Mr. Nitze whether personnel from DOD could provide some knowledgeable people formerly employed by them as attachés. There seemed to be general consensus that this source would not be too useful.

A discussion was held as to the need for authority to remove people who are employed in the L.A. programs without regard to existing statutes. The President was informed of the current evaluation team headed by George Train travelling through L.A. Mr. Coffin indicated the tentative decision of Mr. Hamilton on not requesting the renewal of the 621 firing authority for the agency as a whole. The President, however, indicated that it might be desirable to pinpoint this for Latin America only. The solution to this matter will be presented to the President in the context of the legislation to be submitted to the Congress.

Action: BOB in clearance of the proposed legislation

On the question of supergrades, it was agreed to withhold further action until Mr. Hamilton completes discussions with the Chairman of the Civil Service Commission on obtaining additional positions from the Civil Service pool.

Mr. Coombs indicated that he had an education program for L.A. totaling $100 million a year. He also indicated some concern over the need to indicate U.S. interest in a forthcoming UNESCO-sponsored conference in Santiago. The President requested that Mr. Coombs' proposal be presented to him after appropriate staffing. A later session may be necessary to review Mr. Coombs' recommendation.

Mr. Nitze indicated to the President that various determinations requiring the President's action have been pending in AID for 4 months. The President directed that these determinations be made available to him for action and if further delays are necessary, to explain the reasons therefor. He indicated that Senator Fulbright reported that views in the Senate have changed considerably on restricting the amount of military aid to Latin America and that it would be possible to provide additional assistance if required.

Action: Bureau of Budget and Department of Defense will review possible needs for additional military aid to L.A.

Mr. Nitze also raised the problems in connection with the Inter-American Defense College and the lagging contributions by other Latin American countries.

Action: Bureau of the Budget with State and Defense will report to the President on the problem of moving ahead in establishing the college

---

42.   Memorandum of Conversation

Washington, March 9, 1962, 10:15–11:20 a.m.

SUBJECT

Conversation with the President on AID Matters

PARTICIPANTS

The President	Mr. Lingle
Mr. Ball	Mr. Coffin
Mr. Bell	Mr. Gaud
Mr. Dungan	Dr. Chenery
Mr. Hamilton	Mr. Nicholson

[Here follow paragraphs 1–4, a discussion of AID administrative matters.]

5. There was an extensive discussion of the Alliance for Progress and the difficulties in getting it properly organized. Mr. Lingle stressed the need for a clear directive from the President to AID so that responsibility would flow in a direct line through the Office of the Administrator to the Coordinator of the Alliance (and a definition of responsibilities for the Alliance within the Department of State). The President explained his reaction to the chaotic picture that was presented in the previous meeting on the Alliance two weeks ago,[1] but agreed with Mr. Hamilton and Mr. Lingle as to the desirability of the Alliance remaining within AID. It was

---

Source: Department of State, Presidential Memoranda of Conversation: Lot 66 D 149, January–March 1962. Confidential. Drafted by Chenery on March 10 and approved by the White House on April 20. The time of the meeting is from the President's Appointment Book. (Kennedy Library) The meeting took place at the White House.

[1] See Document 41.

agreed that the Alliance should be visible as a separate entity but not otherwise become a separate agency. The President said that the other AID regional bureaus would have to recognize the special position of Latin America in the AID program at this time and not feel neglected because of the emphasis being put on the Alliance. It was generally agreed that the main problem in getting the Alliance organized was to find a strong deputy for Mr. Moscoso who could take over most of the administrative work and leave him free for program decisions, negotiations, and external representation of the Alliance. The possibility of Mr. Nicholson's being available as a Special Assistant to Mr. Hamilton to help organize the Alliance for Progress was discussed.

[Here follows paragraph 6, a discussion of AID administrative matters.]

43.   Memorandum From the Deputy Assistant Secretary of State for Inter-American Affairs (Goodwin) to President Kennedy

Washington March 14, 1962.

SUBJECT

Historical Genesis of the Alliance for Progress

The statement of the *N.Y. Times*[1] that the Eisenhower Administration thought of the Alliance for Progress and you merely named it is wholly inaccurate and will certainly come as a surprise to those Latin American leaders—such as Kubitschek—who desperately tried to get previous administrations to adopt some such policy without success.

1. For the first seven years of the previous administration there was no policy toward Latin America—merely a continuation of old practices, policies and attitudes.

2. In 1960—alarmed by the growing deterioration of the situation in Latin America and under the prodding of Doug Dillon—we supported

---

Source: Kennedy Library, President's Office Files, Goodwin. No classification marking.

[1] Reference is to a *New York Times* editorial of March 13, which read: "It is often forgotten, by the way, that while President Kennedy gave the program [Alliance for Progress] its name, the concepts were enunciated—and the $500,000,000 committed—by the Eisenhower Administration in 1960."

the Act of Bogota and asked Congress for $500,000,000 to implement it. This Act was a step forward, but a limited step. It was restricted to U.S. assistance in the field of social progress—the construction of schools, homes, waterworks, public health facilities, etc., and it said that Latin American nations must help themselves in these fields. It was a program of social development, and social development only, on a limited scale with the $500 million to be spent over a period of two years and the fund to be mostly administered ($400 million worth) by the Inter-American Bank.

3. The Alliance for Progress, it is true, incorporated the principles of the Act of Bogota, but went far beyond this Act to a new concept of Inter-American cooperation. A few specifics will serve to illustrate this.

a. The Alianza was based on a long-term program of economic development, a program to increase productive capacity, accelerate rates of growth and make a permanent increase in standards of living. It envisaged a decade-long plan of hemispheric development leading to the stage of self-sufficient growth. The entire program of long-term economic development—the keystone of the Alianza—was new to this Administration.

b. The Alianza introduced the concept of long-term planning and programming. This was absent from previous U.S. policies and yet must be considered the basis for today's development efforts.

c. The entire institutional structure, including the OAS Experts, the Planning Institute, etc.—with the exception of the Inter-American Bank—has been newly created by the Alianza.

d. The stress on social reform as a condition of development aid—although first intimated in the Act of Bogota—has become a matter of central emphasis under the Alianza. It was impossible to demand social reform as a condition of long-term development financing before this, because long-term development financing was not available.

e. The entire program of commodity stabilization is new since our previous policy actually opposed the idea of stabilizing commodity prices.

f. The Alianza was the first to put U.S. support behind programs of economic integration in Latin America.

g. The magnitude of the plans is incomparable—this year we spent approximately three times as much as previous administrations ever spent in any one year.

h. Almost all the political components of the Alianza represent new thought, including our current stress on political democracy (and coldness toward dictatorial governments) and, more important, our basic decision to identify the United States with the progressive democratic forces in Latin American countries.

If the Alliance for Progress had a predecessor it was Brazil's Operation Pan-America and not the policies of previous administrations. The bitterness of the Brazilian government at our failure to seriously consider Operation Pan-America is the surest evidence of how much things have changed in the last year.

In addition to the specifics of your policies the entire atmosphere of our relations to Latin America, our attitudes, our progressiveness, our receptivity to Latin needs, has shifted dramatically since last January. No one would be more surprised to hear that we were simply following past policies than the democratic leaders of Latin America who have viewed the Alliance—in both public and private statements—as a new breakthrough in Inter-American relations, and the last, best hope of democracy in this hemisphere.

Dick

44.   Memorandum by the Deputy Assistant Secretary of State for Inter-American Affairs (Morales-Carrion)

Washington, April 9, 1962.

This memo aims to focus attention on the Alliance for Progress as essentially a political and ideological force in the Hemisphere. It summarizes some of the difficulties the Alliance is facing in the ideological field and sets forth some operational guidelines.

A. The Ideological Gap

1. Ideologically, the Alliance is facing stormy weather. Its avowed aim is to bring about in Latin America a free, open, prosperous society, democratically oriented and capable of great cultural creativeness. Its instrument is an intense developmental effort in the social and economic field.

Source: Department of State, S/P Files: Lot 69 D 121, American Republics, 1962. No classification marking. Sent to Rostow by Teodoro Moscoso, U.S. Coordinator of the Alliance for Progress, under cover of a May 1 memorandum. Rostow sent copies to McGhee, Johnson, Nitze, William Bundy, Rowan, Parker, Fowler, Helms, Cline, McGeorge Bundy, and Kaysen under cover of a May 3 memorandum. According to Rostow's covering memorandum, Moscoso referred to this paper in a meeting with this group on May 1. No record of the meeting was found.

2. To many a Latin American eye, the Alliance is simply a money-lending operation in the fiscal or financial fields. The publicity which surrounds each loan or grant helps to underscore the "money-lender" image. And no money-lender in history has ever evoked great enthusiasm. We have yet to see a charismatic banker.

3. The Alliance presupposes certain basic notions of economic development and national planning. These are sophisticated notions with no mass-appeal, unless they are given a heavily political flavor. The present lingo of economic technocracy simply does not reach the average Latin American. His slogans come from the world of nationalism, not the world of technocracy. Hence, the ideological gap.

4. The Alliance is increasingly seen in Latin America as a U.S. policy. It is basically linked with the United States and not with its Latin American background or, indeed, with its Latin American origins. It does not seem to have an autochthonous flavor, in spite of the fact that most of its conceptual framework is derived from recent Latin American economic and social thinking. It still looks "foreign" and "imported", it still looks as a "Made in U.S.A." product.

5. The biggest psychological obstacle the Alliance is facing is that it has not been wedded to Latin American nationalism. The single, most powerful, psychological force now operating in Latin America is nationalism. It provides the emotions and slogans for political action through the ideological spectrum. It animates the military and the extreme left. It dominates the universities and the labor unions. Unless the Alliance is able to ally itself with nationalism, to influence it in a constructive direction, to translate the abstract terminology of economic development into familiar concepts related to nation-building, the Alliance will be pouring money into a psychological void.

6. Washington thinking about the Alliance has mainly centered on the urgency of its economic and administrative problems. Immediate action in streamlining aid has been the goal, as witnessed by the White House meetings. The professional economists have been summoned to do a job. But there is lack of a similar effort to think through the political and ideological problems. Furthermore, an impressive array of top Latin American economists (Prebisch, Herrera, Sol, etc.) has been available for constant consultations on the economic phase. But no equivalent group has steadily worked on the political and ideological aspects. And yet the Alliance can only be wholly successful if it is politically and ideologically successful. Again, this is the present *ideological gap*.

B. Some Operational Guidelines

A warning is in order: It is easier to devise an economic development program than a political or ideological offensive. Statistical facts are easier to understand than human emotions. A great psychological gulf has separated the U.S. from Latin America. Its magnitude is greater than the economic gulf to which it is, nevertheless, closely related. No easy formula is available. What follows are just a few pointers of urgent priority, with due recognition to the fact that the action proposed will probably involve action outside the usual government channels.

1. Help to progressive, democratically-oriented political parties

This is an order of the first magnitude. We have committed ourselves to a $20 billion effort in economic development. Have we asked ourselves how much are we willing to invest in political development? Fifty thousand dollars to help a party like the APRA might go a longer way than a $100 million loan to an Odria-type government in Peru.

2. Need to Create a Political Apparatus

We have a seminal experiment in the Costa Rican Political Institute. This could be expanded into four centers: the present one in Costa Rica; an Institute for the Andean region, geared to the Indian heritage; an Institute for the River Plate; an Institute for Brazil. These Institutes, besides developing young cadres of political leadership, could become active centers in the distribution of the ideological literature so badly needed at present. Furthermore, the Institutes could establish close cooperation with progressive parties and help in providing economic support.

3. Need of an Offensive on the Intellectual Front

We can have no ideological breakthrough unless we fully understand the role of the intellectual in Latin American society and his influence on public opinion. A cultural or literary society in Latin America could have, sometimes, more of a revolutionary impact than a political party. A well written article might destroy the initial impact of a hundred million loan. We need a special program geared to the intellectuals wherever they are—a program that would support their magazines and their newspapers, that would publish their books and would grant them due recognition through awards, travel grants, etc. Here we will have to face up to the communists who are doing, in many places, a terrific job. While we concentrate on the loans, they concentrate on the minds. Some of the top Latin American writers, poets, and artists have been converted to Marxism. They are now the prestige symbols of the Red putsch.

4. Need of a Massive Book Program

We need a paperback breakthrough in Latin America. We have to challenge the communists in the popular bookstands, in the "barracas del estudiante," now swamped by Marxist literature in all fields. The problem is not simply to translate American books. Latin America is part of the Western world, of the Atlantic community. We have to marshal the best thought of the West to engage in this offensive, and this effort has to be undertaken with full Latin American participation; indeed, under Latin American direction, wherever possible.

5. Need of Participation by Private Institutions

We have to help develop a new type of institution, more flexible than the present foundations and institutions, which could deal with parties, political institutes, publishing firms, student groups, literary and cultural societies, etc., and do things beyond the scope of government.

---

45.   Department of State Guidelines Paper

Washington, May 1962.

LATIN AMERICA

GUIDELINES OF UNITED STATES POLICY AND OPERATIONS

I. Basic Approach

1. The importance of Latin America to United States policy is older than the Monroe Doctrine and stems from the position of two continents whose security is interdependent. Today, three factors of Latin American development are intimately interlinked and together define the challenge facing the United States.

(a) In many countries, social tensions are mounting, and growing public dissatisfaction is directed against privileged groups who have ruled for generations without successfully dealing with major social and economic problems.

(b) There is a growing desire on the part of important governments to demonstrate that their foreign policy is independent of US control.

(c) Using Cuba as a major base of operations, Communist organization is attempting with purpose and skill to capture both of these movements and turn them against the United States.

2. Our strategy in this situation is: a) to lead and assist Latin America, through the Alliance for Progress and other means, in a major effort to satisfy basic human wants, to effect agrarian and tax reforms, and to promote self-help, cooperative efforts; b) to frustrate the efforts of Com-

---

Source: Kennedy Library, Schlesinger Papers, Latin America, Blue Label, May 1962–February 1963. Secret.

munists to gain control of the movements demanding reforms, to strengthen Latin Americans' will and capacity to resist Communist subversion, and to isolate and promote the downfall of the Communist beachhead in Cuba; and c) to strengthen the inter-American system and cultivate closer relations with all the Latin American countries and peoples, especially with those key nations which appear destined to play an important role in the hemisphere and in the world, such as Brazil, Argentina, and Mexico.

3. In this enterprise we must exert positive leadership. We must cooperate to the fullest with the self-help efforts of countries seeking to modernize themselves. We must disassociate ourselves from reactionary forces which decline to respond to the needs of the people, and learn to discriminate between legitimate expressions of dissatisfaction with the existing social order and Communist-inspired agitation. We must influence and help the military to become guardians of constitutional order and agents of constructive change. We must be patiently understanding of the growing pains of countries which, in striving to establish their national identity, are feeling a temporary need to dramatize their independence from us. We must commit the resources required for the task.

4. During the next decade, our problems will become more complex, rather than less. The tide of change is bound in the short run to work against certain of our immediate interests. Old power groups will be increasingly estranged from us as we press for basic reforms. New groups in power will often be more difficult to deal with than leaders of the past. Through these years, we will have to keep our long run interests clearly in mind—a continent to the south made up of viable political societies capable of maintaining their independence and of dealing adequately with their own internal problems.

[Here follow the remaining 70 pages of this paper consisting of four additional sections: II, "Background," III, "Objectives," IV, "Lines of Action," and V "Contingencies."]

46.   Memorandum From the Deputy Assistant Secretary of State for Inter-American Affairs (May) to the Assistant Secretary for Inter-American Affairs (Martin)

Washington, August 13, 1962.

SUBJECT

Recommendations for IA–ECOSOC Meeting in Mexico City

It is almost certain that the meeting will be convened on October 1 at the expert level and on October 22 at the Ministerial level. On the assumption, therefore, that one of the subjects to be covered at the expert level meeting will be preparation for decisions to be reached at the Ministerial meeting, we have about seven weeks in which to prepare our positions and, to the extent necessary, to obtain general understandings from the other participating countries so as to preclude serious conflicts at Mexico City. Two suggestions are summarized below, with the thought that steps should be undertaken as soon as possible to reach a general inter-American understanding with regard to those suggestions prior to the meeting:

I. That certain IA–ECOSOC subcommittees be constituted for the purpose of creating a multinational mechanism for evaluating the progress attained in Latin America under the Alliance for Progress, as well as for the purpose of promoting a more rapid rate of progress throughout the area. I believe it is obvious that the United States has accepted an undue share of the responsibility for evaluating and promoting the progress in each of the Latin American countries. The subcommittees suggestion is designed to promote as much responsibility as possible in each of the Latin American countries for the rate of progress in each of the others.

The specific suggestions set forth below may facilitate discussion of this subject:

A. Initially, there might be four subcommittees concerned, respectively, with fiscal reform, agrarian reform, educational reform, and planning.

B. Each subcommittee might consist of 5–7 member countries, each country to be represented by its most highly qualified expert on the subject matter being considered by that subcommittee. Each other country represented on the IA–ECOSOC could send an observer to the meetings of each subcommittee, and the observers would be allowed to participate in the discussions of the meetings, though not authorized to vote.

Source: Department of State, Central Files, 371.8/8–1362. Confidential. Drafted by May. Also sent to the Deputy Assistant Administrator of AID, Graham Martin, and the Assistant Secretary of the Treasury, John Leddy. A copy was sent to William Turnage, Director of the Office of Inter-American Regional Economic Cooperation.

C. Each subcommittee would meet regularly every three months to:

1. Review the quarterly and annual progress reports to be prepared by the Secretariat of the Pan American Union on the progress achieved on the subject in question in Latin America in general and in each Latin American country in particular.

2. Write a quarterly and an annual subcommittee report evaluating the rate of progress in the area concerned. The reports could be on a functional basis, such as the rate of title clearance for agricultural land in all of Latin America. The reports would, as appropriate, refer to progress by country, as for example by extending special commendation to a specific country for the enactment and implementation of agrarian and fiscal reform.

3. Submit quarterly and annual recommendations for steps to be taken to improve the rate of progress. These reports also could be written in terms of function, as by recommending specific steps to be taken to increase the number of cadastral surveys in Latin America. The reports also could recommend specific steps to increase the rate of progress in each country.

D. Each subcommittee could, within limitations, establish its own rules of procedure. Each could determine whether to meet regularly in just one city or to meet in different cities each time. Each could decide whether to have a permanent chairman or rotating chairmanship. Each could determine the number of days and the specific dates for each meeting, provided that the last meeting prior to the annual IA–ECOSOC meeting should be held on dates which would permit the submission of an annual report by each subcommittee to the separate country representatives of the IA–ECOSOC within a period of no less than 2 months prior to the scheduled meeting of the IA–ECOSOC.

(While I am biased against both committees and meetings, I believe they could be useful in this instance for the purpose of getting each country directly involved in the affairs of each of the other countries within the Alliance. I believe this mechanism would be much preferable to reliance upon the staffs of any permanent institutions, whether the OAS, ECLA, or the IDB. I should say also that while I do not expect the multinational committee mechanism to show quick and useful results, I cannot envisage any other mechanism which is as likely to be fruitful.)

II. A "super committee" should be set up for the purpose of inducing each of the various Latin American countries to exert greater effort in achieving the objectives of the Alliance. Ex-President Kubitschek of Brazil has already taken some initiative in this regard. Ex-President Lleras Camargo of Colombia may also be willing to participate in this effort. It has been suggested that this sort of super committee might report to the Council of the OAS in a purely advisory capacity. Alternatively, it might be given general, non-specific, responsibility for consulting with the separate Latin American governments and for formulating suggestions which might be presented at the annual meetings of the IA–ECOSOC.

Obviously, I have no clear idea as to what such a group might in fact do. It seems clear to me that these outstanding statesmen could not be expected to concern themselves with technical matters, nor should they be encouraged to do so. However, two or three men such as Kubitschek and Lleras Camargo might be able to do much, by virtue of their public stature, to help create or to strengthen the *mystique* of the Alliance for Progress through some sort of informal and non-defined association with the Alliance. On the other hand, care must be taken to avoid giving them too much responsibility, lest they make public recommendations conflicting with those emanating from the 9 wisemen or the IA–ECO-SOC. I have no doubt that these men could be useful for promoting the Alliance, but very careful understandings should be reached with them as to the limitations of their responsibilities, before they are given an important public role.

---

47.   Memorandum From the President's Special Assistant (Schlesinger) to the President's Special Assistant (Dungan)

Washington, October 15, 1962.

SUBJECT

Alliance for Progress

I have lost track of the Alliance in recent weeks, but I am a little disturbed by some stray items which have recently crossed my path.

Obviously the Alliance is in the throes of a much needed effort to build the contribution of private capital to Latin American development. This is plainly a necessity: public effort by itself cannot come near doing the job; and, as the need for social overhead capital is met, the private sector must more and more become the main engine of economic expansion. It is also a healthy redressment of what seemed in the first months of the Alliance an excessive commitment to public investment and planning. And it is a natural response to the frustrations of dealing with indolent, inefficient and uninterested governments.

Nonetheless there is surely danger in going overboard in this direction and reverting to the Eisenhower Latin American policy.

Source: Kennedy Library, Schlesinger Papers, Chron File, 1962. Confidential. Copies were sent to Kaysen, Hansen, and Goodwin.

The answer of the United States Government to the problem of hemisphere development in the fifties was to stake everything on bringing about the private investment climate deemed essential to an adequate rate of economic growth. This climate was to be achieved in two ways: (1) in the economic field, through insistence on policies of monetary stabilization; (2) in the political field, through insistence on government committed to the protection of private foreign investment (including, if necessary, military dictatorships).

The Eisenhower policy was a failure. Nonetheless it has its attractions for those (still) in the bureaucracy who shaped the policy and have never been enthusiastic about the public-sector aspects of the Alliance; moreover, it is a policy which wins cheap and unthinking applause and a reputation for "realism" in North American business circles. But the policy is as wrong today as it was in the fifties—more so, because of the churning up of political sentiment in the intervening years. Adolf Berle discusses this point effectively in his new book. If we return to the Eisenhower policy and make the creation of a "proper" climate for foreign private investment our main objective in Latin America, we might as well kiss the Alliance—and the hemisphere—goodbye.

These reflections are stimulated by a number of things which, I trust, are *not* straws in the wind:

1. I attach No. 1120 from Mexico City.[1] Here, at a meeting of experts to discuss the Alliance, a Brazilian cited Argentina as an example of the political pitfalls of rigorous conformity to IMF standards. In response, the representative of the Kennedy Administration "suggested that Frondizi's failure resulted not from following IMF but from failure to do so."

I do not argue that we should applaud 30 percent inflation. But the statement of the U.S. representative is exceedingly questionable so far as facts are concerned; and, if our new hemisphere line is to be the infallibility of the IMF, then we are right back with Eisenhower.

2. I call your attention to Embassy Airgram A–437 from Mexico City[2] entitled "Mexican Discrimination Against United States Investment Threatens Alliance for Progress (An Analysis of Causes, Tactics, Consequences and Remedies)." Obviously Mexican policies which drive away foreign capital are, in the main, bad for Mexico; and obviously an analysis of the techniques of discrimination is well worth having. But the basic presuppositions of this memorandum are (a) that there are no legitimate motives for economic nationalism—its proponents are either demagogues trying to keep in power, crooks seeking to pick up equity ownership in the confusion of Mexicanization and forced industrialization, or

---

[1] Not found.

[2] Dated September 28. (Department of State, Central Files, 812.00/9–2862)

Marxists; (b) that the big failure of the United States in Latin America has been "the failure of both the United States Government and U.S. private business enterprise over a long period of years to protect United States investments"; and (c) that the urgent necessity is "to mobilize United States economic power in both the private and public sectors, so that our economic power, like our military power, will be a threat in being, enabling us in a fair and flexible way to further the objectives of our foreign policy by using it to require of Mexico and other governments cooperation on their part," especially "to improve the investment climate essential to an adequate rate of economic growth."

Some of the specific suggestions in this memorandum sound useful; but the philosophy of the memorandum is completely the philosophy of the Eisenhower Administration and at war, as Berle's book emphasizes, with the realities of life in Latin America.

3. There is the appointment of General William Draper as head of the country team inspection mission to Brazil.[3] I have known Bill Draper for years, and he is a man of certain qualities. Nothing would be more appropriate for the Eisenhower Administration than to send to Latin America a Republican investment banker whose most recent big assignment was as chairman of the Mexican Light and Power Company. It seems to me wholly incongruous, however, for Bill Draper to go as a representative of the New Frontier to a country where even American businessmen are coming to feel that foreign ownership of public utilities is a blind alley.

4. There is the decision to resume military aid to the Peruvian military junta—a decision in terms which allowed the junta to announce on October 11: "The situation will permit us to continue, from now on, the close collaboration of our armed forces with those of the United States in the execution of the plans of continental defense and those of economic and social development of Peru." This announcement, even though qualified from Washington, weakens the argument for withholding economic assistance from Peru and suggests that we are quite prepared now to accept military dictatorship in Latin America—even a military dictatorship which is currently working with Communists in the trade union movement in an effort to destroy APRA leadership of organized labor in Peru.

5. There is an apparent shift in the kind of men we are sending as Ambassadors to Latin America. A good deal of the purchase the Alliance has been able to get has been due to the first wave of ambassadorial appointments—Gordon, Moscoso, Loeb, Stephansky, J.B. Martin. But

---

[3] Reference is to the team composed of Lincoln Gordon, Ambassador to Brazil; Teodoro Moscoso; James Loeb, Ambassador to Peru; and Ben Solomon Stephansky, Ambassador to Bolivia.

the recent tendency has been to send to Latin America men who have no particular sense of identification with the Kennedy Administration and who could live (and in some cases did live) quite as happily with the Eisenhower Latin American policy.

No doubt I am unduly apprehensive. But this apparent recrystallization of elements of the Eisenhower policy within the framework of the Alliance for Progress is troubling and, I believe, will get us nowhere.

Arthur Schlesinger, jr.[4]

---

[4] Printed from a copy that bears this typed signature.

---

48.   Editorial Note

The Inter-American Economic and Social Council of the Organization of American States convened in Punta del Este at the expert level October 1–21 and the Ministerial level October 22–27. The purpose of the meeting was to review the progress of the Alliance for Progress after its first year. Deputy Assistant Secretary of State for Inter-American Affairs Herbert K. May headed the U.S. Delegation to the first series of meetings. Secretary of the Treasury C. Douglas Dillon arrived in Uruguay on October 22 to participate in the Ministerial sessions but was recalled immediately to Washington as the Cuban missile crisis escalated.

Dillon addressed the Council on October 23 before leaving Punta del Este. He acknowledged that Alliance for Progress programs were being implemented more slowly than had been anticipated but expressed confidence that they were moving Latin America in the right direction. He affirmed the support of the United States for economic integration in Latin America and for commodity price support agreements in the region. He confirmed that the United States had fulfilled its pledge to commit $1 billion to the Alliance for Progress before March 1962 and pledged to continue aid to Alliance programs in the year ahead "on the same general order of magnitude." (*New York Times*, October 24, page 23) Before he left Uruguay, Dillon named Teodoro Moscoso to take his place at the final sessions of the conference.

Documentation on the conference is in Department of State, ARA/ IPA Files: Lot 69 D 211, IA–ECOSOC: USDEL to Annual Mtg. of the IA

Econ. and Social Council at the Ministerial Level, Mexico City, October 1962; and ibid., ARA/USOAS Files: Lot 76 D 381, First Annual Meeting Economic and Social Council, Mexico, 1962.

---

49.   Biweekly Summary Report on the Alliance for Progress

No. 23   Washington, undated.

MAJOR COUNTRY AND PROGRAM DEVELOPMENTS

1. Results of Mexico City Conference Encouraging

The Alliance for Progress was considerably strengthened by the first annual review conducted by the Inter-American Economic and Social Council in Mexico City during the month of October. This milestone in the conduct of the AFP was greatly facilitated by the careful advance work of all U.S. executives. Not only were the usual Latin American denouncements of the U.S. absent but the Latin American delegates took the initiative in sponsoring action which demonstrated positive adherence to the principal U.S. objectives.

The experience of the first year of the Alliance had, it seemed, convinced each of the member nations that the Charter of Punta del Este was fundamentally valid. The Conference reflected a growing realization on the part of the Latin American delegations that the success of the Alliance, under the Charter, depends in large part on the efforts of their own countries, and is not merely another US aid effort. As a result, the country presentations and the final reports of both the experts and ministerial level meetings subscribed to the vital need for an increased tempo of self-help and reform. The special problems in each of the reform fields—tax, agrarian, institutional—were studied and analyzed with a candor which reached new highs for Inter-American conferences. The Conference concluded that the Central American integration movement was making real progress, though major actions under LAFTA need to be greatly accelerated. In the area of divergent US and Latin American

---

Source: Department of State, Central Files, 720.5/11–1462. Confidential. Attached to covering memoranda from Graham Martin to the President dated November 9 and from Brubeck to Bundy dated November 13. This report covers the 2-week period ending November 9.

interests—commodity price problems—the final results were at least satisfactory for our purposes, even if temporary.

The Conference came up with some important procedural innovations. First, a committee of two statesmen is to be appointed, to review and make recommendations with respect to the entire Inter-American system in the light of Alliance developments. While this effort is desirable, our primary goal was to provide a platform permitting Lleras Camargo to mount an intensive effort to enlist the younger political leaders in Latin America in more active efforts to implement the principles of the Charter. Secondly, reflecting the strengthened consensus that Latin American efforts were crucial, the Conference established six special groups of responsible government officials, from nine countries each, to review developments in the fields of: planning and project implementation; agricultural development and agrarian reform; fiscal and financial policies and administration; industrial development and financing the private sector; education and training; and health, housing and community development. These groups are to meet at least twice before the next Annual IA–ECOSOC meeting, and will provide real continuity to the review process.

The success of the conference would have received more prominent press coverage both in the U.S. and Latin America had it not been overshadowed by the Cuban crisis. While initially the crisis threatened to sidetrack the Conference, it had a tangible unifying effect on the ministerial delegates.

[Here follow sections 2–9, which discuss miscellaneous Latin American developments during October 26–November 9, 1962.]

50.   Airgram From the Department of State to All Posts in the American Republics

CA–5226   Washington, November 10, 1962, 3:24 p.m.

SUBJECT

IA–ECOSOC Meetings—Mexico City, October 1962

REF

Mexico City's 1221[1]

I. Summary Evaluation

The first Annual Meetings of the Inter-American Economic and Social Council (IA–ECOSOC) conducted a successful review of economic and social progress in Latin America. Meeting for three weeks (October 1–21) at the Experts level and subsequently (October 22–27) at the Ministerial level, frank discussions were held on accomplishments and problems in the first year of the Alliance and future prospects. The fundamental validity of the Charter of Punta del Este was reaffirmed and there was common agreement that the Alliance was primarily a Latin responsibility.

After initial hesitation, a process of self-appraisal and cross-questioning was starting among countries in meetings at the Experts level. For the most part, representatives of Latin governments presented reasonably full accounts of progress and shortcomings in their countries' performances. It is hoped that such confrontation will become a regular feature in the IA–ECOSOC and an important mechanism toward this end was adopted at the meetings. (See Special Committees below.) There was also agreement on the need for high level review of the Inter-American system, to be undertaken by two Latin statesmen.

While the Ministers were of course highly sensitive to developments in the Cuban crisis, the meetings themselves considered only the economic and social aspects of the Alliance, sustaining the non-political tone of the discussions at the Experts level.

II. Major Substantive Issues

There was general recognition that accelerated growth in Latin America will require: 1) well-developed plans which carefully identify investment projects and important structural reforms to be undertaken, 2) greater progress in land reform, taxation and financial discipline,

---

Source: Department of State, Central Files, 371.8/11–1062. Official Use Only. Drafted by Schmukler on November 9.
[1] Dated October 18. (Ibid., 371.8/10–1862)

expanded educational programs and other self-help measures, 3) improved opportunities for exports and 4) continued high levels of external assistance with more flexible procedures (see reftel for the extensive experts-level discussion on U.S. aid). On the other hand, the role of private enterprise (domestic and foreign) was not fully discussed.

Of the three major areas of substantive discussion (progress under the Alliance, integration and trade) trade problems raised by the Latins were the most difficult to reconcile with U.S. positions. The Latins continued to press for concerted action to negotiate elimination of European Economic Community restrictions on meat, a sugar study group directed in part toward recommending changes in U.S. sugar policies and prompt consideration of a regional mechanism to compensate for fluctuations in export receipts. The U.S. abstained on the meat and sugar resolutions and was able to appropriately modify the regional approach to compensatory financing.

The discussion of integration in Latin America was less incisive in highlighting important issues or eliciting proposals for further progress. The substantial steps already taken in Central America were noted but broader and speedier actions appeared necessary among the countries in the Latin American Free Trade Area.

III. Major Actions Taken

Some 40 resolutions were approved by the Council, of which particular attention is called to the following:

Agreement was reached on two important structural innovations to help move the Alliance forward. First, a Committee of two statesmen is to be appointed by the OAS Council to review the Inter-American system in the light of Alliance requirements and to make recommendations for adjustments. Second, the Council established six Special Committees which would meet at least twice a year to discuss their respective subjects, in order to promote self-help and reform. The six committees and their memberships follow:

I. Special Committee of Planning and Project Formulation: Argentina, Costa Rica, Ecuador, Haiti, Honduras, Panama, Peru, United States and Uruguay.

II. Special Committee on Agricultural Development and Agrarian Reform: Chile, Costa Rica, Dominican Republic, Ecuador, Mexico, Paraguay, Peru, United States and Venezuela.

III. Special Committee on Fiscal and Financial Policies and Administration: Brazil, Chile, Colombia, Ecuador, Guatemala, Honduras, Mexico, Nicaragua, and Venezuela.

IV. Special Committee on Industrial Development and Financing of the Private Sector: Argentina, Brazil, Colombia, El Salvador, Guatemala, Mexico, Nicaragua, United States, and Venezuela.

V. Special Committee on Education and Training: Argentina, Brazil, Chile, Colombia, Ecuador, Haiti, Panama, Paraguay and Uruguay.

VI. Special Committee on Health, Housing, and Community Development: Dominican Republic, El Salvador, Guatemala, Haiti, Nicaragua, Paraguay, Peru, Uruguay, and Venezuela.

The United States is a member of three of these committees and expects to cover the other committees as an observer. In order to contribute most effectively to the work of each committee it is necessary that our representatives have available a growing volume of information relevant to the work of each committee. We expect the OAS Secretariat to prepare a list of questions for use by the committees (which will be soon sent to the field), answers to these questions should facilitate the discussions of the committees.

In the field of trade, a resolution was approved which specified the characteristics and rules for the establishment of OAS "Action Groups". The basic US objection to these Groups was the interpretation of their powers, including powers of speaking on behalf of, or negotiating for, the United States. The rules state that these Groups may be created by IA–ECOSOC or the Council of the OAS, that the resolutions creating them must specifically state their powers and that the Groups may represent only those countries which approve their establishment. Thus the Group on Meat, for example, does not represent the United States.

Other resolutions were approved setting up special or "pre-action" Groups, whose functions will be to analyze various problems connected with trade in bananas, coffee and cocoa, follow efforts being made in other international forums to arrive at solutions to these problems and, if appropriate, to present to IA–ECOSOC a plan of action to facilitate solutions which may include recommendation for the establishment of Action Groups. The US will decide at the time these plans are presented whether or not it wishes to approve them. The US will participate in the work of the groups on bananas and cocoa. Resolutions calling for support for the creation of international study groups on bananas and copper under UN auspices were also approved.

IV. The Next Annual Meeting of IA–ECOSOC

It was agreed to recommend to the Council of the OAS that the next regular Annual Meeting be held in either July or August 1963 in Brazil.

[Here follows section V., "Main Documents."]

Rusk

51.   Memorandum From the Director of the Office of Inter-American Regional Economic Affairs (Turnage) to the Assistant Secretary of State for Inter-American Affairs (Martin)

Washington, November 29, 1962.

SUBJECT

Certain Concrete Achievements During First Year of Alliance for Progress

1. Improved Tax Administration

Tax collections in 1961 in Bolivia were 17% greater than in the previous year; in Venezuela tax revenues in 1961 were about 15% greater than in the previous year and tax declarations increased 22%. In Chile, as of mid 1962, 100 officials had completed training courses in the newly established school for tax administrators. In 1962 in Chile the first tax fraud indictment was made. Panama estimates that tax collections in 1962, by doubling its auditing staff, will be increased by $5 million (mainly from income taxes). In Paraguay customs and sales levies increased about 50% during the first 5 months of 1962 as compared with the same period of the previous year.

2. Expanded Education Programs

In Chile 14% of the national budget in 1961 was allocated to education as compared with 9% in 1959 ($129 million compared with $69 million). In Ecuador 17% of the national budget in 1962 was allocated to education as compared with about 10% in previous years. In Peru 21% of the national budget in 1962 was allocated to education as compared to about 17% in previous years. In Mexico education accounted for 21% of the national budget in 1962 as compared with 16% in 1959. During 1961 in Mexico, 8,000 new rural schools were opened. In Guatemala, as of June 1962 in a joint program with AID, 971 class rooms had been completed and 467 were under construction. The National Literacy Campaign in Venezuela resulted during a 3 year period in 675,000 persons under age 10 learning to read and write.

3. Agrarian Reform

In a substantial acceleration of the land reform program begun some years ago 71,000 land titles were issued to farmers during the period August 1960 through December 1961. In Venezuela since 1960 some 2

Source: Department of State, Central Files, 811.0020/11–2962. No classification marking. A copy was sent to May.

million hectares of land have been distributed among 55,000 families. In Mexico, between September 1960 (Act of Bogota) and July 1962, almost 7 million hectares of land had been turned over to approximately 60,000 families in a continuation of the land reform program started several decades ago. In Salvador a decree was issued by the government requiring a day of rest with pay each week for farm workers.

4. Development Planning

All countries have taken appreciable steps toward the preparation of national development plans. Chile and Colombia have completed plans which have already been evaluated by the Panel of Nine. The Panel is now considering plans submitted by Mexico and Venezuela.

5. Other

The Social Progress Trust Fund has extended loans of more than $100 million in 10 countries in support of expanded low cost housing programs. The Trust Fund has also extended more than $100 million in loans in 11 countries in support of improved water supply and sanitation systems.

---

52.   Memorandum of Conversation

Washington, December 13, 1962.

PARTICIPANTS

United States:	*Organization of American States*:
President Kennedy	Senator and former President J. Kubitschek
Assistant Secretary Martin	of Brazil
Assistant Administrator Moscoso	Former President A. Lleras Camargo of
Deputy Assistant Secretary May	Colombia
Mr. A. Jose De Seabra (Interpreter)	
Mr. Ralph Dungan	

President Kennedy welcomed the two former presidents and expressed his gratification over the important task that they were going

---

Source: Department of State, Presidential Memoranda of Conversation: Lot 66 D 149, October–December 1962. Secret. No drafting information appears on the source text, but it was approved in the White House on January 9, 1963. The meeting took place at the White House.

to undertake.[1] He felt that the general situation in Latin America had become worse over the last two years, and that it called for a common and concentrated effort on the part of all the governments. One problem that was a cause of major concern was the drop in the prices of many commodities. At present the U.S. could not give aid to Latin American countries in the same way that it had helped to rebuild Europe with the Marshall Plan. For one thing, U.S. aid at that time was concentrated in one area. Also the United States' current balance of payments deficit amounts to more than three billion dollars a year, and aid programs represent a loss of 1.3 billion dollars a year in balance of payments. The aid given is spread throughout the world, with countries like India receiving very substantial amounts. With regard to Latin America, U.S. aid is not meeting all the needs, and an effort will be made to provide more next year. It is important to consider the limitations on U.S. aid, although it is recognized that aid under the Alliance for Progress is a matter of primary concern and of the highest priority for the U.S.

President Kubitschek agreed that the situation in Latin America had deteriorated in the past two years and that it was particularly serious in Brazil. He stressed the need for a joint concentrated effort so that the Alliance might become an efficient instrument for the rapid economic development of the Latin American countries. He realized that even with present limited resources there was a great deal more that could and should be done. At the time of the talks with Eisenhower and Dulles about Operation Pan America, no one thought in terms of 20 billion and it was felt that a great deal could be accomplished with 10 billion. Since then costs had increased. Nevertheless, if the funds now available and committed were used efficiently, the situation could be improved substantially. In talking with many U.S. government officials, President Lleras and himself had discussed a vital aspect of their mission: that of making the Alliance popularly accepted, thus dispelling the present misgivings and lack of confidence that exist in Latin America. When the Alliance was first announced, there arose a widespread belief that aid would be forthcoming with the utmost speed and efficiency. The many delays in the implementation of aid programs have caused a state of despair, even distrust. To offset such impressions it would be necessary to implement programs in the most urgent manner.

President Kennedy recognized that operations should be speeded up. Yet, one could not overlook the rules laid down by the U.S. Congress regarding the feasibility of each project, the need for engineering studies,

---

[1] In accord with a resolution passed at the First Annual Review Meeting of the Inter-American Economic and Social Council in October 1962, former Presidents Kubitschek and Lleras were appointed by the Council of the Organization of American States to conduct a study of the Alliance for Progress and ways in which its programs could be expedited. See Document 50.

the precise accounting of expenditures, etc. Even in an experienced organization such as the World Bank, which operated at a high level of efficiency, there usually elapsed about two years between the time the application was made and that when the funds were actually used. Of course there were projects for certain purposes of a special nature such as budgetary support and assistance to balance of payments. In the case of Brazil, there had been difficulties on the U.S. side in connection with the recruitment of personnel and although during his administration sizable funds had been committed, there was not yet much to show. In addition there were conflicting pressures within Brazil. The issue was not one of shifting responsibilities, and the U.S. hoped that the desired speeding-up could be achieved. Often delays were caused by the absence of plans, programs or organizational structure, and even hostility as has been the case in the Brazilian Northeast.

President Kubitschek made some remarks on the specific situation in Brazil. The last time he had visited the U.S. in March of this year he had noticed a feeling of distrust of Brazil and a fear that the country would turn communist. Now, he was running into the same attitudes, only stronger. This feeling of fear on the part of the U.S. was a very serious matter indeed, because it might be translated into a holding back of aid. In the present situation the U.S. should be willing to run the risk of giving effective aid to Brazil, keeping in mind the fact that in Brazil there is a strong and widespread anti-communist feeling. In those circumstances quick and effective aid to Brazil would be of vital importance. President Kennedy, in his latest press conference, had mentioned the grave situation existing in Brazil.[2] The Government of Brazil was well aware of the gravity of the situation and was contemplating measures to combat inflation. Its efforts would be all the more successful if it could count on quick and effective cooperation on the part of the U.S. With regard to the prices of basic commodities in Latin America, it could be said that practically all the aid received from the U.S. was bleeding away through the continuing drop in prices. That matter deserved the most careful study.

President Kennedy pointed out that during the same press conference he had commented on the drop in prices over the last three years, also that he hoped that the Coffee Agreement would bring about some measure of stability in the marketing of that commodity. With regard to the Brazilian situation, he said that the U.S. was no longer in a surplus position on balance of payments. Finance Minister Moreira Salles had visited Secretary Dillon during the Quadros administration and had

---

[2] In a December 12 press conference, President Kennedy noted the high rate of inflation in Brazil, the failure of the Brazilian Government to implement anti-inflationary economic reforms, and the negative impact this had on Alliance for Progress aid from the United States. (*Public Papers of the Presidents of the United States: John F. Kennedy, 1962*, pp. 866–874)

obtained relatively large commitments, which, although not commensurate to the needs were substantial in the light of the resources available. There are two items which have caused much concern to the U.S. One is the fact that no matter how much money was put into Brazil, that money made no impression because of the continued inflation and flight of capital. The other is the strong radical, Marxist or communist influence on labor and other key areas of Brazilian society, which has been a contributing factor to the over-all worsening of the situation.

President Kubitschek said that he shared the same concerns. He explained that left-wing elements, although they did not seem to carry significant weight, were nevertheless sufficiently active and vocal to help make unpopular the Alliance and any form of relationship with the U.S. He added that any Brazilian official coming to this country to discuss better relations between the two countries would invariably be subjected to a great deal of abuse not only in some newspapers but also on the part of certain members of Congress. At the same time the overwhelming majority of the population was firmly attached to Christian and democratic principles, and a strong reaction against radical ideas was inspired and led by the highly influential clergy together with the business and industrialist community. In that context it was essential that the U.S. be willing to give help and support to those who systematically resisted communism. In spite of the 300 million dollars obtained by Moreira Salles, Brazil found itself in serious difficulties with regard to balance of payments. And there was an ever stronger pressure of public opinion on the Government to the effect that positive measures be taken to curb inflation. It should be pointed out in this connection that there had been five changes of government in Brazil during the past year. It was hoped, however, that with the likely return to presidentialism after the plebiscite of January 6,[3] the President would again have full powers and could therefore take the necessary measures to correct a situation which caused him the greatest concern. The fact that the situation was definitely going to improve after January 6 should be one more reason for the U.S. to cooperate fully with Brazil and without delay. He then said that it had not been his intention to delve at such length on the Brazilian situation, but since Brazil played such a key role in Hemisphere affairs it was absolutely essential that Brazil be fully integrated in the solutions envisaged for the common problems.

President Kennedy made four important points:

—It should be emphasized that the Alliance is not a U.S. run or inspired undertaking, but rather a true cooperative effort that had had its

---

[3] On January 6, 1963, a government-sponsored plebiscite, which restored full presidential powers to Brazilian President Joao Goulart, was approved. The constitutional power of the presidency had been reduced before the Brazilian military allowed Goulart to assume office on September 7, 1962.

inception with Operation Pan America and earlier aid programs. As far as the U.S. is concerned, the Alliance provides a method whereby U.S. aid can be effectively channeled and increased on a long term commitment basis. This is in contrast to previous programs that were intermittent and not well coordinated. The countries of Latin America should make a decided effort, singly and collectively, to improve their lot with the assistance of the U.S., but never losing sight of the fact that the Alliance is basically a Latin American concept and reality, instead of being some abstract scheme imposed from the U.S. by remote control.

—The problem of falling commodity prices is being seriously studied by the U.S. and Western Europe with a view to preventing the "hemorrhage" previously referred to.

—The flow of private capital to Latin America should be encouraged. There are investment problems in Brazil and Chile for instance.

—There is a need for the U.S. to improve its own procedures so as to attain more speed and to increase aid whenever possible.

President Kubitschek expressed his appreciation for the excellent definition of the Alliance as given by President Kennedy, the best in fact he had ever heard. He was going to include the four points above in the presentation that President Lleras and himself were to make to the O.A.S. He hoped that President Kennedy would use his prestige with the leaders of Western Europe to obtain assurances of a wider European participation in the Alliance, so that industrialized nations would share the aid burden with the U.S. He himself had had an encouraging talk with de Gaulle on the prospects of increased French participation. He was hopeful that deeds would follow the words. In Western Germany he had also found encouraging signs of an increasing interest in the economic development of Latin America. Japan should also be looked upon as an additional source of aid. As a matter of fact Japan had a long and substantial record of constructive investment in Brazil. His own attitude toward private investment in Brazil was best summed up in the fact that during his administration over 2.5 billion dollars from foreign countries were invested in Brazil, at an average of 500 million dollars per year. That was in marked contrast to the sharp drop in foreign investment in Brazil experienced after he had left office. This last year for instance, a mere 10 million dollars had been invested. He was calling particular attention to that difficult situation in order to emphasize the crucial need for effective cooperation.

President Kennedy mentioned the concern caused by radical policies that pushed strongly in favor of the nationalization of capital and the expropriation of foreign investments, with the result that less and less foreign capital was going into countries where such policies were in force or contemplated.

President Kubitschek referred to the situation in Brazil where a handful of politicians with support from the left was waging a campaign that was scaring away foreign capital. In the Brazilian Congress, where there is absolutely no leadership at present, about ten left-wing congressmen of which two or three are avowed communists, had succeeded in pushing through two items of legislation that were a true calamity: namely, the laws on the remittance of profits and on tax reform. There were certain aspects of the situation that were not too unfavorable, however. The automobile industry, for instance, which many thought was doomed to failure, was facing such a demand for vehicles that buyers had to wait for six months after placing their orders. Also, a great deal was being done to improve the lot of rural populations through the construction of key highways and other facilities. And Brasilia continued to play a major role in getting people to settle the interior of Brazil, with the result that additional employment opportunities were being created.

President Kubitschek added that with regard to the all important task of building confidence in the Alliance, such a task was particularly difficult in Brazil, where the friends of the U.S. remained silent, whereas its enemies and detractors were consistently vocal and active. A case in point was that of the Brazilian Northeast, where there had been made a U.S. commitment amounting to 130 million dollars, which had produced favorable reactions. Subsequently, due to administrative deficiencies and shortcomings on the part of Brazil the money had never been used. Unfortunately, those deficiencies and shortcomings were never presented to public opinion in Brazil; the only known fact was that the promised funds had not come, with understandably adverse effects. That again showed the absolute necessity of prompt and effective implementation of aid programs. In summary, speaking with the complete frankness that exists between friends, President Kubitschek said that he wanted to make a confession, namely, that during the last two years many serious mistakes had been made by Brazil in the area of effective cooperation with the U.S. Then he said that he was looking forward to a statement from President Kennedy showing support for Brazil based on a true understanding of that country's problems. With reference to the proposed visit to Brazil by President Kennedy, he said that Mr. Kennedy would receive a most enthusiastic welcome. It was important for President Kennedy to see with his own eyes what Brazil was like, to realize how much friendly feeling there was toward the U.S., and to discover that Brazil was not as presented in the news. There was no denying, of course, that under the present parliamentary system the country had been without an effective government for the past two years. Miraculously enough the country had managed to survive.

President Lleras commented that he was following very closely the Brazilian situation, as he felt that anything constructive that was going to be done in Latin America had to get off to a good start in Brazil. He was also deeply aware of the fact that Brazil presented a most dangerous situation, which had been a cause of major concern for President Kennedy, even more than the Cuban crisis at its worst.

President Kennedy stated that he recognized the key position and nature of Brazil in Hemisphere affairs. He then voiced the concern of the U.S. and his own over the situation in Brazil, which worried him more than that in Cuba. Cuba after all is a small country which has been contained and where the situation can only improve. Brazil presents a great potential for constructive achievement, but the really effective steps must be taken by Brazil. He would very much like to visit Brazil when the situation shows signs of moving toward greater stability, and when the U.S. would be able to play its proper role in relation to Brazil. He hoped that there would be evidence of greater stability and that the visit could take place in 1963.

President Kubitschek expressed his appreciation for the significant words of President Lleras that reflected his great statesmanship and vision. Talking now more than ever in the tone used by close friends he wanted to urge President Kennedy to display his political acumen to the fullest and talk earnestly like a Dutch uncle to Brazil in the same way that he talked so successfully to the voters of Massachusetts when he was running for the Senate. There was no doubt that the Alliance was destined to be an unforgettable page in the annals of world history, but this page now being written by President Kennedy was not completely written. It should show to future generations that in the same way that the Marshall Plan built a wall that halted the inroads of communism, the Alliance should prevent the downtrodden populations of Latin America from plunging into chaos. He stressed the fact that President Goulart had a genuine liking for President Kennedy and considered the latter as a friend. Kubitschek had been shown by Goulart the last letter that Brazil's Chief Executive had received from Kennedy. Kubitschek felt that such exchanges of letters between the two Presidents are a very good thing. Even telephone conversations could be considered as a further means of gaining and keeping the confidence of the President of Brazil. He described Goulart as a man of sound principles with good political understanding, but added that Goulart needs to feel supported, so as to counteract the many adverse influences such as that of his violently anti-American brother-in-law (Brizola).[4] He felt that this endeavor of bringing the two Presidents closer together in order to enable President Kennedy to win over President Goulart is of paramount importance, even of the utmost urgency, considering the serious situation. The Alliance could not be permitted to fail, for such failure would be catastrophic. He then brought up the matter of the many questions he would

---

[4] Governor Leonel Brizola of the state of Rio Grande do Sol in northeastern Brazil had begun nationalizing American-owned property and businesses in his jurisdiction on February 16, 1962.

be asked about his meeting with President Kennedy: particularly what was Kennedy's position with regard to the Alliance and especially Brazil. Kubitschek asked Kennedy whether he (Kubitschek) could reply that Kennedy had good-will toward Brazil and was willing to cooperate with and assist Brazil.

President Kennedy replied that the U.S. was anxious to help, that he was concerned about Brazil, that country being a matter of constant concern even more than Cuba, and therefore of the highest priority. However, the fact remained that no matter what the U.S. did, the situation might deteriorate.

Assistant Secretary Martin pointed out that President Kennedy had a favorable attitude toward the Alliance as well as toward Brazil. But did Brazil have a favorable attitude toward the Alliance and the U.S.?

President Kubitschek said that there were an overwhelming majority of people in Brazil who were well disposed toward the U.S. At the same time, he granted that there were people in the Brazilian Government who were openly hostile to the U.S. For that reason, it was absolutely essential that the U.S. give strong support to its friends. But if the U.S. were to withhold such support just because of the few in the Government who were unfriendly, then the U.S. would certainly lose the friendship of both the Government and the people of Brazil, and that would be a very grave turn of events.

President Kennedy said that President Kubitschek, when asked about the meeting at the White House, could reply that the U.S. was a very good friend of Brazil and also that the U.S. was giving strong support to the Alliance. He was sure that President Kubitschek had been aware of the deep concern in the U.S. for the problems of Brazil as well as of the sincere desire on the part of the U.S. to assist in working out solutions to those problems. The final solutions, however, rested with Brazil. He pointed out that the U.S. still wished to play the role that Brazil hoped and expected the U.S. would play. But the role of the U.S. was and would be a secondary role, just as it had been at the time of the Marshall Plan. Brazil was the sole master of its own destiny.

President Kubitschek said that he had never intended to ask the U.S. to play the decisive role in the final solutions of Brazil's problems. He pointed out to President Kennedy that during his term of office, he had waged a determined fight for development, having achieved a good deal of success even though he had received almost no assistance from the U.S. Government. There were certain areas of the economy where prompt U.S. cooperation could do much good, such as the balance of payments situation. He wanted to make it emphatically clear that he would never expect the U.S. to come into Brazil and create that country's progress and wealth.

President Lleras said that together with President Kubitschek he was undertaking a thorough study of the Alliance's structure, procedures and operations. A study would also be made of the part played in the Alliance by the U.S. Government.[5] He then asked President Kennedy if someone from outside the Alliance could be made available for liaison and consultation purposes. He hoped that such a person could be of the stature of Acheson or Harriman, as evidence of the interest shown by President Kennedy.

President Kennedy said that he contemplated calling on Acheson, whom he felt to be highly qualified, although most of his experience was with Europe. He also praised the work of Mr. Moscoso as Coordinator of the Alliance. Among certain things to be done he cited the need to determine whether aid procedures under the Alliance could be speeded up. He was aware of the delays in the disbursement of Alliance funds for Brazil and mentioned in that connection the report of the Draper committee.[6] He also invited the two former Presidents to voice any criticism and to formulate any constructive suggestion that would always be welcome. He then pointed out the need to emphasize the positive aspects of the Alliance, such as the efforts made by many countries in carrying out necessary reforms, rather than always to publicize the vast amounts of unfinished business. He recalled that at his press conference the previous day, when asked whether Latin American countries were actually making reforms, he replied that those countries were by and large trying to make reforms, in the face of staggering difficulties that were much greater than anything that a war-ravaged Europe had ever had to experience. He felt that Latin America should organize itself in order to present effectively its views to the European Common Market. He thought that Latin America should speak directly to Europe and with its own voice, so as to dispel the belief often held in Europe that Latin America lies exclusively within the area of interest of the United States. There existed several organizations that could be used effectively to that end, such as the Latin America Free Trade Association and the Central American Common Market. The two former Presidents could also speak very effectively to the European Common Market on behalf of the Latin American community.

---

[5] Kubitschek and Lleras submitted their report to the OAS Council on June 15, 1963 (OAS Document OEA/Ser. G/C–d–1102 and 1103). Their principal recommendation was that the OAS create a Committee for Inter-American Development, an executive body for the Alliance for Progress to oversee its programs.

[6] See Document 228.

53.   Memorandum From the Director of the Bureau of Intelligence and Research (Hilsman) to the Assistant Secretary of State for Inter-American Affairs (Martin)

Washington, December 19, 1962.

SUBJECT

Trouble Spots in Latin America

As of possible interest in connection with your briefing of the Special Group (CI) on December 20, our Latin American office has prepared a rundown on probable trouble spots in the area during 1963.

We expect a number of the many potential trouble spots in Latin America to flare up during 1963. Communists may instigate or benefit from violence in several countries. Violence or developments unfavorable to the US can occur in connection with scheduled elections or changes of government in nine countries. Abrupt change can also bring trouble in almost any one of these countries and in several others as well. Without attempting to predict the exact form these crises will take, we would identify the likely focus of trouble in each country as follows:

The Caribbean

In the *Dominican Republic* there is a strong possibility that the transition to representative government will break down, even if the regime emerging from the upcoming elections is installed. The Duvalier dictatorship in *Haiti* could go during the next year, and give way to political chaos.

Central America

Guatemala will be extremely sensitive throughout 1963. The prospect of Arevalo's victory in the December presidential election may cause new coup attempts and one could prove successful. In *Nicaragua* a non-violent termination of the Somoza political dynasty through "free" elections will be hard to achieve. As the lid is loosened, a real explosion may develop.

East Coast

The problem of communist-inspired violence is still more significant in *Venezuela* than in any other country and will continue to threaten serious political instability.

Brazil's problems will be difficult at best. A continuation of leftward slippage under Goulart could lead some elements to seek his ouster. The

---

Source: Department of State, Central Files, 720.00/12–1962. Secret.

prospect for a successful coup of the classic Brazilian bloodless pattern is remote, and widespread civil strife would probably accompany the overthrow of the Goulart regime. Although there is still a good chance that Brazil will follow a relatively moderate political course, the potential for internal violence is at a new high.

Even if *Argentina* returns to representative civilian government, the country will probably still have to deal with recurrent crises, such as those which have marked its political life in recent years. Assimilation of the Peronists could prove too tough a nut to crack and lead to another military solution.

West Coast

In *Chile* there is little danger of violence, but the municipal elections and opening stages of the 1964 presidential campaign will make the political pot boil. The procommunist Popular Action Front in Chile stands a fair chance of coming out ahead.

The deepening divisions within the ruling MNR in chronically troubled *Bolivia* will be aggravated as the question of presidential succession comes to the fore; the possibility of fairly widespread violence is enhanced in the short run.

Communists have made alarming progress in labor during the tenure of the military junta in *Peru*, and the junta's failure to permit APRA to take power if it proves victorious in the promised elections could lead to violence.

Opposition to the Arosamena regime in *Ecuador* is likely to increase, and its overthrow may come during the year.

Summing up, we find that serious threats to domestic social order or to good relations with the US may appear in perhaps eight countries (Bolivia, Venezuela, Chile, Brazil, Ecuador, Guatemala, Dominican Republic, Haiti) in the coming year. In another three (Argentina, Peru, Nicaragua), the problems of government succession may bring a violent or at least unconstitutional response from the security forces of the country.

54.   Memorandum From the Assistant Secretary of State for Inter-American Affairs (Martin) to Secretary of State Rusk

Washington, February 4, 1963.

SUBJECT

Latin America in 1962—Institutional Changes

As an effort to stimulate more qualitative thinking on the part of all of us, I asked the Desk Officers, in cooperation with the Office Directors and the Embassies, to come up, as part of the 1962 review exercise, with a list of the three most important institutional changes which took place in their countries in 1962, and the three that we should most seek to accomplish in 1963.

The results, which are attached,[1] are not wholly satisfactory, despite several attempts. It is not easy to define what is an institutional change, nor what is one institutional change as distinct from a bundle of measures with a similar objective, nor am I sure that we have really gone deep enough in picking what are the most important things to seek in 1963. A year from now we should know more and be able to do better.

A rough summary of the attached papers indicates that we have been, and will be, concentrating on agrarian and fiscal measures, those which have received the most publicity as objectives of the Alliance for Progress. In 1962 there were a dozen items each in these fields. In 1963 there is a step-up in the fiscal reform field with 16 listed, but still only a dozen for agriculture. I should emphasize that these cover a wide range of measures in these fields and do not refer only to higher taxes and break-up of landed estates.

There has been also a commendable emphasis on better planning for the use of scarce resources with 8 major achievements listed for 1962 and 9 projected as desirable for 1963.

While it has not been quite clear that non-governmental changes should be listed as "institutional" changes, it is significant that despite this limitation there were 4 achievements in 1962 and 5 projected for 1963, which deal directly with expanding the role of private enterprise, largely in the industrial field. Agricultural credit and technical assistance for farmers, as well as promotion of home ownership are also, of course, efforts in the direction of expanding the private stake in the community.

Source: Department of State, Central Files, POL LA. Confidential. The memorandum and the attached report are companion pieces to a February 1 study entitled "Latin America—Political Progress." (Ibid.) Both bear marginal notations indicating that the Secretary read them.

[1] Not printed. The 23-page report discusses institutional changes in each Latin American nation.

In view of the fact that the shortage of trained personnel for private and public enterprise is a crucial bottleneck in the program of the Alliance, and that educating leadership is necessarily a relatively long term job, it is disappointing that in this first full calendar year of the Alliance for Progress only one is reported in the educational field. However, six are projected for 1963. I am still not sure we are giving adequate emphasis to this area, though it may be that the need is for many small steps, rather than big ones which could be listed as one of 3 major targets.

55.   Memorandum of Conversation

Washington, February 7, 1963.

SUBJECT

> Conference of Central American Presidents, the President of Panama and President Kennedy in San José, March 18–20

PARTICIPANTS

> *United States Government*:
> The President
> Mr. Ralph A. Dungan, Special Assistant to the President
> Ambassador Angier Biddle Duke, Chief of Protocol
> Mr. V. Lansing Collins, Director, Office of Central American and Panamanian Affairs
>
> *Costa Rican Government*:
> His Excellency Daniel Oduber, Foreign Minister
> His Excellency Gonzalo Facio, Ambassador to the United States

President Kennedy opened the meeting by asking Foreign Minister Oduber what arrangements are being made for the meeting in San José.[1] Mr. Oduber said that a schedule was being worked out which he reviewed in brief with the President. He stressed that it was his hope to avoid bilateral talks in which demands would be made of the United States. He said that the substantive topics would be the economic integration of Central America and the threat posed to the economic and social development of Central America by the "reactionary" Soviet dom-

---

Source: Department of State, Presidential Memoranda of Conversation: Lot 66 D 149, Jan–Mar 63. Secret. Drafted by Collins and approved by the White House on February 12.

[1] Reference is to President Kennedy's meeting with the Presidents of the Central American Republics and Panama in San José, Costa Rica, March 18–20; see Document 58.

inated Castro regime. Mr. Oduber described in some detail the eventual hope of the Central Americans that in the next few years a customs union and a monetary unit in Central America could be established and that in ten years a Central American and Caribbean customs union could include the Dominican Republic, Jamaica, Trinidad, and even eventually Colombia and Venezuela. The Central American and Caribbean customs union would have a population of nearly 40 million people and would afford an opportunity for a vast economic and social program. Mr. Oduber described this 10 year plan as the dream of the liberal group in the Caribbean, of which he and his friends in Costa Rica were a part, as were Presidents Betancourt, Villeda and President-Elect Bosch with Governor Munoz-Marin as senior statesman. Mr. Oduber, in reply to a question from the President, said that the six Central American Presidents would meet in San José the day before President Kennedy arrived and that, furthermore, the Central American Foreign Ministers and Ministers of Economy planned to meet in Tegucigalpa, Honduras, February 12 and 13. He indicated that out of the Tegucigalpa meeting should come a report of Central American integration so far, a statement of the intention to achieve customs union and a monetary unit within a few years, and an assertion that this indicated that the Central American countries were faithfully and promptly carrying out the directives of Punta del Este and were thus deserving of special treatment. The Tegucigalpa paper would conclude with a request to the President of his opinion of this program and of his support for the program and further social and economic development in the area. The position in the document will be taken that the Castro regime in its present form under Soviet domination with Soviet troops, etc., in Cuba represented a reactionary threat to the Alliance for Progress and the social and economic development of Central America.

Mr. Oduber indicated that he felt the Cuban situation could become dangerous. The President replied saying that though Mr. Khrushchev had promised to remove Soviet forces in Cuba only a relatively small number had been taken out so far. The President said that we might see a diminution of these forces in the next month or so but that it was equally possible that a new Cuban crisis might involve an even greater confrontation than had the last. The President said that in any event the support of the Latin American countries in the OAS, as in October,[2] was vital. President Kennedy then asked Mr. Oduber what the Central Americans thought should be done about Cuba. Mr. Oduber said that there were a number of views. Presidents Ydígoras of Guatemala and Somoza of Nicaragua favor an outright invasion while Oduber and his friends favor the

---

[2] Reference is to Latin American support for the United States during the Cuban missile crisis of October 1962.

strengthening and increasing of present non-military pressures and the training and equipping of guerrillas and saboteurs in the hope of bringing down Castro within the year. The President injected a word of caution at this point saying that the Soviets had helped Castro establish a police state which was highly efficient and that we had not had too much good fortune with guerrillas and saboteurs. The President also expressed the hope that the Central American nations could make some kind of declaration about Cuba prior to his arrival in San José so that it could not be alleged that the Central Americans were being drawn by the United States into an attack on Cuba. Mr. Oduber agreed to try to get something like this out of the Foreign Ministers' meeting in Tegucigalpa which might be issued by the Presidents in Central America the day before President Kennedy arrives there or might be issued by the Foreign Ministers after Tegucigalpa. In any event it was agreed that the theme would be recaptured in the Declaration of San José but in the sense of Soviet-Castroism impeding the social and economic revolution in Central America under the Alliance for Progress.

Mr. Oduber also expressed the hope to the President that he would address the students of the University of Costa Rica.

The President expressed the hope that we could discover some new themes to emphasize in the Declaration of San José, falling back on the re-emphasis of old themes if necessary. It was generally agreed that a number of new themes could be found.

In discussing the question of the association of other areas to the Central American Common Market President Kennedy asked Mr. Oduber whether President Bosch of the Dominican Republic was going to attend the San José Conference. Oduber said that it had been his intention to invite him but that Guatemala had refused to consider this as there were no diplomatic relations between Guatemala and the Dominican Republic. Mr. Oduber went on to say, however, that there was a little bit more to it than that. Guatemala is opposed to Jamaica and Trinidad joining the OAS because of its fear that this will prejudice its rights to British Honduras and consequently Guatemala is at the moment opposed to any further extension of the Central American Common Market system. Mr. Oduber hoped to be able to change this position soon.

56.   Summary Record of the 509th Meeting of the National Security Council

Washington, March 13, 1963, 4:30 p.m.

SUBJECT

Latin American Policy

[Here follows discussion of Cuba and Haiti; see volume XI and Document 377.]

Turning to the economic side, the President asked whether there was anything we could do to halt the flight of capital out of Latin America.

Secretary Dillon responded at length and made these points: All of Latin America, minus Cuba, is one problem. We are not making as good use of the Alliance resources as we should for political purposes. We must always move in an overall framework and help the countries that are friendly to us more than we now do. Putting one country against another in solving an immediate problem hurts us; i.e. Brazil, which we have to help economically, does little to help us politically. We must tie aid programs and politics closer together. One way to do so would be to give AID Administrator Bell a larger political role in addition to making him Alternate Governor of the Inter-American Development Bank. We are trying to arrange tax rebates in order to increase the profitability of U.S. investments in Latin America. Such rebates will not do the job alone and we should continue the investment guaranty program in those countries where it is acceptable.

Director McCone asked why the Latin American countries could not do more to protect private investments. Mr. Martin said investments were affected by inflation, by political instability, and by plain bureaucratic harassment.

(Ambassador Stevenson arrived at this point.)

Under Secretary Ball pointed out that the OECD was drawing up an investment code for use in underdeveloped countries.

Secretary Dillon acknowledged that private businessmen in Latin America had been very remiss and had thought only of their selfish interest rather than the national interest. He cited instances in which local Latin American businessmen were now getting into politics to the extent of persuading their governments to act so as to increase internal stability. Mr. McCone said that private businessmen were very helpful in Vene-

---

Source: Kennedy Library, National Security Files, Meetings and Memoranda Series, NSC Meetings, No. 509. Top Secret. Drafted by Bromley Smith.

zuela and Nicaragua and that we should do all we can to promote similar interest by businessmen in other Latin American countries.

In response to Mr. Rusk's comment that we could not permit Brazil to get away with violating all our economic criteria, Secretary Dillon agreed. He pointed out that the better a country performs economically, the harder our policy toward that country becomes. He thought that we should be easier with those countries which followed economic policies which made sense to us.

Mr. Martin responded to a comment of the President's which referred to earlier complaints of Ambassador Mann about coordination by citing the close cooperation which now exists between AID and the State Department on Ex-Im Bank matters. As regards the IDB, we do not have a complete veto. Private banks which had been lending heavily to Mexico, responded to our suggestions that they hold down further lending.

Under Secretary Ball called attention to the fact that AID Administrator Bell was now being brought into the main stream of policy as Under Secretary, and that he, in fact, was serving as head negotiator for the Brazilian and Argentine deals.

Secretary Dillon commented that Bell should become a full political officer and it should be understood by Latin America that he is such, not merely an aid dispenser.

[Here follows discussion of independence for British Guiana and Cuba.]

Bromley Smith[1]

---

[1] Printed from a copy that bears this typed signature.

57. Memorandum From the Attorney General's Administrative Assistant (Symington) to the President's Special Assistant (Schlesinger)

Washington, March 15, 1963.

RE

Alliance for Progress—Promotion

I remember in the early organizational days that there was a consensus among the representatives of State, USIA, and other Inter-Agency spokesmen that action should precede words, and that promotion features should take a back seat to accomplishment. This philosophy has been carried out too successfully. Among the intelligentsia attitudes range from whimsy to cynicism as a new form of U.S. imperialism. Among the masses there is hardly any attitude at all.

It seems the Latin governments feel they can benefit from the Alliance without promoting its concepts—perhaps because some of them are revolutionary. But, I think the story could be told in each country in a way appropriate to the times and tides.

Even in the worse barriadas people have a number of transistor radios. I think it would be useful to stimulate a hemisphere conference of leaders in the Broadcasting Industry on the subject of the Alliance and the need to explain its purposes, its direction, and its results to-date. It should be held not here but in Latin America and perhaps Leroy Collins and some colleagues could attend it on our part, with USIA observing but not participating.

I have heard many Latin announcers selling soap, and beer, and reporting soccer games; they do this with gusto and excitement. I think it was time the Alianza receive this kind of treatment across the board.

I read the much edited yet very interesting report on the Inter-American Symposium you attended. I think we need much more of this kind of effort in the private sector.

Jim

Source: Kennedy Library, Schlesinger Papers, Writings, Alliance for Progress—General Memoranda. No classification marking.

58.   Editorial Note

President Kennedy attended a summit of the Presidents of Central America and Panama in San José, Costa Rica, March 18–20, 1963. The meeting had been suggested by President Miguel Ydígoras Fuentes of Guatemala the previous July. The Kennedy administration viewed the meeting as an opportunity to promote the Alliance for Progress, stimulate Central American economic integration, and consolidate support for the diplomatic isolation of Cuba.

President Kennedy opened the summit on March 18. The following day he flew to El Bosque, outside San José, to visit a housing project being built with Alliance for Progress funds. On March 20 he addressed students at the University of San José before returning to Washington. Under the terms of the Declaration of Central America, signed by the Presidents on March 19 and released publicly on March 20, President Kennedy pledged $6 million for a survey to determine the quality and timing of U.S. aid to Central America. The text of President Kennedy's remarks during the summit as well as the text of the Declaration of Central America are in Department of State *Bulletin*, April 8, 1963, pages 511–520, and *American Foreign Policy: Current Documents, 1963*, pages 231–238. Documentation on the San José Conference is in Department of State, Conference Files: Lot 66 D 110, CF 2228–2233.

59.   Telegram From Secretary of State Rusk to the Department of State

San José, March 19, 1963, 11 p.m.

Secto 3. Highlights First Plenary Session (public). Rivera (El Salvador) Chairman.

Rivera. Emphasized economic integration, political unification. Integration a form of self help under Alliance for Progress. Asked CA Presidents commit selves to: (1) customs union; (2) free movement labor; (3) mobilization available capital; (4) regional coordination national poli-

---

Source: Department of State, Conference Files: Lot 66 D 110, CF 2229. Official Use Only; Priority.

cies, plans; (5) stable higher prices for primary commodities; (6) self help and reform, including good private investment climate, more public investment. Asked more foreign assistance. Noted Cuban subversive impedes accomplishment Alliance goals.

Orlich (Costa Rica). Must improve political, social conditions. Called for: (1) greater civic conscience; (2) better living conditions; (3) ample employment opportunity; (4) equality of opportunity; (5) elimination economic inequities between nations as well as between classes of people; (6) willingness to accept results of democratic processes. Noted US power shields Latins from Soviets, enabling Latins devote selves to economic and social progress, asked reduced Latin military budgets. Hoped for early international disarmament, reallocation funds to help under-developed areas. Asked early completion Inter-American highway.

Ydigoras (Guatemala). Seeks: (1) a Republic of Central America; (2) solution of some economic and social problems; (3) control of Belize (British Honduras). Expects US help, especially on Belize.

Villeda (Honduras). Emphasized harmful effects on CA politics, society, economy of filibusters, old foreign investors such as fruit companies. Conceded foreign businesses not now as bad as once were. Said major CA problems are: (1) need for political unity; (2) population pressures; (3) precarious economy—poor terms trade with industrial areas, lack development capital (said free enterprise socially and politically most desirable, but lack of resources demands large government role in development); (4) lack of civic conscience which leads to Caudilloism; (5) Cuba and Castroite subversion; (6) need for rapid CA economic integration (requires external help); (7) advance under Alliance for Progress, better living standards, sacrifices by all (especially CA elites), perhaps some radical solutions.

Somoza (Nicaragua). Called for CA unity, better security arrangements against Cuba, support for Guatemalan claim to Belize, CA economic integration. Under economic integration asked: (1) industrialization, foreign investment, currency stabilization; (2) more import substitution; (3) better living conditions for all; (4) flexible foreign financing which helps pay local currency costs of development; (5) uniform regional foreign trade policy; (6) Panamanian association with CA common market. Deteriorating terms of trade, lack of education and housing, poor land distribution, poor health impede economic integration movement.

Chiari (Panama). Panama expects from meeting (1) more aid under Alliance for Progress, (2) better control of subversion. Economic development requires (a) greater mass market, (b) correction inequitable terms trade, (c) success of Alliance for Progress. Re Alliance he feared failure because U.S. and Latins dissatisfied with contributions of each other, lack of spectacular progress gives Latins sense of hopeless impotence. Noted Panama's special trade and economic relationships, nevertheless supported full economic integration of five CA countries, asked associate membership.

Schick (President-elect Nicaragua) spoke, covered same ground as others in general way.

President Kennedy cited (1) common American heritage, brotherhood; (2) Inter-American system and past joint actions keeping extracontinental powers out of hemisphere; (3) non-intervention; (4) joint hemispheric effort in Alliance for Progress, CA accomplishments and needs, need for equality of opportunity for all; (5) hindrances created by Castro–Communist subversion. Reference to defeat of William Walker and pledge of U.S. support for CA economic integration brought ovations.

Rusk

60.   Summary of Meeting

Washington, March 20, 1963.

INTERDEPARTMENTAL COMMITTEE OF UNDER SECRETARIES ON FOREIGN ECONOMIC POLICY

Problems Related to Private Participation in the Alliance for Progress

I.   Attendance

[Here follows a list of participants. Under Secretary of State McGhee chaired the meeting.]

II.   Problems Related to Private Participation in the Alliance for Progress

A paper on this subject had been prepared by Commerce and circulated prior to the meeting. Mr. Behrman made the initial presentation,

Source: Department of State, Bureau of Economic Affairs, Policy Reporting Staff Files: Lot 65 D 68, Interdepartmental Committee of Under Secretaries on Economic Policy, Private Participation in the Alliance for Progress. Official Use Only. Prepared by Ruth Donahue, Chief, Policy Reporting Staff, Bureau of Economic Affairs, on March 25.

discussing specific problems, issues and questions which had been raised by the report of the Commerce Committee for the Alliance for Progress (COMAP) to Secretary Hodges. Comments were then made by most of the agencies represented.

The COMAP Report.[1] COMAP is an advisory group of about 25 businessmen which Commerce asked to look into the matter of private participation in the Alliance for Progress last spring. The original idea was to have task forces do feasibility studies of industries in specific countries in Latin America. As the Committee got under way, it concluded that the problem was not so much that of identifying specific investment opportunities but rather of getting the obstacles cleared away and, if that could not be done, to find ways of meeting the situation so as to generate more private investment.

The COMAP report does not represent a consensus of the Committee but is almost wholly that of Peter Grace, who contributed some fifteen people from his firm to work on it. It might be added that Mr. Grace is addicted to statistics and the report is full of them. There have been a good many comments on the report from other members of the Committee. Most of them have been in favor of its conclusions, although some exceptions were taken to certain points. Only one was clearly opposed to the tax credit idea. Messrs. Rockefeller, Collado and Wriston[2] wrote a long letter commenting on and concurring in the report. Unfortunately, this letter became public and has raised some serious objections in relatively conservative circles in Latin America.

The report concludes that the decline in American private investment in Latin America has become so serious that the situation cannot be remedied by our trying to persuade the Latin Americans to alter their investment climate themselves but that the United States Government should take unilateral action to neutralize or offset the risks to investment there. The report speaks of four main categories of risks: low profit rate, foreign exchange losses suffered by American subsidiaries that are not suffered by local companies, no earnings at all, and loss of the investment capital itself. The report has about twenty-five recommendations which can be grouped under the following headings: 1) tax recommendations; 2) local currency recommendations; 3) investment guaranty recommendations; and 4) general recommendations.

Tax Proposals. Treasury studied the COMAP tax proposals and found most of them not very helpful. Treasury sent a reply to Mr. Grace on most of the proposals, but has not yet had a comment from him. We

---

[1] Not found.

[2] Reference is to David Rockefeller, Chairman of the Chase International Investment Corporation, Emilio Collado, Director of the Standard Oil Company, and Walter Wriston, Executive Vice President of City Bank of New York.

already have a pretty liberal system of taxation for investments in Latin America and all developing countries, but COMAP is asking for something more than we have now as an incentive to investment in Latin America.

The report asks for tax sparing, but that would pull money out of the countries as it operates only when the money comes back to the United States. We have generally gone on the assumption that any incentive that operates to induce profits to come out of Latin America is not the best kind but that incentives should encourage money to go to Latin America. So the United States Government has decided against action in this regard.

In the United States there is a 5% credit against U.S. taxes for investment. Treasury has thought that could be extended to investment in Latin America. Mr. Grace and others think that is not enough, and have suggested a 25% credit for new investments in Latin America. This is the proposal that is being considered by the Executive Branch. If something like this is necessary to make the Alliance work, Treasury believes it could be added appropriately to the tax system. Whether the Congressional Committees will agree is another question.

We have not been able to come up with any estimates as to just how much investment would flow to Latin America as a result of such action but it may be that this device will transform what might have been a marginal investment proposal into something viable. It may, of course, give a windfall to investors who would be going down anyway.

Treasury has worked out a mechanism with the other agencies which, while complex, should work. The tax credit would not apply to investment in the extractive industries, both because such industries do not seem to need it as an inducement to go in and because politically it would be unwise to do so. This is about ready to be submitted to the President with a recommendation that he submit it to Congress. Responding in this way with something concrete should enhance the Government's relationship with the public committee and may create a psychological effect that will lead to a broader economic effect.

Local Currency Proposals. COMAP did not seem to understand that under the PL–480 agreements where we have counterpart funds, we must negotiate with the countries on their use. Where we have a shortage of PL–480 funds, which is chronic in Latin America, we have an allocation of 25% and it would not help to raise it to 50%.

COMAP's chief interest was to find other sources for local currency which could be loaned to investors so they could use it as a hedge against devaluation.

It was suggested that counterpart from balance-of-payments loans be considered for this purpose. On that suggestion we can point to Colombia as a response. A portion of the local currency from the $60 million balance-of-payments loan is being lent through the Central Bank down there to international firms that want to borrow. (COMAP recognizes that such funds must be available to other investors as well as American.)

Investment Guaranty. The recommendations of the COMAP report in the investment guaranty field are not too helpful. AID is already working on this and is making progress. Within AID, it is being recommended that in the next few months diplomatic pressures be used wherever feasible to get the agreements signed. AID is updating the ground rules for investment guaranties and is asking for increases in the ceiling on investment guaranties along the lines of the COMAP recommendation. It will streamline and simplify contracts. We are considering a multilateral risk guarantee but think that we should get other things settled first before pursuing this.

Criticism at the Meeting of the COMAP Report. AID felt that the COMAP report didn't take cognizance of the difference between two things: a) efforts to improve the climate, which is a very gradual process on which more progress is being made than either the COMAP report or the Rockefeller–Collado–Wriston letter indicate; and b) the impossibility of waiting until we have reached the optimum climate before we become operative.

There is a fallacy in using the statistics and averages in the COMAP report—low return, no return, etc. A businessman does not make an investment in Latin America—he makes an investment in a specific business in a particular town in a selected country because he thinks he will make a profit. Use of the term "Latin America" is misleading, because there are so many differences among the countries and within the countries. Also it is fallacious to speak of the business community as a single entity. There are all kinds of differences of opinion within the community, and the twenty business committees concerning themselves with Latin America do not speak with one voice.

There were comments to the effect that the COMAP report exaggerated the problem—that the investment climate is not as unattractive as the report made out; that some investment is taking place; and that the rate of return is not as low as the report indicated. The major problem is in the Latin American countries themselves and is something we cannot influence in a major way either by agreements, exhortation, or U.S. legislation. The real problem is doubt on the part of the investor deriving from Latin American revolutions, expropriation in Cuba, inflationary conditions, and mismanagement. It is largely psychological, and the only way to offset it is to have it become generally realized that people are doing business in Latin America and doing well there.

Agriculture had a strong reaction against the COMAP report's desire to back away from land reform. Agriculture agreed with the comments in the Commerce paper that the basic objectives of the Alliance, including land reform, health and educational programs, must go on if the Alliance is to have widespread support in Latin America itself.

Some of the statistics in the COMAP report were criticized as not presenting the true picture. For example, the report shows that in the first nine months of last year there was a net outflow of U.S. capital from Latin America. The other months of that year show a different trend. Also, no account is taken of the Japanese and European investment in Latin America which is considerable.

How to Use the Private Sector in the Alliance. The report, which one official characterized as the worst blow yet to the Alliance, raises a question as to how to use the private sector in approaching a problem that involves the private sector. The COMAP experience is one which would lead a good many to be wary of participating in this kind of an effort. It is a serious problem to bring a group in on an advisory basis. Now we have quite a problem in getting Mr. Grace squared away in testimony.

The longer-range issue is how to mobilize the private sector for the Alliance in Latin America as well as in the United States. This is one of the most difficult problems in the Alliance. The private sector is very disaffected and doesn't feel it has been adequately consulted. In this regard, one of the problems discussed in Committee IV at Buenos Aires was the place of industrial promotion centers and getting the private sector to take responsibility for doing basic industry feasibility studies to find opportunities for investment which should be pursued and then finding the financing for the investment, through the IDB or elsewhere.

Mr. Rostow said that we should be thinking not merely how to encourage private investment but how our leadership in private enterprise can make a contribution to the structural problems of Latin American countries. Private enterprise activities in the fabrication sector tend to be confined to cities and the middle class urban market. Behind lays the hinterland and the vast slums. A central problem is to break the private enterprise activities out of their limited urban markets and offer on a mass basis the means for increasing productivity in the form of agricultural tools, equipment, fertilizer as well as the incentives in the form of consumer goods. A major contribution of American private enterprise would be to make common cause with those Latin American businessmen who have the energy and potential to break out of the present situation and think in terms of a mass market.

The Problem of Relating Stability and Development. Mr. Rostow spoke of the difficulty of marrying fiscal and banking measures designed to produce stability which have a deflationary effect with development projects which involve government-to-government investment for social overhead projects. There is danger of throttling the private sector. He hoped that problem could be discussed sometime, in this forum.

Need to Improve the Image of American Investment. It was suggested at the meeting that there needed to be a real campaign to remove the bad and unfair image that has been created with respect to American investment. People should be made aware that American private investment has put into less developed countries good housing, schools, hospitals, roads, and other things which improve the standard of living. The Latin Governments should give credit for the benefits, and the American companies themselves should do something about improving their image. Officials of American subsidiaries should take part in the community, for example, participating in the local Chambers of Commerce as well as in the American Chambers of Commerce.

It was noted that enough material was available to make an effective reply to criticisms of the Alliance and misconceptions concerning business; someone high in the Administration should make a speech on this subject.

Summation. Mr. McGhee noted that the discussion had brought out several very important points. The Latin American countries themselves have much to do. We have limited means to induce them.

It is important that we should not be talked out of our basic philosophy on the Alliance for Progress by Mr. Grace. The San Jose meeting of Presidents made clear that we are going forward with social measures at the same time as with the private sector, and that we haven't changed our philosophy. In individual cases, we have to consider how far to press, but the general basis and objectives are the same as outlined at Punta del Este.

III. Next Meeting

The next meeting is scheduled for April 4, and Governor Harriman will preside. The subject will be "Problems of Foreign Aid: Alternative Means of Helping Nations to Achieve Self-reliance". AID is preparing a paper which will be circulated.

C. W. Nichols[3]
Executive Secretary

---

[3] Printed from a copy that bears this typed signature.

61. **Memorandum From the Executive Secretary of the Department of State (Brubeck) to the President's Special Assistant for National Security Affairs (Bundy)**

Washington, March 25, 1963.

SUBJECT

Implementation of Agreements Reached at San Jose

In response to the President's written inquiry of March 22[1] to Assistant Secretary Martin, there is enclosed an initial report on measures being taken to implement agreements reached at San Jose.

D. Rowe[2]

Enclosure

Memorandum Prepared in the Department of State

SUBJECT

Implementation of Agreements Reached at San Jose

A. *Security Measures Against Subversion in the Isthmian Countries:*

1. We have notified Nicaragua we will be represented at a meeting of Ministers of Interior at Managua on April 3.

2. We circulated to our Embassies in the Central American Isthmus on March 23 a telegram outlining the range of measures we might wish to take up at Managua on April 3, and requested comments and suggestions from the field.[3]

3. Major General Krulak has been assigned responsibility for substantive preparations for the Managua meeting. He is preparing for the consideration of the Department an outline of our objectives for the conference, suggested agenda, and delegation membership, all of which will be cleared with Mr. Ralph Dungan.

Source: Department of State, Conference Files: Lot 66 D 110, CF 2233. Confidential.

[1] Not found.

[2] Rowe signed for Brubeck above Brubeck's typed signature.

[3] Reference is to Department of State Circular 1641; Department of State, Central Files, POL 7 NIC/FM.

The head of our delegation has not yet been named; Deputy Attorney General Katzenbach or Deputy Assistant Secretary of State Cottrell are under consideration.[4]

B. *Alliance for Progress:*

1. Managua Conference

a. Mr. Moscoso will lead a delegation of State and AID officials from Washington and US AID Directors in the Isthmian countries to a conference with Isthmian Ministers of Economy, Finance, Public Works, etc., at Managua April 4–6.

b. State/AID circulated to our Embassies in the Isthmus on March 23 a suggested agenda for the meeting, and solicited comments and suggestions.

c. The proposed agenda is designed to give maximum acceleration to formulation and execution of development projects in the Isthmus, both regional and national, and will be the major follow-up operation.

d. After the Managua conference an AID/W team will visit each capital to complete action on loan projects and applications which may not have been concluded at Managua.

2. Other

a. AID on March 21 obligated $75,000 to the Disabled Persons Institute at Tegucigalpa. President Villeda Morales received notification on arrival at Tegucigalpa airport from San Jose.

b. AID is prepared to grant $130,000 in support of the Children's Hospital in San Jose as soon as the Ambassador notifies us as to the appropriate timing.

c. We are examining the record of the bilateral talks at San Jose to identify other commitments made so that we may follow up on them without delay.

---

[4] The Meeting of the Ministers of Government, Interior, and Security of Central America and the United States met in Managua, Nicaragua, April 3–4. The U.S. delegation was led by Deputy Attorney General Nicholas Katzenbach. The Final Act of the meeting is printed in *American Foreign Policy: Current Documents, 1963*, pp. 239–242.

62.   Circular Telegram From the Department of State to All Posts in the American Republics

Washington, March 27, 1963, 11:36 a.m.

1667. During San Jose conference Secretary met various US newsmen regularly stationed Latin capitals. He impressed by their ignorance Alliance for Progress. Some these same correspondents in recent stories explained at great length why Alliance is failing. In aggregate, they have contributed significantly to negative image of program being formed by US public and Congress.

With concern over problem increasing at highest level administration, Department feels ARA country teams from Ambassador on down have special, urgent responsibility provide maximum positive guidance to resident US correspondents as well as casuals passing through. Without gilding facts or minimizing problems, Department feels there are enough Alliance accomplishments which, if pointed up, would moderate reporters' preoccupation with program failures and shortcomings.

Evidence of this was seen during San Jose meeting when stories began appear in US press sounding gee-whiz note that in fact there has been considerable and even surprising progress under Alliance.

In laying on guidance, posts should (1) emphasize fact Alliance not US aid program but rather US pledge aid these countries willing make sacrifices and provide great bulk of total investment required in economic, social development programs, (2) deal with self-help projects undertaken without reference to Alliance or without US funding as Alliance projects as long as they are within spirit of Punta del Este and (3) based on materials provided from Washington keep newsmen informed on Alliance as whole and not just your country.

It would be most helpful intensify Latin American identity with Alliance and its goals. Most convincing display of success in Alliance is active participation and involvement in it by Latin leadership.

Rusk

Source: Department of State, Conference Files: Lot 66 D 110, CF 2229. Confidential. Drafted by King; cleared by Phillips, Martin, and Goldmann; and approved by King.

63.   Memorandum From the Secretary General of the International Peace Corps Secretariat (Goodwin) to President Kennedy

Washington, September 10, 1963.

In the last couple of weeks (while on vacation) I have given considerable thought to the Alliance for Progress in my recent capacity as disinterested observer.

I believe this is the most important on-going program of your Administration (as distinct from critical decisions such as Cuba, test ban etc.). Moreover it is a new and significant initiative in U.S. policy toward an area of the world which has been of historic and intimate concern to us; an area which is second in importance only to Europe. Its success would be viewed as one of the great achievements of U.S. policy ranking with the Marshall Plan, the Good Neighbor policy etc.; policies which now have the gloss of past triumphs but which were intrinsically no more path-breaking or significant than the Alianza.

It is increasingly disappointing that a program which is sound in conception and historically right is operating at about one-half effectiveness. (And that may be a generous estimate.) I have continual self doubts about this estimate since Washington is a city filled with reassurances and self-justification; but every time I get involved or go to the field (I was recently in Bolivia) my dismay and alarm keep crowding back. As an example: about a year ago we suggested the state-to-country program using California and Chile as a pilot. Everyone concurred in this idea. Several times you indicated your personal interest in it. Yet one year later a person is being placed on the staff to implement the project. This, I submit, is inexcusable and, as a result, we have lost not only time in the Alianza but all hope of political benefit in time for Congressional actions on the AID request. Another example: The AID Director in Bolivia has been waiting six months for a qualified loan officer despite the fact that he has one of the largest, if not the largest, loan program in Latin America. Individual instances of this sort can always be explained and justified; but they are part of a pattern of lack of imagination, daring, administrative efficiency etc. which is critically damaging the program.

Much of the delay etc. is explained on the grounds of the necessity to be careful about what Congress thinks. But all the cautions in the world have not only failed to win over those hostile to the Alianza; but the consequent failures and delays and inefficiencies have helped to alienate our friends. A dynamic, successful program—well-publicized—is the way to win congressional support rather than the building of an intricate net-

---

Source: Kennedy Library, President's Office Files, Staff Memoranda, Goodwin. No classification marking.

work of safeguards which protect the individuals running the program, but not the program itself. The fact that obvious failures cannot be blamed on anyone is itself a bad sign. For people unwilling to take chances of personal failure will never run the risk of success.

Probably the most serious single problem is personnel. The Alianza has the same trouble as the Washington Nats—they don't have the ball-players. There are, of course, some very good people, but there is also a tremendous amount of mediocrity in high places. No program is better than the people who run it. The reasons for this are many and too detailed to go into here, but they include: complete lack of a good recruiting effort, impossible personnel procedures, a structure which discourages individual initiative and responsibility, a careerist mentality, and inability to recognize mediocrity when it is seen. There are good people available, and they can be recruited. I know this for several reasons: (1) I know enough people to know there are good people available; (2) Shriver's success at recruiting people, some of them formerly among the best of AID. The Alianza is intrinsically more exciting, bigger and more glamorous than the Peace Corps and there is no reason why it should not attract as good or better people; (3) A year and a half ago I proposed to Moscoso that we should try and recruit the brightest young men from Wall Street law firms etc. to come to Washington to work in the Alianza. We would give them a six months' training program to prepare them to become development desk officers for various countries. He thought this was fine. I organized a cocktail party in New York (our intention was to follow it up with similar gatherings in other cities). About thirty-five young lawyers and businessmen attended. They were nearly all men with outstanding scholastic records at major law or business schools; of high caliber personally and rising in their firms. I talked with them about the Alianza and asked those who were interested in joining the training program to send a letter with a résumé. Twenty-two sent letters. Their quality can be judged by the fact that Bicks (the antitrust chief under Ike) told an acquaintance of mine that the Alianza was getting all the bright young lawyers in New York. I sent the names and letters to the Alianza. No action was taken to my considerable personal discomfort. But it did prove the people are there.

I can think of only one answer to all of this: to tell Shriver he must run the Alianza for at least a year, get it on its feet and recruit a successor. This does not mean that he is the only one who can do it. But he is the only one I know; especially since to put a new man, no matter how good, into the existing situation who lacks the personal muscle and experience to destroy the bureaucratic obstacles will not do the job. Shriver must also get what he thinks he needs to do the job. This will mean radical organizational and personnel changes. Many people, including some of your best and most trusted people, will object. It will run afoul of all sorts of theoretical administrative objections, and some serious practical difficulties. All I can say to this is: (a) We have had two and one-half years trying to do the job the other way; (b) If you expect a good man to try a difficult job you must give him the tools he thinks he needs to do it, not what others think he needs; (c) For whatever it's worth it is my judgment that this is the only way to do the job, and I disagree with those who think it is not; (d) It is a good idea to break up a losing ball club.

This approach will conflict with many ambitions, desires and the considered views of thoughtful and dedicated people. It will hurt Moscoso, whom I admire and like deeply. But I feel so strongly about the importance of this program to the country and to your Administration, that I am confident everything must be tried. We will be judged on whether we won or lost, and not how we played the game.

There will also be some feeling that things are not going so badly. I submit that much of this is because we have lived so long with existing shortcomings, lack of imagination etc., that we regard them as part of the nature of things and lower our sights accordingly. The Peace Corps has helped show what an overseas program can be when approached with great imagination and skill. I think we could do as much for the Alianza, although I recognize the great difficulties involved.

I also believe action of this sort should be taken quickly. Latin America will probably be a foreign policy issue in the campaign; and the Alianza is likely to be a principal target both in Congress and outside unless it can be raised above too much reproach rather quickly. Otherwise we will be in a weaker position on it, to say nothing of the very real danger of losing much of it in the Congress. This year is really the "year of truth"—to paraphrase a Latin phrase.

I do not want to sound as if I have all the answers, or that I am sure that this approach is the right one. But I have felt this with increasing strength for a long period of time, and would be remiss toward you if I did not relay my thought.

It would be helpful if you did not circulate this memorandum since I have to deal with many of the people affected; but I leave that entirely to your judgment as to the best approach.

Dick

Frankfurter always told me that I would only be of use as an assistant as long as I was willing to say unpleasant things.

P.S. Of course, I have told Sarge about this memo.[1]

---

[1] The last two sentences are handwritten by Goodwin on the source text. Reference is to Supreme Court Justice Felix Frankfurter, for whom Goodwin clerked in 1958–1959, and to Sargent Shriver, Director of the Peace Corps.

64.   **Editorial Note**

On Sunday, October 6, 1963, the New York *Herald Tribune* published an article by Assistant Secretary of State for Inter-American Affairs Edwin Martin that outlined U.S. policy toward military governments in Latin America. In the piece, Martin emphasized U.S. support for constitutional civilian governments in the region. He stated that the military in Latin America must play an active and constructive role in support of these governments. Martin noted further that the militaries of some Latin American nations had played critical roles in dislodging dictators from power, instituting progressive reforms, and returning their countries to more democratic civilian control. Still, Martin continued, military governments established by coups d'état must be condemned as anti-democratic. Martin cautioned that the United States could not be expected to intervene militarily or economically against any military government in the region established by coup d'état. Rather, it was the responsibility of the Latin Americans to create conditions in which such regimes could not survive and in which democracy could prosper. The text of the article is in Department of State *Bulletin*, November 4, 1963, pages 698–700. It was repeated to all Latin American diplomatic posts in Department of State Circular 637, which described it as having been cleared "at highest levels" of the U.S. Government. (Kennedy Library, National Security Files, Regional Security Series, Latin America, July–November 1963)

A July 14 article in *The New York Times* quoted Department of State officials as lauding the "sense of mission" displayed by the Ecuadorean military on July 11 when it overthrew the Arosemena government, which had opposed many Alliance for Progress reforms. The article caused consternation in Latin America and prompted a concerned letter from Venezuelan President Romulo Betancourt to President Kennedy, which was delivered personally by the Venezuelan Ambassador on August 2. (Department of State, Central Files, POL 26 LAT AM) President Kennedy, in his reply of August 16 assured the Venezuelan President that the Department of State officials had been misquoted and that it was the "unalterable position of the Government of the United States to support representative, constitutional processes" in Latin America. (Ibid.)

The New York Times incident prompted administration thinking about the proper posture of the United States in relation to military governments in Latin America and led directly to the drafting of the Martin article.

65. Memorandum From the President's Special Assistant (Schlesinger) to President Kennedy

Washington, October 8, 1963.

SUBJECT

The Martin Doctrine

I hope very much that at your press conference tomorrow you will be able to clear up some of the fears aroused by the Martin statement in the *Herald Tribune* Sunday[1] and the Martin backgrounder as reported in today's *Post*. The Venezuelan Ambassador called me this morning and said that the "Martin Doctrine" was causing "consternation," that it was being interpreted as a "very serious reversal of policy," that he feared it would "trigger all sorts of bad reactions though the hemisphere," and that the Venezuelan Foreign Minister had returned to Caracas yesterday "very apprehensive and gloomy." I assured him that there was no change in policy, that the Martin statement was to be read in the context of our total Latin American policy, that it dealt with only one aspect of that policy, that it did not repeal the Secretary's statement of Friday, etc. I think, however, that a more authoritative declaration to this effect is required if the Martin statement is not going to begin to cause damage. The points, I think, which should be made are:

a) there has been no change in Administration policy

b) our main reliance in Latin America continues to be on the forces of progressive democracy, and our essential hope lies in the establishment and extension of civilian, democratic regimes

c) the Martin statement does not constitute a "doctrine"; it was wrongly and misleadingly headlined by the *Herald Tribune* as "Official U.S. Policy for Latin America"; it is simply a sober and realistic description of certain conditions and problems which the struggle for democracy is bound to encounter along the way.

Since I have had some involvement in Latin American affairs, I hope you will not mind if I add a few words about the Martin statement. I think Ed Martin had done a first-class job in running ARA; and I recognize the need for cooling down those in the press and Congress who suppose that military coups constitute definitive evidence of the failure of the Alliance. I do think, however, that the Martin statement needlessly laid itself open to misinterpretation. The notion that the statement means a

---

Source: Kennedy Library, National Security Files, Regional Security Series, Latin America, July–November 1963. Confidential.

[1] October 6; see Document 64.

reversal of U.S. policy is only partly to be explained by the *Herald Tribune* headline. It is also to be explained by the way the Martin statement said some things and by the way it omitted other things.

The signal contribution of your Administration to Latin American policy has been to make an implicit alliance with the forces of progressive democracy in Latin America. You have become a rallying-point for these forces, which in past years have been disorganized, dispersed and discouraged. Your coming to Washington has meant a new voice, a new position, a new opportunity. It has altered the relationship of the United States to the rest of the hemisphere by identifying Washington with moral and progressive leadership. The Alliance for Progress is really based on this implicit alliance.

Now obviously we have been disappointed by the weakness of progressive democracy in many countries, but only what Ed Martin calls "impatient idealists" would have expected these forces to triumph overnight. The trouble with the Martin statement is that it gives the impression that, since they have failed to triumph overnight, we have lost interest in them and are now looking to military rule to produce progressive regimes. This impression is conveyed especially by what seems to me a gross exaggeration of the merits of military rule in Latin America and of its "contribution to political freedom and stability in many countries." Thus the Martin statement says of Ecuador and Guatemala that "military regimes have announced reform programs of substantial importance." What is the advantage of going on the record in praise of regimes which we know are not much good? Everyone knows that the Guatemalan regime has been quite regressive and repressive, and that the Ecuador regime is falling apart, and our praise must therefore convey to many the implication that, if military regimes "announce" nice programs, they will be forgiven everything else. Similarly the Martin statement says that military government in Argentina has produced "one of the most progressive regimes" that Argentina has ever had—a striking feat of clairvoyance, since the new regime in Argentina has not yet taken office. I see no gain in committing ourselves to so glowing a description of a government which has not even been inaugurated.

Everyone in Latin America accepts the necessity of dealing with military regimes for tactical purposes, so long as there is fundamental faith in our democratic purpose. The Martin statement has alarmed some about the constancy of that purpose by appearing to transform a pragmatic necessity into a new policy departure—or rather into a reversion to old and familiar U.S. policies which for a moment Washington seemed to have abandoned. Because the statement does not reaffirm in any vivid way our preference for the forces of progressive democracy, and because it detects so many notable virtues in military rule, it seemed to be signaling, say, to the Venezuelan military that, if Leone turns out to be weak, it is OK to throw him out so long as the military regime "announces" reform programs and observes the proper etiquette. The Martin statement even calls for "military participation in the formation of some national policies." A Chilean diplomat says sadly, "We have struggled for years to keep our military out of politics. You are weakening the democratic structure in Chile by inviting them in."

I don't want to prolong this memorandum, but I should add that the tone of the statement also seems unduly cold and condescending and to suggest a lack of sympathy with the problems of Latin American democracy and with the dignity of the Latin American people. The suggestion that "the traditional method of transferring political power has been by revolution or coup d'etat" is offensive to countries like Chile, Uruguay, Mexico, Costa Rica, Brazil, Argentina, etc., where this has *not* been the traditional method. The suggestion that the goal of the Alliance is to "strengthen in each society the power of the educated middle class" suggests that we have forgotten all our fine words about helping the *campesinos*, and the workers and that our basic concern is with the business community. And there is altogether too much flourish of the word "we"—"*we* must strengthen in each society . . ."; "*we* cannot aim to reduce them to impotence in the national life . . ."; "*our* efforts to train the military in their most valuable role . . ."—all this suggesting to sensitive Latinos an unconscious paternalism and contempt in American policy.

For all these reasons, I think it would be most important for you to strike a note of reassurance in tomorrow's press conference.[2]

Arthur Schlesinger, jr.[3]

---

[2] At his October 9 press conference, President Kennedy was asked whether he had cleared the Martin article and whether it represented a reversal of U.S. policy in Latin America. He replied that he had not personally cleared the article but was generally aware of its content and that the United States remained opposed to governments in the region imposed by coups d'état. Assistant Secretary Martin, he said, was "merely attempting to explain some of the problems in Latin America, why coups take place, and what problems they present [the United States] with." (*Public Papers of the Presidents of the United States: John F. Kennedy, 1963*, pp. 767–775)

[3] Printed from a copy that bears this typed signature.

66.   Scope Paper

São Paulo, October 24, 1963.

UNITED STATES DELEGATION TO THE ANNUAL MEETING OF
THE INTER-AMERICAN ECONOMIC AND SOCIAL COUNCIL
AT THE MINISTERIAL LEVEL

São Paulo, October–November 1963

Main U.S. Objectives at São Paulo Meetings

1. Since the Alliance is a long-term effort, and this is only the second annual meeting of the IA–ECOSOC, the character of the conference itself is of great importance. USDel will strive to make this annual assembly of the Alliance the forum where all problems are discussed honestly, and constructively. The resolutions which are adopted should be few, and meaningful.

The evaluation by IA–ECOSOC of the progress of the Alliance is contained in a brief report issued by the ministers; a longer report (La Marcha de la Alianza) is prepared by the experts. USDel will seek to make these reports of the highest quality.

2. The USDel should support a meaningful Latin American initiative to establish CID along the lines approved by the President.

The establishment of the new committee will provide an entity with a wider coordinating function than heretofore exercised by any agency within the Alliance.

The committee's activities, as well as those of the Panel of Nine, should not be limited to review and recommendations relating to national development plans but should also include studies and recommendations concerning foreign trade and integration policies and programs both with respect to their effectiveness and their consistency with national development plans as well as to their consistency with the plans and programs of other countries in the region. The creation of such a committee offers perhaps the best means of strengthening the multilateral character of the Alliance and of increasing pressures on member countries to adopt sounder and more constructive policies.

3. Explain or clarify U.S. assistance data and operations under the Alliance, including major problems which have affected these opera-

Source: Department of State, ARA/IPA Files: Lot 69 D 211, IA–ECOSOC (Ministerial Level), Position Papers and Background Papers. Limited Official Use. Drafted by Elac and cleared by Rogers, Turnage, Tragen, Luzzatto, Weintraub, Wilson (RPA), Barcroft (USIA), Rendall (Treasury), and Monyihan (Labor).

tions. USDel will express willingness to review possibilities of streamlining procedures, and will point out the improvements made since the Mexico City Meetings.

4.   USDel will support, or co-sponsor, a resolution on a study leading to the establishment of methods and institutions for promoting the trade of OAS members (including the U.S.), e.g., undertaking market research, promoting knowledge of trade opportunities, providing a variety of services to exporters, etc. A major new effort toward export promotion is sorely needed.

5.   The U.S. will press for approval of a plan to secure Latin American financial support, starting in January, 1965, for the expenses of the expanded Pan American Union activities in support of the Alliance now financed by a U.S. grant.

Background

The purpose of these meetings is to conduct the Second Annual Review of the Alliance for Progress. The First Annual Review was held in Mexico City during October 1962.[1] The Mexico City meetings are considered to have been highly successful, since the debates were quite frank— in contrast to traditional Inter-American gatherings which have been characterized by florid oratory, avoidance of the difficult issues, and too much formality. It is in the interest of the United States that in the São Paulo meetings there be a thorough discussion of all the problems confronting the Alliance, a realistic evaluation of the progress made in its first two years, and that resolutions be adopted which will lead to constructive action to further the aims of the Alliance.

It is anticipated that during the two weeks of the meeting at the expert level the agenda will be covered completely. As a result, the ministerial meeting will receive from the expert meeting a general analysis of the Alliance, plus an analysis of those important issues which the experts either have not been able to resolve, or simply prefer to leave to the discretion of the ministers.

The usual focus on the alliance relates to its basic approach as expressed in the Charter of Punta del Este. Since the United States was the only "external" source of support signatory to the Charter of Punta del Este, much of the discussion at IA–ECOSOC inevitably centers around what the countries of Latin America have done for themselves, and what the U.S. has or has not done to support them. Thus, we can expect that our Latin partners will tend to emphasize U.S. shortcomings. The U.S. delegation will be prepared to clarify and explain our operations over the past two years. The report prepared by the U.S. Government for the IA–ECOSOC will perhaps reduce considerably the amount

---

[1] See Documents 48 and 50.

of time spent by the conference in determining what in fact was done by the U.S. over the past year under the Alliance, and permit more attention to be given to the problems encountered by the Latin American countries, individually and collectively, in meeting their own responsibilities under the Charter of Punta del Este.

Special Note—The discussion of any agenda item which has program or budget implications should be brought to the attention of USDel spokesmen on budget committee.

Agenda

The provisional Agenda will probably be adopted without major changes.

Under Topic I–A (Planning, Reforms and Financing) there will be general presentations made by the heads of delegations—at the expert level—followed by a discussion of results obtained in the countries and in the region in 1962 and the first half of 1963. There will probably be much interest shown by the Latin American delegations in the adequacy of external financial and technical assistance, both in terms of quantity and quality. The data will show that the total availability of external resources was smaller in 1962 than in 1961, even though the amounts provided by the U.S. Government were roughly at the same level.

A more detailed debate on sectorial and functional development problems will be conducted under Topic I–B of the Agenda. Here most of the emphasis will be on internal measures taken by the Latin American countries. The U.S. Delegation will be in a position to show that our support has been substantial in most of these areas. Special attention will be given to agrarian and tax reforms.

Topic I–C might receive the greatest attention by newsmen in the United States and in Latin America, as well as by the delegations to IA–ECOSOC. It is important, however, that action on the Lleras–Kubitschek proposals not be made the sine-qua-non for the success of the São Paulo meetings. There is a well documented story to tell about substantial achievements under the Alliance for Progress in the member countries and several other proposals for future action have potentially great merit. The establishment of CID must not be allowed to appear as a second beginning of the Alliance; rather, it should be considered a further, if dramatic, step in the evolution of an ongoing program which was already judged in Mexico City to be intrinsically sound.

Topic II (Latin American Foreign Trade and its Significance for the UNCTAD) may well turn out to be as important to many delegations as I–C. Indeed, the title of the topic was officially proposed by the governments of Argentina, Brazil and Chile. The São Paulo meetings present an opportunity to begin a dialogue between the U.S. Government and the Latin American governments on the many issues that may be debated at the UNCTAD. It is probable that Latin American delegations will be anxious to get U.S. assurances of support for some of their projects. While sympathetic interest can be shown the Delegation will doubtless be unable to support all proposals fully at this time.

Topic III (Regional Integration) may provide a more substantive debate than there was in Mexico City. There is increasing concern in the various countries with the limited opportunities for national development. The São Paulo meetings may turn out to be place and time for regional integration to be given a real push forward. Some general principles for an acceleration of the integration movement—which is at the heart of the Alliance—may be discussed. USDel should seize the opportunity to make clear its support of genuine steps for economic integration and the fundamental importance of promoting competitive forces to maintain and sustain economic growth.

Topic IV (Programs and Budgets) may be the most troublesome of the Agenda items, in that perhaps an insufficient number of delegations will assign a member, and those who are assigned may not be competent to the task. The regular budget of the Pan American Union for those activities within the sphere of competence of IA–ECOSOC must be given a preliminary analysis as a basis for recommendations to the Council of the Organization of American States. The activities and budget of the Program of Technical Cooperation will receive final approval by the IA–ECOSOC, and the pledges of financial support will be requested at a designated session at the ministerial level. Other delegations should be prodded into giving these OAS programs and budgets the attention they deserve. At the Mexico City meetings, the analysis was only cursory. The experience should not be repeated in São Paulo. Finally, consideration will be given to the establishment of a new OAS fund for the Alliance for Progress, in which a special U.S. contribution would be matched, in an agreed proportion, by Latin American contributions.

67.   USIA News Policy Note

40–63   Washington, October 25, 1963.

IA–ECOSOC Meeting in Sao Paulo

The Inter-American Economic and Social Council's conference at Sao Paulo, Brazil, October 29–November 15, will be the second Annual Review Meeting of Alliance for Progress members. Expert-level sessions are scheduled October 29–November 10; ministerial sessions, November 11–15.

Treatment

We want coverage to show that Alliance for Progress has made a good beginning—but only a beginning—toward its long-range goals of economic progress and social reform. As evidence, cite AFP achievements and firm AFP plans and projects which member countries report. Points for emphasis:

(1) The Alliance for Progress is a multilateral effort of twenty American nations. Its success depends primarily on the nineteen Latin American members. It is not a U.S. aid program.

(2) The Alliance's Charter (of Punta del Este) calls for the processes of national growth, governmental evolution and social reform to move forward together, simultaneously.

(3) The United States welcomes Latin American initiative in proposing a Committee for International Development (CID) which would function as a full-time IA–ECOSOC sub-committee to strengthen AFP programs.

(4) The United States is meeting its obligations under the Charter of Punta del Este. In 1961–62, U.S. economic assistance commitments to Latin America amounted to $1,038,000,000—$4.82 for each Latin American. In the same period Latin America's share of the total U.S. foreign assistance budget was twenty-five per cent—as compared with seven per cent for the period 1946–60. (See U.S. Report to the Inter-American Economic and Social Council, 1963.)

Caution: The Latin American countries are seeking a common position on control of commodity prices, specifically for coffee, cocoa and tin. They may attempt at Sao Paulo to enlist U.S. support. The U.S. attitude is one of sympathy and cooperation in the problems of trade and commodity prices, but it is unlikely that the U.S. delegation will be drawn into a

---

Source: Kennedy Library, Schlesinger Papers, Writings—Alliance for Progress, 1963 Memoranda. Limited Official Use. Drafted by Needham. Sent by Pauker to Clarke, Sayles, Vogel, LeClair, and Ehrman.

definite position at this conference. Official U.S. statements should guide us in whatever minimal treatment of the subject credibility may require.

Background

This year's IA–ECOSOC meeting is expected to develop a modest amount of evidence indicating effective beginnings of the Alliance for Progress—more signs of progress than were available at last year's sessions in Mexico City. However, the U.S. wants to keep these in the perspective of "a good beginning."

In evidence of that "good beginning" will be such steps as institutional, agricultural and industrial development, economic stabilization, and integation, private enterprise development (domestic and foreign), fiscal reform, commodity markets and expanded trade opportunities, and improvements in AFP planning and administration.

Ex-President Lleras Camargo of Colombia and Ex-President Kubitschek of Brazil have recommended establishment of a Committee for Inter-American Development. The U.S. will support the recommendation if the Latin American countries on their own initiative evince a strong majority desire for CID. The committee would operate full-time to provide a continuing review and coordination of Alliance activities. It would include representatives from all AFP member countries of the Alliance, with a seven-man executive committee on which the United States would be represented at all times. The other six memberships would rotate among the Latin American countries.

---

68.   Memorandum From President Kennedy to Secretary of State Rusk

Washington, October 29, 1963.

I would like to create the position of Under Secretary of State for Inter-American Affairs.[1] This would be the fourth ranking position in the Department. Its occupant would have responsibility for the Alliance for Progress as well as for the Bureau of Inter-American Affairs (each of

---

Source: Department of State, Rusk Files: Lot 72 D 192, White House Correspondence. Confidential.

[1] This recommendation dates to the Report from the Task Force on Immediate Latin American Problems to the President-elect of January 4, 1961; see Document 2.

which would continue under officers at the level of Assistant Secretary). In addition, he would have general concern with all government activities relating to Latin America. Obviously he would have no supervision over Assistant Secretaries of State outside Latin America.

I am familiar with the argument that, if we do this for Latin America, other geographical areas must receive equal treatment. But I have come increasingly to feel that this argument, however plausible in the abstract, overlooks the practicalities of the situation.

1) The top officers of the Department, for good and sufficient reason, are absorbed in the problems of Europe, Asia, and East-West relations. It seems to me inevitable that this should be so, but the consequence is that Latin American policy does not get the day-to-day, high-level attention which our national interest demands.

2) There are, moreover, strong reasons for distinguishing Latin America from the other regions of the world. Historically Latin America has been the area of primary U.S. interest. Currently it is the area of the greatest danger to us. It is the area where the U.S. is most intimately involved in day-to-day operations, and where it is held most accountable for the results. All these considerations would seem amply to justify a special place for Latin American affairs.

Since I am familiar with the arguments against the establishment of the Under Secretaryship, I would like this time to have a positive exploration of its possibilities. If we decide to move quickly on this, it would be advantageous for the new post to be announced in Washington during the period of the IA–ECOSOC meetings at Sao Paulo. Such an announcement at such a time would drive home the seriousness of our commitment to Latin American affairs.

John Kennedy

69.   Editorial Note

The Second Annual Meeting of the Inter-American Economic and Social Council of the Organization of American States convened in São Paulo, Brazil, October 29–November 16, 1963, to review the accomplishments of the Alliance for Progress. The Council met at the expert level October 29–November 10. Under Secretary of State W. Averell Harriman represented the United States at Ministerial-level sessions of the conference November 11–16. Addressing the Council on November 13, Harriman said that the United States had dispensed $2.3 billion in development assistance to Latin America since the establishment of the Alliance for Progress in August 1961. He urged the Latin American governments to develop well-conceived and technically sound projects within the framework of the Alliance. Before adjourning, the Council created an Inter-American Committee on the Alliance for Progress (CIAP) to police the operations of the Alliance and make financial recommendations within it. For text of the resolution establishing CIAP, see *American Foreign Policy: Current Documents, 1963*, pages 342–347. Documentation is in Department of State, ARA/IPA Files: Lot 69 D 211, IA–ECOSOC: USDel to Annual Mtg. of the IA Econ. and Social Council at the Ministerial Level; Sao Paulo, Oct.–Nov. 1963, and ibid., ARA/USOAS Files: Lot 76 D 381, Second Annual Meeting Economic and Social Council, Sao Paulo, Brazil, 1963.

---

70. Memorandum From the Executive Secretary of the Department of State (Read) to the President's Special Assistant for National Security Affairs (Bundy)

Washington, November 14, 1963.

SUBJECT

Political Atmosphere at Inter-American Economic and Social Council Meeting

Perhaps the most significant fact which detaches itself from the IA–ECOSOC meeting to date is the tendency manifested by Brazil to pursue an independent course possibly involving a re-evaluation of its relationship to the United States. This was reflected, in particular, in President Goulart's speech on the opening day. Governor Harriman characterized it as "essentially a bid for Brazilian leadership of the 'Latin American
• continent' which would, by implication, exclude a major U.S. role." There was a single passing reference in Goulart's speech to the Alliance for Progress and none whatsoever to the United States, the President, economic assistance, investment, or inter-American cooperation. On the other hand, our delegation has reported that the Goulart speech has not

---

Source: Department of State, ARA/IPA Files: Lot 69 D 211, IA–ECOSOC, General, 1962–1963. Confidential. Drafted by Gonzalez and cleared by Cottrell, Chapin, and Woolf.

been well received by a majority of other delegations and that other country presentations have been generally quite favorable to the United States and to the Alliance. In addition, Governor Harriman reports that his own speech in which he was rather blunt on some points was warmly received. The U.S. delegation further reports that a friendly atmosphere has prevailed in its contacts at all levels with other delegations noting, however, that there has been some concern expressed over recent Senate amendments to the Foreign Aid Bill.

A major issue before the conference is the examination of the Alliance machinery in the form of the proposal to create an Inter-American Committee for the Alliance for Progress (CIAP). The terms of reference for this multi-national body and its authority over AFP programming and utilization of funds will be decided by the Ministers. Brazil initially opposed this proposal and wished instead to submit an alternative which would create a multilateral fund in which a major U.S. contribution would be matched by Latin American contributions. Appropriations would be approved by the national legislatures and disbursement would be made through the Inter-American Bank for Development in such a way as to preclude present U.S. control. Brazil found little support for its alternative and has now withdrawn it with the explanation it wished only to give the Alliance greater long-term continuity and truer multilateralization. At the same time, Brazil also informed us that it would not obstruct the CIAP proposal, which they recognize as a step forward although more modest than they would have wished.

Another major Latin American concern evidenced during the meeting has been the problem of deteriorating terms of trade. The failure of world prices for primary products to keep pace with prices for finished goods coupled with increased import requirements for developmental purposes was singled out by Goulart as a main cause for balance of payment difficulties which have resulted in the need for underdeveloped countries to negotiate loans and re-finance debts under unfavorable conditions. The Latin American countries have shown a keen interest in coordinating their positions at the forthcoming United Nations Conference on Trade and Development (UNCTAD). Brazil is seeking support for a proposal to establish a Latin American Coordinating Committee for Trade which would be headquartered in Rio and serve as a focal point for Latin American trade positions at UNCTAD and thereafter as a coordinating point for Latin American trade matters. Some of the more extreme positions on matters to be discussed at UNCTAD have been propounded by Brazil and the U.S. delegation has been instructed to oppose the creation of a permanent Latin American coordinating committee. At the experts meeting, Argentina proposed an interim coordinating committee to prepare for UNCTAD. The United States is prepared to participate as an observer in such a group. Furthermore, Governor Harriman stated in his speech that the United States shares the concern for the trade problems of developing countries and pledged the "constructive role" of the United States at the UNCTAD meeting in Geneva. He also pointed to the efforts made by the United States to have Western Europe do away with tariffs, quotas and excise taxes which tend to limit consumption of tropical products.

H. Gordon[1]

---

[1] Gordon signed above Read's typewritten signature.

---

71.   Memorandum From the Assistant Secretary of State for Inter-American Affairs (Martin) to Secretary of State Rusk

Washington, November 27, 1963.

SUBJECT

Important Problems in Latin America

Attached are brief outlines of the following important problems faced by the Bureau of Inter-American Affairs:

1. Inter-American Committee for the Alliance for Progress.
2. Foreign Ministers Meeting of the OAS.
3. Principal Problems of U.S. Private Investment.
4. Brazil.
5. Recognition of Dominican Republic and Honduras.
6. Cuba

   a) Arms cache in Venezuela
   b) NSAM 220 (shipping).

7. Venezuela—Elections and Violence.
8. Panama—Treaty Problems.

Source: Department of State, Central Files, POL LAT AM. Confidential. Drafted by Cottrell.

Attachment No. 1

THE INTER-AMERICAN COMMITTEE ON THE ALLIANCE FOR PROGRESS (CIAP)

The committee created by the Inter-American Economic and Social Council (IA–ECOSOC) in Sao Paulo, Brazil, is a major step forward for the Alliance for Progress.

1. The committee will consist of a chairman—hopefully ex-President Lleras—and seven representatives of OAS member countries (one of which will permanently be the United States). It will meet at periodic intervals yet to be agreed, with the chairman acting for the committee in the interim. The meetings will be held for the most part in Latin America although the seat of the committee will be Washington.

2. It is designed to implement the Alliance as a cooperative development, and destroy its image as just another U.S. AID program. The committee is empowered to make a continuing review of Latin American country development efforts such as tax reform, land reform, modernization of government, budgeting for growth and to make recommendations to the member countries with respect to improvements. Then, always within the limits of what is available, it is to make proposals on the distribution of the totals of the external resources which each country can use effectively and meaningfully in support of its own development efforts. Thus, foreign assistance will come more and more to depend on Latin American evaluation of Latin American efforts. At the same time assistance will be tied even more directly to development.

3. Present thinking is that the committee will begin in March. Representatives will be chosen by their respective governments and a chairman will be elected by the Council of the OAS in January.

Attachment No. 2

FOREIGN MINISTERS MEETING OF THE OAS

Following the Council of the OAS decision of November 12 to convoke a Meeting of Foreign Ministers (MFM) on strengthening representative democracy, a Committee was appointed to recommend the date, site and agenda. The Committee, which includes the United States, decided to postpone fixing the time and place until more of a consensus on the agenda is reached. A working document, based on an informal

United States draft declaration, is under informal discussion as are other suggestions which the MFM might consider regarding affirmative actions to promote democracy, human rights, and preventive measures against coups.

Little progress has been achieved in reaching a consensus as to what resolution should come out of an MFM meeting. As a practical matter, it does not seem likely an MFM can be called before mid-January. As the time for the MFM extends into the new year, it is quite possible that there will be increasing sentiment not to hold the MFM at all, but to consider the matter at the Eleventh Inter-American Conference, scheduled to meet in Quito, Ecuador April 1.

Attachment No. 3

PRINCIPAL PROBLEMS OF UNITED STATES PRIVATE INVESTMENT

It is impossible to generalize about the climate for U.S. investment in Latin America. The rising tide of nationalism has created antiforeign sentiment which is often directed against foreign investment, particularly when it dominates the economic life of the country as copper does in Chile and oil in Venezuela. The political leadership of the left combines its own antagonism to the private enterprise system and the U.S., as the main representative of it, with a synthetic nationalism to belabor this issue unceasingly. In some countries these elements are joined by certain parts of the local business community who resent foreign competition as disturbing their comfortable high profit, low volume enterprise. There are, however, increasing elements in every country that recognize the value of the capital and the technical skills which foreign enterprise brings.

In practical terms both through the Alliance for Progress commitment and the continuing public statements every country welcomes private enterprise and foreign investment. Several of them have taken new initiatives recently to encourage it, including opening offices in New York to make contact with potential investors.

On the other hand several governments have taken action with respect to a few specific kinds of foreign investment which, despite their disclaimers of any intent to discourage investment, generally have in fact been discouraging to the world investment community. These involve oil contracts or concessions in Argentina or Peru, public utility and mining investments in Brazil and Chile and drug operations in Colombia and Brazil. Public utilities are, of course, a border line issue everywhere as are extractive industries like petroleum and mining which demagogues can allege are taking national wealth away without adequate reinvestment. The drug problems are similar to, and in part stem from, the activities of Senator Kefauver in this country.

In addition to these specific actions there are, of course, a wide variety of irritating difficulties faced by foreign firms in dealing with most Latin American governments which reflect in part a negative attitude toward such investments and in part the inefficiency of the bureaucracy. There is no evidence, however, that this problem has worsened in recent years.

As a result of anti-investment publicity, of the actions in the limited number of situations referred and of a general concern about the political stability of Latin America in the face of Castro communism and of both political and economic instability in Argentina and Brazil, where U.S. investments had been moving in large volume, new funds have not been directed to Latin America by U.S. firms in the past two years in the amounts hoped for. However, new investment in manufacturing alone has been substantial and reinvestment of earnings of firms already operating in Latin America has been large and is increasing.

There is considerable evidence that European and Japanese capital have been less timid about investing in Latin America in recent years than U.S. business.

There follows a thumbnail sketch on each of the major problems referred to above.

Oil

Argentina Cancels Oil Contracts. Argentina's new Government announced the annulment of all oil exploration and production contracts on November 15. The oil companies involved (six of which are American) are discussing compensation and possible new working arrangements with Argentine officials. We warned the Argentine Government repeatedly before it acted that annulment of the contracts would have serious repercussions in the United States and we are currently seeking to promote a settlement of this problem which would protect the United States interests involved.

International Petroleum Company of Peru. Following failure of negotiations with the company, the Peruvian Government has submitted to the Congress a bill to establish an entirely new operating regime for the IPC, a subsidiary of Standard Oil of New Jersey with an investment of about $190 million in Peru. The Bill provides that, if the regime is not acceptable to the company, it would be taken over by the Government. The company maintains that the proposed regime would be confiscatory. Thus the question of the applicability of the Hickenlooper Amendment could arise. The Government insists it wishes the company to continue operating, and there are some hopeful signs that it would not be averse to a modification of the Bill in the Congress, although this may be difficult. IPC officials are at present talking to Congressional leaders.

Utilities

The American and Foreign Power Company (AMFORP) Case. On April 22, 1963, AMFORP reached an agreement with the Brazilian Government on the terms to be incorporated into a subsequent contract, details of which are still under negotiation, although very recently the Minister of Mines announced that negotiations would be postponed until such time as the company inventories are completed which, he said, may take up to as much as twelve months. The April agreement provided for the purchase of all AMFORP interest in all of its utility subsidiaries in Brazil for $135 million, 75 per cent of which would be reinvested by AMFORP in Brazil in nonutility enterprises.

The AMFORP agreement has become the target for political demagoguery and it is obvious that the Brazilian Government is reluctant to move ahead with it. A new problem has arisen in connection with a recent request of the Brazilian Government to AMFORP to install $30 million worth of new generators at AMFORP's Peixoto power plant. The company is unwilling to proceed in view of its present uncertain situation.

Mining

The Hanna Mining Company Case (Brazil). In September 1963, the Hanna company lost its appeal to a Federal Appeals Court for an injunction against cancellation of several of its iron ore mining concessions in Minas Gerais. The company has appealed this decision to the Supreme Court of Brazil. The Minister of Mines recently announced that the Brazilian Government would not authorize cancellation of Hanna concessions pending a final decision by that Court. The outcome of this case is an important precedent for the future development of mineral resources and foreign private investment in Brazil.

The Copper Problem in Chile. American copper mines in Chile are currently being taxed at high and discriminatory rates, but there is no immediate prospect of nationalization. The taxes coupled with general unease regarding the Chilean political situation have made the American companies extremely reluctant to increase investment. Anaconda owns two large mines, and Kennecott owns another; the total investment is around $500 million. A law passed in 1955 gave these companies assurances of lower taxes as they increased investment and production. Part of that law was reversed when extraordinary taxes were imposed in late 1961. Both companies (but particularly Anaconda) have negotiated with the Chilean Government for a reduction of taxes and a bill for that purpose is soon to go to the Chilean Congress. However, we doubt that the bill can be passed since the Presidential election is only 10 months away.

Speeches by Senator Morse critical of Chile have irritated Chilean public opinion and alarmed Government officials. We believe the current tax problem is just one aspect of the unfavorable situation confronting these wholly-owned United States companies as nationalism rises in Chile. We are submitting the entire "copper company problem" to the Randall Committee, probably in early December, asking the Committee for suggestions as to how we can help the companies and what the companies might do to improve their political position.

Drugs

   Drugs in Colombia. The Colombian Government has issued permissive decrees providing for the marketing of drugs under their generic names at low prices. Most of the United States and Colombian drug industry have strongly opposed this program. The Government of Colombia's reaction has been to introduce legislation requiring compulsory licensing of drug patents and reducing the duration of drug patent protection. Neither the draft bill nor the previous decree appear to infringe on rights of the United States companies. The draft law is similar to legislation introduced by Senator Kefauver in the United States Congress. Senator Hart's sub-committee is considering whether to continue investigations which may involve Colombian operations of United States companies. With the help of the Randall Committee, we hope to work out with the United States drug industry some positive response to the growing Latin American demand for cheaper drugs and better public health programs.

   Discrimination Against Foreign Drug and Pharmaceutical Companies in Brazil. There is a definite discriminatory trend against foreign drug and pharmaceutical companies in Brazil. Recently, an executive government body called GEIFAR was created to oversee the prices of drugs and pharmaceuticals, promote national production of essential drug products and supervise a research fund for nationally-owned laboratories. The foreign companies believe that GEIFAR will be used against them. The Minister of Health, Wilson Fadul, recently charged certain foreign laboratories with over-invoicing imports in order to remit profits abroad clandestinely, a charge which the foreign companies have vigorously denied. Recent legislative measures have been introduced into the Brazilian Congress which would increase discrimination against foreign drug firms. One such measure would create FARMACOBRAS, which would be a monopoly on all drug and pharmaceutical imports. Another measure would freeze pharmaceutical prices for one year.

   [Here follow attachments 4–8.]

72.   Airgram From the Department of State to All Posts in the American Republics

CA–6009   Washington, December 10, 1963.

SUBJECT

IA–ECOSOC Meetings in São Paulo

The Second Annual Meetings of the Inter-American Economic and Social Council were held in São Paulo, Brazil between October 29 and November 16, 1963. The meeting at the Expert Level was from October 29 through November 9; the meeting at the Ministerial Level was from November 11 through November 16.

At the Expert Level meeting 34 resolutions were approved in final form in addition to 14 draft resolutions for submission to the Ministerial Meeting, as well as a draft agenda for the Ministerial meeting. The IA–ECOSOC meeting at the Ministerial Level adopted 28 resolutions including those transmitted by the Experts.

A summary of the substantive analysis and conclusions of the IA–ECOSOC at the Expert Level is contained in a 225 page report on the Alliance for Progress. The Ministers issued a very brief report entitled "The Alliance for Progress and its Outlook".

The final reports of the IA–ECOSOC meetings at the Expert and Ministerial Levels, as well as the two substantive reports—The Alliance for Progress: its Second Year (225 p.), and The Alliance for Progress and its Outlook (10 p., included in final report of the Ministerial meeting), will be sent to all Missions ASAP.[1] Secretariat expects them to be reproduced in about two weeks.

The São Paulo meetings can be considered to have been most successful, not just because of the specific actions taken, but more importantly, because after two years of existence the Alliance for Progress has enlisted the support and the open commitment of responsible Latin American governments.

The U.S. press (though, significantly, not the Brazilian press) foresaw dire consequences from the implied downgrading of the Alliance by Goulart, in his speech, and from the inadequate performance of the Brazilian delegation. The major point was missed: the rest of Latin American delegations stood solidly behind the Alliance, thus forcing Brazil to go along or face isolation.

Source: Department of State, ARA/IPA Files: Lot 69 D 211, IA–ECOSOC, General, 1962–1963. Limited Official Use. Drafted by Elac.

[1] Texts of these documents are ibid., ARA/USOAS Files: Lot 76 D 381, Second Annual Meeting of the Economic and Social Council, São Paulo, 1963.

On the specifics:

1. We went to São Paulo expecting a strong Latin American initiative for the creation of a Committee to provide a more multilateral character to the Alliance for Progress. The expectations were fully verified. The Inter-American Committee on the Alliance for Progress (CIAP) is to be constituted at a special meeting of IA–ECOSOC which is scheduled to convene in Washington January 15, 1964, to designate the chairman and the seven members of CIAP. Separate Airgram on CIAP has been sent to all posts.[2]

2. The ministers approved in principle the establishment of an OAS fund to support special Alliance programs undertaken by the Pan American Union. Thus by January 1, 1965, the U.S. unilateral grant to the OAS will be multilateralized through voluntary contributions from the member governments.

3. Much emphasis was given to the participation of private groups in the preparation of development plans and their implementation. A special committee of IA–ECOSOC was created to deal with labor matters. Also, a resolution was adopted calling for the establishment of National Trade Union Advisory Committees for the Alliance for Progress.

4. The Latin Americans showed their usual concern with trade problems, and expressed great interest in the UNCTAD. We demonstrated our sympathy for their problems, and sponsored a resolution creating a special committee of IA–ECOSOC which will recommend new or improved methods or institutions to promote exports, especially of manufactured and semi-manufactured products. Also in reference to trade, a temporary special committee of IA–ECOSOC will hold a meeting in Buenos Aires, February 24–March 14, 1964, to coordinate, so far as feasible, the positions of the Latin American countries at the UNCTAD; the U.S. will be an observer. Brazil had apparently wanted instead a gathering of Latin Americans outside of IA–ECOSOC.

The consensus of the U.S. delegation is that the cause of the Alliance has been much further advanced because of the meetings in São Paulo.

IA–ECOSOC decided to accept the offer of Peru, so that the Third Annual Meetings of IA–ECOSOC will be held in Lima in late 1964.

Rusk

---

[2] Not further identified.

LATIN AMERICAN SECURITY

73. Editorial Note

At a meeting of the President and the Joint Chiefs of Staff on February 23, 1961, there was some discussion of Latin America during a general discussion of guerrilla and counter-guerrilla warfare. According to a memorandum of the meeting by Defense Liaison Officer Brigadier General C.V. Clifton, USA, dated February 27, JCS Chairman General Lemnitzer reported briefly on a meeting with Latin American military representatives, and the President asked Lemnitzer to try to find out "how these military Latin Americans feel about Castro; from a military viewpoint, what would they do from their countries to offset his regime; and does Castro represent a threat to their countries?" The President requested a JCS analysis of what the United States could do around the world to build anti-guerrilla forces, and indicated that he especially wanted comments on each Latin American country. (Kennedy Library, National Security Files, Clifton Series, JCS Conferences with the President) The text of Clifton's memorandum of the meeting is printed in volume VIII, Document 18.

---

74. Editorial Note

At the 478th meeting of the National Security Council on April 22, 1961, the Council discussed U.S. policy toward Cuba and, in NSC Action No. 2406, approved by the President on April 24, took several actions relating to Cuba. In NSC Action No. 2406–f, the Council

"Noted that an interdepartmental study group would be considering an increase in U.S. assistance to Latin American countries in matters relating to internal security and counter-guerrilla activities, and agreed that a representative of the Department of Justice should be added to this group."

In NSC Action No. 2406–h, the Council

"Noted the President's directive that the possibility be studied of creating a Caribbean Security Agency, to which we and the other Caribbean countries would contribute forces, and to whom any nation attacked could appeal for help." (Department of State, S/S–NSC (Miscellaneous) Files: Lot 66 D 95)

In National Security Action Memorandum No. 44, from the President's Special Assistant for National Security Affairs McGeorge Bundy to Secretary of State Rusk and Secretary of Defense McNamara, April 25, Bundy called attention to NSC Action No. 2406–h and requested that they undertake the study as soon as possible and present their preliminary views at the next NSC meeting. (Department of State, NSAM Files: Lot 72 D 316, NSAM 44)

At the 483d meeting of the National Security Council on May 5 the Council discussed U.S. policy toward Cuba and, in NSC Action No. 2422, approved by the President on May 16, took several actions relating to Cuba. (Department of State, S/S–NSC (Miscellaneous) Files: Lot 66 D 95) For text of NSC Action No. 2422–k, see Document 113. The complete texts of NSC Actions No. 2406 and 2422 and related material are printed in volume X.

75. Circular Telegram From the Department of State to Certain Diplomatic Posts in the American Republics

Washington, May 10, 1961, 4:14 p.m.

1761. One of decisions taken at high level review of problems posed by Castro regime (Depcirtel 1755)[1] was to explore possibility of establishing Caribbean Security Arrangement within OAS framework to improve capabilities of Caribbean countries to protect themselves against both external and internal threats of Castro-Communism. Given below is brief description of essential elements of arrangement. Before

---

Source: Department of State, Central Files, 737.00/5–1061. Confidential; Limit Distribution. Drafted by William G. Bowdler of the Office of Inter-American Regional Political Affairs and Jamison; cleared in draft by Coerr, Task Force on Latin America Chairman Adolph A. Berle, and Assistant Special Counsel to the President Richard N. Goodwin; and approved by Achilles. Sent to Guatemala, Tegucigalpa, San Salvador, Managua, San José, Panama, Bogotá, Caracas, and Port au Prince and repeated to Mexico City, Ciudad Trujillo, London, Paris, The Hague, Ottawa, and USUN for Stevenson.

[1] Circular telegram 1755, May 8, sent to all Embassies in Latin America, stated that a decision had been made "to seek as promptly as possible inter-American program to condemn, isolate, and weaken Castro regime and assist other governments to counter its subversive activity." (Ibid., 737.00/5–861) The text is printed in volume X.

preparing plan for presentation to foreign officials we desire soonest views of Embassy in consultation with Defense members country team on its feasibility as well as probable receptiveness local government.

1. *Rationale*. Primary US objective in Latin America and only long-term solution to basic problems of area is to advance as rapidly as possible in social and economic development, thereby giving mass of people greater stake in functioning of their own government. This process will take time. Castro-Communism in meantime can be expected attempt infiltrate and subvert established governments and to disrupt positive development program. It is essential build up defenses against this danger so Latin American countries can get on with development plans.

Area most immediately vulnerable to Castro-Communism is Caribbean. States bordering Caribbean basin have special interest adopt new techniques to cope with this threat.

2. *Membership*. Arrangement would include governments which have demonstrated awareness of danger posed by Castro-Communism and which USG has reason to believe would be interested in joining with US in such arrangement: Guatemala, El Salvador, Honduras, Nicaragua, Costa Rica, Panama, Haiti, Colombia and Venezuela. Given its attitude on Cuban situation, Mexico undoubtedly would not be interested in plan. Dominican Republic under present conditions would not be invited to participate until acceptable post-Trujillo government is formed. Parties to arrangement would make known, however, that one of its purposes was to protect entire island of Hispaniola. Arrangement also might be elaborated provided concurrence metropol governments obtained, to place protective arm around West Indies.

3. *Commitments*. Each participant in arrangement would:

a) Pledge to assist at their request other participants threatened by indirect aggression and subversion directed or supported by Castro-Communism.

b) Each state would earmark and train military units for a Caribbean Security Force. In event of emergency stemming from such a situation this force could be used in whole or in part at request of threatened state and with approval of state contributing elements.

4. *Immediate Steps*. While details of arrangement are worked out among participating countries, USG would be prepared, at request of any threatened participating state, to establish a system of surveillance in Caribbean to seek out and prevent, in territorial waters of requesting state, landing on part of Castro-Communist elements of armed forces or supplies, and otherwise assisting governments to identify and frustrate armed assistance to subversive elements. Such a system could subsequently form part of operations plan for the Caribbean Security Force with participation of units from other states parties to arrangement.

5. *Intermediate Steps*. Arrangement would have bilateral and eventually multilateral aspects. Intermediate phase would involve bilateral

agreements between USG and other participating states, incorporating commitments specified in paragraph 3 above. Depending upon Congressional authorization where additional funds are involved, USG prepared to negotiate agreement with each participant to help build up internal security and military capabilities for internal and external defense, or, in cases of governments with which US already has MAP agreements to redefine "missions important to the defense of the Western Hemisphere" to indicate maintenance of constitutional order in existing cases. Assistance would be pursuant to requirements determined by survey team now in area.

6. *Long-range Relationship to OAS*. Eventually bilateral commitments could be multilateralized through agreement, negotiated among participating states, establishing arrangement under OAS as one of "special treaties" on collective security referred to in Article 25 of OAS Charter. It would be given further OAS context by having states participating in arrangement reach agreement in advance on salient points and submit these to OAS when it meets to consider Cuban problem. OAS could take note that Castro regime presents special threat to Caribbean area countries and authorize them to work out special measures among themselves to insure their own security. Participating states could utilize Inter-American Defense Board to develop security plan built around Caribbean Security Force.

Bowles

---

76. Draft Paper Prepared in the Department of Defense

Washington, May 19, 1961.

U.S. POLICY FOR THE SECURITY OF LATIN AMERICA IN THE SIXTIES

Part I—Introduction

Latin America is militarily important to the security of the United States. It is an area on which we are dependent for bases and strategic

Source: Department of State, Central Files, 720.5/6–2861. Secret. The source text incorporates revisions after May 19 and is filed with a covering memorandum of June 28 from Deputy Assistant Secretary of Defense for International Security Affairs Haydn Williams to Berle. Williams recommended sending the draft to the National Security Council for consideration, but other attached memoranda indicate that it was not sent.

resources in peace and war. The Cuban experience makes it plain that the fall of additional Latin American nations to the Sino-Soviet Bloc would jeopardize the entire Inter-American system; and that the establishment of a military foothold in Latin America by Bloc powers would pose a direct threat to the security of the U.S. itself.

The purpose of this paper is to review current U.S. military policies and programs concerned with the security of Latin America and project them in the light of the threat, the resources available to meet it, and the adjustments which may be necessary during the 1960's. The focus will be on the strategic concepts, collective security arrangements, military assistance and other military programs, and arms control policies applicable to the security of the Western Hemisphere during the decade.

Parts II–IV of the paper will discuss three principal security problems: (1) the problem of extra-continental aggression; (2) the problem of aggression by one State against another; and (3) the problem of indirect aggression and subversion. Examined under each will be the nature of the threat; existing strategies and policies; and existing capabilities to cope with the threat. Part V of the paper proposes strategy and policy for the future. The last two sections of the paper set forth conclusions and recommendations in the military field for furthering the goals of our "Alianza para Progreso" and meeting successfully the challenge we face in the decade of the 1960's.

The long-range goals of hemispheric security are dependent not only on military capabilities but also on a carefully phased approach to such complementary needs as political stability, social and economic development, and the encouragement of the people of Latin America toward what the President has called "an historic decade of democratic progress" and a "hemisphere where all men can hope for the same high standard of living". Where directly relevant to the military requirements and resources, other factors—economic, political, and psychological—will be discussed. Basically, however, this paper is limited to an analysis of the military aspects of hemispheric security.

[Here follow Parts II through V.]

Part VI—Conclusions

1. Latin American nations collectively are essential to the security of the U.S., and certain Latin American countries, individually, are important to its security. The fall of individual Latin American countries to the Soviet Bloc will jeopardize the security of the United States.

2. The Western Hemisphere has a sound strategy and sufficient capacity at this time to guard against the least likely threat to its security, an armed external attack, and an ineffective strategy and insufficient capability to guard against the most likely threat—the threat to internal security.

3. Existing military policies and programs for the security of Latin America will have to be modified to meet the shifting nature of the security problem, giving priority to the internal security threat and new emphasis to military programs contributing to economic development and the strengthening of representative government, while at the same time, maintaining an effective strategy to secure the Western Hemisphere against external attack.

4. Modifications in existing programs will have to be brought about gradually, taking into account the sensibilities of the Latin Americans on these matters. The goal should be to give Latin American states a sense of more vital and more dignified partnership with the U.S. in the overall defense of the hemisphere from attacks from without and within.

Part VII—Recommendations

1. Encourage acceptance of the concept that the U.S. has primary responsibility for the defense of Latin America against external attack, that the role of the Latin American nations in this mission is to be de-emphasized, and that the internal security mission of Latin American nations is to be accorded increased emphasis.

2. As further means of coping with indirect communist penetration of the hemisphere, the U.S. should:

a. Seek to create increased awareness on the part of Latin American countries of the danger to hemispheric security posed by Castroism and communism in general and of the need to take prompt multilateral action, when necessary, to eliminate this danger.

b. Negotiate, or renegotiate, as may be required, bilateral agreements designed to provide assistance to countries requesting help in defending themselves against indirect aggression and subversion directed and sustained by communists from within or without the hemisphere.

3. Explore the establishment of an Inter-American Security Force, and, as an initial step, promote the establishment of a Caribbean Security Arrangement, by means of which Caribbean countries would cooperate with the U.S. and one another in maintaining the security of any Caribbean country, at its request, against bona-fide communist-directed aggression or subversion.

4. Make efforts to strengthen the IADB through such means as: (1) closer relationship with the COAS, (2) increased joint defense planning, (3) greater responsibility for planning and advising on internal security matters (including a system of surveillance in the Caribbean to identify and frustrate armed assistance from Cuba to subversive movements in other countries).

5. Promote the establishment of the proposed Inter-American Defense College at an *early date*.

6. In our military assistance programs, give first priority to measures designed to meet the threat to internal security and seek to eliminate missions which may no longer be valid. In this connection seek the repeal of the Morse Amendment.

7. Increase and strengthen the training of Latin American military personnel in anti-subversion, anti-guerrilla, and riot control techniques.

8. In accordance with the President's Special Message on Foreign Aid, place new emphasis on military assistance programs which contribute to the civic improvement and economic development of the countries of the area, and at the same time to the development of improved social responsibility and better public acceptance of the local military.

9. In order to give additional emphasis to the internal security and civic action missions of Latin American forces, seek a modest increase in the level of U.S. military assistance programs.

10. Encourage and support Latin American initiatives toward regional arms limitation agreements.

---

77.   Memorandum From the Deputy Coordinator for Foreign Assistance (Bell) to Secretary of State Rusk

Washington, June 26, 1961.

SUBJECT

> Proposed Presidential Determination under Section 105 (b)(4) and 451(a) of the MSA of 1954, as amended, permitting the use of funds to furnish military assistance to Panama, Costa Rica, Nicaragua, El Salvador, Honduras, Guatemala and Haiti

There are attached (Tab A)[1] a proposed memorandum to the President and a Memorandum of Determination by the President which would permit the use of funds to provide grant military aid to Panama, Costa Rica, Nicaragua, El Salvador, Honduras, Guatemala, and Haiti.

The military assistance proposed is for the purpose of internal security, which, as you know, requires a decision by the President under the

---

Source: Department of State, Central Files, 720.5–MSP/6–2661. Secret. Sent through Ball who initialed, indicating his approval. Drafted by Joseph B. Kyle of Bell's office with revisions by Bell.

[1] None of the attachments is printed.

terms of the Mutual Security Act. You are aware of the fact that the proposed Fiscal Year 1962 aid bill seeks the deletion of the requirement that the President make these findings. This has been strongly opposed by those in both the Senate Foreign Relations Committee and the House Foreign Affairs Committee who have spoken on the subject. This opposition has been based on the conviction of the speakers that aid to nondemocratic Latin American regimes to assist the maintenance of internal security will be equivalent to the maintenance in power of harsh and repressive regimes. Senator Morse, in particular, has spoken vigorously to the effect that decisions on such matters should be made only by the President. There is no question but that the reason for this provision of law is to make plain the view of the Congress in opposition to aid to dictatorships and the belief that the President will be less likely to make exceptions if a determination by him was required.

The proposed determination which is attached (Tab A) would provide internal security military assistance to seven countries, two of which, Nicaragua and Haiti, can hardly be said to have democratic regimes. ARA's argument as to the necessity for the determination is set forth in the Memorandum to the President and in the case of Haiti, is elaborated in a memorandum from Mr. Coerr at Tab B. ICA has recorded a dissent which appears at Tab C. You are also aware of the particular opposition voiced by Senator Humphrey to giving any aid to Haiti, even economic, under the present circumstances. I am sure that his reaction to military assistance to Haiti would be even stronger as would be that of Senator Morse and such members of the House of Representatives as Mr. Hays. Thus, my feeling is that Congressional reaction to this determination would be seriously adverse to the legislation which we are trying to obtain. Whether this attitude on the part of the Congressional leaders could be overcome by conversations seems to me doubtful and, in any case, there is very little time since this determination to be effective would have to be approved by the President in the next few days.

Since the issue is one of the political necessity as against the assumed adverse effects on aid legislation, I believe you should personally review this proposal and indicate whether you wish it advanced. If so, the Memorandum to the President should be signed.[2]

---

[2] A June 29 memorandum from Under Secretary Bowles' Special Assistant Samuel W. Lewis to Executive Secretariat Director Battle states that Bowles concurred with the recommendation, provided that no action should be taken on aid to Haiti until it could be incorporated in the overall aid package for Haiti. Coerr had assured Bowles that any decision on Haiti could be kept confidential for the time being. (Department of State, Central Files, 720.5–MSP/6–2961) A June 29 note from Rusk's Special Assistant Emory C. Swank to Rusk, attached to the source text, noted that it might not be possible to keep any decision on Haiti confidential since the Department was required by law to furnish the Speaker of the House and the Chairman of the Senate Foreign Relations Committee copies of all Presidential determinations. Rusk did not sign the memorandum to the President.

78.   Telegram From the Embassy in Honduras to the Department of State

Tegucigalpa, July 23, 1961, 5 p.m.

54. In informal meeting in advance of Joint Session[1] this morning at which US observers presented GOUS views, CA and Panamanian Foreign Ministers expressed to US group their undivided and joint support for Colombian plan[2] in face of Communist-Castro threat to hemisphere. Agreement will be kept confidential in order avoid counter-productive effects of untimely publicity but Foreign Ministers emphasized solidarity their six governments in support this initiative at appropriate moment. (Later, in plenary session, Foreign Ministers approved strongly-worded public resolution deploring Communist penetration and recommending reaffirmation of democratic principles and the adoption of measures to stop the spread of Communism but omitting all reference to Cuba or Castro.)

Foreign Ministers voiced their conviction and deep concern that Central American area was weakest flank, must expect receive brunt of Castro-Communist attack and subversion. Consequently this area should be extended most immediate and meaningful support, economic and otherwise. Deep appreciation was expressed for recognition shown by GOUS to importance of region by attendance high ranking mission at meeting of Ministers.

At least four of six in stressing danger of direct attack by Castro-Communist forces, perhaps on July 26, spoke of arms caches that had been found in their countries and of plans of subversive elements to overthrow governments. Goodwin replied to effect US recognizes treaty obligations and prepared extend aid if required and requested.

Embassy and visiting group assumes US forces in area have been properly alerted for July 26 potentialities.

Burrows

Source: Department of State, Central Files, 713.20/7–2361. Confidential; Priority. Repeated to Bogotá, Guatemala City, Managua, Panama City for POLAD CINCARIB, San José, San Salvador, and USUN.
    [1] Reference is to an informal meeting of Foreign and Economic Ministers of Central America and Panama, held July 21–23 in Tegucigalpa.
    [2] See Documents 111 and 114.

79.   **Memorandum From the Deputy Director for Operations of the International Cooperation Administration (FitzGerald) to the General Counsel of That Agency (Rubin)**

Washington, August 21, 1961.

SUBJECT

Provision of Military Assistance to Central American Countries; your memorandum of August 16, 1961[1]

I am very skeptical of the proposal to furnish military assistance to Panama, Costa Rica, Nicaragua, El Salvador, Honduras, and Guatemala. There is no demonstration that the provision of this equipment will significantly increase the capabilities of the armed forces to deal with Castro-Communist type of infiltration or subversion. The addition of the equipment contemplated inevitably will raise the operation and maintenance cost of the armed forces and further divert local government resources from constructive economic development. The draft determination contains no estimate of this additional cost nor whether the countries concerned are willing and able to meet it. Finally, even if they are so willing, there is no evaluation of the relative priority of the use of the country's resources for its military establishment as compared to its use for economic or social development.

The same considerations apply also to the proposal to furnish Haiti with almost a million dollars worth of military equipment. In addition, there is the question of our posture in supporting such a repressive regime as that of President Duvalier. Finally, the draft determination states that "the present regime has decimated and humiliated the armed forces by frequent purges . . ." In this situation it hardly seems likely that the armed forces could make any effective use of the proposed equipment but rather it would be used by Duvalier for the purpose of supporting his own regime.[2]

Source: Department of State, Central Files, 720.5–MSP/8–2961. Secret. Filed with an August 29 memorandum from Rubin to Kyle.

[1] Not found.

[2] Rubin's August 29 memorandum, cited in the source note, states that the ICA position was as stated in FitzGerald's memorandum, but that ICA would concur if the Department of State judged that political considerations required the proposed Determinations, which Kyle had sent to Rubin with an August 15 memorandum. (Department of State, Central Files, 720.5–MSP/8–2961)

80.   National Security Action Memorandum No. 88

Washington, September 5, 1961.

TO

The Secretary of Defense

SUBJECT

Training for Latin American Armed Forces

I would appreciate hearing what steps we are taking to train the Armed Forces of Latin America in controlling mobs, guerrillas, etc. In addition, as the events of the past week have shown in Brazil, the military occupy an extremely important strategic position in Latin America. I would like to know how many officers we are bringing up from Latin America to train here and whether we could increase the number. Also, what other steps we are taking to increase the intimacy between our Armed Forces and the military of Latin America. It has been suggested that we set up a camp in the United States similar to the FBI Academy which brings in police from all over the United States. We would bring up a good many officers from the different countries of Latin America for a period from 1 to 2 months; we would have FBI people there who could talk to them about the techniques they have developed to control communism, subversion and we could have our military coming in to teach them how to control mobs and fight guerrillas. In addition to increase their effectiveness it would also strengthen their ties with the United States. Will you let me know your view of this?

John F. Kennedy[1]

Source: Department of State, NSAM Files: Lot 72 D 316, NSAM 88. Secret.
[1] Printed from a copy that indicates Kennedy signed the original.

81.   **Memorandum From the President's Assistant Special Counsel (Goodwin) to President Kennedy**

Washington, September 6, 1961.

The Cuban Task Force met at the White House on Thursday, August 31. Present were Under Secretary Ball, Assistant Secretary Woodward, two members of the ARA Bureau, Dick Bissell, Tracy Barnes and myself.

The following decisions were made:

1. We would proceed immediately to discuss with other Caribbean governments the possibility of organizing a Caribbean Security Force. This could be organized on the basis of informal understandings within the framework of existing treaty arrangements, as a series of new bilateral treaties, or a formal, multilateral treaty. It was thought that the basis of organization would depend on the judgment of other Caribbean countries as to how they could accomplish the objective of establishing the force without running serious internal political risks. The United States, for its part, would prefer the formal multilateral arrangement. Such a Caribbean Security Force would have at least four major aspects:

(1) Advance commitment to come to the aid of other signatories threatened by Castro revolutions and, perhaps the designation of specific units for participation in necessary multilateral actions.
(2) The establishment of a pool of intelligence information concerning subversive activities with provision for exchange of such information.
(3) The establishment of a Caribbean air and sea patrol to watch for suspected infiltration of Castro arms or agents.
(4) A training program in combatting subversive tactics, police organization and procedure, etc.

It was conceded that the substantive aspects of this arrangement could, if necessary, be achieved informally. However, the decision to seek a more formal arrangement was primarily arrived at on the basis of internal political considerations in the United States.

[Here follows discussion of other aspects of U.S. policy toward Cuba; for text, see volume X.]

Richard N. Goodwin[1]

Source: Kennedy Library, Schlesinger Papers, Box 31, Cuba 1961. Secret. Another copy of this memorandum, ibid., National Security Files, Countries Series, Cuba, General, is dated September 1.
[1] Printed from a copy that bears this typed signature.

82.   Memorandum From Attorney General Kennedy to President Kennedy

Washington, September 11, 1961.

In furtherance of our conversation on the plane last week, I believe it might be advisable for a team made up of representatives from the FBI plus the military to make a survey of the security situation in the countries of Central and South America.

Shortly after Cuba we made arrangements for an FBI man to accompany a group which was making a tour of Central America. When he returned he wrote a confidential report for me which indicated that security arrangements in a number of the countries were extremely deficient.

I think that if a group of this type went down into these countries they could determine whether all necessary steps are being taken by the internal police to deal with communist infiltration and whether the military or police are prepared to deal with mob riot, or guerrilla bands that may become active. Also, as we learned in the Dominican Republic crisis, that the communications system with the State Department and the CIA was inadequate. Steps should be taken to determine what is needed in this field and this problem remedied. I am sure that reports are coming in from various embassies that touch on this situation but I think it should receive top priority.[1]

Source: Kennedy Library, National Security Files, Meetings and Memoranda Series, NSAM 88. No classification marking. The source text bears the notation in Kennedy's handwriting, "OK JFK".

[1] A September 12 note from White House staff member Mildred Zayac to Goodwin, filed with the source text, states that Bundy had asked her to send it to Goodwin with the message that "the President would like to get it going right away."

83.   Letter From the Deputy Assistant Secretary of Defense for
       International Security Affairs (Williams) to the Assistant
       Secretary of State for Inter-American Affairs (Woodward)

Washington, September 12, 1961.

DEAR MR. WOODWARD: At a meeting on 5 May 1961, the National
Security Council agreed, inter alia, that the United States should at once
initiate negotiations to enlarge the willingness of other American states
to join in bilateral, multilateral, and OAS arrangements against Castro.
Listed among the possible measures were:

a.   Creation of a Caribbean Security Force; and
b.   Initiation of a naval patrol to prevent Cuban invasion of other
states in the Caribbean.

The Department of Defense recognizes that there are desirable political benefits in establishing a Caribbean Naval Patrol (CNP) and a Caribbean Security Force (CSF). However, so that the Department of State is
fully informed of all aspects of the matter, I wish to convey the following
comments made by the Joint Chiefs of Staff in which I concur.

Briefly, the Joint Chiefs of Staff hold the opinion that, militarily, the
advantages in establishing a CSF and a CNP would not be significant.
Nevertheless, the Joint Chiefs of Staff, in support of the NSC decision,
have furnished guidelines for use in creating a CNP and a CSF. Those
guidelines are attached herewith.[1]

Military opinions of the Joint Chiefs of Staff follow:

Comment on a proposed Caribbean Naval Patrol (CNP): The U.S. Atlantic Fleet is fully capable of conducting necessary naval patrols in the
Caribbean. In the past, the U.S. Navy has operated with combined Latin
American Naval forces in the Caribbean for other purposes. From a U.S.
military point of view, there are no apparent military problems incapable
of solution which would be generated by the establishment of a multi-
national naval patrol to prevent a Cuban-sponsored invasion of other
Caribbean states. The stopping of clandestine shipment of arms and men
is complicated by the restrictions of international law against boarding
and searching ships on the high seas. The CNP could stop, board and
search suspicious ships in the territorial and/or customs waters of those
Caribbean countries which are willing to grant such authority to CNP

Source: Washington National Records Center, RG 330, Records of the Office of the
Secretary of Defense, OSD/ISA Files: FRC 64 A 2382, 381 Caribbean. Secret.

[1] Two memoranda from the Joint Chiefs of Staff to McNamara, both dated August 18,
are attached to the source text. JCSM–560–61 concerns a possible Caribbean Security Force;
JCSM–561–61 concerns a possible Caribbean Naval Patrol. Each has an attached appendix
setting forth guidelines.

forces. With such authority the CNP could intercept some clandestine shipments of areas and men destined for Caribbean countries.

Comment on a proposed Caribbean Security Force (CSF): Latin American military contributions to such a force, would, of necessity, be small. Hence the U.S. contribution should be sufficiently great to ensure successful military action. However, from a U.S. military point of view there would be no apparent military problems incapable of solution which would be generated by the establishment of a multi-national CSF.

Castro Threat: Cuban military forces lack the capability to launch a meaningful military invasion against any Latin American country with the possible exception of Haiti. In the case of Haiti, the capability is limited to a lightly armed invasion using a few aircraft and/or small boats.

Castro possesses the capability to export the Cuban revolution through support and provision of "volunteers" and/or arms to indigenous revolutionary groups in other countries and is more likely to choose this alternative than military ventures which could be identified as being instigated by the government of Cuba.

General Comment: Before a political decision is reached for the establishment of a CNP and CSF, consideration should be given to the possible legal effects on the treaty with Cuba for use of the U.S. Naval Base at Guantanamo[2] lest Castro gain grounds for legal termination of the treaty. Following a political decision to create a Caribbean Security Arrangement and prior to initiation of operations thereunder, international agreements providing for combined operations, rights of entry of forces, and overflight authority will be required.

If arrangements go forward for a CSF and a CNP then supplemental funding arrangements will have to be provided in appropriate programs.

Sincerely,

Haydn Williams[3]

---

[2] Signed at Havana February 16, 1903, and at Washington February 23, 1903; for text, see 6 Bevans 1113.

[3] Printed from a copy that indicates Williams signed the original.

84.   Memorandum From the Assistant Director of the Bureau of the Budget (Hansen) to the Under Secretary of State (Bowles)

Washington, September 28, 1961.

SUBJECT

Presidential determinations for Caribbean Countries

As you requested, I have made a hurried appraisal of the proposed MAP determinations and have discussed this with Dick Goodwin in the White House. We came out on the matter as follows.

1. From a review of the WAT report[1] we are concerned as to whether the team did the type of thorough review of the problem with regard to each country which appears required for such a determination by the President. Our main concern stems from whether or not the right questions have been asked with regard to the nature of the internal security threat in each country (i.e., there appears to be a standard finding that such a threat exists), and as to whether this particular addition of military hardware represents the optimum use of our resources to meet such actual or potential threat (i.e., if the country team had their "druthers" would they choose this particular means of meeting the threat?). The process of evaluation and the rather hasty manner in which the evaluations appear to have been made do not inspire our confidence. On the other hand, we do not know the team members and might have a quite different reaction had we reason to believe that the exercise was conducted in a hard-headed, objective manner by personnel who were required to make a judgment as to whether this form of assistance was of the essential nature which would require a *Presidential* determination of this type, at this time.

Frankly, the impression left by the report is that this was a rather narrow inquiry to establish deficiencies in military armed strength against stereotyped or presumptive findings of threats to internal security.

2. A second aspect of these proposals is the very real question of what we are buying with the arms, not only in terms of the immediate security problem but also the pattern of supplying assistance to these countries in this unilateral manner. From the viewpoint of the Presidential determination, it would appear preferable that such arms aid, if

---

Source: Department of State, Central Files, 710.5–MSP/9–2861. Secret. No drafting information appears on the source text.

[1] Reference is to a Washington Assessment Team, with State, ICA, and Defense representatives, that visited Central America in April and May. No report has been found. Related documentation is ibid., primarily under 620.37 but also under 611.20, 710.5, and various country numbers.

granted, be given in the context of some Caribbean security force or in attribution to a framework of cooperation by the Caribbean countries to meet the Castro threat. This does not mean that the arms aid would be granted to a collective organization, but that presumably it would be done in response to a collective agreement that the internal security of member nations should be strengthened in the face of their joint determination to resist Castro subversion.

3. It is not clear from the information available to us that the provision of these arms is in satisfaction of commitments already made by the United States, but presumably the general political noises we have been making in that area following the Cuban crisis would lead these countries to believe that we were going to be forthcoming in assisting them to meet internal security problems. It is not clear that our various program actions to create and train more efficient police forces are far enough along to indicate that more than those efforts are currently required, although in sifting through these proposals some of the items appear to be of obvious utility related to these efforts.

4. Finally, we have seen no indication that the request for approximately $7 million assistance for these areas has been reviewed against the global total of MAP assistance provided for all of Latin America, i.e., $57 million. We are not sure that present MAP planning for Latin America is far enough advanced to indicate a clear priority for the use of this $7 million requiring Presidential determination. (In this connection there is no legal need for urgency on this matter, since the passage of the new Act requires that the funds be paid out of the total $57 million allowance, under Sec. 511 of the new Act,[2] and determination now would not count these grants against the earlier authorized ceiling.)

In summary, and based on brief study, we are extremely uneasy as to the adequacy of the process by which these determinations have been proposed to you. But at the same time, we cannot document that the conclusions of these earlier studies are not valid. This puts the issue to whether or not you have confidence that the judgments you are being asked to endorse have been made in a responsible, accountable manner. If you do not feel that this is the case, we would suggest that you place a review of the matter in the hands of Assistant Secretary Woodward, with the requirement that he review this with the assistance of staff in whom you both repose high confidence as to the results. This is not to say that we like to recommend that the answer to one study is another study, but we clearly cannot judge the competence and comprehensiveness of the original review of this problem by the WAT.

---

[2] The Foreign Assistance Act of 1961, approved on September 4; for text, see 75 Stat. 424.

If you determine to your satisfaction that these determinations (except the one for Haiti, which is subject to much more substantive political argument) should go forward to the President, we suggest that the determinations be posed in the context of regional action rather than dealt with as purely bilateral actions addressed to the internal security problems of each individual recipient.

I hope these considerations will prove helpful, although I must confess they represent "second guessing" of a nature that I do not ordinarily indulge. Dick Goodwin or I will be glad to discuss this further with you if you so wish.

Kenneth R. Hansen

---

85.   Memorandum From Acting Secretary of State Bowles to President Kennedy

Washington, September 29, 1961.

SUBJECT

Determinations under sections 511(b) and 614(a) of the Foreign Assistance Act of 1961, as amended, permitting the use of funds in order to furnish military assistance to Panama, Costa Rica, Nicaragua, El Salvador, Honduras, and Guatemala

The purpose of this memorandum is to recommend that you make the requisite determinations under sections 511(b) and 614(a) of the Foreign Assistance Act of 1961, as amended (hereinafter referred to as "the Act"), to permit the use of funds in order to furnish military assistance up to $6,500,000 to Panama, Costa Rica, Nicaragua, El Salvador, Honduras and Guatemala.

The proposed military assistance is needed for purposes of internal security to increase the capability of these countries to defend themselves against Castro-communist subversion. The considerations relevant to this recommendation are as follows:

1.   Washington agencies which have primary interest in the maintenance of effective internal security forces by the Latin American nations

Source: Kennedy Library, National Security Files, Subjects Series, Presidential Determinations. Secret. No drafting information appears on the source text.

are aware of the serious threat to the security of the area generated by growing social unrest and the intent of the Castro movement, in alignment with the Sino-Soviet bloc, either to promote or use this unrest to overthrow governments by internal subversion. In May, 1961, these agencies determined that the most effective way to assess the internal security requirements of the area and to develop specific United States programs aimed at assisting American Republics to develop a capability to counter subversion was to appoint an interagency Internal Security Assessment and Programming Team to hold on-the-spot discussions with each United States Government country team. It was determined that the Internal Security Assessment and Programming Team should visit initially only Panama, the five countries of Central America, and Haiti. All of these countries are considered prime targets for Castro-communist subversion. Near to Cuba geographically, they do not have the capability to prevent the clandestine entry of men or arms into their national territories. Because of unstable political institutions, enormous social differences, and retarded economic growth, many groups in their societies feel isolated from the main currents of national development, and are easy prey to Castro-communist propaganda and organizers. Forces responsible for maintaining law and order have neither the equipment nor the trained personnel to counter well-conceived and well-executed plans to subvert the state, either by mob action, guerrilla warfare, terrorism and sabotage or by armed invasion.

2.   The Internal Security Assessment and Programming Team held discussions with the United States Government country teams in Panama, Costa Rica, Nicaragua, El Salvador, Honduras, and Guatemala from April 27 to May 12, 1961. It was determined that serious threats to internal security exist in these countries; that these threats are likely to take the form of direct and/or indirect Castroist action, either unilaterally or in conjunction with local communists, exiles, or dissident opposition groups. It was further determined that the action might take the forms of actual invasion, strikes, guerrilla action, sabotage, terrorism, or mob action.

3.   The Internal Security Assessment and Programming Team and the country teams are of the opinion that the six countries do not possess the effective capability to resist invasion or protracted internal subversion. They do agree, however, that with the provision of grant assistance, to include equipment and training, a considerably improved degree of capability can be developed to cope with isolated, spontaneous attempts at internal subversion, to determine the existence and nature of border incursions, and to prevent the small-scale clandestine movement of men and arms across frontiers.

4.   The Internal Security Assessment and Programming Team and the country teams reached the conclusion that the major deficiencies

within Panama, Costa Rica, Nicaragua, El Salvador, Honduras, and Guatemala for coping with the internal security threat were in the fields of transportation, communications, and maintenance; in leadership and intelligence techniques; and, to a somewhat lesser degree, in serviceable and appropriate arms, and in certain types of consumable goods. Recommendations, in consequence, follow the general lines of, for mobility, such items as jeeps and trucks, transport aircraft, and Coast Guard-type patrol vessels. Similarly, for communications, there were endorsed essentially a certain amount of fixed, or automobile transported, and of "walkie-talkie" types of radio apparatus. In terms of arms, there were endorsed riot control type equipment or light weapons such as the M–1 series. As respects leadership and intelligence techniques, recommendations concerned training and military and civil police advisory assistance. The recommendations took into account the ability of the countries to absorb the equipment and training.

5. If the recommendations of the Internal Security Assessment and Programming Team and the country teams as to the equipment and other requirements referred to above were accepted for funding, it would require the obligation of approximately $6,500,000. In addition to the requirements to be funded from military assistance availabilities, there are equipment and training requirements, for which $726,000 was obligated in fiscal year 1961, to be administered by the International Cooperation Administration through its Public Safety program in Panama, El Salvador, Honduras, and Guatemala.

6. In addition to enhancing the capabilities of local security forces to counter threats to internal security, the provision of grant military assistance will serve an additional purpose. Part of the assistance will consist of tools and/or construction machinery which will enhance the capability of the security forces to participate more fully in social and economic development, thereby contributing to narrowing the gulf that historically has divided the security forces in these nations from the rest of society.

[Here follow paragraphs 7–12, with discussion of the internal security situation in the six countries in question.]

Under these circumstances, it is considered to be important to the security of the United States to promote stability in Panama, Costa Rica, Nicaragua, El Salvador, Honduras and Guatemala by furnishing these nations with military assistance for their internal security upon a determination under the third sentence of section 511(b) of the Act that internal security requirements may be the basis of this program. It is also considered important to the security of the United States to furnish military equipment and materials to Panama, Costa Rica, and El Salvador (which are not parties to general military assistance agreements with the United States) and to Guatemala, Honduras, and Nicaragua (which are parties to general military assistance agreements with the United States, such agreements being applicable, however, only to assistance furnished for Western Hemisphere defense missions), for the purposes described above without regard to the requirements of section 506(a) of the Act requiring agreement to four specific undertakings. It is planned to seek special agreements with the six countries providing all or some of the undertakings in section 506(a) of the Act; however, since the negotiation of these agreements may be protracted in duration or may not be successful, it is considered necessary to waive the requirement for such undertakings in the event that negotiation of these agreements is protracted in duration or not successful.

Enclosed is a detailed statement of the background and justification of this program, the implementation of which is estimated to require the expenditure of up to $6,500,000 of funds available for military assistance.

It is considered that the furnishing of the assistance described above and the use of funds made available for military assistance programs are in furtherance of the purposes of the Act and are important to the security of the United States.

It is accordingly, recommended that you sign the enclosed memorandum, thereby making the determinations required by the Act for the above-mentioned purposes.[1]

The Department of Defense concurs in this recommendation.

Chester Bowles

---

[1] The President signed Presidential Determination No. 62–3 on October 26. (Ibid.)

---

86.   Memorandum From Acting Secretary of State Bowles to the Deputy Assistant Secretary of State for Politico-Military Affairs (Kitchen)

Washington, September 29, 1961.

SUBJECT

Military Aid to Central American Countries

I have today signed the memorandum to the President recommending that a determination be made authorizing up to $6.5 million in grant

---

Source: Department of State, Central Files, 710.5–MSP/9–2861. Secret. Drafted by Bowles' Special Assistant Andrew E. Rice. Filed with Document 84.

military assistance to five Central American republics and Panama to preserve internal security.

If the President makes this determination, a grave responsibility lies on us to insure that the assistance is responsibly administered. I call to your attention the following considerations which appear pertinent:

1) We must make perfectly clear that this aid is not to be used to deter legitimate popular expressions of aspirations for greater social justice and political freedom. This is particularly important since this assistance is not designed to provide the capability to put down any major uprisings but rather is aimed at the control of "spontaneous outbursts". If weaponry identified as coming from the United States shoots down non-violent demonstrators, we would obviously be in grave danger of strengthening the popular appeal of forces unsympathetic to the United States.

2) In Nicaragua—and perhaps in other countries as well—we should be alert to the possibility of conditioning specific elements of our aid upon the accomplishment of specific reforms in police, judicial or other governmental procedures.

3) We should indicate to all the countries that the problem of internal security in Central America should be a matter of joint rather than unilateral concern. Our goal, I think, should be the development of a coordinated plan for defense against clandestine border crossing and coastal landings so that our aid supports the common determination of these countries to resist Castro subversion, rather than treating each country separately.

4) We should emphasize again the high importance we attach to "civic action" by the security forces of each country. The recommendation to the President points out that part of the assistance will consist of tools or construction machinery which will enhance the capability of these forces to participate in economic and social development. We should not fail in this respect.

I should like to be kept informed of the major steps which are taken to implement the Presidential determination, keeping in mind the above considerations, and to this end should appreciate your staff keeping Andrew Rice of my office advised.

87.   Memorandum From the President's Military Representative (Taylor) to President Kennedy

Washington, October 7, 1961.

The Secretary of Defense has responded (Tab 2)[1] to your memorandum of early September (Tab 1)[2] requesting information on the steps being taken to train the armed forces of Latin America in controlling mobs, guerrillas, etc., as well as your suggestion that a camp be set up in the United States similar to the FBI Academy.

We have also received memoranda from the Secretary of State (Tab 3)[3] and the Director of Central Intelligence (Tab 4)[4] who have submitted information on their programs for attacking this overall problem.

A brief summary follows:

a.   Mr. Gilpatric informs you that the military schools in the United States and in the Canal Zone are giving considerable emphasis to courses in internal security for Latin American officers. For example, 600 officers attended such courses in FY–61. In addition, the U.S. military school system is training just about as many Latin Americans in these and general military courses as the countries concerned are able or willing to make available for this purpose. As you know, many Latin American countries utilize their armed forces for performing the basic internal security mission as well as to officer their police forces. Thus our military schools afford a direct way of reaching this influential element of the governments in Latin America. The officers concerned gain an appreciation and understanding of the U.S. more or less by absorption while attending these courses. The extent of direct political indoctrination in these courses is probably very small, if not non-existent. Mr. Gilpatric is favorably disposed to the idea of setting up an FBI-type academy.

b.   The memorandum from the Central Intelligence Agency indicates that they have a modest program for training selected, high-level security officers from Latin America in the U.S. They have resident advi-

---

Source: National Defense University, Taylor Papers, Box 17, T636–71. Secret.

[1] The tabs were not attached to the source text. Reference is to a September 11 memorandum from Acting Secretary Gilpatric to Kennedy. (Kennedy Library, National Security Files, Meetings and Memoranda Series, NSAM 88)

[2] Document 80.

[3] Reference is to a memorandum of September 30 from Acting Secretary Bowles to Kennedy. (Kennedy Library, National Security Files, Meetings and Memoranda Series, NSAM 88) A second memorandum of that date from Bowles to Kennedy urged that more should be done in U.S. training programs for foreign military personnel to foster an appreciation of democratic values and that U.S. aid programs should place more emphasis on rural reform. (Ibid.)

[4] Reference is to a memorandum of September 12 from Acting Director General Charles P. Cabell to Kennedy. (Ibid.)

sory officers in a few Latin American countries, [5 *lines of source text not declassified*].

c. The State Department memorandum describes the AID/ICA program for police training. This program is rather comprehensive, and involves in-country assistance and advice as well as training programs in the U.S. itself. It will be noted that the budgetary support for this worldwide program has been reduced from $10 million in 1961 to about $9 million in 1962, with a corresponding amount of counterpart funds being used in the host countries. About 20% of this is used for Latin America. AID is currently considering a proposal to establish a U.S. police academy, preferably in a Caribbean location such as the Canal Zone. This would allow them to train greater numbers of Latin American police officials at a reduced cost.

It is not apparent in the memoranda, which are quite straightforward, but there is a certain amount of friction between the various Departments in the implementation of these programs. This is particularly true in areas where civil disturbance is such a major problem that normal police measures are not adequate to cope with it. It is also found in areas where the Army or some para-military agency discharges or controls the basic police function. I would suggest the advisability of sending all of these memoranda to the Secretary of State and ask that he have the relationship of these programs studied and redefine the responsibilities for such programs in countries where it may be a matter of contention.

If this suggestion meets with your approval, I will inform the Secretary of State, Secretary of Defense, and Director of CIA that you have noted their memoranda and are asking the Secretary of State to study this overall problem and clarify responsibilities for such programs in countries where it is in dispute.

Maxwell D. Taylor[5]

---

[5] Printed from a copy that bears this typed signature.

88.   Circular Airgram From the Department of State to Certain Posts

Washington, November 2, 1961.

CA–388. Depcirtels 1761, May 10;[1] 196, August 1, 1961.[2]

The Department, after careful consideration of the Caribbean Security Arrangements Plan in the light of your replies to the reference Depcirtels and developments throughout the Latin American area, has concluded it is more desirable at present to pursue the objective of strengthening the defenses of the Central American and Caribbean countries against the Castro-communist threat of indirect aggression through a less formal approach than previously envisaged.

Benefits to be derived from formalization of the Plan through a series of bilateral agreements do not at present appear to be great enough to offset possible consequences of the fact that several governments would deem it necessary to seek congressional approval. This would give Castro-communist elements greatly increased opportunity to exploit nationalist sentiments, anti-Americanism, and other Castro-communist themes with a resulting possibility of failure of the governments to join in the Plan which would seriously detract from its psychological impact and effectiveness.

As you are aware, the most obvious methods by which the United States Government can contribute to the strengthening of security in the Caribbean and Central American area against indirect aggression—that is, incitement to revolt, and infiltration of men, matériel, funds and propaganda for creating disturbances, terrorism and sabotage—are the following:

1. Helping to equip and train local forces;
2. Offering to provide immediately, upon request, air-sea surveillance;

Source: Department of State, Central Files, 710.5/11–261. Confidential. Drafted by Woodward, Jamison, and Bowdler; cleared by Charles Maechling, Jr., Director for Internal Defense in the Office of the Deputy Assistant Secretary of State for Politico-Military Affairs, Captain Paul B. Ryan, USN, of the Office of the Assistant Secretary of Defense for International Security Affairs, and Goodwin; and approved by Woodward. Sent for action to Mexico City, Guatemala City, San Salvador, Tegucigalpa, Managua, San José, Panama City, Bogotá and Caracas.

[1] Document 75.

[2] Circular telegram 196, August 3, instructed recipient Embassies to give the President and Foreign Minister assurances of U.S. support and to indicate that the United States was prepared to establish a system of air-sea surveillance in case of need upon request. The telegram is missing from Department of State, Central Files, 713.00/8–361. The information here is from a copy of the first page on a microfilm index and from follow-up telegrams to and from Guatemala City, San José, San Salvador, and Tegucigalpa, all ibid., under 713.00 and 713.5.

3. Attempting to promote more useful exchange of information among all the countries, and particularly between neighboring countries, on movements of subversive agents, arms and substantial amounts of propaganda material, known misuse of travel documents, methods of sabotage, espionage, terrorism or agitation and any other pertinent information which government officials consider useful to their colleagues in other governments for the purpose of detecting and preventing subversion.

The Department expects to be able soon to inform the Ambassadors in the Central American capitals and Panama, and in Bogotá, that Presidential determinations have been given for the provision of matériel for the internal security of the Governments to which those Ambassadors are accredited.[3] (It is considered that the Government of Venezuela does not require this type of assistance at this time. Serious question has been raised as to whether matériel and other kinds of assistance against indirect aggression in addition to that already being made available to the Haitian Government should be given in present circumstances, particularly because of the apparent aspiration of President Duvalier to perpetuate himself in office indefinitely.)

In those countries in which the Governments have not already been given assurances that the U.S. Government would provide air-sea surveillance upon request—when there appears to be good reason to believe that this might help to prevent landings of armed forces, agents or supplies by Castro-communist elements—the Department believes that the Ambassador should take occasion to give this assurance at the time when he personally informs the Chief of State to whom he is accredited concerning the fact of the availability of the additional matériel for security against indirect aggression. In those countries where assurances have already been given pursuant to Depcirtel 196, the Ambassador should repeat the assurances, alluding to the previous offer of air-sea surveillance in time of emergency. If any of the Ambassador addressees in such countries which have not previously been given these assurances wish to suggest some alternative procedure, it would be appreciated if they would inform the Department. At the same time, the Department would appreciate the comments of the Ambassadors at Caracas and at Port-au-Prince, in their separate and different circumstances, concerning the appropriate timing of such assurances to the Chiefs of State to whom they are accredited. You should mention to the Chiefs of State, when discussing this subject, that as beneficial effects of the Alliance for Progress appear and as there develops a more widespread conviction that economic and social progress can really be brought about more rapidly by

---

[3] The President so authorized in Presidential Determination No. 62–9 on December 14. (Kennedy Library, National Security Files, Subjects Series, Presidential Determinations)

democratic methods, it can be expected that subversive activities will be stepped up by Castro-communist elements.

At the same time that discussions are initiated on the above subjects in the respective countries, it would be appreciated if the Ambassadors would consult with the Chiefs of State to whom they are accredited concerning the problem of improving exchange of information. The object is, of course, to promote the rapid flow of practical information between the particular officials most directly able to use it for the purpose of revealing plans or preparations for indirect aggression and therefore of preventing it should it occur. We believe that the exchange of information can better be handled if the GUS and the Government to which you are accredited were to designate an official (or officials) in their respective countries who would be primarily responsible for sending and receiving such information. Similar arrangements could be made by each government with the other governments of the area. The transmission of information between the designated officials could then be carried out through diplomatic channels. We believe that this type of system is preferable to establishing a new centralized organization for this purpose which would probably only slow down the transmission, although we would not want to give the impression of impeding the establishment of a Central Intelligence Service as envisaged by the recent meeting of Chiefs of Staff of the Central American countries and Panama if these states want to set up such a body.

Department recognizes possibility that security of individual countries can be enhanced by collective measures whereby countries work out joint defense plans and establish procedures for dealing with subversive activities, and Depcirtel 707[4] authorized Ambassadors emphasize this line. While hoping that CADC may perform actively in this role, Department aware some divisive tendencies within CADC, such as : Col. Lopez' (Honduras) statement he doubted advisability of central intelligence exchange, particularly with Nicaragua; Minister of Government Robles' (Panama) statement in the National Assembly that Panama has no obligation toward CADC; President Echandi's (Costa Rica) as yet uncertain attitude toward the participation of the Costa Rican Guardia Civil officers in the meetings so far. Ambassadors accredited countries which participated recent meeting Guatemala of Chiefs of Staff[5] may at their discretion again refer to Depcirtel 707 provided they believe such repetition would be helpful in achieving reftel objective and would not

---

[4] Dated October 14; sent to six Embassies in Central America and Panama. (Department of State, Central Files, 713.5/10–1461)

[5] The meeting of Central American Armed Forces Chiefs of Staff, held September 19–23, called for coordinated defense efforts, including the creation of a Central American Defense Council. (Despatch 147 from Guatemala, September 26; ibid., 713.5/9–2661)

be a meaningless or harmful gesture. Advise if you believe renewed approach 707 would be helpful.

Your comments and suggestions would be appreciated.

For Embassy Mexico City: Given the Mexican attitude toward the defensive measures contemplated in this instruction, the decision on how to approach the GOM and how much of the foregoing to use in the approach is left to the Embassy's discretion.

For Embassy London: Further instructions re UK Caribbean territories will follow.

Bowles

89.   Memorandum From the Joint Chiefs of Staff to President Kennedy

JCSM 832–61   Washington, November 30, 1961.

SUBJECT

Military Actions for Latin America (U)

1. On 12 October 1961, in your conversation with General Decker at Fort Bragg, you asked what additional contribution the US Armed Forces could make in conjunction with indigenous military forces toward the attainment of US national objectives in Latin America. As a result of consultations, the Joint Chiefs of Staff submitted an interim report on 9 November,[1] in which you were advised that a comprehensive program was being prepared for later submission to you. This program is submitted herewith in three parts.[2] It is intended for use in conjunction with and in support of existing US political, economic and social measures and in implementation of the concept of the Alliance for Progress. It is designed to maximize the contribution of the US military in the achievement of over-all objectives for Latin America.

Source: Kennedy Library, National Security Files, Departments and Agencies Series, Department of Defense, Joint Chiefs of Staff, Vol. I, Military Actions for Latin America. Secret.

[1] JCSM–768–61; not printed. (Ibid.)

[2] Parts II and III are not printed.

2. Part I summarizes recommendations for increasing the effectiveness of the military program and the contribution of the US Armed Forces for the achievement of US national objectives in Latin America. Implementation of some of these recommendations will require additional funding and personnel.

3. Part II is a detailed presentation of the recommendations with supporting data. Included therein are some military actions that will require coordination by other US agencies and acceptance by allied governments. Part III is factual data, including US and Latin American military capabilities in the Southern Hemisphere.

4. It is recommended that you approve the suggested programs as a matter of policy guidance governing the future role to be played by the US Armed Forces in Latin America.

5. It is further recommended that detailed Diplomatic Mission plans reflecting this guidance be developed and implemented as a matter of priority.

For the Joint Chiefs of Staff:
L. L. Lemnitzer[3]
Chairman
Joint Chiefs of Staff

Appendix A

MILITARY ACTIONS FOR LATIN AMERICA

Part I

1.   Recommendations

The following recommendations are submitted for consideration as means for increasing the effectiveness of the US military program in Latin America and the contribution of the US Armed Forces for the achievement of US national objectives in Latin America and in support of the Alliance for Progress.

Of paramount importance is the necessity to convince the Latin American Governments of the significance of this program and encour-

---

[3] Printed from a copy that indicates Lemnitzer signed the original.

age and prevail upon them to accept it in good faith and assist in its implementation and success. These governments should be made to understand the importance of the educational phase in particular, and persuaded to accept it and fill all available quotas in US schools. Latin Americans must also discard the philosophy that a corps of US trained country personnel are dangerous to the indigenous governments because of the radical changes they could impose as a result of their exposure to the US and the US way of life.

  a. *For Increased Internal Security*

  (1) Seek congressional action to make less restrictive those provisions of the Military Assistance Act which limit military support in the internal security area.

  (2) Orient the Latin American armed forces to accept the apolitical role of the military. All US Government representatives in Latin America should continue to stress to their counterparts that the military is an instrument responsive to democratic government and should act in support of the constitutional principles of that government.

  (3) Expand the provision of US military technical assistance to develop more efficient Latin American military establishments.

  (4) Broaden and expand the capability of indigenous forces to conduct counter-insurgency, anti-subversion and psychological warfare operations.

  (5) As the emphasis on our military assistance to Latin America shifts from hemispheric defense only to internal security, anti-submarine warfare, counter-insurgency, and civic action programs insure that means are available and methods are developed to guarantee the rapid provision of the necessary training, equipment and material.

  (6) Improve the US/LA combined intelligence capability.

  b. *For Hemisphere Defense*

  (7) United States act to increase the effectiveness of the Inter-American Defense Board.

  (8) The United States lend full support to the early establishment and subsequent contribution to the operation of the Inter-American Defense College.

  (9) United States encourage frequent US/LA Defense Conferences.

  c. *For Economic Development*

  (10) Encourage and assist the indigenous armed forces to devote more effort and influence toward internal development.

  (11) Increase the number of US military advisors and mobile training teams in Latin America to provide a broader scope and an accelerated advisory effort in civic action programs.

  (12) Establish Latin American Civilian Conservation Corps Programs.

(13) Strengthen the Latin American Military Air Transport Capability.

(14) Increase the activities of the Inter-American Geodetic Survey (IAGS) to accelerate the production of critically needed maps of Latin America.

(15) Encourage and support a Latin American military contribution to indigenous communications improvement programs.

(16) Encourage Latin American services to convert more strictly combat units to dual purpose units which will contribute to the countries' military capabilities, and also to their economic development.

(17) Expansion of Latin American shipyard capabilities.

d. For Information and Education

(18) Encourage and assist Latin American armed forces to establish their own Military Information and Education Programs.

(19) Establish and support a Western Hemisphere Military Speakers Program.

(20) Expand the US/LA officer exchange program.

(21) Increase the language training and proficiency both for US personnel going to Latin America and for Latin Americans undergoing training in the United States.

(22) Increase US interest in the more junior-ranking Latin American military personnel who will later emerge as their countries' leaders. Increase the number of US orientation tours for those young officers.

e. Miscellaneous

(23) Encourage the revision of archaic Latin American per-diem laws which provide excessive allowances and serve to restrict the numbers of Latin American military personnel able to come to the United States for training.

(24) Appoint retired US career military personnel to positions in the US diplomatic missions in Latin America.

(25) Establish and support alumni associations for Latin American officers who have attended US service schools and academies.

(26) Encourage Latin American military sponsorship of youth programs such as Boy Scouts, Girl Guides, YMCA, church groups, and sports activities.

(27) Provide training and indoctrination for the Latin American services in disaster relief.

2. The Problem and Need for Action

a. The US military capability in furthering US national objectives in Latin America is greater than the actual utilization made of the US Armed Forces in this respect. Efforts of the US military within Latin

America have done much to strengthen the US position. However, because of existing circumstances, opportunities are being missed in which the US Armed Forces could do much more to foster Latin American resistance to Communist penetration of the hemisphere and, at the same time, enhance the US image.

b. The importance of encouraging the Latin American services to organize and train for internal security and antisubmarine warfare as their most effective contributions to Western Hemisphere defense is recognized and appreciated.

c. Of almost equal importance is the requirement to demonstrate to the Latin American governments the potential of their own military services to support their own economic and social development. An analysis of the situation now existing in each of the Latin American countries, and an attempt to establish what could be done by the military to assist these countries in furthering their own economic development programs reveals certain over-all similarities. In most of the countries, a large majority of the population leads only a marginal existence. The reasons are primarily institutional and technical. Current programs of the Agency for International Development, aimed at overcoming these conditions, are broad in scope and catalytic in nature. However, in every country there are problem areas susceptible to attack by indigenous military forces in a civic action role.

d. Illiteracy encompassing the majority of Latin American populations is perhaps the greatest obstacle to development. In many countries, entire areas are without educational facilities. Construction of village schoolhouses and other buildings of public assembly is within the capabilities of indigenous troops. These same forces could provide teachers, as well as the physical facilities for an expanded program of public education.

e. As stated in the 9 November memorandum of the Joint Chiefs of Staff, an increased US military program in support of US objectives in Latin America should be established on a broad base of information and education for the Latin American military man. Annex D to Part II of the present report amplifies this.

f. Departure from the previously purely military roles by US and Latin American armed forces in implementing these recommendations will result in some resentment and criticism from certain power groups in Latin America. However, integrated policy direction at the US national level plus continued close coordination of approved programs by the US Ambassadors in their country programs will minimize this risk.

g. The US Armed Forces have done much in their combined operations, and in other contacts with the Latin American services, to reduce the traditional distrust and animosity between the Southern Hemisphere countries. Continued effort in this respect will contribute heavily to the establishment of the cooperation required between the Latin nations (as well as between them and the US) in the battle against communism.

h. Funding and additional personnel for the program presented cannot be determined until specific recommendations are approved, at which time the services will submit estimated requirements. Resources required will be justified by the value of the results achieved. Parts of this program will require no more than a change of attitude and direction.

i. The US military in Latin America are doing a good job in strengthening internal security in the Southern Hemisphere. With positive direction from the top and with coordination and cooperation between the military and the other executive agencies of the Government, from the top down, the US Armed Forces can do much more to help accomplish US objectives and help the Latin Americans derive greater benefit from the Alliance for Progress and country resources.

---

90.   Report and Recommendations of the Washington Assessment Team on the Internal Security Situation in South America

Washington, January 10, 1962.

[Here follows a table of contents.]

SUBJECT

Report of Assessment Team on Internal Security Situation in South America

Between November 15 and December 21, 1961, a special inter-agency survey team visited the ten South American countries to assess the internal security situations in these countries, and to report their views for transmittal to appropriate officers of the United States Government. The team consisted of the following members:

C. A. Boonstra (Chairman), Department of State
E. C. Townsend, Colonel, USA, Department of Defense
H. L. Downing, Colonel, USAF, Caribbean Command
H. O. Hardin, Agency for International Development
S. J. Papich, Federal Bureau of Investigation

Source: Department of State, Central Files, 611.20/8–461. Secret.

N. L. Ferris, Federal Bureau of Investigation
[*name not declassified*] Central Intelligence Agency
[*name not declassified*] Central Intelligence Agency

Background

The capabilities of nations in Latin America to maintain law and order in situations where violence is instigated, or supported, by Communist and Castro agents or sympathizers is vitally important to hemisphere defense. In late 1960 the American Embassies in these countries were instructed by a joint State–Defense–ICA directive to prepare detailed reports assessing the internal security situations. A follow-up in Central American and Caribbean countries was made by a traveling inter-agency assessment team in April–May 1961.

Scope of Survey

The South American Assessment Team (SAAT) was instructed to report on (1) the nature and extent of the Communist threat in each country; (2) the capacity of the police and armed forces of each country to maintain internal security, and the will of government and society to back them up; (3) any organizational changes needed in each country to improve the maintenance of internal security; (4) the capabilities of the U.S. agencies within the country to assist the local government in internal security, and to keep Washington informed; (5) prospects for exchange of intelligence information; and (6) requirements for U.S. advice, equipment and training.

Latin American problems are such that almost all actions by the local governments, and by the U.S. exert influence on the internal security situations. Particularly important are courses of action relating to economic and social development, now embodied in the Alliance for Progress, and those affecting education, health, and information. The survey team considered its specific assignment, however, as being the complex of police, military, and intelligence activities which bear directly on the suppression and control of subversion and politically-motivated violence.

Visits were made by the team to each of the South American countries, beginning in Venezuela and proceeding thereafter to Brazil, Uruguay, Argentina, Paraguay, Chile, Peru, Bolivia, Ecuador and Colombia. In each country the team consulted with U.S. personnel and reviewed pertinent documents.

General findings and recommendations are summarized in the first part of the report. The second part presents the individual country assessments. The review of intelligence activities, for which Mr. S.J. Papich of the Federal Bureau of Investigation had primary responsibility, comprises the third part of the report and is being forwarded separately through appropriate channels.[1]

Summary of Findings

In general the internal security forces of the South American countries have the capability, when there is a will to do so, for maintaining order and for suppressing outbreaks of violence in those principal urban centers where, so far, the strength of subversive forces has been concentrated. In none of the countries are the Communist parties capable at this time of seizing power, or of sustaining a large-scale campaign of organized armed struggle, through efforts involving only their own members and sympathizers.

The primary threats to internal security come from the capabilities of Communists and Communist sympathizers to utilize the forces of other political groups in advancing their programs. Unrest and disorder stemming from these diverse other sources provide opportunities for the use of violence, not in the previous pattern of palace coups, but in broadly based political and social movements. The Communists are able to cooperate with and to supply leadership to the extremists of the left, and to provoke violence on the part of the extremists of the right. Emphasis is placed on discrediting, outflanking, and outmaneuvering those internal security forces which the Communists cannot successfully combat. Their courses of action include the now-familiar techniques of pressure, infiltration, and division in weakening the will of governments for taking effective action, and of initiating violence principally in rural areas and on issues where the internal security forces are vulnerable.

Countries having already critical problems in internal security accompanied by violence that requires urgent attention are Colombia and Bolivia. Political and class divisions are developing in Peru and Ecuador which soon could place these countries in a similar category. Venezuela, Brazil and Argentina are maintaining internal security through a delicate balancing of political forces which involve risk of sudden deterioration. In Chile, where internal security is supported by relatively good police forces, Communist capabilities are being strengthened through constitutional processes and accelerated by a deteriorating economic situation. Uruguay, which is a relatively stable country in spite of being the base for much Soviet bloc activity, will find its problems serious if situations in Brazil and Argentina grow worse. Finally, Paraguay is unique among the South American countries in that its primary internal security threat is not aggression from within, but from exiles outside its borders who are motivated by highly diverse political objectives.

Even in those countries where internal security problems are the most serious, there is time still for the construction of forces adequate to

---

[1] Part II is not printed. Part III was not found with the source text.

deal with them. Recognition of the urgency to do something now is the principal problem.

Past military and intelligence programs of South American countries, and those for providing U.S. assistance, have been relatively small and slow-moving and have dealt principally with unrealistic requirements for defense against external aggression. Under previously prevailing priorities and attitudes, lags and obstacles were not considered of serious import. Such approaches are now incompatible with the urgent need to improve internal security capabilities.

Since much of the Communist threat is based on the exploitation of disorders developing from economic and social pressures, the foundation of the internal security programs must be the effort to remedy these underlying causes. To be successful, however, such programs must in themselves disturb the existing structures of nations and their societies, and they increase accordingly the need for internal security forces capable of assuring the stability essential to their implementation.

The fact that military strength has long been a principal supporting factor in South American governments is misleading with respect to the capability of these forces, during this period of rapid changes, to assure internal security. In most countries the armies are little more than professional officer corps controlling masses of poorly trained conscripts. Such forces have been effective frequently as a political factor, and when used on a mass basis, have been able to control principal cities and to repel attacks on garrisons. The value of such forces for internal security action against subversive forces, however, is highly questionable. Officers and enlisted men share few common objectives. The forces can be easily divided on political issues; they lack the training, light arms, communications, transport and small tactical units which would be necessary to control widely scattered disorder or guerrilla attacks. What is needed today is the shift of South American military effort away from the principal cities and from the traditional political role, to the establishment of small tactical forces stationed strategically where internal security is threatened.

This would require concurrently an increase in police capabilities within these principal cities. The South American countries best equipped today to use their Armed Forces effectively for internal security purposes are those with relatively strong police forces. Deficiency in day-to-day maintenance of public order in the populated areas provides an ideal climate for subversive action throughout the entire country. Those countries relying on strong armed forces with little emphasis on police thereby reduce their capabilities to move where needed against wide-spread subversive effort and indirect aggression.

Equally vital to internal security are adequate facilities for investigation and for intelligence collection. The internal security efforts of South American countries are deficient in these respects.

To a large extent these situations exist because the will of government and society is such that the necessary improvements are not considered urgent or demanded. The U.S. is endeavoring now to stimulate will toward remedying basic causes of social unrest and civil disorder. There is required equally the stimulation of will to erect internal security structures capable of dealing with subversive activity and violence. This will require drastic modifications in the structure, equipment, and training of South American armed forces, in the strengthening of police forces, and in intelligence collection.

The first systematic United States effort toward development of internal security capabilities in the South American armed forces was made in the 1962 military assistance program, but because top-level approval still is lacking, the program is not yet fully in operation. In the interim there have been grants of several special "packages" of internal security equipment and training. Aside from this, any increase in internal security capabilities derived by the South American armed forces from past programs has been a fringe benefit.

Another benefit, often considered to be the principal U.S. asset derived from the past programs, is the existence of a generally pro-U.S., well-oriented, and reasonably well-educated officer corps. Influential officers are to be found within each country today who recognize the need for reconstruction of the armed forces to meet subversive threats of the type which in the future may appear. Although each of the countries for its own reasons will endeavor to support some conventional, prestige type forces, there exists today a far better opportunity than ever before to exert U.S. influence toward orienting these forces to the internal security concept.

Along with military aspects of internal security programs, most of the South American countries are studying the advisability of utilizing their armed forces on construction projects and other programs characterized as civic action. Such effort is commendable provided it does not detract from the internal security capability. The first, and most important, task is the transition from conventional forces to those trained and equipped primarily for internal security. The South American armed forces at present do not have the trained manpower to do this and simultaneously to divert their resources into widespread civic action. Initial emphasis should be given to those functions which serve areas where they provide simultaneously an internal security and construction force.

U.S. efforts to cope with internal security problems are hampered by lack of unity in working out programs at the country level and in Washington. This is strongly evident in the South American military assistance programs. U.S. military training missions to the South American countries are individually and independently established on service lines. At present, although one U.S. officer in each country has responsibility for coordination and for implementation of the military assistance program, he does not have command authority except over officers of his own service. Communications with the Canal Zone headquarters of the unified command, and with other agencies, and with Washington are limited by inadequate procedures and facilities. The result is a cumbersome, slowly moving effort lacking the unified command and influence needed for adequately coordinated assistance to the armed forces of the host country.

If U.S. military influence is to be used more effectively toward improving the internal security capabilities, what is most needed today is an adequate revision of the entire U.S. military program in South America including the basic bilateral treaties and the force structures agreed to therein, the command and support organization of the U.S. MAAGs and military training missions, the intelligence effort of the armed forces attachés, the legislation which hampers systematic planning of internal security assistance and a clear cut assignment of responsibility and authority as compared to the present diffused system.

To assist in strengthening police capabilities, the AID at present has police assistance and training programs in four of the South American countries. These programs are making a notable contribution toward internal security in proportion to the relatively small resources being utilized. The emphasis has been on organization, administration, records, investigations, and non-lethal tactics of riot control, all based on the public service concept.

Questions have been raised in the past as to whether police assistance and training is properly an AID function. The survey in South America indicated clearly that AID should continue to have responsibility for administering the police assistance programs. This, along with financial support for modest civic action programs of the military forces, provides to AID an important role in the overall internal security effort.

Intelligence capability is the third principal area of deficiency which can benefit by U.S. assistance. This by its nature is delicate and sensitive. Attachment of intelligence advisors to U.S. military missions, already underway, is a useful contribution. Training and assistance for the investigative branches of the police forces is another. Encouragement and assistance should be given to those countries which are trying to organize national intelligence systems.

The adequacy of U.S. intelligence collection, mainly to keep the U.S. informed, but also to support where desirable the internal security capabilities of the South American countries, is assessed in the separately distributed annex to this report.[2]

Finally, the several U.S. agencies administering internal security programs within South American countries require better coordination. The country team as presently constituted in the larger Embassies

---

[2] Reference is to Part III.

imposes too broad a span for the Ambassador to coordinate and control effectively the multitude of U.S. programs. For internal security programs there is need to fix responsibility in a small working group headed by a senior officer with responsibility and adequate authority. The size of working groups from that now required could be drastically reduced by the previously suggested simplification of the command structure for U.S. military personnel within the country.

An urgent need exists for coordinated inter-agency guidance to the Country Teams on internal security programs. At present there is no directive authorizing the Country Teams to carry on joint military planning with the host countries for such purposes. Restrictions continue to exist on the use for internal security of equipment delivered within the hemisphere defense programs of past years. Guidance is inadequate respecting sources of supply, types of equipment and policies to be followed in responding to requests for riot control equipment.

Recommendations for U.S. Action

1. All aspects of the U.S. military assistance programs including authorizing legislation, bilateral agreements, MAAG and Mission organization, and U.S. policy objectives should be revised to conform with the concept that maintenance of their own internal security is the primary contribution that South American armed forces can make to Western Hemisphere defense.

2. Responsibility and authority should be consolidated and specifically assigned in Washington to provide for the continuing direction, control and coordination of the internal security program for Latin America. Within the Country Team of each Embassy, responsibility and authority similarly should be consolidated and assigned.

3. AID, the Department of Defense and the Central Intelligence Agency should agree on a joint program for each country defining the weapons, tactics, and forces to be encouraged for use in control of mobs and violence and the means for assuring adequate stocks of riot-control equipment and appropriate police weapons.

4. Effectiveness and flexibility of military assistance should be improved by combining the Training Missions and Military Assistance Advisory Groups (MAAG's) in each country into one unified command directly subordinate to Commander-in-Chief Caribbean Command (CINCARIB), by providing adequate communications systems, by systematic planning of internal security assistance, and by prompt and orderly implementation of agreed programs.

5. AID should give much higher priority in South America to the support of police assistance and training, both in country and regional projects.

6. The Department of Defense, CIA, and AID should increase and coordinate their efforts to improve intelligence capabilities of South

American countries, particularly in the areas of intelligence advisors, intelligence exchange, police investigative personnel, technical equipment and training.

7. The USIS, the Department of Defense and AID should make a coordinated effort to foster a constructive information and indoctrination program for personnel of the South American armed forces and police forces.

8. Participation of South American military forces in civic action, and in economic and social development programs, should be encouraged only to the extent that such efforts contribute to, or do not interfere with, the reorganization and urgently needed training of forces for internal security.

9. AID, in addition to police assistance, should coordinate with the Department of Defense on civic action programs contributing to internal security, including in some cases the recognition of improved living standards for the armed forces as an economic and social need.

[Here follows Part II of the report.]

---

91.   Special National Intelligence Estimate

SNIE 80–62   Washington, January 17, 1962.

THE THREAT TO US SECURITY INTERESTS IN THE CARIBBEAN AREA

The Problem

To estimate the threat to US security interests in the Caribbean area over the next two decades.

The Estimate

1. US security interests in the Caribbean relate principally to the maintenance of independent and friendly states in the Western Hemisphere. The Caribbean is not only the basin around which are located a

---

Source: National Archives and Records Administration, RG 59, S/P Files: Lot 69 D 121, American Republics, 1962. Secret. A note on the title page indicates that the estimate was submitted by the Director of Central Intelligence and that the U.S. Intelligence Board concurred on January 17. The CIA and the intelligence organizations of the Departments of State, Defense, the Army, the Air Force, the Joint Staff, and the National Security Agency participated in the preparation of the estimate. All members of the board concurred except the AEC representative and the Assistant Director of the Federal Bureau of Investigation, who abstained on the grounds that the subject was outside their jurisdiction.

large number of American republics, but it is the link between the US and the larger American republics in the southern continent. In addition, the US is concerned with keeping its southern flank free of hostile military power, and with maintaining the unrestricted operation of the Panama Canal and of other US installations.

2. Threats to US interests could arise from a variety of sources: the vulnerability of the area to attack from outside the hemisphere; the establishment of a military presence within the area by hostile powers; attempts by the Communist powers, with the help of the present Cuban Government, to spread Communist revolution to other parts of the area by military action or subversion; the growth of indigenous radical nationalism; and instability rising from attempts by governments in the area to interfere in the affairs of their neighbors or to impose their will upon them. A discussion of each of these threats follows in the paragraphs below.

3. *Vulnerability to outside attack.* The area of the Caribbean is within range of Soviet ICBMs and long-range bombers, and cities, canals, and military installations could also be attacked by missile-carrying submarines. In the event of general war, some US installations, such as the canal and air and naval bases, probably would be subjected to Soviet attack.

4. *Establishment of a hostile military presence.* Cuba and any other Caribbean state which fell under Communist control could be used by the USSR as areas in which to establish missile, submarine, or air bases, designed to bring North America under attack or to add to the deterrents to any conceivable US military action in the Caribbean or elsewhere. On the whole, we believe the establishment of such Soviet bases is unlikely for some time to come. Their military and psychological value, in Soviet eyes, would probably not be great enough to override the risks involved.

5. The Soviet leaders would be concerned lest steps toward the establishment of such bases would provoke the US to overthrow the Castro regime before bases could become operational and would generally heighten the risk of war. Moreover, Soviet bases in Cuba could involve the USSR in difficult political and control problems with the Cuban Government; the Soviets have been very careful to retain control over situations which involve them in any serious degree of risk, and they would be mindful of the danger that Cuban initiatives could expose the USSR to serious risks of general war. Finally, the Soviet leaders, for the present at least, appear to prefer not to make their presence too obvious or apparent, lest they discourage rather than encourage the spread of communism to other Latin American countries. Since their essential aim in Latin America is not military conquest but Communist revolution, we believe they will prefer to use Cuba as a symbol of spontaneous popular revolution and as a base for subversive operations.

6.   Nevertheless, the USSR can and probably will augment its naval, air, and communications capabilities in the area by the development of arrangements or facilities not openly identifiable as Soviet military bases. For example, the improvement of Cuban naval and air installations would provide facilities suitable for Soviet use, and special installations and arrangements could be set up for intelligence collection or subversive purposes.

7.   This reluctance to establish military bases might not extend over the entire period under review. If communism spread to other countries in the area, and if the US appeared to be weakening in world power and national will, the Soviet leaders might be emboldened to buttress their gains by openly establishing Soviet military bases in the area, with the object of further weakening US prestige and further strengthening and protecting their local satraps. If such bases were established, the first step might be the establishment of jointly-operated submarine or air bases, on the theory that the establishment of such bases would be less likely to incur risk of US reaction than would the establishment of missile bases, while at the same time constituting a demonstration of Soviet presence and protection.

8.   *Possibilities of the spread of communism in the area.* The area of the Caribbean presents a picture of great variety, in terms of social structure, economic organization, and political direction. A few states have had or are passing through full-fledged social revolutions; in others the pressures for revolution are building up. Some states have very backward economies, while others are moving toward modern industrial societies. Many are single crop or commodity exporters; others are moving toward more balanced economies. In each country there are groups seeking to overthrow the existing order; even Mexico, which can be considered to have completed its revolution, harbors groups who believe that the revolution has been arrested and that a new leftward movement should be set in train. Some of these revolutionary groups are Communist led; some are not.

9.   It appears to us very likely that during the next decade or two the Communist element among the revolutionary forces will grow in size, although its growth in influence would not necessarily be proportionate to the growth in size. The important question is not whether communism grows, but whether the non-Communist revolutionary forces can grow more rapidly, can control the revolutionary movement, and can achieve an acceptable level of momentum and progress in social, economic, and political change. This question cannot be answered at this stage of Latin American history; much depends upon such factors as the degree of success of the Alliance for Progress in achieving real social change, the skill and determination of local non-Communist leaders, and the activities

and achievements of Castro's Cuba and of the local Communists in exploiting and subverting revolutionary unrest.

10. We believe that Castro's Cuba will continue to do what it can to export its revolution. It has to some degree handicapped itself by openly espousing Marxism-Leninism, but to the extent that it can capitalize on the failure of non-Communists to achieve real reform, it may yet succeed in bringing sympathetic forces to power elsewhere. For some of these countries, Venezuela for example, the critical choice between communism and non-communism may come within the years immediately ahead. For some of the others it may come later. During the next two decades, all could escape communism, but some may fall under Communist control. Local factors of an unforeseeable character, such as the quality of emerging leadership, may prove more decisive than existing political trends or degree of backwardness. In addition, factors external to the area, such as Communist successes or reverses in other underdeveloped countries, developments within the Communist Bloc itself, or changes in the appreciation of the general power balance between the Communist Bloc and the Free World will play a part.

11. *Growth of indigenous, non-Communist, radical nationalism.* Those states which experience a profound social, economic, and political transformation without coming under Communist control will almost certainly develop a greater sense of national identity and a stronger impulse to assert political independence. As broad-based political movements replace military or personal rule, there will develop a much stronger feeling that the Latin American states can be masters of their own destinies, and the new political leaders will be obliged to stress their devotion to national sovereignty and especially their independence of US policy. In some instances national sovereignty may come to mean that anything can be attempted with little concern for US reaction.

12. This is not to say that the growth of nationalism will necessarily be accompanied by a rise of anti-US attitudes. To the extent nationalism succeeds, it will tend to reduce the antagonism toward the US among the broad mass of the people, but at the same time it will win the enmity of established elites. In any event, the very emergence of new forces, and the identification—rightly or wrongly—of the old order with the US will tend to promote suspicion of US motives and policies and will encourage the new leaders at least to strike a pose of independence and self-determination. As a consequence, the US role in the control and operation of canals or other US installations will almost certainly come under heavy attack, and the US freedom of action will probably become increasingly restricted. In the event of open differences with the US, an opportunity might be presented for hostile extra-hemispheric powers to gain a measure of influence.

13. Such a trend toward radical nationalism appears to us to be unavoidable, although it will probably move at a variable and indeterminable pace. In some countries it probably will gather force more slowly than in others. In Panama today, where the Canal Zone offers a visible target for agitation, it appears to be particularly strong; in some of the more isolated countries of the area it may mature only after major reforms have occurred and a new sense of self-confidence develops.

14. *Rivalries and tensions within the area.* Historically, the Caribbean area has been rife with personal feuds and petty tensions between states. Conspiracies and revolts against some leaders or countries have been organized, armed, and initiated on the soil of others. Combinations and alignments have been developed among groups of countries or leaders against others. We believe this kind of activity will continue in the years ahead, although it may take a somewhat different form than in the past. The pace of social, economic, and political change will not be uniform. Oligarchs cut off from power in one state may move to others and may receive aid and comfort in their plots to reassume control at home. Similarly, frustrated revolutionists will, as in the past few years, use asylum in sympathetic countries to organize and plan revolutions in their home countries. While the form may be the same as in the past, the ultimate stakes will not be personal power so much as the social and economic structure of the nation itself.

92.   Memorandum From the Executive Secretary of the Department of State (Battle) to the President's Special Assistant for National Security Affairs (Bundy)

Washington, February 5, 1962.

SUBJECT

> National Security Action Memorandum No. 118—Participation of U.S. and Latin American Armed Forces in the Attainment of Common Objectives in Latin America[1]

This report is in response to NSAM 118. It was prepared in collaboration with the Department of Defense and has the concurrence of that department.

I.   Policy

The implementation of our Latin American policy is taking place within a framework of rapid evolutionary change. Throughout Latin America social tensions are mounting. The reforms generated by the Alliance for Progress are likely to weaken, rather than strengthen, the fabric of society in most Latin American countries by increasing these tensions during the period before the long term programs of the Alliance become effective. We must expect the Communists and other extreme left-wing political factions to try to exploit this situation to their own advantage.

A key element in preserving the internal stability of Latin American countries during this critical period will be the position and attitudes of the Latin American military. Historically, the military in Latin America has played a major role in local political life. In only a few countries is there any tradition of civilian control. Frequently, the armed forces have exercised degrees of open control varying from outright military dicta-

---

Source: Department of State, NSAM Files: Lot 72 D 316. Secret. Drafted by Maechling and Brigadier General W.A. Enemark, USA, Regional Director for Western Hemisphere Affairs in the Office of the Assistant Secretary of Defense for International Security Affairs, with concurrences by Deputy Under Secretary of State for Political Affairs U. Alexis Johnson and Deputy Assistant Secretary of Defense for International Security Affairs William Bundy, and in the Agency for International Development.

[1] NSAM 118, from McGeorge Bundy to Rusk and McNamara, dated December 5, stated that the President was "favorably impressed" with the general approach and content of the proposals in JCSM 832–61 (Document 89) and desired their further refinement and development into specific programs for action. It further stated that the President had assigned primary responsibility for formulating a policy guidance paper on this subject to the Department of State and responsibility for developing general and specific programs for implementation to the Department of Defense and that he requested a brief consolidated report on February 1 outlining actions that were underway. (Department of State, NSAM Files: Lot 72 D 316)

torship to situations where they influence the political balance of power, either by dictating the limits within which a civilian government is permitted to operate or by swinging their support from one faction to another.

In the past there was a strong tendency on the part of Latin American military establishments to support conservative political institutions. Even though the officer corps in Latin America is predominately of middle and even lower-class origin, it has usually identified its interests with those of the upper-class landowning and commercial oligarchy that has dominated the political scene in Latin America since the wars of independence. Today, however, the same factors which are revolutionizing the civilian environment are affecting the military establishments of Latin America. In nearly every country the rising generation of younger officers is sympathetic to social and economic reform. In a few cases, their social and economic tendencies are beginning to introduce a new and unpredictable element into already unstable local political situations.

From the standpoint of military policy, our current strategy calls for the United States to assume primary responsibility for defense of the Western Hemisphere against external attack. Our policy objectives, therefore, require military establishments in Latin America which are capable of contributing to the defense of the hemisphere by maintaining internal security against the threat of Castro or communist-inspired insurgency. We also want military establishments that will evolve in a way that contributes to the political stability and economic development of their respective countries. In this connection, it should be noted that most Latin American armed forces are capable of maintaining internal security in urban areas only; they are not generally capable of coping with uprisings or guerrilla actions in rural areas.

In order to align Latin American military establishments with United States military policy, and to train and equip them for their contribution to the defense of the hemisphere, the United States must be the paramount foreign military influence in Latin America. A favorable political orientation on the part of the Latin American officer corps is vital to our interests. This calls for continuous effort in solidifying the bonds between our military forces and those of Latin America.

In achieving the foregoing objectives, we must recognize, however, that some kinds of action to strengthen Latin American military forces are fraught with hazardous political consequences. In nearly every Latin American country the political balance is a delicate one, with the armed forces capable of tipping the scales. Most governments are carefully nurturing the principle of civilian control. We cannot afford to be identified with any step backward either to repressive dictatorship or military intervention in political life.

Accordingly, every move we make to strengthen our ties with the Latin American military must be done on a selective basis with careful attention to the sensitivities of the country concerned and their effect on the political balance in that county. With this qualification, we are implementing the proposals made in JCSM 832–61, along the following lines.

II. Implementation

Nearly all the proposals in JCSM 832–61 have been under way for some time. Nevertheless, we have reviewed the entire list carefully to determine which proposals should be continued at their present level, which should receive increased emphasis, and which should be rejected as not feasible or undesirable.

Our review disclosed that of the twenty-four specific proposals that the Joint Chiefs of Staff submitted to cover their original twenty-seven recommendations, nineteen are already in operation. We believe that eleven of these should continue at present levels and nine should receive increased emphasis. The report being prepared in connection with NSAM 119 (on civic action)[2] will include recommendations on the degree of emphasis for these nine. Four of the twenty-four proposals (Nos. 1, 9, 12 and 24) have been carefully reviewed and found to be either unfeasible or of such questionable value that they are being returned for further study. The Enclosure[3] lists the twenty-four proposals with the current status and degree of emphasis recommended for each.

The civic action recommendations of JCSM 832–61 deserve special mention. Action is now being taken pursuant to NSAM 119 to expand civic action programs in underdeveloped countries throughout the world, including Latin America. The Department of Defense has reviewed the FY 1962 military assistance equipment program with a view to expediting certain projects for selected military forces in Latin America which can contribute substantially to economic and social development, and to determine whether other purely military projects can be deferred without significantly lowering the military effectiveness of Latin American forces. $2.9 million in the FY 1962 Military Assistance Program is being authorized for these projects, and another $5.0 million may also be allotted for the same purpose.

To determine what funds can be obligated for civic action type projects in FY 1962, and to program other such projects in FY 1963, a DOD–AID team will soon visit selected Latin American countries. The specific programs resulting from this visit will be listed in the report on NSAM

---

[2] See vol. VIII, pp. 231–232.

[3] Not printed and titled "Specific Projects Submitted by the Joint Chiefs of Staff to Cover the Recommendations Contained in Their Paper No. JCSM–832–61, with Comment on the Current Status, Desirability, and Degree of Emphasis Required for Each"; undated.

119, due on March 31.[4] We therefore recommend that with this memorandum action on NSAM 118 be considered completed.

William H. Brubeck[5]

---

[4] Dated March 30.

[5] Printed from a copy that indicates Brubeck signed the original above Battle's typed signature.

---

93.   Memorandum From Secretary of State Rusk to President Kennedy

Washington, February 20, 1962.

SUBJECT

Report and Recommendations of Washington Assessment Team on Internal Security Situation in South America

I am enclosing a copy of the Report and Recommendations of the Washington Assessment Team (SAAT)[1] which visited South American countries, during the period November 15–December 21, 1961, to assess the communist threat, the local Government's capability to meet and overcome it and U.S. Country Team capabilities for rendering internal security assistance. Also enclosed is a copy of a Staff Study of the Report prepared by this Department.

The following steps in implementation of the Report are being taken: (1) each concerned agency is being requested to review the nine recommendations in Part I and to state its views concerning them; (2) the Special Group (Counter-Insurgency) is being provided a copy for such action as it may deem appropriate; (3) each concerned Ambassador is being provided a copy for his use and comment.

In the meantime, the following actions consistent with the recommendations in the Report already have been initiated:

Source: Kennedy Library, National Security Files, Meetings and Memoranda Series, NSAM 134. Secret.

[1] Document 90.

1. The Defense Department has taken steps to unify the Service Missions in each South American country into a single MAAG under the command of the Commander-in-Chief Caribbean Command;

2. AID is engaged in reviewing the current Public Safety Program for Latin America to insure that it is responsive to the critical needs of Latin American countries for police assistance;

3. Pursuant to NSAM 119, AID and the Defense Department are acting jointly in the development of civic action projects, additional to those now underway, that might usefully be undertaken in Latin America;

4. Pursuant to NSAM 118, an expanded program of collaboration between the U.S. and Latin American military is underway.

Dean Rusk[2]

Enclosure

Department of State Staff Study

SUBJECT

Report and Recommendations of Washington Assessment Team (SAAT) on the Internal Security Situation in South America

The Report is the product of an inter-agency team, which visited each of the ten South American countries during the period November 15–December 21, 1961, to assess the communist threat, the local Government's capability to meet and overcome it and U.S. Country Team capabilities for rendering internal security assistance. The Report is based on interviews and briefings by Country Team and other U.S. personnel only; there were no contacts with local nationals.

The first seven pages (Part I) summarize the Team's general findings and recommendations. These are followed by detailed country reports (Part II). Part III, the sensitive intelligence annex which reviews local government and U.S. intelligence capabilities, is in the custody of the Director of the Central Intelligence Agency.

I.   *Team's Basic Findings*

(a) *The Threat.* The primary threat is posed by the growing capacity of a communist minority in each country to exploit others, particularly

---

[2] Printed from a copy that indicates Rusk signed the original.

extremist factions of the right and left, for the promotion of communist programs and goals. In order to reduce the deterrent capability of security forces, communists are placing emphasis on the discrediting, out-flanking and outmaneuvering of such forces. These tactics include the policy of fomenting violence in rural areas, where security forces are weak, and of promoting disorders over issues on which security forces are vulnerable.

(b) *Security Force Capabilities*. Although each country maintains substantial military and police forces supposedly capable of maintaining internal security, these are deficient in the quality, orientation, organization, training and equipment they require to meet and overcome the threats that reasonably may be anticipated. Police forces, in particular, require strengthening.

(c) *Country Team Capabilities*. U.S. efforts to furnish governments the guidance and assistance they require to maintain effective security are hampered by inadequate coordination of the total U.S. internal security effort at the Country Team, CINCARIB and Washington levels. In particular, the entire U.S. program and overseas representation require review and revision. Reorientation of the program is necessary if it is to become a fully effective instrumentality for improving the internal security capabilities of South American countries.

II.   *Team's Recommendations and Analysis of Security Situation*

(a) Part I of the Report contains nine recommendations, which are set forth in enclosure 1 of this memorandum.[3] These should be endorsed, in principle, except recommendations numbered 1 and 8.

(1) The revisions of U.S. programs proposed in recommendation 1 should be limited to those determined, in consultation with concerned Ambassadors, to be politically practicable. For example, bilateral military assistance (MAAG) and military training mission agreements are not now wholly in conformity with the concept that the primary role we envisage for Latin American armed forces in hemisphere defense is the maintenance of internal security. In some cases, it may not be possible to persuade the local government to adopt this concept and to agree to the revisions necessary to bring existing bilateral agreements into conformity. Moreover, in some cases it may be juridically necessary for revised agreements to obtain local Congressional ratification or approval. Extreme leftists and nationalist opposition elements might prevent, and would delay, such approval in certain countries. This would place in jeopardy not only the revised or new agreements, but also our existing military agreements and defense arrangements.

---

[3] Not printed.

(2) In recommendation 8, the Team has too severely restricted conditions under which South American military forces should be encouraged to participate in civic action. The participation of South American military forces in civic action and in economic and social development programs should be encouraged, whenever such participation does not detract from, or interfere with, the reorganization and urgently needed training of internal security forces.

(b) Additional recommendations appear in each country report (Part II). These represent, for the most part, the Team's judgment on how the nine recommendations in Part I should be translated into specific U.S. actions at the country level. While most have some merit, they should not be endorsed prior to the receipt and review of each concerned Ambassador's comment.

(c) The Team's analysis in each country report (Part II) of the internal security situation is as comprehensive and accurate as might reasonably be expected, in view of the limited time spent by the Team in each country. On the basis of information available to the Department, the country analyses are not wholly accurate, nor are the conclusions in the country reports entirely valid. However, these discrepancies do not, by themselves, necessarily nullify the recommendations included in the country reports, the majority of which are consistent with the Department's appraisal of the local security situation.

III. *Implementation*

(a) Each concerned agency (Defense, AID, CIA, USIS) should be requested to review the nine recommendations in Part I which affect its policies, programs and activities, and to state its views concerning them.

(b) The Special Group (Counter-Insurgency) should be provided a copy of the Report for such action as it may deem appropriate.

(c) Each concerned Ambassador, in consultation with other members of the Country Team, is in the best position to assess the merit of the Team's recommendations set forth in Part II, inasmuch as they relate to matters largely in his jurisdiction. Accordingly, each Ambassador should be sent a copy of the Report for his own use and requested, in consultation with other members of the Country Team, to transmit his comments.

In the meantime, the following actions consistent with the recommendations in the Report are already in process of implementation:

(1) The Defense Department has taken steps to unify the Service Missions in each South American country into a single MAAG under the command of the Commander-in-Chief Caribbean Command (recommendation 4);

(2) AID is engaged in reviewing the current Public Safety Program for Latin America to insure that it is responsive to the critical require-

ments of Latin American countries for police assistance (recommendation 5);

(3) Pursuant to NSAM 119, AID and the Defense Department are acting jointly in the development of civic action projects, additional to those now underway, that might usefully be undertaken in Latin America (recommendation 9);

(4) Pursuant to NSAM 118, on which a report was forwarded to the President on February 5, an expanded program of collaboration between the U.S. and Latin American military is underway.[4]

---

[4] NSAM 134, from Bundy to Rusk, dated March 12, stated that the President had noted his "interim report" enclosing a copy of the SAAT report and requested that the Department of State coordinate the report with the departments and agencies concerned and recommend a governmental position based on its recommendations in a paper to be forwarded no later than May 1. (Kennedy Library, National Security Files, Meetings and Memoranda Series, NSAM 134) A July 16 memorandum from Taylor to U. Alexis Johnson indicates that no paper was sent. (Ibid.)

---

94.   Memorandum From the Executive Secretary of the Department of State (Battle) to the President's Special Assistant for National Security Affairs (Bundy)

Washington, February 28, 1962.

SUBJECT

National Security Action Memorandum No. 118—Participation of U.S. and Latin American Armed Forces in the Attainment of Common Objectives in Latin America

This constitutes a revised report in response to the State Department's responsibility under NSAM 118 to provide policy guidance on collaboration between U.S. and Latin American military forces.[1]

Source: Kennedy Library, National Security Files, Meetings and Memoranda Series, NSAM 118. Secret. The source text bears no drafting information, but the Department of State record copy indicates that it was drafted by Officer in Charge of Inter-American Security and Military Affairs George O. Spencer and cleared by U. Alexis Johnson and Haydn Williams and in the Agency for International Development.

[1] The text of the undated memorandum omitting the introductory paragraph, and entitled "United States Policy for Participation of U.S. and Latin American Armed Forces in the Attainment of Common Objectives in Latin America," was circulated with NSAM 140, from Bundy to Rusk and McNamara, March 26, which states that the President had approved it. (Ibid., NSAM 140)

The fundamental objective of U.S. military activities and programs in Latin America is the establishment of a Latin American military leadership dedicated to the tasks of: (1) preserving democratic constitutional order; (2) maintaining internal security; (3) contributing to collective defense on a scale commensurate with Latin American military and economic capabilities; and (4) promoting social and economic development. Pursuant to this objective, it is our policy to encourage the Latin American military to reorient their military establishments in the following manner:

1. Encourage acceptance and fulfillment of the concept that each of the Latin American countries is responsible for contributing to the defense of the hemisphere by:

a. Maintaining security against the communist-Castro threat of violence and subversion, including guerrilla warfare, and the movement of armaments and men clandestinely across land, sea and air borders for subversive purposes.

b. Maintaining security, against overt external aggression, of their ports and coastal waters, bases and strategic areas within their territories, but placing maximum reliance on effective application of the Rio Treaty with full U.S. military cooperation to deter or counter such aggression.

c. Contributing to overall hemispheric defense capabilities in adjacent areas of the Caribbean Sea and the Atlantic and Pacific Oceans, e.g. anti-submarine warfare, patrol harbor defense, and related functions.

d. Contributing patrol or combat forces, or other feasible assistance, for any Caribbean Security arrangements that may be negotiated and for implementing any OAS decision that collective military action be taken to maintain the peace and security of the hemisphere.

2. Encourage, to the maximum extent consistent with needs and capabilities of each Latin American nation, standardization along U.S. lines of military doctrine, unit organization and training.

U.S. military programs developed in implementation of the foregoing policy objectives should be so designed as to win the support of non-communist civilian elements, both for the programs and for the local military. To this end, U.S. programs should:

1. Consist of types of assistance that can be justified to non-communist elements of the population as a bona fide security requirement for them and for their constitutional governments.

2. Whenever possible without losing primary military capability, include assistance having some visible economic utility, e.g. assistance for dual-purpose units which contribute to economic development as well as security.

3. Acquaint the Latin American military with the complete portfolio of communist techniques, including the communist tactic of alienating the military from the support of the civilian population by depicting it as a repressive, extravagant and irresponsible element in public life.

It is particularly desirable that the foregoing policy objectives and guidelines be used in the development and conduct of military training and exchange programs, military conferences and other forms of military collaboration which bring U.S. and Latin American military personnel into close professional and personal association. Inasmuch as such programs and activities provide particularly effective channels for promoting U.S. interests, U.S. military personnel engaging in them should be made fully cognizant of U.S. policy objectives.

Finally, it is essential that U.S. military programs be carefully tailored to the individual requirements of Latin American countries. Neither Latin American military nor civilian authorities should be stimulated to request a particular program prior to a careful determination by our Ambassador, confirmed by the State Department, that the program would serve U.S. foreign policy interests in that country.

ML Manfull[2]

---

[2] Manfull signed for Battle above Battle's typed signature.

---

95.   Editorial Note

On February 19, 1962, AID Administrator Fowler Hamilton recommended in a memorandum to President Kennedy that he make a determination required by section 511(b) of the Foreign Assistance Act of 1961 that internal security requirements might be the basis for the furnishing of grant assistance of defense articles to Bolivia, Brazil, Chile, Colombia, Ecuador, Haiti, Paraguay, Peru, and Uruguay. On February 28 President Kennedy signed Presidential Determination No. 62–17, which permitted furnishing defense articles on a grant basis up to approximately $20.2 million to those countries. (Kennedy Library, National Security Files, Subjects Series, Presidential Determinations)

96.   Memorandum of Conversation

Washington, April 11, 1962, 5:40 p.m.

SUBJECT

Inter-American Defense College[1]

PARTICIPANTS

The President

Mr. Edwin M. Martin, Assistant Secretary of State, ARA

His Excellency Dr. José Antonio Mayobre, Ambassador of Venezuela

Ambassador Mayobre indicated that all he wanted to talk about was the Inter-American Defense College. He expressed previously known views that to bring senior officers to Washington for nontechnical, political training would, in the Latin American climate, inevitably stimulate their interest in taking political power. He also thought that bringing just a group of Latin Americans together might establish a mutually supported network of Latin American military interested in taking power. Apart from these objections of principle he thought this was a particularly bad time to set up such an institution in view of the Argentine crisis and that leftist elements would attack it most vociferously.

He went on to say that, while in the recent discussions and in the vote this morning, only Brazil and Mexico had stood with Venezuela, he knew for a fact that many other governments were strongly opposed to the proposition but had only voted for it because of strong outside pressures, and in view of their unwillingness to stand up to their own military, which very much wanted the College. In response to a request from the President he listed at least half the countries of Latin America as being in reality opposed.

Assistant Secretary Martin pointed out that this was not what the governments had told the United States and there might be some difference of view between delegations and governments. He also pointed out that while we had a real appreciation of the problem with which the Ambassador was concerned, we felt that the curriculum could be so handled as to have the opposite effect and that he knew the people involved and was sure they would be quite happy to work in this direction.

Source: Department of State, Central Files, 371.7553/4–1162. Confidential. Drafted by Martin and approved by the White House on April 19. The meeting was held at the White House.

[1] The Inter-American Defense Board agreed on December 19, 1961, to establish an Inter-American Defense College at Fort McNair in Washington. On April 11 the OAS Council approved a resolution finding no impediment to the establishment of the Defense College, thus overruling the position put forward by Mexico and Venezuela that the Board lacked authority to create it and that the OAS Council thus had no responsibility to fund its operating expenses. Documentation on this subject is ibid., 371.7553.

The President felt it of great importance to get the American military and the Latin American military better acquainted with each other so they could work together better on the common hemispheric problems in the military field. The President said he could not help but believe that close association with American military, who understood so well the need to subordinate the military power to the civilian, would be helpful in dealing with the problem with which the Ambassador was concerned.

On the other hand, we would not want to push through a project which was in reality opposed by a substantial number of Latin American governments. He knew that many of them had soldiers up here for training at Bragg and many other places and this seemed to be helpful. He felt that some way should be found to review the organization and curriculum of the new College in a way to avoid the difficulties which the Ambassador's Government feared. He felt the institution had a role to perform and it would be very unfortunate to abandon the project at this stage by confessing that we could not reach agreement. He asked the Ambassador to consult some of the other governments which were concerned and then talk to Assistant Secretary Martin and see if some solution could not be worked out which would meet the problems which had been raised.

[After he had left the President's office, the Ambassador indicated to Mr. Martin that one helpful move might be a carefully worded statement at the time the OAS announces that the College is to be established, which would emphasize the democratic and civilian objectives of the training to be provided. He told Assistant Secretary Martin that he would consult his colleagues and be in touch with him in about a week.][2]

---

[2] Brackets in the source text.

97.   Circular Telegram From the Department of State to All Posts in the American Republics

Washington, April 18, 1962, 8:30 p.m.

1781. Following is guidance to assist Ambassador carry out internal security program responsibilities cited President's letter last May.[1] Following applicable particularly to counter-insurgency, civic action, military indoctrination and other programs bearing US military "cold war" label.

As general rule US should encourage and whenever in US interest assist LA military and/or police to: (1) improve their capability to maintain internal security against communist inspired or exploited subversion and violence; (2) engage in those high-impact civic action projects which are necessary primarily for security reasons, i.e. projects required to improve image of local military and thereby improve military's ability to maintain public support, particularly at village and campesino level, for necessary security measures; (3) engage in larger-scale, longer-term civic action projects which serve broad nation-building goals more than narrow security objectives, provided such projects consistent with and make practical contribution toward Alliance for Progress, are within local government's economic capabilities to finance and/or US budgetary limitations to support, and do not substantially detract from required reorganization, training and equipping of necessary internal security forces.

However, each US movement into these relatively new fields of collaboration must have Ambassador's prior assessment of its political-economic-military impact on country. To insure such assessments, Amb requested keep informed, in consultation Country Team members and CINCARIB, all current and proposed internal security activities of US departments. Whenever necessary, Amb should consult Dept for additional information or advice he requires for their adequate evaluation.

In particular, local civilian, police and military authorities should be stimulated by members Country Team, or US personnel visiting country, to request or accept only those US programs or activities which Washington has approved after full consideration Ambassador's views. Dept desires that timing and channeling of such stimulation be subject Ambassador's approval in every case.

Source: Department of State, Central Files, 720.5/4–1862. Secret. Drafted by Spencer, cleared in draft by Maechling and with the Agency for International Development and the Department of Defense, and approved by Martin. Repeated to CINCARIB and CINCLANT.

[1] Reference is to a letter of May 29 from Kennedy to all U.S. Ambassadors. For text, see the Department of State *Bulletin*, December 11, 1961, pp. 993–994.

In developing his recommendations to Dept re any internal security program, Amb should, unless he considers inadvisable or is otherwise instructed, obtain views pro-US, anti-communist civilians who Amb believes are in position make sound judgments re possible adverse impact of program on genuinely democratic developments and who he believes can be relied on to provide frank advice on pitfalls to avoid.

In developing recommendations re assistance to local police and/or paramilitary forces, particularly counter-insurgency training and equipment, Amb should evaluate risk of pro-communist municipal, provincial or other authorities using such forces against efforts of national military to maintain security against communist subversion and violence. In assessing this risk, Amb should, unless he considers inadvisable or is otherwise instructed, consult pro-US, anti-communist civilians or military authorities who can be relied on for objective and disinterested judgment on likelihood of any such misuse.

Rusk

98.   Circular Telegram From the Department of State to Certain Posts in the American Republics

Washington, August 10, 1962, 8:51 p.m.

230. Influential members Congress, wide segment press and some LA civilians severely criticizing MAP program, alleging: (1) close association of U.S. with LA military promoted by MAP and other joint activities contributes little or nothing to developing LA military respect for constitutional principles, e.g. Peru, Argentina; (2) U.S. equipment utilized largely to increase military prestige and capability to suppress non-communist democratic elements; (3) military establishments, budgets and arms acquisitions already too large; (4) MAP should include only minimum equipment and training critically required for internal defense defined in narrowest terms (e.g. police-type assistance) and civic action.

Source: Department of State, Central Files, 720.5/8–1062. Secret; Priority. Drafted by Spencer, cleared in the Department of Defense, and approved by Martin. Sent to all diplomatic posts in the American Republics except Lima and repeated to CINCARIB and CINCLANT.

Following assumptions believed to underlie this criticism: (a) LA military have no legitimate hemisphere combat mission and U.S. armament only stimulates arms race; (b) long history military coups and caudillos likely to continue; (c) military largely oriented toward right and generally oppose social and economic reform; (d) military not significantly engaging their resources in economic and social development; (e) because military's right-wing orientation militates against danger it will affiliate with local communists or Sino-Soviet Bloc, U.S. can, without jeopardizing its security interests, severely limit assistance it grants or sells to that which U.S. determines unilaterally to be critical LA requirement; (f) restrictive U.S. arms policy would promote reduction military expenditures and divert savings to economic development, but if not, would benefit U.S. public image by disassociating U.S. from LA military extravagance and irresponsibility.

Embassy requested cable soonest thoughtful comment re validity criticism and assumption. Include judgment whether adoption of more restrictive grant and sales policy would result in net U.S. gain or loss in terms our across-board foreign policy objectives in country.

Rusk

99.   Circular Telegram From the Department of State to Certain Posts

Washington, September 10, 1962, 7:38 p.m.

442. In discussing Cuban situation several Central American Governments have again expressed fears of Castro aggression as result of current buildup in Cuba. General line of action we are proposing has been indicated in circular telegrams 377 and 378.[1]

However, you should, as appropriate remind CA Govts of special US concern in past over threat of such aggression, direct and indirect,

---

Source: Department of State, Central Files, 737.00/9–1062. Confidential. Drafted by Director of the Office of Central American and Panamanian Affairs Katherine W. Bracken, cleared in draft by Assistant Legal Adviser for American Republics Affairs Marjorie M. Whiteman and with the Office of International Security Affairs in the Department of Defense, and approved by Martin. Sent to Guatemala City, Managua, Panama City, San José, San Salvador, and Tegucigalpa; repeated to POLAD/CINCLANT and POLAD/CINCARIB.

[1] Both dated September 2. (Both ibid., 737.56/9–262)

and our efforts to strengthen CA countries' defenses against Castro attempts in this connection. Point particularly to ninth paragraph of President Kennedy's statement of September 4.[2] ("It continues to be the policy of the United States that the Castro regime will not be allowed to export its aggressive purposes by force or the threat of force. It will be prevented by whatever means may be necessary from taking action against any part of the Western Hemisphere.") Reiterate assurances given in circular 196 (August 3 1961)[3] that we are prepared to assist, upon request, in identification, interdiction or frustration of armed assistance to Castro-Communist elements.

Complementary to this potential assistance is strengthening of their own internal defense capability in which we are cooperating through MAP programs, particularly in efforts during past year to shore up weaknesses in current internal security capability of these countries.

Although inflammatory broadcasts from Cuba are continuing we have no reliable indication that Castro-Communists at this time are capable of, or intend, armed raiding parties in Central America. It appears to us they depend, instead, on ability of local Communist parties to exploit local issues, particularly sabotaging of the Alliance for Progress. We thus hope that governments will respond to our expression of special concern and special efforts we have been making to deter action toward Central America by Castro-Communists, with realistic estimates of areas in which Communists are most active locally and measures to control their attempted subversion of legitimate progress by Communist groups responding to Castro's radio calls.

You may add that we would, if your host government desires, be glad to consult on practical problems involved in arms smuggling on Atlantic Coast in an attempt to develop a better control with resources now available to our two countries.

Rusk

---

[2] For text of the statement, see Department of State *Bulletin*, September 24, 1962, p. 450.

[3] See footnote 2, Document 88.

100. Letter From Secretary of State Rusk to the Chairman of the Subcommittee on American Republic Affairs of the Senate Foreign Relations Committee (Morse)

Washington, September 15, 1962.

DEAR MR. CHAIRMAN: This is in response to your letter of August 3, 1962,[1] in which you requested that we examine in depth the policies underlying our military assistance program for Latin America and provide you answers, with supporting data, to several questions which you raised regarding this program. As I indicated our intention to do in my initial response of August 10,[1] Secretary McNamara and myself, the members of our staffs and our Ambassadors in the field have been engaged in a careful and serious re-examination of these policies and programs. Your thoughtful letter, together with recent political developments in Latin America, have been helpful in stimulating a fresh look at this important area of policy. This explains the delay in responding to your request.

In historical perspective, our program of military collaboration with Latin American Governments has not developed haphazardly. It has constituted, since the beginning of World War II, a calculated United States response to three major historical military developments bearing in their wake direct and serious challenges to the security of the United States: (1) the threat of Axis domination, represented by World War II; (2) the threat of global war, brought into sharp focus by the Korean conflict; and (3) the threat represented by the appearance in Cuba of a Marxist-Communist regime committed to promote subversive, Castro-communist movements throughout Latin America. Our military programs have developed and altered in response to these threats. Our current programs have a three-fold objective: (1) improving hemispheric defense, principally through continuing to develop Latin American ASW capabilities; (2) internal defense, where necessary; and (3) a growing civic action program of direct civilian benefit.

Thus, broadly speaking, our programs are designed to contribute to hemispheric stability, to the maintenance of political democracy and to the principles of the Alliance for Progress. Notwithstanding occasional, deplorable military actions which have temporarily set back the progress of democracy, I am convinced that our programs are making a substantial contribution to all of these objectives.

Source: Department of State, Central Files, 720.5/8–362. No classification marking. Drafted by Director of the Office of Inter-American Regional Political Affairs Ward P. Allen and Spencer.

[1] Not printed. (Ibid.)

The basic causes of the problem of violence in Latin America are to be found not in the military, but in basic weaknesses in the political, economic and social fabric of Latin American societies. Clearly the ultimate solution requires nothing less than the establishment of political, economic and social stability, under democratic institutions, throughout Latin America. In this process, an examination of history since World War II shows that the Latin American military have in general been a force for good and have played a leading and often decisive role in unseating dictators and helping to maintain political stability against revolutionary efforts to impose totalitarian regimes. Moreover, as we work toward the ultimate, evolutionary solution to the violence problem, we dare not disregard the current, most serious challenge I have mentioned above—the threat posed by the intention of the Castro-communist movement to utilize subversion and military force, whenever necessary, to retard or prevent democratic development. Thus a primary purpose of our military program must necessarily be to provide Latin American countries with the training and military equipment they require to frustrate such efforts.

In connection with our re-examination of our policy and programs, we asked each of our Ambassadors in Latin America to appraise the local impact of our military assistance policies and programs and to inform us whether, in his best judgment, a more restrictive policy with respect to the furnishing of military assistance would result in a net gain or loss in terms of United States foreign policy objectives in the country.[2] Their replies, without a single exception, take the view that a more restrictive United States arms policy would not be in our national interest.[3]

It is to be borne in mind that these programs of which we speak, although important to our national objectives, are not large. Our total military assistance effort for Latin America is less than five percent of our world-wide program. It represents less than six percent of the military budgets of the Latin American nations themselves and thus is not responsible for the size of Latin American armed forces, which, in their turn, are not distorted in size compared with those of most other developing countries, accounting for only about ten to fifteen percent of total Latin American budgets.

In short, our re-examination of our current three-pronged program in the perspective of our over-all policies and objectives, leads us to conclude that the program is basically sound.

[2] See Document 98.
[3] Detailed replies are in Department of State, Central File 720.5.

The foregoing comments and conclusions emerge from a detailed Staff Study which we have prepared in response to your request and which I enclose.

Your letter also requested information covering five specific points which I am happy to provide. This information is set forth in Part II of the enclosed Staff Study and the supporting material appended thereto.[4]

Sincerely yours,

Dean Rusk[5]

---

[4] The September 2 staff study and its enclosures are not printed.

[5] Printed from a copy that indicates Rusk signed the original.

---

101.   Circular Telegram From the Department of State to Certain Posts

Washington, September 25, 1962, 3:55 p.m.

517. Based on paragraph 2e. of Depcirtel 508[1] Department has been considering courses action which countries bordering Caribbean can take demonstrate their determination work collectively resist attempts direct or indirect aggression by Castro regime. Current planning runs along following lines:

A.   *Courses of Action*

1.   Establishment system air-sea surveillance around Cuba and along coast Caribbean countries. Surveillance would serve inhibit Castro regime from sending clandestine shipments of arms and men to other countries of area and would strengthen capabilities those countries intercept such shipments. We would assume primary responsibility for Cuban patrol while other countries would cover own coasts with such assistance from us as may be necessary. Our conducting Cuban patrol

---

Source: Department of State, Central Files, 710.5/9–2562. Confidential. Drafted by Bowdler, cleared by Martin and Legal Adviser Abram Chayes, and approved by Allen. Sent to Bogotá, Caracas, Guatemala City, Managua, Mexico City, Panama City, Port-au-Prince, San Salvador, San José, Santo Domingo, and Tegucigalpa and repeated to USUN, POLAD CINCARIB, POLAD CINCLANT, Asuncion, Buenos Aires, La Paz, Lima, Montevideo, Quito, Rio de Janeiro, and Santiago.

[1] Document 151.

would not rule out contributions by other Caribbean countries (e.g. naval units or support facilities for such units).

2. Intensification efforts counter Castro-communist subversion including control of travel to and from Cuba, shipment subversive propaganda from Cuba and transfer funds from Cuban sources for subversive purposes. Governments could also agree on system for exchanging information on Castro-communist subversive activities.

3. Issuance by governments of Caribbean area, including United States, of joint declaration that extension by Castro regime of its Marxist-Leninist system by force or threat of force to any part of Caribbean area or creation or use of a Soviet supported offensive military capability endangering security of any country in area, will call for taking of any necessary measures to protect security of countries concerned. This declaration would be accompanied by announcement that discussions will be held at military level to plan for defensive measures for meeting these contingencies.

B.   Timing and Forum

1. Paragraph 2e. of Depcirtel 508 if approved at informal MFM would constitute additional hemispheric acknowledgment that Caribbean countries are particularly vulnerable Castro-communist subversion and consequently justified taking special defensive measures. This would serve minimize criticism Rio Treaty being bypassed or that inter-American system being fractionized.

2. Based this paragraph we would seek have President Caribbean country (e.g. President Betancourt) invite Ministers Defense and Interior Caribbean countries meet during second or third week of October to consider special measures which should be taken. Courses action outlined A. could constitute program to be approved. Inclusion Interior Ministers would emphasize that problem of dealing with Castro-communist threat is not purely external but one in which internal measures are equally important.

Comment:

Department aware foregoing plan presents certain problems, particularly (1) whether Haiti and Mexico would want to join in action contemplated and (2) probability agreement patrol activities will give rise to requests for further military assistance. Would appreciate your evaluation receptivity of local government to plan and additional problems you can foresee in its execution. Foregoing is exclusively for information of addressees and should not be discussed with local officials until specifically authorized by Department.

Ball

102. Special National Intelligence Estimate

SNIE 85–4–62   Washington, November 9, 1962.

CASTRO'S SUBVERSIVE CAPABILITIES IN LATIN AMERICA

The Problem

To describe and evaluate Castro's capabilities, with Soviet help, for carrying out subversion and sabotage in Latin America after satisfaction of all US conditions relative to the withdrawal of strategic weapons systems from Cuba and a consequent US commitment not to invade.

Note: In this estimate we have considered Castro's raw capabilities, taking note of, but not working out in detail, US and Latin American capabilities for counteraction.

Summary

A. The dangerously unstable situation that prevails throughout much of Latin America is the product of fundamental inequities and historic circumstances; it is not the creation of Castro and the Soviets. Castro's efforts, with Soviet help, to exploit this situation by means of subversion and sabotage have not produced significant results. Propaganda exploitation of Castro and Cuba as symbols of revolution has probably been more effective to date than other subversive activities. Castro's influence in Latin America had waned by the time of the missile base crisis and was further reduced by the revelation that he had accepted Soviet strategic missile bases on Cuban soil and by the manner of the Soviet decision to withdraw them.

B. Implementation of an agreement between the US and the USSR whereby the strategic weapons systems would be withdrawn and the US committed not to intervene in Cuba with force will leave Castro with a new immunity and a greater freedom for subversive actions throughout Latin America. The extent to which this potential is realized will depend upon the situation in Cuba, Soviet policy toward Cuba, and the policies and performance of the other Latin American governments and of the US with respect to the Castro threat. There are many targets in the hemi-

---

Source: National Archives and Records Administration, RG 59, S/P Files: Lot 69 D 121, Cuba, November–December 1962. Secret. A note on the title page indicates that the estimate was submitted by the Director of Central Intelligence and prepared by the CIA, and the intelligence organizations of the Departments of State, Defense, the Army, the Navy, the Air Force, and the National Security Agency. All members of the U.S. Intelligence Board concurred on November 9 except the AEC representative, who abstained on the grounds that the subject was outside his jurisdiction.

sphere vulnerable to Castro-Communist subversion and sabotage, and the Soviets are likely to assist Castro in reaching them by contributing both to his security at home and to his capability for action overseas. As in the period before the missile base crisis, the effect of Castro's subversive activities will depend not only upon his capabilities but upon the attractiveness of the Cuban example and the willingness of the American governments to take determined counteraction. This willingness will probably be weakened by fulfillment of the US commitment not to invade Cuba.

C. We have examined how Castro's subversive potential would be affected by alternative courses of Soviet policy regarding Cuba: (1) virtual withdrawal of support; (2) continuation of economic and military support ranging from present up to substantially increased levels. We believe that course (1) would considerably reduce Castro's subversive potential, and that the Soviets are unlikely to elect it. We conclude that Soviet course (2) would maintain Castro's potential for subversive action at least at present levels or actually raise it to the point where he could undertake amphibious and/or airborne subversive operations against close-in targets.

[Here follow the remainder of the estimate; Annex A, "Highlights of Cuban Subversive Activities in other Latin American Countries to Date"; and Annex B, "Estimated Military Equipment in Cuba After Withdrawal of Strategic Missiles."]

---

103. National Security Action Memorandum No. 206

Washington, December 4, 1962.

TO

> The Secretary of State
> The Secretary of Defense
> The Chairman, Joint Chiefs of Staff
> The Director of Central Intelligence
> The Administrator, AID

SUBJECT

> Military Assistance for Internal Security in Latin America

The President has signed a determination authorizing the grant of up to $34.9 million of military matériel for internal security purposes in

---

Source: Department of State, NSAM Files: Lot 72 D 316, NSAM 206. Secret. Copies were sent to the Attorney General and the Director of the Bureau of the Budget.

Latin America.[1] In this connection, the President underscored his concern with the need for the most challenging scrutiny of the justifications advanced for providing items under this determination.

In the complex and rapidly shifting circumstances in Latin America, it is essential that our military aid program be a carefully tailored and constantly updated part of our overall strategy aimed at development and security in the hemisphere. The program development and review process must assure that the specific items furnished under MAP are appropriate to solving the key internal security problems to which our overall country planning is addressed; and that this program in fact strengthens and supports the other objectives of the U.S. effort in each country, including the development of popularly supported civilian governments and effective civil police authorities.

The President recognizes that considerable effort has already been made to reorient military assistance in Latin America. But because this program is so sensitive in relation to the whole gamut of Latin American problems, he wishes to be assured that you continually stress the need to screen MAP items against the full range of intelligence, political analysis, policy evaluation, and other U.S. programs on a current basis.

Specifically:

Are jet aircraft really justifiable items for the internal security mission, or are they included essentially for political reasons? If so, do we have a clear idea of the full political ramifications, and are they clearly to our advantage?

Does the design of the MAP internal security program reflect our current efforts to strengthen the roles and capabilities of civil police in the same countries?

Is there explicit division of missions between the military and police units we support in each country?

Does the projected level of MAP in Latin America reflect a consciously measured balance between our military and police efforts in the internal security field?

Is an adequate contribution made by the intelligence community in the review of internal security programs?

In this connection, the President desires that careful consideration be given to intensifying civil police programs in lieu of military assistance where such action will yield more fruitful results in terms of our primary internal security objective. Should AID funds be insufficient to meet total requirements, a transfer from military assistance should be seriously considered.

Will you please take whatever steps are necessary to assure that the FY 1963 MAP program for Latin America is appropriate in terms of these

---

[1] Presidential Determination 63–7, December 1. (Kennedy Library, National Security Files, Subjects Series, Presidential Determinations)

criteria. The President wishes to have the Administrator of AID, in his role as coordinator of foreign assistance, submit a report, in cooperation with the Secretary of Defense, on the steps being taken to assure that MAP has the desired effects on our total efforts in Latin America. He also desires a report later in this fiscal year on the scope and character of the program which is finally implemented under the determination which has just been made.

McGeorge Bundy

104. Editorial Note

At the daily White House staff meeting on January 18, 1963, there was some discussion pertaining to Latin America. The relevant portion of a January 18 memorandum of the meeting by Colonel Lawrence J. Legere of the NSC Staff reads:

"Chuck Johnson had recently sent Bundy a paper recommending that consideration be given to the creation of some kind of multilateral military force for the Latin America nations, or perhaps only for those Latin America nations in the Caribbean area. Of course, by this he did not mean a multilateral MRBM force or even necessarily a multilateral seaborne force, but was merely trying to underline the advantages of getting the Latin Americans to associate themselves in some kind of common military enterprise. The discussion on the Johnson memorandum per se got no place, but it did prompt a side discussion of the military forces of the Latin America nations, with emphasis on the military assistance which the US furnishes them. Komer delivered himself of a few brief but sarcastic outbursts alleging that the US military was all too prone to listen sympathetically to Latin American requests for 'submarines, aircraft carriers, jet fighters, etc.,' (a bit of Komer hyperbole). At this point, Ralph Dungan, a Latin America expert and, because of his closeness to the President, a big gun at these staff meetings, cut Komer off very sharply. Dungan said that he had found the US military very much aware of the nonsense involved in over-sophisticated weaponry for these countries, and that they had 'really put the clobber' on such requests for FY 63. In short, as Dungan put it, the whole direction of MAP for Latin America has 'turned around very well.' In another context later in the meeting, Bundy indicated that he had been absolutely unaware of how military assistance programs to Latin America had 'turned around'; it was apparent, however, that he approved of what Dungan had said." (National Defense University, Taylor Papers, Box 25, Daily Staff Meetings)

105. Memorandum for the Record

Washington, February 18, 1963.

SUBJECT

Meeting with The President on 18 February 1963

Present at the meeting were: Ambassador Raymond L. Thurston, Sterling J. Cottrell, Robert Hurwitch, J.C. King, Ralph Dungan, Cyrus R. Vance, Major General Victor H. Krulak, USMC, and the undersigned.[1]

In the meeting, the President discussed the attached summary of proposed actions with respect to Cuban-based communist subversion in Latin America.[2]

In connection with Section V of the attached summary,[3] the President stated that we should go to Congress for a larger military assistance program keyed to subversion in Latin America and the Cuban situation.

With respect to Section VI. B.,[4] the President approved in general terms a selected exchange of intelligence with Latin American governments.

With respect to Section VIII,[5] the President said that he was not yet ready to carry out such activities, but that they should be thought out and plans should be developed.

With respect to Section IX.A.2.,[6] the President approved in general terms the establishment of a clearing house for information about communist activities based in Cuba. However, it was left open whether such a clearing house would be within or without the OAS and whether it would be the SCCS.

In addition, the President asked Secretary Vance to review our counterinsurgency contingency plans for Latin American countries, particularly with respect to the reaction time of the U.S. military and with respect to the extent of non-U.S. participation contemplated in such plans.

Source: Washington National Records Center, RG 330, Records of the Office of the Secretary of Defense, OASD/(C) A Files: FRC 71 A 2896. Top Secret. The source text bears no drafting information except that it was drafted on February 22.

[1] Those not yet identified include Deputy Coordinator of Cuban Affairs Hurwitch, Secretary of the Army Vance, and Major General Krulak, Special Assistant for Counterinsurgency and Special Activities to the Director of the Joint Staff.

[2] The attachment, unsigned and undated, titled "Elements of an Expanded U.S. Program to Combat Cuban-Based Communist Subversion in Latin America," is not printed.

[3] Section V is titled "Military Measures."

[4] Section VI is titled "Expanded Intelligence Effort."

[5] Section VIII is titled "Special Measures to Obtain Greater Support for the Anti-Subversion Campaign."

[6] Section IX is titled "Increased Multilateral Effort."

The President read the attached memorandum which presented the DoD position on the basic paper submitted by Ambassador Thurston[7] and then left the room to attend another meeting. Subsequent to his departure, the persons present discussed the question whether a single point of contact should be designated for supervising the execution of the total counter-subversion program in Latin America.[8]

Joseph A. Califano, Jr.[9]
Special Assistant to the
Secretary of the Army

---

[7] The memorandum by Vance, February 18, on the subject "Cuban Based Communist Subversion in Latin America," is not printed. The basic paper was apparently the paper cited in footnote 2 above.

[8] Cottrell stated in a February 27 memorandum to Vance and others that he was establishing a subcommittee of the Interdepartmental Coordinating Committee of Cuban Affairs, to be called the Sub-Committee on Cuban Subversion; it was to be chaired by Krulak. (Filed as an attachment to a March 4 memorandum from Califano to Colonel Francis J. Roberts; ibid.)

[9] Printed from a copy that indicates Califano signed the original.

---

106. Circular Telegram From the Department of State to Certain Posts

Washington, February 27, 1963, 6:01 p.m.

1491. Joint State/AID/Defense message. Subject: Military Assistance for Internal Security in Latin America.

In connection with Presidential approval of the use of military assistance funds for internal security purposes in Latin America for FY 63, the Executive Branch has been directed to apply the most challenging scrutiny to the justification of items proposed to be provided to Latin American countries under the Military Assistance Program. In this connection, the following guidance shall control the development of Military Assistance Programs hereafter. All such programs shall be carefully tailored and constantly updated so that they are interrelated parts of our

Source: Department of State, Central Files, DEF 19 US–LAT AM. Secret. Drafted by Deputy Assistant Administrator for Politico-Military Affairs in the Agency for International Development Joseph J. Wolf; cleared by AID Administrator David E. Bell, Martin, Maechling, Enemark, and Dungan; approved by Wolf. Sent to 19 Embassies in the American Republics and CINCARIB.

overall strategy aimed at development and security in the Hemisphere. They should be related to the concepts of approved Country Internal Defense Plans where such are in effect. The MAP program and the Alliance for Progress programs are mutually supporting elements of U.S. foreign policy. Internal security and civic action are the primary purposes of our Military Assistance Programs in Latin America. At all levels, both in the field and in Washington, the program development and review process must assure that the specific items furnished under MAP are appropriate to solving the key internal security problems to which our overall country planning is addressed. In this connection, it is clear that the internal security question is composed of political, military, and economic factors, which are closely interrelated. Specific evaluation of these factors is an integral part of the justification of any proposed Military Assistance Program, even when programs are politically motivated. The program justification must also, in addition to major item justification, set forth the interrelationship of the proposed program with other objectives of the U.S. in the country, so that program justification makes it apparent that the proposed program would strengthen and support the overall objectives of the U.S. in the country concerned, including the development of popularly-supported civilian governments and effective civil police authorities. In those cases wherein the communist threat or other local circumstances make it impossible to justify a full compatibility between the Military Assistance Program and the longer-range goal of encouraging the development of popularly supported civilian governments, the relevant and controlling facts should be expressly set forth.

Military elements as a political force in the country concerned may, in the U.S. national interest, require support because of this political consideration. To the extent that this is a factor in the formulation of Military Assistance Programs, it should be expressly analyzed and recognized in program submissions. In this connection, the current and desired role of each of the military services should be expressly analyzed, and the proposed levels of MAP support for each service should be specifically justified.

It is U.S. policy that the thrust of MAP programs to Latin America should be to cope with the internal rather than the external threat. This determination is based upon the evaluation of the immediacy of the respective threats, the necessity of the most careful marshalling of the resources of the United States and its Latin American allies, and in light of the role of the United States in Hemisphere defense. Internal security, as a justification for Military Assistance Programs in Latin America should not be used as a catchall justification for the continuation of military assistance which cannot be soundly justified as being related to the actual or potential internal security threat. Pressures for the continuation of programs at previously existing levels and composition cannot be accepted as automatic justification for the inclusion of items as internal security items. There is a continuing requirement to screen all MAP items against the full range of intelligence, political analysis, policy evaluation and other U.S. programs on a current basis. Thus, deviations from previously submitted programs could at any point in the programming cycle be directed in order to insure consonance of program composition with policy objectives.

Some specific points which require express justification are the following:

1. The inclusion of jet aircraft in Military Assistance Programs as items justified for internal security missions and training should be supported by express evaluation of both political and military considerations involved. The external as well as the internal implications of providing jet aircraft should be specifically discussed. In this connection, the regional interrelationship of country programs requires special comment by all levels above the Country Team level, in order to avoid the inclusion of items in country programs simply because they have been included in other country programs.

2. The interrelationship between MAP internal security programs and the current efforts of the U.S. to strengthen the roles and capabilities of civil police should be the subject of express consideration. There should be a notation of the correlation of missions between the military and police units of a country, and particularly those supported by the U.S., and the degree to which the internal security problem requires the support of complementary strength. The possibility of political elements in the country using military or police forces in struggle, one against the other, should be discussed. The projected level of MAP should expressly reflect a consciously measured balance between our military and police efforts in the internal security field, related to the concepts of approved Country Internal Defense Plans when such are in effect. On these issues, as well as on the whole subject of civic action programs, both the AID element and the political element of the Country Team will have important contributions to make.

3. It is U.S. policy that careful consideration be given to intensifying civil police programs wherever such action will yield more fruitful results in terms of our internal security objectives. While Military Assistance Programs and Police Assistance Programs should not be treated as being necessarily substitutional, Country Team evaluation in depth and judgment of the respective requirements is an essential part of the programming justification process.

4. It is the responsibility of all elements involved in the programming process to insure, by careful consideration and express evaluation of the factors concerned, that each Military Assistance Program sub-

mitted promotes internal security and stability. The Chief of the Diplomatic Mission should insure that all related aspects of the internal security problem are evaluated and coordinated at all stages in the development of proposed programs, including not only submissions made in the annual programming cycle, but spot recommendations made from time to time.

In light of the foregoing, programs for FY 1965 and subsequent years should be accompanied by justifying statements clearly covering the foregoing points.

With respect to MAP programs for FY 1963, Missions are directed to review approved programs and promptly submit by March 25 any comment as to whether the delivery of any of the items included therein should be questioned. Specific comment is requested on the inclusion of jet aircraft in these programs.

With respect to FY 1964 programs, all Missions are requested to prepare and submit statements dealing with the points covered by this instruction, to reach Washington by March 25.

It shall be the continuing responsibility of Missions to be guided by the foregoing with respect to ongoing as well as future programs, bearing in mind the situation as it may develop in the country concerned and the continuing nature of military assistance programming.

Rusk

---

107.   Memorandum From the Secretary of the Army (Vance) to Secretary of Defense McNamara

Washington, March 15, 1963.

SUBJECT

Interdepartmental Coordinating Committee of Cuban Affairs: Movement of Subversives and Subversive Trainees

REFERENCES

(a) NSAM No. 213 dated January 8, 1963[1]

Source: Washington National Records Center, RG 330, Records of the Office of the Secretary of Defense, OASD/(C) A Files: FRC 71 A 2896. Secret. No drafting information appears on the source text. Also sent to the Secretaries of the Navy and Air Force, the Chairman of the Joint Chiefs of Staff, and the Assistant Secretary of Defense (International Security Affairs).
[1] The text of NSAM 213, entitled "Interdepartmental Organization for Cuban Affairs," is printed in volume XI.

(b) Memo for McGeorge Bundy from DepSecDef dated January 10, 1963, subj: Interdepartmental Organization for Cuban Affairs[2]

The attached Program on the Movement of Subversives and Subversive Trainees to and from Cuba was approved by the President on March 8, 1963.

For implementation in the Department of Defense, the Program has been divided under two major headings:

A. Actions Within the Primary Responsibility of the Department of Defense, and
B. Actions Within the Primary Responsibility of a Department or Agency Other Than the Department of Defense.

[Here follow assignments of actions within the primary responsibility of the Department of Defense.]

Attachment

PROGRAM ON THE MOVEMENT OF SUBVERSIVES AND SUBVERSIVE TRAINEES APPROVED BY THE PRESIDENT ON MARCH 8, 1963

A.   Actions Within the Primary Responsibility of the Department of Defense

1. Continue current U.S. sea and air surveillance of the Caribbean area contiguous to Cuba.

2. Continue the development, at high priority, of U.S. communications in Latin America, in order to improve alerting, reporting and control capabilities.

3. Study, on a priority basis, the feasibility and desirability of establishing intelligence centers at Caribbean Command and Caribbean Sea Frontier Headquarters for rapid processing and dissemination to countries concerned, via the American Ambassadors, of intelligence on the movement of subversives.

4. Establish a coordinated Caribbean surveillance system involving:

a. Continued close-in surveillance of Cuba by U.S. forces.
b. A U.S. military alerting system, by which intelligence of subversive movement will be rapidly transmitted to the American Ambassa-

---

[2] Not printed.

dors to countries concerned (contingent upon the decisions made as a result of the study under A. 3, through intelligence centers at Caribbean Command and Caribbean Sea Frontier Headquarters of the Atlantic Command).

c. A unilateral surveillance and interception effort by each country in its own territorial waters.

d. U.S. assistance in final interception in territorial waters, upon request by the country concerned.

5. Establish Military Assistance objectives and planning guidance to provide selected countries, especially in the Caribbean and Central American area, with the necessary small patrol craft, and training and logistical support, to enable these countries to establish an effective patrol of their own coasts. Provide necessary funds in addition to present programs.

6. Provide U.S. Navy, Air Force and Coast Guard training assistance, as required, to develop or improve coastal patrol capabilities of Latin American military forces. This may take the form of a Canal Zone training activity, employment of mobile training teams, or a combination of both.

7. Urge the accelerated improvement of internal security forces and police forces in Latin American countries and the intensification of patrol and intelligence activities aimed at preventing clandestine departures and apprehending returned trainees. Provide equipment, training and advice as required.

B.   *Actions Within the Primary Responsibility of a Department or Agency Other Than the Department of Defense*

1. Intensify U.S. intelligence efforts in each country to identify persons who have travelled, or intend to travel, to Cuba, and report selected information promptly to the host government, as consistent with our own intelligence program, and the requirement to protect our sources.

2. Intensify our action in making available to each country selected intelligence concerning the extent, nature and implications of Cuban subversive activities, as consistent with the requirement to protect our own intelligence program.

3. Utilize U.S. intelligence capabilities to determine the nature and extent of clandestine aircraft and small boat traffic between Cuba and other countries in the Caribbean area, with special attention to Mexico, Honduras, Jamaica, Haiti and the Dominican Republic. Use evidence obtained to persuade governments concerned to institute surveillance and other control measures.

4. Increase greatly our penetration and other intelligence efforts to identify persons engaging in illegal travel to Cuba, and determine routes and methods employed. Report selected information, consistent with

the requirement for protecting our own intelligence program to host government.

5. Intensify current efforts to introduce [*less than 1 line of source text not declassified*] from each country into the Cuban training program.

6. Both through the OAS and bilaterally, induce each Western Hemisphere country to:

a. Stamp passports or other travel documents issued to own nationals "not valid for travel to Cuba."

b. Refuse exit permits for Cuba to any national of a third country who cannot produce a valid permit issued by his own country for travel to Cuba.

c. Refuse to honor any visa for Cuba which is not an integral, non-detachable part of the travel document issued by the country of which the traveller is a citizen.

d. Require accurate manifests of all carriers departing for or arriving from Cuba, and furnish copies of these manifests to diplomatic missions of other Western Hemisphere countries which are affected.

7. Persuade Mexico to fingerprint, in addition to photographing, all persons leaving for or arriving from Cuba, and to provide data to the parent country of the nationals involved.

8. Make [*less than 1 line of source text not declassified*] arrangements [*2 lines of source text not declassified*] to impose administrative impediments and harassment on suspicious Cuba-bound travellers, in order to increase the difficulty of travel and thus discourage prospective travellers.

9. Both through the OAS and bilaterally, request Latin American countries to deny their ports to ships of Cuban registry.

10. Pursue a campaign to expose the scope and purpose of Cuban training of the nationals of other countries for subversive purposes, in order to discourage prospective trainees and impress the governments and the peoples concerned with the urgent need to halt the travel of Latin American nationals to Cuba.

11. Through bilateral negotiations press countries with inadequate legal restrictions on travel to Cuba to adopt laws enabling the prohibition of such travel and providing severe penalties for evasion. Recommend that rewards be offered for identification of evaders.

12. In separate diplomatic approaches to each country, reiterate the need for full and effective cooperation with appropriate OAS bodies, and bilaterally among the several states, in the interchange of information concerning travel of persons to Cuba and other Castro-Communist subversive activities.

13. Propose periodic regional or sub-regional meetings of ministers of Government of the American Republics to review the implementation of steps taken by them to combat movement of subversives in the Caribbean.

14. Urge other Latin American nations to negotiate separately and/or collectively with Mexico, Uruguay, Brazil, Bolivia and Chile in order to enlist cooperation in adopting specific measures to prevent the movement through their countries of third country personnel to and from Cuba.

15. Encourage Latin American governments to institute administrative procedures, such as exhaustive examination of manifests, air-worthiness checks of aircraft, baggage inspection and inspection of health and other documents, all designed deliberately to delay and otherwise make difficult the carrying of passengers to Cuba.

16. Request governments of Latin American countries which persist in maintaining diplomatic relations with Cuba to expose the falsification of travel documents by Cuban embassies or consulates, and take punitive measures, such as the expulsion of Cuban diplomatic personnel, to bring such illegal activity to a halt. Provide U.S. technical assistance as requested.

17. Intensify technical assistance to Latin American countries in improving immigration and customs controls.

18. Persuade Mexico to halt Cubana Airlines service. If unable to do so, seek to persuade Mexico to refuse the introduction of Soviet-made aircraft in the Havana–Mexico City route on technical grounds. This will create an obstacle to Cubana, since the Britannia aircraft now used are falling into disrepair.

19. Request again of Great Britain, Canada and any other potential supplier that they cut off the supply of spare parts for Cuba's Britannia aircraft.

20. Conduct negotiations with the Netherlands, Mexico, Canada and Spain to persuade those countries to stop, or refrain from reestablishing, commercial air flights to Cuba. Enlist the cooperation of other Western Hemisphere countries normally providing terminal service for any of the airlines involved, such as Venezuela and Trinidad, in applying pressure.

21. Intensify [less than 1 line of source text not declassified] input of propaganda in Latin American public information media discrediting the Cuban training effort, exposing the hazard which it holds for Latin American tranquility, and discrediting persons who have undergone subversive training, in order to discourage possible volunteers and develop popular opposition to such activities.

22. Identify returned trainees who are dissatisfied with their Cuban training experience and exploit their capabilities for provision of intelligence and propaganda material for exposing and discrediting Castro-Communist subversive activities.

23. Initiate a publicity campaign throughout Latin America, not attributable to the United States, which focuses unfavorably on the use of

Mexican, Uruguayan, Brazilian and Chilean transit facilities for movement of persons of other countries to and from Cuba for subversive purposes.

24. Propose recommendations by the OAS to member governments of a program of steps, on both the national and international levels, to control travel by their nationals to Cuba, utilizing the proposals in the report by the Special Consultative Committee on Security (SCCS) as well as the specific recommendations set forth herein.

25. Once the initial comprehensive program in 24 above is undertaken, utilize the appropriate OAS bodies to follow up on implementation through such means as multilateral exchange of information, meeting of experts, and utilization by individual countries of the services of the Special Consultative Committee on Security.

---

108.   Memorandum From the Executive Secretary of the Department of State (Read) to the President's Special Assistant for National Security Affairs (Bundy)

Washington, August 17, 1963.

SUBJECT

Review of U.S. Military Policy Toward Latin America

In response to Mr. Dungan's memorandum of May 1 (Tab A),[1] we have reviewed our policy covering our military relations with Latin American countries. The most recent statement of this policy is contained in the Military Assistance Manual of May 5, 1963 (Tab B).[2] Considering that this policy has been developed for regional application, as well as for countries with military establishments of varying degrees of sophistication, we consider the policy to be essentially sound and realistic—sound because it contains reasonable flexibility, and realistic because the goals established therein appear to be achievable.

Source: Department of State, Central Files, DEF 19 US–LAT AM. Secret. Drafted by Spencer; cleared by Martin and U. Alexis Johnson.

[1] Not printed; it expressed concern that the United States did not have a consistent military assistance policy in Latin America and recommended discussion of the subject by the Latin American Policy Committee.

[2] Tabs B through F were not attached to the source text.

During this Administration we have devoted our efforts in the military field primarily to the task of leading Latin American countries away from the concept of hemispheric defense and to developing an effective stance of deterrence and capability against internal threats of communist subversion and insurgency. Our grant military assistance program (Tab C) provides us our principal and perhaps most effective leverage in promoting this objective. Due to the modifications of supportable missions, present policy guidance now limits our grant assistance to internal defense, including Civic Action (65% of the program), naval defense (20%), miscellaneous training (10%), and packaging, crating, and handling costs (5%). Our efforts to provide guidance to the Ambassador and Country Team on the formulation of grant programs have included our Circular Telegram of February 27 (Tab D),[3] letters to each of our Ambassadors (Tab E) and a proposed follow-on instruction which it is planned to discuss in the LAPC in the light of comments by AID and Defense.

It is not clear how successful we shall be, especially as present equipment becomes more and more obsolete from the standpoint of professional combat standards, in selling this program to the Latin American military. A discussion in the LAPC of the longer-term prospects would seem to be in order.

While our efforts to encourage Latin American countries to concentrate their military programs on internal defense also extend to our military sales program, our influence in the latter sector for obvious reasons is somewhat less controlling. We are convinced, however, that our present sales policy strikes a reasonable balance between our interest of promoting a reduction of unnecessary Latin American arms acquisitions on the one hand and on the other of realizing the dollar benefits of U.S. sales when we are unable to discourage unnecessary purchases from non-U.S. sources. A letter to this effect has been sent to Defense (Tab F).

In addition to those aspects of our policy discussed above, we have in preparation a policy guidance instruction to all of our Ambassadors on the problem presented by the increasing interest of Third Countries (both European and Latin American) in expanding their military relations with particular Latin American countries. While this matter has received considerable study and attention both Departmentally and inter-Departmentally, interagency agreement on this matter has proved difficult.

Finally, we recently sent to our Ambassadors proposals for the reorganization of our MAAG-military missions structure in Latin America, which we believe will serve to improve the capabilities of the military components of our Country Teams to achieve U.S. policy objectives. Our

---

[3] Document 106.

Ambassadors' reaction to these proposals when received will be reviewed by the LAPC as soon as all Ambassadors have submitted their comments.

In summary, while we believe our current U.S. arms policy toward Latin America is essentially sound, there are several pending issues on which there is not complete agreement within the government. In order that these may again be reviewed looking toward their resolution, they will shortly be presented in a memorandum to the Latin American Policy Committee.[4]

Robert Kent[5]

---

[4] Not found.
[5] Kent signed for Read above Read's typed signature.

THE CUBAN QUESTION IN LATIN AMERICA

109. Editorial Note

On April 23, 1961, in circular telegram 1661, the Department of State instructed all U.S. Embassies in Latin America to discuss with the highest available authorities the problems flowing from the situation in Cuba. The telegram stated that the United States considered that the situation was that of "intrusion of extra-continental power into Hemisphere menacing Hemisphere peace and security and calling for measures of Hemispheric defense, defense of neighboring countries threatened and conceivably of self-defense of US." It stated that although hemispheric defense was a matter for consideration under the Rio Treaty and other inter-American procedures, the defense of threatened countries might be the subject of unilateral or bilateral action or group agreement; if the Organization of American States failed to take multilateral action or authorize action by one or more powers, those governments, which were threatened or prepared to assume responsibility to oppose extra-continental aggression, might act singly or in concert. It drew a distinction between "'intervention' in the internal affairs of another state" and "defense against widening area of domination by extra-hemispheric powers".

The telegram instructed the recipients to "obtain and report views of government to which accredited and get feeling regarding either (1) meetings of Foreign Ministers or (2) special session OAS or (3) organization consultation Rio Treaty under Article 6 on ground capture and use of Castro government by bloc threatens security of American states and peace of Americas." It stated that the Department would carry on parallel conversations with Ambassadors in Washington. (Department of State, Central Files, 737.00/4–2361) The complete text of the telegram is printed in volume X.

The text of the Rio Treaty, or Inter-American Treaty of Reciprocal Assistance, done at Rio de Janeiro, September 2, 1947, is in 4 Bevans 559.

110. **Editorial Note**

At the 483d meeting of the National Security Council on May 5, 1961, the Council discussed U.S. policy toward Cuba and, in NSC Action No. 2422, approved by the President on May 16, took several actions relating to Cuba. In NSC Action No. 2422–k, the Council:

"Agreed that the United States should at once initiate negotiation to enlarge the willingness of other American states to join in bilateral, multilateral and OAS arrangements against Castro, such as (1) breaking diplomatic relations with Cuba; (2) controlling subversive activities of Cuban agents; (3) preventing arms shipments to Castro; (4) limiting economic relations with Cuba; (5) creating a Caribbean security force; (6) initiating a naval patrol to prevent Cuban invasion of other states in the Caribbean; and (7) denunciation of Castro as an agent of international communism by all nations of this hemisphere." (Department of State, S/S–NSC (Misc) Files: Lot 66 D 95)

The complete text of NSC Action No. 2422, along with related documents, is printed in volume X.

---

111. **Telegram From the Embassy in Colombia to the Department of State**

Bogotá, May 6, 1961, 6 p.m.

518. Embtel 506.[1] Foreign Minister visited me last evening to deliver promised memorandum on Cuban situation. Free translation follows:

"In present circumstances Colombia considers it indispensable consolidate inter-American system and make it operative rather than permit it weakened or refuse its responsibilities. If system's unity preserved and efficacy stimulated, American States can avert risks Cold War and prevent Communism's advance, penetration and infiltration in rest of hemisphere.

Within criteria making system operative it is indispensable modify impression produced among LA people and governments by abortive

---

Source: Department of State, Central Files, 737.00/5–661. Confidential; Priority.

[1] Telegram 506, April 27, reported that Foreign Minister Julio Cesar Turbay had informed the Ambassador that he would soon receive a memorandum with the Colombian Government's analysis of the Cuban situation and possible OAS action as mentioned in circular telegram 1661; see Document 109. (Department of State, Central Files, 737.00/4–2761)

Cuban invasion and by publicity giving details its preparation, organization and development. Independently of whatever act Cuba may commit in future, such as attacking American nation or intervening in internal affairs to foment revolts, which would permit rapid collective action within terms Rio Pact, Colombia conceives a procedure which would be as follows:

Convoke soonest IA–ECOSOC with object defining extent new programs and placing them in operation. Perhaps would be convenient for Foreign Ministers as well as Ministers Economy attend this meeting order enhance its political importance, reinforce contacts among themselves and commit their governments even more to execution plans for reform and social welfare. Meeting would be called to create Mistica of revitalization and progress which would permit governments obtain generous response their people for better fulfillment their national and international obligations.

Beginning now careful preparations could be initiated for FM meeting acting as organ consultation so that, soon as very bad impression caused by frustrated invasion dissipated, meeting could be convoked examine evident threats to peace deriving from present situation and to indicate measures which should be taken in face specified foreseeable acts aggression by Cuba or through her intervention against integrity and autonomy American States.

As inter-American system runs risk collapse if it proven inefficient this case or if limits itself to making non-obligatory recommendations it should not choose easy road of FM meeting under act 39 of Charter nor for meeting OAS Council which due limited competence might result in debate on procedure.

Meeting organ consultation should not take measures authorized by Rio Pact as sanctions against Cuba for events that have occurred up to now. Emphasis would be on threat American security rising from possible action of country placed within Soviet orbit. In consequence recognition these threats, organ consultation could specify various types of typical cases aggression against continental security; for example, establishment of Sino-Soviet military bases on American territory; acquisition nuclear arms; sending arms to any American country; intervention to promote subversion in another American state; aid to subversive movements against legitimate governments. In this way acts of legitimate self defense by one or various countries would be authorized in such cases and a vigilance committee could be created to denounce any activity preparatory to any of those acts defined as aggression.

Earlier or simultaneously aforementioned determinations, organ consultation should reaffirm solidarity inter-American system and its essential principles. Should declare that any country which does not submit itself to existing treaty and agreement obligations could not claim rights or prerogatives which system extends to those who live within it in good faith. Cuba should be invited abandon any military or political alliance with Sino-Soviet nations and to submit itself to system's discipline. In improbable case Cuba should accept invitation ad hoc committee created San Jose could function. If rejects invitation its attitude would serve persuade all sectors opinion of undisguised political ties between Cuba and Communist Powers.

Would not be difficult for American states reach agreement re what acts would characterize aggression in future given present conditions in hemisphere. Would be little less than impossible agree on what acts were aggression in past.

Colombia is optimistic on prospects for policy to correct common faults and error. There is no American state that has not committed them. But it is not too late to correct them nor to adopt line of conduct wedded to principles that have made OAS admirable experiment.

Ministry has given precise instructions its Ambassadors to OAS and White House order that they may have complete information re manner which Colombia conceives of how these ideas should be developed. They have authorization to deliver copy of these instructions to State Department if it so desires." *End Verbatim Text.*

After reading document Turbay urged me to transmit it in toto rather than to attempt summary. He said Salaxar Santos returning Washington Sunday night with copy memo and detailed instructions for Ambassadors Santamaria and Xuleta Angel to carry forward further consultations with Department. He appeared very anxious obtain our reactions but I begged off commenting until I had had time study document and of obtaining Department's reactions except to say I believed no added evidences of Cuban alliance with Soviet Bloc needed for OAS to tackle problem. Turbay emphasized that Santamaria authorized show Department his detailed instructions.

This GOC memo obviously prepared with full concurrence President Lleras. As matter of fact Turbay was on phone with him reading text memo when I entered his office.

Spanish text will reach Department by pouch Tuesday night.

Wells

112.   Telegram From the Department of State to the Embassy in Colombia

Washington, May 18, 1961, 10:39 p.m.

700. Re Depcirtel 1755.[1] Berle and Department officers met with Colombian White House and OAS Ambassadors May 18. Essential points Deptel 692[2] conveyed to them. Sanz[3] expressed special interest following:

1. Possible presence FonMins at Extraordinary IA ECOSOC Meeting Uruguay as means achieve informal consensus on subsequent OAS action on Cuba. He was informed Department not in position make commitment re presence Secretary; would appear essential effective advance agreement be achieved before FonMins consider Cuban problem jointly either formally or informally, and some feeling exists even peripheral consideration political aspect might prejudice outcome economic meeting.

2. Timing possible OAS action on Cuba. Sanz was informed we do not wish exclude possibility political action prior IA ECOSOC although at this moment it may appear doubtful.

3. Importance Colombians attach to view that OAS actions should be those addressed to possible Cuban aggressive acts in future and not condemnatory of past. Our view that while past cannot be ignored, important thing now is to isolate Cuban-communist danger and prevent its extension.

Sanz inquired whether there are proposals for dealing with Cuban problem other than theirs and was told we knew of none except our own and that of Venezuela[4] which now appears dormant.

Bowles

Source: Department of State, Central Files, 737.00/5–1861. Confidential. Drafted by Director of the Office of Inter-American Regional Political Affairs Edward A. Jamison, cleared by Chairman of the Task Force on Latin America Adolph A. Berle and Officer in Charge of Colombian Affairs Sam Moskowitz, and approved by Acting Assistant Secretary for Inter-American Affairs Wymberley DeR. Coerr.

[1] Circular telegram 1755, May 8, sent to all U.S. Embassies in Latin America, stated that a decision had been made "to seek as promptly as possible inter-American program to condemn, isolate, and weaken Castro regime and assist other governments to counter its subversive activity." (Ibid., 737.00/5–861) The text is printed in volume X.

[2] Telegram 692, May 15, instructed the Ambassador to give U.S. views on the Colombian proposal to the Foreign Minister. It argued that a basis for action already existed, although advance agreement would be essential and might not be immediately obtainable, and urged more specific measures than the Colombians were suggesting, but it stated that the United States did not object to Colombian consultations with other governments about their proposal. (Ibid., 737.00/5–661)

[3] Colombian Ambassador Carlos Sanz de Santamaria.

[4] The Venezuelan proposal for a meeting of Foreign Ministers to urge sanctions short of armed intervention against Cuba was reported in telegrams 3072 and 3089 from New York, dated May 9 and 11. (Department of State, Central Files, 737.00/5–961 and 737.00/5–1161, respectively)

113.   Telegram From the Department of State to the Embassy in Venezuela

Washington, May 19, 1961, 8:28 p.m.

1085. Embtel 1080.[1] Meeting May 19 with Ambassador Mayobre Berle reviewed substance Depcirtel 1755[2] and indicated problem seems to be narrowing to questions: (1) timing and procedures for MFM and (2) substantive actions to be taken. Said might be disadvantages mixing political question with objectives Montevideo meeting IA–ECOSOC and consensus necessary for meaningful action prior July 15 seems unlikely. Expressed view attitudes LA Governments and public opinion must be allowed jell favor multilateral action respect Castro.

Berle mentioned Colombian proposals of which Venezuelans aware and said appears most LA Governments could agree course compatible thinking Betancourt, Lleras Camargo and US. Exceptions Brazil, Mexico, Ecuador and Chile. Suggested Gov might help persuade Brazil and perhaps others adopt more positive viewpoints.

Bowles

Source: Department of State, Central Files, 737.00/5–1861. Secret; Priority; Limit Distribution. Drafted by Officer in Charge of Venezuelan Affairs John J. Ingersoll, cleared by Jamison and Berle, and approved by Director of the Office of the East Coast Affairs Harvey R. Wellman. Repeated to USUN for Stevenson.

[1] Telegram 1080 from Caracas, dated May 18, reported that President Betancourt had decided that a Foreign Ministers meeting on the Cuban problem should be postponed until after the IA–ECOSOC meeting. (Ibid., 737.00/5–1861)

[2] See footnote 1, Document 112.

---

114.   Circular Telegram From the Department of State to All Posts in the American Republics

Washington, June 24, 1961, 6:47 p.m.

2094. FYI. Colombian President Lleras Camargo in May gave USG note and memorandum containing considered analysis Cuban problem

---

Source: Department of State, Central Files, 737.00/6–2461. Confidential. Drafted by William G. Bowdler of the Office of Inter-American Regional Political Affairs and approved by Coerr. Repeated to USUN and to CINCARIB for POLAD.

and offering specific course of action for dealing with it. Additional memorandum elaborating proposal given Stevenson on recent trip.[1] Copies being airpouched.

Essential points Colombian analysis are:

(1) Record which led to Cuba's "formal introduction into Soviet orbit" is paralleled by series US unilateral measures culminating in support invasion attempt.

(2) Internal political situations and public opinion on Cuban problem in LA affected in manner which prevents governmental support effective OAS punitive action.

(3) US should reject unilateral action and "force regional organization to act." OAS action program on Cuba should deal with present and future and not with past.

(4) Essential that OAS action deal with strengthening inter-American system for future by demonstrating its ability deal with problems of underdevelopment as well as security.

(5) Alliance for Progress and Rio Treaty collective measures offer means for accomplishing these objectives. For present priority must be given to social and economic progress, unless Cubans commit major provocative acts such as attack or intervention which would call for immediate OAS action.

Colombian proposals contemplate specific program which includes following:

(1) Successful IA ECOSOC Ministerial Meeting as indispensable to creation propitious atmosphere for subsequent MFM under Rio Treaty on Cuba. Position that USG adopts to assist LAs accelerate economic development and radically improve social conditions will be "absolutely decisive." Amount assistance required and clarification criteria under which it will be granted important. Equally or more important is action improve and stabilize prices of LA basic commodities because any new weakening of prices will "completely" annul USG monetary aid.

(2) Shortly after IA ECOSOC meeting there would be convoked Meeting of Foreign Ministers (MFM) under Rio Treaty with these objectives:

a. Examine political and juridical obligations inter-American system and reaffirm intention of American States strictly adhere to them.

---

[1] A copy of the memorandum that Lleras Camargo gave Stevenson on June 21 is in the Princeton University, Seeley G. Mudd Manuscript Library, Stevenson Papers, Previously Embargoed Files, Box 2, Cuba. For Stevenson's report to the President on his June 4–22 trip to South America, including his summary of South American views concerning a possible Foreign Ministers meeting, see Document 14. Information on his visit to Colombia is in telegram 638 from Bogota, June 21, and despatch 806 from Bogota, June 27. (Department of State, Central Files, 721.00/6–2161 and 120.1520/6–2761, respectively)

b. Examine incompatibility inter-American system with policy of neutralism toward threats posed to system or individual member by direct or indirect aggressive action international communism.

c. Declare that in event any such aggressive actions or threats of aggression are substantiated by OAS vigilance committee would justify automatic intervention by inter-American system.

3. Pursuant these objectives, MFM would adopt three basic resolutions:

a. First would contain synthesis meaning inter-American system and obligations and rights its members; reaffirm intention states respect all obligations; imply that state which failed respect obligations would voluntarily place itself outside system; affirm "that any irrevocable attachment of American State to Communist orbit would be incompatible with OAS obligations". Accompanying resolution would invite Cuba abandon ties with Sino-Soviet bloc (manner not specified).

b. Second would make clear that inter-American system does not permit neutralist position in face of threats to system or one of its members and that intervention international communism constitutes permanent threat to hemisphere peace and security.

c. Third would specify certain acts which would constitute aggression or threats aggression within terms of Articles 6 and 9 or Rio Treaty including: establishment of Sino-Soviet military bases on American territory, acquisition of nuclear weapons from Communist bloc, sending Communist bloc arms to any American state to promote subversion in other American states (sic), support to subversive movements which seek to overthrow legitimate governments and establish communist regimes. OAS vigilance committee would be set up to watch situation and convoke Organ of Consultation on perceiving threats to peace and security of hemisphere.

Colombian analysis and proposals being given immediate careful study. GOC has already discussed initiative with various LA governments. Foreign Minister Turbay currently on trip to Panama, Brazil and Chile to enlist support. Action requested: Treat this material on Colombian initiative as background. Report any local reaction. Instructions will follow. End FYI.

Rusk

115. Memorandum of Conversation

SecDel/MC/43   New York, September 25, 1961, 1 p.m.

SECRETARY'S DELEGATION TO THE SIXTEENTH SESSION OF THE UNITED NATIONS GENERAL ASSEMBLY
New York, September 19–24, 1961

PARTICIPANTS

US   *Colombia*
President Kennedy   Ambassador Turbay[1]

SUBJECT

Lleras Plan

Before the Secretary's lunch today for the Latin Americans, there was a short exchange of views between President Kennedy and Ambassador Turbay (Colombia). The President was interested in the progress of the Lleras Plan. Ambassador Turbay said it consisted of three resolutions, designed to test Cuba's willingness to conform to and remain within the Inter-American System. His exposition of this substance was as he gave it to Secretary Rusk on September 22.[2] The texts had not yet come from Bogota.

Ambassador Turbay then said he hoped the President would speak of the Plan to President Frondizi, since Turbay had the impression the Argentine position was not as clear as it had seemed to be. President Kennedy asked whether in Ambassador Turbay's opinion a conference of Foreign Ministers could or should be called. The reply was that unless Argentina, Brazil, and Ecuador were in line (it was useless to hope Mexico would be), the bulk of the OAS members would abstain. It was true that if fourteen members were in agreement on a subject, the rest had to go along, but in this case, without these key members' approval, there would not be fourteen votes. President Kennedy inquired whether Argentina was the key to this problem. Turbay replied in the affirmative,

---

Source: Department of State, Conference Files: Lot 65 D 366, CF 1957. Confidential. No drafting information appears on the source text. Approved by the White House on October 3. The conversation took place before a luncheon at the Waldorf Astoria. The time and place are taken from Kennedy's Appointment Book. (Kennedy Library)
    [1] Former Foreign Minister Turbay.
    [2] Turbay met with Rusk on September 21 and 22. Memoranda of the conversations are in Department of State, Conference Files: Lot 65 D 366, CF 1957.

saying good support by Argentina would surely bring Brazil and probably Ecuador along.[3]

President Kennedy expressed the U.S. appreciation for Colombia's and Ambassador Turbay's initiative in the Cuban matter.

---

[3] Kennedy raised the subject on September 26 with Frondizi, who was noncommittal but indicated that a meeting of consultation might be possible in early 1962. (Ibid., Central Files, 720.5–MSP/9–2761) A memorandum of the conversation is printed in volume X.

---

116. Memorandum of Conversation

SecDel/MC/45   New York, September 25, 1961, 5:30 p.m.

SECRETARY'S DELEGATION TO THE SIXTEENTH SESSION OF THE UNITED NATIONS GENERAL ASSEMBLY
New York, September 1961

PARTICIPANTS

US	Brazil
The Secretary	Amb. Afonso Arinos de Melo Franco
Mr. Achilles	Minister Geraldo de Carvalho Silos
Mr. Woodward	
Mr. Braddock	

SUBJECT

Situation in Brazil and Brazilian Attitude toward Cuban Problem

The Secretary opened the conversation by asking how Brazil was adjusting to the change in its Constitution and its Government. Ambassador Arinos launched into a lengthy discussion of Brazil's constitutional form. He said that Brazil followed more the Greek concept of the state than the Anglo-Saxon and that whereas in the latter the idea was to defend the citizen against the government, in the former it was to integrate him with the state. He said that in Brazil the President is not elected by political parties or institutions (there being twelve political parties) but rather by a plebescite of the people. The President, therefore, feels

---

Source: Department of State, Conference Files: Lot 65 D 366, CF 1957. Confidential. Drafted by Braddock, cleared in draft with Achilles, and approved in S on September 27. The conversation was held at the U.S. Mission to the United Nations.

responsibility to the mass rather than to any institutional groups. Congress, on the other hand, is made up of representatives chosen by parties or other specific organizations. Congress, therefore, tends to be more moderate in its views than does the President.

With this as a background, Ambassador Arinos said that Brazil was experiencing little difficulty in adapting itself to the sudden constitutional and governmental change. He mentioned that Goulart drew much of his strength from his home state of Rio Grande do Sul and from the labor unions, of which he was a national official.

The Secretary asked whether in Brazil, which had great problems and great potentialities, the government did not concentrate more on internal matters than on external. The Ambassador thought this was generally true and stated that the President, and now also the Prime Minister, were so involved with domestic problems and administration that they left the conduct of foreign affairs largely to the Foreign Minister. He said that Brazil did work closely with some of its smaller, weaker neighbors, particularly Paraguay and Bolivia, to help them toward greater economic and political stability. Brazil exercised with them a role, he said, not too unlike that which the United States exercised toward Latin American countries, including Brazil.

The Secretary asked whether it was not difficult to conduct foreign affairs from Rio with the President located in Brasilia. Ambassador Arinos answered in the affirmative. He said that the Foreign Office had forty members of its staff in Brasilia and five hundred in Rio, and that all of the archives and files were in Rio. He thought that coordination with the President's office might be improved by the recent creation of a new position of Under Secretary of Foreign Affairs in Brasilia, which is filled by a member of Congress.

The Secretary brought the conversation gradually around to the subject of Cuba and sought to find out how Brazil viewed the Cuban problem. Ambassador Arinos said that Cuba under Castro was pro-Communist and against the Church, whereas Brazil was anti-Communist and very Catholic. He said that Brazil had some Communists but that thus far they had not gained any ascendency in the drive to relieve human misery in Brazil, notwithstanding the influence of Castro and the Cuban revolution. The Secretary observed that the modern history of the United States was proof that democratic institutions could meet the need for social and economic change and that we did not concede any superiority to the Communists on this point.

Ambassador Arinos stated that Brazil was opposed to intervention and felt that the attitude that should be taken toward Cuba was to try to bring it back as a full member of the American system rather than to put it outside. Asked by the Secretary whether he thought Cuba could be brought back, the Ambassador said that there was a remote chance that it could, provided Cuba were permitted to retain the positive accomplishments of its revolution and were given assurances of assistance with its economic and social problems. The deterioration of the Cuban economy would work in favor of this course, he said.

The Secretary asked what the Ambassador thought of the proposals made by President Lleras with regard to Cuba. The Ambassador said that inasmuch as these proposals were aimed at trying to bring Cuba back into the family, they were fairly close to the thinking of the Brazilian government. He gave no other indication as to whether the Brazilian government would endorse or support the Colombian initiative, or whether he believed that this course was worth pursuing. When asked by the Secretary what he thought about the possible convocation of a meeting of Foreign Ministers, he seemed surprised and asked for what purpose the meeting would be called. The Secretary answered that a meeting if called would be in connection with the Colombian initiative. The Ambassador appeared somewhat relieved but not entirely reassured.

The Secretary said that Cuba represented not just one problem for us but several. There was the problem of Cuba itself. There was the problem of Cuban-U.S. relations. There was the problem of Cuba's efforts to undermine other governments. There was the problem of Cuba as a member of the Organization of American States. And there was the effect of the Cuban problem on American public opinion. Unless the Organization of American States could find a way to deal with the problem, it was to be feared that the American public would lose faith in the Organization. The Secretary explained that in saying this he was thinking not of particular sanctions by the OAS but of recognition by the OAS of the existence and seriousness of the Cuban problem and of a serious effort to deal with it.

117.   Circular Telegram From the Department of State to All Posts in the American Republics

Washington, October 17, 1961, 8:41 p.m.

721. Request by Peru for application Rio Treaty to Cuban situation[1] has precipitated showdown this issue in OAS at time and under circumstances not of Department's choosing. Issue having been planted, however, particularly in such well-reasoned challenging terms as contained Peruvian OAS Representative's statement (Depcirtel 718),[2] Department believes best strategy is endeavor combine surprise Peruvian initiative with Colombian initiative and rally maximum support, including most of large LA states.

In theory easy combine two initiatives. Both contemplate action under Rio Treaty. Peruvian seeks appointment by COAS, acting provisionally as Organ of Consultation, of Investigating Committee to go to Cuba to investigate series of acts falling under categories violation human rights, subversive activities abroad and rejection inter-American commitments by association Sino-Soviet bloc, and submit report. Peruvian initiative does not specifically contemplate further action beyond this, but logical next step would be for meeting Organ of Consultation (i.e. Meeting of Foreign Ministers) to adopt resolutions, based on findings of Committee, along lines of those proposed by Colombia.

In practice may not be so easy combine two proposals and achieve same degree support which Colombian alone might have obtained. Indications are however that President Lleras looking upon situation created by Peruvian initiative realistically and desirous work out combination to move ahead rapidly. Department consulting Colombians and Peruvians on feasibility and best manner coordinate their initiatives.

If queried re US position you may state:

1. USG believes Peruvian proposal and its sound well-reasoned supporting statement warrant most careful consideration.

Source: Department of State, Central Files, 371.05/10–1761. Confidential; Priority. Drafted by Bowdler and Jamison; cleared by William Barnes, John H. Crimmins, Alton W. Hemba, and Samuel O. Lane, Deputy Directors of the Offices of Central American and Panamanian Affairs, Caribbean and Mexican Affairs, East Coast Affairs, and West Coast Affairs, respectively; and approved by Coerr. Repeated to Ciudad Trujillo, POLAD CINCLANT, POLAD SACLANT, and USUN.

[1] Circular telegram 712, October 14, reported that Peru had requested a special meeting of the OAS Council relating to the Cuban situation; the Department had had no advance notice of the move and was considering how it might affect the Colombian initiative. (Ibid., 371.05/10–1461)

[2] Dated October 16. (Ibid., 371.05/10–1661)

2. Of utmost importance any move in COAS on Cuban issue clearly constitutes forward step and not be subject to interpretation OAS inactive or negative on Cuban problem.

3. We are developing views on best means for insuring coordinated OAS steps to contribute to steady progression in OAS action.[3]

Rusk

---

[3] On October 25 the OAS Council voted 19–1, with 1 abstention, to refer the Peruvian initiative to Council's General Committee. The decision was a compromise, worked out after it became clear that the Council was divided. Documentation on this subject is ibid., 371.05 and 737.00.

---

118.   Memorandum From the Acting Assistant Secretary of State for Inter-American Affairs (Coerr) to the Under Secretary of State for Economic Affairs (Ball)

Washington, November 4, 1961.

Problem

To determine U.S. action on the Colombian Proposal regarding Cuba in the OAS.

Discussion

The Peruvian initiative calling for Rio Treaty action on the Cuban situation has, in combination with its resultant publicity and Colombian activities on behalf of its own initiative, put the OAS under strong pressure to decide whether or not it will face up to the Cuban issue. There is an increasing belief that the OAS cannot sidestep the problem much longer without grave loss of confidence and prestige.

The Colombians are actively consulting other governments to determine potential support for their plan to convene a Meeting of Foreign Ministers (see Tab A for brief summary).[1] They believe they have at least fourteen votes—the two-thirds majority required for substantive action—and are hoping to add one or two of the larger countries. The Colombians probably will not move from the stage of consultations to

---

Source: Department of State, Central Files, 737.00/11–461. Confidential. Drafted by Coerr, Bowdler, and Jamison and cleared in the Legal Adviser's Office.

[1] The tabs are not printed.

action in the OAS in the face of the united opposition of the large Latin American countries. We have encouraged them at a high level and consistently in the last few months to pursue their plan, and have informed the other Latin Americans of our basic agreement with its objectives. They consider they have our backing and may be expected to ask for our active support at any time.

We have two courses of action:

1. Limit ourselves to action now being taken on the Peruvian proposal, pressing for investigation by the Inter-American Peace Committee and similar action by the Inter-American Human Rights Commission and withhold at this time the strong U.S. support for the Colombian proposal.

2. Combine with the above action on the Peruvian proposal close cooperation with the Colombians and, should they request it, strongly support the Colombian proposal in talks with all Latin American governments and especially Argentina, Brazil, and Chile.

The first course would avoid a formal showdown on Cuba and would offer some faint appearance of anti-Cuban activity in the OAS. In ARA's opinion, however, this course of action would be so weak as to constitute a clear victory for Cuba.

The second course would run the risk of committing the U.S. to a line of action that might be thwarted by the opposition of several of the larger Latin American countries. This could resolve in a psychological victory for Castro but we believe such a victory would be, although more dramatic, no greater than the one he would gain through continued OAS failure to act affirmatively on the Cuban issue in the face of Peruvian and Colombian initiatives. ARA believes that the issue has been joined in the OAS and that we should take advantage of the momentum started by the impulse of the Peruvian and Colombian proposals by giving our full support to the Colombian effort to gain maximum Latin American backing for the Colombian Plan. We believe that the vigor, tact and timing of our effort will have a substantial effect on the vote, especially if nations now doubtful or opposed are given to understand that the United States is determined to bring the issue to a vote.

The various considerations discussed above are described in greater detail in Tab B.

Recommendation

That you approve the second course of action.[2]

---

[2] Ball approved this recommendation on November 6.

119.   **Memorandum From the Representative to the Council of the Organization of American States (Morrison) to the Assistant Secretary of State for Inter-American Affairs (Woodward)**

Washington, November 15, 1961.

Following extensive personal conversations with a large number of OAS Ambassadors in Kansas City during Friday and Saturday of last week, I have come to the conclusion that we have an excellent chance of getting a vote ranging from 13 to 16—first in favor of calling the meeting of Foreign Ministers and next getting some type of effective action regarding the Cuban issue. In my opinion, this is the most important success that the Kennedy Administration can achieve in foreign policy. By the same token, if we fail, it could be a definite loss for the Administration and, of course, for the U.S. people.

I know that Brazil has gone to work energetically doing missionary work to achieve a negative vote. Although the Mexican Ambassador has stated to me that they will not make a campaign and will be "fatalistic" about having this meeting that they do not want, still we have to realize that these two nations are going to press hard to defeat the Colombian proposal,[1] delay it or "pigeon-hole" it.

My point is we have to act quickly with all resources at our command. I say "quickly" because I am sure that already the Brazilian Foreign Minister is working energetically on Uruguay, Argentina and Chile. These are three countries that with extensive, timely action on our part will support the Colombian proposal. But all concerned must be impressed with the necessity for needed and timely effort to be put forth now in reaching not only the Foreign Ministers but also the Chiefs of State. OAS Ambassador Rivarola (Argentina) stated that he had personally recommended to his government support of the Colombian proposal. OAS Ambassador Clulow (Uruguay) feels the same way. My fear is that before we get our missionary work underway, we may find that as a result of Brazilian urging these three countries may be induced to "play the delaying game" or take a neutral position. In my opinion, Uruguay, Argentina and Chile (the difference between 13 assured and 16 votes) are the key to our diplomatic success and likewise if the situation is ultimately unfavorable, the reason for diplomatic defeat.

I would recommend that you show this memo to Mr. Ball and also to Mr. Goodwin.

Source: Department of State, Central Files, 737.00/11–1561. Confidential. Drafted by Morrison. A note attached to the source text indicates that the memorandum was sent to Ball. Copies were also sent to Coerr, Jamison, Hartwick, and Crimmins.

[1] At the OAS Council meeting on November 14, the Colombian representative presented a request to convoke a meeting of Foreign Ministers under the Rio Treaty. The Council was scheduled to meet on December 4 to consider and act upon the Colombian request.

120.   Telegram From the Embassy in Argentina to the Department of State

Buenos Aires, November 22, 1961, 7 p.m.

905. At lunch today Under Secretary of Foreign Affairs Camilion said GOA not in accord use Article VI Rio Treaty and believes action on Cuba should be under OAS Charter (Article 39). Reaffirmed other points made in Embtel 898.[1] GOA talking to both Brazil and Cuba [*Chile*]. Says latter two will both vote against calling MFM under present Colombian initiative and GOA would probably do so also. GOA impressed and agrees with Mexican arguments against Colombian initiative on juridical grounds.

Camilion said December 4 date too early and that it might be possible convene December 4 and then declare recess until full consultations can be held. He did not answer categorically my question as to whether GOA prepared take action at this time on Cuba if consultations could be held but instead referred back to need for consultations. Camilion stressed GOA not interested whether its name appears in connection with new proposals but very obvious to me this question of thou dost protest too much and the GOA very much interested in being in the forefront of any proposals.

Hoyt

Source: Department of State, Central Files, 737.00/11–2261. Confidential; Priority. Repeated to Bogotá, Rio de Janeiro, and Santiago.

[1] Telegram 898, November 21, reported on a meeting between Senator Hubert Humphrey and Foreign Minister Carcano, in which the latter stressed that Frondizi wanted to talk to a high-level U.S. emissary during his forthcoming visit to Trinidad. (Ibid., 737.00/11–2161)

121. Circular Telegram From the Department of State to All Posts in the American Republics

Washington, November 30, 1961, 2:30 p.m.

1028. Secretary and Woodward today informed Argentine Foreign Minister in Canada of acceptability to President Lleras of compromise formula suggested by Argentines to Stevenson at Trinidad November 26–27.[1] Argentine formula calls for COAS decision December 4:

1. Agree that MFM be held;
2. That COAS decide before December 31 (a) whether meeting to be held under Article 6 Rio Treaty or Article 39 OAS Charter; (b) date and place of MFM.

Following was clearly understood as part of formula: (a) Argentina would vote favorably this resolution and obtain support other LA governments. FYI. Argentina would concentrate Chile Uruguay Brazil and if feasible Mexico. End FYI. If support for Argentine formula should prove to be limited, US would have to weigh carefully possible advisability of return to full support Colombian initiative under Rio Treaty; (b) period between December 4 and 31 would be used to reach agreement on whether MFM would be convoked pursuant Rio Treaty or OAS Charter and to seek maximum possible advance agreement on substantive action to be taken at MFM in hopes this would be sufficient to obtain support of practically all member governments. Should there be apprehension lest US abandoning view that Rio Treaty applicable you should make it clear that we continue to believe nature of threat such that it clearly falls within terms Rio Treaty Article 6.

Argentine Foreign Minister told Secretary he would immediately have Argentine embassies take up formula with OARS, particularly Brazil Chile Uruguay, while Argentine Ambassadors to White House and OAS would discuss formula with LA Ambassadors Washington. Secretary agreed we would support Argentine formula with countries that already have indicated support Colombian proposal or favor stronger action but effective outcome will depend primarily on Argentine initiative this matter. Woodward urged Foreign Minister come Washington work on this matter with Colombian Foreign Minister due arrive here

Source: Department of State, Central Files, 371.05/11–3061. Confidential; Niact. Drafted by Jamison and Bowdler; cleared by Bracken, Crimmins, Wellman, and Director of the Office of West Coast Affairs Taylor G. Belcher; approved by Woodward. Repeated to USUN, Ciudad Trujillo, POLAD CINCARIB, and POLAD SACLANT.

[1] A memorandum of Stevenson's meeting with Frondizi is filed ibid., 737.00/11–2761. Telegram 346 from Bogotá, dated November 28, reported that Ambassador Freeman had presented the compromise formula to Lleras and that the latter had agreed to the formula with some modifications. (Ibid., 737.00/11–2861)

November 30 or December 1. Foreign Minister said he would consult immediately with Argentine Ambassadors to White House and OAS as well as President Frondizi on this point.

FYI. We have acquiesced in Argentine move in expectation achieving equally good substance of OAS action on Cuba with more support than that contemplated Colombian proposal, including possibly even Brazil and Mexico. Other factors are real or dissembled disgruntlement indicated by several governments, with Argentina in lead, over precipitate formal presentation Colombian proposal to COAS (Depcirtel 997)[2] and alleged lack prior consultation on exact texts Colombian draft resolutions. Views other governments so far received on substance resolutions, except for Mexico and on one or two important points Brazil (both of which obviously would prefer no MFM) do not reveal major differences on type of anticipated MFM substantive action and some of these views appear essentially constructive. End FYI.

Request you seek earliest opportunity convey foregoing orally to President or Foreign Minister. Report reaction soonest.

Rusk

---

[2] Dated November 24. (Ibid., 371.05/11–2461)

---

122.   Circular Telegram From the Department of State to All Posts in the American Republics

Washington, December 3, 1961, 5:11 p.m.

1047. Depcirtels 1028[1] and 1041.[2] Consultations here clearly show Argentine formula has failed to add support deemed essential and in particular has not proved acceptable Brazil, Chile and Mexico. Under

---

Source: Department of State, Central Files, 371.05/12–361. Confidential; Niact. Drafted by Bowdler and Jamison; cleared by Crimmins and in draft by Woodward; approved by Jamison. Repeated to USUN, Ciudad Juarez, POLAD CINCARIB, and POLAD SACLANT.

[1] Document 121.

[2] Circular telegram 1041, December 1, sent to 13 Embassies in Latin America, instructed them to make it clear that unless the Argentine formula could obtain a "substantial majority" in the OAS Council on December 4, the United States would support the Colombian proposal. (Department of State, Central Files, 371.05/12–161)

these circumstances GUS returning full support Colombian proposal convoke MFM under Rio Treaty on which vote will be taken COAS meeting afternoon December 4.

Request you inform President or FonMin of foregoing if you deem it appropriate and useful, stressing importance we attach to favorable vote, particularly in light Castro's recent public admission he confirmed Marxist-Leninist who deliberately deceived and used non-communists to gain his ends, as well as because of regime's alignment Sino-Soviet bloc; also if necessary expressing our hope COAS Delegations will be given instructions support Colombian request convocation MFM under Rio Treaty.[3]

Rusk

---

[3] On December 4 the OAS Council approved a resolution convoking a meeting of consultation of Foreign Ministers under Articles 6 and 11 of the Rio Treaty. The vote was 14–2 with 5 abstentions. The text of the resolution is in *American Foreign Policy: Current Documents, 1961*, pp. 323–324.

---

123. Circular Telegram From the Department of State to All Posts in the American Republics

Washington, December 11, 1961, 7:41 p.m.

1104. Colombian FonMin while in Washington recently (Depcirtel 1079)[1] stated Colombian Embassies would be instructed take up soonest with respective governments substance Colombian draft resolutions, copies of which he said had been handed to Foreign Ministries in all countries with which Colombia has diplomatic relations. (Mentioned possibility special mission to Guatemala.) Requested our support Colombian-USUN [New York] efforts achieve maximum possible agreement these drafts.

Source: Department of State, Central Files, 371.05/12–1161. Confidential. Drafted by Jamison; cleared by Whiteman, Bracken, Hemba, Lane, and Crimmins; and approved by Woodward. Repeated to USUN, POLAD CINCARIB, and POLAD SACLANT.

[1] Circular telegram 1079, December 7, summarized a meeting between Woodward and Colombian Foreign Minister Caicedo Castilla. (Ibid., 371.04/12–761)

USG has proposed certain changes Colombian projects, circulated in English (CW–4207)[2] and summarized Depcirtel 952.[3] Furthermore events since drafts prepared, particularly Castro December 1 identification himself and regime as Marxist-Leninist, strongly suggest drafts require strengthening or change in certain respects as outlined second paragraph Depcirtel 1079.[4] Specific suggestions this effect being made to Colombians.

Request you approach FonOff soonest, coordinating your approach with Colombian colleague where appropriate, and report our firm support for essentials Colombian proposals, as well as our feeling that in certain respects they now require strengthening. If question raised, you should make it clear that we do not in present circumstance plan raise question application specific Art 8 measures (i.e. sanctions). Request you inquire as to acceptability Colombian drafts to FonOff and elicit any suggestions they propose to make for amendment. Make clear we not necessarily seeking definitive views but interested at least in preliminary reaction as means initiating consultations on Colombian drafts.

Ball

---

[2] Not found.

[3] Circular telegram 952, November 16. (Department of State, Central Files, 371.05/11–1661)

[4] Woodward told Caicedo that in the U.S. view Castro's speech made it advisable to consider. "(1) ways make more specific exact nature Castro-communist danger; (2) advisability changing 'invitation' to Cuba to break Sino-Soviet ties to firmer call or demand; and (3) definition specific steps which would be required for Cuba demonstrate conclusively compliance with that call." He also suggested that the MFM might authorize the OAS Council to observe and report on Cuban compliance with the above-mentioned call and to recommend possible action in case of compliance or non-compliance.

124. Memorandum of Conversation

Caracas, December 16, 1961, 5:15 p.m.

SUBJECT

Conference Between President Kennedy and Venezuelan President
Betancourt—Cuban Problem—OAS Foreign Ministers Meeting

PARTICIPANTS

The President
Ambassador Chester Bowles
Mr. C. Allan Stewart, Chargé d'Affaires ad interim
Mr. Robert F. Woodward, Assistant Secretary of State for Inter-American Affairs
Mr. Teodoro Moscoso, Assistant Administrator for Latin America of the Agency
    for International Development
Mr. Richard Goodwin, Deputy Assistant Secretary of State for Latin American
    Affairs
Mr. Harold Linder, President of Export-Import Bank of Washington
Mr. Fernando van Reigersberg, LS staff interpreter

President Romulo Betancourt of Venezuela
Dr. Marcos Falcón Briceño, Foreign Minister of Venezuela
Dr. Andres German Otero, Minister of Finance of Venezuela
General Antonio Briceño Linares, Minister of Defense of Venezuela
Dr. Jose Antonio Mayobre, Venezuelan Ambassador to the United States
Dr. Alejandro Oropeza Castillo, Governor of the Federal District of Venezuela
Dr. Manuel Perez Guerrero, Chief, Office of Coordination and Planning,
    Venezuelan Government

The meeting convened at 5:15 p.m. on December 16, 1961, at Los
Nuñez, President Betancourt's residence in Caracas, Venezuela. Several
unrelated matters were discussed at this conference, including the subject covered in this memorandum.[1]

Cuban Problem—OAS Foreign Ministers Meeting

President Kennedy brought into the conversation the OAS Foreign
Ministers' Meeting (MFM) scheduled on January 10 to deal with the
Cuban problem. He said the Panamanian Government had offered Panama City as site for the Meeting but had indicated that circumstances
made it necessary to hold the meeting in February. President Kennedy
asked President Betancourt whether a delay would be advisable or
whether the meeting should be held as scheduled in the Pan American
Union headquarters in Washington.

Source: Department of State, Central Files, 737.00/12–1661. Secret. Drafted by Stewart, van Reigersberg, and Moskowitz. Approved in the White House on February 6. President Kennedy traveled to Venezuela December 16 and 17.

[1] See Document 334. Other memoranda of conversation are in Department of State,
Conference Files: Lot 65 D 366, CF 2016.

President Betancourt replied that he had discussed this point with Foreign Minister Falcón Briceño and Ambassador Mayobre and had concluded that the important point was not the site but whether the necessary two-thirds votes could be obtained to vote sanctions against the Castro regime. He said the Governments of Colombia and Venezuela were working a "pincers" movement against Ecuador. He had written a letter to the Ecuadorean President and might send an emissary to converse with President Arosemena about changing his country's policy in favor of voting sanctions. He is also considering a possible trip to Venezuela by the Ecuadorean President.

President Betancourt added that when President Frondizi of Argentina stopped briefly in Venezuela he was of the opinion that Argentina planned to vote favorably for the Meeting of Foreign Ministers, but actually had abstained.

President Betancourt also said that as a result of a trip of President López Mateos of Mexico to Caracas, personal contact was established between the two Presidents. The Government of Venezuela was considering the possibility of sending a special envoy to Mexico in order to try to convince that country to modify its stand vis-à-vis Cuba. Of course, there were internal political factors and a traditional attitude on the part of the Mexican Foreign Ministry that would make such a change extremely difficult to achieve.

When President Kennedy asked again whether the timing of the MFM was vital President Betancourt responded that time was not as important as having the necessary 14 votes.

President Kennedy expressed the view, which was corroborated by Assistant Secretary Woodward, that it would be difficult to obtain a resolution imposing sanctions on Cuba but thought that one would pass asking the Castro regime to sever its ties with the Sino-Soviet bloc and return to the inter-American family. He felt that the strongest possible resolution should be passed.

President Betancourt agreed with this. He added that Venezuela would vote for sanctions or for any other resolution such as the one that had just been indicated by the President. President Betancourt observed that the resolution against the Dominican Republic, voted at San José, did not go very far but it was of great moral assistance in paving the way for downfall of the Trujillo regime.

President Kennedy asked for Mr. Woodward's comments on the MFM meeting and the latter stated that it was not likely Chile, Brazil, Argentina, Mexico and possibly Bolivia and Ecuador would vote for strong sanctions. Mr. Woodward thought that we should support the Colombian resolution strongly and attempt to pin down Castro to break with the Sino-Soviet bloc or face sanctions.

At this point President Betancourt observed that any unilateral action against Cuba would destroy the inter-American system and President Kennedy assured him the United States did not intend to take unilateral action against the Castro government.

President Kennedy added that the United States hoped to get as strong a resolution against Cuba as it was possible to get; but even if one calling only for a break with the Sino-Soviets were obtained, it is certain Castro would refuse to do so and thus place Cuba in a most difficult position. He said if we lower our aim from the outset the final result might well be a watered-down resolution that would not be very effective. Perhaps we would not be able to agree on sanctions at this meeting but we could lay the groundwork for them in the future. Castro will obviously reject the OAS request and his refusal could be the basis for another Meeting of Foreign Ministers later on. Because it will take some time to line up the necessary votes and the Christmas holidays are near, President Kennedy expressed the view that the February meeting was most logical.

Mr. Woodward added that President Kennedy would have an opportunity on December 17 to obtain President Lleras Camargo's judgment on the timing of the meeting and the type of resolution which could be obtained. President Kennedy said Mr. Woodward would stay an extra day in Bogotá to go over the proposed resolutions which are to be presented at the MFM meeting. He thought the revised drafts would be ready for consideration in 10 days.

President Betancourt stated that Venezuela would support strong action against Cuba but cautioned that it might be necessary to go by easy stages, as was done with the Dominican Republic. He expressed the conviction that Castro's days were numbered and he based this on his residence in that country for two years. Castro has insulted everyone and brought about rupture of relations with most of the OAS members. He said that the resistance movement in Cuba must be strongly supported and Venezuela is so doing within its resources. President Betancourt indicated that the situation in Cuba is different from that in the Soviet Union because the Cuban people had known freedom and the Russians never have. He hoped that the Cuban people will eventually be able to get rid of Communism. Any unilateral action on the part of the United States would be extremely harmful.

President Kennedy replied that the police system in Cuba was very powerful and that it would make it difficult for the Cubans to revolt. On the other hand, the United States would not act unilaterally but only on a hemisphere-wide basis. In view of Castro's recent speeches and of the economic and social structure he was trying to impose on Cuba it would seem that it would be difficult for the Latin American governments to oppose a resolution that urged Castro to return to the inter-American family of nations. Castro has shown himself to be a Communist rather than a great American revolutionary leader. President Kennedy thought it would not be likely that Castro would return to the inter-American family and therefore action against his regime would be easier once he had refused to break his ties with the Sino-Soviet bloc.

President Betancourt expressed his total agreement with the President's views.

125.   Memorandum of Conversation

Bogotá, December 17, 1961, 5:30 p.m.

SUBJECT

Developments in the Dominican Republic Planning for Foreign Ministers' Meeting on Cuban Problem

PARTICIPANTS

U.S.	Colombia
President Kennedy	President Lleras Camargo
Mr. Chester Bowles, President's	Foreign Minister Caicedo Castilla
Special Assistant	Minister of Finance Mejia
Ambassador Moscoso	Director of National Planning Dept.
Assistant Secretary Woodward	Gutierrez
Deputy Assistant Secretary Goodwin	
Ambassador Freeman	
Mr. Henry Dearborn, Counselor of	
American Embassy, Bogota	

President Kennedy called at President Lleras's office at 5:30 p.m. on December 17. Each President was accompanied by advisers as recorded above. Press photographers were invited in and pictures taken. President Kennedy then suggested that the group sit down for conversations and the Presidents, together with their advisers, held a discussion for over an hour.

[Here follows discussion concerning the Dominican Republic; see Document 335.]

Source: Department of State, Conference Files: Lot 65 D 366, CF 2016. Confidential. Drafted by Dearborn on December 20 and approved by the White House on January 8, 1962.

Planning for Foreign Ministers' Meeting on Cuban Problem

The Presidents devoted most of their conversation to the pending Foreign Ministers' Meeting to consider the Cuban problem. The points discussed were: 1) the timing of the Meeting; 2) the place where it should be held; 3) the need for additional support; and, to some extent, 4) the substance of the resolutions to be presented.

President Kennedy raised the question of timing. President Lleras stated that before President Kennedy went to Venezuela and Colombia he favored holding the Meeting on January 10, as proposed earlier. Since the visits, and owing to their extraordinary success, he was even more firmly opposed to postponement. He thought the momentum derived from the visits should not be lost. President Kennedy agreed and said that preparations should be aimed at an early holding of the conference. He said that Ambassador Woodward and Mr. Goodwin would remain in Bogota for another day to join Ambassador Freeman in an effort to reach an agreement with Foreign Minister Caicedo and President Lleras on the texts of the resolutions to be presented.

In considering where the Meeting might be held, President Lleras stated that he was not one of those who was worried about adverse reactions if Washington should be chosen as the site. He remarked that no one could reasonably say that because the Meeting was held there, its action would be dictated by the U.S. Government. Washington was, after all, the seat of the OAS and what could be more logical than for important questions to be considered there. He doubted, for example, that many really believed the UN was under the domination of the United States because its headquarters was in New York. If the Meeting could be held elsewhere, President Lleras suggested that Bariloche in Argentina would be a good place. He added that Montevideo, Santiago, or "even Brasilia" would also be acceptable. He did not think El Salvador would be satisfactory, but he was in favor of Costa Rica if that Government were amenable. It was agreed that a site must be chosen before the end of the week, and it was the consensus that if no other place were available Washington should be the place.

President Lleras expressed the opinion that at least one other country should be brought into the group of those favoring action since Uruguay was doubtful. He believed that of the countries which abstained on the vote of December 4, Chile would be the most easily won over. He said he knew that President Alessandri was 100 per cent in agreement with him and that the reason why Chile had abstained was that Alessandri had lost the last elections and had bowed to political pressure. Argentina, Dr. Lleras thought, might be brought around, especially if it could be made to appear that the Argentine Government was playing a leading role. He asserted that he would be glad to have Argentina think it invented "the whole thing" if only it would adopt a constructive attitude. Dr. Lleras urged that President Kennedy work on President Fron-dizi, President Alessandri and also on the Bolivian Government. Mr. Woodward noted confidentially that Mexico had let the United States know that it would break relations with Cuba if all the other American States did so. President Kennedy replied that the United States would work especially on Presidents Frondizi and Alessandri and would do what it could to influence Brazil, Bolivia and Ecuador. He also urged President Lleras to concentrate consultive efforts on these Governments.

Regarding the substance of the resolutions, President Lleras empha-sized that he thought the word "sanctions" should not be used as this would draw all manner of objections from various countries. He favored simply noting at the chosen time that the Cuban Government had identi-fied its interests with the Sino-Soviet bloc and had reneged on its inter-American commitments, and therefore the nations of the inter-American system were breaking off relations with it. President Kennedy stated that he would prefer not to give Cuban relations with the Sino-Soviet bloc as a reason for the break, but rather that the Cuban Government was engaged in subverting the democratic governments of the western hemisphere in implementation of the policies of Moscow. President Lleras enthusiasti-cally supported this suggestion.

President Lleras explained that Colombian strategy would be to hold firmly at first to an insistence that a special vigilance committee be set up to follow Cuban performance and to report to the COAS. He wished to assure President Kennedy, however, that Colombia would ultimately agree to having the COAS itself to perform this function. He said Colombia was adopting this strategy in order to sidetrack the numerous changes in the resolutions which other countries might pro-pose. He hoped they would devote their efforts to convincing Colombia to give up its vigilance committee, thereby diverting them from seeking changes in more vital parts of the resolutions. Dr. Lleras suggested that the United States might inform other Governments that it was working on Colombia to dissuade it from insisting on a vigilance committee. He urged President Kennedy to meet with President Frondizi on the latter's way home from the Far East, but also urged that Colombia's strategy on the vigilance committee not be divulged. President Kennedy suggested that the U.S. might suggest that Argentina too attempt to convince Colombia to give up this committee idea.

President Kennedy asserted that it was now urgent to reach an agreement on the draft resolutions with Colombia and that he hoped this could be done the following day. Then consultations with the other Gov-ernments could begin promptly. He stressed again that a definite time and place for the Meeting should be set before the end of this week. Dr. Lleras was entirely in agreement and an appointment was set up for Mr. Woodward, Ambassador Freeman and Mr. Goodwin to meet with Foreign Minister Caicedo and President Lleras on December 18.[1] Mr. Jamison, who had just arrived in Bogota for these conversations, would be present. President Kennedy stressed that the strategy should be to draft fairly strong resolutions and then modify them if necessary.

---

[1] Telegram 422 from Bogota, December 18, reported on the meeting. (Ibid., Central Files, 737.00/12–1861)

---

126. Circular Telegram From the Department of State to All Posts in the American Republics

Washington, December 20, 1961, 7:27 p.m.

1141. Depcirtel 1104.[1] During conversations with Department officials Bogota, President Lleras said Colombian Fonmin Caicedo arriving Washington December 21 to confer and negotiate with representatives other governments, particularly those which abstained on December 4 convocation re substantive action to be taken at 8th MFM. Rather than conducting consultations on basis existing Colombian drafts, Caicedo would point out new circumstances created by Castro's open identification himself and Cuba with communist ideology and policies Sino-Soviet bloc, and in effect seek suggestions for action which might go beyond that contemplated in present Colombian drafts, including possibility agreement on specific measures (sanctions) under Article 8. As result such consultations Colombia would prepare new draft or drafts upon which widest possible area of agreement to be sought prior to opening MFM.

FYI. We prepared and left with Colombians draft single combined resolution[2] representing changes which in our view would substantially

---

Source: Department of State, Central Files, 737.00/12–2961. Confidential. Drafted by Jamison; cleared by Assistant Legal Adviser for Inter-American Affairs Marjorie M. Whiteman, Director of the Office of Central American and Panamanian Affairs Katherine W. Bracken, Hemba, Belcher, and Crimmins; and approved by Woodward.

[1] Document 123.

[2] Reference is apparently to a "hypothetical draft" transmitted in circular airgram CA–715, December 22. It called on Cuba to renounce Marxism-Leninism, break with the Sino-Soviet bloc, and cease all attempts to subvert or overthrow the governments of other American Republics, and called on the governments of the American Republics to break diplomatic relations with Cuba unless it complied within 30 days. (Department of State, Central Files, 371.04/12–2261)

strengthen and clarify steps contemplated in present Colombian drafts and would also respond to certain comments made to our Missions on Colombian texts. Copies this draft being forwarded airmail for possible use in event it or similar draft becomes basis pre-MFM negotiations. End FYI.

Ball

127.   Telegram From the Department of State to the Embassy in Argentina

Washington, December 26, 1961, 1:14 p.m.

1151. In December 24 conversation, President Kennedy explained to President Frondizi[1] that conversations between Colombian Government and several other governments have revealed a general view that Castro's recent frank admission of Marxist-Leninist convictions and intention to make Cuba into a communist state now require action beyond that originally contemplated by Colombian draft resolutions. President Frondizi was given a copy of a new Colombian draft (substituting for the former third resolution) providing forthrightly for obligatory breaking of diplomatic and economic relations, and also a Colombian-US preliminary draft of a single combined resolution which also incorporates this provision.[2]

President Frondizi indicated no receptivity to applying sanctions; he emphasized that political difficulties in Brazil and Chile and to a lesser extent in Argentina make it impracticable to consider such sanctions; he asserted that it is much more important to preserve a high degree of unanimity of action and solidarity in the inter-American system than it is to try to enforce such sanctions against Cuba; he thought that the inter-American system might become seriously divided and weakened by

---

Source: Department of State, Central Files, 737.00/12–2661. Confidential. Drafted by Woodward, cleared by the President, and approved by Woodward.

[1] Frondizi and Kennedy met at Palm Beach.

[2] A Colombian draft of a combined single resolution, given to the Department on December 22 by the Colombian Foreign Minister, was transmitted in circular airgram CA–735, December 29. (Department of State, Central Files, 371.04/12–2961)

possible refusal of Brazil and other countries to comply with a two-thirds vote that did not include Brazil and Mexico which have over half of the population of Latin America (plus presumably Argentina and Chile); he emphasized the great importance he attributes to the U.S. and Argentina working and consulting together on this and all other important Hemisphere matters; he and particularly Minister Carcano thought that a strong resolution condemning Cuba for becoming an accomplice of the Soviet Bloc might provoke Cuba into separating itself from the inter-American system without obligatory sanctions; and he offered to send President Kennedy a draft of such a resolution.

President Kennedy told President Frondizi we would be glad to receive and consider such a draft resolution; he agreed that the US should work as closely as possible with Argentina; he agreed that it is important to maintain the solidarity of the inter-American system; he stated that the US of course wishes to weigh carefully the danger of causing a division in the inter-American system and internal political problems to Argentina, Brazil and other countries against the need for the most effective action possible to isolate Cuba and set up safeguards against Soviet bloc subversive influences from Cuba; but that he suspected that there would be less unfavorable reaction in Brazil and other countries if sanctions were applied against Cuba than President Frondizi considers likely.

(On the airplane to and from Palm Beach, Woodward emphasized to the Argentine delegation that the countries favoring obligatory breaking of diplomatic and economic relations with Cuba are beginning a concerted effort to obtain maximum support for these measures and believe they have at least 14 votes. After the conversation with President Kennedy, Woodward therefore urged that the Argentines formulate a suggested resolution as soon as possible. Minister Carcano and Ortiz de Rosas said January 2 was the earliest they could submit a draft to President Kennedy and that they would do so through the US Embassy in Buenos Aires.)

President Frondizi expressed concern regarding pressures from Argentine armed forces on GOA for more emphatic action against Cuba which he said he suspects is accentuated by stimulation US intelligence sources.

Please hold information this telegram in confidence and take advantage of opportunities to urge expeditious preparation suggested resolution by GOA and express US hope that GOA will exert leadership in conversations other governments.

Rusk

128.   Telegram From the Department of State to the Embassy in Brazil

Washington, December 26, 1961, 8:37 p.m.

1776. Embtels 1499[1] and 1500.[2]

1. While approach outlined point 7 reftel[3] which you propose taking with Brazilians appears satisfactory, we believe you should make it clear to them that there is considerable pressure from governments which are urging positive action on Cuban problem for obligatory rupture of diplomatic and economic relations under Article 8 Rio Treaty. Inclusion reference to diplomatic break in draft forwarded WIROM 1733[4] was in fact made after preliminary consultation Bogota with FonMin Caicedo and President Lleras during which they suggested this as a logical reaction to recent frank Castro declarations. At later meeting on December 18 they read to us and handed us a resolution prescribing rupture both diplomatic and economic relations. Caicedo subsequently informed us in Washington that several governments favor these more drastic sanctions.

2. USG desires promote widest possible agreement in advance of MFM on actions which will achieve moral isolation Castro regime and contribute to defensive capacity independent OAS governments protect themselves against Castro communist subversive design and activities. While we anxious consult to maximum with reluctant governments, USG obviously does not wish to put itself in forefront in opposing desire for strong action of governments deeply concerned and perhaps more immediately affected by Castro communist threat than those which abstained December 4 vote. Since Brazil and others of these governments

---

Source: Department of State, Central Files, 371.04/12–2461. Confidential. Drafted by Jamison, cleared by Pezzullo, and approved by Woodward.

[1] Telegram 1499, December 24, reported a conversation with Foreign Minister Dantas and stated that his position had "progressed substantially." (Ibid.)

[2] Telegram 1500, December 24, expressed concern at the latest draft resolution on Cuba. Ambassador Gordon stated that he had been making progress in his efforts to bring Brazil to a course in line with U.S. views, but "without previous warning, I find that our own position has apparently moved forward a good deal without giving Brazil or other southern South American Governments a chance to catch up." (Ibid.)

[3] Paragraph 7 of telegram 1500 urged that the draft resolution should not be circulated in any way until Gordon and Deputy Assistant Secretary Goodwin, who had just arrived in Rio de Janeiro, could fully explore the Brazilian position.

[4] Not found. A draft resolution calling on Cuba to renounce Marxism-Leninism, break with the Sino-Soviet bloc, and cease all attempts to subvert or overthrow the governments of other American republics, and calling on the governments of the American republics to break diplomatic relations with Cuba unless it complied within 30 days was circulated to U.S. Embassies in Latin America in circular airgram 715, December 22, which stated that it was a "hypothetical draft" intended for "possible use" by the Colombian Government. (Department of State, Central Files, 371.04/12–2261)

apparently now recognize need for OAS action, we would hope they will themselves make genuine effort convince governments desiring strong action that less drastic OAS steps necessary and likely in long run to have greater effect in counteracting danger.

3. We would be most grateful opportunity review carefully draft, which as mentioned item 5 of reftel, Dantas indicated he would prepare, and hope also Brazilians will consult on such draft with other governments particularly Colombia. From what we know here of Brazilian viewpoint as previously outlined, it appears Brazilian draft, as Embtel suggests, likely include much of substantive material now contained in US combined draft (WIROM 1733).

4. Consultation with FonMin Dantas should be highly useful in achieving better understanding respective viewpoints and hope he will be able visit Washington during week beginning December 31.

5. FYI only. Both Colombian revision US draft forwarded WIROM 1733 and more drastic Colombian draft providing merely for break in diplomatic and economic relations discussed with and handed to Argentine President and FonMin on strictly confidential basis December 24. Argentines promised give President Kennedy by January 2 draft resolution containing their views on appropriate action. End FYI.

Rusk

129. Telegram From the Department of State to the Embassy in Colombia

Washington, January 3, 1962, 8:56 p.m.

535. FonMin Caicedo stopped briefly Washington on return Paris to Bogota, where scheduled arrive January 4. Woodward saw him twice review prospects 8th MFM and handed him copies comparative revision Colombian draft he left with us in December (text revision circulated CA–715[1] as amended Depcirtel 1200).[2] This most recent draft contains provision for obligatory break diplomatic and economic relations Cuba after 30-day waiting period observe compliance.

Source: Department of State, Central Files, 371.04/1–362. Official Use Only. Drafted by Jamison, cleared by Belcher and Morrison, and approved by Woodward.

[1] Reference is apparently to CA–735; see footnote 2, Document 127.

[2] Dated January 3. (Department of State, Central Files, 371.04/1–362)

Caicedo indicated this revision seemed generally satisfactory but needed consult President Lleras before giving final view.

Principal additional questions discussed were: (1) whether necessary 14 votes obtainable for resolution containing obligatory measures and (2) whether even if attainable such action would be preferable approval by larger majority of resolution like that contained Depcirtel 1200 but with obligatory feature amended to make it recommendation. Caicedo appears personally favor all-out effort obtain 14 or more votes for obligatory measures.

Unfortunately Argentine draft which is presumably aimed at strongest feasible action short of obligatory measures (BA tel 1133 rpt Bogota 39)[3] not available prior Caicedo's departure. We plan keep Colombians informed of any developments that respect.

Rusk

---

[3] Dated January 3. (Ibid., 737.00/1–362)

---

130.   Telegram From the Embassy in Brazil to the Department of State

Rio de Janeiro, January 4, 1962, 4 p.m.

1551. Woodward from Goodwin. Upon arrival in Buenos Aires I had an hour talk with Camilion, I was then taken to meet with Frigerio and Musich. Afterwards to an hour meeting with Carcano and later to talk with Frondizi in the Casa Rosada.

During the entire trip I was followed by a car full of military intelligence agents. The visit received press coverage. My talks left no doubt in my mind that Frigerio is at least the second most powerful man in Argentina, with enormous influence on Frondizi. In foreign policy his voice is the only one that counts while Carcano is an intelligent sincere fellow with very little meaningful influence or authority.

The essence of the Argentine position is: 1. Sanctions are impossible because they are unacceptable to Brazil, Chile etc., and to force them would be to disrupt the inter-American system. 2. It is vital to have a united front of the American nations on this question, because a serious division between the large nations and the small nations plus US would be a serious defeat for American policy and a victory for Castro.

Source: Department of State, Central Files, 371.04/1–462. Confidential; Niact. Repeated to Buenos Aires and Montevideo.

3. Argentina's position is based on these two factors since its own internal situation is strong enough to permit Argentina to do anything it wishes, including the imposition of sanctions. 4. It is vital to reaffirm the Alliance for Progress and restate the basic principles of the inter-American system in order to give the MFM a wider scope than a mere effort to condemn Castro.

They then showed me their resolutions[1] which consisted of: A. A long resolution stating the principles of inter-Americanism and saying that all must adhere to those principles if they were to be members in good standing of the system. Cuba is not mentioned by name but would clearly be excluded under the criteria. (I assume you now have the resolutions and so will not discuss in detail); B. Two other resolutions adopted from Colombia (1) and (2) but with much of the anti-Cuba language watered down.

I informed the Argentines that, as a strictly personal reaction, I found nothing wrong with the ideas of restating the principles of inter-Americanism, although I would want to suggest much modification in the detailed wording of their draft. I went on to say that there was a great deal of feeling in favor of imposing mandatory sanctions. I said we agreed that it was important to achieve agreement between the big nations, and that not to do so would be a serious blow to the system. However, I said, if it was a choice between (A) lack of agreement and the passage of a strong resolution or (B) agreement on a weak and meaningless resolution, then the US would have to choose the former. The ideal solution, of course, would be agreement on a strong and meaningful resolution. I said I realized the problems raised by sanctions and, if we could get agreement among the big nations, perhaps other nations could also agree on a resolution which fell just short of sanctions. If this was not possible then I was afraid the US would be in the same position it found itself before the convocation vote. We would be compelled to vote with the more militant nations; since the only justification for not voting sanctions now would be the agreement of the large nations. I said that a strong resolution would have to have at least three elements: 1. A strong condemnation of Cuba for subordination of sovereignty and attempts to overthrow other governments; 2. Calling upon Cuba, in the strongest possible terms, to renounce these practices etc. (Both these would be along lines contained in the resolutions Woodward and I left with Lleras Camargo.); 3. A strong reporting provision calling for a report, within a specified period of time, as to whether Cuba had complied with the resolution.

---

[1] Three Argentine draft resolutions were enclosed with a letter of January 2 from Frondizi to Kennedy. (Kennedy Library, National Security Files, Countries Series, Argentina, General) Telegram 1218 to Buenos Aires, January 5, reported that the letter had been delivered to the White House on January 4. (Department of State, Central Files, 737.00/1–362)

They said the elements of all these were in their resolutions. I agreed, but said they had not stated them forcefully enough or with enough specifics. They said that they thought there was no real difference in principle, but a difference in language only and that they would be willing to accept our stronger language since they realized our public opinion problem etc. I actually showed Carcano the language of condemnation and the call for renunciation contained in the combined draft we left in Colombia. He thought it was a little strong but thought they could accept it, and perhaps sell it to the Brazilians. I did not show him the reporting provisions contained in your latest telegram instructing me to go to Argentina.[2] But I continually referred to the necessity of provisions along those lines. (Please have that section of the resolution translated into English.)

In sum, I believe there is a substantial chance that the Argentines will accept a strongly worded resolution which should be acceptable to us. This means a considerably strengthened version of the resolutions they sent to you, very much along the lines we had been considering. I foresee some difficulty with the thirty-day provision. In turn, I believe we should be able to accept their resolution restating the provisions of inter-Americanism. Of course, their version requires considerable editing; especially to avoid the implication that we are buying political support. This resolution is central to their position, does no harm to the other resolutions which are our real interest, and, in fact, will give the conference a broader political base. As to whether there should be one resolution, which we prefer, or three, as they prefer, I do not have a strong view.

Today we are talking with the Brazilians. In the next two days I also expect to have another talk with Dantas and, probably, with Goulart. I urge not precipitous rejection to the Argentine resolution until we have had a chance to strengthen it, and try it on them. I believe they will send Camilion to Washington some time next week. It looks probable that Dantas also will come to Washington about January 9 or 10; although his health situation is still precarious.

Gordon and I are preparing a general commentary on the US position which we will send before the end of the week.

I also spent three hours in Montevideo talking with Sparks. Of course, the Uruguayans have no clearly defined position. However, after talking with Sparks and the Argentines (who are in constant contact with the Uruguayans) I believe it is probable that they will follow Argentina and Brazil.

Gordon

---

[2] Reference is to telegram 1806 to Rio de Janeiro, December 30. (Ibid., 371.04/12–2961)

131. Telegram From the Embassy in Brazil to the Department of State

Rio de Janeiro, January 7, 1962, 11 a.m.

1570. 1. Goodwin and I met Thursday with Bernardes and Valle, and Saturday with Foreign Minister Dantas, Bernardes, and Renato Archer to discuss GOB views forthcoming MFM. (Deputy Archer is new Undersecretary in Foreign Office under terms Parliamentary amendment.)

2. Dantas states as basic premises (A) need to secure maximum unity and strengthening inter-American system in face Cuban problem and (B) need to avoid sharp conflict and division with Brazilian public opinion. Immediate or slightly deferred but automatic diplomatic or economic sanctions continue to be outside framework Brazilian thinking, although we made clear these possibilities under increasingly active discussion in Washington and warmly supported by smaller countries closer to Cuba.

3. With respect condemnation Cuban past and present, Dantas continues prefer idea of resolution confronting Cuban official statements and actions with restatement of principles of inter-American system, drawing conclusion that such statements and acts are clearly incompatible with system. Against this background, Brazilians would introduce new idea that declared Marxist-Leninist state can coexist peacefully with rest of hemisphere only if it accepts a form of "neutralization", which would include arms limitation, avoidance types military actions set forth Colombian drafts, foreswearing of subversive radio broadcasts to other LA countries, and refraining from subversive infiltration by other means. MFM would appoint a special committee to define terms of neutralization in detail and discuss with Cubans, and to report results to COAS within definite time period. If no positive results, Cuba then would clearly be engaged in acts under Article 6 Rio Treaty and could be subjected to sanctions under Article 8. To our surprise Dantas said such sanctions might include if necessary even armed force.

4. This idea appears to have a double origin (A) Bernardes belief after long talks with Olivares that if assured that US will not invade, Cuba would in fact accept rigorous limitation, and (B) Dantas conviction that no juridical definition is feasible of "breaking ties with Soviet bloc", whereas neutralization is an accepted juridical status which could be defined unequivocally.

5. Dantas also considering some means coupling above plan with MFM declaration that Cuban actions and statements warrant determina-

Source: Department of State, Central Files, 371.04/1–762. Confidential; Priority. Repeated to Buenos Aires, Montevideo, Santiago, and Bogotá.

tion by rest of OAS that Cuba has taken itself out of system and is no longer entitled to its rights and privileges. This might be immediate or automatic within fixed time period unless Cuba radically altered her posture and policy. Further discussion tentatively arranged for Sunday, although not firm date.

6.   We regard Bernardes idea paragraph four (A) above as pipe-dream, but see some real merit in idea reading Cuba out of system, possibly losing OAS membership thereby, as MFM action result, immediate or deferred, rather than formal sanctions which we do not believe Brazil can accept at this time. Neutralization concept, if defined with enough rigor, may come to much same thing as breaking military ties Soviet bloc and refraining any form subversion other LA countries. Discussions are making Dantas aware that US also faces major problem public opinion which he and other southern country Foreign Ministers must weigh. We believe position should be kept sufficiently flexible to accommodate at least part Brazilian approach if it develops in concrete manner.

7.   Dantas still troubled recent chest operation but believes may be able to come Washington by mid-week, e.g. January 10 or 11.

8.   Goodwin will be back Monday and will discuss further.

9.   Goodwin concurred in draft.

Gordon

---

132.   Circular Telegram From the Department of State to All Posts in the American Republics

Washington, January 9, 1962, 9:16 p.m.

1230. Department's current analysis positions OAS governments re possible action 8th MFM indicates:

Group of governments constituting most if not all thirteen which clearly supported Rio Treaty convocation appear favor obligatory rupture diplomatic and economic relations perhaps with 30 to 60 day waiting period demonstrate Cuban noncompliance. Certain these governments such as Guatemala and Peru would support measures having appearance even stronger action including some type air-sea sur-

---

Source: Department of State, Central Files, 737.00/1–962. Confidential. Drafted by Woodward and Jamison; cleared by Belcher, Whitman, Bowden (SOV), Bracken, and Charles K. Johnson; and approved by Rusk.

veillance Caribbean area or denial Cuba's right participate OAS. On other hand Argentina, as reflected in consultations possible actions resulting Kennedy–Frondizi December 24 meeting, emerging as leader in group which opposes or unreceptive obligatory rupture diplomatic and economic relations, but willing support or favorably consider non-mandatory action, including insistence Cuba clearly define its position within OAS system or suffer at least moral consequences. Argentina also desires inclusion exhortation drastic emphasis on and acceleration Alliance for Progress program. This group would probably also support continuing COAS responsibility maintain vigilance and recommend means strengthening capacity defense against Cuban-communist intervention. Although positions all governments not clear, Chile, Brazil, Bolivia, Ecuador might follow Argentine lead. Uruguay uncertain, Mexico will probably oppose on "juridical" grounds.

Principal immediate questions are:

(1) Whether necessary majority fourteen votes obtainable for obligatory measures; and

(2) Whether, even if such bare majority obtainable, it is not preferable seek agreement additional governments on action not involving obligatory measures but clearly achieving moral isolation Castro regime and agreement on strengthening defense against its penetration.

In these circumstances our position should be described as follows:

(1) US favors MFM action which will accomplish most conclusive possible definition OAS position against Castro regime's making itself accomplice Sino-Soviet bloc.

(2) Resolution or resolutions containing principal points draft forwarded CA–735,[1] and that developed on basis Depcirtel 1200[2] including obligatory diplomatic and economic break (after waiting period), would accomplish this purpose particularly if substantial majority for it achieved.

(3) We continue prepared consult on ways in which basic objective effective OAS isolation Cuba can be achieved, but we consider it extremely important that countries favoring obligatory measures be urged consult with countries not favoring such measures and vice versa since most imminent danger from Marxism-Leninism-Castroism is to Latin countries and USG judgment cannot substitute for their judgment in deciding on MFM actions in relation their individual country situations and danger from Cuba.

FYI. While maintaining obligatory measures as "basic position" we do not wish preclude outcome which would clearly accomplish isolation

---

[1] See footnote 2, Document 127.

[2] See footnote 2, Document 129.

Castro without forcing reluctant countries into obligatory break at this time. End FYI.

Please discuss US position with FonMin (except Brazil, Argentina and Colombia) and report his views. Mention that US does not have a specific proposal but has drafted tentative articles to be of assistance in recording consensus when substantial majority views are known.

Rusk

---

133.   Telegram From the Department of State to the Embassy in Argentina

Washington, January 11, 1962, 12:55 a.m.

1246. Verbatim Text. Transmit following message from President Kennedy to President Frondizi:

"Dear Mr. President:

I am grateful for your letter of January 2, 1962[1] and for the frank expression of your viewpoint regarding the prospective actions to be taken at the forthcoming Meeting of Foreign Ministers in Punta del Este. You may be certain, Mr. President, that I share your preoccupation regarding the urgent necessity that both the solidarity of the hemisphere and the internal unity of the Member States be strengthened rather than weakened as a result of that Meeting. Naturally, I welcome your emphasis upon the program of the Alliance for Progress, and I share your view that the spirit of that program—the fulfillment in peace and freedom of the aspirations of the peoples for economic and social progress should characterize the Meeting.

I am confident that all of our Governments are deeply concerned over not only the need for rapid and effective demonstration of the achievements which can be made in economic and social development, but also the need for finding means to prevent the inroads in this hemisphere of the power bloc and system of which the Cuban Government

---

Source: Department of State, Central Files, 737.00/1–1162. Confidential; Niact. Drafted by Woodward and Jamison, cleared in draft by Rusk and with the White House, and approved by Woodward.

[1] See footnote 1, Document 130.

has become an accomplice. A substantial number of our Governments, including those which are threatened most closely by the principal source of the present infection, are so greatly concerned over the existing danger that they would strongly support OAS action for the application of some, at least, of the mandatory measures which are available under the Rio Treaty. Some of these Governments indeed seek mandatory action of an even stronger nature. To ignore the concern of these immediately threatened Governments—which compose the majority of the inter-American community—incurs the grave risk that our system would be confronted with a division at least as wide and as deep as that which might result from the adoption of steps which they deem important and urgent.

I must emphasize in all frankness that the Government of the United States shares their view concerning the importance and urgency of applying effective measures under the Rio Treaty against the existing and potential threat posed by the alignment of Cuba with the Sino-Soviet Bloc, dedicated as it is to eventual subversion of the Governments of this hemisphere and to the denial of every value for which the Alliance for Progress stands. It appears that a majority of the American States are in agreement that it would be desirable that these measures take the form of the obligatory imposition of sanctions. I recognize, however, the advisability of seeking to avoid a probable rift in solidarity if this can be accomplished by achieving unanimity, or virtual unanimity, on a program which would include the concepts of great importance contained in your proposals. There are, however, certain modifications in those proposals which my Government wishes to suggest.[2] The suggested modifications are largely changes in the third proposed resolution. However, my Government would also wish to suggest modifications in the first resolution to place greater emphasis on the mutual nature of the pledge taken in the Charter of Punta del Este. I should like to emphasize that these modifications—which are primarily changes of language and not changes of principle—represent the minimum position which we could expect that a substantial number of American Governments, including my own, would be able to accept.

The penetration of this hemisphere by international communism has endangered the security of the American nations and evoked the strongest possible feelings of the people of the United States, as well as of the people of other American States. I believe that this Meeting offers the OAS an unparalleled opportunity to demonstrate that collective action, through the inter-American system, can deal with this threat. The future unity and vitality of the Organization of American States depends upon

---

[2] The modifications were transmitted in telegram 1247 to Buenos Aires, January 11. (Department of State, Central Files, 737.00/1–1162)

taking the strongest possible action with respect to Cuba which commands the support of a substantial consensus of the hemisphere. We consider it still possible that such a consensus might be achieved in favor of the imposition of sanctions. If so, we would hope to pursue this course together with your Government.

In view of the limited time remaining before the opening of the Meeting in Punta del Este, I am requesting the Secretary of State to transmit the suggested modifications to you through our Embassy at Buenos Aires. I shall be very much interested to know your opinion of these suggested modifications, as well as your latest views as to the possibilities of imposing diplomatic and economic sanctions. I would also be pleased to learn the responses which you may receive from the proposal of these modified resolutions to the Governments that are not now supporting the idea of a collective break in diplomatic and commercial relations.

In the meanwhile, my Government is informing the other Governments that the United States is prepared to support the firmest effective action for which there is a substantial majority, and we are discussing with those Governments illustrative phraseology for action which might receive the support of such a majority.

In conclusion, I should like to express my appreciation for the leadership which you and your Government are displaying in this most important effort. If we achieve a satisfactory decision at Punta del Este and, at the same time, maintain the essential unity of the hemisphere, you will have made a highly significant contribution to that result. This fruitful collaboration between our two countries will, I am confident, be extended and strengthened in all fields of hemispheric political and economic activity. The important role which Argentina is playing in Latin America will be one of the most important forces in bringing us closer to our mutual goals for the freedom and prosperity of the Americas.

With pleasant recollections of your visit to Palm Beach and with cordial best wishes,

Sincerely yours,

John F. Kennedy"

Rusk

134. Telegram From the Department of State to the Embassy in Brazil

Washington, January 14, 1962, 5:09 p.m.

1922. Brazilian proposals 8th MFM action as set forth in memorandum Valle brought[1] and Foreign Minister's January 12 statement discussed by Secretary, Woodward and Goodwin with Valle and Campos morning January 13.[2] Our discussion largely aimed at clarification their ideas. No commitment was made for other than further study, but it was suggested that they might wish discuss with Argentines. We also emphasized strong feeling of many other OAS members in favor vigorous action and strength of feeling within US on Cuban problem.

Seems clear that Brazilian program, while fostering notion that Cuba can or should have its right to "neutral" status recognized by OAS, contemplates no action by MFM beyond some kind of preliminary indication of incompatibility between declarations (not acts) of Castro regime and OAS principles and that all other aspects working out "statute of relations" between Cuba and hemisphere would be left to Foreign Ministers group or other "special organ" which would hear all parties and report to COAS. Valle vague on precise terms reference for such group.

Principal questions raised with them were: 1) Whether their formula does not contemplate possibility permanent acceptance neutral status for Cuba, i.e. permanent acceptance accomplice of Soviet bloc; Valle's reply was that things couldn't go on there indefinitely as they are (he conceded that a "communist state" is "by definition interventionist"). 2) Effect within Brazil of MFM decision on obligatory measures; Valle said result would be [to] greatly accentuate existing tensions. 3) Whether neutralization not the same as isolation other programs contemplate; Valle said isolation would inevitably widen gap between Cuba and other American states, while their program could lead to its being narrowed (even to consideration of resumption of US-Cuban trade).

Source: Department of State, Central Files, 737.00/1–1462. Confidential; Niact. Drafted by Jamison, cleared by Woodward and Rogers, and approved by U. Alexis Johnson.

[1] Not found, but summarized in telegram 1593 from Rio de Janeiro, January 9. (Ibid., 737.00/1–962)

[2] A more detailed record of the conversation is ibid., Secretary's Memoranda of Conversation: Lot 65 D 330.

Valle produced copy of the illustrative draft (Depcirtel 1236)[3] which we are making available other COAS representatives here (but not by us to Brazilian pending your reaction Deptel 1903).[4] We explained carefully to him the basis on which it was prepared and is being used for consultative purposes.

Valle queried whether Secretary would be able stop off in Brasilia on January 19 en route to Punta (when he will be receiving four other Fon-Mins including Roa) and he explained that unavailability aircraft before evening January 20 would make that impossible.

Rusk

[3] Circular telegram 1236, January 11, instructed recipient Embassies to give the Foreign Minister in confidence a draft prepared on the basis of circular telegram 1200 (see footnote 2, Document 129) emphasizing that it was not a U.S. proposal but an example of a position that might have substantial support. (Department of State, Central Files, 737.00/1–1162)
[4] Telegram 1903, January 11, instructed the Embassy to give the Brazilians the draft resolution on the basis set forth in circular telegram 1236, unless it perceived objections to doing so. (Ibid., 371.04/1–1162)

---

135.   Memorandum of Conversation

Washington, January 18, 1962, 4:13 p.m.

SUBJECT

Redrafts of Argentine Resolutions for 8th MFM[1]

PARTICIPANTS

The Secretary	Ambassador del Carril of Argentine Republic
ARA—Mr. Goodwin	Dr. Oscar H. Camilión, Argentine Under Secretary of
RPA—Mr. Jamison	Foreign Affairs
RPA—Mr. Bowdler	Mr. Ortiz de Rozas, Director General, Political Division,
	Argentine Foreign Office

After an exchange of amenities during which the Secretary expressed appreciation to the Argentine emissaries for having come all the way to Washington, Under Secretary Camilión explained the pur-

---

Source: Department of State, Central Files, 371.04/1–1862. Confidential. Drafted by Bowdler and approved in S on January 20. The time of the meeting is taken from Rusk's Appointment Book. (Johnson Library)

[1] The Argentine redrafts are filed with a memorandum prepared in the Department of State summarizing the Argentine position as presented at the January 18 meeting. (Department of State, Central Files, 737.00/1–1862)

pose of their visit. He indicated that at President Frondizi's request the Foreign Office had reviewed very carefully the observations made by President Kennedy in his letter and the suggested modifications to their resolutions. They had found these very useful and had reworked their earlier drafts in the light of them. However, there were certain aspects of the changes recommended by the United States, particularly with respect to sanctions, that in their opinion would not command the support desired and hence would threaten the unity of the hemisphere to which President Frondizi attached the greatest importance. He emphasized the need to maintain a united front in the Americas not only against Castro but as a demonstration of purpose within the Free World.

The Secretary stated that there were several ways in which unity could be disrupted. He said we should not lose sight of the fact that the countries geographically close to Cuba are very concerned about the danger to them from Cuba and because of this feel very strongly about the need to take effective measures. Another aspect of unity is that if President Kennedy does not give the American people and the Congress an adequate formula for dealing with the Cuban problem, this could have an erosive effect on our capacity to work with the OAS. Still another consideration is the implications which go beyond the Continent. For example, it is difficult for the United States public to understand our concern over communist penetration in other distant areas of the world and the need to act against it if nothing is done about penetration within our own hemisphere. Also, other countries on the periphery of the Soviet bloc are watching to see how resolutely we handle a problem, such as Cuba, in our own back yard as an indication of how determined we would be to assist them in a difficult situation.

Under Secretary Camilión recognized the validity of these considerations but questioned whether the solution we advanced based on sanctions would really achieve what is being sought. He said that the problem was not one of definition—we are all agreed that Cuba is communist and that this is incompatible with Cuba's continuation in the OAS—but of the efficacy of the action contemplated. Argentine thought that the more effective measure would be to find a way to suspend Cuba's participation within the inter-American system.

The Secretary interrupted to say that he wanted to mention another consideration making it very important that decisive action be taken at Punta del Este. He said he had not mentioned this matter to any other Latin American government and did not want to be misinterpreted for bringing it up in this context. He explained that the latest reports from Ambassador Thompson in Moscow on his conversations with Premier Khrushchev show that if the Soviets persist in their current policy on the Berlin problem we are on a collision course which will lead to war. Given this circumstance, it is of the utmost importance that no weakness be shown in Punta del Este lest the Soviets interpret this as a lack of determination on our part. The Secretary went on to say that if suspension of Cuba from the OAS can be worked out, then it might be a substitute for sanctions. He added that if it could not be put into effect quickly, however, we would find it difficult to accept as an alternative.

In an exchange of comments on the effectiveness of sanctions, the Secretary expressed the view that such measures would have a profound impression on the Cuban people and would help us in getting other members of the Free World to align their policies with those of the hemisphere on Cuba and Dr. Camilión again expressed his doubts as to their efficacy. The Secretary then asked Department officers present to try to work out with the Argentine emissaries a formula which might accomplish an effective provision leading rapidly toward exclusion of the Cuban Government from the inter-American system, and to check back with him.

136.   Telegram From Secretary of State Rusk to the Department of State

Punta del Este, January 23, 1962, 1 a.m.

Secto 6. Daily Summary Cable. Secretary saw Foreign Ministers Argentina, Chile and Mexico morning of January 22. Argentine Foreign Minister Carcano maintained view it would be inadvisable press for sanctions and favored Charter amendment permit expulsion Cuba. He said most Argentina could do is abstain on sanctions and comply if approved. He stressed OAS unity theme and argued Central Americans should not force other countries accept sanctions. He said Argentina not committed to sticking with Brazil, but showed no indication shift in direction of strong resolution based on sanctions or explicit statement endorsing suspension.

Chilean Foreign Minister Martinez, while making no new comment on substance although opposing sanctions, appeared eager to take lead in bringing positions of reluctant and negative countries more nearly

Source: Department of State, Central Files, 371.04/1–2362. Confidential; Priority. Repeated to Buenos Aires, Rio de Janeiro, Santiago, Mexico City, Port-au-Prince, and USUN. Received at 1:20 p.m.

into line with that of US and others. He said he was holding a meeting this group immediately following the Secretary's call and would inform Secretary its outcome. He emphasized that since Chile had not taken public stand it is in good position to assume leadership in such conciliation efforts. Furthermore, he claimed Chile not subject to same internal pressures as other countries, mentioning specifically Brazil. Hoped to achieve, if not unanimous, at least nearly unanimous support for resolution which would strengthen rather than weaken OAS system.

Secretary emphasized (1) importance that as part of responsibilities under system, Governments not believing themselves to be so directly affected support Rio Treaty action requested by other Governments directly in line of Castro's Communist fire; (2) intense interest US public opinion Cuban problem and its inability understand why OAS should be reluctant take definite stand on issues as well as possible effect this would have on ability US support OAS; and (3) that in view of current trend Soviet policy on Berlin essential that free world in no way indicate to Khrushchev any weakening of determination to resist, and that therefore what occurs at eighth MFM in relation Communist threat has impact on that situation.

Most notable development in conversation with Mexican Foreign Minister Tello was latter's unequivocal assertion that Mexico prepared support clear pronouncement incompatibility between Communist Government which Cuba has become and Inter-American principles and agreements. Otherwise, repeated several of now familiar Mexican juridical arguments against Rio Treaty action. Suggested nevertheless that US advisers and Ambassador Sanchez Gavito join forces to endeavor to work out general resolution containing specific points for some of which Mexico might be able to vote favorably.

Haitian delegation issued statement which, as explained in backgrounder to French press representative, was interpreted to mean that Haiti intends give no support to even moral sanctions on Cuba and that its attitude at this meeting will conform strictly to that of the Mexican delegation. Foreign Minister later made completely ambiguous statement to informal meeting of 14 described below.

In informal meeting called at US instance of 14 countries which voted for holding MFM all except Uruguay and Haiti either pressed for or expressed willingness endorse immediate application diplomatic and economic sanctions. Uruguay urged need to work out action commanding wide support. Haiti took equivocal position it would study proposals in light of principles non-intervention and self-determination. Repeating basic US position in support strong action, Secretary said there were indications other six countries seeking work out formulas which would bring two groups closer together, beginning with what now appears clear consensus that Communist character and alignment Cuban Government incompatible with OAS principles and agreements.

Brazilian Foreign Minister in intimate conversation late January 22 shows deep concern re difficulty attaining common agreement and gives indications willingness take more direct approach. For example, he broached idea possible call on Cuba at this MFM to state whether Cuba will confirm standards such as those listed in Brazilian[1] (unsatisfactory) providing now for application sanctions after 60 or 90 day waiting period. He also indicated acceptance possible removal Cuba from IADB by this MFM; prohibition movement arms from Cuba to OARS; and possible creation special committee IADB or subordinate directly to COAS intensify protection against Castro-Communist infiltration particularly in Caribbean area.

US inscribed at eighth place in order of speaking.

Cuba (inscribed at fifteenth place) requested meeting Secretariat use one of meeting rooms to mount "exhibit" which will be open to press and other delegations immediately after "FonMin" Dorticos speaks.

Substance above may be used in general terms for Congressional briefings as appropriate.

Rusk

---

[1] The source text here indicates an omission and states that a correction will follow. No corrected copy has been found, but on the transmission copy, the relevant passage is "Brazilian formula and then (if action unsatisfactory)". (Ibid., Conference Files: Lot 65 D 533, CF 2038)

---

137. Telegram From Secretary of State Rusk to the Department of State

Punta del Este, January 23, 1962, 5 p.m.

Secto 8. Eyes only for the President and Acting Secretary. No Other Distribution.[1] Have concentrated during first day of Conference on intensive consultation with other Foreign Ministers singly and in groups to get direct sense of situation and to discuss with them US political and other problems related to the Conference results.

Source: Department of State, Central Files, 371.04/1–2362. Secret; Niact. Received at 7:15 p.m.

[1] An unnumbered telegram of the same date from Punta del Este, filed with the source text, instructed that this should be interpreted to mean distribution to "top echelon Department and ARA."

On issue of obligatory diplomatic and economic sanctions there is strong support among 14 who voted December 4 to call this meeting, except for Uruguay and Haiti who, for different reasons, are wobbling. Situation which Haedo would readily resolve on cash basis of aid. Haiti is holding aloof possibly because of Duvalier's disgruntlement over recent aid discussions as well as from nervousness that Haiti may be next in terms of outside intervention against dictatorship.

It seems clear that Mexico, Brazil, Argentina, Chile, Ecuador and Bolivia have been moving significantly in recent weeks but still too early to determine exact basis on which broad consensus might be reached.

Have used in private talks fact that President Kennedy is now calling upon US people and Congress for greater support of OAS than has any President. This includes massive Alliance for Progress program, trade authority to negotiate common market external tariffs downward on most favored nation basis and commodity arrangements. This means President needs OAS support to demonstrate to American opinion that such support is both needed and deserved. Have also spoken frankly with Foreign Ministers key larger countries about necessity OAS deciding whether such problem as Cuba can be handled multilaterally or whether we revert to unilateral action and law of jungle in hemisphere. Have also discreetly indicated what action taken this Conference could have significant bearing on Khrushchev's estimate determination of free world in decisions he must be making about such matters as Berlin and Southeast Asia.

Believe there are many points on which there could be near unanimity, including basic proposition that communist country is incompatible with membership in and obligations of hemisphere system. Even Mexico seems prepared join in some such declaration. There will also be strong support for certain detailed steps such as exclusion Cuba from Inter-American Defense Board, embargo of arms traffic between Cuba and rest of hemisphere and strengthening of Peace Committee to give it vigilance functions regarding security questions posed by Cuban activity.

As result these consultations, my present thought is that we might substitute for obligatory breach of diplomatic relations, the exclusion of present government of Cuba from participation in organs of OAS. This would, in fact, be more drastic action than breach of relations remaining countries having Ambassadors Havana. On economic side, I would be prepared to use exactly the formula used with Dominican Republic, namely, to start now with arms trade and ask COAS to recommend additional steps.

Congressional advisers naturally want strongest possible line although they recognize complications, including fact that there may not be 14 votes for simplest form of obligatory diplomatic and economic sanctions applied at this meeting.

Will have specific recommendations for President's consideration after Tuesday's consultations during which we will be getting results discussions among Argentina, Brazil and Chile as to how far they think they can go to meet our position. One important element is passionate determination Central Americans and Panama to get immediate and drastic sanctions to which they consider themselves entitled because they are countries under most direct attack.

Will advise later.

Rusk

---

138. Telegram From the Department of State to the Embassy in Ecuador

Washington, January 24, 1962, 8:10 p.m.

389. Please deliver soonest following message[1] from President Kennedy to President Arosemena:

"Dear Mr. President:

My latest information from Punta del Este is that the governments of the hemisphere are moving rapidly toward agreement on what the Conference of Foreign Ministers should do with regard to the Cuban question. Among the elements of such an agreement are (a) procedures to suspend the present Government of Cuba from participation in the various organs of the inter-American system, and (b) the application of economic sanctions using the same formula that was applied in the case of the Dominican Republic, that is, immediate suspension of trade in arms with other items to be added only by further decision of the Council of the OAS.

I am sure that you are well aware of the intense preoccupation of the people and Congress of the United States with the Cuban problem and

---

Source: Department of State, Central Files, 711.11–KE/1–2462. Confidential; Niact; Limit Distribution. Drafted by Deputy Director of the Office of Inter-American Regional Political Affairs John M. Cates, Jr., cleared by Deputy Special Assistant to the President for National Security Affairs Carl Kaysen, and approved by Walter Collopy.

[1] The message was drafted in Punta del Este and transmitted in Secto 19, January 24, from Rusk to Kennedy, recommending that he send a message along these lines to Arosemena. (Ibid., 371.04/1–2462) Telegram 375 from Quito, January 25, reported that the message had been delivered. (Ibid., 711.11–KE/1–2562)

that we are most concerned not to leave other and smaller countries in the Caribbean area under the impression that we are indifferent to what they consider to be a genuine threat to their national security. I am confident that you would not wish Ecuador to be isolated from the large majority of the OAS who are concerned to deal with this threat to the hemisphere in order that they might release their attention and energy to the great promise of the Alliance for Progress and other efforts which all of us are making to advance the welfare of the people of the hemisphere.

I do hope you will find it possible to give your distinguished Foreign Minister broad authority to join with the very substantial majority which is rapidly forming at Punta del Este. Solidarity with the United States at this critical time in world affairs would be especially appreciated.

Please accept my very best wishes for your personal well-being and for the prosperity and progress of the Ecuadorean people.

Sincerely, John F. Kennedy."

FYI. Department hopes publicity can be avoided. End FYI.

Ball

---

139. Telegram From Secretary of State Rusk to the Department of State

Punta del Este, January 25, 1962, 1 a.m.

Secto 23. Daily Summary Telegram. At first meeting General Committee Venezuelan Foreign Minister Falcon Briceno and Costa Rican Foreign Minister Vargas Fernandez elected chairman and rapporteur respectively.

Colombia, Mexico and Guatemala spoke during morning session and Chile, Bolivia and Brazil in afternoon.

Colombian Foreign Minister gave carefully reasoned speech explaining juridical basis Colombian initiative for MFM under Article 6 Rio Treaty. He traced development inter-American collective system indicating application this system is not intervention and failure could lead to unilateral action. He called for break diplomatic, economic and consular relations with Cuba, COAS maintaining vigilance over situa-

Source: Department of State, Central Files, 371.04/1–2562. Confidential. Repeated to Bogotá, Mexico City, Guatemala City, Santiago, La Paz, Rio de Janeiro, Buenos Aires, Caracas, and USUN.

tion and prompt handling of problem incompatibility Cuba's continued participation OAS.

Mexican Foreign Minister Tello repeated familiar juridical arguments Rio Treaty not applicable this type situation but closed with strong statement asserting incompatibility between a government's adopting Marxism-Leninism and continued participation in OAS. He said membership in OAS irreconcilable with adoption governmental system characteristics of which not those representative democracy.

Guatemalan Foreign Minister Unda Murillo made sharp and at times telling attack on Castro regime for its association with Sino-Soviet bloc, promotion subversive activities and violation human rights. Effectiveness of speech blunted by length and repetitiveness.

Chilean Foreign Minister Martinez Sotomayor concentrated on general review inter-American principles and need for strengthening inter-American system by overcoming threat of misery and underdevelopment in Latin American countries; said we should focus on preserving unity and strengthening of inter-American system; recognized that Cuba by adopting Marxism-Leninism has separated itself from inter-American system but thought sanctions were not answer to making Castro regime change policies; said political sanctions should not be applied this problem and economic sanctions not effective in view Cuban trade pattern with Sino-Soviet bloc aid certain western nations.

Bolivian Foreign Minister Fellman traced history Bolivian Revolution and described internal matters of interest to Bolivia, such as commodity prices, economic development assistance and access to sea. He stressed principles self-determination and non-intervention arguing meeting should not take punitive action, but urge governments organize themselves on basis free elections and representative democracy.

Burden long speech by Brazilian Foreign Minister Dantas was that door should be left open for Cuba return to American family of nations instead of adopting measures which would only serve to push it irrevocably into Sino-Soviet bloc. He described Brazil's formula for "neutralization" of Cuba through set of negative conditions that would govern future relations between Cuba and inter-American system.

Secretary met at midday with Argentine and Chilean Foreign Ministers who brought memorandum said to represent views themselves and five others (Brazil, Bolivia, Ecuador, Haiti and Mexico). Memorandum contemplates resolution which after restatement certain principles focuses on incompatibility between present Cuban regime and inter-American system and prescribes means for regulating resulting relationship, with implication this might require amendment OAS Charter. Additional items on inter-American defense board and traffic in arms not spelled out. Memorandum asserts above would offer "adequate" basis MFM action, and insisted no sanctions should be approved either now or after fixed period.

In response Foreign Minister Carcano's question whether US would support resolution on above basis, Secretary stated while he felt it offers certain possibilities, it did not meet minimum requirements in at least two important respects: (a) absence obligatory diplomatic and economic break or an alternative such as expulsion Cuba from system, and (b) a formula on suspension economic relations in manner this done Dominican Republic. Secretary said that he believed time had come endeavor bring together governments favoring firmest action and those supporting above formula in order start building bridge of agreement instead of walls between two groups OAS members. Carcano and Martinez agreed this would be good idea and said that after checking with other members their group steps would be taken create informal working group with representatives Argentina, Chile, Uruguay, Colombia, Venezuela, US and one from Central American and Panama group. By arrangement with Uruguayan chairman of meeting, such group being formed and US delegation planning provide it with draft forwarded Department (Secto 18).[1]

Above may be used in Congressional briefings as required and appropriate.

Rusk

---

[1] Secto 18, January 24, called for excluding Cuba from participation in the bodies of the Inter-American system, excluding it from the Inter-American Defense Board, and partial interruption of economic relations of all member states with Cuba, beginning with the immediate suspension of trade in arms and implements of war. (Ibid., 371.04/1–2462)

---

140. Telegram From Secretary of State Rusk to the Department of State

Punta del Este, January 28, 1962, 2 a.m.

Secto 36. Eyes only for President and Acting Secretary. No Other Distribution.[1] General speeches were concluded last evening and For-

---

Source: Department of State, Central Files, 371.04/1–2862. Secret; Niact. Received at 4:49 a.m. and passed to the White House.

[1] An unnumbered telegram of the same date from Punta del Este, filed with the source text, instructed that if necessary this should be interpreted to mean distribution to "top echelon Department and ARA."

302 Foreign Relations, 1961–1963, Volume XII

eign Ministers have spent today in intensive consultations to try to draw conference to prompt and satisfactory conclusion. One striking aspect here is to see how much hemisphere has moved, including such countries as Brazil and Mexico, since similar conference at San Jose sixteen months ago.

There is practically unanimous agreement on (1) a general declaration about communism in relation to principles and purposes of hemispheric system; (2) a short but strong reaffirmation of Alliance for Progress to make point that Castro–Communism is not the answer to economic and social development; (3) a clear declaration that the present Marxist-Leninist Government of Cuba is incompatible with the obligations and privileges of hemispheric system; (4) the immediate expulsion of Cuba from the Inter-American Defense Board; (5) the immediate interruption of trade and traffic in arms and strategic items to and from Cuba and the hemisphere; (6) the establishment of a special security committee to the COAS to recommend measures for protection against subversion, espionage, etc., etc.

Remaining points of difference turn on exact solution to (a) expulsion or suspension of present Government of Cuba from organs and agencies of the OAS; (b) authorization to COAS to recommend, in terms of Dominican precedent, suspension of trade in other items.

Differences by end of day have become narrow but deep since it is an underlying juridical difference about whether we can or should invoke the Rio Treaty against Cuba.

I wish to emphasize that the problem now is not the US position but that of reconciling sharply divergent views between the two principal wings of this conference. If we move slightly in one direction we lose support from the other. We are searching for a solution in the practical realm which will leave delegations to weave their own juridical theories. We are not overlooking possibilities of getting near complete unanimity on a satisfactory basis but we shall be during Sunday in the somewhat tense final phase which is normal to such multilateral negotiations.

I have been surprised by the distance which Brazil and Mexico have moved since early December. My sharpest difficulty might be to get certain intransigents such as Ydigoras and Prado to take a firm but reasonable rather than an extremely belligerent view.

Congressional advisers have given us understanding and loyal support. I have not departed from position authorized by President in discussions with them but I am not unmindful of fact that if they come back reasonably satisfied our Alliance for Progress and other programs affecting Latin America will have strong and crucial support.

We are very close to a good result but not yet out of danger of a bad one. At end of day I am moderately optimistic.

Rusk

141. **Telegram From the Department of State to the Delegation at the Meeting of Consultation of Ministers of Foreign Affairs of the American Republics at Punta del Este**

Washington, January 28, 1962, 2:38 p.m.

Tosec 48. For Secretary from Ball. In conversation with President last night he reflected concern way press was playing Punta del Este conference as defeat for United States if anything less than full sanctions approved. He thought you might wish consider backgrounder in Punta del Este for United States correspondents pointing out limited character of results we had originally hoped for and progress you were making in equalling or surpassing initial realistic expectations. He feels that press here is representing our original expectations extravagantly and consequently any result less than sweeping sanctions may be interpreted as defeat. At same time he is fully aware of sensitivity of situation in Punta del Este and need to avoid any suggestion in press stories as to views of United States Delegation which might adversely affect course of negotiations.

I pass these comments on for your consideration, in the light of the situation as you appraise it on the spot. Meanwhile I have spoken to Fulbright who believes that suspension from OAS organizations far more significant than economic sanctions. I feel confident that if you obtain suspension resolution he would be prepared to announce he regards this as triumph. Along same line believe it possible to arrange for other similar expressions of opinion and as soon as probable shape and form of resolution becomes clear we shall take steps here to prepare ground for appropriate statements to be made once resolution finally adopted.

Example of press treatment specifically called to my attention by President is today's *New York Times* article by Tad Szulc headlined "Split on Cuba is Blow to U.S." Main burden of article is that US did not prepare ground sufficiently and was unrealistically optimistic about results.

Ball

Source: Department of State, Central Files, 371.04/1–2862. Secret; Priority. Drafted by Ball.

142. Telegram From Secretary of State Rusk to the Department of State

Punta del Este, January 30, 1962, 4 a.m.

Secto 41. Eyes only for the President and Acting Secretary. No Other Distribution. Deliver White House for President before 8:00 a.m. Conference has reached point where there is general agreement on every element of a fine result, except matter of expulsion or suspension of Cuba from OAS organs and agencies. Full day and night of most intensive negotiations has failed to produce a formula on which there can be more than 13 votes. What I have been working for is an answer which could get at least 18 if not 20 votes in order not to give Castro the satisfaction of having more important Latin American countries appear to be defending him. Bear in mind that exclusion or suspension from OAS organs is substitute for diplomatic sanctions which can probably get only 13 votes.

Argentina and Chile are more pliable but are unwilling to leave Brazil and Mexico completely in lurch. Latter two are ready to see Cuba expelled from most OAS organs but find it difficult for internal reasons to say so at this meeting. On other side, Colombia is leading Central American and rightist LA group but Colombian Foreign Minister is taking exceedingly stubborn position that this meeting must make executive decision to exclude Cuba from OAS now. Colombian FM is making no effort to find formula to produce unity on this point. Prospect is, therefore, that entire program is jeopardized because failure to agree on exclusion will mean no voting on all other items now agreed. I myself agree we must solve this question in order to make acceptable package meeting general support.

Have not had chance to consult Congressional advisers after tonight's consultations going well past midnight but will see them first thing Tuesday morning. I will emphasize to them importance you and I attach to avoidance of split of OAS on basis bare 14 votes if possible, particularly since we have only 13.

Believe it would be of inestimable value if you could telephone Lleras Camargo immediately to ask him to instruct his Foreign Minister to give me maximum cooperation to find formula which could unite OAS on satisfactory basis rather than suffer fatal breakdown this conference and devastating split OAS. As former Secretary General OAS he should be responsive this appeal. Time is of essence because this tempest in teapot is making US and OAS look ridiculous.

Source: Department of State, Central Files, 371.04/1–3062. Secret; Niact. Received at 3 a.m. and passed to the White House.

Will meet with Central American and hard-line LA countries early Tuesday morning to attempt moderate their views. But what is needed is a genuine desire particularly by Colombia to find generally acceptable formula.

Regret this situation but it is consequence of bare majority of 14 which called this meeting over serious objections of other important countries and insufficient time for intergovernmental preparations before conference convened. As background your talk with Lleras Camargo, recall that Colombia precipitated December 4 action and this meeting without prior consultation with us. They have special obligation to do everything possible to make it outstanding success it could be if we could solve this particular deadlock.

Request you not instruct me to attempt proceed with remainder agreed program without solution to this problem because resentment would be so high among many delegations that conference would collapse without tangible results. Lleras Camargo should telephone his Foreign Minister to give us maximum time advantage.

Have had diplomatic undercover evidence here of deep jealousies between most small Latin American countries and few larger more important ones, as reflected earlier conference here on Alliance for Progress. Am confident that if we can settle this one remaining question, conference could provide startling demonstration unity of hemisphere and strong movement on communism and Castro during past several weeks and months.

Rusk

---

143. Telegram From the Department of State to the Embassy in Colombia

Washington, January 30, 1962, 10:18 a.m.

604. President Kennedy talked briefly with President Lleras Camargo this morning with regard to possibility of Colombia cooperating with US in reaching agreement on Cuban exclusion from OAS. The President felt somewhat constrained in view open telephone circuit and requests you present following message to President Lleras soonest:

Source: Department of State, Central Files, 371.8/1–3062. Confidential; Niact. Drafted by Cates, cleared by McGeorge Bundy and Brubeck, and approved by Ball. Repeated to Punta del Este.

"In confirmation and amplification of our telephone conversation this morning I wish to emphasize what we firmly believe to be importance of reaching conference decision which will have broadest possible support.

Current situation at Punta del Este Conference is that we have only thirteen sure votes for exclusion Cuba from OAS and feel that if we do not reach as near unanimity as possible result will be victory for Castro and weakening of inter-American system.

We believe possible develop formula which moves toward exclusion of Cuba by subsequent action of Council and possibly Inter-American Conference and which will meet views Argentina Chile Brazil Mexico.

We recognize and greatly value energy and firmness Colombian stand throughout Conference but realize danger of grave split in OAS system if we insist on full exclusion Cuba now. Your FonMin is key man and we are disturbed by prospect of disagreement with him. That is why I have asked for your help in obtaining his cooperation work closely with Rusk in favor of compromise which can attract widest support. Unless we reach some such agreement I fear inter-American system will suffer serious blow and Alliance for Progress will be set back.

I feel an agreement on incompatibility of Cuba with principles of OAS, exclusion of Cuba from Inter-American Defense Board and establishment special watch dog committee plus agreement in principle appropriate steps to be taken to exclude Cuba from OAS would add up to successful conference.

As I said on the telephone I am most grateful for your willingness to help me in this matter and feel confident that your representative and mine working together can assure a highly successful result. John F. Kennedy"[1]

Ball

---

[1] Telegram 546 from Bogota, January 31, reported that Lleras had telephoned Caicedo, who told him that Uruguay had now accepted the Colombian/Central American resolution with a minor modification, making 14 votes, and that Argentina and Chile had decided to abstain. (Ibid., 721.00/1–3162)

144. **Telegram From Secretary of State Rusk to the Department of State**

Punta del Este, January 31, 1962, 5 a.m.

Secto 47. Eyes only for the President and Acting Secretary. No Other Distribution. Six resolutions representing our six-point program were passed by conference early this morning with twenty votes for strong declaration on Communist offensive in hemisphere, Alliance for Progress and expulsion Cuba from Inter-American Defense Board. Establishment of security committee received nineteen votes, one abstention. Economic measures sixteen votes, four abstentions and exclusion Cuba from organs and agencies OAS fourteen votes, six abstentions.[1]

Only disappointment was exclusion vote with Mexico, Brazil, Argentina, Chile, Ecuador and Bolivia abstaining on resolution as whole although joining with majority to give twenty votes on first two operating paragraphs underlining incompatibility Marxism-Leninism and present Cuban Government with inter-American system. Efforts to find formula to bridge gap continued up to final stage. Uruguay played courageous and key role in providing fourteenth vote. Keenest disappointment was emphasis abstainers on juridical arguments to such an extent as to imply majority was acting illegally. They let us down not so much by their votes as by way they handled it. In each instance severe internal problems were cited privately as determining their attitude and in all countries except Argentina I must confess these factors obviously dangerous and important. Brazil has especially vulnerable internal factors with government which manages to stabilize the left and which is anxious not to provide Quadros liberal and leftist support.

I would suggest general theme your press conference this subject ought to be program as a whole indicating remarkable movement in hemisphere in past several months in recognizing dangers of Communist penetration program in startling contrast to results San Jose conference sixteen months ago and far more than could have been reasonably expected as late as early December. Would try to get specific point of difference into context entire achievement and context of unanimous recognition of incompatibility Cuban regime with inter-American system. You might point out that smaller countries especially in and around

---

Source: Department of State, Central Files, 371.04/1–3162. Confidential; Eyes Only; Niact. Received at 4:49 a.m. and passed to the White House.

[1] The texts of the resolutions are printed in the "Final Act of the Eighth Meeting of Consultation of Ministers of Foreign Affairs, Serving As Organ of Consultation in Application to the Inter-American Treaty of Reciprocal Assistance, Punta del Este, Uruguay, January 22–31, 1962" (OAS doc. OEA/Ser.C/II.8), and in Department of State *Bulletin*, February 19, 1962, pp. 278–283.

Caribbean feel themselves to be under direct Castro–Communist pressures and that US felt it important that OAS give these countries its full support. Countries at greater distance from Cuba feel less directly threatened by Castroism. Would urge caution in discussing questions of diplomatic victory or defeats as between friends in OAS; OAS itself scored a most significant victory looking at program as whole. Most important you not show irritation or annoyance those abstaining expulsion vote since we must proceed on basis closest cooperation with them.

Congressional advisers pleased with results but naturally upset about countries abstaining expulsion vote. But I know they will return with better appreciation realities Latin American scene and with conviction that conference succeeded.

Rusk

---

145.   Memorandum for the Record

Washington, February 6, 1962.

SUBJECT

Daily Staff Meeting, 6 February 1962

1. Mr. Bundy presided. Although the main purpose of the meeting was to listen to Walt Rostow's summary of the Punta del Este conference, Bundy did mention

[Here follow references to two unrelated matters.]

2. Rostow's discussion of Punta del Este was, as are all his presentations, interesting but perhaps a little discursive compared to his usual style. Perhaps the most significant part of his discussion was a small byplay between him and Bundy on the degree of unanimity achieved for the final resolution of the conference. Bundy seemed to think that, given the President's desire for as nearly a unanimous outcome as possible, we might have done better than to squeak by with the minimum fourteen votes for a bare two-thirds majority. Rostow, however, said he felt strongly that Secretary Rusk, who worked like a Trojan night and day, had done the best he could do in conscience. It was true that at one point

---

Source: National Defense University, Taylor Papers, Box 24, Daily Staff Meetings. Secret. Drafted by Colonel Lawrence J. Legere.

the Argentine delegation proposed a mealy-mouthed anti-Communist compromise resolution which might have achieved unanimity or close to it, but the Secretary felt that a more meaningful outcome was to secure the fourteen votes he got for a resolution that meant something.

3. Rostow feels that all delegations gained something by the conference outcome. The United States succeeded in deflating the Cuban issue in domestic politics (the Congressional delegates were able to see at first hand how tough the going was to achieve the end result obtained), plus a goodly gain in good will among all the Latin American delegations for having put forth an honest, conscientious, polished try. In a rather contemptible manner, the big conservative powers such as Argentina and Chile could record a gain because they had opposed Uncle Sam and placated the left wing oppositions in their own countries.

4. Rostow noted the potential importance of the five-man security committee[1] which the Alliance had agreed to establish as a watch dog over the development of insurgency situations or even actual arms shipments. This committee should be under strong political control for obvious reasons. The Pentagon has under consideration the question of who will be the US member, and Rostow personally feels that General Thomas White might be a good bet, given his broad outlook, sophisticated background, and command of at least Spanish and maybe Portuguese.

5. DefCons—no change.

LJL

---

[1] Resolution II called for the creation of a Special Consultative Committee on Security.

---

146. Memorandum of Conversation

Washington, April 4, 1962, 6 p.m.

SUBJECT

Cuban Situation

PARTICIPANTS

Brazilian Foreign Minister San Tiago Dantas
The Secretary

Source: Department of State, Central Files, 737.00/4–462. Secret; Eyes Only. Drafted by Wilson and approved in S on April 12. The conversation was held in the Secretary's office.

Ambassador Lincoln Gordon
Mr. J. W. Wilson, Officer in Charge of Brazilian Affairs

In the course of a conversation on other matters, the Cuban situation was discussed.

In response to the Secretary's inquiry as to his opinion on the Cuban situation, the Foreign Minister replied that there is a rapid daily deterioration. Castro is in a fight with the Communists, who have increased the strength of their apparatus, and is in danger of being discarded by them. He has appealed to the esprit de corps of the barbudos. The food situation is bad. He cited as significant the recent action of the Cuban Government in exporting to the USSR appliances, etc. taken from private homes in order to pay for food imports.

The Foreign Minister said Brazil is in a good position to follow and influence the situation. (The Secretary interjected that this may soon be a "unique" position.) For this reason he is interested in what the U.S. views are of this evolution in Cuba—of getting Fidel away from the Communists. The Foreign Minister said there can be no thought of retreating from the Cuban revolution, of return to the Cardonas and the like, the status quo ante. It would be easier to create the conditions for a new form of democratic revolution. In response to a question by Ambassador Gordon, the Foreign Minister indicated that this might be something on the model of Yugoslavia. He asserted that it is clear that Khrushchev despises Fidel.

The Secretary said that, while their conversation was speculation, of course, he wanted to make sure it was understood clearly that from the U.S. viewpoint two things are not negotiable: (1) the direct Cuban ties with Moscow, such as arms and the Communist apparatus; and (2) Cuban subversive actions elsewhere in the hemisphere. If the situation inside Cuba should involve a clear break with Moscow and the concentration of Cuban activities in Cuba, then the possibility would be opened for a change of the policies of other countries. We have known of some top level defections and discontent (among those still in Cuba) over the embracing of the Communist apparatus.

The Secretary emphasized that, as President Kennedy has stated publicly, it is not the expropriations nor the internal changes in Cuba which are our concern; it is the ties with Moscow and the subversion elsewhere in the hemisphere. If Castro had support free from the Communist apparatus and cut the ties to Moscow, this would create a new situation.

The Foreign Minister then inquired whether the Secretary thought the idea of trying to wean Castro away from the Communists had some merit. The Secretary responded by pointing to the fact that we have never asked Brazil to break relations with Cuba, an omission which is not due to accident.

In recapitulating the Secretary's two points of U.S. policy on Cuba, the Foreign Minister said it was his understanding that these were tied to formal Communist participation in the Cuban regime and that, if these were removed, other points would be negotiable. He stated parenthetically that Castro is not weak internally. The Secretary said evidence of cutting the ties with Moscow would be, for example, reconciliation with Castro's early supporters who have left him on the Communist issue and the dropping of the language of Communism. When the Foreign Minister inquired if the U.S. made a distinction between diplomatic relations and ties with the U.S.S.R., the Secretary said that a change such as breaking ties would probably bring on a break in relations.

The Secretary mentioned the problem of asylees in the Ecuadoran Embassy and wondered if the Cubans would let some of them out of Cuba for Brazil. The Foreign Minister said the Brazilian Embassy was taking them in liberally and commented on the numbers in various Embassies. Some had been let out of the country in the past, he said.

In concluding the discussion of Cuba, the Secretary said he wished to make two more points. (1) There will be no military invasion of Cuba except in the event of fighting with the Soviet Union over something elsewhere, such as Berlin. (2) We do not take seriously the threats of Khrushchev to support Cuba. Khrushchev will not sacrifice the Soviet Union for Cuba.

With regard to an appointment to continue their discussion upon the Foreign Minister's return from Mexico, the Secretary said he was free all Thursday afternoon, April 12. He proposed that, should the weather be good, they take a cruise on the Potomac in the President's boat, having lunch on board and talking during the afternoon.

The Foreign Minister said he intended to summon the Brazilian Ambassador in Habana to Mexico City during his visit there. When the Secretary cautioned on the need for holding closely knowledge of their discussion, the Foreign Minister assured him of the Ambassador's discretion.

147. Memorandum of Conversation

Mexico City, June 29, 1962, 4:45 p.m.

SUBJECT

 Communism in Latin America

PARTICIPANTS

 President Kennedy
 President Lopez Mateos
 Foreign Minister Tello
 Ambassador Mann
 Mr. Martin
 Ambassador Carrillo Flores

President Kennedy brought up the subject of the danger of the spread of Communism in Latin America, particularly in the Caribbean basin, as a result of Sino/Soviet influence in Cuba and the use of Cuba as a springboard.

President Kennedy first asked whether President Lopez Mateos thought that the Cuban people would be able in the foreseeable future to recover their sovereignty from the Castro regime. President Lopez Mateos expressed the opinion that while the Castro regime had lost ground with the Cuban people because it had perverted the original purposes of the revolution and had come under the influence of the Communist bloc, it seemed doubtful, as a practical matter, that the Cuban people would be able to do very much about it in the foreseeable future because of the nature and military strength of the Castro regime. President Lopez Mateos doubted that the Communist revolution could gradually become a national type of revolution such as the one which took place in Mexico.

There was some discussion about the ability and disposition of the Soviet Union to give meaningful aid to Cuba.

President Kennedy, following up on President Lopez Mateos' appraisal of Castro's chances for survival, then asked what President Lopez Mateos thought could be done to prevent the spread of Soviet power and doctrine via Cuba to other American Republics. President Kennedy mentioned his concern with Soviet activities in countries like Venezuela, Colombia, Guatemala and Ecuador. Guerrilla activities in

---

Source: Department of State, Central Files, 611.12/7–662. Secret. Drafted by Mann on July 3 and approved by the White House on July 10. The source text, marked Part II, is filed with a July 6 covering memorandum from Department of State Executive Secretary William H. Brubeck to Bundy, which also enclosed a memorandum of Part I of the conversation.

Colombia and the recent revolts in Venezuela were specifically mentioned.

President Lopez Mateos acknowledged that this was a very difficult question. He said that Mexico had the ability to deal with Communist subversion and implied each country should take whatever measures are necessary to defend itself. Mr. Tello suggested at this point that it is important that Latin American countries prevent their territories from being used as a base of operations against other American Republics.

President Lopez Mateos repeated the familiar Mexican thesis: The important thing is to create better economic and social conditions and especially to provide jobs. When the people were better off, he thought it would not be easy for the Communists to lead them astray. He stressed his opinion that the Alliance for Progress is the best way to combat Communism.

President Kennedy replied that he did not underestimate the importance of economic growth and social progress; nor was he suggesting that Communism was an immediate danger in the United States or Mexico. But he pointed out it would take a decade to achieve the objectives of the Alliance for Progress even under the best of conditions. In the meantime, the question was: What did Mexico think should be done to prevent the spread of Communism in other American Republics? President Kennedy pointed out that, as Cuba shows, once a Communist regime has fastened itself on a country, it is most difficult for the people to rid themselves of it.

The Foreign Minister then recalled that Mexico was the first country at Punta del Este to openly espouse the doctrine of incompatibility between Cuba and the inter-American system and argued that this was a very substantial contribution to the success of Punta del Este because this was the thesis that prevailed rather than the Colombian or Peruvian doctrines. He explained again the Mexican juridical doctrine of the necessity for amending the Charter of the OAS so that there would be a sound legal basis for collective action.

The Foreign Minister went on to say that the Castro regime had made many "mistakes" and in his opinion would continue to make mistakes. He said that Chile, for example, had recently been on the verge of breaking relations with Cuba. [3-1/2 *lines of source text not declassified*]

President Kennedy returned again and again to his question of what President Lopez Mateos thought was the best way to deal with the obvious danger of an expansion of Communist influence in Latin America. President Lopez Mateos each time repeated his view that rapid economic development and social progress was the answer. In the end he said he would give the matter more thought.

In the course of the discussion, President Kennedy stated that the United States wished to deal with the problem of Communist penetration in the hemisphere in cooperation with other Latin American states like Mexico. He said he wanted to keep in close touch with Mexico on this point and to reach agreement on practical measures which could be taken by American states to deal with the threat. He said the United States had no plans at the present time for unilateral military action against the Castro regime.

148. Memorandum From the Assistant Secretary of State for Inter-American Affairs (Martin) to Secretary of State Rusk

Washington, August 30, 1962.

SUBJECT

Informal Meeting of OAS Foreign Ministers

Discussion

Enthusiasm for the United States resolution on Latin American military coups[1] is lagging with the general resumption of relations with Peru. After considerable negotiating of text, we can still not be sure of a majority. The Argentine Ambassador has indicated that his government cannot vote for our resolution but would think it useful to have an informal meeting of Foreign Ministers to discuss this subject. This would substitute an informal meeting in the immediate future for the formal meeting in the indefinite future as proposed in the United States resolution. Moreover, such an informal, private meeting, precedent for which was established in 1958,[2] would have the advantage of demonstrating our continuing concern with the problem of coups but without public debate or voting of resolutions on the subject.

In addition, there is widespread concern in Latin America about news accounts of recent arrivals of Soviet arms and men in Cuba. The

---

Source: Department of State, Central Files, 371.04/8–3062. Confidential. Drafted by Director of the Office of Regional Political Affairs Ward P. Allen and Martin.

[1] Reference is to a U.S. draft resolution presented to the OAS Council on August 16. The text of the operative portions is printed in *American Foreign Policy: Current Documents, 1962*, p. 308. Related documentation is in Department of State, Central Files 371.04 and 371.05.

[2] Reference is to an informal meeting of Foreign Ministers of the American Republics held in Washington September 23–24, 1958. The text of the communiqué issued at the conclusion of the meeting is printed in Department of State *Bulletin*, October 13, 1958, pp. 575–576. See also *Foreign Relations, 1958–1960*, vol. V, p. 37, footnote 2.

Guatemalan Government has suggested a meeting of the OAS Foreign Ministers to consider what action should be taken. This could be better handled at an informal meeting.

You could also give them a general briefing. The Berlin crisis is serious. The Geneva disarmament negotiations have been the scene of important new Western proposals. These are both matters in which there is much interest in Latin America and should be more. It is in our interest to give the Latin American Foreign Ministers a greater sense of participation in these developments.

The XI Inter-American Conference scheduled for Quito in 1960, in accordance with the OAS Charter, has been twice postponed. Meanwhile an agenda of over 40 items has accumulated. It would be desirable to decide whether or not this series of Conferences at 5-year intervals should be continued, replaced by something else or abandoned. This, too, could be taken up at the informal meeting and a manageable agenda of five or six items could be worked out for the Quito Conference.

In addition to the above matters, such a meeting could discuss and perhaps resolve the pending problem of the admission of Jamaica and Trinidad to the OAS.

Everything considered, it would appear highly desirable for the United States to issue invitations for an informal two-day meeting of Foreign Ministers in Washington[3] during the last ten days of September or early October when many of the Foreign Ministers will be in the United States for the UN General Assembly opening.

Recommendations[4]

1. That we respond favorably to the Argentine suggestion and informally seek to develop support for such a meeting with the other American Republics.

2. That, assuming generally favorable response, the United States take the initiative in arranging such a meeting.

3. That you secure the approval of the President for taking up these matters in this way.

---

[3] At this point on the source text, the words "or New York" were handwritten in the margin. Rusk crossed out Washington and wrote "in N.Y.", which he underscored twice.

[4] Rusk initialed his approval of recommendations 1 and 2 on August 31. He wrote in the margin next to recommendation 3, "Not necessary to bother him. DR".

149.   Circular Telegram From the Department of State to Certain Posts in the American Republics

Washington, September 16, 1962, 12:45 p.m.

468. Please convey following to FonMin soonest:

Response various FonMins to consultation initiated by Secretary September 5[1] indicates general receptivity to idea informal MFM. Taking into account wishes and convenience largest number, Secy therefore wishes invite his colleagues meet with him in Washington Tuesday and probably Wednesday, Oct 2 and 3. In view informal nature gathering, no formal agenda necessary. Meetings would be closed. Secy would initiate meeting with general review world situation with emphasis on Berlin and other major problems. He would follow with appraisal Cuban situation on which we hope there will be general exchange views. We also expect at least Argentina, Venezuela and US will have comments to make on international aspects general question coups d'état in American Republics as they may affect political tensions in hemisphere and success Alliance for Progress. There also some indications FonMins may want consider desirability COAS review agenda 11th IA Conference order eliminate all items except those major importance. However this matter, as well as any exchange views on possible date of Conference, may well take place outside meeting.

There would be no voting or any resolution emerging from meeting, but if a consensus develops on any subject this might be expressed in public communiqué to be issued close of meeting.

Secretary hopes all his colleagues will be able attend and dates have been arranged in order facilitate maximum attendance. However Secretary understands of course that in few cases attendance FonMin may prove impossible, in which event it hoped FonMin could deputize special high-level representative attend in his place.

Secretary desires invite those attending to informal dinner October 2.

Following points for your background and use your discretion:

Source: Department of State, Central Files, 371.04/9–1662. Confidential. Drafted by Allen, cleared in substance by Deputy Director of the Office of International Conferences Richard S. Wheeler, and approved by Martin. Sent to all diplomatic posts in the American Republics except Kingston and repeated to USUN, POLAD/CINCLANT and POLAD/CINCARIB.

[1] Circular telegram 388, September 5, summarized a meeting that day between Rusk and Latin American Ambassadors, in which Rusk discussed the Cuban situation and suggested an informal meeting of Foreign Ministers in New York, where many would be attending the U.N. General Assembly. (Ibid., 737.00/9–562) A record of the meeting was transmitted in Document 153.

(1) Consultations indicate probable attendance all FonMins above dates except Mexican (who agreeable to meeting but committed accompany President Far East tour), Peruvian, Uruguayan and Chilean, whose attendance uncertain.

(2) While Secretary does not plan stress problem coups, we believe it desirable not overlook question, in view position taken by US in its pending COAS resolution that discussion by FonMins appropriate, in view fact original Argentine initiative proposed informal meeting for this explicit purpose[2] and in view strong feelings Venezuelan FonMin and others that problem must be raised. Any discussion will not refer to Peruvian situation. Moreover, informal discussion this matter would make it unnecessary for US to press its resolution in Council.

(3) On balance we think it undesirable meeting take up question Bolivian withdrawal which inextricably mixed with Rio Lauca dispute which might well make Chilean attendance impossible.

(4) In view Ecuadorean desire that question postponement Quito Conference not be discussed because of domestic political repercussions, we do not wish press this issue but believe corridor talks re streamlining agenda should not embarass Ecuadoreans. Quito may assure FonMin communiqué if any will not contain any reference this matter without their approval.

(5) In view fact question admission new members now in process consideration COAS and in deference Guatemala's desire it not be discussed at meeting, US does not propose raise it.

(6) SYG Mora will be invited attend.

(7) Meetings will be held in Department conference rooms and not in PAU, but this does not preclude possibility some ceremonial session after meeting at PAU with FonMins acting as Council members if this desired.

Rusk

---

[2] The Argentine suggestion was made in an August 21 aide-mémoire, the text of which was transmitted in telegram 553 from Buenos Aires, August 21. (Department of State, Central Files, 371.04/8–2162)

150. Memorandum of Conversation

Washington, September 18, 1962, 11:49 a.m.

SUBJECT

   Mexican policy towards Cuba

PARTICIPANTS

   The Secretary
   Antonio Carrillo Flores—Ambassador of Mexico
   Mr. Martin—Assistant Secretary for Inter-American Affairs
   Mr. Sayre—Officer in Charge, Mexican Affairs

The Ambassador called at the Secretary's request. The Secretary inquired about the projected trip of President López Mateos to the Far East. He said that the United States wanted to do whatever it could to assist the President while he was in the country. The Ambassador expressed appreciation for this offer. He thought the President would make a technical stop at Los Angeles on October 4, would stay over night at Honolulu on October 5, and make another technical stop at Guam on October 6.

The Secretary then turned to a discussion of the Cuban situation.

The Secretary said that he had little to add to the facts which he had described earlier to the Latin American Ambassadors. In response to the Ambassador's question, he said that the weapons received by Cuba were normally used in a defensive system. He noted, however, that they had offensive capability if targets came within range, e.g., if a U.S. aircraft flying outside Cuban territorial waters came within the 17-mile range of ground-to-air missiles it could be shot down. He acknowledged that the weapons did not constitute a direct military threat to the U.S. and that they would require minimum attention if the U.S. had to move into Cuba. He said that the United States of course had no intention of permitting Cuba to export any of these to other Latin American countries.

The Secretary said that the American republics had to recognize that the Castro regime could not be permitted to continue in the Hemisphere for an extended period because it was incompatible as the Foreign Ministers had said at Punta del Este. He said that the United States is concerned about Cuban subversive activities, the large number of Latins receiving training in Cuba, and the amount of money being provided from Cuba for activities in other countries. He said that the people of the United States are seriously concerned about Cuba, as are the other

---

Source: Department of State, Central Files, 612.37/9–1862. Secret. Drafted by Sayre and approved in S October 12. The conversation was held at the Department of State. The time of the meeting is taken from Rusk's Appointment Book. (Johnson Library)

republics. He said that some might consider these feelings irrational, but that these feelings are a fact and the United States Government had to deal with the situation with them in mind. The Ambassador said that he could confirm from his own experience that the people of the United States viewed the Cuban issue with considerable emotion. He said he is unable to make a speech anywhere without the question arising. The Secretary said that in explaining this situation to the NATO parliamentarians he had told them that all the money their countries are spending on publicity campaigns in the United States would be to no avail so long as ships carrying their flags participated in the Cuban trade.

The Secretary said that the U.S. considers that extra-continental intervention in the Hemisphere is a fact. We believe that Cuba intends to export its system to other countries. We view Castro-Communist activities as deeply antagonistic not only to the OAS Charter but to the values and systems of each of the republics. He urged that Mexico review its position on Cuba, giving the most solemn consideration to Mexico's own interest, to the views of Mexico's neighbors who look to her for leadership, to Mexico's commitment in the Hemisphere, and to what Cuba really means to Mexico and to the Hemisphere.

The Secretary said that he did not want to make any specific proposals to Mexico. These would occur to Mexico as it studied the problem. He did want to mention that Mexico's neighbors are preoccupied by the large number of their citizens who are passing through Mexico enroute to Cuba. The use of Mexico in this manner is disturbing to them and they are frustrated in dealing with the problem. He noted that a Mexican airline provides part of the service. He said that the U.S. feels that a strict watch should be kept on activities in the Caribbean. The American republics could not afford secrecy in this area. He said he knew Mexico maintained some surveillance against possible movements to and from Cuba. He expressed the hope that this could be increased and Mexico could announce publicly its action. The Secretary mentioned the subversive activities of the Cuban Embassy and consular personnel in Mexico. The Ambassador referred to the strict controls which his Government maintains at the Mexico City airport as an example of surveillance over Cuban diplomatic and consular personnel. The Secretary said he referred to Cuban diplomatic activities only as a point which Mexico might want to consider. Maybe such activities could be controlled by limiting the number of Cuban personnel in Mexico.

The Secretary emphasized again that he was not proposing or asking for any specific action but did want to suggest that Mexico earnestly explore what was in its own best interest and that of the Hemisphere. The Ambassador inquired whether he could say that the sense of the Secretary's remarks was that Mexico should show it is preoccupied and not indifferent to the problem. The Secretary hoped that Mexico could go further, and show that it is deeply concerned. He said Hemisphere leaders had to look forward, and see where continuance of the present situation would lead. He noted that this is the first time that people now living have had to deal with the problems of a vicious form of intervention in the Hemisphere. The Secretary said he thought everything should be done to isolate Cuba and was afraid Mexico was not conveying an impression of solidarity.

The Ambassador said that he had not previously been confronted with so difficult and complex a problem in US-Mexican relations. He thought it was a political and not a military problem. He understood the Secretary to be urging that Mexico consider how it could best establish that it had a sense of solidarity with other republics on the Cuban issue. He recalled that President López Mateos had said in meeting with President Kennedy that Castro was no longer a popular figure and was now a tool of the Soviets. Mexico also recognized Cuba might be a greater problem for Mexico than the U.S. The problem was to find a solution that would not boomerang. Mexico was limited by its own political situation and upcoming presidential election. President López Mateos is seeking to avoid an open fight between the extreme left and right. Steps by Mexico on the Castro regime therefore would have serious political consequence. Thus President López Mateos had to make concessions first to the right and then to the left in order to maintain harmony. He noted Mexico's relations with Spain were a concession to the left. Assistant Secretary Martin suggested the Mexican President might consider making concessions to the right on Cuba.

The Secretary said that the problem for the U.S. is not just political or one of public opinion in the U.S. or Congress. In a real sense, it involved the future of Cuba and of the Hemisphere. Cuba is the first point of confrontation with the Soviets in the Hemisphere. He noted that the U.S. has a million men on duty outside the U.S., with casualties a weekly occurrence.

The Secretary said that the Soviets are investing substantial sums in Cuba. He noted that the Soviets are not investing this for Cuba alone, but with the thought that Cuba is a bridgehead to the rest of Latin America. If the American republics could demonstrate that the investment will not pay off, the Soviets might reconsider the value of Cuba because the Soviets cannot afford such an investment on Cuba alone.

The Ambassador inquired as to the possibility of a meeting between President Kennedy and Premier Khrushchev and whether Cuba would be discussed. The Secretary indicated that he thought not, because the Soviets would link Cuba to Turkey or some other spot. Assistant Secretary Martin noted that agreement by the U.S. to discuss Cuba with the Soviets would be in keeping with Khrushchev's view that the Monroe Doctrine is dead.

151.   Circular Telegram From the Department of State to Certain Posts in the American Republics

Washington, September 21, 1962, 8:23 p.m.

508. Depcirtel 468.[1] Department believes that informal MFM at conclusion its deliberations should issue public communiqué containing meaningful statements regarding increased danger Cuban subversion and aggression and specifying defensive measures which American community should take meet it.

We believe communiqué might include following elements:

1.   Recognition recent Cuban arms build-up with Soviet military personnel and equipment intensifies dangers hemispheric peace and security. FonMins view with increasing seriousness Soviet intervention in building up Cuba as vanguard for assault on institutions of American Republics. This requires governments keep situation under constant review and renew efforts, individually and collectively, guard against further communist penetration this hemisphere.

2.   Agreement work through appropriate OAS organs as necessary in pursuing following courses of action:

a.   Reexamine trade relations with Cuba to see what additional steps affecting trade in items other than food and medicines could be taken limit capacity Castro regime subvert institutions OARs or threaten peace and security individual country or hemisphere.

b.   Act to prevent vessels under their control from carrying to Cuba arms, implements of war, other items strategic importance.

c.   Appeal all other independent nations take similar action with respect trade with Cuba and use vessels under their control.

d.   Intensify efforts prevent Castro-communist agents and groups within their respective countries from subverting their established institutions.

e.   Recognize Caribbean is area most immediately vulnerable to subversion from Cuba and consequently governments of area, pursuant paragraph 3 Resolution II of 8th MFM, have special interest take defensive measures prevent clandestine shipment men and material from Cuba to their countries for subversive purposes.

f.   Agree that in this hemisphere cloak of secrecy should not be used cover up military buildups supported by extracontinental powers

---

Source: Department of State, Central Files, 371.04/9–2162. Confidential. Drafted by Bowdler, cleared by Martin, and approved by Allen. Sent to all diplomatic posts in the American Republics except Kingston and Port-of-Spain and to USUN, and repeated to POLAD CINCARIB and POLAD CINCLANT.

[1] Document 149.

threatening peace and security of Americas and consequently intensify their individual and collective surveillance of delivery of arms and implements of war and all other items strategic importance to Cuba from any source and exchange information on such deliveries.

g. Request COAS undertake, pursuant Resolution II of 8th MFM and using SCCS as necessary, urgent and thorough investigation of: (1) transfer of funds from Cuban sources to OARs for purpose subverting peoples and governments in interest of international communism, (2) flow of Cuban subversive propaganda to OARs, (3) utilization Cuba as base for training and indoctrination of persons from OARs in techniques communist subversion and as staging area of movement of persons from OARs to Sino-Soviet bloc countries for further training. Investigation should include recommendations to governments on how combat these dangers, bearing in mind laws and constitutional provisions of respective countries.

3. Reaffirmation by FonMins their determination invoke Rio Treaty to counter immediately and effectively by whatever means may be necessary, including use of force, any threat from Castro regime or Sino-Soviet bloc powers to safety of American Republics and peace and security of hemisphere.

4. Declaration that FonMins look forward to time when freedom-loving Cuban people will establish government compatible with principles and purposes inter-American system which will be quickly recognized, assisted and welcomed back into family American nations.

Foregoing is exclusively for information of addressees. No mention should be made to local officials until specifically authorized by Department. We recognize this is ambitious program and may not be possible to secure agreement of FM's at informal meeting this character to commit themselves this far. Will be exploring very informally with them individually in NY next week. Meanwhile would appreciate your comments.[2]

---

[2] Printed from an unsigned copy.

152. Circular Telegram From the Department of State to Certain Posts in the American Republics

Washington, September 25, 1962, 3:55 p.m.

517. Based on paragraph 2e. of Depcirtel 508[1] Department has been considering courses action which countries bordering Caribbean can take demonstrate their determination work collectively resist attempts direct or indirect aggression by Castro regime. Current planning runs along following lines:

A.   Courses of Action

1. Establishment system air-sea surveillance around Cuba and along coast Caribbean countries. Surveillance would serve inhibit Castro regime from sending clandestine shipments of arms and men to other countries of area and would strengthen capabilities those countries intercept such shipments. We would assume primary responsibility for Cuban patrol while other countries would cover own coasts with such assistance from us as may be necessary. Our conducting Cuban patrol would not rule out contributions by other Caribbean countries (e.g. naval units or support facilities for such units).

2. Intensification efforts counter Castro-communist subversion including control of travel to and from Cuba, shipment subversive propaganda from Cuba and transfer funds from Cuban sources for subversive purposes. Governments could also agree on system for exchanging information on Castro-communist subversive activities.

3. Issuance by governments of Caribbean area, including United States, of joint declaration that extension by Castro regime of its Marxist-Leninist system by force or threat of force to any part of Caribbean area or creation or use of a Soviet supported offensive military capability endangering security of any country in area, will call for taking of any necessary measures to protect security of countries concerned. This declaration would be accompanied by announcement that discussions will be held at military level to plan for defensive measures for meeting these contingencies.

B.   Timing and Forum

1. Paragraph 2e. of Depcirtel 508 if approved at informal MFM would constitute additional hemispheric acknowledgment that Carib-

Source: Department of State, Conference Files: Lot 65 D 533, CF 2171. Confidential. Drafted by Bowdler, cleared by Martin and Chayes, and approved by Allen. Sent to Bogotá, Caracas, Guatemala City, Managua, Mexico City, Panama, Port-au-Prince, San Salvador, San José, Santo Domingo, and Tegucigalpa, and repeated to USUN, POLAD CINCARIB, POLAD CINCLANT, Asuncion, Buenos Aires, La Paz, Lima, Montevideo, Quito, Rio de Janeiro, and Santiago.
[1] Document 151.

bean countries are particularly vulnerable Castro-communist subversion and consequently justified taking special defensive measures. This would serve minimize criticism Rio Treaty being bypassed or that inter-American system being fractionized.

2. Based this paragraph we would seek have President Caribbean country (e.g. President Betancourt) invite Ministers Defense and Interior Caribbean countries meet during second or third week of October to consider special measures which should be taken. Courses action outlined A. could constitute program to be approved. Inclusion Interior Ministers would emphasize that problem of dealing with Castro-communist threat is not purely external but one in which internal measures are equally important.

Comment:

Department aware foregoing plan presents certain problems, particularly (1) whether Haiti and Mexico would want to join in action contemplated and (2) probability agreement patrol activities will give rise to requests for further military assistance. Would appreciate your evaluation receptivity of local government to plan and additional problems you can foresee in its execution. Foregoing is exclusively for information of addressees and should not be discussed with local officials until specifically authorized by Department.

Ball

---

153. Telegram From Secretary of State Rusk to the Department of State

New York, September 26, 1962, midnight.

Secto 21. Informal MFM. Following based on uncleared memcon:[1]

Secy met Sept 25 informally with FonMins Bolivia, CR, DomRep, Guat, Nic and Panama for discussion Cuban problem in preparation informal MFM next week. He briefly reviewed situation, pointing out while recent Sov shipments supplied at Castro's urging have neither increased power of Cuba as offensive military threat nor increased Castro's ability control own people, do represent increased Sov involve-

---

Source: Department of State, Central Files, 737.00/9–2662. Confidential; Limit Distribution. Repeated to all posts in Latin America except Trinidad and Jamaica, and to POLAD CINCLANT, and POLAD CINCARIB. Received at 1:19 a.m. on September 27.

[1] A memorandum of the conversation is ibid., Conference Files: Lot 65 D 533, CF 2152.

ment. Secy repeated unequivocal assurances US will under no circumstances permit any raids or attacks of any kind by Cuba on LA countries and stated so far Castro acting cautiously in this area. Recent Sov bluster still gives no indication Soviets contemplating actions of type President warned against in press statement.

Secy made clear US not prepared accept Cuban situation as permanent. Although military action remains eventual possibility, we must think of ways solve problem without recourse to arms. Objective should be actions which increasingly isolate Cuba so as make abundantly clear to Soviets Cuba is unprofitable enterprise for them, either in itself or as basis Communist penetration other ARs.

Such steps, which worthy discussion informal MFM, would include review of minimal trade relationships with and shipping to Cuba (this matter we also discussing with our NATO allies); measures to control flow of small arms, propaganda, money, agents from Cuba and movement of groups of Latin nationals to Cuba for training in subversion; measures of increased surveillance Carib area; and measures control Commies in each country.

In making clear our determination isolate Cuba, we naturally hope for complete hemisphere solidarity, at least on general approach. In addition we prepared move on more intensive steps tightened surveillance and controls with those ARs willing do so, particularly Caribbean nations whose special right take extra measures was recognized at Punta del Este (para 3 res 11).

In ensuing discussion (Bolivia and El Salvador silent) Central Americans expressed agreement Secy's approach; showed real interest in moving forward in Carib concert, but did not suggest any radical or belligerent action. They showed general concern (to which Secy agreed) that one serious impact in their countries of recent Cuban buildup has been to increase confidence and insolence local Commie groups who intensifying their subversive nibbling tactics. Guatemalan suggested all should urge those ARs still maintaining relations with Cuba to break them. Considerable emphasis placed by Latins on importance of intensive combined efforts educate peoples OARs on actual conditions Cuban people to counteract heavy Castro propaganda.

Separate meeting of Central American and Caribbean FonMins (excluding Mexico) held 3 pm September 26 with Martin[2] for more concrete exploration possible steps. Secy met 5 pm same day with FonMins South American Reps present for similar initial review of situation.

Rusk

---

[2] The meeting was summarized in Secto 41 from New York, dated September 28. (Ibid.)

154.   Telegram From Secretary of State Rusk to the Department of State

New York, September 27, 1962, 7 p.m.

Secto 28. I. Secretary met September 26 with Foreign Ministers Chile, Haiti, Peru, Venezuela and ex-Foreign Minister Arinos of Brazil.[1] Reviewed Cuban situation along lines reported Secto 21,[2] amplifying following points:

1.   Re Soviet military build-up. If it should be necessary US take military action, only 3-4 hours preparation would be required reduce effectiveness of material so far received since July. If should be necessary use force, US would employ maximum, non-nuclear violence order minimize time and casualties, but we most anxious avoid this course since would leave long lasting wounds in Cuba and elsewhere.

2.   This is why we pursuing objective of making Soviet involvement in Cuba as expensive and unprofitable as possible for USSR by measures which will further isolate Cuba and exert maximum pressure on USSR.

3.   Made clear US not objecting to whatever type social or economic system Cuban people may freely choose, but only to Soviet intervention there and Soviet-Cuban intervention OARS. Stressed US unwilling negotiate Cuban problem with USSR. Due special IA relationships and agreement, Cuban situation no way comparable to or linkable with situations elsewhere, i.e., Berlin or US MAP relations with other free world countries such as Turkey. Stressed US not seeking import cold war into hemisphere or drag OARS into problems not their responsibilities. Cold war direct result Soviet efforts subvert true independence national states. It they who have now brought cold war to hemisphere through Cuba.

4.   Also pointed out intense preoccupation American people with Cuban problem is political fact that must be taken into account—as must public opinion situation OARS as well.

II. Venezuelan Foreign Minister, agreeing Secretary's approach, pointed out fight against Castro-Communist gangsterism OARS closely relation promotion democracy.[3] In Venezuelan own experience Communists gained strength under dictatorships. Peruvian Foreign Minister,

---

Source: Department of State, Conference Files: Lot 65 D 533, CF 2171. Confidential; Priority. Repeated to all posts in Latin America except Trinidad and Jamaica, and to POLAD CINCLANT, and POLAD CINCARIB.

[1] A memorandum of the conversation is ibid.

[2] Document 153.

[3] A note on the source text indicates that this sentence reads as received and was confirmed by the originator.

though agreeing desirability meeting on Cuban problem, opposed distracting attention by reference other issues and stated if any their problems (i.e., coups d'état) discussed, Peru would not attend.

Secretary responded by stressing informal nature meeting outside institutional framework OAS. US thought has been take advantage presence Foreign Ministers in US (originally preferring New York as locus) to talk about problems hemisphere interest, foremost among which, in US view, is Cuba. All realize are various problems within family, such as US-Panama differences re Canal to which Panamanian Foreign Minister referred in GA, and US-Mexican border problem. One country not participating OAS meetings due differences with another. Upcoming Brazilian elections may complicate Brazilian discussion certain matters. However, view our common interests, obligations and objectives, US strongly hopes will be possible Foreign Ministers can gather to talk without regard for various problems within hemisphere and without raising the difficult and divisive question of what we must formally discuss.

While in situation of complete informality it not possible impose conditions on what any Foreign Minister might mention or call any one to order, this should not pose real problem if we all relatively relaxed and not try give institutional effect to an agenda when there is no agenda.

Chilean and Brazilian made mildly helpful statements re general desirability of meeting. Arinos stated Brazilian information confirms Secretary's description Soviet build-up, but little evidence indicate Castro-directed efforts infiltrate Brazil. Indicated some concern re how reach and express conclusions of meeting, referring to possible press communiqué. Secretary gave impression probably will be communiqué but stated at moment US has no flat suggestions re content.

III. We intend follow up this and previous meeting with further talks New York and Washington, exploring more concretely ideas contained Department Circular telegram 508.[4]

View absence or late arrival in US Foreign Ministers of Ecuador, Honduras, Paraguay and Uruguay Embassies those countries requested consult Foreign Ministers soonest, drawing on background presentation of problem by Secretary reported above and in Secto 21 and stressing US desire discuss at meeting steps indicated paragraph three Secto 21. Unless Department perceives objection recommend Department authorize other addressees utilize information both telegrams for discussion Foreign Offices as appropriate.

Rusk

---

[4] Document 151.

155. Memorandum From the Assistant Secretary of State for Inter-American Affairs (Martin) to Secretary of State Rusk

Washington, September 30, 1962.

SUBJECT

Latin American Attitudes re Informal MFM

As a result of your meetings with the Latin American Foreign Ministers and additional conversations with them during the last few days, the following is our appraisal of their positions at present:

1. The *Central American and Caribbean countries* (except Mexico and Haiti whose views are unknown) are interested in taking some joint action among themselves to strengthen their defenses. Some of them are toying with a separate declaration, but due to their dispersion and lack of leadership, this has not jelled. All are receptive to the idea of a later Caribbean meeting of the Ministers of Defense and Interior to establish joint air and sea patrols for coastal surveillance and to set up some system for exchanging information. The major points in our proposed communiqué are all acceptable to them.

In addition, one or more have suggested the following steps, none of which is generally acceptable to all (nor to us):

a. Creation of a government in exile. (Guatemala will push this.)
b. Convocation of a formal MFM under the Rio Treaty to take binding decisions on severance of diplomatic and economic relations.
c. In addition, there have been press reports that some countries favor the creation of a Caribbean NATO-type military alliance. However, they have not proposed this in discussions with us.

2. *Venezuela* likes the points contained in our proposed communiqué but insists on adding a reference to the importance of strengthening representative democracy. *Colombia* is sympathetic and cooperative, but somewhat concerned that any separate action by the Caribbean group would appear as a division within the OAS.

3. *Brazil's* position is encouraging. They agree to the desirability of firmer action to control the flow of funds, propaganda, agents and trainees; agree to the right of the Caribbean countries to take special measures; agree that some public declaration is desirable and Arinos did not object to any of the basic points contained in our proposed draft.

4. *Bolivia* will probably follow Brazil. The Bolivian and Chilean Foreign Ministers have engaged in informal conversations regarding the Lauca controversy. They will keep this subject out of the MFM.

Source: Department of State, Central Files, 371.04/9–3062. Confidential. Drafted by Allen. The source text bears Rusk's initials indicating that he read it.

5. *Argentina's* position is uncertain due to the lack of a Foreign Minister, but we believe they will be generally helpful. *Mexico's* views are unknown.

6. *Chile* poses a serious problem. The Foreign Minister feels strongly there should be no communiqué at all. His position is based on the Chilean domestic situation and on his alleged promise to the legislature in return for permission to participate in the meeting, that there would be no agreement or declaration emerging from the meeting. If, however, we have the support of Brazil and Argentina, the Chileans can be isolated and perhaps brought along.

156. Editorial Note

An informal meeting of Foreign Ministers of the American Republics was held October 2–3, 1962, in Washington. In addition to Secretary Rusk, the participants included 17 Foreign Ministers or Acting Foreign Ministers, Special Representatives from Argentina and Brazil, and the Chairman of the Council of the Organization of American States. No formal, agreed records of the meetings were made. U.S. memoranda of conversation recording the four sessions are in Department of State, Central Files 371.04/10–262 and 371.04/10–362. The texts are scheduled for inclusion in the microfiche supplement to volume XI. See also Document 157. Related material is in Department of State, Conference Files: Lot 65 D 533, CF 2168–2171.

157.   Circular Telegram From the Department of State to Certain Posts in the American Republics

Washington, October 4, 1962, 8:21 p.m.

596. Department regards informal MFM as highly successful. Communiqué[1] is strongest unanimous statement on Cuban problem yet to emerge from gathering of all American governments. Both by itself and as impetus for follow-up action on 8th MFM decisions it should have helpful political and psychological, and to limited extent economic, impact in promoting our twin objectives of (1) making it as expensive as possible for USSR to maintain Cuba and (2) isolating Cuba and thereby reducing subversive, political and psychological usefulness of Cuba to Soviets. Re US opinion communiqué helpful in meeting criticism of OARs and OAS for disinterest and inaction.

Discussions characterized by friendly and cooperative spirit and high degree of frankness which reflected in communiqué. Strength of communiqué lies not only in content but also fact it reflects unanimous agreement with no abstentions or reservations. Document contains all essential points we desired. If phraseology not as strong or specific as we would have preferred on some aspects, particularly in condemning Castro regime, this due stand taken by countries maintaining relations with Cuba. They agreed oppressive nature Castro regime and suffering Cuban people but feared adverse effect their relations if meeting too outspoken this matter.

Features of communiqué which further USG objectives re Cuba are:

1. Recognition of Soviet effort convert Cuba into armed base for penetration of Hemisphere and subversion its democratic institutions.

2. Agreement OAS bodies should intensify efforts to carry out assignments regarding Cuban situation and be ready move quickly if situation calls for additional action. (This refers particularly to action under Rio Treaty.)

3. Consensus that studies on subversive travel, funds and propaganda should be done pursuant Resolution II of 8th MFM without delay.

4. Consensus that recent events in Cuba warrant action under Resolution VIII of 8th MFM including use of American Republic ships in Cuban trade, accompanied by appeal to other independent countries to review their Cuban trade and use of ships.

Source: Department of State, Central Files, 371.04/10–462. Confidential. Drafted by Bowdler and Allen, cleared by Martin, and approved by Allen. Sent to all diplomatic posts in the American republics except Kingston and Port-of-Spain and to USUN and repeated to POLAD CINCARIB, POLAD CINCLANT, Kingston, Port-of-Spain, London, and Paris.

[1] For text, see Department of State *Bulletin,* October 22, 1962, pp. 598–600.

5.   Recognition that Soviet intervention in Cuba is not analogous to, and cannot be justified by, defensive measures which other Free World countries have taken against Soviet imperialism (e.g. bases in Turkey).

6.   Recognition that threat of Cuban subversion manifests itself differently in different areas of Hemisphere calling for special measures to deal with it pursuant paragraph 3 of Resolution II of 8th MFM. (Caribbean generally recognized as area of greater danger although this not specifically stated.)

7.   Voicing of deep sympathy with the Cuban people over their plight. Views expressed in communiqué provide us with basis for pressing for action in COAS, joining with Caribbean countries in special measures along lines Depcirtel 517,[2] and urging NATO and other Free World countries support American Republics in their efforts isolate Cuba.

Text of communiqué carried in wireless file.

Ball

---

[2] Document 152.

---

158.   Memorandum of Conversation

Washington, November 30, 1962, 11 a.m.

SUBJECT

Communism, Cuba and Caribbean Security

PARTICIPANTS

President Kennedy
Ambassador Charles R. Burrows
Assistant Secretary of State Martin
Assistant Administrator of AID Moscoso
Mr. Ralph Dungan, The White House

President Villeda Morales of Honduras
Honduran Ambassador to the United States and the OAS Céleo Dávila
Honduran Foreign Minister Alvarado Puerto
Honduran Finance Minister Bueso Arias

Source: Department of State, Central Files, 611.15/11–3062. Confidential. Drafted by Edward M. Rowell of the Office of Central American and Panamanian Affairs and approved by the White House December 28. The source text is marked "Part 1 (of 7)." The meeting was held at the White House.

The conversation was long and involved.

President Villeda Morales made the following points:

United States efforts leading to withdrawal of Soviet missiles from Cuba were magnificent, but there is no way to be sure whether or not underground bases still threaten hemispheric security and peace. In the Cuban crisis Honduras offered facilities in accordance with its obligations under the Rio Treaty and the decision of the Council of the OAS.[1] The United States can always rely on unlimited Honduran cooperation.

The problem of Cuba and security transcends nuclear arms and purely military operations. Every Communist is dangerous. Cuba directly affects all the small nearby countries. These countries must develop socially and economically to offset Marxist propaganda. Communism will be no menace if countries are ruled democratically, and if assistance under the Alliance for Progress is forthcoming.

It would be suicidal for the Communists to take over a Central American Government, because they could not isolate a mainland country as they did Cuba. The Communists recognize this. Also, it is easier to generate instability from outside a Government than from within. Hence, the Communists are not interested in taking over any Central American Government, and the menace of communism is not imminent in the region. It is a mistake to ascribe to the Communists disturbances such as the recent one in Guatemala, since this exaggerates their truly limited power.

In Honduras communism is in a state of lethargy and communism is weaker than in any other Central American country. This is because the Government profoundly believes in human dignity and the elimination of repressive measures.

The constitution forbids participation by non-democratic parties in elections. Eighty per cent of the electorate supports the present administration. Communists are kept under close control. Five years ago they generated street fights, but since then their activities have dwindled. They are no danger in Honduras.

The situation may be different in other Central American countries, and what affects one affects all.

Villeda introduced the possibility of a Caribbean force, and likened "Operacion Fraternidad" to a group of firemen ready to answer an alarm. However, an alliance of armies (which would be used against guerrilla or insurgent groups) should be preceded by creation of a civil-

---

[1] Reference is to a resolution approved by the OAS Council on October 23 calling for the withdrawal from Cuba of all missiles and other offensive weapons and recommending that member states take all necessary measures to ensure that Cuba could not continue to receive Soviet military supplies and to prevent the missiles from becoming an active threat. (OAS doc. OEA/Ser.G/III/C–sa-463 (1); also printed in Department of State *Bulletin*, November 12, 1962, pp. 722–723)

ian force. This two-stage establishment of forces should not be revealed to the Communists. Villeda noted that three years ago he met Presidents Lemus of El Salvador, Ydígoras of Guatemala and Somoza of Nicaragua, and suggested the creation of a civilian security system to fight communism.

The question of an army to defend the democracies can be raised in Honduras, preferably after the elections. In this connection, it was suggested that an air base be built near San Pedro Sula.

Relations between the Central American Governments are propitious for the discussion of a joint military force. The situation should remain good after the Nicaraguan election in February, 1963. Villeda believes he can coordinate such an effort. He said the other Central American Governments had "indicated their confidence in his ability to reflect the common hopes and ideals of them all".

President Kennedy made the following points:

Castro is still an aggressive element. President Kennedy has been considering creation of a Caribbean force which could be used against guerrilla or insurgent groups. President Villeda's reference to such a force mentioned in connection with "Operacion Fraternidad", is interesting. President Kennedy hoped Villeda would continue to think of a joint force or army. Care must be taken to see that it would not support dictatorships (e.g., Haiti), and that it would not appear to interfere in elections. Possible Communist gains in turbulent Guatemalan elections would tempt such interference. The force would have to be established within the framework of the OAS to avoid the stigma of "U.S. imperialism". An example of successful joint action is that taken by the United States, Colombia and Venezuela to prevent a Communist take-over in the Dominican Republic following Trujillo's death.

The United States will study the matter of common military action with the Central American Republics, and will keep in touch with Villeda.

President Kennedy cautioned Villeda, saying experiences with Jagan, the Chinese and Castro demonstrate that Communists frequently take over a Government in the guise of enlightened, democratic, revolutionary leaders, and not as Communists per se.

It is essential to recognize that present Hemisphere problems pit the Hemisphere and the United States against communism, and are not just reflections of bilateral conflict between the United States and Castro. Should Castro convince people that the matter is purely bilateral, he will draw greater sympathy, and the eradication of the Communist menace will be more difficult.

159.   Memorandum of Conversation

Washington, March 12, 1963, 12:30 p.m.

SUBJECT

Cuba and Communist Activities in Latin America

PARTICIPANTS

U.S.	Brazil
The Secretary of State	Finance Minister Dantas
Asst. Secretary Martin	Ambassador Campos
Ambassador Gordon	Ambassador Bernardes
A.J. DeSeabra (Interpreter)	

The Secretary, referring back to the conversations on Cuba held last year,[1] recalled that there were two points that were not negotiable:

(1) the military and political connection between Cuba and Moscow;

(2) the attempts by Cuba to foment subversion in other Hemisphere countries.

The first point was brought to a dramatic climax last October. Since then the missiles and bombers have gone, some troops have left. Since it is not exactly known how many troops will remain in Cuba, the problem is still very much with us. The U.S. was gratified at the unanimity shown in the O.A.S. on the quarantine, the Brazilian position being particularly significant. It was such unanimity that made possible a peaceful solution of the missile problem. Had there not been unity in the O.A.S. or in N.A.T.O., Khrushchev might have made a different judgment on the missile situation.

The second point was still troublesome. While Cuba was not the sole channel used by the communists for subversive activities in Latin America, Cuba was extensively used for the supply of funds, the movements of persons, propaganda broadcasts, etc. The U.S. was concerned with measures to reduce or eliminate that subversive pressure from Cuba, which has been felt especially in Venezuela, as in other parts of the Hemisphere. The Secretary went on to say that there appeared to be no serious interest in Havana in a reconciliation with the rest of the Hemisphere. During the Mikoyan visit, several points of view were apparently expressed within the Cuba regime, one favoring continued ties with Moscow, another advocating a closer tie to Peking, and a third which

---

Source: Department of State, Central Files, CSM 10 LAT AMER. Confidential. Drafted by A.J. DeSeabra of the Division of Language Services.

[1] See Document 146.

might be termed a Titoist approach. The fact remained that there was no thought being given to a reconciliation with the rest of the Hemisphere. The Secretary asked Minister Dantas to comment on the two points raised, as well as to give his impressions, on the basis of information obtained from the Brazilian Embassy in Havana, on the present state of affairs in Cuba and on the present attitudes of the leadership in that nation.

Minister Dantas said he had had no recent contact with sources of information on Cuba, and asked Ambassador Bernardes to make some comments.

Ambassador Bernardes said that the impression of the Brazilian Embassy in Cuba was that there had been some training in subversion of individuals from Latin America. There was no knowledge of any Brazilians having been trained, leaving the possibility that the number had been so small that the Embassy had no knowledge of it. Such training was aimed particularly at Venezuela and the Caribbean area, but did not seem to present a serious problem with regard to Brazil, Argentina or Uruguay for instance. The economic situation was deteriorating daily in Cuba, with severe shortages and strict rationing. Just the same Castro was still getting a hard core support, and there was no prospect of a popular uprising at this time. There were divergencies inside the Cuban Government between the followers of Moscow and those of Peking. But Cuba was so economically dependent on Moscow that it could not afford to go over to the Chinese.

Ambassador Gordon asked whether there had been any change in the Brazilian attitude in the O.A.S. toward possible collective action against Cuba-subversion.

Ambassador Bernardes mentioned that the proposed resolution on that matter might be made acceptable, although there should be a reference to respecting constitutional procedures, since there are in Brazil constitutional limitations on interference with the movement of people in and out of Brazil. He also said that Brazilian support would be much easier if there were some known cases; so far there had been no known case of Brazilians who had actually been trained in Cuba in subversive techniques.

Ambassador Gordon mentioned the Lima documents that contained some evidence.

Ambassador Bernardes indicated that the individuals in question had not been trained in Cuba.

The Secretary asked whether communists in Brazil made their contacts with Moscow through Cuba.

Minister Dantas explained that communist contacts with Moscow were made mainly through Czechoslovakia, although the pro-Peking faction had a closer contact with Cuba. In Brazil the orthodox communists were now denouncing those who had close ties with Cuba, such as Francisco Juliao. As for Carlos Prestes, his actual status within the communist party of Brazil is not very well known. He still enjoys some prestige, but he no longer appears to be the effective leader. The activities of communist groups in Brazil are not very important in the domestic scene. Communists concentrate their efforts mainly on endeavoring to maintain positions of leadership in the labor unions, where they are being challenged by non-communist labor leaders.

Turning to the initial remarks made by the Secretary, Minister Dantas recalled that ever since the first talks about Cuba, the major concerns of the Brazilian Government were identical to those of the U.S. Government; to wit, to eliminate Cuba's military ties with the Soviet Bloc and to eliminate the promotion from Cuba of subversive activities in the Hemisphere. The only significant difference between the U.S. and Brazil was in the methods to be used to obtain the ends mentioned above. Early in 1962, it had been thought in Brazil that it would be possible to arrive at an agreement with Cuba to eliminate these two dangers while respecting the evolution of the Socialist regime in Cuba, by securing a commitment on the part of Cuba to abstain from military ties with the Soviets as well as refraining from further subversive activities in the Hemisphere. Those are the objectives to which the Brazilian Government had remained, and still remains, faithful. Since then there have occurred two events, one more important than the other, which show the consistency of the continued Brazilian position. The first important event was that at the time of the quarantine, Brazil gave its support to the blockade so as to avoid any military danger from Cuba, military ties with the Soviets, and the introduction of nuclear weapons in other countries of the Hemisphere. The other more recent event had to do with subversive activities. For some time, pro-Cuba groups in Brazil had been organizing and publicizing a Congress for Solidarity with Cuba, to be held in Rio with participants from all over the world. In the last few weeks, the Brazilian Government had voiced its disapproval of the Congress, its untimeliness, and had instructed its Consular offices to refuse visas to anyone desiring to attend the Congress.

The Secretary asked whether there had ever been any information or complaints from neighboring countries regarding any subversive activities based in Brazil.

Ambassador Bernardes mentioned that he did not know of any such complaints. He added that at the time the documents had been found in Peru, there had been comments in the Peruvian press about possible international ramifications. But there had been no official complaint on the part of the Peruvian Government.

Ambassador Gordon mentioned that there had been rumors of subversive activities in Bolivia and Paraguay, but Ambassador Bernardes said nothing more had transpired.

---

160. Circular Telegram From the Department of State to Certain Posts in the American Republics

Washington, March 13, 1963, 8:23 p.m.

1564. In meeting March 18–20 with six Presidents Central America and Panama, there will be discussion of measures which should be taken to reduce travel between Cuba and Isthmian countries and flow of funds, propaganda and arms to them from Cuba.

We expect in course of discussion to offer consult with Central American and Panamanian Governments on additional U.S. training and other assistance which may be required to develop or improve border and coastal patrol capabilities of their respective security forces.

Action addressees should inform Govt of foregoing and state that we desire make this offer also to addressee govts. Advise soonest if govt to which you are accredited is interested in principle.

Consultations will be arranged later.

Necessary there be no publicity on this exchange until further word.

Separate message on Jamaican request for patrol boats being sent.

FYI. U.S. desires establishment of a coordinated Caribbean surveillance system involving:

a.   Continued close-in surveillance of Cuba by U.S. forces.

b.   A U.S. military alerting system, by which intelligence of subversive movement will be rapidly transmitted to the American Ambassadors to countries concerned through intelligence centers at Caribbean

---

Source: Department of State, Central Files, POL 36 CUBA. Secret; Priority. Drafted by Deputy Assistant Secretary for Inter-American Affairs Sterling J. Cottrell and Deputy Director of the Office of Central American and Panamanian Affairs John W. Fisher; cleared by Martin, Deputy Assistant Secretary of Defense for International Security Affairs Frank K. Sloan, Special Assistant to the Joint Staff Director for Counterinsurgency and Special Activities Major General Victor H. Krulak, and in substance by Special Assistant to the President Ralph Dungan; and approved by Director of the Office of Central American and Panamanian Affairs Lansing Collins. Sent to Bogotá, Caracas, Santo Domingo, Kingston, and Port of Spain, and repeated to Guatemala City, Managua, Panama City, San José, San Salvador, Tegucigalpa, CINCARIB POLAD, and CINCLANT POLAD.

Command and Caribbean Sea Frontier Headquarters of the Atlantic Command.

c. A unilateral surveillance and interception effort by each country in its own territorial waters.

d. U.S. assistance in final interception in territorial waters upon request of the country concerned. End FYI.

Rusk

---

161.   Circular Telegram From the Department of State to Certain Posts in the American Republics

Washington, March 14, 1963.

1572. President plans make following points re Cuban problem CA and Panamanian Presidents Meeting March 19. Although only restatement present policy in view likelihood leaks you requested convey orally and confidentially to FonOff no earlier than March 18.

1. Cuba not merely Caribbean or hemispheric problem: Soviet involvement makes it complex and delicate East-West problem;

2. We do not favor initiating military action at present; however we fully support our hemispheric treaties and obligations and no commitments have been made inhibiting our ability do so including taking military action against Cuba if necessary;

3. Cuban economy in poor condition, economic measures by free world nations having their effect;

4. Cuba's political isolation increasingly uncomfortable for Castro regime;

5. US has told USSR we not satisfied with rate of withdrawal troops; we will not countenance military action by Soviet troops in Cuba against Cubans.

6. Our best courses action at present are:

a. Assure offensive weapons not reintroduced into Cuba;

Source: Department of State, Conference Files: Lot 66 D 110, CF 2229. Confidential. Drafted by Allen and approved by John M. Cates. Sent to Bogotá, Buenos Aires, Caracas, Kingston, La Paz, Montevideo, Port-au-Prince, Port of Spain, Rio de Janeiro, Santiago, and Santo Domingo.

b. Bring about removal remaining Soviet military personnel;

c. Prevent Cuba from taking any aggressive military action against other Caribbean states;

d. Reduce its capabilities to direct and support subversion and insurrection within other hemisphere states;

e. Intensify resistance to and counter attacks of Castro propaganda throughout LA;

f. Increase IA cooperation within OAS, continuing to work through collective action;

g. Increase isolation of Castro regime from political life of hemisphere;

h. Maximize cost to Soviet Bloc and ChiComs of supporting Castro regime;

i. Reduction in movement of nationals LA countries to Cuba for training in subversion, terrorism, guerrilla warfare, and control those returned from Cuba.

7. Isthmian countries and US can accomplish something together on these courses, especially last one.

8. (We support in discussion program for reducing movement of Communist subversives between Cuba and CA Isthmus along general lines SCCS report.)[1]

Rusk

---

[1] See footnote 1, Document 162.

---

162. Circular Telegram From the Department of State to Certain Posts in the American Republics

Washington, March 14, 1963, 9:22 p.m.

1573. Presidents' Meeting. We hope that, in discussion of Cuba and subversion problems at San Jose, there will be useful exchange of views on measures which Isthmian Governments themselves can take to restrict movement of people between their countries and Cuba which serve subversive purpose.

Source: Department of State, Central Files, POL 36 CUBA. Confidential; Operational Immediate. Drafted by Fisher; cleared by Allen and Cottrell; and approved by Collins. Sent to Guatemala City, Managua, Panama, San José, San Salvador, and Tegucigalpa.

We will be prepared to endorse and offer support to suitable program this end. Program should come up in discussions at San Jose as much as possible under Isthmian auspices, rather than come as U.S. proposal.

You should convey following outline of program to Government to which accredited, and without undertaking to "negotiate" program with Government, you should express strong hope that latter will take opportunities to propose and support points contained in it at Presidents' Meeting. Specific proposals are drawn largely from SCCS report to COAS[1] and we now urgently seeking have them embodied in action program to be recommended to all AmReps. However, will be impossible complete COAS action prior meeting.

You may express our gratification at quick negative response on rumor of Isthmian announcement on Cuba just before San Jose.

Collins[2] will be prepared discuss further with Foreign Ministers in San Jose March 16–17.

Proposed program follows:

1. Appropriate Ministers countries Central America, Panama, and U.S. meet periodically to review measures adopted and progress made to control Castro-communist subversive movements between Cuba and Central American Isthmus.

2. Institute full and effective cooperation our countries with appropriate bodies of OAS, and bilaterally among our several states, in interchange of information concerning travel of person to Cuba and other Castro-communist subversive activities.

3. Initiate bilateral talks with other countries to enlist their cooperation in adopting specific measures prevent movement through their countries of persons to and from Cuba.

4. Agree to support action by COAS to recommend program of controls of travel along lines of proposals presented by COAS Committee, and meanwhile so far as possible, to implement such program, principal elements of which are:

   a. Adopt appropriate legal restrictions on travel to Cuba and provide severe penalties for evasion. Through bilateral talks we should urge other countries to do the same.

   b. Stamp passports or other travel documents issued to own nationals "not valid for travel to Cuba."

---

[1] Reference is to a report by the Special Consultative Committee on Security to the Committee to Study Resolutions II.1 and VIII of the Eighth Meeting of Consultation of OAS Foreign Ministers, February 8, 1963. For text, see OAS doc. OEA/Ser.L/X/II.3; its conclusions are printed in *American Foreign Policy: Current Documents, 1963*, pp. 254–255.

[2] Lansing Collins.

c. Refuse exit permits for Cuba to any national of third country who cannot produce valid permit issued by his own country for travel to Cuba.

d. Refuse to honor any visa for Cuba which is not integral, non-detachable part of travel document issued by country of which traveler is citizen.

e. Require accurate manifests of all carriers departing for or arriving from Cuba, and furnish copies of these manifests to diplomatic missions of other Western Hemisphere countries which are affected.

f. Intensify intelligence efforts in each country to identify persons who have traveled or intend to travel to Cuba and report selected information promptly to own government.

g. Pursue campaign expose scope and purpose of Cuban training of nationals of our countries for subversive purposes, in order discourage prospective trainees and highlight urgent need halt subversive travel of our nationals to Cuba.

h. Utilize our intelligence capabilities to determine nature and extent of clandestine aircraft and small boat traffic between Cuba and other countries in area.

i. Institute unilateral surveillance and interception efforts by each country in its own territorial waters to stop this traffic. U.S. prepared upon request to assist in final interception in these territorial waters.

Rusk

---

163. Editorial Note

President Kennedy met with the Presidents of Central America and Panama in San José, Costa Rica, March 18–20, 1963. The Declaration of Central America, which they issued on March 19, stated their agreement that ministers of the seven countries should meet as soon as possible to develop and put into effect "common measures to restrict the movement of their nationals to and from Cuba, and the flow of matériel, propaganda and funds from that country." The text is printed in Department of State *Bulletin*, April 8, 1963, pages 515–517. Documentation concerning the meeting is in Department of State, Conference Files: Lot 66 D 110, CF 2228–2233. See also Documents 58, 59, 61, and 62.

164.   Memorandum From Secretary of State Rusk to President Kennedy

Washington, April 1, 1963.

SUBJECT

My Memorandum of March 12, 1963 Regarding Next Steps in OAS on Cuban Problem[1]

I enclose a copy of the referenced memorandum which was transmitted to the White House March 12.

With respect to the COAS report on subversive activities referred to in paragraph 1, the Committee has now completed preliminary approval of its program of recommendations, and although these have not yet been submitted to the full Council, they will be available for use at the April 3 meeting in Managua.

Paragraph 2 of the March 12 memorandum recommends that we seek further action in the OAS on economic measures against the Castro regime. I am informed that no action has yet been taken on this recommendation. In the light of our overall Cuban policy, this problem remains important and the recommendation is not affected by the San Jose meeting. Indeed, the recommendation that further economic measures be taken against the Castro regime would be quite consistent with the general attitude of the other Presidents as expressed in that meeting. I renew my recommendation, therefore, that you authorize the Department of State to seek action by the COAS along the lines of paragraph 2 of my memorandum of March 12.[2]

Dean Rusk[3]

Source: Department of State, Central Files, POL 3 COAS–IA. Secret. Drafted by Allen.

[1] Copies of the March 12 memorandum from Rusk to Kennedy and its enclosure, an undated memorandum by the Coordinator of Cuban Affairs, are attached to the source text. A March 30 note from David Rowe of the Executive Secretariat to Rusk's Special Assistant Emory C. Swank, attached to the source text, states that the White House had lost the March 12 memorandum and had requested a copy with an update of its recommendation concerning OAS action.

[2] An April 5 memorandum from Dungan to Rusk, attached to the source text, states that the President concurred in Rusk's recommendations and left the question of timing of implementation to the Department.

[3] Printed from a copy that indicates Rusk signed the original.

Enclosure[4]

Memorandum by the Coordinator of Cuban Affairs (Cottrell)

SUBJECT

Next Steps in OAS on Cuban Problem

1. Subversive Activities (Movement of Persons, Propaganda and Funds).

The COAS Committee charged with maintaining vigilance against subversive activities has been working for the last several weeks on a practical program of recommendations to the governments for the control of travel, propaganda and funds, basing its work in part on the recent SCCS report which had been prepared at its request. (The United States member is also drawing upon material prepared by Subcommittee chaired by Major General Victor Krulak, USMC.)[5]

We are accelerating this work so that, if possible, the Committee's report may be sent to all members of the Council by March 15. Then the consideration of this hemisphere-wide problem by the seven Presidents at San José may be within the hemisphere-wide framework of the OAS.

2. Further Economic Measures against the Castro Regime.

The following three considerations militate against strong immediate OAS punitive measures against Castro:

a. Dissipation through time and circumstance of the crisis-stimulated willingness to take strong action;
b. United States concern lest the impending partial withdrawal of Soviet troops be prejudiced; and
c. The importance attached to preserving unanimity in the OAS.

Nevertheless, it is important that some forward movement be made in the OAS toward our ultimate objective (other than the above defensive action against that part of the problem represented by subversive activities).

Recommendations:

1. I therefore recommend that, prefaced by consultations with members of the COAS Committee and others, we seek to have the COAS adopt by the last week in March a resolution which would:

---

[4] Originally enclosed with Rusk's March 12 memorandum to Kennedy, cited in footnote 1. Both were enclosed with Rusk's April 1 memorandum to Kennedy.

[5] Reference is to the Counter-Subversion Subcommittee of the Interagency Cuban Coordinating Committee.

   a. Extend the arms embargo imposed by Resolution VIII of Punta del Este to include "all items of trade except foodstuffs, medicines and medical supplies";
   b. Recommend that Member States prohibit the use of their vessels to carry to Cuba any embargoed items;
   c. Recommend that Member States deny overflight and landing rights to Soviet aircraft on bloc-Cuban runs; and
   d. Call upon the rest of the free world to take similar measures.

Such a resolution is consistent with United States objectives and practice, should be welcomed domestically, would have slight economic, but appreciable psychological advantages, stands a good chance of obtaining unanimous or near unanimous support, and seems unlikely to affect Soviet willingness (if any) to remove its troops.

   2. After the recovery of the United States prisoners, and after observing further withdrawals of Soviet troops, we can consider additional measures for adoption by the OAS.

---

165. Memorandum Prepared in the Department of State

Washington, undated.

SUBJECT

   Implementation of Agreements Reached at San José

   The initial report of March 25 indicated that a meeting of Ministers of Government would take place at Managua, Nicaragua, on April 3 to draw up security measures against subversion in the Isthmian countries. Deputy Attorney General Katzenbach headed the United States Delegation to this meeting and results were considered most successful.

   The most significant of the resolutions promulgated at the end of the meeting April 4[1] were the following:

   1. To recommend to their governments that they adopt, within the limitations of their respective constitutional provisions, measures to be

---

Source: Department of State, Central Files, POL 7 COSTA RICA. Confidential. Drafted by Collins and O.L. Sause of AID. Filed as an attachment to an April 22 memorandum from Brubeck to Bundy, which stated that it was a further response to the President's March 22 written inquiry to Martin. Kennedy's March 22 memorandum to Martin asked Martin to let him know that steps he was taking to implement "the testament of San Jose." A copy is filed with a March 25 memorandum from Brubeck to Bundy enclosing an initial report. (Ibid.)
   [1] The resolutions are printed in Department of State Bulletin, May 6, 1963, pp. 719–721.

put into effect immediately to prohibit, restrict and discourage the movement of their nationals to and from Cuba. To this end, the Meeting proposes the adoption of the following measures:

a. Provide, as a general rule, that every passport or other travel document which may be issued carry a stamp which indicates that said passport is not valid for travel to Cuba.
b. Declare officially that nationals who are permitted to travel to Cuba should have the permission duly inscribed in their official travel document.
c. Promulgate regulations restricting the granting of visas to foreigners who have travelled to Cuba within a stipulated period of time.

2. To recommend that their governments take action to impede the clandestine movement of arms into the Isthmian countries, including specific instructions to border control forces to intensify port, airfield and border inspection of incoming and outgoing cargo in order to prevent contraband shipment of arms; establish strict security and accountability with respect to arms and ammunition issued to their armed forces and law enforcement agencies.

3. To recommend to their governments the adoption as soon as possible and to go into effect immediately, of effective measures to prevent activities for subversive purposes that may be instigated by Castro-Communist propaganda or agents in each of the Central American countries.

4. To recommend to the Governments of Central America and Panama the establishment, as soon as possible, of an organization in each state, with the sole purpose of counteracting Communist subversion in the Central America-Panama area. These organizations will be primarily responsible for:

a. Detecting, controlling and counteracting actions and objectives of the members, organizations, sympathizers and collaborators of the Communist Party.
b. Lending mutual support to each other and continually exchanging information regarding movements of persons or groups, propaganda, funds and arms for Communist subversive purposes.

These resolutions do not represent commitments on the part of governments but only recommendations to governments. In order to assist the Central American Governments to put these recommendations into effect and in order to find out what technical or material assistance the United States should offer, a team with Immigration Service, AID, Joint Chiefs of Staff, CINCARIB, USIS, CIA and State representation will visit each of the Central American countries starting from Panama around

April 23 and ending in Guatemala. The report of this team[2] will be used to persuade the Central American Governments to put more recommendations into effect and also as a basic paper for the United States Delegation to the next regular meeting of Ministers of Government of Central America which, at Managua, was set for 90 days hence, i.e., July 5.

[Here follows discussion of the implementation of decisions on economic matters.]

---

[2] The report of the Interdepartmental Team on Counter Subversive Measures in Central America and Panama, which visited Central America and Panama April 23–May 11, is in the Kennedy Library, National Security Files, Regional Security Series, Latin America.

---

166. Memorandum From Acting Secretary of State Ball to President Kennedy

Washington, May 24, 1963.

SUBJECT

Mexican Position on Imposing Economic Sanctions Against Cuba

In a memorandum of May 17[1] you asked for comments on the report that Mexico has agreed with Brazil to oppose any OAS effort to tighten Hemisphere restrictions on trade with Cuba, particularly in light of the many ways we have recently been trying to be helpful to Mexico.

The Mexican position is not unexpected. In a long conversation with Assistant Secretary Martin at the end of January on a variety of possible measures with respect to Cuba, President Lopez Mateos made quite clear that Mexico would give its public support to any action against Cuba necessary to prevent a serious and direct threat to the security of the United States or the Hemisphere, as it did in the missile crisis. It was also prepared to support measures which would clearly contribute to [less than 1 line of source text not declassified] a significant diminution of his power in Cuba or in the Hemisphere, though it would strongly prefer to do so quietly rather than publicly. It was not prepared to collaborate in

---

Source: Kennedy Library, President's Office Files, Cuba, Security. Secret. The source text bears no indication of the drafter.

[1] A copy is filed as an attachment to a copy of Ball's memorandum, ibid., National Security Files, Countries Series, Cuba, General.

actions whose value was largely symbolic or psychological and particularly where a public position was required. He felt the domestic difficulties that such measures would cause him would far outweigh any possible contribution they might make to achieving agreed Hemisphere policy objectives.

He is particularly concerned at the present time about domestic impacts of public actions vis-à-vis Cuba because of the current necessity to secure and maintain the support of all elements of his party in the difficult task which he must complete by the fall of choosing the next Presidential candidate. This responsibility traditionally belongs to the outgoing President, and he is most anxious to perform it. He is also equally anxious to maintain the solidarity of the party behind the candidate selected. With the tensions increasing each year between the left and right wings of the party, these objectives can only be secured by avoiding public positions which would tend to alienate either group or by balancing gestures to one by gestures to the other. He is personally closer to the left and will be particularly careful not to alienate unnecessarily this source of his greatest strength. In these circumstances Lopez Mateos can be expected for the next year to be extremely cautious about taking public positions on the question of Cuba unless really major security issues are involved.

It will be exceedingly difficult for us to demonstrate that further controls on Latin American trade with Cuba will have any but a psychological effect on the viability of the Castro regime. Exports are currently limited pretty much to foods and medicine. A recent analysis is enclosed.[2]

It may be noted that, pending consideration by the OAS Council of the report of the Vigilance Committee on measures to limit Cuban subversive activities in Latin America, the United States has not made any proposal with respect to trade limitations, and therefore the Mexican position is not formally in opposition to any existing United States proposal. The Vigilance Committee report is expected to be submitted to the Committee this week but action may not come for several weeks.

George W. Ball

---

[2] The enclosure, a May 6 memorandum prepared in the Department of State, is not printed.

167. Memorandum From the President's Special Assistant for National Security Affairs (Bundy) to President Kennedy

Washington, May 25, 1963.

SUBJECT

> A possible declaration against further Soviet penetration of the Western Hemisphere

At your direction, I have had a small group of people working on this problem outside the normal channels in the last three weeks. We have now produced two papers which we think are worth your attention. One is a draft Declaration (Tab A).[1] The other is a set of possible situations in which a prior Declaration of this sort might prove helpful (Tab B).[2]

We are still working on a third problem, which is to analyze the alternative ways and means of getting such a Declaration on the record with a minimum amount of opposition within the hemisphere. While the Declaration, as this preliminary draft will show, can be surrounded with a good deal of hemispheric mood music, it would nevertheless be a major unilateral U.S. move, and we could count on a lot of Latin American twittering—especially from Brazil and Mexico; it would be important to reduce this if possible.

The easy way to get this Declaration on the record would be to have it issued in the context of some crisis in which in fact our decision to act would be generally approved. The hypothetical British Guiana case in the scenario is an example.[3] There is, however, little point in solving such

---

Source: Kennedy Library, National Security Files, Regional Security Series, Latin America, Kennedy Doctrine. No classification marking.

[1] Tab A, May 24, is entitled "Draft Declaration Against Further Soviet Penetration of Latin America." After discussion of the Monroe Doctrine and the inter-American system, it stated that "extension, by any means, of the political domination or military presence of the Communist powers within this hemisphere is hostile to the basic principles of the life of the Americas." It further stated, "Such intrusion cannot be accepted, and we will take the steps to prevent it that may be required in the interest of freedom. This is the obligation of all free nations of the hemisphere under the Rio Treaty, as we understand it, and it is the policy of the United States."

[2] Tab B, entitled "Draft Scenario for Statement Embodying Kennedy Doctrine," dated May 23, did not describe possible situations; it was a scenario of actions to be taken, such as consultations with other American governments and advance notice to Congressional leaders, before the President made such a statement. It began with an ARA note stating that it was assumed that the proposed statement meant that the United States would take unilateral military action if necessary to prevent a Communist takeover of a Latin American government, but that such a step would raise grave problems in U.S.-Latin American relations.

[3] The attached scenario does not mention British Guiana, nor does it describe any background events leading to the scenario it sets forth.

easy and relatively unlikely cases now. We can meet them readily as they come. The hard problem is to lay a groundwork against a repetition of something like the Cuban case as it actually developed, so that we would have had support and not general opposition to drastic action as early as 1960.

One possibility is to precede the Declaration by a meeting of OAS Foreign Ministers in which the Secretary of State, without tabling a resolution that could not pass, would make very clear the concern of the United States and its own determination to leave no doubt of its own position. Quite possibly a new and somewhat stronger resolution of concern could be passed which might help as a cover for a new U.S. Declaration. But what is more important is that such a meeting would be a highly visible form of consultation which might ease the problem of a unilateral statement shortly afterward.

It is also possible to express U.S. concern in a preliminary way through press conferences and Executive Branch testimony on the Hill. And our concern can also be orchestrated in different ways before the UN and in NATO, although these are less important centers for this particular problem.

The consensus of this small working party is, first, that some declaration or affirmation of this sort is desirable and possible, and second, that it would be well to take plenty of time to get it done right, with all appropriate preparation. Our inclination is to believe that it is something that can be done more effectively when Congress is not in session, and our tentative recommendation is that we plan toward a major statement which might be made in October or November. We believe that the Declaration should be made on some important hemispheric occasion, and that plans should be made now to make sure that such an occasion is on the calendar well ahead of time.

Members of the working party will value your guidance for further staff work.

McG. B.

168. Memorandum From Gordon Chase of the National Security Council Staff to the President's Special Assistant for National Security Affairs (Bundy)

Washington, June 6, 1963.

SUBJECT

Kennedy Doctrine

1. You wanted to be reminded about the possibility of setting up a meeting on the Kennedy Doctrine.

2. Bob Hurwitch[1] tells me that State has dropped its plans to stir up an OAS resolution focussing on the presence of Soviet troops in Cuba. Ed Martin and others feel it is a non-starter—there is no sense in passing a resolution unless the OAS is prepared to act on it. If the OAS is not prepared to act, the resolution will simply highlight the impotency of the OAS.

3. I talked to Bill Bowdler about the OAS tactics involved in taking a first jump towards a possible Kennedy Doctrine. (In the past, Bill had been in touch with Walt Rostow on the Doctrine.) Bill's feelings are generally as follows:

(a) The OAS will be a difficult forum, especially at this time. For one thing, we have let Cuba cool down substantially; at this point, many Latin Americans feel that the U.S. is really not interested in doing much about Cuba. For another thing, elections in Latin America in the near future (Peru, Argentina, Mexico, and Chile) do not help matters. Mexico's key primary in September, which determines the next president, will make Mexico especially tough to deal with; Chile is presently ginning up for next year's election and will be similarly difficult to handle.

(b) It would not be easy to call a meeting of Foreign Ministers under the prevailing tepid atmosphere. A call for a meeting, as a reaction against the recent Castro visit and Khrushchev speech about national liberation movements, would not be credible. The OAS countries are really not concerned with subversion and "another Cuba." About the only credible issue you could conceivably use now to gin up a Foreign Ministers meeting is the presence of Soviet troops in Cuba.

(c) Bill doubts that we could get an OAS resolution on intervention which is any stronger than the Punta del Este resolution. The OAS countries probably would not even buy a resolution stating that we don't

---

Source: Kennedy Library, National Security Files, Regional Security Series, Latin America, Kennedy Doctrine. Secret.

[1] Deputy Coordinator of Cuban Affairs Robert Hurwitch.

want another Cuba. They would immediately think in terms of the next step, which they are not willing to face—actions to prevent another Cuba.

(d) Bill said that, in about a month, the COAS will meet to consider the Lavalle Committee's report on subversion.[2] This context might provide a useful forum for a small jump towards the Doctrine.

4. Assuming we want to condition the OAS for the Kennedy Doctrine (maybe we don't) there seems to me to be 2 ways we can do it—dramatically (e.g. a Foreign Ministers meeting without much softening up) or subtlety. The subtle method would seem to involve the use of a series of statements to create an atmosphere which reflects our concern about another Cuba in the hemisphere. If we decide to take the subtle road, we should probably use every chance we get to take a jump, no matter how small, towards the Kennedy Doctrine. In this regard, a reaction to the Castro visit and the Khrushchev speech seems to me to be in order—perhaps a speech in the COAS by the Secretary or one of the Under Secretaries. Also, it would seem appropriate to say something in the COAS at the time when the Lavalle Committee submits its report on subversion. It should be noted that the small steps would not preclude a Foreign Ministers meeting; in fact, they might create a more credible atmosphere for one.

5. In view of the fact that we are getting close to the operational stage of the Kennedy Doctrine, you might want to consider inviting an ARA type or two to the next meeting of the Kennedy Doctrine group.[3]

GC

---

[2] Reference is to the report of the Special Committee to Study Resolutions II.1 and VIII of the Eighth Meeting of Consultation of Ministers of Foreign Affairs, submitted to the OAS Council on June 4. (OAS doc. OEA/Ser.G/IV/c–i–605 Rev. 3, July 3, 1963; printed in part in *American Foreign Policy: Current Documents, 1963*, pp. 271–276) The OAS Council voted on July 3 to transmit the report to member governments urging them to implement its recommendations to the extent that they had not already done so within the limits of their constitutions. (Circular telegram 23 to ARA diplomatic posts, dated July 3; Department of State, Central Files, POL 3 COAS–IA)

[3] A memorandum of February 21, 1964, from Bundy to Robert Kennedy and others, states that Bundy's May 25 memorandum to the President (Document 167) and its attachments were developed outside regular channels at President Kennedy's direction. It states, "The actual policy result of all this was a few sentences in the President's November 18 speech, which was blanketed almost immediately by his death." The text of Kennedy's speech is printed in Department of State *Bulletin*, December 9, 1963, pp. 900–904.

169. Memorandum From Secretary of State Rusk to President Johnson

Washington, November 27, 1963.

SUBJECT

Venezuelan Announcement of Cuban Origin of Discovered Arms Cache

On November 3 the Venezuelan Government discovered a large arms cache buried on a beach of the Paraguana Peninsula in northwestern Venezuela. A careful examination of the weapons revealed them to be of Cuban origin. The Venezuelan Government has advised us that it plans to make the evidence public on November 28.

When we learned the Venezuelans had conclusive evidence that the arms cache was Cuban and planned to announce it, we urged President Betancourt to do two things: (1) as a minimum to present the evidence to the OAS and (2) as a highly desirable maximum to combine the disclosure with an appeal to other governments of the Caribbean area for cooperation in multilateral surveillance under Resolution II of the 8th Meeting of Foreign Ministers (Punta del Este) to detect and thwart further attempts by the Castro regime to export arms and men for subversive purposes. President Betancourt agreed to report the incident to the OAS but he was decidedly cool to the suggestion of an appeal for surveillance cooperation. His coolness is attributable to domestic political considerations, particularly the December 1 national elections and the implications of having publicly to request foreign assistance.

The Venezuelan intention to publicize the Cuban origin of the arms cache, read in conjunction with previous statements made by President Kennedy and me (compilation enclosed)[1] about insuring that the Castro regime does not export arms and men in this hemisphere, makes it important that we comment promptly and publicly on the announcement. Even though the public statements which President Kennedy and I made were quite clearly referring to Cuban military action against other American Republics, they are susceptible of being interpreted as applicable to this type of incident.

A contingency press statement is enclosed. Depending on the terms of the Venezuelan announcement, it may need some adjustment, although I anticipate that the changes will be minimal. It is designed to emphasize Castro's growing interventionist activities in the hemisphere

---

Source: Department of State, Central Files, DEF 12 CUBA. Confidential. Drafted by Bowdler. President Kennedy was assassinated in Dallas, Texas, on November 22.

[1] The enclosures are not printed.

and to call for greater cooperation in watching for and thwarting these activities, without generating a sense of alarm. The statement makes clear our willingness to cooperate in surveillance but leaves the initiative to the Latin Americans from where it must come if we are to obtain their participation.

In keeping with the objective of calling attention to Cuban subversion without causing alarm, I plan to have the Department Press Officer volunteer the statement at the regular noon press briefing following the Venezuelan announcement.[2]

Dean Rusk[3]

---

[2] For text, see Department of State *Bulletin*, December 16, 1963, pp. 913–914.

[3] Printed from a copy that indicates Rusk signed the original.

---

170. Circular Telegram From the Department of State to Posts in the American Republics

Washington, December 4, 1963, 7:59 p.m.

1016. Depcirtels 983,[1] 986,[2] 1004.[3] Department now making careful assessment of options for COAS/OC action in Venezuelan complaint on Cuban arms cache case. Options being weighed in terms practical effects of measures in further isolating Cuba and degree of support which can be achieved, particularly from those countries maintaining diplomatic relations with Cuba.

Source: Department of State, Central Files, POL 3 COAS–IA. Confidential; Immediate. Drafted by Bowdler; cleared by Allen, Belcher, Collins, Director of the Office of East Coast Affairs Daniel F. Margolies, and Acting Director of the Office of Caribbean and Mexican Affairs Kennedy M. Crockett; approved by Martin. Sent to all Embassies in the American Republics except Kingston and Port-of-Spain and repeated to Kingston, Port-of-Spain, USUN, and POLADs CINCLANT and CINCSO.

[1] Circular telegram 983, November 29, outlined a Venezuelan proposal to invoke the Rio Treaty, call a meeting of Foreign Ministers, and appoint a commission to investigate the Cuban arms cache. (Ibid.)

[2] Circular telegram 986, November 30, instructed recipient Embassies to consult the Foreign Ministries in their respective countries and urge support of the Venezuelan proposal in the OAS Council. (Ibid.)

[3] Circular telegram 1004, December 3, reported that the OAS Council, acting provisionally as the Organ of Consultation under the Rio Treaty, had authorized a committee to investigate the arms cache. (Ibid.) For text of the resolution, see OAS doc. OEA/Ser.G/III/C–sa–526; also printed in *American Foreign Policy: Current Documents, 1963*, p. 286.

Initiative on proposed action rests primarily with Venezuela and to some extent with Investigating Committee which in addition to determining facts may also include recommendations in its report. At present moment we have no clear picture what Venezuelan intentions are. President Betancourt in press conference Nov 29 reportedly said it has become "necessary to have joint definitive action to finish with this bridgehead of communism in America." He apparently did not specify what action he had in mind. On Dec 3 he reportedly told press Venezuela would seek partial air and naval blockade of Cuba to prevent export of arms and rupture diplomatic relations with Cuba by OAR's still maintaining them. Venezuelan COAS Representative at COAS/OC session confined himself to asking for investigation after which "Venezuela will demand a clear and heavy judgment."

We view range of options of COAS/OC in this situation as including following:

1.   air and naval blockade to prevent shipment of arms to Latin America from Cuba;
2.   break in diplomatic and consular relations;
3.   break in economic relations (embargo already authorized by Eighth MFM);
4.   complete or partial interruption of communications;
5.   endorsement of system of cooperative surveillance by interested Caribbean countries against clandestine shipment of arms and men from Cuba.
6.   condemnation of Castro regime for interventionist activities;
7.   call for increased vigilance by OARs and implementation Lavalle Committee recommendations on control of travel, propaganda and funds.

Assuming Venezuela case is airtight (which we believe it is) and Venezuela makes determined bid for effective action as it did in case against Trujillo, request urgently your own assessment (without going beyond Embassy staff) of degree of acceptability of each of these options to government to which you accredited.

Rusk

171. **Record of Actions by the National Security Council Standing Group**

Washington, December 10, 1963.

Meeting No. 16/63, December 10, 1963—5:00 PM

Deputy Under Secretary of State Johnson summarized a draft State Department paper dealing with possible measures which might be taken in the OAS to prevent Cuban arms exports to Latin America.[1] Following a discussion, the group asked the State Department to prepare a memorandum for the President's decision covering the two preferred alternatives.[2]

a. Requiring OAS authorization for the use of force in connection with visit-and-search in international waters against selected Cuban vessels and selected vessels of OAS countries.

b. Not requiring OAS authorization for the use of force because visit-and-search would take place only within the territorial waters of an OAS country agreeing to cooperative interception.

Because the attitude of Mexico and Brazil toward the use of force is critical in any effort to obtain OAS approval for such action, the State memorandum will recommend that our Ambassadors in Mexico City and Rio de Janeiro be authorized to find out informally the probable view of these two governments toward an OAS resolution authorizing the use of force if a visit-and-search in international waters were challenged by a Cuban vessel or selected vessels of any OAS country.[3]

Source: Johnson Library, National Security File, Agency Files, NSC Standing Group, Vol. I. Secret. No drafting information appears on the source text.

[1] Not printed. (Ibid.)

[2] A memorandum of December 13 from Ball to Johnson set forth the alternatives. (Department of State, Central Files, POL CUBA)

[3] The instructions were sent in telegram 1071 to Mexico City, also sent to Rio de Janeiro and Caracas, December 17. (Ibid., POL 3 COAS–IA)

ARGENTINA

172. Telegram From the Department of State to the Embassy in Argentina

Washington, May 24, 1961, 10:52 p.m.

1701. Following based on uncleared memorandum of conversation:[1]

Argentine Economic Minister Alemann called on President today accompanied by Ambassadors del Carril and Rubottom.[2]

Alemann said that Frondizi hoped to meet the President on occasion IA–ECOSOC Conference, either in Montevideo or in Buenos Aires, should President plan to stop at one or more countries en route. President said he too would most warmly welcome such a meeting although he unable at this time make decision on visiting Montevideo, in view of possibility his presence might be needed in Washington during July when Congress would probably be very active on many of the Administration's important bills.

Alemann referred with pride to hard-won economic successes Frondizi Government has already achieved. He referred also to GOA's political success in most recent local elections. He declared GOA now approaching point where Frondizi's sound economic practices will produce basic economic success and political recognition, but that GOA needs immediate help. Alemann declared he not in Washington to seek "aid package" but rather to obtain informal but firm assurance, for political purposes, of USG's intent to extend loans to GOA when requested on sound project basis. He cited specifically need to finance rehabilitation of railroads which running at deficit approximately equal to fiscal deficit.

Alemann said GOA fully understood and approved US aid to Brazil as significant contribution Brazil's economic and democratic stability which extremely important to Argentina and US and Latin America as a whole.

Source: Department of State, Central Files, 735.5–MSP/5–2461. Confidential. Drafted by Coerr; cleared with Goodwin, O'Conner, Barall; and approved by Coerr.

[1] Not found.

[2] The meeting was held from 4:28 to 4:57 p.m. at the White House. (Kennedy Library, President's Appointment Book) In the briefing memorandum to the President prepared for Alemann's call, May 22, the Department of State stressed that by receiving the new Argentine Economic Minister, President Kennedy could provide useful support of Argentina's economic stabilization and recovery program. The austerity program had won international approbation, but was very unpopular in Argentina. (Ibid., National Security Files, Countries Series, Argentina, General, 1/61–7/61)

President mentioned USG's traditional difficulty in making long-range aid commitments. He said he understood Alemann had had useful meeting with Dillon. He asked Goodwin of White House staff to coordinate urgent study and action by State, Treasury and other interested agencies both on trade and aid matters that Alemann had raised.[3]

Rusk

---

[3] No further documentation on this prospective study has been found.

---

173. Telegram From the Department of State to the Embassy in Argentina

Washington, September 27, 1961.

575. 1. President Kennedy and President Frondizi talked privately on September 26 for about two hours[1] and with their advisers for almost two hours more.[2]

2. Argentines submitted a long memorandum in advance requesting following loans:[3]

(a) $146.7 million for El Chocon–Los Colorados hydroelectric project, estimated to cost a total of $262 million;

Source: Department of State, Central Files, 711.11–KE/9–2761. Confidential. Drafted by Woodward, cleared by Goodwin, and approved by Woodward. Repeated to USUN.

[1] The memorandum of the private conversation, held at the President's suite in the Hotel Carlyle, New York City, 9–10:15 a.m, is ibid. Kennedy and Frondizi were at the United Nations for the General Assembly session.

[2] The second meeting with advisers (Rusk, Woodward, Martin, and Goodwin for the United States; Foreign Minister Caraco, Ambassador del Carril, Minister of Economics Alemann, Ambassador Arnaldo Musich, and Cecilio Morales for Argentina) also took place at the Hotel Carlyle from 10:15 to 11:30 p.m. (Johnson Library, Rusk Appointment Book) The memorandum of conversation of the meeting, September 26, is in Department of State, Central Files, 611.35/9–2661.

[3] Rusk sent President Kennedy a memorandum, dated September 26, explaining that the Argentine request totaled over $1 billion. He noted that only a small percentage of the projects had been mentioned before and "the new ones appear to have been hastily conceived and haphazardly presented—apparently for the purpose of affording us an opportunity to provide financial assistance if we are anxious to do so." Rusk recommended that Kennedy give Frondizi only a general commitment for assistance. The specific projects would have to be discussed with U.S. advisers. (Kennedy Library, President's Office Files, Countries Series, Argentina, General, 1961)

(b) Equipment and construction to renew entire meat-packing and meat transportation system with several items totaling $220 million;

(c) Ditto for poultry raising and processing industry, totaling $15 million;

(d) Ditto for fruit storage and transportation industry, totaling $65 million;

(e) For savings and loan and other low cost housing credit institutions, $200 million;

(f) For fish storage and processing, $20 million. (Appended to memorandum were lists of other hydroelectric projects totaling $149 million, and irrigation projects totaling $187 million.)

3. President Frondizi said his Government determined to proceed with El Chocon complex and wished "political" if not financial commitment from US. President Kennedy agreed to favorable response concerning US participation this project, conditioned on favorable recommendations by current IDB survey.[4] Final communiqué[5] also included statement of US favorable disposition toward additional assistance in low-cost housing field and manifested sympathetic attitude toward good projects in other categories, although no indication was given that assistance in agricultural processing industry could go beyond medium term credits for equipment.

4. Argentines emphasized their concern for larger US markets for meat. President Kennedy assured that scientific recheck by independent scientists on basis for US quarantine on pickled and cured meats now proceeding completely objectively.

5. President Kennedy offered to talk personally with Moore of Wilson Packing Co. to determine possibilities of constructive action.

6. In response to Secretary Rusk's direct query, Foreign Minister Carcano said that he did not know enough about the bilateral aviation agreement to be able to discuss it usefully. No mention was made of possible airport loans.

7. Only passing descriptive comments were made by Argentines concerning steel production projects, and comments concerning railroad re-organization were even more casual.

8. President Frondizi emphasized his belief that multilateral action concerning Cuba should be postponed because it would be extremely difficult until practical results could be shown to the people from Alliance for Progress projects.

9. President Kennedy emphasized that striking self-help measures, such as in taxes and land reform, will be necessary if his Adminis-

---

[4] Not found.

[5] The text of the communiqué is in *Public Papers of the Presidents of the United States: John F. Kennedy, 1961*, pp. 627–629.

tration is to obtain additional large appropriations required from US Congress for assistance in economic and social development.

10. Argentines appeared to be comparatively unimpressed with documents (Deptel 561) and doubted their authenticity.[6] Department arranged to have a complete set of photostats delivered by de la Torre directly to Argentine visitors, since Cuban exiles are very anxious to release texts of the documents and this direct contact would relieve Department of responsibility for repercussions from such publication.

Bowles

---

[6] Reference is to documents obtained by a member of the Cuban Embassy staff in Buenos Aires, who defected. The documents allegedly provided evidence of Cuban subversive activities in Argentina. (Memorandum from Goodwin to the President, undated; Kennedy Library, National Security Files, Countries Series, Argentina, General, 1/61–7/61) Telegram 561, September 25, is not printed. (Department of State, Central Files, 373.00/9–2861)

---

174. Memorandum of Conversation

Palm Beach, Florida, December 24, 1961.

SUBJECT

Summary of Conversation between President Kennedy and President Frondizi at Palm Beach, December 24, 1961, on subjects other than the Prospective Meeting of Consultation of Ministers of Foreign Affairs Scheduled for January 22, 1962

PARTICIPANTS

President Kennedy
President Frondizi
Argentine Foreign Minister, Dr. Miguel Angel Carcano
Argentine Ambassador to Washington, Sr. Emilio Donato del Carril
Argentine Under Secretary of Foreign Affairs, Dr. Oscar Camilion
Argentine Chief of Political Section of Foreign Office, Dr. Carlos Ortiz de Rozas
Assistant Secretary of State, Robert F. Woodward

1. President Frondizi expressed pride and satisfaction in the economic gains his Administration has made, with the result that public

---

Source: Kennedy Library, National Security Files, Countries Series, Argentina, General, 8/61–12/61. Confidential. Drafted by Woodward, and approved by Bundy at the White House on December 26. Frondizi's visit to Palm Beach was an informal one.

attention in Argentina has become focused on constructive economic developments and away from the former unproductive discussions of "nationalization" of utilities and industries and on largely theoretical and impractical discussions of social problems and labor benefits.

2. He pointed out that this had made it possible for the Argentine Government to weather a 40-day strike of railroad workers and discharge 40,000 of them who had been working absurdly short hours and were unneeded. The Argentine Government gave these workers full termination pay and would have discharged up to 40,000 more if the Government had the money to pay termination pay to them. Now the Government badly needs to show the public improvements in the railroads and wants to purchase freight cars and other equipment in the United States with a requested Eximbank loan. President Kennedy said he would speak with President Linder of the Eximbank about this, recognizing that the Eximbank has been awaiting action on the request for a World Bank loan for rehabilitation of the railways and that the World Bank has been awaiting the study of its mission in Argentina on this subject which will be completed next month.

3. President Frondizi spoke with satisfaction of the provincial elections in Santa Fe and other provinces in which his supporters won large majorities and the "Peronists" had a surprisingly small showing. Despite this showing, he thought it would be decidedly disadvantageous to the Government in the March elections if the voters were stirred up with publicity about debate on possible application of sanctions against Cuba at the Punta del Este meeting in January.

4. President Frondizi mentioned his hope for success in the efforts of the US mission going to Argentina next month to study ways in which cured and pickled meats can be prepared for shipment to the United States without any danger of foot and mouth disease. President Kennedy expressed a similar hope.

5. President Frondizi alluded to the continuing Argentine desire for financing of the El Chocon–Los Colorados hydro-electric and regional development project. President Kennedy stated, as he had in September 1961,[1] US willingness to give the most careful and sympathetic consideration to participation in the financing when the proposal is formulated and presented and when indications of the other sources of financing are ready.

6. President Kennedy reviewed briefly with President Frondizi the status of the interest of the US Steel Corporation in possible establishment of a steel mill in Argentina as evidenced by a study now in process.

---

[1] See Document 173.

7. President Frondizi commented that he was pleased that a new US Ambassador in the confidence of President Kennedy is being sent to Argentina and expressed the hope that he would come soon. President Kennedy said he would come just as soon as the question of his confirmation by the Senate can be worked out with the Senate which reconvenes in about two weeks.[2]

8. President Frondizi said that the Argentine Ambassador to Cuba, who had come to New Orleans to report to him, had asserted that there is steady economic deterioration in Cuba and that the recent Castro declarations are for the purpose of attempting to compel the Soviet Bloc to take on greater responsibility for economic support of Cuba—and also for the purpose of enabling Castro personally to compete with old-line Communist leaders who appear to be competing seriously with him within Cuba. (For example, a speech by Blas Roca two days before Castro's speech of December 1 received much more publicity in the press than Castro's.) The Argentines asserted, also, that they considered Castro's provocation of diplomatic breaks with Venezuela, Colombia and Panama—and his speech of December 1—were designed to force a vote on a "hard line" at the Meeting of Foreign Ministers which would divide the inter-American system and thus increase Cuba's chances of retaining a degree of cooperation and support from Brazil, Mexico, Chile and a few other countries.

9. President Frondizi said he did not consider the situation in Brazil to be very stable and he considered that any agitation, such as debate over sanctions against Cuba, which might precipitate movements in Brazil of the right or left, would be harmful.

10. President Frondizi asserted that there is no need for land reform in Argentina which provides for any division of present land ownership, but that increased productivity of agriculture is badly needed. He implied that he thought there might be some need for land division in countries such as Chile where the rural population is a larger percentage of total population. President Kennedy said he hoped that the "Operation Beef" technical assistance program was helping with increased productivity, and President Frondizi said appreciatively that it is.

11. President Frondizi remarked on his impression that the Japanese with whom he talked a week ago did not consider Red China a threat because they believe Red China's internal problems are so great. He said he thought Argentina might be able to sell grains, meat and wool to Red China. President Kennedy said that Red China constitutes such a great and unpredictable threat to all of us in the Western World—and will more so as it obtains nuclear weapons—that it would be very unfortu-

---

[2] Robert McClintock was appointed Ambassador to Argentina on February 6.

nate if anything were done to help the Government in the face of even a remote chance that internal forces may be developing in opposition to the present Peking Government.[3]

---

[3] On February 1 Frondizi sent Kennedy a long letter detailing economic progress and problems in Argentina, and requesting "in concrete terms" $50 million credit from the U.S. Treasury "without the presently required provision of total prior utilization of the $100 million contingent credit granted by the International Monetary Fund." Frondizi also requested $100 million with the program of the Alliance for Progress to finance the transfer of 200,000 public employees to "new productive occupations in national development sectors." (Kennedy Library, National Security Files, Countries Series, Argentina, General, 1/62–2/62)

---

175. Telegram From the Department of State to the Embassy in Argentina

Washington, February 10, 1962, 4 p.m.

1436. Reference Embassy's telegram 1350[1] and Department's telegram 1391.[2] Department shares Embassy's concern internal political crisis may result in destruction of balance between civil and military forces and subordination of constitutional elected executive to military. We welcome foreign policy changes brought about by internal pressures mainly from military.[3] We believe however continued and extreme military pressure upon government would be contrary to US interests.

You have taken position with our approval that this is Argentine internal matter in which we are resolved not to intervene but that we would deplore overthrow of constitutional government by military. If consistent with this position you have opportunity in contacts with military to point out advantages of relieving pressure on Government in

---

Source: Department of State, Central Files, 735.00/2–862. Secret. Drafted by Wellman, cleared by Goodwin, and approved by Rusk.

[1] In telegram 1350 from Buenos Aires, February 8, the Embassy reported increasing tension between the Frondizi government and the Argentine military. The Embassy noted fears that either the military would demand the ouster from the government of certain Frondizi supporters, placing him in an inferior political position, or might even overthrow him. (Ibid.)

[2] In telegram 1391 to Buenos Aires, February 2, the Department noted it "would deplore overthrow by armed forces of constitutional government." (Ibid., 735.00/2–162)

[3] Reference is to the breaking of relations between Cuba and Argentina on February 8.

interest of moderate solution, now that foreign policy changes have been achieved, you are encouraged to do so.[4]

Rusk

---

[4] In telegram 1389 from Buenos Aires, February 15, the Embassy reported that it had on several occasions used U.S. officials to inform the Argentine military that overthrowing Frondizi "would indicate a regression in Argentine political affairs and could not but help affect adversely our relations." (Department of State, Central Files 735.00/2–1562)

---

176. Telegram From the Embassy in Argentina to the Department of State

Buenos Aires, March 19, 1962, 3 p.m.

1661. This telegram is in nature of a contingency paper and in consequence I do not wish it to be taken as a cry of alarm. Other telegrams going out from Embassy this morning will analyze results of elections, submit biographic data on Framini and company, and summarize Embassy opinion on psychological, political, and economic impact from yesterday's balloting.[1]

Purpose of this telegram is to point out various contingencies which may arise from an unsatisfactory situation.

1. Ironic paradox is that national elections which by every index were clean and honestly run will lead to one of three alternatives, none palatable to Argentina nor ultimately to US:

A) Election results are allowed to stand "as is" with Peronists thus gaining control of seven to nine provinces, including vitally important

---

Source: Department of State, Central Files, 737.00/3–1962. Top Secret; Niact; Limit Distribution. Repeated to POLAD CINCARIB.

[1] National elections were held in the federal capital and 16 provinces. Fourteen provinces elected governors along with provincial and local officials. Fifteen provinces and the federal capital elected members of the National Chamber of Deputies. Eighty-seven of the 192 seats in the National Assembly were at stake. The Peronists ran first in 11 provinces, winning 9 governorships and were second in the federal capital. Voting for seats in the National Chamber resulted in the following distribution (including hold-over members): Unión Cívica Radical Instransigente (UCRI), Frondizi's party, 74; Unión Cívica Radical del Pueblo (UCRP), 56; Peronists, 47; and 14 seats were distributed among minor parties. Documentation on the election is ibid., 735.00.

Buenos Aires province, as well as materially increasing their representation in Chamber of Deputies. Such control could easily prepare a way for election two years hence of a Peronist president.

B) To prevent foregoing alternative, Frondizi (as Morales told me last night—Embtel 1656)[2] might intervene against Framini in Buenos Aires province and other Peronist Governors in remaining six provinces. This, although constitutionally "legal" since Argentina still remains in state of siege, would of itself negate democratic process as carried out by elections.

C) Military, incensed at what they regard as a gigantic miscalculation by Frondizi, may use their power not merely to insist that he have recourse to intervention as outlined above, but might as well ask themselves "why not go the whole hog?" "Why not throw out Frondizi?"

2. Our own attitude toward these three alternatives initially should be one of "no comment" although here and there we could make noises about hope that constitutional procedures will be followed in one of Latin America's most politically advanced countries.

3. If, however, military do oust Frondizi they will certainly not stop short of getting rid of Frigerio at same time and will place Peronists, at least for time being, beyond the pale. Their coup d'état will undoubtedly have window dressing to make it seem an anti-Communist, anti-Castro measure. It is perhaps early to discern whom they would entrust with power as an eventual provisional president, but it seems clear that Aramburu would most likely fill requirements of that position. If he is appointed I believe we should give him prompt recognition with stress on fact that it was he who intervened against Peron and succeeded in bringing nation to restoration of a constitutional regime. General Fraga, Secretary of War, might be another possibility.

Foregoing is responsive to last sentence Deptel 1668[3] although drafted before receipt that telegram.

McClintock

---

[2] Dated March 18. (Ibid., 735.00/3–1862)

[3] The last sentence of telegram 1668 to Buenos Aires, March 19, reads: "Your evaluation election results including probable effect on position and policies GOA and US-Argentine relations eagerly awaited particularly in view Congressional interest." (Ibid.)

177. **Telegram From the Department of State to the Embassy in Spain**

Washington, March 21, 1962, 4:22 p.m.

914. Refs urtel 1209 and Buenos Aires to Dept 1680 repeated to Madrid niact 9.[1] We appreciate considerations raised urtel 1209 and also doubt any approach to GOS would be effective. We would like to give sympathetic response to President Frondizi however and have consequently asked our Ambassador to tell him we have requested our Embassy Madrid to explore what it may be possible to do in response to his request.[2] If upon further consideration you feel that approach at appropriate level in Spanish Government might be helpful in situation described BA telegram 1680 you are authorized in your discretion to make it.

Despite statement Foreign Office official (Embtel 1299 June 7, 1961)[3] Peron so far had kept his word to refrain political activity, we have received reports he has remained in contact with Peronista organizations in Argentina with some Peronista leaders having visited him in Spain.

You will understand any approach to GOS should be handled so as to minimize possibility public disclosure U.S. interest.

Report your conclusions and any action you may take.[4]

Ball

Source: Department of State, Central Files, 735.00/3–2062. Top Secret. Drafted by Wellman, cleared in EUR/WE, and approved by Martin. Repeated to Buenos Aires.

[1] In telegram 1680 from Buenos Aires, March 20, McClintock reported a conversation with Frondizi who asked the United States urgently to approach Generalissimo Franco. Frondizi wanted Franco to prevent Juan Perón, in exile in Spain, from sending instructions to Peronist militants in Argentina to incite riots, strikes, bombing incidents, or other demonstrations against the Frondizi government. In telegram 1209 from Madrid, the Embassy recommended against direct representation to Franco as it was unlikely to lead to success. Instead, the Embassy proposed to make the approach to the Foreign Office. It was not hopeful of strong Spanish cooperation. (Both ibid.)

[2] In telegram 1701 to Buenos Aires, March 21. (Ibid.)

[3] Not printed. (Ibid., 735.00/6–761)

[4] In telegram 1246 from Madrid, March 23, the Embassy reported that it took up the "Perón problem" with Foreign Minister Fernando Maria Castiella who agreed that Perón should maintain silence, assured the Embassy that Perón had agreed to do so, and that Perón was not sending instructions to Peronists in Argentina. Castiella stated that Spain was sympathetic to Frondizi. (Ibid., 735.00/3–2362)

178.   Memorandum From the Assistant Secretary of State for Inter-American Affairs (Martin) to Acting Secretary of State Ball

Washington, March 26, 1962.

SUBJECT

Argentine Situation

For Frondizi (not in order of priority)

1. Essentially accepts our domestic economic objectives.
2. Is legally President.
3. No good alternative visible.
4. Replacement by military apt to loose Peronista violence.
5. Military coup bad example for Latin America.
6. He has courage, at least as far as staying in office is concerned.

Against Frondizi

1. In foreign and domestic political matters it seems sometimes difficult to know what he really believes.
2. Has made deals with Peron.
3. Has no important supporting group in country which will help him govern and solve future urgent problems; if he stays it will be because of principle of constitutionality only.

On balance, and especially looking beyond the next few weeks, it is a close thing and our instructions have been accordingly restrained. The FYI on Friday's cable[1] was FYI. Its positive clause was a negative instruction against any encouragement to military to take over. It did not revoke our earlier instructions[2] or my telephone conversation of Tuesday night with Ambassador[3] when we agreed he should personally stay out of crisis and only pass views through [*less than 1 line of source text not declassified*]. It only changed previous endorsement of constitutional processes

---

Source: Department of State, Central Files, 735.00/3–2662. Top Secret; Eyes Only. Drafted by Martin.

[1] Reference is to telegram 1738 to Buenos Aires, March 23. An FYI message in the cable reads: "It is our strong desire and policy that Frondizi not be forced to resign by military and nothing should be done that might in any way encourage the military to take such action." (Ibid., 735.00/3–2362)

[2] Apparent reference to telegram 1668 to Buenos Aires, March 19, in which the Department stated that the United States must "avoid any intervention in Arg internal affairs, and this is particularly advisable in view uncertainty regard game Frondizi is playing vis-à-vis Peronists and others. (Ibid., 735.00/3–1862)

[3] No other record of this telephone conversation, March 20, has been found.

to an FYI expression of our support for Frondizi because by Friday two seemed to have merged and success of Frondizi seemed only way to prevent military coup. But this was a statement of our views and not an authorization to move to open and active support.

His initial reported response was not wholly inappropriate relay of US views through [*less than 1 line of source text not declassified*]. Action on Frigerio was first open intervention and while good advice to Frondizi, could put us in bad spot in future with Frigerio group; and ploy along this line through McCloud to military was bad tactics also in relations with Frondizi. On Sunday he openly stepped in with authority to Frondizi to quote FYI US view to Navy and in his own meeting with Navy. Subsequently he met with Air Force and General Aramburo and revealed to Frondizi the General's personal plans to replace Frondizi.

I do not now feel able to pass judgment on actions of man on spot in crisis of this urgency.

This report in No. 1779[4] on Sunday's activities also underlines that even with the title of President, Frondizi will not have the support necessary to govern. The large Peronista vote makes it even more important than would normally be the case that there be a firm government in Argentina with a clear policy which it is able to carry out.

Recommendations:[5]

1. That we concur in Ambassador McClintock's recommendation in the second section of No. 1779 that he take no further action but let events take their course for the immediate future.

---

[4] In telegram 1779, March 25, McClintock reported that Frondizi told him that he was under heavy pressure from the Argentine Navy to resign. Frondizi asked McClintock to talk with the admirals. McClintock reported that Chief of Naval Operations Admiral Penas and Navy Chief of Staff Rear Admiral Palma informed him that unless Frondizi resigned, there would be a coup in 48 hours. McClintock encouraged the admirals to work with Frondizi in reorganizing the government. McClintock saw Frondizi again that afternoon and agreed to speak to key members of the Argentine Army and Air Force. After these meetings, McClintock met General Aramburu who was firmly in favor of Frondizi's voluntary departure to avoid a coup. McClintock reported to Washington that he had discharged his "moral obligation" to aid Frondizi, had discouraged an outright coup d'état, and that Frondizi was a spent force. McClintock recommended that the United States sit tight and "let the Argentines work out their own salvation." (Ibid., 635.00/3–2562)

[5] There is no indication on the source text whether Ball approved or disapproved these recommendations but in telegram 1767 to Buenos Aires, March 26 at 8:49 p.m., the Department told McClintock that it concurred that the "best course of action is to let events take their course," and that the prohibition against the United States "not intervening in open fashion still stands." The Department reminded McClintock that other initiatives should not be taken without instructions from Washington. The cable also suggested that once the situation stabilized, the United States should try to help secure a government with sufficient support to govern effectively and to meet the challenge of the Perónists vote. (Ibid.) According to an attached note, Ball did not see this memorandum until after telegram 1767 was sent.

2. That we should turn our attention to the need for a government in Argentina which can govern effectively and vigorously and with some degree of popular support, particularly to deal with the issues raised by the Peronista vote. What the US can do to promote this objective will require very careful examination.

---

179. Memorandum From the President's Special Assistant (Schlesinger) to President Kennedy

Washington, March 30, 1962.

SUBJECT

Attitude Toward the Argentine Situation[1]

Problem. Should the State Department or the White House issue a statement disapproving of the action of the Argentine military in interrupting constitutional processes in Argentina (without, of course, closing the door to eventual relations with the new government)?

Arguments Pro. The failure to do this will lead the military in other countries to suppose that they have a green light to stage coups of their own. Loeb in Peru, Stewart in Venezuela, Bernbaum in Ecuador and now John Martin in the Dominican Republic have all reported ominous stirrings in their local military establishments. Betancourt, who is obviously greatly alarmed, has pulled most of his people out of Buenos Aires and, according to radio reports, has sent a telegram to you and other Latin American Presidents concerning the Argentine situation. (We are checking, but the Betancourt message apparently has not yet arrived, the radio report did not describe its contents.)[2]

Great concern is reported throughout Latin America from the particular friends of the Alliance for Progress.

It is further contended that making such a statement, far from prejudicing future relations with the new Argentine government, may have a

---

Source: Kennedy Library, National Security Files, Countries Series, Argentina, General, 3/16/62–3/31/62. No classification marking.

[1] On March 29 Argentine military forces removed President Frondizi from power claiming that he had reduced Argentina to a critical state by his errors and justifying their actions by the need to protect the constitution and the aims of the revolution which overthrew Perón in 1955. For the immediate U.S. reaction, see Document 182.

[2] See footnote 1, Document 185.

sobering and salutary effect (as similar statements may have had in the case of South Korea).

Arguments Con. We do not yet know enough about the situation to take a public attitude of disapproval; and, if we do so, it may make it more difficult for us to influence the direction of the new government. We should deal with the situations in Peru, Venezuela, Ecuador and the Dominican Republic by specific means adapted to each country rather than by comment on the Argentine situation. In some cases (El Salvador in the past, perhaps Cuba in the future), we have welcomed military coups. Given the uncertainty of the situation, it would be safer to move with caution, let our disapproval be made evident by delaying formal relations with the new government and refrain at this point from going out on the limb.[3]

Arthur Schlesinger, jr.[4]

---

[3] At the daily White House Staff meeting, the coup in Argentina was discussed. According to Ewell's memorandum for the record, March 30, the discussion was as follows:

"Arthur Schlesinger brought up the fact that we had not reacted yet to the Argentine situation. The President evidently decided that we would say nothing yesterday (Thursday), but had issued no guidance as to today or subsequently. Schlesinger's primary interest is for us to tell the other Latin American countries that we are opposed to military takeover. Bundy is in the middle as he sees no need for unnecessarily antagonizing the new Government. It was accepted by all that we would sooner or later recognize the new Government." (National Defense University, Taylor Papers, Daily Staff Meetings, January–April 1962)

[4] Printed from a copy that bears this typed signature.

---

180. Circular Telegram From the Department of State to Posts in the American Republics

Washington, March 31, 1962, 9:33 p.m.

1657. Relations with new Argentine Government.

1) Particularly in view repercussions Argentine developments throughout Hemisphere and interest already expressed by certain governments in US position we wish to exchange information and views

---

Source: Department of State, Central Files, 735.00/3–3162. Secret; Priority. Drafted by Wellman and approved by Martin. Repeated to Buenos Aires, London, USUN, Madrid, and POLAD CINCARIB.

with Government to which you are accredited. You are requested to confer with Government at high level promptly for this purpose.

2) Following is summary of current governmental situation in Argentina based on reports from our Embassy which should be conveyed to Foreign Office:

Constitutionally elected President Frondizi removed from office on March 29 by Argentine military forces after he had persistently resisted strong military and civilian pressures to resign. Jose Maria Guido, President of Senate, took oath office as President on March 29. He reaffirmed assumption office in public ceremony March 30 before Supreme Court in presence Members of Congress and military leaders. New government claims right legal succession under Article 75 Argentine Constitution as implemented by Law of Congress 1868. This provides that 1) in event Republic without a head due to lack of a president in certain contingencies (in this case absence from capital) and Vice President (resigned) executive power shall be vested in President of Senate, and 2) new President shall within thirty days call for new election of President and Vice President.

Reportedly Senate President was at first reluctant to serve but took Presidential office at personal sacrifice to himself with consent or perhaps even request Frondizi and at urging of leaders UCRI (Frondizi's) party in order to avoid installation of military government. UCRP (which was principal opposition party in Congress) has reportedly announced support for him. Military commanders accepted Guido after initial reluctance and some leading military have reportedly asked to be retired.

Cabinet not yet formed. Guido is civilian and although military will probably have much to say about composition of Cabinet, it seems likely to be largely non-military in character. Congress will probably be called into session within next few days to enact electoral and other urgent legislation.

3) You are requested to state that it will always be source of regret and concern for USG when a democratically elected government which is cooperating in the OAS and with the Alliance for Progress is replaced at insistence of military forces. We hope however that a civilian government will be established in Argentina which will command support from the Congress, democratic political parties and majority populace, as well as military forces, that this Government will operate within democratic constitution and that it will observe its international and inter-American obligations including those under Alliance for Progress. If a government of substantially this character is organized by Guido, it should be in the interest of all states with the interests of Argentine people at heart to assist it in strengthening democratic institutions in

Argentina and resuming the social and economic programs called for by our mutual commitments under Alliance.

4) You should state that USG therefore intends to watch developments in Argentina very closely over next several days, and in particular will be interested in composition new Cabinet when formed, congressional support of new government, plans for new election pursuant to constitution and other indications of policies it will follow. In this connection USG will be pleased to receive such information and views as foreign government may have on Argentine situation.

5) Report promptly Government's reactions together with any comments you may have.[1]

Rusk

---

[1] The responses are ibid., 735.00.

---

181. Telegram From the Department of State to the Embassy in Argentina

Washington March 31, 1962, 9:33 p.m.

1866. Ref BA Embtel 1902.[1]

1. We would like to study Argentine situation further before making decision on relations with new government and in particular on question of timing. We would like first to have your report and evaluation of new Cabinet when selected by provisional President. We are also interested in reaction to new government in special session of Congress proposed to be called almost immediately, which should provide evidence degree of Congressional support, as well as an indication from new Government of its plans, including those for new elections. In other words we wish to be sure new government is in effective control and to consider degree to which it is able to act along constitutional lines. We

---

Source: Department of State, Central Files, 735.00/3–3062. Secret; Niact; Limit Distribution. Drafted by Wellman; cleared by Walter L. Cutler (Rusk's Staff Assistant), Rusk, and the White House (paragraph 3 only); and approved by Martin.

[1] In telegram 1902 from Buenos Aires, March 30, the Embassy described secret negotiations between Guido and the military to enact measures to control the Perónists, modify labor union legislation, and enact a bill for proportional representation in future elections. In this telegram the Embassy recommended that the United States continue relations with the Guido government. (Ibid.)

also need to exchange information and views with other Latin American Governments. Cirtel for this purpose being repeated to you.[2]

2. We appreciate and share your interest in supporting a civilian government and forestalling outright military dictatorship. On other hand too prompt action might reassure military that they can act as they choose in future without fear of US disapproval. We trust procedures outlined above will not result in undue risk on this score.

3. You have noted repercussions of Argentine situation in other Latin American countries particularly those where democratic governments have only recently succeeded military regimes. In order reassure democratic elements in Latin America and to discourage military adventures the President is considering a public statement in general terms on role of military in government, perhaps in connection with a further decision on our relations with Argentine Government.

4. We hope you can find early opportunity to explain privately to responsible military elements supporting new government that we are concerned over possible adverse effects of reports on Argentine developments upon political stability of democratic and constitutional regimes elsewhere in Hemisphere. This may require US to make public statement this subject. It would not be directed primarily at Argentine situation, where civilian government under a democratic constitution is now in office, but designed to influence situation in certain other American countries where continuance any form of democratic regime may be endangered if military elements not warned. We hope they will understand Hemisphere conditions which seem to call for some such statement by us. FYI only. We have in mind for example at present time DR, Venezuela, Peru and Ecuador. End FYI.

5. We shall appreciate further information when available on following: a) composition of Cabinet and competence and reputation new Ministers; b) extent support new government outside Peronists and communists; c) plan for convening special session Congress; d) intention re new elections; e) effect of proposed proscription totalitarian parties on 1) recent elections to Chamber of Deputies and 2) continuance and extension of interventions of provincial governments; f) nature and effect of proposed modification of basic labor law; g) probable reaction of Peronists to new Government and proscription totalitarian parties, and ability new Government to cope with them; h) reliability of reports Frondizi approved Guido acceptance Presidency.

Rusk

---

[2] Document 180.

182. Editorial Note

At the White House daily staff meeting on April 2, 1962, presided over by the Deputy Assistant for National Security Affairs, Carl Kaysen, Argentina was the last topic of conversation. According to an April 2 memorandum for the record by Colonel Julian J. Ewell of General Maxwell Taylor's staff, the discussion was as follows:

"Schlesinger reported that our policy on Argentina is still up in the air. Secretary Rusk and the Country Desk, as well as the Ambassador, are for recognition, the Assistant Secretary and Schlesinger are against. There was mention of a reputed message from Betancourt which proposed that no one recognize a military government put in place by a coup. No one has seen this message as yet. Bromley Smith will make inquiries to see if it was delayed in transmission. Schlesinger philosophized a little bit on the possibility that the Peronista element might not be as bad as has been painted. He pointed out that the International Monetary Fund has had a complete lack of success in stabilizing economies in Latin America without the Government falling from power. He inferred that perhaps we needed a different approach, that such harsh economic medicine resulted in killing the patient. I asked Schlesinger if he was saying that we shouldn't have economists in Government, and he said he had always been against it. This was after Kaysen had left the room." (National Defense University, Taylor Papers, Daily Staff Meetings, Jan–April 1962)

Regarding President Betancourt's message, March 29, see footnote 1, Document 185.

---

183. Memorandum From the Director of the Agency for International Development (Hamilton) to President Kennedy

Washington, April 6, 1962.

SUBJECT

Effect of Alliance for Progress on Argentine Election Results; NSAM No. 141, March 27, 1962[1]

Source: Kennedy Library, National Security Files, Countries Series, Argentina, General, 4/62. Confidential.

[1] NSAM 141, entitled "Analysis of Frondizi's Political Reverses," is in Department of State, NSAM Files: Lot 72 D 316, NSAM 141. The NSAM is paraphrased in the first paragraph of section 1 below.

1.   You requested an analysis be made of the extent to which President Frondizi's recent political reverses were due to (a) exploitation by his opponents of the fact that he arranged to accept United States aid, or (b) exploitation by his opponents of reforms undertaken or promised by him and associated with the Alliance for Progress. After consulting our Embassy in Argentina, we believe the answers are as follows:

President Frondizi's opponents did not attempt to exploit Argentine acceptance of United States aid and his political reverses were not ascribable to such acceptance. An emissary from President Frondizi emphasized, quite to the contrary, that Frondizi's defeat would have been of almost catastrophic proportion if announcement of the $150 million Alliance for Progress loan had not come when it did.[2]

President Frondizi's election opponents did not openly seek to exploit the reforms he had initiated or promised to initiate in connection with the Alliance for Progress. Frondizi's austerity program designed to bring about the financial stability necessary for sound economic development, which the United States supported, was a factor in the elections, however. An important reason for Frondizi's defeat was that his reforms and development program had not gone far enough or deep enough to reach the common man as yet.

As the Embassy observed,[3] the persistent favorable after-image of Peron in the public mind was a fundamental factor in the election.

2.   You asked the question as to whether it is advisable to channel more Alliance aid through the Inter-American agencies. Until we have obtained more experience with these agencies, I do not believe it advisable to increase the amounts above our current plans for the Inter-American Development Bank and the Organization of American States programs. Under our current plans, these two organizations, in FY 1962, will have utilized slightly more than one-half of the $400 million portion of the $500 million appropriation provided by the Congress last year with the remainder available in FY 1963.

Our experience to date with the Inter-American agencies has been rather limited and produced equally both good and bad results. In a number of cases, the agency has been most useful and successful in dealing with the local government to bring about reforms. In other instances, we have found that because of the newness of the task the Inter-Ameri-

---

[2] On February 25 the White House announced that the United States was making a loan of $150 million to Argentina for its economic development under the Alliance for Progress. The money was for specific development projects and balance of payments assistance. (White House press release, February 25; Department of State *Bulletin*, March 19, 1962, p. 470)

[3] The Embassy made this observation in telegram 1699 from Buenos Aires, March 21, in its assessment of the significance of the March elections. (Department of State, Central Files, 735.00/3–2162)

can agency's performance has not been adequate in the implementation of projects and in assisting countries to develop sound programs and plans.

Walter L. Lingle[4]

---

[4] Lingle signed for Hamilton above Hamilton's typewritten signature.

---

184. Memorandum From the Assistant Secretary of State for Inter-American Affairs (Martin) to Secretary of State Rusk

Washington, April 13, 1962.

SUBJECT

Recommendations for Regularizing Official Relations with Argentina

Discussion

I. The following considerations favor regularizing official relations with the Guido Government without substantial further delay.

1. It has effective control of the machinery of government in accordance with the Argentine Constitution.

Upon Frondizi's arrest and removal by the military, Guido as President of the Senate assumed office of President as next in line under Argentine Constitution. He was sworn in before the Supreme Court with members of Congress present, and the Supreme Court later reaffirmed the constitutionality of the succession. Frondizi also approved his succession after-the-fact. Guido has constituted a cabinet of civilians (except three armed forces secretaries) who are of conservative-bent but generally respected. He has convened a special session of Congress to meet between April 12 and 25 to reform the law of succession to provide for the calling within 180 days (rather than 30 days) of a new presidential election at a future date deemed advisable under the circumstances.

2. It is in office with general acquiescence if not support.

Source: Department of State, Central Files, 611.35/4–1362. Secret. Drafted by Wellman on April 12 and cleared by Whiteman.

All political groups except the Peronistas and Communists support or acquiesce in government, although differing on the desirability of honoring recent congressional elections and other major policy questions. UCRI (Frondizi's party) deputies and provincial governors demanding the return of Frondizi do so largely for the record, as political maneuvering with eye toward future electoral prospects, in our Embassy's opinion. Indications are that the Peronistas would prefer civilian government to military dictatorship though of course outlawing this party or too reactionary economic measures might force them into more active opposition. Moderate military leaders who are in majority in armed forces accept and support government.

3. Any considerable further delay by U.S. Government in regularizing relations would increase substantially the risk of a military dictatorship.

The moderate military leaders now appear to be in the ascendancy in the armed forces. Extreme military leaders who were influential in bringing about Frondizi's removal distrust the civilian government and would prefer a military dictatorship. The danger of a further military coup increases if through delayed U.S. action the Guido government should lose public confidence and support.

4. Clarification of major policy issues involving elections, Congress and Peronists is not likely in near future.

The special session of Congress called for some time between April 12–25 is limited to considering reform of the constitutional succession (see above). It is probable new presidential elections will be held in 1963 at the earliest. To avoid having to choose between seating the elected Peronist Congressmen (which the military would resist) or nullifying the recent election (which major democratic parties oppose) the government will probably not convene Congress on May 1 or soon thereafter. It will not likely soon terminate the intervention of the five important provinces which elected Peronist governors, in particular Buenos Aires province. It may seek to work out a compromise acceptable to the Peronists and the military for some limited participation by the Peronists in electoral matters in lieu of the proscription of the neo-Peronist parties, e.g. accession to provincial governships not intervened, and right to vote in new presidential election.

5. The Guido government provides the best and the only present possibility for gradual return of Argentina to democratic processes.

Guido is ostensibly a constitutional president. Frondizi's return is not a real possibility; the military would not accept him, and he has lost the confidence of important civilian elements of the nation. The only alternative appears to be a military dictatorship possibly accompanied by disorders and even civil war. The best hope for return to democratic constitutionality is through action of the present government, supported by moderates, taking a center course between extremes, and seeking by negotiation to extract concessions from both the Peronists and the military.

6. Argentina is facing an incipient financial crisis, which a new political crisis would precipitate and worsen.

7. Other western governments, including some in Latin America, have moved to continue relations, and others are considering doing so.

The following governments are among those which have continued relations: Colombia, Haiti, Honduras and El Salvador from Latin America; and UK, France, Netherlands, Belgium, Italy, Spain, Switzerland and China.

8. The Guido government has indicated it intends to pursue the economic stabilization program of the Frondizi government, a program which had our support. It is now negotiating a new stabilization agreement with IMF, is prepared by new import surcharges and freeing of the peso to reduce the balance of payments deficit, and by increased taxes to reduce the budget deficit.

II. The following considerations indicate caution and favor further delay.

1. The future support of or opposition to the government will be affected by its policy on certain difficult and unresolved political issues of which the most important appear to be the following:

a) whether Congress will be convened or the government will rule by decree.
b) whether Congressional elections will be honored or nullified in law, or in fact by not convening the Congress.
c) whether the provincial interventions will be maintained and other provinces intervened where Peronists won governorships.
d) whether the Peronist parties will be proscribed.
e) whether the labor law will be amended to terminate the monopoly of national labor confederation which Peronists effectively control, in labor representation.

Action by the government or even its failure to take action on these issues will create internal conflicts.

2. The extent of the support by the democratic political parties might be more clearly indicated at the special session of Congress to be convened between April 12 and 25.

3. Depending on the policies of the government and the reaction of the Peronists, the latter may incite disorders in which the Communists would join and other labor elements might participate. Although the military forces are disposed to maintain order and could probably do so, it would be at the expense of democratic liberties and return to democratic processes would be retarded.

4. The government though civilian in form will be subject to strong military influence, which could become dominant depending upon how the situation develops.

5. The government is conservative and in the economic field tends to be orthodox. There is no indication it will give adequate attention to social reform and immediate improvement of the economic and social conditions of the lower classes. It will probably be less inclined than the previous government to reach an accommodation with the Peronists and to seek to integrate them into the democratic framework, especially because Frondizi's unsuccessful attempt to do this brought about his deposition by the military. Yet the Peronists cast 35% of the total vote in the recent Congressional elections.

6. Of the Latin American governments which have not continued relations with the Argentine government, most are following our policy of watchful waiting and would follow our lead if we should decide to continue relations. Brazil, however, is inclined to withhold action until it is able to ascertain what action GOA will take on seating Peronist governors-elect, and what Argentine public reaction will be. Venezuela, while sympathetic to action by U.S. Government to continue relations, intends to adhere firmly to its policy not to recognize a government resulting from overthrow by military of constitutionally elected regime.

III. On balance it is believed in United States interest to take action to confirm continuance of relations with the Argentine government without any considerable further delay.

Recommendations[1]

A. That the United States Government continue official relations with Argentina on the basis that the Argentine government has effective control in accordance with the Argentine Constitution of the machinery of government and Argentine territory with general acquiescence of the Argentine people, provided important Latin American countries (i.e. Brazil, Chile, Uruguay) also decide to do so simultaneously or in coordination with us. (Failure of any such important Latin American countries to agree to this would not preclude a subsequent U.S. decision to continue official relations if the U.S. so desired.)

B. That following this action, with view to helping the situation in those Latin American countries where civilian democratically elected governments may feel weakened by the example of military intervention in Argentina, an official U.S. spokesman make a statement to the press, preferably in reply to a press question, along lines of expressing regret at the interruption of the democratic processes in Argentina and

---

[1] Rusk approved recommendations A–D on April 14 on the condition that the press statement in recommendation B would be softened.

encouragement to the Argentine people and government to maintain and strengthen democratic institutions in order that Argentina may resume and intensify the social and economic programs called for by the Alliance for Progress.

C. That with reference to the special situation of Venezuela, a letter be sent to President Betancourt by the President in reply to the former's letter, along the lines suggested and approved by our Ambassador in Caracas. A proposed form of letter is attached.[2]

D. That following announcement of continuance of relations, the United States upon request from Argentina for the economic assistance it will continue to need, announce its willingness to provide aid under the $150 million aid package of March 1962, subject to (1) Argentina's carrying out the self-help and reform measures (railway reforms, financial stabilization and national development planning) accepted at that time by the Argentine government, which would be publicized, and (2) increasing attention by the Argentine government to the aspirations of the average man in Argentina for social justice, social reform and improved living standards.

---

[2] Attached to this memorandum, but not printed, are a proposed reply from President Kennedy to President Betancourt's March 29 message on the ramifications of the change of government in Argentina, a memorandum of a conversation between Martin and Foreign Minister Dantas of Brazil on the same issue, and an advance copy of telegram 2063 from Buenos Aires, April 13, in which McClintock argued that the only way to keep Argentina from outright military dictatorship was to recognize the Guido government, the "least objectionable of alternatives in the limited choice we have."

---

185. Memorandum From the Executive Secretary of the Department of State (Battle) to the President's Special Assistant for National Security Affairs (Bundy)

Washington, April 14, 1962.

SUBJECT

Reply to President Betancourt's telegram on Argentina's situation

On March 29, President Betancourt sent to the President and various other Chiefs of American states telegrams in which he strongly criticized

---

Source: Department of State, Central Files, 735.00/4–1462. No classification marking. Drafted by Martin and Wellman on April 14.

the overthrow of the legal Government of Argentina and stated Venezuela would not grant recognition to the new Argentine Government. (Tab B)[1] The Venezuelan Government ordered all the personnel in its Embassy in Buenos Aires to return to Caracas. In subsequent consultations with our Ambassador in Caracas, President Betancourt has indicated that although he would view sympathetically our continuance of relations with the Argentine Government, Venezuela would adhere to its position of nonrecognition in view of its plan to propose at the next Inter-American conference that there be prior consultation before recognition of de facto regimes in this hemisphere. This policy has strong backing in Venezuela.

The Venezuelan Government is especially sensitive to removal of a civilian President by the military forces as took place in Argentina. After three years it has held office longer than any previous elected government in Venezuelan history. Extremes on both left and right threaten to overthrow it by subversive activities and plots. It will endure as long as the military forces continue their support of constitutional government. It is understandably anxious therefore that nothing encourage military elements to think that they could move against the government with impunity. We have sought to make clear we support Betancourt, would deplore his overthrow and would have to review our policies toward Venezuela if he were overthrown.

Our Embassy has recommended that a reply to the Betancourt letter to the President would be desirable before we take any step toward regularizing relations with Argentina.

We agree that it would be helpful to Betancourt and to US-Venezuelan relations for the President to reply to his letter in advance of our continuance of relations with the Argentine Government. The attached proposed reply (Tab A)[2] for your approval would assure President Betancourt we appreciate his position, share his concern that constitutional and democratic processes be observed and are considering the matter of relations with the Argentine Government in the light of what we can do to help strengthen democratic institutions there. If after our continuance of relations with Argentina, Betancourt should wish to release the text of the President's message, we believe we should agree.

The Secretary believes this reply should be dispatched now. Events of the past week have led the Department to the conclusion that the present confused political situation in Argentina is not apt to be cleared up for several weeks. Nevertheless, there is a civilian government in power which has called the legislature into session. There are also disturbing

---

[1] Attached, but not printed. Sent via commercial channels.

[2] Not attached, but sent as telegram 1104 to Caracas, April 17. (Department of State Central Files, 735.00/4–1762)

reports of dissatisfaction among some elements of the military and of plotting to overthrow Dr. Guido. If recognition by us can strengthen civilian authority, it seems best to act promptly.

We have delayed long enough to make clear our disapproval of the military pressures which forced Frondizi from office. Some 34 governments, including Colombia, have acted to continue relations.

Earlier in the week we informed key governments in Latin America that we thought the time might be approaching for us to regularize relations. We received no protests and almost a sympathetic response from Betancourt.

Assistant Secretary Martin discussed the possibility with Brazilian Foreign Minister Dantas Thursday might. The latter was doubtful if Brazil would move yet but did not protest our acting. He requested time to consult President Goulart. Mr. Martin assured him we would wish President Goulart's views. We are sending a message to Ambassador Gordon to follow up with Minister Dantas.

We are now also seeking a reaction to a definite proposal to move from Uruguay, Chile and Peru, and are also asking them whether or not they would wish to coordinate the timing of any action on their part with that by us.

We hope that on April 17 we may be in a position to decide what to do.

A. E. Breisky[3]

---

[3] Breisky signed for Battle above Battle's typed signature.

186.   Memorandum From the President's Special Assistant (Dungan) to President Kennedy

Washington, April 17, 1962.

SUBJECT

Resumption of Relations with Argentina

As I told you last night,[1] most of the European countries have already resumed normal relations with Argentina.

Of the Latin American countries, Mexico will not make any formal reply to the Argentine note because their procedures permit resumption of relations without any formal notification. Chile will resume relations at 6 P.M. this evening; Peru is ready to announce concurrent with our announcement, if it comes. Peru requires 4 hours notice. Gordon has already talked to the Foreign Office in Rio and will be seeing Dantas later this afternoon.[2] It is unlikely that Brazil will take any action until after the Lower House of the Argentine Legislature acts on the Succession Bill. The Lower House of the Argentine Legislature will meet this afternoon and refer the Bill to a committee, thus deferring action until after the Easter holiday. It appears unlikely that the UCRI (Frondizi) will oppose the measure in the Argentine Legislature.

The Secretary will probably call you this afternoon suggesting that we move ahead promptly and reply to the Argentine note,[3] thereby resuming normal relations with the Guido government. I think that there is no need to rush into this and that we would not want to complete this action before your press conference tomorrow morning.[4] The announcement could be delayed until next week without any damage.[5] I think you

---

Source: Kennedy Library, President's Office Files, Countries Series, Argentina, General, 1962.

[1] According to an April 17 memorandum from Martin to Rusk, President Kennedy told Dungan on the night of April 16 that "he was reluctant to move until one of the big countries, like Brazil or Mexico, had moved. He was also unwilling to have the letter to Betancourt go out, even though it did not commit us, until we decided to move." (Department of State, Central Files, 611.35/4–1762)

[2] Ambassador Lincoln Gordon in Brazil.

[3] In the note of March 30, the Argentine Government informed the Embassy that the office of the President was vacant and that Guido had taken the oath of office before the Supreme Court and had assumed the Presidency of the Republic. (Telegram 2037 to Buenos Aires, April 17; Department of State, Central Files, 735.11/4–1762)

[4] Reference is to the President's press conference of April 18, in which Argentina was not discussed; for text, see *Public Papers of the Presidents of the United States: John F. Kennedy, 1962*, pp. 331–339.

[5] According to Press Release No. 257, April 18, Ambassador McClintock that day acknowledged receipt of the Argentine note of March 30, thus continuing relations with the Government of Argentina.

already know that all of the Latin American governments have been put on notice that we will probably move to resume normal relations with Argentina. I might say all have either indicated no opposition or approval. In every case, there was an expression of satisfaction that we have consulted with them on this matter.

RAD

187. Memorandum From the Director of the Bureau of Intelligence and Research (Hilsman) to Secretary of State Rusk

Washington, April 27, 1962.

INTELLIGENCE NOTE

Prospects for Argentina—Political Repression and Military Rule

Argentina will probably be ruled by the military until May 1964. Annulment of the March 18 election results and federal intervention in all Provinces leaves the country without an effective Parliament and with government completely in the hands of the central Executive, installed and controlled by the military. Since the remnant which remains in the Chamber of Deputies will barely exceed a constitutional quorum, even token dissent will prevent legislative action, and the expectation is that Argentina will be ruled by decree for the next 24 months.

Little hope is seen for the liberalization of the present military regime. Violence and repression are likely if Peronists and other labor groups strike against the economic austerity program which has already substantially increased the cost of living. The Peronists might well extend strikes and demonstrations to protest against cancellation of their election victories, the probable proscription of Peronist parties, and restrictions on labor union activities. However, military forces appear to be strong enough to control the country, although there will likely be some deaths and many arrests. The economy will be slowed by strikes and a loss of business confidence at least in the short run.

In Italy and France at the close of World War II as large a part of the electorate supported Communism as now supports Peronism in Argen-

Source: Kennedy Library, National Security Files, Countries Series, Argentina, General, 4/62. Confidential. Copies were sent to Schlesinger, Dungan, and Thomas Parrot of CIA.

tina. However, the Communists in Italy and France were not proscribed from political participation and thus were not limited to strikes, demonstrations, and terror for political expression. Instead the existence of the Communist group in Parliament and in the electorate encouraged the non-Communist forces, which were divided on many issues, to work together. Frondizi was pursuing such a course in Argentina, before the military reversed the trend on March 29.

The hard-line military group now in control have no constructive plan for the political future of Argentina. Some military probably hope to break the Peronist movement by suppression; but this tactic did not work between 1955 and 1958. Others assume the military will proscribe the Peronists in the 1963 election and guarantee the election of their candidate. However, in any free election in which the Peronists are proscribed from presenting their own candidate they hold the balance of power in choosing among the major candidates. The ability of the Peronist organization to direct about two million voters was demonstrated in 1957, 1958, 1960 and 1962. Thus in the 1963 elections the military might well be confronted, as they were in 1958, by a situation in which the leading candidates appeal for Peronist support despite military objection.

Implications for U.S. Policy. The United States can have little effect on immediate developments in Argentina. However, the nature of our relations with the government will be an important factor in determining the strength of those forces which want a rapid return to fully democratic government. Such forces are already considerable in the political parties, in apolitical groups, and even in the military. Considerations for U.S. policy are:

1) the nature of official U.S. contact with members of the present government, especially with the Argentine military;

2) the extent of our contacts with the political parties, including the Peronists;

3) whether to disburse or withhold the announced $150 million in Alliance for Progress aid; and

4) if aid funds are released, whether to channel them through the government or directly into projects which immediately benefit the people.

188.   **Letter From the Ambassador to Argentina (McClintock) to the Assistant Secretary of State for Inter-American Affairs (Martin)**

Buenos Aires, May 31, 1962.

DEAR ED: In response to your letter of May 8,[1] may I say how welcome it is to know that you have set up informal working groups in ARA closely to study the trend of recent events in Argentina, to draw conclusions therefrom, and to advocate a line of policy which may make it possible for us to achieve our objectives in relation to Argentina. I also note that you share the views expressed in our telegram No. 2233,[2] that our policy and endeavor should center on economic measures to palliate the crisis and give hope of social reform, and on political measures designed to speed the transition between democracy in word and democracy in deed. You will recall that I ended that telegram with the statement that although the price of victory would be high, the cost of defeat would be even greater.

We have accepted your suggestion that our recommendations on possible new courses of action should be cast in the format of a revision of the Department's Guidelines paper on Argentina dated March 1962.[3] With the full collaboration of the entire Country Team, we have prepared such a revision and enclose it herewith.[4] For the convenience of the various elements in the Department who will study the paper I am likewise sending the original hectograph mat to facilitate reproduction. We have sought to stay as close to the March issue of the Guidelines paper as possible but have not hesitated to depart where necessary from its language. We have also been happy to draw here and there on phraseology from the first draft of the Strategic Studies Group on Argentina prepared in S/P.[5] I shall, however, wish on a separate occasion to comment on that valuable paper and in particular some of its suggested courses of action with which I do not agree.

Within the Procrustean bed of a bureaucratic policy paper it is difficult to impart the flavor of the present situation in Argentina.

Source: Kennedy Library, National Security Files, William Brubeck Series, Argentina, '61–'62. Secret.

[1] Not found.

[2] Dated May 4. (Department of State, Central Files, 735.00/5–462)

[3] This paper, prepared in consultation with interested Departments and Agencies, was issued under the authority of the Department of State for guidance of all concerned in the conduct of foreign policy. (Ibid., 611.35/3–3162)

[4] Not found attached.

[5] This draft study, April 14, is 85 pages long. (Department of State, S/P Files: Lot 69 D 121, Argentina)

As I pointed out in Embassy telegram No. 1977,[6] the revolution which overthrew Frondizi was the result of, and also the explanation of, a number of paradoxes. Fair and free elections supervised by the military returned a Peronist vote which many construed as the threat of a return to Peronist dictatorship. Even in advance of any request from the military that he negate the results of the elections, President Frondizi intervened the provincial governments where the Peronists had won on March 18, 1962; yet despite his zeal in this direction, he was thrown out by the military. Although Frondizi was physically deposed, the Supreme Court piously declared that his successor, Guido, was in fact constitutional President. The military themselves, although they could easily have reached for overt power and still in the background exercise the negative power of veto, undertook their revolution in the firm conviction that they were acting in the name and spirit of democracy. However, as I have pointed out, we are in the case of Argentina using the same vocabulary but different dictionaries.

Fundamentally the recent crisis in Argentina was an emergency in morality. It was the inability of President Frondizi to move for any length of time on a straight course and his inability to follow a consistent policy of telling the truth which aroused many elements of the population against him and particularly the military who thought that he was either a front man for Peronism or, worse, a Judas who would eventually betray the country to Communism. Their suspicions of Frondizi were deepened by the utterly amoral, and frequently immoral, activities of Frondizi's eminence grise, Frigerio, who thought that every man had his price and who himself had his own price, frequently a high one. This crisis of morals in the political leadership, the absence of morals in that part of the economic community which paid bribes to Frigerio, and the cynical apathy of the people which will be noted below, caused a moral bankruptcy which was the basic cause of the recent coup d'état. Whatever remedies we seek to apply must in essence begin on a moral basis.

In what I sometimes ironically refer to as "the constitutional revolution", I have also remarked to Argentine friends that the nation is suffering from a political disease called acefalía. This is a word taken from the 1868 Law of Presidential Succession aptly termed la ley de acefalía, or headlessness. This ultimate paradox finds us with a tacit dictatorship lacking a dictator. In effect, a committee of three high military officers, the Secretaries of War, Navy and Air, act as a triumvirate with power of veto and suggestion over the civilian government headed by President Guido. (This they also exercised from time to time over the government of Frondizi.) However, within the civilian Cabinet there are men of ability and power who have a wide range of liberty of action and are a more

---

[6] Dated April 6. (Ibid., Central Files, 735.00/4–662)

positive counterpoise to the military. Principal of these is Alsogaray, the decisive, imaginative and bold Minister of Economic Affairs. Second to him is Del Carril, the Minister of Foreign Affairs, whose sense of historical perspective and whose ability to write have given him an increasing ascendancy with the somewhat illiterate military. A third figure yet to be tried, but who impresses me favorably, is Cantilo, the civilian Minister of Defense. This hybrid government, a camelopard of many spots, also operates without two of the hallmarks of dictatorship: both the judiciary and the press of Argentina are free.

Yet all of these elements, both civilian and military, seem to be suffering from this political disease of acefalía or headlessness. The disease extends likewise to the leadership in the political parties. Although officially placed in an "estado de asamblea", an Argentine legalism for suspension of activities, the various party leaders and the members of Congress whose sessions have been suspended by decree, still vociferate and grumble at their impotence. I do not discern in the congressional leadership nor in the political parties as now constituted any real emergent chief. In consequence, some of the easy recommendations for us to encourage a fusion of the two Radical Parties, or to bring about the creation of a Labor Party utilizing sanatized Peronist strength, seem in the shape of wishful thinking. In politics, as in the government itself, the disease of acefalía is rampant.

I have frequently pointed out that Argentina at present exhibits a perilous political vacuum. In the absence of leadership there is a terrible apathy in the Argentine public which in reality is not a true apathy of "I don't care", but the more dangerous apathy born of an absolute cynicism. The Argentine people, and particularly the inhabitants of Buenos Aires, inherit the anti-government sentiments of their Spanish and Italian progenitors plus the "me first, the devil take the hindmost" attitude of the Italian immigrants who came to Argentina for the sole purpose of making money. After a generation of military rule in one form or another, their natural distrust and disgust of government has reached the point of utter cynicism not yet tinctured by utter despair.

With this aching void in a mass of people who have yet not reached the point of suffering where they will take great personal risk, the time will inevitably come when new leadership will emerge. The danger is that the new leader will be an adventurer masked in the old Argentine tradition of the caudillo. Whether he comes mounted on a horse or a tank is a matter of detail.

However, there are certain assets on which one can build. In their halting and groping way most of the Argentine military are sincere in their patriotism and in their desire to make way for a truly democratic state. They are also, mark you, friendly to the United States at the present time and find it difficult to understand why we should look down our noses at the military who are as fervently anti-Communist as we. The Argentine military, in my judgment, should be regarded as an asset by the United States (if rightly used) and not as a liability as some people in Washington seem to believe. In this connection, see the nuclear contingency I added to the Guidelines paper on Argentina.

The Argentine military in the background and the Ministers of the civilian government in the foreground need help in trying to rebuild the political machinery of the state. If some manner could be devised to divest Argentina of its self-serving present politicians and to replace them with younger and more enlightened elements, I see no reason why a new democratic political era should not dawn in Argentina. Much will depend upon who emerges as the next President and upon the degree of enlightenment coupled with leadership he will show. It is clear to me, however, that at the present time the key vote in Argentina is the Peronist vote, that this bloc of voters has by far the best discipline, and that it should not be beyond the range of ingenuity to canalize this element into new courses which will lead to a new and effective party with which we could get along. I am less confident, unless the present leadership is removed, of the ability of anyone to get the two warring factions of the Radical Party to get together.

All of these contingencies in the political field are deeply affected by the current economic crisis. Unless measures can be taken to increase productivity, to bring the national economy more into balance, to make possible markets for Argentine agriculture and to alleviate the pang of the rising cost of living on the workers, the chances of achieving political democracy will be correspondingly diminished. In the economic field we probably have more practical resources at hand to guide the course of events than in the political field. However, I do not despair of the resources of personal diplomacy nor of the ability of this Embassy to influence the course of political events.

Forgive the length of this letter. It was merely that I wished to give a certain sense of perspective and an intimation of direction that seemed easier of expression by this means than in the more stilted phrases of a policy paper. We have an exceedingly difficult task ahead but we are not bereft of assets and we are dealing with a proud and intelligent people. In fact, as I have said in my telegrams, I think the present crisis in Argentina affords us a unique opportunity for showing that the principles of the Alliance for Progress can be made to work and produce tangible results.

In consequence, let me conclude on a note of confidence. Over the long range I am bullish on Argentina. With the exercise of diligence, the use of our heads, and that essential ingredient of diplomacy, "a little bit of luck", I think we can succeed.

Cheers,

RM

189.   Plan of Action for Argentina

Washington, undated.

SUBJECT

Argentina—Plan of Action Over Period From Present to April 1964

A.   Objectives

1.   Maintenance of the present civilian regime to the end of its declared tenure: April 30, 1964 at the latest.

2.   Strengthening of the prospects for continued democratic civilian government through early elections held without undue military pressure or dictation.

3.   The election and installation in office of an administration that

a.   holds promise of a social outlook and program sufficient in scope and appeal to permit a gradual weaning of the Peronists and other dissidents from adherence to extremist solutions to national problems.

b.   is basically committed to wise use of foreign or domestic economic resources for national development, the maintenance and expansion of a favorable environment for private enterprise and friendly cooperation with the U.S.

4.   Seek to assist the Argentine Government in its efforts to reverse the trend and mitigate the consequences of the presently adverse economic situation.

C.   [sic] Plan of Action

I.   Intelligence

1.   Strengthening [*less than 1 line of source text not declassified*] intelligence collection on activities of the far left.

a.   Determine the extent of Communist involvement with Peronism and its reaction to the movement by Peronist leaders to the left.

b.   Clarify importance in Peronist movement of leaders John Cooke (in Cuba) and Americo Barrios (in Montevideo) and their links with Peron despite his reported disavowal of them.

Source: Kennedy Library, National Security Files, Countries Series, Argentina, General, 7/62. Secret. Transmitted by Brubeck to McGeorge Bundy under cover of a July 4 memorandum which indicated that it was for his approval. According to Brubeck the plan was based on the decisions of the Latin American Policy Committee at its June 21 meeting. Bundy wrote the following note on the covering memorandum: "Ralph: I doubt if we want to 'approve' anything as detailed as this. We might simply note it & leave responsibility in Dept.—unless you want to disapprove. McGB." Bundy sent Brubeck a memorandum on July 17, noting that he had reviewed the plan, that it did not require Presidential approval, and that the NSC staff should not undertake to give formal approval or disapproval to Department of State documents. He also noted that Dungan had comments on some of the points and would communicate directly with relevant officers at the Department; see footnotes 1, 3, and 4 below. (Ibid.)

c. Determine if Castro followers have increased activities since March, 1962 . . . and to what immediate ends.

d. Provide additional information concerning Peron's quasi-Communist stance and whether he is promoting a coalition for elections or for an attempt on the government.

e. Follow activities of Frigerio group and especially watch for possibility of its organization of a combination with civilian and military elements of extreme left.

2. Increase capacity and efforts of service attachés [*less than 1 line of source text not declassified*] to gather intelligence on political activities of the military as their highest priority task.

a. Identify leaders of hard line military group.

b. Determine the specific issues between Guido Government and this group and particularly those measures against the Peronists and Communists it would have the government take.

3. Evaluate the support, program and intentions of the National Social Front. Specifically seek to ascertain

a. judgment of suitable Church authorities on likelihood of participation by members of the hierarchy.

b. whether Christian and anti-Communist tendencies and present divisions in the Peronist parties may have induced Peronists like Framini to adhere to the National Social Front.

c. if any "62 Bloc" Peronist union leaders look with favor on the National Social Front idea or are more likely to adhere to a Peronist-left popular front.

d. if National Social Front has support of so-called "Nasserite" army group.

e. whether the National Social Front has produced a program indicating the extent to which its objectives coincide or conflict with those of the U.S.

f. whether the front would be permitted to operate as a political party for the coming elections.

II.   Political and Military

1. Cooperate with and support the Guido Government in all feasible ways in order to strengthen it vis-à-vis the military.

a. Continue quietly but firmly to indicate to key personalities in and behind the Guido Government that the U.S. would find it extremely difficult to cooperate with any government installed as the result of a new military coup.

b. Communicate the foregoing sentiment . . . very discreetly . . . to Peronist leadership to forestall any extremist Peronist link with military "Nasserites."

2. Avoid any association with policies or action by the government, military or political parties which might in the popular mind identify us with anti-popular elements. Our deep interest in and commitment to assuaging social discontent should be promoted on every feasible occasion through personal diplomacy, our public statements and our aid program.

3. Explore quietly and judiciously with non-extremist political groups the possibility of the formation of the middle groups in Argentina into a broad if loosely organized political movement or voting coalition and the manner in which Proportional Representation might benefit or adversely affect electoral prospects for such an amalgamation.

a. Seek out those factions of the UCRI and the UCRP most closely identified in the past with doctrines generally sympathetic to U.S. objectives and most disposed to carry their party name and/or followers into a "Center Front." These leaders or factions are most likely to be acceptable to the government and the military and without them prospects for a broad center alignment would founder.

b. Identify moderate political groups not conspiciously linked to Old Line Parties which might be persuaded to take the initiative in forging a center coalition.

c. Urge upon the target party leaders a search for an Argentine of large stature as a presidential candidate, possibly a man of letters or an educator of the mold (if not the substance) of a Sarmiento not previously identified firmly with a given party or partisan faction.

d. Analyze relations between Peronist voters and leaders and identify issues on which working class might be brought into center or center-left grouping.

4. Explore the advantages and disadvantages as they bear on our policy objectives, of the early release of former President Frondizi bearing in mind his possible return to politics in Argentina; communicate our conclusions to the Guido Government should we conclude a greater degree of freedom . . . including residence abroad . . . for Frondizi is desirable.

5. Refrain from supporting or promoting the candidacy during the foreseeable future of any of the incipient presidential candidates now on the scene (i.e., Alsogaray, Aramburu, del Carril, Alende, etc.). Wait for younger leaders to emerge.

6. Determine whether the Guido Government or its moderate military backers will seek to shape and control a political movement or party and the names of those individuals it would in those circumstances support as Presidential and Vice Presidential candidates.

7. Maintain a "correct" attitude in our relations with the military and do nothing which is likely to accentuate the deep divisions among them. Insure when possible that our actions, whether in the field of mili-

tary cooperation or in our desired contacts in the political-labor arena, will not contribute to further divisions among the military or a hardening of the resolve of any of its factions to overthrow the civilian government.

8. Encourage within the possibilities of the Argentine situation civic action by the Argentine military forces.

9. Examine the wisdom, should threat of a military coup prove imminent, of covert and pointed indication to hard line military leaders of U.S. concern with a view to forestalling the adventure and fortifying the resolve of the moderate military to prevent it.

III. Labor

1. Urge upon Guido Government that it take on sweeping action against Peronist unions or leaders which would penalize pro-democratic unions and leaders or drive the latter into full cooperation with militant Peronists.

2. Consult discreetly with democratic labor leaders to obtain their judgment regarding formation of a democratic labor party which might in present circumstances attract softcore Peronist support.

a. Approach Church authorities to find if there might be Church interest in supporting creation of a democratic labor party.

b. Assess the likelihood of such a party's participation in a center coalition.

3. Give priority to greatly increasing our contacts with labor but not without assessing the possibility of adverse military or government reaction.[1]

a. Improve and enlarge our labor exchange programs, seminars, round-tables and informational activities.

b. Enlist support of Department of Labor and U.S. trade unions to enlarge measurably the scope and depth of the latter's contacts with Argentine labor including its Peronist elements. Specifically seek to encourage expansion of leader exchange, attention to worker education and provision of technical assistance in union administrative activities.

IV. Informational and Youth

1. Augment our efforts to work with and influence youthful members and potential leaders in the Peronist formations.

2. Increase efforts of U.S.I.S. and the Embassy's political and economic sections to extend contacts with student and youth organizations.

---

[1] In a July 12 memorandum to McGeorge Bundy, Dungan commented on this recommendation: "I do not believe we should be inhibited in making contact with labor groups in Argentina or elsewhere by excessive anxiety about disturbing the government's power or elements within it. If it is important for us to maintain substantial and good contacts with labor or any other group we should go ahead and do it even if it has to be done on a covert basis." (Ibid.)

3. Greater participation by political and economic officers in the selection of information and exchange program target groups and of exchange candidates.

4. Insure greater attention as target groups to professional organizations receiving large numbers of university graduates.

5. Rapid action in the book translation and publication program.

6. Promote with the Guido Government the rapid creation of an Argentine Peace Corps for domestic purposes, to focus the energy and social consciousness of youth into constructive channels, providing them a sense of participation in the solution of the country's pressing needs. Our Peace Corps might provide administrative assistance.

7. Expand assistance to Argentine educational institutions and encourage similar assistance by private U.S. educational and philanthropic organizations.

V. Economic—(The following general statements complement the AID/LAPC paper.)[2]

1. Express to Guido Government our general satisfaction with self-help measures it has undertaken but continue to press upon it that more remains to be done.[3]

2. Press for arrangement for private professional U.S. assistance to National Development Council and to continue USG efforts through A.I.D. to assist with special studies, statistical services and other appropriate technical aid.

3. Recognize the possibility that the GOA may not find it possible to remain within the credit expansion ceilings established by the June, 1962 IMF Standby Agreement. Be prepared to provide sympathetic consideration to requests for revision by the Guido Government and a parallel extension of the U.S. Treasury Agreement.

4. Impress upon Minister of Economy Alsogaray the rapid need for undertaking negotiations with the Europeans to reschedule short-term financial obligations.

5. Seek to secure a cut-back in Argentine military expenditures, and discourage particularly expenditures for large items.

6. Encourage the Guido regime to consult with labor groups before undertaking specific wage-price decisions of national import.

---

[2] Not found.

[3] In the July 17 memorandum to Bundy, Dungan commented that "we should direct State–AID to conduct as quickly as possible an examination of the Argentine budget, analyze its present monetary policies and come up with a specific list of so-called self-help measures which we think to be in their interest and consistent with our objectives under the Alliance. Unless we have this basic analysis we have no way of knowing whether it is prudent for us to advance dollars to create local currency for public works or other types of projects or whether it is possible to fund some of the local currency costs themselves." (Kennedy Library, National Security Files, Countries Series, Argentina, General, 7/62)

7.   Devote highest priority to plans for low-cost housing in Argentina by both U.S. Government and international lending agencies.[4]

a.   Accelerate our investigations (A.I.D.) of the methods by which assistance may be provided labor union and other cooperative organizations for the financing of low-cost housing without direct Argentine Government participation.

8.   Explore with the Export-Import Bank the manner in which its $50 million segment of the $150 million February, 1962 loan package should be used, particularly whether any portion might be devoted to infra-structure or impact project purposes.

9.   Establish a government-wide consensus regarding the extent to which the U.S. wishes to encourage increases in both production and productivity of Argentine agriculture given its largely competitive role with U.S. plant and animal products.

a.   Arrive at this decision with particular reference to the meat import problem.

10. Reach policy conclusion regarding the timing and scope of personnel reforms of the Argentine national railways, bearing in mind the severe repercussions ill-advised or rash action might have on the stability of the regime.

11. Explore the possibility of A.I.D. providing technical assistance in the field of labor-management relations.

---

[4] In the July 17 memorandum to Bundy, Dungan queried, "On what basis have we decided to place our highest priority on low-cost housing in Argentina?" (Ibid.)

190.   Memorandum of Conversation

Washington, July 19, 1962, 4:03 p.m.

SUBJECT

Argentine Economic Situation[1]

PARTICIPANTS

Argentine Minister of Economy—Alvaro Alsogaray
Vice President, Argentine National Development Council—Admiral Francisco Castro
Argentia Ambassador—Roberto T. Alemann
The Secretary
The Under Secretary
Assistant Secretary—Edwin M. Martin
Deputy Coordinator—Alliance for Progress—Graham Martin
Deputy Assistant Secretary—Herbert K. May
Chief, Latin American Division, Treasury Department—Henry Costanzo
Officer in Charge, Argentine Affairs—Bruce M. Lancaster
Department of State Interpreter—Donald Barnes

After he had been welcomed by the Secretary, Minister Alsogaray gave a detailed review of the current Argentine situation and his plans to bolster the Argentine economy. He stated that under his Government's newly announced political plan, elections would be held next June and a new President and Congress inaugurated in October 1963. In the meantime, the present Government would have considerable freedom of action to work on economic problems and he hoped that the economy of Argentina could be brought to a state where elections would take place under favorable circumstances.

The Minister stated that in his opinion the announcement of the Alliance for Progress had ushered in a period in which the Argentine people took a particularly favorable attitude toward the U.S. It was his hope that the Alliance would be able to offer the right aid at the right time. A long range development program for Argentina was very necessary, but his Government needed immediate support for projects which had already been undertaken and which could not be completed because

---

Source: Department of State, Secretary's Memoranda of Conversation: Lot 65 D 330. Confidential. Drafted by Lancaster and approved by Swank in S on July 31. The time of the meeting, which lasted until approximately 5 p.m., is from Rusk's Appointment Book. (Johnson Library)

[1] At the White House daily staff meeting, July 19, Kaysen briefed the staff on Argentina: "Kaysen reports that a crisis is momentarily expected in Argentina, probably in the form of an outright military takeover. The immediate problem is that the Argentine finance minister is in town and the US has to take some firm position, or lack thereof, in regard to the Argentine financial crisis." (Memorandum by Ewell, July 19; National Defense University, Taylor Papers, Daily Staff Meetings, May–Sept. '62)

of budgetary difficulties. If the U.S. could help with these projects within the terms of the $150 million aid package there would be three desirable consequences: necessary projects could be completed, Argentina's own efforts to reduce its federal budget would be buttressed and financial stability could be maintained. Many of the projects which he had in mind were as much as 80 per cent complete, with the entire cost to date having been borne from Argentine funds. A memorandum regarding such projects would be ready in several days.

The Minister added that he was not seeking assistance from the U.S. which would be designed for or publicized as emergency aid, but as part of a continuing program of cooperation under the Alliance for Progress. He mentioned the need for housing to replace Buenos Aires slum districts as of particular importance.

(In concluding his remarks, Minister Alsogaray referred to several miscellaneous subjects, including the possibility of P.L. 480 aid in providing forage for cattle producers in drought areas, the desirability of completing the investment guarantee agreement between the U.S. and Argentina and the highly favorable reaction in his country to the U.S. arrangement for providing a sugar quota for Argentina.)

The Secretary asked what the political atmosphere might be like in Argentina during the year preceding the elections. Would people take a wait-and-see attitude or would there be active cooperation with the present Government? Minister Alsogaray replied that at present the Argentine public was much more preoccupied with economic than political problems. The man-in-the-street in Argentina knew about and was very interested in the present financial negotiations with the U.S. He believed that his Government could maintain a mutually agreed truce with rank and file union members. Even though union leaders, many of whom were actively involved in politics, could be expected to attempt to stir up trouble, he did not expect to have acute political difficulties with the unions. Indeed he believed that, considering the economic difficulties which most Argentines had had to cope with in the past few months, labor had been remarkably restrained.

The Secretary then asked if there had been recent capital flight from Argentina and whether Argentine capital could be mobilized for the development of the country. In response the Minister stated that capital flight had been a problem after Frondizi was deposed. The peso had gone as high as 137, but capital flight had now largely stopped and he believed that the peso could be stabilized at around 114. The attitude of the Argentine public during the next few weeks would be crucial. A favorable aid arrangement with the U.S. would evoke a very good reaction.

The Secretary commented that he hoped that Alsogaray's discussions with the IMF would proceed to a successful conclusion. An agreement with the IMF would generate confidence abroad which would be transmitted back to Argentina and thus increase the confidence of the Argentine people in their own economy.

(At this point the Secretary and the Under Secretary withdrew to keep other appointments.)

At the suggestion of Mr. Edwin Martin, Mr. Graham Martin commented on the Minister's interest in AID support for uncompleted projects, stating that his agency would want to examine details before expressing its views. Mr. May referred to the $50 million portion of the aid package which was an Eximbank commitment, stating that these funds could only be used to cover purchases in the U.S.

Minister Alsogaray agreed that this was the case. He said that he was interested additionally in talking to the Eximbank about a loan for highway construction equipment which had been granted some time ago. A good portion of this loan had not been used and he was hopeful that it could be released for other purposes. [An Eximbank official stated later that only $20 million of this $40 million loan had been drawn to date.][2]

Mr. Edwin Martin stressed the U.S. view that Argentina should reschedule its debts with the Europeans as soon as possible. He asked whether these debts were to be extended by their present holders or whether they would be refinanced by European financial institutions. Minister Alsogaray replied that his Government would be talking to the Europeans very soon about extensions of the debts of the Government of Argentina as well as those of Government-owned enterprises. He still did not know the extent of private indebtedness to the Europeans or to U.S. banks. He believed that some private debtors who had undertaken excessive obligations would have to learn a lesson. Mr. May said that he believed that the Europeans were very receptive to the idea of rescheduling Argentina's debts and might perhaps even provide new money. He was sure that the Argentine Government did not want to get into a position where private debtors (including even those who had incurred unwise obligations) would place a heavy burden on Argentina's foreign exchange reserves by rushing in to purchase foreign currencies.

Mr. Edwin Martin said that in the process of straightening out the Argentine economy prior to the elections, it appeared highly important to avoid any sort of inflation which would place an undue burden on the wage earner. Minister Alsogaray agreed, and stated that U.S. help with a low-cost housing program would be particularly helpful in meeting the desires of labor.

---

[2] Brackets in the source text.

Minister Alsogaray concluded by stating that Argentine financial experts were arriving Sunday[3] who would provide the IMF with detailed information and proposals on credit stabilization during the early part of the coming week. He hoped to be able to complete negotiations with the IMF by Wednesday.[4] Mr. Edwin Martin said that, after the Argentine position with the IMF had been clarified, he and senior officers of the Alliance for Progress and Eximbank would like to sit down with the Argentine group and review U.S. programs.

Mr. Martin then added that he understood that Minister Alsogaray was interested in calling on the President before he left. The Minister stated that he was indeed anxious to do so and hoped that this might be arranged for the latter part of the coming week. Mr. Martin said that the President had an extremely tight schedule but that the State Department would see what it could do.[5]

---

[3] July 22.
[4] July 25.
[5] See Document 191.

---

191.   Memorandum of Conversation

Washington, July 27, 1962, 9:30–9:48 a.m.

SUBJECT

   Minister Alsogaray's Appointment with President Kennedy

PARTICIPANTS

   President Kennedy
   Mr. Ralph Dungan, Special Assistant to the President
   Mr. Edwin M. Martin, Assistant Secretary of State for Inter-American Affairs
   Minister Alvaro Alsogaray, Argentine Minister of Economy
   Ambassador Roberto Alemann, Argentine Ambassador to the United States

Minister Alsogaray opened the discussion by making three points. First, he explained the history of Frondizi's attempt to maintain himself in power by favoring first one group and then another with the eventual

---

Source: Kennedy Library, National Security Files, Countries Series, Argentina, General, 8/62. Confidential. Drafted by Martin. The time of the meeting is taken from the President's Appointment Book. (Ibid.)

result that he was distrusted by all. Next, he described briefly the electoral situation which had been the final straw in securing the deposal of Frondizi and his replacement by a civilian government, headed by the next in line of succession. Lastly, he stressed the importance of dealing with the Peronistas as individuals but not dealing with their leaders who were just like Fascists or Nazis.

He then gave a brief summary of the broad economic policies of his regime, stressing its encouragement of private enterprise and freedom from government intervention and activity. He also described his recent discussions to try to reduce the burdensome debt in Argentina resulting from a too rapid expansion. He said they had been entirely successful, resulting in making available some $500 million from public and private sources, none of it new money.

The President expressed his happiness at having a chance to talk to him. He emphasized the importance of the Government's showing an interest in the welfare of all the people and not maintaining too much of a hands off attitude. He expressed some concern that a too conservative and cautious and deflationary policy would meet the interests and desires of the privileged groups and the bankers but not serve the needs of all the people. A program, which would seem to the people to be meeting their needs was essential, he thought, politically as well as economically.

Minister Alsogaray said he agreed entirely and the Government has its own program for controlling economic developments. It was working closely with unions and was anxious to develop a big housing program to help the masses of people. He was stressing the attitude toward private enterprise of the new Government only in contrast to that under Peron.

---

192.   Memorandum From the Director of the Bureau of Intelligence and Research (Hilsman) to Secretary of State Rusk

Washington, August 15, 1962.

INTELLIGENCE NOTE

Argentina Threatened by Military Take-over

Guido government weakened by Cabinet crisis. Argentina's Minister of Defense, Cantilo, has resigned amid criticism of his failure to resolve the

---

Source: Kennedy Library, National Security Files, Countries Series, Argentina, General, 8/62. Confidential. Copies were sent to Bromley Smith, Schlesinger, and Taylor.

dispute between rival factions of the Army. The "hard-line" faction, which now has the upper hand over forces loyal to the Guido government, is pressing for more authoritarian rule and repression of Peronism. It is demanding the resignation of other key Ministers and reportedly intends to force the resignation of President Guido himself.

"Hard-line" faction extends control over Army. Several officers in key command posts, who remained loyal during last week's rebellion, have been replaced by supporters of "hard-line" leader Gen. Toranzo Montero. The "hard-line" now controls the Cavalry garrison at Campo de Mayo, the government's major source of strength up to now.

Move to install military junta considered likely. The events of the past week-end, when the Guido government backed down from an armed fight with the rebel generals, revealed the government's inability or unwillingness to mobilize enough support to block the "hard-line" thrust. Many formerly loyal officers now view the installation of a junta—in which they might still have some voice—as the only alternative to one-man rule. Even with across-the-board military participation, such a junta would incline toward "hard" policies which would postpone return to democratic processes and eventually provoke violent reaction from the Peronists, probably in alliance with the far left.

---

193. Telegram From the Department of State to the Embassy in Argentina

Washington, October 13, 1962, 3:23 p.m.

982. Department agrees with analysis Buenos Aires telegram 1079[1] that Peron, who is almost unique among twentieth century dictators in that he retains a large following because he was deposed at a time when many of his followers were still unaware of extent to which he had debauched their country, remains most difficult and pressing political problem confronting GOA. It seems likely that he will remain a major problem as long as he lives unless in the meantime bulk of his followers decide they have nothing to gain by continuing heed his orders. Blatant manner in which these orders issued and important role he assumes per-

---

Source: Department of State, Central Files, 735.00/10–1062. Secret; Limited Distribution; No Distribution Outside Department and CIA. Drafted by Lancaster, cleared by Wellman, cleared in substance with H. Freeman Matthews of EUR/WE and Albert E. Carter of INR/DDC, and approved by Martin. Repeated to Madrid.
[1] Dated October 10. (Ibid.)

sonally even in documents such as action program (Buenos Aires telegram 1074)[2] given out to non-Peronists indicate continuing boldness of his plans. Argentine political situation is of course further complicated by immaturity, selfishness and lack of desire cooperation other parties and politicians. In this situation we believe that if USG attempts any action at all vis-à-vis Peron it should be designed reduce his authority by encouraging his present followers to look elsewhere for leadership.

It is our view that an approach by US to Peron along lines which Interior Minister Martinez appears to suggest in first reftel would probably accomplish following:

1. Enhance personal position of Peron.
2. Convince both political and military leaders in Argentina that US approves of deals with Peron.
3. Leave major role in choice of person who would be elected next President of Argentina to Peron, thus confronting Argentine military with situation which they might well believe required their renewed intervention to annul elections.
4. Indicate US thought Peron could now be trusted. (Do addressees have any reason believe Peron would honor any agreement made with US unless it in his opinion would in long run assist groups under his personal control regain power in Argentina?)

In our view some or all of above would take effect as immediate result any indication US interest in acting as intermediary between GOA and Peron. We therefore do not desire become in any way involved in such dealings with Peron.

Unless you perceive strong objections you are requested convey these views to Interior Minister at early date and use this US position at your discretion in discussions of Peron problem with other Argentine leaders. At same time you should point out that US policy makes clear distinction between exiled dictator and great bulk of his current following, stressing our support reasonable objectives of Argentine labor.

We also believe it would be well to speak directly to GOA at this time regarding increasing number of hints from senior Peronists (as well as certain of their would-be collaborators such as Frigerio) that Peron will actively seek Communist support unless US begins negotiations with him. It is our firm view that greatest opportunity international Communism could currently hope for in Argentina would be restoration of Peronism or some similar authoritarian government. Role Communism could hope to play when such a regime were finally brought down would in all likelihood be much more dangerous than anything Communist Party could hope to accomplish otherwise. In addition we are confident Peron realizes any significant enlargement of his current flirtation

---

[2] Telegram 1074, October 9, contained a statement delimiting actions necessary by the Guido government to comply with the spirit of Peronist demands. (Ibid., 735.00/10–962)

with Communists would result in serious differences within Peronist Party.

We would appreciate your report of Interior Minister's reaction to our rejection of first of two alternatives he has put forward[3] keeping in mind possibilities for other action discussed in Deptel 901 and difficulties set forth Madrid's 443.[4]

We are sending separate instructions[5] regarding dealings with Peronists who wish to establish contact with US officials.

Rusk

---

[3] In telegram 1079 from Buenos Aires, McClintock reported that Interior Minister Rodolfo Martinez had suggested that Argentina would ask the Spanish Government "to put Peron under wraps." A second alternative, according to Martinez, was to get an agreement from Perón to instruct his following in Argentina to cooperate in elections designed to return a representative form of government.

[4] In telegram 901 to Buenos Aires, October 4, the Department suggested that although the approach to the Spanish Government should come from the Government of Argentina, the United States would give immediate assent and support. This support would not be kept secret since it would reassure the hard-line military and might help to detach some of the less doctrinaire Perónists from their "erstwhile leader." (Department of State, Central Files, 735.00/10–462) In telegram 443 from Madrid, October 9, Ambassador Robert F. Woodward stated, that Spain was unlikely to agree to quarantine Perón during the Argentine pre-election period. (Ibid., 735.00/10–962)

[5] Not further identified.

---

194. Memorandum of Conversation

Washington, November 6, 1962.

SUBJECT

Meeting Between President Kennedy and General Pedro Aramburu, Former Provisional President of Argentina—The White House, 6:30 P.M., November 6, 1962[1]

PARTICIPANTS

The President
General Pedro E. Aramburu, Former Provisional President of Argentina
Assistant Secretary Edwin M. Martin—ARA

Source: Department of State, Central Files, 611.35/11–862. Confidential. Drafted by Barnes and Charles A. Gendreau of EST/A and approved in the White House on November 28.

[1] In an October 18 memorandum to Bundy, Executive Secretary Brubeck requested an appointment for a meeting with President Kennedy for Pedro Eugenio Aramburu. Brubeck noted General Aramburu's role in facilitating the elections of 1958, his attempt to mediate (unsuccessfully as it turned out) the dispute between Frondizi and the military in March 1962, and suggested that he might be "the sole Argentine who might command sufficiently widespread backing as a presidential candidate." For these reasons, the Department recommended that the President see him. (Ibid., 735.11/10–1862)

Mr. Ralph Dungan, Presidential Adviser
Ambassador Roberto T. Alemann, Argentine Ambassador
General Aramburu's Aide de Camp (name not recorded)
Mr. Donald F. Barnes, Division of Language Services, Department of State

The President expressed warm appreciation for Argentina's Cuban quarantine cooperation as the first nation to offer material assistance. Aramburu observed that not only was Argentina pleased to cooperate but would, if necessary, provide additional equipment and personnel. He wholeheartedly agreed with the President that it was vital to stop Communist penetration in the Hemisphere.

Political stability in Argentina was a matter of concern to the United States, the President stated, since Argentina was important not only in itself but because of its influence in neighboring countries, particularly Chile and Brazil, the futures of which were in some doubt. Aramburu indicated he was hopeful and optimistic about Argentina's future stability and recognized his country's spiritual leadership in South America. Although the Chilean picture was indeed clouded he did not believe the situation to be as somber as has been painted. The problems of Brazil date back many years. Gradual Communist penetration in this period had affected even the armed forces: the Brazilian Communist leader Luis Prestes was a former Army officer. Although Argentina is indeed concerned over events in Chile and Brazil, and does not wish to have foci of Communist infection on its borders, he was not personally concerned over prospects for the Communists in Argentina where party membership is small.

In response to a question by the President, Aramburu estimated that the Peronists represent about 25 to 30 per cent of the voters. The significance of these figures, he added, has to be interpreted against the circumstance that among the several currents in the Peronist movement, most could be drawn into legal and constitutional political life, although some might incline towards the Left. Peron himself is not the leader of the Peronist masses but is himself inclined to follow their lead before fixing his own position. Peronist strength in the March, 1962 elections has been exaggerated, said the General, since they had been joined by numerous Argentines who were unhappy with the Frondizi Government which had defrauded them. He was, all in all, optimistic about Argentina's return to orderly constitutional life and emphasized that the United States could count on his country being a friend and a bulwark against Communist penetration.

The President observed that the next twelve months would be critical in Latin America with respect to renewed Communist attempts at penetration: all countries should be alert to this danger. He asked that the General transmit to the Argentine Government the appreciation of the United States for Argentine assistance in the Cuban quarantine. Aramburu acknowledged he would be glad to return to Buenos Aires with this message.

195.   National Intelligence Estimate

NIE 91–62   Washington, November 21, 1962.

THE SITUATION AND PROSPECTS IN ARGENTINA

The Problem

To analyze the political and economic situation in Argentina and estimate the prospects over the next year.

Conclusions

A. The central political problem in Argentina is how to integrate the Peronists into a democratic political system. Seven years after Peron's overthrow, Peronism remains a political force representing perhaps one-quarter of the electorate. The Peronist masses, whose strength is concentrated in labor, view Peron as a symbol of the economic advantages and social prestige which they achieved under his rule. Peron's continuing influence over the voting habits of his followers enables him to affect the outcome of any free election. The conservatives and many moderates fear a return to the radicalism, corruption, and economic irresponsibility of the Peron era. (Paras. 1, 14–15)

B. The military, largely conservative and mindful of its subjugation under Peron, is determined not to allow the Peronists to return to political power. The military is split, however, on how to cope with Peronism. The "legalist" faction, currently predominant and the force behind Guido and his cabinet, favors early elections with safeguards against a Peronist resurgence. The "hard line" faction favors stern repression of Peronism and several years of authoritarian government before elected government is reinstated. (Paras. 2, 5–10, 41)

C. The non-Communist political parties provide only unsteady foundations for civilian government. They are generally divided internally by personal rivalries, ideological positions, and disagreements over future political tactics. They are unable to cooperate with each other and are in various degrees bidding for the support of the Peronists. Some Peronists are inclined to make a peaceful effort to secure legal participation in government; more radical elements favor use of Peronist power in

Source: Central Intelligence Agency Files, Job 79–R01012A, ODDI Registry. Secret. According to a covering sheet, this estimate was prepared by the Central Intelligence Agency and the intelligence organizations of the Departments of State, Army, Navy, Air Force, and the Joint Staff. All members of the Board concurred with this estimate on November 21, except the representatives of the AEC and FBI, who abstained on the grounds that the subject was outside their jurisdiction.

many key labor unions to engage in militant opposition, and even alliance with the Communists to gain their ends. The Communists, also well established in the labor movement, have had some success in allying themselves with the leftwing Peronists. (Paras. 17–24, 42)

D. Guido and the "legalist" military faction have announced presidential and congressional elections for 16 June 1963, with a new President to take office the following October. At best, the problem of electing and installing a civilian government will be difficult. Militant Peronists—probably with Communist support—will resist restrictions on their political activities and may resort to strikes and violence. On the other hand, much of the military opposes any concessions to Peronism, and as elections approach, military apprehensions over the risks will increase. These sentiments could lead to a preventive coup against Guido and the "legalists" in advance of elections, or a military move to negate the elections if they should result in significant Peronist successes, or a coup against a newly elected government unacceptable to the military. The great majority of Argentines favor holding elections and we think that, in spite of the obstacles, there is at least an even chance that they will take place. Any new government will live under the shadow of being ousted by the military if the latter believes the evils of the Peron era threaten to recur. (Paras. 9, 12–13, 17, 42–45)

E. Solution of the Peronist problem is also complicated by the country's economic stagnation and the dim prospects for an early recovery. Longstanding neglect of the agricultural sector and decline in overseas demand for Argentine exports have severely reduced the country's export earning capacity. Despite promising basic resources, Argentina is plagued with critical balance of payments problems, inflation, budget deficits, and a high unemployment rate. (Paras. 27–29, 31–32)

F. Guido's Minister of Economy, Alsogaray, has sought strenuously and with some success to impose a mild austerity program, to improve the climate for private investment, and to obtain foreign assistance. His methods, however, have antagonized influential political and military elements and his room for maneuver is dangerously narrow. The government will probably succeed in obtaining some new loans and other outside assistance, but it seems unlikely to undertake the many basic reforms necessary to begin economic recovery. (Paras. 11, 33, 35–37, 40)

[Here follows a "Discussion" section of 12 pages.]

196. Memorandum of Conversation

Washington, January 22, 1963, 10–11 a.m.

SUBJECT

    Call of Argentine Foreign Minister on President Kennedy

PARTICIPANTS

    The President
    Argentine Foreign Minister Carlos Manuel Muniz
    Argentine Ambassador Roberto T. Alemann
    Mr. Ralph Dungan
    Assistant Secretary Martin
    Ambassador McClintock

The Argentine Foreign Minister called by appointment on President Kennedy at 11 a.m., January 22, 1963, and had an interview lasting one hour.[1] He presented Mrs. Kennedy with a painting by a well-known Argentine modern artist and gave the President a very finely woven vicuna poncho, receiving in turn the President's autographed portrait.

The President commenced the conversation by expressing appreciation for the prompt participation of Argentina in the Cuban quarantine. This had been particularly helpful because it prevented propaganda images being portrayed of the United States ganging up against a small Latin American nation which stood alone against a great power. The Argentine participation encouraged other Latin American countries to come in and thus gave convincing proof that the nations of the Western Hemisphere were united in preventing communist infiltration and aggression.

The Foreign Minister responded that Argentina had clearly seen the hemispheric danger and that his Government's prompt action was supported fully by an overwhelming majority of the Argentine people.

The President then asked the Foreign Minister to give him a description of the present situation in Argentina and if possible an indication of what the situation might be in neighboring countries such as Brazil and Chile.

Source: Kennedy Library, National Security Files, Countries Series, Argentina, General, 1/63. Secret. Drafted by McClintock and approved in the White House on January 26. The meeting was held at the White House. The time and place of the meeting are taken from the President's Appointment Book. (Ibid.)

[1] Muniz met with Department of State and AID officials on January 21, at 3:40 p.m., with Assistant Secretary Martin on January 23, at 11:30 a.m., and with Secretary Rusk on January 23, at 2:30 p.m. At the three meetings the Argentine economy was the main topic of conversation. (Department of State, Central Files, 611.35/1–2163, 611.35/1–2363, and 611.35/1–2363, respectively)

The Foreign Minister then launched into a very lengthy description of the political and economic situation in which Argentina finds itself. He emphasized that the present Government is trying to re-establish a republican constitutional regime. He likened the existing Cabinet to a sort of New Frontier of Argentina.

Elections have now been called for on June 23 for a new president, vice president, provincial governors and legislators. It is the earnest hope of the Argentine Government that there will be a peaceful return to constitutional government supported by the military.

However, Argentina is currently in a period of deep crisis. The working masses had been waiting eight years since the revolt of 1955 which overthrew Peron. Although the costs of living have gone up wages have not kept pace during the past year, and in many cases salaries have not been paid. It is nothing short of a miracle that the working class had remained calm in the face of increasing adversity. The masses still believed in democracy but there was a limit to their patience.

The Foreign Minister then said he had a personal message for President Kennedy from President Guido. It was as follows: The team of economic ministers who had been in office now for a month and a half and who worked earnestly to maintain a free enterprise economic system are presently in a state of desperation and alarm. They and President Guido are under increasing pressure for a change in the present free enterprise economy with its insistence on orthodox finance, to change to a directed economy with exchange controls and all the other indices of a controlled economy. Such a change in Muniz' view would be disastrous. He hoped it would not affect the holding of elections. If some form of aid were not received promptly the present economic team would be forced to resign and the consequences would be grave. This was a transitory problem but an emergency one. Objectively the Argentines themselves had the principal responsibility for meeting the crisis. But they needed help to find a solution in order to give a feeling of alleviation to the masses. Already in Argentine public opinion the example of Brazil was being cited and the man in the street was beginning to wonder if a directed economy like that in Brazil would not lead to a better life for him and his family.

Here the Foreign Minister digressed to speak of the effect on neighboring countries of what happened in Argentina. He cited the dependence of Paraguayan economy on that of his own country and the instantaneous effect on Uruguay and Bolivia of what took place in Argentina.

Muniz went on to estimate that the current budgetary deficit of Argentina is in the neighborhood of 30 billion pesos or 238 million dollars. This deficit was exactly equivalent to last year's loss of the state railways to say nothing of other losses by the YPF, the state petroleum monopoly. The Argentina Minister of Economic Affairs was now confronted by a demand by the IMF for the immediate reduction of 15 billion pesos in this year's budget and an increase of taxes by the same amount. However, just how the Minister of Finance could chop the budget to the extent of 15 billion pesos and discover new sources of revenue totalling 15 billion pesos was a mystery.

Furthermore, said Muniz, Argentina had had four years of consecutive drought in Buenos Aires Province and to some extent in the province of La Pampa. There was thus an immediate need for aid in these drought-stricken areas. Again the Minister reiterated that Argentina needs aid, perhaps modest in amount and limited in terms of the time a credit would be extended, but above all, immediate in its impact.

At this point the Minister handed President Kennedy a letter signed by President Guido together with an English translation but did not divulge its contents. Subsequently Muniz made available a copy of the English translation which is appended herewith.[2] The letter is couched in very general terms and is not to be confused with the oral message which Muniz conveyed to President Kennedy as coming from President Guido.

President Kennedy then asked what kind of assistance would the Foreign Minister have in mind. The President recalled the dangers of inflation and the need for controls to see that, if aid were forthcoming, it would go to the people who really needed it. What for example was the status for negotiations with the IMF?

The Foreign Minister replied that reforms of the state railways and the YPF had almost been achieved. The appointment of new and able administrators had been announced to the IMF team now in Buenos Aires. However, when it came to cutting the budget by 15 billion pesos and increasing taxes by an equal sum this was almost beyond the realm of possibility, given the current economic crisis in Argentina. Nevertheless, the Government had followed a stern policy. The salaries of public employees had not been raised despite the increase in the cost of living and Government salaries were still weeks, if not months, in arrears. The tax moratorium decreed by a recent government had been rescinded. However, none of these measures was sufficient to meet the immediate problem. Somehow the economy, the Government and the people had to survive until the elections took place.

The President asked what the Government proposed to do with the Peronist vote. Muniz replied that in the eight years since Peron had been overthrown changes had taken place in the Peronist movement. He knew of conversations which were going on between the Peronist leaders and the heads of other political parties. It seemed probable that the

---

[2] Attached, but not printed.

Peronists would give their vote to various parties. He had been told recently by a prominent Peronist leader (and this corroborated the information of the Minister of Interior) that the Peronists would refrain from putting up their own candidate for president, vice president and various other provincial governorships. (He did not add what Interior Minister Martinez has informed the American Ambassador, which is that the Peronists will, however, endeavor to return a sizable bloc of their supporters to both houses of Congress.) Despite their dislike of Peronism, said Muniz, the armed forces were agreed on the necessity to back civil authorities and return to constitutional government through elections.

The Minister then reverted to the oral message he had been instructed to convey from President Guido. He quoted the President as saying that the existing Cabinet has been given a deadline of 15 days either to improve the economic situation or else give over to a new team which would install a directed economy with exchange controls. Muniz admitted that this was an ultimatum from the military chiefs. (Later Muniz confided to Ambassador McClintock that the ultimatum had come from Secretary of War Rattenbach and Army Commander-in-Chief Ongania. Furthermore the time limit was not 15 days as stated by the Minister but until the end of the present month.) Muniz continued to say he hoped the present system of free enterprise could be continued but many people would not understand economic and financial problems and the wave of disillusionment was spreading.

President Kennedy pointed out that the United States, despite its great resources, would not have sufficient aid funds to bail out every country in Latin America or for that matter, the world. Even if we could find funds to help Argentina they might be devoured by inflation or leak away in payments to European or other creditors. Certainly the United States would not be able to find means to help Argentina unless it could make arrangements with its European creditors, with the United States banks, and also take steps to guard against inflation.

The Foreign Minister said that his Government would not need much but it needed help now. An IMF renewal of the standby agreement would permit a roll-over of the European debt and there was the further possibility of renewing the 75 million dollar composite bank credit which recently had been repaid to 55 European banks in eight different countries plus a number of other banks in the United States. Furthermore, he hoped that Argentina could arrive at an Investment Guaranty Agreement with the United States against expropriation and war risk. However, these measures, while useful, would not serve to meet the immediate crisis (the 15 day ultimatum) which had come up so quickly that it had transpired even after the departure of the American Ambassador from Buenos Aires for Washington.

Assistant Secretary Martin asked Muniz just what is needed in the next fifteen days.

The Foreign Minister replied that first renewal of the IMF standby was essential. Second, aid was needed for the drought areas on an emergency basis. Third, and basic, was the need to help the public Treasury which was empty. Asked as to what amount he thought was needed, Muniz said he was not a financier or economist but he guessed the amount requested was not more than between 50 and 70 million dollars. However, he could not specify as to what uses this sum would be put other than that it would go into the public Treasury.

The President said that a reply would be forthcoming to the letter from President Guido and as to other matters that had been discussed, he would have to talk to his advisers and also find out the attitude of the IMF. The Secretary of State would be in touch later with the Minister.[3]

As the interview was closing the Foreign Minister said he would like to inform the President of the readiness of Argentina to provide assistance under the Alliance for Progress and within the framework of the OAS in the field of Latin American education. Argentina might have deficits in the budget but at least it had a surplus of teachers. There were ten thousand extra teachers that might be available elsewhere in Latin America. Likewise Argentina had good normal schools and could offer ten thousand places to Latin American students seeking education as teachers. Argentina was also an important source of text books in Spanish. The Minister handed the President a portfolio apparently containing a summary of Argentine export educational resources.

As a final gesture the Foreign Minister handed the President the text of a decree signed by President Guido conveying to the United States a plot of ground in Buenos Aires near our Embassy residence for use in the eventual construction of an Embassy Chancery. The President expressed his thanks as well as his general pleasure in having had such a lengthy and candid interview with the Foreign Minister.

---

[3] On March 28 the Department of State announced that the United States was extending an additional 4 months to its outstanding exchange agreement with Argentina, thus providing Argentina with an additional $25 million through October 6, 1963. The IMF was making available to Argentina $50 million through October 1963. Subject to completion of Argentine bilateral accords with European governments for refunding agreements, the Export-Import Bank would refinance $92 million of Argentine debt owed to it and other U.S. creditors. (Department of State Press Release 154, March 28; Department of State *Bulletin*, April 22, 1963, pp. 617–618)

197. Memorandum From the Executive Secretary of the Department of State (Brubeck) to the President's Special Assistant for National Security Affairs (Bundy)

Washington, April 12, 1963.

SUBJECT

Suggested Message to President of Argentina

Stalwart support by loyal Army and Air Force units has enabled President Guido to survive the latest abortive revolution in Argentina[1] and allowed the Argentine Government to continue with its plans to hold elections this summer.

In the midst of this latest revolt Ambassador McClintock recommended that a message be sent from the President to President Guido congratulating him on his steadfastness and that of loyal military elements in insisting on elections as a proper basis for a new government in Argentina (Tab A).[2]

After the revolt had been put down, the Ambassador continued to counsel that such a message would be useful in strengthening the desire of President Guido and progovernment military forces to persist in their support for elections (Tab B).[3]

In order to avoid even a small possibility that a written message conveying these views and sent at this time might be regarded as U.S. intervention in a domestic problem, and since it is believed that our Ambassador could achieve virtually the same results by transmitting a message from the President orally, it was decided that a verbal message would be desirable in these circumstances.

It is recommended that Ambassador McClintock be authorized to transmit the verbal message from the President to President Guido con-

---

Source: Department of State, Central Files, POL 14 ARG. Secret. Drafted by Bruce M. Lancaster, Officer in Charge of Argentine Affairs; cleared by Daniel F. Margolies, Deputy Director of the Office of East Coast Affairs, and Assistant Secretary Martin.

[1] The abortive coup took place on April 2–3. According to joint reports from Buenos Aires, the attempted overthrow was part of the tension between "Colorados" ("reds" or more reactionary elements in the armed forces) within part of the Navy and the "Azules" ("blues" or more moderate elements) within the Army and Air Force. Situation reports from Buenos Aires during the attempt are ibid., POL 26 ARG.

[2] Tab A, not attached, was telegram 2031 from Buenos Aires, April 3, in which McClintock recommended "now may be the psychological moment for us to do something to sustain lonely little Guido who must be maintained in office with his government if these elections are to be held as scheduled or even with an acceptable delay of a few months." McClintock suggested that while the message need not be made public, it could be spread privately among military leaders and politicians. (Ibid., POL 14 ARG)

[3] Tab B, not attached, was telegram 2067 from Buenos Aires, April 9. (Ibid., POL ARG–US)

tained in the telegram attached at Tab C.[4] No publicity has been planned for this message, since it is designed solely as a private means of strengthening the resolve of the Argentine Government.[5]

Jackson Lloyd[6]

---

[4] Tab C, not attached, was a draft, which was approved and sent as telegram 1847 to Buenos Aires, April 17. The verbal message in telegram 1847 reads: "I want you to know of deep impression made on American people by your steadfastness of purpose during recent period of trouble and by position of loyal military elements who since last September have firmly ranged themselves on side of constitutional solution through civilian government of your country's political problems. This reinforces our confidence in devotion of Argentine people and their leaders to democratic heritage which sustains Argentine Republic." (Ibid., POL ARG–US)

[5] In telegram 2141 from Buenos Aires, April 19, McClintock reported he conveyed the President's message to Guido, who was "exceedingly appreciative" and confident that there was not real danger of another coup. McClintock also reported that he had invited the Army Commander in Chief, General Juan Carlos Organía, and Secretary of the Air Force Eduardo McLoughlin to his house to tell them in confidence the gist of the President's message. McClintock thought both military men were "heartened by this evidence of US moral support." (Ibid.)

[6] Jackson Lloyd signed for Brubeck above Brubeck's typed signature.

---

198.   Memorandum From the Acting Executive Secretary of the Department of State (Little) to the President's Special Assistant for National Security Affairs (Bundy)

Washington, July 6, 1963.

SUBJECT

The Argentine Elections

The enclosed memorandum[1] summarizes developments in the Argentine electoral campaign, which reaches an initial climax on Sunday, July 7, when the public goes to the polls. It explains why it is

---

Source: Department of State, Central Files, POL 14 ARG. Confidential. Drafted by Lancaster and approved by Wellman and Martin.

[1] Attached, but not printed.

unlikely that any Presidential candidate will receive a popular majority,[2] on July 31 will be of crucial importance. In case of a stalemate in the Electoral College, the new Congress will meet on August 12 to have the final say in picking a President.

There has been a continuing series of shifts on the part of important groups as the Peronists sought to find loopholes in decrees promulgated by the government and designed to prevent their obtaining a controlling role in the new government. Peron's latest instructions to his followers have been to vote in blank as a protest, and it is possible that he may also be planning to have them precipitate strikes and riots.

This memorandum is based on information available in Washington as of 10:00 a.m. Friday, July 5, and should provide the background needed to interpret last minute developments as well as the outcome of the popular vote. A previous memorandum dated June 10 provided more detail on the political parties and the complex election mechanism.[3]

D. Rowe[4]

[2] According to telegram 47 from Buenos Aires, July 8, the elections of July 7 "took place in an atmosphere of complete calm but not of apathy as indicated by surprisingly low percentage of blank votes cast." The majority victory of Arturo Illía and the UCRP and the strong showing of Oscar Alende and his faction of the UCRI led the U.S. Embassy to believe that "two radical parties now stand at point of historic opportunity for fusion and reform of Argentina's traditional radicalism." (Department of State, Central Files, POL 14 ARG) In telegram 61 from Buenos Aires, July 10, the Embassy noted that Argentines were indulging in "surprised self-congratulations and genuine enthusiasm" over Illía's victory. "Military, which masterminded electoral strategy, are flushed with success," the Embassy noted, "their prestige at new heights." (Ibid.)

[3] Not printed. (Ibid.)

[4] David Rowe signed for Little above Little's typed signature.

199. Memorandum From the Director of the Bureau of Intelligence and Research (Hughes) to Secretary of State Rusk

Washington, October 11, 1963.

INTELLIGENCE NOTE

Political Ramifications of Oil Issue in Argentina[1]

Issue Reflected in Illía's *Cabinet Selections.* Influential members of President-elect Illía's newly announced cabinet apparently stand solidly behind his party's campaign promise to annul Argentina's contracts with US and other foreign oil companies. Those who stand out in this respect are Foreign Minister Miguel Angel Zavala Ortiz, Economy Minister Eugenio Blanco, and Justice Minister Carlos Alconada Aramburu. Alconada resigned as Interior Minister in 1958 in a clash with the conservative Minister of Commerce and Industry, who sought to have private capital participate in oil development. At that time Alconada came out for "absolute nationalization."

Illía evidently wishes to take as moderate a course as is politically feasible on the contracts. He has suggested the possibility of renegotiating the contracts that his government finds unsatisfactory. Illía, nevertheless, almost certainly felt obligated to take into account strong sentiment against the contracts in his own party and other popular groupings when he selected his cabinet.

Public Attitude Toward the Contracts. Former President Frondizi's contracts with the foreign companies have realized considerable savings in foreign exchange, but the public bias against them—in part a reflection of deep-seated nationalism—remains. When Frondizi negotiated the contracts in 1958, they were opposed by nearly all political parties, organized labor, and important elements of the military. The contracts helped to undermine Frondizi's public support and to pave the way for his ouster by the military in 1962.

The Military Viewpoint. The present attitude of the military on the contracts is not known. Some officers, however, have already indicated dissatisfaction with the incoming President, who has made known his plans to reestablish firm civilian control. They are probably apprehen-

---

Source: Kennedy Library, National Security Files, Countries Series, Argentina, General, 10/63. Secret.

[1] On September 20 Executive Secretary Read sent McGeorge Bundy a paper explaining in detail the Argentine petroleum contracts issue. In this paper, the Department characterized the U.S. fundamental objective as a solution "which would avoid lasting damage to U.S.-Argentine relations" and "protect the legitimate rights and interests of U.S. oil companies." (Library of Congress Manuscript Division, Harriman Papers, Kennedy and Johnson Administrations, Argentina)

sive about Illía on a number of counts. Should Illía's policy on oil arouse strong public dissatisfaction and thereby weaken his position, they might regard this situation as creating an opportune atmosphere for intervention.

---

200. Telegram From the Embassy in Argentina to the Department of State

Buenos Aires, November 8, 1963, 11 p.m.

835. For President and Secretary from Harriman.[1] I delivered your letter[2] to President Illia this evening. He was warmly pleased at its expression of friendship and said he would like to have translation released to press. He likewise spoke warmly of his high regard for you and the objectives of your administration.

I covered same ground made with FonMin this morning but dwelt largely on oil contract problem and political effect in United States and Argentina of contemplated annulment contracts.

President listened carefully to my exposition and then gave me rationale of his feeling of compulsion that contracts must be annulled.

Illia said that although he had been elected with less than thirty per cent of popular vote, other parties joined with his own in electoral college to vote him into presidency. All parties were unanimous on one point; that 1958 oil contracts had to be annulled. Illia clearly feels he has mandate from Argentine people and there can be no question that contracts must be annulled. As for political impact in United States, he recalled that his party's consistent attitude on foreign contracts had been known at least five years back when contracts were signed and when political situation in U.S. was different from what it is today.

Source: Department of State, Central Files, PET 15 ARG. Confidential; Limit Distribution. Passed to the White House on November 9.

[1] Harriman was en route to São Paulo for the second annual meeting of the Inter-American Economic and Social Council at the Ministerial level, November 11–16. Harriman met with Argentine officials to discuss the oil contracts issue.

[2] Dated November 3, the letter was an attempt to convince the Illía government to reexamine or delay its expected decision to annul its contracts with U.S. oil companies; in effect, to expropriate them with undetermined compensation to be decided later. The text of the letter was attached to a memorandum from Read to Bundy, November 3. (Department of State, Central Files, PET 15 ARG)

Speaking with great deliberation President said that, although he would regret if action on contracts might injure Alliance for Progress, diminish chances of passage of a satisfactory foreign aid bill and reduce opportunities for future U.S. investment in Argentina, he nevertheless had to carry out mandate of his people. This was not a caprice or a decision taken lightly but one arrived at only after carefully matured deliberation and study.

President did, however, say companies whose contracts would be annulled would have opportunity to be heard and to arrive by judicial means at what he called "a mutual estimation" of proper indemnification—and the companies would be paid. He mentioned figure of $200 million as his approximation of amount involved. When I pressed Illia as to any possibility of some means being found to minimize unfortunate repercussions of his act, he said that he did not exclude possibility that once annulment had taken place Argentine Government might consider negotiating with companies to use their technical skills on basis of service contracts.

In answer to his question, I said that without knowledge as to precise nature of decrees forthcoming, it was difficult for me to give advice on what to do. President authorized me at Embassy dinner this evening with his Minister and other high officials to explore more precisely nature of these decrees. He also authorized me to discuss with his Ministers question of renegotiation of contracts after annulment. Fact this authorization was given in presence of Central Bank President Elizalde, who acted as interpreter for President, may give opportunity to explore modifications of pending decrees. Elizalde has been leader of Firebrand group insisting on immediate annulment.

(Illia also agreed to see us tomorrow for report on tonight's talks and further consideration.)

My present estimate resembles that of a prisoner condemned to capital punishment who at least knows appeal for reprieve has gone to governor.

McClintock

201.   Paper Prepared in the Department of State

Washington, November 15, 1963.

SUBJECT

The President's Meeting with the Argentine Vice President

Dr. Carlos Humberto Perette, Vice President of the Republic of Argentina, has accepted an invitation from Mayor Robert King High of Miami, Florida, to visit Miami from November 17 to 23 to participate in "Argentine Week", sponsored by the City of Miami. Perette will be seated on the platform at a dinner given in President Kennedy's honor in Miami at 7:00 p.m. Monday, November 18. Perette has been informed that the President will see him for a brief, informal conversation in a manner convenient to the President. We believe it important to our relations with the new Argentine Government that the President meet with Perette, as Ambassador McClintock has recommended.

Perette's political career has been notable for the opportunism and extreme nationalism he has displayed. Although the Vice President in Argentina does not usually play a major policy-making role, Perette is a controversial politician who has been the leader of the ultranationalist elements who are pressing Argentine President to take immediate action to annul the oil contracts.

Dr. Perette speaks English.

The following are enclosed for use by the President in connection with Perette's visit to Miami. The Secretary has not had an opportunity to review this memorandum.

Ben H. Read[1]

Attachment

SUBJECT

Talking Points to Use With Carlos H. Perette, Vice President of Argentina

1. The United States was gratified that the Argentine elections last July were conducted in accordance with the highest traditions of repre-

---

Source: Department of State, Central Files, POL 7 ARG. Confidential. Drafted by Lancaster and approved by Margolies and Cottrell.

[1] Printed from a copy that indicates Read signed the original.

sentative democracy and we wish the new Government of Argentina well.

2. We believe the revival of public confidence following the elections and the installation of the new Argentine Government provide an opportunity for the country to work its way rapidly to improve its economic situation and resume a position of leadership in the hemisphere. We respect and admire the declaration in President Illia's inaugural address that the Argentine Government is determined to make better use of its own resources. We were also pleased that at the same time he expressed such strong support for the Alliance for Progress. We believe it is clear that it is not President Illia's intention to take the ultranationalistic view that Argentina should "go it alone". While this view might appeal to some political groups in Argentina, it would have unfortunate long-term effects on both Argentina and all her friends in the hemisphere, as the history of the Perón era demonstrated.

3. We believe the record of United States relations with Argentina, particularly during the difficult year and a half preceding the inauguration of the Illia–Perette Government indicates our real desire to be helpful. Dr. Perette may not be aware that the United States Government provided more than $290 million in loans or refinancing arrangements to Argentina during this period. We also encouraged private United States as well as foreign governmental and international lending institutions to help Argentina during this difficult period. These actions on our part undoubtedly helped the interim Argentine Government prevent the country's economic recession from spreading into a deep depression. This stabilization of economic conditions also had important political results as well, since it made it possible for elections to be held in a reasonable atmosphere.

4. It is our hope that Argentina, as a leading power in the hemisphere and as a country which has maintained an exemplary reputation for its actions relating to international business, will continue to set a good example for other countries which are less well endowed.

The appropriation bill for our contribution to the Alliance for Progress is now before the United States Congress. The Congress and the people of the United States are deeply concerned over the fact that, while the United States Government has been fulfilling its financial commitments ($1 billion a year) made at Punta del Este, private funds considered necessary to support an adequate level of growth in Latin America have not been forthcoming. The fact of the matter is that actions motivated primarily by domestic political considerations in a number of Latin American countries have seriously diminished the flow of private foreign investment to Latin America and have caused domestic Latin American investors to send large sums abroad.

In these circumstances, we would regard it as a great misfortune if Argentine Government's action on the oil contracts would take a form which the United States people and Congress would regard as expropriatory.[2]

5.   The United States Government would like to continue to be helpful to Argentina. We know that other friendly Governments take a similar view, and we understand that private United States firms would increase their investments in Argentina if they were assured of political stability and reasonable treatment.

We have never questioned the right of Argentina to manage its own natural resources. However, if this is done in an unwise way and American firms do not receive just treatment, the United States Government can not call on its taxpayers to get the Argentine Government out of economic difficulties.

6.   We have no indication that Perette will wish to discuss civil aviation matters. However because of his special interest in this subject and as a result of a request by Mr. Feldman a background paper on United States-Argentine civil air relations is enclosed.[3]

---

[2] Following the assassination of President Kennedy on November 22 in Dallas, Texas, Perette and Foreign Minister Zavala Ortiz met with Rusk, Harriman, and Martin on November 27, from 9:30–10:15 a.m. Rusk stated that he hoped the oil contracts issue would be handled in a way to preserve opportunity for private investment in Argentina. Perette stated that the oil issue was in the courts, but he recognized Rusk's point. The oil companies would be compensated and "foreign investment had nothing to fear from Argentina." (Telegram 526 to Buenos Aires, November 28; Department of State, Central Files, POL 7 ARG) The memorandum of conversation of this meeting is ibid.

[3] This undated paper is attached, but not printed.

202.   Memorandum of Conversation

Washington, December 3, 1963.

SUBJECT

US-Argentine Relations

PARTICIPANTS

Argentine Ambassador Alemann
Under Secretary Harriman
Mr. William H. Sullivan, Special Assistant to the Under Secretary
Mr. Bruce M. Lancaster, Deputy Director, ARA:EST

The Under Secretary turned over a letter to Vice President Perette which Ambassador Alemann had undertaken to deliver when he went to Buenos Aires on the inaugural Pan American flight December 5 (copy of letter attached).[1] The Under Secretary recalled that, just as he was putting on his hat after an informal Thanksgiving Day lunch at the Argentine Embassy, Perette had stated his hope that the oil contract issue would be resolved equitably and mentioned the possible desirability of concluding new contracts through the process of open competitive bidding.[2] Perette had been on the point of leaving for New York and lack of time had prevented the Under Secretary from responding directly. He did not, however, want the Argentine Government to believe that his failure to comment immediately should be construed as agreement with the suggestion regarding open competitive bidding. The letter which he had prepared for Vice President Perette set forth, in general terms, the US view that new oil contracts which would be equitable could best be worked out by direct informal negotiations between the oil companies and the Argentine Government.

Ambassador Alemann commented that it was his belief that any new bidding process arranged by the Argentine Government would take previous investments already made by the companies into account. For example, every company bidding for a new contract on an oil field which had already been partially developed should be required in their bid to agree to compensate the developer of the field for previous investment. The necessity to compensate for previous investment would in most instances leave the company which had made this previous invest-

---

Source: Department of State, Central Files, POL ARG–US. Confidential. Drafted by Lancaster and approved in Harriman's office on December 4.

[1] Dated December 2; attached, but not printed.

[2] The memorandum of conversation of that meeting, November 28, was drafted by Harriman. According to Harriman, Perette "spoke of opportunities for future relations with oil companies as contractors, possibly on a competitive bidding basis." (Department of State, Central Files, POL ARG–US)

ment and had already worked the field in the best competitive position when bids were called for.

The Under Secretary pointed out that the risk which the companies had taken in opening up new fields had to be considered when the value of their investment was evaluated. He believed that as a result of talks here Perette had a better knowledge of the deep US concern over the new Argentine Government's action in annulling the oil contracts.

Ambassador Alemann agreed that Perette had gained a better understanding of international features of the problem. The latest reports received from Buenos Aires indicated that informal negotiations between the companies and his Government were going quite well. If nothing untoward happened during the next ten days, the long Argentine Christmas vacation lasting until the end of January would begin and these informal negotiations could continue without the burden of the previous public pressure and publicity in Argentina. It should be recognized that the negotiations could be upset from the US side too, as the reaction to the new Hickenlooper amendment[3] had shown.

All the members of the Argentine delegation, according to the Ambassador, were deeply impressed by the courtesies accorded them during President Kennedy's funeral. Their visit here had given them a chance to discuss many subjects on which Argentina and US had a strong community of interest. The Ambassador realized that some actions of the new Government had upset US public opinion greatly, and there were still those in this Government who were pressing for unusual solutions to problems before they had had time to profit from the understanding of the complex nature of many issues which would come with experience in power. The US would have to be very patient initially with this group, which had been out of office so long, and be prepared for some noisy and unpleasant speech making. It should be recognized, however, that the UCRP was fundamentally democratic in outlook and had been friendly to the US even during World War II when most other Argentine parties were not. After referring to the Argentine support during the Cuban quarantine last year the Ambassador said that he believed the new Government would stand very strongly with the US on Cuba and other important world problems and that Argentina continued to show good prospects of becoming the most dependable ally of the US in the hemisphere.

The Under Secretary agreed that the Perette visit had been useful and said that the US was very appreciative of the continuing support we had received from Argentina in international bodies.

---

[3] The Hickenlooper amendment to the Foreign Assistance Act of 1963 required the President to suspend assistance to any country that nationalized or expropriated U.S.-owned property without compensation. (P.L. 88–205, enacted December 16, 1963; 77 Stat. 386)

Ambassador Alemann then went on to make a strong personal plea for continued efforts to strengthen ties between the US and Argentine military. He regarded early conclusion of an arrangement to provide military equipment to Argentina as essential. He recalled the remarks of the Argentine Secretary of Army, General Avalos, to the Under Secretary about his discussions in the Pentagon and the Department. General Avalos wanted to proceed as rapidly as possible to conclude an agreement under which Argentina could obtain equipment from the US. The Ambassador hoped that the US could meet the General's desire to avoid possible difficulties with sensitive Argentine politicians which would arise if the US insisted that the new agreement be extremely lengthy and be couched in terms of a "mutual defense pact".

The Under Secretary said that he favored close ties between the military of the two countries and asked how negotiations for military aid stood. The Ambassador said that conclusion of an agreement to supply equipment was not possible prior to the elections of last July because of US concern over the role of the Argentine military in politics. General Ongania had, in the course of preparations for the elections, provided leadership for a demonstration of fundamental support by the military for democracy. General Avalos now wanted to help Ongania reorganize and streamline Argentine forces and some US equipment and training were needed to do this. In response to a question from the Under Secretary, Mr. Lancaster stated that training at a greatly increased level was already being provided. The US was awaiting specific suggestions on the form of an agreement for military assistance, which General Avalos had stated would be put forward initially by Colonel Castro Sanchez as a preliminary to formal negotiations to be undertaken by the Argentine Foreign Affairs. The fact that Congress had not yet completed action on the military aid appropriation for FY 1964 had to be kept in mind. The Under Secretary stated that he would maintain a continuing interest in this question and asked to be kept informed as negotiations for an agreement proceeded.

Before the Ambassador left, the Under Secretary gave him a Spanish translation of his book "Peace with Russia" to be delivered to Vice President Perette. He said that the State Department was considering means of meeting the Argentine Foreign Minister's request for special training of Argentine diplomats assigned to Communist countries. He hoped to be able to provide initial information on what we could do before the Ambassador left on the inaugural flight. In any event the Ambassador could assure the Foreign Minister of our active desire to meet this request.

BRAZIL

203. Paper by the Operations Coordinating Board

Washington, February 1, 1961.

ESTABLISHING RELATIONS WITH NEW BRAZILIAN ADMINISTRATION

Problem

To establish close and friendly relations as soon as possible with the new Brazilian President Janio Quadros and with his administration which assumed office this week.[1] In addition to bilateral considerations, the Brazilian role in current hemispheric problems is of critical importance to the United States. President Quadros' avoidance of contact with U.S. officials thus far and reports of his inclination toward an independent foreign policy adds to the urgency of the problem.

Current Action

The Bureau of Inter-American Affairs in the Department of State believes it is extremely important that the United States take the initiative to quickly establish good relations with the new Brazilian administration by offering U.S. assistance in meeting Brazil's balance of payments problem through an Eximbank line of credit and through the "Food for Peace" program, and to help Brazil to meet the problem of its depressed Northeast territory through the new Social Development program. State believes this U.S. offer of assistance will be more effective if recognized as a friendly U.S. action disconnected from any pressure from President Quadros. Assistant Secretary Thomas C. Mann has incorporated these proposals in the form of an instruction to Ambassador Cabot to offer such assistance to President Quadros, and is currently attempting to secure the necessary clearances in State and from Treasury, Agriculture, and the Eximbank.

Background

Brazilian leaders believe that their country is destined to become one of great world powers. Brazil has been resentful in the past with being treated by the United States as if it were just another of the Latin

---

Source: Kennedy Library, National Security Files, Countries Series, Brazil, January 1–February 24, 1961. Secret. Drafted by Marotta.

[1] Janio Quadros became President of Brazil on January 31, 1961.

423

American "banana" republics. It has sought a special relationship with the United States, desiring to be consulted by the U.S. on matters affecting the hemisphere. Also, Brazil has led the demands that the United States embark on a large-scale aid program for Latin America on the same scale as the Marshall Plan. It feels the $500 million social development program proposed by the United States is a step in the right direction although it is disappointed by the magnitude. A Governor of one of the economically depressed provinces of Northeast Brazil has recently requested U.S. assistance on an urgent basis to combat growing Communist influence in that poverty-stricken area through a rural land development program.

204. Telegram From the Department of State to the Embassy in Brazil

Washington, February 3, 1961, 10:51 p.m.

1010. Critical importance of Brazilian role in current hemisphere problems along with bilateral considerations makes evident urgent need establish effective and productive understanding with Quadros soonest possible. For this purpose Department recognizes your need in initial contacts to have available constructive suggestions and proposals dealing with economic and financial problems of probable chief immediate concern to Quadros.

United States Government handicapped this regard by Quadros avoidance so far of substantive contacts with us and by inability assess clearly probable Quadros policies either within country or abroad. On other hand this provides opportunity to make exploratory suggestions designed draw out and influence Quadros positions. In this connection we particularly concerned such aspects as chaotic GOB financial situation, unconfirmed reports Quadros inclination toward independent foreign policy, and position re Castro and associated hemisphere problems. Our objectives require constructive GOB postures these issues and avoidance tendency GOB to bargain political cooperation against financial assistance.

Source: Kennedy Library, President's Office Files, Brazil—Secretary 1961. Confidential; Niact; Limit Distribution. Drafted by Boonstra. Approved by Ball. Cleared by Mann, Martin, and S/S in the Department, Dillon for Treasury, Goodwin for the White House, and by Agriculture and the Export-Import Bank.

Judging from Embdes 627[1] and other sources the magnitude of GOB financial problem and scope of desirable assistance during 1961 cannot be ascertained until detailed studies requiring weeks or months after Quadros inauguration. However appears certain that GOB will solicit and expect substantial assistance to help maintain essential imports and reschedule existing debts owed to United States, European and other major creditors. At that time it would be appropriate to link such assistance to specific action on part of GOB with respect to its internal and external financial problems.

In view present situation U.S. Government believes our objectives best served by tangible immediate expression our willingness assist Quadros during initial months his government so that he will have time study problems and adopt constructive solutions. This move obviously most effective if recognized as friendly action unconnected any pressure from Quadros and preliminary to consideration more detailed program he may subsequently draw up.

Accordingly you instructed seek appointment with Quadros soonest and make known following U.S. Government view:

1. U.S. Government cognizant difficulties GOB facing this year in external payments and in maintenance essential imports. We assume that GOB will be engaged during next several weeks in study of problem and formulation of constructive program. Representatives U.S. Government agencies will be available for consultation to extent GOB may desire.

2. If Quadros indicates that immediate U.S. Government financial assistance would assist him in gaining time for establishment of constructive program and if you believe that an offer of such assistance would be warmly received you are authorized to say on behalf of President Kennedy that Eximbank would be willing to extend a credit line of 100 million dollars to assist GOB in financing essential imports of capital goods from U.S. as required and thus to conserve remaining foreign exchange.[2] Early consultation necessary in this case between GOB technicians and Eximbank regarding procedures for utilization of credit and negotiation of repayment terms.

3. Reference wheat, other commodities (FYI—not including sugar—End FYI), and local currency problems, President Kennedy in State of Union Message January 30 announced that Food for Peace mission will be sent to Latin America immediately. This mission will be pre-

---

[1] Dated January 23. (Department of State, Central Files, 832.10/1–2361)

[2] In a February 3 memorandum to the President, Secretary Rusk stated that the Department did not know the desires of President Quadros with respect to the loan. If he did desire the money, arrangements could be made for the President to make any such announcement. (Kennedy Library, President's Office Files, Brazil—Secretary 1961)

pared to discuss with Brazilian officials the means for assuring orderly PL–480 shipments following expiration present extended agreement, including possibilities partial grant of funds, as well as loan, if GOB prefers, as well as other possibilities of increasing and rationalizing production and distribution of food.

4. In economic and social development problems, U.S. Government is vividly aware of distressed region in Northeast Brazil and, subject to GOB desires, suggests the early exploration of joint remedial projects in that area.

Rusk

205.   Telegram From the Embassy in Brazil to the Department of State

Rio de Janeiro, March 3, 1961, 1 p.m.

1130. Berle[1] had talk with Janio yesterday which lasted almost two hours. Talk at first centered on Brazilian financial difficulties. Berle again mentioned our willingness to grant $100 million loan. President was doubtful whether Brazil should accept this since in itself it would not solve Brazil's financial problems. Janio again spoke of his intention to undertake drastic program which would make him very unpopular but which was necessary because country was on brink of bankruptcy. He strongly intimated his need for solid backing from US to enable him carry out program. He said he would send Moreira Salles shortly as special Ambassador to prepare way for mission headed by Ministers of Finance and Foreign Affairs.

Berle then introduced Cuban topic and pointed out grave danger that early explosion will take place in Caribbean area probably starting with Dominican Republic and Haiti. He indicated that inter-American action was essential to meet this threat and urged Brazil join US in undertaking such action. Janio's reply to which he stubbornly clung was he

---

Source: Department of State, Latin America Task Force Files: Lot 61 D 298, Brazil 1. Confidential.

[1] Adolf Berle, chairman of the President's Task Force on Latin America, visited Brazil from February 27 to March 3.

could not undertake any bold maneuver in foreign field until he had financial and social crisis now confronting nation under better control. He said if he were to undertake any such action under present circumstances it would result in explosion here. At one point he commented he did not have majority in congress and was glad of it because majority would be too expensive. He did, however, seem to be in complete agreement with Berle's analysis of Cuban situation. Berle and I got impression he was sincere in his position.

At another point in conversation Janio mentioned his anxiety to meet President Kennedy at unspecified date. Berle made no comment.

Of possible interest we noted on Janio's table unsigned photo of Tito and ebony statue sent Janio by Che Guevara and presented by *Prensa Latina* representative. These have been added to engraving of Lincoln presented by Rockefeller which was only decoration there at time my first visit.

Cabot

206. Memorandum From Secretary of State Rusk to President Kennedy

Washington, March 21, 1961.

SUBJECT

Your Appointment with Special Emissary of President Quadros of Brazil

You have agreed to receive President Quadros' special emissary, Ambassador Walther Moreira Salles, who wishes to deliver to you a letter from President Quadros. The Department does not know the contents of the letter.

The Ambassador probably will mention that he is in the United States for preliminary financial talks with United States and international agencies preparatory to a visit by the Brazilian Finance Minister.

Source: Kennedy Library, President's Office Files, Brazil—Secretary 1961. Confidential. Special Ambassador Moreira Salles met with President Kennedy and Mann on March 22 from 4:50 to 5:16 p.m. No record of their conversation was found.

President Quadros is taking constructive action to deal with the financial crisis which he inherited from the Kubitschek administration. On March 13 he simplified Brazil's chaotic foreign exchange system. This action met with quick approval, as a temporary measure, by the International Monetary Fund. Ambassador Moreira Salles has begun discussions with the Fund looking toward a full stabilization program, and has approached us concerning financial support for such a program. Brazil desires the remaining $140 million of its IMF quota, $400 million balance of payments assistance from the Export-Import Bank, and a stretch-out of payments on its $2 billion medium and long-term debt to official and private institutions here and elsewhere.

We have recognized the seriousness of Brazil's financial difficulties and through Ambassador Cabot and Mr. Berle have made known to President Quadros our willingness to assist. Important questions, however, are still to be resolved. These include the help which Brazil can obtain from its European creditors, the completion of drawing arrangements with IMF, the budget and credit policies to be pursued within Brazil, and the measures to be used in financing Brazil's huge coffee surpluses.

The recent moves of President Quadros in carrying out his "independent" foreign policy have raised the issue of just how far Quadros intends to go in moving Brazil away from its traditional policy of cooperation with the United States and support for the Inter-American system. This makes it desirable to couple our expressions of helpfulness with allusions to cooperative action in the mutual interest of both countries.

Dean Rusk

207.   Telegram From the Embassy in Brazil to the Department of State

Rio de Janeiro, April 12, 1961, midnight.

1384. For the President from Secretary Dillon.

Dear Mr. President:

This report is dictated Wednesday afternoon on the plane returning to Rio from Brasilia, where I have just had cordial and interesting hour's conversation with President Quadros. Since our arrival the Brazilians have gone out of their way to be friendly and President Quadros made his personal Viscount available to me for transportation to and from Brasilia. Prior to our meeting we had received yesterday morning a comprehensive memorandum from Brazilian Finance Minister Mariani regarding Brazil's financial needs and hopes. Mariani and Ambassador Moreira Salles accompanied us to Brasilia and were present during our meeting with Quadros. I was accompanied by Ambassador Cabot, Assistant Secretary Leddy, Mr. Linder, representing the Export Import Bank, and Dick Goodwin.

[Here follows 1-1/2 pages of general discussion of the political situation in Latin America.]

Regarding the Brazilian situation I told Quadros I had not been able to discuss the problem in detail with you since we had only received the Brazilian memorandum after my arrival in Rio. I said the U.S. Government, and you in particular, were full of admiration for his courage in moving toward the stabilization of the domestic economy in Brazil. We wished to give Brazil and him whatever support we could. We agreed with Brazil that it would be necessary to stretch out the excessively large current foreign indebtedness. We also recognized that substantial new funds would be required. I said we felt that primary emphasis should be placed on stretching our existing debts because this would be easier to do than to obtain new money in the amounts that would otherwise be required. I told him that it was most important to us that Brazilian debts to Europe be extended on the same basis as similar debts to the U.S. I expressed our gratification at the news that there would be a meeting in Paris at the end of this month to discuss a stretch-out of the Brazilian debt to Europe. I said that we wished to be helpful in pressing the Europeans for a maximum stretch-out. I said we would also like to do what we could to urge the Germans, as part of their newly announced program of assist-

Source: Kennedy Library, President's Office Files, Brazil, Security, 1961. Secret; Priority; Eyes Only. Treasury Secretary Dillon saw President Quadros while in Rio de Janeiro to attend the second annual meeting of governors of the Inter-American Development Bank, April 10–14.

ance to developing countries, to make a substantial sum available to Brazil. I pointed out the importance of an agreement with the IMF since the IMF has a great influence with the European countries and since there was $140 million available in the IMF which would be badly needed in meeting Brazil's needs.

I said that it was our intention immediately on returning to Washington to study the Brazilian memorandum intensively and to prepare a concrete proposal of our own which would be available for discussion with the Brazilians prior to the meeting in Paris on April 28. This would be necessary since the Europeans would undoubtedly wish to know what the U.S. would do before taking action on their own. I said that after the Paris meeting we hoped that we could rapidly come to a conclusion with the Brazilians and that then Minister Mariani could come to Washington some time in May to finalize the agreement. I closed by repeating our wish to be helpful.

President Quadros started speaking in Portuguese with Ambassador Moreira Salles interpreting. Part way through the conversation he switched to English speaking slowly and carefully but very competently. He said that he had come to power pledged to preserve democracy and the free way of life in Brazil. He said the economic problem of Brazil could only be understood in terms of the political and social problems. Unless the economic problems of Brazil could be solved, which meant putting an end to the ruinous inflation of the past years, he felt his government would probably be the last free and democratic government in Brazil. He was determined to take whatever action was necessary to stabilize the situation. This meant that he had had to take unpopular measures but this did not give him pause. He and all his ministers were determined to carry through since they felt it was their mission to save democracy in Brazil. The burdens left them by the outgoing administration were very heavy and his problem was compounded by the fact that although he had been elected by the greatest margin in Brazilian history, in a repudiation of the previous administration's policies, there had been no simultaneous congressional election. Therefore, he was still operating with the old congress in which he did not have a majority. While he would do his best to proceed no matter what other countries did it was clear that there was little hope for success unless Brazil's foreign debts could be rearranged. This was a most urgent problem and he hoped for the full understanding of the U.S.

It was at this point that Quadros changed to English to make the most important point of the meeting. He said he believed he had the right to ask the U.S. to put confidence in him. He had been brought up in the free and democratic tradition and believed whole-heartedly in the same ideals that had made the U.S. a great nation. It was his objective to make these ideals triumphant in Brazil. His record as mayor and later governor of Sao Paulo was proof of his fiscal soundness. He was determined to give the same kind of administration to Brazil in putting an end to inflation and to deficit financing. Most importantly he could assure me there was no cause whatsoever for any political difficulties between U.S. and Brazil. He said that we should understand the situation in which he came to power. He did not have a fully free hand. In proportion as his domestic position strengthened due to the success of his domestic program he could take a stronger position on external political matters in the hemisphere. He again said that we should not fear a strengthened position on his part since there was no reason for political difficulties between our two countries as our ideals and objectives were completely parallel.

Comment: While Quadros did not directly say so he very obviously intended to give the impression that his neutralist political activities in the international arena were designed to strengthen his position against the Brazilian left in the battle over his domestic program. He repeated this thought on two separate occasions to be sure we got his point. This same thought had been put to me very directly earlier by the Brazilian Finance Minister. It was interesting that Quadros himself desired to make the same sort of statement. *End comment.*

Quadros then, in an aside, asked Mariani whether he should discuss details of the Brazilian refinancing proposal and Mariani told him this was not necessary. It was obvious that he was fully informed on details. He did, however, mention the importance of a substantial sugar quota for Brazil. He said this was important not only from foreign exchange standpoint but because sugar was the main product of the depressed northeast.

Comment: I agree and hope we will make real effort here. It will be far easier than giving the aid directly. *End comment.*

We then had some further discussion on time schedule and it was agreed that Moreira Salles would return to Washington before the April 28 meeting in Paris to receive our proposal. We would return to Washington after the Paris meeting and we would attempt to reach a final conclusion as rapidly as possible after which Mariani would come to Washington. Quadros seemed fully satisfied with this schedule.

Since Quadros had not mentioned our overall development program I asked him if he had any comment on that which he wished to pass on to you. He replied that the new administration in Washington seemed to perfectly understand the problems of Latin America. These were many and included some difficult ones, such as Cuba and Ecuador. However, in his view the overriding problem in the hemisphere was the question of what would happen in Brazil during the next three or four years. There were 70 million people in Brazil and if the situation should be righted Brazil would become a strong force for stability throughout the hemisphere. If Brazil went the wrong way there was no doubt but what the whole of Latin America would sooner or later go with her. Therefore, in working to stabilize the situation in Brazil he felt that he was working for the future of democracy throughout the hemisphere. Quadros then thanked me and asked me to convey his best wishes to you and the meeting came to an end. As the meeting broke up he asked Dick Goodwin to stay behind for a few minutes of personal conversation which Dick will no doubt report directly to you.

Comment: My overall impression of Quadros is of a vigorous, hard-working, forceful personality. He is obviously fully aware of all the details involved in his domestic policies. He is clearly a zealot. His missionary zeal must be a source of strength to him in domestic matters but it also makes for unpredictability. I believe he was sincere in his professions regarding foreign policy but the fact that he looks on foreign policy primarily as a tool to help him out with his domestic problems can make for unexpected and at times unpleasant results. I think it is important for us to fully inform him in advance regarding specific issues such as China policy, in which American public opinion is deeply engaged. I feel the meeting was a useful one and that he undoubtedly wishes to cooperate with the U.S. to the full extent that he considers politically possible. *End comment.*

The bank meeting is proceeding uneventfully. It has been marked by a very genuine acceptance of the concepts of your new foreign aid program and of the Alliance for Progress. Member countries are also very obviously pleased by the speed with which the bank has got its operation under way. I will be stopping in Brasilia again on Saturday when President Quadros will receive the bank governors and their alternates, after which I will go on to Puerto Rico for the night, returning to Washington Sunday afternoon.

Faithfully yours, Douglas.

Cabot

208. Memorandum From the Deputy Assistant Secretary of State for Inter-American Affairs (Coerr) to Acting Secretary of State Bowles

Washington, May 14, 1961.

SUBJECT

President Quadros' Attitude on Neutralism and Cuba

I have prepared the following summary with attached documents in response to the White House's urgent request of this afternoon to receive them today:

As a presidential *candidate*, Quadros visited Cuba in April 1960 and initially voiced praise of it and saw no Communist infiltration in it, and later indicated displeasure that it had deviated from its initial inspiration to the point of endangering hemispheric security. He announced in October that, should he be elected, Brazil would pursue a policy of "absolute independence" and renew relations with the USSR and Bloc countries. He again praised Cuba in January 1961.

As *president*, Quadros devoted his inauguration speech of January 31 (Appendix A)[1] chiefly to stating economic and financial difficulties and affirming sound policies to meet them. On February 3, however, he took steps to establish diplomatic relations with Bloc countries. On February 15, he exchanged friendly telegrams with the Presidents of Yugoslavia and Cuba as well as with Khrushchev. He also said Brazil would vote in favor of including in the UN agenda the question of admitting Communist China. In February 1961, Quadros granted an interview to the Director General of Cuba's *Prensa Latina* and accepted from him a picture of Che Guevara (for preceding items, see Appendix B).

In his message to Congress in March 1961 (Appendix C), Quadros declared that Brazil 1) would assume a "more affirmative and independent" foreign policy; 2) would remain democratic and have a duty of "contributing toward . . . reduction of international tensions"; 3) believed the best way to do so would be to establish advantageous contacts between "countries of divergent ideology"; 4) could not ignore the "vitality and dynamism of the socialist states"; and 5) would remain loyal to the inter-American system.

Source: Department of State, Central Files, 732.5–MSP/5–1261. Secret. A copy was sent to the Latin American Task Force on May 15.

[1] Appendixes A–C are not printed.

On May 10, Quadros issued a press release on foreign policy (Embassy Rio telegram No. 1567, Appendix D)[2] that, with regard to the Cuban situation, asserted Brazil would 1) support "self-determination" of Cuban peoples; 2) oppose any "foreign intervention, direct or indirect, to impose upon Cuba any form of government" and would consider military as well as economic and ideological intervention to be improper; 3) not recognize in any American state a political regime which results from clearly manifested interference by a foreign power (Embassy Rio telegram 1571).[3] Our Ambassador commented that Brazil is continuing to sit on the fence, but "perhaps more on the western than eastern side."

In April, Quadros joined with Argentine President Frondizi in a statement that, inter alia, praised the Alliance for Progress and urged the repelling of "direct or indirect interference of extra-continental factors" (Embassy Rio telegram No. 1480, Appendix E).[4] In early May, he urged Cuban President Dorticos to treat the revolutionary prisoners with clemency, and he tacitly refused to respond to Dorticos' ensuing condemnation of the United States (Embassy Rio airgram No. G–380, Appendix F).[5] On the other hand, Quadros has sent a Brazilian trade mission to Moscow, has agreed to receive a Soviet cultural mission (Embassy Rio telegram No. 1558, Appendix G)[6] at Rio and has invited President Tito to Rio.

Comment

In Embassy Rio telegram No. 1579 (Appendix H)[7] of May 12, 1961, Ambassador Cabot expressed concern at the tendency to assist Quadros despite Quadros' constantly manifested indications of neutralism. ARA believes it may be possible to exert pressure on Quadros against neutralism and in favor of a more pro-western attitude, but that the extent of United States commitment and Brazilian expectations regarding the currently considered financial package is so great that to cancel or delay it at this stage would result in Quadros' becoming more rather than less neutralist. Quadros will continue to want our help, especially in the form of loans and PL–480. Working in our favor is a rising feeling in Brazil against Quadros' foreign policy. We should carefully study how to strengthen this feeling and how to get the best use of our total bargaining position.

---

[2] Dated May 10. (Department of State, Central Files, 737.00/5–1061)
[3] Dated May 11. (Ibid., 737.00/5–1161)
[4] Dated April 25. (Ibid., 632.35/4–2561)
[5] Dated May 3. (Ibid., 737.00/5–361)
[6] Dated May 9. (Ibid., 033. 6132/5–961)
[7] Dated May 12. (Ibid., 732.5–MSP/5–1261)

209. Memorandum of Conversation

Washington, May 16, 1961.

SUBJECT

Brazilian Finance Minister's Call on President Kennedy

REFERENCE

Deptel 1694 to Amembassy Rio de Janeiro d–5/18/61[1]

PARTICIPANTS

The President
Finance Minister Clemente Mariani of Brazil
Secretary Dillon of Treasury
Special Ambassador Moreira Salles of Brazil
Chargé d'Affaires Bernardes of Brazil
Assistant Secretary John Leddy of Treasury
Acting Assistant Secretary Coerr of State

Brazilian Minister of Finance Mariani, accompanied by Mr. Carlos Alfredo Bernardes, Chargé, and Special Ambassador Moreira Salles, called on the President to express his deep personal appreciation of the U.S. Government's handling of the Brazilian loan.[2]

In the course of the conversation, the President emphasized that in the negotiations the U.S. Government had completely avoided mention of political factors. He said the purpose of the United States in extending financial assistance to Brazil was to assist it to achieve economic progress and financial stability. This objective was doubly important because Brazil, in addition to being a friend of the United States, is the largest nation in Latin America. Now, however, that the decision on the loan had been taken, the President wanted Minister Mariani to consider some political difficulties that he faced. The President said he realized that Quadros had political problems in Brazil but he wanted the Finance Minister to know that he, too, had problems in the United States with relation to Brazil. He showed the Minister some press clippings, particularly an article from the *Philadelphia Inquirer* contrasting the U.S. loan to Brazil with Brazil's recent assertion of neutrality vis-à-vis Cuba, and a *Washington Post* editorial of May 16, entitled "Raspberry from Brazil." The President said

---

Source: Kennedy Library, National Security Files, Countries Series, Brazil, February 25–May 31, 1961. Confidential. Drafted by Coerr.

[1] Reference is incorrectly dated; it should be dated May 16. (Department of State, Central Files, 732.5–MSP/5–1861)

[2] On May 17 Treasury Secretary Dillon and Finance Minister Mariani issued at Washington a joint announcement granting new and extending existing credits to Brazil by the United States and the IMF totaling $338.5 million. For text, see *American Foreign Policy: Current Documents, 1961,* pp. 355–357.

the United States was interested in the Castro regime because it is a weapon used by international communism in its efforts to take over additional Latin American countries by internal subversion. The President pointed out that the primary threat is not to the United States but to Latin American nations. He declared that the U.S. view is that Castro is not a free agent or a traditional Latin American revolutionary but is for all practical purposes an agent of international communism. The President said that we recognized Quadros' objections to the idea of military intervention in Cuba and that we understand those objections. We strongly believe, however, that this hemisphere must isolate Cuba and frustrate its use by international communism against other Latin American nations. He said that nations of the inter-American system obviously cannot achieve this objective unless they agree on the basic analysis of the situation in Cuba, and that such agreement is seriously prejudiced when the leader of the largest nation in Latin America asserts a strongly divergent view.

The Finance Minister said he thought that the U.S. newspapers' view of Brazil's "neutralism" was exaggerated. He pointed out that Quadros had publicly recognized and opposed the threat of "ideological intervention" in Cuba, which would indicate certain agreement with the U.S. view, and that the Brazilian Government was well aware that Castro's May 1 description of Cuba as a "socialist" state actually meant, in communist parlance, a nation in a stage approaching communism. The Minister said that Quadros has to deal with considerable communist and leftist strength within Brazil. He declared that timely U.S. aid will give Quadros needed financial strength and will improve his ability to take a firmer political position vis-à-vis the communists. He emphasized that Quadros had been moving with increased rapidity away from his pre-electoral position in favor of Castro.

The President tore off a half sheet with the *Philadelphia Inquirer* clipping and gave it to the Finance Minister for Quadros.

The Finance Minister thanked the President for the frank expression of views which he said was most fitting between friends. He said he would fully report the conversation to President Quadros who would be keenly interested.

210. Telegram From the Embassy in Brazil to the Department of State

Rio de Janeiro, May 31, 1961, 4 p.m.

1733. Despite Mariani's statement to President Kennedy that Quadros "had been moving with increased rapidity" away from pro-Castro position (Department telegram 1694)[1] we believe it would be mistake to expect rapid reorientation Quadros policy vis-à-vis Cuban problem under present circumstances. While we do not by any means exclude possibility eventual shift Quadros Cuba policy in our favor, we believe he regards considerations which gave rise to present policy as still largely valid and that he will endeavor exhaust benefits this policy before moving to new ground. Although one of these considerations is almost certainly that cited by Mariani—i.e. that Quadros has felt obliged appease left through foreign policy concessions in order keep them off his back in field domestic policy—we suspect this justification may have been worked for more than it is worth. There are in our view other factors of at least equal importance which behind Quadros Cuba policy and which will conduce to its continuance, at least over short term. Principal among these factors are following:

1) Cuba policy conspicuously at variance with that of US suits Quadros purpose of dramatizing new-found "independence" of Brazil in international field;

2) While he undoubtedly finds certain aspects Castro's conduct reprehensible, Quadros is instinctively attracted by revolutionary nature Castro regime and by its swashbuckling defiance of "colossus of north";

3) He does not yet consider Cuba real threat to Brazil or to hemisphere (despite statement made to me recently by Secretary General Foreign Office that Quadros "much more alive to dangers of Castroism than he generally given credit for");

4) Pressures generated by domestic opposition to his Cuba policy not yet sufficiently strong to force him to alter that policy (in this connection recent announcement massive US aid to Brazil without political conditions has at least temporarily undercut opposition efforts discredit Quadros "independent" foreign policy);

5) He aspires serve as mediator in peaceful settlement Cuban problem, which he continues regard as bilateral one between US and Cuba, and therefore feels Brazil must maintain viable relationship with Cuba as well as US until time is ripe for such mediation.

Source: Department of State, Central Files, 732.5–MSP/5–3161. Secret. Drafted by Bond.

[1] See footnote 1, Document 209.

Any significant future shifts in GOB Cuba policy (and same could be said of GOB foreign policy in general) are likely be determined by President himself on basis of his own assessment his and Brazil's self-interest (which he will define in terms his desire make himself world figure and Brazil major power). In this situation changes in existing policy in our favor might result from developments such as following:

1) Consolidation of anti-Castro opinion within Brazil to point where continued benevolence toward Castro would clearly be political liability instead of asset, particularly to extent of endangering Quadros internal stabilization and reform programs;

2) Conclusion on Quadros' part that Cuba is in fact under control of international communism and that continuance existing situation would pose genuine threat to security Brazil and hemisphere—if, in other words, he should conclude that threat of Cuba-based Communist subversion outweighs political advantages his present "independent" stance;

3) Conclusion on his part that Castro, whether Communist or not, in position successfully to challenge Quadros' own aspirations for hemisphere leadership.

Until he sees clear advantage to be gained from change of policy, for foregoing or other reasons, believe we may expect Quadros continue take independent line on Cuba, playing up to leftist and ultra-nationalist opinion in his public statements while making occasional concessions to US point of view and never fully committing himself to either side.

Bond

211.   Memorandum of Conversation

Washington, July 14, 1961.

SUBJECT

Call of Celso Furtado on the President

PARTICIPANTS

The President
Celso Furtado—SUDENE[1]
Carlos Bernardes—Minister Counselor, Brazilian Embassy
Under Secretary Chester Bowles
Robert F. Woodward—Assistant Secretary for Inter-American Affairs, Department of State
Richard Goodwin—White House
Leonard J. Saccio—Director USOM Brazil
Milton Barall—Deputy Assistant Secretary for Inter-American Affairs, Department of State

After greetings, Dr. Furtado handed the President a letter from President Quadros which the President read immediately.[2] The President instructed Mr. Goodwin to try to prepare a reply prior to Dr. Furtado's departure on July 15. He told Dr. Furtado that if the letter is not ready on that date, it will be transmitted to President Quadros through the Embassy. The President also accepted a copy of the master plan for the Northeast, on which he said he already has some information.

The President asked for Dr. Furtado's judgment on whether the Brazilian Congress would approve the plan and appropriate the funds, and his estimate of the impact of implementation of the plan. Dr. Furtado replied that the lower House has already approved the plan. He said the impact must be enormous for it is intended to change the area in a 3 to 5 year period. The entire future of Brazil depends on success in this area, he said. The President asked several questions with respect to population, the percentage of arable land, square miles, etc. to which Dr. Furtado replied. On the question of the percentage of people who own land, Dr. Furtado replied that ownership was highly concentrated in the hands of a few people and for this reason he hoped to increase efficiency in cane production and reduce the number employed in the cane fields through the mass migration program. He explained his proposal to trade irriga-

---

Source: Kennedy Library, National Security Files, Countries Series, Brazil, June–July 1961. Official Use Only. Drafted by Barall. Approved in U on July 24 and in the White House August 2.

[1] SUDENE: Superintendency for the Development of the Northeast (Brazil). [Footnote in the source text.]

[2] Not found.

tion for land which would then be turned over to the people in the form of small holdings for the production of scarce foodstuffs. He believes the land owner would be willing to trade land in this way because cane operations are now uneconomical and non-competitive with sugar grown in the south. Dr. Furtado also provided some explanation of the sums he seeks from foreign sources.

President Kennedy said he had become aware of the problems of the Northeast which were now a matter of great interest and understanding in the U.S. He said we would have to move toward a solution and that the U.S. desires to be helpful. He commended Dr. Furtado for his sound judgment in making use of his experience to plan for the solution of the problems of this area. The President said U.S. assistance would, of course, be conditioned by what is available here. He referred to the present fight in Congress on the Aid Bill, but said we would nevertheless want to be associated with implementing Dr. Furtado's plan.

The President mentioned the forthcoming trip to Brazil to be made by his brother[3] and expressed the hope that he would be able to visit the Northeast. Dr. Furtado said he would be delighted to show him around the area, at least the East coast humid zone, and to give him a first-hand explanation of his plan.

Dr. Furtado then provided some explanation of the severe problems of the Northeast and his hopes for the ultimate migration of up to 1 million persons. He said the major difficulty is to create hope in people who now have none. This, he said, can be accomplished only by immediate action which would make the people of the area aware of the fact that help was in sight. The President replied that he sensed that migration was an essential feature of the plan. He asked whether the peasant leagues gave land to the people. Dr. Furtado replied that they promise land and this promise alone was very effective because land is what the people most desire. He said that initially land would be made available by the Government, but in later stages through the exchange of land from the sugar cane plantations in payment for irrigation, and through the land reform bill now being prepared.

The President asked about the size of SUDENE. Dr. Furtado replied that he had about 200 technicians now but that he had an active program for training additional professionals and he hopes to reach 500 within a year.

When the President expressed concern for the people of the area who suffer from a shortage of food, a high rate of infant mortality and other symptoms of acute depression, Dr. Furtado replied that it is awareness of this situation which makes President Quadros accept the

---

[3] Edward M. Kennedy visited Brazil July 30–August 4.

improvement of the Northeast as the number 1 task of his Administration.

The President read the press release which he approved and subsequently issued.[4]

After closing remarks, the party was escorted to another part of the White House for a private showing of a Bell and Howell film on the Northeast in which Dr. Furtado played a prominent role.

---

[4] See *Public Papers of the Presidents of the United States: John F. Kennedy, 1961*, pp. 508–509.

---

212. National Intelligence Estimate

NIE 93–61   Washington, August 8, 1961.

THE OUTLOOK FOR BRAZIL

The Problem

To estimate the situation in Brazil over the next few years, with emphasis on the character of the Quadros government and its foreign policy orientation.

Summary and Conclusions

1. In Brazil the pace of change is greater than in any other Latin American country except Cuba, and its national sense of achievement sets it apart from the rest of the continent. Brazil is conscious of its growing strength and population, and powerful drives for more development and international standing underlie the nationwide political and social ferment. Consequently, Brazil's relationships with the US and the rest of the world are changing swiftly. (Para. 11)

2. Janio Quadros assumed the Presidency in 1961 following five years of headlong economic development under President Juscelino

---

Source: Central Intelligence Agency Files, Job 79–R01012A, ODDI Registry. Secret. According to a covering sheet, this estimate was prepared by the Central Intelligence and the intelligence organizations of the Departments of State, Army, Navy, Air Force, and the Joint Staff. The Director of Central Intelligence submitted this estimate to the U.S Intelligence Board on August 8, and all members of the Board concurred except the representatives of the AEC and FBI, who abstained, the subject being outside their jurisdictions.

Kubitschek which went far toward modernizing Brazil, but cost the country economic stability. The flamboyant and free-wheeling Quadros was the popular choice to rescue Brazil from its economic difficulties, to set the financial and administrative house in order, and to enhance greatly Brazil's international prestige through an "independent" foreign policy. He has restored a measure of economic stability—aided by considerable external assistance—and has made a good start toward introducing administrative reform and reducing corruption. (Paras. 17–20)

3. The financial problems the Quadros government inherited include a large foreign and domestic debt, and serious pressures on the balance of payments. However, Quadros will probably be able to engineer some improvement in the Brazilian financial and economic situation over the next year or so. He is certain to press for additional large-scale external assistance from the West and will also accept Bloc trade and development offers when he thinks it will be advantageous. (Paras. 40–44)

4. Despite his auspicious start Quadros is finding it difficult to make rapid progress on Brazil's main problems, and the period through October 1962, when congressional elections are scheduled, will be critical. He has already encountered criticism from conservative forces, especially the military, the press, and the Church, primarily on the ground that his foreign policy favors the Bloc. In Congress, he cannot count on a working majority and he faces other difficulties in dealing with labor, and the fellow-traveling Vice President, Joao Goulart. Both the political parties and the labor movement are fragmented and can mount only comparatively weak opposition. Also, his conservative foes will probably be unwilling to run the risks of immediate action against him. On balance, however, we believe Quadros will be able to maneuver more or less as a free agent until after the 1962 elections. (Paras. 21–27, 51, 53–54)

5. The outlook beyond the 1962 elections is less certain. The congressional election will be the administration's first major political test; should the outcome constitute a vote of confidence, Quadros will be less dependent on manipulation of existing political groups, and will almost certainly step up his efforts to reorganize and reform crucial phases of Brazilian national life. We believe that he will be successful in carrying out substantial administrative reforms in an atmosphere of financial stabilization. Moreover, it is likely that he will obtain sufficient foreign assistance so that he can claim that he is maintaining a reasonable rate of development. Also, Brazil has been for many years one of the most politically mature countries in Latin America and its record in this respect weighs heavily in favor of Quadros. On balance, therefore, it is probable that the Quadros administration will stay in office until the completion of its term in 1965. (Paras. 55–56, 58)

6. The Communist Party (PCB) and its pro-Castro allies will probably be able to keep the poor, rural northeast in ferment. There, the 25,000-member Peasant Leagues, led by pro-Communist, pro-Castro Francisco Juliao, have become a powerful force for social agitation among the rural laborers and tenant farmers. In general, the Communists will probably come into increasing conflict with the administration, particularly on stabilization and other matters of domestic policy. Quadros, however, will probably bear down on them whenever necessary to maintain order. In view of this watchfulness, the Communists and their pro-Castro allies are unlikely to pose a serious threat to Brazil's political stability over the next several years. (Paras. 28–32, 57)

7. The largely pro-US armed forces will continue to be the major limitation upon Quadros' freedom of action, although they will continue to support his administrative and economic reforms and probably will tolerate a considerable degree of neutralism in his foreign policy. Quadros' authoritarian bent probably constitutes the most serious threat to his survival as President. His determination to impose his own policies, together with his high-strung temperament, could lead to some hasty action on his part which might cause the military to lay aside their preference for constitutional order and oust him. This would be a likelihood should he move recklessly to reduce the special position of the armed forces, or to abandon Brazil's ties with the West, or should he take definite steps to perpetuate himself in power beyond 1965, in contravention of the constitution. (Paras. 52, 58)

8. Quadros will almost certainly continue his unorthodox methods to attain a more important role for Brazil in world affairs. Although he is unlikely to adopt a full-fledged neutralist position, he will probably drive hard bargains in future negotiations with the US. It will be difficult to persuade him to renew the agreement, expiring in January 1962, giving the US rights for a guided missile tracking facility on Fernando de Noronha. However, Quadros is unlikely to jeopardize the basically close ties existing between the US and Brazil, although he may risk subjecting them to considerable strain. Should his ventures into world affairs prove unrewarding, he may be disposed, from time to time, to improve his relations with the US. (Paras. 45–47)

9. Quadros is committed to respect Brazil's inter-American obligations, and seems certain to insist on a key role in any important community action, although his ambitions as a statesman extend beyond the continent. He will almost certainly continue to oppose OAS or US intervention in Cuba, and is unlikely to turn on Castro as long as the issue provides him with considerable leverage with the US. He also hopes to develop closer ties with the underdeveloped nations, especially the Africans; thus, Brazil is likely to demonstrate a more anticolonialist spirit in the future. (Paras. 49–50)

10. Quadros' efforts to demonstrate independence of the US have resulted in expanded trade and diplomatic relations with the Bloc. He will almost certainly re-establish diplomatic relations with the USSR before the end of 1961. He may instruct Brazil's delegate to vote for the seating of Communist China at the September 1961 session of the UN; eventually he may go so far as to establish formal diplomatic relations with Peiping. To the extent that Quadros can obtain substantial trade and economic assistance both from the Bloc and the West he will, by his example, encourage other Latin American states to seek closer relations with the Bloc. (Para. 48)

[Here follows the 9-page "Discussion" section of this estimate.]

213. Editorial Note

President Janio Quadros abruptly resigned on August 25, 1961, declaring that his government had been "overcome by the forces of reaction." Speaker of the Chamber of Deputies Ranieri Mazzili was sworn in as interim President.

Vice President Joao Goulart was in transit to Brazil from a trade mission to the People's Republic of China when Quadros resigned. Goulart was an unpopular figure with both the military and the conservative political leadership, and it was not certain whether he would be allowed to assume the presidency in accordance with the Brazilian constitution. On August 28, Mazzili announced that the military would not accept a Goulart presidency "for reasons of national security."

In an August 30 press conference, President Kennedy said of the crisis, "I think it's a matter which should be left to the people of Brazil. It is their country, their constitution, their decisions, and their government." (*Public Papers of the Presidents of the United States: John F. Kennedy, 1961*, page 578)

A compromise solution to the crisis was reached on September 2, when the Brazilian Congress passed a constitutional amendment curbing the power of the presidency and establishing a parliamentary form of government with a strong Prime Minister. Goulart was sworn in as President on September 7, and fiscal conservative Tancredo Neves was named Prime Minister the same day.

214.   Telegram From the Embassy in Brazil to the Department of State

Rio de Janeiro, September 8, 1961, 6 p.m.

713. Reference: Embtel 702.[1] Embassy believes US policy concerning financial aid to Brazil should differ somewhat as between making new aid commitments, on one hand, and complying with commitments already made, on other.

Embassy believes US should be particularly slow in entering into new aid commitments. Goulart's past associations with Communists and his anti-US positions are matter of public record and well-known through Latin America. Haste in offering US aid, in absence convincing disavowal those associations and positions, would undoubtedly weaken political strength of US friends throughout hemisphere and particularly in Brazil.

Embassy believes fact is USG is in excellent posture. No new aid commitment should be expected from it. Those commitments already made are sufficient, e.g., stabilization support and Alliance for Progress as reached Punta Del Este. We should and can avoid debate Mariani implication commitment finance Plano de Emergencia, reference despatch 140, 1499.[2]

With respect financial commitments already made by US, comprising $338 million new money, Embassy considers harm could be done to fundamental Brazil–US relations if there is any suggestion US does not intend comply fully with agreements establishing those credits. Such suggestions would undoubtedly be interpreted in Brazil as proof US opposition to Goulart. Many, possibly including Goulart himself, might even use such "proof" of US opposition to Goulart to support thesis, being widely spread by Communists and others, that USG was behind movement Brazilian military frustrate will of people that Goulart take office as President. On other hand, Embassy recommends that in talks with Brazilian officials, as soon as advisable, we give emphasis to fact US financial commitments predicated on GOB policy pursue self-help measures, as manifested GOB letter and memo to IMF, and that Embassy be authorized convey to new officials desire of USG ascertain whether new GOB intends follow stabilization program described in memorandum to IMF, since $338 million credits approved on understanding GOB

Source: Department of State, Central Files, 732.5–MSP/9–861. Secret.

[1] Dated September 6. (Ibid., 732.11/9–661)

[2] Reference is to Despatch 140, August 22, and telegram 1499, April 27. (Ibid., 732.5–MSP/8–2261 and 737.00/4–2761)

economic program would be pursued "under conditions of financial stabilization." (Dillon–Mariani press release May 17).[3]

Following additional factors considered pertinent:

A. Importance that Finance Ministry be strong and be allowed
operate under firm orientation toward financial stability is greater than
ever now that Parliamentary form of government in effect. Likelihood
that inexperienced, if not irresponsible, legislators will undermine
Finance Minister's policies will probably be magnified unless new government, including Prime Minister and legislators, understand importance financial stability.

B. Bank of Brazil foreign exchange position fairly strong at present;
reference Embtel 696.[4] Accordingly, US can delay authorizing drawings
on loans without endangering Brazilian balance of payments position at
this time. However, GOB clearly cannot postpone such drawings indefinitely.

Bond

---

[3] See footnote 2, Document 209.
[4] Dated September 6. (Department of State, Central Files, 832.14/9–661)

---

215. Telegram From the Department of State to the Embassy in Brazil

Washington, September 12, 1961, 7:13 p.m.

815. Your 713.[1] Embassy should seek early, appropriate opportunity
to explain to Finance Minister Moreira Salles, and to other GOB officials
as Embassy considers desirable, that while we intend to fulfill our financial commitments to Brazil under the international financial stabilization
arrangements (Dillon–Mariani announcement May 17, 1961), our intention to do so is based on the understanding that Brazil intends to go

---

Source: Department of State, Central Files, 732.5–MSP/9–861. Confidential. Drafted
by Hembra; approved by Woodward; and cleared by Martin, Springsteen, the Export-Import Bank, and Treasury.
[1] Document 214.

ahead with the stabilization program described in its standby arrangement of May 17 with the IMF. Begin FYI. Department explained foregoing position to Brazilian Chargé Bernardes September 11 prior his departure for Brazil on consultation. Treasury suggested to Bernardes that Finance Minister might wish attend Vienna IMF meeting which would provide opportunity for discussions with IMF and US officials. *End FYI.* Embassy should state it would be pleased to receive, for transmittal to USG, any assurances which Finance Minister can give respecting Brazil's intentions to maintain its stabilization program.

Begin FYI. Understand that Brazil has not kept its commitments to IMF to adhere to specific ceilings on currency issue, bank credits, budgetary deficits and expenditures on coffee. End FYI.

Rusk

216.   Memorandum From the Assistant Secretary of State for Inter-American Affairs (Woodward) to Secretary of State Rusk

Washington, October 3, 1961.

SUBJECT

Suggestion that we might reinforce instructions to all U.S. Representatives to try to dissipate the idea that the U.S. Government heads a "Bloc", as distinct from the exertion of U.S. leadership of democratic countries all seeking the same objectives

The Brazilian statement of foreign policy, reported in the attached telegram,[1] impresses me anew with the idea that it might be very useful for you to reinforce present instructions to all U.S. Representatives by asking that they try to dissipate the impression that the United States is the leader of a "bloc", as distinct from the exertion of U.S. efforts to lead democratic nations toward the attainment of similar objectives.

Source: Department of State, Central Files, 611.32/10–361. Confidential. Drafted by Woodward and cleared with Cleveland and McGhee.

[1] Telegram 863 from Rio de Janeiro, September 30, reported that at a meeting of the Council of Ministers of the OAS on September 29, the Brazilian delegate presented a policy statement that described Brazil's foreign policy as independent from all politico-military blocs and dedicated to economic development in the Third World. Brazil would pursue normal political and economic relations with the Communist nations and would oppose outside intervention in the affairs of Cuba.

More specifically, I think it might be useful if you were to mention at a staff meeting:

1) that we should try to relate every suggestion that the U.S. Government makes to another government concerning foreign policy positions to the interests of the nation to which the suggestion is made, and

2) that we should carefully avoid "thanking" the governments of other countries for their support of the same points of view that we support, but rather

3) that we should express our admiration of their wisdom in adopting such policy positions and emphasize our support of the same objectives that they have.

This suggestion may be elementary but I submit it for your possible use.

217.   Telegram From the Embassy in Brazil to the Department of State

Rio de Janeiro, October 21, 1961, 8 p.m.

1022. At President Goulart's request, I spent hour and half with him today in Rio in informal discussion US-Brazilian relations. (Bond only other person present.) Conversation was entirely cordial and exceedingly frank throughout, with frequent reiteration by Goulart that he speaking with utmost candor because of seriousness situation in Brazil.

Goulart stressed at outset that, whatever I might be told by other members of government, political crisis resulting from Quadros resignation has by no means been resolved. He said present phase represents merely political truce between forces of moderation (represented by his government) and forces of right and left extremism which are threatening existence of regime. He estimated government might have another 60 to 90 days of grace in which to find solutions basic social and economic problems presently afflicting Brazilian people but that if it not able to do so, or at least to reverse present deteriorative trend, extremist forces would move against government precipitating crisis which would be much more serious than that of August–September and might even lead

---

Source: Department of State, Central Files, 611.32/10–2161. Secret.

to revolution. He added that in view evident disposition Cubans, Soviet, ChiComs etc to intervene in such a situation, result might well be "another Korea". He said he had accepted mixed presidential-parliamentary regime precisely in order avoid revolution, which his stopover in Rio Grande do Sul had convinced him was real possibility, since he convinced that revolution (even if he himself assumed its leadership) would be disastrous for Brazil.

Goulart emphasized situation particularly dangerous because prevailing economic injustices and social discontent being exploited by small but well-organized Communist minority to create pre-revolutionary situation. In this connection he said Fidel Castro has been tremendous asset to Communists, external as well as internal, by providing dramatic symbol of revolutionary aspirations of underprivileged masses throughout Latin America. He stated both Soviets and ChiComs making effective use this symbol, particularly in Brazilian Northeast. (At this point he remarked ChiComs now more interested in Cuba than in Formosa.) Regarding Cuban problem itself, Goulart expressed opinion Cuba retrievable and that time will be increasingly on side of US provided latter has patience to wait for situation Castro regime deteriorate under its own weight. If US will be patient, he said, time will prove to be more effective weapon than any missile. He expressed view US does itself great disservice by agitating Cuban problem since Latin American masses are instinctive on side of tiny Cuba whenever it menaced by colossus to North.

Principal point foregoing remarks clearly to underscore importance continued large-scale US assistance, without which he said his government could not survive present critical period. While expressing full awareness and appreciation past US aid to Brazil, Goulart said unfortunately such aid has not gained US any appreciable credit with masses of Brazilian people. He said he entitled speak for masses since he himself is man of people, who has consistently drawn his political support from working classes. He stated lower economic strata in Brazil have never been aware of US aid, fruits of which have never filtered down to their level in any form they could recognize. They consequently have had no defense against anti-US propaganda directed against alleged economic imperialism, trusts, profiteering, et cetera with which many Brazilian politicians (and he admitted he did not exclude himself from this category) have found it politically advantageous to associate themselves. He said it avails US nothing to have its case presented to Brazilian people by industrialists and other elements pro-US elite (i.e. Entreguistas) who have no credibility among lower classes. What is needed is to have US case, including facts regarding US aid, presented by spokesmen who belong to and are trusted by Brazilian working classes. He emphasized it is these elements which must be cultivated by US if it is to make any significant impact on course of events in Brazil today, since they are elements which, although still largely uncommitted, are in serious danger being won over by Communists. He urged that US therefore not only continue "massive" aid to Brazil but also that it do so in form and manner intelligible to Brazilian masses. In latter connection he emphasized importance applying such aid inter alia to meeting urgent social needs of lower economic classes in Brazil.

On basis his knowledge conditions in Uruguay and Argentina, he said he believed comparable conditions prevail throughout South America.

In further discussion Communist interest in Brazil, Goulart said he has received steady stream of proposals from Soviets since he took office looking toward expanded USSR-Brazil relations and he has also received during this period 20 invitations visit Cuba, none of which he has accepted.

On subject proposed visit to US, Goulart said he anxious meet with President Kennedy but that he preferred not try set definite date at this juncture. He acknowledged, however, that late January or early February might prove to be feasible from his point of view and he expressed hope President Kennedy could also pay early visit to Brazil, where he said he would be received with same popular acclaim as was President Roosevelt.

Gordon

---

218.   Letter From the Deputy Assistant Secretary of Defense for International Security Affairs (Williams) to the Assistant Secretary of State for Inter-American Affairs (Woodward)

Washington, November 7, 1961.

DEAR MR. WOODWARD: Since the resignation of President Quadros and the ensuing politico-military crisis of September, the trend of events

---

Source: Department of State, Central Files, 732.00/11–761. Secret. Woodward replied to Williams' letter on November 15. (Ibid., 732.00/11–1361) He welcomed the offer of the Department of Defense to consult with the State Department on the Brazilian situation. He hoped to do so after consultation with the Embassy in Rio de Janeiro and following the completion of a new Special National Intelligence Estimate on Brazil (Document 219). Ambassador Gordon, in telegram 1280 from Rio de Janeiro, November 25, wrote, "Embassy greatly disturbed at evident breakdown in communication among agencies US Government implicit in Williams' letter." The Embassy, he continued, was aware of the developments in Brazil described in the Defense Department letter. (Department of State, Central Files, 732.00/11–2561)

in Brazil has caused increasing concern in this Department. The immediate and most obvious result of the crisis was the psychological and political defeat suffered by anti-Communist leaders in the Brazilian Armed Forces. At the same time, the emergence of Governor Brizzola[1] of Rio Grande do Sul as a potential national leader, the steps taken by him in forming paramilitary nuclei with Communist assistance, and his activities in connection with Communist leaders in other regions of the country since the crisis are disquieting.

According to our Embassy in Rio de Janeiro, the new Government of Brazil so far appears to have functioned in essence as a presidential system, with President Goulart executing full powers and the cabinet in effect by-passed. For several years there have been recurring and reliable intelligence reports that the Communist Party of Brazil regards Goulart as "their man", and it is known that the party attempted to obtain his nomination for the presidency in the Labor Party conventions prior to the presidential elections of both 1955 and 1960. At the same time, Goulart's considerable influence in the Brazilian labor movement has been marked by increasing Communist infiltration of labor organizations and by the removal, with government cognizance and at times connivance, of anti-Communist trade union leaders.

Since Goulart's accession to the Presidency an extensive shake-up has occurred in the Brazilian armed forces. Those officers best known as enemies of the Communist movement have been scattered and demoralized, either by retirement or by reassignment to positions where they can exercise little influence on military or political affairs. These officers have been replaced by others who are in most instances without experience in or proven capacity for their new posts and who in some instances are suspected of being Communist sympathizers or even secret agents. The appointment of an officer in this category to head the Federal Public Security Department in Brazilia seems cause for alarm. While this process has occurred in the military services, a parallel infiltration of the civilian branches of the government is reportedly taking place. In this connection, the appointment as Attorney General of an individual who seems best described as a Communist sympathizer appears significant.

In the field of foreign policy, while there has been relatively little opportunity so far to assess the long range orientation and objectives of the present government, there are initial indications that these may not be compatible with the national interests and security of the United States. We have already observed the efforts of the Brazilian Ambassador in Buenos Aires to strengthen the determination of President Frondizi and the Argentine Foreign Office to resist pressure from the Argentine

---

[1] Reference is to Leonel Brizzola, brother-in-law of President Goulart.

military and press to break relations with Cuba. The Brazilians also rallied the opposition to the recent Peruvian initiative on Cuba in the Organization of American States.

From these and other indications, it would seem that we may be faced in Brazil with a foreign policy oriented increasingly toward the Soviet Bloc in world affairs and toward the Castro regime in inter-American affairs. At the same time, we must reckon with the domestic policies of the Vargas elements who have ruled Brazil almost without interruption since 1930, whose economic and political irresponsibility is notorious, and whose collaboration with the Communists is amply documented.[2] In the present case, these elements have produced a government in which Communist infiltration and influence exceed anything of the sort previously known in the country. They apparently plan to force the U.S. to finance this inimical regime. This is occurring at a time when the basis for paramilitary uprisings exist in both north and south, and when the nation's financial straits are critical. Meanwhile, the power and influence of the anti-Communist and largely pro-U.S. armed forces are at their lowest point.

In these circumstances, the Department of Defense has serious misgivings as to the trend and possible effects of the current situation in Brazil on U.S. strategy for the security of the Western Hemisphere. In our judgment, this trend is serious enough to require the coordinated use of all available U.S. assets.

It would therefore be greatly appreciated if the Departments of State and Defense could review together the policies, programs, and actions contemplated with respect to Brazil and how the resources available to the Department of Defense could be employed in conjunction with the plans of the Department of State to assist in meeting an increasingly dangerous situation. We should particularly like to explore the value of maintaining and strengthening the relationship between the Brazilian and U.S. Armed Forces as a factor of equilibrium, and to consider such questions as the effects on the solidarity and defensibility of the hemisphere of Brazil's neutralist policy.

Sincerely,

Haydn

---

[2] Reference is to the followers of Getulio Dornelles Vargas, who was President 1930–1945 and 1951–1954.

219. Special National Intelligence Estimate

SNIE 93–2–61   Washington, December 7, 1961.

SHORT-TERM PROSPECTS FOR BRAZIL UNDER GOULART

The Problem

To estimate the outlook for Brazil up to the October 1962 elections, with special reference to the orientation and prospects of the Goulart government.

Conclusions

1. The constitutional compromise which enabled Goulart to succeed to the Presidency after Quadros' resignation in August 1961 has left a confused atmosphere in which the locus of executive power is uncertain. Nevertheless, Goulart has emerged as considerably more than a figurehead President and his principal concern will be to maintain and, if possible, to increase the prestige and power of the Presidency and of his Brazilian Labor Party (PTB). To this end, he will exploit his influence in labor and leftist circles while seeking to avoid undue offense to conservative elements, particularly the military, who continue to view him with suspicion because of his long record of collaboration with the Communists. Meanwhile, the various political forces will be jockeying for control of the executive power and for victory in the October 1962 election. (Paras. 5–11, 15–16, 19, 23–24)

2. In these circumstances the short-range prospects for the growth of Communist influence in Brazil are favorable. The Communists will benefit by the tolerance not only of Goulart but of many other Brazilian political leaders. They will probably encounter little effective competition or governmental restriction in their efforts to entrench themselves in areas where agrarian and social unrest is most acute and will also benefit to some extent by the entry of additional party members or sympathizers into the bureaucracy. However, it is unlikely that Communist infiltration of the government will go so far as to give the Communist Party a significant influence on the formulation and execution of policy within the period of this estimate. (Paras. 12, 18, 25–26)

Source: Central Intelligence Agency Files, Job 79–R01012A, ODDI Registry. Secret. According to a covering sheet, this estimate was prepared by the Central Intelligence Agency and the intelligence organizations of the Departments of State, Army, Navy, Air Force, and the Joint Staff. All members of the USIB concurred in this estimate on December 7 except the representatives of the AEC and FBI, who abstained, the subject being outside their jurisdictions.

3.   The initial indecisiveness of the new government and the blow to national confidence engendered by the succession crisis have caused a new decline in Brazil's economic and financial situation. Nevertheless, given the continued disbursement of the credits called for in the May 1961 aid package, the government can probably keep going financially until the fall of 1962, though no substantial improvement in the basic causes of the country's financial disequilibrium is likely. Although legislation on the reforms promised by Quadros and espoused by the current administration will probably be enacted, it is not likely to be sufficient to assuage popular discontent. Thus the regime is likely to be plagued by recurring political crises and possibly by breakdowns in public order. On balance, however, we believe that Goulart and the present constitutional system will probably survive up to the October 1962 elections. It is less likely that the present Council of Ministers will last that long. (Paras.20–22, 27–29)

4.   The present government will continue to emphasize the "independent" character of its foreign policy, but the need for US financing, as well as domestic political considerations, will probably render it less truculent toward the US than was the Quadros administration. Although Brazil has already re-established diplomatic relations with the USSR, development of diplomatic and economic ties with Bloc countries will probably not go much beyond the existing framework. Brazil will almost certainly continue to oppose sanctions against Castro, though if most major Latin American states were disposed to take some limited action, it would probably go along. (Para. 31)

[Here follows the 5-page "Discussion" section of this estimate.]

220.   Memorandum From the Administrator of the Agency for International Development (Hamilton) to President Kennedy

Washington, February 9, 1962.

SUBJECT

Aid to Brazil

In response to your memorandum of February 5[1] about aid to Brazil before their elections next fall, I am happy to report that we are about to conclude agreements with Brazil calling for three important programs in the crucial northeast area: (a) a $33 million immediate impact loan-grant program; (b) a $62 million long-range development program; and (c) a very substantial program for emergency food, wheat, corn and dry milk. We also hope to initiate projects elsewhere in Brazil which will have impact before October.

The programs for northeast Brazil derive from the recommendations of the survey team[2] which we sent to Brazil last October following up your talk with Dr. Celso Furtado on the Northeast Brazil Development Agency last summer.[3] These programs are as follows:

a. *Immediate impact.* This program is primarily social in purpose and directed to the centers of greatest discontent in the northeast. The main elements are: water supply—public fountains, wells and water systems in cities and towns; labor centers and community self-help development projects; rural electrification; literacy and simple industrial training for those just entering the labor force; and mobile health units. This multiple program will be financed by $15 million in dollar loans and grants plus about $18 million of U.S. local currency. The target is to have these items physically in place before the October elections, so far as possible, with "Alliance for Progress" markers.

b. *Long-range development.* We plan to participate in a longer range program to attack some of the fundamental social economic problems of the northeast. The accent will be on irrigation, roads, power, primary education, community water supply and agriculture. We are thinking now of a two-year commitment of about $62 million of loans and grants, plus local currency aid with later participation depending on results. Final negotiations will take place within the next few days.

Source: Department of State, Central Files, 811.0032/2–962. Official Use Only. A February 9 covering memorandum from Hamilton to Bundy indicates the memorandum is a response to a February 5, request from the President for information on U.S.-sponsored economic projects being implemented in Brazil prior to the October 1962 Congressional, state, and municipal elections there.

[1] Not found.

[2] The report of this survey team was not found.

[3] See Document 211.

c. *Food programs*. There are presently two substantial PL 480 food programs being carried on in northeast Brazil and two additional ones about to be initiated. Last December we agreed to supply 40,000 tons of dry milk on a grant basis over a two-year period to be consumed by almost 4 million people, the majority being school children. Shipments have started and the program will be in full operation in a few months. U.S. voluntary agencies are conducting a food distribution program on a grant basis which has already amounted to $6 million thus far in FY 1962.

We are now ready to move on an emergency food supply program consisting of about 25,000 tons of food on a grant basis to be used in kind as partial pay for work relief projects to help people suffering from this year's unusually bad drought conditions. Brazil has not yet agreed to accept a standard agreement for this type of program. In addition, a sales agreement for 800,000 tons of wheat and some corn is now being negotiated.

Ted Moscoso and I would appreciate your comments about these proposed programs and any others which may seem appropriate to you; and we hope to have the opportunity to discuss them with you.

Fowler Hamilton

---

221. Memorandum of Conversation

Washington, February 19, 1962.

SUBJECT

The Expropriation of the IT&T Properties in Rio Grande do Sul, Brazil

PARTICIPANTS

The Secretary
Ambassador Roberto Campos, of Brazil
Minister Arnaldo Vasconcellos, Brazilian Embassy
ARA—Mr. Barall
EST—Mr. Wilson

In the course of Ambassador Campos' call, the Secretary mentioned the problem created for the two Governments by the action of Governor

---

Source: Department of State, Secretary's Memoranda of Conversation: Lot 65 D 330. Official Use Only. Drafted by Wilson of ARA/EST. Approved in S on February 28.

Brizzola, of Rio Grande do Sul, in expropriating the properties of the IT&T in that state.[1] He said we know that the Brazilian Government is concerned about the matter also. It is a problem we could both do without. The Secretary indicated he believed the eventual solution might be for the Government of Brazil to underwrite the settlement on compensation. Ambassador Campos agreed that the expropriation is embarrassing for the Brazilian Government and for President Goulart, who has intervened in the problem. He said he thought evaluation of the properties might eventually have to be set by the courts, with payments to be made by the State or Federal Government. He pointed out the autonomy of the state governments in Brazil in such matters.

With regard to the statement made to the press by the Department on Saturday,[2] Ambassador Campos said he thought this action by the Department was premature. It may have repercussions in Brazil, though he has not yet heard of any. He thought it would have been better to delay any statement while the Federal Government of Brazil was taking action. The Secretary replied that the expropriation created a problem for us too. The State Department had to make an indication of interest and concern with the problem in order to forestall possible strong pressures in this country from the business community and the Congress. He said an action such as the expropriation was contrary to our efforts to mobilize the capital available for development.

Ambassador Campos referred favorably to the proposals of American and Foreign Power to arrange for sale of its properties with the intent of shifting its investment into less controversial fields, as was done in Colombia and Mexico. Such an arrangement prevented the loss of capital investment in the country through the sale. The Ambassador commented that he thought Brizzola had jumped the gun by his expropriation action and that the timing had been most unfortunate. The Secretary said we hope to maintain the morale of U.S. investors abroad in order for them to take part in development. Expropriation without adequate compensation makes this very difficult. The Ambassador agreed.

---

[1] On February 16 Governor Leonel Brizzola ordered the expropriation of the Companhia Telefonica Nacional, a subsidiary of the American firm International Telephone and Telegraph. The Brazilian Government compensated the company in the amount of $140,000. ITT valued CTN's assets at between $6 and $8 million.

[2] On February 17 the Department of State issued a statement condemning the actions of Governor Brizzola and stating that the adequate, just, and prompt compensation that must accompany such an expropriation had not been made to ITT. (*Keesing's Contemporary Archives*, 1961–1962, p. 18815)

222.   Memorandum From Secretary of the Treasury Dillon to President Kennedy

Washington, April 3, 1962.

SUBJECT

U.S.-Brazilian Financial Discussions

This will supplement the information I gave you by telephone on our financial discussions with Brazil.

After several days of negotiations in which the U.S. side was represented by the Export-Import Bank, the AID, the State Department and the Treasury, we reached full agreement last night on U.S. financial support for the new Brazilian stabilization program. I believe this agreement is fully satisfactory to the U.S. and that it will provide adequate support to Brazil's new program while assuring that U.S. funds will be made available only as progress is achieved under that program.

Last May we had agreed to provide $338 million in new money to support stabilization under the Quadros regime. Additional funds were provided by the International Monetary Fund and by Brazil's European creditors. After the breakdown of the stabilization program connected with the resignation of President Quadros, Brazil's drawings from the IMF were halted. By the turn of the year drawings from the Europeans and from the U.S. were also discontinued. Of the original $338 million committed by the U.S., Brazil drew $209 million, leaving a balance of $129 million. Of this, $59 million were in Eximbank funds, $35 million in AID funds and $35 million in the Treasury Exchange Stabilization Fund.

On March 15, 1962 the Council of Ministers approved a new stabilization program designed to bring a halt to the serious inflation which has amounted to about 50% over the past 12 months. The new program marks a hopeful beginning, but its effectiveness will depend importantly on action still to be taken by the Brazilian Congress, as well as on the willingness of the Brazilian Government to adopt additional and alternative measures in the event that the program initially approved will not prove adequate. *The principal unknown quantity is the degree to which President Goulart will himself pursue stabilization efforts with the necessary vigor in the face of inevitable domestic political opposition.*

Because of the uncertainties regarding future Brazilian performance the IMF was unwilling to give its full approval to Brazil's program at this time and accord to Brazil a further standby. However, the IMF has agreed

---

Source: Kennedy Library, National Security Files, Countries Series, Brazil, April 1962. Confidential.

to postpone repayment of Brazil's debt to the Fund of $20 million, to work with Brazil in the next 2 months in perfecting its program and to invite the European creditors to release some $20 million from the remaining standby of about $80 million from Europe.

The agreement we have now reached with the Brazilians consists of: (1) a letter to me from Minister Moreira Salles outlining the new program approved by the Council of Ministers and (2) my response to the Finance Minister stating that the U.S. is prepared "to effect releases out of the $129 million balance of the funds earmarked for Brazil in May 1961, as the financial program is effectively carried out and as may be mutually agreed between the two Governments."

We have agreed to release immediately (this week) an initial amount of $35 million—$16 million to be provided by the Eximbank and $9.50 million each from AID and the Treasury. Minister Moreira Salles was strongly urged by his delegation to ask for an immediate release of at least $50 million. He called on me last night to ask whether this would be possible but assured me that he did not wish to press the point. He was entirely satisfied with the explanation I gave him to the effect that a larger release in the absence of Brazilian performance, as distinct from plans, would be seriously criticized by our Congress which was now considering the large appropriation which we were proposing for the Alliance for Progress. I do not believe that Minister Moreira Salles will recommend to President Goulart that he pursue this matter further with you, but it is always possible that other members of the Brazilian delegation here will do so. I do not believe that any further concessions are desirable or necessary.

We have kept the IMF fully informed of our discussion and Managing Director Jacobsson is in full agreement with the arrangements we are making.

The exchange of letters between Moreira Salles and myself will be completed today and a short statement will be released to the press.

We have also agreed on a paragraph which might be included in the communiqué which you and President Goulart plan to issue sometime tomorrow.[1] A copy of this text for your consideration is attached.[2]

Douglas Dillon[3]

---

[1] For text of the communiqué, see *Public Papers of the Presidents of the United States: John F. Kennedy, 1962*, pp. 287–289.

[2] Not found.

[3] Printed from a copy that indicates Dillon signed the original.

223. Memorandum of Conversation

Washington, April 3, 1962, 2:30 p.m.

SUBJECT

Conversation between President Goulart and President Kennedy—Various Topics

PARTICIPANTS

U.S.   Brazil
President Kennedy   President Goulart[1]
A. Jose DeSeabra (interpreter)

[Here follows discussion of the situation in Argentina.]

President Goulart replied that he had taken over at the height of one of the most serious crises in Brazilian history. Thus far he said he has managed to earn and keep the confidence of the masses, but didn't know how much longer he could do so. Thanks to his efforts, a substantial amount of political stability had been secured, but it can only be lasting if true social peace is attained, he added. He feels confident of receiving continued support from the people, but he feared that they could endure only so much hardship. He said that in order not to betray the people's trust it was imperative that basic reforms be undertaken, which in turn would bring about greater social stability. This position appears to be understood by conservative elements, he said, which may be more or less sincere in their attitude. In President Goulart's opinion, the most urgent need in Brazil is to find a solution for its many pressing social problems. The U.S. may help greatly, not only by money, but through an effective cooperation that will help Brazil to develop and solve its social problems. He said that a solution to these problems was the only way to maintain democracy. With regard to communism in Brazil, he said that, as a party, it is relatively weak and furthermore divided on many issues. He reiterated that Latin America was plagued by serious social problems and if no solution was found, democracy would be in great danger. He declared that Brazil looks to President Kennedy with great expectations, as he is the leader of a liberal party with advanced ideas. President Goulart added that effective cooperation from the U.S. would help Brazil to solve major problems, but economic liberalization had to be attained first

---

Source: Department of State, Presidential Memoranda of Conversation: Lot 66 D 149. Official Use Only. Drafted by DeSeabra of L/S. Approved by S on April 12 and by the White House on April 16. The meeting was held at the White House. The time of the meeting is from the President's Appointment Book. (Kennedy Library)

[1] President Goulart visited the United States April 3–7; he spent April 3–4 in Washington, April 5–6 in New York City, and April 7 with President Kennedy at Offutt Air Force Base in Omaha, Nebraska, before departing for Mexico.

and foremost through Brazil's own efforts. The government, he said, is trying to curb inflation, but it was impossible as yet to achieve complete stabilization. He affirmed that the struggle for development had to continue, and therefore inflation had to be faced for a long time. He feared that if the strict measures advocated by the International Monetary Fund were to be applied in Brazil, there would result a situation possibly similar to that of Argentina.

President Kennedy asked whether inflation was up to about 50% per year.

President Goulart replied that it was around 40% to 42% and that efforts were being made in earnest to reduce it gradually. Again he brought up the point that stabilization at this time would create serious social problems.

President Kennedy said that the IMF had done well with inflation in Bolivia. He then inquired whether a reduction of inflation from 40% to 25% would require action from Congress on the stabilization program and whether such program would be adopted.

President Goulart replied that part of the stabilization program was being carried out by action of the government in reducing its budgetary expenditures by 20% to 22%, but that there also would be action by Congress, with a majority supporting the program.

President Kennedy referred to the talks between Secretary Dillon and the Foreign Minister.[2] He said that Dantas also mentioned that sustained growth would bring about a reduction in inflation, while avoiding the danger of widespread unemployment. According to Dantas, unemployment would deprive the government of labor support.

President Goulart interjected that Argentina was known throughout Latin America as the most faithful disciple of the IMF.

President Kennedy said that it was the hope of the U.S. that the governments in Latin America would all have true popular support, and that it was the intention of the U.S. to continue to support President Goulart and his government. The U.S. realizes that Brazil has had internal difficulties, and that it is a complex matter to maintain the proper balance between stability and deflation on the one hand and growth and development on the other.

President Goulart stated that Brazil was inclined to follow the latter path.

President Kennedy then brought up the subject of labor organization in the Hemisphere and the concern of the U.S. over an emerging Latin American trade union movement that would exclude the U.S. and Canada, while including Cuba. The President said that this is fraught

---

[2] See Document 222.

with danger and that strong ties between U.S. and Latin American labor organizations are essential to the survival of democracy.

President Goulart responded that the attitudes of labor in Latin America are bound together with development and the ever present social problems. He added that he counted on strong support by the workers of Brazil. He admitted that the left was strong and particularly active in the labor movement, but that its strength varied in direct ratio to the seriousness of social problems. He emphasized that he maintained a good relationship with all areas of the Brazilian labor movement.

President Kennedy stated that stronger and continuing ties between U.S. and Latin American labor organizations would help substantially to keep the Latin American labor free. But, he said, if Cuba were to be brought into a new Latin American labor organization, this would multiply considerably the danger of communist infiltration and subversion, and that therefore, a decided effort should be made to improve the relations between U.S. and Latin American labor organizations.

President Goulart commented that the Cuban phenomenon in its early stages was supported not only throughout Latin America, but even in the U.S.

President Kennedy said he recognized that Castro started out with a popular program which he did not follow.

President Goulart commented that up to the time Castro came out as an outright Marxist, the Cuban leader was in fairly good standing in Latin America.

President Kennedy then inquired about the possibility of Clodsmidt Riani and others trying to form a separate Latin American labor organization. He felt that stronger ties between U.S. and Latin American labor organizations would be a source of strength not only for labor but for democracy in general. And if those ties were broken, and the U.S. and Canada were to be kept out while Cuba came in, there would be a strong increase in radical left and communist influence on Latin American labor.

President Goulart replied that such a separate movement had been tried, but nothing concrete had happened, and that he himself was not in favor of it. He said that he has recommended to Ambassador Gordon that there be a greater exchange of labor leaders between the countries, as it is obvious that by and large, Brazilian labor leaders do not know sufficiently about the U.S. labor movement. He said that at the time the Soviet Bloc countries are making a successful effort in wooing Latin American and Brazilian labor leaders.

President Kennedy stated that such exchanges would be increased. He also mentioned that there was dissatisfaction on both sides with the AFL–CIO representatives in Latin America. The importance of good contacts between labor leaders cannot be overemphasized, since business and government contacts are only a part of the contacts between nations and peoples, he added.

President Goulart commented that the part played by the respresentatives of U.S. labor organizations in Latin America was very significant. If their attitude was one of understanding and friendly cooperation, he said better relations would result; but if they interfered too openly in internal affairs, there would be conflicts.

President Kennedy hoped that President Goulart would have the opportunity to discuss fully labor problems in his subsequent meetings with labor leaders and with the Secretary of Labor. He also expressed his concern over the need to strengthen labor relations, so that no break would occur. He would like to receive from President Goulart a memorandum suggesting how best to promote greater harmony in the United States-Latin American labor relations.

President Goulart said that the labor situation as heretofore discussed did not present any unsurmountable difficulties. He then mentioned that labor attachés at the U.S. Embassy often intervened too directly in the affairs of Brazilian labor organizations. He said, by the same token, caution should be exercised in implementing Alliance for Progress programs, so that feelings of national pride were not hurt. It must be borne in mind, he said, that the poorer people are the prouder they are and that such interventions were particularly strong under the Eisenhower administration. He said that it did not appear that the representatives of the AFL–CIO in Latin America were fully aware of the different approach that must be adopted. He noted that it was also necessary to make a joint effort to dispel many misunderstandings existing about the U.S. which are prevalent among certain significant areas of public opinion. As for the misconceptions about Brazil, he said, it sufficed to mention the many accusations of communist sympathies leveled at him.

He concluded by expressing the certainty that these minor difficulties could be easily solved.

> *Note:* At this stage the two Presidents joined the Foreign Minister, Secretary of State and other aides in the next room.

224. Memorandum of Conversation

Washington, April 4, 1962, 10:16–11:13 a.m.

SUBJECT

US-Brazilian Relations

PARTICIPANTS

For Brazil:
President Goulart
Minister of Foreign Relations Francisco Clementino San Tiago Dantas
General Amaury Kruel, Head of the Military Household
Mario Gibson Barbosa, Head of the Cabinet of the Ministry of Foreign Affairs
Ambassador Campos, Brazilian Ambassador to the U.S.

For the United States:
The President
Mr. Arthur Schlesinger, White House
Ambassador Gordon, U.S. Ambassador to Brazil
Assistant Secretary of State Edwin Martin
Deputy Assistant Secretary of State Richard Goodwin
Mr. Teodoro Moscoso, AID

[Here follows discussion of public utilities questions.]

He then asked Ambassador Campos to go through a series of points, largely in the economic field. Campos covered the following:

1. President Goulart is anxious to have emergency economic assistance while his reform proposals are before the Brazilian Congress, in order to insure confidence in the future. He needs things like the Northeast project to get the support and help of the people generally.

2. They were anxious to proceed with a three-year wheat agreement and thought there would be no Argentine objection.

3. They welcomed United States support for a worldwide coffee agreement of a long term character. They also were glad to have the United States help with respect to discrimination against coffee by the Common Market and against the excise taxes in Germany and elsewhere. They would need United States assistance in financing the eradication of excess coffee trees. They welcomed the encouragement they had had in this matter so far. They had a plan ready which should bring the surplus under control and will give it to the Department of State. They hoped they could have the President's personal support.

Source: Department of State, Presidential Memoranda of Conversation: Lot 66 D 149. Official Use Only. The meeting took place at the White House. The time of the meeting was taken from the President's Appointment Book. (Kennedy Library) Approved in S on April 12 and in the White House on April 16.

4. The Brazilian Government was disappointed in the recent allocation of sugar under the barter arrangement. They could have sold 300 thousand tons but were only permitted to sell 50 thousand tons. They hoped for a permanent quota under the new law, though they are not sure what form the law will take.

5. They were disturbed that, while the United States heretofore supported the idea of a regional compensation scheme for fluctuations in export earnings while an international one was being worked out, we had now abandoned this position in favor of working only on a global scheme. They felt it would take too long to work out a global arrangement.

The Brazilian Finance Minister expressed their satisfaction with the understanding reached with Secretary Dillon and his confidence that the program for financial recovery would proceed successfully. They had not sought the approval of the Fund for this program but believed they could, nevertheless, control inflation and then come back for further discussions with the Fund.

Ambassador Campos continued that the previous difficulties with the Eximbank with respect to releases under the May 1961 agreement had been solved. However, some Brazilian applicants for export financing were coming back with reports that the Eximbank said they were closed for business with Brazil and this was bad for Brazil's credit generally. They had also been frozen out of the IBRD with no loans since 1958, while $400 million had gone to other Latin American countries and another $400 million to South Asia. They felt that these were not constructive attitudes and hoped the United States Government would try to change them.

With respect to the European Common Market, Brazil welcomed the lowering of trade barriers which might result from our trade legislation and negotiations, and expressed appreciation for our efforts to secure a lowering of barriers against Latin American exports. They also supported Nigeria in the proposal to eliminate tariff barriers entirely on tropical products, especially coffee. The UK negotiations may present a new problem in terms of securing discriminatory treatment for coffee from Tanganyika and Kenya. Brazil is looking forward to the forthcoming meeting in Geneva on tropical products and hoped they would have our strong support on matters of interest to Brazil and Latin America.

President Kennedy replied that we had a great interest in the Northeast program and hoped it would have immediate and visible effects. Our aid last year was in large part really appreciated only by bankers and the program it was supporting did not have readily visible results even though it did limit the balance of payments troubles. Last year's effort was a major one and it was essential that what we do from here on out really have an impact, not only in the Northeast but elsewhere in the country as well.

He reviewed the general history of our financial transactions with Brazil and expressed satisfaction with the result of the Dillon–Moreira Salles discussion. The President emphasized the necessity of getting Congress to go along with our actions and, therefore, we must show results from the use of our money. We realized that Brazilians need funds to get a stabilization program going but after the discouraging results of last year, we have to reach a balance and keep a proper relation between the use of our funds and Brazilian action in order to keep Congress in a mood to support us and if possible to secure IMF support as well. He understood the Brazilians were in agreement with Dillon that this really should be carefully worked out by stages. The Brazilian Finance Minister said there was agreement. President Kennedy continued that if they implemented the program it would become easier for the IMF to enter the picture and we would continue to press them, but the Brazilians must act first.

With respect to wheat he emphasized the need to consider the export position of other countries but agreed to look right away into the prospects for a multi-year agreement.

He endorsed the general lines of the coffee program, emphasizing the importance of production controls by all countries, not only Brazil.

With respect to sugar the President emphasized the desire of United States producers to take over more of the United States market. He thought 50,000 tons, which was about one-third of what was available, was not bad for Brazil in view of the competition.

The President thought it was wrong to think the Eximbank closed to Brazilians, although they do have heavy commitments in Brazil. He said he would seek to clarify this. He asked if they were seeing Mr. Linder and Mr. Black to discuss the Eximbank and IBRD problems and they said they were.

The President went on to say that we were trying our best to protect Latin America with respect to the Common Market. The possibilities for preferences for French and UK African territories was of great concern to us. He personally had talked to Erhard, DeGaulle, Mende, and others about this and would continue to do so. Our real interest in all this, of course, is its effect on Latin America.

Deputy Herbert Levy was asked to comment on the coffee situation by President Goulart. He called attention to the fact that Brazil had carried the burden of world over-production as she was the only country which had kept surpluses off the market. Brazil could not carry this umbrella over the market indefinitely and the burden must be shared on a global basis. He also pointed out the contribution that this policy had made to inflation in Brazil. The President agreed fully with this analysis.

Ambassador Gordon mentioned that the Embassy had received the eradication plan two weeks ago and had made preliminary recommendations. It looked promising on first review.

The President commented that he assumed the IBRD problem had to do with the balance of payments situation. The Brazilian Finance Minister agreed.

Foreign Minister Dantas mentioned that they had been discussing the need for measures to implement the Alliance for Progress in Brazil and had been thinking of reviving the joint commission which had once existed. In discussions the day before with Ambassador Gordon, the latter had suggested a more simplified arrangement which they thought now might be preferable. The President suggested they continue to talk to Ambassador Gordon and see what could be worked out. The old joint commission was successful but the conditions and problems are somewhat different now and there are hemispheric organizational arrangements to take into account. We certainly do need better priorities and better-prepared applications from Brazil for specific development projects. The President then asked Mr. Moscoso to comment.

Mr. Moscoso said that we will be happy to study the question of better means for cooperation on our side, but that the first problem is one of effective Brazilian machinery for program coordination, establishment of priorities, and preparation of projects. President Goulart agreed.

Foreign Minister Dantas emphasized that their thought now is not so much one of a joint commission, but rather the permanent availability in Brazil of representatives of the main outside financing agencies, U.S. and international, to work closely together with the new Brazilian machinery which they would establish.

225. Memorandum Prepared by Director of Central Intelligence McCone

Washington, April 4, 1962.

MEMORANDUM OF DINNER [CONVERSATION] HELD ON EVE-
NING OF APRIL 4, 1962, AT BRAZILIAN EMBASSY FOR PRES-
IDENT GOULART

In attendance were the President, Brazilian Ambassador Campos, Foreign Minister Francisco san Thiago Dantas, Former Brazilian Ambassador and now Minister of Finance Walther Moreira Salles, Secretary McNamara, Mr. John McCone, Ambassador Galbraith, Mr. Arthur Schlesinger, Mr. Richard Goodwin, Mr. Ted Sorensen, Mr. Walter Rostow, Mr. Ralph Dungan.

The meeting was informal. No serious general discussions took place. The atmosphere was very friendly and pleasant.

The following statements of significance were made to me.

1. The Minister of State (Foreign Minister) desires to discuss with us some facets of the organization of an intelligence service. What seems to concern him is the establishment of Bloc Embassies in Rio, and later in Brazilia, and steps that he should take to protect Brazilian security. Minister Dantas is leaving today with President Goulart but will return from Mexico City on Wednesday, April 11, and will be in Washington through April 13, and desires an appointment with us to discuss the above question.

Action: Two or three qualified people should be selected to prepare a presentation and discussion with the Minister. Either Assistant Secretary Martin or Dick Goodwin should also be present.

2. Dantas expressed concern over CIA. He said this concern is shared by most officials of Latin American countries and the root of concern was a feeling that the fundamental purpose of CIA was to create a worldwide secret police force strong enough to influence and affect countries in which they operated. I assured him that CIA had no such purpose but the intelligence apparatus of the Soviet Union definitely had such purpose in mind.

Action: In connection with the meeting mentioned above, a presentation should be made, to the extent possible, of the operations of the Soviet foreign intelligence apparatus, most particularly the evidences we have of its penetration in Brazil.

Source: Central Intelligence Agency, Job 80–B01285A, DCI/McCone Files, Memoranda to the Record. Secret. Drafted by McCone on April 5. Copies were sent to General Carter and to Helms, Earman, and Elder.

3. The Foreign Minister expressed concern over the forthcoming elections, indicating a wave of liberalism that could very possibly place in the House of Representatives and the Senate undesirable people. He expressed particular concern over the actions of Julio who he felt to be a dangerous character.

In this connection, Dantas stated that a considerable quantity of Czechoslovakian arms had been sent into Northeast Brazil by Castro. He had investigated because the original reports were that arms were "old muskets" and therefore not useable; however, he was now under the impression that they were very modern, effective light arms and this action by Castro, if true, concerned him greatly.

Action: We should discuss this matter further and then arrange through WH for a thorough and immediate verification.

4. As an opposing point of view on the political situation, the Minister of Finance, Mr. Walther Moreira Salles (former Ambassador), felt there was a very strong "swing to the right" in Brazil and therefore in all probability a number of right wing representatives would probably be elected and this would be a bad thing for the country because, in his opinion, their presence in the government would be resented by the extremes on the left who would stir up the masses and cause great trouble.

5. Neither Dantas nor Salles felt that the Communist Party was a strong influence in Brazil, that Brazil would ever succumb to Communism, that the free enterprise system would be preserved, and that such utilities as transportation facilities, etc., as might be nationalized, which would be a step necessary to their social and economic development, would be done on a proper reimbursable basis. Incidentally, it was stated that the takeover of IT&T was a result of a deadlock in the negotiations and not an arbitrary action on the part of the State.

Action: I believe the above and many other subjects of interest can be explored at the time of the meeting mentioned above.

Note: I would be happy to arrange a small stag dinner at my home for the Foreign Minister and the Ambassador, which should follow the conference mentioned above.[1]

John A. McCone[2]

---

[1] No record of this meeting was found.

[2] Printed from a copy that bears this typed signature.

226.   Memorandum of Discussion With Secretary of State Rusk

Washington, April 10, 1962.

SUBJECT

Brazilian Foreign Minister Dantas

1.   Rusk explained that he had had confidential discussion with Dantas concerning Cuba and had told Dantas that Castro's affiliation with International Communism and his efforts to subvert or otherwise influence other Caribbean and Latin American countries were not negotiable as far as the United States was concerned. Rusk indicated other matters such as compensation for American properties, etc. were in his opinion negotiable.

2.   Dantas has told Rusk that the Castro regime was split at the top and that his Ambassador had reported a serious conflict existed between Castro and his followers on the one hand and the hard-line Communists on the other. Dantas felt that this split might be capitalized on and the Communist regime disposed of. Rusk encouraged this thinking and urged me to explore carefully with Dantas [less than 1 line of source text not declassified].

3.   Rusk envisaged a two-stage operation; first the rupture between Castro and the Communist [less than 1 line of source text not declassified]. At one point Rusk intimated that Castro might be acceptable if free of Communist influence. McCone disagreed.

4.   Rusk felt we should attempt to develop a direct unattributable contact with Castro as the ability to reach him might be important at some future time.

5.   Rusk denied any involvement in policy on Food for Prisoners. McCone expressed great concern over AG's talks with Perrez and President's meeting this afternoon with Cardona, which Rusk knew nothing about. Apparently probing in this area is being done outside of State.

6.   In summary, Rusk felt we should recruit Dantas' assistance to split Castro and the Communists but should not under any circumstances reveal our decision reference Castro.

John A. McCone[1]
Director

Source: Central Intelligence Agency, Job 80–B01285A, DCI/McCone Files, Memoranda to the Record. Secret. Drafted on April 11.

[1] Printed from a copy that bears this typed signature.

227. Memorandum of Conversation

Washington, April 12, 1962, 1 p.m.

SUBJECT

Mexican-Brazilian Communiqué

PARTICIPANTS

For Brazil:
Foreign Minister Dantas
Head of Cabinet of Ministry of Foreign Affairs Gibson
Ambassador Campos, Brazilian Ambassador to U.S.

For the United States:
Secretary Rusk
Ambassador Gordon, U.S. Ambassador to Brazil
Mr. Edwin M. Martin, Assistant Secretary, ARA

During luncheon the Secretary pointed out some of the difficulties it created for American public opinion to read in the Goulart–Mateos[1] communiqué that the two governments had no "ties with any political-military group." It was the view of many Americans that we were participating together in an inter-American system which included defense arrangements under the Rio Treaty.

Our public could even less understand the need or the appropriateness of this kind of denial when they read in the immediate next paragraph the commitment to observe the arrangements in force for "mutual assistance for the Hemisphere's defense."

There ensued a discussion of what the Brazilians meant by an independent foreign policy as distinguished from systematic neutralism in which Dantas emphasized that they were supporting a policy which was in Brazil's interest and would reach conclusions on international issues independently and as a reflection of their interests after careful examination of both sides. They would not be systematically neutral, which he interpreted to mean a member of a bloc which always advocated the middle position between the Soviet bloc and the Western bloc. In other words, they would exercise judgment and choose sides on specific issues.

The Secretary emphasized the importance in this respect of careful appraisal of the validity of the respective positions, pointing out that

---

Source: Department of State, Secretary's Memoranda of Conversation: Lot 65 D 330. Confidential. Drafted by Martin.

[1] Following his visit to the United States, President Goulart flew to Mexico City on April 8 where he held talks with President Adolfo Lopez Mateos. They issued a joint communiqué reaffirming the independence of Brazilian and Mexican foreign policies from any political or military bloc.

those who sought regularly for a middle ground merely encouraged the West to take an extreme position rather than a conciliatory one, since any concession by us merely moved the middle point over more closely to the Soviet position. Dantas seemed to understand this and agree with it.

The Secretary finally said that we would not object to an independent policy, in fact he wanted our friends to be independent but he thought that, if it were one that did reflect real judgment between the two camps, our common background and heritage and beliefs would bring them to our support more often than not.

228. Report From the Inter-Departmental Survey Team on Brazil to President Kennedy

Washington, November 3, 1962.

DEAR MR. PRESIDENT: In accordance with your wishes, the Secretary of State appointed us a survey group to visit Brazil and to submit appropriate recommendations. Our briefings in Washington started on October first; we spent ten days in Rio de Janeiro, a day in Brasilia, two days in Sao Paulo and three days in Northeast Brazil.

We learned that Brazil is on the verge of financial collapse. Since you then expected to visit Brazil in November, we dispatched preliminary reports on October 23 and October 25 to the Secretary of State.[1] Although you have now postponed your Brazilian trip, we confirm our preliminary recommendations, and repeat them later in this report.

Scope of Our Discussions

Our discussions in Washington included meetings with most of those concerned with Brazil in the several departments of our govern-

---

Source: Kennedy Library, National Security Files, William H. Brubeck Series, Brazil, November–December 1962. Secret. Under the provisions of NSAM 173, "Interdepartmental Field Visits," July 18, the Special Group (Counter-Insurgency) approved the creation of a joint survey team, headed by General William H. Draper, Jr., to examine the effectiveness of the cooperation of the Country Team in Brazil and the departments and agencies in Washington with which they worked. The Draper Commission spent 16 days traveling throughout Brazil in October 1962. (Department of State, NSAM Files: Lot 72 D 316)

[1] The preliminary report of October 23 was transmitted in telegram 912 from Rio de Janeiro, October 24. (Ibid., Central Files, 732.00/10–2661) The text of the other preliminary report was not found.

ment, and with the heads of the Export-Import Bank, the World Bank and the International Monetary Fund. In Brazil Ambassador Gordon and his entire Country Team in the cities we visited gave us every possible cooperation, advice and help. We talked there with many officers of all the U.S. agencies represented in Brazil.

One or more members of the group met with President Goulart, the Prime Minister, Finance Minister, Minister charged with Planning, Superintendent of Money and Credit (SUMOC) and with officials of the Banco do Brasil and of the Northeast Development Agency (SUDENE), as well as with several Governors, Military Commanders and other officials.

We met with groups from the American Chamber of Commerce in both Rio de Janeiro and Sao Paulo and with a number of other American and Brazilian businessmen and bankers. We had discussions with both the local and foreign heads of the two large utility companies, American Foreign Power and Brazilian Light and Power, which the Brazilian government proposes to take over. In Panama, where we prepared much of this report, we had the benefit of the views of the Military Commander in the Caribbean area, whose interests include Brazil, and of his Political Advisor.

You will recognize that we could not check all the aspects of the problems involved in the time available and that our conclusions and recommendations, which are all unanimous, are necessarily largely based on a synthesis and analysis of the information and opinions given us by those with whom we talked.

[Here follows a section entitled "The Country Team."]

The Image of the United States

There is in Brazil a long established and still effective tradition of special friendship with the United States, as between the two great, progressive, and non-Spanish powers of the Western Hemisphere. This tradition is still powerfully supported, especially within the military establishment, by pride in the fact that Brazil was the only Latin American state to make a substantial military contribution in World War II, as a loyal ally of the United States.

Since 1945 this favorable image has been clouded by a Brazilian feeling that the United States tends to take Brazil too much for granted, in particular that the United States has denied to Brazil the aid urgently required for its development while granting lavish aid less important allies, and even to neutralists. This feeling that the United States has disregarded Brazil's needs and importance has been vigorously exploited by Communists and ultra-nationalists to whip up anti-American sentiment. These efforts have not materially affected the bulk of the population, but criticism of the United States and a sympathetic attitude toward

Castro's Cuba have received increasing acceptance in political and intellectual circles.

The recent forceful action of the United States with respect to Cuba, and the revelation of the extent of the Soviet presence in that country, is doing much to restore a more favorable image of the United States in Brazil. The friends of the United States have been emboldened to speak up. Even such a violent critic of the United States as Brizola has now found it expedient to denounce Khrushchev's exploitation of Cuba in the face of the resurgence of pro-U.S. and anti-Castro sentiment.

The Political Situation

The Brazilians are convinced that theirs is a great country with a great future and that they are competent to manage their own affairs. They are disposed to claim U.S. financial support as a matter of right in consideration of Brazil's importance to the United States, but are highly sensitive to any implication of U.S. tutelage or direction. This nationalistic attitude is not a new thing attributable to the perversity of the present Brazilian administration. It has been growing for a generation, but is now more acute than ever.

The parliamentary system which was improvised as a condition precedent to Goulart's accession to the presidency has failed to function. Since then Brazil has been virtually without an effective national government; all concerned have attempted to evade responsibility for the political drift and rapid financial deterioration which have characterized the period. Goulart has been obsessed with his struggle to recover full presidential powers.

The recent election was peaceful enough but it was not conclusive—both left and right had gains and losses, and the presidential issue was not directly involved. Almost certainly, however, the presidential system will be restored through the plebiscite to be held in January.

Goulart's political career has been based on demagogic leadership of organized labor, after the fashion of Vargas and Peron. His future course is unpredictable. He is essentially a clever opportunist, with no strong motivation save his craving for popularity and personal power. He is facile in political maneuver, but plays by ear according to the need and inspiration of the moment. It is unlikely that he fully comprehends or is competent to cope with Brazil's desperate financial situation. He is not likely to take drastic remedial measures which would adversely affect his popularity so long as he can avoid them. If faced with a financial crisis which threatened his tenure of office, he would take whatever course seemed best calculated to ensure his retention of power and would have no personal conviction or inhibition against turning to the Soviet Bloc. The present deterrents to that course are (1) continuing hope of greater U.S. aid, (2) reduced Soviet prestige since the backdown in Cuba, and (3) fear of provoking a military coup.

A significant consequence of Goulart's political opportunism is the favor and patronage which he has shown to Communists and suspected Communists throughout his career, in return for their political support. Almost certainly Goulart believes that the men he has appointed to key positions in his administration are personally loyal to him, but his tolerance and patronage have been affording the Communists an unprecedented opportunity to infiltrate the Federal bureaucracy.

The policy of the Communist Party in Brazil is calculated to make the most of this opportunity. The Party is numerically weak; it has no significant capabilities for revolutionary or guerrilla action. With the apparent sanction of Moscow, it has chosen to pursue its purposes by political action—by identifying itself with and fomenting anti-U.S. nationalism and radicalism, by infiltrating the bureaucracy and the leftist political parties, by extending its influence and control in organized labor and student groups, and by working to regain legal status as a political party.

Traditionally, the Brazilian armed forces have considered themselves the guardians of constitutional order, above considerations of party politics. The unsuccessful attempt of the high command to prevent Goulart's succession spread confusion in the military establishment and weakened the unity essential to this traditional role. Goulart has now appointed to high command officers on whom he believes he can rely, because they share his political views, or because they are personally committed to uphold his constitutional authority. Although the bulk of the officer corps remains highly dissatisfied with the political tendencies of the Goulart regime, a military move to overthrow the regime is highly unlikely, except in the event of an extreme provocation or a severe national crisis.

In consequence, Goulart may well serve out the remaining three years of his term, unless the rapidly deteriorating financial situation and resulting popular discontent should become so acute that the military, with substantial political support, would conclude that a political change was imperative.

As long as Goulart remains in office, the United States should continue its efforts to make him realize the gravity of Brazil's financial and economic situation, and continue to urge the adoption of adequate remedial measures which would justify our large-scale financial help. At the same time we should attempt to influence his political orientation in directions better calculated to serve U.S. interests.

The United States should also intensify its intelligence concerning, and unobtrusively maintain contact with, any military and political elements of a potential and more friendly alternative regime, and should be prepared to act promptly and effectively in support of such a regime, in case the impending financial crisis or some other eventuality should result in the displacement of Goulart.

Assuming Goulart's continuation in office, the United States should begin now to identify those political elements which it would wish to see prevail in the election of 1965, and to consider ways and means of discreetly supporting them in that election.

[Here follow sections entitled "The Financial Crisis," "The Alliance for Progress," "The Population Problem," "Other Economic Problems," "The Military Assistance Program," and "The Information Program."]

Summarized Recommendations

Political

Washington should issue clear policy guidance setting forth the United States attitude, strategy and tactics toward the Goulart Administration.

Financial

Ambassador Gordon should immediately inform President Goulart of the U.S. assessment of the Brazilian financial situation, should explain that the size of the 1963 external deficit is too large for U.S. resources alone to meet, should nevertheless offer our help, if a workable stabilization plan is made effective, and should recommend that Brazil adopt a stabilization plan acceptable to the European creditors and to the International Monetary Fund, whose help will also be required.

We suggest that you confirm this position and offer of help in a personal letter to President Goulart for the record and for possible future use.

Because the Brazilian Constitution requires that legislation making structural tax changes be enacted before November 30, 1962 and making changes in tax rates before December 31, 1962, if the legislation is to become effective during 1963, we believe these recommended actions should be taken at the earliest possible moment.

If the Goulart Administration accepts these suggestions, and the Brazilian Congress enacts the necessary tax legislation, the United States should do everything possible to negotiate a stabilization plan acceptable to the Brazilian Government and to the International Monetary Fund.

If, however, no satisfactory plan is worked out and the Brazilian Government is unable to meet its maturing obligations, the United States should still offer limited help, such as PL 480 wheat and an Export-Import loan for oil, while the Brazilian situation is being clarified, attempting to use aid and other U.S. resources to orient the Brazilian Government as closely as possible toward U.S. objectives.

Alliance for Progress

The overriding need for financial stability in Brazil should be given precedence over new Alliance for Progress projects, except as counterpart funds become available which are not needed for budgetary support.

All presently approved Alliance for Progress programs, and particularly the Northeast Program, should be reduced to specific, funded projects within the next six months and implemented as rapidly as possible. The Ambassador should be given ample authority to accomplish this.

Population

We recommend that you appoint a Commission to study the implications of rapidly growing populations and their relationship to economic development, particularly in underdeveloped countries, and to recommend to you the related policies best suited to accomplish the aims of the United States in its foreign economic assistance programs.

Economic

The United States should stress the need for increased Brazilian exports of both agricultural commodities and industrial goods, and should encourage Brazil to increase its production of wheat to reduce its future dependence on PL 480 wheat from the United States.

Military

Every effort should be made to increase the number of Brazilian officers assigned for training in U.S. Military Schools, as only a small percentage of available vacancies have been filled during the past two years.

Our Mission in Brazil should bring pressure at the earliest appropriate time on the Brazilian Navy and the Brazilian Air Force to resolve the controversy that now makes the only Brazilian aircraft carrier inoperable and which has caused a serious rift between these two services.

Conclusion

The political and economic future of Brazil is of tremendous importance to the United States. Its orientation toward or away from the West will greatly influence the other Latin American Republics.

While the present difficulties in Brazil are primarily financial, they stem from what we believe is an incorrect economic philosophy.

Brazil has given the expansion of her economy highest priority among her economic objectives, and has counted on inflationary governmental spending and United States aid to make up any resulting deficit. Nationalistic policies have put up bars to the vital capital from abroad that otherwise would have eased Brazil's problems.

Economic laws eventually operate in the same way throughout the world. Brazil is no exception to the fact that a depreciating currency robs the population generally of its savings and that inflation, if uncontrolled, eventually leads to financial disaster.

Germany and Japan are examples of war shattered economies which adopted sound measures to rebuild their currencies and to restore their prosperity. In both countries the spirit of the slogan "Export or Die" became the dominant force that led to the solution of their balance of payments difficulties, which were much greater in 1945 than Brazil's similar difficulties are today.

France, Greece and Spain are other examples of countries which have overcome their internal budgetary difficulties and their external deficits by adopting sound but harsh measures and then strictly enforced them.

Political calm and economic sanity are both essential to solve Brazil's difficulties.

In Germany, Adenauer and Erhard have made up the politico-economic team. In Japan it was Yoshida and Ikeda. In France General de Gaulle held the fort while Pinay carried out the economic program.

If we could persuade President Goulart of this thesis—this economic philosophy—and he could keep Brazil calm politically while some man of his choosing laid down and enforced the necessary financial and economic measures, Goulart could become the saviour of his country's economy.

Perhaps this is too much to expect or even to hope for, but as the traditional and sincere friend of Brazil, and in our own interest as well, we should do our utmost in this direction.

Respectfully yours,

William H. Draper, Jr.
Chairman

Douglas V. Johnson
Department of Defense

Ludwell L. Montague
Central Intelligence Agency

Thomas E. Naughten
Agency for International Development

C. Edward Wells
United States Information Agency

Henry J. Costanzo
Treasury Department

William B. Connett, Jr.
Department of State

229. Memorandum From the Executive Secretary of the Department of State (Brubeck) to the President's Special Assistant for National Security Affairs (Bundy)[1]

Washington, November 30, 1962.

SUBJECT

Brazilian Situation

The Department has been deeply concerned for some time with political and economic developments in Brazil. Following the return of the Draper Mission and the consideration of its report, the Department in collaboration with other interested agencies instructed Ambassador Gordon to take up with the President of Brazil our concern with both the political orientation of the Brazilian Government and the deterioration of its financial situation. (Telegrams attached at Tab A.)[1]

The Brazilian Government subsequently planned to send to the United States for financial discussions the ex-Foreign Minister, who is to be the new Minister of Finance, Santiago Dantas, and we had intended to raise with him also important political questions. The Brazilian Government has now determined to postpone Dantas' visit until January because its stabilization program is not complete and therefore it is not yet ready to discuss the need for external financial assistance. We welcome this postponement since it will give us additional time to determine our future policies toward Brazil in both political and economic fields.

As a result of further discussions recently with President Goulart and other Brazilian officials, Ambassador Gordon has been able to

---

Source: Kennedy Library, President's Office Files, Brazil—General, 1962. Secret.
[1] None found attached to the source text.

explore the situation further, to probe President Goulart's position and to confront him on significant issues in which we are in disagreement. We have commented in return on the Ambassador's reports. (Telegrams attached at Tab B.)[2]

Notwithstanding the postponement of the Dantas' visit Ambassador Gordon is arriving for consultations in Washington between December 4 and December 8, primarily on the Brazilian political situation but also on financial, aid, and other aspects of our relations with Brazil. It is hoped the Ambassador will have an opportunity to review the Brazilian situation with the President before his return to Brazil.[3] As a result of the consultations with Ambassador Gordon we hope to have recommendations regarding our Brazilian policy, particularly in the short term, to submit to the President for his approval early in the week of December 10.[4]

PW Kriebel[5]

---

[2] None found attached to the source text.
[3] No record of any such meeting appears in the President's Appointment Book. (Kennedy Library)
[4] See Document 230.
[5] Kriebel signed for Brubeck above Brubeck's typed signature.

230. Memorandum Prepared for the National Security Council Executive Committee Meeting

Washington, December 11, 1962.

U.S. SHORT-TERM POLICY TOWARD BRAZIL

Recommendation

It is recommended that

1. Within the next two weeks, i.e., before Christmas 1962, there be a discussion with President Goulart in general terms, which would reflect the views of President Kennedy and which would emphasize (a) U.S. concern over political and economic developments in Brazil; (b) U.S. desire to collaborate with Brazil in both political and economic fields; and (c) U.S. conviction that such collaboration will be impaired as long as certain difficulties persist. A proposed speaking paper to initiate such a discussion is contained in the draft at Tab A[1] (it is left open whether the discussion on behalf of the President should be by a representative sent specially for that purpose or by the U.S. Ambassador speaking for and on instruction from the President).

2. Thereafter there be conducted with President Goulart a continuing personal dialogue on behalf of President Kennedy (in which Presidential letters could be used as well as personal representations by the Ambassador) on selected specific issues of major importance. It is probable that the major immediate issues will concern Brazilian internal decisions in the economic field (economic stabilization and climate for private foreign investment). However, these will also have substantial political significance and internal political repercussions.

3. If President Goulart's initial reaction to these discussions should be favorable and he should begin to change accordingly the orientation of his government, the U.S. should avoid ostentatious favoritism toward those elements in Brazil friendly to us but hostile to President Goulart.

4. Actions which the U.S. should initiate in the OAS with respect to Cuba for the purpose of protecting national and hemispheric interests

---

Source: Kennedy Library, National Security Files, Countries Series, Brazil, November 16–30, 1962. Secret. The meeting was scheduled for December 11 at 10 a.m. A December 12 memorandum from Brubeck to Martin, Gordon, and Moscoso, excerpts NSC Executive Committee Record of Action for this meeting. It concluded that the President "accepted the recommendation that our best course of action is to seek to change the political and economic orientation of Brazilian President Goulart and his Government" and decided to send a special envoy to Brazil to speak with President Goulart. (Department of State, Central Files, 611.32/12–1262) Attorney General Kennedy met with Goulart in Brasilia on December 17. A memorandum of their conversation, December 19, was transmitted in airgram A–710 from Rio de Janeiro, December 19. (Ibid., 033.1100–KE/12–1962)

[1] Not printed.

should not be avoided for fear of adverse Brazilian reaction. At the same time, otherwise unsound actions should not be initiated merely for the purpose of isolating Brazil.

5.   The question of the date of a Presidential visit to Brazil should be deferred for the time being.

6.   Any further large-scale assistance to Brazil in connection with an economic stabilization program should be considered only after Brazil had taken certain significant positive steps, both economic and political, and should be phased in accordance with Brazilian performance under such a program. Specific precondition should include satisfactory settlement of the IT&T Case, a clear Brazilian Administration position on remedying the defects in the present profits remittance law, and a public posture of collaboration in the Alliance for Progress, in addition to the necessary measures for economic stabilization.

Reasons

1.   The existing alternatives for the United States are:

A. To do nothing and allow the present drift to continue.
B. [2 *lines of source text not declassified*]
C. To seek to change the political and economic orientation of Goulart and his government.

2.   Alternative A is rejected because the Brazilian internal and external financial crisis, with exhaustion of foreign exchange reserves, will require a United States reaction, either positive or negative, to the new Brazilian economic stabilization program to be presented in January. The present situation, in short, is unstable, and will have to turn soon either for the better or for the even worse. (See Tab B for description of present political and economic situation.)[2]

3.   [7 *lines of source text not declassified*]

4.   Alternative C is selected as the only feasible present approach and as one having a reasonable chance of success. [1 *line of source text not declassified*]

5.   The following considerations indicate that representations should be made to President Goulart within the very near future:

(a) The Brazilian critical foreign exchange problem is imminent and the Dantas mission to the United States to seek large-scale economic assistance is expected in mid-January.

(b) President Goulart will be making decisions on new government appointments in anticipation of the restoration of the presidential system following the January 6 plebiscite.

(c) U.S. prestige and credibility are high and Soviet reliability correspondingly low as a result of the Cuban crisis. (This, however, may be a diminishing asset with the passage of time.)

---

[2] Not printed.

6. Confrontation of President Goulart on internal and external policies may produce a change of trend, but is unlikely to bring a total one-shot conversion. It will be necessary to maintain pressure and continually to join issue with him on specific topics. Having in mind our evaluation of President Goulart and our past experience with him this can best be accomplished by:

A. Creation of a personal relationship between President Kennedy and President Goulart with repeated personal approaches to President Goulart on behalf of President Kennedy.

B. Simple ad hoc approaches related to specific issues and situations.

C. Seeking to influence key Goulart advisers receptive to our views.

D. Continuing to encourage Brazilian moderate democratic elements in Congress, the Armed Forces and elsewhere who advocate domestic and foreign policies which we can support.

E. Adjusting U.S. assistance and cooperation to Brazilian performance.

F. Making any financial assistance required to meet immediate foreign exchange shortages available on a short-term basis on conditions implying no long-term commitment.

G. Pressing President Goulart to take public positions on issues which are critical for U.S.-Brazilian cooperation.

H. Large tolerance of Brazilian differences with us on non-essential matters.

7. With the passing of the Cuban crisis, Cuba is not a major issue in Brazil. Actions with respect to Cuba in OAS should not be contrived merely to challenge Brazil. But essential hemispheric decisions on Cuba can be utilized to apply pressure and force choices.

Discussion

In January or soon thereafter representatives of President Goulart, led by the new Finance Minister San Tiago Dantas, will be coming to this country to explore with us a large-scale, long-term program for bringing under control their deteriorating financial situation. They will be asking us for substantial financial assistance and for support in obtaining help from other governments and international agencies. However, it is undesirable to address ourselves seriously to this important problem without some clearing of the air with the Brazilian Government on recent adverse political developments in Brazil. Also we need to present our views on the political front immediately so that we can bring our influence to bear on important near-future political decisions (e.g., appointments to the new cabinet). A political confrontation and developments flowing from it could help clear the air sufficiently so that we will know in which direction to move not only in the matter of broad financial assistance but also in various other dealings with the Brazilian Government. Such a political confrontation now would be especially timely in view of the foregoing factors.

Unconditional support to the Goulart administration without a political confrontation might be justified now only if we wanted to gain time against a strong expectation that events within the country would bring about either the early overthrow of President Goulart or a near-future change in his policies. We might then continue unqualified support to maintain a favorable image of the U.S. in Brazil and to deny ammunition for diversionary tactics by President Goulart and his supporters. However, such unconditional support cannot be justified because (a) there is not sufficient expectation that either of the alternatives will come to pass without some positive action on our part; (b) our unconditional support could in fact encourage President Goulart and extremists around him to continue their present course and we would thus contribute to a further deterioration of the political and economic situation.

There are limited possibilities of confronting President Goulart on the international front. Unless Brazil should make a clear break with the rest of the countries of this hemisphere, an effective confrontation will be difficult. While the Brazilian position was ambiguous and deliberately confused during the recent Cuba experience, they did vote along with the other American Republics. It is possible that Brazil might be forced to shift its policy to avoid putting itself in isolation in the hemisphere. In this regard, however, we can only continue our firm policy in the OAS and confront or isolate Brazil only as Brazil makes such action necessary. We should not, however, overlook opportunities to deny prestige to Brazil's "neutralist, peace-making" role insofar as it encourages resistance to U.S. policy objectives in this hemisphere.

One should not expect that a major political confrontation with President Goulart will bring about his sudden and complete conversion. He will still maintain at least some of his alliances with leftist elements. He will still be limited by his own ineffectiveness and excessive pre-occupation with political power maneuvers. A major political confrontation could, however, influence President Goulart toward a more moderate and more constructive political course, including much heavier reliance on center forces in the country willing to collaborate with him if he acts responsibly, in which more harmonious U.S.-Brazil relations could be maintained.

If there is such a political confrontation, it is unlikely that President Goulart will react violently against the representations or against the U.S. unless our posture is too drastic. It will be necessary to avoid any suggestion that President Goulart is incompetent or ineffective. It may be necessary in the discussion to acknowledge some of the leftist developments of the past eight months as part of an understandable past political strategy even while we object thereto in terms of their adverse impact on U.S.-Brazil relations. It may be necessary to stress the importance of key government personnel more fully representative of Brazilian political thinking as a basis for effective Brazil-U.S. relations, rather than directly criticizing the quality and character of recent cabinets. In short, the confrontation must be phrased so as to avoid any avoidable offense to President Goulart.

The confrontation must also offer positive inducements. Not only might there be a citation of the unhappy experience of other nations which have trusted the communist nations too much, but there should be positive expressions about President Kennedy's great hopes for the future of Latin America; about the need for hemispheric solidarity in improving, and accelerating advances under, the Alliance for Progress; and about the special leadership role of Brazil as the southern giant. It would be useful, too, to cite the precedent of President Goulart's early political patron, Getulio Vargas, who in the early '40s made the wise decision of putting Brazil unequivocally on the side of the Allies and who developed a special relationship with President Roosevelt in so doing. Additionally it would be desirable to hold forth the promise of serious consideration to their request for help on their larger financial program, based on a serious effort to promote development within a framework of financial stabilization. All of this would be phrased as contingent upon the expectation that obstructions to effective Brazil-U.S. relations would be removed.

From past experience it is probable that President Goulart will appear reasonably responsive in any confrontation along the lines suggested above. However, experience has also demonstrated that President Goulart can be glib on general assurances and weak on specific performance. It would therefore be desirable for the U.S. Ambassador to follow up and discuss one at a time in subsequent conversations with President Goulart all of the important items covered in the general confrontation. One meeting, for example, might be on the subject of positive steps being taken by the U.S. to move ahead on the Alliance for Progress and the matching steps which should be taken by the Brazilian Government to give positive constructive support to the Alliance as a joint Latin American-U.S. venture. Another meeting might be devoted to the climate for private investment and obstructions thereto. There will be many other specific issues for similar follow-up.

The foregoing course of action could discourage, but is not designed specifically to cope with, the possibility that President Goulart may have decided, or may decide, to move toward a left-wing dictatorship or toward other undemocratic developments, with the support of his extreme leftist allies. This might involve suspending the Congress or intervention in the government of various states. [3-1/2 lines of source text not declassified]

231. Memorandum of Conversation

Washington, December 26, 1962.

SUBJECT

   United States-Brazil Relations

PARTICIPANTS

   Ambassador Roberto Campos of Brazil

   ARA/P—Mr. J. F. King

Last night Ambassador Roberto Campos called to quiz me about a "press campaign" against Brazil being inspired by the United States Government, particularly the State Department. His main concern in the 30–45 minute conversation was that United States Government officials, by "overblowing" current United States-Brazil differences, were creating a situation where "animal reactions which cannot be controlled" might result. He made this point several times in the talk, insisting that the situation is getting dangerous.

He said that in the past week or so three reputable newsmen have come to him to express shock that State Department officials were talking so freely about the deterioration of United States-Brazilian relations. One, he said, indicated that his department sources (I'm pretty sure he was referring to me) seemed to be goading the reporter to take a hard line in his stories on the Attorney General's visit to Brasilia.

I asked for specifics but what really seemed to be bothering him was President Kennedy's comments on Brazil earlier this month, both at his press conference and during the questions and answers following his speech in New York to the Economic Club.[1] As to who in the Department might be fomenting the hard line against Brazil, the Ambassador said it isn't just Department officials but A.I.D. and Eximbank too. He said the three major newsmagazines and the major un-struck papers (with the exception of the *Christian Science Monitor*) had all taken the hard line against Brazil in recent weeks. This criticism was becoming "too humiliating," he said.

The Ambassador at another point in the talk referred to the negotiations for a United States loan of $30 million to tide Brazil over the thin

---

Source: Department of State, Central Files, 611.32/12–2662. Official Use Only. Drafted by King on December 27.

[1] At his December 12 press conference President Kennedy expressed his "strong concern" with Brazil's high rate of inflation, which he said was raising the Brazilian cost of living, reducing the effectiveness of U.S. economic assistance, contributing to the flight of capital from Brazil, and diminishing the stability of the state. (*Public Papers of the Presidents of the United States: John F. Kennedy, 1962*, p. 871) At the Economic Club of New York on December 14, President Kennedy repeated these concerns. (Ibid., p. 549)

part of the new year. He said he sensed some foot-dragging by the United States Government on this, but conceded that holiday leaves may be responsible.

Throughout the talk the Ambassador kept referring to the United States Government's preoccupation with inflation in Brazil and repeated his contention that we overlook his country's solid growth in real terms, etc.

232.   Memorandum of Conversation

Washington, December 26, 1962.

SUBJECT

United States-Brazil Relations

PARTICIPANTS

Ambassador Roberto Campos of Brazil
ARA/P—Mr. J. F. King

This is chapter 2 of the memcon on my talk with Campos.[1] In urging the Ambassador to believe there is no calculated campaign by USG to blackguard the Brazilian government in the US press, I told him that our line to the press has been that we are waiting for action on the Goulart Administration's promises, not just the rephrasing of old promises. I said you had made this very point to Henry Raymont just yesterday evening. So this morning Henry called me to report that Campos had got him out of bed to pick his brains. Henry was at a loss to figure out what was going on, but he wondered why Campos was so upset.

Before I could digest this, Marcilio Moreira, second secretary at the embassy, called to discuss the "very dangerous situation that is blowing up just at the moment when we see most hope for definite improvement of relations." He mentioned that the Rio papers have been playing AP and UPI stories from Washington which comment darkly on the state of US-Brazil relations.

More important, Moreira said Campos is beginning to feel shut out of USG and that "he can't get through to anybody anymore." He men-

Source: Department of State, Central Files, 611.32/12–2662. Official Use Only. Drafted by King on December 27.

[1] See Document 233.

tioned in this connection that Rusk failed to telephone Campos as the Secretary had promised he would, and that Dillon has kept him waiting "weeks and weeks" for an appointment. "It looks like a policy decision to ignore the ambassador," said Moreira.

He added that Campos is going to Brazil January 2 and that if he comes back here without any word on his interim aid request or a general improvement of relations, Campos is finished as Ambassador. USG, said Moreira, was responsible for getting Campos fired once "and you saw what happened. I don't think you would want it to happen again."

233. Policy Guidelines Paper Prepared in the Department of State

Washington, undated.

GUIDELINES OF U.S. POLICY AND OPERATIONS

Brazil

I. *Basic Approach*

A stable, friendly, democratic Brazil is in the U.S. interest. In terms of population, area and economic potential, it stands in the front ranks of the nations of the world and is by far the largest and most populous nation in Latin America, comprising roughly one third of that region. In it are centered all of the political, economic and strategic problems to which the Alliance for Progress is a response.

We wish to see Brazil achieve orderly economic and social progress as a solid foundation for and as a means of strengthening its political democracy. We try to stimulate and support Brazilian efforts to accelerate sound economic development, more equitable distribution of resources, and social advances. We hope thereby to encourage resistance to the undemocratic extremes of both right and left. If U.S. policy fails on Brazil, it will become extremely difficult to achieve success elsewhere in Latin America.

Source: Department of State, S/P Files: Lot 69 D 121. Secret. The source text was transmitted by Brubeck to Ford of S/P under cover of a memorandum dated February 7, 1963, which stated that the paper was being disseminated on a need-to-know basis for use within the Executive Branch and at U.S. missions abroad.

We recognize Brazil's potential and ambition to achieve world-power status, as well as its position of leadership in Latin America, and we seek to channel Brazil's activities in world and hemispheric affairs into a constructive role for Free World interests.

[Here follows section II entitled "Background" comprising 23 pages.]

III. Objectives

A. Long Term

1. Assist Brazil to move toward economic and social progress under a democratic system to the end that it may become a strong member of the community of free nations.

2. Preserve Brazil's traditionally friendly orientation toward the United States and channel its growing "independence" in international affairs into support of U.S. foreign policy objectives and a constructive role for the free world.

3. Assist Brazil in the development, under conditions of financial stability, of a modern, dynamic competitive economy, which will form a solid foundation for democracy in a nation which has the potential of becoming a world power.

4. Assist Brazil in relieving widespread social pressures arising from chronic poverty and economic depression, especially in the potentially explosive Northeast.

5. Guide Brazil's youth into constructive programs to advance Brazil's freedom and progress.

6. Seek to maintain a favorable climate in Brazil for the investment of U.S. capital and to secure maximum participation of U.S. private investment in the Alliance for Progress program in Brazil.

7. Protect the right of U.S. enterprise to fair, prompt and adequate compensation in case of expropriation.

8. Increase the export and import trade between the two countries.

9. Encourage Brazil to extend financial, technical and other assistance to neighboring, less economically developed countries.

B. Short Term

1. Demonstrate the effectiveness of the Alliance for Progress by concrete accomplishments.

2. Insure continued U.S. access to and use of those facilities and sites in Brazilian territory which are determined to be required in our military and space programs, including the following:

a. airport, dock and communications facilities at Recife needed to support the Atlantic missile range and other operations in the area;

b. continued operation by the United States of Radio Rio (in the Brazilian Navy Ministry) as part of the U.S. naval communications system.

3. Strengthen the determination and capability of the Brazilian armed forces to detect and cope with Communist infiltration and subversion, and other civil disorders.

4. Obtain removal by Brazil of the existing discriminations against foreign, including U.S., shipping.

5. Secure Brazil's continued respect and application of the principles contained in our Air Transport Agreement with Brazil.

6. Preserve mutually satisfactory trade relations with Brazil under the GATT.

7. Enlist Brazil's diplomatic assistance (within or without the UN) in influencing the Government of Portugal to institute reforms in her colonial policy in Africa.

[Here follow sections IV and V entitled "Lines of Action," and "Contingencies" comprising a total of 13 pages.]

---

234.   Special National Intelligence Estimate

SNIE 93–63   Washington, February 27, 1963.

THE CHARACTER OF THE GOULART REGIME IN BRAZIL

The Problem

To estimate the character of the Goulart regime and the courses of action it is likely to take with respect to the financial problems confronting Brazil.

Note

This summary estimate is based on extensive research done in preparation for a more elaborate national intelligence estimate on the situation and prospects in Brazil. This summary treatment is presented now in view of the impending visit of the Brazilian Minister of Finance. The more extensive estimate will be produced later, when the results of his visit can be taken into account.

Source: Central Intelligence Agency Files, Job 79–R01212A, ODDI Registry. Secret; Controlled Dissemination.

The Estimate

1. President Goulart is essentially an opportunist. Although his political career has been based primarily on association with organized labor and radical nationalists, including associations with known and suspected Communists, there is little reason to believe that he is dedicated to a radical transformation of Brazilian society or to a radical reorientation of Brazil's independent foreign policy. He appears to be interested in political power primarily for the personal prestige, popularity, and perquisites to be gained thereby. If he believed it to be politically feasible, he would probably seek to establish a more authoritarian government along the lines of Vargas' *Estado Novo* (1937–1945) or the Peron regime in Argentina.

2. The circumstances of his accession to the presidency of Brazil have given Goulart a deep distrust of actual or potential opposition, particularly in the military establishment. He has taken care to appoint to high civil and military offices men on whose continuing personal support he has felt he could rely. A considerable number of them have been notably pro-Communist or anti-US in attitude. Nevertheless, Goulart has also among his advisers men of more moderate views. In domestic and foreign policy he has shifted from moderate to radical attitudes and back again according to his calculation of the political requirements of the moment.

3. Until recently Goulart has been preoccupied with his campaign to recover full presidential powers, to the neglect of the problems presented by Brazil's runaway inflation and by mounting budgetary and foreign exchange deficits. Having recovered full powers, he is now addressing himself to these problems. His principal advisers on these matters are Celso Furtado,[1] author of a three-year plan for economic development, and San Thiago Dantas,[2] the new minister of finance, whose task it is to obtain urgently needed external financial support.

4. Since 1950 Brazil's expansionist economic policies have produced a claimed growth in GNP averaging 6 percent per year, or nearly 3 percent on a per capita basis. These policies have also led to large deficits in the balance of payments and to domestic inflation, which in 1962 exceeded 50 percent per year. Inflation has in turn tended to aggravate the balance of payments problem, partly by its adverse effects on the

---

[1] Furtado is a reputable economist and planner with an eclectic, but predominantly statist attitude. He was formerly active in the Communist movement and still retains close associations with radical leftist and nationalist elements. [Footnote in the source text.]

[2] San Thiago Dantas is a political opportunist. Originally a Brazilian fascist, he perceived the political potential of Goulart's Labor Party and became one of its principal leaders. Although best known for his opposition to the US at Punta del Este, he is currently urging Goulart toward an accommodation with the US in order to obtain US financial support. [Footnote in the source text.]

flow of private capital; it has tended to stimulate remittances and to reduce new foreign investment. To some extent inflation has also discouraged exports, notably of meat, and has encouraged large-scale smuggling to the detriment of government tax and exchange income. At the present time Brazil has an external debt totaling about 3 billion dollars. Payments of over 900 million are due in 1963, of which an estimated 200–300 million dollars is owed to private and official US creditors. Of the estimated 1963 balance of payments deficit of 825 million dollars about 500 million remains uncovered by financing now in sight.

5.   As indicated in Furtado's three-year plan of economic development, the government gives priority to maintaining rapid economic growth, but also proposes a gradual attack on domestic inflation. According to the plan, GNP is to grow at 7 percent per year, supported by annual foreign loans and capital investment of 500 million dollars to maintain developmental imports at the level of recent years. The rate of inflation is to be reduced to 25 percent in 1963 and 15 percent in 1964 through various measures of internal reform, including decreases in government expenditures and increases in revenue, the reduction of subsidies, and the use of "non-inflationary" means to finance government deficits. Steps have already been taken to increase taxes on income and consumption and to remove subsidies on imported wheat, newsprint, and petroleum.

6.   The Furtado plan appears to have been designed with Goulart's political needs very much in mind and in an effort to solve Brazil's financial problems without austerity. It attempts the difficult feat of reducing the rate of inflation and at the same time maintaining a high rate of economic growth, and relies on extensive foreign assistance to make these both possible. Although the plan calls for certain unilateral Brazilian actions, it provides little evidence of any disposition to face the hard realities of the Brazilian situation or to make decisions of a politically difficult character.

7.   Negotiations in recent months appear to have shaken the belief of the Goulart regime that the US is so deeply committed that it must come to an arrangement satisfactory to Brazil. The Brazilians now appear to realize that the US will not meet all of Brazil's financial needs, and to recognize that agreement with the US and the IMF is prerequisite to satisfactory arrangements with European and private creditors. Dantas has said that the Brazilian government is willing to go beyond the stabilization measures contained in the Furtado plan. However, Goulart is most unlikely to make any concessions that he would consider prejudicial to the maintenance of a high rate of economic growth in Brazil, a matter of prime political concern, and this will seriously limit his ability to attack effectively inflation and the balance of payments problem.

8. If the financial assistance which Dantas is able to obtain from Western sources falls far short of that which Brazil now seeks, a substantial default on Brazil's external obligations would be inevitable and severe economic disruption and hardship would ensue. In such circumstances, Goulart would probably adopt a radical leftist, ultranationalist policy line and intensify efforts to obtain aid from the Soviet Bloc. While the Bloc could make considerable contributions to Brazilian development over the longer term, it is unlikely that it could render much effective aid on short notice. Goulart would seek to blame the economic deterioration on US hard-heartedness, probably with considerable success. He would seek to control the internal situation through the imposition of authoritarian political and economic controls, and to disarm any opposition by appeals to Brazilian patriotism.

9. If Dantas does obtain sufficient financial assistance to support substantially the Furtado plan, Goulart may conclude that it would be to his political advantage to pursue a moderate political course for the next year or two. His constancy cannot be relied upon, however. His course will be determined by the pressures exerted upon him from all sides as the political situation develops. If it appeared to him that he was losing his basic support on the left without gaining any reliable compensatory support at the center, he would be likely to revert to a leftist, ultranationalist course.

10. Should Goulart embark on an extreme radical-authoritarian course, he would risk provoking a military-conservative coup against him, a factor which would be taken into account in his calculations. Such a coup's chances of success would depend to a considerable degree on how the issue was defined and the lines drawn, as well as on the timing. As time passes, Goulart will have the opportunity to establish more of his personal supporters in key military positions, thus strengthening his control over the military establishment and reducing the likelihood of a successful coup.

11. Under even the most favorable conditions, Brazil faces the prospect of serious economic difficulties and recurrent political crises during the next year or two.

235.   Memorandum From the Ambassador to Brazil (Gordon) to President Kennedy

Washington, undated.

SUBJECT

Brazilian Political Developments and U.S. Assistance

I.   The Problem

Brazil's new Finance Minister, Dr. San Thiago Dantas, is now planning to engage in talks in Washington for a week to ten days beginning March 11 with high officials of the U.S. Government, the Managing Director of the IMF and representatives of other international financial institutions. He will be seeking external financial assistance to support the Goulart administration efforts to reduce substantially and progressively the rate of inflation in Brazil while maintaining a high rate of economic development. His aim will be an assistance package, including debt postponement, short term balance of payments assistance, and long term development assistance within the Alliance for Progress, if possible backed jointly by the U.S. Government, European governments and Japan, the IMF, and perhaps the Inter-American Development Bank and the World Bank.

Our preliminary analysis of the Brazilian stabilization and development effort, which is still being reviewed in technical bilateral and IMF talks, indicates that it does contain the essential ingredients of an effective program, although a large number of technical and policy questions have yet to be resolved. Actions have already been taken by the GOB under this program, including tax increases, elimination of major import subsidies, restraint of excessive credit expansion, and formal adoption of a program for large-scale budget cuts. The program is being pursued with an apparent firmness of purpose unmatched in Brazil in recent years. The GOB has also taken steps to eliminate certain specific areas of friction between Brazil and the U.S., including a satisfactory interim

---

Source: Department of State, Central Files, POL 1 BRAZ–US. Secret. Drafted by Gordon. The paper was sent with a second paper (not printed), which summarized recent Brazilian political developments, under cover of a memorandum from Brubeck to Bundy dated March 6. The covering memorandum stated that the document was discussed on March 5 by senior representatives of the Departments of State and Defense, AID, and CIA all of whom had contributed to the documents considered at the December 11 meeting of the NSC Executive Committee (see Document 230). At their March 5 meeting they agreed that the approach described in the undated memorandum from Gordon was sound and that the decisions reached at the December 11 meeting were still valid.

settlement of the IT&T expropriation case,[1] tentative agreement to reasonable voluntary purchase terms for the AMFORP electric utility properties, and the removal of discrimination against import of sulphur from the U.S.

At the same time, although there has been some improvement since last December, there is a continuing problem of communist and other extreme nationalist, far left wing, and anti-American infiltration in important civilian and military posts within the government, and governmental tolerance or even encouragement of communist and other extreme left wing influence in trade union and student organizations. The foreign policy of the Goulart administration, likewise, although showing some sense of greater cooperativeness with the U.S. is still equivocal, with neutralist overtones, on various issues including Cuba, arms control, and trade and aid relations with the Soviet bloc.

Assuming agreement by the GOB on an effective economic program for stabilization and development, therefore, the question remains whether Brazil's domestic and foreign political trends warrant U.S. economic support and if so, on what terms. If the answer is negative, there arises the subsidiary problem of whether Finance Minister Dantas should not be advised to cancel his now scheduled mission.

Our preliminary analysis indicates that, if an agreement can be worked out between Brazil and the IMF, and if reasonable European support can be secured, the U.S. resources required for aid to Brazil during the 12 months of April 1963–March 1964, apart from the release of $84 million remaining from the May 1961 "stabilization support package," would be in the general magnitude of $200 million.

II.   Recommendations

It is recommended that support be given to a technically satisfactory Brazilian program for economic stabilization and development, but on a "short-leash" basis permitting periodic review and making possible the withdrawal of support on either economic or political grounds. The support program should be scaled over time in relation to balance-of-payments needs and should be contingent upon explicit standards of GOB performance in implementing the necessary economic policies. At the same time, continuous diplomatic pressure should be maintained for the reduction of communist and other extremist influences within the government and for the pursuit of policies favoring democratic development, strengthening the private sector of the Brazilian economy (both

---

[1] At their meetings April 3–5, Presidents Kennedy and Goulart agreed that in cases involving the nationalization of foreign companies by the Brazilian Government, "the principle of fair compensation with reinvestment in other sectors important to Brazilian economic development" would be maintained. See *Public Papers of the Presidents of the United States: John F. Kennedy, 1962,* pp. 287–289, and Documents 223 and 224.

domestic and foreign), and progressively shifting the "independent foreign policy" toward more systematic collaboration with the U.S. and the free world.

Parallel with the basic relationship with the Brazilian government summarized above, efforts should be maintained to strengthen and encourage democratic anti-communist forces outside the government. The principal organizations involved are the Congress, the vast majority of the state governors, the military officer corps, the Sao Paulo industrial community, mass media of public information, the Church, and labor and student groups. This effort should be directed at reducing the likelihood of a further leftist-nationalist swing by Goulart and, if this proves impossible, to prepare the most promising possible environment for his replacement by a more desirable regime in the event that conditions deteriorate to the point where coups and counter-coups are attempted.

The basic strategy, in short, should continue to be one of encouraging Goulart to constructive courses of action, strengthening the forces restraining him from undesirable courses of action, and strengthening the prospects for a favorable successor regime if the constitutional order breaks down.

As an immediate step, the Dantas mission should be received on March 11 and the program for economic stabilization and development should be encouraged. During the Dantas visit, appropriate occasions should be used to restate our continuing concern with the political problems pointed out to Goulart by the Attorney General in December.

[Here follows section III entitled "Considerations."]

IV. *Alternative Courses of Action*

Support by the U.S. for the Brazilian effort at economic stabilization and development involves two dimensions: time and quantity. There is considerable flexibility as to the lengths of time for which we might make a forward commitment, the circumstances for periodic review, and the associated conditions of performance on the Brazilian side. In the dimension of quantity, however, there is less flexibility, since effective support requires that the combined external sources—U.S., European, Japanese, and international institutions—be sufficient to permit Brazil to maintain the inflow of raw materials, capital goods, oil and wheat required for continued growth while also meeting its external financial obligations. In the first phase, therefore, which includes the immediate balance-of-payments needs pending negotiation of an accord with the IMF, followed by nine to twelve months of combined balance-of-payments and development support related to assistance from the IMF and from other creditor countries, the realistic alternatives are *adequate support* or *no support*. In a later phase, implying a well thought through development program under the Alliance for Progress, there might be a much wider range of choice on the volume and sources of support.

The alternative of withholding support is advocated by a few conservative Brazilian political leaders and by some U.S. businessmen with long experience in Brazil. Their argument is that Goulart is absolutely untrustworthy, anti-American by instinct, and consciously or unconsciously inclined toward putting the country either under outright communist control or under some form of national-socialist, Peronist, syndicalist dictatorship—which would be almost as bad from the viewpoint of U.S.-Brazilian relationships. If we refuse support, they argue, the resultant combination of debt defaults and import shrinkage will bring about such a deterioration in social and economic conditions as to entail serious internal disorder permitting a right wing coup to replace Goulart by a more satisfactory regime. The bulk of the Brazilian business community, and some portion of the American, are disposed to give some margin of confidence to the Dantas' effort, although they are deeply suspicious of both him and Goulart.

The Embassy has sought to appraise carefully the strength of center and right wing opposition to Goulart and the likelihood of a successful coup against him. Our present view is that, in the absence of overtly unconstitutional action by Goulart himself there does not now exist in Brazil adequate leadership, organization, or strength to carry out such a coup successfully. The military attitudes are crucial in this regard. The bulk of the officer corps, although suspicious of Goulart, retain their deeply rooted Brazilian tradition of support for legally constituted civilian authority. If an obviously illegal initiative were taken by Goulart, there is a substantial prospect of a successful center-right reaction. The mere deterioration of confidence as a result of non-support for the economic program by the U.S., however, cannot be relied upon to lead to a successful center-right action against Goulart.

The exact nature of a Goulart reaction to a refusal of U.S. support is not easy to predict. At one point last November, he indicated as the alternative a kind of blackmail threat of turning to the Russians, as well as denouncing the U.S., defaulting on debt payments, nationalizing foreign enterprise, and tightening the Brazilian belt through a radical socializing program. Subsequently he has carefully eschewed the repetition of such threats.

In recent weeks, the Soviet Ambassador has been actively courting Goulart, but we are not informed on the details of their conversations. Apart from the dubious question of large scale Soviet support, it is plausible to expect a violently nationalist reaction against the stabilization effort in the event of American non-support, combined with a debt moratorium and adverse action of many types against American business interests. The Alliance for Progress in Brazil would come to a quick and sticky end. Although Brazilian economic conditions would be gravely impaired, the nationalist impulse toward closing ranks behind Goulart might keep him in power for a substantial period.

Given the presence of an apparently constructive and genuine effort at economic stabilization and development, modest (though still far from satisfactory) improvement in domestic political orientation, and at least a temporary disposition for collaboration with the U.S. under the Alliance for Progress and in other ways, the superior alternative clearly appears to be as recommended in Section II above.

236. Memorandum of Conversation

Washington, March 12, 1963, 12:30 p.m.

SUBJECT

> Brazilian Political Situation

PARTICIPANTS

U.S.	Brazil
The Secretary of State	Finance Minister Dantas
Asst. Secretary Martin	Ambassador Campos
Ambassador Gordon	Ambassador Bernardes
A.J. DeSeabra (Interpreter)	

Minister Dantas then presented a broad picture of the Brazilian situation. It was his impression that Brazil had entered a phase of its political evolution whose importance could not be ignored by the U.S. Government. Following two years of instability and efforts to find the right road that marked the parliamentary experiment, the present Government was in a position of firm authority derived from the will of the people as expressed in the recent plebiscite. That Government was now ready to carry out a financial policy that would have significant political consequences. That policy, as already explained to Secretary Dillon, to the President himself and to other U.S. officials had as its objective monetary stability with continued economic development. If that policy were successful in attaining those goals, then Brazil could consolidate its position

---

Source: Department of State, Central Files, POL BRAZ. Confidential. Drafted by DeSeabra of L/S and approved in S on March 26.

as one of the truly important democracies in the Western World. Brazil was fully aware of the fact that on today's world stage there was something else in addition to the U.S.-Soviet conflict. That was an emerging European force wanting to be independent and to attract into its sphere of influence the new African nations. The fact that Brazil was a democracy with a solid foundation of private enterprise was a historical event whose importance should not be minimized. The efforts of the present administration in Brazil were aimed at the preservation of free enterprise, and there was no move to increase government intervention in the nation's economy. What there was was a concerted and integrated effort to create a neo-capitalism unlike anything that ever existed before in Brazil. That fact was more important than any isolated pronouncement by this or that political leader. The situation in Brazil had to be viewed as a de facto situation and all its consequences realistically gauged. The very geographic position in Brazil involved ties with the U.S. that should never be a source of concern to Brazil or to the U.S. There were left-wing movements and trends in Brazil and that was something to be expected in a country where the economy was still weak, which was beset by many unsolved social problems, and which was still in the process of consolidating its democracy. However, the development of Brazil as contemplated in the present historical context could not help but bring ever closer together the destinies of the Brazilian and the U.S. democracies. It must be borne in mind that if Brazil were to fall prey to any subversive movement fostered and abetted by the Soviets, it would then lose its opportunity to carry forward its national emancipation, because it would become a mere battlefield of the cold war where the events would be dictated by U.S. and Soviet moves. It was Minister Dantas' firm conviction that Brazil is sincerely oriented toward effective cooperation with the U.S. But that cooperation would become a reality only to the extent that Brazil would be able to attain its objectives of political and economic stability in the shortest possible time. Following the conclusion of Minister Dantas' statement, the Secretary and his callers went to lunch.

237. Telegram From the Department of State to the Embassy in Brazil

Washington, March 13, 1963, 8:21 p.m.

1677. Subject: Conversation between President and Brazilian Fin-Min Dantas 3/11/63. Following uncleared interpreters' memorandum of conversation for information only and contents should not be disclosed to foreign officials. It is uncleared and subject to amendment upon review.[1]

President welcomed Minister Dantas and said thought he had come at most useful time for discussion matters concern both countries.

Dantas thanked President, presented Goulart's greetings and handed him two letters from Goulart.[2] He expressed Goulart's hope President Kennedy would visit Brazil. President Kennedy replied that such a visit must certainly take place during the present terms of office of himself and Goulart, and they would have to consider a satisfactory time for such a visit.

Dantas explained purpose his call was to discuss Brazil's economic and political situation in all frankness and clarify some aspects of situation which are objects of concern to United States, including some aspects which already discussed during Attorney General Kennedy's visit Brazil. He particularly wanted bring President up to date on how things stand now that government has retuned to Presidential system, thanks to plebiscite.[3]

Plebiscite has enabled Goulart establish government of solid authority, marked by unity of purpose. Plebiscite was categorical in extending overwhelming popular support to Goulart. Consequently, Goulart believes he will now be able deal with Brazil's problems along lines he had already described to President Kennedy.

Goulart feels present situation Brazil such that he will be able bring about a democratic consolidation of country. Best way to do this is through government that has great popular support and enjoys confi-

---

Source: Kennedy Library, National Security Files, Countries Series, Brazil, March 12–21, 1963. Secret; Priority; Limit Distribution. Drafted by Burton and Crane; cleared by Gordon, Wellman of ARA/EST and S/S; and approved by E.M. Martin.

[1] No formal memorandum of conversation was found in Department of State, Presidential Memoranda of Conversation: Lot 66 D 149. A place-holding card in this file directs the reader to telegram 1677 for a record of the conversation. The card notes that the telegram's account had been reviewed by the White House and cleared.

[2] Both letters dated March 8; for full texts, see ibid.: Presidential Correspondence: Lot 66 D 204.

[3] Reference is to the January 6 plebiscite that restored to the Brazilian Presidency those powers curtailed by the September 2, 1961, amendment to the Brazilian constitution. See Document 213.

dence of working class. This was case of Vargas administration. Vargas exercised type leadership that attracted progressive and liberal elements and Goulart believes he can do same, i.e., have a democratic government supported by working classes.

[Here follows discussion of Brazil's economic stabilization plan.]

Next question Dantas raised was US concern that Communists have infiltrated GOB. Dantas said this infiltration greatly over-estimated, and added that label of "Communist" has been attached to people who have leftist tendencies but are not members of Communist party.

[Here follows discussion of left-wing elements within Brazilian Government and society.]

Dantas then brought up Brazil's view of Cuban situation. This already discussed by representatives of US and Brazil, but he felt it worthwhile go over it again. Goulart government must maintain consistent relationship with public opinion, particularly left of center groups that support it. Public opinion on Cuba varies considerably in Brazil, but there is no doubt that when there is danger of military aggression based on Cuba, the government's stand is fully supported by people. This was clearly shown at the time of naval quarantine last October and Brazilian vote on this in OAS. When, however, it is matter of hostility towards regime itself, situation is different. Dantas assured President Kennedy that in the case of real security threat from Cuba, Brazilian people will support US fully, and this support will in turn yield positive policy decisions on part of GOB.

[Here follows a discussion of public utilities in Brazil and Communist infiltration of the Brazilian labor movement.]

In conclusion, Dantas stressed Goulart's belief that this is decisive moment which will define Brazil's future role in Latin American framework. Brazil's democratic position is definite; Brazil is a friend of US and will remain so, with or without international cooperation. But effectiveness of Brazil's role in Latin America will depend on whether or not in 1963 & 1964 it succeeds in stabilization program and in strengthening private enterprise.

If Brazil succeeds, it can play important role in maintaining strength of West. If it fails, while there will be no shift in Brazil's ideological position, Brazil's effectiveness will be greatly reduced. Therefore, Goulart believes it is very important for United States and Brazil to come to understanding so as to assure success of stabilization plan.

President Kennedy thanked Dantas for his presentation and said he was pleased that a man of Dantas' experience and ability was working to solve major problem of obtaining stability plus growth. He wished Mr. Dantas success, adding that we in US have stability but not enough growth.

Details of how US can assist Brazil are to be discussed at later meetings with other officials of the Administration, but he assured Dantas that US wants to help. He explained it is becoming increasingly difficult for US to support efforts of other countries, adding that it is a bad mistake to set up a good plan which then fails owing to lack of adequate implementation and support. Therefore we hope American aid to Brazil will be used to meet Brazil's real needs.

President Kennedy then raised other matters which concern US, assuring Dantas that his comments were not to be taken as interference in Brazil's affairs, but simply as an expression of our interest in Brazil.

[Here follows discussion of Communist influence in the Brazilian labor movement.]

President Kennedy commented that he did not think it would be possible to bring complete social peace to Brazil in near future. (Even France, with great prosperity in recent years, has not been able to solve its social problems, witness current miners' strike.) He believes that it is most important to get rid of Communists in Army, labor movement, and Goulart's household. The Government is bound to have problems, and Communists will exploit them.

As for American aid to Brazil, we have various preoccupations here owing to expropriation of American firms in Brazil, certain aspects of Brazil's foreign policy, Brizola's activities, and situation in labor movement.

Furthermore, Alliance for Progress has been attacked in Brazil. Alliance for Progress is an effort by United States to help Latin America with hope that our aid will succeed. If we cannot hold out this hope, it is difficult to get American people to support long-range aid to Latin America. Attacks on Alliance by Brazilians make it difficult for us to help Brazil, and give impression that whatever we do it won't make much of a difference. The United States wants to help Brazil, provided we feel that our help can make a difference.

Ambassador Campos said reports here about Communists in Goulart's household are exaggerated. It is difficult to distinguish between various shades of leftism and communism. He said there are no communists in key positions of authority. Problem of Communist infiltration in labor movement is serious however. Situation arose because government tolerated their presence because it needed support of labor. Now, with split in labor over stabilization plan, Communists will be eliminated. Process may be more gradual than United States might like, but Campos believes there will be an erosion of Communist influence.

Dantas said government should remove all Communists because they present a danger to government. However, government cannot go so far in removing leftist elements that it appears to be a conservative government. If that happens, it would lose support of people.

President Kennedy said he had no objection to an "opening to the left," but that it should stop short of Communists. He also understands difficulty in distinguishing between Communists and leftists. He also knows that this is a matter that has been discussed by Ambassadors Campos and Gordon.

President stated his belief that situation in Latin America is critical to West. Latin America is a key element, and Brazil is key country in Latin America. He then wished Dantas success in his undertaking stressing once more his pleasure that a man of Dantas' capacity and experience had taken on very difficult task of promoting economic stabilization and development in Brazil. He suggested that they meet again to continue their talk, and a date was provisionally arranged for Thursday, March 21.[4]

Rusk

---

[4] President Kennedy and Minister Dantas met again at the White House March 25, 11–11:35 a.m., according to the President's Appointment Book. (Kennedy Library) No memorandum of their conversation has been found. At that time AID Administrator David E. Bell and Dantas signed an agreement by which the United States would provide Brazil with $385.5 million in economic assistance. See Department of State *Bulletin*, April 15, 1963, pp. 557–561.

---

238. Memorandum From the Officer in Charge of Brazilian Affairs (Burton) to the Assistant Secretary of State for Inter-American Affairs (Martin)

Washington, May 14, 1963.

SUBJECT

Proposals for Reducing Brazilian Resistances to U.S. Hemispheric Polices

1.   Brazil has shown an increasing tendency to reject the OAS or various key actions in the OAS and to seek action (a) in the UN, (b) in concert with other Latin America Republics, or (c) in an organization, such as

---

Source: Department of State, Central Files, POL BRAZ–US. Secret. Drafted by Burton and cleared in draft by Allen of ARA/RPA.

LAFTA, of which the U.S. is not a party. Other LA's, including major ones such as Chile or Mexico, have often been in agreement with Brazil.

2. Brazil has increasingly expressed its concern that the OAS (a) is being converted into an instrument for intervention into the internal affairs of individual nations, (b) is being used as an instrument for the imposition of U.S. objectives.

3. Brazil has become increasingly sensitive about its position as a major power in world affairs and increasingly resentful, it seems, of its "dependence" on the U.S. U.S. purchase of coffee and U.S. aid are, to many in Brazil, elements of a kind of dependence of which they would like to free themselves. This attitude can at some point provoke a kind of defiance and opposition which can give us very serious trouble.

4. While we can oppose and pressure Brazil vigorously on OAS, Cuba, and related issues—and I have strongly advocated this in various instances there may come a time when such tactics will work against us, when we will regret not having resorted more to other tactics, when we will find it imperative to win over Brazil and yet find it impossible because we started too late.

5. What I am suggesting is a more active effort to win Brazil over (and others in the process) by a vigorous consulting with Brazil in order to reach a greater meeting of minds on hemispheric problems. In this context we might sort out a number of things we are doing and decide that they are not worth the strains and cleavages they engender. Even if we agree on only limited measures of accommodation, the fact that we treat Brazil's views with respect by resorting to a greater exchange of views for the purpose of achieving a greater meeting of minds could bring a greater responsiveness on the part of the Brazilian Government.

6. While I would disagree vigorously with any suggestion that we are carrying on any kind of "war" against Brazil in hemispheric affairs, I would agree even more vigorously with Ambassador Gordon's recent efforts to initiate a more extensive exchange of views with the Government of Brazil on hemispheric matters—in which he needs our support.

7. My own limited background and exposure suggest that a rather serious reappraisal of our hemispheric measure—perhaps by a special group—would be desirable to decide whether certain of these measures generate dissensions and resistances which deter or destroy cooperation to major objectives far more than they contribute thereto. (Not an inter-agency group, but a committee of statesmen of the caliber of Bunker and Merchant.)

8. My more immediate concern is to obtain a greater measure of consultation between the U.S. and Brazil on hemispheric matters (a) to obtain a better understanding in the Brazilian Government of U.S. policy, (b) to make such accommodations to Brazil's views as may be appropriate, (c) to give Brazil a feeling that we accept and respect her position as a

major hemispheric power, (d) to win, in the process, a greater measure of responsiveness from Brazil in hemispheric matters. Such consultations, for maximum impact, must be carried on through our Embassy with the Brazilian Government. I think it would be generally agreed that the chief impact has to be on the government in Brazil, not the Brazilian representatives in the OAS or the UN.

Recommendations:[1]

That we take steps in cooperation with our Embassy in Brazil to initiate a more active and continuing dialogue with the Brazilian Government on hemispheric problems for the purposes set forth in 8 above. This is consistent with recent views and recommendations of Ambassador Gordon. (Recent Deptel 1939,[2] attached—particularly paragraph two—is a move in the direction recommended.)

That RPA have primary responsibility in ARA for the foregoing and that the Office of Brazil Affairs give supporting assistance.

---

[1] Martin approved both recommendations.
[2] Dated April 26. (Department of State, Central Files, CSM 9–6 LAT AM)

---

239. Telegram From the Department of State to the Embassy in Brazil

Washington, August 16, 1963, 5:37 p.m.

234. For Ambassador from Martin. In reviewing recent developments in Brazil as reported by Embassy, I am increasingly concerned that US image in Brazil, rightly or wrongly and probably largely wrongly, is dominated by three things: (1) pressure for financial austerity in support of IMF; (2) protection of US investments especially in public utilities; and (3) support for Governor Lacerda in his opposition to Goulart.

The first two are charges we must of course accept as we feel these objectives are in the long term interest of Brazil even more than US. The third, which is of course not well-founded, probably stems from the con-

---

Source: Kennedy Library, National Security Files, Countries Series, Brazil, August 21–31, 1963. Secret; Priority; Limit Distribution. Drafted by E.M. Martin; cleared by Weismann of ARA/BR, U.A. Johnson, and S/S; and approved by E.M. Martin.

servative image we have as a result of the first two points, as well as the probable tendency of the US business community in Brazil, a large and noticeable one, to take positions consistent with those of Governor Lacerda. It is probably also due in some part to erroneous claims of support by Lacerda, and to even more erroneous charges of support by irresponsible leftists. While I accept the impossibility of a public repudiation of Lacerda, I continue to feel that his general approach is too far on the right and too fanatically anti-Goulart to be accepted as a useful contribution to US objectives, and his tactics are equally irresponsible and unacceptable.

Regardless of the reasons, however, this is a false picture of US policy both in Brazil and in the Hemisphere. Its continuation can damage our position not only in Brazil but in other countries. It seems to me that we must seek means for impressing on Brazilian people and Government a better rounded picture of our objectives for Brazil. What I have in mind are stronger means of conveying this broader message supplementary to your speeches throughout the country with respect to economic development.

The lead is given, I think, in President Kennedy's August 2 press conference statement[1] which was picked up so avidly by President Goulart as if it were news. We should find additional means for emphasizing more clearly and widely by word, and insofar as possible by action, that we favor social and economic reform and development just as strongly as we favor financial stability and protection of foreign investment. You have shown that though it is more subtle point to get over to a mass audience, stability as a means to reform and development can also be defended. Such an emphasis would balance out the two rather negative parts of the image and by the difference which they would publicize between our views and those of Governor Lacerda on reform issues, indirectly accomplish much to disassociate ourselves from him without need for direct repudiation.

I realize the risks we may run in coming out in Brazil for reform in the same forthright way we do in other countries in view of the careless and often misdirected talk about reform which comes from Goulart and his entourage. I should think however that we could find means to prevent our reform objectives from being too readily confused with the demagoguery which stems from these sources, though we would have to confess that our ultimate objectives are similar to those which he and his associates announce.

---

[1] Reference is apparently to President Kennedy's August 1 press conference in which he emphasized the commitment of the United States to help Latin Americans implement "revolutionary," although peaceful, social and economic reforms through the Alliance for Progress. (*Public Papers of the Presidents of the United States: John F. Kennedy, 1963*, pp. 612–619)

I am sure such a program will not be an easy one to develop but it seems to me to be of early and crucial importance. I know we have discussed this general subject previously but I feel we must discuss it again. I would like urgently your views and recommendations.

In this connection a significant means for broadening the picture of the US could of course be a visit by President Kennedy, for his speeches would clearly have to stress in Brazil as elsewhere the revolutionary aspects of the Alliance as we see it. What are your views?

Rusk

240. Policy Paper Prepared in the Department of State and the Agency for International Development

Washington, September 30, 1963.

PROPOSED SHORT TERM POLICY—BRAZIL

The following assumptions, objectives, and lines of action are intended to provide guidelines for the conduct of U.S. relations and programs vis-à-vis Brazil up to the closing months of 1964 when the campaign for the Presidential succession will be getting into full swing, looking toward elections in October, 1965. These elections, apart from other developments on the national scene, should compel a fresh look. General assumptions are set forth at some length in the belief that a very extensive change can occur on very short notice in a country situation as viable and uncertain as that in Brazil; and if this happens, guidelines will need to be reexamined. In any event, a further comprehensive review should be made early in 1964 to consider the need for possible revisions in these guidelines.

Source: Department of State, Central Files, POL 1 BRAZ–US. Secret. A covering memorandum from Read to Bundy, October 1, explains that the paper was prepared jointly by Ambassador Gordon, ARA, and AID/LA for consideration at an October 3 meeting of the Latin American Policy Committee. No record of this meeting was found. ARA suggested that the paper be circulated to the members of the NSC Standing Group for their October 1 meeting. The Standing Group declined to discuss the paper at the meeting. Another covering memorandum, also dated October 1, from Stephen Wailes of S/S–S to Read indicates that the paper was circulated to Harriman.

Assumptions:

1. Goulart will continue his shifting game of political agitation, accommodation and manipulation with the objectives of (a) blunting the attack and winning at least the passive accommodation of the opposition (mainly of the center and right); and (b) maintaining his control over supporting elements in labor, the military, and other sectors (mainly of the left) while destroying or weakening those who would threaten or contest this control.

2. The demonstrated disinterest and incapacity of Goulart outside of the realm of tactical political manipulation, and the absence since last June of forceful leadership among Goulart's principal associates, makes it unlikely that he or his government will mount, much less follow through on, any substantial program of constructive economic and social betterment, especially where it involves significant measures of unpopular discipline, self-restraint or self-denial which would subject Goulart to serious political criticism.

3. While leftists and ultranationalists of various shades have for decades played significant parts in Brazilian politics and government, such individuals will continue to enjoy particular favor under the Goulart regime. Goulart will not be disposed to sacrifice the political support derived from his long-standing ties with extreme-leftist (including Communist) and ultranationalist elements, and he will continue to give them position and opportunity from which they can carry on their anti-U.S., and in some cases Moscow, Peking, or Havana Communist-line, advocacy in Brazil.

4. There is of course a possibility that the extreme left, or some elements thereof, may be tempted to break with Goulart because his manipulations to stay in power will also involve accommodations to the center and right, because he does not consistently collaborate in their own efforts to achieve and consolidate power, or because he is not achieving, at least formally, alleged social betterments. Goulart's capacity for accommodation and manipulation, plus extreme leftist reluctance to give up significant benefits, plus the fact that both would lose substantial strength in separating from each other, makes this an unlikely prospect.

5. Goulart himself will probably not be prepared to abandon his accommodations with more moderate political elements, and will probably seek to curb his extremist following on occasions when their excesses provoke strong reaction in the military and other quarters. Goulart's abandonment of this line in favor of unequivocal alignment with his extremist following is unlikely unless he comes to believe that they are so strong that this step offers the best opportunity for his political survival, or that other forces are so unequivocally opposed to him that he has no alternative base of support.

6. Ultranationalism (whose strong manifestations in Brazil can be traced back to the 30's and earlier, and which has periodically erupted since then) will continue to find strong support in many sectors in Brazil from left to right and will continue to present problems for American diplomacy and for U.S. private enterprise in Brazil, which is currently the main target of nationalists as were British interests in earlier years.

7. Goulart will continue to reassign and promote military officers within what he judges to be the limits of political feasibility in order to strengthen his supporters and to weaken those forces which might mount a political opposition to him within the armed services. While promotions and assignments have undoubtedly weakened anti-Goulart elements and in varying degrees strengthened pro-Goulart forces, opportunists, nationalists and leftists (including extremists in the latter two categories) in the Brazilian armed services, there continues to exist in the armed services a strong advocacy of law and order, and a substantial preference for orderly democratic processes which will react against extremist excesses either by the left or the right. This has been at least temporarily strengthened by the recent Sergeants' revolt. This means that while the already limited military capability to overthrow Goulart on purely political grounds has been further weakened, the capability for resistance to any clear-cut move against constitutionalism or against the military hierarchy as a body will probably continue and be capable of expressing itself not only against Goulart but also against any uncon-stitutional move against Goulart either from left or right.

8. There is still a significant reservoir in the armed services of actual and potential good-will toward the U.S.

9. The military appear to be the only force capable of maintaining and restoring public order—and, if necessary, orderly government—should the political and economic deterioration produced by the policies of the present regime "get out of hand."

10. While Goulart and the extreme leftists among his supporters have not demonstrated the capacity to pursue truly constructive courses of action (and Goulart himself probably lacks the desire to do so), they will continue to identify themselves in their public relations with pro-gressive and "popular" change (e.g., "basic reforms") while labelling the opposition as negative, reactionary, status quo, etc.

11. Goulart—to the extent that circumstances and his political manipulations might permit him to do so at minimum political risk—will seek to restrict and might even attempt to stifle democratic opposi-tion forces and processes. He would probably like to achieve a dictatorship on the models of Vargas or Peron, closing the Congress and intervening all the State governments.

12. Goulart's own ineptitude and political manipulations, coupled with increasing inflation and other economic deterioration, may create

sufficient political and social tensions as to bring about his "removal" or "withdrawal" from the Office of President, probably at military "urging," without his having taken obviously unconstitutional steps.

13. While Goulart will probably attempt to liquidate or weaken political forces which directly and seriously attack or threaten him, he will very likely stop short of such action against other democratically-oriented forces which do not offer this direct, personal threat. He will be motivated by fear of alienating too broad a spectrum of opinion and power, and also by the desire to retain some forces which can move against excesses by his own extremist supporters or be used as a counterweight against such supporters when they get out of hand.

14. Goulart may from time to time condone or even encourage in labor and other sectors, democratic elements opposed to the extreme leftist and ultranationalist elements who ordinarily support Goulart and enjoy his direct and indirect support—this to discourage the latter from "getting out of hand."

15. Key areas of activity in which one can have maximum impact on developments in Brazil, political and otherwise, include (a) government, including the State Governors and the Congress, (b) the military, (c) labor, (d) students, (e) the Catholic church, particularly church-sponsored community services and activities, (f) business and industry, and (g) the press, radio, and other media influencing general public opinion.

16. In the OAS and the UN, and in its foreign relations generally, Brazil will continue to pursue its "independent" foreign policy line, overreacting at times against U.S. and OAS "intrusions" into national sovereignty, seeking to realize its pretensions to world power status by providing leadership among the new and the underdeveloped nations as a kind of new "third force" in relation to the major powers and the developed nations. It will also continue to maneuver for the leadership of the Latin American nations through exclusively Latin American organs or arrangements from which the U.S. is excluded.

17. As part of the foregoing general policy, Brazil will continue to expand its relations with Communist nations, will overreact against identity with the free world "bloc"; but will at the same time stress its dedication to christian democracy and continue to work with the U.S. on a wide range of specific international issues in the UN, the OAS, and elsewhere.

18. Barring clear indications of serious likelihood of a political takeover by elements subservient to and supported by a foreign government, it would be against U.S. policy to intervene directly or indirectly in support of any move to overthrow the Goulart regime. In the event of a threatened foreign-government-affiliated political takeover, consideration of courses of action would be directed more broadly but directly to

the threatened takeover, rather than against Goulart (although some action against the latter might result).

19. While there are continuing efforts among them for reconciliation and coordination, there are many schisms and disagreements among the extreme left, the ultranationalists, and the Communists which can produce conflict within as well as among these various groups, and which can alienate from them the more moderate nationalists and leftists.

20. While the Goulart Government will continue to tolerate and nourish elements opposed to the U.S. and its objectives, Goulart's own friendship or antagonism toward the U.S. can temper or stimulate the behavior of such elements or the degree of official tolerance or acceptance of U.S. operations in Brazil.

Objectives:

1. Promote and strengthen in all sectors of Brazilian life democratically oriented forces which can restrain undemocratic or anti-democratic excesses by Goulart or his extreme leftist or ultranationalist supporters (and also, to the limited extent it threatens, by the extreme right as well), and facilitate the most favorable possible succession in the event that a crisis of regime leads to Goulart's removal, and in any case in the elections of 1965.

2. Promote the formulation and vigorous advocacy of constructive reform programs by the democratically oriented forces in Brazil so that they can compete more effectively against the rabble-rousing demogoguery of Goulart and his extremist supporters.

3. Maintain and build in Brazil a favorable image of the United States through all possible channels to counteract nationalist and ultranationalist attacks.

4. Weaken or soften by seduction as well as by opposition the opportunistic, ultranationalist or extreme leftist forces in Brazil in their affiliation with or support of antidemocratic or undemocratic agitations or causes.

5. Discourage counter-productive maneuvers by forces opposed to Goulart of a type which can be exploited by Goulart and his extremist supporters either to pursue their own demogogic political aggrandizement or to weaken the forces capable of restraining their undemocratic or antidemocratic excesses.

6. Avoid insofar as possible measures or policies by U.S. Government or U.S. business interests which can be exploited by anti-U.S. elements either to stir up nationalist antagonisms against the U.S. or to jeopardize the legitimate interests of the U.S. or its citizens by stimulating nationalistic hostility to them.

7. Maintain a friendly, helpful, posture toward Brazil and its government in order to maximize our ability, limited as it sometimes may be,

to carry forward our own programs and to protest more effectively against undemocratic elements and actions, especially as they are unfriendly to the U.S., U.S. business or U.S. nationals.

8. Build a more extensive consultation on U.S.and Brazilian foreign policy objectives, particularly as between the U.S. Embassy and the Brazilian Foreign Office, with a view to promoting a more receptive psychological climate in Brazil toward cooperation with the U.S.

9. Promote division and conflict within and between extreme leftist and ultranationalist groups and attempt to alienate other leftists and the more moderate nationalists from them.

10. Promote the formation of an effective coalition of politically effective forces which will present a viable alternative to the demagoguery of the extreme left and to the reactionary proposals of the far right.

11. Strengthen the basically democratic and pro-United States orientation of the military.

12. Weaken the influence of the Communist and other extremist anti-U.S. elements in both labor and student organizations.

[Here follows a section entitled "Lines of Action."]

BRITISH GUIANA

241. Memorandum of Conversation

Georgetown, February 16, 1961.

PARTICIPANTS

His Excellency Sir Ralph Grey, K.C.M.G., Governor of British Guiana
Mr. Rockwood H. Foster, West Indies Desk Officer, Department of State
Mr. Everett K. Melby

Mr. Foster called on the Governor of British Guiana on Thursday, February 16, and was later entertained at lunch by him.

In a brief discussion of the political situation in British Guiana before lunch, the Governor asked whether Mr. Foster had had an opportunity to talk with Dr. Jagan and then proceeded to give some of his own views on him and other B.G. political leaders.

The Governor throughout tended to minimize, if not discount, the view that Jagan was a communist. [1 *line of source text not declassified*] and his greatest weakness was his lack of appreciation of the responsibility of public office and his capacity to administer effectively [*4-1/2 lines of source text not declassified*].

Whatever the reasons for it, Sir Ralph said that in British Guiana politicians are forever looking for excuses why they cannot do something; it is the only country he knew in which a plausible excuse for inaction was an acceptable substitute for action.

As far as his Government was concerned, its primary objective was to leave the country as capable as possible to run its own affairs when it becomes independent. The U.K. has fully accepted the fact that the days when it can run British Guiana are over and it would like to get out of the business of running the country as gracefully and honorably as possible. He spoke of this as an obligation which was being discharged with no particular pleasure, implying that the U.K. had never had much out of the colony (though certain interests, of course, had made handsome economic profits), and that he did not feel it had the natural potential to compete successfully as an independent country with other former colonial areas of the U.K. Sir Ralph stated later in the meeting that B.G. in its present condition was hardly a good showpiece for what the "old imperialism" either had accomplished or was capable of accomplishing.

Source: Kennedy Library, Papers of Arthur M. Schlesinger, Jr., British Guiana—Jagan. Confidential. No drafting information appears on the source text. Transmitted to the Department of State as enclosure 5 to despatch 96.

242.   Special National Intelligence Estimate

SNIE 87.2–61   Washington, March 21, 1961.

PROSPECTS FOR BRITISH GUIANA

The Problem

To estimate the political situation and prospects in British Guiana, with particular reference to the coming elections and Communist potential in the colony.

The Estimate

1.   British Guiana is a small outpost of empire with a population of over half a million, about half East Indian in origin and about a third of African descent. The remainder of the population includes small numbers of British, Portuguese, native Indian, and Chinese residents. Partially self-governing since elections in 1957, the colony is scheduled to assume increased responsibilities for its own affairs following new elections on 21 August 1961 and, if all goes well, to gain full independence two or three years thereafter.

2.   The politics of British Guiana is dominated by the Communist-led People's Progressive Party (PPP) of Cheddi Jagan. Jagan is an East Indian, and his party draws its support almost entirely from East Indians, including not only poverty-stricken rural and urban workers, but also a considerable number of small businessmen in Georgetown and other centers. Jagan's US-born wife, who exercises very strong influence over him, is an acknowledged Communist. She shares with Jagan control of the PPP, and is a government minister. Several other PPP leaders are believed to be Communists. Jagan himself is not an acknowledged Communist, but his statements and actions over the years bear the marks of the indoctrination and advice the Communists have given him. While there is no Communist party per se in British Guiana, a number of the leaders in the PPP have been members of, or associated with, Communist parties or their front groups in the US and the UK.

3.   Moreover, these individual leaders maintain sporadic courier and liaison contacts with the British and US Communists and with Communist Bloc missions in London. Both Jagans have visited Cuba in the

Source: Central Intelligence Agency Files, Job 79–R01012A, ODDI Registry. Secret. A note on the cover sheets indicates that this SNIE was prepared by the Central Intelligence Agency and the intelligence organizations of the Departments of State, the Army, the Navy, the Air Force, and the Joint Staff, and concurred in by all members of the U.S. Intelligence Board on March 21 except the representative of the AEC and the Assistant Director of the FBI, who abstained because the subject was outside their jurisdiction.

past year and have since chosen to identify the PPP with Castro's cause. However, neither the Communist Bloc nor Castro has made any vigorous effort to exploit the British Guiana situation.

4. The principal opposition to Jagan's party is the People's National Congress (PNC), a socialist party made up largely of city negroes. It is under the ineffectual leadership of Forbes Burnham, a negro and a doctrinaire socialist. Like most British Guiana politicians he was at one time allied with Jagan, and indeed was second to Jagan in leadership of the PPP. The United Force (UF), a party made up largely from businessmen of various ethnic groups, was recently organized and has not demonstrated any wide popular appeal. Neither it nor the PNC is disposed to work with the other to present Jagan with a united opposition; previous efforts at coalition have failed.

5. The elections scheduled for August 1961 will be one of the last steps preparatory to independence, which the British have agreed to grant approximately 18 months after The West Indies achieves independence in 1962 or 1963. With the next elections not due for another five years, the winning party in this year's contest will carry the government through independence. During the transition period, the local British officials will retain ultimate authority for external affairs (including defense), but their present over-all veto power will be narrowed to these matters. After the elections, the local government will assume full control of the police.

6. The election seems likely to hinge mainly on personalities and to be decided by voting along ethnic lines—though racial antagonisms have not been deliberately stirred up. Social and economic problems, though they will certainly be issues in the election, have not yet made as much popular impact in British Guiana as they have in most of the Latin American area. The PPP has promised to put through various schemes of economic development, but has been ineffectual in fulfilling its promises, partly through lack of technicians and funds. It wants to get more money out of the US-developed bauxite resources of the country. The good rice crop of the past year has made the economic situation seem improved and for the time being has tended not only to obscure PPP shortcomings, but even to redound to the party's credit. The PNC stands for anticommunism and the desirability of joining The West Indies (in contrast to Jagan's antifederation stance), but these are not popular issues. The UF's appeal against communism and for a businessman's government is even less effective.

7. Of the 35 districts from which members of the Legislative Council will be elected next August, the PPP appears certain of victory in 13; the PNC, in 15 or 16. Thus, control of the government will be determined by the electoral outcome in a half dozen or so of the 35 districts. A PNC–

UF coalition could take enough of these to assure itself a majority in the Legislative Council; but it is unlikely that such a coalition will be formed. Without such cooperation between the opposition parties, Jagan is almost certain to win in most of the pivotal districts. Accordingly, we believe that Jagan's PPP will probably succeed in winning the right to form the next government.

8.   From time to time Jagan has threatened to boycott the elections, on the grounds that a redrawing of the boundaries of electoral districts, carried out by a British-appointed commissioner, was adverse to PPP interests. We think it highly unlikely that he will carry out his threat; and certainly he will not do so unless he believes his party is going to lose the elections.

9.   Jagan's election as Chief Minister in the preindependence phase would not be likely to result in a dramatic and sudden shift to the left, since he would probably seek to avoid action which would discourage the granting of independence by the British and recognizes that he would lack sufficient support for a revolutionary attempt to force the British out. He is almost certainly mindful of the effectiveness with which the British moved in with force in 1953, when they feared he might try to set up a Communist regime.

10. However, with a new electoral mandate, Jagan will probably make a more determined effort to improve economic conditions than he has heretofore. This will entail pressure on the UK—and the US—for economic assistance considerably above present levels. If he feels that economic aid from the West is not adequate to fulfill requirements for development, he will go elsewhere being careful not to provoke the British. He has already indicated interest in an alleged Cuban offer of an $8.5 million low-interest loan. At the same time, he may threaten nationalization or confiscation of foreign and local businesses to extract additional revenues and benefits.

11. How far a Jagan government might go after eventual achievement of independence is obscured by uncertainty about the nature and extent of his actual commitment to Communist discipline and about the tactical aims of the Bloc with respect to British Guiana. We believe that British Guiana will obtain membership in the UN upon independence, and that it will align itself under Jagan with Afro-Asian neutralism and anticolonialism. At a minimum, we would expect his government to be assertively nationalistic, sympathetic to Cuba, and prepared to enter into economic and diplomatic relations with the Bloc, although such a government would probably still be influenced by the desire to obtain economic help from the UK and the US. A good deal will depend on how far the spirit of social revolution has spread in nearby areas of Latin America. We think it unlikely that Jagan would give up his opposition to joining the federation of The West Indies (TWI), which would offer few

economic rewards and would subordinate his regime to outside and predominantly conservative influences.

12. It is possible that Jagan, once he had a free hand, would proceed forthwith with an effort to establish an avowed Communist regime. However, we believe that he would consider this undesirable, even if he were fully committed to eventual establishment of such a state, in view of the lack of trained cadres in British Guiana, the territory's primitive state of political and social development, and the likelihood of adverse international reactions. We consider it more likely that an independent Jagan government would seek to portray itself as an instrument of reformist nationalism which would gradually move in the direction of Castro's Cuba. Such a regime would almost certainly be strongly encouraged and supported by Castro and the Bloc.

13. Before independence, the attitude and actions of the British will bear heavily on the situation in British Guiana. Thus far the British seem to have been motivated chiefly by a desire to see British Guiana independent. They have tried to get along with Jagan and to overlook his Communist associations because he has seemed to them the only man capable of running the country. Since their intervention in 1953 to halt Jagan's first bid for power, they have refrained from actions which would antagonize him; the Governor's veto power has never been used. Even though they retain the capability for controlling Jagan, we believe they will do little to interfere with political developments in British Guiana.

---

243. Memorandum From the Executive Secretary of the Department of State (Battle) to the President's Special Assistant for National Security Affairs (Bundy)

Washington, May 19, 1961.

SUBJECT

British Guiana

The draft record of actions at the NSC meeting of May 5, 1961 contains the following:

Source: Kennedy Library, National Security Files, Countries Series, British Guiana, May 19–Aug. 23, 1961. Secret. Two typed notes by Bromley Smith appear at the bottom of the source text: "Mr Battle: I have not yet tied up this loose end. Before I do, has time altered your recommendation? 7/17" and "8/1 Mr. Goodwin: Where is this subject now being discussed—in the Task Force?"

"5. U.S. Policy Toward British Guiana

Agreed that the Task Force on Cuba would consider what can be done in cooperation with the British to forestall a communist take-over in that country."

The Department of State has been actively working with the British on this question for some weeks. In the discussion between Secretary Rusk and Lord Home at which the Acting Secretary was present on April 6, the following interchange occurred on British Guiana.

"Mr. White reported that at the present time a joint appraisal of the situation in British Guiana is taking place in London. Later in the month Sir Ralph Grey, the Governor, and Mr. MacKintosh, of the Colonial Office, are passing through Washington. At that time we are to consider possible programs. Sir Frederick frankly conceded that the UK does not know what to do about the U.S. concerns about British Guiana. Lord Home thought they could give us a note on the problem. Mr. White commented we were familiar with the Colonial Office's views and that the UK is committed to a date for British Guiana's independence. Mr. Kohler observed a fixed independence date was all right assuming there will be a reasonable government at that date. Isn't there some way we could encourage the moderates? Ambassador Caccia felt the Jagans provided the most responsible leadership in the country and they would be difficult to supplant. Mr. White stressed that we ought to work in the direction of getting the people in British Guiana interested in British Guiana's joining the Federation. Lord Home agreed and said the UK would like to see British Guiana in the Federation and would be willing to consult with us to further them in this direction."

Subsequent to that discussion arrangements were made for a high level meeting in London between Colonial Secretary MacLeod and Under Secretary Fraser on the British side and Ambassador Bruce aided by Ivan White and Jack Bell on the American side. This conference is to be held on May 26 and 27. In addition to discussing federation matters it is planned to examine the situation in British Guiana with a view to coming up with a jointly approved program. [*5 lines of source text not declassified*]

The Acting Secretary agrees with the Bureau of European Affairs' request that the responsibility for the preparation of recommendations on British Guiana be transferred from the Task Force on Cuba to the committee on which you both serve.

Melvin L. Manfull[1]

---

[1] Printed from a copy that indicates Manfull signed above Battle's typed signature.

244.   Telegram From the Department of State to Secretary of State Rusk, at Paris

Washington, August 5, 1961, 2:55 p.m.

Tosec 8. President suggests that if suitable opportunity presents itself you may desire briefly express to Lord Home our continued concern over forthcoming election in British Guiana which presently seems likely will result in Jagan victory.

FYI. President briefly raised matter with Macmillan in April and you discussed it with Lord Home. Subsequently Ivan White and Ambassador Bruce raised matter with McLeod. However British have not been willing to undertake any operation or permit us undertake operation to prevent Jagan victory and generally take view that Jagan is probably "salvagable." While now too late undertake any meaningful action prior to election August 21 and alternatives to Jagan not attractive or strong, suggest your remarks to Home might pave way for more meaningful future U.S.-U.K. cooperation on problem.

Also FYI. At Senator Dodd's request Alex Johnson is seeing him Monday with respect his August 3 letter addressed to you expressing hope "some action will be possible in this situation before we have another Castro regime in Latin America".

Ball

Source: Kennedy Library, National Security Files, Countries Series, British Guiana, May 19–Aug. 23, 1961. Top Secret; Eyes Only. Drafted by U. Alexis Johnson, cleared in substance in INR, and approved by Johnson and William C. Burdett. The first paragraph was cleared in substance by Schlesinger in the White House. Repeated to London eyes only for the Chargé.

245.   Telegram From the Department of State to the Embassy in the United Kingdom

Washington, August 11, 1961, 7:14 p.m.

708. For Ambassador Bruce from Secretary. Due to extreme shortness of time I have today given Lord Hood a letter to Lord Home of which following is text:

Source: Kennedy Library, National Security Files, Countries Series, British Guiana, May 19–Aug. 23, 1961. Top Secret; Priority. Drafted by Rusk.

"Dear Alex: There was one matter of deep concern to us which I find that I did not take up with you in Paris. This has to do with the forthcoming elections in British Guiana and the prospect that Jagan may have a working majority in the new government.

My colleague Ivan White went to London at the end of May to discuss this matter with your colleague Mr. McLeod and others. Although your and our information about Jagan seems to be much the same, as is to be expected from our close collaboration, I believe that our estimates may differ somewhat about the man himself and the implications of his future leadership in British Guiana. No doubt you would expect us to show considerable sensitivity about the prospect of Castroism in the Western Hemisphere and that we are not inclined to give people like Jagan the same benefit of the doubt which was given two or three years ago to Castro himself. However, we do believe that Jagan and his American wife are very far to the left indeed and that his accession to power in British Guiana would be a most troublesome setback in this Hemisphere.

Would you be willing to have this looked into urgently to see whether there is anything which you or we can do to forestall such an eventuality? Even if the electoral result was sufficiently confusing to lay the basis for another election, this could give us a little more time. But the difference in four or five seats in the new legislature might well be decisive.

Since this question is, as I understand it, largely one for the Colonial Office at this stage, I am taking the liberty of urging you to have a look because of the foreign policy ramifications of a Jagan victory. It would cause us acute embarrassments with inevitable irritations to Anglo-American relations. I do not refer in this last point to official circles but to problems of public and Congressional opinion. Cordially yours, Dean Rusk."

Rusk

246.   Message From Foreign Secretary Home to Secretary of State Rusk

London, August 18, 1961.

DEAR DEAN, Thank you for your message of the 11th of August[1] about the elections which are to be held in British Guiana next Monday. Your people and ours have looked very carefully into the possibilities of taking action to influence the results of the election. You may recall that your Ambassador went over the whole ground with Fraser not long ago. I am convinced that there is nothing practical—i.e., safe and effective— that we could do in this regard and that if we tried anything of this kind, we should only make matters worse. In any case, there would not now be enough time at our disposal.

I can well understand your concern and the situation has its difficulties for us as well. Basically, and this is true over the wide field of our Colonial responsibilities, we have had to move faster than we would have liked, but now the choice before us in situations like this is either to allow the normal process of democracy and progress towards self-government to go ahead and do our best to win the confidence of the elected leaders, and to wean them away from any dangerous tendencies, or else to revert to what we call "Crown Colony rule." It is practical politics to take the latter course only when it is quite clear that a territory is heading for disaster. We have done this once already in British Guiana—in 1953. But since the restoration of the democratic process in 1957, the elected government has behaved reasonably well and we have had no grounds which would justify a second attempt to put the clock back. If we do have grounds in future, and they would have to be really serious if we were to have any possibility of justifying our action to world opinion, we have full power under the new constitutional arrangements to suspend the new constitution. We have also incorporated in the new constitution a number of checks and balances which limit the freedom of action of British Guiana Ministers, and we have, of course, reserved to the Governor responsibility for defence and external affairs.

No one can say for certain how Jagan will behave if he is returned to power. He is a confused thinker and his mind is clogged with ill-digested dogma derived from Marxist literature. But he has learnt a good deal in the last eight years; he has not, since 1957, proved as difficult to deal with as he was earlier. It is true that he has during the election campaign made it clear that he expects to strengthen his relations with Cuba, and he has at

---

Source: Kennedy Library, National Security Files, Countries Series, British Guiana, May 19–Aug. 23, 1961. Secret.

[1] See Document 245.

times shown an interest in the possibilities of both trade and aid with the Soviet bloc. But he has also, during the election, promised to seek further aid from the United States; and, if we in the West show a real willingness to try to help, we think it by no means impossible that British Guiana may end up in a position not very different from that of India.

This situation will not be without its anxieties and embarrassments, but we are convinced that the only possible policy we can follow, and the most fruitful one, is to treat British Guiana like any other dependency and to try to "educate" its elected leaders unless and until we have clear justification for doing otherwise. It would be of the greatest possible help to us if we could have your support in this policy. I realise the difficulties that you face; if there is anything we can do to help you overcome those difficulties, you know that we should be very ready to do what we can.

Yours ever,

Alex[2]

---

[2] Printed from a copy that bears this typed signature.

---

247.   Telegram From the Department of State to the Embassy in the United Kingdom

Washington, August 26, 1961, 4:54 p.m.

977. Eyes only Ambassador Bruce. Unless you perceive objection please deliver following message from Secretary to Lord Home as soon as possible:

"Dear Alex:

As we feared, Cheddi Jagan's party emerged from the August 21 election in British Guiana with a majority of the seats in the Legislative Council. Unpalatable as the result is to us, our task now is to determine where we go from here. In your letter of August 18 you mentioned that our support for your policy would be of great help.

Source: Kennedy Library, Papers of Arthur M. Schlesinger, Jr., British Guiana—Jagan. Top Secret; Niact. Drafted by Burdett and approved by Rusk and U. Alexis Johnson.

If agreeable to you, I suggest that representatives of our two governments again sit down to discuss the situation. They might start with a review of the intelligence assessment, then go on to consider courses of action in the political, economic and information fields. I also attach importance to the covert side and recall that in June Hugh Fraser told David Bruce you would have another look at what could be done in this field after the election.

Should you think well of my proposal, I am prepared to send two or three officers to London to assist David Bruce in talks which I would ask him to hold with you, Mr. MacLeod and your colleagues. I am impressed by the desirability of starting promptly whatever program we may decide upon. Therefore, we might try to commence the discussions the week of September 4.

Cordially yours, Dean Rusk"

Rusk

248. Memorandum From the President's Special Assistant (Schlesinger) to President Kennedy

Washington, August 28, 1961.

SUBJECT

British Guiana

Melby, our Consul in Georgetown, is in Washington this week; and he is working with the State Department on an action program for British Guiana. The thought is that this program would be taken up with the British next week in London.

Alexis Johnson tells me that State will have its recommendations ready for you by Thursday. Would you like a meeting on British Guiana on Thursday or Friday? If you do not wish a meeting, Rusk will give you the program in writing by Thursday.

Melby, who seems a reasonably astute observer, feels that we should take the gamble of trying to be friendly to Jagan. In view of the fact that

Source: Kennedy Library, National Security Files, Countries Series, British Guiana, Aug. 23–Sept. 4, 1961. Confidential.

friendliness (e.g., bringing Jagan into the Alianza) would probably alarm Tom Dodd, do you think it might be a good idea for Melby to go and talk with Dodd sometime this week?

Arthur Schlesinger, jr.[1]

---

[1] Printed from a copy that bears this typed signature.

---

249. Memorandum From the President's Special Assistant (Schlesinger) to President Kennedy

Washington, August 30, 1961.

SUBJECT

British Guiana

The State Department feeling about British Guiana (which I share) is that we have no real choice but to feel Jagan out and see what we can do to bring (keep?) him into the western camp.

State accordingly recommends:

(1) that we offer Jagan technical and economic assistance;
(2) that we prepare the way for the admission of an independent British Guiana to the OAS and the Alliance for Progress;
(3) that Jagan be given a friendly reception during his visit to the US in October, including an audience with you.

At the same time, State also recommends (4) a covert program to develop information about, expose and destroy Communists in British Guiana, including, if necessary, "the possibility of finding a substitute for Jagan himself, who could command East Indian support."

The idea, in short, is to use the year or two before independence to work to tie Jagan to the political and economic framework of the hemisphere, while at the same time reinsuring against pro-Communist developments by building up anti-Communist clandestine capabilities.

Source: Kennedy Library, National Security Files, Countries Series, British Guiana, Aug. 24–Sept. 6, 1961. Top Secret.

This program depends in large part upon British cooperation. Accordingly State would like to send a State–ICA–[*less than 1 line of source text not declassified*] group to London next week to agree upon a program of action.

The main issues involved in the policy recommendation are:

A. The covert program proposed in (4) might conflict with the friendship policy proposed in (1–3). This means that the covert program must be handled with the utmost discretion and probably confined at the start to intelligence collection.

B. The size of the aid program must be carefully reviewed to make sure that it is not out of proportion to what we are doing elsewhere in Latin America (lest we seem to be rewarding Jagan for his pro-Communist reputation).

Final decisions on points A and B need not be taken immediately. The question to be decided now is: is it all right for State to send its group to London to discuss things with the British along the above lines? Or do you wish a meeting next week with Rusk, Dulles and Murrow before the State group goes? (No reply has yet been received to Rusk's cable to Home of August 26.)

Also, do you want to see Melby, our Consul in Georgetown, before he goes back? I found him quite illuminating on Jagan and the situation. He is scheduled to return to British Guiana on Friday; but he could, of course, stay over if you wanted to see him. (On the other hand, the sooner he gets back, the better from the viewpoint of observing, and even perhaps of influencing, the movement of events in British Guiana.)

Presumably the decision about sending a special US envoy to talk to Jagan would be made after the London conversations.

You will be interested in reading the attached clipping[1] in which Jagan sets forth his own avowed views on the subject of Communism.

Arthur Schlesinger, jr.[2]

---

[1] Not printed.

[2] Printed from a copy that bears this typed signature.

250.   Memorandum From the President's Special Assistant (Schlesinger) to President Kennedy

Washington, August 31, 1961.

SUBJECT

British Guiana Paper

I attach herewith the State Department paper on British Guiana.[1] I have communicated to Alexis Johnson your assent in principle to points 1–5 on page 2 of Secretary Rusk's memorandum.

I have also communicated to Johnson your particular concern over the covert program and your desire to know more detail before the State Department group goes to London. The present covert program is set forth under Tab B in the attached file. You will note that the first emphasis is (properly) on intelligence collection, with covert political action to come later. Part II (if Jagan should turn sour) seems to me pretty feeble, but it is also pretty tentative. Johnson emphasizes that the [*less than 1 line of source text not declassified*] paper is "only a basis for planning and discussion, as appropriate, with the British, and specific action will be subject to the usual Special Group consideration and approval."

I think you need look at only the Rusk memorandum and Tab B.

Arthur Schlesinger, jr.[2]

Source: Kennedy Library, National Security Files, Countries Series, British Guiana, Aug. 24–Sept. 6, 1961. Top Secret.

[1] Not printed.

[2] Printed from a copy that bears this typed signature.

---

251.   Telegram From the Department of State to the Embassy in the United Kingdom

Washington, August 31, 1961, 8:01 p.m.

1086. Eyes only Ambassador Bruce. Embtel 876.[1] FYI. We agree on desirability focusing attention "first team" in Colonial Office on British

---

Source: Kennedy Library, National Security Files, Countries Series, British Guiana, Aug. 24–Sept. 6, 1961. Top Secret; Priority. Drafted by Burdett, cleared by Tyler, and approved by U. Alexis Johnson.

[1] Dated August 29. (Department of State, Central Files, 741D.00/8–2961)

Guiana. However, we uneasy at postponing talks which would oblige us delay discussion we plan to have with Jagan until after mid-September. Also we desire involve Foreign Office and Lord Home personally in problem whose ramifications clearly extend beyond colony of British Guiana and which could have abrasive effects on Anglo-American relations. Lord Home will be away from London latter part week September 11 attending FonMin meeting here. End FYI.

Under circumstances, appears to us best procedure is that suggested by Colonial Office, e.g., that you have preliminary talk with MacLeod week of September 4. We hope you could include Lord Home. You could outline to them general lines of our thinking and seek agreement in principle. More intensive talks could be held early week of September 11.

If you consider this approach feasible, we prepared to send on short notice Department officer (Burdett) brief you on our proposed program. ICA [less than 1 line of source text not declassified] reps could arrive subsequently for talks week September 11.

Intelligence estimate referred to is one submitted Embassy despatch 1966.[2]

Rusk

---

[2] Dated April 19. (Ibid., 741D.00/4–1961)

---

252. Telegram From the Department of State to the Embassy in the United Kingdom

Washington, September 2, 1961, 2:28 p.m.

1147. Eyes only Ambassador Bruce. Embtel 947.[1] Following message from Lord Home to Secretary received Sept 1:

"Dear Dean,

Thank you for your message of August 26 about British Guiana. We welcome your suggestion that we should have talks in London to define the courses of action best suited to support our policy, which I hope will be your policy also, of persuading the new British Guiana Gov-

---

Source: Kennedy Library, National Security Files, Countries Series, British Guiana, Aug. 24–Sept. 6, 1961. Top Secret; Verbatim Text. Drafted by Burdett, cleared by Cutler (S), and approved by U. Alexis Johnson.
[1] Dated September 1. (Department of State, Central Files, 741D.00/9–261)

ernment that the West is still its best friend. We, too, are impressed by the desirability of starting promptly whatever programme emerges and would like to make an early start with the talks. I am afraid that the first date on which we on our side could assemble the right team would be September 11. Our difficulty here would not preclude a preliminary talk between David Bruce, Iain MacLeod and Hugh Fraser if that would help. I would be ready to come in later if need be. We will put this to David Bruce at once and hold ourselves in readiness.

I would just like to say that my colleagues and I will enter these talks with the firm conviction that the emphasis must be in the political and economic spheres if we are to expect rewarding dividends."

We do not plan to reply and will leave arrangements for discussions to you.

We will provide guidance for your meeting with MacLeod Sept 6. Advise when you wish Washington group to arrive.

Rusk

253. Telegram From the Department of State to the Embassy in the United Kingdom

Washington, September 4, 1961, 3:51 p.m.

1165. Eyes only Ambassador Bruce. Following letter from Secretary contains instructions for talks with UK on British Guiana:

"Dear David:

We have now completed a review of our policy towards British Guiana, and the enclosed action program, in its general outline, has been approved by the President. Specific steps under the program, of course, are subject to subsequent decisions.

As the first move in executing the program, I am asking you to undertake with the British Government the discussions mentioned in my letter of August 26 to Lord Home. I realize the delicate relationships

---

Source: Kennedy Library, National Security Files, Countries Series, British Guiana, Aug. 24–Sept. 6, 1961. Top Secret; Priority; Verbatim Text. Drafted by Burdett and approved by Johnson (S/S).

involved but hope that you will find a way to bring Lord Home and the Foreign Office into these talks. As you know, we believe the ramifications of this problem extend far beyond British Guiana as a colony.

You will see from the program that we are prepared to accept as a working premise the British thesis that we should try to 'educate' Cheddi Jagan. We have carefully studied the various reports of Communist connections on the part of Jagan and his People's Progressive Party and are fully aware of the pitfalls of proceeding along this path. However, it is our judgment that an across-the-board effort to 'salvage' Jagan is worth attempting. A factor in our conclusion is the unattractiveness of the available alternatives.

At the same time, it is only prudent to put out certain anchors to windward. Thus, our program also calls for [1 line of source text not declassified] discussion with the British of the feasibility of another election prior to independence, and reassurances from the British regarding their willingness to use their "reserve powers" as a last resort. We envisage these various components as parts of an inter-related package. Officers from the Department, ICA, [less than 1 line of source text not declassified] assigned to assist you in the talks will be in a position to elaborate on our thinking.

Clearly, the closest Anglo-American cooperation is essential. We also hope to bring in the Canadians and possibly others.

We would like to see the following emerge from your talks with the British: (1) A brief, agreed intelligence assessment; (2) British acceptance of the general concept of our action program; (3) Agreement ad referendum on a coordinated aid program; (4) [1-1/2 lines of source text not declassified]. The covert program described in the enclosure is only a basis for planning and discussions at this time [less than 1 line of source text not declassified]. Specific actions under the program would be subject to further high-level U.S. Government consideration and approval. (5) Agreement on tactics.

I leave to your discretion the manner of presenting our ideas to the British, taking into account the importance of moving rapidly. If, during your discussions, you believe we could be of assistance to you from Washington, please let me know.

Cordially yours, Dean Rusk"

Paper setting forth action program pouched Ambassador September 2.[1]

Rusk

---

[1] Not found.

254. Telegram From the Department of State to the Embassy in the United Kingdom

Washington, September 5, 1961, 9:45 p.m.

1181. Eyes only Ambassador Bruce. Deptel 1165.[1] Following comments supplementing letter of instructions from Secretary for talks with UK on British Guiana submitted as background for your discussion with MacLeod.

(1) We continue have serious reservations about British assessment Jagan as set forth in London talks in April (London Despatch 1966)[2] and in conversation here with Governor Grey (Memcon of April 26).[3] In our view, we should keep in mind possibility Jagan is Communist-controlled "sleeper" who will move to establish Castro or Communist regime upon independence. Particularly ominous is number of Communist-connected persons assigned safe constituencies by PPP and thus assured of seats in Legislative Council in August 21 election.

(2) We believe too much attention to Jagan at this stage would serve to inflate his ego and make dealing with him more difficult. Also it would smack of insincerity.

(3) We have deliberately refrained up to now from intimating to British we prepared to try their prescription for handling Jagan. We hope this card will serve as leverage to obtain British agreement to our action program as whole.

(4) [less than 1 line of source text not declassified] You may wish to emphasize importance [less than 1 line of source text not declassified] of current and continuing intelligence on developments in general and especially Communist activities. [1 line of source text not declassified] You may desire to play down covert political action program.

(5) We would like to see UK maintain and if possible expand level its economic assistance. Conversely, we wish avoid British assumption US will pick up total tab. We expect to explore fitting our aid into British Guiana's own development program and possibilities involving Canadians and others.

(6) We concerned about possible adverse effects on Federation of West Indies of spectacular program for British Guiana. Over-generosity and over-attention to Jagan could tempt TWI imitate his tactics.

Rusk

Source: Kennedy Library, Papers of Arthur M. Schlesinger, Jr., British Guiana—Jagan. Top Secret; Niact. Drafted by Burdett; cleared by U. Alexis Johnson, INR/DDC in draft, and Johnson (S/S); and approved by Tyler.

[1] Document 253.

[2] Dated April 19. (Department of State, Central Files, 741D.00/4–1961)

[3] Not further identified.

255. Memorandum From the President's Special Assistant (Schlesinger) to the Deputy Under Secretary of State for Political Affairs (Johnson)

Washington, September 7, 1961.

SUBJECT

British Guiana

I don't want to become a bore about cables on British Guiana; but I do not think that #1165, Eyes Only, to Bruce reflects Presidential policy as I understand it.[1] I would have rephrased (1) to read: "We continue to have serious reservations about British assessment as set forth [etc.][2] . . . In our view, we should keep in mind possibility Jagan will move to establish Castro-style regime upon independence. Particularly ominous [etc.] . . . Nevertheless we see no alternative at this point to testing whether situation salvageable by exploring policies designed to tie an independent British Guiana politically and economically to hemisphere."[3]

I would have omitted the bit about Jagan as a possible sleeper. Sleeper is a technical term meaning a disciplined agent who pretends to be one thing and then, at a given moment, tears off his mask and reveals himself as something entirely different. I have not heard this seriously suggested about Jagan, and I hope that David does not, on the basis of this cable, convey to the British the idea that our government seriously entertains this idea. [2 lines of source text not declassified] Also I would have added the last sentence because the cable nowhere states what we are trying to achieve in British Guiana.

I think I would have omitted (2) or reduced it to a tactical point. Is it really our policy to keep Jagan dangling? My guess is that the President has been thinking in terms of a cordial try at bringing British Guiana into the hemisphere. Nothing is worse than a half-hearted courtship.

(3)–(6) seem to me fine.

I feel that the omission of any positive statement of our policy, of the sort suggested in the last sentence of my revised (1), plus the inclusion of (2), might give David Bruce a misleading impression of our present thinking on the subject.

Arthur Schlesinger, jr.[4]

Source: Kennedy Library, Papers of Arthur M. Schlesinger, Jr., British Guiana—Jagan. Secret.

[1] Document 253.

[2] All brackets in this paragraph are in the source text.

[3] Quote is from telegram 1181, Document 254, not telegram 1165.

[4] Printed from a copy that bears this typed signature.

256.   Memorandum From the Deputy Under Secretary of State for Political Affairs (Johnson) to the President's Special Assistant (Schlesinger)

Washington, September 9, 1961.

SUBJECT

British Guiana

I have spoken to Bill Burdett about your memorandum of September 7, 1961[1] commenting on our telegram to David Bruce for his talks with the British on British Guiana. Burdett is leaving for London on Sunday to assist the Ambassador in these discussions, and I have asked him to keep your points very much in mind and to make sure David Bruce is under no misapprehension regarding the President's thinking.

As guidance to David Bruce, we sent to him three documents: the action program for British Guiana as transmitted to the President under the Secretary's memorandum of August 30, 1961;[2] a telegram containing a letter of instructions for the talks from the Secretary;[3] and the telegram to which you refer intended to supplement the Secretary's letter.[4] We intended the three documents to be parts of one package. While read in isolation the telegram you mention could be misconstrued, I hope you will agree that read in conjunction with the other two documents it will not mislead David Bruce.

Regarding your specific points, the Secretary's letter to David Bruce, particularly his third paragraph, states explicitly what we are trying to achieve. Before submitting our recommendations to the President, we considered carefully the possibility that Jagan, having in mind what happened in 1953 when he acted too openly, is now deliberately masking his real intentions. We do not think it is prudent to dismiss the possibility that he is dissembling. Given the British inclination to brush aside reports of Jagan's communist connections, we thought it advisable to flag this aspect for David Bruce. Our point 2 is, as you suggest, in large part tactical. We want to tread warily both to avoid making Jagan personally more difficult to work with and to prevent adverse repercussions in the Federation of the West Indies.

I can assure you that Burdett will emphasize to David Bruce that basic to our entire program is the determination to make a college try to tie Jagan to the West.

Alex

Source: Kennedy Library, Papers of Arthur M. Schlesinger, Jr., British Guiana—Jagan. Secret.

[1] Document 255.

[2] For a summary of this paper, see Documents 249 and 250.

[3] Document 253.

[4] Document 254.

P.S. As of possible interest, I am enclosing two papers on the situation in French Guiana and Surinam which I asked to have prepared. I would appreciate their return.[5]

UAJ

---

[5] Not printed.

---

257. Information Airgram From the Department of State to Certain Posts

CA–263   Washington, October 4, 1961, 1:40 p.m.

US Program for British Guiana

In consultation with the British, we have developed an action program for British Guiana to meet the situation following the grant of internal self-government to the former colony and the victory of Dr. Jagan in the recent election. The basic concept of the program is a wholehearted across-the-board effort to work with the new Jagan Government and to foster effective association between British Guiana and the West. Among the factors contributing to the decision to adopt this policy were 1) the impracticability of any alternative course of action; 2) the dearth of effective political leadership in British Guiana apart from Jagan; and 3) recognition that coldness toward Jagan and withholding of aid could only result in his gravitation toward the Soviet-Castro bloc. The decision was made with full recognition of the risks involved in view of the known Communist associations of British Guiana leaders. Our Consul in Georgetown has offered Jagan our cooperation in the political and economic fields; suggested an early visit by ICA representatives to discuss certain facets of an aid program; and invited Jagan to call on the President during the Premier's forthcoming visit to Washington. Jagan expressed appreciation for our willingness to work with him and was

---

Source: Kennedy Library, Papers of Arthur M. Schlesinger, Jr., British Guiana—Jagan. Secret. Drafted by Staples (EUR), cleared by Foster (BNA), and approved by Burdett. Sent to Bonn, The Hague, London, Moscow, Ottawa, Paris, New Delhi, Barbados, Belize, Hamilton, Kingston, Nassau, Port-of-Spain, Georgetown, and all posts in the American Republics.

gratified over the invitation to see the President. He much concerned about problem his public relations since he felt image world had of him as Communist was a major stumbling block to his plans for BG. Jagan said aware US was of two minds about him, but all he asked was to be judged by actions he took from now on.

258.   Memorandum From the Director of the Bureau of Intelligence and Research (Hilsman) to the Deputy Under Secretary of State for Political Affairs (Johnson)

Washington, October 17, 1961.

SUBJECT

US Policy in British Guiana

In reviewing materials recently on Jagan and his associates, we have multiplied our doubts about the feasibility of the policy adopted for British Guiana. Our position is set out below and, though it has been discussed with BNA, it is very much INR's point of view.

The current US program for British Guiana is based upon general agreement with the UK for a coordinated effort to get along with Jagan. At the same time resources are to be built up to enable a harder line to be put into effect if, after a reasonable time (but before British Guiana becomes independent), it is clear that British Guiana is going the way of Castro Cuba.

This approach is based upon such considerations as (1) Jagan's apparently firm hold on British Guiana politics; (2) the lack of cohesive opposition; (3) the unwillingness and stated inability of the UK to resist pressure for British Guiana's independence at this time; (4) the hope that the assumption of political power by Jagan under the new constitution will be followed by the exercise of political responsibility in a manner acceptable to US-UK interests; (5) the belief that Jagan himself is not a controlled instrument of Moscow; that he is instead a radical nationalist who may play both sides of the street but will not lead British Guiana into

Source: Department of State, ARA/NC Files: Lot 67 D 77, Br. Gu.—US Policy Toward Jagan. Secret. Drafted by Bernard S. Morris and Philip C. Habib and cleared with Richard H. Courtenaye and Charles G. Bream.

satellite status; and (6) the assumption that regardless of Jagan's orientation, the mass of people in British Guiana are not and will not become communist.

Without debating the pros and cons of these considerations, it is another matter to accept the general thesis that we should support and live with a British Guiana under Marxist leadership with what this implies for the structure of the economy and the character of its political and social institutions. Moreover there is the possibility, if not the probability, that strong, direct ties with Moscow will emerge as British Guiana achieves independence. Yet a successful US policy in British Guiana should start from the assumption that the Bloc must be precluded from a position of direct or indirect control or even substantial influence.

The UK, which remains the responsible power in British Guiana, is not willing to take a hard line. So long as HMG is prepared to try and get along with Jagan, the United States is faced with a dilemma in its own approach—whether to take a line contrary to the UK, or to accept the UK thesis and hope for the best while seeking to build in safeguards in the form of contingency plans for a reversal of policy. Because of the strength of UK conviction, and given the international climate regarding colonial status, the United States has apparently had no option but to agree with the major lines proposed by the UK.

If, as we suspect, the UK policy cannot be successful in the short time that remains before independence, then US planning should be directed to converting the UK to a program of direct anti-Jagan action. The safeguards built into the US-UK working party report should be strengthened and become the focal point for US policy. The time factor—independence for British Guiana is proposed in 1963 at the latest—has not been sufficiently weighed in the current program. It does not seem realistic to expect the institutional, political and economic readjustment of Jagan's thinking in so short a time.

Our pessimism as to the chances of success for the UK approach is also based upon the expected dissatisfaction (already evident) of Jagan with proposals to aid British Guiana's economic development. It is on this question of economic aid to British Guiana that there is likely to be a clash between Jagan's expectations and US-UK plans. A key factor in the proposals to get along with Jagan has been the hope that cooperation in British Guiana's development will bring the US and UK into a position of influence while at the same time Jagan and his government would be seized of their internal problems and concentrate their efforts on economic development. This seems a forlorn hope (again given the time factor), and it is more likely that irrational and Marxist dissatisfaction with our methods and deliberateness will work against achievement of our objectives. Certainly the amount of aid which has been offered to Jagan is not sufficient in his eyes. It may be better to stop talking about a fixed sum of money and talk more about the orderly progression of economic planning and assistance on a phased basis. The $5 million in aid being offered is not enough to engage Jagan. We should recognize that it is going to take a lot more money if we pursue a course so heavily dependent upon economic blandishments.

The testing period for this conclusion is the next few weeks. If Jagan is unshakeable and insatiable in his expectations, we will be in a better position to judge our course of action. We should not feel bound by the US-UK working party agreement if the premises and the chances of success are shaken. If the possibilities remain obscure after Jagan's visit, we should still seek to strengthen the safeguards which we have built in, and be prepared on short notice to re-cast our approach. In the final analysis we should plan for the possibility that we will have no reasonable alternative but to work for Jagan's political downfall, which would have to precede the granting of independence. To bring about such a result will require an extensive and carefully coordinated effort, for which much planning has already been done.

It is, therefore, proposed that the present policy for British Guiana be reviewed immediately following the visit of Jagan to Washington. If it develops that the premises underlying policy are clearly questionable, we should be prepared to re-open the matter with the UK.

---

259.   Memorandum of Conversation

Washington, October 25, 1961, 11 a.m.

SUBJECT

Call of Premier Jagan of British Guiana on the President

PARTICIPANTS

The United States:	*British Guiana*
The President	Premier Cheddi B. Jagan
Under Secretary of State Ball	
Professor Arthur Schlesinger	
Mr. Richard Goodwin	
Mr. William R. Tyler, Acting Asst. Sec.,	
EUR	

The greater part of the meeting was taken up by an extensive presentation by Premier Jagan of the economic and social problems of British Guiana and of the plans and goals which Premier Jagan's government has under consideration.

Source: Kennedy Library, National Security Files, Countries Series, British Guiana, Oct. 21–Nov. 6, 1961. Secret. Drafted by Tyler. The meeting was held at the White House.

Premier Jagan described himself politically as a socialist and a believer in state planning. At the same time, he was at pains to emphasize the guarantees for political freedom which he had personally incorporated into the British Guiana constitution, such as the democratic freedoms, an independent judiciary, and an independent civil service in the British tradition. While professing to be a follower of Aneurin Bevan, he was evasive on all ideological and doctrinal issues, claiming that he was not sufficiently familiar with theory to distinguish between "the various forms of socialism", within which he appeared to include communism. He spoke at all times of the cold war as an issue in which he did not feel himself engaged or committed, but he stressed repeatedly his determination to keep British Guiana free and politically independent. The terminology he used was less forthright than in his speech, and in answer to questions, at the National Press Club luncheon on October 24.

Premier Jagan analyzed the political composition of British Guiana and the antecedents of the recent elections. He said that his political rivals (Burnham of the PNC and D'Aguiar of the UF) had made wild promises of obtaining vast sums of aid, if elected. He said that they had done this irresponsibly and that in the case of D'Aguiar he had undoubtedly received aid from the United States in his campaign. The President interjected to say that the United States Government had certainly not intervened in any way, directly or indirectly, in the internal affairs of British Guiana. Premier Jagan said that he had not intended to imply this, but that certain "forces" had subsidized the political campaign with his opponents. He alluded to certain films "shown on street corners by USIS" during the campaign, which were directed against Castro and communism in general, and which had been exploited by his political opponents against him and his party. He said he had no objection to USIS carrying out its program in normal times, but that these particular activities during the pre-election period had constituted intervention against which he had protested. He said he must obtain aid to carry out his urgent domestic program, and that this was a political necessity for him, as he was "on the hot seat."

The President stressed to Premier Jagan that the internal system and the political and economic philosophies of a country were, to us, a matter for it to decide. The important thing for us was whether a given country, whether we agreed with its internal system or not, was politically independent. The President pointed out that we had given very considerable sums of aid to Yugoslavia, which is a communist state. He also referred to the considerable amount of aid we had given to Brazil and to India.

Premier Jagan asked whether the United States would consider as a hostile act a commercial agreement between British Guiana and the communist bloc whereby British Guiana would export bauxite in return for the importation of commodities.

The President pointed out that the United States and its allies were engaged in trade with the communist bloc, thus we would not consider trade per se to have political significance. However, if the nature and the extent of trade between British Guiana and the Soviet bloc were such as to create a condition of dependence of the economy of British Guiana on the Soviet bloc, then this would amount to giving the Soviet Union a political instrument for applying pressure and trying to force damaging concessions to its political interests and goals. Under Secretary Ball emphasized the experience of Guinea in this connection.

The President concluded the formal discussion by saying that he understood and sympathized with the political, economic and social problems which Premier Jagan was facing, and that the United States was disposed and willing to help British Guiana to move toward its economic and social goals within a framework of political freedom and independence. He pointed out that our resources were limited and that we had worldwide commitments, all of which made it necessary for us to examine very carefully specific projects on which we might be in a position to help. The President said that he had made it a rule not to discuss or offer specific sums of money, but that the United States would be prepared to send down to British Guiana as soon as feasible experts who could work with Premier Jagan's government and make recommendations which we would consider sympathetically in the light of our other commitments and of our financial resources.

---

260. Memorandum of Conversation

Washington, October 26, 1961.

SUBJECT

　　U.S. Assistance to British Guiana

PARTICIPANTS

　　Dr. Cheddi B. Jagan, Premier of British Guiana
　　Mr. Henry J.M. Hubbard, Minister of Trade and Industry
　　Mr. Clifton C. Low-a-Chee, Permanent Secretary to the Ministry of Development
　　　Planning and Secretary to the Council of Ministers
　　Mr. Lloyd A. Searwar, Assistant Head of Government Information Services
　　Mr. John Hennings, Colonial Attaché, British Embassy
　　Dr. Arthur Schlesinger, Jr., Special Assistant to the President
　　Mr. William C. Burdett, Acting Deputy Assistant Secretary of State

---

Source: Kennedy Library, National Security Files, Countries Series, British Guiana, Oct. 21–Nov. 6, 1961. Confidential. Drafted by Burdett. The meeting was held at the Dupont Plaza Hotel.

Dr. Schlesinger called on Premier Jagan to deliver a personal note from the President regretting his inability to accede to a request made by the Premier for a further meeting. The President referred to his crowded schedule including a Cabinet Meeting and official luncheon. He asked the Premier to speak frankly to Dr. Schlesinger who had his complete confidence.

Upon reading the President's letter, Premier Jagan expressed his thanks and his understanding of why the President was unable to receive him. He then made clear his disappointment that the United States was unable to be more responsive to his request for economic assistance. He described British Guiana's development program along the lines used with Mr. Fowler Hamilton earlier in the day. The Premier said that frankly speaking he felt that British Guiana was getting "a run around". He detailed the numerous surveys and missions which had visited his country. He asserted that the refusal of the United States to make a specific money offer placed him in an impossible political position. He inquired whether the United States attitude should be attributed to his failure to make a satisfactory "political" impression. The Premier referred to a figure of $5 million mentioned by the recent ICA Mission. He asked if the United States could at least undertake to provide this sum.

Dr. Schlesinger assured the Premier that we were most sympathetic to his desire to help the people of British Guiana develop an economic and social program. He recalled that the President had said that the internal system and political and economic organization of a country were for each country to decide for itself. We insisted only that a country remain genuinely free and independent. Dr. Schlesinger explained the necessity for universal standards in the administration of our aid program. We were not able to commit any specific figure until we had an opportunity to examine British Guiana's development program as a whole and the details of the various projects. We would be glad to help British Guiana perhaps in cooperation with Hemisphere organizations to formulate a development program and to work out the details of agreed projects. We would be willing to send a mission of economists and planners down to British Guiana. The United States definitely was not stalling.

The Premier asked whether we could finance part of the gap in the Berrill Plan which had been prepared with British advice. He recognized that we might not be able to accept the expanded Guianese program. Dr. Jagan said he would be glad to receive a mission, but did not want it to take up a lot of time. It was pointed out to him that even the Berrill Plan had not been reviewed in detail by U.S. technicians.

Premier Jagan asked what was he to say when he returned to Georgetown. He would be severely criticized. Was there some statement which he could make? Dr. Schlesinger responded that it might be possible to agree on a statement. Minister Hubbard asked if we had a draft. Dr. Schlesinger circulated a possible statement which might be issued by the State Department.

At this point the Premier had to leave for the airport to catch a plane for New York. The discussion was continued in the car. Dr. Jagan made several suggestions about the draft. He insisted that the mission should only "review" British Guiana's own plans. He wished to avoid any inference that the Guianese had not been able themselves to produce a plan. He asked who would decide about the composition of the mission.

After the Premier's departure Minister Hubbard and Mr. Hennings returned to the Department of State and met with Mr. Burdett and Mr. Foster to adjust the draft, taking into account the Premier's suggestions. Agreement was arrived at subject to confirmation by the Premier from New York on October 27.

Note: Agreement on the wording of the statement was reached by Dr. Jagan and Dr. Schlesinger by telephone on October 27.

261. Memorandum From the President's Special Assistant (Schlesinger) to President Kennedy

Washington, January 12, 1962.

SUBJECT

British Guiana

On January 11, State and AID representatives met with George Ball to decide on British Guiana policy.

At this meeting, State and AID agreed (a) that technical assistance be expanded immediately to approximately $1.5 million; (b) that an economic mission be sent to Georgetown by February 15; and (c) that the Jagan Government be informed of these steps. The remaining question was whether, in addition, we undertake to finance the construction of a road from Atkinson Field to Mackenzie at the cost of $5 million over a couple of years. (George Ball, by the way, is going to make one more effort to draw the Canadians in by asking them to assume part of the cost of the road, if we eventually decide to go ahead on it; Mackenzie is an important ALCAN center.)

State advocated this project on the ground that the key element in the British Guiana action program (as approved by you on September 4) was an across-the-board, whole-hearted effort to work with Jagan; that the delay in starting the economic program has given rise to the impression in Georgetown that we are not interested in helping; that this has substantially increased the risk that our action program may not achieve its objectives; that some dramatic commitment is necessary to reestablish credibility and confidence; that expanded technical assistance will not do it, since British Guiana has had a technical assistance program for seven years; that the acid test from their viewpoint is in the field of economic development; and that therefore if we are to recover the momentum achieved at the time of Jagan's visit in October and have a reasonable prospect of achieving the objectives of our policy, we should make an immediate commitment to build the road.

AID opposed the road because (a) the AID statute says that (except in case of waiver) no commitments to such projects be undertaken until feasibility studies are completed, (b) AID doubts that we shoot so much of our wad on a single project, (c) AID is still reluctant to expose itself to congressional criticism or to strengthen Jagan by making early demonstrations of support to his government.

Undersecretary Ball took the AID position, and the road project has been deferred until feasibility studies are completed.

While State/EUR will of course loyally carry out the decision, I believe that it regards the program as, in effect, a reversal of the September policy of a whole-hearted try. Their feeling, I think, is that knocking out the road (or some comparable demonstration that we mean business in aiding British Guiana development) means the evisceration of the British Guiana action program and virtually guarantees its failure. They also feel that this will create serious difficulties with the British who have [1 line of source text not declassified] assurance on our part that we were serious about providing economic assistance to British Guiana.

I agree with State/EUR that the decision against the road increases the chance that our action program will fail. On the other hand, I do not believe that it makes failure certain. I believe that other steps, if taken with adequate speed and conviction, will do much to restore our credibility; and that, so far as the road is concerned, if our mission recommends it, the commitment of funds to the road may be postponed only from January to June.

However, further delay in the other steps will certainly doom our program in British Guiana. So, in order to make sure that these other steps are taken immediately, I recommend that you send the attached memorandum to Fowler Hamilton.[1]

Arthur Schlesinger, jr.

---

[1] Not printed.

262. Memorandum From President Kennedy to the Administrator of the Agency for International Development (Hamilton)

Washington, January 12, 1962.

SUBJECT

British Guiana

I wish immediate steps to be taken to get an economic mission to British Guiana by February 15 and to expand technical assistance to the level of $1.5 million. I am also requesting immediate action to intensify our observations of political developments in British Guiana and by this and other means extend our program of reinsurance in case the situation should show signs of going sour.

Could you report to me as soon as possible concerning your action on this matter.[1]

Source: Kennedy Library, National Security Files, Countries Series, British Guiana II. Secret.

[1] Printed from an unsigned copy.

---

263. Memorandum From the Assistant Secretary of State for European Affairs (Tyler) to Secretary of State Rusk

Washington, February 18, 1962.

SUBJECT

British Guiana

Discussion

1. U.S. policy towards British Guiana as approved by the President on September 3, 1961, has had two principal components: (a) an effort to work with Premier Cheddi Jagan; [2 lines of source text not declassified].

Source: Kennedy Library, National Security Files, Countries Series, British Guiana II. Top Secret. Sent through U. Alexis Johnson.

2. Agreement was reached with the British in September on a coordinated program in accord with this policy. The British attached major importance to a wholehearted effort by the U.S. to work with Jagan involving, among other things, his visit to the U.S. and a U.S. economic assistance program. [5-1/2 *lines of source text not declassified*]

3. In implementation of this program the President received Premier Jagan in October[1] and a real effort was made by top U.S. officials to impress Jagan that we sincerely wish to work with him. Jagan came with exaggerated expectations of what economic assistance we might provide. He was disillusioned by our unresponsiveness. Since October, for a variety of reasons, we have been unable to get our economic assistance program off the ground.

4. In response to pressure from Jagan including action at the UN, the British have announced readiness to hold a conference in May to approve a constitution and set a date for British Guiana's independence. Independence would presumably occur before the end of 1962. We concurred reluctantly in the British timetable for independence, but in doing so strongly stressed the hope that new elections would be held. The timetable may be stretched out as a result of the current disorders.

5. A strike broke out in Georgetown the week of February 12 in protest against an austerity budget proposed by Jagan sharply increasing rates of taxation. The budget was bitterly attacked by the business community and included measures which would bear upon the low income groups. Our information on the situation in Georgetown is incomplete. However, matters have worsened, the British have moved troops in from Jamaica and flown in two companies from the UK at Jagan's request. The first disorders occurred on February 16 and two people were reported killed when police fired on demonstrators. A series of fires and looting occurred in the main business district. According to the latest report (noon, February 17) the security situation was under control. It should be noted that the strike so far has been limited to Georgetown, the stronghold of the UF and PNC. It has not extended to the country areas where Jagan's strength lies.

6. We asked the British Embassy on February 16 to obtain if possible by February 19 HMG's assessment of the situation including implications for future policies.

Conclusions

1. The policy of trying to work with Jagan has not been really applied in practice subsequent to Jagan's visit to the U.S. Economic assistance was an indispensable part of this program and the U.S. has not carried out the agreement on economic assistance reached during Jagan's visit. Factors beyond the control of State have also intervened.

---

[1] See Document 259.

Latest reports indicate that Jagan is increasingly suspicious of the U.S. It is now doubtful that a working relationship can be established with Jagan which would prevent the emergence of a communist or Castro-type state in South America.

[*10 paragraphs and 1 heading (2-1/2 pages of source text) not declassified*]

3. That you sign the attached telegram to London containing a message to Lord Home.[2]

---

[2] See Document 264.

---

264.   Telegram From the Department of State to the Embassy in the United Kingdom

Washington, February 19, 1962, 5:16 p.m.

4426. For Ambassador Bruce from Secretary. Please deliver following message to Lord Home as soon as possible: "Dear Alex: You know from our correspondence in August of last year of my acute concern over the prospects of an independent British Guiana under the leadership of Cheddi Jagan. Subsequent to his victory in the August elections we agreed to try your policy of fostering an effective association between British Guiana and the West and an Anglo-American working party developed an appropriate program. At our request safeguards, including consultations about new elections, were included in case matters went awry. In pursuance of this program the President received Jagan on his visit to this country in October.

I must tell you now that I have reached the conclusion that it is not possible for us to put up with an independent British Guiana under Jagan. We have had no real success in establishing a basis for understanding with him due in part to his grandiose expectations of economic aid. We have continued to receive disturbing reports of communist connections on the part of Jagan and persons closely associated with him. Partly reflective of ever growing concern over Cuba, public and Congressional opinion here is incensed at the thought of our dealing with Jagan. The Marxist-Leninist policy he professes parallels that of Castro which the OAS at the Punta del Este Conference declared incompatible with the Inter-American system. Current happenings in British Guiana indicate Jagan is not master of the situation at home without your sup-

---

Source: Kennedy Library, National Security Files, Countries Series, British Guiana II. Top Secret; Priority; Eyes Only. Repeated to USUN.

port. There is some resemblance to the events of 1953. Thus, the continuation of Jagan in power is leading us to disaster in terms of the colony itself, strains on Anglo-American relations and difficulties for the Inter-American system.

These considerations, I believe, make it mandatory that we concert on remedial steps. I am anxious to have your thoughts on what should be done in the immediate future. In the past your people have held, with considerable conviction, that there was no reasonable alternative to working with Jagan. I am convinced our experience so far, and now the disorders in Georgetown, makes it necessary to re-examine this premise. It seems to me clear that new elections should now be scheduled, and I hope we can agree that Jagan should not accede to power again. Cordially yours, Dean Rusk."

Rusk

---

265. Letter From the Representative to the United Nations (Stevenson) to Secretary of State Rusk

New York, February 26, 1962.

DEAR DEAN: I appreciate receiving a copy of your February 19 message to Lord Home about British Guiana, but I am concerned by what may be its implication.

I am of course in agreement that the emergence of British Guiana as an independent state under Cheddi Jagan would be a calamity—from various points of view.

Without knowing any details of the situation in British Guiana, or of the degree of our involvement to date, however, I should like to suggest that the following considerations are among those worth keeping in mind:

1. Action by the United Kingdom which could be pictured as arbitrarily "stalling" on an independence date for British Guiana would probably strengthen Jagan's position. Cancellation, or even deferral, of the scheduled May conference would seem to be in this category.

Source: Kennedy Library, National Security Files, Countries Series, British Guiana. Top Secret. A copy was sent to the President.

2. Substantial U.S. involvement in the situation would probably be impossible to conceal over a period of time.

3. Disclosure of U.S. involvement would (a) probably strengthen Jagan, (b) undermine our carefully nurtured position of anti-colonialism among the new nations of Asia and Africa, (c) grievously damage our position in Latin America. (Against this, I suppose that a *successful* operation, if discreet, might enhance our standing in some Latin-American quarters.)

4. The damaging effect of such disclosure would be magnified if the U.S. involvement disclosed were of the character which might be inferred from the last sentence of your letter.

If our best intelligence is that new elections would result in the ouster of Jagan, then certainly we ought to encourage the U.K. to arrange for such elections, to be conducted under U.K. supervision, with effective protection against intimidation and rigging by Jagan's people. Whatever part the U.S. might play should, it seems to me, be carefully considered in the light of the risks mentioned above.

I would be grateful if you could keep me au courant with the situation, and I would in particular appreciate having an early CIA briefing on what their role may have been or what may be contemplated.

Sincerely,

Adlai E. Stevenson

---

266. Letter From Foreign Secretary Home to Secretary of State Rusk

London, February 26, 1962.

MY DEAR DEAN, Thank you for your letter on British Guiana.[1] From our past discussions we have known your pre-occupations and you have known the efforts which we have made despite setbacks to provide for the orderly development of this territory. We are studying what best to do now to discharge our responsibilities and when we have decided, we shall be glad to see in a more official way what can be done to concert our action and yours.

Source: Kennedy Library, National Security Files, William H. Brubeck Series, British Guiana, Jan. 1961–April 1962. Top Secret.

[1] See Document 264.

Meanwhile there are some general thoughts which I should like to put to you privately and with the same frankness with which you wrote. I do so not only because I think this is right between us, but because you have often shown in the conversations which the two of us have had, that you recognise the sustained efforts over long periods that we have made in our dependent territories to try to ensure that they have a reasonable chance of using and not abusing freedom when they get it. This must depend to a large extent on the progress of each different territory and its readiness to run its own affairs. But once this process has gone as far as it now has, there is bound to be an added risk over timing in the remaining dependent territories which are still either backward or have peculiar racial or other difficulties. This was inherent in the problem from the beginning.

Now it was your historic role to have been for long years the first crusader and the prime mover in urging colonial emancipation. The communists are now in the van. Why? Amongst other things because premature independence is a gift for them.

What I do not think possible is to beat them by cancelling the ticket for independence and particularly if this is only to be done in the single instance of British Guiana. You say that it is not possible for you "to put up with an independent British Guiana under Jagan" and that "Jagan should not accede to power again". How would you suggest that this can be done in a democracy? And even if a device could be found, it would almost certainly be transparent and in such circumstances if democratic processes are to be allowed, it will be extremely hard to provide a reasonable prospect that any successor regime will be more stable and more mature.

So I would say to you that we cannot now go back on the course we have set ourselves of bringing these dependent territories to self-government. Nor is it any good deluding ourselves that we can now set aside a single territory such as British Guiana for some sort of special treatment.

This of course does not mean that we should not try to mitigate the dangers in British Guiana as elsewhere in the areas of the Americas and elsewhere. You will know our present concern over Kenya, the Federation and other territories in East Africa. I take comfort from your letter to think that you will be ready to understand and support us in solving these problems. I do not want to go into them further here. But I should like to draw your attention to another territory in the area of the Americas, British Honduras. It will be difficult enough to provide for the future well-being of this territory. We now have in addition the President of Guatemala using language reminiscent of Hitler to press his claim. "The Guatemalans", he said publicly on February 20, "would maintain their unshakeable determination to regain Belize." As the present regime in Guatemala would hardly have come into being without your support in

1954 and since, I shall be asking you to use your good offices at the right time to prevent another possible misadventure on your doorstep.

Let us by all means try and do what is possible to prevent the communists and others from perverting our common aim of doing our best to assure a timely and orderly development of independence in the remaining dependent territories. But we must do this across the board and you will realise that while territories like British Guiana may be of special concern to you in your hemisphere, there are others of at least equal importance to us elsewhere.

Yours ever,

Alex

267. Memorandum From the President's Special Assistant (Schlesinger) to President Kennedy

Washington, March 8, 1962.

SUBJECT

Memoranda on British Guiana to State and CIA[1]

The point of these two memoranda is that both State and CIA are under the impression that a firm decision has been taken to get rid of the Jagan government.

The desired effect is to make sure that nothing is done until you have had a chance to talk with Hugh Fraser.

The attached memcons will give you an impression of current British attitudes.

British Guiana has 600,000 inhabitants. Jagan would no doubt be gratified to know that the American and British governments are spending more man-hours per capita on British Guiana than on any other current problem!

Arthur Schlesinger, jr.[2]

Source: Kennedy Library, Papers of Arthur M. Schlesinger, Jr., British Guiana—Jagan. No classification marking.

[1] Neither printed.

[2] Printed from a copy that bears this typed signature.

Attachment[3]

Memorandum From the President's Special Assistant (Schlesinger) to the Ambassador to the United Kingdom (Bruce)

February 27, 1962.

SUBJECT

British Guiana

I had lunch today with Iain MacLeod and Reginald Maudling. The subject of British Guiana came up; and MacLeod made the following assertions:

1. Jagan is *not* a Communist. He is a naive, London School of Economics Marxist filled with charm, personal honesty and juvenile nationalism.

2. The tax problem which caused the trouble was *not* a Marxist program. It was a severely orthodox program of a "Crippsian" sort appropriate for a developed nation like Great Britain but wholly unsuited for an immature and volatile country like British Guiana.

3. If another election is held before independence Jagan will win.

4. Jagan is infinitely preferable to Burnham. "If I had to make the choice between Jagan and Burnham as head of my country I would choose Jagan any day of the week."

Maudling was rather silent during this conversation not, I think, because of disagreement, but because he preferred to let MacLeod take the initiative. He did say jovially at one point, "If you Americans care so much about British Guiana, why don't you take it over? Nothing would please us more." As we were breaking up Maudling expressed privately to me his puzzlement over the Secretary's letter to the Foreign Minister. I said I was returning to Washington at the end of the week. He said it might be a good idea for us to have a talk before I go back.

Arthur M. Schlesinger, jr.[4]

---

[3] Confidential.
[4] Printed from a copy that bears this typed signature.

Attachment[5]

Memorandum From the President's Special Assistant (Schlesinger) to the Ambassador to the United Kingdom (Bruce)

March 1, 1962.

SUBJECT

British Guiana

I had a talk this afternoon with Maudling, the Colonial Secretary, on the subject of British Guiana. He expressed total bafflement as to what the next steps might be. So far as independence is concerned, he thinks that the preparatory conference should be held as scheduled in May but that actual independence will certainly be postponed, perhaps as long as a year. He sees no point in holding elections before independence because he believes that an election campaign would only rekindle the racial animosities without changing the composition of the British Guiana Government.

[*less than 1 line of source text not declassified*] He does not regard Jagan as a disciplined Communist but rather as [*less than 1 line of source text not declassified*]. He says that he would not trust Jagan [*less than 1 line of source text not declassified*]. He added that it is his understanding that Burnham is, if possible, worse. He is reluctant to take any action which will make Jagan a martyr. He does not feel that Britain can consistently dislodge a democratically elected government.

His general view is that Britain wants to get out of British Guiana as quickly as possible. He said that he would be glad to turn the whole area over to the United States tomorrow. [*1-1/2 lines of source text not declassified*] He added that he is thinking of sending his Parliamentary Secretary, Hugh Fraser, over there next week to make an on-the-spot report. This has not been cleared with the Prime Minister but if Fraser should go he would probably stop in Washington on his way back.

Maudling said at one point that while he himself thought it "inconceivable," "responsible people" had said that CIA had played a role in stimulating the recent riots. I said that this of course was inconceivable and that I could assure him that this was not the case.

He mentioned the Foreign Secretary's letter and conveyed the impression that it had given the Cabinet great pleasure. He repeated

---

[5] Secret. A typed note at the bottom of the last page of the source text reads: "(Page 2 was not proofed by Mr. Schlesinger)."

with particular relish the sentence that the British might be willing to delay the independence process in British Guiana if the Americans would not insist on expediting it everywhere else. I took the occasion to correct Lord Home's apparent belief that the revolution of 1954 had brought the Ydigoras regime into power in Guatemala.

We also had some conversation about Trinidad. Maudling, [1 *line of source text not declassified*] warned me to expect more trouble over the Chagoramas Base. Maudling said that he had taken a drive past the base and could not see why we needed it so desperately. He also said that Williams was disturbed over what he regarded as the American failure to finance certain projects mentioned in the Agreement with Trinidad. Though the language of the Agreement commits the United States only "to participate" in the financing, Williams insists that Ambassador Whitney assured him that this was a form of language adopted to make things palatable to Congress and that the United States would in fact underwrite the project completely. Maudling says that the failure of the language to state the extent of participation leads him to believe that Williams may be correct on this point.

Arthur M. Schlesinger, jr.[6]

---

[6] Printed from a copy that bears this typed signature.

---

268.   National Security Action Memorandum No. 135

Washington, March 8, 1962.

TO

The Secretary of State

SUBJECT

British Guiana

No final decision will be taken on our policy toward British Guiana and the Jagan government until (a) the Secretary of State has a chance to

---

Source: Department of State, NSAM Files: Lot 72 D 316. Secret. Copies were sent to Attorney General Kennedy, McNamara, McCone, and General Maxwell D. Taylor.

discuss the matter with Lord Home in Geneva, and (b) Hugh Fraser completes his on-the-spot survey in British Guiana for the Colonial Office.

The questions which we must answer before we reach our decision include the following:

1.   Can Great Britain be persuaded to delay independence for a year?
2.   If Great Britain refuses to delay the date of independence, would a new election before independence be possible? If so, would Jagan win or lose? If he lost, what are the alternatives?
3.   What are the possibilities and limitations of United States action in the situation?

John F. Kennedy[1]

---

[1] Printed from a copy that indicates Kennedy signed the original.

---

269.   Letter From the Assistant Secretary of State for International Organization Affairs (Cleveland) to the Representative to the United Nations (Stevenson)

Washington, March 9, 1962.

DEAR ADLAI: We had hoped to brief you during your visit to Washington March 8 on all aspects of our present thinking about British Guiana as you requested in your letter of February 26 to the Secretary.[1] The Secretary plans to discuss this delicate problem with Lord Home in Geneva. Until we know the outcome of this discussion and have learned of the results of the on-the-spot survey which Hugh Fraser, Parliamentary Under Secretary at the Colonial Office, is making we will not reach any final policy decisions. CIA, by the way, was in no way involved in the recent disturbances in Georgetown.

We are bringing again to the Secretary's attention your pertinent comments about the effects of actions we might take on the position at the UN.

Source: Kennedy Library, National Security Files, Countries Series, British Guiana II. Top Secret; Eyes Only. Drafted by Burdett.
[1] Document 265.

On your next trip down I hope we will have a chance to fill you in completely on this rapidly moving situation.

Sincerely,

Harlan Cleveland[2]

---

[2] Printed from a copy that bears this typed signature.

---

270. Telegram From Secretary of State Rusk to the Department of State

Geneva, March 13, 1962, midnight.

Secto 28. Eyes only Acting Secretary. Re Secto 22 sent London 690.[1] Lord Home and I discussed British Guiana. He fully understands and sympathizes with our basic plan that Britain must not leave behind another Castro situation in this hemisphere. Fraser will return through Washington to see President. Home said Fraser would recommend a commission to study causes of recent disorders in British Guiana. Such a commission would delay independence and its report would muddy situation sufficiently to reopen Britain's present commitments as to schedule. Home seems ready to accept continuation British responsibility for a period despite their anxiety to settle troublesome and expensive problem.

[1 paragraph (3-1/2 lines of source text) not declassified]

For present I do not believe covert action with or without British is indicated. Home does not want to go down that trail until overt possibilities of delay are fully exploited. It is quite clear, however, that he does not exclude such action if delay and procrastination do not succeed.

I am convinced that he fully understands seriousness our view and wants to cooperate as intimate ally in finding answer which is acceptable to us.

Dept please have Wisner advised not to pressure matter for time being.

Rusk

Source: Kennedy Library, National Security Files, William H. Brubeck Series, British Guiana, Jan. 1961–April 1962. Secret; Priority. Repeated to London eyes only for the Ambassador and Wisner.

[1] Not found.

271. Memorandum From Acting Secretary of State Ball to President Kennedy

Washington, March 15, 1962.

SUBJECT

British Guiana

The British Ambassador is bringing Hugh Fraser, Parliamentary Under Secretary at the Colonial Office, to call on you at 5:00 P.M., March 16, to discuss British Guiana.

The press quotes Mr. Fraser as stating in Georgetown: (1) racialism is a greater danger than political differences; (2) all political parties must accept the inevitability of independence; (3) Britain was not aware of any Communist threat to British Guiana.

In his talk with the Secretary in Geneva about British Guiana, Lord Home seemed ready to accept a continuation of British responsibility "for a period." The Secretary reported that he did not believe covert action with or without British participation was indicated for the present. He added it was clear [1-1/2 lines of source text not declassified]. The Secretary's report on this conversation is enclosed (Tab A).[1] There may be differences between the Foreign Office and the Colonial Office about British Guiana.

In seeking Mr. Fraser's assessment you may wish to inquire about: (1) the extent of Communist association on the part of Jagan and his colleagues; (2) alternative leaders to Jagan; (3) the probable outcome of any new election; (4) how long might independence be delayed; and, (5) what might be done prior to independence to alter the difficult situation we now face. Unless steps are taken Jagan and the PPP are likely to remain in power.

You may wish to say: (1) the Secretary's talk with Lord Home was reassuring, particularly the indication the British are ready to accept a postponement of independence; (2) the British are well aware of our views on Jagan and his colleagues; (3) we should jointly examine in detail the possibilities open to us and the repercussions of alternative courses.

Staff papers are enclosed giving a chronology of events (Tab B) and comments on possible courses of action (Tab C).

George W. Ball

Source: Kennedy Library, National Security Files, William H. Brubeck Series, British Guiana, Jan. 1961–April 1962. Secret; Eyes Only.
[1] None of the tabs is printed.

272.   Paper Prepared in the Department of State

Washington, March 15, 1962.

SUBJECT

Possible Courses of Action in British Guiana

This paper points out the possibilities and limitations bearing on three possible courses of action and notes a fourth. Many permutations are possible. An early decision on U.S. policy is desirable because events are tending to constrict our options.

I.   Support Jagan in the hope of associating a British Guiana under his leadership with the West, particularly the Inter-American system. This would be a continuation of the policy agreed to with the British in September 1961.

A.   The advantages are—Jagan is now in power. He leads the largest and most cohesive party in the country. He is the ablest leader in British Guiana. This course is favored by the UK. The disadvantages arise from the Communist associations of Jagan and his colleagues. However, there is no conclusive evidence that Jagan in under Communist control. Also, during the recent disturbances he appeared incapable of controlling the situation without the support of British troops.

B.   Jagan's suspicions of the United States have grown since his visit here in October because of our failure to implement the economic agreements reached with him in October and the activities of private American individuals and organizations in the February disturbances. CIA was not involved. It is now much more difficult than ever to convince Jagan that we are sincerely prepared to support him. The prospects for success of a policy of trying to associate a British Guiana led by Jagan with the West have thus decreased substantially since September.

C.   A vocal section of the U.S. public, several members of Congress and U.S. labor unions are strongly opposed to working with Jagan. We have received since Jagan's visit 113 Congressional letters and 2,400 public letters critical of a policy of working with him. A high level effort would be required to obtain public support for such a policy. We would need to find ways to prevent private Americans, e.g. individuals, labor unions, large companies having investments in British Guiana, and right-wing groups (such as the "Christian Anti-Communist Crusade") from intervening in British Guiana contrary to this policy.

Source: Kennedy Library, National Security Files, William H. Brubeck Series, British Guiana, Jan. 1961–April 1962. Secret; Eyes Only. Transmitted to the White House.

D. We would need to carry out our economic agreement of October 1961 and be prepared to extend economic development assistance on a continuing basis at a figure in excess of $5 million per year.

E. This course would be generally favored in the UN.

II. Postponement of independence by the UK for a substantial period, say until 1964. (The "period" mentioned by Lord Home to the Secretary is probably much shorter. We probably could persuade the British to delay independence for one year from now, i.e., the spring of 1963.)

A. This would defer the decision on whether we should take steps to remove Jagan. It would provide a further period of British tutorship during which the splits within the colony might heal and more responsible leadership might emerge.

B. The Jagan Government would vigorously oppose postponement in the UN and elsewhere. Burnham and D'Aguair favor postponement.

C. The UK is strongly opposed to substantial postponement.

1. Lord Home in his letter of February 26 to the Secretary stated that HMG cannot make an exception in the single instance of British Guiana to its world-wide decolonization policy.

2. The UK would be faced by strong attacks in the UN from the Afro-Asians and possibly some Latin Americans. Just before the recess of the last General Assembly Sir Hugh Foot stated in the Fourth Committee that no decision had been made to postpone the independence conference in May despite the February riots. This was done to avoid debate on an item calling for early independence for British Guiana. Although the resumed session of the 16th General Assembly decided to limit its session in June "exclusively" to the question of Ruanda–Urundi, we and the UK must be prepared for the addition of British Guiana to the agenda if independence is postponed. The Soviets and extreme Afro-Asians would be severely critical. However, this situation might be manageable in the UN if a reasonable rationale for delay in independence can be developed. The key would be whether the Latin Americans can be convinced through discreet consultations that premature independence could result in a Castroist toehold in British Guiana. The French Africans might also be alerted to the consequences for the negro population if a Jagan–East Indian independent Government emerges which might not maintain democratic Government. Nevertheless, the U.S. would find itself in a very awkward position and if this course of action is decided upon careful and extensive consultations would be required.

3. There might be opposition from the Labor Party in the UK.

4. The UK would be faced with continuing heavy expenditure estimated roughly at $20 million a year.

5. A portion of the limited British strategic reserve might be tied down indefinitely in British Guiana.

D. In return for delay the British probably would ask:

1. Public support for postponing independence including active lobbying and voting in the UN.
2. A quid pro quo with respect to other British colonies, that is, U.S. support should Britain for its own reasons judge it desirable to slow down progress towards independence, e.g., in Kenya.
3. Shouldering part of the financial burden.
4. Account of the diversion of troops to British Guiana when pressing the UK about military commitments elsewhere.

E. Instead of announcing a postponement of independence the British could just stall for a limited number of months by such devices as a Commonwealth Commission to investigate the February disorders (the press has announced its appointment) and thorough airing of the Venezuelan claim. Such strategems probably would provoke adverse world reactions, notably in the UN. Unless accompanied by other moves Jagan probably would remain in power.

III. A program designed to bring about the removal of Cheddi Jagan.

A. The program should fit within the framework of existing democratic institutions and would probably result in some slippage in the independence day, e.g., to the first half of 1963.

B. Covert U.S. political action would be required and we would be obliged to follow up by a continuing aid program.

C. Disclosure of U.S. involvement would undermine our carefully nurtured position of anti-colonialism among the new nations of Asia and Africa and damage our position in Latin America. It could also strengthen Jagan over the long term if he became a "martyr of Yankee imperialism".

D. A non-PPP Government probably would accept a postponement of the independence date thus somewhat easing problems in the reconvened General Assembly.

E. Before proceeding on such a course of action we would need reasonable assurance of positive answers to the following questions:

1. Can we topple Jagan while maintaining at least a facade of democratic institutions?
2. Can the PPP be defeated in new elections without obvious interference?
3. Can alternative leaders better than Cheddi Jagan be found?

F. A prerequisite should be at least British acquiescence.

G. We would have to be prepared to pay a heavy price in terms of world public opinion in the UN if evidence were presented showing any

U.S. covert activities. Even if the extent of U.S. covert involvement were not disclosed, the Soviet bloc and Castro would make the most of "another Guatemala" and "another Cuba". While we probably could escape censure in the UN, our anti-colonialist image would be severely damaged, our position in Latin America undermined, and our credibility as a supporter of the principle of non-intervention would be severely diminished.

IV. Radical Solution

A. Some drastic solutions might be considered such as establishment of an OAS trusteeship for British Guiana.

B. The UK would be delighted to be relieved of responsibility; we could postpone a decision on Jagan; we would be relieved of public uneasiness and opposition both domestically and internationally.

C. However, great practical difficulties would be faced, e.g., the OAS charter makes no provision for trusteeships. Considerable additional study would be required.

---

273. Memorandum of Conversation

Washington, March 17, 1962.

SUBJECT

British Guiana

PARTICIPANTS

George C. McGhee, Under Secretary for Political Affairs, M
U. Alexis Johnson, Deputy Under Secretary for Political Affairs, G
William R. Tyler, Acting Assistant Secretary, EUR
Woodruff Wallner, Deputy Assistant Secretary for International Organization Affairs, IO
William C. Burdett, Acting Deputy Assistant Secretary, EUR
Thomas Hughes, Deputy Director for Intelligence and Research, INR
Loren Walsh, Special Assistant, INR/DDC
Rockwood H. Foster, Acting Officer in Charge, West Indian Affairs, BNA

Arthur Schlesinger, White House
Ralph Dungan, White House

Hugh Fraser, British Parliamentary Under Secretary of State for Colonies
D.A. Greenhill, Head of Chancery, British Embassy

Source: Kennedy Library, National Security Files, Countries Series, British Guiana II. Secret. Drafted by Foster and approved in G on March 21.

Mr. Johnson welcomed Mr. Fraser and asked if he would give his analysis and forecast of the situation in British Guiana.

Mr. Fraser expressed his appreciation for the opportunity of talking with officials of the United States Government. He explained, however, that he was in a difficult position since he had not yet been able to report his findings to the British Government. He asked, therefore, that anything he said be taken as preliminary and subject to modification by his Cabinet colleagues in London.

He said that the situation in British Guiana was tricky. The affairs of the colony were puffed up out of all proportion to their true importance. He felt that this was partially the fault of the British in sending troops and suspending the constitution in 1953. Jagan's visit to the United States and the hostile American reaction to him had also contributed to the inflated importance of the colony. [*1-1/2 lines of source text not declassified*] He felt we should all keep a sense of humor and proportion in considering the situation. Mr. Johnson interjected to say that Jagan had at least symbolic importance for us and we would not think it funny if another country in South America were to go communist.

Mr. Fraser stated that the racial tension between Africans and East Indians in the colony was the central problem. This made matters particularly difficult for the United Kingdom which planned to get out of the colony as soon as possible. He felt that the elections of August 1961 had been the last chance for Burnham and the Africans in the colony. From now on there would be more Indians of voting age than Africans. It was his understanding that by the middle of the 1970's there would be a ratio of almost 2 Indians to 1 African in the population.

Mr. Fraser said that he felt British Guiana was in the United States' sphere of influence. The danger lay in the real possibility that chaos would come to the colony and bring communism after it. He did not feel that communism would come first and then bring chaos with it. He believed that the Indians were not naturally inclined towards communism. They were an acquisitive people and had a strong ethnic loyalty to their own kind. This racialism had been stimulated by Burnham's African bias and by the actions of D'Aguiar.

Mr. Fraser felt that Jagan was a nice man but he was surrounded by a mildly sinister group of advisors, several of whom were the worst kind of anti-colonialist. He did not take Benn seriously and thought Jacob to be a theoretical Marxist. Kelshall was in his opinion a smart adventurer but not necessarily a communist. Rai was definitely anti-communist but not a very staunch person.

He thought it likely that the PPP would win another election since there was no clear alternative to Jagan's leadership. He thought that the United States was now unpopular with the leaders of all the parties. The United States had promised to send a mission to British Guiana but had not done so. This failure of the United States to act tended to throw the Indian merchants behind Jagan since the recent riots give them no moderate alternative. If the United States continues to stay out of the situation he believed all moderate Indian elements would increasingly tend to back Jagan. Mr. Fraser believed that both Burnham and D'Aguiar want the U.S. aid mission to come to the colony before Jagan's control becomes even tighter.

He felt that the Indian commercial community might well put pressure on Jagan to move to the right if the United States adopted a more friendly attitude. Mr. Fraser had urged Jagan to move to the right and to indicate publicly that private capital was welcome in British Guiana. He had urged Jagan to consider himself as the premier of a country and not just the head of a political party.

Mr. Fraser felt that the main contribution of his recent visit to Georgetown was to get the agreement of Jagan, Burnham and D'Aguiar to sit down together and discuss the constitution. He explained that the conference in May which would be held in London was to set a date for independence and to work out the method by which independence for the colony will be achieved. All political leaders in British Guiana want independence but each has a particular timetable and certain requirements for it. D'Aguiar wants it delayed and a referendum held, Burnham wants it soon but with some form of proportional representation and Jagan wants it immediately without provisions which diminish his present political advantage.

Mr. Fraser said he had assured all three leaders that the conference would be held in May as previously scheduled. He expected, however, that this conference might well break down on the question of an agreed constitution. In that case, the matter would have to be given to a U.K. appointed commission to consider. He felt that the constitution would have to contain certain safeguards for minorities in the colony. Both Burnham and D'Aguiar seem to favor some form of proportional representation. Mr. Fraser himself had not reached a decision on this matter but was favorably inclined to the idea at the moment. He mentioned the possibility of establishing a second legislative chamber. He was considering the idea of sending a constitutional expert from the United Kingdom to British Guiana to advise the three leaders as appropriate on the details of constitutions worked out in other countries with similar problems.

Mr. Fraser emphasized his feeling that a delay in British Guiana's independence would not help matters. He did not believe that the Jagan regime was communist. He did feel, however, that there were certain sinister implications in the apparatus being set up to penetrate the trade union movement and the educational institutions. Even these actions were not necessarily communist inclined but could be largely a result of

Indian chauvinism. He emphasized that the danger lay in chaos rather than in communism. Jagan himself had said to Fraser that the Africans would never accept a communist-dominated Indian Government and that he would never accept a communist-dominated African Government.

Mr. Fraser explained that the independence conference to be held in May would discuss two things; a date for British Guiana's independence and the means for achieving it. Essentially it would be a constituent assembly of all parties whose recommendations were only advisory to the British Government. It was necessary to produce a constitution which was not only agreeable to all three political parties but consistent with British democratic tradition.

In discussing Burnham, Fraser said that he was intelligent and opportunistic. He was, however, an African and would lose out in the long run unless he broadened the base of his support. He pointed out that Burnham had campaigned almost entirely on a racial basis during the last election. He had not even bothered to issue an election manifesto.

It had become clear to Fraser in his discussions that Jagan thinks D'Aguiar and the CIA were probably responsible for the recent riots. D'Aguiar believes Jagan instigated the civil disorder deliberately. Burnham damns all parties concerned. Mr. Fraser felt nevertheless that all elements were shocked by the racial factor in the recent riots. He pointed out that Jagan could easily have called in the Indian cane-cutters from the field to attack the African rioters. This was probably prevented by the rapid British action in bringing troops to the city. The violence in Georgetown had been directed mainly against Indian shops. The demonstrations had begun as a non-racial, public protest against Jagan's budget. The causes of the rioting would be determined by the Commonwealth Commission of Inquiry which had recently been announced.

In response to a question, Mr. Fraser did not believe that there was an alternate Indian leader within the PPP who could command support equal to Jagan. Rai had been spoken of in this connection but Fraser seriously doubted whether he had the capacity to lead the PPP.

In discussing the Commonwealth Commission of Inquiry, Mr. Fraser emphasized that its terms of reference were deliberately being kept narrow. Jagan had initially asked for a United Nations commission which would have placed the problem squarely into a cold war situation. Mr. Fraser had talked him out of this and obtained his agreement to a commission appointed by the United Kingdom. He explained that the United Kingdom had strong moral obligation to hold such an inquiry in view of the presence of British troops in the colony. He did not feel that this inquiry would damage Jagan's position. He emphasized that it would not in all probability delay independence.

In response to a question, Mr. Fraser expressed the opinion that independence would come possibly at the end of 1962 but more probably in early 1963. He emphasized strongly that it would be madness to attempt to delay independence and maintain British Guiana's colonial status with British bayonets. He felt the situation would not improve and delaying independence would make things worse.

Mr. Johnson said that we were worried about things getting worse in the colony and wondered what would happen when the troops were pulled out. Mr. Fraser said that the police force which was now largely African would have to be strengthened. Safeguards would be put into the constitution. He felt that British troops should be pulled out as soon as possible and that the number should be cut down to two companies immediately.

Mr. Fraser said he was aware of the recent offer by Cuba to take a large number of British Guiana students. It was clear to him that an independent British Guiana would have a neutralist foreign policy.

Mr. Fraser urged in the strongest possible terms the importance of the United States sending the economic mission to British Guiana as soon as possible. He said that the time was psychologically right for such a mission and it would have a most favorable impact on the people there. Mr. Johnson expressed his concern at the amount of aid which Jagan demanded from the United States. Since this amount was so disproportionate with that available to be given he wondered whether the dispatch of a United States mission and the provision of a very modest amount of money would only cause more trouble. Mr. Schlesinger added that we must also think of the effect on other Latin American countries of aid to British Guiana. He pointed out that on a per capita basis a significant grant of United States aid to British Guiana would place our program out of balance with that being given to an important country such as Brazil.

Mr. Fraser indicated that Jagan was desperate for money. He had tried to get it from the United States, Canada and the Soviet Bloc with no success. The key to the situation in his view was some alleviation by the West now of Jagan's financial problem. The arrival of a U.S. mission would make people in the colony feel that they belonged to the free world and had not been cast into outer darkness. Jagan himself liked strutting on the world stage and was probably bored with the prospect of tending to his internal domestic knitting.

Mr. Fraser indicated that the British planned to leave British Guiana quickly but they hoped to leave conditions there as tidy as possible. He said the British companies in the colony were not worried about this and that Bookers and Alcan were not worried about nationalization. He indicated that the United Kingdom upon leaving the colony would probably agree to providing to British Guiana the balance of the Colonial Development and Welfare commitment already made. This commitment was approximately 8 million pounds sterling.

Mr. Fraser thought it was [*less than 1 line of source text not declassified*] to send his wife Janet up to Canada wearing a red shirt. He thought it unlikely that Canada would make a substantial economic contribution.

Mr. Johnson said that the United States would like to feel more confident that the withdrawal of British troops and the granting of independence to British Guiana would not bring chaos and a communist controlled government. He reminded Mr. Fraser that we thought of this situation partly in terms of our Cuban experience. Castro had originally been presented as a reformer. We do not intend to be taken in twice. He felt it important that the United States and the United Kingdom work very closely at all levels on the problem of British Guiana in order to prevent catastrophe from taking place there. Mr. Fraser agreed entirely but expressed the opinion that the problem of communism would get worse if a United States mission did not go to the colony soon. He felt there was a real possibility that the Soviets might decide to send such a mission if there was no constructive action by the West. Mr. Johnson suggested the advisability of discussions between the U.S. and U.K. about a political action program. Mr. Fraser did not respond.

Mr. Schlesinger and Mr. Dungan mentioned the difficult domestic problem which the United States faced with regard to Jagan. The provision by the United Kingdom of a constitutional advisor would not help to allay fears in Congress and among the American people about the future of the colony. The Administration would be subject to severe criticism particularly from the right wing along the lines that a United States mission was being sent to help Jagan, the communist. The activities of Mr. Sluis of the Christian anti-Communist Crusade made matters worse. The Administration was already facing considerable opposition to the foreign aid legislation before Congress. Criticism of aid to Jagan would not help politically in getting this important legislation approved. Jagan has made things very difficult by his behavior in the United States. It would be helpful if he would take some action to better his United States public image and destroy the parallel in the American public mind with Castro. It would help a great deal if Jagan would do something about this or if some other figure were to arise as the leader of British Guiana.

Mr. Fraser felt that neither Bookers nor Alcan would wish to get involved in British Guiana's politics. Bookers probably considered Jagan to be the best leader of the lot. Any attempt to dump Jagan or to manipulate the political molecules in the situation would be tricky and apt to be counter-productive. If proportional representation became part of the British Guiana constitution this might help in affecting the outcome of a new election. He stressed, however, that such a solution could not be imposed either by the United States or the United Kingdom. We must maneuver British Guianese opinion into wanting some kind of an adjust-ment in the present political machinery.

Mr. Johnson ended the meeting by expressing his thanks to Mr. Fraser for his comprehensive presentation and analysis of the situation. He urged that the closest contact between United States and the United Kingdom Governments be maintained. He promised that the United States Government would take a hard look at the possibility of sending the economic mission to British Guiana. There might be some possibility of connecting it with the recent disaster in Georgetown and placing it in a humanitarian frame of reference.

274. Special National Intelligence Estimate

SNIE 87.2–62   Washington, April 11, 1962.

THE SITUATION AND PROSPECTS IN BRITISH GUIANA

The Problem

To estimate the short-term outlook for British Guiana, with particu-lar reference to the political orientation of Jagan and his party, the likely outcome if new elections were to be held, and the nature of possible alter-natives to the Jagan government.

Conclusions

1. Racial conflict is likely to continue to be the basic factor in the political situation in British Guiana. The two major political parties rep-resent the nearly equal East Indian and Negro communities and party rivalry has increasingly taken on a racial character. The British, who have exercised a stabilizing influence, will almost certainly withdraw and grant independence not later than mid-1963, since they apparently fore-see strong adverse reactions with unpleasant international connotations if they try to extend the period of their authority in the colony. (Paras. 5, 13–14)

Source: Central Intelligence Agency Files, Job 79–R01012A, ODDI Registry. Secret; Noforn. A note on the title page indicates the SNIE was submitted by the Director of Cen-tral Intelligence and concurred in by the U.S. Intelligence Board.

2.   Premier Cheddi Jagan and the People's Progressive Party (PPP) represent the East Indians, who are more numerous than the Negroes and who have been consolidated politically by the February 1962 disturbances. Jagan and the PPP are likely to maintain control of the government, whether or not new elections are held. However, any one of a number of likely developments could precipitate another period of violence. (Paras. 5, 11,15, 18)

3.   The PPP leadership has a clear record of Communist association and of Communist-line policies, but the evidence does not show whether or to what extent they are under international Communist control. We believe, however, that Jagan is a Communist, though the degree of Moscow's control is not yet clear. A Jagan government in the postindependence period would probably follow a policy of nonalignment in international affairs, but would probably lean in the Soviet direction. Its associations with East and West would be highly opportunistic and strongly influenced by its interest in obtaining aid for British Guiana. Its domestic program would be radically socialist and reformist. (Paras. 6–7, 19)

4.   The People's National Congress (PNC), led by L. Forbes Burnham, is supported by a large proportion of the Negro population but by almost no one else. A PNC majority in the legislature, even with the support of the small United Force Party (UF), is unlikely under presently foreseeable circumstances. If the PNC were to come to power its policies would probably be leftist and neutralist, though somewhat less radical and pro-Bloc than those of the PPP. (Paras. 8–9, 15)

Discussion

I.   Background

5.   For over a decade political life in British Guiana has been marked by the racial split between East Indians, who make up about half of the population, and Negroes, who account for a somewhat smaller proportion. The most powerful political force has been the People's Progressive Party (PPP), led by the government's East Indian Premier, Cheddi Jagan. The PPP derives its strength mainly from East Indians, most of whom live in the countryside, but also has found some support among the Negroes. In the August 1961 election, the PPP won about 43 percent of the popular vote, thereby gaining a 20–15 majority in the legislature.[1] Since the elections it has demonstrated considerable political ineptitude and has failed to make headway against the enormous economic difficulties of the colony.

[2 paragraphs (1 column of a 2-column format) of source text not declassified]

---

[1] The election in one constituency was set aside by court decision as a result of irregularity and the PPP majority is now 19–15. [Footnote in the source text.]

8. The principal opposition party is the People's National Congress (PNC) of L. Forbes Burnham, a Negro who is a radical reformer and who until 1954 was one of Jagan's lieutenants in the PPP and an advocate of extremist measures in government. The PNC is supported by most of the colony's Negro population in the cities (including most government employees) and in the bauxite mining areas. Outside Negro ranks it has virtually no following, and among many middle class Negroes its support is not firm. In the 1961 election it polled 41 percent of the vote and won 11 seats in the legislature. PNC policy has been largely that of opposing the PPP. What we can say of PNC policy if it were to form a government must be based largely on Burnham's statements and on the content of his party newspaper. The PNC in office would probably feature a more moderate policy of domestic socialism than the PPP. Likewise, in the foreign field it would also be neutralist but somewhat less pro-Bloc than the PPP. [4-1/2 lines of 2-column format source text not declassified]

9. An additional opposition party is the United Force (UF), which seeks to be multiracial. It is based largely on the small commercial class (including the Portuguese minority) which fears that Jagan would transform the country into a Communist state after independence. It won four seats in the 1961 election. Had the UF not run, the PNC might have won some of these seats but probably not all. In any case it would not have gained a majority.

II. February Riots

10. A tremendous increase in the racial tension in British Guiana and in the potential for conflict came as a result of a week of strikes and riots which shook the capital city of Georgetown in mid-February 1962. The immediate cause of the strikes was Premier Jagan's budget bill, but the riots were also rooted in the longstanding racial antagonism and in the dissatisfaction of many urban groups, notably public service employees and businessmen, with the policies of the PPP government. As the disturbances spread, they took on the character of a struggle between the Negro urban community and the East Indian Government and its rural supporters.

11. Paradoxically, the February crisis strengthened Jagan by consolidating the support of his East Indian followers. At the same time, it reduced his stature and tarnished his prestige as a national leader. His economic and financial problems are more acute now than before the riots. His government is hard pressed to meet current expenditures. Whereas before the riots almost 20 percent of the labor force was out of work, an even larger number are now unemployed as a result of the destruction in Georgetown. Jagan's plans for economic development have been set back, partly because he has been forced to trim his tax measures and partly because uncertainties about his country's political stability are inhibiting the flow of outside public assistance, on which

development is heavily dependent. The February events have discouraged foreign investment.[2] Extensive capital flight is in progress and foreign investors are doing no more than attending to existing operations. A good many city merchants, East Indians among them, are inclined to cut and run rather than to stay and rebuild.

12. On the other hand, the crisis also left the opposition with reduced prestige. Its several leaders acted recklessly and in the end tended to neutralize each other. Those unions which are predominantly Negro actively collaborated with the opposition parties, but the rank and file of the largest single union, chiefly East Indians, did not. There have been rumors of dissension in the PPP and reports that the opposition might try to win some of Jagan's legislators away from him, but sufficient defections to cause the legislative defeat of the Jagan government are not considered probable in the near future under existing circumstances.

III. Prospects

13. The British presence is a check on the violent political forces that seethe near the surface in British Guiana. British departure will be the prelude to a period of uncertainty and possibly of violence during which the country will be establishing its international orientation. Nevertheless, the British appear determined to get out. They are not anxious to continue to put money into British Guiana, and they calculate that the present cost to them of $7 million a year would be increased to $20 million per annum if they reimposed direct government. They assert in private that British Guiana is in the US, not the UK, sphere of interest and they probably consider that its future is not properly their problem, but one for the US. At the same time, London is less inclined than is the US to believe that communism will achieve dominance in the colony. Finally, it fears that to delay independence very long would arouse indignation in many parts of the world where colonialism is a sensitive issue.

14. The British may see fit to hold on for a time by postponing the May 1962 conference, which was to have discussed plans and timing of independence. Even if the conference is held on schedule, independence may be deferred. Jagan has agreed to an investigation of the recent riots by a Commonwealth commission, but the the scope of the inquiry is such that it is not likely to necessitate much delay. Independence might also be delayed by the failure of Jagan and opposition leaders to get together on a new constitution. A vote of no-confidence in the government could also hold up proceedings, but we believe that Jagan will move cautiously on

---

[2] British foreign investment in Guiana amounts to between $400 and $500 million and is mainly in sugar production. Canadian investment (about $80 million) and US investment (about $30 million) is mainly in bauxite and sugar. [Footnote in the source text.]

matters of domestic policy to assure control of his majority in the legislature. In any circumstance, however, we do not anticipate that the British
will delay much beyond the end of 1962.

15. For any of the above reasons, the UK may find it desirable to hold
new elections. New elections held on the same basis as were those in
August 1961—with the same parties and same electoral system—would
probably return a Jagan government again, even in the face of a PNC–UF
electoral coalition. The PNC is urging a proportional representation system, under which it believes it could turn the PPP out, but the latter is
unlikely to accept any form of proportional representation that would
seriously prejudice its electoral chances.

16. After independence Jagan [3 *lines of 2-column format source text
not declassified*] will probably seek to move toward consolidation of his
control over the country. [2-1/2 *lines of 2-column format source text not
declassified*]

17. Nevertheless, Jagan will be under some restraints not to ride
roughshod over the wishes of the public—Negro as well as East Indian.
The size and potential strength of the Negro community were well demonstrated by the February riots, and Jagan will fear to bring the Negroes
into the streets against him again. He is also aware that the rank and file
of his party—and indeed the East Indian community as a whole—is not
Communist and may react against unpalatable Communist or socialist
measures. Furthermore, he has the problem of developing and controlling a security force.[3] He has apparently been considering a largely East
Indian security force of some kind, but must be aware of the dangers
implicit in such a move, especially since the existing police force is principally made up of Negroes. Jagan's [*less than 1 line of 2-column format source
text not declassified*] enthusiasm for his own reform programs and the
temptation to work through and for the East Indian community may be
moderated by the realization that, if the country is to be held together,
important concessions must be made to the Negroes. [2 *lines of 2-column
format source text not declassified*]

18. We do not believe that we can project our estimate very far
beyond the period of independence. Jagan will almost certainly maintain his predominant position in the PPP, and can probably prevent an
opposition government from taking over. However, any one of a number
of likely developments could precipitate another period of disturbances
like that of last February. We see no prospect for a coalition of moderates
of both parties and both races.

---

[3] In addition to the 1,500-man local police, the security forces in the colony now
include a Volunteer Guard of about 500, some 200 British troops normally stationed near
Georgetown, and about 600 of those brought in at the time of the disorders. Jagan has
threatened to recruit his own police or to create a national army and in response the British
are proposing to enlarge the local police by 500. [Footnote in the source text.]

19. We believe a Jagan government in the postindependence period would be likely to identify itself—as it has in the past—with anticolonialist and independence movements. It would probably follow a policy of nonalignment and seek to benefit from relations with both the West and the Communist countries, but would probably lean in the Soviet direction. For some time Jagan has been seeking trade and aid from the West and he has expressed interest in joining the Organization of American States and in participating in the Alliance for Progress. He has also been seeking trade and aid from the Bloc. He has just signed a trade contract with East Germany and other deals with Bloc countries are likely to follow.

---

275. Memorandum From the President's Special Assistant (Schlesinger) to President Kennedy

Washington, April 27, 1962.

[Source: Kennedy Library, Papers of Arthur M. Schlesinger, Jr., British Guiana. Secret. 2 pages of source text not declassified.]

---

276. Telegram From the Department of State to the Embassy in the United Kingdom

Washington, June 7, 1962, 5:48 p.m.

6512. Eyes only Ambassador Bruce. Following is text of letter to President from Macmillan dated May 30:

"Dear Friend: When we met in Washington last month we did not find time for any full discussion of the problems of Colonial policy. I am

---

Source: Kennedy Library, National Security Files, Countries Series, British Guiana II. Top Secret; Verbatim Text. Drafted and approved by Burdett.

however conscious that Colonial problems can be so presented as to weaken the Western position generally, both at the United Nations and with neutral opinion elsewhere. In the course of our discussion you referred briefly to this, and said you were thinking of taking steps to secure closer co-ordination on this question between the various agencies of your Government, both in Washington and in New York. You also said that you would be glad to have fuller information on some of our own Colonial problems. I agree that there is room here for closer consultation between our two Governments; and, if you should decide to establish a single focus of co-ordination for this in Washington, we should be very glad to feed into it fuller information on our own Colonial problems and our views on the Colonial problems of our Allies. On these questions it seems best that Anglo-American consultation should be centered in Washington; and, if you would care to tell our Ambassador what arrangements you have in mind for this purpose, I will see that he is kept fully supplied with the necessary information and views from this end.

Meanwhile, there is the rather separate question of British Guiana on which, at your suggestion, representatives of the State Department had some talk with the official advisers who accompanied me to Washington. The suggestions then made on behalf of the State Department were partly general and partly particular. Their general request was that we should keep you more fully informed of the probable course of political and constitutional developments in British Guiana. [3 lines of source text not declassified]

Since my return to London I have considered these requests in consultation with the Ministers concerned. We all recognise that developments in British Guiana—and, for that matter, in British Honduras—are of special concern to the United States Government. When these territories become independent, as they must before very long, they may well be of more direct concern to you than to us. We hope that you will continue to interest yourself in their future: indeed, in the case of British Guiana, we have been pressing you to contribute towards the cost of economic development. In these circumstances we fully agree that, in these last stages of their advance to independence, you should have full opportunity of expressing your views on the shaping of their future.

We are therefore ready to make special arrangements for consultation with you on the affairs of British Guiana and British Honduras. In this case, as we shall be going into greater detail, I think it would be better that the consultations should be held in London. I envisage a series of informal meetings which, though held at the Foreign Office, would include representatives of the Colonial Office, and also, when necessary, the [less than 1 line of source text not declassified] other Departments concerned. If you agree that this would be helpful, perhaps you will arrange for your Ambassador here to nominate the representatives who would regularly attend these meetings. I know you will feel, as I do, that we ought to keep these meetings secret.

[*1 paragraph (16-1/2 lines of source text) not declassified*]

Finally, you may like to have an indication of our latest thinking on the course of constitutional development in British Guiana. Previously, we had been thinking in terms of an Independence Conference in May, to be followed by independence within a few months. We have now decided to postpone the Conference until July, and we intend to try to persuade the leaders of the political Parties to agree that elections should be held before the territory becomes independent. This will give us a little more time and also, perhaps, a further opportunity to establish whether, under a democratic system, there is any alternative to Dr. Jagan's Government. If, however, it becomes clear, by a further expression of electoral opinion, that Dr. Jagan's Party is the choice of the people, I hope we shall be able to persuade you that the best line for both our Governments to follow is to do our best to keep that Government on the side of the West by co-operating fully with it and giving it the economic support which it requires."

Rusk

277. Memorandum for the Special Group

Washington, June 13, 1962.

[Source: Kennedy Library, National Security Files, William H. Brubeck Series, British Guiana, Aug. 1962. Secret; Eyes Only. 6 pages of source text not declassified.]

278.   Memorandum From the President's Special Assistant (Schlesinger) to President Kennedy

Washington, June 21, 1962.

SUBJECT

British Guiana

I attach a collection of papers from the State Department.[1] They include [3 *lines of source text not declassified*] and (c) a report from Harry Hoffmann on the British Guiana political situation.

[3 *paragraphs (18-1/2 lines of source text) not declassified*]

At the same time, the Secretary recommends that we go ahead with the economic studies proposed by the Hoffman–Mayne mission on the ground that action on the economic aid front will indicate good will, [*less than 1 line of source text not declassified*] and lay the groundwork for a development program when we have a friendly government.

I agree that the evidence shows increasingly that Jagan's heart is with the Communist world. He is quite plainly a Marxist nationalist, who sees the west in terms of the old stereotypes of capitalism and imperialism and who is deeply persuaded of the superiority of Communist methods and values. There is no convincing evidence that he is a disciplined member of the Communist party, but then neither is Castro. [8 *lines of source text not declassified*]

The alternative to Jagan is Forbes Burnham. [5-1/2 *lines of source text not declassified*] Burnham, moreover, as an African, is the representative of the ethnic group deemed by its low birth rate to minority status in British Guiana. On the other hand, Burnham is regarded more favorably by the AFL–CIO people who have had British Guiana contacts and by some people in the British Labour Party (among them Gaitskell). He made a generally good impression in his visit to Washington.

All alternatives in British Guiana are terrible; but I have little doubt that an independent British Guiana under Burnham (*if* Burnham will commit himself to a multi-racial policy) would cause us many fewer problems than an independent British Guiana under Jagan.

[4 *paragraphs (25-1/2 lines of source text) not declassified*]

On a three-day trip to the Berbice and Corentyne last week, I found considerable unrest and suspicion—even fear—of Jagan's leanings among middle-class East Indians, even in Jagan's home village of Port

---

Source: Kennedy Library, Papers of Arthur M. Schlesinger, Jr., British Guiana. Top Secret.

[1] None printed.

Mourant. They expressed respect and admiration for Rai—but to the man they said in an election showdown the masses would flock to Jagan. Rai was described as too new on the political scene, compared with Jagan, and lacking in the mass appeal that belongs to Jagan, who could make political hay by characterizing Rai as a traitor to the cause. In the end, they said, the East Indians would vote race—and Jagan would get the votes of even many of the doubtful ones as the East Indian most likely to win.

This situation would be changed, of course, if there were a uniting of the Burnham and D'Aguiar forces behind Rai. But, so far, Burnham is so impressed by his own importance and self-analysis of popularity that this is not likely to happen. He is convinced in his own mind that his PNC would win any new election, and until such time as he can be persuaded otherwise the chances for any reasonable and effective unification are remote. Also, there is considerable feeling here, which I am inclined to share, that British Guiana would be worse off with Burnham than with Jagan.

[4 paragraphs (13 lines of source text) not declassified]

Arthur Schlesinger, jr.[2]

_____

[2] Printed from a copy that bears this typed signature.

---

279. Telegram From the Department of State to the Embassy in the United Kingdom

Washington, July 2, 1962, 5:49 p.m.

10. Eyes only for Ambassador Bruce. Request you reply to portion of Macmillan's letter to President of May 30[1] dealing with consultations on

_____

Source: Kennedy Library, National Security Files, Countries Series, British Guiana II. Confidential. Drafted by Burdett; cleared by Sweeney (BNA), Cleveland (IO), Tasca (AF), Furnas (S/S), and McGeorge Bundy; and approved by U. Alexis Johnson. Repeated to USUN eyes only for Stevenson.
[1] See Document 276.

colonialism. At your discretion you may pass our views as given below to either Macmillan or Lord Home indicating they have approval of President:

1.   We are happy to see from Macmillan's letter of May 30 to President that US and UK agree on desirability closest liaison on colonial problems. Generally speaking there are two somewhat overlapping aspects involved—detailed consideration of individual problems and exchange of views on broad policy issues. It might be helpful if you were to feed into your Washington Embassy fuller detailed information on individual problems. We would also welcome as much advance indication as feasible of the trend of your thinking on over-all developments. We of course are glad to share our ideas with you. By this approach we could avoid misunderstandings arising from different assessments of factual situation and would be fully aware of each other's policy thinking and the reasons therefor even though we might be obliged to agree to disagree in specific instances.

2.   On reflection we believe further formalization of methods of consultation is unnecessary. We are already in constant touch through our Embassies in London and Washington and US and UK Delegations to the UN. These consultations are supplemented periodically by high-level exchanges on broad policy issues. Governor Williams will be in London this month for general discussion of colonial policy and Mr. Cleveland for talks on UN aspects. This combination of day to day consultation supplemented by periodic high-level exchanges seems to us to offer most effective utilization of expert knowledge and senior policy level consideration. We would welcome, of course, your further views and any further suggestions you care to make.

3.   Essential point in our opinion is that all concerned should know that President and Prime Minister firmly believe in value of close and continuing consultation.

Rusk

280.   Memorandum From Secretary of State Rusk to President Kennedy

Washington, July 12, 1962.

SUBJECT

British Guiana

We have reassessed the probable orientation of an independent British Guiana under Cheddi Jagan's leadership and I attach for your consideration a paper describing the program we propose to follow (Enclosure 1).[1]

A Special National Intelligence Estimate dated April 11, 1962,[2] concluded "We believe ... that Jagan is a Communist, though the degree of Moscow's control is not yet clear. A Jagan government in the post independence period would probably follow a policy of nonalignment in international affairs, but would probably lean in the Soviet direction." [5-1/2 lines of source text not declassified] We have also been given by the FBI a report of the American Communist Party's intention to seek for Jagan economic assistance from the Soviet Bloc (Enclosure 3). Attached is a study we have prepared of contacts by the People's Progressive Party (PPP) with communists, communist fronts and the communist bloc since September, 1961 (Enclosure 4). During cross examination before the Commonwealth Commission of Enquiry into the causes of the February riots Jagan admitted on June 22, 1962 that he was a communist. This admission came after much muddled explanation by Jagan as to what the term "communism" meant and was qualified by his definition that communism was a system based on "from each according to his ability and to each according to his needs". Further questioning on Jagan's political beliefs was cut short on June 26 by the British Chairman of the Commission with the ruling that it was useless to pursue the subject since it had "already been established beyond peradventure" that Dr. Jagan was a communist.

In the light of all the evidence which has now accumulated, I believe we are obliged to base our policy on the premise that, once independent, Cheddi Jagan will establish a "Marxist" regime in British Guiana and associate his country with the Soviet Bloc to a degree unacceptable to us for a state in the Western Hemisphere. Such a development would have severe adverse effects in the foreign relations field and obvious undesirable repercussions within this country.

Source: Kennedy Library, National Security Files, Countries Series, British Guiana II. Top Secret.

[1] None of the attachments is printed.

[2] Document 274.

It is also my view that a policy of trying to work with Jagan, as urged by the British, will not pay off. Jagan is already too far committed emotionally and suspicious of our intentions.

[1 paragraph (3 lines of source text) not declassified]

I propose that we transfer the locale of the discussions with the U.K. on British Guiana to Washington and that I call in the British Ambassador and speak to him along the lines indicated in the attached paper. My thought in transferring the locale to Washington is to enable us to deal through a sympathetic British Ambassador with the Foreign Office and the Prime Minister rather than sending messages to our Embassy in London which in practice usually discusses British Guiana with the not so sympathetic Colonial Office. It is further helpful to us to talk in Washington because we have available here people with the most up-to-date U.S. information on British Guiana and we would be able to provide nuances of our current thinking to the British Ambassador.

Recommendations

I recommend that you approve specifically the following:

[4 paragraphs (12 lines of source text) not declassified]

5. That you approve my talking with the British Ambassador along the lines of Section I of the attached paper and that we try to maintain Washington as the venue for any further discussions on British Guiana in the immediate future. This would constitute a reply to Prime Minister Macmillan's letter to you of May 30[3] (Enclosure 6).

Dean Rusk[4]

---

[3] See Document 276.

[4] Printed from a copy that bears this typed signature.

281. Memorandum From the President's Special Assistant for National Security Affairs (Bundy) to President Kennedy

Washington, July 13, 1962.

SUBJECT

British Guiana

Here is a paper from Dean Rusk which comes out hard for a policy of getting rid of Jagan.[1] It is a careful and thorough argument of one side. It has more energy than most State Department papers.

These documents seem to me to demonstrate that Jagan will indeed go the way of Castro, if he is not prevented. He would be weaker than Castro, because he is even more inefficient, but he would also probably be more easily controlled from Moscow.

But while the papers make a clear case against supporting Jagan, or even trying to sustain peaceful coexistence with him, the case for the proposed tactics to be used in opposing him is not so clear. In particular, I think it is unproven that CIA knows how to manipulate an election in British Guiana without a backfire.

My immediate suggestion is that when you have read this, we should have a pretty searching meeting on the details of the tactical plans, in which you can cross-examine those who are really responsible for their development. I do not think the Secretary of State should go to the British Ambassador with the proposed talking paper until we are a little more sure of our own capabilities and intentions.

There is also a real question whether Dean Rusk is the man to talk with the British on this. The last time he told Home "we could not put up with Jagan" the British simply dug in their heels. Since British support for an anti-Jagan policy would be the most powerful single force for its success, I think you may want to go all out with David yourself on this one.

McG. B.

Source: Kennedy Library, National Security Files, William H. Brubeck Series, British Guiana, June 1–Aug. 15, 1962. Top Secret.
[1] Document 280.

282.   Memorandum From the President's Special Assistant (Schlesinger) to the President's Special Assistant (Dungan)

Washington, July 19, 1962.

SUBJECT

British Guiana

I return herewith the BG dossier.[1] I agree with Mac's memorandum and with my earlier memorandum[2] on the initial version of the plan (which I think you have). In short, I agree that there is no future in Jagan; and that the Burnham risk is less than the Jagan risk; but the CIA plan makes me nervous; [1 line of source text not declassified]. I also share Mac's doubts as to whether the Secretary is the man to talk to Ormsby Gore on the subject.

I would suggest that you bear down hard on two points:

1) Does CIA think that they can carry out a really *covert* operation— i.e., an operation which, whatever suspicions Jagan might have, will leave no visible traces which he can cite before the world, whether he wins or loses, as evidence of U.S. intervention?

2) If we lose, what then? The present suggestions are pretty bleak— especially when our chances of winning are probably less than 50–50.

Arthur Schlesinger, jr.[3]

Source: Kennedy Library, National Security Files, William H. Brubeck Series, British Guiana, June 1–Aug. 15, 1962. Top Secret.

[1] Not printed.

[2] Documents 281 and 278.

[3] Printed from a copy that bears this typed signature.

---

283.   Memorandum Prepared in the Central Intelligence Agency

Washington, July 20, 1962.

[Source: Central Intelligence Agency, DCI/McCone Files, Job 80–B01258A, Box 6, 7/1/62–12/31/62. Secret; Eyes Only. 2 pages of source text not declassified.]

284. Draft Telegram From the Department of State to the Embassy in the United Kingdom

Washington, undated.

FYI. During weekend July 20 the President spoke along following lines to UK Ambassador Ormsby Gore in reply Macmillan's letter May 30[1] re British Guiana:

The President welcomed the PM's suggestion for special consultations about BG and suggested they be held in Washington. [*3 lines of source text not declassified*] Commenting that an independent BG under Jagan's leadership seriously disturbed him, President said US cannot afford to see another Communist regime established in this hemisphere. It is obvious Jagan is distrustful of US motives, that there is little chance of our obtaining his confidence and that it therefore seems unrealistic to hope now that BG could be kept on side of West by policy of cooperation. [*1-1/2 lines of source text not declassified*]

Stating he was glad to know that UK envisages new elections in BG, the President said they would provide opportunity for government of different complexion to come into power through democratic processes. [*8 lines of source text not declassified*]

In conclusion the President told Ormsby Gore that in economic field we are going ahead with the additional detailed studies recommended by our survey mission recently returned from BG. He said our idea is to let people of BG know we are serious about helping them and to be that much further along with preliminary work by the time a new government comes into power in BG. End FYI.

Source: Kennedy Library, National Security Files, Countries Series, British Guiana II. Top Secret; Limited Distribution; Eyes Only. Drafted by Rewinkel on August 1; cleared by Burdett, Scott (INR), and Little (S/S); and approved by U. Alexis Johnson. There is no indication on the source text that this telegram was sent, nor was an outgoing telegram found in Department of State files.

[1] See Document 276. The President and Ormsby Gore met in Hyannis Port, Massachusetts, July 21 and 22.

285. Memorandum From the President's Special Assistant for National Security Affairs (Bundy) to the Acting Deputy Assistant Secretary of State for European Affairs (Burdett)

Washington, August 6, 1962.

As I told you I would on the telephone, I spoke briefly with Lord Hood, at the President's instruction, to comment on the British response to the President's proposals on British Guiana. Lord Hood told me that he had not been informed of the response on this other channel. I told him its general nature and indicated the President's concern that a study of this sort might imply a long delay in reaching an agreed U.S./U.K. position. I told Lord Hood that from our point of view there was considerable urgency in this matter, and while much the best scheme would be to proceed in agreement with the U.K., we would be sorry to have action hampered by prolonged discussion back and forth. [3 lines of source text not declassified] Nevertheless, I said that the President had asked me to convey this point to Lord Hood for such onward communication to the Ambassador or to the Foreign Office as he might think useful.

[1 paragraph (5 lines of source text) not declassified]

I am sending this memorandum only to you [less than 1 line of source text not declassified] and will count on you to arrange for any essential limited distribution in your respective empires.

McGeorge Bundy[1]

Source: Kennedy Library, National Security Files, Countries Series, British Guiana II. Secret.

[1] Printed from a copy that bears this typed signature.

286.   Memorandum From the President's Special Assistant for National Security Affairs (Bundy) to Director of Central Intelligence Helms

Washington, August 6, 1962.

The President has received the message conveyed in your memorandum of August 6th,[1] and requests that the following reply be made through [*less than 1 line of source text not declassified*]:

"The President has received the message [*1 line of source text not declassified*] and is quite willing that discussions on British Guiana be conducted [*less than 1 line of source text not declassified*]. The President would like to emphasize, however, that in his view the first object of these discussions would be to determine whether our two governments can reach agreement on their assessment of the situation in British Guiana and the urgency of taking action to improve it. The President approves of the plan to have a team of four officers come to Washington on August 14th, but he hopes that these discussions can be followed promptly by a policy assessment which will permit him and the Prime Minister to come to a clear understanding on which action can be based."

McGeorge Bundy[2]

Source: Kennedy Library, National Security Files, Countries Series, British Guiana II. Secret.

[1] Not found.

[2] Printed from a copy that bears this typed signature.

---

287.   Memorandum From the Department of State Executive Secretary (Brubeck) to the President's Special Assistant for National Security Affairs (Bundy)

Washington, August 8, 1962.

SUBJECT

British Guiana

At a meeting this afternoon between Mr. Johnson and Mr. Helms it was agreed that we would propose to the British a specific agenda for the

---

Source: Kennedy Library, National Security Files, Countries Series, British Guiana II. Top Secret. A copy was sent to Burdett.

talks next week on British Guiana. The objective is to bring matters to a head by forcing a consideration of political factors [1 *line of source text not declassified*].

The agenda is as follows:

1. Assessment of the situation in British Guiana.
[4 *paragraphs (4 lines of source text) not declassified*]

E.S. Little[1]

---

[1] Little signed for Brubeck above Brubeck's typed signature.

---

288. Memorandum From the President's Special Assistant (Schlesinger) to President Kennedy

Washington, September 5, 1962.

SUBJECT

British Guiana

On September 5 a meeting was held at Mr. Moscoso's office to discuss the aid program to British Guiana. Mr. Burdett represented the State Department.

The following considerations were involved:

1) the Administration can not be put in the position of working to strengthen a quasi-Communist regime in British Guiana—and this is all the more true in view of recent developments in Cuba;

2) our covert plans in British Guiana will be much facilitated [1 *line of source text not declassified*], which requires a minimum of continuing contact with the Jagan regime; and

3) should our covert program succeed, we would wish to be in the position of being able to give the successor regime immediate aid, which requires the completion before that time of certain economic and engineering feasibility studies. (The question of the covert program was not, of course, brought up at the meeting, but was very much in Burdett's mind when he set forth State's position.)

Source: Kennedy Library, National Security Files, Countries Series, British Guiana II. Secret. Copies were sent to McGeorge Bundy and Dungan.

The conclusion, agreed to by everybody, was as follows:

a) that we should go ahead with certain economic feasibility studies as follows:

Hydro-electric economic feasibility	$ 75,000
Topographic and geological survey at Tiger Hill (engineering feasibility)	150,000
DEB Highway Development	100,000
Ebini Agricultural Area (Support to UN Soil Survey—Preplanning of Land Settlements—Water Conditions)	100,000
Economic Study of New Amsterdam	60,000
Architectural Study for Outpatients Clinic for Georgetown Hospital	80,000?

This amounts to about half a million dollars. The AID bill budgets about $1.5 million for assistance to British Guiana. Moscoso brought this British Guiana item up on two occasions before committees on the Hill this summer, and no one asked any questions about it. The feasibility studies are invisible so far as immediate impact is concerned, and if anyone heard about them, going ahead with them would be defensible in terms of congressional clearance and approval.

b) that we should postpone until mid-November the asking of bids for the test cut of the Berbice Bar at New Amsterdam. This project, which would cost $860,000, would require a public call for bids in the U.S. and would be highly visible in British Guiana. The feeling was that we should go ahead with the project *after* November on the ground that this would show what U.S. aid could do if there were a government we really wanted to aid.

c) that certain engineering studies required for the DEB Development Scheme be started as soon as the preliminary economic feasibility studies are completed. These studies are necessary if we are to have an aid program ready for quick action in the event of a Jagan defeat.

Arthur Schlesinger, jr.[1]

---

[1] Printed from a copy that bears this typed signature.

289.   Summary of Developments

Washington, January 18, 1963.

[Source: Kennedy Library, National Security Files, Countries Series, British Guiana, 1/63–5/15/63. Secret; Eyes Only. 3 pages of source text not declassified.]

---

290.   Airgram From the Consulate General in Georgetown to the Department of State

A–250   Georgetown, March 14, 1963.

SUBJECT

   Time and Jagan: The Consulate General's Appraisal

REF

   A–249, March 14, 1963[1]

[Here follows a table of contents.]

General

   It seems to be generally agreed by the Department, HMG and the Consulate General that Proportional Representation (PR) as an electoral system for British Guiana (BG) represents the most practical electoral device for replacing Premier Cheddi Jagan and the People's Progressive Party (PPP) with a more democratic and reliable government. It is generally conceded that PR should be put to a referendum. The most advantageous timing for a referendum and election—in the very near future, or after a delay which may extend for as much as one year—is not so readily apparent.

   Based on an appraisal of the local scene, the Consulate General believes that, unless definite action is taken, time favors Jagan. The longer the delay the more difficult it will be to dislodge Jagan and Jagan's

---

   Source: Department of State, Central Files, POL BR GU. Secret; Limit Distribution; Noforn. Repeated to London. Drafted by Rosenthal.

   [1] Not printed. (Ibid.)

brand of "socialism" from Government; extended delay presents the possibility of Cuba-like situation. Since it is definitely not in the best U.S. interests to have either British Guiana or an independent Guyana ruled by Jagan's PPP, the U.S. Government should strive for an HMG decision for an immediate referendum on PR, either by itself or as a combined referendum-election.

Recent Memorandums of Conversation and other reports reaching this Consulate General indicate that HMG states it believes that the PPP government is "ragged and running down hill" and may be forced from office, either by popular uprising or a Legislative Assembly vote of "no confidence." In the Consulate General's opinion, this is unrealistic and perhaps reflects wishful thinking. Sufficient British troops are present to prevent any recurrence of the February 16, 1962 disorders, even if Government were to allow conditions which would permit passions to rise as in February 1962. In view of the Guianese temperament, the possibility of a flash riot seems remote. As for a "no confidence" vote, it must be stressed that while the form of the BG Legislative Assembly is that of UK parliamentary democracy, its substance is not. On all but the most trivial of issues Legislative Assembly voting is on straight party lines. The PPP legislators are zealots, political hacks, or opportunists—or combinations thereof—in varying degrees. Although Balram Singh Rai defected on ideological grounds (or so he now stoutly claims), he was a comparative newcomer (circa 1956) to the PPP, and has a rich wife. No other PPP legislator, except possibly Fenton Ramsahoye, appears to question the advantages of defecting. It could be that Ramsahoye, an opportunist, and possibly one or two backbenchers could be induced to defect for private gain of one type or another. However, such gain would have to be greater than the patronage and other awards which the ruling PPP can now offer. With the situation currently favoring the PPP there is no practical reason why potential defectors would bolt on their own initiative. Thus, the PPP cannot be expected to fall on a "no confidence" vote. If the Government is dissolved, it will be because Jagan believes it can effect some political advantage. Dissolution will be as a result of the ruling clique's decision.

Comments on HMG Position as Seen from the Consulate General

The UK will have no major political interest in an independent Guyana, although comparatively small—by British standards—commercial investment will remain. HMG wants to shed BG quickly, consistent with as graceful a departure as possible. The private views of one Colonial Officer seem to stress more the awkwardness of an Order in Council for PR than its utilization to remove Jagan.

It appears that for most of the last decade it has been the British approach to present the Guianese situation as one which, while neither tranquil nor in the best free world interest, is not as serious as might be supposed.

In 1953 HMG believed that the various actions and declarations of the PPP government demanded suspension of the Constitution and the internment of some PPP leaders, including both Jagans. A subsequent White Paper stated that this was necessary since the PPP was attempting to establish a communist state. In the late 1950's it became HMG policy to consider Cheddi Jagan and the majority of the PPP hierarchy as neither communist nor particularly bloc oriented. Rather, they were considered misguided and politically immature. There was no firm evidence to indicate a change of PPP philosophy, although the Party became somewhat less blatant in its support of communism and communist causes. This may have been due to the leaders' honest, albeit unstated, change of heart. However, given that the Party has maintained and even increased its bloc contacts, the evidence would indicate that the PPP hierarchy realized that, even though the largest political grouping, it would be impossible to head any pre-independence government without British tacit approval. Hence, the softening of the public line. The UF has given wide circulation to what is purported to be Cheddi Jagan's "Secret Address to the 1956 Party Conference." The text states that until 1953 the Party "committed deviations to the left" which had to be corrected due to the need for a "flexible and well considered policy" (allegedly a quote from Stalin). Whether the speech was Jagan's or an excellent fraud has never been ascertained. However, PPP policy certainly corrected the "deviationism to the left" in its public approach (excluding its continued strong support for Castro), although, as noted, there was no decrease in communist ties. At the risk of over-simplification, there appear to be four possible explanations for the British approach during the last decade.

1) Self-deception, based in part on the subconscious recognition that HMG had failed to instill basic democratic principles in some of BG's major political figures, or to create a viable economy.

2) An effort to delude the U.S., "temporarily," until such time as HMG had evolved a solution which would allow withdrawal with some degree of dignity, and without U.S. Government pressure or criticism.

3) A combination of 1 and 2, based upon HMG's inability to recognize the need for actions which might be embarrassing internationally.

4) They are instinctively correct.

The current HMG position seems to be one of outlining the administrative or parliamentary problems involved in proposing PR, on the assumption that Jagan will somehow, sometime soon, disappear due to his own incompetence. This approach appears to avoid the unpleasant reality that few Governments fall through stupidity. Jagan might not possess "nimbleness of intellect" but his is sincere to his own ends. Janet Jagan and some of the men surrounding her can probably provide the intelligence needed to keep Cheddi propped up.

U.S. Interest in a Solution for British Guiana

Granting that spheres of influence exist, an independent Guyana will be within the U.S. sphere. It is not in the national interest to have a communist government on the mainland of South America. An independent Guyana with Jagan and the PPP in office represents such a threat and as such should be removed.

Politically, Jagan remains firm under the status quo and may well be improving his position. The Civil Service, the Ministries, government corporations and the public information media are all being used to PPP advantage. By what could be described as "administrative subversion," PPP actions are eroding the principle of a democratically oriented government with an a-political Civil Service. Economically, BG's position is worsening but Jagan may well be able to avoid any serious government financial crisis. The longer the delay in firm action which will remove Jagan, the greater must be the eventual U.S. efforts required to correct the damage. If undue delay results, at best it will be most difficult to unscramble and re-assemble the Guianese egg; and at worst a communist state will be established.

The Need for Strong Efforts Now to Attempt Forcing HMG Action on PR

Failure to act quickly provides Jagan a chance to assume the initiative. For example, if the present situation continues he might demand new elections under first-past-the-post. With the existing electoral districting, he would probably win a majority of seats. This would permit him to present a "fresh mandate" for independence, without PR.

Lack of action probably provides the PPP with a morale boost and simultaneously tends to dishearten further the opposition.

The presence of a British army battalion makes the possibility of renewed mass urban disorders most unlikely. Also, having learned its lesson in January–February 1962, the government can take preventive action to avoid creation of the tension-filled situation which preceded February 16, 1962.

A British Labour Government could be expected to be more inclined to grant independence under the existing government than would a Conservative one. Therefore, U.S. actions should be taken while the UK Government of the moment could be expected to be more receptive to the PR concept.

Two Areas of U.S. Action

1. At appropriate levels, efforts should be intensified to create a greater British awareness that, although it may be temporarily unpleasant and awkward, a PR decision should be quickly implemented. A new PR election would probably force Jagan from office, lead to some revitalization of internal economic activity, speed the date of independence and

allow time to correct and eradicate communist influences. If, conceivably Jagan wins a PR referendum, it would force recognition that he would probably head an independent Guyana, at which time other measures could be considered.

2.   The U.S. should be able to develop better information on political parties in BG. The Consulate General has fairly reliable sources within the PNC, fewer and less good contacts in the UF, and virtually none in the PPP. Information provided by the British—for whatever reasons—is inadequate and unsatisfactory. This gap in basic data should be filled.

The Current Scene

   A. Political Factors

In British Guiana, as elsewhere, domestic politics requires full-time devotion and is not a field to be cultivated only before an election. The PPP (or at least the Janet–Benn–Bhagwan core) recognizes and exploits this far more effectively than do the opposition. In so doing, the PPP has the tremendous advantage of being the party in power.

After an initial period of inactivity following the failure at London, the PPP has resumed full-scale politicking. Party leaders, including the Premier (but apparently not Janet), are constantly in the country and often in the urban centers. The PPP approach continues to be that immediate independence—without PR—means economic advancement, that colonialism and "big business" are the causes of BG's lack of progress and that growth under "socialism" can only be accomplished by the PPP. When the question of communism is raised, the Party equivocates although after several months of silence on Cuba, it is returning to somewhat cautious praise for Castro. Strong organizational efforts continue among youth and women through the PPP, the PYO and the PWO.

The PPP continues to infiltrate all levels of the bureaucracy. In the main, the Civil Service, while probably opposed to Jagan as individual voters, is still a-political. However, as the older civil servants retire or resign, they are being replaced by either Party supporters or bureaucratic nondescripts. In some cases, PPP watchdogs are placed in government enterprises as rewards to the faithful and as implied threats to the others. New government units, such as the Central Planning Division, are staffed with handpicked native or expatriate personnel, who—whatever their other qualifications—are selected for their compassionate views toward the PPP. Plans for a National Army continue and it is believed by many locally, including the Consulate General, that PPP/PYO cadres, including those now in Cuba, will play a significant role. While great emphasis has been placed on the Army's multi-racial character, it will be difficult if not impossible to ascertain the political philosophy of future troops. The same may be the case for the BG Volunteer

Force (militia). Several months ago, an expatriate police officer remarked that a considerable number of East Indians had suddenly come forth expressing a desire to join the Volunteer Force with the identical reason: "to serve my Queen and Country." The officer assumed that they had been ordered to join by the Party.

In the meantime the PPP appears to be accepting some salary and fee kickbacks from government coffers to help support the party. All ministers of government are obliged to contribute BWI$100 from their monthly salaries of BWI$800. Mooneer Khan, Chairman of the Rice Marketing Board, is understood to be taking kickbacks on the sale of rice bags, although who gets the money is unknown. The PPP also receives whatever profits (or other funds) are forthcoming from Guiana Import-Export and the New Guiana Corporation. While the PPP may or may not be receiving funds directly from the bloc, it is most certainly in a better financial position than either the PNC or the UF.

The PPP Government is effectively using the public information media to strengthen the Party hold on BG. By law Government is entitled to free radio time for informational purposes and much of this is being effectively utilized for Party interests. Despite some sniping, Jagan's weekly press conference is little more than a propaganda forum which is rebroadcast twice over the weekend. It is accepted practice that the tape is edited before release. Other Government Information Services press releases and programs exhort Government's deeds, with particular references to PPP ministers or the accomplishments of socialist (never communist) countries.

Although the broadcasting company is privately owned, it is under strict corporate injunction not to antagonize the government. This is carried to such an extreme that local news reports do not mention Legislative Assembly debates which are critical of Government. Scripts (including USIS material) for such programs as "Viewpoint" are vetted to ensure that they will not "embarrass" Government.

On the press side, the PPP weekly *The Mirror* (printed on Cuban-confiscated U.S. presses given to the PPP) is becoming consistently more newsworthy since it has private access to ministerial decisions. It is rumored to become at least a bi-weekly shortly. The other papers are ineffective as sources of anti-government news. The *Evening Post*, and its Sunday edition, *Argosy*, exist on a shoestring. Circulation is down, bills are up. Content is mainly boilerplate and the small amount of local reporting is devoid of intelligent, or even particularly factual, presentation. The *Chronicle* is so rabid in its attacks on the PPP government that at times it almost assumes an anti-East Indian bias in some of its stories. It has no special reputation for accuracy. Worse, it is ineffective. The expatriate-owned *Guiana Graphic*, like the radio stations, follows such an a-political course in working with the government of the moment that at times it appears to be pro-government.

Probably to ensure that it becomes even less of a threat, Government has announced that a Press Council will be established. When queried, Jagan said initially the Council will not have punitive powers, although these might be subsequently necessary.

Through Government the PPP is also effectively creating the groundwork for greater control over education. To cite two examples: creation of a University of Guyana and withdrawal from UWI; release of the long-standing Board of Governors of a major government high school after it had refused to allow the PPP to use the school for a political meeting. A new board is to be named.

All these activities are indicative of the degree to which the PPP is spreading tentacles into Guianese life. All will become increasingly more difficult to eradicate the longer the Party is in office.

The situation might be ameliorated if the political opposition showed signs of increasing its effectiveness but if anything the reverse seems to be the case.

PNC organizational activities appear to be almost non-existent. Most of the PNC effort seems to be directed toward its signature campaign for a PR referendum. However, the fact that the campaign continues well past the original closing date in January indicates that it is not going well, despite recent UF support. A certain amount of time is spent by Burnham and others exhorting the faithful in Georgetown and (once) in New Amsterdam but there seems to be little PNC activity in the rural areas, sections which will become particularly important if PR becomes a reality. Far too often the PNC attacks Jagan for courting the rural areas at the expense of the urban. While this may serve as a sop to the PNC urban supporters, it only tends to alienate further the rural voter.

While the PPP obviously courts and actively recruits youth with Freedom House lectures, strong influence at ITABO, scholarship offers and the prize of a college degree through the University of Guyana, as far as can be determined the PNC is doing little if any proselytizing among this group. With some 6,000 school leavers a year searching for opportunities, the PNC either through ignorance or indolence is overlooking a significant segment of the potential electorate.

The United Force is probably losing much of whatever appeal it may once have had for the non-white, non-Amerindian voter. After 2 years, Peter D'Aguiar has failed to develop any political intelligence and the UF is merely his political reflection. Instead of attacking Government on the selected well-documented evidence which abounds, the UF tactic is to swing against the PPP with wild charges, while making the most preposterous of claims as to what it would accomplish in office (i.e., $500,000,000.00 of new foreign investment). As noted, the *Chronicle* has become little more than a daily political rag, and one which unfortunately often is almost anti-East Indian in tone as it attacks Government. Equally bad is the *Chronicle*'s habit of printing foreign source information about BG which it knows to be misleading, if not patently false. To cite one example: the *Chronicle* printed U.S. columnist Victor Riesel's story on BG starting with a lead sentence to the effect that the U.S. and UK had forgotten "abandoned" Atkinson Field, but the Russians had not. A quote of Janet's supporting the Berlin Wall, later verified, was buried in the story but was generally discounted locally.

UF supporters may be losing heart. Ann Jardim, the only UF leader with any sense of political realities, has been ailing, is discouraged, and considering leaving the colony. The UK Entry Certificate Officer (i.e. visa man) commented privately that many of the middle and upper classes (from which the UF draws the bulk of its support) have taken out departure insurance in the form of UK entry certificates. Thus, in its initial electoral bid in August 1961 the UF, as presently oriented, probably gained as large a percentage of the electorate as possible. Its total voting strength could well decline as time passes. The only group which will remain firm is the numerically small Amerindian, who can still be controlled by Melville, with an assist from the Church.

A PNC–UF working arrangement might be possible with a combined electoral majority under PR—if only to keep Jagan out. However, a PPP–PNC coalition is possible if Burnham believes the chances for a PR referendum are fading.

Balram Singh Rai has been inactive politically for the last few months and there has been more speculation recently in the U.S. and UK than in BG on his political future. Whatever electoral potential Rai may hold or be expected to gain, either by himself or in conjunction with other center-left personalities or the UF, is yet to be tested. However, the longer the status quo, the farther from public awareness Rai will be. The Consulate General would hazard that there are two basic criteria for Rai's motivation; a specific electoral target and, possibly, financial support. Public moral support might also help.

Thus, on balance, the PPP is strong and working to solidify its political position. As the party in power, it recognizes all the advantages this carries. While it cannot yet fully implement its policies, it can create the understructure needed to do so on short notice. While its ability to conduct foreign affairs is proscribed, it has started to sever its traditional West Indies ties, and to commence initial ("economic") ties with the bloc. Against this background the political opposition, which lacks motivation, seems to be becoming somewhat less effective.

B. Economic Factors

Jagan's government potentially is weaker on the economic side than on the political. There are two issues, the general status of the internal economy and the particular weakness of the government's financial position.

The internal trade sector remains bad. Imports do not appear to have risen and inventories remain down. However, these factors affect the urban areas, particularly Georgetown, far more than the rural. Even if conditions do not improve there will be little adverse effect on Jagan's electoral popularity. While some urbanites may work more actively against Jagan, others show signs of surrendering and leaving BG. In any case, it is well known that Jagan's urban voting strength has been negligible. These factors tend to cancel each other—excluding the very remote possibility of a sudden, truly spontaneous riot in the comparatively brief time before British troops could be mobilized.

The export market is good. Bauxite workers are the highest paid in the colony, have reasonable job security by local standards and continue to support the PNC. The sugar workers support Jagan politically, although the anti-PPP MPCA represents them on trade union matters. Currently, MPCA is negotiating a new contract and another "once for all" bonus. While a strike may develop, the ultimate result will be some sort of bonus and possible increased daily wages and fringe benefits. Any dissatisfaction at the settlement will probably be generated by the Guiana Agricultural Workers Union (formerly BG Sugar Workers), the PPP union which is attempting to depose MPCA. GAWU will claim, regardless of what MPCA gets, that they could have done better had they possessed bargaining rights.

Rice could be Jagan's major weakness over a long period. While crop expectations for 1963 are excellent and the price to farmers has improved, at present the 26,000 ton Trinidad market may have been lost. Also, Cuba will absorb only some 15,000 tons in 1963, instead of an expected 36,000. There could be a considerable surplus. Also, through mismanagement and entanglement in bloc arrangements, the Rice Marketing Board may be in serious trouble. The Consulate General's A–242 of February 21, 1963[2] explores this in some detail, and notes the possible effects of Jagan's electoral popularity.

Government's financial position presents the greatest potential weakness for Jagan, although not necessarily a fatal one. The 1963 Recurrent Budget predicted a major increase in imports over 1962 and a BWI$4.5 million revenue increase through new taxes and the increased tax rates. If Government is overly optimistic about these levels, a finan-

---

[2] Not printed. (Ibid., 741D.00/2–2163)

cial crises is possible. While it could incur some deficit spending and draw down its General Revenue Balance (reserves which were only $3.4 million at the end of 1962), there still could be insufficient funds to pay the Civil Service. Any work stoppage could be considered the "grave emergency" needed by the UK to suspend the Constitution.

While the potential for a financial crisis is present, there are three possibilities which could forestall it:

1) When a similar situation arose in 1962, the UK rescued the Government with a vitally needed short-term loan. The British might well do so again to avoid the charges that one of their colonies faced financial difficulties resulting from colonialist rule (and the lack of independence).

In late 1962 the Governor, Sir Ralph Grey, stated privately that the UK was unwilling to allow Jagan to wreck the country financially, even if this demanded saving the PPP government. It would be most interesting to know what the UK would do if BG again faced the problem.

2) If a crisis threatened, the Government could request the large expatriate firms to pay immediately all or part of their 1963 taxes (due in 1964). The expatriate firms, who must attempt to work with the government of the day, would not refuse such a request. This device, utilized in other countries, might provide the Opposition with some political ammunition, but the danger is far less serious for Government than a financial breakdown.

3) A quick local loan might be floated. Ordinarily such a loan in BG at this time would be badly undersubscribed. However, if the bloc decided to risk a comparatively small sum for future gains, it could channel funds either through Guiana Import-Export or the New Guiana Corporation, who could then subscribe all or part of the loan.

The Threat of Jagan Out of Office

The argument has been entered, particularly by HMG, that Jagan out of office is more dangerous than Jagan in power, particularly while BG is a colony. This is not valid. Admittedly, Jagan would attack the existing government, the "colonialist-imperialist" group, the West and big business. He would also preach his various themes on the need for bloc ties. However, in power, *as he is now,* he can, and does, follow this approach with a minimum of restraint while entrenching the PPP and laying the framework for even closer bloc connections. The point that Jagan out of office might resort to violence should not deter efforts to remove him; appropriate common criminal action can always be initiated—provided his removal precedes heavy concentrations of the PPP in civil and (proposed) military organizations.

U.S. Long Term Objectives

The immediate objective is the replacement of the PPP in office. A long term objective should be to impress upon the average Guianese the desirability of a democratic government oriented to free world philosophy and objectives, as well as to the dangers of bloc ensnarement.

The need for this immediate objective is outlined in this paper. Parts of the longer term goal, once this is accomplished, can be considered through USAID and USIS programs. In addition, the Consulate General will shortly present an outline of several projects which, after PPP removal, may be effective in discrediting Jagan with some of his supporters.

Conclusion

Continuation of the status quo permits Jagan to consolidate his gains in establishing PPP domination over all facets of BG life. To the degree which the U.S. Government and HMG fail to move to counteract this trend, they are providing implicit support for his rule. Such support is dangerous.

EK Melby
American Consul General

---

291.   Memorandum of Conversation

Washington, March 20, 1963, 4 p.m.

[Source: Department of State, Central Files, POL BR GU. Secret. 2 pages of source text not declassified.]

292. Letter From Premier Jagan to President Kennedy

Georgetown, April 16, 1963.

DEAR MR. PRESIDENT, It will be recalled that as a result of my talks with you and U.S. Government officials in October 1961,[1] your Government in response to my request for aid, undertook to take the following steps:

(i) To provide as early as possible in consultation with the British Guiana Government, and unilaterally or in cooperation with Hemisphere organisations, economists and other experts to assist the Government of British Guiana to bring the most modern economic experience to bear upon the reappraisal of its development programme.

(ii) To provide technical assistance for feasibility, engineering and other studies concerning specific development projects.

(iii) To determine as soon as possible after the steps mentioned in paragraphs one and two, and on the submission of suitable projects within the context of the British Guiana Development Plan, what assistance the U.S. can give in financing such projects, taking into account other U.S. commitments, available financial resources, and the criteria established by applicable legislation.

(iv) To expand its existing technical assistance.

2. In the period since my visit, U.S. technical assistance has been expanded, and feasibility and engineering studies for certain specific development projects are in train. On the other hand progress with the reappraisal of the development programme has been far less satisfactory. Following on the cancellation of its proposed visit early in February, the Economic Planning team led by Mr. Harry G. Hoffman eventually visited British Guiana in May of last year. It is now very nearly a year since the visit of that mission but I have so far been unable to obtain any certain information regarding the progress of its report. (It is understood however that when the AID Desk Officer visited British Guiana two months ago he stated in a newspaper interview that the Mission's report had then been sent to the printers.) I am naturally anxious about the fate of the Hoffman report as it appears that U.S. assistance in the financing of development projects is conditional on the completion of it.

3. My request for aid in October 1961 was only the latest request of the many made over the years for U.S. assistance with development proj-

---

Source: Kennedy Library, National Security Files, Countries Series, British Guiana III. Secret. Transmitted to McGeorge Bundy by Brubeck on May 18 under cover of a note that indicates an advance copy of the letter was sent to the White House on May 1 and that the Department of State would submit a recommendation concerning a reply as soon as possible.
[1] See Documents 259 and 260.

ects. Early in 1958, an application was made to the Development Loan Fund (DLF) for aid for financing road and drainage and irrigation projects. I visited Washington in the summer of 1958 and 1959 and held talks with officials of the World Bank and U.S. Government Agencies. At a meeting with State Department officials in 1959 in Washington, I was told that a sum of about $6 to $8 million (U.S.) would be made available to my Government toward the cost of the construction of an interior road from Parika to Lethem. Such aid did not in fact materialise. A request was also made to the Commodities Division Office of International Resources in the State Department to see if this country's imports of flour and stock-feed from the U.S.A. ($3.5 million U.S. per annum) might be given under United States Public Law 480 and the proceeds of the sale used for development projects. This request was turned down as it was explained that any assistance under the law must be over and above the existing volume of imports. The Export-Import Bank was then asked to assist with the financing of equipment for a flour mill and a feed mill but the response was not encouraging.

4. At one stage a U.S. AID official in British Guiana indicated that economic assistance might be forthcoming for a Land Reclamation Project (the Tapacuma Drainage and Irrigation Scheme). But later, when the Project Report was ready my Government was informed that assistance was not likely to be available because of possible Congressional objections to a scheme which would be solely devoted to the cultivation of rice, a commodity of which the U.S. had a large surplus.

5. An application to the Export-Import Bank in June 1961 for rice milling equipment—cleaning, drying and storage—amounting to about $2 million B.W.I. has not yet been considered.

6. It will thus be seen, that leaving technical assistance aside, valuable though such assistance is, my efforts to obtain U.S. assistance have so far yielded little material result. It was against a background of growing unemployment and lack of adequate overseas assistance that I resolved on my return to British Guiana from the U.S.A. in November, 1961, to embark on a programme of fiscal reform designed to mobilise local resources for development. I was encouraged in this step by the fact that the criteria for AID assistance appeared to stress self-help efforts by the less developed countries themselves. I had noted that it had been stated in the Summary Presentation of an Act for International Development, 1961 (page 14) that the major areas of self-help include "The effective mobilizing of resources. This includes not only development programming, but also establishing tax policies designed to raise equitably resources for investment; fiscal and monetary policies designed to prevent serious inflation; and regulatory policies aimed to attract the financial and managerial resources of foreign investment and to prevent excessive luxury consumption by a few."

7. Unfortunately this self-help or austerity budget was used as an excuse for disturbances inspired by opponents of the Government. These disturbances have since been thoroughly investigated by a Commonwealth Commission of Inquiry and it is worth recording the views of that Commission on the Budget: "It will be seen" stated the Commission on page 15 of its report "that there was nothing deeply vicious or destructive of economic security in the budget. It had been drawn up on the advice of an experienced economist, who could not be said to have any Communist prepossessions. The budget won immediate approval from many persons. *The New York Times* said in an editorial that the budget was courageous and economically sound. The *London Times* in a leading article observed 'The immediate problem for the Prime Minister, Dr. Jagan, is how to win some acceptance for his economic proposals which are courageous and certainly not far from what Guiana must have.' Sir Jock Campbell, Chairman of Booker Bros., the largest industrial and agricultural concern in British Guiana, said 'It clearly was in intention a serious attempt by the Government to get to grips with the formidable economic problems of the country by a hard programme of self-help. It was radical—what have the people of British Guiana got to be conservative about—but not confiscatory.' Senator Anthony Tasker, Chairman of Bookers Group Committee in British Guiana, gave his own opinion about the budget by saying 'We assessed it as a realistic attempt to grapple with the economic problems of British Guiana.'"

8. I venture to suggest that an objective consideration of these Budget proposals and the overall programme of my Government leads to the conclusion that they meet, to a high degree, the criteria which have been laid down by your Government for disbursements under the Alliance for Progress:

(a) *Long range plans based on the application of programming techniques must be drawn up for both private and public sectors:*

My country as compared with many under-developed territories has had a comparatively long history in the planning of economic development. A development programme prepared as long ago as 1948 by the then Economic Adviser to Government the U.K. economist Col. O.A. Spencer, introduced ideas which later influenced planning within the Caribbean region and exercised a considerable influence in other British colonial territories. In 1952–1953 a Mission from the World Bank considered afresh and reported on the problems of the economic development of the territory. Then in 1959 a Cambridge University Economics Don, Mr. Kenneth Berrill, at the request of my Government, advised on the preparation of the Development Programme which is now in progress. My Government has also had from time to time the benefit of the advice of many distinguished economic experts who have visited for short periods. It will thus be seen that the Hoffman Mission is only the most recent study of our economic problems.

(b) *The fiscal system should be reformed both in order to increase the level of tax revenue in relation to national income and to make the tax structure more progressive. At the same time the machinery for the collection and assessment should be completely overhauled:*

This was what the budget of 1962 mainly sought to do. It is also to be noted that this budget reflects the major conclusions reached at the Conference on Fiscal Policy held in Santiago, Chile last December and which was attended by fiscal experts from all over the Americas. In a release made in Washington by the Pan American Union Secretariat of the Organisation of American States it was stated among other things that it had been agreed that the reform of Latin American tax system should include progressive personal income tax which included the taxation of capital gains both on mobile and immobile property, complemented by a net wealth tax where feasible and the strengthening of a system of inheritance and gift taxation. Those recommendations also envisaged the establishment of an objective and coordinated system of tax administration—all features of my 1962 Budget. This budget also proposed a number of measures including Pay-As-You-Earn which were calculated to improve the efficiency of tax collection and to prevent tax evasion. Although certain of the budget proposals were subsequently withdrawn the present position is that all the fiscal requirements mentioned have been met.

(c) *Measures should be instituted to increase domestic savings and these should be applied to productive investment:*

The budget already referred to introduced a National Development Savings Levy. Under this scheme, persons earning more than $300 a month (a better than middle class salary) are asked to contribute 5% of that part of their incomes above $300 to a National Savings Scheme. The scheme also applies to companies which contribute 10% of their income before tax. The monies which accrue in this way are safeguarded by being directly chargeable on the revenues and assets of the country, and are being put into development fund and drawn upon for the financing of concrete and high earning schemes calculated to have an immediate impact on development, especially in the urban areas.

(d) *Certain basic social reforms must be implemented such as the breaking up of large latifundia—the old plantation type economy—for the purpose of distributing unused or under-utilised land to peasants who will be required to put the land to good use:*

Since 1957, my Government has succeeded in persuading the foreign owned sugar companies to release some of their non-utilised lands leased from the Crown. Attempts are still being made to secure additional lands for use by individual farmers. The distribution of unused land to individual farmers is one of the objectives of my Government and has been pursued constantly. Nevertheless, the problem in this country is not one of maldistribution but of lack of financial resources to bring undeveloped land into cultivation.

(e) *Development programmes should lay as much stress on improving the quality of the people, for example by expenditure on education and training, as on increasing the stock of physical capital:*

My Government is now embarked on an educational programme which aims at promoting a national system of education which will provide all Guianese with the opportunity of developing their educational and personal potential and of sharing in all the educational facilities available regardless of race, religion or economic circumstances. To this end the educational system is being reorganised—so as to provide for secondary and university education, after the pattern of your own country, for all who can benefit from it. My Government has also gone a long way towards providing health facilities throughout the country and a start has been made in certain areas on the provision of free medical services for the people.

(f) *Democratic regimes in Latin America should be encouraged:*

I have achieved power in the political life of my country by virtue of three successive General Elections which my Party won. I have often stated and now wish to re-affirm my adherence to parliamentary democracy by which I recognise the rights of opposition parties, freedom of speech, freedom of worship, regular and honest elections, an impartial judiciary and an independent public service. The draft constitution which my government proposed for an independent Guyana specifically provided for the protection of the rights of citizens by the Courts of Law along the lines enshrined in the U.S. Constitution and moreover provided for the impartial conduct of elections and the review of boundaries of constituencies by an Electoral Commission. On this point may I venture to remind you of remarks ascribed to you in a U.S.I.S. release of the 7th December, 1961. In the course of your interview with the Editor of *Izvestia* you are reported to have said ". . . the United States supports the idea that every people should have the right to make a free choice of the kind of Government they want . . . Mr. Jagan . . . who was recently elected Prime Minister in British Guiana is a Marxist, but the United States doesn't object because that choice was made by honest election, which he won."

(g) *Aid should be guaranteed over the period of the plan:*

I have long supported this idea as it is only on this basis that the Government of any under-developed country can plan development on sound lines.

Trade Policy:

9. As the trade policy of my Government and its attitude to private enterprise has been widely and deliberately misrepresented in the U.S.A. I should like to deal briefly with these subjects. I am aware that the thinking which inspired your Act for International Development recognised the trade problems of the less developed countries. Thus on page 25 of the Summary Presentation already referred to, it is stated inter alia:

"Export capacities of most of the less developed countries are limited. In many cases, especially in Latin America and Africa, exports are heavily dependent on one or two primary products of either agricultural or mineral origin. For most of these products, world markets are expanding only slowly. The prices of these products are subject to volatile fluctuations which greatly affect the exchange available to producing countries. In some instances, there appears to be a long-range trend for prices of primary commodities to fall in comparison with the prices of the industrial goods for which they must be exchanged. Moreover, the advance of science and technology presents for some commodities the prospect of displacement by synthetics (as had happened in some measure for rubber) or competition from substitutes."

It is these considerations which compel nations such as my own as a matter of economic necessity to seek markets or capital equipment wherever they may be obtained most advantageously. Such trading arrangements do not mean however that my Government has become part of any international conspiracy.

Attitude to private enterprise:

10. My Government is committed to a mixed economy in which private and public enterprise would exist side by side as is the case with India. For reasons inherent in the nature of this country, my Government must enter as quickly as possible into the industrial sector of development, either alone or in joint ventures with private enterprise. It is however the policy of my Government to give protection where necessary to new undertakings both public and private, in order to make them viable and competitive.

11. The expropriation of private property is not in my Government's programme. The provisions for safeguarding the Fundamental Rights in our present Constitution and in the Constitution for an independent Guyana will provide adequate protection for private property.

12. On nationalisation, no Government can tie its hands but it is not our intention to nationalise the bauxite and sugar industries. I am also prepared to guarantee that if any private enterprise should be nationalised there will be adequate and fair compensation to be decided by the Supreme Court of Law in cases of dispute as laid down in the Constitution.

13. A United Kingdom Trade and Industrial Mission led by the English Industrialist Lord Rootes, which visited British Guiana in 1962 concluded that:

"On the political front, there is no exceptional risk to be faced by industry in British Guiana beyond that of nationalisation inherent in any socialist country. It must be said also that sound reasons can be found in the condition of the country for Dr. Jagan's concept of a mixed economy, with the Government providing some of the initiative in development."

14. Again as recently as March this year, Sir Jock Campbell, Chairman of Bookers Bros. McConnell and Company Limited, a group of companies which represent one of the large investments of private capital in this country, while on a visit stated that he saw no danger of a Communist dictatorship being established in British Guiana. He was confident that the Premier, Dr. Jagan had no intention of setting up such a dictatorship and further, that the conditions were not present in British Guiana to make a communist dictatorship viable. "I do not believe," Sir Jock Campbell said, "that there is a corrupt Government now in British Guiana against which the people will rebel and I do not think that the people can feel that they will be better off if there was a Communist Government." He added, however, that he did not think the people of British Guiana would vote for a Government whose stated policy was to pander to private enterprise.

15. In my country, we are now embarked on the creation of a just society based on the ideas and forms most suitable to the needs of this country and which would enable its citizens to develop themselves to the full in a free country. We have nothing to hide. Because of hostile, uninformed and unsympathetic speeches and comments made in the U.S. Congress and press, I have already invited through your Consul General in Georgetown, members of Congress and of the press to visit from time to time. Such visits would be welcome. I cannot but think that the American people who first began that revolution in social and political thought which still moves our world will find sympathy with the ideas and aspirations of my people and Government.

16. As I am sure you are aware, a Government such as mine has inherited the problems of poverty and under-development which are characteristic of colonial territories. To these problems have been added the problem of a high post-war population growth. In the face of growing unemployment and all that it means in discontent and the waste of human resources, the political Opposition and other local leaders hostile to the Government have openly charged that U.S. assistance will not be forthcoming once my Government remains in office. The long delay in the completion of the Hoffman Report has tended to lend substance to this charge. In addition, the Trade Union Congress which on the whole aligns itself with the political Opposition has recently announced that it

has been able to arrange substantial assistance for a housing scheme through the American Institute for Free Labour Development, a body which, one senior local Trade Union Official stated in a broadcast, derives the major part of its funds from the Agency for International Development. Earlier a generous Scholarship Scheme announced by the U.S. Consul General had apparently been designed to bypass my Government which had not been notified or taken into consultation.

17. These are only the most recent of the series of events which have created the impression that your Government is unwilling to assist the presently elected Government of this country and has served to embolden the Opposition to embark on irresponsible courses which are aimed at the forcible overthrow of my Government and which are likely to undermine the future of democratic government and the maintenance of peace in this country.

18. Thus, U.S. citizens, Dr. Schwartz and Dr. Sluis openly interfered in the domestic affairs of the country during the 1961 election campaign when they supported the Defenders of Freedom and the United Force. They later admitted spending the sum of about $76,000 B.W.I. during this campaign. (It is to be noted that Section 53 of Cap. 57—the Representation of the People Ordinance 1957—limits the expenses which may be incurred by a candidate to $1,500 and there were only 35 seats.) Dr. Sluis visited British Guiana six times between 21st February, 1961 and 26th April, 1962, including a two-month visit just prior to and during the 1961 Elections.

19. You will recall that I complained to you about the activities of U.S. Government Information Services during the 1961 election campaign when film shows were held at street corners. The U.S.I.S. had never before arranged for such shows in the public. These film shows highlighted anti-Castro and anti-communist propaganda. It happened that this line of propaganda coincided with the smear campaign then being conducted against the Government by the Opposition.

20. While no economic assistance was given to the Government, the impression was and is still being created in the country by Mr. Peter D'Aguiar and the United Force that they will be able to secure substantial financial assistance from the U.S. Government. During the election campaign the United Force cited a figure of one billion dollars, half a billion dollars as loans to the Government for "infra structure" development and half a billion for industrial development by private U.S. investors. So far as I am aware, these statements met with no denial from your Consulate General, or any other U.S. official.

21. Press reports had stated that Dr. Claude Denbow, President of the League of Coloured Peoples and close associate of the People's National Congress had contacted, during a visit to the U.S.A. immediately prior to the 1961 August elections, a group of prominent Guianese

professional men now resident in New York, some of whom had interviews with State Department officials at which, it was reported offers of assistance were made to help the Opposition to "liberate" British Guiana from my Government.

22. Since the elections it appears to be the policy of the United States State Department to refuse visas to members and known supporters of the governing party, People's Progressive Party, who wish to visit the United States. This has been the case even with well known and eminently respectable members of the business community.

23. I cite these observations because I share your deep concern not only about the problems of world poverty but also of the growing tendency of the usurpation by reactionary elements of the democratic rights and liberties of free peoples. I am sure you would not want it said that in British Guiana, the objectives of your administration were not being realised and fulfilled.

24. In the light of the points made above I shall be grateful if urgent consideration may once again be given to the question of what assistance may be made available for the financing of development projects.

25. I have noted that you have been able in spite of the heavy burden of your office to visit a number of Latin American countries, so as to meet their people and to find out at first hand about their problems. I am aware that my own small country must rate low on the scale of priorities, but my Government nevertheless wishes to invite you to visit this country as soon as may be convenient to you. In the meanwhile my Government wishes to invite your personal aide, Mr. Arthur Schlesinger Jr. who I understand has been entrusted with the study of the problems of this country to visit us as soon as possible.

Yours sincerely

Cheddi Jagan

293.   Memorandum for the Record

Washington, June 21, 1963.

SUBJECT

White House Meeting on British Guiana

ATTENDANCE

The President
For Department of State: Messrs. Rusk, Johnson, and Burdett
For AID: Mr. Bell
For the White House: Messrs. Bundy, Dungan, and Kaysen
For CIA: Messrs. McCone and Helms

1.   The meeting opened with a briefing by Helms on the current situation in British Guiana. [2 *lines of source text not declassified*] and the hard position being taken by Jagan in the negotiations for a return to work on the part of the TUC.

2.   There followed a discussion of the AID aspects of a paper submitted to the President entitled "Instructions for Official Level Talks with UK on British Guiana". Rusk and Bell pointed out that we were proposing financial support to British Guiana which was significantly in excess of anything given to a country of comparable size under the Alliance for Progress. There was some comment about the resentment this might cause in Latin America, but it was clear that the President was prepared to accept unfavorable reaction if the United States Government was able to secure a favorable resolution of the political problem in British Guiana, [*less than 1 line of source text not declassified*]

3.   The meeting turned to a general discussion of the President's scheduled talk with Macmillan at Birch Grove. It was clear that the President regards British Guiana as the most important topic he has to discuss with the Prime Minister. There was some debate as to the desirability of inviting Duncan Sandys to Birch Grove since he is a significant figure in any decisions which HMG may take. Rusk indicated that he would be better able to advise the President after he had met with Sandys and Home a day or two earlier.

[2 *paragraphs (11-1/2 lines of source text) not declassified*]

6.   This meeting clarified the significant extent to which British Guiana has become a major policy issue between the United States and Great Britain.

Richard Helms[1]
Deputy Director (Plans)

Source: Central Intelligence Agency, DCI/McCone Files, Job 80–B01285A. Secret; Eyes Only. Drafted by Helms.

[1] Printed from a copy that indicates Helms signed the original.

Attachment[2]

British Guiana—Points the President might make to Senator Fulbright

1. Call his attention to the statement on June 20 by Mrs. Janet Jagan, Minister of Home Affairs in charge of Security—British Guiana will establish closer relations with Russia and Cuba when it becomes independent. British Guiana Government is "deeply grateful" to Fidel Castro's Cuba for "helping us out when we were stuck."

2. The British have in fact supported the Jagan Government during the current strike. For example, the Cold Stream Guards were used to guard Cuban ships which arrived carrying food and fuel to break the strike. They also guarded the loading of a Russian freighter.

3. We understand that additional Cuban ships are on their way.

4. The strike was called in protest against a labor relations bill introduced by the Jagan Government which would have given the government control over the British Guiana labor movement. The strike has been supported by labor organizations in the US, UK, and the Caribbean.

5. Colonial Secretary Sandys stated in the House of Commons on June 18—"The struggle is now more political than industrial and it has become clear the two sides are evenly balanced." He then urged the people themselves to work out a widely acceptable settlement of the dispute. This is not only a misrepresentation of the nature of the strike, but illustrates the unwillingness of the UK to cope with the Jagan Government.

---

[2] Confidential.

---

294. Telegram From the Department of State to the Embassy in the United Kingdom

Washington, June 21, 1963, 7:03 p.m.

6918. Eyes only for Ambassador Bruce from the Secretary. President wants you to know high importance he and I attach to reaching under-

---

Source: Department of State, Central Files, POL 19 BR GU. Secret. Drafted by Burdett; cleared in draft by Rusk and U. Alexis Johnson and cleared by Hilliker (S/S); and approved by Burdett.

standing with UK on British Guiana. This is principal subject President intends raise with Macmillan at Birch Grove and is main reason for my talks in London with Home and Sandys.

Our fundamental position is that the UK must not leave behind in the Western Hemisphere a country with a Communist government in control. Independence of British Guiana with government led by PPP is unacceptable to US. Our objective in London is to get HMG to take effective action to remove Jagan Government prior to independence. As you know there has been long series high-level exchanges this subject. Last fall Macmillan agreed to this objective but he has now reverted to view UK should wash its hands of British Guiana by granting early independence, leaving the mess on our doorstep.

I hope you will let it be known to Alec Home and the Prime Minister that President and I intend to focus on this subject while in England. I think it most important that we involve Alec Home. This is not just a Colonial problem but one with the highest foreign policy implications.

I would welcome your thoughts on how best to convince our British friends of deadly seriousness of our concern and our determination that British Guiana shall not become independent with a Communist government.

I also ask your views on what might be done with labor leaders. George Brown while in Washington seemed to sympathize with our position, but Patrick Gordon Walker was less receptive. Would you advise frank talks with Labor leaders. If so, by whom? What we wish to avoid is Labor's committing itself publicly to early independence to British Guiana from ignorance of true facts and in effort to needle government. This of course would make it extremely difficult for them to reverse course once they come to power.

I am looking forward to talking this whole problem over with you on June 27.

Rusk

295. Memorandum of Conversation

US/MC/21   Birch Grove, England, June 30, 1963, 10 a.m.

SUBJECT

British Guiana

PARTICIPANTS

United States	United Kingdom
The President	Prime Minister Macmillan
The Secretary of State	Lord Home
Ambassador Bruce	Sir David Ormsby Gore
Mr. McGeorge Bundy	Lord Hailsham
Mr. William R. Tyler	Sir Harold Caccia
	Mr. Duncan Sandys
	Mr. Peter Thorneycroft
	Lord Hood
	Mr. Philip de Zulueta

The Secretary reviewed his talks with Lord Home and Mr. Sandys. [4-1/2 lines of source text not declassified]

Mr. Sandys then spoke and confirmed the Secretary's account of the conversations which had been held in London. He said he thought that, theoretically, there were four courses open: (1) To muddle on as we are now doing, which he thought should be rejected as a choice; (2) To move forward by granting British Guiana independence now (he said that although this would be a move forward it obviously presented grave problems); (3) To suspend the constitution and institute direct colonial rule (he said that this would be a move backward politically); (4) to establish a Burnham–D'Aguiar government and then grant British Guiana independence.

He said that if we were to persevere with the present exercise and succeed, we could perhaps give British Guiana independence. [2-1/2 lines of source text not declassified] On the whole he thought that a referendum on proportional representation would have a favorable outcome, though this was not certain. The reaction of the people was problematical. If the referendum was successful, there would have to be new elections. He said another factor in the situation was the predictable increase in support for Jagan as time went by. He said that presumably Burnham, if he came to power, would make a defense agreement with the United States, and that the US had the legal right to reactivate the base in British Guiana, [1-1/2 lines of source text not declassified]. He thought that a Burn-

---

Source: Department of State, Central Files, POL BR GU–US. Secret; Eyes Only; Limited Distribution. Drafted by Tyler.

ham–D'Aguiar government would certainly wish to have a defense agreement with the United States.

The President asked Mr. Sandys how long he thought the UK could string out the process of establishing proportional representation. Mr. Sandys said he was not sure, as it depended on the outcome of the present strike situation. He said there was a financial problem if the UK was prepared to keep Jagan going. In the meantime, the UK could string out the process for a number of months. He said we had to be careful that Jagan should not be put in a position where he would ask for dissolution and new elections, because he would certainly win again. Under the present constitution he had the right to ask for dissolution, and the governor would have to grant it. He said that under direct rule, two serious problems would emerge, apart from the financial one: (1) it was not certain that after five years we would be any better off than we are now, (2) it was quite likely that Jagan would take off and create a movement of underground resistance of the Malayan type. Mr. Sandys said he did not know whether in this case the Indians and the Negroes would fight against each other, or band together against us. There was also the consideration that, in the event of the UK resuming direct rule, it would be greatly criticized. "Its image would be pretty severely tarnished," said Lord Home. "There would also be the effect on Southern Rhodesia. People would say that if the UK could resume power in British Guiana, why would it not be able to do the same thing in Southern Rhodesia."

The President said he thought that Mr. Sandys had made a very good and fair presentation. It was obvious that if the UK were to get out of British Guiana now it would become a Communist state. He thought the thing to do was to look for ways to drag the thing out. The situation was inflammatory at this time. He thought that Latin America was the most dangerous area in the world. The effect of having a Communist state in British Guiana in addition to Cuba in 1964, would be to create irresistible pressures in the United States to strike militarily against Cuba. There would be great US resentment against the UK for having pulled out. He thought the UK should say that it could not make British Guiana independent because of the danger of unleashing a racial war, and that the UK should not say that it was because of the danger of British Guiana becoming Communist. The Prime Minister asked whether it was not worth while going on with the present strike pressure. Mr. Sandys asked what the US reaction would be to the UK granting independence to a Burnham–D'Aguiar government. Under present conditions, such a government would collapse by itself. However if the United States Government was prepared to shore it up, this would change the situation, specifically if the US could provide money [1-1/2 lines of source text not declassified]. The Secretary pointed out that Africans control the police and the towns, so that Jagan would be relegated to agitating in the countryside. The President asked Mr. Sandys if the UK could tell Jagan that HMG was going to hold on for another two years. Mr. Sandys said that Jagan would then ask for dissolution. The Secretary asked whether, in this event, the UK could insist on holding a referendum on proportional representation. Mr. Sandys said that this would be in the worst circumstances, because it would be clear to everyone that we were only doing this because we were afraid of the outcome of elections.

The President said he agreed with the analysis of all the difficulties, but that these still paled in comparison with the prospect of the establishment of a Communist regime in Latin America. Mr. Sandys said he thought the best solution was that of a Burnham–D'Aguiar government to which the UK would grant independence. [5 *lines of source text not declassified*] The President again repeated his view which he had previously expressed, that the great danger in 1964 was that, since Cuba would be the major American public issue, adding British Guiana to Cuba could well tip the scales, and someone would be elected who would take military action against Cuba. He said that the American people would not stand for a situation which looked as though the Soviet Union had leapfrogged over Cuba to land on the continent in the Western Hemisphere. Mr. Sandys asked whether the United States Government was prepared to give the UK real support in the United Nations and publicly, if the UK were to resume direct rule in British Guiana. "It would be a pleasure," said the President, "we would go all out to the extent necessary." "You didn't give us that much support on Southern Rhodesia," piped up Lord Home. "Well, for that matter," said the President, in a light tone of banter, "you haven't given us that much support on the MLF." The President added that we would be willing to review our stand on the resolution of the Committee of Twenty-four. He said he thought that the aspects of the situation in British Guiana which we should stress were its instability and the danger of racial strife.

296. Memorandum for the Record

Washington, August 15, 1963.

[Source: Central Intelligence Agency, DCI/McCone Files, Job 80–B1285A. Secret; Eyes Only. 2 pages of source text not declassified.]

297. Telegram From the Consulate General in Georgetown to the Department of State

Georgetown, September 5, 1963, 5 p.m.

103. Called on Jagan this morning at his request. We had hour-long meeting during which Jagan earnestly discussed general problem U.S.-BG relations and means of reversing steady deterioration these relations.

Jagan said he was much concerned about the rate this deterioration and unnecessarily harmful effects this was having on both countries. As far as developments in U.S. were concerned, he reluctantly had been forced to conclusion that administration had now adopted as its policy attitude of right extremists, namely, Jagan must go. He cited as evidence Tyler testimony last March before sub-committee of Committee on Appropriations (only portions he has seen are extracts woven into news story in August issue of *Thunder*). Jagan said up to present he has steadfastly defended President in face of attacks by extremists in PPP, arguing that President remained true to assurances he gave Jagan in 1961, but that as politician he of course had to be responsive to vocal sections of U.S. public opinion. Now in light of Tyler testimony Jagan wonders if administration has changed its policy.

This change also having important effects in BG. Present state of U.S.-BG relations is one of causes of lamentable condition BG economy and fact that "our best people are leaving country."

Sir Jock Campbell recently wrote Jagan asking if steps could not be taken to prevent wildcat strikes which were reducing sugar production. Jagan said he was obliged to reply this was aspect of BG affairs which he no longer controlled; hotheads and extremists in party no longer looked to him but acted on their own.

His real worry, Jagan said, was expressed in his press conference remarks on nuclear test ban treaty, though his remarks then had been misrepresented and he apparently had not fully put his meaning across (A–26, August 18).[1] America, Jagan said, is worried about BG becoming another Cuba. Castro once in reference to BG laughingly asked if socialism had ever come about without revolution. Jagan said he had openly discussed his socialist ideals with President as well as his determination to bring this about by peaceful means. All he is asking of U.S. is understanding and assistance so that he can make BG first example of socialist state created by non-violent means.

Source: Department of State, Central Files, POL 1 BR GU–US. Secret; Limit Distribution. Repeated to London.

[1] Not printed. (Ibid., POL BR GU–US)

Alternative to himself, Jagan said, is violence because if he were pushed aside extremists in party would take over and then U.S. would have Castroite situation it is now so strenuously seeking to avoid.

I of course made no specific reply to Jagan's question as to what could be done to improve U.S.-BG relations. I noted that when matters had deteriorated to the extent he described it was usually a long road back to more normal relations, an observation which seemed to depress him. I also briefly reviewed usual points about doubts in U.S., both public opinion and government, on his ultimate objectives, his relations with Cuba and Communist bloc. As he talked much about his socialism, I said question in mind many Americans was precisely that, whether it was his socialism or socialism controlled by another power. To this Jagan said he had once invited representatives of U.S. press and government to see for themselves who ruled BG, he was thinking of renewing this invitation.

Comment: This is third time in past 10 days that approach has been made to us about improving U.S.-BG relations, third time we have had fairly reliable indication of divisions within PPP, and first time Jagan has intimated to U.S. official he might be in serious trouble in his own party. I do not believe Jagan's calling me in for this discussion was merely a trick (which would have been fair conclusion if it had been made only by [garble]); he was as serious today as when we discussed his Washington trip in September–October 1961.

We cannot assess whether Jagan is really in real trouble with his socialist friends here and abroad, and whether this is a last ditch plea for help before more extreme members of PPP take over. We feel, however, there must be some fire behind this smoke and we believe we should not let opportunity to explore it, and possibly exploit it, slip by.

We therefore suggest that contact be made with Jagan during his stay in New York, by U.S. official fully briefed on BG situation and of sufficient rank to speak with authority. Jagan in effect has asked us to tell him what is wrong with U.S.-BG relations and what should be done to improve them. We believe that we should talk to him openly and bluntly. Completely frank discussion which he has asked for at least should give us some insight into present state of PPP, which we feel will be extremely valuable for future operations here.

Melby

298.   Memorandum From the Director of the Bureau of Intelligence and Research (Hughes) to Secretary of State Rusk

Washington, September 6, 1963.

INTELLIGENCE NOTE

Jagan's Pitch for Improved US-BG Relations

Jagan called in our Consul General in Georgetown, September 5, expressed his concern about the deterioration of US-BG relations, and asked what could be done to improve them. Jagan said he had concluded that the US had adopted a policy of "Jagan must go." He warned that if he were pushed aside the extremists in his party would take over and the US would then have the Castroite situation it was seeking to avoid.

Jagan's Sincerity Doubted. Jagan's concern about the deterioration of US-BG relations seems highly inconsistent with (1) the vicious attacks he and his party paper have been making on the US and President Kennedy in the last several weeks, and (2) a series of actions since mid-summer resulting in closer links between BG and Cuba.

Ability of Extremists Questioned. Furthermore, Jagan's analysis of his possible succession by extremists seems questionable. We do not deny that the extremists may have subjected Jagan to increasing pressure. We are inclined to doubt, however, that there is any individual or group among Jagan's lieutenants that could command sufficient popular support to run the party and the government without Jagan.

Jagan's Probable Motivation. It seems probable that Jagan's pitch has been motivated by his apparent failure to get aid from the Soviet Bloc in the face of his great need for such assistance. Although his government has recently obtained a $1 million dollar loan from Cuba, and there have been disputed reports of fund transfers from the USSR to BG, the Guianese economy and the government's finance are in poor, though probably not yet disastrous, shape.

Source: Kennedy Library, National Security Files, Countries Series, British Guiana III. Secret; No Foreign Dissem; Limited Distribution.

299.   Telegram From the Department of State to the Consulate General in Georgetown

Washington, September 7, 1963, 2:55 p.m.

92. Re Georgetown's 103.[1] We have considered suggestion reftel for approach to Jagan for discussion US-BG relationships and have concluded that disadvantages and potential misinterpretations outweigh possible advantages to US. Jagan's alleged concern about deterioration of relations with US seems inconsistent with attacks PPP paper has been making on US and President personally in last few weeks and with series of steps resulting in closer links between BG and Cuba. We also inclined doubt there any individual or group among Jagan's lieutenants that could command sufficient popular support seriously to challenge his control of party.

We wish to avoid creating any impression, or enabling PPP to do so, that there exists real possibility of improving relations between PPP and USG.

Accordingly, we plan adhere to guidance set forth Deptel 88[2] and keep contacts with Jagan at as low level as possible.

Rusk

Source: Department of State, Central Files, POL 1 BR GU–US. Secret; Limit Distribution. Repeated to London.

[1] Document 297.

[2] Dated September 3. (Department of State, Central Files, POL 19 BR GU/UN)

THE DOMINICAN REPUBLIC

300. Telegram From the Consulate General in the Dominican Republic to the Department of State

Ciudad Trujillo, January 4, 1961, 1:20 p.m.

818. Not since last August has Dominican Republic been such beehive of reports and rumors. Subjects deal with precarious GODR finances, action against Venezuela, action by government against GODR including invasion, commercial and POL developments between GODR and Soviet bloc, proposed action against US and its citizens, dissident plots for overthrow Trujillo, and GODR plots to annihilate dissidents. Yesterday Consulate officer was asked by underground contact to furnish him with four hand grenades to be passed on through several intermediaries to ultimate destination for use against Generalissimo this weekend. He was of course informed we were not in that business. This request renewed however my fervent hopes that no hotheads will assassinate Trujillo—or at least not before US takes widely publicized action which will convince even most doubtful dissidents USG is in sympathy with termination Trujillo dictatorship and eventual establishment representative government. Principal point for Department be aware of this connection is assassination plotters are increasingly active and period of relative quiescence is over for time being at least. No organized uprising in sight but ambush of Trujillo considerably more likely than month ago.

Dearborn

Source: Department of State, Central Files, 739.00/1–461. Confidential; Priority.

301. Telegram From the Consulate General in the Dominican Republic to the Department of State

Ciudad Trujillo, February 4, 1961, noon.

923. Rumors circulating Trujillo plans expropriate American properties and terminate US consular relations if Dominican Republic deprived of Cuban windfall sugar. Rumors likewise circulating these reports inspired by GODR for purpose preventing adverse US Congressional action on Dominican Republic.

Consulate believes GODR may take retaliatory action if Dominican Republic deprived share Cuban windfall. While it would not appear be in Trujillo's long range interest further cut ties with US neither has his progressive alienations of US over past two years been wise if considered from view his own interest. His problems are of own making and if it were not for his unrelenting military and financial efforts replace representative Latin American governments with dictatorship and his exacerbation Caribbean tensions by persistent violation generally accepted human rights his regime could today be enjoying degree prosperity and tranquillity enjoyed by few Latin American countries. USG should therefore be prepared for Trujillo follow course leading to destruction his own regime—namely further separation from US and other OAS members and suicidal sponsorship Communist-type propaganda and commercial contacts with Communist countries.

Consulate reiterates its previous judgment that position of US security and business interests in Dominican Republic will continue deteriorate with every additional day Trujillo remains in office. He is increasingly reorienting political and commercial policies along line which run counter US objectives. Most important be cognizant fallacy of Trujillo sponsored argument that US driving GODR to its present course. Nothing further from truth. Trujillo himself is unconscionable violator OAS non-interventionist and human rights principles and his objective is allowed continue these violations without interference from US or OAS. If OAS interferes he threatens associate self with its enemies and this is blackmail from any angle which cannot be tolerated if OAS to be political force in hemisphere.

Dearborn

Source: Department of State, Central Files, 611.39/2–461. Confidential.

302.   Memorandum From Secretary of State Rusk to President Kennedy

Washington, February 15, 1961.

SUBJECT

The Dominican Republic

You have inquired regarding the assertion that the elimination of the Dominican Republic's windfall sugar quota will lead to the downfall of Trujillo and his replacement by a Communist-oriented regime.[1]

Economic Aspects

It is true that the Dominican Government is faced with serious economic difficulties. Foreign exchange reserves are kept secret by the Dominican Government but they are believed to be low. Similarly, the current budgetary position is secret but we assume that by reductions which have been made in the public works program and other civilian costs and by the increased taxes which have been placed on imports and exports and budget will be nearly in balance. The level of business activity is low, credit is scarce, unemployment high and the cost of living has risen.

The principal causes of Trujillo's economic difficulties are not to be found in our U.S. sugar policy but rather in his excessive military and propaganda expenditures coupled with unwise fiscal, financial and investment policies and his systematic milking of the Dominican economy for his own personal gain. While increasing U.S. purchases of sugar six-fold (the estimated windfall quota for the Dominican Republic between April 1 and December 31, 1961 is about 466,000 tons which at the U.S. price would bring a premium of approximately $22.6 million over the price which could be obtained on the world market) would doubtless help the Dominican economy, it is not proposed to eliminate his historic share of the U.S. market (the Dominican basic quota for the April 1–December 31, 1961 period is approximately 83,000 tons which represents a premium of approximately $4 million over what could be obtained on the world market).

Since Trujillo owns directly or indirectly about 60 percent of the sugar-producing properties in the Dominican Republic, a large part of the

---

Source: Kennedy Library, National Security Files, Countries Series, Dominican Republic, General, January–June 1961. Top Secret.

[1] National Security Action Memorandum 17, approved February 13, directed Secretary of State Rusk to prepare a memorandum setting forth the status of U.S. relations with the Dominican Republic and to analyze the effect of a possible elimination of the Dominican Republic's sugar quota on the stability of the Trujillo regime. (Department of State, NSAM Files: Lot 72 D 316)

windfall accrues not to the Dominican economy but to Trujillo personally. Furthermore, with a personal fortune estimated to be somewhere in the neighborhood of $500 million, a substantial part of which consists of liquid holdings abroad, Trujillo has the personal resources, if he wishes to use them, to provide substantial amounts of capital to the Dominican economy.

Political Aspects

In spite of economic difficulties there is no solid evidence that Trujillo's fall is imminent. Trujillo rules by force and will presumably remain in power as long as the armed forces continue to support him. While there is evidence of dissatisfaction on the part of a few officers there is as yet no cogent evidence of large-scale defection within the officer corps.

The underground opposition to Trujillo composed of business, student and professional people is believed to by predominantly anti-Communist. They have substantially increased in numbers in recent years but have been unable to move effectively against Trujillo. In addition to opposition groups in the Dominican Republic, there are numerous exile groups located principally in Venezuela, Cuba, United States and Puerto Rico. In some cases these groups have been infiltrated by pro-Castro or pro-Communist elements.

In the event the Trujillo regime should fall the degree of danger of a communist takeover would, according to our intelligence, depend on whether the domestic or the exile groups succeeded in gaining dominance. The danger would be less if the domestic opposition gained power, and it would be increased substantially if infiltrated exile groups should emerge as the next government.

Finally, account must be taken of the adverse effect on our position of leadership in the hemisphere if we support tyranny in the Dominican Republic. Our ability to marshal Latin American support against the Castro dictatorship would be impaired; Venezuela has made it clear that action against Trujillo is a condition precedent to Venezuelan support of collective action against Castro.

Comments have also been requested concerning the progress which has been made in assuring an orderly takeover by anti-Communist elements should Trujillo fall.

Our representatives in the Dominican Republic have, at considerable risk to those involved, established contacts with numerous leaders in the underground opposition. These leaders look to the United States for assistance. They believe in a free enterprise economic system, plan the nationalization of public utilities with compensation to the owners, intend to institute a land reform program based on agricultural cooperatives and the nationalization of idle agricultural land, and intend to confiscate all of Trujillo's properties. They have agreed on a president to lead them, propose to prevent the re-entry of Communist and subversive agents and to hold elections within a two-year period during which they plan to carry out their program. No financial assistance has been given these underground leaders [2-1/2 lines of source text not declassified].[2]

These leaders are believed to have considerable support within the country and while they plan immediately to seize control of the government if Trujillo falls, their ability to carry out their plans obviously depends to a large degree on the attitude of the Dominican armed forces. They believe they have important support in the officer corps.

With respect to Dominican exile groups, [less than 1 line of source text not declassified] has established useful working relationships and attempted to distinguish between democratic and undemocratic elements. Conversations with them continue. These exile groups have received limited financial assistance and propaganda assistance in the form of certain radio broadcasts.

Should the underground leaders with whom we are in contact fail to obtain the support of the Dominican armed forces and should they call on the United States for assistance, a question arises as to whether the United States would be prepared to intervene militarily either unilaterally or collectively with other American States. This question needs study and a review of the entire plan is desirable. It is recommended that Mr. Berle's Task Force be assigned this task.[3]

There is enclosed a memorandum containing additional background information.[4]

Dean Rusk

---

[2] The January 12 decision to authorize such deliveries is described in the Interim Report of the Select Committee to Study Government Operations with Respect to Intelligence Activities, United States Senate, "Alleged Assassination Plots Involving Foreign Leaders," November 20, 1975, pp. 196–197.

[3] A footnote in Rusk's handwriting reads: "This has been done." No record of the Task Force's deliberation on this matter was found.

[4] Not found.

303.   Telegram From the Consulate General in the Dominican
        Republic to the Department of State

Ciudad Trujillo, February 24, 1961, 9:56 p.m.

994. Businessmen and administrators who have been collaborators in Trujillo regime were asked in last few days by chosen representatives of dissidents what Trujillo's reaction would be if convinced Kennedy administration would definitely not follow conciliatory policy toward his regime. They replied Trujillo would in their opinion do practically nothing against USG or Americans because he fully realizes he still has basic sugar quota and US market for other important exports to safeguard. These collaborators believe Trujillo will attempt smooth things over with USG once convinced his blustering tactics no avail. He may criticize but will soft pedal. In discussion on Cuban windfall sugar Ramfis reported have said recently "what is all the excitement about? Loss of the windfall is not so important. It was something we never had before". Further reasoning behind observations of collaborators is Trujillo has failed in strenuous and costly efforts change US policy toward him, break solidarity OAS, and exchange missions with additional countries western Europe, UAS and iron curtain nations. He now knows he has no place to turn and in play to salvage his power and preserve his wealth will play down attacks on US and turn conciliatory. (Noteworthy he has not yet attacked Kennedy administration on its position re purchases Dominican sugar though Rusk letter to Rayburn was publicized February 21.)[1]

Responsible dissident businessmen who are in contact with mentioned collaborators are developing consensus foregoing may be accurate prognostication.

Close adviser of Trujillo recently remarked to friend of former in veiled way Trujillo more preoccupied by another development than over sugar problem. Best informed dissidents are guessing this greater problem connected with reported disloyalties at home (Consulate telegrams 987 and 991)[2] and fear of activities anti-Trujillo Dominican exiles abroad. Dissidents reason if anything worries Trujillo more than his sugar sales this concern probably results from knowledge of some physical threat to his regime.

Source: Department of State, Central Files, 739.00/2–2461. Confidential; Priority.

[1] In a February 17 letter to Speaker of the House of Representatives Sam Rayburn, Secretary Rusk asked that Congress consider amending the U.S. Sugar Act to empower the President to deny the Trujillo government any of the sugar quota previously alloted to Cuba.

[2] Dated February 23 and February 24. (Department of State, Central Files, 739.00/2–2361 and 739.00/2–2461, respectively)

Comment: Source of foregoing is of utmost reliability and group for whom he speaks is comprised of pro-US moderate dissidents. If views expressed are correct, my interpretation is Trujillo tried by sound and fury (threats expel all Americans, terminate Consular relations, tie up with iron curtain, etc.) prevent USG from taking steps adverse his interests. He may now realize his strategy has failed and may try save his regime by only course left—namely convince US and OAS to tolerate him. I have been interested in several comments by contacts during past week that Ramfis is one who is restraining Generalissimo from taking drastic action against Americans. Last night [*less than 1 line of source text not declassified*] who I consider be practically agent of Trujillo and son (though perhaps less so than formerly) told me Ramfis is one who could give further good advice and US should talk with him. These developments may [*sic*] than Trujillo family hopes save skins by persuading US businessmen and USG that reconciliation can be worked out through Ramfis. My advice is Ramfis is most unstable, ruthless, US-hating, untrustworthy and cynical occupant of whole Trujillo nest and we should avoid him like bubonic plague. This opinion borne out by such important source as President Balaguer who remarked to high ranking friend of mine who made some complimentary remarks about Ramfis "Ramfis is the worst of the lot" (this information given me in utmost confidence).

I wish emphasize Trujillo is short-term proposition in Dominican Republic, that future US interests here lie in building goodwill among moderate elements of dissidents, and that if USG gives slightest indication of softening toward Trujillo US security and business interests in Dominican Republic will suffer consequences for years to come. In own interest I believe US should do all possible within non-interventionist commitments to hasten turnover of GODR to elements which will respect guiding principles of OAS.

Dearborn

304. Airgram From the Consulate General in the Dominican Republic to the Department of State

Ciudad Trujillo, March 22, 1961.

G–105. This Airgram is on the subjects of "What is the Trujillo Opposition?" and of "The nature of the U.S. Choice in the Dominican Republic today". It does not contain details since they have already been supplied to the extent that they are available in the Consulate's previous reporting.

The Trujillo opposition.

There is no well organized unitary opposition to Trujillo. On the other hand, on the basis of the judgment of our best sources 80 to 90 per cent of literate Dominicans are anti-Trujillo and would like to have a representative form of government oriented toward the west, one which would not intervene in the affairs of its neighbors and which would respect basic human rights. The strongest unifying force of the anti-Trujillo Dominicans is their hatred of the dictator.

While most anti-Trujillo Dominicans are not even considering any action against the Generalissimo owing to a combination of the Generalissimo's highly organized repressive machinery, their long experience of domination through fear, their lack of capability, their lack of courage and their generally recognized docile nature, there are small nuclei of Dominicans who are planning to overthrow him. Their very lack of a large well defined opposition is a defensive condition, since in the past whenever a conspiratorial group became large or well defined, it was caught and ruthlessly suppressed. It was usually exposed by torture and rendered ineffective by assassination of the most courageous elements. These circumstances have led the nuclei of which I speak to view liquidation as the only way to accomplish their ends. Political assassination is ugly and repulsive, but everything must be judged in its own context. The United States used the atom bomb on Hiroshima and that was ugly and repulsive—unless one stops to consider that it was used to save thousands of lives in the long run. One cannot regard those Dominicans who favor the assassination of Trujillo as morally bankrupt, criminals, etc. Some of them are in fact, and this is a sobering thought, the people with whom we ourselves would be identified if we had the misfortune to be Dominicans. The nuclei who are friendly to the U.S. have spurts of courage, they are pro-U.S., they subscribe to the principles of the OAS, and they are the hope of the D.R.

There are probably other nuclei against Trujillo than those of which we are informed.

Source: Department of State, Central Files, 739.00/3–2261. Secret; Limit Distribution.

The Consulate believes the communists have been working here at least since August through the Generalissimo and Radio Caribe in pursuit of the ends of Moscow. The Consulate cannot prove it. Like so many dictators, Trujillo does not see the danger to his own way of life in playing with these elements. He thinks he is using them, but in reality is being used. It is quite possible at this stage he no longer cares as long as they are anti-U.S. and anti-Catholic Church. Whatever communist led nuclei there may be, the Consulate does not believe they are in a position to take over the country. The campesino has not yet been politically awakened. He will be the pawn of whatever element takes over. The people with education, control over economic life, control of the professions (doctors, lawyers, engineers) are mostly in our camp. The military is a question mark despite all our efforts to discern its innermost thoughts. The Consulate suspects we cannot discern their thoughts because they do not have any beyond staying out of trouble and living as well as possible. We are informed some of the military would follow quickly if an anti-Trujillo outbreak began, but we cannot prove this with firsthand testimony. It is probably true, if it becomes evident that a revolution has a chance. The military are used to following a leader and the Consulate believes they will continue to do this. The big question is, "What leader?" If the Jefe disappeared they might go with Balaguer; more likely they would set up a junta but someone would emerge as leader, probably eventually a civilian. It seems reasonable to suspect that under the conditions which prevail here the people with brains and influence would come out on top. Those friendly to us have a near monopoly on those commodities. This is not to say they will do everything our way. There are lots of changes to be made here and there will be no singlemindedness on how to make them. As must be expected, trial and error will be a principal method of progress and not even the U.S. can know all the answers of what is good for the D.R. in its own peculiar circumstances. Patience and understanding will be highly important.

The nature of our choice.

The Consulate doubts there will be *chaos* after the fall of Trujillo, but this depends somewhat on what one means by chaos. There will probably be some bloodshed and there will be many difficulties of adjustment, both economic and political. How much of this there will be will depend in large part on the Dominicans, but also partly on the U.S. and the OAS. The OAS must be prepared to give help promptly if requested and the U.S. must be prepared immediately to be the agent of the OAS.

Ever since August 1960 Trujillo has, wittingly or not, been softening up the D.R. for leftist extremists. Consulate reporting has pointed this out clearly and repeatedly and it was in large part the basis for our argument for effective sanctions against Trujillo's exports last August. Our theme has been that the longer Trujillo continues to dominate the D.R.

the more susceptible the country is becoming to leftist extremists, and that, therefore, Trujillo's overthrow in the near future would be in the interest of the U.S. The situation is not as favorable to us as it was last August because of the softening up that has gone on in the meantime. It is, however, more favorable to us than last December, and I believe if Trujillo should be overthrown today we would come out of the situation better than we ever will again. This is because since early January our stock with the dissidents is high. If we were free to choose our alternative, our choice would not be simple. As often occurs in international relations, it would be a choice between two difficult alternatives. If the U.S. should decide that Trujillo is bad but that it should, for the sake of momentary expediency, work with him in a keep-your-distance sort of way, the prestige and influence of the U.S. in the Dominican Republic would disappear with Trujillo, and he cannot last much longer in any event. If, on the other hand, the U.S. is known to be using its influence toward the establishment of a representative government in the Dominican Republic which subscribes to the principles of the OAS, it has a good chance of maintaining a position of influence in the government that succeeds the Generalissimo. Let no one, however, think that the transition from a thirty-one year old dictatorship is going to be accomplished with anything approximating the orderliness of a mere administrative shift in personnel and the type of policy deliberations one would find at a meeting of the National Security Council.

Dearborn

---

305. Telegram From the Department of State to the Consulate General in the Dominican Republic

Washington, April 28, 1961, 9:05 p.m.

683. If confronted with sudden political instability or violent overthrow of Trujillo regime, ranking US representative in Dominican Republic should until receipt of further instructions be guided by following principles:

Source: Department of State, Central Files, 739.00/4–2961. Secret; Priority. Drafted by Devine, cleared by Coerr, ARA/CMA, ARA/RPA, ARA/WST, ARA/EST, S/S, L, L/ARA, CIA, DOD/ISA, and CINCLANT, and approved by the Secretary. Repeated to CINCLANT.

(1) US cannot afford and will not permit external imposition on Dominican Republic of pro-Communist or pro-Castro regime as successor to present GODR;

(2) US strongly hopes any succeeding government will be broadly acceptable to people of Dominican Republic, will be oriented toward US, and will promptly commit self to establishment democracy and firm scheduling of free elections.

(3) US influence in Dom Rep should be exercised toward achievement above objectives.

(4) At time of replacement of present GODR or significant change in present control you should on any appropriate occasion convey clear impression that US recognition and/or assistance to Dominican Republic would necessarily be influenced and determined by degree government's disassociation from unacceptable personnel, policies and practices of Trujillo regime and by clarity its dedication to principles listed item 2 above.

(5) As opportunity presents self under circumstances outlined above you should encourage formulation realistic coalition civilian and military elements capable holding power as provisional government friendly toward and disposed work with US.

(6) Should a provisional government which in your judgment satisfies foregoing criteria request US armed assistance in face of real or anticipated threat from abroad, you should submit such request together with your recommendation soonest, suggest it may wish request assistance other democratic governments such as Venezuela and Colombia and inform OAS.

(7) Please keep Department currently informed.

Rusk

306. Memorandum From the President's Special Assistant for National Security Affairs (Bundy) to President Kennedy

Washington, May 2, 1961.

Here is a report from Bob Murphy about his visit to Trujillo with Igor Cassini.[1]

Murphy's conclusion is that our hostility to the Dominican Republic is unwise; he thinks we should "walk back the cat and initiate a policy of guidance." He thinks that the groups at Ciudad Trujillo are willing and eager "to be taken by the hand and to institute democratic reforms."

I know nothing of the Dominican Republic except by heresay, but I think there can be little doubt that the whole concept of the Alliance for Progress would be gravely shadowed in the eyes of Latin Americans if we were to move to anything like a policy of "friendly guidance" toward Trujillo.

At the risk of misunderstanding, I think I ought to add that if the public were to know that Igor Cassini is providing public relations help to Trujillo, your own personal position as a liberal leader might be compromised. I cannot help thinking that your own position should be fully disengaged from any venture of this sort.

McG. B.

Attachment

April 16, 1961.

Accompanied by Igor Cassini, I had private and informal talks at the Palacio Nacionale, Ciudad Trujillo, April 15 and 16, 1961, with Dr. Joaquin Balaguer, President of the Dominican Republic, Foreign Minister Porfirio Herrera Baez, Personal Assistant to President Balaguer, Otto

---

Source: Kennedy Library, National Security Files, Countries Series, Dominican Republic, Murphy Trip, May–July 1961. Secret.

[1] In April President Kennedy sent veteran U.S. diplomat Robert D. Murphy to the Dominican Republic to discuss with Trujillo the political situation there. Murphy was accompanied by Hearst newspaper reporter Igor Cassini, an acquaintance of the Kennedy family who had ties to Trujillo and acted as an unregistered agent for him in the United States.

Vega, and Generalissimo Rafael Leonidas Trujillo Molina. Protocol was carefully observed at both meetings to mark the status of the Generalissimo as a private citizen; we were first received for a few minutes by the President and the Foreign Minister for perfunctory conversation. Then we were joined by the Generalissimo who acted as Dominican spokesman.

It developed from the conversations that conditions on the Island are stable and calm; that there is no suffering or actual inconvenience resulting from the OAS embargo. The effect of it is disturbing in the psychological and political sense and of course it is deeply resented.

My approach was that of asking questions in order to explore the situation, seeking a solution, with emphasis on the traditional friendship between our two countries. I suggested that while it is perhaps true that the vast majority of North Americans are uninformed about and little interested in the affairs of the Dominican Republic, a minority are highly critical of the "Trujillo dictatorship". They, I suggested, were better judges than I of sentiment in Latin America.

During the course of the conversations there were frank references to the 6th OAS meeting at San Jose; to the feud between Betancourt and Trujillo;[2] to the necessity of free elections in the Dominican Republic with some form of OAS supervision; to the question of the Dominican future should the Generalissimo disappear from the scene, for example, as a result of illness or accident; and to the urgent need for better communication between the D.R. and other American Republics, including the U.S. as well as the U.N. I referred to a certain preoccupation in Washington and elsewhere of stories regarding alleged tortures, brutalities and suppression by the regime. I stressed the hostility in certain quarters and among sectors of the press against what they believed to be a cruel dictatorship which did not disdain corrupt methods in its dealings. I referred also to the concern that the D.R. not become another Cuba as a result of a vacuum created by the eventual disappearance of Trujillo, and the possible entrance of elements antagonistic to the U.S.

I found an alertness regarding all these problems. The following emerged from our talks:

The Generalissimo not only does not intend to leave the D.R. as Batista left Cuba but he and his associates see no reason to do so. He is certainly no Batista. Trujillo in his seventieth year seems in excellent health and spirits. He manifests what appears to be genuine confidence in the stability of the position. He pointed to the fact that the Republic's

---

[2] Reference is to the Sixth Meeting of Foreign Ministers of the Organization of American States in San José in August 1960. The Ministers approved economic sanctions against the Trujillo government, which had supported an assassination attempt against Venezuelan President Romulo Betancourt in June.

constitution requires Presidential elections in May, 1961. He and his associates said that it would be most difficult to amend the constitution to require earlier elections. However, Trujillo declared that he is prepared to accept OAS observers and the full publicity. He seemed persuaded that the situation required freer contact with the press. Mr. Cassini provided a helpful and convincing account of President Kennedy's handling of this important problem, especially the feature of open conferences, and the acceptance of the fact that there would be inevitably critical and even hostile elements attending. The Dominicans seemed to agree that there was wisdom in meeting these openly in the hope that as they feel their case is sound, sympathetic support would be forthcoming from many sectors of the press who are not prejudiced a priori.

The Generalissimo expressed vigorous confidence in the stability of the Dominican situation, believing that the population stands wholeheartedly behind the present program and approved what has been achieved in the past to improve the living conditions of the mass and to provide better opportunities for the average man. He stated his belief that if he should disappear, constitutional processes are adequate to maintain the position. He emphasized that he has no plans to perpetuate a Trujillo dynasty, confirming what his son had recently said on the subject.

According to the Generalissimo he intends to stand on the side of the U.S. regardless of the present difficulties.

Trujillo authorized Mr. Cassini to work out a plan of improved communications including the selection of a professional public relations expert from the U.S. to work in the D.R. for a better public image of the D.R. abroad. An attack would be made on baseless and distorted stories regarding the regime and the light of day thrown on the allegations frequently of obscure origin concerning brutalities and suppression. The intention would be to open the D.R. to a truly free press recognizing that a controlled press is a liability.

The Foreign Minister read to us a draft of an informal and personal letter he planned to send to Secretary Rusk and fifteen other L.A. Foreign Secretaries. In essence it was an historical account of the D.R.'s foreign policy and an expression of regret over the OAS resolution and attitude. He asked for my reaction. I replied that my personal reaction was unfavorable because if I were an addressee of such a letter I would not know what to do with it. I might interpret it wrongly as an expression of anxiety whereas I had gained the impression that they did not so intend it. They all agreed that it would be more effective to institute a series of informal representations by qualified persons in the various capitals. They said they would be grateful if I would discuss it at a convenient moment with Secretary Rusk.

Comment:

It might be useful to compare American policy vis-à-vis other countries in different areas—countries which are similar in size and presenting various interpretations of democratic government. Three analogies occur to me: Tunisia, Guinea and the Republic of the Congo (French).

In the case of the Dominican Republic, the U.S. has broken diplomatic relations for hemispheric reasons no doubt which are arguable, but certainly having some relationship to the Betancourt–Trujillo feud, and specifically for the consideration of the pallid OAS resolution at San Jose on Cuba. Yet there is no question that the D.R. has provided consistent support of U.S. policies especially in the field of E-W relations, than any of the three countries mentioned. Also as distinguished from the D.R., the U.S. has extended substantial material aid to the other countries mentioned.

The U.S. maintains friendly diplomatic relations with the "democracies" of Bourguiba, of Sekou Toure, and of Abbe Youlou. Tunisia has approximately the same size population and is if anything poorer than the D.R. Surely no one would suggest that when it comes to strong arm methods, Bourguiba would yield any ground to Trujillo. Sekou Toure's approach to democracy is of course several degrees less liberal than either Bourguiba or Trujillo. Sekou Toure of course has to deal with a more primitive population whose ideas of democracy are hazier than Tunisian or Dominican, and whose economy is also more primitive.

The case of Abbe Youlou at Brazzaville is that of a classic approach of a tribal leader coming to power by the massacre of opposing tribal leaders. He is now in apparently absolute control as a result of brutal methods for which there is a tradition in the area. By no stretch of the imagination is Brazzaville the capital of a democracy in our sense of the word, and yet quite properly we maintain diplomatic relations with that country, as we do with Guinea and Tunisia. Yet we have broken with the D.R. which is close to our shores and very close to Cuba. I am frankly puzzled as to the wisdom of our position. Should we not walk back the cat and initiate a policy of guidance. The moment would seem ripe for it. The present situation does not seem to call for harshness and public condemnation but rather a process of friendly leadership. It seems to me that the group at Ciudad Trujillo are eager and willing to be taken by the hand and to institute democratic reforms.

307.   **Memorandum From the Cuban Task Force of the National Security Council to the President's Special Assistant for National Security Affairs (Bundy)**

Washington, May 15, 1961.

SUBJECT

The Current Situation in and Contingency Plans for the Dominican Republic

The Trujillo regime in the Dominican Republic is in the most serious trouble of its 30-year history. It has been condemned and isolated by the action of the 6th Meeting of Foreign Ministers at San Jose in August 1960. The economic position of the country has weakened seriously. Opposition to the regime is expanding and becoming more determined, and recent reports indicate Trujillo's removal may be imminent.

The paramount interest of the U.S. is to prevent Castro-Communist or other unfriendly elements from taking control and to insure that Trujillo is succeeded by a friendly, democratic government. These objectives can best be achieved by cooperation with and encouragment of those elements in the Dominican Republic and elsewhere who share them and oppose Trujillo.

Opposition to Trujillo is divided into two main groupings: (a) the exile movements centered in the U.S., Venezuela and Cuba, and (b) the internal dissident movements. The facts that the various exile groups have little unity or cohesion, to some extent have been infiltrated by Communists and Castroites, and are generally not acceptable to the Dominican people make them a poor risk for the U.S. to support.

During the past year a moderate group of internal dissidents who appear to meet U.S. requirements has been identified and encouraged in its efforts by the U.S.

While it is highly desirable in the present Dominican situation for the U.S. to be identified with and to support democratic elements seeking to overthrow Trujillo, we necessarily run some risks in doing so. If Trujillo is overthrown with U.S. support, we may well be criticized by world opinion for subverting an existing government, albeit a highly

Source: Department of State, NSC Files: Lot 62 D 1, Cuba and the Dominican Republic. Top Secret. Drafted by Hoover (S/O), cleared by Acting Secretary Bowles, Acting Assistant Secretary Coerr, Consul General Dearborn, Berle, S/O, IO, L, CIA, DOD/ISA, and DOD/J–t. According to a covering memorandum from Battle to Richard Goodwin, May 15, the report had been requested of the Cuban Task Force at the 483d Meeting of the NSC, May 6. Another covering memorandum from Theodore C. Achilles, State Department Operations Center Director, to the Secretary, dated May 26, stated it had been shown to the President who approved it on May 24 "in the absence of NSC consideration in view of the reported imminence of an attempt to assassinate Trujillo."

unpopular one. A miscalculation of the capabilities of the moderate group could mean that U.S. support for an unsuccessful attempt against the Trujillo regime would be exposed, and following on the recent Cuban experience U.S. prestige would plummet. If we were to misread the intentions of the moderates or they were deliberately concealed from us, we might find ourselves in the position of having created a Dominican Castro. An additional factor for consideration in deciding the amount and timing of further U.S. support to the moderate anti-Trujillo group is the possibility that our support may prompt this group to take action before it or we are ready.

There is attached a paper dealing with various contingencies that may arise in the near future in the Dominican Republic and setting out various recommendations for the President's approval.

In this connection it may be mentioned that Castro-Communist control of the Dominican Republic would almost certainly lead to a similar takeover in Haiti.

Attachment

DOMINICAN REPUBLIC—CONTINGENCY SITUATIONS AND RECOMMENDATIONS

I. Trujillo Removed and Succeeded by Friendly Internal Elements.

Recent reports indicate that the internal Dominican dissidents are becoming increasingly determined to oust Trujillo by any means, and their plans in this regard are well advanced. This group is believed to have support among the various sectors of the population and their leadership includes members of the Dominican military, although the degree of support they can command in the armed forces is uncertain.

Once Trujillo is overthrown this moderate group plans to establish a provisional junta and to begin to create a democratic government and society in the Dominican Republic. It appears to have the best chance of establishing a stable government oriented toward the US. No other group which combines an effective organization with an acceptable political philosophy has been identified. The pro-Trujillo elements do not hold any promise of being able to establish a post-Trujillo government which would be acceptable to the US. Over the past year our Consulate at Ciudad Trujillo has been in touch with the leaders of the moderate group and encouraged them to look toward the US both as a model and for support in their efforts. If it is successful in ousting Trujillo, it will merit prompt United States recognition and support.

In addition to recognition and moral support, a provisional government format by this moderate group will probably urgently need outside military force to assist it in maintaining internal order and resisting internal and external attempts at subversion. Subversive initiative could be expected to come from Cuba and/or from the Dominican exile groups. Approved plans for the employment of US military forces in the Dominican Republic have been prepared and are sufficiently flexible to permit various degrees of force to be applied under Presidential authority. An amphibious force, with Marines embarked, normally operates in the Caribbean area and other forces in the continental US are available on relatively short notice if required. From the point of view of US posture in Latin America and the world, military intervention in the Dominican Republic should to the extent possible be taken through the OAS or at the request of a provisional government in conjunction with selected Latin American countries rather than by the US alone. In any event, the OAS should be notified of the action taken.

Recommendations:

1. That the US Consul General at Ciudad Trujillo when so authorized inform the moderate group of pro-US dissidents that if they succeed at their own initiative and on their own responsibility in forming an acceptable provisional government they can be assured that any reasonable requests for assistance from the US will be promptly and favorably answered.

2. That in the event Trujillo is overthrown and an acceptable provisional government is established:

a) The US swiftly recognize such a government.

b) Upon receipt of a request from this government for military assistance against a real or anticipated external threat, we dispatch such aid, up to and including the landing of US forces, recognizing at the same time that a concomitant objective will be the stabilization of an internal situation acceptable to the US.

c) The US encourage the provisional government also to request the assistance or the presence of other friendly democratic nations, such as Venezuela and Colombia, with notification to the Organization of American States of the action taken and a request that the measures adopted at the Sixth Meeting of Foreign Ministers be discontinued. (For this purpose OAS observers might be invited into the Dominican Republic.)

d) The US take steps to screen the departure from the continental US and Puerto Rico of all Dominican exiles attempting to return to the Dominican Republic for as long a period as may be desirable and feasible, and request the Venezuelan Government to take similar action.

3. That the US send immediately to Caracas a special emissary to:

a) Obtain from President Betancourt a commitment to immediately earmark specific forces which would be prepared to act jointly with US forces and to commit such forces to joint operations in the event actions envisaged in this paper are ordered.

b) Request President Betancourt to approach President Lleras of Colombia with a view toward a similar commitment for participation of Colombian forces.

c) Explore with President Betancourt, and ask him to discuss with President Lleras, the possibility of a prompt, affirmative response to an appeal from an acceptable provisional government, which might include a joint declaration by the three heads of state disclaiming political or territorial ambitions in the Dominican Republic and expressing readiness to lend moral and material support for the specific purpose of assuring to the Dominican people opportunity to carry through necessary reforms and establish democratic institutions and practices free from the threat of externally supported invasion or subversion.

This emissary should speak only with President Betancourt and emphasize secrecy, urge the same treatment by Lleras, and make clear that the US is only planning against a possible contingency.

II. Trujillo Removed and Unfriendly Elements Take Over.

It is possible that the plans of the moderate group of dissidents may be frustrated. Unfriendly elements, either Trujillo supporters or possibly Castro-Communists, may remove Trujillo themselves and seize power. Or, once Trujillo had been removed by the moderates, these unfriendly elements might grab control in the resulting confusion. In any of these situations the group supported by the U.S. may be unable to establish themselves. It is also possible that the removal of Trujillo would result in a total breakdown of the power structure, leaving the country in a chaotic state of anarchy with no group or individual able to stabilize the situation.

Recommendations:

1) That the US Consul General when so authorized discuss with leaders of the acceptable dissident group the advisability of having in his possession a pre-signed request for US, Venezuelan and OAS help in the event of a quiet takeover by unfriendly elements or of a situation in which friendly leaders would be unable to expose or establish themselves. If they agree, such pre-signed request should be obtained.

2) The US Consul General should have stand-by instructions to urge the moderate pro-US group to declare themselves to be the provisional government and to request help from the US and the OAS.

3) Upon notification by the US Consul General that Trujillo has been removed from power, or that his removal seems reasonably certain the

appropriate US military forces be immediately positioned to be able to reach Dominican territory with a minimum of delay.

4) Upon receipt of a request for military assistance from an acceptable group which has declared itself and taken any reasonable or plausible steps to constitute itself a provisional government, or upon notification by the US Consul General that he has received such a request, US forces should move into the Dominican Republic immediately.

III. Trujillo Remains in Power.

Despite the difficulties he faces Trujillo may manage to maintain himself in power for an indefinite period. During this time it would be in the interests of the US to continue to give encouragement to the internal dissidents in order to buttress their position in the anti-Trujillo movement and hold their loyalty.

Our attitude toward Trujillo is a continuing foreign policy test before Latin American and world opinion of US support for democracy and social reform. In view of the criticism that has been leveled at the US in the past for its alleged support of Trujillo, it is imperative that the US public posture be unequivocally in favor of the return of the Dominican Republic to the inter-American community under a government committed to democratic principles. It is important, therefore, that the US avoid any action that would imply support or toleration for Trujillo and that we continue to express publicly our distaste for the oppressive undemocratic nature and policies of his regime.

Recommendations:

1. The Voice of America, and all other media, should carry more information highlighting the anti-US, pro-Communist, anti-OAS, anti-Catholic Church line of the Trujillo press, and editorial comment condemning Trujillo's constant violations of human rights and his interventions in the affairs of other nations.

2. High ranking US public officials should make appropriate and timely statements critical of the excesses and undemocratic practices of the Trujillo regime.

3. The US should present to the appropriate committees of the OAS information reflecting Trujillo's violations of OAS principles.

4. The US should expose through public media attempts which Trujillo is now preparing to hoodwink the American community into believing that he is preparing to hold free elections.

5. In pursuing actions along the above lines, the US should maintain flexibility of application in terms of current developments.

308. Editorial Note

At approximately 10 p.m. on May 30, 1961, three cars stopped the limousine of Generalissimo Trujillo about 9 kilometers outside Ciudad Trujillo on the highway to San Cristobal. Eight assailants from the cars fired 70 rounds of machine gun ammunition into Trujillo, killing him and putting an end to his more than 30 years of rule in the Dominican Republic. (Joint WEEKA No. 23 from Ciudad Trujillo, June 6; Department of State, Central Files, 739.00(W)/6–661)

---

309. Telegram From the Department of State to the Consulate General in the Dominican Republic

Washington, June 1, 1961, 11:54 a.m.

760. Trujillo's death leaves Joaquin Balaguer in key position as continuing President and head of recognized Dominican State. Anti-US elements such as Abbes–Ramfis clique will probably attempt subject him their exclusive influence. US interests would best be served should he accept support from and represent pro-US dissidents and acceptable military elements. Following paragraph based on absence thus far any realistic prospect that pro-US dissidents can make successful effort take over Government and our understanding that in past they have indicated their possible readiness work with Balaguer in such contingency.

Request your opinion as to advisability and feasibility your obtaining (personal and non-recorded) interview with Balaguer alone in which you would (1) emphasize deep significance his actions at this crucial point in Dominican history may have for Dominican Republic and its relations with Inter-American System; (2) discuss substance above paragraph and attempt ascertain his intended political course; (3) inform him US attitude toward GODR and willingness consider reestablishment diplomatic relations, and any possibility US assistance would depend heavily on degree to which GODR rejects dictatorial regimes and prac-

---

Source: Department of State, Central Files, 739.00/6–161. Secret; Niact. Drafted by Coerr; approved by Rusk; and cleared by Bowles, Goodwin, ARA/CMA, L/ARA, S/S, and S/O. Repeated to Port-au-Prince, Bogota, Caracas, POLAD CINCARIB, and Paris (where the Secretary was accompanying President Kennedy on a State visit).

tices whether of Trujillo or Castro origin and degree to which GODR demonstrates determination move toward re-vitalization democratic principles and friendship for Free World; (4) tell him we are confident that Dominican leadership, including leaders of armed forces, would wish prevent domination of Dominican Government by Communists or Castroites or other elements basically hostile to the Inter-American System and that moderate coalition headed by Balaguer might open way to brighter future for Dominican Republic without serious civil strife; (5) assure him USG would consider promptly and favorably written request by GODR to assist, in case of need, in air and sea within limits of GODR jurisdiction to seek out and repel any Castro-Communist attack from abroad. Tell him US forces positioned for such assistance; (6) discuss with Balaguer, if he appears react favorably to above points, possible consideration ways and means arrange good-will visit US naval force which might provide influence in favor of stability.

Info posts submit comments, if any.

Rusk

310. Memorandum by the Under Secretary of State (Bowles)

Washington, June 3, 1961.

NOTES ON CRISIS INVOLVING THE DOMINICAN REPUBLIC

In mid-May we had our first indications that a group in the Dominican Republic might be plotting against the life of Generalissimo Trujillo. Dissident groups communicated with American officials in the Dominican Republic to inform them that the assassination was imminent and that they would like help, in the shape of arms, recognition, and general support.

Dick Goodwin, who had spent considerable time studying the problems involving the Dominican Republic was in favor of both granting

---

Source: Yale University Library, Bowles Papers, Box 392, Folder 154. Personal. The editors have not been able to account for certain chronological discrepancies in this memorandum.

arms and guaranteeing support. However, I and others in the Department of State took a strong position that we had no real knowledge of who the dissidents were, their views, or depth of influence. Nor was it proper for the United States to be involved in an assassination, directly, indirectly, or in any other way.

The first plans for a contingency paper were developed during the week of May 24th.[1] When I left for Connecticut (my first trip outside the District of Columbia since February), this paper had not taken shape. However, I was sufficiently concerned about developments not only in the Dominican Republic but also in Haiti to ask Alexis Johnson before I left the office to move into both situations and to recommend a constructive plan for whatever may occur.

Shortly after I took office I asked Tom Mann to send an economic mission to Haiti to find out what we could do to help relieve the massive malnutrition which existed there. Although I followed this up on two or three occasions, the pressures on Mann, myself, and others were so great that there was no follow through on this effort.

Early Wednesday morning I received a telephone call from the Secretary before I left for New York for a luncheon with Anna Rosenberg and Bill Benton. The Secretary told me he thought it was essential that I come back immediately for reasons which would become evident when I arrived. I managed to get the 10:26 plane out of Bridgeport, and Sam Lewis and Joe Scott[2] met me at the airport with the news that Trujillo had been assassinated the night before.

They had with them the contingency paper which had been prepared over the week end. The immediate impression I had was that it was a dangerously inadequate document, which broadly interpreted, could throw us into a war in the most casual fashion.

For instance, one of the provisions was the statement that if we receive [sic] from a dissident element in the Dominican Republic to intervene, and if the Consul General should concur in this request, we would immediately send in American forces to take over the island without regard for the Organization of American States, treaties, or common sense.

After arriving back in Washington, I went into the Secretary's office and called these sections of the contingency paper to his attention. I am not clear whether or not he had previously gone over it with any great care, but it is my impression he had not, since he agreed immediately with my own concern.

---

[1] Apparent reference to Document 307, which was approved May 24.

[2] Reference is to Samuel W. Lewis and Joseph W. Scott, Special Assistants to the Under Secretary of State.

It was completely clear following this conversation that he agreed that this contingency paper would have to be interpreted with the greatest care.

The Secretary had intended to leave that day (May 31) to join the President in the conference with DeGaulle.[3] However, he waited over until the following day, leaving at noon. In the meantime, the situation remained calm.

On Thursday afternoon about 2:30 Dick Goodwin called to say he thought we should have a high level meeting to discuss "what we should do about the Dominican Republic." I told him I would discuss this with some of our people working on the problem and get in touch with him.

Alexis Johnson, Ted Achilles, and Wyn Coerr all agreed that no meeting was called for, and I asked Wyn Coerr to call Goodwin to tell him. About an hour later Bob McNamara called to suggest a similar meeting in my office at 6:45. It was obvious he had been called by Dick Goodwin.

In the meantime the Vice President wanted to report to me on his trip to Southeast Asia. He arrived about 5:45 and our talk lasted for forty-five minutes. I told him about the meeting and asked him if he would like to attend. The Vice President, Bob Kennedy, Secretary McNamara, Dick Goodwin, General Lemnitzer, Wyn Coerr, and Ted Achilles were here. Bob McNamara and Lemnitzer stated that under the terms of the contingency paper, they were required to be prepared to move into the island on short order if required to do so, and this, in their opinion, called for substantially more troops that we had in the area. After some discussion we considered two more aircraft carriers, some destroyers, and 12,000 marines should be moved into a position some one hundred miles off the Dominican Republic shore.

I underscored that this troop movement should be accomplished with the minimum of publicity, the minimum of maneuvers, that the fleet be spread out over a wide area so that it would not appear to be in formation.

Lemnitzer estimated that this force would be in position by Sunday. After some discussion, I further agreed that we would authorize the destroyers and other vessels within sixty miles of the coast, still well out of sight of land.

The tone of the meeting was deeply disturbing. Bob Kennedy was clearly looking for an excuse to move in on the island. At one point he suggested, apparently seriously, that we might have to blow up the Consulate to provide the rationale.

---

[3] Secretary Rusk accompanied President Kennedy to Paris May 31–June 3.

His general approach, vigorously supported by Dick Goodwin, was that this was a bad government, that there was a strong chance that it might team up with Castro, and that it should be destroyed—with an excuse if possible, without one if necessary.

Rather to my surprise, Bob McNamara seemed to support this view. I took the opposite view that our whole world position was based on treaty rights, that it would be a catastrophic mistake to take them lightly, and that in acting in a reckless manner in the Dominican Republic, we would only be compounding the mistake of Cuba, and that while I thought it was necessary to take all possible measures for the protection of American lives, we should not move beyond that point.

There was then further discussion about the need to stimulate movement among some of the dissident movements which might as a dissident government and propose American assistance so that we would have this kind of excuse in case we wished to move [sic].

I said I thought this was a mistake since a request of this kind, stimulated by us, would almost make us react favorably, if we were to provide a reasonable measure of good faith.

After some argument, this was put aside.

The entire spirit of this meeting was profoundly distressing and worrisome, and I left at 8:00 p.m. with a feeling that this spirit which I had seen demonstrated on this occasion and others at the White House by those so close to the President constitutes a further danger of half-cocked action by people with almost no foreign policy experience, who are interested in action for action's sake, and the devil take the highmost.

The next morning I learned that in spite of the clear decision against having the dissident group request our assistance Dick Goodwin following the meeting sent a cable to CIA people in the Dominican Republic without checking with State or CIA; indeed, with the protest of the Department of State.[4] The cable directed the CIA people in the Dominican Republic to get this request at any cost. When Allen Dulles found this out the next morning, he withdrew the order. We later discovered it had already been carried out.

When the meeting broke up, it was suggested that another meeting be held at 9:00 the next morning. I asked that it be postponed until 11:00, in order to give me an opportunity to consult with people here in the Department and Dean Rusk in Paris.

Immediately following the staff meeting, I called in George McGhee, Ed Murrow, and George Ball, and told them the full story. They were startled and shocked as I was, and I was gratified to find them in full

---

[4] Not further identified.

agreement on the position I had taken. Indeed, they were even more out-spoken in outlining the disastrous consequences of this kind of action.

I also talked with Dean Rusk on the telephone, told him the general developments, and outlined the position I had taken, and as I expected, I found him in close agreement.

At the meeting at 11:00,[5] Bob Kennedy was again present together with Arthur Schlesinger, Dick Goodwin, Allen Dulles, Alexis Johnson, Bob McNamara, Walt Rostow, Wyn Coerr, Ed Murrow, George McGhee, George Ball, Colonel King, Lyndon Johnson, General Wheeler. I later discovered that Adlai Stevenson was in the building and sent to call for his attendence.

Bob Kennedy was in an even more aggressive, dogmatic, and vicious mood than the previous meeting. He turned directly to me and said, "What do you propose to do on the situation in the Dominican Republic?" I answered that I thought we had taken the necessary military precautions, and the next order of business was to find out what was going on.

Cablegrams that morning from Dearborn expressed some of the horror stories of assassination and retaliation which were reported going on behind the scenes at the Dominican capital.[6] I pointed out that while these stories were probably correct and everyone knew the vicious character of the young Trujillo who would take over the government, there was still a great deal which needed to be taken in.

For instance, there was no evidence whatsoever that any American had been harmed or threatened, or any evidence of aggressive acts against Haiti or any other country.

Bob Kennedy's response was vicious, unpleasant, and dogmatic. Dick Goodwin supported his position, although in somewhat more polite language. To my surprise, they were joined by Arthur Schlesinger, who was almost as outspoken as Bob Kennedy and Dick Goodwin, although in more pleasant terms.

Bob McNamara went along with their general view that our problem was not to prepare against an overt act by the Dominican Republic but rather to find an excuse for going into the country and upsetting it.

Walt Rostow spoke only once or twice and I did not get any clear impression of where he stood. I then called on McGhee, Ball, and Murrow to express their views, and each of them did in the most vigorous and outspoken manner.

---

[5] No record of this meeting was found.

[6] Telegram 1917, from Santo Domingo, June 1. (Department of State, Central Files, 739.00/6–161)

Ed Murrow said that the effect of any such act would be entirely catastrophic on world attitudes to the United States. McGhee gave a stiff statement on the importance of treaty rights, and George Ball said he could not believe people talking in these terms were really serious.

This strong counterattack, plus the fact that I had asked George McGhee to talk privately with Lyndon Johnson before the meeting resulted in Johnson taking a much more moderate view.

At that point Adlai Stevenson came in, listened a while to the somewhat subdued proposals of Kennedy, Goodwin, and Schlesinger, and expressed his own amazement that these proposals were being seriously talked about.

During the course of the meeting, Dean Rusk called me back and I brought him up to date and he seemed in general agreement, although, as usual, he did not say very much.

After a good deal of discussion I again stated that I was against our stimulating any appeal by a dissident group for support, which we were not prepared fully to give, and this was generally accepted, although with considerable snarling from the White House contingent.

At that point Wyn Coerr came up with a very imaginative suggestion which grew out of a statement which Bill Fulbright made to me before, i.e. to send in an OAS fact-finding team. A basis of action was developed out of the San Jose conference in September, 1960 which called for a fact finding group to visit the Dominican Republic if there was any basis for relaxing the sanctions which were imposed.

Although the situation did not seem to justify the relaxation of sanctions, it seemed the only way we could get an OAS team on the island. Steps were also taken to intensify the effort to find out what the full facts were, to exchange views with the British, Canadians, and others with ties in the Dominican Republic.

Since this was Friday and just before a summer weekend and with the likelihood that many members of Congress would be out of town, I decided to go to Capitol Hill to describe events as we knew them in the Dominican Republic and describe the action we had taken.

This meeting was held at 5:00 with Mike Mansfield, Hubert Humphrey, Bill Fulbright, Everett Dirkson, and other Congressional leaders. They all emphasized the need for working with OAS.

Late in the evening on Friday, strongly prodded from Dick Goodwin, Alexis Johnson, who I had set up to keep on top of the whole problem, called a meeting to determine if any further action was necessary. Although in my opinion this was a serious mistake, I believe Alexis was justified because of the pressure which the White House people brought on him. Although I did not attend the meeting, I telephoned two or three times during the evening to keep in touch.

The only new development was an appeal from General Estrella in response to our prodding (unauthorized), asking for American troops to assist the opposition troops but with no indication whatsoever of any strength or substance.

Early Saturday morning I had a telephone call from Ellis Briggs, who was assigned to go to Latin America with Adlai Stevenson, saying that Stevenson[7] was so alarmed about the meeting on Friday that he was about to call off the trip on the impression that we were about to go to war. I reassured Briggs that this was not the case and told him Adlai should go along with his plans.

At 10:00 Alexis Johnson told me Dick Goodwin was holding a background press conference on the viciousness of the regime. This, of course, would have eliminated the possibility of the OAS team going into the Dominican Republic to find out what the conditions are. It was too late to call off the backgrounder, but with a good deal of telephoning back and forth, I was able to modify the tone and to avoid any statements that the Dominican Republic might have considered provocative.

---

[7] Reference is to Stevenson's trip to Latin America June 4–22; see Document 14.

---

311.   Telegram From the Department of State to Secretary of State Rusk, at Paris

Washington, June 5, 1961, 6:29 a.m.

Tosec 39. Dearborn summoned by Balaguer noon June 4. ForMin Herrera Baez and Luis Mercado (Consul General in NY) present.

Balaguer denied existence violence and reign of terror in Dominican Republic. Action being taken only against those directly involved in assassination. Said Ramfis appointment made to unify armed forces and he had promised to support government, particularly in international matters.

Balaguer emphasized he was eminently anti-Communist and would fully support western democracies. Said GODR would respect all treaties and agreements. Firm intention to prepare for democratic elections May 1962 in which all groups guaranteed freedom.

Source: Department of State, Central Files, 739.00/6–561. Secret; Niact. Drafted by Stone, cleared by Braddock, and approved by Achilles. Also sent to Caracas, Bogota, CINC-LANT, CINCARIB, and the Commander of the Second Fleet for POLAD.

Dearborn thanked President and lauded objectives but observed adverse impression abroad caused by brutal SIM methods and belief people punished for guilt by association. Number Americans concerned about their safety. Balaguer replied Americans need have no concern if not directly implicated in assassination.

At that time ForMin left and Dearborn told President he would have do something drastic convince world GODR would not tolerate police state methods. Suggested he get rid of Abbes and Espaillat. [*less than 1 line of source text not declassified*] In reply further question Balaguer said he aimed create situation where those who opposed Trujillo could speak out freely within six months.

Dearborn assured Balaguer USG would consider promptly and favorably written request assist militarily seek out and repel Castro or Commie attack. Balaguer interjected question "attack from abroad"? Dearborn took this as veiled invitation for support against internal attacks and replied US prepared help militarily any time at his request if sectors Dominican military attempted to prevent progress toward democracy. Balaguer replied should assume Ramfis promise sincere until proved otherwise. Appeared grateful Dearborn statement.

Balaguer in reply question on relations with Bishops said he had offered resign rather than expel them as requested by armed forces.

[*1 paragraph (2 lines of source text) not declassified*]

Bowles

312. Memorandum From the President's Special Assistant (Goodwin) to the President's Special Assistant for National Security Affairs (Bundy)

Washington, June 8, 1961.

RE

June 7 meeting at the White House Mansion

Present at the meeting were: The President, Secretary Rusk, Secretary McNamara, Vice President Johnson, Attorney General Kennedy,

---

Source: Kennedy Library, National Security Files, Meetings and Memoranda Series, Meetings with the President. Secret.

Allen Dulles, General Lemnitzer, Admiral Burke, Alexis Johnson, Wyn Coerr, Henry Dearborn, Arthur Schlesinger, and Richard Goodwin.

1.   Dominican Republic.

Alexis Johnson gave a brief review of the current Dominican situation. He pointed out that the OAS inspection team had gone with the mandate to inspect and come back with a recommendation whether current sanctions against the Dominican Republic should be lifted, retained or strengthened.[1] He told of Dearborn's conversation with Balaguer (fully reported in cables). He pointed out that Bill Pawley had talked with Trujillo's daughter prior to her departure for the Dominican Republic and she had since communicated that Ramfis, et al., wanted to move toward a more moderate form of government.

Dean Rusk added that Porfirio Rubirosa had talked to Murphy and told him that Ramfis desired to stay on a little while and help move the country toward Democratic government; that he then intended to leave the country, having no great desire to live in the Dominican Republic. Ramfis is also reported to have suggested his willingness to grant an amnesty to current political prisoners.

Dearborn, reinforced by a few others, said that these promises, e.g., free elections, amnesties, even the firing of Abbes, were the same moves that Trujillo had always made without any intended impact on the structure of his regime.

The President asked what our immediate goals in the Dominican Republic were.

Alexis Johnson replied that we would like an immediate move toward dissolution of the secret police—the principal instrument of coercion.

In response to another Presidential question Dearborn indicated that he felt it would be possible to have a Democratic regime in the Dominican Republic without a communist takeover—that pro-Democratic, pro-United States forces were present and could run a government. He told of Radio Caribe—run by Ramfis, Abbes et al.—which has taken a strong anti-United States and a moderate pro-Soviet line over the past several months. This instrument had been one of the most dangerous in promoting a pro-communist viewpoint on the island.

Bob Kennedy expressed the view that we should give the current regime a chance to do what they promised to do; that it was worth our while to wait out the situation.

---

[1] Ambassador Gerald Drew, Inspector General of the State Department, represented the United States on the OAS inspection team that toured the Dominican Republic June 7–14.

It was pointed out that anything we did should be in concert with Venezuela, that we would do ourselves great harm if we appeared to be making a deal with Ramfis without consultation and concurrence by our Caribbean Allies, and perhaps by the OAS itself.

The President said that we wanted a Democratic regime in the Dominican Republic; failing that we would prefer a friendly dictatorship, and the last thing we wanted was a Castro type regime.

Dearborn said that our goal over six months should be a situation in which Democratic pro-United States forces were not afraid to organize a party, speak in public places, etc.

Decisions: It was decided (a) that all our contacts would be informal ones through Murphy and Alexis Johnson should remain in contact with Murphy; (b) that we would have no contacts through Pawley—that if he carried out his plans to go to the Dominican Republic we would be glad to hear his reports but he was in no way to involve State, CIA, the White House, etc., i.e. not to indicate that we approved what he said or authorized his visit. Secretary Rusk was detailed to communicate this to Pawley; (c) our military forces would remain in their current state of readiness for a few days at least—no decision was made as to when they should lift the current alert status; (d) we would re-examine the situation in a week or two and see where we are.

---

313.   Memorandum of Conversation

Washington, July 10, 1961.

PARTICIPANTS
    President John F. Kennedy
    Mr. Robert F. Woodward

President Kennedy said that he would like to have Mr. Hill[1] come up from Ciudad Trujillo so that the President can have a thorough conversation with him and become well acquainted with him. The President is particularly interested in having Mr. Hill's personal appraisal of the kind of people who are in the various opposition groups.

Source: Department of State, Central Files, 739.00/7–1061. Confidential. Drafted by Woodward. No mention of this meeting was made in the President's Appointment Book.
    [1] John Calvin Hill replaced Dearborn as U.S. Consul General in Ciudad Trujillo.

The President said that any day would be all right with him and that arrangements can be made for the specific appointment through Mr. O'Donnell, the appointments secretary, but it was clear that the President would like to see Mr. Hill at the end of this week or the beginning of next. Naturally, it would be risky for Mr. Hill to count on seeing the President either on Saturday or Sunday.

President Kennedy said that he would like to have a personal conversation with the officer that we are trying to find who could establish a close liaison with student groups; I had explained to the President that we were endeavoring to find an officer who had highly proved his ability in this respect. The President would also like to see the officer that I told him we were trying to find with similar qualifications for establishing relationships with labor groups.

President Kennedy said that he thought we should be in a position to suggest to President Balaguer a specific program of action for bringing about the democratization of the country. What the President has specifically in mind is the possibility that it would be useful for the Dominican Government to take steps to call a constitutional convention if an examination of the constitution indicates that its present form does not allow for the conduct of political campaigns by political parties. He mentioned the possibility that the country might, for example, need a new constitution, and he suggested that we find out what the Pakistani Government is doing in its efforts to work out its transition from a military government to a more democratic form of government. He mentioned that the Legal Adviser should be able to give some legal advice along this line. He said "He's from Harvard and a smart guy."

[Here follows discussion of preparations for the Punta del Este Meeting of the IA–ECOSOC.]

314.   Memorandum From President Kennedy to the Assistant Secretary of State for Inter-American Affairs (Woodward)

Washington, July 10, 1961.

Do we have any evidence of Communist activity or Castro activities in the Dominican Republic today? Have they infiltrated the "popular Dominican movement"? Which refugees have come back and what are their political history? I want to make sure that our people there are the best people we can get, that their judgment is good and that they are not emotionally committed to one group or another and not carrying out a crusade for anything but the United States. Would you check and give me your assurances that those are the kind of people we have because a great deal will depend on their judgment. We don't want to have another Cuba to come out of the Dominican Republic.

Previous to your return I stated that our objective was (1) have a democracy (2) to continue the present situation. I also said that if we could not have a democracy with some hope of survival I would rather continue the present situation than to have a Castro dictatorship. That is our policy and we want to make sure that in attempting to secure democracy we don't end up with a Castro-Communist island.

We should indicate that we are opposed to permitting refugees to come back from Cuba or any Communist-controlled country. I note this is what Balaguer said, but we should indicate our approval. I want to watch this situation carefully and get a copy of all important reports coming in.

Source: Department of State, Central Files, 737.00/7–1161. No classification marking. A covering memorandum from Goodwin to Woodward, July 11, reads: "The President dictated this before his meeting with you. I thought it might be useful as a reminder of your conversation."

315. Paper Prepared in the Department of State

Washington, July 17, 1961.

COURSES OF ACTION IN THE DOMINICAN REPUBLIC

Objective:

To prevent Castro/Communism from developing or taking control of the Dominican Republic and to promote the establishment there of a friendly government as democratic as possible.

Situation:

1. After the assassination of Generalissimo Trujillo, his son Ramfis moved swiftly and effectively to establish control over the armed forces and to pledge his backing of President Balaguer in the latter's program for gradual reform and liberalization of the Trujillo system. Law and order have been maintained in the country. Ramfis' control of the military has thus far gone unchallenged, although it cannot be taken for granted that this will be the case over a protracted period. Likewise Ramfis has emerged as the dominant figure over the Trujillo family and over the Trujillo economic interests which encompass an estimated two-thirds of the nation's productive economic activity.

2. President Balaguer, within the scope allowed him by Trujillo and the military, has undertaken a series of reforms, the principal of which are:

(a) The secret police SIM has been renamed and drawn into the background. Tortures have apparently stopped. The notorious Abbes, who directed SIM activities, has been sent abroad but little progress has yet been made in purging subordinate secret police personnel.

(b) Legitimate political activities, including opposition activities, have been guaranteed. Public meetings have been held, a few self-proclaimed anti-Castro exile leaders have returned, and a Constitutional opposition is forming.

(c) The President, and presumably Ramfis, are aware of the Castro danger. An anti-Communist law has been sent to the Congress, the entry of exiles from Cuba and other Communist countries barred, and steps initiated to disband the Castro-line party which was set up by the late Generalissimo. The Government has announced a pro-Western policy and anti-American material has virtually vanished from press and radio.

Source: Kennedy Library, National Security Files, Countries Series, Dominican Republic, July–August 1961. Secret.

(d) A new Cabinet, better than the old, has been appointed.

(e) Measures have been taken to liberalize the economy. Businessmen have been taken into economic policy-making positions. Export controls, administered through Trujillo-controlled monopolies, have been relaxed and some of the monopolies broken up. Some prices, particularly of consumer items used by the lower classes, have been lowered by decree. The Trujillo family has given away, as a token, its holdings in two enterprises.

3. These reforms have not yet affected the core of the Trujillo family's power. Ramfis is still in control of the armed forces and the family remains in a dominant economic position. The Government Party, Partido Dominicano, supports the Trujillos and their circle rather than Balaguer: it operates a large portion of the government's social welfare program and its membership includes virtually every adult Dominican, since government jobs and services could only be obtained by exhibition of a party card.

4. Opposition to the Trujillos—which is extensive in the upper and middle classes—remains deeply skeptical that human rights can be assured and fair elections held as long as the family retains this core of military, economic and political power. For the moment, however, they have decided to try to oust the Trujillo family by political means in an orderly manner, and anticipate the support of the United States in this enterprise. Most, but not all, middle and upper class opposition elements are aware that revolutionary and subversive activity at this time could bring disorder and other openings for a Castroist take-over. However, to the extent that efforts to effect a withdrawal of the Trujillos before the May 1962 elections by political means fails to achieve results, the temptation to resume revolutionary and subversive activities will grow.

5. There is emerging a weak, poorly organized, somewhat divided, but widespread movement in opposition to either the restoration of a full-fledged Trujillo dictatorship or a Castro-Communist take-over. The spectrum of this movement includes:

(a) President Balaguer and the more moderate elements he has brought into the government. The President and these elements, however, do not yet have the full confidence of the opposition.

(b) The Union Civica Nacional (UCN), an opposition political movement (not party) whose formation was made public on July 16. Comprised initially of several hundred of the outstanding Dominican business and professional leaders, it has pledged itself to peaceful action and taken an anti-Communist position. However, hidden within it, are apparently elements who were the intellectual authors of the Trujillo assassination, and its present determination not to participate in the elections and resume revolutionary activities unless the Trujillos are out should not be taken lightly.

(c) The "14 of June" Movement, a younger somewhat more radical group composed of persons who participated in or morally supported an abortive plot in 1959/60 to overthrow Trujillo. Although it has agreed with the UCN (some members belong to both organizations) not to make common cause with the Castro-lining MPD, it appears somewhat more fuzzy on the Castro danger.

(d) The Partido Revolucionario Dominicano (PRD), which is being established in the Dominican Republic by three returned exile leaders. Its public position is one of peaceful rather than revolutionary action and it has taken an open stand against Communism and Castroism and in favor of change on the pattern advocated by Betancourt and Figueres. As the first new opposition party to come into the open, it has created a good deal of excitement in the Dominican Republic but does not as yet have strong or organized support. Its leader, Juan Bosch, who remains outside the Dominican Republic is a close friend of Betancourt and Figueres who support him. (However, an FBI report has cited him as a Communist and the Department is urgently attempting to secure an evaluation from the intelligence community to clarify this point.)

The above, broadly speaking, comprise the middle-of-the-road, pro-American political forces in the Dominican Republic. The twenty-odd Dominican movements still abroad have little following and many of them are infiltrated by pro-Communist and pro-Castro elements.

6. Within the Dominican Republic, pro-Castro sentiment is centered in the Movimiento Popular Dominicano (MPD). Until recently the MPD had no real significance or organization; it was established by Trujillo when he was piqued by the OAS sanctions against him and sought to prove to Dominican and world opinion that opposition to him was Communist. Although its leadership was authentically Castroist imported from Cuba, its membership was heavily infiltrated by secret police agents and the secret police earlier this year suppressed it altogether for some months. However, the Castro-line MPD leaders were quick to use the liberties granted by Balaguer to agitate and to incite to mob action with considerable success. The President has indicated his intention to shut the MPD down but this has not yet been done.

7. The situation in the Dominican Republic is, then, precarious. From the U.S. point of view, it would be desirable to strengthen President Balaguer and moderates within the government and to encourage and support an anti-Castro, middle-of-the-road opposition. These elements are weak and untested. They are faced by unreconstructed Trujillista elements (probably not including Ramfis himself) who want to continue the Trujillo era with as few changes as possible. However, since Ramfis himself is not even attempting to play his father's role and since opposition to the Trujillos is widespread, it is doubtful that an attempt to maintain the status quo could long be successful and the chances are high that if

the Trujillos try to hang on, a revolutionary movement will develop. On the other hand, pro-Castro elements are ready to move into the vacuum created by any abrupt relinquishment of power by the Trujillos and will do so unless non-Communist civilian and military elements are prepared to step in.

Problems:

1. The basic political problem facing the U.S. is how to encourage and foster a stable government, resistant to Castroism, constructed from Balaguer's moderate wing of the existing government, the middle-of-the-road opposition elements and the armed forces. An effort to prolong the control of unreconstructed Trujillista elements beyond an adequate transition period would be to invite revolution and disorder at a time when there is no one to exercise the controlling role formerly played by the Generalissimo. To act precipitately to remove the Trujillos before firm foundations are established for a more representative government would be to invite a collapse of authority if not civil war. On the other hand, U.S. identification with the Balaguer Government while the Trujillos retain essential control could have the disadvantages of (a) giving other countries the impression that we are condoning dictatorships which they consider too slow, (b) reassuring the Balaguer Government so it might move *more* slowly, and (c) leading the embryonic middle of the road oppositionists to believe that the U.S. has accepted continued Trujillo dominance and thus encouraging the more active among the opposition to turn to revolution and assassination.

2. Thus the immediate problems in the Dominican Republic are:

(a) How to encourage the Balaguer Government, with Ramfis' support, to make further modifications without excessively identifying the U.S. with it.

(b) How to increase the strength and cohesiveness of the middle-of-the-road elements and to prevent the opposition moving towards Castroism and

(c) Whether arrangements can be made for the orderly step-by-step withdrawal of the Trujillos at a stage not so early as to create a collapse and not so late that the opposition—in despair—turns to revolutionary activities.

3. On the economic front, discontent is likely to rise in the next few months and find political expression, since it is improbable that the current depression will not end until confidence is restored and the economic system is made more rational.

4. A problem also arises in the OAS, where 14 votes are required to restore diplomatic relations with the Dominican Republic and lift other sanctions. It is unlikely that such action will be forthcoming soon. The OAS Subcommittee that visited the Dominican Republic to determine

whether the government there still constitutes a "threat to the peace and security of the Hemisphere" returned to Washington and has now issued a report[1] which notes certain constructive moves but concludes that it is too early to determine the extent of change and that observation by the OAS should continue. While the presence of the Subcommittee might inspire somewhat more rapid evolution toward democracy, the Subcommittee would be confronted with the serious problem of either awaiting some significant *new* development, which might require a long stay, or returning and issuing another inconclusive report which could be harmful to the Balaguer Government. Therefore, if OAS technical advisors are requested, and an OAS "presence" can thus be assured, it would be wisest to await a significant new development that might warrant a more favorable conclusion by the Subcommittee before encouraging its return to the Dominican Republic.

5. A problem also arises in determining how far the U.S. is willing to intervene to prevent a Castro take-over. President Balaguer has been assured of U.S. military action if there should be a Castro invasion *from abroad*. But the precarious situation contains potentialities of a take-over *from within*; for example, through the assassination or sudden flight of Ramfis coupled with a breakdown of law and order. Should such a situation arise, our representatives will have to know immediately how far the U.S. would be willing to commit itself to Balaguer and other anti-Castro elements and what the U.S. position with respect to the Trujillos would be in such an event.

Actions Already Taken:

1. We have assigned as Consul General a very experienced officer who did superb work in Guatemala during the fall of Arbenz and who has been Latin American Bureau liaison with CIA for several years during which time he worked on the Dominican problem.

2. Measures to prevent a Castroist take-over:

(a) We have assured President Balaguer privately that we would upon request give prompt military support within Dominican jurisdiction if there should be a Castroist invasion from abroad.

(b) We mobilized a considerable military force immediately after the assassination of the Generalissimo and still retain forces nearby.

(c) We have firmly encouraged President Balaguer to adopt an anti-Communist law, to ban the entry of exiles from Cuba and Communist countries, and encouraged his proposal to shut down the MPD.

(d) We have consistently advised opposition elements against Castroism and encourage them to take anti-Communist positions.

---

[1] OAS doc. OEA/Ser.G./CE/RC.VI–10.

3.   Measures to reform and humanize the Trujillo system.

(a) We have assured Balaguer privately and publicly that his reforms have our support.

(b) We have specifically urged him to clean up the security police, to make electoral reforms, and to allow legitimate, non-Communist opposition groups to operate openly and within the Constitution.

(c) We have urged Balaguer and the Partido Dominicano's new leader to stress the future and gradually reduce the divisive emphasis on the late Generalissimo.

(d) We were instrumental in persuading the OAS to send a Subcommittee to the Dominican Republic and in keeping a corps of U.S. newsmen there to exercise a moderating influence immediately following the assassination.

(e) We have encouraged Balaguer to ask for OAS technical advisors for the elections.

4.   Measures to bring forth an anti-Castro political force.

(a) We took a key role in encouraging the business and professional leaders to establish the UCN.

(b) We urged the Betancourt-oriented PRD to take a moderate position and to come forth openly with their anti-Castro and anti-Communist position.

(c) We have urged all non-Communist opposition groups to work in harmony, to avoid efforts of the Castroists to form a "united front" opposition, and to give President Balaguer's reforms a chance however much they distrust them.

Proposed Future Actions:

1.   To continue to press on all of the above points wherever progress lags and whenever we think action is likely to be productive.

2.   To continue to encourage the sending of an OAS technical advisory group to assist the government in preparing for elections. Action by the OAS special committee should await significant new developments before again sending the present or "new subcommittee to the Dominican Republic even though the Dominican Government has sent the Subcommittee an invitation to return. In these and other ways, continue to give emphasis to the OAS role in the Dominican Republic.

3.   To give encouragement and assistance to acceptable opposition movements on the condition that they make every effort to act in concert with other acceptable groups.

4.   To exert special efforts by discreet means to become acquainted with and influence student and labor groups. The visa officer in our Consulate in Ciudad Trujillo has special aptitude for relations with students and we are assigning him to this work, sending in another visa officer. We are seeking an outstanding labor officer.

5. To identify lines of authority and influence in the Armed Forces in order to be able to understand and influence individual leaders, and to gain intelligence on the intentions of individuals and factions within the military.

6. To explore the possibilities of inducing Ramfis and the Trujillo family to effect a step-by-step, orderly transfer of their control of military and economic power at a stage not so early as to run a high risk of collapse and not so late as to encourage the opposition to abandon Constitutional activities in favor of renewed subversive and revolutionary actions.

7. To refine contingency planning in order to be prepared to act promptly and appropriately in any sudden adverse change in the situation.

8. To develop contingency plans to take promptly effective economic and political action to stabilize and strengthen an anti-Castro Government when and if the Trujillos withdraw.

9. We have examined the political experience of some countries, who are in a transitional stage following dictatorships, but have not found any aspects of their experience which would be applicable to the Dominican situation. We will continue this examination.

316. Memorandum From Secretary of State Rusk to President Kennedy

Washington, July 19, 1961.

SUBJECT

Dominican Republic

There is enclosed for your review and approval a suggested telegram confirming the oral instructions which you gave on July 18[1] to John Hill, our Consul in the Dominican Republic.

Dean Rusk[2]

Attachment

SUGGESTED MESSAGE

For Hill

Confirming President's oral instructions to you July 18, you should convey following President Balaguer upon your return:

During consultation Washington, you were asked to meeting with President attended by Assistant Secretary Woodward, Robert Murphy and others having interest in or responsibility for relations with DR.

President expressed himself as encouraged by measures President Balaguer had taken towards establishment representative democracy DR and orderly exercise political rights by all non-Communist elements. He asked you convey this President Balaguer.

Source: Department of State, Central Files, 611.39/7–1961. Secret. Drafted by Vallon. A marginal notation indicates that Goodwin approved the telegram's content and that it was sent on July 21 as telegram 94. (Ibid., 611.39/7–2161)

[1] Consul General Hill met with President Kennedy on July 18 from 6 to 6:30 p.m. according to the President's Appointment Book. (Kennedy Library) Also in attendance were Assistant Secretary of State Woodward, Deputy Assistant Secretary Arturo Morales-Carrion, Robert Murphy, Richard Goodwin, and Edward Jamison. No record of the meeting was kept. Hill conveyed the President's message to Balaguer in a meeting on July 23. (Telegram 159 from Ciudad Trujillo, July 22; Department of State, Central Files, 611.39/7–2261)

[2] Printed from a copy that indicates Rusk signed the original.

President also directed Department issue appropriate statement reflecting USG encouragement at steps thus far taken in hopes this would be useful President Balaguer (FYI. This to be used on confirmation statement issued. End FYI.)

President thought it of utmost importance transition towards exercise democratic rights continue and orderly democratic life be established for all who willing act within responsibilities Constitutional democracy.

President questioned you closely about progress anti-Communist law in Dominican Congress, measures taken exclude return Communism and Castroist exiles, and other actions taken prevent infiltration and agitation by Communist/Castroist elements. He noted with particular satisfaction President Balaguer's stated determination prevent pro-Communist and pro-Castro activities, pointing out danger DR, US and Hemisphere if Castroists should establish themselves in DR.

President emphasized that development of solidly based representative democracy provides only alternative to either repression, which would eventually bring on revolt, or uncontrollable disorder and violence which would open way for exploitation by Castro/Communist elements. President wished President Balaguer well in this enterprise and is personally following situation closely.

FYI. You are also reminded that the President instructed you to inform democratic opposition of substance your conversation with President Balaguer explaining this move intended further to encourage President Balaguer on road to representative democracy and increase guarantees for democratic political groups. End FYI.

317.   Special National Intelligence Estimate

SNIE 86.2–61   Washington, July 25, 1961.

THE DOMINICAN SITUATION

The Problem

To examine the political situation in the Dominican Republic and to estimate the prospects for an orderly transition to a more representative political system.

The Estimate

1.   The heirs of Trujillo are seeking to regain international acceptance by relaxing the late dictator's stringent political controls and permitting the development of democratic political activity. With the return of several opposition leaders from exile—with government guarantees for their safety—opposition forces within the country have surfaced and begun to crystallize. The violence incited by pro-Castro elements in early July has demonstrated that the liberalization of political controls involves some risk for the security of the regime.

2.   The real power in the Dominican Republic is still held by the Trujillo family through Ramfis' control of the armed forces and the police. The family also continues to dominate the economic life of the country. Ramfis is resolved to preserve what he can of his family's economic interests, but has apparently concluded that some political relaxation is necessary for this purpose. Contrary to expectations, he has permitted the titular president, Balaguer, to encourage the open development of political opposition groups. He has also permitted Balaguer to institute important reforms in the economic field, including the dissolution of the Trujillo family monopoly in coffee and cocoa exports and a reduction in utility rates and the prices of certain foodstuffs. Balaguer has also appointed a reputable cabinet, indicated his willingness to consider the return of the OAS investigating subcommittee, and declared that he was prepared to have OAS representatives observe the national elections scheduled for May 1962. Both men probably estimate that the well-established machinery of the government-controlled Partido Dominicano will suffice to sweep the election, even if OAS observers are in attendance. Publicly organized opposition so far consists of four groups: the Dominican Revolutionary Party (PRD), the Dominican Popular Movement (MPD), the National Civic Union (UCN), and the 14th of June Movement.

Source: Central Intelligence Agency Files, Job 79–R01012A, ODDI Registry. Secret.

3.   The PRD is a long-established organization of Dominican exiles led by Juan Bosch,[1] with branches in New York, San Juan, and Caracas. Its leaders have associations with ex-President Figueres of Costa Rica and President Betancourt of Venezuela. At recent rallies the party has demonstrated some drawing power among city workers, other elements of the lower class, and poorer segments of the middle class. However, the majority of the middle class, which suffered most under the tyranny, is critical of PRD leaders as men who have remained out of the country for decades and escaped hardship and abuse. Many in the middle class do not trust the PRD, some believing that it has sold out to the Balaguer government and others suspecting it of extreme leftist or Communist tendencies. At the same time PRD leaders are being denounced by the Cuban radio as agents of the US.

4.   The MPD was originally organized in Cuba by Maximo Lopez Molina, a pro-Communist Dominican exile. At the time of the San Jose Conference, in 1960, Trujillo permitted Lopez to return to the Dominican Republic and establish the MPD there. He probably did this in order to demonstrate both tolerance of political opposition and a Castroist threat. Within a short time the party was suppressed, but it has recently been reactivated. It is aggressive and Castro/Communist in character, though probably still small in size. Following the early July disturbances the government threatened to suppress the MPD and took occasion to have the legislature enact an anti-Communist law.

5.   The upper and middle classes were the principal victims of the Trujillo dictatorship and have a corresponding interest in the establishment of civil liberties and representative government. Until recently, however, opposition elements from these classes have remained underground because of the brutal repression which members of their group suffered at the hands of the late dictator. With the continuation in power of the Trujillos, and lacking US or OAS guarantees of their safety, they hesitated to surface until the return of the PRD leaders and the activities of the MPD showed that some political agitation could be conducted openly and convinced them that, if they did not move, political leadership would pass to extremists by default. They have established the UCN, an organization composed largely of respectable business and professional men headed by long-time Trujillo oppositionist Viriato Fiallo. They still defensively deny that the UCN is a political party, but nevertheless it does provide a rallying point for moderate elements anti-

---

[1] Juan Bosch was at one time a member of the Caribbean Legion, a motley assortment of professional revolutionaries and idealists devoted to the overthrow of dictatorship. He is presently in San Jose, Costa Rica, although he makes his headquarters in Caracas. The principal PRD leaders now in the Dominican Republic are Angel Miolan and Ramon Castillo. The latter and another PRD leader, Nicolas Silfa, are naturalized US citizens. [Footnote in the source text.]

pathetic to the Trujillo regime, on the one hand, and to the leftist PRD and pro-Communist MPD on the other. We believe that the UCN is predominantly pro-US, despite a public statement opposing foreign, particularly US, intervention. This statement was probably designed for internal political effect.

6. There is also the 14th of June Movement,[2] originally a clandestine middle class organization composed largely of younger persons. It was smashed by the late dictator in early 1960, but the remnants have recently emerged as an open political movement and have attracted support from the burgeoning student movement. The membership is divided between those who would go along with pro-Castro activists and those who favor moderation. In these circumstances some of the adherents of the 14th of June Movement may eventually merge with other opposition groups.

7. In the political vacuum created by the 30-year dictatorship, the PRD, MPD, UCN, and the 14th of June Movement are competing for leadership of the dissatisfied elements of the population. None of them has been in the open long enough to have developed an extensive political organization for electoral purposes. An evident danger is that, unless the anti-Communist opposition bestirs itself, the more aggressive MPD may capture the leadership of popular dissidence.

8. So far, political ferment is confined largely to the capital city and the larger towns. The mass of the peasants remains unaffected; the government-controlled Dominican Party is still the only political organization in effective contact with them.

9. The rapid development of open political opposition, and the potential for violence demonstrated on 7 July, put in question the feasibility of President Balaguer's apparent plan to conduct a controlled transition to a more representative political system. The opposition parties almost certainly realize that, even with the degree of political freedom now permitted, they have little or no chance of prevailing in an election to be held only nine months from now. To gain more time for organization and campaigning, they are likely to demand postponement of the election, and might refuse to participate if it is held on schedule. Moreover, instead of relying upon the election as the means of replacing the present regime, each opposition group is probably seeking to subvert a sufficient segment of the armed forces to be able to seize power by a coup. To this end, the more moderate oppositionists would urge that the elimination of the Trujillos was necessary in order to establish a stable

---

[2] The movement draws its name from the date in 1959 on which a Castro-supported invasion group made an abortive attempt to initiate revolution against Generalissimo Trujillo. However, a member of the movement has said that its name is intended to exploit the event, not to emulate Castro's 26th of July Movement. [Footnote in the source text.]

democratic political system and to head off the Castro/Communist threat represented by the MPD.

10. The more moderate opposition groups are not likely to seek to incite popular violence against the regime, for fear that this would work to the immediate advantage of the MPD and would provoke the eventual suppression of all political activity. In the tense circumstances, however, spontaneous disorder is a constant possibility.

11. The mechanism of the police state remains intact and, if put to use, is probably still capable of suppressing all opposition. To do this, however, would destroy the impression which both Balaguer and Ramfis have been at pains to create, of an evolution toward a more democratic system. We therefore believe that while Ramfis will act forcefully to prevent or suppress violence and disorder, he will be disinclined to suppress moderate political opposition.

12. As the political situation develops, much will depend on reactions within the Trujillo family and within the armed forces. Some members of the family are determined to defend their property and position and would resist any further political or economic concessions on the part of Ramfis which they thought would seriously jeopardize their interests. In such circumstances, they could probably count on the support of elements in the armed forces, particularly among senior officers, who see peril for themselves in any change in the political system. On the other hand, there are some junior officers who desire reform, or who are interested in the promotions which they could expect from an overturn of the system, and might therefore be open to subversion by one or another of the opposition groups. Thus Ramfis could lose control of the situation through a move from within the Trujillo family to displace him and restore the status quo ante, or through a move from within the armed forces, in conspiracy with one of the political opposition groups, to expel all the Trujillos. In either case, Balaguer's attempt at a political finesse would have failed and a sanguinary struggle for power among many diverse elements would probably ensue.

13. In view of the flexibility and skill which Balaguer and Ramfis Trujillo have shown, the power at their disposal, and the rudimentary character of the political opposition, we believe it likely that the present Dominican Government will be able to retain control of the situation, at least until the May 1962 election. However, on the separate issue of an orderly transition to a more representative political system, we believe that there is no more than an even chance of a moderate program being carried out in view of the possibilities of a return to more forceful repression as opposition activity increases or of a power struggle among present leaders. In any case the scale and nature of US support is likely to have an important effect upon the success of the Balaguer program.

318.   Telegram From the Department of State to the Consulate General in the Dominican Republic

Washington, August 3, 1961, 12:18 a.m.

137. Congentel 213.[1] Following courses of action decided upon at meeting called by President at White House today to discuss Dominican problem:

(1) You should continue to urge that Communists and pro-Castro elements be deported.

(2) Department will explore technical and political problems involved in partial lifting of OAS economic sanctions other than those affecting sugar and arms.

(3) Department will (a) explore whether Dominican people suffering any food shortage, (b) what private agencies available for distributing food in Dominican Republic, (c) feasibility and desirability undertaking PL–480 food distribution program through private agencies.

(4) Department will study desirability consult Venezuelan Government regarding desirability above lines of action as acceptable firm evidence U.S. support for Balaguer and U.S. concern for Dominican people.

Rusk

Source: Department of State, Central Files, 739.00/8–161. Secret; Priority; Limit Distribution. Drafted by Coerr, cleared by Vallon and S/S, and approved by Woodward. At 6:15 p.m., the President met with Woodward, Goodwin, Coerr, and Robert T. Morrison of the State Department Bureau of Intelligence and Research according to the President's Appointment Book. (Kennedy Library) The meeting ended at approximately 8 p.m. No record of the meeting has been found

[1] Not printed. (Department of State, Central Files, 739.00/8–161)

319. Draft Memorandum From Secretary of State Rusk to President Kennedy

Washington, August 24, 1961.

In preparation for your meeting on August 25[1] on the Dominican Republic, I enclose a memorandum assessing our problem there and recommending courses of action. These courses are designed to strengthen President Balaguer in his program of democratization, induce the moderate opposition, Ramfis Trujillo and the military establishment, to support Balaguer's program and avoid violence, and assist in resolving the question of the departure of the Trujillo family and the disposition of their properties, particularly their large sugar holdings. I also enclose a memorandum summarizing action already taken or under way toward these objectives.[2]

Dean Rusk

Attachment

THE DOMINICAN SITUATION

I. Problem

To take action which will relieve the present tension in the Dominican Republic and will at the same time promote the basic United States objectives of (a) preventing Castro-Communism from developing or taking control, and (b) establishing a friendly and stable government as democratic as possible.

II. Discussion

Tension in the Dominican Republic is increasing. Elements of the military fear for their future and are reacting with violence to political activities, some of them provocative, by the newly emerging political

---

Source: Department of State, Central Files, 739.00/8–2461. Secret. Drafted by Coerr and Crimmins. Marginal notations indicate that this document was to be revised; however no later version was found.

[1] The meeting, in fact, took place August 28; see Document 320.

[2] Not found.

opposition. Some of the military elements have also threatened to "turn to the left" and are reportedly favoring Castro-Communists. Ramfis appears to be weakening in his initial declared intention to control the armed forces and give Balaguer effective support. Military elements may overthrow Balaguer at any time.

If the Trujillo and military elements achieve or continue seriously to threaten a coup, the currently non-Communist opposition can be expected to reject moderate leaders and tactics, undertake widespread strikes and covert revolutionary activities, and seek alliance with Castro-Communists. They may also gain support from some of the military.

Should such a coup occur, the new regime could probably impose temporary order but would almost certainly lead to an explosion that would give the Castro-Communists ideal conditions for gaining strength and assuming power. Such a regime also could expect intense Venezuelan hostility and OAS disapproval and would be most difficult for the United States to support.

To reduce this threat, we must seek means of easing the transition for the military and other Trujillo-associated elements from the Trujillo system to a freer society. These means must be compatible, however, with our support of the Balaguer program and the moderate opposition, which represents our best hope for reaching our objectives.

These means must take into account the economic power of the Trujillos, which is a critical aspect of the problem. For example, under existing United States legislation, the Trujillos would stand to gain $28 million from the sale to the United States of their sugar under a windfall quota, which would automatically be assigned to the Dominican Republic upon resumption of diplomatic relations.

III. Recommended Courses of Action

A. Immediate

We should:

1. Publicly and privately make clear that we support President Balaguer and his program of democratization, and where possible identify our programs as expressions of that support and of our interest in the Dominican people.

2. Inform Ramfis Trujillo at the earliest opportunity that we (a) would view with serious concern the overthrow of Balaguer by force or intimidation; (b) urge that security and military forces seek common cause with the moderate opposition and avoid abuses against it; and (c) recommend that the military and security forces recognize that they would be certain victims of a Castro-Communist take-over and that they avoid supporting Castro-Communist elements.

3. Take steps toward establishing a small United States military mission at field-grade level, commencing with the assignment of military liaison officers to the Consulate.

4. Inform the moderate opposition that we (a) consider it a key factor in the future of the Dominican Republic; (b) urge it to pursue its objectives peacefully and seek a constructive relationship with the military; and (c) urge it to exclude rigorously and oppose Castro-Communists.

5. Informally assist the Balaguer Government in contracting for, or through the OAS, a police mission to improve the attitudes and methods (especially in intelligence techniques and crowd control) of the security forces.

6. Once President Balaguer has made a request, urge and assist voluntary relief agencies to make the necessary survey leading to a PL 480 food distribution program for needy Dominicans.

7. Move in the OAS to remove sanctions on petroleum, trucks, and spare parts.

8. In order to induce the Trujillos to relinquish power and, in some cases, leave the country in a constructive manner, with their self-respect and some small part of their holdings within the Dominican Republic, obtain their consent in principle to the establishment of a foundation which would take over the bulk of their holdings (including all sugar properties) within the Dominican Republic and administer them for the benefit of the Dominican people. Once consent is obtained, have a qualified U.S. lawyer and an economist work out the details.

9. Persuade Balaguer to agree to a statement, and Ramfis to support it, (a) expressing the intention to continue the democratization program; (b) offering the moderate opposition representation in the government; (c) eliminating the PD assessment on salaries; and (d) announcing the Trujillos' agreement to a foundation.

10. Seek Venezuelan support for or acquiescence in our plans, emphasizing the divestment of the Trujillos of their properties.

B. Subsequent

Following on the above actions, we should:

11. Move for the return of the OAS Sub-Committee to receive the declaration outlined in paragraph 9.

12. Move in the COAS for the rescission of Resolution 1 of the VI MFM, i.e., for the restoration of diplomatic relations.

320. Editorial Note

According to his Appointment Book, President Kennedy met on August 28, 1961, from 5 to 6:15 p.m. with Assistant Secretary of State for Inter-American Affairs Woodward, Deputy Assistant Secretary Coerr, Office of Caribbean and Mexican Affairs officers Edwin Vallon, John Crimmins, and Charles Torrey, Director of the Office of Inter-American Regional Political Affairs Edward Jamison, Ambassador Robert Murphy, Barnes [text not declassified] of the CIA, and Presidential Special Assistants Stephen Smith, Goodwin, and Schlesinger about the Dominican situation. (Kennedy Library) No memorandum of the conversation was found.

A State Department memorandum of a conversation among Under Secretary Ball, Woodward, Crimmins, and Jamison, dated August 29, details actions to be taken as a result of the meeting. (Department of State, Central Files, 739.00/8–2961)

U.S. Ambassador to the Organization of American States DeLesseps Morrison was to condemn the repressive incidents that had marred the Balaguer government's democratization program. Consul General Hill would make clear U.S. support for this program and inform Ramfis Trujillo that the United States would view with serious concern an overthrow of the Balaguer government. Additionally, a field-level U.S. military mission was to be established in the Dominican Republic, and Deputy Assistant Secretary of State Arturo Morales-Carrion was to be dispatched with Ambassador Murphy "to explain our plans and gain consent to them from the various elements."

321. Memorandum From the Director of the Bureau of Intelligence and Research (Hilsman) to Acting Secretary of State Bowles

Washington, September 20, 1961.

SUBJECT

Assessment of Dominican Situation

Let me call your attention to T–588 of September 17 (received yesterday),[1] from Ciudad Trujillo, a marked copy of which is attached. I feel that the analysis contained in this three-part message, especially regarding the effects of continued US support for the present Dominican government, confirms a viewpoint which INR has held since the Trujillo assassination but which has not, until now, received widespread appreciation.

Paragraphs 4–10 of the subject telegram are especially pertinent. In essence, the Consul General emphasizes that the present Dominican government is transitory, that the demand for the Trujillos to leave "has become an obsession," and that longer term US interests dictate that a friendly, anti-Castro, anti-Communist government succeed the present one. The attainment of the latter objective hinges upon the state of US relations with the opposition which are deteriorating because of the latter's belief that the US is, in effect, supporting the present government. With growing dissatisfaction in the Dominican Republic over OAS and US policy, Castro-minded influence in the opposition is increasing.

Our analysts in INR strongly agree with this analysis. *We believe that the US, by unintentionally identifying itself with an unpopular cause through its "transition" policy, is seriously jeopardizing its long-term interests in the Dominican Republic.* A continuation of present trends will increase the likelihood that a successor to the Balaguer government will be Castroist. Parenthetically it should be noted that the Consul General's estimate that Balaguer and Ramfis cannot control the situation for more than a few months, a judgment in which we concur, modifies the Intelligence Community's estimate contained in the final paragraph of SNIE 86.2–61, "The Dominican Situation," July 25, 1961.[2]

In view of the above-described situation, it seems somewhat surprising to us that the Consul General continues to endorse, albeit hesitantly, even the partial lifting of OAS sanctions. Given the heated political climate of the Dominican Republic, the removal of OAS sanc-

---

Source: Department of State, Central Files, 739.00/9–2261. Confidential. A covering memorandum indicates that this paper was sent to Bundy on September 22.

[1] Not printed. (Ibid., 739.00/9–1761)

[2] "We believe it likely that the present Dominican Government will be able to retain control of the situation, at least until the May 1962 elections." [Footnote in the source text. SNIE 86.2–61 is Document 317.]

tions would surely be widely interpreted, both in the Dominican Republic and in Latin America generally, as further, conclusive evidence that the United States is committed to an indefinite continuation of the present regime.

---

322.   Memorandum of Conversation

New York, October 3, 1961.

PARTICIPANTS

Dr. Joaquin Balaguer, President of the Dominican Republic
The Honorable George Ball, Under Secretary of State
The Honorable George McGhee, Counselor of the Department of State
Mr. John Calvin Hill, Jr., Consul General, Ciudad Trujillo

SUBJECT

Program for the Dominican Republic

President Balaguer came alone, at the request of the United States, to Ambassador Stevenson's suite in the Waldorf Astoria for an informal and confidential conversation which lasted from 9 p.m. until about 11 p.m. No notes were taken during the meeting in order to preserve the atmosphere of confidence.

Mr. Ball opened the conversation by telling the President that we welcomed the opportunity to discuss the Dominican situation with him informally and frankly as the United States was, within a few days, going to take further specific decisions with regard to its Dominican policy. He stated that the objective of the United States was the reincorporation of the Dominican Republic in the inter-American system.

He noted that President Balaguer had taken certain preliminary measures toward creating the conditions which would make reintegration possible. While recognizing that the problem was not simple and that President Balaguer was faced with formidable difficulties he felt it necessary to say frankly that so far the rate of progress had seemed to the United States Government to be disappointingly slow.

After the United States Government had fully developed its policy within the next few days it would be able to make clear with precision the nature of the steps which it regarded as an indispensable prelude to the lifting of sanctions. Certain of these steps would have to be taken by President Balaguer as the head of the Dominican state. Other steps would have to be taken by General Ramfis Trujillo as head of the Trujillo family. When the United States position was fully defined the precise nature of

---

Source: Department of State, Central Files, 739.00/10–361. Secret. Drafted by Hill and Ball.

the required steps would be made known both to President Balaguer and General Trujillo.

Meanwhile he could say in general that the United States regarded the following as among the pre-conditions to the lifting of sanctions:

(1) The deconcentration of the political and economic power of the Trujillo family, including the early departure of General Arismendi and Generalissimo Hector Trujillo, and

(2) Appropriate arrangements for the disposition of the Trujillo properties.

(3) Cessation of repressive measures by the repressive groups and progress towards observance of human rights.

(4) Arrangements with the moderate opposition, such as a coalition government, and

(5) Effective action against repressive and Communist elements which sought to undermine the democratic system.

President Balaguer replied to these points as follows:

(1) Trujillo family.

He agreed with the United States position on the Trujillo family. It was essential that Arismendi go as he was the most reactionary of them and [*less than 1 line of source text not declassified*]. Hector had withdrawn from politics but as long as he remained in the country he would be a natural focus for reactionary elements in both the civilian and military sectors. Balaguer noted, however, that the United States position, which asked only for the key members of the Trujillo family to leave the country, was different from that of the opposition which demanded that the whole family go.

He thought that it was essential for Ramfis to stay for the time being to assure the unity and support of the armed forces which was necessary for the stability of the nation and the government. He described Ramfis as desiring to retire and go abroad as soon as the situation permitted. He said that there was no problem about arranging for him to leave when the time came.

Later in the conversation, Mr. Ball raised the question as to what would happen if Ramfis were to leave the country now. Would General Sanchez then be able to control the Armed Forces and would he be likely to undertake repressive action against the opposition?

The President replied that, if Ramfis should leave the Dominican Republic at the present time, he did not believe that General Sanchez could maintain his position with the Armed Forces. Sanchez, the present Air Force Chief of Staff, was, he said, only 32 years old. [*1-1/2 lines of source text not declassified*] If Ramfis were to leave now, the Armed Forces would be likely to break up into warring groups as various officers made their bids for power. Anarchy would result.

The President suggested that, when the time came for Ramfis to leave, [4 *lines of source text not declassified*].

(2) *Trujillo properties.*

The President indicated that while the book value of the sugar enterprises was $170,000,000—$140 million for the Rio Haina complex and $30 million for the northern mills—this was exaggerated. Under present conditions a more realistic price would be $80 million. They were subject to debts owed the Dominican Government aggregating $48 million.

As a result Balaguer stated that, if the properties were sold, the Dominican people would benefit by the repayment of these debts. Ramfis proposed, he said, to dispose of the properties in the following way:

(a) He proposed to sell the northern properties, on which the Government-owned Banco Agricola held a note, for $30 million to Dominican businessmen—[2 *lines of source text not declassified*]. The sale price would be $30 million. The purchasers, however, would not put up any money on their own. They would borrow $30 million from the Banco Agricola and repay the indebtedness owed by the northern properties to the Banco Agricola. The transaction would thus be a "wash sale".

(b) He proposed to sell Rio Haina to foreign investors for $50 million. He hinted that the purchaser would be George Pappas. Of this $50 million, $18 million would be applied to repay a note owed by Rio Haina to the Banco Central.

President Balaguer emphasized the fact that if these transactions were completed the Dominican Government would thus receive $48 million through the repayment of the notes owed by Trujillo on the sugar properties. This money could be used for badly needed public works such as the CIBAO irrigation project.

Mr. McGhee pointed out that if the transactions were undertaken as described by President Balaguer the net benefit to the Dominican Government would be only $18 million, since the $30 million repaid to the Banco Agricola would be offset by a new loan by the Banco Agricola to [*less than 1 line of source text not declassified*] who were not putting in any equity capital. The President replied that these were "fictitious" paper transactions. Mr. McGhee asked if it might not create a more favorable impression on the opposition if the northern properties were taken over by the Banco Agricola directly. He pointed out that under the proposed arrangements [*less than 1 line of source text not declassified*] would in effect acquire the properties without putting up any money of their own. The President agreed that this was the case and that it might be better to have the transaction handled in the manner suggested by Mr. McGhee.

Mr. Ball pressed the President as to whether he thought Ramfis Trujillo would be willing to contribute a substantial portion of his net receipts from the proposed transaction ($32 million) to a foundation. The President replied that if the properties were sold he thought that the General might be willing to give a portion of the proceeds to a foundation, mentioning the Instituto de Auxilios y Viviendas.

In the discussion of these financial matter problems the President seemed [*2 lines of source text not declassified*].

The President stated that, in his view, it was more important, as part of the conditions, to concentrate on assuring that the greater portion of the current *income* of the properties be made available for the Dominican Government and people than to concentrate on *titles* which could be left in suspense. He agreed that the Trujillo family was "on its way out" and that, when it lost its position in the country, the state would almost certainly move to take over the properties.

(3) Measures by repressive groups.

The President said that repressive measures would in large part automatically cease with the departure of Arismendi—which he reiterated was urgent—since he was responsible for most of them. He also stated that a program was being undertaken to purge the armed forces of undesirable elements.

(4) Coalition Government.

The President expressed the view that, while the PRD and 14 of June were flexible, the UCN was inflexible and radical in its demands. The President was entirely willing to have them come in to the government; some concessions could be made; and the climate would be better when Arismendi and Hector had departed. He acknowledged that the UCN was opposed to Ramfis' remaining, but this was a necessity that they would accommodate to because it was a reality that he was needed in the armed forces.

Mr. Ball stated that in his opinion conditions would not be propitious for elections in May 1962 and that the elections should be postponed. The President replied that there would be no problem about postponing the May 1962 elections if there was a coalition government. The members of the government could then agree on when they should be held.

At this point, the President entered a strong plea for gradual but progressive action by the United States with respect to lifting the sanctions, starting with lifting the January sanctions (on petroleum, petroleum products, trucks and spare parts) and going on to full lifting the sanctions as progress was made. He argued that inaction at this time had the effect of making the opposition more intransigent and the military more alarmed and he did not know what could happen.

(5) Subversive elements.

The President pointed out that the FNR had already been deported and it was planned to take similar action with others, including (the MPD's) Lopez Molina.

Mr. Ball raised the subject of the OAS Human Rights Committee, suggesting that the Dominican Republic should issue an invitation for it to the Dominican Republic. Mr. Hill explained that it was possible to issue such an invitation under the Statute and highly desirable to do so promptly as the Committee itself was considering Cuba and the Dominican Republic and that the expected refusal of Cuba to cooperate would contrast to the favor of the Dominican Republic. The President demurred, saying that the Dominican Republic had already taken action to put itself on the same footing as the other American Republics, that no other country had invited the Committee, and that the matter would have to be studied closely on his return to Ciudad Trujillo to see if it would be possible to extend an invitation without giving the Committee a power of "vigilance" intruding on the country's sovereignty.

Mr. Ball alluded to the President's possible acceptance of the candidacy of the Partido Dominicano, pointing out that it would be difficult to reach an understanding with the opposition if he were a candidate. The President said that he had been under great pressure to accept the nomination because the party needed a candidate but that September 24 Convention had been postponed indefinitely. He said it could be made a condition that he not accept, since he personally hoped to retire to private life at the end of his term in August 1962. However, if no progress is made (towards the lifting of sanctions) a new and dangerous situation would arise and he would have to judge what was best for the nation in that circumstance.

Asked by Mr. Ball if he had any questions of his own to raise, the President asked for a personal estimate on when it might be possible to lift these sanctions. Mr. Ball replied that, primarily, it depended on progress in fulfilling the conditions which would be spelled out in greater detail in the next few days and replied he could not be more precise at this time. He said a high official, authorized to be a spokesman for the United States Government, would meet with the President and with General Trujillo shortly.

Prior to the meeting, when Mr. Hill picked President Balaguer up at his hotel to escort him to the Waldorf, Sr. Luis Mercado was in the President's suite talking long distance with Ramfis. He told Ramfis that we were leaving for the meeting and he would call him back after it was over.

In the car going to the meeting, the President expressed distress that sanctions could not be lifted for two or three months, according to the plan. On the return trip, he reiterated that it was more important to assure that the income from the Trujillo properties go to the State than to concentrate on the titles and indicated Ramfis was waiting to see some evidence that the United States was going ahead before taking action on Lopez Molina.

323. Memorandum From the President's Special Assistant (Goodwin) to President Kennedy

Washington, October 3, 1961.

John Martin's return from the Dominican Republic,[1] and his excellent reportage, clarifies considerably the situation in that country and confirms the suspicions of those of us who have believed that our previous view was unreal. Based on Martin's trip, the other information which has come to our attention, and our previous knowledge of the people involved, I would summarize the situation thusly:

The opposition is well-meaning but as yet has not displayed any capacity for effective government. No political figure, around which activity could be centered, has emerged from the opposition ranks. There is general reliance on the United States to solve all problems. This is all very understandable in light of 30 years of harsh and brutal repression; but nevertheless it is an inescapable fact in the formulation of our policy. I believe that in time figures will emerge and competence will develop. But it hasn't happened yet.

As for the regime there is also an inescapable fact. The power to control the country resides in the hands of the military and especially the Air Force. The Air Force is modern and well-equipped and in the hands of General Sanchez, a Trujillista, a supporter of Ramfis and a brutal, right-wing figure. He is interested only in power. To a lesser extent the same sort of figures are in effective control of the Army. The Navy is not important. Ramfis Trujillo has no intention of giving up effective power. Talk along these lines is probably nothing but an effort to string us along; and if he did he would probably be replaced by Sanchez who has no intention of letting the UCN or any other opposition group run the country. Unless

---

Source: Kennedy Library, National Security Files, Countries Series, Dominican Republic, Murphy Trip, August 1961–May 1963.

[1] John Bartlow Martin, a free-lance writer with previous experience in the Dominican Republic, had written speeches for Kennedy during the 1960 election campaign. As a result of the August 28 White House meeting (see Document 320), President Kennedy sent Martin to the Dominican Republic on a fact-finding mission. Martin arrived in Ciudad Trujillo on September 10 and spent 3 weeks examining the political situation throughout the country. His 110-page report, October 3, was read in its entirety by the President. It recommended the United States send a high-level envoy to the Dominican Republic to negotiate an end to Trujillo family economic power in the country, help establish a broad-based provisional government until free OAS-sponsored elections could be held, convince the Trujillos to leave the country peacefully, and arrange for a gradual repeal of OAS sanctions against the island. (Kennedy Library, National Security Files, Countries Series, Dominican Republic, Murphy Trip) Kennedy met with Martin at the White House on October 5 to discuss these findings. No formal record of the conversation exists. Director of the State Department Policy Planning Staff McGhee was dispatched immediately to Ciudad Trujillo in accord with the recommedations of the report. (John Bartlow Martin, *Overtaken by Events*, 1966, pp. 64–83, and Schlesinger, *A Thousand Days*, p. 770)

we are prepared to use military force—and we are not—then we cannot escape the fact that the Trujillo–Sanchez group has the guns and is prepared to use them to stay in power. Therefore I believe—sad as it makes me to say this—that any solution which involves an actual relinquishment of authority by Trujillo is not practical or possible or even desirable at this time. (Sanchez would be no improvement.)

Nevertheless we have considerable bargaining power since recognition, relinquishment of sanctions, trade with U.S., etc. are essential to the success of the government. We can, in my estimation, use this bargaining power much more effectively if we use it with a realization of the realities of the situation.

1. The primary and overriding objective of the U.S. in the Dominican Republic is the prevention of the establishment of a pro-Communist or neutralist state. We can see two primary dangers to this objective:

A. Overt U.S. support for Trujillo will dishearten the opposition, causing it to re-group around a radical-left, anti-U.S. resistance resulting in an eventual Castro-type revolution.

B. The regime itself, under Ramfis, moves in a leftward direction. Here the danger is not so much Communism as Nasserism or Titoism. There is a very real danger here. Nasser is Ramfis' hero; and in the pre-assassination days he was noted for his anti-Americanism and leftward leanings. It is an over-simplification to attribute this all to pique at being thrown out of school here—and it is a dangerous assumption to assume that all has changed now that he is in power and needs us for a while.

There is no pleasant answer to this problem. But I believe we should do the following: Accept the fact of Ramfis remaining in power and bargain to create an acceptable democratic facade which will win the confidence—if reluctant confidence of the opposition—and create the conditions under which future democratic government may be possible. We should negotiate with Ramfis under the shadow of the U.S. Fleet. He does not realize just how non-interventionist we have become and the more doubt he has about our willingness to send in the Marines the easier it will be to bargain.

The actual negotiation should take the following lines:

1. A property settlement—most of the Trujillo property going into a public foundation with a good, healthy, liquid share for Ramfis. This is the most complex to work out but probably the easiest to achieve basic agreement on.

2. A political settlement—This would involve the departure of the uncles (Arismendi and Hector) which would please Ramfis; disbanding Arismendi's private army; the formation of a coalition government under Balaguer; the end to other private armies and to the secret police; guarantees of basic civil liberties; an end to the terror generally; a postponement of the elections (no one can be ready for anything but a farcical

election in May), etc. These steps will do much to satisfy the opposition and create a healthy climate for the growth of effective political groups for the future. At the same time it is important to note that this leaves Ramfis in control of the armed forces and the real power in the country.

3. When these things are announced and done—not before—we will lift sanction, resume diplomatic relations, etc.

4. We will send a series of missions to the Dominican Republic—economic development, agriculture, organization of public administration, even a constitutional government mission—to help re-establish a viable society. The presence of these missions and their work is the surest short-term guarantee of some sort of stability.

5. When these negotiations move ahead, Arturo Morales Carrion should be sent to talk to the opposition; tell them what a great job we are doing for them, and persuade them to accept the results of this negotiation. I think this can be done.

6. It should be left reasonably clear in Ramfis' mind that if he begins to move to the left or towards neutralism we would find a pretext for coming in with the Fleet.

7. This leaves the question of who should negotiate. George Ball has suggested George McGhee. I share Arthur Schlesinger's thought that Ellsworth Bunker would be best for this kind of mission. John Martin should be used as Bunker's staff assistant on this mission.

Richard N. Goodwin[2]

---

[2] Printed from a copy that bears this typed signature.

324. Airgram From the Department of State to the Consulate General in Ciudad Trujillo

A–20   Washington, October 13, 1961.

Following are instructions for McGhee's oral use in discussions with President Balaguer and General Trujillo[1] and for Hill's guidance in follow-up.

1. Political and economic matters (other than property) should be negotiated with Balaguer, but they should be given Ramfis as part plan and commitment to support them should be obtained from him. Actual negotiations with Ramfis should be limited to questions concerning Trujillo family, property, armed forces and internal security.

2. As introduction to specific program described para 4, you should outline basic considerations governing US policy toward present Dominican situation as follows. These essentially same points contained in talking paper for New York meeting with Balaguer. You may draw on them in discussions as you see fit.

(a) US objective with respect Dominican Republic is its early reincorporation in inter-American system with a democratic government and free from any threat Castro-communism. US regards this as essential to security and peace in Caribbean during period increased world tension.

(b) US has noted efforts made last four months by Balaguer, with support Ramfis, to initiate program to effect difficult transition to democracy but progress in some respects has been distressingly slow. US has also noted measures to realign foreign policy of GODR in manner friendly to the other American republics, including US; to cooperate with OAS Special Committee, to align DR with Free World against world communism; and to cooperate with US and US officials.

(c) US seeks no economic, commercial or political advantage and looks to Dominican people to settle own internal affairs, but US is prepared assist in any way helpful successful completion democratization program.

(d) US would like a situation to develop which would make it possible for sanctions to be lifted and diplomatic relations restored by end 1961. However, in view hemisphere and US opinion, as well as internal

---

Source: Department of State, Central Files, 739.00/10–1361. Secret; Limit Distribution. Drafted by Hill, Martin, Crimmins; cleared by Coerr, Martin, Hill, McGhee, ARA/RPA, ARA/REA, S/S; and approved by Ball.

[1] Accounts of McGhee's meetings with Balaguer and Ramfis Trujillo are ibid., 739.00/10–261 through 739.00/11–1661.

situation in DR, US cannot support these steps until and unless there is visible progress on following critical points:

(1) Deconcentration of political, economic, and military power Trujillo family, including especially early departure Arismendi and Hector Trujillo, removal other members of family from positions of government, and departure further members family.

(2) Arrangements for benefit Dominican people, through foundations or other instrumentality not controlled by Trujillos, which would end domination Dominican economy by Trujillo family and would assure that Trujillo family did not profit from resumption relations and lifting sanctions. You should point out US Dept. Agriculture apportions sugar quota for first quarter 1962 by end first week December.

(3) Cessation extra-legal repressive measures and further visible progress towards observance human rights.

(4) Arrangement of modus vivendi, preferably through genuine coalition with moderate non-Communist opposition. This, in our view, will require President Balaguer stand above party politics and not be candidate.

(5) Effective action by GODR to prevent political activity by any totalitarian elements including Communist, pro-Communist, or pro-Castro. This especially involves carrying out President's July 8 statement to Hill that leaders MPD would be deported.

3. You may recall to Ramfis discussions which Hill has had with him in recent weeks on plan intended to meet requirements of situation as USG views it. You should refer specifically to Hill's conversations with him of September 10 and 11 (which were based on Deptels 284 and 306)[2] and tell him your purpose is to carry forward these conversations by further defining plan, which, you may emphasize, has been approved at highest level USG. (To Balaguer you may cite Hill's conversation with him Sept. 9.) You should state USG believes it urgent there be dramatic further public evidence of progress in implementation plan outlined by Hill and will probably find it necessary issue statement clarifying basic considerations governing United States policy. Statement will probably be made not later than October 25 in order prepare ground for announcing US position on steps it may support on basis OAS Sub-committee report expected late October. Since statement must touch on key question US attitude on progress made toward breaking up concentration political, economic, and military power characteristic of previous regime, it is to interest all concerned that visible progress be made along these lines and other aspects of plan in next two weeks. You should tell Ramfis and Balaguer that Hill will be pursuing matter with them after your departure.

---

[2] Neither printed. (Department of State, Central Files, 739.00/9–161 and 739.00/9–661)

[Here follow a detailed description of proposals to be made to the Balaguer government and the timetable for their implementation.]

---

325. Telegram From the Consulate General in the Dominican Republic to the Department of State

Ciudad Trujillo, November 16, 1961, 11 a.m.

950. Return of Trujillo brothers, Generals Hector and Arismendi, on 15 November has precipitated behind-the-scenes national crisis. American ConGen has stated flatly that Hector and Arismendi must leave today or US will be confronted with decision to withdraw support in OAS for partial lifting sanctions. General Ramfis Trujillo, head of Dominican armed forces, submitted offer of resignation to President Balaguer yesterday and has withdrawn to Bocachica villa. President Balaguer has stated he himself will resign if brothers do not leave. Resignation or withdrawals of Ramfis and Balaguer will leave country without actual or titular head. In this event, power struggle likely between older officers headed by Hector and Arismendi and younger officers headed by Sanchez and Leonestevez.

In view of above, ConGen requests estimate of forces available and reaction times to execute phase one, two, and four of OPN 05–61.[1]

This does not constitute expectation activation these phases at this time. This information needed for contingency planning here.

Hill

Source: Department of State, Central Files, 739.00/11–1661. Secret; Niact; Operational Immediate.

[1] Not further identified.

326. Telegram From the Consulate General in the Domincan Republic to the Department of State

Ciudad Trujillo, November 17, 1961, 10 a.m.

964. Presented plan (Deptel 601)[1] to President Balaguer at his residence at 7:15 a.m. this morning. He thoroughly agreed with concept and every point as only way out and undertook do his best to convince Trujillos to comply.

He had strong doubts, however, that Hector and Arismendi would leave. He had tried all day yesterday persuade Trujillo family this only thing to do, but they just as determined to remain as Ramfis is determined to leave. They were reconciled that sanctions would remain in force and that DR would not receive additional sugar quota but thought they could maintain friendly regime in power.

President said Ramfis ostensibly trying assist him persuade uncles to go [10 lines of source text not declassified].

President urged maximum US pressure be brought on Hector and Arismendi to leave, including imposition additional sanctions and threat to use armed force, if his efforts today did not succeed. I authorized him say US Government's firm position and demand was that they leave according to plan I presented; that sanctions would not be lifted if they here and that, at best, normal sugar quota would probably be smaller; that we doubted any government could survive these conditions; that in case of threat of Fidelismo or situation such as breakdown or disorders leading to same, US would act preserve its essential interests. I offered to tell anyone, including uncles, directly of our position if it would help. President thanked me, urged that permanence of uncles' departure not be stressed to them, as this only made them more determined to stay, but leave open possibility their eventual return. I replied evident that after transitional period, whether they could return depends on government here, and they should be told best way assure any future was to cooperate now by leaving.

In light foregoing, stressed military leaders should be acceptable but I did not mention names specific officers who might be suitable chiefs services and/or council so as not imperil them. Am reserving this aspect for time, if ever, that there is clear agreement on plan.

Discussed with President possibility his resigning or threatening resign as additional pressure on uncles if current efforts fail, making

---

Source: Department of State, Central Files, 739.00/11–1761. Secret; Niact; Limit Distribution.

[1] Not printed. (Ibid., 739.00/11–1661)

clear, however, that as matters now stood, we strongly wished him to stay. His mind now inclining in direction staying in office, letting Ramfis leave, and then bringing maximum pressure on uncles. Said he would have think through consequences any action he took.

Believe our course during day should be arm me with additional specific pressures which can bring to bear to re-enforce President. Can I say we will propose additional sanctions and, if so, specifically in what categories? Have we any influence which would curtail Dominican sugar sales to Europe and world market and/or future reduce Dominican income from US market? Can I threaten use every means our disposal expose to Dominican Armed Forces and people that they would be sacrificing selves and honor for Trujillo family interests and would have support hemisphere if they rid themselves of Trujillos? Can US military show of force be prepared for use if we judge would be useful? Believe we should act as quickly and decisively for inherent danger in situation is that installation of regime under influence Hector will drive opposition into radical and uncontrollable channels which can only favor development of Castro-like movement sooner rather than later.

FYI: Reason Rodriguez Echavarria placed ahead Rodriguez Mendez and Montas ahead Hermida in our 955[2] is that all indications are first named have enough toughness to maintain discipline and latter considered possibly too easygoing. End FYI.

Hill

---

[2] Dated November 16. (Ibid.)

---

327. Telegram From the Department of State to the Consulate General in the Dominican Republic

Washington, November 17, 1961, 9:49 p.m.

606. Contel 964.[1] Our ability arm you with additional specific pressures limited at present to positioning one to three naval units at point

---

Source: Department of State, Central Files, 739.00/11–1761. Secret; Niact; Limit Distribution; Verbatim Text. Drafted by Crimmins, cleared by Coerr, and approved by Woodward.

[1] Document 326.

just below horizon from Ciudad Trujillo, on call to move within sight of shore immediately should you so request. Ships will be on station morning eighteenth. You should not make this known for present.

Secretary made following voluntary statement in press conference today:

"In OAS there are two questions immediately in front of us. One has to do with the Dominican Republic. Question before OAS is whether there could be now a partial lifting of so-called sanctions against Dominican Republic. This possibility is directly related to events in Dominican Republic itself. Those turn on events which may change on hour-to-hour basis.

On one side we have been encouraged by tendencies in Dominican Republic to move toward more moderate and constitutional government embracing broader elements of population in political and constitutional affairs and moving toward kind government which Dominican people themselves could respect and which would win esteem international community states. Just as there has been some confusion in last few hours as to exactly what is happening in Dominican Republic I would not anticipate that OAS would feel itself in position act immediately upon suggestions which our representative made this week that subject."

We are urgently considering other means pressure and will advise you further.

Rusk

---

328. Editorial Note

On November 18, 1961, the Department of State issued press release 799, a statement by Secretary of State Rusk, which reads as follows:

"It has been confirmed that leading figures who were closely associated with the repressive measures of the former dictatorship in the Dominican Republic and who had departed from that country returned to Ciudad Trujillo on November 15.

"Moreover, it appears that they may be planning an attempt to reassert dictatorial domination of the political and economic life of that country, threatening the recent gains of the Dominican Government and people toward democratization.

"On the recommendation of the United States, the Special Committee of the Organization of American States has already postponed further consideration of a proposal on withdrawing the suspension of trade with the Dominican Republic in certain products.

"In view of the possibility of political disintegration and the dangerous situation which could ensue, the Government of the United States is considering the further measures that unpredictable events might warrant." (Department of State *Bulletin*, December 4, 1961, page 931)

The Department of State subsequently released two similar statements of concern: press release 829, November 30, and a statement read to the news correspondents by a Department press officer. The texts of both those statements are ibid., page 1003.

---

329. Telegram From the Department of State to the Consulate General in the Dominican Republic

Washington, November 18, 1961, 7:12 p.m.

609. Embtel 976.[1] Department today determined following actions in response your telegrams present situation:

1. Secretary has issued statement confirming our opposition to reimposition dictatorship and continuing support democratization (unclassified Deptel 608).[2]

2. You should immediately inform Balaguer we would respond affirmatively and promptly should he request courtesy visit US Naval unit. Cruiser now in position below horizon out of ground sight. (Code word "hospitality." We would suggest covering statement by USG along following lines "President Balaguer who has been playing an active role in working toward the democratization of the DR has invited units US Navy which have been on maneuvers in nearby waters pay courtesy call at CT. This invitation has been accepted." We would gear release of such statement to your recommendations which would of course take into account optimum timing from point of view of Balaguer's safety. *Com-*

Source: Department of State, Central Files, 739.00/11–1761. Secret; Niact; Limit Distribution. Drafted by Coerr; cleared by Jamison, Achilles, Crimmins, Schlesinger, L, and S/S; and approved by Woodward.

[1] Not printed. (Ibid.)

[2] Not printed. (Ibid., 739.00/11–1861) For text of the statement, see Document 328.

ment: We prefer courtesy visit at invitation GODR as more immediate, more moderate and more generally acceptable measure than USG show of force. Obviously it would also serve show US strength soonest. (Personnel would not go ashore without further instructions.) We tend to believe presence Naval unit in harbor might have calming effect and might provide element of security for President Balaguer whose physical safety highly important to successful USG operations this difficult situation.

3. You are authorized request Navy make active demonstration force "Wave High" in international waters (not within DR jurisdiction) at your discretion. You may make request directly to Navy with info Washington or to Navy through Washington. Navy will respond soonest. Planes on strip alert commencing dawn 19th. You are authorized similarly request Navy move vessels into sight international waters. (Code word "Sea Gull.")

4. We would be prepared consider active demonstration of force such as "Grass Cutter" within Dominican jurisdiction only if President Balaguer explicitly requests (preferably in writing).

Rusk

---

330. Editorial Note

On November 19, 1961, following the appearance of U.S. warships off the coast of the Dominican Republic, Dominican Air Force General Rafael Rodriguez Echavarria declared in favor of the Balaguer government. Hector and Arismendi left the country on November 20. It was learned afterward that Ramfis, who had resigned as chief of the Dominican armed forces and police on November 14, had slipped away on his yacht the night of November 17. U.S. talks with the Balaguer government resumed on the questions of ending sanctions, establishing a provisional government leading to OAS-sponsored elections, and the resumption of full U.S. diplomatic relations with the Dominican Republic. The talks bogged down due to civil unrest in the Republic and the reluctance of Balaguer to leave office. (Department of State, Central Files, 739.00/11–2261 through 739.00/12–1561; Martin, *Overtaken by Events*, pages 82–83)

331. Telegram From the Consulate General in the Dominican Republic to the Department of State

Ciudad Trujillo, November 19, 1961, 9 a.m.

990. Situation as of 0700.

1. Ships now visible and making two runs before city.

2. Alvarez[1] came in to say UCN has word that their contacts with military in Cibao area have been successful and there is now joint military opposition understanding which controls Santiago–San Francisco–LaVega. UCN also has news from Sanisidro General Rodriguez Echavarria, who still there took charge in middle night and issuing communiqué—this not verification or direct news of situation.

3. Yesterday Vidal Torres, Governor Santiago, appointed Secretary Interior and Pedro Jorge, popular with moderate opposition. Vidal replaces Herrera Bellini, moderate, who took over Partido Dominican of Rommercado who took off for Miami and reportedly Europe on Thursday 16.

4. Military liaison officer has just called R/Admiral Valdezvidaure who assures Navy behind Balaguer and that Trujillos have to go. He is certain he is in effective control Navy. Has not been in touch with Sanisidro but believes Air Force also behind Balaguer.

5. Remaining question is Army.

Hill

Source: Department of State, Central Files, 739.00/11–1961. Secret; Niact. Relayed to the White House, OSD, Army, Navy, Air Force, and CIA.

[1] Braulio Alvarez Sanchez.

332.   Telegram From the White House to the Department of State

San Juan, Puerto Rico, December 16, 1961.

PRWHO5. From Naval Aide to the President. To Mr. Bundy, WashDC, Sec Rusk, State Dept. Following instructions were given to Mr. Hill by the President.

Memorandum for John Calvin Hill, Consul General, Santo Domingo

For your use immediately on your return to Santo Domingo on December 16, 1961, there are attached:

1) Instructions for a conversation with President Balaguer on my behalf.
2) Instructions for a conversation with General Rodriguez Echavarria.
3) General instructions for your guidance in these conversations.

s/John F. Kennedy

December 16, 1961
La Fortaleza
San Juan, Puerto Rico

1. The President has personally instructed that you make the following known to President Balaguer.

The Government and people of the United States have great admiration for President Balaguer's heroic and courageous efforts to effect a peaceful transition to democratic government in the Dominican Republic whatever the feelings of the moment in the Dominican Republic. The President is confident that if Balaguer's efforts are successful he will endure as one of the great figures of his country's history and an important figure in the history of this hemisphere. Because of this admiration for President Balaguer the President is greatly disturbed at the current course of events in the Dominican Republic. If the current impasse is allowed to continue then violence and terror are certain to rise—the problems of peaceful transition will be complicated—and the efforts to achieve democracy will be endangered. As long as President Balaguer continues without indicating a definite decision to turn over the office of President to a successor—then the entire atmosphere in the Dominican

Source: Department of State, Central Files, 739.00/12–1661. Secret. No time of transmission is indicated on the source text. President Kennedy, en route to Venezuela and Colombia, met with Woodward, Bowles, Morales-Carrion, Hill, and Goodwin at the Governor of Puerto Rico's mansion, La Fortaleza, to discuss the Dominican negotiations.

Republic will continue to grow hostile and dangerous—and distrust for the regime and for President Balaguer will increase. Thus, unless immediate steps are taken to set a date for departure the dangers of a new dictatorship will increase and the prestige of President Balaguer will decline. If he leaves early and on his own initiative then he undoubtedly will be known as one of the few men in any country to have brought about a peaceful transition to democracy. If he does not do this, and if he is forced out at some later date, then his prestige and his position in history will be damaged or even destroyed.

We realize the difficulties which President Balaguer faces. And we admire the skill with which he has handled the enormous problems of his country. Therefore we have, at all times, supported his efforts to bring about constitutional government. We believe that the following suggested course of action will bring final success, after which we are confident President Balaguer can return to an important official position of some prestige—as well as to a secure position in the history of his country and of western democracy:

(A) We suggest that the President make it clear that the announcement of his final solution was not forced on him by others—but was arrived at his own free will and after careful thought for the welfare and future of his country.

(B) That the President announce his intention to resign on February 27, 1962. He should state that in the interim he intends to carry out the program of establishing the Council of State, reorganizing the cabinet etc. To create a government of national unity. We believe it is essential to announce a definite date for President Balaguer's resignation. Not to do so would create distrust of his intentions, make it impossible to form a bona fide coalition government, and make it very difficult for the United States to lift sanctions or recognize the government until after his departure. On the other hand, if he announces a date the sincerity of his intentions will be recognized. His position and prestige in his own country and elsewhere will be strengthened, and it will be his government that will achieve not only democratic government, but the restoration of diplomatic relations and an end to sanctions. If he does not announce a date then it will appear as if he were forced out, as if others had made the decision as to when he should leave, whereas if he does set a date then he will appear to be in control of the situation, to have made his own decision, and be shaping his country's future.

(C) Balaguer should also announce—on his own initiative—his intention to create a Council of State, a representative cabinet, and to take other measures necessary to assure a government of national unity with elections.

(D) That President Balaguer announce the appointment of these bodies including the appointment of the members of the Council of State as advisors to the President pending enactment of the necessary constitutional and legal change to establish the Council. That he also announce his intention to resign February 27, 1962 in favor of the person who will be elected Vice-President of the Council.

(E) The United States will then proceed to move to lift sanctions and re-establish diplomatic relations so that these things will be accomplished before President Balaguer leaves office.

2. The President has instructed the Consul General of the United States, in his discretion, to seek an interview with General Rodriguez Echavarria and state the following points on behalf of the President:

(A) The United States believes the Armed Forces of the Dominican Republic are deeply interested in supporting the democratic evolution of the republic and in its reincorporation into the Inter-American community at the earliest possible time.

(B) The United States considers that the support of the armed forces to a political and constitutional solution as may be reached between President Balaguer and the responsible opposition will greatly help in overcoming the present crisis and will pave the way for quick international action on behalf of the government and people of the Dominican Republic.

(C) Were the armed forces to give their unequivocal support to the solution accorded by President Balaguer and the responsible opposition, the United States, on its part, will:

(1) Take or support an initiative in the OAS to revoke immediately the sanctions imposed by the San Jose conference.
(2) Restore diplomatic relations as soon as formal action is taken by the COAS and,
(3) Consequently authorize the additional "windfall" sugar quota for the Dominican Republic.
(4) Give immediate and sympathetic consideration to bilateral programs between the United States and the Government of the Dominican Republic under the Alianza Para el Progreso, with particular reference to the social development of the Dominican people.
(5) Be prepared to discuss, upon request by a government of national unity of the Dominican Republic the conclusion of a suitable military agreement for military cooperation including the provision, if desired, of a United States military mission.

(D) Were the Armed Forces of the Dominican Republic to deny their support to the political solution reached by President Balaguer and the responsible opposition, the United States will be unable to support the lifting of sanctions or will consider inadvisable to grant the "windfall" quota or enter into any agreements related to the extension of the Alliance for Progress to the Dominican people.

3. The President instructed the Consul General of the United States in the Dominican Republic to seek an immediate interview with Presi-

dent Balaguer on his return to Santo Domingo on December 16 and to convey the message which he has been instructed to give to President Balaguer. In addition, the Consul General may make any or all of the following points:

(1) The United States is anxious that there be an early solution to the political impasse between the Government of the Dominican Republic and the anti-Communist opposition at the earliest possible date.

(2) When an accord is reached, the United States is prepared to take, or support, an initiative in the OAS to revoke the sanctions imposed by the Conference of San Jose, to restore diplomatic relations and, consequently to authorize the additional ("windfall") sugar quota for the Dominican Republic. The United States, upon the restoration of diplomatic relations, is further prepared to give sympathetic and immediate consideration to bilateral programs between the United States and the Dominican Republic, under the Alianza Para Progreso program, in such fields as economic, cultural and military cooperation as well as give sympathetic support to Dominican requests to international institutions for the financing of sound programs and projects for the economic recovery and development of the Dominican Republic.

(3) The United States, however, considers that it will not be in a position to take these actions in benefit of the Dominican Republic until such time as the Dominican Government is broadly representative of national opinion on the basis of an accord between the government and the main political groups representing the Dominican people. Therefore, the United States believes that reaching such an accord is of the greatest urgency.

(4) The United States further considers that delay in reaching an accord not only enhances the possibilities of the growth of leftist and Castroist agitation and disturbances or of the growth of military influence in the civil affairs of the Dominican Republic, but also does serious damage to the international reputation of the United States, of President Balaguer and of the Dominican Armed Forces. The United States, and its President, fully recognize and appreciate the role which President Balaguer has taken in setting the course of his nation towards a democratic system and towards the restoration of good relations with the United States and other American Republics. The United States is prepared to use its influence in order to assure that, upon leaving office, President Balaguer is treated with the consideration due to the efforts he has made towards these objectives.

(5) While recognizing that the nature of an accord between the government and the opposition is essentially an internal matter, the United States is prepared to lend its support in the OAS and bilaterally to a government consisting of

(a) A President.

(b) A Council of State composed of distinguished citizens mutually acceptable to the opposition and to the government including the armed forces.

(c) A cabinet divided among nominees of the present government and the opposition and

(d) The armed forces, responsible under the constitution solely to the President and responsible under him for their own self-administration without political interference.

(6) The United States does not consider that the completion or non-completion of President Balaguer's term of office should be an obstacle to reaching an agreement. On the contrary, the United States believes that President Balaguer has a unique opportunity to successfully set his country on the road to democracy, but that his position would become untenable in the eyes of the hemisphere if insistence on completing his term of office became the sole obstacle to reaching an accord and that such serious damage would be done to the reputation of the President and to the present Dominican Government that it would be impossible for the United States to lift sanctions or resume diplomatic relations.

(7) *Note:* In reporting the results of this conversation and of other developments in the Dominican Republic, the Consul General will forward his recommendations on the desirability of having Deputy Assistant Secretary Morales Carrion return to the Dominican Republic and on the advisability of having OAS Secretary General Mora go there.[1]

---

[1] Printed from an unsigned copy.

---

333. Telegram From the Department of State to President Kennedy, at Caracas

Washington, December 16, 1961.

707. Presidential Visit. Following from Santo Domingo, is repeated "Number 1298,[1] December 16, 2 p.m., signed Hill". Niact. Presidential Handling. Limit Distribution.

Source: Kennedy Library, National Security Files, Countries Series, Dominican Republic, September–December 1961. Secret; Niact; Eyes Only. The President was in Caracas December 16–17 to meet with President Betancourt.
[1] Not printed. (Department of State, Central Files, 739.00/12–1661)

In accordance President's instructions, called on President Balaguer late this morning and—after generally describing talks in San Juan and President Kennedy's great personal interest in early solution which would preserve President Balaguer's stature before history—conveyed to him the President's message. Only change from text was substitution of "a date in January or February" for "February 27" since, on my return, was informed opposition negotiators still hopeful of January retirement and I did not wish place President Kennedy in position of undermining it by firmly suggesting a later date.

President Balaguer expressed appreciation for President's message, which he said accorded with his own thinking except that point re announcement of his resignation unresolved. He listened attentively to passage in President's message and to my amplifying explanations, including allusion to fact that President had found in 15 years experience that it was better to retain initiative with clear-cut solution than to be exposed to continuing pressures which would make decision, when finally announced, appear to have been taken under pressure. I also added that it was my own judgment that leaving this key question open would at same time make it difficult present clear-cut convincing solution to OAS and result here in continuing attacks by opposition which could be avoided if definite decision announced.

President Balaguer indicated he was personally convinced, but would have to talk to Armed Forces because it was they, not he, who opposed naming a fixed date, but he thought they could be persuaded. He was disposed to make speech and send necessary constitutional changes to Congress concurrently. He described negotiations as being in advanced state, with only unresolved issues being who should succeed him, [less than 1 line of source text not declassified] and when his withdrawal should be announced.

During conversation, General Rodriguez Echavarria sauntered in on another matter, and joined talk. He was obviously relaxed and on his best, most respectful manners with President. After President and I had briefed him, I conveyed to him President Kennedy's message which obviously pleased him and also flattered him. In ensuing discussion, General neither approved nor disapproved of President making announcement but indicated generally he would agree to whatever President decided about plan and offered to make concurrent public announcement Armed Forces supported solution. However, he quietly firm that Rafael Bonelly not only should be but must be "Vice President of Council of State and President Balaguer's successor as the person having confidence of Armed Forces". [2 lines of source text not declassified]

As President and General saw it, agreement could be announced and sent Congress on Monday if opposition negotiations agreed to above. I myself am not sure Bonelly's name will sit well with UCN because of his friendship with General.

Amiama, Bonelly and possibly Imbert to see President later in day and we shall see then whether agreement in sight and whether or not it would be desirable for Morales Carrion to return."

Ball

334. Memorandum of Conversation

Caracas, December 16, 1961.

SUBJECT

Conference Between President Kennedy and Venezuelan President Betancourt—Dominican Republic Situation

PARTICIPANTS

The President
Ambassador Chester Bowles
Mr. C. Allan Stewart, Chargé d'Affaires ad interim
Mr. Robert F. Woodward, Assistant Secretary of State for Inter-American Affairs
Mr. Teodoro Moscoso, Assistant Administrator for Latin America of the Agency for International Development
Mr. Richard Goodwin, Deputy Assistant Secretary of State for Latin American Affairs
Mr. Harold Linder, President of Export-Import Bank of Washington
Mr. Fernando van Reigersberg, LS staff interpreter

President Romulo Betancourt of Venezuela
Dr. Marcos Falcón Briceño, Foreign Minister of Venezuela
Dr. Andres German Otero, Minister of Finance of Venezuela
General Antonio Briceño Linares, Minister of Defense of Venezuela
Dr. Jose Antonio Mayobre, Venezuelan Ambassador to the United States
Dr. Alejandro Oropeza Castillo, Governor of the Federal District of Venezuela
Dr. Manuel Perez Guerrero, Chief, Office of Coordination and Planning, Venezuelan Government

The meeting convened at 5:15 p.m. on December 16, 1961, at Los Nuñez, began with a discussion of the Dominican Republic situation and the Cuban problem. Other subjects were discussed subsequently.

Source: Department of State, Central Files, 739.00/12–1661. Secret. Drafted by Charles A. Stewart of the Embassy, Fernando van Reigersberg (LS), and Sam Moskowitz (ARA/ESA) and approved in the White House on February 6, 1962.

Dominican Republic Situation

The Dominican question was the first topic discussed. President Kennedy outlined United States efforts to bring the Dominican Republic toward a provisional democratic government, which would rule until free elections could be held later in 1962. He said that he had talked to Deputy Assistant Secretary Morales Carrión and Consul John Hill the night before in Puerto Rico, that they had returned to Santo Domingo immediately afterwards and that Mr. Hill was to meet with President Balaguer this very day. He discussed the difficulties in bringing the democratic opposition parties into agreement with the Balaguer government and said that agreement appeared to be near for naming a provisional junta. President Kennedy thought that the opposition parties should unite and agree to present a common front and that President Balaguer should form a provisional junta immediately. He should also make a speech to the nation stating that he would resign on a certain date but that his resignation would be the result of his own decision and not forced on him by the opposition parties. After a coalition government is formed, the United States would support the lifting of economic sanctions and the resumption of diplomatic relations.

President Kennedy indicated that it was very useful for the United States, Venezuela, and Colombia to work together in this matter. In twenty-four or forty-eight hours he would know more about the success or failure of Mr. Hill's mission. The United States would keep in touch with President Betancourt and keep him informed of the latest developments. Unquestionably, the difficult man to deal with would be General Rodríguez Echevarría. It would be necessary to persuade Balaguer and Rodríguez of the need for Balaguer to resign. The opposition parties would have to be persuaded to form a workable coalition and a date for Balaguer's resignation would have to be set. If Balaguer refused to resign or if General Rodríguez opposed the plan, the problem would be much more serious and acute than at the present time.

President Kennedy said there would be, in any case, a waiting period before sanctions were lifted and in the meantime, efforts would continue to be made by the United States to induce Balaguer to leave the presidency some time during the winter if the provisional junta idea were accepted by the negotiating factions. He requested President Betancourt to use his influence to persuade Balaguer to leave office and to persuade the opposition groups to cooperate in reaching a satisfactory solution.

President Betancourt stated that he had followed Dominican developments very closely. His prediction that the death of Trujillo would not be followed by Castroism had proven to be correct. When the United States sent its destroyers to the Dominican Republic, Venezuela considered sending some of her ships but decided that it would not be necessary.

President Betancourt said the procedure indicated by President Kennedy met with the approval of the Venezuelan Government. He said he was disposed to send a personal message to President Balaguer and General Rodríguez Echevarría urging them to accept the proposal presented by the opposition parties with United States approval. He stated that General Rodríguez is a very ambitious man. There is a clear and present danger that he may wish to follow in Trujillo's footsteps. It is very fortunate that the three main parties opposing Balaguer are on excellent terms with him (Betancourt) and have written to him on several occasions. He had sent his personal envoy to Santo Domingo recently to inquire into the situation and would send him again if it were necessary to induce Balaguer to remain as President only transitorily. It was decided to wait at least 48 hours before any action be taken in view of present indications that some arrangement might be reached between Balaguer and the opposition parties.

---

335. Memorandum of Conversation

Bogotá, December 17, 1961.

SUBJECT

Developments in the Dominican Republic
Planning for Foreign Ministers' Meeting on Cuban Problem

PARTICIPANTS

U.S.
President Kennedy
Mr. Chester Bowles, President's
    Special Assistant
Ambassador Moscoso
Assistant Secretary Woodward
Deputy Assistant Secretary Goodwin
Ambassador Freemen
Mr. Henry Dearborn, Counselor of
    American Embassy, Bogota

Colombia
President Camargo Lleras
Foreign Minister Castilla Caicedo
Minister of Finance Mejia
Director of National Planning Dept.
    Gutierrez

President Kennedy called at President Lleras' office at 5:30 p.m. on December 17. Each President was accompanied by advisers as recorded

---

Source: Department of State, Central Files, 721.00/12–1761. Confidential. Drafted by Dearborn on December 20 and approved in the White House on January 8, 1962.

above. Press photographers were invited in and pictures taken. President Kennedy then suggested that the group sit down for conversations and the Presidents, together with their advisers, held a discussion for over an hour.

Developments in the Dominican Republic

President Kennedy had just been handed a cable from the Consul General in Santo Domingo[1] with information on developments there and the Dominican situation was the first item of conversation. He gave President Lleras information from the cable to the effect that President Balaguer had agreed to announce his withdrawal from the presidency before the end of February, actually intending to leave on January 26. Balaguer had agreed in the meantime to set up a Council of State consisting of Jose Maria Cabral Bermudez as First Vice President, Dr. Rafael Bonelly as Second Vice President and with the following as members: Monsenor Perez Sanchez, Sr. Amiama Tio and Sr. Imbert. Presidents Kennedy and Lleras and others present discussed the characteristics of this group and it was generally agreed that the information in the telegram was encouraging.

[Here follows discussion of the preparations for the Eighth Meeting of Foreign Ministers of the Organization of American States; see Document 128.]

---

[1] See Document 333.

---

336. Editorial Note

On December 17, 1961, following U.S.-brokered negotiations between the Government and the Dominican opposition parties, President Balaguer announced that a 7-man Council of State would take power in the Dominican Republic January 1, 1962, pending OAS-sponsored elections for both the legislature (August 16) and the Presidency (December 20). The Council took office with Balaguer as its President. The other members were Rafael Bonelly, Eduardo Read Barrera, Antonio Imbert Barrera, Nicolas Pichardo, Luis Amiama Tio, and Elisco Perez Sanchez. On January 4 the Council of the OAS voted to lift the sanctions imposed on the Dominican Republic on August 20, 1960. On January 6 the United States reestablished full diplomatic relations with the Dominican Republic. John C. Hill remained as Chargé d'Affaires ad interim.

On January 16 Balaguer resigned as President of the Council following street demonstations in the capital by those opposed to his continued participation in the Dominican Government. Later the same day General Pedro Rafael Rodríguez Echavarría ousted the Council of State and established a military civilian junta. (Department of State, Central Files, 739.00/1–1662 through 739.00/1–1962)

337. Telegram From the Embassy in the Dominican Republic to the Department of State

Santo Domingo, January 16, 1962, 9 p.m.

1494. Imbert called Shaw[1] urgently to Palace at 6 p.m. to inform that as result afternoon's incidents (Embassy telegram 1490)[2] Balaguer had informed entire Council he would resign immediately. Formal commitment will be taken at Palace meeting in session now, of Balaguer, entire Council, Rodriguez Echavarria and other armed forces chiefs. Amiama and Pichardo (who later joined conversation) plus Imbert all agree situation has reached decisive moment: Balaguer would definitely go and Rodriguez Echavarria—who they said [would] either accept or not accept Bonelly as chief of state. Latter case would result in military coup. Asked point-blank whether senior military would support General in takeover, Amiama gave fairly firm negative. Obvious that he and others nervous though self-possessed. They all agree, however, that General plans eventual complete takeover. Net impression was they feel better than even chance exists Bonelly will be accepted for moment at least.

Imbert privately urged that Embassy Service Attachés encourage General to obey constitutional authority, they urged US fleet again be displayed to insure he did so. Amiama, just entering, agreed with latter. Was answered that no country could continue to rely on foreign solutions to its internal problems, to which both agreed. Further indicated that critical factor was lack of confidence by general inability and disposition of Council to maintain order, which all three recognize. They

---

Source: Department of State, Central Files, 739.00/1–1662. Secret; Niact. Passed to the White House, OSD, CIA, CNO, CINCLANTFLT, COMCARIBSEAFRON, Chief of Staff USAF, Chief of Staff USA, COMNAVBASEGTMO, COMSECDELT, and CMC.

[1] David G. Shaw, political officer.

[2] Not printed. (Department of State, Central Files, 739.00/1–1662)

said would attempt guide meeting to create best possible impression on General. Conversation closed as military chiefs arrived with massive bodyguard heavily armed officers and NCOs numbering in dozens.

Hodge[3]

---

[3] Charles L. Hodge, consular and economic officer.

---

338. Telegram From the Department of State to the Embassy in the Dominican Republic

Washington, January 17, 1962, 7:41 p.m.

885. As soon as possible upon your return and unless your estimate current situation suggests different course action (in which case you should advise Dept immediately) you should speak to Rodriguez Echavarria along following lines:

We believe that with departure Balaguer he may be only man in position to move DR rapidly along road to democratization. This is great historical opportunity which we are hopeful he will take. Any other course will inevitably lead to increasing tension, unrest, etc., and make it impossible for US follow through on intention assist social and economic development DR. These conditions will not only prevent him from gaining stature in hemisphere as friend of democracy, but, by setting the military against the people, will seriously endanger position of military establishment when, as is inevitable, civilian rule is restored. On other hand, if he acts rapidly to restore civilian rule he and military will be credited for having preserved order and constitutional government.

His action in removing six-man council and setting up new council evidently under his control is compelling us to reconsider entire range of our political and economic policies toward DR. Raises such basic questions as recognition of government established by apparently unconstitutional means; desirability and legal possibility, under existing circumstances, of authorizing further purchases under windfall quota,

---

Source: Department of State, Central Files, 739.00/1–1762. Secret; Niact; Limit Distribution. Drafted by Goodwin and Crimmins, cleared by McGhee, and approved by Ball.

which once lost cannot be recaptured by DR; and desirability furnishing economic and military assistance. You may indicate that we are giving serious study to immediate withdrawal AID mission currently in DR, and plans for military assistance now in abeyance. In this discussion, you may draw on substance your conversation with General after your visit San Juan.

You should add that, although we have taken note his anti-Communist statements and his intention have Punta del Este delegation[1] take firm anti-Castro stand, we are convinced his actions which appear constitute military coup without any popular support will strengthen Castro-Communists in DR, drive moderate opposition in desperation into alliance with them, and gravely weaken, if not destroy, effectiveness posture at MFM of GODR. You should state that several democratic nations hemisphere will almost certainly raise present Dominican situation at MFM, including civil rights situation, particularly arrests and deportation non-Communist leaders. You may draw parallel between current situation and that created by return Hector and Arismendi.

You should state our belief best solution present situation would be restoration former Council under presidency Bonnelly. This return status quo ante would enable us proceed with programs already at point execution. At minimum, solution must be found that permits genuine participation moderate opposition in government. You should emphasize that we recognize necessity maintenance effectiveness armed forces, and that he may have legitimate basis for fears of future status of armed forces under civilian rule by opposition. Accordingly we prepared assist both sides in working out appropriate guarantees re armed forces role and rights. You may add that as first step this effort we prepared receive from him definition guarantees sought by armed forces. However, we strongly believe his continuance present line action, by setting armed forces against people, can only destroy former, open country to Castro-Communism and thwart indefinitely hopes for orderly progress in DR.

You should also inform leaders moderate opposition who still free (including, as you see fit, Amiama and Imbert) we are attempting restore situation. However, in order have any chance success, our efforts must be accompanied by exercise by them of flexibility and moderation, avoidance provocative actions and recognition necessity for guarantees to armed forces.[2]

Rusk

---

[1] Reference is to the Eighth Meeting of Foreign Ministers of the OAS at Punta del Este, January 22–31.

[2] On January 18 General Echavarría's coup ended when he was arrested by his own men. The original Council of State was reinstated and Rafael Bonnelly was sworn in as its President.

339. Telegram From the Embassy in the Dominican Republic to the Department of State

Santo Domingo, March 4, 1962, noon.

1860. Upon relinquishing responsibility for US-Dominican relations here after nine months, should like record following observations and recommendations:

1. Government of this country is now in hands of moderate, anti-dictatorial and anti-Communist group which if anything is over-friendly to and dependent on US in this age of nationalism. It is accepted or supported by vast majority of politically conscious elements of population as transition to elections at end of year.

2. Sentiment toward US is, on whole, good. US is widely credited with having played key role in ending Trujillo dictatorship and its vestiges and with being principal bulwark against a possible new Communist dictatorship. Active anti-American feeling and actions have been concentrated in juvenile delinquent groups receiving exaggerated publicity in downtown area, whose unrepresentative character demonstrated by recent success of anti-Communist students in gaining control of university. This, however, should not obscure equally important fact that there is deep seated and growing nationalism which resents patronism or bear-hug by US and which could flare up into more active anti-American feeling.

3. Stability of Council of State is reasonably well assured against any direct attempts to overthrow. The extreme left does not have control of or significant influence over labor unions, students or civic organizations, or armed forces and thus does not have instrument to take power. The Union Civica National (UCN) and Partido Revolucionario Dominicano (PRD) which control upwards of 85 percent of organized political party members are both avowedly anti-Communist though some lower echelon leftist infiltration exists in both through country offsetting to some degree government's ineptness to date in internal security matters since destruction Trujillo's security apparatus. The Castro-lining "14 June" party is currently torn by internal dissension though maintaining a high degree of Communist infiltration, while the Castroist MPD is underground with its leader Lopez Molina fugitive from police. However, firm and sometimes unpopular measures will be required by Council of State with US support if sparks of Communist infiltration in this

---

Source: Department of State, Central Files, 611.39/3–462. Confidential. John Bartlow Martin was sworn in as Ambassador to the Dominican Republic on March 2; he presented his credentials on March 9.

volatile transitional period are not to set off a conflagration. Softness and timidity can be fatal.

4. The armed forces profess complete loyalty to constitutional government and to the Council. Experience of General Rodriguez Echavarria's attempted January coup has provided officers corps with convincing evidence that neither Dominican people or USG would support military government at this time. However, armed forces remain uneasy, disoriented, in need of restraining [*retraining*?], reorganization, and some regroupment but most of all in need of feeling that Council State, Dominican populace and USG support them in their constitutional role of preserving security of state. At future date, should civilian government stumble and population become tired of disorders and inefficiency some elements of armed forces will be ready to move in.

5. The economic situation of Dominican Republic is manageable and vigor and imagination can make it into a showcase of democratic as against Communist revolution. Our 25 million dollar credits should tide country over balance payments difficulties caused by Trujillo family's looting. Difficult problem will arise in maintaining internal fiscal soundness in view of $35 million plus (almost quarter of budget) deficit if taxes not raised by May and of wage increase of 100 percent in sugar industry, perhaps 40 percent nationally in what must be greatest redistribution of income this year in any country participating in Alianza para el Progreso. Against manageable danger of inflation, however, must be set politically-stabilizing upspurt in commerce and business.

6. In international relations, present Dominican Government can be counted on to remain firmly aligned with us on key international security questions although it may well have tendency to show token independence on lesser issues and on issues in which developing countries stand against industrialized countries. The success of regime is dependent on cooperation with US and it knows it.

7. I foresee following as areas which will spell success or failure of US policies here:

A. US sugar quota: if US adopts global sugar quota paying world market prices this year, in my judgment results would be psychologically, politically and economically virtually disastrous to our policy objectives here. Even to attempt to press for this would hand Castro/ Communist one thing they most lack, a convincing issue on which to sell Dominican opinion on thesis US is working against Dominican interests and imposing a new, exploiting colonial occupation on country. Loss of sugar income cannot be compensated for [by] government to government loans and grants under Alianza para el Progresso, since sugar industry under new wage structure cannot break even without US premium price.

B. Return of $22 million of sugar preferential "withheld" by USG under sanctions which Dominicans view as being rightly theirs. Dominican opinion across spectrum unlikely acquiesce in "retention" this money and left is sure exploit issue as long as it lasts. As setting country on feet likely cost another $22 million, we would be well advised move forward swiftly to restore this money.

C. Anti-Communist measures. Council of State may hesitate from time to time to take energetic measures to control Communist infiltration and agitation because of public sensitivity to any methods reminiscent of Trujillos. However, a strong hand in this field is a must and GODR will need extensive encouragement and help in reorganizing its security services and policies along modern humanitarian lines within the framework of constitutional democracy adapted to local conditions.

D. Armed forces are in need of immediate US encouragement and help in reorientation and adaption to new missions under Council. Military assistance agreement should be signed early this month, missions arrive immediately afterward, and grant-aid uniforms and other soft goods be airlifted in as soon as possible.

E. Labor organizations are divided and FOUPSA, originally intended as free labor movement, has been infiltrated by anti-American leftist elements at top. Although these have cagily not yet brought in significant number leftists at lower echelons and are strongly opposed by FOUPSA libre, creation of unified, independent and anti-Communist labor movement should be first objective and one from which we should not be diverted because of agitation re AFL–CIO or Embassy personalities or tactics.

While above and other pressing problems will require energetic US actions in coming weeks, leave these responsibilities with basic sense of optimism that both Dominican nation and USG have already demonstrated ability to meet greater challenges in effort thus far successful to prevent reversion to Trujillo-type tyranny or Communist take-over.

Hill

340. Memorandum of Conversation

Washington, April 2, 1962, 3:30–4:22 p.m.

SUBJECT

The Secretary's Conversation with Dr. Jose A. Bonilla Atiles, Dominican Secretary of State for Foreign Affairs

PARTICIPANTS

The Secretary
Dr. Jose A. Bonilla Atiles, Dominican Secretary of State for Foreign Affairs
Mr. Edwin Martin, Assistant Secretary, ARA
Mr. C. P. Torrey, O-in-C, Dominican Republic Affairs, CMA

The Secretary opened the conversation by expressing his appreciation for Dr. Bonilla's helpful position at the Eighth Meeting of Foreign Ministers and Punta del Este and for his more recent initiative in the OAS which resulted in a Resolution calling for fair treatment for the Cuban prisoners captured following the April 17, 1961 invasion of Cuba. Dr. Bonilla stated that he felt it was his duty to initiate action on the latter point and that he intends to try to obtain the same resolution at the United Nations. He said these efforts would be based on humanitarian rather than political grounds. The Secretary commented that Dr. Bonilla's efforts in the UN would be more difficult because of the Afro-Asian countries which have little interest in or do not understand the Cuban problem.

Dr. Bonilla brought up the question of the return to the Dominican Republic of the $22 million in fees levied by the United States against the importation of Dominican sugar in 1960–61 stating that the Dominican Government is under heavy pressure from the Dominican leftists concerning these fees. The Secretary and Mr. Martin explained that the return of the money was complicated by the law suits pending against the United States Government. They stated, however, that the return of the fees was under study and that the money may be made available to the Dominican Government from FY 1963 AID funds.

Dr. Bonilla inquired about the status of the soft-goods which the United States had promised to provide the Dominican armed forces. It was explained to Dr. Bonilla that the shipment was at present in New Jersey awaiting shipment and that it should arrive in the Dominican Republic in a very short time.

Source: Department of State, Secretary's Memoranda of Conversation: Lot 65 D 330. Confidential. Drafted by Torrey and approved in S on April 13. The time of the meeting is taken from Rusk's Appointment Book. (Johnson Library)

The Secretary and Dr. Bonilla discussed briefly the situation in Haiti and Haitian-Dominican relations. Dr Bonilla stated that the situation in Haiti is serious and that the activities of Haitian President Duvalier and former *Trujillistas* in Haiti are a source of great concern to the Dominican Government. Dr. Bonilla said that he is thinking of taking the Haitian problem to the OAS Human Rights Commission but that he would do nothing until the United States has had a chance to consider the situation. The Secretary agreed that the conditions in Haiti are not satisfactory and said that the Department is now studying the situation.

On the general political and economic situation in the Dominican Republic, Dr. Bonilla stated that conditions are slowly improving. He said that the morale of the armed forces is better and that jobs are becoming available to civilians. He said that he wanted the Secretary to understand the problems involved in holding elections in December of this year as now scheduled. Dr. Bonilla said that there are now five main political parties in the Dominican Republic—the National Civic Union, the Dominican Revolutionary Party, the 14th of June Party, Dominican Revolutionary Vanguard, and the Revolutionary Social Christian Party—in addition to about fifteen other smaller parties none of which are well organized. He said that most of the parties realize that fair and democratic elections cannot be held this year. He has been authorized by the Council of State to request the same OAS Electoral Committee which visited the Dominican Republic last fall to advise on whether the necessary conditions can be established in time to hold elections this year. He said the Council of State is willing to follow the advice of the Electoral Committee. Dr. Bonilla stated his belief that national elections should be postponed for at least one year to enable elections to be held first for municipal and provincial offices and thereby establish a firm base for a true democracy.

341.   Memorandum of Conversation

Washington, April 4, 1962, 12:56 p.m.

SUBJECT

Dominican Republic: President's Conversation with Dominican Foreign Minister

PARTICIPANTS

For the United States:
The President
Assistant Secretary Edwin Martin,
   ARA
Also present:
Mr. Francisco Aguiere

For the Dominican Republic:
Secretary of Foreign Affairs Bonilla Atiles

In reply to a question by the President as to what the prospects were for elections, Dr. Bonilla replied that at present the situation was confused. He said that he would like the OAS Election Committee to help draft an election law and prepare election procedures. He said that under present conditions the success of elections was questionable. Dr. Bonilla said that he would prefer that elections be held after the Government had made progress in reducing unemployment, improving economic conditions, and in providing housing for peasants under the "Techo, piso y letrina" program.

The President said that he was aware that the present time might be a difficult one for election purposes.

Dr. Bonilla said that the Unión Cívica had originally sought a two-year period before holding elections, but that Balaguer had set the one-year period. He said that the Government's hope was to be able to set up local municipal elections prior to national elections. The work of the Peace Corps would be very useful in preparing for municipal elections.

The President inquired about the work of the Peace Corps in the Dominican Republic. Dr. Bonilla praised Mr. Hernández, Director of the Corps in his country, and said that Mr. Hernández had picked fifteen young Dominicans to study municipal government at the University of Puerto Rico.

The President said that he was interested in seeing that the sugar money should reach the Dominican people, and that the United States was willing to have it reach them through the aid program. He realized the problem of the suit brought by the South Puerto Rican Sugar Company.

Source: Department of State, Presidential Memoranda of Conversation: Lot 66 D 149. Confidential. Drafted by Donald F. Barnes (LS) and approved by the White House on April 16. The meeting was held at the White House.

Dr. Bonilla said that this was more a political than a technical problem for his Government, which was only interested in getting the money as soon as possible. This was important in view of Communist pressure concerning this matter. He said that any solution put forward by the United States Government would be satisfactory.

The President said that if it were said that the money would go to the company, it would mean that $7 million would not reach the Dominican people. He said that the Dominican problem would seem to be met if the United States made this money available to the Dominican people.

Dr. Bonilla said that the Government could exert pressure on the company to prevent this money from being distributed among its stockholders and to have it go to the Dominican people instead. They were under pressure from the Communists to see that this was done promptly.

The President said that the United States, together with the other Governments of the Hemisphere, had taken measures against the previous Dominican Government of its own volition. He said that the United States Government was under no compulsion to pay the subsidy, and had no reason to apologize to the Communists for its stand.

Dr. Bonilla said that in referring to Communist pressure, he had meant that his Government wanted to use the money for the benefit of the people, to improve their standard of living and to reduce unemployment, in order to deprive the Communists of issues they could exploit.

Dr. Bonilla said that with regard to elections, a satisfactory outcome for democracy was in doubt at the present time, in view of emotional pressures on the people and of the need for providing more employment and housing. He said that the outlook for democracy would be brighter if the people had an opportunity to see achievements by the Government before they went to the polls. He said that in any case, he did not want to have in his country anything like what had taken place in Argentina.[1] Dr. Bonilla said that his Government's project was to have elections to local and municipal offices before the Presidential elections, in order to have the people accustomed to casting votes.

The President asked if the people would be opposed to a postponement of Presidential elections, and Dr. Bonilla replied in the negative, adding that this postponement had been requested by the political parties themselves.

The President inquired as to the position of the 14th of June Movement, and Dr. Bonilla replied that it was in open opposition to the Government and was following a Castro line, and that its leaders were pro-Castro.

---

[1] On March 29 the Argentine military replaced the government of President Arturo Frondizi with one led by Senate President Jose M. Guido. See Documents 179 ff.

342. Telegram From the Department of State to the Embassy in the Dominican Republic

Washington, April 4, 1962, 8:32 p.m.

1332. Deptel 1331.[1] In conversations with President, Councillors, leaders moderate parties and possibly military leaders, you should draw on following as appropriate:

(a) As its actions have demonstrated, USG supports and intends continue support present GODR as representing best hope for further progress toward viable free society. FYI. This of course does not imply we committed present composition Council. End FYI.

(b) USG would view with grave concern replacement present Government by elements of, or allied with, far left or far right.

(c) In event overthrow Council from any direction, USG would be obliged reexamine its entire policy toward DR.

(d) In view current uneasy situation created in part by ill-considered and demagogic actions by moderate elements which have only given opportunities for exploitation by extremists, it appears essential these elements, in their own interest and in interest country in general, should assume more responsible attitude.

(e) Instead of exacerbating situation, UCN as principal democratic party has special obligation to follow realistic and moderate course.

(f) While opposition to Government natural and desirable in democratic society, such opposition should be responsible, reasoned and constructive. In present circumstances, neither country nor moderate parties can afford luxury of indiscriminate, destructive attacks against Council nor can Council afford actions of its own which justify such attacks.

(g) In view common interests Council and moderate parties and threat to both from extremes, basic orientation of both should be to seek accommodation of differences rather than magnify them.

(h) Release of energies now expended by Council members in political maneuvering and in defense against attacks from those who should be its friends would permit Council to settle down to task governing country and enable it confront its and country's real enemies.

(i) Violent attacks against armed forces can only increase current tension and impede progress toward acceptance by them of their legitimate role in a free society.

Guidance for speech will follow.[2]

Source: Department of State, Central Files, 739.00/4–462. Secret; Niact. Drafted by Crimmins and approved by Martin.

[1] Dated April 4. (Ibid.)

[2] Printed from an unsigned copy.

343.   Editorial Note

On May 1, 1962, President Kennedy chaired a White House meeting on the Dominican situation according to the President's Appointment Book. (Kennedy Library) Present were Under Secretary of State McGhee, Assistant Secretary of State for Inter-American Affairs Edwin Martin, Ambassador to the Dominican Republic John Bartlow Martin, Rafael Pico, temporary U.S. coordinator of economic aid to the Dominican Republic, Teodoro Moscoso and Newell Williams of AID, [text not declassified] of CIA, and Ralph Dungan of the White House staff. No formal record of the meeting was kept. During the meeting, which lasted from 4:30 to 5:27 p.m., the President inquired about the Dominican sugar quota, the upcoming Dominican elections, the activities of the recently established MAAG in Santo Domingo, and the chances of a military coup in the Dominican Republic. He asked that the Dominican police force receive U.S. instruction in riot control techniques. (Martin, *Overtaken by Events*, pages 121–122)

---

344.   Department of State Policy Directive

PD/ARA–5   Washington, May 15, 1962.

DOMINICAN REPUBLIC: PLAN OF ACTION FOR PERIOD FROM
PRESENT TO FEBRUARY 1963

A.   *Reference:*

National Security Action Memorandum No. 153 of May 15, 1962, Subject: Policy Statement on Dominican Republic.

B.   *Objectives:*

1.   The maintenance of the Council of State in effective power until it is replaced by an elected government;

2.   Control of the threat from the far left (Castro/Communist) and the far right (Trujillistas);

Source: Kennedy Library, National Security Files, Departments and Agencies Series, Department of State Policy Directive, 1961–1963. Secret; Limit Distribution. President Kennedy approved this plan of action at a White House meeting on May 1. It was originally attached to NSAM 153, May 15. (Department of State, NSAM Files: Lot 72 D 316)

3. Resolution of the current Dominican economic and financial difficulties;

4. Sound preparation of the Dominican people for participation in the electoral process.

C. *Plan of Action:*

1. *Immediate* (within 2–4 weeks)

(a) Go beyond the present statement of the U.S. position in the event of the overthrow of the Council to make clear to all concerned, especially key military figures and Amiami and Imbert, that the United States Government would find it extremely difficult to recognize and to provide assistance to any government installed as the result of a coup against the Council.

(b) Advise the Council to proceed carefully on the "purge" of Trujillista elements in the armed forces, to assess closely the risks involved before moving, and to establish if possible a definite cut-off point for a "purge" so as to avoid unnecessary apprehension and consequent reaction among the military.

(c) Continue to press the Council to act on: agrarian reform (if the new law is sound), holding elections as scheduled, and the establishment of a specific administrative entity to receive claims against the Trujillo properties.

(d) Urge the Dominican Government to request the immediate return of an OAS electoral mission whose first task would be to assist in preparations for the August and December elections, and whose subsequent task would be to observe the elections.

—Be prepared to consider very carefully a delay in the elections, if the OAS mission so recommends.

—Be prepared to seek a delay in the elections if it becomes apparent that the results would be contrary to our interests, and attempt to influence the OAS mission in that direction.

—Encourage the political parties to hold their conventions and begin normal political work in preparation for the elections.

—Urge that the Dominican electoral law be so drafted as to avoid the creation of a multi-party system with consequent political fragmentation.

(e) Urge the Council to use the administrative entity set up to receive claims as a means of relieving pressure against it and of avoiding any further claims settlements until an elected government has established a sound procedure for financing payments against claims.

—Advise the Council to announce, simultaneously with the creation of the claims tribunal, that a percentage (perhaps 25 percent) of the net profits, if any, from all the Trujillo properties will be placed in escrow to be used for payments of claims when an elected government has taken the action mentioned above.

—Urge the Council to cease the sale of any Trujillo properties except those which are generally recognized as uneconomic.

(f) Complete immediately the consultations with Congress on the use of AID FY 1963 contingency funds as the equivalent of the $22 million in sugar fees so as to enable Ambassador Martin soon after his return to the Dominican Republic (May 3) to advise President Bonnelly confidentially of the United States Government decision.

—Make no public announcement of the decision before the Dominican reaction is received. (The announcement, which must be carefully worded, should be released simultaneously by Ambassador Martin and AID headquarters.)

(g) [1 *line of source text not declassified*] improve intelligence collection on the activities of the far left and the political attitudes and activities of the military as their highest priority task. [*less than 1 line of source text not declassified*]

—Have the Service Attachés and senior MAAG personnel increase their efforts to gather intelligence on the political activities and attitudes of the Dominican military as their highest priority task.

(h) Assign competent, Spanish-speaking AID experts in riot control procedures to Santo Domingo immediately.

(i) Arrange for a public relations adviser to the Council (preferably, he should be a qualified Latin American under contract to the Council: failing that, an American under contract to the Council; and only as a last resort, an American paid from AID funds).

(j) Take immediate steps to reduce Embassy Santo Domingo's visa backlog to the point where it is no longer a political liability.

2. *Continuing* (present to February 1963)

(a) Promote an agreement between the Council on one side and the UCN and PRD on the other on a minimum program of action by the Council which the parties would at least not oppose. (Such a consensus might encompass initially the principle of agrarian reform, specific economic and social projects under the Alliance for Progress—perhaps with special reference to the $22 million—and the OAS role in the preparations for elections.)

(b) Maintain pressure on the Council to continue to move forward, suggesting new tasks as the Council demonstrates its ability to perform.

—Publicize in the Dominican Republic through U.S. information channels positive accomplishments by the Council.

(c) Begin immediately to develop an anti-guerrilla capability in the Dominican armed forces.

—Bring about a reduction in the size and cost of the Dominican armed forces consistent with the provision of suitable internal security, coastal surveillance and anti-guerrilla capabilities.

(d) Maintain pressure on the Council for prompt action to reduce the budget deficit by sound tax measures and by the elimination of unnecessary expenditures.

(e) Urge the Council to rationalize the present control structure for the Trujillo properties. (An appropriate breakdown would appear to be an agency for the sugar properties, another for non-sugar agricultural lands, another for industrial enterprises, and a fourth for commercial and service enterprises.)

—Arrange for a request from the Dominican Government to the IDB or AID to finance a thorough inventory and analysis, by a first-class U.S. management group, of all the Trujillo properties. (The group would be expected to determine the present condition of each of the properties and its future earning prospects. This report would furnish the factual basis for sound decisions by an elected government concerning the final disposition of the properties.)

—Help the Dominican Government in obtaining technical assistance to operate the properties efficiently, and provide such assistance through AID, if private consultants are not available or desired.

—Discourage U.S. interests from seeking to invest in the Trujillo properties until an elected government has made basic decisions on disposition.

—Discourage U.S. management of (as distinct from technical assistance to) politically sensitive properties such as the sugar holdings, until an elected government has made basic decisions on disposition.

—Keep constantly before the Government the necessity that the properties should be so operated as to maximize the economic and social benefits they can provide the Dominican people whose patrimony they are.

—If, as is likely, the new constitution contains provisions concerning the handling of claims against the Trujillo properties, urge that these provisions be kept general in order to assure the new, elected government maximum flexibility. (Subject to conditions existing at the time of the drafting of the constitution, provision might be made in the constitution for the creation of a claims tribunal or commission which would begin operations under the new government and to which the administrative entity previously set up would turn over the claims it had received.)

(f) Be prepared to meet, and, if necessary, stimulate a Dominican request for a well-qualified adviser for the constitution-drafting process. (The adviser should be a Latin American jurist of suitable experience and acceptable political background. If no appropriate Latin American can be found, any American chosen would have to have extensive background in Latin American constitutional law.)

(g) Be prepared to provide very substantially increased economic assistance to the Dominican Government if, as a result of changes in U.S. sugar legislation, Dominican sugar ceases to earn the U.S. premium price.

—If such changes are not made, impress upon the Dominican Government the necessity for planning its economic and financial policies so as to take into account the temporary nature of the preferential U.S. market.

(h) Country team collaborating with Washington agencies develop promptly an outline of social and economic objectives and specific programs to reach them.

—Allocate responsibility for implementing programs to various agencies cooperating in the Alliance for Progress (AID, IDB, OAS, etc.) and set up mechanism to insure follow through.

(i) Expand, coordinate and improve the technical assistance and training programs of the Alliance organizations in the economic and financial agencies of the Dominican Government, as the priority element of a public administration program.

(j) Continue to press the IMF to raise the Dominican quota in the Fund so as to make available $13.5 million to bolster the Dominican reserve and foreign exchange positions.

(k) Provide AID financing for a privately prepared and presented "political literacy" course to teach, through radio and television, the basic principles and procedures of democratic government.

(l) Continue, with all available means, to control and reduce Castro/Communist influence in the student and labor movements.

(m) Assign without delay one or two political officers to Santiago to cover the important area of political activity centered on that city.

(n) Assure that all U.S. personnel assigned to the Dominican Republic be of the highest quality obtainable.

Action By:

Immediate

Department

(d)—paras 2 and 3
(f),(g)—para 1
(i),(j)

AID

(f),(h),(i)

[*2 lines of source text not declassified*]
Embassy Santo Domingo Country Team

(a),(b),(c),(d),(e),(f),(g),(i),(j)

DOD

(g)—para 2

Continuing

Department

(e)—paras 3 and 4
(f),(g),(h),(j),(m),(n)

AID

(e)—paras 2,3,4,5
(g),(h),(i),(j),(k),(l),(n)

USIA

(b)—para 2
(k),(l),(n)

Embassy Santo Domingo Country Team

All paragraphs

DOD

(c),(n)

[*2 lines of source text not declassified*]

345.   Editorial Note

On May 16, 1962, the Kennedy administration moved to abandon the country quota system for the purchase of sugar abroad by having legislation introduced in the House of Representatives that would establish a world quota system. Negative reaction in the Dominican Republic was immediate and voluble. Dominican sugar had been purchased at a premium price above the world price and its quota had been protected under the current Sugar Act (set to expire June 30). The new legislation would drastically reduce the Republic's quota and profits. On June 15 the House Agriculture Committee, chaired by Harold Cooley, passed its own sugar bill significantly different from the administration's but still unsympathetic to the Dominican Republic.

On June 17 Ambassador Martin spoke with Second Vice President of the Council of State Donald Reid Cabral. Reid said that in the absence of a favorable sugar bill, the Council would cancel all AID agreements made under a $25 million loan the United States had made to the Dominican Government in January. All Alliance for Progress reforms in the country would be suspended. On June 19 the House voted in favor of the Cooley Bill. (Martin, *Overtaken by Events*, pages 161–164)

346.   Telegram From the Embassy in the Dominican Republic to the Department of State

Santo Domingo, June 20, 1962, 5 p.m.

2460. For Assistant Secretary Martin from Ambassador Martin pass to White House. Embtels 2438, 2439, 2444, 2448, 2455 through 2459.[1] Would be difficult to overstate the depth, power and danger of Dominican reaction to the Cooley sugar quota legislation and the continuing uncertainty over the $22 million.

Even our best friends here feel betrayed. They feel the US Executive has, by its promises of help, put them out on a limb—and now Congress has sawed the limb off.

Despite sporadic riots led by leftist agitators, the Dominican people at large are basically friendly to us. They have clung to their somewhat

---

Source: Department of State, Central Files, 411.39/6–2062. Confidential; Niact.
[1] Telegrams 2438, 2439, 2444, 2448, 2455–2459, dated June 18–20, are ibid., 411.396/6–1862 through 411.396/6–2062.

childlike faith in us despite the Marine occupation and what many regard as our support of Trujillo. More, they have looked to us almost desperately for help. They tend toward dependency. Their history since 1844 is replete with their attempts to make themselves the protectorate of a larger power—Spain, France, England, US. This spring their most constant theme has been, "you must help us."

President Kennedy said in January he would. Pico came and did.[2] So did the Embassy. News stories pointed with pride. The shaky Council of State, with our guidance, survived and began to grow stronger. Of late uneasiness has spread because neither Council nor AID has made any improvement in the daily life of ordinary Dominican. To counteract this we had planned to present to Council Friday important program to put Dominican fiscal house in order and crash program in housing and roads to speed progress and create employment during critical September lay-off period. We cannot do so now. For now in the Dominican view the worst has happened: the quota is being cut.

According to Finance Secretary Ramon Caceres Troncoso, proposed quota would reduce GODR revenue this year by RD $20,000,000. This is made up of RD $14,000,000 in reduced income from sugar, estimated RD $5,000,000 from reduced customs duties due to lower imports, and RD $1,000,000 in reduced income from other taxes due to lower level of economic activity. Figures assume that DR expected to sell 950,000 tons to US in 1962, that DR would have received the $22 million in any case, that DR would sell only 175,000 tons to US in the second half 1962, and that prices would be 5.29 cents per pound on US market and 2.66 cents on world market. These estimates depend on costs, and no one really knows what they are. Also they do not allow for shortfalls and may anticipate too low world price. Bramble[3] says the Cooley quota would bring total this year $82,000,000 and shortfalls might raise total to $89,000,000, a reduction of $11 million, not the $20 million Caceres estimated. (A 950,000 ton quota would yield $100 million.) Next year, Cooley quota would yield only $77 million, a drop of $23 million from what Dominicans had expected this year. Whole question of course is greatly complicated by heavy ownership of government itself in sugar industry, a legacy of Trujillo. Bramble concludes overall that the purely economic effects of Cooley quota are not so serious as represented in public statements here. Responsible Dominicans know they must diversify out of sugar. But they need time (5 years, most say).

---

[2] Following its resumption of full diplomatic relations with the Dominican Republic, the United States, through the Agency for International Development, made a loan of $25 million to the Dominican Government. Puerto Rican banker Rafael Pico was sent to administer the aid temporarily.

[3] Harlan Bramble of AID was sent to administer the $25 million loan in late spring.

But economic effects aside, the political effects are all but disastrous.

The Council of State has staked everything on US support. Now that that support has, in Dominican view, been suddenly withdrawn, some Councillors instinctively feel that Council can save self only by setting its face against US and going it alone. Others do not go so far but feel need to somehow disentangle Council from US. Councillors therefore propose to shut the sugar mills, cut wages, tighten belts, and go it alone. They propose to stop—and in fact have already stopped—spending any more of the $25 million US loan made in January on ground they cannot obligate future government to debt it cannot pay since its sugar quota is cut. They propose to repay that portion of the loan already spent from the $22 million. This has not been voted formally by Council but is sense of Councillors and they have already stopped projects. President Bonnelly is attempting stave off formal vote and frozen position. If vote taken now, Council would probably vote to stop projects.

Formal vote or no, this stops Alliance dead. It threatens suicide of Council, since if Council tries to go it alone, it will probably fail. Austerity—isolation policy can bring only more unemployment, misery and unrest. Will open door to left, and if left rises, military right probably would take over. So ends moderate democracy here.

Of course, if AID had gotten off ground and projects were already actually employing people, Council would have difficulty stopping them. But AID has not. So Dominican pressure to continue program—which might be termed by critics only a pile of papers anyway—is likely to be minimal.

But although this amounts to a strike by the Council against the Alliance and against itself, it would be mistake to regard it as calculated attempt to blackmail Congress. Method of going about it refutes that theory. Moreover, explanation lies in Dominican character, history and current political situation. Like children, they feel betrayed, and so are sulking. Danger is their sulk may carry them to suicide. Time and again in their history they have shown unconscious tendency to destroy their country when unable give it away. And they genuinely fear foreign debts, for once foreign debts led to Marine occupation and previously had several times led to deep trouble. In current politics, left has recently made headway with anti-American campaign. Council has resisted, aligning self with US. Now its position has been totally undermined. So is ours. In past when $22 million seemed in jeopardy or when world quota system was proposed, I have reassured Dominicans that US would never abandon DR. These assurances sound hollow now. Our policy has envisaged further loans or grants if needed. Council now would reject further loans and perhaps even grants.

Amid near-panic here, President Bonnelly is attempting to hold firm, restrain impetuous Councillors and get through next 2 weeks. He alone is keeping head.

Best thing that could happen from Dominican standpoint would be stalemate in Senate, with present legislation extended. Impossible estimate effect here if world quota bill wins out. Passage Cooley bill as stands would be disaster. (If Cooley bill fails, we must move with lightning speed to salvage the $22 million provision by separate bill or by immediate (repeat immediate) aid grant, for Dominicans working to defeat Cooley bill overlook fact it alone at present contains their $22 million.)

Whatever happens in Senate, much of the damage done this week cannot be undone. For faith in our support has been eroded, and Dominicans, who thought all would be well when Trujillo fell and thought we would not let them down once they got rid of him, will not now feel quite the same firm faith in us.

We may not like Dominican emotionalism. But all we have here are Dominicans. And it is really too much to expect any people, after 31 years of tyranny, in the world today, with communism on the move, to build democratic society without massive US guidance and support.

We face here dangerous forces. The Castro-Communist forces are mobilizing. The military right is biding its time. Only the Council is on democracy's side. And however much it may fumble and disappoint and irritate us, it is nonetheless democratic government which sees the Dominican future alongside the US. We helped create it. If it falls, we may not get another such chance.

Congressional action on sugar has dealt an extremely heavy blow to our efforts to build democratic bastion in the Caribbean. We could scarcely have handed better weapon to Castro and Moscow. They must be delighted. They have said all along that only bloody revolution, not peaceful democratic evolution, could solve Latin America's problems. To those on sidelines at times like this we must appear to be helping prove them right.

I understand something of complexities and difficulties of sugar legislation. I am confident Congress understands the vital importance to us of this republic in our own back yard. But I wonder if Congress understands fully how seriously its current action is undermining our policy here.

Martin

347. Editorial Note

Ambassador Martin kept President Bonnelly apprised of the U.S. sugar bill as it made its way through Congress. The political repercussions of the legislation were made clear to the Ambassador by Council members Imbert and Amiama who on June 25, 1962, told him that if the sugar problem were not resolved he "had better find them a home outside the Dominican Republic." (Telegram 2486 from Santo Domingo; Department of State, Central Files, 411.396/6–2562) The same day the Senate Finance Committee passed a sugar bill much like the Administration's but which contained a special quota for the Dominican Republic. On June 30 a conference committee sugar bill still unfavorable to the Dominican Republic was passed. On July 2 Ambassador Martin was authorized to make a compromise proposal to the Dominican Government. "It said, in substance, that the conference bill's quota, plus the Cuban windfall, was worth, at current prices, about $31 million less in profit than the Republic would have received [that] year under the present law. President Kennedy, recognizing the special case of the Republic, would undertake to make up the difference—to establish a special economic readjustment fund over three years . . . provided the Consejo [Council] would use this special 'Kennedy Fund' to diversify out of sugar. As for the $22 million, it would be paid as a grant, probably out of AID funds." (Martin, *Overtaken by Events*, page 169) On July 4 a slightly refined proposal was accepted. Ambassador Martin's memoirs trace the progress of the "Great Sugar Crisis" on pages 161–163.

348. Telegram From the Embassy in the Dominican Republic to the Department of State

Santo Domingo, October 15, 1962, 8 p.m.

570. Policy. Reference: Airgram A–173.[1]

Part One: Background

1. Political situation still fluid but developing rapidly. Deadlines approaching. By this Saturday, October 20, any Council member intend-

---

Source: Department of State, Central Files, 739.00/10–1562. Secret; Limit Distribution.

[1] Not printed. (Ibid., PER)

ing run for president or vice president should resign in accordance with gentlemen's agreement among themselves. UCN held national district convention and PRSC organizational convention last weekend. UCN will hold provincial nominating conventions October 19. PRD will hold national nominating convention this Friday–Sunday, October 19–21. All candidates must declare selves by November 5. Political tensions rising. Strikes occurring or threatened various places. Saturday October 13 Fiallo meeting Puerto Plata stoned and UCN photographer shot dead, possibly by sniper actually aiming at Fiallo himself.

2. Cass, Fandino, and I spent long weekend aboard yacht *Exangelita* with President Bonnelly, Imbert, Reid, Freitas, Ramon Caceres, prosecutor Garcia Vasquez, General Luna, Commodore Rib, President's daughter and son-in-law, an Imbert chum, others, and the wives of most. Collective impressions, supported by other recent observations and interviews, are that (a) Imbert and Amiama are in effect virtually running country; (b) Bonnelly knows they are; (c) Bonnelly has not joined them nor begun actively supporting them but probably does not intend oppose them and is only trying maintain tranquility to end; (d) Imbert indifferent to Bonnelly; (e) Bonnelly joins all aboard in appallingly deep contempt [*less than 1 line of source text not declassified*] and all political parties, hardly mentioning Bosch at all; (f) all seem to assume neither Fiallo nor Bosch will become President; (g) Imbert controls police; (h) Imbert controls administration criminal justice; (i) military dislikes Imbert but is afraid of him and unless rapidly stiffened may not stand up to him in any move he may make; (j) Imbert and Amiama maneuvering furiously to try to put together coalition ticket possibly including Vanguardia, Juan Isidro Jimenez Grullon's party, and minor parties; (k) candidate unknown, though Imbert himself, Fernandez Caminero, Tabare Alvarez, and others have been mentioned; (1) Imbert determined not relinquish power in any case; (m) Amiama working with Imbert, though keeping in background; (n) they emerging publicly as strongmen who can maintain order.

3. Military, always the key, has been suddenly deprived of its own defenses and its non-political role by (a) Fiallo's blunder of two weeks ago (Embassy telegram 515)[2] and (b) Bonnelly's blunder in response to that blunder and (c) Bonnelly's semi-withdrawal from power. This appears to give Imbert opportunity to move in on military.

4. Imbert's intentions uncertain except that he does not intend relinquish power. He has several roads open: (a) Put together coalition

---

[2] Not printed. (Ibid., 739.00/10–362) "Fiallo's blunder" refers to Viriato Fiallo's speech of September 30 to the UCN Women's convention in which he said that he had been in contact with senior military figures who had assured him that they would "guarantee" the December elections. Bonnelly, angered, threatened to fire the chiefs of the military services or resign himself.

and try to win or steal the election, or, failing to win or steal, cry "fraud" and knock over winner; (b) abstain from election then confront winner with his control of police and military and demand government posts making his control official; (c) direct coup before or after elections; (d) create sufficient bloodshed and terror in streets and in strikes, with or without help extreme left, to force Council to declare state siege and suspend elections, with possible new Council of State including perhaps himself, Amiama, Bonnelly. He is now trying (a). If it fails, he may try (b). We can probably continue to deter (c). He could try (d) as alternative to (b). Either (b) or (d) would confront us with extremely difficult situation. We do not believe he himself knows just what his moves will be. We had hoped he could reach accommodation with one or, preferably, several parties. But he is not negotiating with them and has indicated to me he will not.

Part Two: Immediate Action

1. In this situation, we can (a) support Imbert; (b) support free election contest between PRD and UCN; (c) stay out completely. I favor (b).

I would much prefer to reach an accommodation with Imbert. But if that proves impossible because he is intransigent and bent on total power, as he seems, I would prefer to oppose him than to yield, even if we lost.

2. After much difficult maneuvering, it now appears possible to hold meeting of Fiallo and Bosch, plus aides, at which they will agree that (a) the loser will support the winner; (b) the winner will permit the loser to exist as loyal opposition; (c) the winner will offer Cabinet posts to the loser. It may prove necessary for me to participate as mediator. If so—but only if my presence is essential—I propose to do this no later than Thursday, October 18. (Imbert and Bonnelly know I favor such an agreement. They consider it impossible.)

3. At this meeting, I would also hope that Fiallo and Bosch could agree on making their best joint offer to Imbert. (They have separately offered him pension, bodyguard, honors. They might go higher but it is doubtful they will give him more than senate seat or ministry without portfolio; and they might not offer that much.)

4. I consider it desirable after this meeting that Imbert understand immediately that this meeting was held, that we support free elections, and that we intend to see that the winner takes office and the loser survives. (Others also should know that this is our position, to avoid any impression we supporting Imbert.)

5. Concomitantly, we will do what we can to make it difficult for Imbert to put together his coalition by trying to keep the lesser parties out of his hands.

6. Obviously I am proposing we stand up to Imbert (since no one else, with possible exception Fiallo, will). To make it stick, we should work to (a) encourage the military to resist any effort by Imbert to enlist them for his cause; (b) give moral support to Bonnelly as he confronts Imbert's increasing encroachment on his power; (c) make clear to all hands, including Imbert and Amiama, that we oppose their taking power and support an honest election between PRD and UCN. Rumor says Imbert is about to remove Rivera Cuesta, commander army. This would increase Imbert's power and fear of Imbert among the officers. I propose we immediately tell military leaders, Imbert, Amiama, and Bonnelly we would look with disfavor upon any further arbitrary changes in high military command before next government takes over. I propose we tell them now that we support free elections, including elections free from pressure by anyone in present government.

7. We shall probably need to take further steps later. These represent what we deem present needs.

Martin

---

349. Telegram From the Department of State to the Embassy in the Dominican Republic

Washington, October 17, 1962, 7:33 p.m.

433. Your 570.[1]

1. On basis your analysis, we concur in course action outlined Part Two reftel. Wish make following comments which you should bear in mind in executing steps called for your plan.

a. Support free election contest between PRD and UCN clearly only one of three alternatives posed which serves our current interests.

b. We consider it essential thwart efforts by Imbert (with or without Amiama) to : (1) interfere with holding of elections; (2) nullify results of elections (if they are satisfactory to us); and (3) dominate elected government.

Source: Department of State, Central Files, 739.00/10–1562. Secret; Niact; Limit Distribution. Drafted by Crimmins and approved by Martin.

[1] Document 348.

c. It is most important Imbert and his associates be informed unequivocally of our position that we support free elections held in as calm an atmosphere as possible, that we intend to see the winner (provided he is not committed to left extremists or Trujillistas) take office, and that we expect to use our influence to see that the elected government can govern free of domination by the military or police or by elements controlling them. It should again be made unmistakably clear to Imbert that we would find it extremely difficult to recognize and provide assistance to any government installed by a coup against the Council or its elected successor. If you consider it helpful, Assistant Secretary Martin prepared go Santo Domingo to reinforce your approaches. In addition, we will work on Freites here on grounds he may be able influence Imbert, his cousin and associate. We believe we should avoid playing too heavily with Imbert and Amiama on theme GODR, Dominican people and parties owe them special debt because of danger this may only confirm intransigency.

d. Our position should also be made known critical elements in Council, parties, military and police.

e. On three-point agreement between UCN and PRD, we assume second point (survival of loser) will be presented not as special concession by winner but as natural feature democratic system. We also hope that Social Christians can still be brought into agreement.

f. Re best joint offer to Imbert, we consider agreement by parties to name him or Amiama Secretary for Armed Forces or Secretary Interior would put elected government at their mercy. We recognize Imbert may not settle for less, in which case clear warning of our general position would be only brake on his plans.

g. Not only should we do what we can to keep lesser parties out of Imbert's hands but we should also try to induce acceptable parties (PNR clearly not acceptable and Vanguardia and perhaps others presumably so) which are potential participants in coalition manipulated by him to align themselves with UCN or PRD. Efforts with Social Christians particularly important, although we assume chances their association with Imbert coalition comparatively small.

h. We believe military should be encouraged to maintain neutrality and to resist not only Imbert's but any other's efforts embroil them in elections. We agree further arbitrary changes military high command should be strongly discouraged. Is Imbert hold over police so strong as to make efforts break or weaken it fruitless?

i. We consider that you should take every appropriate occasion to build up Bonnelly's stature and stiffen his spine gainst Imbert's encroachments. As we read Embassy's reporting, only Council member clearly resisting Imbert is Reid. Can he play any significant further role in our confrontation with Imbert? Where does Pichardo stand in relation to Imbert?

2. Your current estimate voting strength in percentages total vote of UCN, PRD, PRSC, far left (14 June, MPD, PNR, FNR, PSP) and possible Imbert coalition would be very helpful. We recognize, of course, that any such estimate would have to be at best very rough guess subject to substantial change.

Rusk

350. Memorandum From the Deputy Assistant Secretary of State for Inter-American Affairs (Goodwin) to the Under Secretary of State (McGhee)

Washington, December 4, 1962.

[Source: Department of State, Central Files, 739.00/12–462. Secret; Sensitive. 5 pages of source text not declassified.]

351. Airgram From the Embassy in the Dominican Republic to the Department of State

A–261   Santo Domingo, December 9, 1962.

SUBJECT

Interim Political Assessment

[Here follow sections entitled "The Campaign," "Amiama and Imbert," "The Extreme Left," "The Trujillos," and "The Government."]

As to *our own position:* Cuba helped us here, unquestionably. The left faltered, the government rallied, the people applauded. A certain letdown occurred when it became clear we were not going to invade

Source: Department of State, Central Files, 739.00/12–962. Secret; Priority; Limit Distribution.

immediately, as many had at first surmised; but although we have to restrain the warhawks and counsel patience, we have not yet heard accusations of paper-tigerism, and everyone agrees Castro's position has been seriously eroded while the forces of democracy, under firm U.S. leadership, have advanced far.

"U.S. intervention" in Dominican affairs has not yet become an issue in the electoral campaign to any significant extent. We have heard that one candidate, Horacio Julio Ornes, intends to make it so.

Except for support of President Bonnelly, we intend to lie low till after the elections, when we must make clear our support of his successor-elect.

I am encouraging responsible U.S. journalists to come here and cover the elections. We should prod the OAS to send its observors in for the same purpose. In every way possible, we should remind Amiama-Imbert, the candidates, and the Council that the world is watching them these days, and expects them to behave responsibly. Forlorn hope, I fear; but we should try.

In sum, I think we have a reasonably good chance of standing aside while the Republic holds reasonably clean and peaceable elections; I think we shall then face a dangerous interregnum when we must be prepared to move in; and I think we stand a fair to reasonably good chance of getting the president-elect into the Palace without bloodshed.

Summary of Recommendations

1. Except for previous recommendations and commitments, stand aside and let anybody win.

2. Work now among all political parties, military, and government to persuade them to recognize the winner as the president of all the people.

3. Work now to moderate such dangerous issues as de-Trujillization and to stop attempts to lay a foundation for a charge of fraud.

4. Lay plans to make our support of the winner publicly clear immediately the result is known, including perhaps an invitation to the White House.

5. Continue our policy of containing Amiama-Imbert if necessary.

6. Be prepared to give new evidence of our support for Bonnelly.

7. Continue our attempts to frustrate plans of Balaguer, the Trujillos, and Echavarria.

8. Encourage journalists to come here now and to stay.

9. Get OAS observers here for the election.

10. Lie low ourselves till time to congratulate the winner.

John Bartlow Martin

352. Memorandum From the President's Special Assistant (Dungan) to President Kennedy

Washington, January 10, 1963.

Dr. Juan Bosch, the newly elected president of the Dominican Republic (60% plurality), has been visiting the United States since before Christmas. He is now concluding about a week's conversations with various people in Washington, both in and out of the Government.[1]

In general, these conversations have gone very well, particularly those with Government people. I believe that Bosch feels that his reception here has been warm and friendly. I believe that it is accurate to say that most of us feel somewhat tentative about making an appraisal of Bosch at this point. He is undoubtedly sincere about his desire to raise the standard of living of the Dominican people but he does seem to be quite confused on a variety of important points and, most importantly, seems to lack any sense of the administrative or operational difficulties involved in the kind of a program which his philosophic notions indicate are necessary in the Dominican Republic. He appears to be totally bereft of any substantial and well-trained people ranging from public relations advisors to economists and lawyers—it is strictly a one-man show.

From our point of view, there are certain encouraging signs. For instance, he has most strongly indicated his desire to have us assist in the training of his internal security force upon which he places a high priority. He recognizes the danger of Communist subversion and, although he desires to maintain an open society (see comments below on internal security), he does believe in the maintenance of a strong internal security system.

Points which might be brought up by Bosch in your discussion:

1. The Imbert problem

Bosch is very preoccupied with Antonio Imbert who is a member of the Council and, as you will recall, one of the Trujillo assassins. Imbert has been a bad actor during the whole period prior to the election—he has been involved in graft and is driven to assume as much power as he can. He now controls the police but is intensely disliked by the military. He and his cohort, Amiana, have recently been made Generals of the Army. There is a possibility, although I think remote in view of the heavy

---

Source: Kennedy Library, President's Office Files, Countries Series, Dominican Republic, Section B. No classification marking.

[1] In Washington and New York January 4–11, President-elect Bosch met with Secretary Rusk and other State Department officials, members of the Supreme Court, Attorney General Robert F. Kennedy, and, informally, with U.S. Permanent Representative to the United Nations Adlai Stevenson, among others.

vote and the obvious support which Bosch has gotten in the United States, that Imbert might try to take power before Bosch's inauguration on February 27th.

2. *The Internal Security*

In addition to requesting training for his own internal security force, Bosch has requested of the Secretary, Defense and me assistance in a Naval patrol of his northern coast. He is also interested in strengthening the entire guerrilla capability of his Army and the coastal patrol capability of his Air Force.

3. *Economic Aid*

In keeping with his independent attitude, Bosch is not entirely satisfied with our aid program. Naturally, as a politician, he emphasizes strongly impact type projects although, at the same time, he talks very strongly about the need for infrastructure—roads, heavy industry, etc. He has no clear idea of what his priorities are although he quite sensibly will set up a planning board in the Presidency at an early time. He has no idea as to whom he will ask to serve in this capacity.

4. *Standard Oil Refinery*

He may bring up the question of a contract between the Council and Standard of New Jersey to build a refinery. This contract, he maintains, he will have to overturn. We are already working with him and Standard to see if this potential trouble spot can be moderated.

RAD

353. Memorandum of Conversation

Washington, January 10, 1963, noon.

SUBJECT

    Conversation Between the President and Dr. Juan Bosch, President-Elect of the Dominican Republic

PARTICIPANTS

U.S.	Dominican Republic
The President	Dr. Juan E. Bosch
Mr. Ralph Dungan—Special Assistant	
Assistant Secretary Martin—ARA	
Ambassador Duke—U/PR	
Mr. Van Reigersberg—LS	

The President congratulated Dr. Bosch on his campaign victory.

Dr. Bosch replied that it was now up to the new Administration to prove to the people and to the whole hemisphere that democracy really works. He briefly analyzed his political campaign, stressing its educational contents and objectives. He said that, economically, the situation in the Dominican Republic was better than that of other countries since its balance of payments situation was good and its public financial standing reasonably sound. He added that the main problem was the lack of "working capital" which is needed to increase employment and production as soon as possible. He described himself as "cautiously optimistic" with regard to the economic future of his country.

The President asked what the United States could do to assist the Dominican Republic.

Dr. Bosch responded with a strong endorsement of the Alliance for Progress, emphasizing the value of its long-term goals. He noted, however that the country had short-term needs as a result of unemployment, under-investment, a lack of farm-to-market roads and inefficient and slow production. Continuing, he said that if the Dominican Republic could obtain from 35–40 million pesos (1 peso is equal to $1) to begin with, it would be able to handle effectively most of these problems. He referred to the inflationary pressures that would be created by the recent increase in the Dominican budget from 136 million pesos to 168 million pesos, while production remained static. Clearly, production must be increased substantially. Dr. Bosch cited a recent conversation with the Director of the Dominican Agricultural Bank who had suggested that he needed from 20–24 million pesos for small loans to farmers, whereas the

Source: Department of State, Central Files, 739.00/1–1063. Secret. Drafted by Crimmins and Van Reigersberg. Approved in the White House on February 15.

bank had only 9 million pesos. He pointed out that during 1962, the Agricultural Bank, with the assistance of the Inter-American Development Bank, had made 47,000 loans of 100–250 pesos each for a total of 11 million pesos. Dr. Bosch argued that although five million pesos had not yet been recovered and this might appear as a loss to the bank, it also represented a net gain to the people. If the bank were to operate at a level of 24 million pesos, it could make 100 thousand loans in 1963, and while it might lose from 6–8 million pesos, the people would gain 18 million pesos. He indicated that he realized that the Alliance for Progress did not intend to lose money, but that, in certain circumstances, money had to be lost as had been the case in the United States during the first Franklin Roosevelt Administration, when the Treasury lost money but the American people had gained it.

The President observed that the Dominican Republic was now getting some 40 million pesos in loans and grants and asked whether this assistance was effective enough.

Dr. Bosch replied affirmatively, but declared that most of it was devoted to long-term projects. Two million pesos he said, had been devoted to small loans to farmers but more money would be needed to satisfy the farmers' need for credit. He referred to his conversations with Mr. Moscoso and indicated that there appeared to be a possibility that 12 million pesos out of the 22,750,000 pesos grant could be set aside for small farm loans. He added that although he had not yet received a final answer from Mr. Moscoso, he expected it to be favorable.

The President briefly discussed the American balance of payments problem and the sizable gold and dollar drain of the last few years. The United States, he said, finds it easier to provide assistance that does not represent a net gold loss. Therefore, loans devoted to the construction of roads are more difficult to provide.

The President then asked what would happen to the former Trujillo properties.

Dr. Bosch stated that the sugar mills would be placed in the hands of the workers and administered through cooperatives. He expressed concern about the sugar situation and the gradual decrease in preferential prices on the U.S. market. He commented that the basic property question was complicated by such factors as the high cost of Dominican sugar production, world competition, domestic corruption and the Dominican people's firm belief that the properties should not return to private hands. He added, that each enterprise would be considered on its own merits. He stated that some of the Trujillo land would be administered by the Development Corporation, some would be devoted to the agrarian reform program and some would be placed in the hands of the Property Recovery Ministry. He explained that the measures to be taken would have to be eclectic. The guiding philosophy would be that while these properties should not be in government hands, they could not be in private hands, therefore, they would be run "in a way that is similar to that of a private enterprise which is not completely private."

The President inquired as to the military needs of the Dominican Republic.

Dr. Bosch indicated that he needed equipment and training scholarships for members of the Armed Forces. Specifically, he said that there was a need for patrol vessels and Grumman (amphibious) aircraft for coastal surveillance, and helicopters for transporting troops into mountainous areas where roads were not available. The number of helicopters, he added, could be small. Dr. Bosch insisted that the U.S. Military Mission could and should play a vital role in stressing to their Dominican counterparts the need to support democracy. This concept should be extended to the police whose situation was very delicate. He pointed out that police strength had more than doubled since Trujillo's time so that it now includes some 15,000 members. This expansion, he stated, had been the result of General Antonio Imbert's desire for power and of his need for a group of armed men who will be personally loyal to him. In this connection, Dr. Bosch declared that the police item in the new budget had been increased by $10 million over 1962. Dr. Bosch stated that the most delicate and urgent task for his administration would be to reduce the size of the police force and to appoint new leaders for it. He recognized that this might well lead to a crisis, and, if so, the sooner it came the better. In Dr. Bosch's judgment, Imbert considers himself the natural heir of Trujillo not only as a political leader but also with respect to his wealth, methods and allegiances.

Returning to military needs, Dr. Bosch stated that the Armed Forces also need communication equipment, such as micro-wave and telephone facilities, and transport. He pointed out that he wants to decrease the number of men in the Armed Forces and increase their efficiency. In this context, he referred briefly to the very bad situation in Haiti and to President Duvalier's readiness to destroy everything he has rather than to act rationally.

The President asked whether the military forces were stronger than the police.

Dr. Bosch replied that the police, spread out in the countryside, were in close touch with the people and that the armed forces were on their best behavior and very discreet. He explained that there was nothing intrinsically wrong with the police unless they are used by Imbert to further his own ambitious purposes. Commenting that the whole question was an internal political affair, Dr. Bosch expressed the belief that he could cope with it.

[Here follows discussion of the proposed Standard Oil refinery in Santo Domingo and of Cuba.]

354.   Airgram From the Embassy in the Dominican Republic to the Department of State

A–308   Santo Domingo, January 13, 1963.

SUBJECT

U.S. Policy in Dominican Republic

The year 1962 was a critical one in Dominican history and for our policy in that country. This is a recap on 1962 and a look ahead at 1963—at what lessons we can derive from past crises, at what future problems may arise. (It is written without knowledge of what happened when Mr. Bosch went to Washington. I assume the Department will wish to assess his visit and may want to put this local piece into the assessment pot.)

Results: 1962

We started the year with three basic objectives—to keep the provisional government in power, to hold free elections, and to install the winner in the Palace.

We have accomplished the first two. As of now, the prospects for the third are good.

We can take some satisfaction in these results, considering that they were constantly imperiled by the Castro-communist left and the Trujillista right, that they had to be undertaken in the enormous vacuum created by the crashing fall of Trujillo, that there was almost nothing but wreckage and rubble to build on—a stagnant economy a looted treasury, vast unemployment, no free voluntary institutions, no democratic tradition, few experienced people in government, an ignorant submerged populace, and a miasmatic fear which prevailed everywhere, for Trujillo had destroyed people's confidence in each other and in themselves.

[Here follow sections entitled "The Council of State," "Crises and Lessons," "Successes and Failures," "The Election's Meaning," "Bosch's Opportunity," and "The Opposition."]

Our Role—and Our Dangers

We have a whole new ballgame. We may have as many problems now as under the provisional government—but they will be different problems. (Of one thing we can be sure: we can never really predict what our problems will be. Who would have thought that the only bloodshed of this year would have been the Palma Sola massacre? Incidentally, I do not think we have heard the last of that sect.)

Source: Department of State, Central Files, 611.39/1–1363. Secret; Priority; Limit Distribution. Drafted by J.B. Martin.

The perils from left and right that plagued the Council are likely to subside for a time in the face of Bosch's mandate—unless he stumbles badly and loses popular support. Then look out.

This seems unlikely to happen soon, perhaps not this year. Therefore, our real problem is the PRD and Bosch himself. We do not know nearly enough about them—especially about the party directorate, the provincial leaders, the candidates, the Senators, the Deputies, and the local leaders of the PRD. We do not know whether Bosch has commitments to the extreme left.

It seems to me that Bosch presents us with several possible dangers. I am aware that our agencies have been checking on Bosch and Miolán[1] for many years. But after Castro, nobody can ever be really sure of anything. So I would list all these as possible dangers:

1. That Bosch has been a deep-cover communist for many years.

2. Ditto Miolán.

3. That Bosch and Miolán might lose control of the PRD to the Castro-communists. (But Miolán is a pro, thank God.)

4. That for unforseeable reasons Bosch might turn toward support of Castro.

5. That Bosch's campaign demagogy might turn into presidential charlatanism, transforming him ultimately into a personal homegrown nationalistic extremist who, though neutral and not tied to Havana or Moscow, would almost surely be anti-American as well as ruinous to the Republic. (I can easily envisage his using us as a whipping boy if things go wrong. He must maintain the underdog role to hold the masses. And having smashed the oligarchs, and being afraid to whip the military, he can only turn on us.)

6. That Bosch, a plunger, might miscalculate, lose a fight, and resign.

How do we defend against these possibilities? I think we do several things. We hang onto the military. We save Imbert and Amiama as an ace in the hole. And of course we do all the nice things to build for the future and strengthen democratic institutions—Peace Corps, CARE, CARITAS, schools, university, voluntary institutions, all by way of going over the head of the government to the people themselves, to align ourselves with them. We should, of course, support Bosch until he goes wrong. We should help him lead, should never impede, his advance into his own revolutionary new frontier. We should hope he goes straight, and takes the people with him, and us too.

But if he ever goes wrong—and I mean if his basic loyalties ever belong to another country than his own—we had better have the military

---

[1] Angel Miolán, Party Chief of the Parti Revolucionario Dominicano.

on our side and, if it happens soon, Imbert and Amiama as well. That might pit us against the people, and the results would not be pretty to contemplate. But we can have no new Castro in the Caribbean.

Let me say at once I do not believe this will happen. But I think we would be foolish to ignore the possibility.

Meanwhile, we should tie him so closely to us that he cannot wriggle loose. At the same time, however, we should try to avoid tying ourselves too tightly to him—should not build him up too much, should not bet on him too heavily, should not propagate the idea that the Alliance is sure to succeed here if anywhere. The prospects here seem dazzling—but we must not be bedazzled, for the inherent difficulties are still enormous. Let us not, and let us hope the Dominican people will not, repeat the mistake of a year ago. All the Republic's problems were not solved because Trujillo fell. Nor are they solved because Bosch won. In every province, in every town, in every village, in the Dominican character itself, you can see the ruin Trujillo wrought. You do not repair in one year, nor perhaps in five, the ravages of 31 years. And we do not yet really know whether Bosch is up to the task at all.

We rejoice, with the people, at the victory of the people's hero. We are grateful for his strengthening the democratic left in Latin America. We can work with him, and we will. But we must not forget what we know about him—[5-1/2 lines of source text not declassified]. He won—but he is still the same man. As a candidate, he was an enigma. As a president, he is an unknown quantity.

All this means, I suggest, that we avoid in the American press over-optimistic statements about the prospects here. It means that in the Dominican press we express our confidence in the future of Dominican democracy and our support for Bosch in his efforts to build a better life for his people.

Moreover, it means we really do support him here. I consider that during the months ahead the emphasis of our work will shift from the political to the economic. Alongside Bosch, the Alianza should do better than alongside the Council of State—the Council was a semi-caretaker, and its oligarchs shrank from some Alianza goals. Tactically, however, I believe we must guard against smothering Bosch with advice and help. We should offer him everything—and not press too much on him. He reacts badly to pressure—though he will take it if forced to in a real crisis. At least at the outset, he will not operate as the Council did, seeking our help at every turn. A prima donna, he will try to do it himself, suffering us to assist. We should accept this role gracefully. And when he makes mistakes and comes to us for advice, we should give it in a spirit of magnanimity.

None of this will be easy. But if we can help him pull it off, we can create a better life for the Dominican people and a modest triumph for ourselves in the Caribbean.

John Bartlow Martin

---

355. Telegram From the Department of State to the Embassy in the Dominican Republic

Washington, January 19, 1963, 8:05 p.m.

682. During Bosch conversations in Washington (full accounts being pouched) it became evident he and his associates have not yet developed concrete plans for positive action in economic and social field to be put into effect upon assumption power. Bosch, however, extremely conscious need make maximum impact immediately. When pressed for info, Bosch usually limited himself to reference to various portions PRD program of govt. which as Embassy knows is little more than generalized statement broad intentions.

As result our concern that in absence establishment of at least basic outlines specific programs new government will flounder about badly in critical initial period, and in order seize opportunity that planning vacuum affords us to shape Bosch course, further conversations were held in New York in effort pin Bosch down and get him and associates started on hard task of getting concrete plans in condition for execution very early in new administration.

Bosch agreed to our assisting him officially or unofficially in at least blocking out plans for action in major fields, although he remained quite vague regarding his own ideas on actual targets and priority among them.

Specifically Bosch agreed to having technical advisers made available from US to PRD "planning committee" to work on plans in several areas. He stipulated that association these experts (who might come from Embassy or AID mission Santo Domingo, USG agencies here or pri-

---

Source: Department of State, Central Files, 739.00/1–1963. Secret; Priority. Drafted and approved by Crimmins and cleared by Dungan and S/S.

vate sources) with PRD "planners" would have to be handled carefully and quietly, that joint group would not discuss plans with or request any assistance from present government except as agreed by Miolan and that consequently group would have to rely largely on published data and resources Embassy and AID Santo Domingo. He said he would inform Miolan of this understanding and instruct him to take personal charge PRD side joint effort. Embassy/AID would be expected use Miolan as point contact this undertaking.

Since New York talks[1] we have learned Bosch has taken to Europe with him Mario Diza, Venezuelan official IDB who has been in Santo Domingo working with Banco Agricola. Diaz designated by Felipe Herrera following Bosch request for economic advisor. Not clear whether he supposed provide general economic advice or deal only with agricultural credit. In addition, Bosch made number approaches various international agencies and private groups (including foundations) for technical assistance. Although precise nature and status these requests not clear, most if not all, will take effect only in post-inauguration period.

While we recognize great difficulties (not least of which is uncertain qualifications PRD personnel) in working this out in short time before inauguration, we consider it essential in our own interest that vigorous effort be made. We prepared take special steps to carry out our part arrangement.

On basis Bosch statements and our own appreciation requirements, we believe areas listed below should be attacked by joint group. Country team requested provide own views soonest on general concept, suggested areas, and personnel and information resources available in Country Team to meet requirements. In its evaluation, Country Team urged indicate other areas, even if outside present AID programs, which in its judgment should be given higher priority attention by Bosch administration. In reviewing list, Country Team should assume no increase present or projected FY 64 funding levels.

On receipt these comments, which should be furnished by opening business Jan 22, we will revise list and instruct Embassy approach Miolan referring to New York understanding, offering proposed list as reflection New York talks, and stating our desire and readiness to meet Bosch's request for cooperation. Meanwhile, we will be arranging for experts on standby basis.

Suggested list follows:

1. *Impact programs:* As indicated above, Bosch wants be able announce immediately impact program or programs that would give substance to his promises of improved economic and social levels.

---

[1] See footnote 1, Document 352.

Tended emphasize road construction (particularly farm-market) on which he said PRD engineers in Ministry Public Works have necessary data. Hopes be able cite on inauguration specific links to be constructed. Also wants put into immediate effect "people's dining room" idea.

2. *Public finances:* Bosch very concerned short-term difficulties this sector: IMF debt, commercial arrears, sharp increase in FY 63 budget, large internal debt which he believes to be 41 million, and Central Bank policies (compounded in his view by antonomy issue). Appears recognize need advice in developing coordinated policy in budget, currency and foreign exchange management and in tax reform and collection. (Has arranged for IBM survey of possibility mechanization revenue collection and expenditure control.)

3. *Agrarian reform:* Bosch acknowledges progress made but wishes step up pace. Wants exempt grazing, mineral and coffee lands from reform in order promote diversification.

4. *Trujillo properties:* FYI. This not specifically agreed to and represents our own suggestion. End FYI. Bosch intends use non-sugar land in agrarian reform program, with sugar properties organized along cooperative lines. Wants use best Puerto Rican experience in sugar coops.

He is very indefinite on industrial and commercial enterprises except for general emphasis on cooperative approach. Claims he wants government out of business.

5. *Diversification:* Heavy Bosch emphasis on development cattle and minerals industries, with accompanying technical skills (e.g. veterinarians). Considerable but less emphasis on poultry and fishing industries. (Made formal request for 26 Peace Corps Volunteers to assist in developing fishing.)

Rusk

356.   Memorandum Prepared in the Central Intelligence Agency

OCI No. 1564/63   Washington, June 14, 1963.

PRESIDENT BOSCH AND INTERNAL SECURITY IN THE
DOMINICAN REPUBLIC

President Juan Bosch of the Dominican Republic rightly considers that he has a popular mandate to bring about a radical transformation of political, economic, and social conditions in the Dominican Republic. He hopes to accomplish this purpose by such measures as agrarian and tax reform, economic development primarily through private foreign investment, and a more equitable distribution of earnings than has been the case hitherto.

There is currently under way a concerted campaign to discredit Bosch by charging that he is himself a crypto-Communist engaged in establishing a Communist dictatorship, or else that his ineptitude will lead to a Communist take over in the Dominican Republic. Manifestly, this campaign represents the reaction of vested interests who see their privileged position threatened by Bosch's revolutionary purposes. It also reflects genuine concern regarding Bosch's remarkably tolerant attitude toward Communist activities.

With reason, Bosch believes that the principal immediate threat to the accomplishment of his mission is the possibility of a reactionary coup. In this context, he has not hindered Communist organizational and agitational activities, so long as the Communists have avoided direct interference with him. He argues that to crack down on these activities would only precipitate a campaign of urban terrorism and guerrilla resistance like that in Venezuela, which would hinder the accomplishment of his constructive purposes.

Bosch understands that the security of his regime depends ultimately upon continued US support, particularly as a restraint upon the Dominican military. At the same time, he is nationalistic, egotistic, and aware of the political inexpediency of appearing to be a US puppet. Consequently, he is not readily amenable to US advice regarding his policy with respect to Communist activities.

The Communist danger in the Dominican Republic is not immediate, but potential. It is none the less serious. Given present freedom to organize and agitate, the Communists will become better prepared to exploit some future opportunity. If Bosch should fail to satisfy the expectations of the Dominican masses, or if he should be overthrown by

---

Source: Kennedy Library, National Security Files, Countries Series, Dominican Republic, June 14–July 31, 1963. Secret.

a reactionary coup, the Communists would have an opportunity to seize the leadership of the popular revolutionary movement. This does not mean that they would directly come to power—the Dominican military have the will and ability to prevent that for the foreseeable future. It does mean that the Communists would have gained the advantage of identification with the popular side in a continuing class struggle.

[Here follows a table of basic facts on the Dominican Republic.]

357. Airgram From the Embassy in the Dominican Republic to the Department of State

A–131   Santo Domingo, September 22, 1963.

SUBJECT

Six Months in a Qandary

[Here follow 13 pages concerning the domestic politics of the Dominican Republic.]

What Next

We are entering—indeed, we are in—quite a delicate period. Bosch has to decide whether to try to regain the initiative by enacting serious substantive legislation at this time—high political legislation that would redistribute wealth (or at least appear to do so, such as land expropriation), and/or put people to work—or, alternatively, whether to lie low a while longer (as he has been doing in the last few weeks.) He has to take this decision at a time when unemployment is high, the cost of living is high, and the military is restless. It is not an easy decision, and probably will depend on his estimate, on returning, of the military problem.

If he should show signs of trying to regain the initiative by spectacular revolutionary legislation, such as land expropriation, I intend to exert what influence I can to avoid explosions both here and in the United States. In this connection, a long memorandum from Abram Chayes[1] will be very helpful—and I may need more help if things really seem to be headed that way.

The Prospect Before Us

As of now, we have a hard way to go, for we confront Bosch's personality, the long-run leftist threat, the imminent rightist danger, and the

---

Source: Department of State, Central Files, POL 2 DOM REP. Secret; Air Priority; Limit Distribution. Drafted by J.B. Martin.

[1] Reference is to the Legal Adviser to the Department of State. No memorandum was found.

problems endemic in the Republic. And we confront our own limitations, principally in two areas: Financial assistance (AID and Congress), and intelligence (CAS).

I think the difficulties are likely to increase in the next two months. Seasonal unemployment is upon us, and we have done little or nothing to help. It will get worse. Military pressures are rising.

I think if Bosch survives this calendar year, he may survive for four—but I emphasize: Prediction beyond tomorrow is ridiculous in this country.

I think that at best his tenure is likely to be a holding operation—not the peaceful democratic revolution we had hoped, certainly not the "showcase" some had advertised.

Although in the present political milieu it is difficult to envisage what comes after a four-year term for Bosch, I think we should regard Bosch's government as a transition government. Under him we will likely never really make a nation here. But we should try to lay the groundwork for one.

Our Present Position

In spite of everything, I continue to believe at this time that our interests lie in supporting the Bosch Government. It is non-communist, tied to the West, friendly to the United States; it is committed to the principles of the Alliance for Progress (though Bosch blows hot and cold in public on the Alianza); it is the freely elected and the constitutional government; it respects individual liberties, human rights, and freedom of expression.

Furthermore, the alternatives are unacceptable.

I agree fully with Deptel 172[2] and have for the second time laid down its line to all Embassy section chiefs and mission component chiefs.

We are paying something for holding firmly to our position.

Some individuals in the mission disagree with it. (I have no firm evidence that any are downright disloyal to it, though Bosch tells me some members of AID and MAAG are. I have told him if he gets me a name and proof, I will send the individual home. I have discussed the question with the AID and MAAG chiefs, and they are cooperative.)

A good many American private citizens think we are mistaken (or worse).

The attachés report that increasingly the Dominican military will not talk to them, since they simply replay the record: "We support constitutional government." We are arming the attachés with economic and political facts for rebuttal.

---

[2] Dated September 13. (Department of State, Central Files, POL 26 DOM REP)

I have, as said above, been attacked publicly as a communist. (Other mission members have been accused privately.)

It is becoming increasingly difficult for us to get information out of opposition political leaders and out of the important business-professional group.

All this is not to say that we are now isolated. We have good ties to the oligarchy; good ties to the PRD; good ties to the PRSC; reasonably good ties to the labor movement; reasonably good ties to the military (I think); good ties to Bosch and his government. We are weak with students, campesinos, the far left, the far right, and some important business-professional men.

There is no question that we are losing contacts and even some support. (So are the Nuncio and others who work with us.) But we are far from isolated.

What I hope to do is to split off the rightist extremists now, while they are active, and the leftists extremists later, when they become active, leaving Bosch and me a broad center. This is probably an unattainable ideal; but it's worth a try.

There have been for months almost no signs of anti-Americanism. I regard this as ominous; it simply confirms my view that the Castro/communist left as going along with Bosch and, so, with us. To gain time, they will permit him short-term victories over FENEPIA and the Electricidad and short-term association with us. When it behooves them, they will move hard. I would like to precipitate this, unless unemployment worsens seriously.

Our ability to influence events is probably waning. It was far greater in 1962 than in 1963—memories of the fleet (November, 1961) and the Echavarria coup (January, 1962) were fresh; we had helped install the provisional Council of State and everyone knew it. But today, time has passed, memories of 1961–2 are fading, and, moreover, Bosch was not installed by us, he was elected by the Dominican people. So, as time passes, our influence declines. And events elsewhere—Peru, Guatemala, Cuba, and, especially, Haiti—tend to undermine our influence here, for regardless of whether our policies in those places were wise, Dominicans see them as evidence of our growing reluctance to send the fleet.

Nevertheless, barring some reckless adventure, anyone who thinks to overthrow Bosch will, if he takes thought at all, find himself obliged to consider our views in advance. If he has a map.

In the final analysis, our ability to influence events here depends upon our willingness to bring the fleet to the horizon. By saying this, I do not mean we are at that point, or near it. I do mean to say that it was one thing to bring the fleet to eject the Trujillos; it would be quite a different thing to bring the fleet to stop an anti-Bosch coup. Unhappily, things are not so simple as of yore.

Simple or not, I reiterate that I believe at the present time that our policy interests are best served by maintaining Bosch in power. (A contingency paper accompanies this piece.)[3]

Recommendations

As a general policy, I believe that we should recognize Bosch is not much of a president, that we should recognize most of his opposition is almost equally incompetent, and that we should attempt to take his government away from him, insofar as possible. This involves what amounts to an extension of activist diplomacy. That is to say, we should woo his own supporters, ministers, and advisors ardently; use every means—or *almost* every means—to get rid of those whom we cannot control; exert every pressure to put our own people close to him and the other levers of power and, to the extent possible, though these people run his government without his knowing it. (Carried to its furthest length, this would mean subverting his government. That would require a most elaborate clandestine apparatus. Even should we decide to give this country the highest priority in Latin America, I doubt we could do it. And even so, such a policy would entail grave risks, enormous difficulties, and considerable likelihood of failure.) Nevertheless, somewhere short of such an elaborate exercise lies an extended activist diplomacy that should be possible now.

I recommend that we:

1) Move immediately on intelligence problem as I outlined in my recent [*less than 1 line of source text not declassified*] telegram.[4]

2) Step up immediately our [*less than 1 line of source text not declassified*] effort. It is not good enough. We do not know enough about the far left, the ministries, or the military. We are preoccupied by Haiti. I continue to believe, as I have said previously, that our single most urgent need here is for surveillance of the left now and [*less than 1 line of source text not declassified*], for it is our only safeguard against communist infiltration. I welcome the advent of the [*less than 1 line of source text not declassified*].

3) Make every effort to split [*2-1/2 lines of source text not declassified*].

4) [*1-1/2 lines of source text not declassified*]

5) [*less than 1 line of source text not declassified*]

6) Identify people and elements of the other shattered parties with the hope that we can build an alternative party. [Action] Embassy.

---

[3] Not found.

[4] Not further identified.

7) Survey and, if feasible, develop the Yaque del Sur, as envisaged in Embtel 236 and Deptel 154.[5] I feel very strongly that TVA should take this on and it should become ours. We badly need a major U.S. project here. And the people here need the valley.

8) Get AID approval if possible, at least on a standby basis, of either the $15 million or the $ 17 million loan applications. Action AID/W.

9) Kill Luna's Hawker–Hunter deal. Action Embassy.

10) Get coastal patrol boats. Action Embassy MAAG/SD, Dept/DOD.

11) Get MAAG agreement ratified. Action Embassy.

12) Straighten out Haina. I will keep pressing Bosch on this. If he asks us for technical help, I may want to request a change in our former policy preventing U.S. management of ex-Trujillo properties. Action Embassy.

13) Get hold of the only three really strong men I have been able to identify in the Republic—Wessin y Wessin, Imbert, and Miolan. Action Embassy.

14) If travel between here and Moscow, Havana, or Prague increases, I propose to press Bosch hard to stop it, pointing out that it contravenes United States policy and is very dangerous to his own government. Action Embassy.

15) Press Bosch to close Dato Pagan's school. Action Embassy.

16) If Bosch tries to regain the initiative through legislation involving private property, I intend to exert what influence I can to avoid explosions both here and in the U.S. Action Embassy.

17) Work for establishment of a Dominican Peace Corps. Action Peace Corps and AID, Washington.

18) Watch Haiti. Action Embassy–[*less than 1 line of source text not declassified*] and Washington.

19) Work to help the Parvin Foundation carry out its program. Action Embassy.

20) Try continuously to get better people into the Bosch Government. Action Embassy.

21) Perhaps bring the Boxer in and take Bosch and his military aboard for lunch as splashy evidence our support.

Tactics

As above, I recommend a stepped-up effort at activist diplomacy. I envisage this as a long-range policy, something we will have to pursue for the forseeable future, perhaps even throughout Bosch's term.

---

[5] Embtel 236, September 11, not printed. (Department of State, Central Files, POL 15–1 DOM REP) Telegram 154, September 4. (Ibid., AID (ALLIANCE FOR PROGRESS) DOM REP)

However, in the short run, as a temporary policy tactic, I am inclined to think we should, in the near future, execute briefly a contrary policy of pulling out. Let me explain.

Right now things seem to be stuck on dead center, with opposing forces in balance and at stalemate. Our influence appears in danger of waning, in part because we have so continuously exerted it in the last 2-1/2 years. Perhaps if we were to withdraw for awhile, the contentious Dominicans might all surrender to each other. They look to us too much. We are a lightning rod. And our continual intervention gives them a sense of importance they do not intrinsically possess or deserve. Tensions get screwed tight in part because of our presence. They have no conception of what our withdrawal, our relaxation of pressure, would do. I think they would be shocked. I think they would miss us. They might even come to us. I would like to give them a taste of it.

Therefore, once we get through, say, the next month, I think we should seriously consider a sudden tactical withdrawal. I want first to set in train certain of the above recommendations—[*less than 1 line of source text not declassified*], the TVA–Yaque del Sur, the patrol boats, Luna's Hawker Hunter fighter deal. This done, we might execute a sudden tactical pullback—adopt a policy of hands-off for a period of, say, three or four weeks or even longer. It would deprive both left and right of a target, force the military to look to its own problems; and might even force Bosch to govern.

To be effective, this policy would have to go all across the board— MAAG, AID, USIS, Embassy (not CAS or Peace Corps). For several weeks, we would all just stop pressing. The public symbol of this policy would be my own departure. I could accept, for example, a long-deferred invitation to visit General O'Meara's headquarters in Panama, perhaps in the last half of October, and I might extend this trip to visit our base at Guantanamo and several democratic countries around the Caribbean with ties to Bosch—Costa Rica, Honduras, Colombia, Venezuela, Puerto Rico.

All this of course would be subject to the Department's approval and to unfolding events here during the next month. But as of now, I think such a sudden relaxation of pressure might have a cold-shower effect that could prove healthy. This would be, I wish to emphasize, only a temporary tactical deviation from the long-haul activist policy.

John Bartlow Martin

358. Memorandum From President Kennedy to Secretary of Defense McNamara

Washington, October 4, 1963.

The events of the past few days in the Dominican Republic and Honduras[1] show that the situation could develop in the Caribbean which would require active United States military intervention. I am not sure that we are prepared for this satisfactorily as there is a large area involved; for example, how many troops could we get into the Dominican Republic in a 12–24–36–48 hour period? How many into Honduras? How many into Venezuela?

I think this matter deserves the highest priority. The State Department should be informed of the results of your study as they may be under the impression that we are prepared—which might be unwarranted.

After you have surveyed the matter I think we should have a meeting on this.[2]

J.F.K.[3]

Source: Department of State, Central Files, POL 26 DOM REP. Top Secret. The source text was transmitted under cover of a memorandum from Department of State Executive Secretary Read to the Secretary for his information.

[1] On September 25 Air Force Chief of Staff Miguel Atila Luna and Colonel Elias Wessin y Wessin ousted President Bosch from power. They cited Bosch's ineptitude, corruption, failure to keep electoral promises, and the growth of Communist influence within the Dominican Government as reasons. The following day it was announced that a "Triumvirate" composed of Emilio de los Santos, Ramon Tapia, and Manuel Tavares would assume power in the Republic. On September 28 Ambassador Martin; Newell F. Williams, Director of the AID mission in Santo Domingo; and Colonel David C. Wolfe, Chief of the Military Assistance and Advisory Group were recalled to Washington. Spencer King, Deputy Chief of Mission, was left as Chargé d'Affaires. On October 3 the government of President Ramon Villeda Morales in Honduras was overthrown.

[2] No record of any such meeting was found.

[3] Kennedy's initials appear in an unidentified hand, indicating he signed the original.

359. Telegram from the Department of State to the Embassy in the Dominican Republic

Washington, October 4, 1963, 10:06 p.m.

237. Re Department circular 629.[1] Following is for Santo Domingo distribution only to King and Shlaudemann. Sections E and F are for Embassy action now; remainder is FYI only at present.

A. USG objectives in DomRep are:

1. Return the Dominican Republic to constitutional representative democracy as soon as possible.

2. Give the Dominican people the best possible government meanwhile, with particular reference to preparations for a new election.

3. Prevent an open military dictatorship or the growth of communist strength.

4. Discourage the military in the Dominican Republic and in the Hemisphere from military attacks on constitutional and free democracies.

B. To achieve these multiple objectives, you should open informal negotiations with representatives of present regime (probably through Reid to Tavares, then to Triumvirate plus Reid, at your discretion), to secure their agreement prior to our recognition or resumption of aid on following main points:

1. Free political activity of all non-Communist parties in preparation for OAS supervised elections in not more than one year, with provision for drafting new constitution thereafter.

2. Restoration of some semblance of constitutionality to present regime and recognition of normal role of PRD in DomRep by substituting for one member of the triumvirate Juan Casasnovas as President.

3. Reconstitute present cabinet to include some of best members of Bosch cabinet and others.

4. Restoration of military to proper role by removal from country of Luna, Wessin y Wessin, and such other changes in command structure as country team may propose (e.g., send Rib abroad, replace Vinas,

---

Source: Department of State, Central Files, POL 26 DOM REP. Secret; Priority; Limit Distribution. Drafted by J.B. Martin, cleared by E.M. Martin, and approved by Cottrell. This telegram constitutes a revised version of a Department of State policy proposal contained in a paper submitted to the President on October 4. (Ibid., POL 20 DOM REP) The proposal was discussed the same day at a meeting chaired by the President from 5:05 to 6 p.m. Present were Under Secretaries of State Ball and Harriman, Assistant Secretary Martin, Ambassador J.B. Martin, David Bell and Teodoro Moscoso of AID, and Colonel J.C. King of CIA. No minutes were kept. (Kennedy Library, President's Appointment Book)

[1] Dated October 4. (Department of State, Central Files, POL 26 DOM REP)

upgrade young US-trained officers, transfer Armed Forces Training Center and Air Force Infantry to Army).

5. Decrees to control communist and Trujillo threats.

6. Assurances of appropriate controls to improve honesty and efficiency of government activities, including especially of Trujillo properties.

7. Commitment to institutional reforms of AFP including agrarian reform and stimulation private enterprise, domestic and foreign.

C. In opening these discussions, you should state clearly and emphatically that USG will not recognize or deal with this regime as it stands. This regime and the politicians who named the cabinet represent a minority of the Dom people. Regime must find some way to return toward representative constitutional democracy.

D. Timing of essence. Dept believes at present that these negotiations should be initiated in a week or ten days and then pursued to a conclusion promptly, i.e., in a month. Regime should be given some time to sit and worry. However, too long delay may result in deterioration of situation in DomRep and Hemisphere; specifically, non-recognition for several months could result in bloody struggle between military and people led by leftist extremists, with military dictatorship winning. Dept requests Embassy's comments and recommendations on when to start negotiations.

E. Because of our sympathy and friendship for Dom people, who should not suffer from misdeeds of golpistas, we will continue CARE, CARITAS, and Peace Corps. FYI, means of continuing food shipments under PL–480 without giving financial assistance to regime being sought.

F. Embassy general view on entire program requested.

Ball

360. Telegram From the Department of State to the Embassy in the Dominican Republic

Washington, October 13, 1963, 10:45 p.m.

264. For Chargé from Under Secretary.

1. Cables received today from Casasnovas addressed to President and Secretary state that Casasnovas has been designated by the National Assembly as provisional President during absence of Bosch.[1] Diplomatic recognition is requested and agrement for del Rosario as Ambassador.

2. Bosch cabled President last night and suggested this compliance with constitutional provisions makes Casasnovas provisional President and therefore legitimate head GODR with which US already has relations.

3. We do not know who has put together this Bosch–Casasnovas–Assembly maneuver, and it is essential you get firmest evidence possible on this point. We are particularly concerned lest it reflect effort by the PSP or other Castro-Communist elements. If you are satisfied, however, that this is basically a PRD operation and that Casasnovas is not being used, knowingly or unknowingly, as tool of Castro-Communists, this appears to create new situation requiring revision of time schedule. Possibly it offers a chance for immediate restoration higher degree constitutionality than we had envisaged.

4. We recognize considerations which lead you to conclude that waiting a few days more will not materially harm our interests. However, as result of PRD action, positions may rapidly polarize. Situation appears to be that triumvirate represents power without legitimacy whereas Casasnovas represents color of legitimacy without power. The problem is to fuse two elements before irrevocable polarization. To this end approach to triumvirate should be made now.

5. Against foregoing background, you are instructed to approach Tavares unofficially as soon as possible Monday morning along following lines:

A. You should state that it is possible the triumvirate has been misled by Lear Reed. We have just become aware of his unauthorized activities. He is a private citizen, purely a volunteer with no official or unofficial standing with USG and he does not and cannot represent views of USG. Whatever has been said to Lear by triumvirate, he has not

---

Source: Department of State, Central Files, POL 15–1 DOM REP. Secret; Immediate; Limit Distribution. Drafted by J.B. Martin, Cottrell, and Ball; cleared in draft by the President; and approved by Ball.

[1] Not printed. Telegrams 262 and 263, from Santo Domingo, October 13. (Ibid.)

passed along to USG, and any opinions he has expressed as to USG position should be totally ignored.

B. As indicated in Secretary's statement of October 4,[2] USG will not collaborate or normalize relations with de facto government under existing conditions. There should be no ambiguity on this point. Actions taken by USG for removal of personnel are continuing and will be continued unless prompt return to constitutionality assured.

C. USG would like to know plans of present de facto government to return to constitutionality.

D. If Tavares describes triumvirate position as you have predicted, that a constitutional assembly will be elected within a year, followed by joint municipal and constitutional elections, with presidential election at end of triumvirate term, you should say that this whole proposal inadequate and unacceptable and that USG could not work with triumvirate on this basis.

E. You should state that USG has been asked to recognize Casasnovas as legitimate provisional President under constitution given substance by action of Assembly. This matter being seriously studied by USG. FYI: However, we are not anxious to act in manner that could exacerbate confusion and polarization or provoke civil disorders. End FYI.

F. We would be interested, therefore, in attitude triumvirate to acceptance of Casasnovas as head of government on assumption Bosch and Gonzalez Tamayo will not return to Dominican Republic. Triumvirate would dissolve and Casasnovas would then have right to select own Cabinet.

G. This would mean immediate restoration of constitutional government with military withdrawing from political control and resuming proper constitutional role. Would also mean withdrawal of certain political parties or party leaders who have forced themselves or their men into key cabinet posts.

H. If triumvirate and their military backers would agree to this arrangement prompt restoration of USG cooperation could be effected.

I. You should make clear to triumvirate that if they agree to Casasnovas takeover, triumvirate will be publicly recognized as having preserved civilian control in most difficult circumstances and provided bridge back to constitutionality thus performing indispensable service of statesmanship to Republic. You should make clear to triumvirate that we would insist that Casasnovas take effective measures to closely restrict Communist travel and internal activities and ensure country against Communist infiltration and subversion, which together with ousting Bosch, was after all ostensible reason for coup. If you think it

---

[2] For text, see Department of State *Bulletin*, October 21, 1963, p. 624.

helpful as sweetening for Triumvirate, we should have no objections to your suggesting that we might try to persuade Casasnovas to make use their talents in new cabinet.

FYI: Throughout discussions, you should bear in mind that important objective is to bring about an effective as well as a constitutional government, at cabinet level and below. You should hold strongly all major points of position. However, if Tavares or other spokesmen for triumvirate indicate possibility of accepting national government in which Casasnovas would agree to include representation of some other parties in Cabinet, we would be prepared to canvass this with them as possible alternative solution. End FYI.

6. Since key appears to be military acceptance, immediately after talking to Tavares on Monday you should approach Vinas Roman (in company with other DR military leaders if you deem others' presence advisable) and make same points to him or them as you made to Tavares (Para 5 above).

Rusk

---

361. Telegram From the Department of State to the Embassy in the Dominican Republic

Washington, October 17, 1963, 6:33 p.m.

290. A. Subject your discretion suggest attachés draw on following explanation of what lies behind our position in informal discussions with Dom military:

Secretary statement and President press conference mean exactly what they say[1] but should be understood in light of following background—we have our problems too.

Coup raised important questions far beyond DomRep involving not only Dom democracy but cause of constitutionality and representative

---

Source: Department of State, Central Files, POL 15 DOM REP. Confidential; Priority. Drafted by J.B. Martin. Approved by Cottrell.

[1] References are to the Secretary's statement of October 4 (see footnote 2, Document 360, and the President's press conference of October 9 (see footnote 2, Document 65).

democracy—right of people to choose own ruler—throughout hemisphere and indeed beyond.

US was deeply involved, materially and morally, in agonizing transition from dictatorial oppression to representative democracy in DomRep. Transformation achieved remarkably quickly and peaceably (with help Dom military—which makes present situation doubly tragic).

Although USG had misgivings about Bosch as ideal president, nevertheless, he won that office with overwhelming majority in a free election which was great source satisfaction to hemisphere and to Dom and Am people in particular. US pointed with pride to its role in these historic events, predicting that in DomRep would arise a clear demonstration of advantages to common man of peaceful democratic evolution as contrasted to violent communist revolution.

Perhaps in time US would have become completely disenchanted with Bosch's fumbling mismanagement and fully alarmed over freedom he allowed Castro/Communists. But even some his severest US critics felt that seven short months provided wholly inadequate basis for final judgment. And coup seriously set back cause democracy throughout hemisphere. These are salient considerations for US, and nothing gained now by arguing whether coup "necessary." Problem is what next.

Military's dominant role in coup presents special problems for US. Regardless of merits, fair or unfair, LA military are seen in US as arbitrary perpetrators of endless series of coups against elected civilian government, thus preventing progress and democratic evolution. Timing of Dom coup made matters far worse—it followed Peru, Guatemala, and Ecuador, and Honduras followed it, arousing widespread alarm in US of chain reaction that might endanger democracy in other struggling LA nations.

Therefore, US reaction against coup very strong, as reflected in editorials and Congress. Moreover, some distinguished members Congress who in past have opposed military assistance to Latin America were so outraged they are now pushing for legislation denying both US military and economic assistance to any government springing from a military coup. Their feelings are understandable, for they represent precisely the same forces which have been most disposed to extend generous helping hand to Dom people in efforts to build a democracy on ruins tyranny.

Dominicans should not understimate strength or importance of public reaction to coup. USG can never disregard public opinion, as Dom military trained here can appreciate.

US does not seek to impose unacceptable—or any single—solution in DomRep. We recognize Communist dangers; we will insist on its being curbed, in our own interests as well as DomRep's. But we must ensure in so far as realistically possible that would-be golpistas in other LA countries take no encouragement from Dom coup, and we must ensure that any solution to present impasses takes fully into account the desire of Dom people (and US people) that control over their destiny shall be returned to hands of a government responsive to their will.

In this connection, well to remember that all PRDers, just like all military, not bad per se, and not "brainwashed" (JANAF 162116Z).[2] We must stop thinking in labels and bogeymen, face realities and individuals.

Finally, DomRep, for historical, geographic, cultural reasons occupies special position vis-à-vis US. US feels nothing but friendliness and sympathy for Dom people and Dom problems.

B. This background, of course, does not in any way presage a new "softer" position. It is an attempt to explain our present firm position, and to give attachés something to keep talking to military, especially, perhaps, junior officers, about.

Rusk

---

[2] Not found.

---

362. Memorandum of Conversation

Washington, November 1, 1963.

SUBJECT

Presidential Meeting on Honduras and DR—November 1—5:00 p.m.

PARTICIPANTS

The President
AID—Mr. David Bell, Mr. Reuben Sternfeld
Defense—Dr. Mountain
CIA—Mr. Richard Helms, Col. J.C. King
State—Mr. Edwin M. Martin
White House—Mr. McGeorge Bundy, Mr. Ralph Dungan

The current situation in the Dominican Republic and Honduras was discussed.

With respect to Honduras, it was observed that the conversations with regard to the return to constitutionality are still going on in the country, that an orderly withdrawal of U.S. personnel is underway, that

---

Source: Kennedy Library, National Security Files, Countries Series, Dominican Republic, October 31–November 22, 1963. Confidential. Drafted by Dungan.

there is no imminent threat of counter-coup or insurgent activity, and therefore our posture for the moment should be to stand pat.

With regard to the DR, it was decided (1) to dispatch Colonel Simmons and the President approved a general instruction for his mission, (2) the President requested a memorandum to be drafted for use in our Latin American embassies in the event that we recognize the new regime in Saigon, and (3) the President directed that the Chargé in Santo Domingo be brought back to the U.S. for consultation early next week.

RAD

---

[1] Lieutenant Colonel Ed Simmons, former U.S. military attaché in the Dominican Republic, was dispatched from Washington to New York to talk to General Rodriguez Echavarría and to the Dominican Republic to talk with representatives of the Dominican military. (Martin, *Overtaken by Events*, pp. 612–613)

---

363. Telegram From the Department of State to the Embassy in Venezuela

Washington, December 13, 1963, 8:15 p.m.

516. Embtel 725.[1] We can assure you decision recognize Honduran and Dominican regimes at this time only after exhaustive consideration all foreign and domestic aspects.[2] In cases both countries our principal objective in withholding recognition has been return at earliest possible date constitutionally elected government. We have also sought (a) give pause incipient plotters in other parts hemisphere, (b) minimize violence and opportunities for extreme leftists expand their strength and (c) secure fullest possible respect for civil liberties and non-communist party activity pending new elections. While our non-recognition has yielded some success, we convinced that prospects for further influencing situation by non-recognition both countries in direction our objectives are virtually nil and continued non-recognition likely nullify gains thus far achieved.

We airpouching for your information detailed memoranda setting forth basis on which decision reached.[3] Meantime following are factors

---

Source: Department of State, Central Files, POL 16 DOM REP. Secret; Immediate. Drafted by Moskowitz; cleared by Cottrell, ARA/EST, ARA/CMA, ARA/OAP, and S/S, and approved by E.M. Martin. Also sent to San José as telegram 226.

[1] Dated December 13. (Ibid.)

[2] The United States recognized the new Dominican Government on December 14.

[3] Not found.

in addition those cited Depcirtel 1065[4] favoring proposed US recognition which you may draw upon in further discussions with Betancourt and Oduber and/or Orlich to clarify our position:

Dominican Republic

1. Our ability influence DR developments along course we favor during short and mid-term future will tend decrease if we continue withhold recognition since high world sugar prices and lack general Dominican popular reaction against coup support conclusion de facto regime does not need US recognition to survive.

2. Regime's personnel are not strong and lack popular support and thus would be easy targets for extreme leftist violence and/or military coup should serious difficulties arise. US recognition and support will significantly increase regime's ability withstand extremists' attacks and maintain commitments on free elections.

3. Withholding recognition can be expected strengthen regime's resistance our suggestions for measures to improve its national and international acceptance making eventual accommodation more difficult and increasing risk seriously damaging basically friendly relations between US and DR.

4. Recognition will significantly enhance prospects for promoting replacement of less desirable elements now in government with more acceptable men since non-recognition is factor which has created cohesive political front against such changes. Triumviate believes US support will enable it take firm stand against party hacks and incompetents in cabinet and enlist able non-party civilians to replace them to improve regime's capabilities for effective government beneficial to Dominicans and for adherence election schedule.

5. Extreme leftists have started small scale guerrilla action against regime supported by suspected arms from Cuba. Recognition will enable us help Dominicans stop possible Cuban arms shipments and strengthen regime's position suppress guerrilla and other extremist-provoked disorders which were being used as pretext by rightist civilian and military elements to suppress free political activity or to seize government and cancel election schedule. Situation this latter respect was deteriorating rapidly.

6. Number of hemisphere governments favor early recognition and have held off this long only in deference our initiatives.

[Here follows discussion of the recognition of the new Honduran Government and instructions to the Embassies in Caracas and San José.]

Ball

---

[4] Dated December 12. (Department of State, Central Files, POL 1 US)

HAITI

364. Editorial Note

Following his election in November 1960, President-elect John F. Kennedy established a Task Force on Immediate Latin American Problems. Former Assistant Secretary of State Adolph Berle chaired the task force, whose members included former Kennedy campaign aide Richard N. Goodwin, Arturo Morales-Carrion and Teodoro Moscoso of the Puerto Rican Government, economist Lincoln Gordon, political scientist Robert Alexander, and historian Arthur P. Whittaker. The task force was charged with evaluating U.S.-Latin American relations and ordering the tasks of the new administration's policy towards Latin America. On January 4, 1961, the task force submitted its report to President-elect Kennedy. The report contained two sets of recommendations for U.S. policy towards Haiti. Under the general heading of "Personnel Changes," the report discussed the question of opposition to President Francois Duvalier. The recommendation from the report reads as follows:

"*Haiti.* The State Department should immediately review the situation of our Embassy in Haiti. This country could explode at any time. Its government is dictatorial but shaky, said to be infiltrated by pro-Communist groups, probably headed for downfall. Probably the tacit temporary working agreement between Castro and the Dominican dictator, Trujillo, includes for the moment non-interference in Haiti by Castro. But any change in the Haitian government might lead to explosion and perhaps invasion from both countries. The American Embassy should seek to draw together the forces for a healthy alternative (including, perhaps, some of the exiles) to the Duvalier government. This is a prerequisite to other action; after [creation of] such organization, consideration might be given to withdrawing support from Duvalier."

Under the heading "Emergency situations requiring immediate action," the report suggested the following action:

"*Haiti.* The State Department should have a 'left hand' in the United States (unofficial relations which do not compromise) and this should be extended to the more responsible Haitian exiles. It should set about and draw together the elements of an eventually effective government. Two possible leaders: Fignolé and Jumelle. There may be better men than either available. Small cadres of Haitians should be chosen immediately who can promptly be trained to deal with governmental problems. (Some Haitians have already studied in Puerto Rico.) Basically, these must be trained to organize, make productive, and insure at least subsistence for more than three million Haitians living in primitive conditions. Puerto Rico seems the best training stage in view of conditions in the

United States and Governor Muñoz Marin has much experience in doing this.

"Unpublicized orders should be given to prevent landing of arms and guerrillas into Haiti and Puerto Rico from Cuba: this means patrol of the Windward Passage; and intimation might be given that if the Dominicans invade, we would respond with any needed help." (Kennedy Library, Pre-Presidential Papers, Transition Series, Task Force Reports, 1960)

365.   Memorandum Prepared in the Department of State

Washington, March 23, 1961.

MEMORANDUM ON UNITED STATES-HAITIAN RELATIONS

Prior to Ambassador Newbegin's departure for Haiti in mid-October 1960, United States-Haitian relations had reached a low point due primarily to the character and uncooperative attitude of the Duvalier government. Following a thorough review of the situation, it was determined that it would be in our interest to avoid creating at this time a political vacuum into which Castro or Trujillo might be tempted to move. Accordingly, in an effort to break the impasse in United States-Haitian relations and contribute to the stability of the Duvalier government, Ambassador Newbegin was authorized to offer an integrated economic aid package intended to demonstrate our intention of carrying on an effective assistance program and even increasing our assistance, subject to the restoration of a satisfactory relationship with the Haitian Government.

In the few months since the Ambassador's arrival, progress has been made in restoring at least ostensibly good relations. However, during this same period President Duvalier's heavy-handed suppression of a student strike, expulsion of a number of Roman Catholic church officials, and arrest and maltreatment of anyone thought to be opposed to

---

Source: Kennedy Library, National Security Files, Countries Series, Haiti, 1/61–6/62. Secret. The Department of State's copy of this memorandum indicates that it was drafted by Abbuhl and was based on despatch 304 from Port-au-Prince, January 30. (Department of State, Central Files, 611.38/1–3061) A copy of the despatch was attached to a March 23 covering memorandum from Battle to Dungan. (Ibid., 611.38/3–2361)

his regime have increased his unpopularity and resulted in an increasing tendency on the part of the general public to blame the Embassy and the United States Government for "support" of a "despised tyrant."

The Ambassador emphasizes that we are faced with two "sorry alternatives." There is no one on the scene now who gives any promise of being able or willing to establish a decent constructive government.[1] Should Duvalier fall, there is a decided danger of chaos and a struggle for power among individuals in whom we would have little ground for confidence. Such a situation might well tempt Castro or Trujillo to intervene in such a way as to jeopardize our national interests, possibly even forcing military intervention. Therefore, unless we are willing to take radical steps (including military intervention, if necessary, after Duvalier's removal), we have little choice but to follow our present course of maintaining friendly and helpful relations with the Duvalier government. This is not an easy task nor one which the Ambassador particularly relishes under present circumstances, but he is perfectly willing to undertake it and believes it to be the less dangerous of two unhappy alternatives.[2]

---

[1] In a February 14 memorandum to Rusk, Berle informed him that it was the conclusion of the Department of State and the Central Intelligence Agency that "the present Haitian Government may linger along for awhile, but it might dissolve into anarchy almost any time." Berle proposed to make contact with the principal members of the Haitian opposition on a cautious basis, making no commitments. (Ibid., Latin America Task Force Files: Lot 61 D 298, Haiti)

[2] In despatch 420 from Port-au-Prince, April 11, Ambassador Newbegin objected to Berle's meeting with Haitian exiles in early March on the grounds that the exiles would assume that the meetings constituted support for Duvalier's overthrow. Newbegin reiterated that the Haitian opposition to Duvalier was so disorganized, disunited, and ineffective that any coup attempt would fail or lead to anarchy. (Ibid., Central Files, 738.00/4–1161) In telegram 274 to Port-au-Prince, April 24, Berle assured Newbegin that his discussions were meant only to establish good relations and guide exile leaders who might eventually play a role in a democratic Haiti. (Ibid.) No other record of Berle's meeting with the exiles has been found.

366. Memorandum From the Acting Assistant Secretary of State for Inter-American Affairs (Coerr) to Secretary of State Rusk

Washington, May 23, 1961.

SUBJECT

Our Policy toward Haiti subsequent to President Duvalier's "Inauguration" May 22

REFERENCE

My draft memorandum of May 22 from Mr. Bowles to Mr. Berle[1]

Background

The reference memorandum (Tab A) describes the decision we took on May 18 to be represented at Duvalier's "inauguration" on May 22 by our Chargé.[2] The *New York Times* today correctly reported our action as a "snub" to the Duvalier regime. Having thus established our position on the dictatorship, we must now attempt to cut our losses by re-establishing adequate working relations with the Duvalier Government. Ambassador Newbegin is at present in Washington on consultation.

We took the difficult decision of May 18, to respond to Duvalier's action with a moderated sign of disassociation, as a calculated risk. To reduce the consequent damage to our foreign policy objectives in Haiti, we must amend our relations with the Government of Haiti in a similar moderate manner. We should try to re-establish effective working relations with the Duvalier regime which is headed by an irrational man who has almost totalitarian power over the island.

I list below with comment the following lines of action that Mr. Berle has told me today he is contemplating:

(1) He has proposed to you that we send a Departmental officer, Mr. John Hoover (FSO–2) to Haiti on a fact-finding mission.

Comment: Mr. Berle and I have agreed on our need for increased information about the situation within Haiti but we have further agreed

---

Source: Department of State, Central Files, 738.00/5–2361. Secret; Eyes Only. Drafted by Coerr, cleared by U. Alexis Johnson, and sent via Bowles.

[1] The attached draft explained to Berle that the decision to send the U.S. Chargé to Duvalier's unconstitutional "self-coronation" represented the middle ground between Berle's contention that non-attendance would demonstrate U.S. support for democracy in Haiti and make a favorable impression within the Western Hemisphere, and Coerr's view that the Ambassador should attend in light of U.S.-Haitian relations and the reaction his absence would cause inside Haiti. These conflicting viewpoints are outlined in memoranda from Coerr to Bowles, May 16 and Coerr to U. Alexis Johnson, May 17, and from Berle and Hoover to Achilles, May 16; ibid., 611.38/5–1616, 611.38/5–1761, and 611.38/5–1761, respectively.

[2] In this memorandum U. Alexis Johnson noted that, as the invitation was addressed to the U.S. Chargé, he and ARA believed that this was a good "out," and that Ambassador Newbegin should remain in Washington until after Duvalier's inauguration. (Ibid., 738.11/5–1861)

that we should at this time make no attempt to get it which would be conspicuous. For us to send a Departmental officer to Haiti now, and before Ambassador Newbegin returns, would, Mr. Berle and I agree, be conspicuous, and Mr. Berle has withdrawn his suggestion.

(2) Mr. Berle was due to leave at 1 p.m. for New York today where he is making a speech this evening. He told me this morning of the possibility that he might be in touch with Haitian exiles, who have quite a colony in New York, with whom Mr. Berle and other interested individuals have maintained an informal contact for some time. He had a supper meeting with a group of Haitian President Duvalier's opponents in New York on March 4.

Comment: It is possible that, although we have no firm evidence to prove it, news of Mr. Berle's March meeting with President Duvalier's enemies in New York has reached Duvalier. If so, this development could account for a series of subsequent actions of the Government of Haiti such as the Haitian delegate's absenting himself from the Cuban debate at the UN and the Haitian President's decision to consolidate his hold on the Government by transforming himself from President to dictator two years before the expiration of his presidential term. Regardless of whether Duvalier has, in fact, heard of Mr. Berle's past meeting or meetings, since he became Chief of the Latin American Task Force, with his exiled opposition, there is no doubt that his reaction would be most adverse should he now hear of such a meeting subsequent to the snub that the U.S. Government administered to him on the occasion of his "inauguration" of May 22.

I pointed out to Mr. Berle that I had assumed a heavy responsibility in recommending the moderated course of action which resulted in our being represented only by our Chargé, that in so doing we assumed the obvious risks of antagonizing the Duvalier regime, with the consequent risks of goading him into excluding the U.S. presence from and facilitating the Castro-Communist penetration into Haiti. I told Mr. Berle I thought that for him or any other easily identified U.S. official to meet under present conditions with the Haitian exiles in New York would be distinctly dangerous. I also told him that should he do so I could not assume any responsibility for subsequent U.S. policy toward Haiti. Mr. Berle said he thought we had to make our stand on dictatorship clear and that he would "take note" of my position.

Recommendations:

(1) That you instruct Ambassador Newbegin to return to Haiti quietly on or about May 26.[3]

---

[3] Rusk approved this recommendation.

(2) That you telephone, or authorize a ranking officer of the Department, or myself, to telephone Mr. Berle today in New York instructing him not to renew contact with the Haitian exiles.[4]

---

[4] According to a note on the source text, Rusk "decided not to intervene here."

---

367.   Memorandum for the Record

Washington, May 26, 1961, 9 a.m.

SUBJECT

White House Conference on Haiti

A meeting under the Chairmanship of Mr. Richard Goodwin of the White House Staff was held in the conference room of the White House at 9 A.M. on May 26, 1961. The following were the participants:

Ambassador Robert Newbegin, U.S. Ambassador to Haiti
Mr. Adolph A. Berle, Department of State
Mr. Theodore C. Achilles, Department of State
Mr. Wymberley Coerr, Department of State
Mr. Daniel M. Braddock, Department of State
Mr Forest E. Abbuhl, Department of State
Mr. John P. Hoover, Department of State
[name not declassified], Central Intelligence Agency
Mr. Maurice J. Mountain, Department of Defense

Mr. Newbegin outlined the situation in Haiti saying that the U.S. interest in that country was chiefly because of its strategic geographic location and that commercial interests in the area were not too important. He said it was desirable from the U.S. standpoint that affairs in Haiti remain quiet at this time so as not to make our general Caribbean situation more difficult than it now is. He said the Duvalier government is stable by Haitian standards and that it appears to be in complete control,

---

Source: Washington National Records Center, RG 330, OASD/ISA Files: FRC 64 A 2382, Haiti, 1961, 000.1—. Secret. Drafted by Maurice J. Mountain, Deputy Director of the Policy Planning Staff, Office of the Assistant Secretary of Defense for International Security Affairs, on May 29. Copies were sent to Bundy, Rowan, and Captain Ryan at the White House.

though it remains so by brutal methods. He said that the Duvalier government at the present time is not doing the United States any harm although it is not doing any good either. There is no democratic replacement for this regime in sight. The population of Haiti is 90% illiterate and while some democracy may be possible among the small literate group, it is probable that their concern would be with the assumption of power and the personal gain to be made by taking over the government.

Ambassador Newbegin said that there was some degree of Communist infiltration. The Minister of Information is undoubtedly a Communist. The Minister of Finance was trained in Rumania and during some time spent in France possibly had Communist associations; he is not now a member of the Party but is an opportunist who would rejoin the Communists if he thought they could win. The Minister of Commerce has leanings toward the Communists. There is believed to be no other serious Communist infiltration. Among the masses Communists are few although one estimate of questionable validity reports it at 4,000.

Mr. Goodwin asked if Castro could cause trouble since Cuba is only 30 miles away. There was general agreement that Castro could cause trouble not through a military invasion but through infiltration of small groups designed to establish a base for subversion. Mr. Goodwin asked about the possibility of patrols of the Haitian coast and whether the United States should try to undertake surveillance against infiltration movements from Cuba. The Department of Defense was asked to look into this matter.

The question of discontent among the Haitian people was discussed. Ambassador Newbegin said that land reform was not an issue. Mr. Berle said that the chief objection the Haitians have to the Duvalier government is its brutality and the point of danger will be reached when the people get sufficiently fed up with being "banged over the head" to take action.

[*less than 1 line of source text not declassified*] of CIA said that intelligence within Haiti was very difficult to obtain since the people were too terrified to talk. A large part of their information comes from Haitian exiles. It is, therefore, uncertain as of now what the Communists have done or are doing within the country. [*less than 1 line of source text not declassified*] pointed to the experience in Venezuela at the time of the fall of Jimenez where a considerable Communist apparatus suddenly appeared though its existence had been discounted prior to the fall of Jimenez. Mr. Goodwin asked that CIA see what could be done to increase our intelligence of Communist or Castro activities within Haiti.

Ambassador Newbegin said that any action taken with regard to Haiti should be very carefully considered since it was clear there would be a reaction forthcoming from Duvalier. He mentioned the fact that Duvalier had been deeply offended by the absence of the U.S. Ambassador at his recent inauguration. This absence was intended to demonstrate U.S. disapproval of the sham through which Duvalier got himself elected to a second six year term. However, none of the Latin American Ambassadors were absent from the inauguration; only the U.S. Ambassador was missing. As a result Mr. Newbegin said he felt the chances were 60 to 40 that Mr. Duvalier would retaliate by declaring Ambassador Newbegin persona non grata. Similar affronts to Duvalier are almost certain to cause reactions which we may not desire. If we become increasingly tough with him, we may drive him toward the Castro-Communist camp. In Mr. Newbegin's judgment we have not identified anyone or any group competent to form a replacement government. Until we do he suggests that we get along with Duvalier as best we can.

Mr. Goodwin said he had learned that the head of the Marine Mission to Haiti was a very able officer and he would like to have him brought to Washington for a few hours of consultation about U.S. relationships with the Haitian military. He suggested Thursday, June 1, or Friday, June 2. Mr. Newbegin said he would like to hold up on this because it too could lead to difficulty with Duvalier if he knew that this officer was being called back. In the discussion which followed it was agreed that Colonel Heinl, USMC, could go to Guantanamo for two or three days of medical check-up during which period he could be flown to Washington. It was agreed that the Department of Defense would arrange this, consulting if necessary [less than 1 line of source text not declassified] for appropriate cover arrangements.

The meeting ended on the note that contingency plans for the Duvalier government continuing in power would not be implemented but that plans for all other contingencies would be kept ready.[1] Another meeting will be held next week.[2]

Maurice J. Mountain
Deputy Director, Policy Planning Staff

---

[1] At the 483d meeting of the National Security Council, May 5, the Council requested the preparation of contingency papers on Haiti and the Dominican Republic given the emergencies that seemed to be developing there. (Memorandum from Coerr to Rusk, June 26; Department of State, Central Files, 738.00/6–2661) The Haitian contingency plan, drafted by Hoover and Abbuhl on May 26 and dated May 29, under cover of a memorandum to McGeorge Bundy, is attached but not printed. The contingencies contemplated included Duvalier remaining in power, an impasse in U.S.-Haitian relations, Duvalier's replacement by death, incapacity, or overthrow, and finally subversion or invasion from without. The Department of State provided recommendations for each contingency. The Department of State copy is ibid., Latin America Task Force Files: Lot 61 D 298, Berle, Task Force Material, Basic Documents.

[2] No record of this meeting has been found. Mountain wrote this last sentence by hand.

368. Telegram From Secretary of State Rusk to the Department of State

Paris, June 2, 1961, 11 a.m.

Secto 5. Eyes only Acting Secretary from Secretary. Have studied Haiti contingency paper submitted May 29[1] by Achilles group and consider it good job within possibilities such papers. As illustrated by many events past and recent history, such papers may have little relevance to unfolding events. Very existence such papers (such as pre-invasion NSP paper on Korea) has narcotic effect through impression we have answered our policy problems and can rest until events fit assumption of paper. I suspect life is more complicated than that.

Haitian paper means to me that we see no good answer and are preparing to look for bad ones. The ways to find better answers is to look for different questions. Following is one attempt which my colleagues can multiply and assess.

Haiti is the cesspool of the Western Hemisphere, under a dictator whom we abhor. The situation is ripe for Castro-type effort and we ourselves cannot in good conscience say that this could be worse for the Haitians however damaging to US and cause of freedom in the Americas.

Since we are already supporting the Haitian economy why not do a good job? Why not talk out with Duvalier our readiness to help Haiti make a major surge forward in economic and social development on the assumption that he will remain in power and might be ready to write a gleaming chapter in Haitian history? His policies cannot help but be modified if he takes up such a dare and the more he advances down such a trail the more pressures are built up to build a decent regime or be forced to get out.

I can imagine a US military development group centered around engineer, medical and signal components which could work with his own armed forces on development projects. Even if Duvalier is initially disinterested in schools, he might be ready to set up a network of simple aid stations and health centers where people would congregate and be available for extension-type information through visual and sound aids.

Suggest we put together ideas which we would wish to see carried out by a decent Haitian Government and then consider whether Duvalier might get on with them. He just might have moments when he yearns to be a decent man.

Source: Department of State, Central Files, 738.00/6–261. Secret. Rusk accompanied President Kennedy on a State visit to France May 31–June 3.

[1] See footnote 1, Document 367.

This might mean changing Ambassadors, eating a bit of crow and enduring a certain amount of criticism. But waiting for a chance to use force is no answer either, because the problem is neither military nor cloak and dagger. Would like report on this upon my return.

Rusk

---

369.   Special National Intelligence Estimate

SNIE 86.1–61   Washington, June 7, 1961.

SHORT-TERM PROSPECTS IN HAITI[1]

The Problem

To assess the short-term prospects in Haiti, with special reference to the likely consequences for Haiti of the assassination of Dominican dictator Trujillo.

The Estimate

I.   The Internal Situation and Prospects

1. In contrast to the Dominican Republic, where the 30 May assassination of Generalissimo Trujillo was preceded by months of unrest, uncertainty, and intensified repression, the situation in Haiti has remained essentially static. President Duvalier has now conferred upon himself a new six-year term in office, two years before the old term was due to expire. In the 30 April parliamentary elections, in which the voters were called upon to choose among various hand-picked pro-Duvalier candidates, Duvalier placed his own name at the top of the ballot, thereafter asserting that he had been unanimously re-elected. Despite the palpable fraud of this procedure, Duvalier was reinaugurated on 22 May

---

Source: Central Intelligence Agency Files, Job 79–R01012A, ODDI Registry. Secret. According to a note on the cover sheet, the Central Intelligence Agency, the intelligence organizations of the Department of State, the Army, the Navy, the Air Force, and the Joint Staff contributed to this special estimate. It was submitted to the U.S. Intelligence Board on June 7 by the Director of Central Intelligence. All members of the Board concurred except the representatives of the AEC and FBI who abstained on the grounds that the subject was outside their jurisdiction.

[1] Supplements and brings up to date SNIE 86.1–60, "The Situation and Prospects in Haiti," dated 27 September 1960, which remains valid and provides a more detailed examination of the Haitian situation. [Footnote in the source text. For text of SNIE 86.1–60, September 27, 1960, see *Foreign Relations, 1958–1960*, vol. V, American Republics, Microfiche Supplement, Fiche 18.]

without protest, in the presence of thousands of peasants brought in from the countryside.[2]

2.   By the forced retirement of some officers and the reassignment of others, President Duvalier has further ensured his control over the military establishment, the principal instrument of political power in Haiti.[3] Although the officer corps as a whole almost certainly resents his divide-and-rule technique, he has put in the key positions men on whom he relies. General Merceron, the army commander, strongly resents the growing influence of Major Raymond, the commander of the Presidential Guard, but has been unable to curb it.

3.   Underlying opposition to Duvalier will of course continue. The President's arrogation to himself of a new six-year term has almost certainly increased the resentment of churchmen, students, military men, and others of the old mulatto elite, which has lost its power and influence since Duvalier came to power. Small exile groups continue to exist in New York, Caracas, and Havana; inflammatory broadcasts in Creole, directed at students and the peasantry, continue to emanate weekly from Cuba.

4.   Nevertheless, the numerous opposition elements, both in and outside Haiti, still appear to lack the strength, vigor, and cohesion to challenge effectively a man of Duvalier's political skill and determination. A four-month strike by students, who had been the most active of Duvalier's critics, collapsed in March 1961. According to the Haitian Government, a small group of Cuban-supported exiles were apprehended when they landed in late April. Although significant pro-Castro sentiment exists among students and other intellectuals, Castroism still appears to have had little impact on the peasantry.

5.   An extremely impoverished country, even by Latin American standards, Haiti has had an unusually poor coffee crop this year, and the dead season is approaching. Nevertheless, the population at large will probably continue to eke out an existence. In November 1960 US financial and technical programs, which had been partially suspended earlier in that year, were resumed and expanded. The present level of US economic assistance (totaling about $13.5 million for the present US fiscal year)

---

[2] Haitian Presidents have invariably sought to perpetuate themselves in office and have as regularly been thrown out at the expiration of their legitimate terms. Although Duvalier has got away with this "re-election" this time, he has laid the basis for a coup attempt at the expiration of his legitimate term in October 1963. [Footnote in the source text.]

[3] The army, which includes the small air force (160 men) and the coast guard (300 men), numbers 5,200, but its small ground forces are scattered over the country in small police and constabulary detachments, except for an 800-man battallion at Port-au-Prince and the Port-au-Prince police (730). The Presidential Guard (400), is an independent command responsible directly to Duvalier. In addition, Duvalier directly controls two paramilitary organizations, a civilian militia in Port-au-Prince (275) and a civilian "secret police" numbering 750–1,000 in the country as a whole. [Footnote in the source text.]

appears sufficient to stave off a foreign exchange or budgetary crisis. Thus, current economic difficulties do not appear sufficient to cause any significant falling away of Duvalier's support. Preliminary indications with respect to the 1961–1962 coffee crop are promising.

6. In sum, we consider it unlikely that the internal opposition will be able to overthrow the Duvalier government in the short run. However, the 54-year-old Duvalier is a diabetic and has suffered at least one heart attack, although his health appears to have improved in recent months. His departure from the scene—whether by natural causes or assassination— would almost certainly be followed by a struggle for power. There is no one leader who could command the quick and widespread support necessary for strong government. The military would be likely to seize control of the government, but probably would not be able to stabilize the situation. The result would probably be a period of disorder similar to the nine-month hiatus preceding the installation of Duvalier, when six provisional governments rose and fell. In such an unstable situation, pro-Castro elements would certainly strive to gain control of Haiti.

II.   Consequences of Trujillo's Assassination

7. The assassination of Generalissimo Trujillo is unlikely to have any important direct effect on the Haitian situation. Despite the psychological encouragement Trujillo's death has almost certainly given to opponents of Duvalier, it has not changed the presently unfavorable situation confronting them in Haiti.

8. If guerrilla operations develop in the Dominican Republic, they might spill over the Haitian frontier, but probably not to such an extent as to involve major clashes or to have a serious unsettling effect on the position of the Duvalier regime within Haiti. We consider it extremely unlikely that either Castro or the present Dominican regime would undertake military operations in or against Haiti in view of the risks of US or OAS counteraction. Major subversive pressures on Haiti from the Dominican Republic would probably arise only in the event that pro-Castro elements gained power in the Dominican Republic.

9. The unsettled state of affairs in the Dominican Republic to his east, coupled with the presence of a revolutionary Cuba to his west, will probably reinforce Duvalier's sense of dependence on US economic, military, and diplomatic support. At the same time, Duvalier will probably attempt to trade on the notion that the US must support him as the only one capable of providing stable government in Haiti. Castro and his Latin American supporters will almost certainly seek to exploit indications of US support for Duvalier as evidence of US affinity for dictators. At present, with the troubles of the Trujillo dynasty focusing hemisphere attention on the island, such Castro propaganda would probably do some damage to the US position in Latin America.

370.   Guidelines Prepared by the Bureau of Inter-American Affairs

Washington, September 18, 1961.

GUIDELINES OF U.S. POLICY TOWARD HAITI

Objectives

United States short-term objectives in Haiti are to keep Haiti on our side and to prevent further economic and social deterioration and political chaos.

In order of priority U.S. intermediate or long-range objectives are:

1.   A stable government aligned with the United States.

2.   Less dishonesty and inefficiency within the Government to permit the U.S. aid program to function more effectively.

3.   Improvement in the economic and social life of the Haitian people through a technical and economic assistance program which will ensure a rate of economic growth greater than that of population growth.

4.   Development of a more reliable, constructive and respected military establishment to fulfill its constitutional role.

5.   An improved climate for foreign private investment.

6.   Settlement of pending claims of private U.S. citizens against the Haitian Government.

Lines of Action

Political:

1.   Continue to live with the Duvalier regime so long as there is no acceptable alternative.

2.   Consciously direct U.S. policy toward the development of a better alternative; to this end increase the flow of intelligence information and identify elements and individuals acceptable to the U.S. as the nucleus of a successor government.

3.   Evaluate and appraise the potential and likely support for an alternative government which might be received from elements within Haiti, including especially the armed forces.

4.   Avoid actions that might precipitate Duvalier's downfall as long as this would create a power vacuum which Castro-Communists could be expected to exploit.

Source: Department of State, Central Files, 611.38/9–1861. Secret. Drafted by Abbuhl, cleared by ICA, S/P, B/FAC, INR/RAR. Sent to Acting Secretary Bowles under cover of a September 18 memorandum from Woodward.

5.   Demonstrate resolution and firmness in dealing with Haitian officials and, whenever possible, take the lead in matters affecting U.S.-Haitian relations.

6.   Urge Haitian officials to avoid excesses and brutality and respect human rights.

7.   Discourage the GOH from its tendency to by-pass the Embassy and USOM and deal directly with Washington agencies.

Economic:

1.   Carry forward as much constructive economic and social development as possible.

2.   Insist that the GOH help itself and demonstrate its willingness and capability to use U.S. aid effectively, by undertaking badly needed reforms designed to improve public administration, particularly budgetary and fiscal procedures.

3.   Undertake, in cooperation with other organizations such as the Pan American Union and ECLA, a comprehensive analysis of the Haitian economy and socio-cultural systems, and the formulation of a national development plan to serve as a basis for Haiti's long-range economic development.

4.   Undertake some projects such as low-cost housing, waterworks, highways and airports to provide large-scale employment and demonstrate the tangible results of U.S. aid.

5.   Extend aid in the form of grants or long-term, low interest loans for projects which are not self-liquidating.

6.   Use the so-called "turnkey contract" procedure for major projects as a means of counteracting the low level of probity and quality of Haiti's administrative machinery and the efforts of many Haitian officials to utilize U.S. aid for purposes not in keeping with our objectives.

7.   Regard budgetary support only as a temporary expedient.

8.   Insist that the GOH include provisions in its budget to service debts owed U.S. citizens.

Military:

1.   Continue, through our present military and matériel assistance programs to develop and maintain a favorable attitude toward the U.S. within the Haitian Army.

2.   Develop roles for the Army to play in the economic development of the country, in coordination with other such activities being undertaken in the country.

3.   Improve the professional capacity, discipline and stability of the Haitian Armed Forces through U.S. training, and encourage more efficient and economical use of these forces within present manpower and funding ceilings.

4. Continue to provide Haiti with the type and quantities of military assistance believed to be required in order to maintain constitutional law and order, giving consideration to the recommendations developed by the country team in consultation with the special inter-departmental team which was recently sent to Central America to assess the internal security situation of each country.

Contingencies

The various contingencies that may arise in Haiti, and recommended courses of action to meet them, are the subject of a separate paper entitled Haiti—Contingency Situations and Recommendations dated May 29, 1961.[1]

[Here follows a section entiled "Rationale," which reported that Haiti had too many people, too little arable land, and scant prospect for economic development since it lacked basic infrastructure. U.S. efforts to aid Haiti had been defeated by corruption of its venal governments. The Rationale section also stated that there were no good prospects for opposition to Duvalier inside or outside Haiti, and that the Duvalier government had little ability to administer joint aid programs, and limited ability to service additional foreign debt. Finally, the section listed five special problems: little capacity for self-government; the legacy of the U.S. Marines' intervention; a tendency to bypass the Embassy and USOM and to try to deal directly with Washington; social and racial tensions; and Duvalier's hypersensitivity to criticism.]

---

[1] See footnote 1, Document 367.

371.   Memorandum From the Executive Secretary of the Department of State (Brubeck) to the President's Special Assistant for National Security Affairs (Bundy)

Washington, June 1, 1962.

Attached is a copy of a memorandum which Mr. Goodwin took with him to the meeting between the President and Ambassador Thurston on Saturday, May 26.[1] I understand that the memorandum was discussed at the meeting and that the President gave his general approval to it.

We would appreciate receiving a memorandum confirming the President's approval of the position set forth in the memorandum or some other indication of the President's decision respecting it.[2]

E.S. Little[3]

Attachment

Our present policy is aimed at the identification and support of a viable alternative to Duvalier and the ultimate dislodgement of the Duvalier regime in favor of such alternative. Our present target date for the completion of this operation is next May, at which time Duvalier's first "elected" term of office expires. (We have never recognized the second "election" at which he extended his term.)

Among the reasons we feel it necessary to dislodge Duvalier are the following:

1. Some of the key people around Duvalier are ultranationalist, anti-U.S. and have communist backgrounds. There is every indication that their influence is increasing. We also believe that they are quietly, and under the very severe limitations of Duvalier's ingrained suspicions of everyone, trying to increase their authority within the government, militia, etc.; hoping to take over when Duvalier goes. The longer that he hangs on the more likely they may be to succeed.

Source: Kennedy Library, National Security Files, Countries Series, Haiti, 1/61–6/62. Secret.

[1] The meeting took place at the White House from 11:02 to 11:20 a.m. Schlesinger also attended. (Ibid., President's Appointment Book) No other record of this meeting has been found.

[2] Not found.

[3] Little signed for Brubeck above Brubeck's typed signature.

2. There is some indication of increasing communist activity in the country. There is no doubt that the longer this repressive regime continues the greater the potential communist strength.

3. Our support of Duvalier inevitably strengthens the hands of those elements of the opposition which are anti-US in orientation.

4. We are convinced that it is hopeless to try to work with Duvalier. He is indifferent to the social and economic welfare of his people, intoxicated with brutality and repressions, unaware or indifferent to the possibility of ultimate communist rule, and hostile to our guidance or advice. All efforts to work with him have met resistance and there seems to be no realistic hope that things will get better in the future.

5. A US role in dislodging Duvalier would, of course, help us with other democratic forces in the Caribbean area and be another significant step in upsetting the old "friendly to dictators" picture which still prevails although lessened by the DR events.

Under no circumstances would we try to dislodge Duvalier without a fairly clear idea who would replace him.

Thus we must use the next year to identify the alternative.

1. The CIA, FBI and INR have completed a dossier of promising Haitian exiles and visible resistance figures[4] from which we are trying to select those most likely to be capable of heading a successor government.

2. We are trying to substantially increase our intelligence on Haiti. [*4 lines of source text not declassified*] Hard as it is to believe, we know far less about Haiti under Duvalier than we knew about the Dominican Republic under Trujillo.

3. Identification of an alternative is the primary mission of our Embassy.

While this is going on we will be publicly cool toward Duvalier and conduct normal personal and private contacts. We are most anxious not to do anything which will precipitate his departure before we are ready. On the other hand a cool public posture, with occasional mild acts of hostility, are essential if we are to encourage the tentative emergence of an opposition and make them willing to be in touch with us.

If we are ready next May it is probable that we will be able to get rid of Duvalier. We are studying plans for this now. The most promising approach would be the withdrawal of recognition at the time when his term expires. This would have a juridical base and we could probably get

---

[4] Reference, at least in part, is to a compilation listing nearly 200 potential oppositionists to Duvalier. The list was attached to a memorandum from Hilsman to Martin, May 7, in which Hilsman noted that Duvalier's repression of dissident elements was so effective that there were no organized opposition groups inside Haiti. Oppositionists were all exiles. Hilsman listed 18 "technicans" who appeared to meet minimum standards of administrative ability, leadership, friendship to the United States or lack of animosity, and absence of Communist sympathies. (Department of State, Central Files, 738.11/5–762)

some other countries (e.g., Venezuela and Colombia) to go along with us. This complete severing of relations on the part of the US and others would make his fall almost inevitable.

I want to stress that this is now a probing operation. We do not intend to move decisively unless and until we feel that we have reasonable control over the future course of events.

---

372.   Memorandum From the Executive Secretary of the Department of State (Brubeck) to the President's Special Assistant for National Security Affairs (Bundy)

Washington, August 8, 1962.

SUBJECT

The Situation in Haiti

As background information for the meeting with the President on Haiti, which is scheduled for Thursday, August 9,[1] the enclosed memorandum on the current situation in that country has been prepared by the Department and concurred in by the Central Intelligence Agency.[2]

E.S. Little[3]

Source: Kennedy Library, National Security Files, Countries Series, Haiti, 7/62–8/62. Top Secret. The Department of State copy indicates that the memorandum was drafted by Abbuhl and approved by Martin. (Department of State, Central Files, 738.00/8–862)

[1] The meeting with the President took place at the White House from 10 to 10:55 a.m. McGeorge Bundy, Edwin Martin, Crimmins, Goodwin, Graham Martin, J.C. King, Richard Helms, and Frank Sloan attended. (Kennedy Library, President's Appointment Book)

[2] No memorandum of conversation of this August 9 meeting has been found, but it was discussed at the White House Daily Staff meeting of August 10. According to Colonel J.J. Ewell's notes of the staff meeting: "State and the White House are, of course, concerned about the situation in Haiti. Someone in State, I think Martin, is for suspending military assistance but Goodwin is against it. He seems to think we had better play this by ear until the situation develops one way or another. He evidently thinks that Duvalier can probably ride this one out and if we have chopped at him, he would then give the U.S. a very hard time. A small Navy/Marine task force is on the alert in the general area." National Defense University, Taylor Papers, White House Daily Staff meetings, May–Sept, 1962) See also Document 373.

[3] Little signed for Brubeck above Brubeck's typed signature.

Enclosure

THE SITUATION IN HAITI

In a country that has had many autocratic, corrupt and incompetent governments, the Duvalier regime ranks among the worst. It maintains itself in power primarily by terrorism, by graft and venality, by the constant removal and rotation of officials who attain any independent stature, and by the President's highly developed ability to ferret out intrigue and play off one group against another. It has consistently demonstrated duplicity in its lip service to constitutional practices, democratic principles and human rights. It frequently indulges in excesses, including harassment, capricious arrest, brutal treatment or summary expulsion of persons thought to oppose it, whether they be church officials, foreigners or Haitian citizens. It has shown no capacity for or interest in improving the lot of the Haitian people.

Since the regime assumed power five years ago, the political situation has deteriorated steadily and the chronically stagnant economy has been further depressed. A partisan civil militia has been developed from among the poorest, and in some cases, worst elements of the population. This militia, which is highly susceptible to political manipulation, may eventually become powerful enough to neutralize the US-trained and oriented regular armed forces, a circumstance which would open the way to a takeover by unscrupulous activists and extremists, including Communist or pro-Communist elements. A small group of ultra-nationalistic and racist advisers, all opportunistic and some receptive to strong Marxist if not Communist influence and some with Communist backgrounds, has gradually consolidated its position within the regime and is exercising a dangerously increasing influence. This group is believed to be trying to expand its authority within the Government and militia, in the hope of taking over when Duvalier goes.

While it is estimated that the strength of the Communist Party has not yet reached dangerous proportions, there can be no doubt but that the continuance in power of Duvalier's brutal, corrupt regime, which despite its propaganda is indifferent to the social and economic welfare of the people and either unaware of or indifferent to the possibility of ultimate Communist rule, is highly conducive to the growth of Communist strength and potential.

On the basis of our experience to date in dealing with the regime, we are convinced that it is hopeless, so long as Duvalier remains in power, to make any further attempt to establish a practical basis of cooperation with it or to carry out successfully the type of aid programs essential to the development of the country and of more enlightened and responsible government.

Accordingly, our present policy is: (a) to look toward the replacement of Duvalier by a more efficient, enlightened and friendly government, but (b) to avoid a premature showdown which might result in failure, elimination or neutralization of the political opposition or the assumption of power by elements no less, or perhaps more, inimical to United States interests than he. Although Duvalier is attempting through unconstitutional means to perpetuate himself in office at least until May 15, 1967, the term for which he was constitutionally elected expires May 15, 1963. The latter date offers special opportunities for pressure and maneuver on our part and is considered a target date for Duvalier's departure.

Since, in our opinion, Duvalier cannot remain in power for any extended period without United States economic and military assistance, these two levers are being used to bring carefully measured pressure to bear on the regime and to influence internal political developments in furtherance of objectives (a) and (b) above.

The decision has been made to phase out quietly two important United States financed regional development projects, which have not succeeded primarily because of the lack of Haitian cooperation, and to reduce over the next several months the range and cost of all other AID activities to about half their present level. It has also been decided to proceed with one rather than both of two pending loans in order to avoid either strengthening Duvalier unduly or provoking him to intemperate action. We are going ahead with a loan to construct a jet-capable airport which will meet a United States military requirement, but not a highway construction loan, approval of which would make it difficult, if not impossible, for us to continue opposing two pending IBRD loans.

On the military side, our Missions are exercising a useful influence on the United States-oriented regular armed forces, but this influence is being offset by Duvalier's deliberate and successful efforts to undermine the armed forces in favor of the potentially dangerous civil militia. At the moment Duvalier appears still to need our Missions and military assistance program as proof of United States support of his regime, but the continued buildup of the militia as the principal instrument for the support of his regime progressively reduces the possibility of using our military assistance to arrest or preferably reverse this unfavorable trend. Consequently, MAP shipments have been temporarily suspended while we still have this leverage, in an effort to elicit improved cooperation from the regime in implementing the Missions' recommendations which are designed to prevent the power balance from changing in favor of the militia.

There are definite indications that awareness on the part of Haitian officials and the public that Duvalier apparently no longer enjoys unqualified United States support has weakened the regime and has helped to stimulate dissident civilian elements, military officers and even former Duvalierists to plot against Duvalier more actively than heretofore. An increasing volume of reports on plots against Duvalier has been received, but the plotting appears to be based largely on wishful thinking and to be vague and uncoordinated. Approaches have been made to us recently by one dissident civilian element for assistance and by a military group (with perhaps some civilian associates) for assurances that the Untied States would not interpose itself against a military coup directed against Duvalier. A spokesman for a pro-American group of former and current Haitian military and civilian officials told our Ambassador as recently as August 1 that they were plotting to overthrow Duvalier not later than October of this year.[4]

While the latter group, which apparently includes some reputable individuals such as the Army Chief of Staff, represents possibly a cohesive and potentially effective challenge to Duvalier, the various currents of opposition activity generally have not yet made any efficacious attempt to organize or agree on future programs or a candidate, and are floundering in little groups out of fear, self-interest and uncertainty. On the basis of present evidence, it appears that the mistrust, treachery and opportunism which are chronic in Haiti make the prospects of Duvalier's overthrow in the near future problematical at best. A cool public posture and occasional mild acts of hostility toward Duvalier by the United States will maintain and probably increase current ferment, but effective opposition action will, in our opinion, probably require at a minimum firm assurances of United States support. Opposition elements at all levels invariably stress that only the United States can come to their relief.

---

[4] As reported in telegram 56 from Port-au-Prince, August 2, Thurston estimated that "this movement of disaffected former Duvalierists represents most cohesive and effective challenge to Duvalier that has yet come to our attention." (Department of State, Central Files, 738.00/8–262)

373.   Letter From the Assistant Secretary of State for Inter-American Affairs (Martin) to the Ambassador to Haiti (Thruston)

Washington, August 11, 1962.

DEAR RAY: I have just read your telegram No. 77[1] and thought perhaps it would be useful to give you some background on our thinking here and on the instructions of the last day or so which seem to have disturbed you. They were based on an hour's discussion with the President Thursday morning, participated in by Defense, CIA and AID, as well as ourselves.[2] No one challenges the basic policy decision that we cannot hope to achieve our objectives in Haiti so long as Duvalier is in power and that we must seek means to secure a change.

However, there is an equally important element in our policy which I think has been made clear throughout that, particularly under present cold war circumstances, it would be against United States interests to have an attempt to unseat Duvalier result in a period of chaos and confusion and perhaps violence, and a government even less effective and able to deal with the Haitian problems, or at worst, a government with Castro-Communist leanings.

The Haitian situation has seemed to us sufficiently confused and the Haitian people sufficiently immature politically, and the country sufficiently weak economically that these consequences could readily result from premature and poorly planned activity.

There was also, of course, a desideratum that any movement against Duvalier have a reasonable prospect of success in order to preserve the relatively few assets Haiti has in terms of effective and well-intentioned leaders.

It has also been clear that the United States definitely wanted any action to be taken to be indigenous and not open us to the charge of intervention. In this connection there are fundamental differences between the Haitian situation and the Dominican situation which must be kept in mind. Action in the case of the Dominican Republic was within the framework of OAS attitudes and positions which in turn stemmed

---

Source: Department of State, Central Files, 611.38/8–1162. Top Secret; Eyes Only; No Distribution.

[1] In telegram 77 from Port-au-Prince, August 10, Thurston reported that he had informed key personnel of his instructions as outlined in telegram 54 to Port-au-Prince, August 9. The Department's instructions were that "all official U.S. personnel in contact with opposition elements should not go beyond that of interested listeners. No encouragement should be given plotting elements." If pressed for U.S. assistance by plotters, Thurston and his relevant staff should only say that the United States would follow its stated policy of nonintervention. In telegram 77 Thurston suggested that these instructions were "too restrictive" and that risks had to be taken to obtain a more enlightened and cooperative government in Haiti. (Ibid., 738.00/8–1062 and 738.00/8–962, respectively)

[2] See footnote 1, Document 372.

largely from Dominican intervention in affairs of other countries, particularly Venezuela. The Haitian Government has taken no such steps and, in fact, there is little interest in Haiti among other Latin American countries with the exception of the Dominican Republic.

In this policy framework we have, as you know, for several months been doing two things. First, both for its effect in Haiti and because it was a correct posture for the United States to take in its own terms and for its position in the Hemisphere, we tried to make clear that we were not friendly to, or supporting in any way, Duvalier and, in particular, his attempts to perpetuate himself in power by the phony election of 1961.[3]

Second, we were stepping up our intelligence activities and contacts in order to appraise the prospects for the organization by the Haitians of a successful coup and the maintenance of a satisfactory government, military or civilian or mixed.

I have had some feeling that the step up of unrest in Haiti was due as much to the increased awareness of the military that time was against them in their competition with the militia as to any actions we have taken to show disapproval of Duvalier.

As I assume you are aware from [less than 1 line of source text not declassified], the Agency reached last week a tentative conclusion, based on such information as was available to them, that there were a number of small plotting groups not in touch with each other and in fact on the whole distrustful of each other and that insofar as they had plans of action, these were on the whole fairly childish in concept. This analysis seems to me consistent with the reports you have been sending in.

It is within the framework of this policy approach and on the basis of this appraisal of the current situation that the President reached the decisions that he did on Thursday. From a timing or tactical standpoint it is perhaps a somewhat more cautions approach than we had had in mind but Crimmins and I agree that it is no change in direction. It was made clear, and, I think, accepted that the continuation of Duvalier in office beyond May 1963 would be a major event in Haitian politics and this date a significant one for Haitian opposition groups.

As you may have heard, or certainly will hear shortly, it was agreed to step up [less than 1 line of source text not declassified] activity by adding

---

[3] Duvalier used the elections of April 30, 1961, for the new unicameral legislature that he created to claim reelection to the presidency. At the top of each ballot for deputy to the legislature was written, "Francois Duvalier, Président de la République." Duvalier claimed that the over 1.3 million ballots for the legislature (most non-Duvalier estimates of those Haitians voting were about 100,000) also constituted his election to the presidency. As the Embassy stated, efforts to give the election an "appearance of constitutionality should stretch the imagination of even the most credulous of the uneducated among the Haitians." (Despatch 469 from Port-au-Prince, May 9; Department of State, Central Files, 611.38/5–961)

one or two people to your post in order to keep in touch more closely with various groups and individuals and know more about their plans, to serve as a better basis for United States policy and action decisions here. There have been no decisions which preclude us from playing an active covert role. There have been no decisions which would prevent us from giving active overt assistance if called upon to do so by a provisional government which was to our liking or, if the situation would develop in a way which would permit OAS sponsorship of action. If this type of situation should develop, we would prefer that United States military activity be associated with military activity of other Latin American countries.

Within the framework of this policy, we shall continue to stress that aid actions have been taken on technical grounds. This reflects our concern about premature action either by Duvalier against us or the opposition or by the opposition against Duvalier. Steps by either side at this time would on the basis of our present information seriously interfere with achieving our fundamental objectives as described above.

The first thing John and I discussed after returning from the White House was the technical problem we, and particularly you, would have in carrying out this policy in the face of the current unrest about which we knew relatively little at the time of the meeting with the President. It is exceedingly difficult for people to keep their courage up to the breaking point over a long period of time, to be uncertain about the future prospects and about the nature or even existence of outside support. On the other hand, and far outweighing these real considerations, is the great damage that could be done to the prospects of success by premature, ill-planned action with a loss of leadership and of prestige that this would involve. Moreover, we must consider as overriding, as I am sure from your reports you have been doing in your contacts, the giving of any basis to any of the opposition groups for thinking that the United States was taking an active role and that they had a claim on us which could be cashed at a time of their choosing. The United States is, and must continue to be, firmly committed to a policy of nonintervention in internal affairs of other countries, even in Latin America, in situations where the security and future of the hemisphere as a whole is not directly involved and where we cannot count on the public support and endorsement of the great majority of other countries in the hemisphere.

While it would be inappropriate to move at this particular time, I am more convinced than ever of the necessity to the carrying out of difficult policy line of an early change in the chief of your military mission. I spoke to Lansing Collins about this on Thursday.

Perhaps I should have written this letter or something like it considerably earlier, but I did not realize that there might be some difference in our concept of the timing factors and the application of what I think has been an agreed basic policy. Nor was I aware until this week exactly how the President looked upon the problem, although I did know from previous conversations of his desire for caution and careful planning.

Sincerely,

Edwin M. Martin[4]

P.S. In reviewing this letter there are two points I may not have made clear. In our understanding we had never, in considering implementation of the basic objective, gone beyond authority to collect intelligence. We still have not done so. Any action by us, covert or overt, can thus only take place as a result of a new decision at the highest level.

I want to stress also that we recognize that we may be faced with very difficult decisions if the evidences of our unfavorable attitude toward the Duvalier Government are taken by Haitians as guarantees of support and they take overt action accordingly. This may be a fairly immediate problem. I cannot, of course, predict what our decisions would be if violence should break out but you should certainly not count on measures beyond those necessary to protect the lives and property of Americans.

EMM

---

[4] Printed from a copy that bears this typed signature and typed initials.

---

374. Memorandum Prepared in the Department of State

Washington, January 21, 1963.

HAITI SITUATION AND UNITED STATES POLICY

The essential elements of the situation in Haiti and our policy towards that country are the following:

1. In his Independence Day address on January 1, 1963, President Duvalier eliminated any remaining doubt that he might hold Presiden-

Source: Kennedy Library, National Security Files, Countries Series, Haiti, 9/62–2/63. Secret. Sent to Bundy under cover of a January 21 memorandum from Brubeck, which noted that this memorandum was prepared as background information for a Presidential meeting on Haiti on January 22. The meeting with the President took place at the White House from 4:15 to 5 p.m.; Martin, Crimmins, Collins, and Dungan attended. Guatemala was discussed in addition to Haiti. (Ibid., President's Appointment Book) No other record of the January 22 meeting has been found.

tial elections before February 10 and step down from the Presidency on May 15, 1963 as he is obligated to do under Haitian law. He stated clearly that he plans to continue in power through 1963 and beyond.

2. The Duvalier regime has not received any substantial assistance from the United States or international lending institutions since July 1, 1962. United States military matériel shipments have been suspended since that time, as has been the greater part of our economic aid. We have also blocked approval of pending AID, IDB and IDA loans totalling some $17 million, because their approval would strengthen Duvalier's position greatly and seriously undermine opposition efforts and morale. We recently approved an AID loan of $2.8 million for a jet airport in order to reduce the risk that our negative attitude toward Duvalier might provoke him to intemperate action before we were prepared to deal with it, and because the airport meets an important United States military requirement for a jet-capable field in Haiti.

3. The fact that the Duvalier regime is now receiving only very limited economic assistance from the United States Government and international lending institutions has served to identify the United States with more enlightened political forces whose cooperation will be required if we are to attain our long-term objectives in Haiti, that is, to keep Haiti aligned with the United States and the free world, and to help overcome its critical economic and social problems in order to establish a broader base for the development of more enlightened, orderly and responsible government. It has also resulted in increased activity on the part of these forces. We estimate, however that the measures taken thus far which are essentially passive in nature, are not likely to provide sufficient stimulus to acceptable opposition elements who are seeking some means of preventing Duvalier from unconstitutionally perpetuating himself in office.

4. In recent weeks, we have been receiving improved intelligence reporting on the organization, internal conflicts, attitudes and activities of Haiti's principal Communist elements. While they now appear to be better organized and therefore potentially more of a threat than we had previously estimated, we do not believe that their strength has reached dangerous proportions. We are, of course, assessing on a continuing basis the relative strength of the Communists and other opposition elements who hope to topple Duvalier.

The most recent comprehensive review of our Haitian policy was made in October when the Latin American Policy Committee approved a Plan of Action (enclosed),[1] the principal conclusions of which were the following:

---

[1] Dated October 23; not printed.

1. The kind of measures, both overt and covert, which would assure Duvalier's departure in favor of an acceptable alternative, were not acceptable to us at that time.

2. We should take advantage of the possible development of circumstances in which the application of further overt measures would tip the balance and result in Duvalier's probable replacement by a more acceptable government. At the same time, we should avoid pin-pricking measures which only serve to make it more difficult to maintain a working relationship with his regime without assuring the desired result.

3. A further review of our policies and programs in Haiti should be undertaken in early 1963 in the light of developments and prospects then existing.

This further policy review is scheduled to be completed the week of February 10 when Ambassador Thurston will arrive here on consultation. The Country Team at Port-au-Prince is forwarding a paper for consideration that is to include, inter alia: (a) a summary of the current situation, (b) Duvalier's prospects of remaining in power beyond May 15, (c) the various courses of action open to us for achieving his departure and the risks involved, and (d) our posture towards the Duvalier regime should it remain in power after May 15.

---

375.   Paper Prepared in the Department of State

Washington, February 20, 1963.

HAITI PLAN OF ACTION FROM FEBRUARY 15 TO SEPTEMBER 15, 1963[1]

[Here follow a discussion of the objectives of the plan (the orderly departure of Duvalier, a working but cool relationship until that time, and preservation and strengthening of the U.S. position with the political

---

Source: Department of State, Central Files, POL HAI. Secret. This paper, which was drafted by Abbuhl, was transmitted to Bundy under a February 21 memorandum from Brubeck. Bundy requested the plan to show President Kennedy en route to Palm Beach, Florida, the night of February 23.

[1] This plan replaced one drafted by Abbuhl on October 16 and October 23, 1962, covering October–May 1963. (Kennedy Library, National Security Files, Countries Series, Haiti, 9/62–2/63)

forces that the United States wanted to see replace Duvalier), a description of the current situation, and an assessment that a change of government in Haiti was likely within the next year.]

Plan of Action

1. Use the implementation of the recently signed loan for the construction of the jet airport as a device for maintaining correct and continuing relations with Haitian officials.[2]

2. At every opportunity in conversations with President Duvalier and other high Haitian officials, exert pressure directed against anti-American, crypto-Communist or Communist elements both in and out of the Government.

3. React with toughness and vigor to any Government excesses involving the violation of the rights of American citizens.

4. Public Law 480, Title III[3] programs should be maintained, with vigorous Embassy support in fighting obstructionism. Appropriate instances of obstructionism should be protested by formal note. If the programs cannot be maintained because of obstructionism, they should be suspended and the reasons for the suspension should be made known publicly.

5. Maintain maximum pressure on the Government to pay its debts both to official American lending institutions and to private American creditors. Particular attention should be given to the satisfactory settlement of private American claims which have been pending for almost a year before the Haitian Claims Commission.

6. American officials should talk fiscal and administrative reform at all levels of contact with Haitians, both in and out of the Government, so that it will be clearly understood that such reforms are a sine qua non for United States aid to Haiti. Mention of such reforms should specifically include the incorporation of all Government revenues into the regular budget, since there is no accountability for the substantial proportion of revenues that are now outside the budget.

7. While limiting its activities to support of the malaria eradication campaign and execution of the jet airport construction loan, the USAID Mission should continue its searching evaluation of United States aid to Haiti in the light of experience, and an attractive and realistic contingency aid program for an acceptable successor government should be prepared.

---

[2] In the "Current Situation" portion, not printed, it was explained that the $2.8 million loan from AID for a jet airport was approved "in order to reduce the risk that our negative attitude toward Duvalier might provoke him to intemperate action before we were prepared to deal with him." See also paragraph 2 of Document 374.

[3] The Agricultural Trade Development and Assistance Act, July 10, 1954, 68 Stat. 454.

8. To offset our retrenchment in other fields, USIS should continue a high level of activities, and the Haitian-American Institute should step up the quantity and quality of United States cultural programs in Haiti in order to raise American cultural prestige. On carefully selected matters where local media for political reasons dare not publish news about U.S. positions regarding Haiti, USIS should be utilized as a channel for distributing this news, bearing in mind, however, the need to protect USIS' relations with local information media and the Haitian Government.

9. United States Military Missions in Haiti should: (a) continue, where possible, to maintain or increase effective contact, private and official, with the Haitian Armed Forces and its leadership, with a view to preventing loss of existing latent assets, and to developing a solid basis for future cooperation; (b) pursue intelligence collection efforts as directed and required; (c) maintain current plans for short-notice resumption of MAP material and training support for the Armed Forces which could be offered to a new and more responsive regime; (d) develop contingency plans for a broader civic action program for the Armed Forces under a successor regime so they may play a more constructive role in the development of the country.

10. Increase the number of visits by units of the United States Navy to the outlying ports of Haiti in order to demonstrate an American presence and sympathetic interest in those areas.

11. The Immigration and Naturalization Service should be requested to issue re-entry (I–512) permits to exile leaders residing in the United States who are attempting to organize a unified movement of all Haitian exiles, both here and in other countries, and need to travel outside the United States to do so. Because of their indefinite residence status as exiles, they are unable without such a permit to re-enter the United States once they leave, except by applying for and obtaining a resident visa from a United States Consul abroad.

12. Consider means of reducing the size of United States military missions in Haiti in such a way as not to violate agreements, hamper United States interests, or provoke Duvalier to demand their complete withdrawal. Planned increases in Military Attaché coverage should be implemented.

13. Continue to block pending AID, IDB, and IDA loans to Haiti which, if approved, would be exploited politically by Duvalier and would support his current effort to portray his regime as progressive, and respected and accepted internationally.

14. Follow closely the financial position of the Haitian Government in order to take advantage of any circumstances in which the United States can exercise any influence thereon in ways furthering our principal objective, i.e., the departure of Duvalier in favor of an acceptable alternative.

15. Assess, on a continuing basis and against the evolving situation, the potential for achieving our objective through a direct approach to Duvalier calculated to encourage him to leave office. Such an approach could be made either through a special emissary or through the American Ambassador, who would point out that there will be no resumption of US aid to Haiti so long as he remains in power, and that it would be in the interests of the Haitian people, U.S.-Haitian relations, and peace and progress in the Caribbean area for him to step down and make way for an orderly succession. In 1956 the then American Ambassador, accompanied by the Papal Nuncio, made such appeal to President Magloire just before he left office.

16. Encourage the international press to publish the facts about Haiti, when this can be done without risk of detection, so that the repressive and illegal nature of the Duvalier regime will continue to be spotlighted on the international scene and so the Haitian opposition will take encouragement from this sympathetic interest in their plight.

17. Publicize by means of background press briefings, statements by appropriate members of Congress, Government officials, etc. that U.S. economic aid has been drastically reduced and military matériel shipments suspended for some time because of the inadequacies of the Duvalier government, its failure to adhere to agreements, and attempts to subvert U.S. aid to political ends. Such briefings and statements should also: (a) deplore the oppressive nature of the Duvalier regime and Duvalier's failure to step down from office at the expiration of his elected term of office, (b) reiterate the desire of the United States to help the Haitian people in accordance with the principles and democratic spirit implicit in the Alliance for Progress, and (c) intimate that substantial U.S. assistance would be forthcoming to a cooperative, responsible government.

18. As the end of Duvalier's constitutionally elected term approaches, consideration should be given to consulting with the representatives in Washington of those Latin American and NATO governments that maintain diplomatic missions in Port-au-Prince, with a view to encouraging them to recall their representatives from Haiti over the period May 15–22, 1963, in order publicly to disassociate their countries from Duvalier's flouting of Haiti's constitution and electoral laws.

19. If Duvalier is still in office on May 15, no actions should be taken to underline the passage of that date or prejudice the continued presence of our Ambassador, except to follow the procedure of the past two years, i.e., call the Ambassador back on consultation before May 15 and have him remain away from Haiti until after May 22, the second anniversary of Duvalier's "reinauguration."

376. Telegram From the Department of State to the Embassy in the Dominican Republic

Washington, March 7, 1963, 6:27 p.m.

788. While Duvalier still maintains firm and effective control of Haiti, opposition to his oppressive regime is widespread and plotting against him has increased substantially since it became evident that he has no intention of voluntarily relinquishing power at the end of his constitutional term of office, May 15, 1963. A sudden coup or act of violence against Duvalier could occur at any time, a possible consequence of which might be an internal armed conflict or a complete breakdown in public authority. Given the degree to which racism has been made an issue by Duvalier, the safety of foreigners would be particularly endangered in such a situation. There could also be danger of a Communist-inspired attempt to move in under cover of a confused or anarchical situation. There could be a request for assistance from a respectable provisional government fighting Duvalier forces.

US contingency planning for Haiti incorporates provision for use of US forces in varying forms as may be required by conditions within Haiti following an outbreak of violence. These possible courses of action range from the bringing of fleet units into Haitian waters to serve as a calming and restraining influence, to the actual landing of troops should the situation degenerate to such an extent that the threat to our interests outweighed the disadvantages of taking such drastic measures.[1]

While some kind of OAS umbrella would be urgently sought for the direct involvement of US forces in any of the contingencies envisioned, it must be recognized that a variety of developments within Haiti could make it encumbent on us to move our forces much more rapidly than it would be possible to obtain any sort of OAS action. Should this prove to be necessary, it would be distinctly advantageous if our actions enjoyed the sanction (and possible participation) of as many as possible of the Hemisphere governments that share our interest in preventing a disaster in Haiti.

Source: Department of State, Central Files, POL 26 HAI. Top Secret; Priority; Limit Distribution. Drafted by Crockett; cleared in draft with Wellman, Deputy Director of the Office of West Coast Affairs Herbert Thompson, Fisher, Allen, Cottrell, and Dungan; cleared in substance with General Enemark of DOD/ISA; and approved by Martin. Also sent to Bogotá, Caracas, Panama, San José, and Tegucigalpa, and repeated to Port-au-Prince, POLAD CINCLANT and POLAD CINCARIB.

[1] The draft contingency plan is in JCS telegram 9018, March 9, sent for information to the Department of State. In telegram 231, March 9, the Department of State sent the JCS plan to the Embassy in Haiti for its comments. In telegram 393 from Port-au-Prince, March 12, Thurston responded that he agreed with the plan, but wanted to be able to assure opposition forces of U.S. assistance in advance of their acting. (All ibid.)

Without approaching host governments, addressee posts are requested to comment on the prospects for obtaining advance commitment of support by the governments to which accredited for utilization of US forces in the manner and degree required by emergency situations that might be expected to arise in Haiti.[2] Such support would consist of public statements calling for or approving US action as well as support in seeking OAS approval.

While the range of such emergency situations is all but limitless, Department has particularly in mind situations resulting from or complicated by Haiti's proximity to Cuba and/or a complete breakdown of law and order, riots and violence such as have attended some previous changes of political power in Haiti.

Rusk

---

[2] The recipient posts estimated that their government's responses to unilateral U.S. intervention in Haiti would be negative. The responses are ibid., POL HAI and POL 26 HAI.

---

377. Summary Record of the 509th National Security Council Meeting

Washington, March 13, 1963, 4:30 p.m.

SUBJECT

Latin American Policy

Present: President, Vice President, Secretary Rusk, Secretary McNamara, Secretary Dillon, Attorney General, General Taylor, Director McCone, Secretary Vance, Under Secretary Ball, Ambassador Stevenson, Administrator Bell, Deputy Secretary Gilpatric, Director Murrow, Director McDermott, U. Alexis Johnson, Assistant Secretary Martin, Assistant Secretary Tyler, Paul Nitze, Mr. McGeorge Bundy, Mr. Sorensen, Mr. Dungan, Mr. Kaysen, General Clifton, Mr. Bromley Smith

---

Source: Kennedy Library, National Security Files, Meetings and Memoranda Series, NSC Meetings, No. 509. Top Secret. No drafting information appears on the source text.

[Here follows discussion of Cuba, for text, see volume XI.]

Secretary Rusk indicated that we must be prepared to move promptly in trouble areas such as Haiti.[1] General Taylor indicated that we could put U.S. Marines ashore in Haiti within 51 hours.

The President reacted sharply to the estimate of 51 hours by saying that this was too long. General Taylor said there was a unit which could be airdropped much sooner if an airfield were available. If we wished, we could keep the Marines aboard ships just over the horizon.

Mr. Martin said our Ambassador in Haiti did not recommend that Marine forces be kept aboard ship just over the horizon. This matter is to be followed closely because of the uncertain situation in Haiti.

[Here follows discussion of other Latin American topics (see Document 56) and further discussion on Cuba (see volume XI).]

---

[1] At the request of the White House, INR prepared an assessment of short-term prospects for Haiti and of possible U.S. actions. It concluded that Duvalier was precariously threatened by opposition groups inside and outside Haiti. These groups were nonetheless ill-equipped to gain effective control of the government should Duvalier be eliminated. Anarchy was the most likely result; and Castro and Haitian Communists would profit most. There were few options open to the United States: direct U.S. intervention would be strongly protested in Latin America, and the Dominican Republic's intervention would raise as many problems as it would solve. OAS intervention would be difficult to sell to the other members, but it was the best option. An OAS mission would have to take responsibility for a remedial economic program and establishing law and order conducive to formation of a successor regime. (Memorandum from Hughes to Rusk, May 8; ibid., 5/7/63–8/63)

---

378. Telegram From the Embassy in Haiti to the Department of State

Port-au-Prince, May 2, 1963.

521. Through situation reports and cables on specific incidents we have attempted to convey accurate picture abnormal situation prevail-

---

Source: Department of State, Central Files, POL HAI. Top Secret; Operational Immediate. Repeated to Caracas and Santo Domingo. No time of transmission appears on the source text. Relayed to the White House.

ing here in recent days.[1] I believe it now essential for US Govt consider urgently what it can do together with other interested govts to get this powder keg under control and turn the crisis to advantage in terms our objectives and interests in Haiti and Latin American generally.

It is difficult to exaggerate the fear, both justified and unreasoning, which now dominates Port-au-Prince. It permeates all elements of the population, Haitians and foreigners, officials and non-officials, rich and poor. Many ordinary Haitians are drifting back to their villages in the hinterland. No curfew has been declared but there is little nocturnal activity because of the fear of being inadvertently shot by army and militia patrols posted around city. Except for violent action by Barbot group (which now believed be ones who killed guardians Duvalier children and to whom is also attributed last night's reportedly successful raid on weapons depot at Martissant area) Duvalier's security forces appear to have everything under control. Yet apprehension persists as crowds of simple people are harangued in inflammatory creole speeches by Duvalier and his henchmen. Duvalier himself in "apres moi le deluge" mood as he continues to crack down on all elements suspected of opposing him.

Both because of personal indignities suffered at hands police authorities and accounts of atrocities reaching them from increasing number asylees in Latin American Embassies foreign diplomats are deeply troubled about situation. To what extent this has as yet had impact on their governments cannot be determined from here, but I would judge that our own general position re Duvalier regime now more widely supported than before recent events.

Arrival OAS commission welcomed here by all except GOH itself which wants it out of town as soon as possible. Our only contact with commission has been through Dean Diplomatic Corps, those Latin American Embassies whose countries are on commission and American journalists. I understand that there are differences in the commission about how broadly they should interpret terms of reference (Emb would appreciate official info from Department on this subject) and how long they should stay in Haiti. Dept should, I believe, use its full influence to keep OAS in this country as long as possible. Appreciate that problem of

---

[1] After the April 26 abortive kidnapping attempt on his family by Haitian dissidents, Duvalier's agents began to arrest oppositionists, many of whom fled to the sanctuary of foreign embassies. The government cordoned off the Dominican and other Latin American Embassies in Port-au-Prince to prevent potential political refugees from obtaining asylum. On April 26 Haitian police forcibly entered the Dominican Embassy. The Dominican Republic called for a special meeting of the Council of the OAS, which in turn created an investigative committee that visited both countries. As a result of the visit and in anticipation of the report, Haiti removed its forces from the Dominican Embassy and allowed some Haitian asylees safe conduct to the Dominican Republic. Documentation on this conflict is primarily ibid., POL DOM REP–HAI. See also John Bartlow Martin, *Overtaken by Events*, pp. 416–447.

intervention in internal affairs presents difficulties, but GODR charges do in themselves afford bridge for OAS to delve into the real factors underlying the fundamentally unsatisfactory situation here and to make recommendations equal to challenge. This is also virtually unanimous view my diplomatic colleagues.

Unless Duvalier removed soon from scene (he shows no signs of voluntary departure) I find it difficult to envisage any solution other than intervention. Under certain circumstances (shooting of US Embassy officials or storming any local embassy to kill asylees) I would recommend unilateral use of US forces. Far preferable however would be collective OAS intervention. Economic sanctions as in Dominican case hardly seem appropriate in country like Haiti so close subsistence level already and might only have adverse propaganda impact. What is required is collective "police" action which would result in effective physical control local situation including if necessary pacification opposing groups. Recognizing that old-fashioned marine type occupation no longer feasible would it not be possible to work on emergency basis towards Venezuelan and Dominican participation, perhaps only symbolic, along with our own forces in OAS sanctioned collective police effort here? I submit that dangers inherent in continued laissez faire policy re Haiti are sufficiently grave to warrant this kind of extraordinary action by our inter-American system.[2]

Thurston

---

[2] In telegram 323 to Port-au-Prince, May 2, the Department reminded Thurston that there was little enthusiasm in Latin America for intervention in Haiti, and that the United States had yet to convince the OAS that a "police action" was needed. Nonetheless, the Department assured Thurston that its policy was "far from one of laissez faire." (Department of State, Central Files, POL HAI)

379. Haitian Situation Report

Washington, May 8, 1963.

1. Reinforced Dominican forces deployed along Haitian-Dominican border during past 48 hours to a total of perhaps 1,200 men.[1]

2. Bosch has assured Ambassador Martin and Ambassador Facio of OAS that he will not take any unprovoked aggressive action outside OAS context.

3. Bosch has informed Ambassador Martin privately of his recognition that Dominican armed forces lack capability to invade Haiti and stated that he is maintaining them along border principally to pressure rapid OAS action.

4. Haiti has been noticeably quieter during the past 48 hours, with a strict 8:00 p.m. to 5:00 a.m. curfew still in effect.

5. The only organized opposition activity is under direction of Clement Barbot, organizer of the TTMs, who has since broken with Duvalier and who claims credit for killing three Palace escorts in recent unsuccessful attempt to kidnap President Duvalier's children. His force is quite small but we have information it probably inflicted around 30 casualties in a clash with TTMs on April 30.

6. 100 U.S. dependents departed for Miami by plane at 11:00 a.m. Another group of about the same size will be evacuated tomorrow, May 9, and a third planeload of private citizens is expected to leave on Saturday, May 11.

7. Haiti agreed to our evacuation and have assured Ambassador Thurston that the Haitian Government has every intention of continuing to guarantee protection of foreigners.

8. This morning the OAS adopted a resolution returning its special investigation committee to Haiti and broadening considerably the terms of reference governing its operation.[2]

Source: Department of State, Central Files, POL HAI. Secret. Sent to the White House under cover of a memorandum from Brubeck to Bundy, May 8. The report of the situation was as of 2 p.m., May 8. It was in response to a request from Dungan.

[1] On May 6 Bosch told U.S. correspondents that he would invade Haiti at 4:30 a.m. on May 7. Ambassador Martin was not convinced that Bosch would invade, neither was he sure that he would not. Martin recommended giving Bosch a firm commitment to help him subvert Duvalier, a flat "no" from the United States implying that the U.S. was withdrawing its support, or some combination of the two alternatives. (Telegram 1364 from Santo Domingo, May 6; ibid., POL DOM REP–HAI)

[2] OAS doc. OEA/Ser.G/V/C–d–1062. The committee made several trips to Haiti an the Dominican Republic. The OAS Council adopted various resolutions in an attempt to facilitate the situation without much success during the remainder of 1963.

9. The UN Security Council will meet at 3:00 p.m. to hear the Haitian protest Dominican aggression.[3] We will try to avoid formal UN action on the basis OAS is currently seized of the problem and dealing with it adequately.

10. The prospective flight of an official Haitian aircraft to Curacao was cancelled at Haitian initiative after authorization for it to land had been given by Dutch authorities. We do not know what the intended purpose of this unusual flight might have been nor the reasons why it was cancelled.

---

[3] That effort was successful. At the end of the discussion of the crisis by the Security Council, May 8–10, the Secretary General ruled that it was a consensus of the majority of the members that the OAS should be given the chance to bring about an amicable solution. (Memorandum from Cleveland to Ball, May 10; Department of State, Central Files, POL DOM REP–HAI)

---

380. Telegram From the Department of State to the Embassy in Haiti

Washington, May 14, 1963, 11:19 p.m.

414. Port-au-Prince and Santo Domingo for Ambassadors, USUN for Amb. Stevenson.

1. In light possibility Duvalier departure[1] a carrier is being instructed move as close to Port-au-Prince as possible while staying in international waters by early Wednesday morning.[2] Whether or not these forces needed appearance may be helpful in calming situation.

2. As soon as you have firm information Duvalier has left from US or other sources you should with such assistance as you consider appropriate from your Latin American colleagues facilitate organization of temporary governmental council composed friendly Haitians now in

---

Source: Department of State, Central Files, POL 15 HAI. Top Secret; Emergency; Limited Distribution. Drafted by Martin; cleared by Rusk, Dungan, Sloan of ISA, and King of CIA; and approved by Martin. Repeated Emergency to Santo Domingo; Priority to USUN; and Operational Immediate to POLAD CINCLANT and POLAD CINCARIB.
[1] According to telegram 413 to Haiti, May, 14, Duvalier's aide made four reservations for Duvalier and others to fly from Curacao to New York to Paris to Algiers via Pan Am Airlines on May 15. (Ibid., POL 15–1 HAI)
[2] May 15.

Port-au-Prince. You should do this regardless efforts by Duvalier to bestow mantle or of unacceptable elements to seize it and claim governmental authority. You should draw upon list available to you. We have in mind particularly [General] Constant, [George] Latortue, and if possible Madhere. Would like at least 5 but 3 would do. Insofar as possible this group should understand that their role is provisional until exiles return and some semblance of order permits organization of wider based governmental council which could be in control pending elections. Would want to get several key exiles like Fouchet, Boucicaut and [Léon] Cantave back and on Council as soon as feasible. Will wait your recommendations as to when.

3.   Leave to your discretion whether it would facilitate maintenance of order to attempt include in such group representatives existing government like President, Supreme Court, who has best title and successor to head of state, or others about whom we inquired [*less than 1 line of source text not declassified*] earlier this week. We see considerable advantages to including one or more of these persons. Would see considerable advantages in Chief Supreme Court serving as very temporary Chairman to add to notion of legitimacy.

4.   Suggest safety of group might be increased if it could operate from a Latin American Embassy, though political reactions of Haitians to such locale would require consideration.

5.   First action this group should be request recognition as provisional government from all countries which have maintained relations with Haiti in past and to invite assistance OAS and its member states individually and collectively in maintenance law and order until Haitians' military and police functions can be returned to normal. Not so immediately necessary but desirable would be indication of their wish for OAS and member state technical assistance on substantial scale in operating Haitian Government pending elections. They should, of course, make public their intention invite participation by other Haitian leaders not presently available in Port-au-Prince in governing committee in very near future. You should on receipt this request telephone it to Washington for conveyance to OAS and use our facilities to repeat to other Latin American governments. We also think it important that they immediately authorize Auguste and Baguidy to act for them at UN and OAS, respectively. Whom we believe may be disposed cooperate.

6.   It is of course desirable that group be able make radio contact with Haitian population at earliest possible moment. If this not feasible from Port-au-Prince facilities, we would like their authority to have Boucicaut broadcast in their name to Haitian people as co-member of group. He is now in Kingston and being held ready for immediate use of this sort. We are working on arrangements to provide him broadcasting faci-

lities either from carrier or aircraft which would appear come from Haitian soil as early as possible tomorrow. Will confirm details later.

7. We would much prefer not to have US forces enter Haiti until request from group for military help received and preferably not until there has been opportunity OAS agree respond favorably which may take 12–24 hours or may never be possible. We would also press for others to join with us on at least token basis as rapidly as possible. However, with or without formation such a group and with or without such an appeal, we are ready at any time, if necessary to protect lives of US and other foreign nationals and asylees, to authorize landing from nearby carrier. It would be of greatest importance if request for such assistance could be made publicly in name not only US Embassy but other Latin American and European Embassies. We will be informing principal European and Latin American capitals early tomorrow of this possibility.

8. Meanwhile, we have been having discussions here today with Cantave, who has plan for entering Haiti from outside which might be made feasible within relatively short period of time if organization provisional government in Port-au-Prince proves impossible. We do feel it necessary to have call for help from such group from within Haiti before we can take anything but most temporary action to maintain law and order or to assist in managing Haitian government. We are holding up action with this group however until we see what happens tomorrow. It seems clear that without such request no sort of OAS action is possible and perhaps not even with it.

9. Telephone on Inter-American phone on receipt this message. You may comment or ask questions by reference paragraph numbers.[3]

Rusk

---

[3] In telegram 663 from Port-au-Prince, May 15, noon, Thurston reported that he had telephoned Martin to inform him that Duvalier was not leaving Haiti. Thurston made comments on the plan outlined above for transition to a temporary government, on the grounds that his views might be useful in the future. (Department of State, Central Files, POL 15 HAI)

381.   Paper Prepared in the Central Intelligence Agency

Washington, undated.

HAITI

I.   Duvalier

1. Apparently Duvalier, in the absence of assassination, will survive the efforts of internal opposition elements (now not organized) will be inaugurated and will continue in control of Haiti. His statements (whether sincere or not) that he will not proclaim a Socialist or Communist state place the United States in the position where we cannot oppose him on political grounds except for the following reasons:

a. Violation of Haitian constitutional processes, thus extending his tenure of office;
b. His administration has not been in the best interests of the Haitian people; and
c. We don't like him and it appears he does not like us.

2. Assuming (a) above to be correct, Duvalier can only be removed by some form of military action by either the OAS, the United States, or an exile group. An alternative would be an uprising by a group from within which might be catalyzed but would require almost immediate external assistance in order to survive.

3. Duvalier has a small Naval force (two sub-chasers and a few small boats, personnel of questionable loyalty) a small Air Force (four P–51s probably inoperable, and a few transports and trainers, and personnel of questionable loyalty). His Armed Forces total 5280 officers and men (including Army, Coast Guard, Air Corps and Police), equipped with light arms, six antiquated tanks and a few field pieces. These forces have been weakened by recent purges of the officer ranks and morale is believed to be low. Although the Army is reinforced by a poorly equipped and badly organized civilian militia, the extent to which these forces would support Duvalier is not known.

4. There appear a large number of refugee or exile groups intent on disposing of Duvalier and taking over the government. Many are former Haitian political figures, who seek restoration of their power or financial positions. Some may be motivated by high principle, others by personal ambition, and there is evidence that some of them are both motivated by

---

Source: Central Intelligence Agency, DCI/McCone Files, Job 80–B1285A, Memos for the Record, 4/15/63–6/4/63. Secret. A handwritten note at the end of this paper indicates that copies were sent to McGeorge Bundy and Ball on an eyes only/personal basis, at the request of McCone on May 20.

and supported by private capital who seek special consideration such as hotels, casinos, etc., in Haiti. There is evidence that some of this support might come from undesirable circles within official endorsement of one or several of these exile groups.

[*1 paragraph (13 lines of source text) not declassified*]

5. The assumption that large segments of Duvalier's military establishment and the Haitian population would immediately defect to the expeditionary force, while a strong possibility, must not be accepted as a certainty in planning such an operation. It is possible that Duvalier might release irresponsible groups throughout Haiti who would unleash acts of terror.

6. [*6 lines of source text not declassified*]

Throughout the history of Haiti's independence there has been a racial problem—95% of the population are negroes and 5% are mulattoes (a combination of negro, French and marines). The mulattoes have been the elite, the successful commercial interests, and the influential forces in government, though seldom the Head of State. They have traditionally had their "hand in the till." When a mulatto has actually headed the government, trouble has resulted. The traditional principle has been to have a negro in the top position in the government. These factors must be taken into account in considering U.S. policy.

7. Whatever is done will be attributed to the United States. It cannot be otherwise. It will be looked upon as United States interference in the internal affairs of a sovereign state (irrespective of how bad that state is). There will be high "noise level" which will be particularly true in many Latin American and African states. [*2-1/2 lines of source text not declassified*]

8. [*less than 1 line of source text not declassified*] Duvalier, despite his statements, is bitter toward the United States. He has disposed of interests traditionally friendly to the United States who have been in Haiti. This has been done by forced exile or assassination. Hence, it can be expected that he probably will turn either to Cuba or to the Bloc for military and economic aid, and this very probably will be forthcoming.

9. We must not overlook the French influence in Haiti and its continued interest in Haiti. Despite difficulties with policy discussions with France at the moment, it might be constructive to explore this entire problem in depth with France because of France's special interest in Haiti and the distinct possibility that they may have an influence in Haiti which we do not have.

Attachment

STRENGTH ESTIMATES

Armed Forces	Officers	Men	Total
	353	4928	5281
A. Port-au-Prince:	259	2627	2886
1. Dessalines Battalion	20	363	383
2. Presidential Guard	20	390	410
3. All other units, including the Police (16/722=738)	16	722	738
Coast Guard (34/278=312),	34	278	312
and Air Corps (25/170=195)	25	170	195
	219	1874	2093
B. Provinces:	94	2301	2395

---

382. Memorandum From the Assistant Secretary of State for Inter-American Affairs (Martin) to Acting Secretary of State Ball

Washington, May 21, 1963.

SUBJECT

Haiti Course of Action

While the understanding of the meeting which we had in Mr. Dungan's office last night[1] was to prepare alternatives for presentation to the

---

Source: Department of State, Central Files, POL HAI–US. Top Secret. Drafted by Martin.

[1] No other record of the meeting has been found. For the policy paper as approved b the President, see Document 384.

President, rather than recommendations, I should like on the basis of that paper to make the following recommendations to you:

1.   Basically I think we should follow courses (b) and (c), maintaining the Embassy under a Chargé but with formal relations suspended and seeking to test the attitude of the Haitian people toward Duvalier through Haitian intermediaries. This is a course which I think we might follow for several months before considering an alternative. Such a course involves certain other steps which follow.

2.   As of the 24th or 25th of May the Ambassador should be recalled for consultation with no immediate attempt to return him there or officially assign him elsewhere. We would put him to work in ARA.

3.   As of about June 1 special alerts would all be stepped down and the major military units withdrawn but patrols in the Windward Passage should be increased somewhat beyond precrisis levels with particular attention to traffic from Cuba.

4.   There should be a slowing routine appearing phase down of the staffs of our military missions.

5.   We should continue the malaria eradication program and proceed on a normal but very strict basis with the airport loan.

6.   We should not have formal relations but the Chargé should be free to talk informally with the Foreign Minister and to use informal channels for routine communication between himself or other members of the country team and Haitian Government.

7.   While one cannot predict OAS potentialities until the Committee files its report, which should be by the end of this week, I think we may assume that with the quieting down of the Dominican-Haitian conflict OAS interest will become rather secondary. The best we can hope for is to stimulate interest in the human right aspects of the Haitian problem and a recognition that glaring violations of human rights can become a threat to peace and security and therefore a matter of international concern.

I do not think this program is one which should be finally adopted for at least 48 hours, namely until we see what develops in the course of the celebrations scheduled for tomorrow and in their immediate aftermath.

A principal problem about this arrangement is the nature of the diplomatic relations we have or don't have with the Duvalier regime. The longer we keep relations in a state of suspension, the more difficult it may be to stay there and to conduct necessary business. On the other hand reestablishing formal relations with the Duvalier regime could create embarrassing difficulties for us in recognizing and assisting a competing regime. Perhaps we might wait a week or so longer before crossing this particular bridge to see what the prospects look like for having such a competing regime problem.

383.   Memorandum for the Record

Washington, May 21, 1963.

SUBJECT

Meeting re Haiti—4:30 p.m., 21 May 1963—Cabinet Room

PRESENT

The President and most of the Principals

1. State presented a paper[1] on the situation advocating the return of our Ambassador, leaving the Embassy with the Chargé, and play the relations with the Duvalier Government on a very low key and await developments.

2. McCone suggested that this looked like the Cuban policy in July 1959 which gave the Soviets an opening into Cuba. I[2] therefore advocated that we conduct a complete diplomatic relationship but that it be on an informal basis. The President agreed, ordered Ambassador Thurston recalled, and reserved the decision as to whether he should be returned or another Ambassador returned.

3. The aid program apparently involves only $3 million or $4 million for airport construction, the administration of which is in the hands of Pan American.

4. CIA was asked to explore the exile group possibilities and to determine what action, if any, should be taken. [7 *lines of source text not declassified*] I pointed out that most insurgents were political has-beens or influential Haitians who desire to regain property that has been lost through expropriation or otherwise.

Source: Central Intelligence Agency, DCI/McCone Files, Job 80–B01258A, Meetings with the President, 4/1/63–6/30/63. Secret; Eyes Only. Drafted by McCone on May 27.

[1] Document 382.

[2] The "I" refers to McCone.

384.   National Security Action Memorandum No. 246

Washington, May 23, 1963.

TO

The Secretary of State
The Secretary of Defense
The Director of Central Intelligence

SUBJECT

Future Policy Toward Haiti

The following conclusions were reached during a meeting with the President on Haiti on May 20, 1963.[1]

1. Ambassador Thurston should be recalled for consultation and a final decision on his return to Haiti will be held in abeyance until the Ambassador can give his views on this matter. (Action: Department of State)

2. Fleet units now positioned off the island of Gonaive may be withdrawn after May 23 if there have been no untoward developments before then indicating reconsideration of this decision. There will continue to be an increased patrol of the Windward Passage to insure against illicit traffic between Cuba and Haiti. (Action: Department of Defense)

3. Involvement in any program to unseat Duvalier should be limited, for the present at least, to encouraging and helping fund an effort by Haitians. Further consideration of the commitment of U.S. prestige or U.S. forces should be deferred until we have fully explored this approach. [1 line of source text not declassified]

(a) Great care should be taken to insure that we control the time frame of any revolutionary action that might involve the United States in any way.
(b) [4-1/2 lines of source text not declassified]

4. A determined effort should be made during the course of the next few months to encourage the development of an exile force that might challenge Duvalier. (The manner in which this decision was reached did not preclude intensified efforts to achieve the same goal by working with oppositionists within Haiti.) [1 line of source text not declassified]

5. It is extremely important that there be no discussion with the press about our plans for handling the Haitian problem.

McGeorge Bundy

Source: Kennedy Library, National Security Files, Meetings and Memoranda Series, NSAM 246. Top Secret.

[1] The President had two "off the record" meetings during the morning of May 20, but his Appointment Book does not indicate the topics discussed. (Ibid.)

385.   Memorandum of Conversation

Washington, May 30, 1963, 11:32 a.m.

SUBJECT

   Haiti[1]

PARTICIPANTS

   The Secretary
   Edwin M. Martin, Assistant Secretary for Inter-American Affairs
   Foreign Minister Freites, Dominican Republic

The Secretary opened the conversation by making four points.

   1.   That we shared the view of President Bosch that the Duvalier regime is a bad thing for the Hemisphere and for Haiti and that we also agreed that it could not be permitted to continue indefinitely and in fact it probably could not do so in view of its repressive policies.

   2.   That under present circumstances the US did not feel that it could intervene unilaterally in any way. In the light of our own history of relations with Haiti and in the light of Latin American attitudes, this would not be helpful. The Foreign Minister indicated that the Dominicans agreed that this would not be desirable.

   3.   That we did not feel that there was at the present time any basis for securing OAS support for an intervention. The Foreign Minister indicated that he had been discussing this question with the Venezuelan Ambassador and that morning with the Venezuelan Foreign Minister and his assessment was the same as ours.

   4.   That mounting an intervention from the Dominican Republic into Haiti as proposed by President Bosch was a very delicate and intricate operation involving a number of risks and would have to be handled with a great deal of care and discretion.

   We would be glad to be kept informed of the development of their program. The Secretary suggested that this could best be done by communicating with Ambassador Martin, who had absolutely secure channels of communications to himself and Assistant Secretary Martin. No one else would see them except the code clerk.

   Source: Kennedy Library, National Security Files, Country Series, Haiti, 6/1–7/14/63. Top Secret. Drafted by Martin on June 4 and approved in S on June 5. The time of the meeting was taken from Rusk's Appointment Book. (Johnson Library)

   [1] In a May 25 memorandum Martin briefed Rusk for his meeting with Freites, which was called at the request of the Dominican Foreign Minister to discuss Haiti. The briefing memorandum, drafted by Abbuhl, reported that the Dominican Republic had recently disbanded a group of 65–70 Haitian exiles training in the Dominican Republic for an invasion of Haiti. Nevertheless, Bosch remained determined to oust Duvalier with or without U.S. cooperation. (Department of State, Central Files, POL HAI)

Ambassador Freites accepted this and made no further requests. He asked whether we had any preference as to individuals. He was told that among the military personnel there was no preference, and probably by now they were better informed about the various military types than we. It was made clear to him that this was not the case with respect to political figures, and in particular he should be clear that we in no way supported the Dejoie–Fignole team.

The Foreign Minister indicated he was somewhat out of touch with recent developments in the Dominican Republic and anxious to get back. For example, two Haitian military personages from Venezuela had arrived since his departure.

The Secretary asked Assistant Secretary Martin if he thought there was any chance of persuading Duvalier to restore the regular army to anything like its previous position of authority. The latter replied that he did not think it was feasible. Freites expressed agreement.

The Secretary asked, if in the light of our limited knowledge of conditions outside Port-au-Prince, there was any chance of finding one or more communities that might declare against Duvalier and form a nucleus of opposition with which we could work. Assistant Secretary Martin, while admitting our information was inadequate, expressed the view that while there was dissatisfaction, there was complete unwillingness to take a stand until tangible evidence of outside support, adequate to ensure that they would be on the winning side, had appeared. Again Freites agreed.

Freites reported that recently a substantial contingent of Haitian military, perhaps as many as 90, appeared at one of the border points and tried to defect into the Dominican Republic. They were told to stay where they were as they could be more useful there.

As the discussion proceeded, the Foreign Minister said there might be some technical assistance we could provide. It appeared that he had in mind facilitating a more vigorous and better oriented program for sabotage and creating disorders of the sort Barbot has been conducting in Port-au-Prince. He felt that, if there were a lull in anti-Duvalier activity, Duvalier would materially strengthen his position, and it was necessary to keep the pot boiling until the Dominican operation was ready. The Secretary said that this was not an easy thing to do technically, but made no commitment one way or the other.

The Secretary raised the question of our information about the geographical origin within Haiti of various of the military people now in exile. He thought perhaps that if there was a particular area where a number of them came from they might have connections there which would make this a likely spot for starting something.

In closing the Secretary repeated our desire to be kept informed, emphasized the importance of not undertaking measures which were not sure to succeed and stressed the need to keep these conversations top secret.

386.   Memorandum of Conversation

Washington, June 1, 1963, 10:25–10:37 a.m.

SUBJECT

Presentation of Credentials

PARTICIPANTS

The President
Mr. Angier Biddle Duke, Chief of Protocol, State
Mr. Edwin M. Martin, Assistant Secretary for Inter-American Affairs, State
Ambassador del Rosario, new Dominican Ambassador to US

[Here follows discusion on the Managua Conference in Central America, April 3–4.]

The President then asked what we were going to do about Haiti. The Ambassador said that the Dominican Republic would prefer to have the OAS act. The President felt they would not do so under present circumstances with which the Ambassador agreed. The Ambassador indicated that they were working directly with some of the Haitian military. The President indicated that this was good, but he guessed there were not very many of them. He pointed out that there were many difficulties about United States intervention, and the history of the Dominican relations with Haiti made it difficult for the Dominicans to get too involved directly in Haitian affairs. Therefore, from both our standpoints, it was desirable to have a strong Haitian group ready to move in case the situation developed in such a way that action was appropriate and not have to rely entirely on Dominican and US forces. The United States wanted to work with the Dominicans on this and support their efforts.

The Ambassador commented on the difficulty in finding a leader that could be trusted and who seemed able. There wasn't much to choose from. The President agreed, but said we had to do the best we could, and he wanted to make sure that, if President Bosch at any time had any requests to make in this regard, he, the President, wanted to know personally about them.

[Here follows discussion of U.S.-Dominican relations unrelated to Haiti.]

Source: Department of State, Central Files, POL 17–1 DOM REP–US. Top Secret; Limit Distribution. Drafted by Martin and approved by the White House on June 14. The time of the meeting was taken from the President's Appointment Book. (Kennedy Library)

387. Memorandum From Secretary of State Rusk to President Kennedy

Washington, June 7, 1963.

SUBJECT

Circumstances Giving Rise to Press Reports that the United States Stopped President Bosch from Invading Haiti

I refer to your Memorandum of June 4, 1963[1] referring to recent press stories about the United States stopping President Bosch from invading Haiti and asking what our role in this matter actually was. The statements in *The Washington Post* and elsewhere that the United States "intervened at least twice against positive steps to remove Duvalier from office with force of arms" are not accurate. The circumstances giving rise to the stories are probably the following:

President Bosch told newsmen Tad Szulc and Henry Raymont the evening of May 5 that he would invade Haiti at 4:30 a.m. May 7, and that he was holding a Cabinet-military meeting the following morning (May 6) at 8:00 a.m., presumably to iron out the final details. Messrs. Szulc and Raymont reported this conversation to Ambassador Martin who in turn reported to the Department, requesting instructions. The Department responded that Ambassador Martin should convey to President Bosch our opinion that he should refrain from moving against Haiti in the absence of OAS sanctions, pointing out that Haitian acts of provocation during the immediately preceding days had seemed insufficient to induce OAS majority approval of military action. At that particular moment, the OAS investigating committee had just returned to Washington to report its findings; the Haitian Government had requested a meeting of the United Nations Security Council; and there was a very real danger that the entire thrust of international concern about President Duvalier might be turned away from him and directed at President Bosch.

Ambassador Martin saw President Bosch on the morning of May 6, before receiving the Department's instructions. President Bosch denied having told Messrs. Szulc and Raymont he would invade Haiti, saying they had deduced this from the general conversation. He admonished

---

Source: Department of State, Central Files, POL DOM REP–HAI. Secret. Drafted by Abbuhl and Crockett and cleared by Martin.

[1] The memorandum, drafted and signed by the President, reads: "I note several references, most recently in *The Washington Post* this morning, about the United States stopping Bosch from invading Haiti. Is this correct? What instructions did we send to our Ambassador to the Dominican Republic? Did we in short 'intervene at least twice against positive steps to remove Duvalier from office with force of arms.'" (Ibid.)

Ambassador Martin not to believe rumors, saying he was merely stirring up the press to prod the OAS and keep the crisis alive. He also told the Ambassador what our military advisers had already learned from Dominican military sources; i.e., that the Dominican military establishment was incapable of mounting a successful invasion of Haiti.

The other incident, which may have given rise to the news stories, occurred on or about May 14. Some 60–70 Haitian exiles, who had reportedly been training at a secret camp on Dominican territory to invade northern Haiti on May 15, were disarmed and forced to disband by Dominican authorities, apparently because the Dominican Government feared the operation would not succeed and a failure might result in unfavorable political repercussions within the Dominican Republic. We became privy to this operation only after it had been called off, but some of the disgruntled participants are known to have alleged (and perhaps believed) that the Dominicans prevented the invasion from taking place at our behest.

Dean Rusk[2]

---

[2] Printed from a copy that indicates Rusk signed the original.

---

388.   Letter From the Assistant Secretary of State for Inter-American Affairs (Martin) to the Ambassador to the Dominican Republic (Martin)

Washington, June 7, 1963.

DEAR JOHN: You will probably have seen by now various memoranda reflecting the general policy line that has been adopted here with respect to Bosch's activities against Duvalier. We continue to work on the question of tactics within the framework of this policy. I want to try to explain in this letter, as closely as I can now, exactly what we have in mind so that you have not only what is in the official papers but what is between the lines, which is, I am afraid, not unimportant in this case.

We continue to be interested in seeing whether there is a possibility of overthrowing Duvalier without causing undue international repercussions. We are quite anxious from the standpoint of international

---

Source: Department of State, Central Files, POL DOM REP–HAI. Top Secret; Official–Informal.

repercussions to keep the United States Government very much in the background.

We see considerable difficulties for Bosch's undertaking a successful operation both from the standpoint of international repercussions and from the standpoint of his own capabilities. We can't avoid the probability that action by him will rub off somewhat on us in view of our close past associations with the Dominican Republic.

There is also considerable sensitivity here to the charge which has been picked up in the United States press that Bosch has more than once been all ready to upset Duvalier but the United States has stopped him. This charge smacks of interventionism or worse and is not accepted easily.

We also take it as an uncomfortable fact of life that the United States activity in support of Haitians, which is undertaken through or in close collaboration with Bosch, is apt to become public. One can't tell when or under what circumstances, but both Bosch and his entourage are not considered to possess undue amounts of security consciousness, to say nothing of the Haitians.

This leads us to want to keep closely in touch with Bosch and the Dominicans on what they are doing on as discreet a basis as possible and in a way which will minimize, though it cannot avoid, difficulties in refusing material or financial assistance. [9-1/2 lines of source text not declassified]

At the same time we hope to be able to get away with this restricted relation with Bosch, we plan to continue working with Haitians directly in order to have a check on what Bosch is doing and what he is saying, in order to have some degree of independent control over the timing of Haitian activities and, if the appropriate occasion should arise, perhaps to be able to give more concrete help to the Haitians without compromising ourselves with Bosch or his associates.

I have no illusions that this is anything but a very tricky and difficult game to play. I think we have no illusions about the prospects of organizing the Haitians to doing anything very helpful in the near future either. But, in order to make the most of it with the least possible damage, I thought it important that you understand, as specifically as I have tried to put it in this letter, what we are trying to accomplish and how we think it best to go about it, so that you can conduct yourself in a way which fits into the program.[1]

---

[1] In a June 12 letter to Edwin Martin, Ambassador John Martin agreed that it would be difficult for Bosch to undertake an operation against Duvalier either successfully, quietly, or without also implicating the United States. Martin also agreed he must distance himself from operational activities, but noted that it was inevitable that Bosch would want to discuss Haiti with him. Martin asked to be fully informed of U.S. activities in the Dominican Republic in conjunction with Haitian dissidents. (Ibid., POL DOM REP–US)

Best of luck.

Sincerely,

Edwin M. Martin[2]

P.S. I have just come back from a visit with Alex Johnson to the JCS, where they wished to discuss the DR situation. I think they are reasonably content with our appraisal and current policies. They have seen your recent long despatch with its 26 recommendations. I told them we were preparing an action paper for the LAPC based on it.[3] This seemed to satisfy them on this score.

---

[2] Printed from a copy that bears this typed signature.
[3] Documents 243 ff.

---

389.   Memorandum of Conversation

Washington, June 18, 1963, 10–10:30 a.m.

SUBJECT

Haiti

PARTICIPANTS

The President
Mr. Ralph Dungan, White House
Ambassador Raymond Thurston
Mr. Edwin M. Martin, Assistant Secretary of State, Bureau of Inter-American
   Affairs

The President asked Ambassador Thurston what we do next in Haiti. Ambassador Thurston replied that he felt we still had a strong interest in changing the regime and that, if we did not do so within two to three years, the dangers of communist activity were substantial. He did not think the communists wanted to move in now but would prefer to wait in order to establish relations with a more popular and secure regime than that of Duvalier.

Source: Kennedy Library, National Security Files, Countries Series, Haiti, 6/1/62–7/14/63. Top Secret. Drafted by Martin on June 21 and approved by the White House on July 12. The time of the meeting was taken from the President's Appointment Book. (Ibid.)

In response to further questioning Ambassador Thurston said that the problem of making a change was becoming increasingly difficult as most of the good leaders were leaving Haiti. It would be desirable to keep in close touch with them, maintain their interest and promote cooperation among them. At the same time we should keep the economic pressure on the Duvalier regime. He mentioned that they were under considerable pressure and were seeking aid from France, Germany and Italy, though he thought it unlikely that any of them would be willing to provide much help. He mentioned the French were thinking of moving slowly on a few technicians. In response to the President's query concerning possible Soviet economic assistance, Ambassador Thurston said that he as well as the experts concerned in the State Department doubted that Soviet bloc was greatly interested in Haiti at this time.

Assistant Secretary Martin commented that Bosch was collecting a good many of the exiled military in the Dominican Republic, and we and the Dominicans were maintaining them. The President said that he thought we should give Bosch a complete green light on building up a Haitian force and give the force any help it needs in money or equipment. He was concerned that we may have held Bosch's hand when he was planning to invade earlier. Mr. Martin pointed out that the Dominican military stopped Bosch first, that they were not capable of acting.

Ambassador Thurston pointed out that it was better for the Haitians with United States support to act than that the Dominicans be publicly involved in view of the long hatred between the Haitians and the Dominicans. The President agreed that we should work very closely with Bosch and keep in close touch with him on this, not only to help, but to keep control over timing. Mr. Dungan raised the problem of creating the momentum by supporting a Haitian exile build-up which might be difficult to control. While this danger was recognized, it was agreed that we should move ahead by assuring control of any decision to initiate action. He did not want an abortive action. He asked how many people were required to upset the regime. Ambassador Thurston thought 500 well-trained Haitians would do it with not more than a battalion of United States forces off shore as back up just in case.

The President asked whether it might not have been better for us to have withdrawn our Ambassador rather than for him to have been asked to leave.[1] The Ambassador thought this was definitely not the case, that a withdrawal would have been interpreted everywhere, but particularly among our Haitian friends, as a move to make our peace with the Duvalier regime, and they would have given up the battle. He thought things had worked out the very best way they could from the standpoint of United States interests.

---

[1] Thurston left Port-au-Prince on May 26; on June 14 the Government of Haiti requested his recall and he did not return to post.

The President suggested that we should send an Ambassador back pretty quickly. Ambassador Thurston thought it ought not be done too quickly, as this would have a bad effect on the friendly Haitians. He recalled that when Stalin declared Ambassador Kennan persona non grata, we did not send a new Ambassador to Moscow for 6 to 7 months. He pointed out that the Chargé was a sound, experienced officer, who could carry on the months ahead without embarrassing United States interests.

The President suggested that Ambassador Thurston might use his time, until a new post abroad became available, to best advantage by serving as a contact point with Haitian exiles and working with them on programs for changing the regime. Ambassador Thurston said he would hope he could have another mission, but meanwhile would be glad to be helpful. Mr. Martin pointed out that the Ambassador had not had leave for four years and deserved some first. The President agreed, but said he then hoped the Ambassador could help with maintaining contact with Haitians outside of Haiti.

Mr. Dungan suggested the possibility of getting some Haitians together in a Haitian-American institute connected with a university in order to finance them and enable them to work out a common program under satisfactory conditions. It was agreed that something like this might be worth exploring.

---

390. **Memorandum From the Executive Secretary of the Department of State (Read) to the President's Special Assistant for National Security Affairs (Bundy)**

Washington, August 14, 1963.

SUBJECT

The Abortive Invasion of Haiti and Its Significance for United States Policy

A brief résumé of the events which took place last week in Haiti[1] and an evaluation of their effect on the Haitian problem follow:

Source: Department of State, Central Files, POL 27–1 HAI. Secret. Drafted by Abbuhl and cleared by Cottrell.

[1] At the daily White House staff meeting of August 7, Haiti was discussed as follows:

"No one is quite sure what is happening, but Bundy dropped the remark that the CIA has a commitment to the failure of this endeavor. Dungan seems to be the key man in the White House, but even he admitted that *The New York Times* is the best source of what's happening. No one seems unduly concerned." (Memorandum by Smith, August 7; National Defense University, Taylor Papers, Chairman's Staff Group, August 1963)

Invasion Facts

Available information about the abortive invasion of Haiti is conflicting and still incomplete. It would appear, however, that the invading force consisted of some 75 or more (perhaps as many as 135) Haitians, few of whom had any previous military experience or training. The invaders were led by former Haitian Army officers, principally, General Léon Cantave, Colonel René Leon, Colonel Pierre Paret, and Captain Emile Wooley. Their jumping off point was Dajabon, a Dominican border town near the north coast. They entered Haiti the morning of August 5, either afoot or by boat, in the vicinity of the village of Dèrac. After disarming personnel at the small Army post there and reportedly shooting several members of the local Ton Ton Macoute group, they moved on to Fort Liberté where the only skirmish between the invaders and Haitian Armed Forces occurred. The invaders were unable to overcome the 25-man Army garrison there; leadership and control failed; and the bulk of the invading force recrossed the border into the Dominican Republic. Some of the invaders apparently remained in Haiti and are hiding out in the hills.

The invasion plan is believed to have called for the invaders to proceed to Cap Haitien, picking up support and recruits en route. It assumed that (1) the appearance on the scene of an invading force would spark a general uprising and (2) resistance from such Government forces as might remain loyal would be nominal and easily overcome. The first assumption was never really put to the test and the second proved incorrect, at least with respect to the Fort Liberté garrison.

The extent of Dominican involvement cannot be determined with certainty on the basis of information presently available, but the fact that the invading force was small, relatively untrained and not well armed, indicates that such involvement was probably nominal and passive in nature. The invaders are believed to have enjoyed some support within Dominican Army circles, particularly the Army Commander at Dajabon.

Invasion Effects

1.   Although unsuccessful, the invasion has given rise to a surprising degree of unity among competing Haitian exile groups who rallied together in support of General Cantave's invasion group. The various groups now appear determined to organize and carry out further incursions of this kind.

2.   Unfortunately, the greatly exaggerated newspaper accounts of the invasion, which the Haitian Government has been careful not to discount, have served to make President Duvalier appear in complete control of the situation and more firmly entrenched in power.

3.   The Haitian Government obviously hopes to use the invasion to bring pressure through the Organization of American States on Presi-

dent Bosch to force him to deny Haitian exiles the use of Dominican territory as a base from which to invade Haiti.

Significance for United States Policy

1. Basic United States policy considerations with respect to Haiti are not believed to have been affected significantly one way or the other by the invasion.

2. The prospects of working with and through the exiles appear improved, and this possibility should be pursued without delay.

3. The principal significance of the invasion for United States policy is that any move at this juncture which could be construed as seeking a rapprochement with Duvalier would be interpreted by both the Haitian opposition and pro-Government forces as evidence that the United States had now given up hope that Duvalier can be forced out and is prepared to do business indefinitely with his regime.

C.C. Moor[2]

---

[2] Moor signed for Read above Read's typed signature.

---

391.   Proposed Plan of Action

Washington, November 13, 1963.

SUBJECT

Haiti: Proposed Plan of Action from November 1, 1963 through April 30, 1964[1]

[Here follow sections entitled "Assessment of the Current Situation," which states that in light of the failures of the invasions by Haitian exiles from the Dominican Republic, the fall of the Bosch government, and Duvalier's purges of the Haitian Army, Duvalier faced little threat to

---

Source: Department of State, Central Files, POL HAI–US. Secret. Drafted by Virgil B. Randolph of ARA/CMA on November 13.

[1] This plan was drafted on November 4 and submitted to the Latin American Policy Committee, which apparently approved it at its meeting of November 7. (Memorandum from Crockett to Martin and Cottrell, November 4; ibid.)

his rule; and "Possible Courses of Action," which states that the United States had four options: continue to isolate Duvalier and attempt to hasten his downfall, establish as near normal relations as possible by considering requests for assistance only as they aided Haitian economic development—as opposed to supporting the Duvalier regime, come to an accommodation with Duvalier, or engage in an all-out effort to remove him and establish an acceptable successor government, using U.S. forces if necessary.]

Conclusions and Recommendations

The situation within Haiti and external factors bearing on the internal Haitian situation have changed materially since Ambassador Thurston was recalled on May 26, 1963. While the United States has been adequately represented within Haiti by its Chargé d'Affaires during the intervening five months, maximum U.S. influence can be exerted only when the leadership and prestige which an accredited Ambassador enjoys can be brought to bear. No decision as to future long-term United States policy toward Haiti should be reached until our new Ambassador[2] has had an opportunity to familiarize himself, on the scene, with current Haitian conditions and to submit his assessments and recommendations. To this end, the new United States Ambassador to Haiti should assume his duties in Port-au-Prince as quickly as possible. During the period of not more than six months which will be required for him to survey the situation, and prepare recommendations, the United States should:

1. Maintain our present cool posture toward Duvalier while denying his government economic or financial assistance other than of a purely humanitarian nature.

2. Disassociate ourselves from any exile attempt to invade Haiti or plot to assassinate Duvalier except under the unlikely circumstances (1) that the prospects for success appear favorable, (2) that public U.S. involvement could be avoided, and (c) that the installation of an acceptable successor group is assured.

3. Keep OAS members currently informed of the situation in Haiti.

4. Continue U.S. participation in the malaria eradication program and PL 480 assistance to voluntary agencies in Haiti. Until Haitian farmers are able to replace crops destroyed by Hurricane Flora, provide a reasonable amount of additional PL 480 foodstuffs.

5. Seek an understanding with the Haitian Government on the size, composition and responsibilities of the MAAG.

---

[2] Benson E.L. Timmons III was appointed Ambassador to Haiti on November 30.

6. Continue blocking AID, IDB and IBRD loans and discourage assistance from Common Market and other non-Communist countries on the grounds that such aid gives prestige and material support to an undesirable dictatorship.

7. Continue to insist that the IMF fully justify on economic grounds its stand-by arrangements with Haiti.

8. Continue to press for payments on debts owed the United States Government even if only on a token basis in deference to the precarious state of the Haitian finances.

9. Discourage visits to Haiti by high-ranking officials of the United States, international organizations or other governments which could be exploited by Duvalier. By the same token, discourage visits to Washington by Haitian officials by receiving them at the lowest level consistent with their rank.

10. Continue to discourage naval visits and tourist travel to Haiti under present conditions

PANAMA

392. National Security Council Report

NSC 6102   Washington, January 10, 1961.

U.S. POLICY ON THE PANAMA CANAL AND A FUTURE INTER-OCEANIC CANAL IN CENTRAL AMERICA

[Here follows discussion of general considerations concerning the Panama canal, a possible sea-level canal and the impact of such a canal on U.S.-Panama relations, and possible solutions.]

Objectives

19. Maintenance at a suitable site of an inter-oceanic canal adequate to meet world-wide commercial and Free World military requirements, as invulnerable to attack as possible, under a form of control adequately protecting U.S. interests and preferably organized on a self-financing basis.

20. A Panama which is politically stable, internally secure, progressing toward sound economic growth, and capable of taking an increasingly constructive role within the Inter-American system.

21. Preservation of at least the present measure of U.S. influence in Panama, and if possible increased influence, so as to (a) deny hostile influence over the region to any other power (especially a non-hemispheric power), (b) exert a constructive influence on radical nationalism and on social evolution in the area, and (c) promote the growth of democratic institutions.

22. Development of U.S. interests in the Isthmian region in a manner which will strengthen the Inter-American system, keep Panama securely therein, and create conditions necessary to successful negotiations for and subsequent operations of a sea-level canal.

Source: National Archives and Records Administration, RG 59, S/S–NSC Files: Lot 63 D 351, NSC 6102. Secret. A January 10 note from NSC Executive Secretary James S. Lay, Jr., to the National Security Council, attached to the source text, states that at the 473d NSC meeting on January 5, the Council adopted the statement of policy in NSC 6026 subject to the amendments set forth in NSC Action No. 2368–b and that on January 10 the President had approved the statement as amended, which was enclosed as NSC 6102. NSC 6026 was dated December 29, 1960. (Ibid., NSC 6026) A memorandum of the NSC discussion on NSC 6026 is in the Eisenhower Library, Whitman File, NSC Records; NSC Records of Action are in Department of State, S/S–NSC (Miscellaneous) Files: Lot 66 D 95.

A note dated January 22, 1963, from NSC Executive Secretary Bromley Smith to all holders of NSC 6102, attached to the source text, indicates that the President had authorized the rescission of NSC 6102.

23. Maintenance of a U.S. military base complex in Panama for so long as it is in the U.S. strategic interest.

Major Policy Guidance

24. Take steps, as outlined below, which hold the greatest hope for assuring the primary U.S. interest in the region—an adequate inter-ocean sea-level canal under conditions of control which are acceptable and advantageous to both the U.S. and the host country.

25. Recognizing that the present Canal will be inadequate in approximately 20 years, proceed on the basis that a sea-level canal should be constructed, that it should be completed by 1980, that a decision as to its preferred location and a construction plan must be made soon and that preferably it should be self-financed.

26. Undertake a comparative study of the economic feasibility of alternate sites for a sea-level canal, giving particular attention to the fact that the present Canal Zone represents territory over which the United States exercises sovereign rights, and to the economic impact upon the Republic of Panama of eventual replacement of the present Canal.

27. Proceed, as consistent with U.S. nuclear testing policy, with a program of research, development and testing to improve nuclear explosives available for excavation purposes; establish as accurately as possible the physical, biological and psychological effects of nuclear explosives under conditions to be encountered at the canal site; and determine the safety and over-all costs of the use of such explosives for a canal project.

28. Formulate promptly a comprehensive program for discussion with the Congress to create the most promising framework for the accomplishment of long-range U.S. objectives in the Isthmian region without relinquishing control of the Zone under existing treaty arrangements.

29. Continue programs to improve community relations between the residents of the Canal Zone and the Republic of Panama.

30. Continue to impress strongly upon the Panamanian Government the urgent necessity, in its own self-interest and the interests of the Panamanian people, of initiating a program of political and socio-economic development utilizing Panamanian resources to fullest possible extent in such fields as (a) land tenure and increased agricultural productivity, (b) housing, (c) taxation, (d) diversification of the economy, (e) public education and administration, (f) political reform, and (g) industrial development.

31. Manage our relations between Panama and the Canal Zone in a manner calculated to establish the politico-psychological framework in which to negotiate satisfactorily for a new canal and for ceasing the operation of the present canal.

32. In seeking to assure the accomplishment of long-range U.S. objectives in the Central American region and of keeping that region securely within the Inter-American systems and susceptible to U.S. influence, continue to contribute to the cost of favorably influencing socio-economic change in Panama.

33. With respect to the present canal:

a. Pending completion of a new canal, maintain in force to the fullest extent feasible, all the rights, power and authority granted the United States by the Convention of 1903 with Panama, as modified by the Treaties of 1936 and 1955.[1]

b. Continue the current Canal improvement program with a view to completing it by 1968.

34. Permit no hostile or lawless actions by individuals or groups within the Canal Zone, and assure that the Government of Panama is made aware that the Zone authorities will take prompt, effective and continuing measures to prevent such disturbances from moving from the Panamanian territory into the Canal Zone and that their full cooperation is desired. To this end be prepared to use U.S. military forces to preserve order in the Canal Zone.

35. Continue to develop the Canal Zone as a center for Inter-American civil and military cooperation.

[Here follow annexes A–D, concerning various aspects of a possible inter-oceanic canal.]

---

[1] For text of the Isthmian Canal Convention signed at Washington November 18, 1903, see 10 Bevans 663. For text of the Treaty of Friendship and Cooperation signed at Washington March 2, 1936, see 10 Bevans 742. For text of the Treaty of Mutual Understanding and Cooperation signed at Panama January 25, 1955, see 6 UST (pt. 2) 2273.

393.   Telegram From the Embassy in Honduras to the Department of State

Tegucigalpa, July 22, 1961, 7 p.m.

52. Limit distribution to Secretary of State, Assistant Secretary Woodward, the White House. From Goodwin. I was met at the conference of CA Finance and Foreign Ministers[1] by David Samudio, Chairman of Panama's National Planning Commission. He said that President Chiari has sent him to the conference to see me and deliver a personal and private message from Chiari to President Kennedy.

The message was, it is necessary for Panama and the US to undertake a fundamental revision of their relations with respect to the Panama Canal. Panama feels that the US should continue to operate and defend the Canal: but the income from operations should go to the GOP (this means the income now devoted to general improvements in the Canal Zone). Chiari wanted to deliver this message to President Kennedy so that the actions of Panama in asking such a revision will not come as any surprise. They want to negotiate an entirely new treaty and not merely renegotiate the existing agreement. This is because the original agreement was made by Secretary Hay and Bunau-Varilla who was a Frenchman acting as the Minister of Interior of Panama in Washington (try that on Abe Chayes). He further stated that Panama would do nothing about this until after Montevideo[2] so as not to embarrass the US by permitting the Communists to use this as a lever with which to attack the conference.

I told him that I would relay his message to the President.

Burrows

Source: Department of State, Central Files, 611.19/7–2261. Secret; Priority.

[1] Reference is to an informal meeting of Foreign and Economic Ministers of Central America and Panama, held July 21–23 in Tegucigalpa.

[2] Reference is to the meeting to be held in August at Punta del Este; see Documents 19 ff.

394. **Telegram From the Department of State to the Embassy in Panama**

Washington, August 31, 1961, 10:18 p.m.

175. Deptel 157,[1] Embtel 198.[2]

1.   Assure Chiari we are sympathetic to his concern for social progress as evidenced his conversation with you reported Embtel 164.[3] We understand his belief, as also expressed in the past by Ambassador Arango, that increased annuity from Canal might provide source funds such purpose.

2.   Discourage Chiari from sending letter requesting treaty negotiations. Inform him US Government is currently making study leading toward decision on sea-level canal and considers any treaty talks dependent on outcome this study; that we are attempting hasten decision. We do not believe mutual interests of either Government would be served by premature forcing of treaty issue leading to needless exacerbations.

3.   In the meantime we would meet with an economic mission from GOP in late September to review social and economic investment plan and study best employment of all available resources for betterment Panamanian people. We believe such a review could result in material benefit to Panama in meeting social progress requirements in immediate future.

4.   We understand Chiari plans personal vacation in Miami late September and return Panama for session Assembly opening October 1. You may indicate that should Chiari wish to visit Washington during his stay, President Kennedy would entertain him at informal luncheon. Because of heavy schedule of visits during September it will not be possible for several days to set date convenient to White House. Protocol difficulties inherent in even informal visit of this nature will be greatly

---

Source: Department of State, Central Files, 611.19/8–2461. Confidential; Niact. Drafted by Katherine W. Bracken, Director of the Office of Central American and Panamanian Affairs; cleared in draft with U/PR, L, H, B, G; and approved by Woodward.

[1] Telegram 157 to Panama City, August 23, instructed Ambassador Farland to discourage President Chiari from sending a letter to Kennedy requesting treaty negotiations, since a study was underway concerning the possibility of a sea-level canal, and the U.S. Government considered the study's completion a prerequisite to any decision to discuss new negotiations. (Ibid., 611.19/8–2061)

[2] Telegram 198 from Panama City, August 24, urged reconsideration of the decisions reflected in telegram 157, which it argued would lead to a deterioration of U.S.-Panamanian relations. (Ibid., 611.19/8–2461)

[3] Telegram 164 from Panama City, August 14, reported a conversation between Ambassador Farland and President Chiari in which the latter stated that talks about the canal were necessary because of Panama's need for additional revenues. (Ibid., 611.19/8–1461)

diminished if President Chiari agrees to this rather than heading economic mission.

FYI only. We are exploring possibility of a unilateral increase in annuity to be deposited to fund for economic and social development along lines recommendation in your May 12 letter to the Secretary.[4] We will advise you further when necessary consultations in Washington have been completed. In meanwhile do not allow Panamanians become aware our efforts in this regard. End FYI.

Since the approach outlined above is designed to meet President Chiari's, rather than the Foreign Minister's, motivations for reopening negotiations, we prefer you talk first with Chiari. However we leave to your discretion how best to discourage transmittal of the draft letter (Embtel 194)[5] within limits of above guidance. Please report soonest.[6]

Rusk

---

[4] Not printed; it made a number of recommendations. (Ibid., 611.19/5–1261)

[5] Dated August 23; it transmitted the text of a draft letter. (Ibid., 611.19/8–2361)

[6] Farland reported in telegram 231 from Panama City, September 2, that he had conveyed the U.S. position to Chiari and Foreign Minister Solis, but that Chiari said he intended to send the letter. (Ibid., 611.1913/9–261)

---

395. Memorandum From the Deputy Secretary of Defense (Gilpatric) to President Kennedy

Washington, September 2, 1961.

SUBJECT

Relations with Panama and the Requirements for a Sea Level Canal

Reference is made to your memorandum of August 30, 1961,[1] concerning the necessity for a sea level canal and current discussions with

---

Source: Washington National Records Center, RG 330, Records of the Office of the Secretary of Defense, OSD/ISA Files: FRC 64 A 2382, 821 Panama. Secret. Drafted in the Office of the Assistant Secretary of Defense for International Security Affairs.

[1] This memorandum referred to recent technical studies indicating that a sea-level canal would not be needed until the year 2000 and requested an early recommendation as to its necessity. (Ibid.)

the Republic of Panama on our relations in connection with the present canal.

Recent technical studies completed under the aegis of the Panama Canal Company indicate that adoption of new techniques for lock over-haul and repair will almost double the present dependable capacity of the canal by 1965. However, recent studies also indicate that the previous forecasts of traffic requiring transit of the canal were conservative. These developments call for a re-study of the concept that commercial require-ments necessitate the completion of a sea level canal by 1980, one of the premises upon which our present canal policy as embodied in NSC 6102 of January 10, 1961, is based. As a result, the Department of the Army has initiated an appraisal of these developments in connection with the requirements for a sea level canal as stated in NSC 6102.

With regard to the preliminary discussions with Panama, the Department of State has drafted a new paper on our policy toward Pan-ama and on a sea level canal.[2] Comments of the Department of Defense have been requested. The paper will reflect the results of the review of recent developments and their effect on the need for a sea level canal, and should make possible final recommendations thereon. Every effort will be made to complete the study and the resulting recommendations at the earliest possible moment.

With reference to your question on the implementation of the "equal pay for equal work" provision of the 1955 Treaty, I am assured by the Sec-retary of the Army that there has been careful and conscientious com-pliance with each element of our commitment. Since Executive Order 10794 assigns to the Secretary of the Army primary responsibility for implementation of these aspects of our treaty obligations, as set forth in Public Law 85–550, I am asking him to prepare for you a statement of the actions taken.

Roswell L. Gilpatric[3]

---

[2] Reference is to a draft Policy Guidelines paper drafted in the Bureau of Inter-Ameri-can Affairs and discussed informally at the working level with the Department of Defense. The paper never received final approval. Drafts dated September 19, 1961, and March 1962, together with related material, are in Department of State, Policy Guidelines: Lot 67 D 396, Panama.

[3] Printed from a copy that indicates Roswell signed the original.

396. Memorandum of Conversation

Washington, September 15, 1961, 10:05–10:20 a.m.

SUBJECT

Call of Ricardo Chiari on the President

PARTICIPANTS

The President
Ambassador Arango of Panama
Mr. Ricardo Chiari, brother of President of Panama, Roberto Chiari
Assistant Secretary Woodward
Mr. Richard Goodwin, Special Assistant to the President
Mrs. Katherine W. Bracken, Director, Office of Central American and Panamanian
   Affairs

The President referred to Ambassador Arango's participation in the work of the OAS Subcommittee visiting the Dominican Republic. He expressed his hope that democracy could be developed there without the country's falling into a military dictatorship, that this was a difficult task, and that a favorable result would be an outstanding achievement.

Mr. Chiari conveyed the greetings of his brother, the President of Panama, and handed President Kennedy a letter from President Chiari.[1] The President read the letter and commented that he recognized that problems exist with regard to the canal, that he would like to discuss with Secretary Rusk and Mr. Woodward how best to go about the questions President Chiari's letter raised. He questioned Mr. Chiari on the principal causes for concern to Panama arising from the Canal treaties. Mr. Chiari mentioned first the sovereignty issue, that the in perpetuity provision was deprecating to the Panamanian people. He said that Panama's economy is in a precarious state and the country needed to exploit its resources, one of which is the canal.

The President asked the amount of the annuity. Mr. Chiari replied $750,000; the Ambassador interposed a correction, to $1,930,000, and pointed out there were two sources: one the annuity, the other the contribution from Canal Zone operations which ran from $40 to $60 million a year, usually the latter, or 1/6 the gross national product of Panama. Mr. Chiari remarked that Canal tolls should be increased since they had remained the same since 1914. Mr. Woodward suggested a survey

---

Source: Department of State, Central Files, 611.1913/9–1561. Limited Official Use. Drafted by Bracken and approved by the White House on September 27. The time of the meeting is taken from Kennedy's Appointment Book. (Kennedy Library)

[1] A translation of this letter, dated September 8, is filed with a covering memorandum of September 28 from Executive Secretary Battle to Goodwin. (Department of State, Central Files, 611.19/9–2861)

should be made to determine what the traffic would bear and at what point it would be cheaper to ship by trans-continental railroad or around the Cape.

In closing, the President said he would consult with Secretary Rusk and Mr. Woodward and would try to have a reply by October 1 since he understood there was some pressure on President Chiari because of the opening of the Assembly. He would like his reply to be responsive. However, he did not believe we should sit down to discuss negotiations without knowing how the discussions were going to come out. He did not want discussions to end in disagreement and felt it was preferable to wait until we were satisfied that we could come to a mutually agreeable conclusion.

397. National Security Action Memorandum No. 95

Washington, September 15, 1961.

MEMORANDUM FOR

The Secretary of State

As you know, the President of Panama has sent me a letter requesting that we re-negotiate our Panama Canal Treaties. It seems to me we should take a careful look at this problem with a view to analyzing what our basic interests are in the Canal Zone, what concessions we could make, and on what terms we could reasonably expect to get a long-term settlement. After we formulate our own views we should discuss them quietly with the Panamanians. We don't want to make a public announcement of negotiations until we have decided what the result of the talks will be.

I think we should establish a special working group with Assistant Secretary Woodward as Chairman,[1] including representatives from

---

Source: Department of State, NSAM Files: Lot 72 D 316, NSAM 95. Secret. A September 15 memorandum from NSC Executive Secretary Bromley K. Smith states that after Kennedy's memorandum had been distributed, it had been decided to include it in the NSAM series and to insert a subject line. Smith's memorandum is filed with a copy of NSAM 95, which includes the subject line, "Renegotiation of Panama Canal Treaty." (Kennedy Library, National Security Files, Countries Series, Panama, General)

[1] A memorandum of September 27 from Battle to McGeorge Bundy indicates that the Department was making arrangements for Under Secretary Ball to chair the study; an attached note states that Bromley Smith had indicated White House approval. (Department of State, Central Files, 611.1913/9–2761)

Defense, the Budget Bureau, Jerry Wiesner[2] and Dick Goodwin. I would like the recommendations of this group within the next two weeks. After that we can go ahead and begin some talks with the Panamanians. You might also bring Farland up for consultation with the group.

John Kennedy

---

[2] Special Assistant to the President for Science and Technology Jerome Wiesner.

---

398. Memorandum From Secretary of State Rusk to President Kennedy

Washington, October 9, 1961.

SUBJECT

Recommendations on Improving Relations with Panama

Your memorandum of September 15, 1961 requests the establishment of a special working group to prepare recommendations on improving relations with Panama.

Such a group, under the chairmanship of Under Secretary George W. Ball, and including representatives from Defense, the Budget Bureau and the White House staff has carefully examined this problem in the last two weeks.

The group has found that an analysis of our basic interests in the Canal Zone, a determination of the concessions we might make to Panama, and the terms on which we could reasonably expect to get a long-term settlement of our problems with Panama, are matters which require far more detailed study than is possible for the group to undertake in such a short period of time.

To formulate a workable policy governing our relations with Panama and the Canal will require an intensive study by a group of experts. To achieve this, it is recommended that you designate the policy group

---

Source: Department of State, NSAM Files: Lot 72 D 316, NSAM 95. Secret. No drafting information appears on the source text, but it was approved by Goodwin on October 18.

under Mr. Ball as an NSC Working Group and authorize the appointment of a special study group of experts, under the chairmanship of the Department, to examine in detail problems confronting us in our relations with Panama. The Department would propose to appoint Ambassador Muccio,[1] who has had extensive experience in treaty renegotiation with Panama in 1955, as Coordinator of this study group. The study group's report would be submitted to Mr. Ball's policy group within 90 days.

Suggested terms of reference for the proposed subgroup are enclosed.[2]

Pending the completion of the report of the NSC Working Group, it is recommended that we proceed on a selective basis with certain administrative actions which can improve our relations with Panama without treaty change, as outlined in the second enclosure.

A draft reply to the letter from President Chiari, requesting that we renegotiate the canal treaties, is also enclosed.

Dean Rusk[3]

---

[1] Ambassador to Guatemala John J. Muccio.
[2] Entitled "Administrative Actions to Improve Relationships." None of the enclosures is printed.
[3] Printed from a copy that indicates Rusk signed the original.

---

399. Memorandum of Conversation

Panama City, January 19, 1962.

SUBJECT

Call of Under Secretary Ball on President Chiari at Casa Presidencial, Panamá[1]

PARTICIPANTS

President Chiari
Under Secretary Ball

Source: Department of State, Central Files, 611.1913/1–1962. Confidential. Drafted by Bracken and approved in U on January 23.

[1] Ball was in Panama to attend a meeting of the Panama Canal Company Board of Directors, on which he represented the Department of State.

ACCOMPANYING PRESIDENT CHIARI

> Foreign Minister Galileo Solis
> Finance Minister Gilberto Arias
> David Samudio, Director General of Planning
> Jorge Riba, Technical Director, Planning Bureau
> Fabian Velarde, Presidential Press Secretary

ACCOMPANYING UNDER SECRETARY BALL

> Ambassador Joseph S. Farland
> Katherine Bracken, Director, Office of Central American and Panamanian Affairs
> George Springsteen, Special Assistant to the Under Secretary

The Under Secretary conveyed the greetings of President Kennedy to President Chiari and indicated that Mr. Kennedy looked forward to seeing Mr. Chiari in Washington in the future.

The Under Secretary said that he had expressed to the Foreign Minister at the airport Secretary Rusk's appreciation of the vigorous action which the Panamanian Government had taken in connection with the Cuban problem and wished to repeat this to the President as well. President Chiari thanked Mr. Ball for his comments.

Mr. Ball then informed President Chiari that, as mentioned in President Kennedy's recent letter to him,[2] a special study group had been set up to assess United States needs with regard to the Canal, and that Ambassador Muccio had been designated to head the group. The importance given the group and the seriousness with which the United States was pursuing the study, the Under Secretary said, was demonstrated by President Kennedy's selection of Ambassador Muccio to direct the activities of the group. Mr. Ball said that the report would provide a basis for a letter to President Chiari and it was hoped that this would come forward in a few months.

President Chiari indicated his pleasure at this information and noted that studies of the Canal had been under way for many years and inquired how this review might differ from already existing reports. The Under Secretary pointed out that there were in effect new conditions and that the present review was a more comprehensive analysis, particularly of the economic and strategic needs, and would take into account the technological advances that have made possible new methods of canal excavation.

President Chiari asked whether the United States was still considering a sea-level canal and the routes already explored. The Under Secretary replied that this is one facet of the total study. President Chiari remarked that he was happy to hear this since he and his Government

---

[2] Kennedy's letter, November 2, replied to Chiari's letter of September 8. For text, see Department of State *Bulletin*, December 4, 1961, pp. 932–933.

had gathered from the extensive improvements under way to widen the cuts that a new canal was no longer considered.

The Finance Minister inquired whether the United States was contemplating a revision of the present canal treaties apart from a treaty regarding a new canal. The Under Secretary responded that this was a part of the total study of a total problem.

President Chiari referred to delay in getting projects implemented under the $9.9 million grant made in October 1961. Mr. Ball referred to the extensive reorganization of the aid programs which had taken place in Washington, but which was just about completed, and added that we could now press on to hasten implementation of the projects. He noted that funds were now allotted and the program could move forward.

President Chiari brought up the question of authorization for Panamanian firms to participate in the school construction projects, particularly since there were well qualified Panamanian firms who could operate in the rural areas to better advantage than foreign firms. The President stressed that Panama is now in the dry season and that unless construction can move forward now, a year of delay would result. The Under Secretary replied that preliminary consideration of the waiver proposal had already begun and that he did not anticipate problems in this connection.

President Chiari expressed his gratification and introduced Mr. Samudio, and Mr. Riba, who had just joined the group. Mr. Samudio described briefly a memorandum he had prepared on the steps, including self-help, taken so far by Panama and the country's expectations under the Alliance for Progress, which President Chiari passed on to Mr. Ball. The Under Secretary indicated he would read the memorandum with great interest.

The Under Secretary then mentioned to President Chiari that one point in the Panamanian scene which had caused some concern had been the inflationary budget just passed by the Assembly and he inquired whether this represented a departure from previous policies. The Finance Minister, at the President's direction, defended that budget as a one-year operation. He explained that while the budget was larger than anticipated, many of the increases in personnel expenditures had been caused by Panama's projects under the Alliance for Progress, mentioning the $600,000 required to set up an electrical authority and a similar sum to support the centralized water authority, both of which were necessary to qualify for hydroelectric and waterworks loans. The financing of the payments to Social Security by bonds in the amount of $2.8 million was, in his opinion, necessary only this year since by 1963 additional revenues possible under the new tax measures would have provided the additional sources needed. The Finance Minister referred to the Chiari Administration's good record in cutting down defaulted payments on current accounts, including the water bill to the Panama Canal Company, and expressed confidence that the improved tax law and better collection methods would begin to ease the situation during the year. He stressed the increase in tax rates, which he personally felt was an important step forward. In response to a question, the Finance Minister indicated that active steps were underway to improve tax collections, noting the addition of 16 internal revenue persons to his staff. He also noted that all Treasury personnel were under Civil Service. The President and the Finance Minister both noted that steps were underway to bring more persons from all branches of government under Civil Service in order to improve Government efficiency. This would be a slow process as standards had to be established and applied. All these added to the budgetary problem.

The Finance Minister explained that one of the problems in increasing revenues was the difficulty in controlling the contraband from the Canal Zone. He suggested that the commissaries in the Canal Zone increase the price of cigarettes, balancing this increase by reductions in other items, so that the Panamanian Government could increase its taxes on cigarettes. He said that as much as $2 million in additional revenue could be realized if this were done. He said that the Republic is faced with a rising volume of contraband each time it endeavors to increase the tax 2 or 3 cents. He noted that the contraband in whiskey had now been brought more or less under control by centralizing sales in certain locations in the Zone. The Under Secretary suggested that Ambassador Farland pursue the matter further with the Panamanian authorities to see what recommendations might be made. The Ambassador indicated that he hoped to have something definitive within ten days.

The Under Secretary inquired of the President whether he had other problems to raise. The President replied that at first he had intended to bring up many problems in connection with the Canal but he had changed his mind after hearing the Under Secretary's comments. Mr. Ball agreed that any attempt to discuss such matters at this time would be premature and would not serve either country's interest.

As the meeting terminated, the Under Secretary informed the President that he would be visiting the self-help housing project at San Miguelito on Saturday. The President expressed his appreciation and wished Mr. Ball well for the rest of his stay on the Isthmus.

400. Memorandum From the President's Press Secretary (Salinger) to President Kennedy

Washington, March 12, 1962.

SUBJECT

United States–Panama Negotiations

Fabian Velarde, Press Secretary to President Chiari of Panama, came to see me today and said he had been directed to communicate with you, through me, rather than through normal diplomatic channels.

In November he said you sent a letter to President Chiari in which you said that you would look into the Panama Canal problem personally and as soon as the needs of the United States with regard to the Panama Canal had been determined you would respond promptly "in a few months."

Mr. Velarde said there had been soundings on the possibility of inviting President Chiari to the United States at which time there might be a chance to start discussions as well as a joint statement on a treaty.

Meanwhile, Velarde said there is a continuing discussion of a sea level canal and arguments as to whether to do it or/and when to do it. Such a canal, of course, would have serious economic consequences for Panama; that continuing discussion on this sea level canal is delaying the start of the negotiations.

Velarde said we should understand that next May schools and universities will open in Panama; he said there are key student groups that are controlled by the extreme left and any further delay would give them an opportunity to stir up problems for the present state of harmonious friendship between the United States and Panama. He said when the Foreign Minister of Panama saw Secretary Rusk in Punta del Este, the Secretary indicated the answer would be forthcoming in March. Velarde said there is impatience to get an answer and that much further delay would cause problems. Mr. Velarde said it is the feeling of the President that an answer must come before May.

Mr. Velarde said that the President should understand that he would be most welcome in Panama and throughout Latin America; it

---

Source: Department of State, Central Files, 611.19/3–1562. Secret. Filed with a March 15 covering memorandum from Charles E. Johnson of the NSC staff to Carol Moor of the Department of State Executive Secretariat, which states that it was to be treated as an unnumbered NSAM, so that the White House would be informed of actions relating to it. A March 12 memorandum from Kennedy's personal secretary, Evelyn Lincoln, to Ball, also attached to the source text, states that the President had asked her to send it to Ball and that he would like an up-to-date report on "these negotiations." A handwritten note indicates that Ball had talked to Special Assistant to the President Ralph Dungan, who would inform the President that the canal study was underway.

would be a source of great satisfaction if you could go to Panama and personally open negotiations. Mr. Velarde plans to remain in Washington for the next 24 hours and then go to New York for a few days. I assured him we would give him some kind of answer as soon as possible.

Pierre Salinger

---

401. Memorandum From the Under Secretary of State (Ball) to President Kennedy

Washington, April 27, 1962.

SUBJECT

Panama Canal Policy and Relations with Panama

The NSC Working Group on Panama has completed consideration of our relations with Panama and the related question of the need for a sea-level canal, pursuant to NSAM No. 95.[1] The Group recommends that the United States:

1. *Defer any decision and avoid any expressed or implied commitment on a sea-level canal for a period of approximately five years while completing those measures which must precede an informed decision,* including:

a. a research program to determine the feasibility, costs and other factors of nuclear construction methods;

b. site surveys to determine the feasibility, costs and other factors of alternative canal routes;

c. economic studies to provide a more complete basis for determining our interest in and requirement for a new canal;

d. quiet preparations, including talks with Panama, and other interested governments as appropriate, to clarify the terms and conditions of a new treaty; and

---

Source: Kennedy Library, National Security Files, Countries Series, Panama, General. Secret. No drafting information appears on the source text. Filed with an April 30 covering memorandum from Deputy Special Assistant for National Security Affairs Carl Kaysen, which commented: "The sum and substance of all this is that we recognize that any firm decision on a second canal cannot be made for as much as five years."

[1] Document 397.

e. studies to clarify the costs and problems of abandonment of the existing Canal, or retention under a new treaty relationship.

2. *Defer any formal treaty negotiations with Panama affecting the present Canal until completion of the foregoing measures.*

3. *Contain Panamanian pressures for treaty renegotiation and strive to improve relations with Panama* by:

a. focusing attention on the research and surveys to obtain data for an informed decision on a sea-level canal;

b. liberal interpretation of existing treaty provisions to satisfy Panamanian aspirations which are reasonable and consistent with the basic interests of the United States, including such unilateral measures as acceding to the Panamanian request for dock facilities in the Zone, and

c. accelerated assistance through the Alliance for Progress to help Panama improve economic and social conditions and reduce its dependence on the Canal.

The basic data and line of reasoning leading to these recommendations are set forth in the *Report of the Coordinator, Special Study Group on Panama* transmitted here as Enclosure I.[2]

I believe that these recommendations, properly carried out, can provide a basis for improved relations with Panama. I wish, however, to introduce cautionary notes with regard to two aspects of the recommended actions.

First, a decision to undertake the construction of a sea-level canal will depend upon many factors, only one of which is that of the means of construction. There should, therefore, be no relationship openly expressed between Operation Plowshare and the construction of a sea-level canal. We have much to learn about the safety of construction by nuclear means and in the absence of demonstrable proof of its infallibility on a project of this scale we could, by over-emphasizing its potential now—and in the absence of an effective information program—provide a golden opportunity for Soviet propaganda throughout Latin America.

Secondly, although the paper correctly recommends deferment of any formal treaty negotiations with Panama for a period up to five years, while we study the need for a new canal, we should not be under any illusions that we can effectively maintain this position over this period. While every effort will be made to maintain our position by exploiting the various proposals outlined in the recommendations, it is doubtful that President Chiari or any chief executive of Panama can long resist normal political pressures to seek renegotiation. The key issue is United States sovereignty over the Canal Zone. Any proposal to abandon our

---

[2] Not printed. A undated copy is filed with a covering memorandum of March 28 from Muccio to Ball. (Department of State, NSAM Files: Lot 72 D 316, NSAM 95)

traditional position with regard to sovereignty would obviously have to be preceded by a great deal of careful work with the Congress.

With these caveats, I submit for your consideration, with the recommendation that you sign or approve them, the following three documents required to carry out the recommended courses of action:

NSAM to carry out the policy decision in accordance with the recommendations;[3]

Suggested letter to President Chiari of Panama, together with copies of his letter of September 8, 1961, and your interim reply of November 2, 1961;[4] and

Preliminary guidelines for discussions with President Chiari on the occasion of his proposed visit to the United States.[5]

George W. Ball

---

[3] See Document 402.
[4] See Document 403 and footnotes 1 and 2 thereto.
[5] Not printed.

---

402.   National Security Action Memorandum No. 152

Washington, April 30, 1962.

TO

    The Secretary of State
    The Secretary of Defense
    The Chairman, Atomic Energy Commission
    The Director of Central Intelligence
    The Director, Bureau of the Budget

SUBJECT

    Panama Canal Policy and Relations with Panama

I have approved the following policy guidance governing the conduct of United States relations with Panama and future actions related to the present Panama Canal and a possible new sea-level canal.

Source: Department of State, NSAM Files: Lot 72 D 316, NSAM 152. Secret. A copy was sent to the Secretary of Commerce. Kennedy apparently revised the draft sent to him with Document 401. Kaysen reported at a May 2 White House staff meeting that the President "had signed off on his Panama papers but had modified them somewhat to indicate his judgment that we would probably be forced to renegotiate the treaty in the not too distant future regardless of any delaying action we might conduct." (Memorandum for the record by Colonel Julian J. Ewell of the White House staff, May 2; National Defense University, Taylor Papers, Box 24, Daily Staff Meetings)

1. The United States will undertake further basic economic and technical investigations to provide the basis for examining the question of the need for and the method of construction, location and cost of a sea-level, interoceanic canal in the Isthmian region. Such investigations will include research to determine within approximately the next five years the feasibility, costs and other factors involved in various methods of excavation.

2. Pending completion of such investigations, the United States is not now prepared to determine as a matter of policy, nor to accept a commitment expressed or implied, that it will at any particular time in the future actually construct a sea-level, interoceanic canal.

3. The United States will not accede at this time to a basic renegotiation of the existing treaties with Panama affecting the present Canal. The Government must recognize, however, that this question cannot be postponed indefinitely and may have to be faced before the studies discussed above are completed.

4. The United States will express a willingness and an earnest intent to consider with the Panamanians specific measures for adjusting our relationships through a liberal interpretation of the existing treaties in order to place U.S.-Panamanian relations on a more mutually satisfactory basis.

5. The United States will give serious consideration to accelerated assistance to Panama through the Alliance for Progress, particularly in support of projects which promise to develop new sources of livelihood for the Panamanian people and otherwise diversify the Panamanian economy.

6. In carrying out these policies:

a. The Secretary of State will:

(1) Consult, in coordination with the Department of Defense and the Atomic Energy Commission, with the appropriate committees of Congress to present and obtain concurrences in the policy guidance and the proposed implementing actions.

(2) Refine the draft set of guidelines for discussions with President Chiari based on the initial Panamanian reaction to my letter and the results of continuing normal diplomatic contacts up to the time of the visit.

(3) Following President Chiari's visit, obtain agreement of the Governments of Panama and Colombia for on-site surveys of potential sea-level canal routes in their respective countries.

(4) Based on the Panamanian reactions to the outcome of our conversations, develop in further detail the U.S. approach to considering with the Panamanians specific measures for adjusting our relationships

through liberal interpretation of the existing treaties and for accelerating assistance through the Alliance for Progress.

(5) Assume leadership, with the participation of other agencies, as appropriate, in conducting in an appropriate time phase with other investigations related to the sea-level canal question: (a) broad economic studies to determine the U.S. interest in and requirement for a sea-level, interoceanic canal; (b) quiet preparations, including talks with Panama and other interested governments as appropriate, to clarify the terms and conditions of a new treaty, and (c) studies to clarify the costs and problems of abandonment of the existing Canal, or retention under a new treaty relationship.

b. The Chairman, Atomic Energy Commission, will establish within the Plowshare Program a research goal to determine within approximately the next five years the feasibility, costs and other factors involved in nuclear methods of excavation. The necessary research program will be a joint responsibility of the Atomic Energy Commission and the Department of Defense in accordance with the mutual agreement between these two agencies.

c. The Secretary of Defense will:

(1) Review, with the Joint Chiefs of Staff, the U.S. requirements for military facilities in the Isthmian region, including the Canal Zone, in the light of the U.S. defense mission in the Western Hemisphere and the need for protection of the present or a new canal.

(2) Arrange, under civil functions, for the participation of the U.S. Army Corps of Engineers in the joint research program with the Atomic Energy Commission as directed above.

(3) Have the Secretary of the Army prepare, as Stockholder of the Panama Canal Company, for submission to the current session of Congress authorizing legislation for on-site surveys by the Panama Canal Company of a limited number of potential sea-level canal routes, including at least one in Panama and one in Colombia. Preparations will be made to fund through normal legislative process survey activities in Panama and Colombia in FY 1963.

(4) Review with the Panama Canal Company the present commercial activities being conducted in the Canal Zone, to determine which of these activities could be discontinued.

(5) Survey with the Panama Canal Company the present land areas and Canal Company facilities and determine which, if any, of them are not essential to the protection, operation and maintenance of the Canal.

John Kennedy

403. Letter From President Kennedy to President Chiari

Washington, April 30, 1962.

DEAR MR. PRESIDENT: In reply to your letter of September 8, 1961,[1] concerning relations between our two countries, I wrote you on November 2[2] that my Government would communicate with the Government of Panama as soon as the various responsible departments and agencies of the United States Government had made a complete re-examination of current and future needs with respect to Isthmian canal facilities. I expressed confidence that representatives of our two Governments, after a frank exchange of views and a careful assessment of mutual needs and interests, could reach fruitful conclusions which would promote the mutual welfare of both countries. A re-examination of current and future needs has just been completed, and I hasten to inform you of the results.

The central question has been the possible future need to construct a sea-level, interoceanic canal in the Isthmian region. I am sure you will agree that the answer to this important question has a fundamental, long-range significance for both Panama and the United States, as well as for all the other countries in the Hemisphere. Because of this fact, a decision should be made only after the most thorough exploration of the problem. In arriving at the answer, particular consideration must be given (1) to the role of Panama Canal traffic in world commerce and global economic development and the possible future impact of the limitations of the present lock canal; (2) to technological advances in transport which may bear importantly on the conveyance by sea of commodities; (3) to the most feasible means of constructing and financing any sea-level canal, route locations and costs; and (4) to the effect which the project itself would have on the countries directly concerned, especially Panama. The examination just completed within the United States Government indicates that much more information on these matters must be obtained before a decision is taken, and that programs should be initiated at once to obtain the necessary data.

We are today living in a world where each day brings new advances in technology and science, particularly in the field of transport. We have, in the last decade, witnessed radical innovations in the conveyance of both people and goods by all modes of transportation. Today we are only beginning to explore the frontiers of space; no one knows yet what

---

Source: Kennedy Library, President's Office Files, Panama, General. No classification marking. Telegram 716 to Panama City, May 1, transmitted the text of the letter. (Department of State, Central Files, 719.11/5–162)

[1] See footnote 1, Document 396.
[2] See footnote 2, Document 397.

impact this mode of travel may have on the future. It is my hope that the studies we propose to undertake will shed new light on the application of new developments to sea travel in the future and hence on the need for a new canal. From these studies we will be better able to reach decisions compatible with the world in which we live and which will further relations between our two countries. The effect of these recent technological advances must be fully evaluated before a decision can be made on the sea-level canal. Our best estimate is that scientific and engineering investigations over a period of years will be needed to complete the evaluation.

In the meantime, I believe that there are a number of interim measures which might be fruitfully discussed by representatives of our two Governments in order to maintain and strengthen relations on a basis of mutual respect and sincere friendship. I would be most pleased and honored if you would accept an invitation to visit the United States early in June. I would suggest if convenient June 12–18. At that time we could personally exchange views on programs for obtaining data relative to a possible future sea-level canal and on areas for discussion by our representatives looking toward the mutual benefit of our two countries.

Sincerely,

John F. Kennedy[3]

---

[3] Printed from a copy that indicates Kennedy signed the original.

---

404. Memorandum of Conversation

Washington, May 21, 1962, 12:55–1:03 p.m.

SUBJECT

Visit of President Chiari

PARTICIPANTS:

Ambassador Arango, Panamanian Ambassador to US

The President

Dr. Carl Kaysen—Deputy Special Assistant to the President for National Security Affairs

Mr. Edwin M. Martin—Assistant Secretary of State for Inter-American Affairs

---

Source: Kennedy Library, National Security Files, Countries Series, Panama, General. Confidential. Drafted by Martin and approved in the White House on July 2. The time of the meeting is from Kennedy's Appointment Book. (Ibid.)

Ambassador Arango delivered to the President separately a letter from President Chiari and a memorandum.[1] In response to the President's request as to whether he had any comments to make, he said his President was very pleased to be able to accept the invitation to visit the United States and would leave it to us to select the precise dates between June 12 and June 18. He also called attention to the final paragraph of the memorandum in which reference is made to the fact that President Chiari hopes that a joint communiqué can be issued in which reference is made to the subjects listed in the memorandum.

The President said that the Assistant Secretary would convey to the Ambassador our suggestions with respect to the date. He then went on at some length to indicate that he thought it extremely important to the success of this meeting, to which he was looking forward with a great deal of pleasure, that there be in advance an understanding of the purposes of the meeting. It would be most unfortunate if he and President Chiari approached the meeting with different purposes, as this would surely involve serious disagreement, and, if these differences became public, might even create bad relations between the peoples of the two countries, something he was sure everyone agreed should be avoided if possible.

President Kennedy said there were a number of things we might be able to do to meet some of the concerns President Chiari had about our relationships with regard to the Canal. On the other hand, there were other things, which required modifications in the treaty, which it would be difficult to do quickly. If it became known that this was even under discussion, there would be a lot of criticism from various US quarters which would create a very bad atmosphere for the visit. He said changes of this sort had to be discussed and fully prepared before it was possible to accomplish them. He did not want to bar discussing the things that were of interest to the Panamanians, but thought it very important to have agreement as to basic purposes so that the publics did not expect concrete results on a wider scope than those apt to be secured. He suggested that the Ambassador get together with Dr. Kaysen and the Assistant Secretary to prepare an agreed statement of the purposes of the visit which would be used for background briefing for the press in the two countries,[2] so that undue expectations would not be aroused. He also

---

[1] Both dated May 17. The texts were transmitted in telegram 919 from Panama City, May 19. (Department of State, Central Files, 719.11/5–1962)

[2] Telegram 761 to Panama City, May 24, reported that Martin and Kaysen had met with Arango and prepared draft points, which described the subjects covered in Chiari's May 17 letter and memorandum and the line the conversations might take without any commitment by either side as to what action might be taken. Telegram 762 to Panama City, May 24, transmitted the draft points. (Ibid., 719.11/5–2462)

indicated that he would cover this point in his reply to President Chiari's letter.[3]

Ambassador Arango said he understood the President's position fully and had made it clear to President Chiari that there were difficulties about getting concrete results immediately on some of the matters in which President Chiari was interested. He said he talked just Saturday[4] with his President and told him it was a very good letter and that he was very glad he had accepted the invitation. He also said he thought the phrasing of the final paragraph of the memorandum left the way open for having these matters referred to as "under consideration" or "subject to further examination" without requiring that definitive results be achieved.

The President welcomed this and said that he hoped in the next 24 hours we could work out the background document to which he referred. He then went on to say he would like Dr. Kaysen to make a visit to Panama sometime in the next few days to discuss with Ambassador Farland and other people the situation there and get a first hand feel for the various political aspects of it and an appreciation of the physical situation in the Canal Zone. The Ambassador said he was sure he would be most welcome.

---

[3] In a May 24 letter to Chiari, Kennedy wrote that he welcomed "the opportunity to explore with you the many aspects of the relations between our countries and to review our mutual concerns and problems as Presidents." (Ibid., 719.11/5–2462)

[4] May 19.

405. Memorandum of Conversation

Washington, June 12, 1962, 4:45 p.m.

SUBJECT

United States-Panamanian Relations

PARTICIPANTS

For Panama:
President Roberto F. Chiari[1]
Foreign Minister Galileo Solis
ex-Foreign Minister Octavio Fabrega
Ambassador A. Guillermo Arango

For the United States:
President Kennedy
Under Secretary Ball
Ambassador Farland
Assistant Secretary Martin
Mr. Carl Kaysen, The White House
Mrs. Katherine W. Bracken (rapporteur)

President Kennedy welcomed President Chiari and suggested President Chiari proceed with any points be wished to make.

President Chiari repeated the burden of his September 8, 1961, letter to President Kennedy on the Panamanian case for renegotiation of the Canal treaties. He suggested that the two countries, in order to bring about a revision of relations, should get to the very bottom of the question and eliminate the clauses that have caused misunderstandings between the two peoples for a great many years. He pointed out the Canal was built not just for one party but to aid international maritime commerce and the security of the United States, as well as to develop the welfare of Panama. He quoted from President Kennedy's letter of November 8 ("When two friendly nations are bound by treaty provisions which are not fully satisfactory to one of the parties arrangements should be made to permit both nations to discuss these points of dissatisfaction") and asked in the name of Panama that the treaties be revised and not considered sacred just because they were signed 58 years ago, that he

---

Source: Kennedy Library, National Security Files, Countries Series, Panama, General. Confidential. No drafting information appears on the source text, but it was approved in U on July 21 and by the White House on August 8. The meeting was held at the White House.

[1] President Chiari visited the United States June 11–16. A memorandum of a brief conversation between Kennedy and Chiari on June 13, when they signed a joint communiqué, is ibid. The text of the joint communiqué is printed in Department of State *Bulletin*, July 9, 1962, pp. 81–82. Memoranda of two conversations between Chiari and Rusk on September 13 are in Department of State, Central Files, 611.19/6–1362. Related material is ibid., Conference Files: Lot 65 D 533, CF 2118–2119.

was certain that with President Kennedy's backing, Congress would agree to renegotiation.

President Kennedy responded that he well understood that the situation was different today than it was in the early 20th century when the treaty was signed and that if the treaty were written today it would be written differently. "The difficulty arises," the President said, "because of our long experience with the Canal. Sovereignty of the Canal by Panama has been recognized; we are there for operating, maintaining and defending it." He continued that he could not see the end of the road in sitting down to rewrite the treaty nor how he could demonstrate to two-thirds of the Senate that such a course had advanced the United States interest. He suggested that since sovereignty is the principal issue and we have recognized Panama as sovereign that we attempt within this framework to work out operation of the Canal along with mitigation of frictions. For example, the contraband problem had been mentioned to him by Finance Minister Arias as well as the problem of Panamanian employees. He noted we were dealing with a tenderly sensitive issue over which any bankrupt politician could arouse emotion. He added that should he try to take any treaty changes through the Senate and fail it would be worse for both countries.

Under Secretary Ball pointed out that the fact that the Canal is 50 years old presents the United States with recognition of changed conditions; that we are seriously preoccupied with the possibility of a sea-level Canal; that it will be some time before we are prepared to make a decision on a sea-level Canal; at that time we would approach Panama for a new treaty and such treaty for a sea-level Canal would be of a different kind. From the point of view of the State Department, Mr. Ball said, an attempt to negotiate on the basis of renegotiation at a time when we are looking toward the strong possibility of going ahead with a sea-level Canal would create greater confusion.

President Chiari noted that studies on a sea-level Canal have been going on for many years, that one must think of the good will of the Panamanian people later toward a sea-level Canal, and repeated his claim for a terminal date, noting that a revision of relations is impossible within the framework of the "in perpetuity" of the present treaty. He described the national feelings involved in seeing the Panamanian flag flying with that of the United States at every place in the Zone.

President Kennedy said he recognized the problems of Panama, how these matters of national sovereignty were sensitive ones and how easily these feelings may be aroused. He stated that he was aware we should take appropriate action but not "at the point of a mob." He pointed out that free movement through the Canal was a part of the folk-lore of the United States on which there were feelings in this country as well. He asked what was considered unsatisfactory in the present arrangement.

President Chiari replied "to recognize sovereignty in the right way" and President Kennedy responded that that had been done in Eisenhower's time. President Chiari repeated that it was a Panamanian right to have flags at every point but this would not mean Panama had jurisdiction over that particular place. President Chiari became frustrated and petulant in his speech at this point. He said his words were misunderstood, that not for a single moment does Panama wish to participate in the maintenance, operation and protection of the Canal, that Panama cannot do it and what happens to the Canal happens to Panama.

Foreign Minister Solis interrupted to state the case more clearly: That Panama would not now attempt to sign a treaty, but that Panama should bring up for discussion points of dissatisfaction over the way the basic treaty now operates; further, that any problem Panama puts up for discussion be subject to thorough consideration and just negotiation. A committee formed of representatives should try to find solutions on points agreed upon. Perhaps the points agreed upon will not need a treaty; what Panama wants is discussion of its point of view.

President Kennedy asked Foreign Minister Solis to clarify his statement, whether he had in mind treaty negotiations or a discussion of issues arising under the treaty.

Foreign Minister Solis, replied: The treaty stipulates all the authority and powers granted by Panama to the United States for the specific purpose of operation, maintenance, sanitation and defense of the Canal. There are manufacturing activities in the Canal Zone that do not relate to those purposes. President Kennedy suggested that in such cases a revision of treaties was not necessary, only an analysis to determine how Panama could benefit more from the market offered by the Canal Zone. Foreign Minister Solis then passed to the demand that jurisdiction over land areas not used should be returned to Panama. President Kennedy replied that if we are holding areas outside treaty purposes, this should be discussed during coming months and resolved in a way that is mutually satisfactory.

Foreign Minister Solis repeated his point that Panama wants consent to discuss all points and to try to find solutions. President Kennedy reiterated his reluctance to become involved in formal discussions which implied renegotiation of the treaty. He repeated his suggestion that we should attempt to see what are major points of concern under present treaties, indicating that 1964, 1965 or 1966 would be a better time to go about a "basic document."

Foreign Minister Solis repeated his suggestion for discussion on points of difference, adding that, if there is agreement, "no harm will be done." President Kennedy replied that an appropriate group should be set up to discuss the problems of Panama. It should not be designated a committee to set the basis for renegotiation; rather it should have as terms of reference improvement of relations with Panama with respect to the Canal Zone. The President repeated his earlier statement that he did not want "to start along a road and three-quarters along the way not see where" he was going. He would like to see the committee set up, to see where we are and start formal treaty negotiations in, say, five to ten years when both the American people and Congress would understand the problem better. If we go ahead with a sea-level canal we would have an entirely different kind of negotiation.

Ex-Foreign Minister Fabrega then presented his version of Panama's case. He said we should be frank and candid; that President Kennedy had stated his problem with regard to Senate confirmation of a treaty but that in Panama there was also a problem of national sentiment that it was difficult to control and postpone. This generation of Panamanian youth does not have the mentality of 1903; new leaders are more aware of rights and are demanding they be granted. Panama should be given a new deal in substantial recognition of its rights. A new treaty would not hamper or limit the need to run or operate the Canal. President Kennedy inquired of Dr. Fabrega what he would like to propose for a treaty. Dr. Fabrega replied : recognition of Panamanian sovereignty and a terminal date.

Foreign Minister Solis repeated the demand for recognition of Panamanian sovereignty with the flying of Panamanian flags, use of Panamanian postal stamps, acceptance of Panamanian exequaturs in the Canal Zone, and mixed courts. Dr. Fabrega interrupted to say that for a clear manifestation of sovereignty it will not be enough to have this done by unilateral act. He then went into the annuity request, noting that Panama was not getting its share of profits, that the annuity is minor compared to the major Panamanian contribution, that Panama has a joint and vital interest in the Canal and that the Canal should be a source of labor in all categories, not only in lower levels.

President Kennedy repeated his offer to begin discussions, particularly to seek to work out a solution of the commissary problem. President Chiari supported Dr. Fabrega's request for more equal opportunity for Panamanian labor in the Canal Zone.

President Kennedy said he desired a just administration of employment policies to bring about improvements within the next twelve months. On the question of mixed courts he said he would have to study the Panamanian proposal. He went on to say that the basic question is the timing, that he was concerned about becoming involved in discussions where there was "no turning back" and public opinion in either country might become overly upset. When we can make a final decision on a sea-level canal it will provide a basis for a more satisfactory arrangement. He asked again whether or not we could work out some immediate improvements.

President Chiari repeated the doubt expressed earlier that any improvement could be worked out without changing the perpetuity clause. President Kennedy asked what time limit Panama suggested and President Chiari suggested a term of something like 50 years.

Foreign Minister Solis repeated his suggestion that Panama put up a list of points for discussion by the joint committee, that the committee would solve those items which could be solved by executive measures, that discussion would not mean a commitment to solutions, that he was not looking for solutions immediately on any point.

President Kennedy suggested that we explore solutions to problems by a more liberal interpretation of present treaties and mentioned the flag issue. President Chiari interrupted to object to the manner in which the Panamanian flag was raised in Shalers Triangle,[2] whereupon President Kennedy countered that although it might have been "raised in the dead of night and in the middle of the woods it was still recognition" of Panamanian sovereignty.

Foreign Minister Solis reiterated his desire for a revision of relations between the two countries to try to reach just solutions. President Kennedy proposed that agreement be sought on some language that would give guidance to a committee. Dr. Fabrega remarked that to revise relations, one must revise treaties; without new treaties there could be no change in relations.

Under Secretary Ball asked what special points of concern the Panamanians had in mind. He added that in his opinion within the framework of cooperation voiced by President Kennedy solutions can certainly be found for some of these problems.

Foreign Minister Solis then interjected that unless they could agree on a revision of all relations and publish it in the communiqué the visit would be a failure.

President Chiari referred again to the perpetuity clause and cited a 19th century example of the United States asking great Britain for a revision of a treaty on the basis conditions and circumstances of date of signing were temporary. He then emphasized Panama's objection to consideration of internationalization of the Canal, that Panama would rather deal with the United States than with 40 or 50 people they did not know, and then launched into a statement of other dissatisfactions about the Canal Zone—the fact that officials did not speak Spanish, that ciga-

---

[2] The United States announced on September 17, 1960, that the Panamanian flag would thereafter be flown together with the U.S. flag on a daily basis in an area known as Shalers Triangle in the Canal Zone. For text of the announcement, see Department of State *Bulletin*, October 10, 1960, pp. 558–559.

rettes sold for 15¢ in the Canal Zone, gasoline for 17¢ per gallon, that Canal Zone residents were given houses and were a "privileged oligarchy." He continued that Zone residents live better than Panamanians and that it hurt Panama's economy, referring to contraband of liquor.

Under Secretary Ball suggested that the matters President Chiari was describing were a matter for solution under the present treaty. President Chiari repeated his request that negotiators not argue about how sacred this or that clause might be, pointing to the 20 months of negotiations for the 1955 treaty. He went on to say that Panama and the United States have a common destiny, that when bombs were expected to blow up the Canal in the last war, the bombs would also have destroyed Panama City, that cooperation in the defense of the Canal was something the Panamanians understood and accepted. However, he urged a new approach to revise relations and then began describing the "filling stations, bakeries, repair shops, furniture factories," etc. operating in the Zone. President Kennedy noted that he understood the problem of contraband from the PX. President Chiari replied that he did not mean "PXes" which are "international" and that on "military bases the world over the same rules apply."

Dr. Fabrega proposed a procedure similar to that followed in the 1932 joint Roosevelt–Arias statement where there was a general statement or agreement to revise treaties, together with a statement of general principles and general guidance, which was followed by 4 years of discussion culminating in the 1936 treaty. He suggested that if the Presidents announce plans for a revision that would not be adopting an extreme position. He repeated his earlier statements on the intensity of the feeling of the present Panamanian generation with regard to the 1903 treaty.

Under Secretary Ball pointed out that one of the main problems in this procedure is that, in the case of whatever revisions President Kennedy submits to Congress, one of the first questions to be asked is the status of plans for the Canal, that it is very difficult to present revisions until there has been a decision on a sea-level canal. One of the things to be done now is go ahead with plans for the study of Canal needs in which Panama might participate. He reiterated his belief that many problems can be solved without revision of treaties.

President Chiari then said that people in Panama were not thinking about a sea-level Canal since it might be built in 2000, may not be built and perhaps not in Panama; for this reason he wanted a change in the 1903 treaty. He then described the importance of symbolism to the Latins, noting that even though a terminal date of 50 years were set the Panamanians would be happy because a date had been set. He then addressed himself to Mr. Ball's comments on studies for a new Canal and said that there is a general impression in Panama that the more money the United States spends in enlarging Culebra cut or improving the Canal the more the suspicion grows that the United States is "going for the third locks" and that the intention to consider a sea-level Canal is not serious.

Dr. Fabrega reiterated his insistence on a "political" solution, asking why Panamanian postal stamps could not be used as they were until 1924.

Foreign Minister Solis interrupted to say that in his opinion the question of presentation of a treaty to the Senate is not an issue since President Kennedy would never sign a treaty he knew would not be ratified and restated the case for discussions of Panama's points, which might end in a treaty and might not. He repeated that President Chiari cannot go back to Panama without agreement to discuss in a negotiation committee all the claims Panama may present; otherwise he will face a political crisis.

President Kennedy replied that he was not in a position to give any commitment that the United States could at this time agree to, sign or ratify a new treaty. He said that he understood the sentiments which the Panamanians expressed, and that passing of time did not improve the features of the 1903 treaty to which the Panamanians objected. He then elaborated on the United States political problem related to any renegotiation of the 1903 treaty and stated that he was not prepared to revise the 1903 treaty, particularly the perpetuity clause, and that he did not intend that we should give the impression that we are engaged in the process of revision. He repeated his belief that we should see what matters could be settled over the next 12 months. He then directed that Assistant Secretary Martin explore with Foreign Minister Solis language for a joint communiqué which would be satisfactory to both sides. He noted that the Panamanian group would be discussing with Secretary Rusk the next morning some of the items that had not been covered in the present conversation. He said he understood there was a division of feeling, that the Panamanians wanted to begin real renegotiation and he was reluctant to begin renegotiation at this time. The key issue was how to deal with the problem so that it did not become explosive, that the best time to deal with the matter of treaty revision was when there was a proper decision on a sea-level canal. He explained that if the canal could be built by nuclear means there was a certain advantage because of the lower costs and, therefore, economic feasibility was easier to establish. Some time was needed for research to establish the practicality of this technique. In addition there was a question of justification of a new canal because of increasing traffic which the present canal could not handle and some additional time was needed to study this factor.

Under Secretary Ball underlined President Kennedy's remarks, and said that the United States proposed to study the problem thoroughly so that within the next four to five years we could reach a decision on whether to build by nuclear or conventional means.

President Kennedy concluded by indicating that the United States would explore and decide the questions brought up with regard to the return of unneeded lands, control of contraband, flying more flags, increased employment opportunities, use of Panamanian postage stamps in Canal Zone post offices, and reduction of commercial activities in the Zone. Foreign Minister Solis said that if action is taken on interim measures they could wait long for the "main purpose."

---

406.   National Security Action Memorandum No. 164

Washington, June 15, 1962.

TO

The Secretary of State
The Secretary of Defense
The Secretary of the Army

1.   As a result of President Chiari's visit we are now committed to a continuing discussion of the problems arising out of our relations with the Republic of Panama from the Canal and the Canal Zone and a search for ways of dealing with them constructively. These discussions should, over time, produce an appropriate flow of concrete results in order to contain Panamanian pressures for immediate and radical treaty revision. This will require some extra attention by the responsible Departments.

2.   As our representatives for the discussions with Panama, I have decided to appoint the Ambassador to Panama, Joseph Farland, and the Governor of the Canal Zone, Major General Robert Fleming.

3.   I request the Secretary of State to take the leadership in organizing a small review group from the appropriate agencies to follow up the discussions between the two governments. This group should also be charged with the responsibility of examining what can be done on all the specific questions which the Panamanians have raised in their recent

---

Source: Department of State, NSAM Files: Lot 72 D 316, NSAM 164. Confidential.

visit. In examining these questions, I think it important to distinguish what can be done by executive authority alone, what can be done by ordinary legislation, and what requires revision of the treaty. In considering specific problems, I think it is desirable to explore methods of dealing with them which could by-pass the traditional concern with the formalisms of sovereignty and concentrate on meeting legitimate Panamanian complaints while maintaining the practical arrangements necessary for the operation of the Canal and for our military activities in the Zone.

Some of the particular points on which the Panamanians have pressed us most are the flying of Panamanian flags on ships going through the Canal, the use of Panamanian stamps in the Canal Zone postage system, change in the jurisdiction of American courts over Panamanian citizens, and the issuance by us of exequaturs to permit Consuls accredited to Panama to function in the Zone. With the exception of the court question, these are largely symbolic matters. In addition, of course, we must continue to examine the more practical problems of U.S. commercial activity in the Zone, labor questions involving equality of treatment for Panamanians, unneeded lands, and direct Panamanian benefits from the Canal.

John Kennedy

---

407. Memorandum of Conversation

Panama City, October 12, 1962.

PARTICIPANTS

President Chiari, Under Secretary Ball,[1] Foreign Minister Solís, Ambassador Farland

SUBJECT

U.S.-Panamanian Relations

Under Secretary Ball opened the conversation by referring to certain difficulties being encountered in the discussions between appointed rep-

---

Source: Department of State, Central Files, 611.19/10–1262. Confidential. Drafted by Farland.

[1] Ball visited Panama to make an address dedicating a bridge across the Panama Canal and to attend a meeting of the Board of Directors of the Panama Canal Company.

resentatives of the two Governments.[2] He said that he understood that the heart of these difficulties lay in insistence by the GOP representatives that the fundamental difficulties between Panama and the United States should be resolved immediately by what amounted to renegotiation of the 1903 Treaty. President Kennedy, the Under Secretary declared, had made very clear the U.S. position on this score during the June meeting in Washington; namely, that the United States could not undertake at this time to renegotiate the basic Treaty until studies were completed which would permit the United States to reach decisions regarding the possible need for a new canal. These studies and surveys might require as much as five years to complete. Furthermore, internal problems with respect to the U.S. Congress made it impossible at this time to successfully put through a new treaty in the U.S. Senate.

President Chiari responded that he understood this fully but had not realized the studies and surveys would require this long a period of time. He said he understood completely, however, that the United States must have all the facts at hand before a decision of such transcendental importance to the United States as well as Panama could be made.

President Chiari then went on to express his keen disappointment over the lack of progress and the absence of results to date of the talks between U.S. and GOP representatives. It was absolutely essential, he said, that progress be made on specific matters within the framework of the agreement reached in Washington, as set forth in the joint communiqué. He had the impression, he said, that the decisions which were being taken in Washington on these matters did not reflect the views of President Kennedy and others at the highest levels of the United States Government who had participated in the June meeting. The Foreign Minister interjected at this point that U.S.-Panamanian relations historically reflected that when discussions were conducted at the highest level between both Governments satisfactory conclusions had always been reached. Conversely, however, when matters were referred to a lower echelon in the United States Government there ensued a lack of progress, further misunderstandings and endless delays. The Foreign Minister also said that the GOP failed to see why matters discussed by the representatives of both Governments could not be mentioned publicly as the talks progressed since, in accordance with the agreement reached in Washington, there was no limitation on the range of subjects which could be brought up by either party.

There then ensued a general discussion of some of the more important matters presently under discussion by the representatives of the two

---

[2] The discussions between Ambassador Farland and Governor Fleming and Foreign Minister Solis and former Foreign Minister Fabrega began on July 13. Documentation concerning them is in Department of State, Central File 611.19.

Governments; namely, (1) raising Panamanian flags in the Canal Zone; (2) recognition of Panamanian exequaturs in the Canal Zone; (3) use of Panamanian stamps; and, (4) increased wages and more employment opportunities for Panamanians in the Zone.

Regarding raising Panamanian flags in the Canal Zone, (1) aforesaid, the Under Secretary said he was under the impression that a satisfactory agreement had already been reached on flags. President Chiari replied that there remained the matter of Panamanian flags on military bases and on ships transiting the Canal. He did not pursue the latter point but did go on with respect to the former by expressing his view that the United States could at least agree to flying the Panamanian flag outside the entrance of military bases without in any way affecting adversely its rights or jurisdiction over the bases. President Chiari remarked that all the issues between Panama and the United States had been well known to the United States for years as a result of prior treaty negotiations and he could not understand why it was still necessary for the United States to commit them all to such lengthy study and consideration at this point. It led him to wonder what the United States Government has been doing while it has been studying these matters for well over a year now.

In the matter of exequaturs, (2) aforesaid, Foreign Minister Solís stated that the GOP saw no reason for the USG's insistence that the word "formal" precede the word "exequatur" in the proposed draft communiqué. He characterized such insistence as unnecessary preoccupation with words and as being too legalistic. He also said that the proposed new language on exequaturs which Ambassador Farland had shown him briefly at the October 10 meeting of the representatives did not meet GOP requirements.

Regarding use of Panamanian stamps and Canal, Zone wages, (3) and (4) aforesaid, Ambassador Farland remarked that the U.S. had a proposal to make on stamps which he hoped the GOP would find acceptable, and gave a brief account of what had already been accomplished by the United States Government in the wage and labor field and commented on some of the improvements under consideration.

President Chiari then moved on to another subject, namely, Panama's need for additional direct revenue from the Canal operation. The President said that under the Alliance for Progress program Panama was engaging in what were, for Panama, extensive projects of a social nature, such as school construction, establishment of new hospitals and public health centers, all of which placed an increasingly heavy financial burden on Panama to operate and maintain. In addition, the needs and demands of the people for services of this kind were increasing, requiring the commitment of further funds for these unproductive although worthwhile projects. He declared that Panama had increased taxes and had improved greatly its tax collections. Further increases in the tax system were under consideration and would probably be proposed in this session of the National Assembly. However, Panama was rapidly reaching a point where further tax increase would be out of the question and its resources were being strained to the breaking point. In view of this and in view, furthermore, that Panama considered the present payment for Canal rights as unjust and antiquated, the GOP felt that it must insist upon a more just and fair compensation from the United States for the Canal rights. President Chiari said that he hoped the Under Secretary would understand Panama's problem and that the United States Government would be sympathetic to it.

408.   Memorandum of Conversation

Washington, November 8, 1962.

SUBJECT

US-Panama Conversations in Panama on Points of Dissatisfaction Concerning the Canal Zone

PARTICIPANTS:

A. Guillermo Arango, Panamanian Ambassador to the U.S.
ARA—Edwin M. Martin, Assistant Secretary
ARA/OAP—John W. Fisher, Acting Director

Ambassador Arango produced a handwritten personal letter sent to him by President Chiari, parts of which he read in translation to Mr. Martin.

President Chiari's letter instructed Ambassador Arango to see the Secretary if possible to apprise him of President Chiari's disappointment in the talks taking place in Panama on points of dissatisfaction concerning the Canal Zone.

President Chiari said that President Kennedy conveyed to him the clear understanding that these talks would proceed rapidly to dispose of Panama's dissatisfactions under the treaty arrangement between the

---

Source: Department of State, Central Files, 611.19/11–862. Official Use Only. Drafted by Fisher on November 13.

two countries. However, in the months since he saw President Kennedy, only the question of flying Panamanian flags over civilian installations in the Canal Zone has been settled. There has been no progress in flying Panamanian flags over military installations or on ships transiting the Canal. There had been talk but no agreement on exequaturs, stamps, and labor. President Chiari was not satisfied with the argument that the U.S. must wait about 5 years for studies on a sea level canal to be completed before undertaking revision of the treaties on the Canal. He emphasized the urgency of prompt action, asserting that his people cannot remain patient much longer.

Ambassador Arango added his own view that dangerous pressures are building up in the absence of satisfaction of Panama's desires concerning the treaty. He referred to the danger of an extremist like Castro getting control of the situation.

Mr. Martin said that President Kennedy made it very clear in his conversation with President Chiari that he would not be able to get the U.S. Senate to agree to changes in basic treaty relations with Panama, such as questions of sovereignty and jurisdiction, perpetuity, etc., at the present time. It would take perhaps five years for the U.S. to prepare itself to make a decision on a sea level canal, which would create a different situation.

Mr. Martin said it had also been made clear in the Washington discussions that the flying of the Panamanian flag on ships transiting the Canal is not an negotiable one. On other questions taken up in the Panama talks, we are now awaiting Panama's response to our proposals. We made suggestions on exequaturs several weeks ago and are prepared to move forward when Panama desires. We understand that the difficulty has been in the wording of the joint announcement of the exequatur arrangement, although there has been prominent public mention made at various times by representatives of both governments concerning adoption of new exequatur procedures.

We made a proposal several weeks ago on stamps and are awaiting Panama's response. On October 16, we made some suggestions on labor practices for further discussion at later meetings. We have announced our readiness to transfer a pier to Panama, and to implement income tax deduction procedures and have had no response from the Panama side at all.[1]

---

[1] An interim joint communiqué concerning the discussions in Panama was issued by the U.S. and Panamanian Governments on January 10, 1963. It stated that it had been agreed that the Panamanian flag would be flown together with the U.S. flag on land in the Canal Zone where the U.S. flag was flown by civilian authorities, that private organizations and persons in the Zone were free to display flags at will over their places of residence or business, and that other aspects of the flag question would be discussed later. The text is printed in Department of State *Bulletin*, February 4, 1963, pp. 171–172.

Mr. Martin thought that President Chiari had a political problem which could be better handled by playing up the solid achievements which can result from the current talks, and playing down the point of basic treaty revision, rather than by doing the reverse.

Mr. Martin said that he provides a detailed monthly report on the progress of the talks to President Kennedy.[2]

---

[2] Monthly reports on actions pertaining to NSAM 152 and NSAM 164, sent from the Department of State to the White House, include brief summaries of the status of the discussions. (Department of State, NSAM Files: Lot 72 D 316, NSAM 152)

---

409.   Memorandum of Conversation

San José, March 20, 1963, 3:05 p.m.

SUBJECT

Meeting Between the President and President Chiari of Panama at San José, Costa Rica[1]

PARTICIPANTS:

U.S.	Panama
The President	President Roberto F. Chiari

There follows the pertinent portions of a Memorandum for the Record dated March 26, 1963 and prepared by Ambassador Farland:

"MEMORANDUM FOR THE RECORD

FROM

Joseph S. Farland, American Ambassador, Panama

SUBJECT

Re Conversation Between President Kennedy and President Chiari at San José and Subsequent Developments Appertaining Thereto

---

Source: Department of State, Central Files, POL 7 COSTA RICA. Secret. Filed with an April 2 covering memorandum from Department of State Executive Secretary William H. Brubeck to McGeorge Bundy. Drafted by McManus, approved in S on April 2 and in the White House on April 4.

[1] President Kennedy met with the Presidents of Central America and Panama in San José, Costa Rica, March 18–20; see Documents 58 ff.

During the initial conferences at San José President Chiari indicated that he was desirous of having a private conversation with President Kennedy. This request was honored and President Kennedy and President Chiari met alone at the temporary White House (Embassy Residence San José) at 2:30 p.m. on Wednesday, March 20. The conversation lasted for approximately 30 minutes.

After the President concluded the conversation with President Chiari and farewells were exchanged, he asked me to return with him to the conference room where we were joined by Secretary Rusk, Assistant Secretary Martin and Mr. Ralph Dungan. There ensued a brief discussion during which the President asked numerous questions pertaining to political, economic and social conditions in Panama. The President also directed his attention to the present financial and economic benefits to Panama ensuing from the Canal, and indicated his preoccupation with the problem posed by the current payment by the United States to Panama of $1,930,000.00 as annuity. This discussion was concluded after the President directed me to return to Washington during the latter part of the month of April for consultation on the question of U.S.-Panamanian relations. In this connection the President asked that I meet with as many Congressmen as possible for the purpose of sounding congressional opinion regarding the problems posed by the Government of Panama. The President also requested that thereafter I meet with him to discuss U.S. policy as related thereto.

During the public exchange of 'farewells' at the airport Secretary Rusk indicated to me that the President had requested him to give particular attention to Panama. In this connection the Secretary expressed his concern lest President Chiari in his public statements upon returning to Panama jeopardize the effort of the Executive Branch to view sympathetically Panama's aspirations. I later spoke with Foreign Minister Solís, Ambassador Arango and other Panamanians to emphasize the importance of Chiari handling with restraint and discretion his public account of his conversation with President Kennedy. In a brief conversation with President Chiari, I said that I was encouraged by the direction Panama's problems had taken and received his assent to my proposal that I call upon him immediately upon his return to Panama.

On Friday, March 22 at 2:30 p.m. accompanied by Mr. V. Lansing Collins, Director Office of Central American and Panamanian Affairs, I met with President Chiari and Foreign Minister Solís at the Presidencia for the purpose of discussing the program for Panama as set forth in

CAM/B–6a of March 13, 1963.[2] This conversation ensued for an hour and a half and ended on a constructive note with President Chiari indicating that his report to the Panamanian people on the developments ensuing from the San José Conference would be moderate and judicious and would not be used as a vehicle for local political advantage. This conversation will be the subject of a separate memorandum."[3]

---

[2] Reference is to a talking paper prepared in the Department of State for Kennedy's meeting with Chiari. It stated that the United States was prepared to consider financial assistance for further acceleration of Panama's industrial development and to propose a major new program in rural development to support Panamanian efforts at agrarian reform. (Department of State, Conference Files: Lot 66 D 110, CF 2228)

[3] Not found.

---

410. Memorandum of Conversation

Washington, May 7, 1963, 10:30 a.m.

SUBJECT

Panama

PARTICIPANTS

The President
Mr. Ralph Dungan, Special Assistant to the President
The Honorable Joseph S. Farland, United States Ambassador to Panama
Mr. V. Lansing Collins, Director, Office of Central American and Panamanian
    Affairs

Ambassador Farland opened the conversation by informing the President that Foreign Minister Solis had visited Washington April 23[1] and that the most important result of his visit was his declaration that President Chiari wanted to stop the United States-Panamanian Commission on July 31 because of the Panamanian political campaign and because Chiari believed it had not accomplished as much as he had hoped. Foreign Minister Solis also said that no Panamanian Government

---

Source: Kennedy Library, National Security Files, Countries Series, Panama, General. Confidential. Drafted by Collins.

[1] A memorandum of an April 23 luncheon conversation between Rusk and Solís is in Department of State, Central Files, POL PAN-US.

could obtain public support for the building of a sea level canal in the Darien region because of the effect on real estate and other values in Panama and Colón. Ambassador Farland went on to say that through diplomatic negotiations during the past week the Panamanian position on both of these two points has been considerably softened. The President asked whether the Panamanian desire to end the work of the Commission was due to dissatisfaction and he was told that this was partly correct. The President indicated that the key question seemed to be the studies on whether the present canal would handle the traffic in the future. He indicated he wanted to know who was going to do the study and was told that the Panama Canal Company would undertake to have the study made but we do not know what specific action is planned by the Company. The President asked whether we had any information on the limitations on leasing piers in Cristobal to Panama based on a proposed bill by Mrs. Leonor Sullivan, Chairman of the House Subcommittee on the Panama Canal of the House Committee on Merchant Marine and Fisheries. Ambassador Farland explained that this had been the sense of the Subcommittee when he testified at the hearings, but that we did not have the details of the most recent amendment which was apparently made yesterday. [It has since developed that no new amendment was entered.][2] Discussing the question of leasing piers Ambassador Farland pointed out that in the 1936 treaty we agreed to go out of the bonded warehouse business as soon as Panama had facilities of its own and that in the 1955 treaty we agreed to turn Panamanian traffic through the piers over to them when they had their own piers in Colon. These treaty obligations mean that if Panama builds a pier of its own we will, under item 10 of the Memorandum of the 1955 treaty, have to give "prompt consideration to withdrawing from" handling cargo for transhipment. We will be left in the Canal Zone with lots of unused pier facilities. Therefore, the leasing of the piers to Panama is a feasibly sound idea. The President indicated that we should find out what Mrs. Sullivan was objecting to and if we could not get her agreement to go ahead. Ambassador Farland noted that the Directors of the Panama Canal Company at their most recent meeting had decided they could not go along with the leasing of the piers to Panama unless they received a Presidential directive to do so.

The President indicated that in his opinion the annuity of $1.93 million we paid Panama every year for the Canal was not enough. Ambassador Farland expressed his agreement with this and stated that the amount of annuity (a treaty provision) had been a major source of conflict over the years; it had been discussed in all previous treaty renegotiations. He went on to state that in lieu of a treaty modification we have perhaps three alternative methods which could be used in adjusting our

---

[2] Brackets in the source text.

relationship with Panama: a) a very active AID program; b) funds obtained by a special Congressional appropriation; or c) funds from the contingency fund. The discussion then centered on the possible renegotiation of the treaty when a decision by the United States had been reached on the question whether or not to build a sea-level canal. The Ambassador reported that the Review Group had met on April 23 and that the consensus is that we should be ready to begin discussions leading to a renegotiation of the treaty to cover present operations in the Canal Zone by late 1964 or early 1965. At this juncture the President indicated his interest in ascertaining what form the Ambassador thought such a treaty might take. The Ambassador stated that the basic aspirations of Panama over the years had been to acquire for Panama a treaty comparable in its provisions to that which the United States had offered Colombia, i.e. the Hay–Herran Treaty.[3] The Ambassador stated that there was good reason to believe that the Panamanian position continues to reflect that view even today. The Ambassador then briefly discussed the points of difference between the Hay–Herran Treaty and the Hay–Bunau Varilla, i.e. 1) a 100-year term; 2) Colombia would retain sovereign rights; 3) zone only six (not ten) miles wide; 4) court system in zone would provide for U.S., Colombian, and mixed courts.

The President then indicated that there was some feeling that Congress might balk at raising the annuity in a special appropriation and asked the Ambassador what had been his observations following his discussion with members of Congress. Ambassador Farland replied that these explorations had convinced him that provided the executive branch kept Congressional leaders completely informed of policy objectives there was good reason to believe there would not be as much opposition as had been previously suspected.

The President then noted that if we are going to have to renegotiate in a couple of years there is not much point in raising the annuity now or trying to get anything like that through Congress now and he asked Ambassador Farland what the Ambassador recommended. The Ambassador said that we should move ahead rapidly on the things under discussion by the Commission that do not cost any money and consider using the mentioned alternative sources of funds for development of, for example, a feeder road program and/or building of a port at Aguadulce and Panama City. Returning to the things that do not cost any money the Ambassador noted that the question of a corridor should be settled soon; that the lease of piers could move ahead once Mrs. Sullivan's objections

---

[3] Reference is to a convention between the United States and Colombia, signed at Washington on January 22, 1903, but never ratified by Colombia. The text is printed in Christian L. Wiktor, ed., *Unperfected Treaties of the United States of America* (Dobbs Ferry, NY: Oceana Publications, Inc., 1977), vol. 3, p. 449.

were met; that we had gone as far as we could in offering to use Panamanian stamps in the Canal Zone and the problem was up to the Panamanians to solve now; that we could look into the question of excess lands in the Canal Zone and we could do something about commercial activities in the Canal Zone. The President noted[4] all of these. The discussion moved on to commercial activities in the Canal Zone. The President noted that the Governor should look into the possibility of having the prices of cigarettes and liquor which he understood were the items the Panamanians complained most about sold in the Canal Zone at prices comparable to those in the United States. There followed some further discussion of the possibility of financing a port at Aguadulce, using either contingency funds or funds especially appropriated by Congress or AID funds. The President felt that this could be done in a way to connect it vaguely to the Canal and make it very clear that this was in effect compensation for the Canal. He directed that this question be looked into. He said that we do not want an explosion in Panama, we must keep the lid on the next couple of years the best way we can. He requested that the possibility of some kind of a Panamanian retail outlet in the Canal Zone such as a store or a cooperative be looked into.

---

[4] The sentence originally read, "The President agreed to all of these." On the source text, the words "agreed to" are crossed out and the word "noted" is handwritten, apparently by Dungan, who initialed his approval on the memorandum of conversation.

---

411.   Telegram From the Department of State to the Embassy in Panama

Washington, July 23, 1963, 9:15 p.m.

49. You are instructed, provided results your efforts required by Embtel 42[1] satisfactory, to deliver following letter at Foreign Office from President Kennedy to President Chiari:[2]

Source: Department of State, Presidential Correspondence: Lot 66 D 476. Secret; Priority; Limit Distribution. Drafted and approved by Collins; cleared by Martin, Springsteen, Kent, and Dungan at the White House.

[1] Not found.

[2] Farland was to deliver this letter if he determined through discussions with Chiari that a plan to provide approximately $3 million in special assistance funds to Panama would be acceptable. Telegram 63 from Panama, July 25, reported that Chiari's reaction was positive, but a handwritten note on telegram 63 states that Farland had been told by telephone not to deliver the letter. (Department of State, Central Files, AID (US) 9 PAN) Telegram 58 to Panama, July 31, transmitted revisions in the letter. (Ibid.) Farland reported in telegram 91, August 14, that he had delivered the letter after further discussion with Chiari and consultation with the Department by telephone. (Ibid.)

"Dear Mr. President:

I am pleased to have the opportunity to exchange views with you again on some of the matters which have been the subject of our previous correspondence and our meeting in San José which I recall with such pleasure. Ambassador Farland's special consultations in Washington following the San José meetings were helpful and I am pleased at the progress which has been made in the resolution of some of the outstanding questions which have been before us.

I know that you continue to share a concern about the threat of Cuban Communist subversion of the Isthmian countries and others throughout the Hemisphere and I noted with gratification the work which was carried on by the representatives of the various governments who met in Managua in April.[3] While certain progress has been made as a result of the follow-up meetings held during April and May in the six countries of the Isthmus, I believe that there are many steps which remain to be taken and I certainly hope that you will be continuing your leadership in this important area.

I recognize the special needs of Panama for assistance in the development of those parts of its economy which have not benefited directly from the operation of the Canal. While Panama's foreign exchange receipts for goods and services sold to the Zone have been sizable, reaching an estimated $84 million in 1962, we are aware that most benefits from the Canal have accrued to that part of the Panamanian economy located close to the Canal.

Your Government has made substantial effort in drawing up a long-range Development Program, and we look forward to discussing it with your representatives after it has been evaluated by the panel established by the Organization of American States. In the interim, as we have already indicated to your Director of Plans, Mr. David Samudio, during his visit to Washington in early May, we are prepared to consider substantial amounts of loan assistance on liberal terms for a number of sound projects. During Mr. Samudio's visit, as you know, the various projects listed in the enclosure to your letter were discussed in some detail, in an effort on our part to provide guidelines on the type of projects that would be eligible for United States financing.

I can understand your desire to draw a conceptual distinction between our cooperative efforts to advance Panama's well being under the Alliance for Progress, and any special measures we undertake to adjust our relations in matters concerning the Canal Zone. I would expect, however, that assistance for the purposes described above could

---

[3] Reference is to a meeting held in Managua April 3–4 to draw up agreed measures against subversion; see Document 165.

be of great and specific benefit to the peoples of Panama, and contribute to the enhancement of friendship between our two countries. Compensation more directly related to our special relationship in connection with the Canal has also been a continuing matter of concern to me. Though the details will have to be worked out, I believe that we may be able, for this year, to provide some special assistance. I have asked Ambassador Farland to discuss with you in detail what we can do.

We were glad to receive your Minister of Foreign Affairs, Dr. Galileo Solis, when he came on your personal instructions to Washington in late April. He left a memorandum with Secretary of State Rusk to which was attached a list of 8 major and 5 subsidiary points which are being or might be discussed by our Special Representatives.[4] I issued instructions that the work on these points, on the United States side, be accelerated with a view to having possible solutions ready by the end of July. The United States Representatives have been discussing these matters with yours and I am confident that constructive progress can be made on most of the major points and several of the subsidiary points. Foreign Minister Solis indicated to Secretary Rusk that it was then your wish to recess the work of the Special Representatives in July. I have since received, in this respect, your letter of July 9[5] requesting an earlier dissolution and as you know I have agreed to do so by means of a joint communiqué.[6] Following such action I would expect that our diplomatic representatives would maintain the forward momentum in finding solutions to the remaining problems which confront us.

With cordial good wishes,

Sincerely,

John F. Kennedy"[7]

---

[4] Translations of the memorandum and the list, both dated April 24, are in Department of State, Central Files, POL PAN–US.

[5] Transmitted in telegram 17 from Panama City, July 9. (Ibid.)

[6] For text of a joint communiqué issued by the U.S. and Panamanian Governments on July 23 announcing the conclusion of the discussions and some of their results, see Department of State *Bulletin*, August 12, 1963, pp. 246–247.

[7] Printed from an unsigned copy.

PERU

412. Memorandum of Conversation

Washington, April 4, 1961.

SUBJECT

    Cuban Situation; Atomic Irrigation Scheme; Economic Survey; Double Taxation

PARTICIPANTS

    The Secretary
    Pedro Beltran, Prime Minister and Minister of Finance of Peru
    Fernando Berckemeyer, Ambassador of Peru
    Theodore C. Achilles, Task Force on Latin America
    Wymberley DeR. Coerr, Deputy Assistant Secretary for Inter-American Affairs
    Richard A. Poole, Officer in Charge of Peruvian Affairs, WST

Cuba and Related Matters

The Secretary welcomed Prime Minister Beltran. He opened the conversation by discussing the grave situation in Laos and then turned to the Cuban problem, which he stated was, of course, a matter of great preoccupation to the United States Government.

Prime Minister Beltran agreed that the situation in Cuba and the ramifications of the Cuban problem throughout Latin America were indeed very serious. It was his feeling that there was no time to be lost, as Castro's hold on Cuba was ever strengthening, with increasing arms from the Soviet bloc, and as Castroist activities throughout Latin America could have grave consequences for the Hemisphere. He felt that the United States would be losing precious time by attempting to get the support of additional Latin American countries for concerted action, as he saw little hope of those countries joining in. He was convinced that action should be taken by the U.S. as soon as possible and that this action should be quick and decisive. He realized that there would be considerable outcry in Latin America against U.S. intervention. However, many of the Latin America leaders who would cry out against us publicly would congratulate us privately. It is an unfortunate fact, he added, that these leaders are so afraid of Castroist, Communist leftist influence on their masses that they feel they have to take such an equivocal position. If our action were quick and decisive, Beltran continued, he felt sure the adverse reaction would not last and that the event would soon be forgotten as a live issue, as in the case of Guatemala and the assassination of Lumumba.[1]

Source: Department of State, Central Files, 737.00/4–461. Secret. Drafted by Poole and approved in S on May 25.

[1] See vol. XX, pp. 16–18, for details on the death of Prime Minister Lumumba.

When the Secretary referred to Peru's break with Cuba[2] and asked what Beltran felt the chances were of other Latin American countries taking similar action, Beltran said Peru had been very disappointed when, prior to the break, it had attempted unsuccessfully to persuade other countries such as Colombia and Argentina to do so concurrently. Here again was an indication of fear of local reactions.

The Secretary then asked what Beltran felt the reactions in Latin America would be if the OAS were to dissolve. Beltran felt that, despite Latin American reluctance to take concerted action, those countries would view with great concern any signs of dissolution of the OAS and would therefore make every effort to prevent this from happening.

Proposed Atomic Explosion to Divert River for Irrigation

Prime Minister Beltran then turned to a subject he had discussed briefly with the Secretary at the University of California in Berkeley.[3] This concerned a scheme which had just been broached to him (Beltran) by Professor Teller to explore the possibility of diverting the waters of the Huancabamba River to flow westward in order to irrigate the barren Pacific coastal desert of northwestern Peru. In response to the Secretary's questions, Beltran explained that the Huancabamba is a tributary of the Marañon, which in turn is one of the two principal tributaries forming the Amazon. Professor Teller's scheme would involve an atomic explosion to blow off the top of the Andean ridge separating the upper reaches of the Huancabamba from the western watershed of the Andes. Professor Teller had guessed this would be about a thousand feet vertically to be removed, although Beltran guessed it would be more like 3,000 feet. Beltran thought that the width at the base of the portion to be removed would be about 3 miles, but he said this too was a pure guess. Professor Teller had told him that this sort of explosion could be precisely regulated not only in terms of the amount of earth and rock to be removed, but also in the direction in which this material could be blown, thus making it possible to deposit it in such a way as to dam the Huancabamba into a lake from which the waters would then drop westward to the Pacific. Beltran said Professor Teller had proposed that two nuclear technicians go to Peru to study the possibility of this project, but that they go under some other guise in order to preserve appropriate secrecy.

---

[2] The Government of Peru severed diplomatic ties with Cuba on December 30, 1960.

[3] Secretary Rusk and Prime Minister Beltran met on March 20. According to a March 21 memorandum made by the Secretary to the files, "Prime Minister Beltran and I met briefly at Berkeley at a reception where private conversation was difficult. He did say he had something 'classified' to discuss with me in Washington; this turned out to be a proposal on peaceful uses of atomic energy he had raised with Dr. [Edward] Teller." (Department of State, Secretary's Memoranda of Conversation: Lot 65 D 330)

The Secretary said he would be glad to have his staff look into the matter.

Economic Survey of Southern Peru

Ambassador Berckemeyer took the occasion to express sincere appreciation for the very thorough economic study of southern Peru accomplished under the supervision of the ICA. (NB: The Ambassador was referring to the thirty-odd volume "Regional Plan for the Development of the South of Peru", dated 1959 and published in 1960, prepared by the joint USOM-Peruvian Servicio Cooperativo Interamericano del Plan del Sur, SCIPA.)

Double Taxation Agreement

Ambassador Berckemeyer also took the opportunity to express his Government's concern over the fact that the double taxation agreement negotiated between Peru and the United States was still in suspense in the Treasury Department.

In response to the Secretary's question as to the status of the matter, Mr. Poole explained that an agreement had been negotiated and initialed in November 1960 in Lima by Peruvian and U.S. negotiating teams, for reference to their respective Governments for signature and ratification, and that, while the Peruvian Government was prepared to go ahead with completion of the agreement, further action on our part was in suspense in the Treasury Department pending a policy study of double taxation agreements in general.

---

413.   Memorandum From the Assistant Secretary of State for Inter-American Affairs (Woodward) to Secretary of State Rusk

Washington, September 20, 1961, 10:05–11:40 a.m.

SUBJECT

Talks between Presidents Prado and Kennedy[1]

We had been prepared to conduct the White House conversations with President Prado along the lines he had requested, i.e., in two parts

---

Source: Department of State, Conference Files: Lot 65 D 366, CF 1963. Confidential. The time of the meeting is from the President's Appointment Book. (Kennedy Library)

[1] President Prado was invited to pay a state visit to the United States in March 1961. Prado visited the United States September 19–22.

with separate agenda items, the first part to be between the two Presidents alone and the second with their respective staffs. Even though the discussions were to be in English, it had been planned that an interpreter would be present ostensibly to help out in case of difficulty but actually for the purpose of taking notes. The interpreter was dismissed, however, when President Prado said he needed none, and as it worked out the entire discussion was between the two Presidents alone. At the termination of the discussion, President Kennedy invited the staffs into his office and briefly reviewed for them the matters discussed, along the following lines:

(1) *Cuba*. President Prado had made three suggestions which President Kennedy thought constructive and worth exploring: (a) He suggested that the COAS recommend that an OAS or Red Cross commission investigate the situation of political prisoners in Cuba. This would probably be refused by the Cubans, but such refusal would doubtless hurt them in Latin America. The initiative for suggesting this COAS action should probably come from a country in the middle of the spectrum (i.e. of attitudes toward Cuba). (b) The Colombian initiative[2] should not be taken up formally until we have all or most countries aligned, including Mexico, Brazil and Argentina. Otherwise the initiative will fail and we will be worse off than before. (c) Meanwhile, we should concentrate on getting additional countries to break relations with Cuba when they have valid reasons for doing so.

President Prado had also suggested the possibility of broadening the Miró Cardona council[3] so that we might recognize it as a government in exile. President Kennedy said we had reservations both because of the difficulty of free Cuban groups and because there are doubts concerning support in Cuba for Miró Cardona and the possible reactions there to recognition; it might even serve to increase support for Castro.

(2) *Double Taxation*. President Kennedy explained that we had the matter under study and that we hoped to have something ready for Congress in January.

(3) *Loans*. The Presidents discussed the various loans the Peruvians are interested in, including the emergency loan for the Puno area, housing, airports, etc. President Kennedy thought it would be a good idea for Minister of Development and Public Works Grieve to get in touch with the various lending agencies on these matters.

(4) *Peru–Ecuador Boundary*. This matter was discussed, but President Kennedy gave no indication of the substance of the discussion.

---

[2] See Document 111.
[3] Reference is to the Cuban exile group led by José Miró Cardona.

(5) *China*. The question of recognition of China was discussed and there appeared to be general agreement. President Prado had submitted a note on the subject from which President Kennedy read a passage[4] stating that Prado had received the impression from his visit last spring to Formosa that Chiang Kai-shek was prepared to invade the mainland alone if he could be assured of arms and moral support. President Kennedy thought this had a familiar ring reminiscent of last April, when we had learned a hard lesson.

President Prado's original agenda was much longer than the above, but as yet we have no further information whether other items were discussed. However, the following additional substantive matters pertaining to the visit may be of interest:

(1) *Loans*. There have been various conversations during the past week between Peruvian officials (including officials sent up independently of Prado's party) and the Department, Eximbank, DLF and ICA pertaining to the above-mentioned prospective loans—to which we should add the Lima water and sewage project. Applications for this loan (to the Eximbank and DLF) and for the aided self-help housing loan (DLF) appear to be in the best position to move ahead fast. The Eximbank cannot handle the airport loan, so the DLF is now studying it; however, we are now thinking in terms of encouraging the German offer but on better terms. The DLF and ICA are continuing discussions on the Puno emergency projects, and there may be a number of small projects that will qualify, although the Peruvians' project preparation is not too adequate.

(2) *Joint Communiqué*. We have had considerable discussion back and forth with the Peruvians concerning the joint communiqué wording on the subject of observance of international obligations and agreements. The Peruvians tried hard for wording we considered pointed too obviously at the Rio Protocol between Peru and Ecuador. We have reached agreement, however, on more general language which we trust will not be offensive to the Ecuadoreans. Other than this there has been no problem in agreeing to the language and substance of the communiqué.[5]

(3) So far President Prado and his party seem happy with the visit.

---

[4] Not found.

[5] For text of the communiqué, see *Public Papers of the Presidents of the United States: John F. Kennedy, 1961*, pp. 611–613.

414.   Memorandum From the Assistant Secretary of State for Inter-American Affairs (Woodward) to Secretary of State Rusk

Washington, September 21, 1961.

SUBJECT

Farewell Meeting between Presidents Prado and Kennedy, September 21

Upon your return from New York,[1] I thought you might wish a brief note on the subject meeting. As in the case of the first meeting (covered in my memorandum of September 20 to you),[2] the two Presidents met alone, after which they met briefly with the accompanying officers on both sides. At this brief meeting President Kennedy mentioned only the following:

(1) *Joint Communiqué.* President Kennedy stated that he had agreed to change the wording in the second paragraph of the joint communiqué in order to indicate U.S. willingness to cooperate in emergency projects in Peru. Our commitment reads as follows:

"With this in mind the Presidents considered various projects of importance to Peru's economic and social development. The United States will participate in emergency projects being initiated by the Peruvian Government in the critical Puno area."

(A copy of the final joint communiqué is attached.)[3]

(2) *Loan Discussions.* President Kennedy said he understood there would be further discussions here concerning the prospective emergency loan. Minister of Development and Public Works Jorge Grieve stated that, with assurance of U.S. participation, the Peruvian Government would start immediately on the emergency program, using funds it has earmarked for this purpose.

Note: Relative to the emergency loan in the Puno area, active consideration is now being given in the DLF, ICA and Department as to method of approach, source of funds, types of projects to be financed and the amount of U.S. financing.

Source: Department of State, Conference Files: Lot 65 D 366, CF 1963. Official Use Only. Drafted by Poole and Belcher on October 4.

[1] The Secretary attended the opening of the U.N. General Assembly in New York September 18–31.

[2] Document 413.

[3] Not printed; see *Public Papers of the Presidents, of the United States: John F. Kennedy, 1961,* pp. 611–613.

415.   Telegram From the Department of State to the Embassy in Peru

Washington, March 24, 1962, 6:01 p.m.

723. Following is summary of conversation with President concerning political situation in Peru:

Ambassador Loeb outlined the political situation in Peru. He said that an APRA victory was possible[1] and that the Peruvian military had indicated that they would not accept such a victory and might attempt to prevent an ARPA assumption of power through military force.

It was agreed that it was not in the United States interest to have a military takeover in Peru if APRA won and that we should try and prevent military intervention in case of an APRA victory.

The President agreed the Ambassador should inform key members of the Peruvian military that we appreciated the traditional friendship of the armed forces with the United States and respected their vigorous and effective anti-communism. However, they had to realize that the United States was committed in the hemisphere, and in the eyes of its own people and Congress, to the support of non-communist constitutional governments throughout the hemisphere. Therefore, if APRA won and the Peruvian military threw them out it would be extremely difficult for us to recognize a government installed by the military or to continue our aid program with such a government.

The President said that the extent to which the US position was pressed would depend upon the discretion of the Ambassador as to the point at which implied threats would become counterproductive of the goal of halting a military takeover in the event of an APRA victory. In line with this the Ambassador was authorized to go as far as stating that it would be "impossible" to recognize a government installed by the military or to continue our aid program with such a government. Furthermore, the Ambassador was also authorized to refer to the fact that he had discussed these matters with the President and other high government officials. If the Ambassador felt it necessary to quote the President directly or to have a Presidential instruction which he could read to Peruvian officials he was to request this from the Department.

Ball

Source: Department of State, Central Files, 723.00/3–2462. Secret; Priority; Limit Distribution. Drafted by Goodwin; cleared by Belcher, Poole, Bromley Smith, and S/S; and approved by E.M. Martin.

[1] Presidential elections were scheduled in Peru for June 10.

416. Telegram From the Department of State to the Embassy in Peru

Washington, May 29, 1962, 9:14 p.m.

860. For Ambassador. Department has held further consultations [*less than 1 line of source text not declassified*] USIA concerning additional steps to be taken in effort prevent military intervention in Peruvian elections using as discussion points informal memorandum prepared during your visit here and your comments by official–informal letter.

1. Agreement reached to proceed immediately with following steps, which we consider to be in consonance your views:

a. APRA should be encouraged again to urge Prado request OAS observer team (request should be made to SYG rather than Chairman COAS). Have you made or do you plan make further approach to APRA, or would you consider it preferable handle through [*less than 1 line of source text not declassified*] (which latter prepared undertake) in order avoid possible leak of your involvement?

b. Department and USIA will encourage US press, radio and TV coverage, including dispatch of correspondents, and off the record will alert key journalists to issues involved in intervention.

c. CAS alerting stations in various LA countries to encourage widespread LA press coverage, including dispatch of correspondents, and will arrange FBIS coverage and playback.

d. USIA will assist in playback but avoid using attributable media.

e. Department will request advance approval of message of congratulations from President to winning candidate to be dispatched immediately if situation warrants.

2. Agreed not to inspire press query to President on US attitude toward possible military intervention.

3. Following suggestions being considered and we would appreciate your views urgently by priority cable:

a. Dispatch of general officer to Peru under suitable pretense (such as inspection trip to include other countries) to serve as additional point of contact and communication with Peruvian military during election

Source: Department of State, Central Files, 723.00/5–2962. Secret; Priority; Limit Distribution. Drafted by Belcher and Poole; cleared by Curtis of INR/DDC, Wellman of ARA/EST, and by S/S; and approved by Goodwin.

period.[1] (View Doig's attitude as revealed Deptel 850,[2] we doubt utility your suggestion in Embdes 622[3] that Gens White and Doig visit Peru ostensibly on SCCS business.)

b. An approach to third countries (i.e. Colombia and Brazil in addition to Venezuela which you report has already taken some action this regard) to suggest they inform Peruvian military that they could not recognize a military takeover while at same time suggesting all three be prepared align selves with US, should coup take place, on policy of at least temporary nonrecognition. (We will discuss with you separately possible courses of action in event elections postponed or nullified because of alleged fraud, actual military coup, etc.)

c. Dispatch of economic mission following elections and prior to inauguration to discuss assistance programs etc. with winning candidate.

3. Are there any other steps you believe you or Washington agencies should take aside from above and steps you have already taken under existing authority? We must bear in mind of course widespread belief in Peruvian military and political circles that you, Embassy and Department favor APRA and resultant fact that, despite our protestations to contrary, overt efforts to prevent coup will be interpreted by many as effort assist APRA and hence be discredited. We must also bear in mind strong possibility of Belaúnde victory and desirability erasing his impression we favor APRA and oppose him as pro-Communist.

Rusk

---

[1] Retired U.S. Army Colonel Clyde R. McBride was sent to Peru for this purpose. A memorandum of conversation between Colonel McBride and Peruvian General Alfredo Rodriguez of May 22 is ibid., 723.00/5–2262.

[2] Dated May 24. (Ibid., 723.00/5–2462)

[3] Dated April 23. (Ibid., 723.00/4–2362)

417. Telegram From the Department of State to the Embassy in Peru

Washington, June 7, 1962, 8:16 p.m.

883. Embtel 951.[1] Request cable summary action suggestions in despatch reftel.

Department now considering proposals for US response to most likely contingencies as follows:

1. Military nullification or postponement elections leaving Prado government in office for remainder term: Continue present recognition GOP; seek convince military of need schedule new election; foster compromise between APRA and military.

2. APRA victory followed by military imposition of new government: Publicly announce we withholding recognition of imposed government; publicly announce suspension aid programs; recall Ambassador for consultation; withdraw at least top aid officials; seek take these steps in concert with LA states; attempt persuade APRA to make deal with military offering military face-saving formula; attempt persuade Belaúnde maintain united front with APRA against military intervention.

3. APRA victory followed by disqualification APRA on charges fraud: Urge Prado to request OAS electoral commission investigation; consider all measures under (2) above recognizing that in confused situation we probably best advised work for Belaúnde–APRA coalition government to avoid civil strife.

4. APRA victory without immediate military intervention: Immediately offer APRA expert assistance in developing its economic program; encourage APRA and Belaúnde to cooperate for social reform; suggest Haya request military support and offer appropriate guarantees security, etc.

5. Belaúnde victory: Increase contact with Belaúnde and make clear we consider his objectives consistent with Alliance for Progress and glad work with him on development of Peru; offer Belaúnde expert assistance in developing his economic program; encourage alliance between APRA and Belaúnde based on trading APRA Congressional support for few key ministries.

We recognize proposals for action would have to be implemented or rejected in light appraisal their effect at time given contingency becomes

---

Source: Department of State, Central Files, 723.00/6–762. Secret; Priority; Limit Distribution. Drafted by Thompson of ARA/WST, cleared by Jamison of ARA/RPA and Robinson of AID/LA-WC, and approved by E.M. Martin.

[1] Dated June 6. (Ibid., 723.00/6–662)

reality. Interpretation of constitutionality of various procedures for solution which Peruvians might adopt likely be important factor our response to various developments under contingencies 1, 2 and 3. We shall be relying heavily on Embassy for these interpretations.

Re contingency 2 above we believe it unrealistic to expect we can bring sufficient pressure to bear to force military to abdicate once they have taken such blatant action. Accordingly object of actions proposed is attempt to influence military acceptance some compromise leading to return to constitutional government.

Request comments.[2]

Rusk

---

[2] The Embassy commented in telegrams 956 and 958 from Lima, June 7 and 8, respectively. (Ibid., 723.00/6–762 and 6–862)

---

418.   Editorial Note

On June 10, 1962, Peru held national elections for President, two Vice Presidents, and the entire Senate and Chamber of Deputies—all for 6-year terms. None of the three major candidates for the Presidency, Victor Raul Haya de la Torre (APRA), Fernando Belaunde Terry (Accion Popular), or Manuel Odria (Union Nacional Odrista), received the one-third of the valid popular vote needed to win the office. The Peruvian constitution stipulated that the new Congress, meeting in joint session, choose the new President when it convened formally on July 28. Charges of electoral graft were immediately exchanged by the candidates.

419. Telegram From the Department of State to the Embassy in Peru

Washington, July 12, 1962, 7 p.m.

22. Eyes only for Ambassador from Secretary. Unless you see strong objections in light of local factors of which I may be unaware, please indicate privately to President Prado that US has great understanding for present difficulties of Peru and his own gallant effort to insure continuity of constitutional government in his great country. If he has any suggestions about any way in which we might be of any assistance in this situation we would be glad to give it the most urgent and sympathetic consideration.[1]

Rusk

Source: Department of State, Central Files, 723.00/7–1262. Secret; Niact. Drafted and approved by Rusk and cleared by Goodwin.

[1] In Embassy telegram 74, July 16, Ambassador Loeb reported to Secretary Rusk that he relayed this message to President Prado ealier in the day. The President thanked the Secretary for his concern and stated that "at the present time he thinks of no specific action USG could take, either privately or publicly, to assist." (Ibid., 723.00/7–1662)

---

420. Editorial Note

The result of the Presidential vote remained disputed for weeks after election day. Haya de la Torre, believing the Peruvian military would not allow him to be elected President, gave his support to Odria's candidacy. Belaúnde demanded on July 12 that the government establish a tribunal to investigate electoral fraud or face violent insurrection (Airgram A–4 from Lima, July 13; Department of State, Central Files, 723.00/7–1362) On July 16 the military demanded that the government annul the results of the elections prompting President Prado's cabinet to resign. On July 18 the military arrested the President and established a 12-man junta under the direction of Army General Ricardo Perez Godoy. The junta declared the results of the elections null and void, announced that free and fair elections would be held in Peru as soon as possible, and asked the world community for official recognition. (Airgram A–49 from Lima, July 20; ibid., 723.00/7–2062)

President Kennedy was informed of the coup at his July 18 staff meeting. (Memorandum for the Record, July 18; National Defense University, Taylor Papers, Daily Staff Meetings, May–September 1962) The Department of State announced that day that the United States was suspending diplomatic relations with Peru and was ceasing all but humanitarian assistance to the country. (Department of State *Bulletin,* August 6, 1962, pages 213–214) Ambassador Loeb was recalled to Washington for consultation on July 26.

---

421.   Memorandum From the Under Secretary of State (Ball) to President Kennedy

Washington, July 27, 1962.

SUBJECT

Relations with Peru

Problem:

1.   What actions should we propose to representatives of the junta as necessary to permit us to resume relations and to recommend such resumption to other countries and what should be our timing in conducting such discussions?

2.   What should be our response to the Venezuelan proposal—supported by several of the Latin American countries—that there be an OAS Meeting of Foreign Ministers to condemn the military takeover in Peru?[1]

Background:

As of today several Latin American countries have broken diplomatic relations with Peru and all the others, except Haiti, have suspended relations, as the United States has. Most of the other western

---

Source: Department of State, Central Files, 611.23/7–2762. Confidential.

[1] On July 18 the Venezuelan Chargé in Washington presented an aide-mémoire to the Department of State expressing the intent of his government to call a special meeting of Foreign Ministers of the OAS to condemn the coup in Peru. Venezuela's Foreign Minister, Dr. Marcos Falcon Bricenos, arrived in Washington on July 24 to ask for U.S. support in this endeavor. He met with Assistant Secretary of State Martin the same day. (Memorandum of conversation, July 24; ibid., 723.00/7–2462) On July 27 he met with Secretary Rusk. (Memorandum of conversation, July 27; ibid., 723.00/7–2762)

world countries, including Canada, France, Germany and Japan, are also in a state of suspended relations. The Argentines have indicated they may resume relations next week. Haiti has recognized the junta.

The press commentary in all the important Latin American countries has been overwhelmingly critical of the junta action in Peru. Press reaction in the United States is beginning to be more mixed, with most United States business interests, particularly the mining interests, pressing for prompt reversal of the United States stand. The Congressional reaction has thus far been entirely favorable to the United States action.

While there is clearly widespread criticism and opposition to the junta action, within Peru, including some public criticism, efforts to create an organized opposition have failed. There has been no significant violence. The attempted general strike was a failure and the major political parties have abandoned attempts to create a common front from which to negotiate with the junta. Parties and leading personalities seem to be rapidly moving toward concentration on jockeying for position in the elections promised for next June.

It seems clear that the sharp reaction of the United States and other Latin American countries has led the junta to take a position with respect to new elections, with respect to current civil rights, with respect to leaders of the previous government and of APRA, and with respect to the private business community and the Alliance for Progress more liberal and more in accordance with United States views than would otherwise have been the case.

While there is also the probability that this prompt and strong reaction has been a warning sign to potential military plotters in other Latin American countries—such as Venezuela and the Dominican Republic—of the difficulties they may face if they act, the Governments of these countries remain deeply concerned about the impact on their situation of premature recognition of the junta and resumption of United States aid. They undoubtedly have some cause for concern.

With respect to the proposal for a Meeting of Foreign Ministers on the Peruvian situation, which is being pressed by Betancourt with varying degrees of support from the Dominican Republic, Costa Rica, Colombia, Panama and Honduras, it seems open to some question whether the necessary eleven votes could be secured to call such a meeting. Even if they could, there would undoubtedly be a major public debate over the desirability of a resolution condemning the junta action, reflecting in part special situations, but largely the nonintervention philosophy of such leading countries as Mexico, Brazil and Chile which was so much in evidence during the recent Punta del Este discussions on Cuba. It seems wholly unlikely that, in the absence of any real resistance to the junta in Peru, OAS action could affect the position of the junta, though it might be a mild warning to future plotters.

On the other hand, the junta and its friends would certainly interpret any difficulty in securing the eleven votes for calling such a meeting and, even more emphatically, a noisy public dispute about a condemnatory resolution, as indication of sympathy and support for their position, support which has heretofore been wholly lacking in the hemisphere. It would therefore be counterproductive.

Without OAS Council action, it would be within the terms of reference of the Inter-American Peace Committee (IAPC) to meet quietly to consider the Peruvian situation in the context of the general Latin American situation and to discuss effective measures which might be taken, including the question of a Meeting of Foreign Ministers. Such a group might be a useful forum to consider on an inter-American basis, rather than on a strictly United States basis, what measures it would be useful to get the junta to take in order to permit resumption of relations with it during the hiatus before new elections take place. It would also enable Venezuela and others concerned to say that their initiative had resulted in some OAS action. The present membership of the IAPC is good for this purpose, inasmuch as it consists of United States, Venezuela, Colombia, Uruguay, and El Salvador, with El Salvador to be replaced by the Dominican Republic on August 6.

Conclusions:

It would seem quite possible that the junta might be persuaded to move up the date of elections from June to February or March. They have stated that timing was dictated by the need to complete a reregistration of all voters to avoid possible fraud. There is no reason why this should not be accelerated.

It is of great importance to have the junta reaffirm, publicly and with emphasis, its intention to hold free elections so that any temptation to continue to enjoy the fruits of power may be discouraged.

It would also be desirable to secure privately a clear indication that the junta will not take actions which would assist the Communists in Peru to extend their influence, particularly over the APRA unions.

Since this is a temporary government and since it is not desirable to make their position too attractive and easy for them, it would seem desirable to resume most economic aid programs, but not to undertake new commitments or to participate in long term planning activities or new project development. It would seem quite incompatible with our condemnation of the action of the Peruvian military, an action which was taken without any serious dissent within the military to resume military assistance until civilian authority has been reestablished.

It would be highly desirable if the present military cabinet could be replaced by a civilian cabinet either representing all parties or of a technical character. It may be quite difficult to persuade the junta to accept this government and it should be sought without becoming a sine qua non of resumption of relations.

In order to conduct an effective negotiation, it is desirable that the junta continue to feel uncertain about its position in international circles, that resumption of relations be kept to a minimum, and that current stories in some segments of the United States press about a reversal of United States position be refuted insofar as possible, perhaps by some small action such as withdrawing the deputy chief of the AID mission and, perhaps, the heads of the military mission.

In opening discussions with the junta, we should not give evidence that we are under pressure for a hasty action. During the course of next week our Chargé should be authorized to initiate discussions with Peruvian civilians who are known to be friendly to the junta, indicating our willingness to consider suggestions of what the junta proposes to do in the direction of restoring civilian control, our policy being guided in these exploratory conversations by the principles outlined above.

In order to persuade the Venezuelans to accept the Inter-American Peace Committee proposal it would be desirable that the President see the Venezuelan Foreign Minister, Marcos Falcón Briceño, who is here with a letter from President Betancourt, and discuss the situation with him. We think all other Latin American countries would accept our view on this if the Venezuelans can be persuaded to do so.

Recommendations:[2]

1. That you authorize an instruction to the United States Embassy to Peru along the lines described above.

2. That you authorize the taking of minor measures of the sort mentioned above to indicate our continued desire to see further moves toward civilian constitutional government in Peru.

3. That you agree to see Marcos Falcón Briceño, the Venezuelan Foreign Minister, on Monday, July 30, and that, subject to the results of that conversation, you approve our arranging the calling of the Inter-American Peace Committee for the purposes described above.

George W. Ball

---

[2] Presumably the President approved all these recommendations although no indication of approval or disapproval appears on the source text.

422. Telegram From the Department of State to the Embassy in Peru

Washington, July 28, 1962, 5:23 p.m.

106. From Loeb. Following is translation of memorandum from Haya, handed me at Lima Airport:

"1. Political line followed by President Kennedy with respect military coup in Peru has produced extraordinarily favorable reaction among people. I think tremendous amount good will has been won among great masses, especially students.

2. Naturally, it is not same among businessmen or among Americans who wish live comfortably and without annoyances. But President must select what is most suitable for United States and democracy: Either have on his side majority of people or have the groups of people who engage in business and live apart from politics. I think we have won battle against Communism through President's firm policy.

3. Solution, it seems to me, may be found in sending OAS committee for purposes 'friendly mediation.' This way out would be very important and constructive. I believe Junta would have opportunity "save face" and we would have good occasion for rapprochement.

4. Composition of Junta could be changed through "friendly mediation" of OAS. At present Junta does not offer any guarantee that will follow democratic line. General Bossio[1] is the most reasonable and certainly the most impartial and "constructive" of its members. Bossio has influence with Torres Matos[2] and Verastegui,[3] but there are dangerous elements such as Llosa,[4] Lindley[5] himself (an extremist in social matters) and another. Perez Godoy is man of limited intellectual resources and prejudiced.

5. Junta should be reorganized and made subject to a statute, at least. If it is to remain in existence, should have some member of the Supreme Court added to it and perhaps direct or indirect representatives of chief democratic parties. I think this is least that can be demanded of Junta, as guarantee of restoration democracy and elections in not distant future (in shorter period than one year), and with assurances human and civil rights will be respected and army will not intervene in next election.

Source: Department of State, Central Files, 723.00/7–2862. Confidential; Niact. Drafted by Poole, cleared by Loeb, and approved by Belcher.

[1] Brigadier General Juan Bossio Colla, Minister of Government and Police.

[2] Admiral Juan Francisco Torres Matos, Minister of Marine.

[3] Brigadier General Maximo Verastegui Izurrietta, Minister of Development and Public Works.

[4] Admiral Luis Edgardo Llosa, Minister of Foreign Affairs.

[5] Nicolas Lindley Lopez, Minister of War.

6. Pretext for coup, that is, "fraud," has been greatly discredited even among army, navy, air force and police themselves. I believe members of Junta themselves do not believe in "the fraud" very much. This circumstance favors possibility of demanding of Junta that it be made more democratic.

7. General Bossio has reiterated his promises of respect for rights of individuals and compensation for damage done to *Casa del Pueblo* and the headquarters of *La Tribuna*. He (who is perhaps brains of Junta) appears well disposed and desirous of 'saving face.' At same time he is very fearful of trend of international public opinion. He is convinced that military coup is extremely *unpopular.*

8. I believe United States is using its prestige in Latin America as 'high card.' This, in my opinion, is fundamental. President Kennedy has gained much in behalf of cause of hemispheric solidarity and anti-Communism. And in my opinion, his policy should be maintained with integrity but without ceasing to consider solutions. But I am sure that President's conduct has met with warm approval on part of great majority of the Peruvian people. For Peru, for cause of Cuba and for sake of hemispheric solidarity, this favorable situation must not be lost. I am sure Peru will accept without protest whatever pressures may be necessary in defense of democracy. Maintaining principle of defense of democracy, I believe Peruvians will accept all that United States may do in clear, energetic way in order not to yield in face of danger of disruption of the American system and of Communist advance.

Lima, July 24, 1962"

Rusk

---

423. Telegram From the Department of State to the Embassy in Peru

Washington, July 30, 1962, 9:17 p.m.

113. Eyes only for Henderson. Deptel 108.[1] As result meeting this morning with President and SecState, following clarification provided for your guidance.[2]

Source: Department of State, Central Files, 723.00/7–3062. Secret; Niact. Drafted by Loeb and Martin; cleared by Belcher, Dungan, S, and S/S; and approved by E.M. Martin.

[1] Not printed. (Ibid., 723.00/7–2762)

[2] No memorandum of conversation for this meeting was found.

We are seriously concerned possible loss US prestige and influence hemisphere affairs as result any outward appearance of failure our efforts. We therefore wish expedite solution in such way as not to leave US isolated or to give appearance US capitulation.

With respect OAS, efforts now being made to put off decision on Venezuelan initiative for MFM at COAS meeting this afternoon for week or ten days without substantive debate, but US definitely opposed MFM. We seeking method handle issue of OAS role without letting down Betancourt too hard.

On recognition issue, appears several European states may resume relations almost immediately but, except for Haiti and possibly Paraguay, Department hopeful no other LA nations will recognize this week.

With view US resumption relations at appropriate time (we waited three weeks in Argentine case) we anxious you intensify negotiations with Junta through appropriate intermediaries looking toward specific restatement, in package to which we could point, of certain concessions of which first two not new but, in our view, not sufficiently understood by world opinion:

1. Guarantee of continued civil liberties.
2. Guarantee of free and fair elections, preferably before June 9 but at no later date, with full rights to all parties under Constitution, and with guarantee that Armed Forces will respect results those elections.
3. Offer by Junta, as indication of good faith, to invite OAS observers during electoral processes. This concession would particularly strengthen Junta's position with respect continental opinion and would also facilitate US recognition. Important that above elements be incorporated in some sort of restatement.

Some civilianizing of Cabinet, provided civilian members were known for dedication to constitutional processes, would make our recognition easier, but our view is not to insist on this as sine qua non of recognition.

Finally, we still consider it important receive private assurances from Junta that communists will not be permitted to use present situation to strengthen their position in Peruvian labor.

Junta should understand that while other countries and US might be willing resume normal relations, this would not imply resumption of aid automatically.

Please communicate soonest any results negotiations.

Rusk

424. Memorandum of Conversation

New York, August 1, 1962.

SUBJECT

>   Peruvian Situation

PARTICIPANTS

>   Former President Prado, Peru
>   Edwin M. Martin, Assistant Secretary for Inter-American Affairs

In order to avoid the press, President Prado chose to remain on his plane. Our conversation of 20 minutes or so was thus entirely private, except for 15 or 20 cleaning people sweeping and dusting around us.

President Prado seemed in excellent health and reasonably good spirits. He condemned the junta takeover and the charges of fraud as equally without justification. He praised the role that Ambassador Loeb had played and thought there was no good reason why he should not go back to Peru. He felt the United States position and the President's statement[1] had been enormously valuable in Peru and to future developments in the hemisphere.

I outlined briefly the conditions we were seeking from the junta as a basis for resumption of relations. He felt they were very sound, though he would have stressed somewhat more than we did the inclusion of civilians in the Cabinet. In response to my question he thought that all one could hope for at this time was technicians rather than politicians.

I outlined our argument against the Venezuelan MFM proposal, and he agreed that we were right.

I indicated our concern about a move by the Communists to take over the APRA Unions. He thought this was one of the most important dangers and deserved all the attention we could give it. He felt the junta was anti-Communist but naive.

I asked him how he felt about General Bossio who had shown himself rather favorably disposed toward APRA. He expressed the view that the General was not to be trusted at all.

He was most effusive in his appreciation for the President's greetings which I had conveyed to him. They obviously touched him very deeply in his present situation. I said it was a personal message which the President did not propose to release and thought best he not give to press, though he could of course say, if he wished, that President had sent him a message of good wishes.

Source: Department of State, Central Files, 723.00/8–1662. Confidential. Drafted by E.M. Martin. The meeting took place at Idlewild Airport, New York City.

[1] For text, see Department of State *Bulletin*, August 6, 1962. p. 214.

425.   Memorandum of Conversation

Washington, August 2, 1962, 10:33–11 a.m.

SUBJECT

Venezuelan Initiative for Meeting of Foreign Ministers on Peruvian Situation

PARTICIPANTS

The President
His Excellency Marcos Falcón Briceño, Foreign Minister of Venezuela
Dr. Carlos Perez de la Cova, Chargé d'Affaires ad interim of Venezuela
Mr. Martin—ARA
Anthony J. Hervas, State Department Interpreter

After the exchange of greetings the Foreign Minister handed to the President a letter from President Betancourt. After reading the letter the President said that he had discussed the matter of the Meeting of Foreign Ministers with Assistant Secretary Martin and that there was agreement that the influence of the nations of the hemisphere should be brought to bear upon the situation in Peru. However, such a meeting might not be successful and he was concerned about the discouragement that might result. He therefore considered that it would be better to wait until August 8[1] and see what measures the Junta adopted in Peru towards the re-establishment of Constitutional Government. In any case there would always be an option to convene the meeting.

The Foreign Minister replied that there were two main problems to consider. Peru had created a very difficult situation and he considered that the United States was doing a wonderful thing by exerting pressure on the Junta so that they would adopt a decent form of Government and call for free elections. However, the Peruvian situation was one that affected the stability of other countries. He had talked with the President-Elect of Colombia, Guillermo León Valencia, in New York recently and the latter had expressed his entire agreement with President Betancourt. He then quoted President León Valencia as having said that "if we do not do something about such a Meeting, how many more days can I remain President of Colombia?"

The Foreign Minister added that the situation in Venezuela was not one of great danger at this moment. A few days ago the Chief of the Navy had publicly stated that he considered that his first duty was to back the Constitutional Government of President Betancourt, and that he was

---

Source: Department of State, Presidential Memoranda of Conversation: Lot 66 D 149. Confidential. Drafted by Department of State interpreter Anthony J. Hervas and approved by the White House on August 15. The meeting took place at the White House. The time and place of the meeting are from the President's Appointment Book. (Kennedy Library)
[1] The Council of the OAS was scheduled to meet August 8; see Document 426.

therefore confident that Betancourt would remain in the Presidency through 1964. However, in his opinion the problem at hand was not one to be considered on a two, three or four year basis, because its consequences would affect the solidarity of the Americas. He added that some years ago military coups were a customary and habitual event in the national life of many countries. However, this was no longer true because now the communist parties are backing these movements, as was the case in Venezuela, in both Carúpano and Puerto Cabello, where known communists were found in uniform during the revolts.

The Foreign Minister further noted that when he was visiting Peru last April he was told that since the beginning of the year there were rumors that if APRA were to win the elections, the Government would be overthrown. The military were aware of the fact that if they did overthrow the Government, the United States would not cooperate, through the Alliance for Progress and other programs, with the new Government of Peru. In spite of this they carried out their coup. This coup was not aimed against APRA or Belaúnde or any political party. Nor was its purpose to correct a fradulent election, based on the charge that many persons had voted twice. The coup was carried out only to satisfy the Army's appetite for power. If the Organization of American States would do nothing about this situation it would greatly affect public opinion in this hemisphere.

The President noted that there was great concern about the situation because of two main reasons: the confusion that had surrounded the vote (the results did not imply a clear mandate, and it had taken a long time to count the votes); and there had been a very small public reaction to the military takeover. According to information received through the press and through the business community there seemed to be a certain acquiescence, which made it difficult for the United States to adopt an attitude of outrage. In view of these events, it became very difficult for the United States to discourage other countries from recognizing the military Junta, especially in the cases of countries such as Argentina, Chile, Paraguay and Bolivia.

In response to the President's question about Bolivia's position, Mr. Martin said that the Government of Bolivia was rather nervous about the whole situation but that it had not, as yet, recognized the Peruvian Junta.

The President then indicated that, considering the prevailing circumstances in Peru, it would not be a very appropriate moment to hold a Foreign Ministers' Conference, especially if other Latin American countries move to recognize the Peruvian Junta. Furthermore if the Meeting were unsuccessful, this would greatly strengthen the military. For these reasons the United States prefers to approach the problem through bilateral means, rather than through the OAS.

The Foreign Minister indicated that for years the principles of solidarity and democracy had been expounded in the Americas. That an organization had been created on the basis of member countries with a democratic form of government. If the Organization's Foreign Ministers could meet, the purpose would be different from the one that was pursued at the Punta del Este meeting. In this case the purpose would not be to seek a direct action, because it would not be possible. In the present circumstances the Foreign Ministers could meet to discuss the situation. No specific mention of Peru need be made in convening the meeting. This would allow other countries to attend, such as Colombia, who have indicated that Peru should not be dealt with pointedly. The holding of the meeting would have a moral and practical effect on the Government of Peru. He added that 11 Governments would vote for the meeting and that recommendations had been presented to prepare an instrument that would consider the adoption of necessary measures in the event of any future military coups in the Americas. Also a study or working group could be formed to consider the situation. He then noted that four countries had requested the meeting and that Venezuela also expected the support of Colombia as had been indicated to him by Foreign Minister Caicedo. Should the meeting take place, the Ministers need not openly condemn the situation in Peru, but could make a general statement of principle condemning military coups as opposed to the principles of the Charter of the OAS.

The Minister further noted, if the U.S. supported the meeting, even in the case of defeat, the United States would lose nothing and on the contrary would have gained a great deal in the eyes of Latin American public opinion.

The President at this point asked the Foreign Minister what were the specific points that he would propose for the agenda of the meeting. Would it be that the OAS would go on record as being against military coups because they constituted a denial of the constitutional practices? Was it a matter of stating a general policy?

The Foreign Minister replied that the United States was the only international power in the Hemisphere and that he understood the world wide implications of any move made by the United States. However, in the case of Latin America this was an action that was expected from the United States.

The President asked the Foreign Minister for his opinion about the situation in Brazil where there was not a direct threat from the military but rather from the radical left as the government is disintegrating. There seemed to be a race between the influence of the military and that of the communists and the mobs in the streets.

The Foreign Minister noted that there are coups from the right and coups from the left. In Venezuela the left had enlisted army support for a coup.

President Kennedy then noted that in Ecuador there seemed to be a conflict between the Army and the Air Force on the one hand and the man in the street on the other, and inquired about the Minister's opinion as to the situation there.

The Foreign Minister stated that there might be some danger in Ecuador. However, it should always be borne in mind that nothing pleases the communist forces more than a military coup from the right especially if it is carried out with the support of the United States.

The President replied that he understood this to mean that the result could be a superficial feeling of stability but that in the end it actually served the purposes of the communist forces. He added that the United States would have to study the final language of the Venezuelan proposal. He clearly understood that it would not be a question of non-recognition.

In response to the President's question regarding the position of the various Latin American countries on recognition of the Peruvian Junta, Mr. Martin replied that Argentina and Chile would probably recognize the Junta early next week. On the other hand Venezuela, the Dominican Republic and Costa Rica would never recognize the Junta.

The Foreign Minister then noted that in matters of politics it is very difficult to use the word never, but that the present position of his country was that recognition would not be extended as long as the Junta remained in power. He further believed that the United States could exert substantial pressure at a Meeting of Foreign Ministers, especially through the lever of the Alliance for Progress and military aid programs.

The President stated that the United States does not wish to appear isolated in its efforts and must be supported by other countries. The United States wants to avoid the labels of intervention and aggression. It would not like to hear the Junta charge that the United States was attempting to dominate the Hemisphere through intervention.

The Foreign Minister indicated that, as was mentioned to him by the Ambassador of Nicaragua, it is important to the success of the Venezuelan proposal that it be supported by the resonant voice of the United States. He added that President Betancourt was deeply concerned not only by his own internal situation but also about the future role of the OAS. He considered it important to go on record against the type of situation the Peruvian coup represents.

The President then requested the Foreign Minister to prepare a written statement of the specific measures that the Venezuelan Government proposes for the Meeting of Foreign Ministers so that the United States Government might study it.[2] He reiterated his understanding that it would not deal with non-recognition but with general principles.

---

[2] Projected draft statement not found.

426.   Editorial Note

At the August 6, 1962, White House staff meeting, Carl Kaysen, Deputy Special Assistant to the President for National Security Affairs related the President's opinion that the United States should grant official recognition to the Peruvian junta. Assistant Secretary of State Martin and Presidential Special Assistant Arthur Schlesinger favored waiting, at least until the August 8 OAS Council meeting. (Memorandum for the record, August 6; National Defense University, Taylor Papers, Daily Staff Meetings, May–September 1962)

At the COAS meeting, the representatives of the Peruvian junta reaffirmed their commitment to respect individual and civil liberties and to conduct free and fair elections as soon as possible. The United States was able to forestall the Venezuelan initiative to call a special OAS Meeting of Foreign Ministers on Peru. On August 17 the Department of State issued a press release announcing the resumption of U.S. diplomatic relations with Peru. (Department of State *Bulletin*, September 3, 1962, pages 348–349)

---

427.   Memorandum From the Assistant Secretary of State for Inter-American Affairs (Martin) to Acting Secretary of State Ball

Washington, October 3, 1962.

SUBJECT

Military Assistance to Peru

Our policy determination to limit the level of military assistance to Peru at this time is based on a number of factors:

1. Last March, in accordance with authorization given him by the President, Ambassador Loeb told top Peruvian military leaders that we would find it very difficult to recognize a government installed by military coup and next to impossible to continue assistance programs, and in doing so he referred to his conversation with the President. The position we took is now public knowledge.

Source: Department of State, Central Files, 723.5–MSP/10–362. Secret. Drafted by Poole and Thompson of ARA/WST.

2. When we announced suspension of diplomatic relations and assistance programs we declared publicly that the coup d'état represented a grave setback to the principles agreed to under the Alliance for Progress.

3. In taking this public position we hoped to demonstrate to the hemisphere our firm support of democratic, constitutional process and to provide a deterrent to potential military coups against democratic, constitutional regimes elsewhere in the hemisphere.

4. In Peru itself it was hoped that witholding full resumption of assistance might serve as an additional inducement toward a rapid return to constitutional government.

We have carefully explained to the Junta our position on limited resumption of military assistance to commence this month, our assurance that, in any case, full assistance would be resumed when the situation returns to "normal" next year, and our disposition to review the situation at some intermediate time, perhaps early next year. (We were prepared to commence limited assistance a month ago, but the White House requested this be deferred until the Congress acts on the 1963 program.) As you know, the Junta has been exercising heavy pressure to induce us to resume full assistance now, accusing us publicly of violating our agreements, threatening to dispense with our military missions, threatening to withdraw from Peru's hemispheric defense mission and generally choosing to confront this issue headlong as a matter of political prestige rather than agree to a gradual approach.[1]

In actuality the grant assistance we have contemplated resuming this month (certain maintenance, spares and training) is not inconsiderable: $6.1 million out of $9 million undelivered in FY '62 and previous programs (i.e. 67%) and $1.5 million out of the $13.8 million FY '63 program, if approved (i.e. 12%), totaling $7.6 million.

I believe the following factors militate against reverting to full military assistance at this time:

1. The deterrent factor in our position against military coups elsewhere in the hemisphere would be impaired, including our credibility should we wish to convey a similar warning.

2. Our posture in the hemisphere and in Peru itself in favor of constitutional process would be weakened by a speedy return to business as usual in military assistance. (The position we took at the time of the coup was generally applauded in the press of the hemisphere and our present position is not out of step in the hemisphere as a whole, where several countries—Colombia, Venezuela, Uruguay, Costa Rica,

---

[1] See, for example, the memorandum of conversation between Secretary Rusk and Foreign Minister Llosa at the U.S. Mission to the United Nations on September 28. (Ibid., Secretary's Memoranda of Conversation: Lot 65 D 330)

the Dominican Republic and Honduras—have not yet even recognized the Junta.)

3. We would permit the Junta to have the satisfaction of seeing us capitulate before threats and pressure from a position carefully arrived at and approved at the highest level. In all probability this would strengthen the extremists in the Junta who have been advocating a hard line and further weaken our already limited influence. (See Lima telegrams 416 and 418 at Tabs A and B.)[2] Disquieting questions have been raised as to the real intentions of the extremists.

4. Congress might well question our tactics in holding the line until adjournment and then suddenly returning to full assistance.

5. Full assistance would be illegal in the absence of a Presidential determination on internal security and the negotiation of an amendment to our mutual Defense Assistance Agreement with Peru. The proposed FY '63 program contains a large internal security component which can be delivered only after those actions. I believe it would be inadvisable to seek to negotiate an amendment of our agreement at this time.

Recommendation[3]

For these reasons I recommend that you speak to the President again in order to secure his agreement that, rather than resuming full military assistance immediately,[4] we modify our position in the following manner, the first three steps to be effective after congressional action (expected shortly) and pending step four:

1. That we permit military purchases on a normal basis rather than the present basis (maintenance and spares only, with certain other items on a "case by case" basis), as sales do not constitute assistance and therefore should not affect our public posture in this regard.

2. That we expand the categories of grant assistance to be provided (now restricted to certain maintenance, spares and training) to include additional training and certain types of non-sensitive end items, e.g. certain civic action items, support items, uniform material, etc. not involving internal security.

3. That we consider other grant assistance only on a case by case basis, using the criterion of urgent necessity.

---

[2] Not printed; dated September 30 and October 1, respectively. (Ibid., Central Files, 723.5811/9–3062 and 10–162)

[3] Ball approved all four recommendations.

[4] A handwritten notation here reads: "This refers to President's decision, made during conversation with Secretary, that full mil. assistance should be resumed immediately."

4.   That we plan full resumption in mid-November—four months after the military coup—and inform the Junta this month that we shall make our promised review at that time instead of early next year.[5]

---

[5] A limited resumption of military assistance to Peru began on October 8 according to a joint State–Defense message transmitted in telegram 281 to Lima, October 8. (Department of State, Central Files, 723.5–MSP/10–862) Telegram 313 to Lima, October 23, reads: "In view need solidarity in face Cuban-Soviet threat to hemisphere security, remaining special restrictions on MAP for Peru (Deptel 281) are removed effective immediately." (Ibid., 723.5/10–2362)

---

428.   Memorandum of Conversation

Washington, January 25, 1963, 12:15 p.m.

SUBJECT

Farewell Call of Ambassador Jones Before Departing for Peru[1]

PARTICIPANTS

The President
Ambassador J. Wesley Jones
Mr. Ralph Dungan, The White House
Mr. Taylor G. Belcher, Director, Office of West Coast Affairs

The President opened the conversation by referring to the many problems which the Ambassador would face in his new post—the forthcoming elections and change of power, the dangers inherent in Leftist agitation, the dispute over territorial waters and the question of submarines for the Peruvian Navy. The President asked whether the Peruvians were claiming the 200-mile limit on territorial waters only with respect to U.S. vessels and it was explained that they were not. Upon learning that the reaction in Lima to our recent approach on behalf of two fishing vessels[2] had evoked a rather negative response based on the alleged tone of our note, the President asked whether in fact the note had been offensive and he was assured that it had not been. The Ambassador spoke of his regret that there were these problems such as the fisheries and the question of submarines to plague him at a time when he felt it was so important to establish a quick sense of mutual confidence and rapport.

Source: Department of State, Central Files, 123 Jones, J. Wesley. Limited Official Use. Drafted by Belcher and approved in the White House on February 18. The meeting took place at the White House.

[1] Jones was appointed Ambassador on November 29, 1962.

[2] On October 28 the tuna fishing vessels *Western Ace* and *Chicken of the Sea* were seized by Peruvian authorities for fishing within the 200-mile territorial limit claimed by Peru.

With regard to the submarines, the President inquired as to why the Peruvian Navy required any submarines, much less new ones. It was explained that the Peruvian Navy had a replacement program set up which provided for two new submarines to replace the two oldest of the four now in commission. A U.S. firm was interested in bidding and we had been informed that the Germans and the British had also been invited to bid. The President said that while it would be better if they did not spend their resources on submarines, if they were determined to purchase them somewhere it would be better if U.S. suppliers had the opportunity than to have the business go to Britain or Germany. It was pointed out to the President that the contrast between the $20 million apparently available for new submarines and the $1.3 million set aside in the budget for the cost of land reform was scandalous and would be likely to evoke embarrassing questions in connection with our aid program for Peru.

The President wished the Ambassador well and asked him to be certain to make it clear to the Peruvians that the U.S. Government was doing all in its power to cooperate with the other governments who were participating in the Alliance for Progress but that they would have to appreciate that our resources were limited and that we did have a balance of payments problem. He added that today Latin America occupies a primary place in our policy considerations. Europe was relatively secure and prosperous while the situation in Latin America required our best efforts and attention.

---

429. National Intelligence Estimate

NIE 97–63   Washington, May 1, 1963.

POLITICAL PROSPECTS IN PERU

The Problem

To estimate the prospect for the establishment of an elected civil government and the basic problems which would confront such a government.

Source: Central Intelligence Agency Files, Job 79–R01012A, ODDI Registry. Secret. According to a covering sheet, this estimate was prepared by the Central Intelligence Agency and the intelligence organizations of the Departments of State, Army, Navy, Air Force, and the Joint Staff. The Director of Central Intelligence submitted the estimate to the U.S. Intelligence Board on May 1, and all members of the Board concurred except the representatives of the AEC and FBI, who abstained on the grounds that the subject was outside their jurisdiction.

Conclusions

A. Peru's present political difficulties are the result of pressures for political and social change generated in a long static society undergoing industrialization and urbanization. These pressures have been building up for a generation. A resolution of the consequent political tensions is not likely to be accomplished for many years. (Paras. 1–6)

B. The present Military Junta seized power in July 1962 in order to prevent direct or indirect accession to power by APRA[1] as the result of the 1962 presidential and congressional election. It has failed in its efforts to develop a political coalition which would ensure the defeat of APRA in the new election which it is committed to hold in June 1963. An election with the candidates now running could be as close and inconclusive as that of 1962. (Paras. 7–11, 20–24)

C. Inasmuch as the military are in a position to control the outcome of the election, they will probably carry out the Junta's commitment to hold it. If, contrary to expectation, Haya should win a undeniable victory, they could still intervene to prevent his inauguration and to establish a military government which would retain power for an unspecified period. There is no doubt that the military have this capability or that they would exercise it if convinced that it was necessary to do so in order to prevent APRA from coming to power. (Paras. 25, 28–29)

D. The Peruvian Communist and pro-Castro groups have little prospect of achieving power in the near future. The Peruvian armed forces and security services are capable of controlling subversive activities short of a well-organized guerrilla movement or a revolutionary uprising on a national scale. (Paras. 16–19)

E. In the past, Peruvian Governments have been unwilling to make the sacrifices or to risk the political liabilities of programs aimed at bringing about fundamental social and economic change. Now, however, Peru faces a situation in which political stability is becoming more and more dependent on the ability and disposition of governments to respond effectively to popular demands for economic well-being and security. This situation augurs a breakup of the existing structure of the Peruvian society and economy. Unless the forces of moderation are able to bring about orderly change, radical leadership will probably get the chance to try its methods. (Para. 34)

[Here follow 9 pages of the "Discussion" section of this estimate.]

---

[1] Alianza Popular Revolucionaria Americana, a radical leftist but anti-Communist party established in 1924. In its earlier days, APRA was violently revolutionary and was repeatedly suppressed by the conservative military. However, in more recent times its program has been considerably moderated and it has sought to achieve power by political action. [Footnote in the source text.]

430.   Memorandum of Conversation

Washington, May 10, 1963.

SUBJECT

Peruvian Elections

PARTICIPANTS

Fernando Berckemeyer, Ambassador of Peru

The Secretary
Richard A. Poole, Officer in Charge of Peruvian Affairs, WST/ARA

Ambassador Berckemeyer said he was calling in response to the Secretary's suggestion in a conversation at a social event earlier in the week, in which the Secretary had expressed his concern over the outlook for the Peruvian elections and had asked the Ambassador to call on him before leaving for Lima. The Ambassador said he would be leaving that same afternoon, accompanying an IFC Mission in his capacity as a Governor of the IFC and that this gave him an opportunity to talk to government leaders and others about the political situation. The Ambassador wished to respond to the Secretary's earlier remarks by stating that the Junta had made a solemn promise to hold free elections and to respect the results, as he himself had had occasion to confirm in Washington. He saw no other course but to live up to this promise and, while he was aware of disturbing rumors to the contrary, he was confident the Junta would do so. He referred to the communiqué issued by the Junta on May 2, in which the Junta stated that there would be no change in the electoral statute and that the elections would be held without fail on June 9.

When the Secretary asked what the outlook for the electoral race seemed to be and whether there was any danger of extremist elements making a strong show, Ambassador Berckemeyer replied that he felt there was no such danger, as the 1962 elections had proven the country to be politically moderate. He said the vote had been very closely divided between the three principal parties, none of which was extremist; and that the three small extreme left parties had shown very little strength; and this year there are the same three principal presidential candidates and only one small party contender. Of the three principal candidates, the Ambassador thought that Odría had gained the most in the interim, having last year won a surprisingly clear victory in the very important Lima–Calloa area where the "quality vote" is cast, i.e., the intellectuals, business, government servants, industrial labor, etc. He mentioned that

---

Source: Department of State, Central Files, POL 14 PERU. Confidential. Drafted by Poole and approved in S on May 15.

Mrs. Odría was a strong asset in the campaign. He thought that there were too many unknowns as far as Belaúnde was concerned and that APRA leadership was now too old.

The Secretary reiterated our interest in the elections and expressed the hope that Peru would get back on the track to progress. He hoped that moderate leadership would emerge to represent the "quality vote" the Ambassador had referred to. He asked the Ambassador to call when he returned from his trip.

(*Footnote:* In an earlier conversation with a Department officer, the Ambassador had expressed himself in strong terms as being very concerned over the outlook for the elections in the face of rumors that they might be cancelled or that there might be some other form of military intervention. He felt that the Junta must live up to its solemn promise or Peru was "finished." He said he had "swallowed the pill" last time, but that there would be no excuse this time. While he found Haya and APRA distasteful and would probably not remain as Ambassador were they to come to power, he nevertheless believed that if they won they should be permitted to take office. He mentioned that, at a recent function for the Grand Duchess of Luxembourg, the President had spoken to him briefly and expressed concern over the outlook in Peru. In the earlier conversation with the Department officer and immediately following his conversation with the Secretary, the Ambassador stated that it was very useful to have these expressions of concern from the President and the Secretary, as he would be able to speak with greater weight in Lima in urging that elections be held and their results respected.)

---

431. Memorandum of Conversation

Washington, May 31, 1963.

SUBJECT

Peruvian Elections

PARTICIPANTS

Fernando Berckemeyer, Ambassador of Peru

The Secretary
Richard A. Poole, Officer in Charge of Peruvian Affairs, WST/ARA

Source: Department of State, Central Files, POL 14 PERU. Confidential. Drafted by Poole and approved in S on June 5.

Ambassador Berckemeyer called on the Secretary pursuant to the latter's suggestion, during their conversation of May 10, that he call after returning from his visit to Peru. (See memorandum of conversation of May 10.)[1]

Ambassador Berckemeyer explained that he had returned from Peru on May 27, following a visit of a little more than two weeks, having gone to Peru with an International Finance Corporation mission in his capacity as a Governor of the IFC. He said he had found the economic situation in Peru to be very healthy, attributable in considerable measure to the marked upswing in sugar prices, the continuing increase in fish meal production and export, and a strengthening in prices of lead, zinc and other metals.

Turning to the political situation, the Ambassador said he had had the opportunity of talking to many people, both in and out of government, about the outlook for the elections. One obvious thing that struck him was the complete freedom of political activity, campaigning and press. He was also impressed by the fact that the candidates showed a general respect for the rights of their rivals to campaign freely and that the candidates and their audiences showed a maturity that had resulted in a relative absence of political incidents and clashes, only a few minor incidents of violence having occurred.

The Ambassador stated that he personally was confident that elections would be held and the results respected regardless of the winner. He had conversations with General Lindley (senior co-President of the Junta), whom he hadn't seen in many years, and developed a high opinion of him, of his integrity and of his determination to hold and respect the elections. He felt certain most of the Junta was equally determined to do so, mentioning the Ministers of Agriculture, Development and Health as particular examples, but he could not say this of all of the members of the Junta, particularly two members whom he did not name. (In a later conversation with Department officers, the Ambassador mentioned specifically Foreign Minister (Admiral) Llosa, who avoids stating his position forthrightly, but who does not convey an impression of confidence as to his feelings about respecting the elections regardless of the results.) The Ambassador added that the overwhelming sentiment he got from talking to a wide cross section of private citizens, business leaders, etc., including staunch anti-Apristas, was that the Junta must live up to its promise even if Haya wins in order that the country might return to constitutional, civilian government.

The Ambassador thought that the elections would be very close, but his impression was that Odría was in the lead, due to several factors:

---

[1] See Document 430.

Odría[2] had made a very good impression with his offer to form a national union with the other parties, even though the offer had not been accepted; the relative prosperity in the country was working in his favor, as it diminished his rivals' appeal to discontented elements; whereas last year Odría had made very few appearances outside of Lima, he this year had been stumping the country with surprisingly good crowds; his wife continues to be a major asset, Belaúnde being divorced and Haya and Samamé being bachelors; while ex-President Prado's party had last year joined forces with the Apristas, most Pradistas this year, who while not numerous were in many cases persons of considerable influence, had joined forces with Odría. APRA, Berckemeyer said, is a strong party and well organized, but there had been some discord among its leaders that had weakened it somewhat. Belaúnde, he felt, was falling behind. The Ambassador was convinced that Belaúnde was not pro-communist although he was not rejecting communist support.

The Ambassador said that some Americans—and he mentioned a priest whose name he could not recall—were claiming that the U.S. Embassy favored APRA. He himself was convinced that this was not so. He had been delighted to find that Ambassador Jones was very well thought of by all the Peruvians he had seen and that he had done a great deal to create an atmosphere of confidence between the Embassy and the Peruvians.

When the Secretary asked how the Castro-communist problem was affecting Peru, Ambassador Berckemeyer mentioned the fact that a group of young Peruvians, mostly university students, had been apprehended entering Peru from Bolivia with arms and subversive plans. The group had proceeded from Cuba, where they had received guerrilla and subversive training. Mr. Poole mentioned that the Department was very interested in this clear-cut case of Castro-communist training, infiltration and subversion and had asked our Embassy to talk to the Peruvian Government about the possibility of greater public use being made of the incident through the Lavalle Committee[3] of the OAS, perhaps with the cooperation of the SCCS,[4] of which General Doig of Peru is a member.

The Secretary expressed his appreciation to the Ambassador for giving his observations on his trip. He said he was glad to hear the Ambassador's expression of confidence.

Footnote: In an immediately subsequent conversation with Department officers Ambassador Berckemeyer mentioned that, at a private social function in the evening of May 28,[5] he had had occasion to talk to

---

[2] Reference is to Presidential candidate Manuel Odria.

[3] See footnote 2, Document 168.

[4] Reference is to the Special Consultative Committee on Security of the OAS.

[5] Reference is presumably to a reception at the house of Hugh Auchincloss in Washington described in the President's Appointment Book. (Kennedy Library)

the President at some length about the Peruvian situation and had expressed his confidence that the elections would be held and respected. He said he did not know how the press learned of the fact that he had talked to the President, but that when he was asked by the press whether the political situation in Peru had been discussed, he had replied that this would be only natural and that he had expressed his feeling of confidence. It had then been reported in the press that the Junta was said to have assured the United States and other friendly governments that elections would be held and respected and that these assurances had been given in person to President Kennedy by him (Berckemeyer). (The UPI correspondent who wrote the story on May 29 had already told a Department officer of this, adding that Berckemeyer had authorized him to use the story without attribution as to source. Comment: In stating this assurance came from the Junta, he must have been trying to interpret the Ambassador's remarks.) The Ambassador mentioned to the Department officers that Foreign Minister Llosa had then issued a statement to the effect that the Junta had given him (Berckemeyer) no message to give to the President and that the Junta's promises had been made to the Peruvian people and not to any foreign government. The Ambassador stated to the Department officers that he felt it perfectly proper for him as Ambassador, after talking to General Lindley, to express his personal confidence to the President and the Secretary.

The Ambassador was confronted by the press when he emerged from his meeting with the Secretary, and in answer to a direct question said he had conveyed no message from the Junta but had reiterated his confidence that the elections would be held and respected; he was careful to add that the Junta had given its promise to the Peruvian people.[6]

---

[6] Fernando Belaúnde Terry was elected President on June 9 and was inaugurated on July 28.

---

432.   Editorial Note

In his inaugural speech of July 28, 1963, President Belaúnde promised to resolve the long-standing controversy between Peruvian interests and the International Petroleum Company (a subsidiary of Standard Oil of New Jersey) over rights to the La Brea y Parinas oil fields. IPC owned the surface and sub-surface drilling concessions to the fields under the terms of a 1922 arbitral agreement. Peru wished to gain control of the fields in the interest of national sovereignty.

Belaúnde discussed the issue with Ambassador Jones and Teodoro Moscoso on August 28 in Lima. Both sides expressed the desire to keep negotiations on the issue private and amicable and to conclude them before October 28. (Airgram A–172 from Lima August 29; Department of State, Central Files, PET 6 PERU)

Negotiations were unsuccessful. On October 28 Belaúnde introduced to the Peruvian Congress a draft law declaring the 1922 agreement null and void. The Congress passed the law on November 1.

On November 8 Ambassador Jones met with Belaúnde to discuss the matter but was rebuffed by the President. The Ambassador made clear that the continued provision of U.S. economic assistance to Peru was contingent on the satisfactory resolution of the issue. (Telegram 572, November 9; ibid.)

Peruvian envoy Manuel Ulloa met with Presidential Special Assistant Ralph Dungan at the White House on November 14 in an effort to reach a compromise solution to the problem. They arranged for renewed negotiations between the Peruvian Government and IPC officials to be held in New York. (Telegram 376 to Lima, November 14; ibid.) The sides held preliminary talks on December 4 and decided to hold more formal negotiations following the December 15 municipal elections in Peru. (Telegram 451 to Lima, December 6; ibid.)

---

433.   Memorandum of Conversation

SecDel/MC/1   New York, September 23, 1963, 11 a.m.

SECRETARY'S DELEGATION TO THE EIGHTEENTH SESSION OF THE UNITED NATIONS GENERAL ASSEMBLY
New York, September 1963

PARTICIPANTS

U.S.	Foreign
Secretary Rusk	Foreign Minister Dr. Fernando Schwalb
Jack D. Neal	Lopez Aldana (Peru)
	Dr. Victor Andres Belaunde, Chairman of Peruvian Delegation

SUBJECT

Peruvian FonMin and Peruvian Chairman of Del Visit with Secretary Rusk

---

Source: Department of State, Central Files, POL PERU–US. Confidential. Drafted by Neal of USUN and approved in S on September 24. The meeting was held at the U.S. Mission to the United Nations in New York.

Foreign Minister Schwalb, accompanied by Dr. Belaunde, called on Secretary Rusk this morning.

The Foreign Minister stated the new Government of Peru was attempting to institute agrarian, corporation and tax reforms. To accomplish these will necessitate the cooperation of the United States. Dr. Schwalb pointed out that the present Peruvian system is obsolete and that it must be changed. He recognizes any alteration will require a fight against the forces of the oligarchy but that President Belaunde Terry, who is an honest, young and strong leader, is determined that the changes must be made—and in juridical and peaceful ways. The Foreign Minister stated his Government will need help from the Alliance for Progress and other United States institutions, particularly in the form of credit and technical assistance.

Secretary Rusk stated we are serious about our faith in the Alliance for Progress and that we can be counted on for assistance. He informed the Foreign Minister we are aware that it is difficult to bring about reforms and changes, but that we are encouraged by Peru's beginning and determination. In reply to the Secretary's question, Dr. Schwalb stated the Government is trying to educate the people to this necessary change by popular appeal and through the Catholic Church which has shown support for the Government's program.

The Foreign Minister told Secretary Rusk that President Belaunde's party has no majority in Congress, and he admitted to the Secretary that the other political parties of Peru have refused to accept cabinet posts in the Belaunde Government. The Secretary reminded him that the development of Peru is for the benefit of all and that possibly the President could get other party help and cooperation in the Alliance for Progress Program.

The Secretary inquired about the activities of private enterprise—not necessarily foreign capital—but particularly what *Peruvian* private enterprise was doing.

The Foreign Minister stated his Government is attempting to stimulate the investment of private Peruvian capital and had invited it to participate. However, he added, the money of Peru is in the hands of a few—the oligarchy—and they are the most difficult opponents of the Government to bring around.

As regards the Peruvian agrarian program, the Secretary sounded a note of caution when he called the Foreign Minister's attention to the failure of the Mexican agrarian reform, when large producing farms were divided into such small units they were not economically productive to the Mexican economy and as a result Mexico became an importing country instead of an exporting nation in several basic food crops.

The Minister stated it was not the intention of the Belaunde program to reduce farm production.

Secretary Rusk told the Foreign Minister Peru had successfully passed through a difficult and important eighteen months. It should capitalize on this opportunity to become one of the leaders in the Hemisphere. He pointed out that investments (both AID and private) are attracted to a given country when it is known these investments will produce results. Peru now has an opportunity to establish a favorable climate and emerge as an example in the Hemisphere.

Both the Foreign Minister and Dr. Belaunde agreed and stated Peru had received favorable comments from other Latin American nations regarding its handling of the recent election.

The Secretary pointed out the favorable public accord which Peru enjoys in the United States. This good will has weathered the past eighteen months without a reduction in popular acclaim. He feels the present Government should do everything possible to maintain this positive position.

The Secretary suggested the Peruvian Government might consider establishing fellowships—at least six—which would encourage college students from the United States to attend some of the better known universities in Peru. He stated the fellowships necessarily would not call for heavy payments to the students, but should cover tuition and modest per diem. Too, he stated the Peruvian Government might consider furnishing some of its literature and publications to institutions in the United States. He feels these steps would have a psychological impact upon certain important segments of this country.

Both the Foreign Minister and Dr. Belaunde were impressed with the idea.

In summing up his thoughts on Peru, the Secretary informed the gentlemen that Peru has a fine opportunity to establish a strong international reputation by mobilizing its own domestic capital in its program of development. He stated it is not necessary to wait 100 years to complete the essential reforms; it can and should be done sooner.

Secretary Rusk turned to the Cuban situation and informed the Foreign Minister of the Russian "move out," but warned him that many were still there. He pinpointed the United States position by informing the Peruvians we cannot accept the present Cuban-USSR relationship and cannot accept the interference of Castro in the Hemisphere.

434.   Telegram From the Department of State to the Embassy in Peru

Washington, October 2, 1963, 7:46 p.m.

243. Ref: Embtel 377.[1] Joint State–AID message. During course of two-and-a-half-day visit here September 25–27, Foreign Minister Schwalb accompanied by Ambassador Berckemeyer and Embassy officers, had informal discussions with Moscoso of AID, Linder of Eximbank and Martin of Department and respective staffs, and with heads of IDB, IBRD, IFC and IMF.

In conversations with US officials Schwalb gave general outline Belaunde Government's reform and development program, budgetary problems and legislative problems. Expressed desire for cordial and fruitful cooperation with US and international assistance agencies. Told Moscoso and Linder that due need for increased revenues to meet present budget deficit and reluctance incur additional opposition by general tax increase, Government relying primarily on foreign lending to finance new development programs.

Moscoso and Linder described loans approved since Belaúnde inauguration and status of those pending, and Schwalb was duly impressed with cooperative attitude he encountered and rapid progress. See Deptel 227[2] re Linder's discussion Eximbank loans.

Moscoso suggested, in interests avoiding providing ammunition to US critics of foreign assistance, that Schwalb attempt in scheduled press conference to correct impression *New York Times* article highlighting his criticism of Alliance red tape in UN speech.[3] (This Schwalb did try to do by pointing out in press conference that his speech as whole was very friendly to Alliance and that criticism was intended as constructive.)

When Schwalb described problems of financing Agrarian Reform, Moscoso suggested GOP look into method adopted in Colombia, where in certain cases land owners pay for improvements provided them by Govt (roads, irrigation, etc., which can be financed by foreign lending institutions) by giving up a part of land holdings to Government for redistribution.

Source: Department of State, Central Files, POL 7 PERU. Confidential; Priority. Drafted by Poole; cleared by Belcher, Allen of ARA/RPA, Moscoso, Lucas of AID/LA, Withereld of AID/LA/WC, and the Export-Import Bank; and approved by Belcher.

[1] Dated September 30. (Ibid.)

[2] Dated September 27. (Ibid., FN 11–1 PERU/XMB)

[3] Reference is to an article of September 25, which described Schwalb's speech at the United Nations General Assembly the previous day in which he criticized the "excessive red tape" he felt hindered the work of the Alliance for Progress.

Schwalb discussed with Moscoso and staff at some length prospective investment guaranty agreement. Agreed wholeheartedly in principle on value of such agreement in attracting foreign capital investment but emphasized public relations, congressional and juridical problem for GOP in provisions pertaining to international arbitration and USG assumption of investors' rights, which he recognized were clauses not likely to come up in practice but nevertheless likely to arouse opposition, especially in view public and congressional sentiment on La Brea y Parinas Arbitral Award. Moscoso and staff explained that 80 countries including 10 LA's had signed agreements with such clauses. In answer Schwalb inquiry about more limited agreements with Colombia and Venezuela, Moscoso explained that former was simply interim agreement pending final action on complete agreement and that latter was due special circumstances. Schwalb was given suggested text contained AIDTO 137,[4] with indication we felt Pastor draft fell short of our requirements largely due omission forementioned controversial clauses. Schwalb promised to study matter further, including possibility resubmission to Consultative Commission on Foreign Relations.

Conversations with Martin and staff followed general lines memorandum of September 27 airpouched to you same date,[4] i.e. with Martin raising following topics: (1) Communism in labor and related political problems as well as Communism among students; (2) International Petroleum Company; (3) IT& T; (4) Discriminatory shipping measures; (5) Agrarian Reform and land invasions, but without discussion specific case of Cerro Crop; (6) COAS chairmanship; (7) Puerto Maldonaldo incident; as well as (8) advisability of further consultations re possible MFM. Fisheries problem and Dominican situation did not arise.

Schwalb gave assurances Government did not favor Communism in organized labor, nor did it favor Aprista-dominated CTP, but rather took position that organized labor and student organizations should be non-political; criticized general strike called by CTP; believed Apristas would support Government reform measures in Congress.

Schwalb was optimistic satisfactory solution to IPC problem could be found, although was not up to date on latest developments. Nor did he have latest information on IT&T and shipping problems. Understood US position on all three questions and stated he would look into them upon his return.

Schwalb was also confident that differences over Agrarian Reform Bill would be ironed out in Congress and that, while doubtless would be dissatisfaction among Odriistas and many landowners, he felt Apristas were in general agreement. Stated problem of land invasions created

---

[4] Not found.

dilemma for Government, which naturally opposed to illegal invasions but wished to avoid violence, which might then be used by opponents of Government's program to defeat it. Government therefore relying on suasion pending passage Agrarian Reform Law.

Schwalb grateful our desire to back Lavalle[6] for COAS chairmanship, but stated question of Lavalle's retention had not yet been decided by Belaúnde. Schwalb had not yet succeeded in getting to Belaúnde on this subject, but would do so on his return. He reiterated interest in making information of Puerto Maldonaldo incident available to COAS. He agreed with Martin that question of holding MFM required further informal consultation among OAS members.

Ball

---

[5] Juan Bautista de Lavalle, Peruvian Ambassador to the OAS.

Index